CAMBRIDGE LIBRAR

Books of enduring scho

Classics

From the Renaissance to the nineteenth century, Latin and Greek were compulsory subjects in almost all European universities, and most early modern scholars published their research and conducted international correspondence in Latin. Latin had continued in use in Western Europe long after the fall of the Roman empire as the lingua franca of the educated classes and of law, diplomacy, religion and university teaching. The flight of Greek scholars to the West after the fall of Constantinople in 1453 gave impetus to the study of ancient Greek literature and the Greek New Testament. Eventually, just as nineteenth-century reforms of university curricula were beginning to erode this ascendancy, developments in textual criticism and linguistic analysis, and new ways of studying ancient societies, especially archaeology, led to renewed enthusiasm for the Classics. This collection offers works of criticism, interpretation and synthesis by the outstanding scholars of the nineteenth century.

The Golden Bough: The Third Edition

This work by Sir James Frazer (1854–1941) is widely considered to be one of the most important early texts in the fields of psychology and anthropology. At the same time, by applying modern methods of comparative ethnography to the classical world, and revealing the superstition and irrationality beneath the surface of the classical culture which had for so long been a model for Western civilisation, it was extremely controversial. Frazer was greatly influenced by E.B. Tylor's *Primitive Culture* (also reissued in this series), and by the work of the biblical scholar William Robertson Smith, to whom the first edition is dedicated. The twelve-volume third edition, reissued here, was greatly revised and enlarged, and published between 1911 and 1915; the two-volume first edition (1890) is also available in this series. Volume 12 (1915) provides a bibliography and general index to the entire third edition.

The Golden Bough
The Third Edition

VOLUME 12:
BIBLIOGRAPHY AND GENERAL INDEX

J.G. FRAZER

CAMBRIDGE UNIVERSITY PRESS

Cambridge, New York, Melbourne, Madrid, Cape Town,
Singapore, São Paolo, Delhi, Mexico City

Published in the United States of America by Cambridge University Press, New York

www.cambridge.org
Information on this title: www.cambridge.org/9781108047425

© in this compilation Cambridge University Press 2012

This edition first published 1915
This digitally printed version 2012

ISBN 978-1-108-04742-5 Paperback

THE GOLDEN BOUGH

A STUDY IN MAGIC AND RELIGION

THIRD EDITION

VOL. XII

BIBLIOGRAPHY AND GENERAL INDEX

MACMILLAN AND CO., Limited
LONDON · BOMBAY · CALCUTTA
MELBOURNE

THE MACMILLAN COMPANY
NEW YORK · BOSTON · CHICAGO
DALLAS · SAN FRANCISCO

THE MACMILLAN CO. OF CANADA, Ltd.
TORONTO

THE GOLDEN BOUGH

A STUDY IN MAGIC AND RELIGION

BY

J. G. FRAZER, Kt., D.C.L., LL.D., Litt.D.

FELLOW OF TRINITY COLLEGE, CAMBRIDGE
PROFESSOR OF SOCIAL ANTHROPOLOGY IN THE UNIVERSITY OF LIVERPOOL

THIRD EDITION, REVISED AND ENLARGED

IN TWELVE VOLUMES
VOL. XII
BIBLIOGRAPHY AND GENERAL INDEX

MACMILLAN AND CO., LIMITED
ST. MARTIN'S STREET, LONDON
1915

COPYRIGHT

PREFACE

THE following Bibliography aims at giving a complete list of the authorities cited in the third edition of *The Golden Bough.* Such a list may be of use to readers who desire to have further information on any of the topics discussed or alluded to in the text. It has been compiled by Messrs. R. & R. Clark's Press Reader from the references in my footnotes to the volumes, and it has been revised and corrected by me in proof. The titles of works which I have not seen but have cited at second hand are distinguished by an asterisk prefixed to them. Throughout the book I have endeavoured to indicate the distinction clearly by the manner of my citation, but lest any ambiguity should remain I have thought it well to mark the difference precisely in the Bibliography. In the case of Greek and Latin authors the editions which I have commonly used are generally noted in the Bibliography ; they are for the most part those which I possess in my own library and have consulted for the sake of convenience.

The General Index incorporates the separate indices to the volumes, but as some of these, especially in the earlier volumes, were somewhat meagre, I have made large additions to them in order to bring up the whole to a uniform standard and to facilitate the use of the book as a work of reference. With this clue in his hand the student, I hope, will be able to find his way through the labyrinth of facts. All the entries have been made by me, but the arrangement of them is in the main due to the Press Reader, whom I desire to thank for the diligence and accuracy with which he has performed his laborious task. The whole Index has been repeatedly revised and freely corrected by me in proof.

In conclusion it is my duty as well as pleasure to thank my publishers, Messrs. Macmillan & Company, for the never-failing confidence, courtesy, and liberality with which they have treated me during the many years in which *The Golden Bough* has been in progress. From first to last they have laid me under no restrictions whatever, but have left me perfectly free to plan and execute the work on the scale and in the manner I judged best. Their patience has been inexhaustible and their courage in facing the pecuniary risks unwavering. My printers also, Messrs. R. & R. Clark of Edinburgh, have done their part to my entire satisfaction; they have promptly responded to every call I have made on them for increased speed, and with regard to accuracy I will only say that in the scrutiny to which I have subjected the book for the purpose of the Index I have detected many errors of my own, but few or none of theirs. Publishers and printers can do much to help or hinder an author's work. Mine have done everything that could be done to render my labours as light and as pleasant as possible. I thank them sincerely and gratefully for their help, and I reflect with pleasure on the relations of unbroken cordiality which have existed between us for more than a quarter of a century.

J. G. FRAZER.

1 Brick Court, Temple,
25th January 1915.

CONTENTS

PREFACE . . . . Pp. v-vi

BIBLIOGRAPHY . . . . . . Pp. 1-144

GENERAL INDEX . . . . . Pp. 145-536

BIBLIOGRAPHY

BIBLIOGRAPHY

N.B.—In the following list an asterisk prefixed to the title of a work signifies that the work in question has not been seen by me (J. G. Frazer), and is known to me only by name or in quotations. Works not marked by an asterisk have been consulted in the originals.

"A Far-off Greek Island," in *Blackwood's Magazine*, February 1886.
"A Japanese Fire-walk," in *American Anthropologist*, New Series, v. (1903).
Abbott, G. F., *Macedonian Folk-lore*. Cambridge, 1903.
Abeghian, Manuk, *Der armenische Volksglaube*. Leipsic, 1899.
Abel, E., *Orphica*. Leipsic and Prague, 1885.
Abēla, Eijūb, "Beiträge zur Kenntniss abergläubischer Gebräuche in Syrien," in *Zeitschrift des deutschen Palaestina-Vereins*, vii. (1884).
*Abelas, *Malta illustrata*, Cintar's Supplements, quoted by R. Wünsch, *Das Frühlingsfest der Insel Malta*. Leipsic, 1902.
Abercromby, Hon. J., in *Folk-lore*, ii. (1891).
    The Pre- and Proto-historic Finns. London, 1898.
Abhandlungen der historischen Classe der Königlichen Bayerischen Akademie der Wissenschaften.
Abhandlungen der historisch-philologischen Classe der Königlichen Gesellschaft der Wissenschaften zu Göttingen.
Abhandlungen der Königlichen Akademie der Wissenschaften zu Berlin.
Abhandlungen der Königlichen Bayerischen Akademie der Wissenschaften.
Abhandlungen der Königlichen Gesellschaft der Wissenschaften zu Göttingen.
Abhandlungen der Königlichen Preussischen Akademie der Wissenschaften.
Abhandlungen der philologisch-historischen Klasse der Königlichen Sächsischen Gesellschaft der Wissenschaften.
Abinal, Father, "Astrologie Malgache," in *Les Missions Catholiques*, xi. (1879).
    "Croyances fabuleuses des Malgaches," in *Les Missions Catholiques*, xii. (1880).
Abougit, Father X., S.J., "Le feu du Saint-Sépulcre," in *Les Missions Catholiques*, viii. (1876).
Abrahams, Israel, *Jewish Life in the Middle Ages*. London, 1896.
    The Book of Delight and other Papers. Philadelphia, 1912.
Abydenus, in *Fragmenta Historicorum Graecorum*, ed. C. Müller, vol. iv.
Academy, The.
Acerbi, J., *Travels through Sweden, Finnland and Lapland*. London, 1802.
Acevado, Dr. Otero, Letter in *Le Temps*, September 1898.
Achilles Tatius. Ed. G. A. Hirschig. Paris (Didot), 1885.
Acosta, J. de, *The Natural and Moral History of the Indies*. Translated by E. Grimston; edited by (Sir) Clements R. Markham. Hakluyt Society, London, 1880.
    *Original Spanish Edition published at Seville in 1590. Reprinted at Madrid in 1894.
Acron, on Horace, *Odes*, quoted by G. Boni in *Notizie degli Scavi*, May 1900.
Acta Fratrum Arvalium. Ed. G. Henzen. Berlin, 1874.

3

Acta Sanctorum. Paris and Rome, 1867.
Acta Societatis Scientiarum Fennicae. Helsingfors, 1856.
Adair, James, *History of the American Indians.* London, 1775.
Adam, J., on Plato, *Republic.* Cambridge, 1902.
Adam of Bremen, *Descriptio insularum Aquilonis,* with the Scholia, in Migne's *Patrologia Latina,* cxlvi.
Adams, John, *Sketches taken during Ten Voyages in Africa between the years 1786 and 1800.* London, N.D.
Addison, Joseph, "Remarks on Several Parts of Italy," in his *Works,* vol. ii. London, 1811.
Adriani, Dr. N., "Mededeelingen omtrent de Toradjas van Midden-Celebes," in *Tijdschrift voor Indische Taal- Land- en Volkenkunde,* xliv. (1901).
Adriani, N., en Kruijt, Alb. C., *De Bare'e-sprekende Toradja's van Midden-Celebes.* Batavia, 1912.
"Van Posso naar Mori," in *Mededeelingen van wege het Nederlandsche Zendelinggenootschap,* xliv. (1900).
"Van Posso naar Parigi, Sigi en Lindoe," in *Mededeelingen van wege het Nederlandsche Zendelinggenootschap,* xlii. (1898).
Aelian. Ed. R. Hercher. Paris (Didot), 1858.
De natura animalium.
Variae historiae.
Aelius Lampridius, in *Scriptores Historiae Augustae,* ed. H. Peter. Leipsic, 1884.
Alexander Severus.
Antoninus Diadumenus.
Antoninus Heliogabalus.
Aelius Spartianus, *Helius,* in H. Peter's *Scriptores Historiae Augustae.*
Aeneas Sylvius, *Opera.* Bâle, 1571.
Aeschines. Ed. F. Franke. Leipsic, 1863.
Contra Ctesiphontem.
Epistolae.
Aeschylus. Ed. F. A. Paley. Third Edition. London, 1870.
Choephori.
Prometheus Vinctus.
Suppliants.
Aetna. Ed. Robinson Ellis, in *Corpus Poetarum Latinorum,* ed. J. P. Postgate. London, 1894–1905.
Afzelius, Arv. Aug., *Volkssagen und Volkslieder aus Schwedens älterer und neuer Zeit.* Übersetzt von F. H. Ungewitter. Leipsic, 1842.
Agahd, R., *M. Terentii Varronis rerum divinarum libri I. XIV. XV. XVI.* Leipsic, 1898.
Agatharchides, in Photius, *Bibliotheca.* Ed. Im. Bekker. Berlin, 1824.
Agathias, *Historia.* Ed. B. G. Niebuhr. Bonn, 1828.
Agerbeek, A. H. B., "Enkele gebruiken van de Dajaksche bevolking der Pinoehlanden," in *Tijdschrift voor Indische Taal- Land- en Volkenkunde,* li. (1909).
*Agriculture of the Nabataeans. ii. 100 and 346.
*Aiton, William, *Treatise on the Origin, Qualities, and Cultivation of Moss Earth,* quoted by R. Munro, *Ancient Scottish Lake Dwellings or Crannogs.* Edinburgh, 1882.
Aiyar, N. Subramhanya, in *Census of India, 1901,* vol. xxvi. *Travancore,* Part I. Trivandrum, 1903.
*Al Baidawî's Commentary on the Koran.
Alberti, L., *De Kaffers aan de Zuidkust van Afrika.* Amsterdam, 1810.
Albertus Magnus, quoted by A. Kuhn, *Die Herabkunft des Feuers und des Göttertranks.* Second Edition. Gütersloh, 1886.
Albîrûnî, *The Chronology of Ancient Nations.* Translated and edited by Dr. C. Edward Sachau. London, 1879.

Alexander, Lieutenant Boyd, "From the Niger, by Lake Chad, to the Nile," in *The Geographical Journal*, xxx. (1907).

Alexander, Sir James E., *Expedition of Discovery into the Interior of Africa*. London, 1838.

Allan, John Hay, *The Bridal of Caölchairn*. London, 1822.

Alldridge, T. J., *The Sherbro and its Hinterland*. London, 1901.

Allegret, E., "Les Idées religieuses des Fañ (Afrique Occidentale)," in *Revue de l'Histoire des Religions*, l. (1904).

Allen, W., and Thomson, T. R. H., *Narrative of the Expedition to the River Niger in 1841*. London, 1848.

Allgemeine Missions-Zeitschrift. Gütersloh.

Allison, Mrs. S. S., "Account of the Similkameen Indians of British Columbia," in *Journal of the Anthropological Institute*, xxi. (1892).

Alpenburg, J. N. Ritter von, *Mythen und Sagen Tirols*. Zurich, 1857.

Alvear, D. de, *Relacion geografica e historica de la provincia de Misiones*, in P. de Angelis's *Coleccion de obras y documentos*, etc., iv. Buenos Ayres, 1836.

Am Urquell. *Monatsschrift für Volkkunde*, N.F.

Amalfi, G., *Tradizioni ed Usi nella penisola Sorrentina*. Palermo, 1890.

Amat, Father E., in *Annales de la Propagation de la Foi*, lxx. (1898).

Ambrosetti, J. B., "Los Indios Caingua del alto Paraná (misiones)," in *Boletino del Instituto Geografico Argentino*, xv. Buenos Ayres, 1895.

Ambrosoli, Father, "Notice sur l'île de Rook," in *Annales de la Propagation de la Foi*, xxvii. (1855).

Amélineau, E., *Le Tombeau d'Osiris*. Paris, 1899.

American Anthropologist. New Series.

American Antiquarian and Oriental Journal.

American Journal of Archaeology.

American Journal of Folk-lore.

American Journal of Philology.

American Journal of Semitic Languages and Literatures.

American Journal of Theology.

American Naturalist.

Amira, K. von, in H. Paul's *Grundriss der germanischen Philologie*. Second Edition. Strasburg, 1900.

Ammianus Marcellinus. Ed. F. Eyssenhardt. Berlin, 1871.

Ampelius, L., *Liber Memorialis*.

Anacreon, cited by Pliny, *Naturalis Historia*.

Analecta Bollandiana.

Anderson, J., *From Mandalay to Momien*. London, 1876.

Anderson, J. D., private communication (ix. 176 *n*.[3]).

Andersson, C. J., *Lake Ngami*. Second Edition. London, 1856.
The Okavango River. London, 1861.

Andocides, *Orationes*. Ed. F. Blass. Leipsic, 1871.

Andree, Dr. Richard, *Braunschweiger Volkskunde*. Brunswick, 1896.
"Die Pleiaden im Mythus und in ihrer Beziehung zum Jahresbeginn und Landbau," in *Globus*, lxiv. (1893).
Ethnographische Parallelen und Vergleiche. Stuttgart, 1878. Neue Folge. Leipsic, 1889.
"Scapulimantia," in *Boas Anniversary Volume*. New York, 1906.
Votive und Weihegaben des Katholischen Volks in Süddeutschland. Brunswick, 1904.

Andree-Eysn, Marie, *Volkskundliches aus dem bayrisch-österreichischen Alpengebiet*. Brunswick, 1910.

Andrews, J. B., *Contes Ligures*. Paris, 1892.

Angas, G. F., *Savage Life and Scenes in Australia and New Zealand*. London, 1847.

Angas, H. Crawford, in *Verhandlungen der Berliner Gesellschaft für Anthropologie, Ethnologie und Urgeschichte*, 1898.

Angelis, Pedro de, *Coleccion de obras y documentos relativos a la historia antigua y moderna de las provincias del Rio de la Plata.* Buenos-Aires, 1836–1837.

Ankermann, B., "L'Ethnographie actuelle de l'Afrique méridionale," in *Anthropos*, i. (1906).

Annales de l'Association de la Propagation de la Foi.

Annales de la Propagation de la Foi (continuation of the preceding).

Annales du Cercle Archéologique de Mons.

Annales du Musée Guimet, Bibliothèque d'Études.

Annales Politiques et Littéraires.

Annali dell' Instituto di Corrispondenza Archeologica.

Annals of Archaeology and Anthropology. Liverpool and London.

Annandale, Nelson, in letter to the Author.

   "Customs of the Malayo-Siamese," in *Fasciculi Malayenses, Anthropology*, Part II. (*a*) (May 1904).

   "Primitive Beliefs and Customs of the Patani Fishermen," in *Fasciculi Malayenses, Anthropology*, Part I. (April 1903).

Annandale, N., and Robinson, H. C., "Some Preliminary Results of an Expedition to the Malay Peninsula," in *Journal of the Anthropological Institute*, xxxii. (1902).

Annual Archaeological Report, 1905. Toronto, 1906.

Annual Reports of the Bureau of American Ethnology.

Annual Reports of the Smithsonian Institution.

Annual Reports on British New Guinea.

"Anonymi Chronologica." Printed in L. Dindorf's edition of J. Malalas. Bonn, 1831.

Antananarivo Annual and Madagascar Magazine.

   Reprint of the First Four Numbers. Antananarivo, 1885.

   Reprint of the Second Four Numbers. Antananarivo, 1896.

Anthologia Palatina. Ed. F. Dübner. Paris (Didot), 1864–1872.

Anthologia Planudea. Ed. F. Dübner. Paris (Didot), 1872.

Anthropological Essays presented to E. B. Tylor. Oxford, 1907.

Anthropological Reviews and Miscellanea, appended to *Journal of the Anthropological Institute*, xxx. (1900).

Anthropos. Ephemeris Internationalis Ethnologica et Linguistica.

Antigonus, *Historiarum mirabilium collectanea*, in *Scriptores rerum mirabilium Graeci.* Ed. A. Westermann. Brunswick, 1839.

Antoninus Liberalis, *Transformationum congeries*, in *Mythographi Graeci.* Ed. A. Westermann. Brunswick, 1843.

Anzeiger der Akademie der Wissenschaften in Krakau.

Apollodorus, *Bibliotheca*, in *Mythographi Graeci.* Ed. A. Westermann. Brunswick, 1843.

   Bibliotheca. Ed. R. Wagner. Leipsic, 1894.

   Epitoma Vaticana. Ed. R. Wagner. Leipsic, 1891.

Apollonius Rhodius, *Argonautica.* Ed. Aug. Wellauer. Leipsic, 1828.

Apostolius, *Proverbia*, in *Paroemiographi Graeci*, i. Ed. E. L. Leutsch et F. G. Schneidewin. Göttingen, 1839–1851.

Appian. Ed. L. Mendelssohn. Leipsic, 1879–1881.

   Bellum Civile.

   Bellum Mithridaticum.

   Hispanica.

   Punica.

   Syriaca.

Apuleius. Ed. G. F. Hildebrand. Leipsic, 1843.

   De magia.

Apuleius—*continued.*
    De mundo.
    Metamorphoses.
Aratus, *Phaenomena.* Ed. E. Maass. Berlin, 1893.
Arbousset, T., et Daumas, F., *Relation d'un voyage d'Exploration au Nord-est de la Colonie du Cap de Bonne-Espérance.* Paris, 1842.
Archaeologia: or Miscellaneous Tracts relating to Antiquity.
Archaeologia, Second Series.
**Archaeologia Aeliana,* N.S., quoted in *The Denham Tracts.* Edited by J. Hardy. London, 1892–1895.
Archaeologia Cambrensis, Second Series.
Archaeological and Ethnological Papers of the Peabody Museum, Harvard University.
Archaeological Review.
Archaeologische-epigraphische Mittheilungen aus Oesterreich-Ungarn.
Archäologischer Anzeiger.
Archäologische Zeitung.
Archias Mitylenaeus, in *Anthologia Palatina,* vii.
Archiv für Anthropologie.
Archiv für Papyrusforschung.
Archiv für Religionswissenschaft.
Archivio per lo Studio delle Tradizioni Popolari.
Arctic Papers for the Expedition of 1875. Published by the Royal Geographical Society. London, 1875.
Aristides (Christian apologist), *Apologia.* Edited by J. Rendel Harris. Cambridge, 1891.
Aristides (Greek rhetorician), *Orationes.* Ed. G. Dindorf. Leipsic, 1829.
    Eleusinius.
    Isthmica.
    Panathenaicus.
Aristophanes, in *Poetae Scenici Graeci.* Ed. G. Dindorf. London, 1869.
    Acharnenses.
    Birds.
    Clouds.
    Ecclesiazusae.
    Frogs.
    Knights.
    Lysistrata.
    Plutus.
    Thesmophoriazusae.
    Wasps.
Aristotle, *Opera.* Ed. Im. Bekker. Berlin, 1831–1870.
    Cited by a Scholiast on Aristophanes, *Acharnenses.*
    Constitution of Athens. Ed. J. E. Sandys. London, 1893.
    De anima.
    De animalium generatione.
    De mundo.
    [*De Mirabilibus Auscultationibus.*]
    De Xenophane.
    Historia de animalibus.
    Meteora.
    Peplos, in *Fragmenta Historicorum Graecorum.* Ed. C. Müller.
    Physica Auscultatio.
    Politics.
    Problemata.
*Arlegui, *Chrón. de Zacatecas,* quoted by H. H. Bancroft, in *Native Races of the Pacific States.* London, 1875–1876.

Armit, Captain W. E., "Customs of the Australian Aborigines," in *Journal of the Anthropological Institute*, ix. (1880).

Arnobius, *Adversus Nationes*. Ed. Aug. Reifferscheid. Vienna, 1875.

Arnold, Matthew, *Essays in Criticism*. First Series. London, 1898.

Arnold, R. A., *From the Levant*. London, 1868.

Arnot, F. S., *Garengauze; or Seven Years' Pioneer Mission Work in Central Africa*. London, N.D., preface dated March 1889.

Arriaga, P. J. de, *Extirpacion de la Idolatria del Piru*. Lima, 1621.

Arrian, *Anabasis*. Ed. R. Geier. Leipsic, 1871.

  Cynegeticus, in *Scripta Minora*. Ed. R. Hercher. Leipsic, 1854.

  Epicteti dissertationes. Ed. H. Schenkl. Leipsic, 1894.

  Indica, in *Scripta Minora*. Ed. R. Hercher.

  Tactica, in *Scripta Minora*. Ed. R. Hercher.

Ars quatuor Coronatorum. The Transactions of a Masonic Lodge of London.

Artemidorus, *Onirocritica*. Ed. R. Hercher. Leipsic, 1864.

Asbjörnsen, P. Chr., *Norske Folke-Eventyr*. Ny Samling. Christiania, 1871.

Asbjörnsen, P. Chr., og Moe, J., *Norske Folke-Eventyr*. Christiania, N.D.

Asclepiades, cited by Porphyry, *De abstinentia*.

Asconius. Ed. A. Kiesseling et R. Schoell. Berlin, 1875.

  In Milonianam.

  In Cornelianam.

Ashe, R. P., *Two Kings of Uganda*. London, 1889.

Asiatick (Asiatic) Researches. Usually quoted in the 8vo Edition. London, 1806–1818.

Asterius Amasenus, *Encomium in sanctos martyres*, in Migne's *Patrologia Graeca*, xl.

Astley, T., *New General Collection of Voyages and Travels*. London, 1745–1754.

Aston, W. G., *Shinto, the Way of the Gods*. London, 1905.

Ateius Capito, cited by Plutarch, *Quaestiones Romanae*.

Athalye, Y. V., in *Journal of the Anthropological Society of Bombay*, i.

Athanasius, *Oratio contra Gentes*, in Migne's *Patrologia Graeca*, xxv.

Atharva-Veda. See s.v. Hymns.

Athenaeum, The.

Athenaeus. Ed. Aug. Meineke. Leipsic, 1858–1867.

  Ed. G. Kaibel. Leipsic, 1887–1890.

Athenagoras, *Supplicatio pro Christianis*. Ed. J. C. T. Otto. Jena, 1857.

Atkinson, E. T., "Notes on the History of Religion in the Himalayas of the North-West Provinces," in *Journal of the Asiatic Society of Bengal*, liii. Part i. Calcutta, 1884.

  The Himalayan Districts of the North-Western Provinces of India. Allahabad, 1884.

Atkinson, Rev. J. C., in *County Folk-lore*, ii. London, 1901.

  Forty Years in a Moorland Parish. London, 1891.

Atkinson, T. W., *Travels in the Regions of the Upper and Lower Amoor*. London, 1860.

Attalus, Letter preserved in inscription at Sivrihissar.

Atti del IV. Congresso Internazionale degli Orientalisti. Florence, 1880.

Aubin, E., *Le Maroc d'aujourd'hui*. Paris, 1904.

Aubrey, John, *Remaines of Gentilisme and Judaisme*. Folk-lore Society. London, 1881.

Augustine, *Opera*. Paris, 1683.

  De civitate Dei.

  De Trinitate, in Migne's *Patrologia Latina*, xlii.

  [*Quaestiones Veteris et Novi Testamenti*,] in Migne's *Patrologia Latina*, xxxv.

  Sermones, in Migne's *Patrologia Latina*, xxxviii.

Aurelius Victor, Sextus. Ed. Franc. Pichlmayr. Leipsic, 1911.

  De viris illustribus.

  Origo gentis Romanae.

Aus der Anomia, Archäologische Beiträge Carl Robert zur Erinnerung an Berlin dargebracht. Berlin, 1890.
Ausgrabungen zu Sendschirli. Berlin, 1902.
Ausland, Das. Wochenschrift für Länder- und Völkerkunde.
Ausonius, *De feriis Romanis.*
  Epigrammata.
Aust, E., *Die Religion der Römer.* Munster i. W., 1899.
  s.v. "Juppiter," in W. H. Roscher's *Lexicon der griechischen und römischen Mythologie*, ii.
Autenrieth, Missionary, "Zur Religion der Kamerun-Neger," in *Mitteilungen der geographischen Gesellschaft zu Jena*, xii. (1893).
Authority and Archaeology Sacred and Profane. Edited by D. G. Hogarth. London, 1899.
Auvergne, Mgr., in *Annales de la Propagation de la Foi*, x. (1837).
Avanchers, Father Léon des, in *Bulletin de la Société de Géographie* (Paris), Vme Série, xvii. (1869).
Avebury, Lord (Sir John Lubbock), *Origin of Civilisation.* London, 1870.
  Fourth Edition. London, 1882.
  Fifth Edition.
  Preface to Sixth Edition. London, 1902.
  Prehistoric Times. Fifth Edition. London, 1890.
Aymonier, Étienne, *Le Cambodge.* Paris, 1900–1904.
  "Les Tchames et leurs religions," in *Revue de l'histoire des Religions*, xxiv. (1891).
  "Notes sur les coutumes et croyances superstitieuses des Cambodgiens," in *Cochinchine française : Excursions et Reconnaissances*, No. 16. Saigon, 1883.
  Notes sur le Laos. Saigon, 1885.
  Notice sur le Cambodge. Paris, 1875.
  Voyage dans le Laos. Paris, 1895–1897.
Azara, F. de, *Voyages dans l'Amérique Méridionale.* Paris, 1809.

Baarda, M. J. van. Cited by A. C. Kruijt, "Regen lokken en regen verdrijving bij de Toradja's van Central Celebes," in *Tijdschrift voor Indische Taal- Land- en Volkenkunde*, xliv. (1901).
  "Fabelen, verhalen en overleveringen der Galelareezen," in *Bijdragen tot de Taal- Land- en Volkenkunde van Nederlandsch-Indië*, xlv. (1895).
  "Île de Halmaheira," in *Bulletins de la Société d'Anthropologie de Paris*, iii. (1892), iv. (1893).
Babelon, E., *Monnaies de la République romaine.* Paris, 1885–1886.
Babrius, *Fabulae.* Ed. W. G. Rutherford. London, 1883.
Bacchylides. Ed. Sir Richard C. Jebb. Cambridge, 1905.
Bachofen, J. J., *Das Mutterrecht.* Stuttgart, 1861.
  Die Sage von Tanaquil. Heidelberg, 1870.
Back, Fr., *De Graecorum caerimoniis in quibus homines deorum vice fungebantur.* Berlin, 1883.
Backer, L. de, *L'Archipel Indien.* Paris, 1874.
Bacon, Francis, *Natural History*, in his *Works.* London, 1740.
Baddeley, St. Clair. Notes sent to the Author (i. 5. *n.*²).
Badger, G. P., Note on *The Travels of Ludovico di Varthema.* Translated by J. W. Jones. Hakluyt Society. London, 1863.
Badham, Rev. Charles, D.D. Cited iii. 156.
Baedeker, K., *Central Italy and Rome.* Thirteenth Edition.
  Palestine and Syria. Fourth Edition. Leipsic, 1906.
  Southern Italy. Seventh Edition. Leipsic, 1880.
Baer, K. F. v., und Helmersen, Gr. v., *Beiträge zur Kenntniss des russischen Reiches und der angrenzenden Länder Asiens.* St. Petersburg, 1839.

Baessler-Archiv.

Baethgen, F., *Beiträge zur semitischen Religionsgeschichte.* Berlin, 1888.

Bagford's letter in *Leland's Collectanea,* i., quoted by J. Brand, *Popular Antiquities,* ii. Bohn's Edition. London, 1882–1883.

Baier, R., "Beiträge von der Insel Rügen," in *Zeitschrift für deutsche Mythologie und Sittenkunde,* ii. (1855).

Bailey, Mabel. Verbal communication (ii. 88 *n.*[1]).

Bailly, J. S., *Lettres sur l'Atlantide de Platon.* London and Paris, 1779.
Lettres sur l'Origine des Sciences. London and Paris, 1777.

Baker, F. B., in *Numismatic Chronicle,* Third Series, xii. (1892).

Balbi, Gaspar, "Voyage to Pegu," in J. Pinkerton's *Voyages and Travels,* ix.

Balfour, Edward, *Cyclopaedia of India.* Third Edition. London, 1885.

Ball, V., *Jungle Life in India.* London, 1880.

Ballentine, Floyd G., "Some Phases of the Cult of the Nymphs," in *Harvard Studies in Classical Philology,* xv. (1904).

Bamler, G., "Tami," in R. Neuhauss's *Deutsch Neu-Guinea,* iii. Berlin, 1911.

Bancroft, H. H., *The Native Races of the Pacific States of North America.* London, 1875–1876.

Banffshire Journal, quoted by R. Chambers, *The Book of Days.* London and Edinburgh, 1886.

Banks, M. M., "Scoring a Witch above the Breath," in *Folk-lore,* xxiii. (1912).

Barber, Rev. Dr. W. T. A., in letters to the Author (iv. 145, 275).

Barbosa, Duarte, *A Description of the Coasts of East Africa and Malabar in the Beginning of the Sixteenth Century.* Translated by the Hon. H. E. J. Stanley. Hakluyt Society. London, 1866.
in *Records of South-Eastern Africa,* collected by G. McCall Theal, vol. i. (1898).

Baring-Gould, S., *Curious Myths of the Middle Ages.* London, 1884.

Barker, W. G. M. Jones, *The Three Days of Wensleydale.* London, 1854.

Baron, R., "The Bara," in *Antananarivo Annual and Madagascar Magazine,* vol. ii., Reprint of the Second Four Numbers. Antananarivo, 1896.

Baron, S., "Description of the Kingdom of Tonqueen," in J. Pinkerton's *Voyages and Travels,* ix.

Barret, P., *L'Afrique Occidentale.* Paris, 1888.

Bartels, M., "Isländischer Brauch und Volksglaube in Bezug auf die Nachkommenschaft," in *Zeitschrift für Ethnologie,* xxxii. (1900).

Bartels, Olga, "Aus dem Leben der weissrussischen Landbevölkerung," in *Zeitschrift für Ethnologie,* xxxv. (1903).

Barth, H., in *Monatsberichte der königlichen Preussischen Akademie der Wissenschaften,* 1859.
"Reize von Trapezunt durch die nördliche Hälfte Klein-Asiens," in *Ergänzungsheft zu Petermann's Geographischen Mittheilungen,* No. 2 (1860).

Barton, Captain F. R., in C. G. Seligmann's *The Melanesians of British New Guinea.* Cambridge, 1910.

Bartram, William, *Travels through North and South Carolina, Georgia, East and West Florida,* etc. London, 1792. *See also s.v.* "Observations on the Creek," etc.

Bartsch, Karl, *Sagen, Märchen und Gebräuche aus Mecklenburg.* Vienna, 1879–1880.

Basedow, Herbert, *Anthropological Notes on the Western Coastal Tribes of the Northern Territory of South Australia.* Separate reprint from the *Transactions of the Royal Society of South Australia,* vol. xxxi. (1907). Printed by Hussey and Gillingham, Adelaide.

Basile, G., *Pentamerone.* Übertragen von Felix Liebrecht. Breslau, 1846.

Basset, R., *Nouveaux Contes Berbères.* Paris, 1897.

Bastian, Adolf, *Allerlei aus Volks- und Menschenkunde.* Berlin, 1888.
"Beiträge zur Kenntniss der Gebirgsstämme in Kambodia," in *Zeitschrift der Gesellschaft für Erdkunde zu Berlin,* i. (1866).

Bastian, Adolf—*continued.*
  Der Mensch in der Geschichte. Leipsic, 1860.
  Der Voelker des oestlichen Asien. Leipsic and Jena, 1866–1871.
  Die Culturländer des alten Amerika. Berlin, 1878.
  Die deutsche Expedition an der Loango-Küste. Jena, 1874–1875.
  Die Seele und ihre Erscheinungswesen in der Ethnographie. Berlin, 1868.
  Die Völkerstämme am Brahmaputra. Berlin, 1883.
  Ein Besuch in San Salvador. Bremen, 1859.
  "Hügelstämme Assam's," in *Verhandlungen der Berliner Gesellschaft für Anthropologie, Ethnologie, und Urgeschichte* (1881).
  Indonesien. Berlin, 1884–1889.
  in *Verhandlungen der Berliner Gesellschaft für Anthropologie, Ethnologie, und Urgeschichte,* 1870–1871.
Bataillon, Father, in *Annales de la Propagation de la Foi,* xiii. (1841).
Batchelor, Rev. John, *The Ainu and their Folk-lore.* London, 1901.
  The Ainu of Japan. London, 1892.
Bather, A. G., "The Problem of the Bacchae," in *Journal of Hellenic Studies,* xiv. (1904).
Battel, Andrew, "Strange Adventures of," in J. Pinkerton's *Voyages and Travels,* xvi. Also published by the Hakluyt Society. London, 1901.
Batten, G. G., *Glimpses of the Eastern Archipelago.* Singapore, 1894.
Batty, Mrs. R. B., and Maloney, Governor, "Notes on the Yoruba Country," in *Journal of the Anthropological Institute,* xix. (1890).
Baudin, Le R. P., "Féticheurs ou ministres religieux des Nègres de la Guinée," in *Les Missions Catholiques,* No. 787 (4 juillet 1884).
  "Le Fétichisme ou la religion des Nègres de la Guinée," in *Les Missions Catholiques,* xvi. (1884).
Baudin, N., Letter dated 16th April 1875, in *Missions Catholiques,* vii. (1875).
Baudissin, W. W. Graf von, *Adonis und Esmun.* Leipsic, 1911.
  Studien zur semitischen Religionsgeschichte. Leipsic, 1876–1878.
  s.v. "Tammuz" in *Realencyclopädie für protestantische Theologie und Kirchengeschichte.* Third Edition.
Baudrouin, M., et Bonnemère, L., "Les haches polies dans l'histoire jusqu'au XIXe siècle," in *Bulletins et Mémoires de la Société d'Anthropologie de Paris,* Vme Série, v. (1904).
Baumann, Oscar, *Durch Massailand zur Nilquelle.* Berlin, 1894.
  Eine afrikanische Tropen-Insel, Fernando Pôo und die Bube. Wien und Olmütz, 1888.
  Usambara und seine Nachbargebiete. Berlin, 1891.
Baumeister, A., *Denkmäler des klassischen Altertums.* Munich and Leipsic, 1885–1888.
  Hymni Homerici. Leipsic, 1860.
Bautz, Dr. Joseph, *Die Hölle, im Anschluss an die Scholastik dargestellt.* Second Edition. Mainz, 1905.
Bavaria, Landes- und Volkskunde des Königreichs Bayern. Munich, 1860–1867.
Bayfield, M. A., in *Classical Review,* xv. (1901).
Bazin, quoted by Breuil, in *Mémoires de la Société d'Antiquaires de Picardie,* viii. (1845).
Beardmore, E., "The Natives of Mowat, Daudai, British New Guinea," in *Journal of the Anthropological Institute,* xix. (1890).
Beatty, A., "The St. George, or Mummers', Plays," in *Transactions of the Wisconsin Academy of Sciences, Arts, and Letters,* xv. part. ii. (October 1906).
Beauchamp, W. M., "The Iroquois White Dog Feast," in *American Antiquarian,* vii. (1885).
Beauchet, L., *Histoire du droit privé de la République Athénienne.* Paris, 1897.
Beaufort, in *Journal of the Anthropological Institute,* xv. (1886).
Beaufort, Fr., *Karmania.* London, 1817.

Beaulieu, L., *Archéologie de la Lorraine.* Paris, 1840–1843.
Beauquier, Charles, *Les Mois en Franche-Comté.* Paris, 1900.
Bechstein, L., *Deutsches Sagenbuch.* Leipsic, 1853.
  Thüringer Sagenbuch. Leipsic, 1885.
Becker, Jérôme, *La Vie en Afrique.* Paris and Brussels, 1887.
Bede, *Historia ecclesiastica gentis Anglorum.*
Beech, Mervyn W. H., *The Suk, their Language and Folklore.* Oxford, 1911.
Beechey, F. W., *Narrative of a Voyage to the Pacific and Beering's Strait.* London, 1831.
Beguelin, M. v., "Religiöse Volksbräuche der Mongolen," in *Globus*, lvii. (1890).
Béguin, Eugène, *Les Ma-rotsé.* Lausanne and Fontaines, 1903.
Beiderbecke, Rev. H., "Some Religious Ideas and Customs of the Ovahereros," in *(South African) Folk-lore Journal*, ii. Cape Town, 1880.
Bekker, Im., *Anecdota Graeca.* Berlin, 1814–1821.
Beleth (Belethus), John, *Rationale Divinorum Officiorum.* Appended to the *Rationale Divinorum Officiorum* of G. [W.] Durandus. Lyons, 1584.
Bell, Charles N., "The Mosquito Territory," in *Journal of the Royal Geographical Society*, xxxii. (1862).
Bellamy, Dr., "Notes ethnographiques recueillies dans le Haut-Sénégal," in *Revue d'Ethnographie*, v. (1886).
Beloch, J., *Der italische Bund unter Roms Hegemonie.* Leipsic, 1880.
Benfey, Theodor, *Pantschatantra.* Leipsic, 1859.
Benndorf, O., "Das Alter des Trojaspieles," appended to W. Reichel's *Über homerische Waffen.* Vienna, 1894.
Benndorf, O., and Schoene, R., *Die antiken Bildwerke des Lateranischen Museums.*
Bennett, George, *Wanderings in New South Wales, Batavia, Pedir Coast, Singapore and China.* London, 1834.
Bensen, quoted by J. Kohler, "Das Recht der Herero," in *Zeitschrift für vergleichende Rechtswissenschaft*, xiv. (1900).
Benson, E. F., in letter to the Author (ii. 52 n.⁴).
Bent, J. Theodore, "A Journey in Cilicia Tracheia," in *Journal of Hellenic Studies*, xii. (1891).
  "Cilician Symbols," in *Classical Review*, iv. (1890).
  "Explorations in Cilicia Tracheia," in *Proceedings of the Royal Geographical Society*, N.S., xii. (1890).
  quoted by Miss J. E. Harrison, *Mythology and Monuments of Ancient Athens.*
  "Recent Discoveries in Eastern Cilicia," in *Journal of Hellenic Studies*, xi. (1890).
  Sacred City of the Ethiopians. London, 1893.
  The Cyclades. London, 1885.
  "The Yourouks of Asia Minor," in *Journal of the Anthropological Institute*, xx. (1891).
*Bentley, R., "Sermon on Popery," quoted in J. H. Monk's *Life of Bentley.* Second Edition. London, 1833.
Bentley, Rev. W. H., *Life on the Congo.* London, 1887.
  Pioneering on the Congo. London, 1900.
Benzinger, J., *Hebräische Archäologie.* Freiburg im Baden and Leipsic, 1894.
Benzoni, G., *History of the New World.* Hakluyt Society. London, 1857.
Béraud, "Note sur le Dahomé," in *Bulletin de la Société de Géographie* (Paris), Vme Série, xii. (1866).
Bérenger-Féraud, L. J. B., in *Bulletins de la Société d'Anthropologie de Paris*, Quatrième Série, i. (1890).
  Les Peuplades de la Sénégambie. Paris, 1879.

BIBLIOGRAPHY 13

Bérenger-Féraud, L. J. B.—*continued.*
 Reminiscences populaires de la Provence. Paris, 1885.
 Superstitions et survivances. Paris, 1896.
Bérenger-Féraud and de Mortillet, in *Bulletins de la Société d'Anthropologie de Paris,* 4me série, ii. (1891).
Bérengier, Dom Théophile, "Croyances superstitieuses dans le pays de Chitta-gong," in *Les Missions Catholiques,* xiii. (1881).
 "Les funérailles à Chittagong," in *Les Missions Catholiques,* xiii. (1881).
 in *Les Missions Catholiques,* x. (1878).
Berg, L. W. C. van den, "De Mohammedaansche Vorsten in Nederlandsch-Indië," in *Bijdragen tot de Taal- Land- en Volkenkunde van Nederlandsch-Indië,* liii. (1901).
Bergk, Th., *Poetae Lyrici Graeci.* Third Edition. Leipsic, 1867.
Bergmann, B., *Nomadische Streifereien unter den Kalmücken.* Riga, 1804–1805.
Berichte über die Verhandlungen der Königlich Sächsischen Gesellschaft der Wissenschaften zu Leipsic, Philologisch-historische Klasse.
Berliner philologische Wochenschrift.
Bernau, Rev. J. H., *Missionary Labours in British Guiana.* London, 1847.
Berosus, in *Fragmenta Historicorum Graecorum,* ed. C. Müller, vol. ii.
 cited by Clement of Alexandria, *Protreptica,* v. Ed. Potter.
 quoted by Eusebius, *Chronicorum liber prior.* Ed. A. Schoene. Berlin, 1875.
Bertrand, A., *The Kingdom of the Barotsi, Upper Zambesia.* London, 1899.
Bertrand, Alexandre, *La Religion des Gaulois.* Paris, 1897.
Bertrand, J., in *Annales de la Propagation de la Foi,* xxii. (1850).
Bessels, E., in *American Naturalist,* xviii. (1884).
Best, Elsdon, "Maori Nomenclature," in *Journal of the Anthropological Institute,* xxxii. (1902).
 "Spiritual Concepts of the Maori," in *Journal of the Polynesian Society,* ix. (1900).
 quoted by W. H. Goldie, "Maori Medical Lore," *Transactions and Proceedings of the New Zealand Institute,* xxxvii. (1904).
Beuster, "Das Volk der Vawenda," in *Zeitschrift der Gesellschaft für Erdkunde zu Berlin,* xiv. (1879).
Bevan, Professor A. A. Private communications (ii. 210 *n.,* iii. 302 *n.*[4], ix. 367 *n.*[2], x. 83 *n.*[1]).
Beveridge, P., "Notes on the Dialects, Habits, and Mythology of the Lower Murray Aborigines," in *Transactions of the Royal Society of Victoria,* vi.
 "Of the Aborigines inhabiting the Great Lacustrine and Riverine Depression of the Lower Murray, Lower Murrumbidgee, Lower Lachlan, and Lower Darling," in *Journal and Proceedings of the Royal Society of New South Wales for 1883,* xvii. Sydney, 1884.
Beverley, Robert, *History of Virginia.* London, 1722.
Bezzenberger, A., *Litauische Forschungen.* Göttingen, 1882.
Biddulph, Major J., *Tribes of the Hindoo Koosh.* Calcutta, 1880.
Biet, A., *Voyage de la France équinoxiale en l'Isle de Cayenne.* Paris, 1664.
Bigandet, Letter, dated March 1847, in *Annales de la Propagation de la Foi,* xx. (1848).
Bijdragen tot de Taal- Land- en Volkenkunde van Nederlandsch Indië.
Bilfinger, Gustav, *Untersuchungen über die Zeitrechnung der alten Germanen,* ii. *Das germanische Julfest.* Stuttgart, 1901.
Binetsch, G., "Beantwortung mehrerer Fragen über unser Ewe-Volk und seine Anschauungen," in *Zeitschrift für Ethnologie,* xxxviii. (1906).
Binger, Le Capitaine, *Du Niger au Golfe de Guinée par le pays de Kong et le Mossi.* Paris, 1892.
Bingham, J., *The Antiquities of the Christian Church.*
 Works. Oxford, 1855.

*Bingley, William, *Tour Round North Wales* (1800), quoted by T. F. Thisleton Dyer, *British Popular Customs*. London, 1876.

Binterim, A. J., *Die vorzüglichsten Denkwürdigkeiten der Christ-Katholischen Kirche*. Mayence, 1829.

Bion, *Carmina*. Ed. Chr. Ziegler. Tübingen, 1868.

Birch, S., in Sir J. G. Wilkinson's *Manners and Customs of the Ancient Egyptians*. London, 1878.

Bird, Isabella L., *Unbeaten Tracks in Japan*. New Edition, 1885.

Birks, Rev. E. B. Private communication (v. 237 *n.*[1]).

Birlinger, Anton, *Aus Schwaben*. Wiesbaden, 1874.

Volksthümliches aus Schwaben. Freiburg im Breisgau, 1861–1862.

Bischof, E. F., "De fastis Graecorum antiquioribus," in *Leipziger Studien für classische Philologie*, vii. Leipsic, 1884.

Bishop, Mrs. (Isabella L. Bird), *Korea and her Neighbours*. London, 1898.

Bisset, Rev. Dr. Thomas, "Parish of Logierait," in Sir John Sinclair's *Statistical Account of Scotland*, iii. Edinburgh, 1792.

in Sir John Sinclair's *Statistical Account of Scotland*, v. Edinburgh, 1793.

Black, Dr. J. Sutherland, in letters to the Author (iv. 260 *sq.*).

Black, W. G., *Folk-Medicine*. London, 1883.

Blackwood's Magazine.

Bladé, J. F., *Contes populaires recueillis en Agenais*. Paris, 1874.

Quatorze superstitions populaires de la Gascogne. Agen, 1883.

Bland, J. O. P., in letter to the Author (iv. 274 *sq.*).

Blandowski, W., "Personal Observations made in an Excursion towards the Central Parts of Victoria," in *Transactions of the Philosophical Society of Victoria*, i. Melbourne, 1855.

Bleek, W. H. I., *A Brief Account of Bushman Folklore*. London, 1875.

Reynard the Fox in South Africa. London, 1864.

Bleek, W. H. I., Ph.D., and Lloyd, L. C., *Specimens of Bushman Folklore*. London, 1911.

Blinkenberg, Chr., *The Thunderweapon in Religion and Folk-lore*. Cambridge, 1911.

Bloomfield, M., *Hymns of the Atharva-Veda*. Oxford, 1897. (*Sacred Books of the East*, vol. xlii.)

"On the 'Frog Hymn,' Rig Veda, vii. 103," in *Journal of the American Oriental Society*, xvii. (1896).

Blumentritt, F., "Das Stromgebiet des Rio Grande de Mindanao," in *Petermanns Mitteilungen*, xxxvii. (1891).

"Der Ahnencultus und die religiösen Anschauungen der Malaien des Philippinen-Archipels," in *Mittheilungen der Wiener Geographischen Gesellschaft* (1882).

"Sitten und Bräuche der Ilocanen," in *Globus*, xlviii. No. 12.

"Über die Eingeborenen der Insel Palawan und der Inselgruppe der Talamianen," in *Globus*, lix. (1891).

Versuch einer Ethnographie der Philippinen. Gotha, 1882. (*Petermanns Mittheilungen, Ergänzungsheft*, No. 67.)

Blümner, H., *Technologie und Terminologie der Gewerbe und Künste bei Griechen und Römern*. Leipsic, 1875–1887.

Blunt, J. J., *Vestiges of Ancient Manners and Customs discoverable in Modern Italy and Sicily*. London, 1823.

Boas, Franz, *Chinook Texts*. Washington, 1894.

"Die Sagen der Baffin-land Eskimo," in *Verhandlungen der Berliner Gesellschaft für Anthropologie, Ethnologie, und Urgeschichte* (1885).

Indianische Sagen von der Nord-Pacifischen Küste Amerikas. Berlin, 1895.

in *Journal of American Folk-lore*, i. (1888).

in *Reports on the North-Western Tribes of Canada*. Separate reprints from the *Reports of the British Association for the Advancement of Science*, 1890–1898.

BIBLIOGRAPHY 15

Boas, Franz—*continued.*
"The Central Eskimo," in *Sixth Annual Report of the Bureau of Ethnology.*
Washington, 1888.
"The Eskimo," in *Proceedings and Transactions of the Royal Society of Canada for 1887*, v. Montreal, 1888.
"The Eskimo of Baffin Land and Hudson Bay," in *Bulletin of the American Museum of Natural History*, xv. part i. New York, 1901.
"The Social Organization and the Secret Societies of the Kwakiutl Indians," in *Report of the United States National Museum for 1895*. Washington, 1897.
Boas, Franz, and Hunt, George, *Kwakiutl Texts.* (*The Jesup North Pacific Expedition, Memoir of the American Museum of Natural History*, December 1902.)
Boas Anniversary Volume. New York, 1906.
Bochart, S., *Hierozoicon.* Editio Tertia. Leyden, 1692.
Bock, C., *Temples and Elephants.* London, 1884.
The Head-hunters of Borneo. London, 1881.
Bodding, P. O., "Ancient Stone Implements in the Santal Parganas," in *Journal of the Asiatic Society of Bengal*, lxx. part iii. (1901).
Bodenschatz, J. Chr. G., *Kirchliche Verfassung der heutigen Juden.* Erlangen, 1748.
Boeckh, Aug., on Pindar, *Explicationes.* Leipsic, 1821.
Boecler-Kreutzwald, *Der Ehsten abergläubische Gebräuche, Weisen und Gewohnheiten.* St. Petersburg, 1854. (The work of two writers, J. W. Boecler and F. R. Kreutzwald.)
Boemus, Johannes, *Mores, leges, et ritus omnium gentium.* Lyons, 1541.
Omnium gentium mores, leges, et ritus. Paris, 1538.
Boers, J. W., "Oud volksgebruik in het Rijk van Jambi," in *Tijdschrift voor Neêrlands Indië* (1840), deel i.
Boetticher, C., *Der Baumkultus der Hellenen.* Berlin, 1856.
Bogle, George. *See s.v. Narratives.*
Bogoras, Waldemar, "The Chukchee," in *Memoir of the American Museum of Natural History, The Jesup North Pacific Expedition*, vol. vii. Leyden and New York, 1904–1909.
"The Chukchee Religion," in *Memoir of the American Museum of Natural History, The Jesup North Pacific Expedition*, vol. vii. part ii. Leyden and New York, 1904.
Boileau, F. F. R., "The Nyasa-Tanganyika Plateau," in *The Geographical Journal*, xiii. (1899).
Boisse, E., "Les îles Samoa, Nukunono, Fakaafo, Wallis et Hoorn," in *Bulletin de la Société de Géographie* (Paris), 6ème Série, x. (1875).
Boissier, G., *La Religion Romaine d'Auguste aux Antonins.* Fifth Edition. Paris, 1900.
Boletino del Instituto Geografico Argentino.
Boni, G., *Aedes Vestae.* Extract from the *Nuova Antologia*, 1st August 1900.
"Bimbi Romulei," in *Nuova Antologia*, 16th February 1904. Separate reprint.
in *Notizie degli Scavi*, May 1900.
Bonnemère, L., "Le Jour des Rois en Normandie," in *Revue des Traditions populaires*, ii. (1887).
Bonney, F., "On some Customs of the Aborigines of the River Darling, New South Wales," in *Journal of the Anthropological Institute*, xiii. (1884).
Bonwick, James, *Daily Life and Origin of the Tasmanians.* London, 1870.
Book of Rights. Edited with translation and notes by John O'Donovan. Dublin, 1847.
Book of Ser Marco Polo. Newly translated and edited by Colonel Henry Yule. Second Edition. London, 1875.

Book of the Dead. Translated by E. A. Wallis Budge. London, 1901.

Boot, J., " Korte schets der noordkust van Ceram," in *Tijdschrift van het Nederlandsch Aardrijkskundig Genootschap,* Tweede Serie, x. (1893).

Boot, J. C. G., in *Verslagen en Mededeelingen der koninklijke Akademie van Wetenschappen, Afdeeling Letterkunde,* III. Reeks, xii. deel. Amsterdam, 1895.

Borchardt, L., " Der ägyptische Titel ' Vater des Gottes' als Bezeichnung für ' Vater oder Schwiegervater des Königs,' " in *Berichte über die Verhandlungen der Königlichen Sächsischen Gesellschaft der Wissenschaften zu Leipzig, Philologisch-historische Klasse,* lvii. (1905).

Borde, Le Sieur de la, " Relation de l'Origine, Mœurs, Coustumes, Religion, Guerres et Voyages des Caraïbes sauvages des Isles Antilles de l'Amerique," in *Recueil de divers Voyages faits en Afrique et en l'Amerique, qui n'ont point esté encore publiez.* Paris, 1684.

Borie, " Notice sur les Mantras, tribu sauvage de la péninsule Malaise," in *Tijdschrift voor Indische Taal- Land- en Volkenkunde,* x. (1860).

Borlase, William, LL.D., *Antiquities, Historical and Monumental, of the County of Cornwall.* London, 1769.

The Natural History of Cornwall. Oxford, 1758.

Bormann, A., *Altitalische Chorographie.* Halle, 1852.

Bosanquet, Professor R. C. Private communication (vi. 250 *n.*[2]).

Boscana, Father Geronimo, "Chinigchinich ; a historical account of the origin, customs, and traditions of the Indians at the missionary establishment of St. Juan Capistrano, Alta California." Appended to [Alfred Robinson's] *Life in California.* New York, 1846.

Bose, Shib Chunder, *The Hindoos as they are.* London and Calcutta, 1881.

Bosman, W., " Description of the Coast of Guinea," in J. Pinkerton's *Voyages and Travels,* xvi. London, 1814.

Bosquet, Amélie, *La Normandie romanesque et merveilleuse.* Paris and Rouen, 1845.

Bossu, *Nouveaux Voyages aux Indes Occidentales.* Paris, 1768.

Bossuet, Bishop, " Catéchisme du diocèse de Meaux," in vol. vi. of his *Œuvres* (Versailles, 1815–1819).

Boswell, J., *Life of Samuel Johnson.* Ninth Edition. London, 1822.

Bottrell, William, *Traditions and Hearthside Stories of West Cornwall.* Penzance, 1870.

Bouche, Pierre, *La Côte des Esclaves et le Dahomey.* Paris, 1885.

Bourien, M., " Wild Tribes of the Malay Peninsula," in *Transactions of the Ethnological Society of London,* N.S., iii. (1865).

Bourke, Captain J. G., in letter to the Author (viii. 178 *n.*[4]).

" Notes upon the Religion of the Apache Indians," in *Folk-lore,* ii. (1891). *On the Border with Crook.* New York, 1891.

" The Medicine-men of the Apache," in *Ninth Annual Report of the Bureau of Ethnology.* Washington, 1892.

The Snake Dance of the Moquis of Arizona. London, 1884.

Bourlet, A., " Funérailles chez les Thay," in *Anthropos,* viii. (1913).

" Les Thay," in *Anthropos,* ii. (1907).

Bowdich, T. E., *Mission from Cape Coast Castle to Ashantee.* New Edition. London, 1873.

Bowring, Sir John, LL.D., *The Kingdom and People of Siam.* London, 1857.

Bradbury, Professor J. B. Private communication (ii. 139 *n.*[1]).

Braga, Theophilo, *O Povo Portuguez nos seus Costumes, Crenças e Tradições.* Lisbon, 1885.

Brand, John, *Popular Antiquities of Great Britain.* London, 1882–1883. Bohn's Edition.

Brandes, J., " Iets over het Papegaai-boek, zooals het bij de Maleiers voorkomt," in *Tijdschrift voor Indische Taal- Land- en Volkenkunde,* xli. (1899).

Brandt, Von, "The Ainos and Japanese," in *Journal of the Anthropological Institute*, iii. (1874).

Brard, "Der Victoria-Nyansa," in *Petermanns Mittheilungen*, xliii. (1897).

Brasseur de Bourbourg, "Aperçus d'un voyage dans les États de San-Salvador et de Guatemala," in *Bulletin de la Société de Géographie* (Paris), IVème Série, xiii. (1857).

Histoire des nations civilisées du Mexique et de l'Amérique-Centrale. Paris, 1857–1859.

*Bray, Mrs., *Traditions of Devon*, referred to by Miss C. S. Burne and Miss G. F. Jackson, *Shropshire Folk-lore*. London, 1883.

Braz, A. le, *La Légende de la Mort en Basse-Bretagne.* Paris, 1893.

Breasted, J. H., *A History of the Ancient Egyptians.* London, 1908.

Ancient Records of Egypt. Chicago, 1906–1907.

Development of Religion and Thought in Ancient Egypt. London, 1912.

Brebeuf, J. de, in *Relations des Jésuites*, 1636. Canadian reprint. Quebec, 1858.

Breeks, J. W., *An Account of the Primitive Tribes and Monuments of the Nīlagiris.* London, 1873.

Brenner, Joachim Freiherr von, *Besuch bei den Kannibalen Sumatras.* Würzburg, 1894.

Bresciani, Antonio, *Dei costumi dell' isola di Sardegna comparati cogli antichissimi popoli orientali.* Rome and Turin, 1866.

Brett, "Dans la Corée septentrionale," in *Les Missions Catholiques*, xxxi. (1899).

Breuil, A., "Du Culte de St Jean-Baptiste," in *Mémoires de la Société des Antiquaires de Picardie*, viii. Amiens, 1845.

Bricknell, J., *The Natural History of North Carolina.* Dublin, 1737.

Brien, "Aperçu sur la province de Battambang," in *Cochinchine Française*: *excursions et reconnaissances*, No. 25. Saigon, 1886.

Brincker, Missionar P. H., "Beobachtungen über die Deisidämonie der Eingeborenen Deutsch-Südwest-Afrikas," in *Globus*, lviii. (1890).

"Charakter, Sitten und Gebräuche, speciell der Bantu Deutsch Südwestafrikas," in *Mittheilungen des Seminars für orientalische Sprachen zu Berlin*, iii. (1900), Dritte Abtheilung.

"Heidnisch-religiöse Sitten der Bantu, speciell der Ovaherero und Ovambo," in *Globus*, lxvii. (1895).

"Pyrolatrie in Südafrika," in *Globus*, lxvii. (January 1895).

Wörterbuch und kurzgefasste Grammatik des Otji-herero. Leipsic, 1886.

Bringaud, "Les Karens de la Birmanie," in *Les Missions Catholiques*, xx. (1888).

Brinton, Daniel G., *Myths of the New World.* Second Edition. New York, 1876.

"Nagualism, a Study in American Folk-lore and History," in *Proceedings of the American Folk-lore Society held at Philadelphia*, vol. xxxiii. No. 144. Philadelphia, January 1894.

"The Folk-lore of Yucatan," in *Folk-lore Journal*, i. (1883).

British Central Africa Gazette.

British New Guinea, Annual Report for 1894–1895.

Broadwood, Lucy E., in *Folk-lore*, iv. (1893).

Brockelmann, C., "Das Neujahrsfest der Jezîdîs," in *Zeitschrift der Deutschen Morgenländischen Gesellschaft*, lv. (1901).

"Wesen und Ursprung des Eponymats in Assyrien," in *Zeitschrift für Assyriologie*, xvi. (1902).

*Brockett, J. T., *Glossary of North Country Words*, quoted by Mrs. M. C. Balfour, in *County Folk-lore*, vol. iv. *Northumberland.*

*First Edition of the *Glossary* published in 1825.

Broeck, T. G. S. Ten, in H. R. Schoolcraft's *Indian Tribes of the United States.* Philadelphia, 1853–1856.

Brooke, Charles, *Ten Years in Sarawak.* London, 1866.
Brown, A. R., "Beliefs concerning Childbirth in some Australian Tribes," in *Man*, xii. (1912).
"Three Tribes of Western Australia," in *Journal of the Royal Anthropological Institute*, xliii. (1913).
Brown, Dr. Burton. Private communication (viii. 100 *n.*[2]).
Brown, George, D.D., *Melanesians and Polynesians.* London, 1910.
"Notes on the Duke of York Group, New Britain, and New Ireland," in *Journal of the Royal Geographical Society*, xlvii. (1877).
quoted by the Rev. B. Danks, "Marriage Customs of the New Britain Group," in *Journal of the Anthropological Institute*, xviii. (1889).
Brown, W., *New Zealand and its Aborigines.* London, 1845.
Brown, F., Driver, S. R., and Briggs, Ch. A., *Hebrew and English Lexicon of the Old Testament.* Oxford, 1906.
Browne, W. G., *Travels in Africa, Egypt, and Syria.* London, 1799.
Bruchhausen, K. v., in *Globus*, lxxvi. (1899).
Brückner, A., in *Archiv für slavische Philologie*, 1886.
Brugsch, H., "Das Osiris-Mysterium von Tentyra," in *Zeitschrift für ägyptische Sprache und Altertumskunde*, xix. (1881).
Die Adonisklage und das Linoslied. Berlin, 1852.
Die Ägyptologie. Leipsic, 1891.
Religion und Mythologie der alten Ägypter. Leipsic, 1885–1888.
Bruguière, Mgr., in *Annales de l'Association de la Propagation de la Foi*, v. (1831), ix. (1836).
Brun-Rollet, *La Nil blanc et le Soudan.* Paris, 1855.
Brunn, H., *Geschichte der griechischen Künstler.* Stuttgart, 1857–1859.
Bruns, C. G., *Fontes Juris Romani.* Seventh Edition. Ed. O. Gradenwitz. Tübingen, 1909.
Buch, Max, *Die Wotjäken.* Stuttgart, 1882.
Buchanan, Francis, "A Journey from Madras through the Countries of Mysore, Canara, and Malabar," in J. Pinkerton's *Voyages and Travels*, viii. London, 1811.
"On the Religion and Literature of the Burmas," in *Asiatick Researches*, vi. London, 1801.
Buchanan, J., *The Shire Highlands.* London, 1885.
Budde, K., *Geschichte der althebräischen Litteratur.* Leipsic, 1906.
Buddingh, S. A., "Gebruiken bij Javaansche Grooten," in *Tijdschrift voor Neêrlands Indië*, 1840.
Budge, E. A. Wallis, *Egyptian Magic.* London, 1899.
Nebuchadnezzar, King of Babylon, on recently-discovered Inscriptions of this King.
"On the Hieratic Papyrus of Nesi-Amsu, a scribe in the Temple of Amen-Rā at Thebes, about B.C. 305," in *Archaeologia*, Second Series, ii. (1890).
Osiris and the Egyptian Resurrection. London and New York, 1911.
The Book of the Dead. London, 1895.
Second Edition. London, 1909.
The Gods of the Egyptians. London, 1904.
Bugge, Sophus, *Studien über die Entstehung der nördischen Götter- und Heldensagen.* Munich, 1889.
Bühler, G., *Grundriss der indo-arischen Philologie.*
in *Orient und Occident*, i. (1862).
"On the Hindu god Parjanya," in *Transactions of the (London) Philological Society* (1859).
*Buléon, Mgr., *Sous le ciel d'Afrique, Récits d'un Missionnaire*, quoted by Father H. Trilles, *Le Totémisme chez les Fân.* Munster i. W., 1912.
Bulletin de Correspondance hellénique.

Bulletin de la Classe historico-philologique de l'Académie Impériale des Sciences de St-Pétersbourg.
Bulletin de l'École Française d'Extrême-Orient. Hanoi.
Bulletins de la Société d'Anthropologie de Paris.
Bulletin de la Société de Géographie (Paris).
Bulletin of the American Museum of Natural History.
Bulletin of the Northern Territory, No. 2. Melbourne, 1912.
Bulletino dell' Instituto di Corrispondenza Archeologica.
Bulletins et Mémoires de la Société d'Anthropologie de Paris.
Bulmer, J., in R. Brough Smyth's *Aborigines of Victoria*, ii. Melbourne, 1878.
Bunbury, E. H., *s.vv.* "Algidus," "Palicorum lacus," "Tifata," "Timavus," in W. Smith's *Dictionary of Greek and Roman Geography.*
Bunsen, Chr. C. J., Baron, *Hippolytus and his Age.* London, 1852.
Bureau of American Ethnology. Annual Reports and *Bulletins.*
Burne, Miss C. S., "Herefordshire Notes," in *The Folk-lore Journal*, iv. (1886).
Burne, Miss C. S., and Jackson, Miss G. F., *Shropshire Folk-lore.* London, 1883.
Burns, Robert, "Hallowe'en."
"John Barleycorn."
Burrows, Captain Guy, *The Land of the Pigmies.* London, 1898.
Burrows, R. M., *The Discoveries in Crete.* London, 1907.
Bursian, C., *Geographie von Griechenland.* Leipsic, 1862–1872.
Burton, Lady. Life of her husband referred to by W. G. Aston, *Shinto.* London, 1905.
Burton, R. F., *Abeokuta and the Cameroons Mountains.* London, 1863.
in *The Captivity of Hans Stade of Hesse.* Hakluyt Society. London, 1874.
["My Wanderings in Africa"] in *Fraser's Magazine*, lxvii. (April 1863).
Burton-Brown, Mrs. E., *Recent Excavations in the Roman Forum.* London, 1904.
Bury, J. B., *The Life of St. Patrick.* London, 1905.
Busk, R. H., *The Folk-lore of Rome.* London, 1874.
Busolt, G., *Griechische Geschichte.* Gotha, 1893–
Bussel, Mr., in Sir G. Grey's *Journals of Two Expeditions of Discovery in North-West and Western Australia.* London, 1841.
*Busuttil, V., *Holiday Customs in Malta, and Sports, Usages, Ceremonies, Omens, and Superstitions of the Maltese People.* Malta, 1894.
Büttikoffer, J., "Einiges über die Eingebornen von Liberia," in *Internationales Archiv für Ethnographie*, i. (1888).
Buttmann, P., *Mythologus.* Berlin, 1828–1829.
Büttner, C. G., "Ueber Handwerke und technische Fertigkeiten der Einge-borenen in Damaraland," in *Ausland*, 7th July 1884.
Das Hinterland von Walfischbai und Angra Pequena. Heidelberg, 1884.
*Buttrick, *Antiquities*, quoted by J. Mooney, "Myths of the Cherokee," in *Nineteenth Annual Report of the Bureau of American Mythology*, Part I. Washington, 1900.
Buxtorf, J., *Synagoga Judaica.* Bâle, 1661.
Byrne, H. J., "All Hallows Eve and other Festivals in Connaught," in *Folk-lore*, xviii. (1907).
Byron, Lord. *Works.* Collected Edition. London, 1832–1833.

Cabaton, A., *Nouvelles Recherches sur les Chams.* Paris, 1901.
Cabeça de Vaca, A. N., *Relation et Naufrages* (Paris, 1837), in Ternaux-Compans's *Voyages, Relations et Mémoires originaux pour servir à l'histoire de la découverte de l'Amérique.*
*Cadamosto, Alvise da, *Relazione dei viaggi d'Africa*, quoted by Giuseppe Ferraro, *Superstizioni, Usi e Proverbi Monferrino.* Palermo, 1886.

Cadière, Le R. P., "Coutumes populaires de la Vallée du Nguôn-So'n," in
    Bulletin de l'École Française d'Extrême-Orient, ii.   Hanoi, 1902.
"Croyances et dictons populaires de la Vallée du Nguôn-son, Province de
    Quang-binh (Annam)," in *Bulletin de l'École Française d'Extrême-*
    Orient, i.   Hanoi, 1901.
Caesar, *De bello Gallico.*
Caland, W., *Altindisches Zauberritual.*   Amsterdam, 1900.
    Die altindischen Todten- und Bestattungsgebräuche.   Amsterdam, 1896.
    Über Totenverehrung bei einigen der indo-germanischen Völker.   Amster-
    dam, 1888.
Calder, J. E., "Native Tribes of Tasmania," in *Journal of the Anthropological
    Institute*, iii. (1874).
Caldwell, Bishop R., "On Demonolatry in Southern India," in *Journal of the
    Anthropological Society of Bombay*, i.
*Calica Puran, The, quoted in *Asiatick Researches*, v.
Callaway, Rev. Canon Henry, *Nursery Tales, Traditions, and Histories of the
    Zulus.*   Natal and London, 1868.
    The Religious System of the Amazulu.   Natal, Springvale, etc., 1868–1870
    (incomplete).
Callimachea.   Edidit O. Schneider.   Leipsic, 1870–1873.
Callimachus, *Hymn to Apollo.*
    Hymn to Artemis.
    Hymn to Delos.
    Hymn to Diana.
    Hymn to Zeus.
    referred to by the * Old Scholiast on Ovid, *Ibis.*
Callone, J. B. de, "Iets over de geneeswijze en ziekten der Daijakers ter Zuid
    Oostkust van Borneo," in *Tijdschrift voor Neêrlands Indië* (1840).
Calpurnius, *Bucolica.*
Calpurnius Piso, L.   Fragments in *Fragmenta Historicorum Romanorum.*
    Ed. H. Peter.   Leipsic, 1883.
Cambridge Bible for Schools and Colleges.
Camden, W., *Britannia.*   London, 1607.
    Britain.   Translated into English by Philemon Holland.   London, 1610.
    Translated by E. Gibson.   London, 1695.
    Ed. R. Gough.   London, 1779.
Cameron, A. L. P., "Notes on some Tribes of New South Wales," in *Journal
    of the Anthropological Institute*, xiv. (1885).
Cameron, Hugh E., in letter to the Author (vii. 162 *n.*[3]).
Cameron, J., "On the Early Inhabitants of Madagascar," in *Antananarivo
    Annual and Madagascar Magazine*, Reprint of the First Four Numbers.
    Antananarivo, 1885.
Cameron, J., *Our Tropical Possessions in Malayan India.*   London, 1865.
Cameron, Miss Morag, "Highland Fisher-folk and their Superstitions," in
    Folk-lore, xiv. (1903).
Cameron, Lieut. V. L., *Across Africa.*   London, 1877.
    in *Journal of the Anthropological Institute*, vi. (1877).
Campana, Father, "Congo ; Mission Catholique de Landana," in *Les Missions
    Catholiques*, xxvii. (1895).
Campbell, Major-General John, *Wild Tribes of Khondistan.*   London, 1864.
Campbell, Rev. John, *Travels in South Africa.*   London, 1815.
    *Travels in South Africa, being a Narrative of a Second Journey in the
    Interior of that Country.*   London, 1822.
Campbell, J. F., *Popular Tales of the West Highlands.*   Edinburgh, 1862.
    New Edition.   Paisley and London, 1890.
Campbell, Rev. John Gregorson, *Superstitions of the Highlands and Islands of
    Scotland.*   Glasgow, 1900.

Campbell, Rev. John Gregorson—*continued.*
Witchcraft and Second Sight in the Highlands and Islands of Scotland.
Glasgow, 1902.
Campen, C. F. H., "De Godsdienstbegrippen der Halmaherasche Alfoeren,"
in *Tijdschrift voor Indische Taal- Land- en Volkenkunde,* xxvii. (1882).
Campion, J. S., *On Foot in Spain.* London, 1879.
Canadian Journal (Toronto) for March 1858, quoted in *The Academy,* 27th
September 1884.
Candelier, H., *Rio-Hacha et les Indiens Goajires.* Paris, 1893.
Candolle, A. de, *Origin of Cultivated Plants.* London, 1884.
Canopic Decree, in W. Dittenberger's *Orientis Graeci Inscriptiones Selectae,*
vol. i. No. 56, and in Ch. Michel's *Recueil d'Inscriptions Grecques,*
No. 551.
Capart, Jean, "Bulletin critique des religions d'Égypte," in *Revue de l'Histoire
des Religions,* liii. (1906).
Les Débuts de l'Art en Égypte. Brussels, 1904.
Les Palettes en schiste de l'Égypte primitive. Brussels, 1908. (Separate
reprint from the *Revue des Questions Scientifiques,* avril 1908.)
Cappellan, S. D. van de Velde van, "Verslag eener Bezoekreis naar de Sangi-
eilanden," in *Mededeelingen van wege het Nederlandsche Zendeling-
genootschap,* i. (1857).
Captivity of Hans Stade of Hesse, in A.D. *1547–1555, among the Wild Tribes of
Eastern Brazil.* Translated by A. Tootal. Hakluyt Society. London,
1874.
Carapanos, C., *Dodone et ses ruines.* Paris, 1878.
Carceri, Stanislas, "Djebel-Nouba," in *Les Missions Catholiques,* xv. (1883).
Cardi, Le Comte C. N. de, "Ju-ju Laws and Customs in the Niger Delta," in
Journal of the Anthropological Institute, xxix. (1899).
Cardus, Father, quoted in J. Pelleschi's *Los Indios Matacos.* Buenos Ayres, 1897.
Carew, R., *Survey of Cornwall.* London, 1811.
Carey, Bertram S., and Tuck, H. N., *The Chin Hills.* Rangoon, 1896.
Carlyle, Thomas, *The French Revolution.*
Early Letters. Edited by C. E. Norton. London, 1886.
Carmichael, Alexander, *Carmina Gadelica, Hymns and Incantations with
Illustrative Notes on Words, Rites, and Customs, dying and obsolete :
orally collected in the Highlands and Islands of Scotland and translated
into English.* Edinburgh, 1900.
Carnoy, E. H., et Nicolaides, J., *Traditions populaires de l'Asie Mineure.*
Paris, 1889.
*Carol, J., *Chez les Hovas.* Paris, 1898. Quoted by A. van Gennep in *Tabou
et Totémisme à Madagascar.* Paris, 1904.
Caron, François, "Account of Japan," in John Pinkerton's *Voyages and Travels,*
vii. London, 1811.
Carpin, Jean du Plan de, *Historia Mongalorum.* Ed. D'Avezac. Paris, 1838.
*Carrichter, Bartholomäus, *Der Teutschen Speisskammer* (Strasburg, 1614),
quoted by C. L. Rochholz, *Deutscher Glaube und Brauch.* Berlin, 1867.
Carter, J. B., *s.v.* "Arval Brothers," in J. Hastings's *Encyclopaedia of Religion
and Ethics,* ii. Edinburgh, 1909.
Carver, Captain Jonathan, *Travels through the Interior Parts of North America.*
Third Edition. London, 1781.
Casalis, Rev. E., *The Basutos.* London, 1861.
Casati, G., *Ten Years in Equatoria.* London and New York, 1891.
Castelnau, Francis de, *Expédition dans les parties centrales de l'Amérique au
Sud.* Paris, 1850–1852.
Castren, M. Alex., *Ethnologische Vorlesungen über die altaischen Völker.* St.
Petersburg, 1857.
Vorlesungen über die finnische Mythologie. St. Petersburg, 1853.

Catat, Dr., in *Le Tour du Monde*, lxv. (1893).

Catlin, George, *Letters and Notes on the Manners, Customs, and Condition of the North American Indians.* Fourth Edition. London, 1844.

O-Kee-pa, a Religious Ceremony, and other Customs of the Mandans. London, 1867.

Cato, *De agri cultura.* Ed. H. Keil. Leipsic, 1884.

M. Catonis praeter librum de re rustica quae extant. Ed. H. Jordan. Leipsic, 1860.

Origines. Fragments in *Historicorum Romanorum Fragmenta*, ed. H. Peter. Leipsic, 1883.

Catullus. Ed. R. Ellis. Oxford, 1878.

Cauer, P., *Delectus Inscriptionum Graecarum propter dialectum memorabilium.* Second Edition. Leipsic, 1883.

Caulin, Antonio, *Historia Corographica natural y evangelica dela Nueva Andalucia, Provincias de Cumaña, Guayana y Vertientes del Rio Orinoco.* 1779.

Cauvet, Éléments d'Histoire naturelle médicale, quoted by Prof. J. Veth, "De Leer der Signatuur," in *Internationales Archiv für Ethnographie*, vii. (1894).

Cavallius, G. O. H., und G. Stephens, *Schwedische Volkssagen und Märchen.* Deutsch von C. Oberleitner. Vienna, 1848.

Cayzac, Le P. P., "La Religion des Kikuyu," in *Anthropos*, v. (1905).

Cecchi, A., *Da Zeila alle frontiere del Caffa.* Rome, 1886–1887.

Cedrenus, G., *Historiarum Compendium.* Ed. Im. Bekker. Bonn, 1838–1839.

Cellini, Benvenuto, *Life*, translated by J. Addington Symonds. Third Edition. London, 1889.

Celsus, *De Medicina.* Ed. C. Daremberg. Leipsic, 1859.

Censorinus, *De die natali.* Ed. F. Hultsch. Leipsic, 1867.

Census of India, 1901, vol. iii. *The Andaman and Nicobar Islands.* Calcutta, 1903.

vol. xiii. *Central Provinces.* Nagpur, 1902.

vol. xv. *Madras*, Part I. Madras, 1902.

vol. xvii. *Punjab*, Part I. Simla, 1902.

vol. xxvi. *Travancore.* Trivandrum, 1903.

Census of India, 1911, vol. iii. *Assam*, Part I. *Report.* Shillong, 1912.

vol. xiv. *Punjab.* Lahore, 1912.

Central Provinces, Ethnographic Survey, I. *Draft Articles on Hindustani Castes.* Allahabad, 1907.

II. *Draft Articles on Uriya Castes.* Allahabad, 1907.

III. *Draft Articles on Forest Tribes.* Allahabad, 1907.

V. *Draft Articles on Forest Tribes.* Allahabad, 1911.

VI. *Draft Articles on Hindustani Castes.*

VII. *Draft Articles on Forest Tribes.* Allahabad, 1911.

Century Bible, The.

Century Illustrated Monthly Magazine.

Certeux, A., et Carnoy, E. H., *L'Algérie traditionnelle.* Paris and Algiers, 1884.

Cervantes, *Don Quixote.* Done into English by H. E. Watts. New Edition. London, 1895.

Cesnola, L. P. di, *Cyprus.* London, 1877.

Chabas, F., *Le Papyrus magique Harris.* Chalon-sur-Saône, 1860.

Chadwick, Professor H. Munro. Notes furnished to the Author.

The Cult of Othin. London, 1899.

"The Oak and the Thunder-god," in *Journal of the Anthropological Institute*, xxx. (1900).

The Origin of the English Nation. Cambridge, 1907.

Chaffanjon, J., *L'Orénoque et le Caura.* Paris, 1889.

Chaillu, P. B. du, *Explorations and Adventures in Equatorial Africa.* London, 1861.

Chalmers, Rev. J., "Notes on the Natives of Kiwai Island," in *Journal of the Anthropological Institute*, xxxiii. (1903).
    Pioneering in New Guinea. London, 1887.
    "Toaripi," in *Journal of the Anthropological Institute*, xxvii. (1898).
Chalmers, J., and Gill, W. Wyatt, *Work and Adventure in New Guinea.* London, 1885.
*Chalmers, W., *Some Account of the Land Dyaks of Upper Sarawak*, quoted in H. Ling Roth's *Natives of Sarawak and British North Borneo.* London, 1896.
Chamberlain, A. F., in *Eighth Report on the North-Western Tribes of Canada.* Separate reprint from the *Report of the British Association for 1892.*
Chambers, E. K., *The Mediaeval Stage.* Oxford, 1903.
Chambers, R., *Popular Rhymes of Scotland.* New Edition. London and Edinburgh, N.D.
    The Book of Days. London and Edinburgh, 1886.
*Chambers, *Edinburgh Journal*, cited by A. Kuhn, *Sagen, Gebräuche und Märchen aus Westfalen.* Leipsic, 1859.
Chambers's Encyclopaedia.
**Chambers's Journal*, July 1842, cited by W. Warde Fowler, *Roman Festivals of the Period of the Republic.* London, 1899.
Chandler, R., *Travels in Asia Minor.* Second Edition. London, 1776.
Chandler, Mrs. Samuel (Sarah Whateley), quoted in *The Folk-lore Journal*, i. (1883).
Chantre, E., *Mission en Cappadoce.* Paris, 1898.
Chapiseau, Felix, *Le Folk-lore de la Beauce et du Perche.* Paris, 1902.
Chapman, J., *Travels in the Interior of South Africa.* London, 1868.
Charax of Pergamus, in *Fragmenta Historicorum Graecorum*, ed. C. Müller, vol. iii.
Charency, Comte H. de, *Le Folklore dans les deux Mondes.* Paris, 1894.
Charlevoix, P. F. X. de, *Histoire de la Nouvelle France.* Paris, 1744.
    Histoire du Paraguay. Paris, 1756.
    Histoire et description generale du Japon. Paris, 1736.
    Voyage dans l'Amérique septentrionale. Paris, 1744. (Continuation in two vols. of *Histoire de la Nouvelle France.*)
Chase, quoted by H. H. Bancroft, *Native Races of the Pacific States*, i.
Chateaubriand, *Voyage en Amérique.* Paris, 1870.
Chatelin, L. N. H. A., "Godsdienst en bijgeloof der Niassers," in *Tijdschrift voor Indische Taal- Land- en Volkenkunde*, xxvi. (1880).
Chautard, Missionary, in *Annales de la Propagation de la Foi*, lv. (1883).
Chavannes, Ed., *Documents sur les Tou-Kiue (Turcs) Occidentaux.* St. Petersburg, 1903.
    Le T'ai Chan, Essai de Monographie d'un Culte Chinois. Paris, 1910. (*Annales du Musée Guimet, Bibliothèque d'Études*, vol. xxi.)
Chémali, L. Abbé Béchara, "Naissance et premier âge au Liban," in *Anthropos*, v. (1910).
Chevron, Missionary, in *Annales de la Propagation de la Foi*, xiii. (1841), xv. (1843).
Cheyne, Professor T. K., in letter to the Author (v. 20 *n.*[2]).
    s.vv. "Messiah," "Moriah," and "Nehushtan," in *Encyclopaedia Biblica*, iii.
Chimkievitch, "Chez les Bouriates de l'Amour," in *Tour du Monde*, N.S., iii. (1897).
China Review. Hongkong.
Chinese Recorder and Missionary Journal.
Chirol, Sir Valentine, in letter to the Author (iv. 274).
Chisholm, Dr. James A., "Notes on the Manners and Customs of the Winamwanga and Wiwa," in *Journal of the African Society*, vol. ix. No. 36 (July 1910).
Choerilus. Greek epic poet. Fragments in *Epicorum Graecorum Fragmenta.* Ed. G. Kinkel. Leipsic, 1877.

Chomé, Father Ignace, in *Lettres Édifiantes et Curieuses*, viii.   Nouvelle Edition. Paris, 1780–1783.

Chouville, Léon, of Rouen and Cambridge.   Private communication (ix. 315 *n.*[1]).

Christian, F. W., *The Caroline Islands*.   London, 1899.

Chronicle of Lanercost for the year 1268.
1 Chronicles.
2 Chronicles.

Church, Colonel G. E., *Aborigines of South America*.   London, 1912.

Church Missionary Record.

Chwolsohn, D., *Die Ssabier und der Ssabismus*.   St. Petersburg, 1856.
   Über Tammûz und die Menschenverehrung bei den alten Babyloniern. St. Petersburg, 1860.

*Ciantar's Supplements to Abelas's *Malta Illustrata*, quoted by R. Wünsch, *Das Frühlingsfest der Insel Malta*.   Leipsic, 1902.

Cicero, *Opera*.   Ed. J. G. Baiter et C. L. Kayser.   Leipsic, 1860–1869.
   Ad Atticum.
   Ad Familiares.
   De divinatione.
   De imperio Cn. Pompeii.
   De inventione.
   De legibus.
   De natura deorum.
   De re publica.
   In C. Verrem.
   In Pisonem.
   In Verrem.
   Paradoxa.
   Philippics.
   Pro L. Flacco.
   Pro Muraena.
   Pro Plancio.
   Tusculanae Disputationes.

Cichorius, *s.v.* "Cincius," in Pauly-Wissowa's *Real-encyclopädie der classischen Altertumswissenschaft*, iii.

Cieza de Leon, Pedro de, *Second Part of the Chronicle of Peru*.   Translated by (Sir) Clements R. Markham.   Hakluyt Society.   London, 1883.
   Travels.   Translated by (Sir) Clements R. Markham.   Hakluyt Society. London, 1864.

Cincius Alimentus, L., Roman historian.   Fragments in *Historicorum Romanorum Fragmenta*.   Ed. H. Peter.   Leipsic, 1883.

Cirbied, "Mémoire sur le gouvernement et sur la religion des anciens Arméniens," in *Mémoires publiés par la Société Royale des Antiquaires de France*, ii. (1820).

*Circular Letter addressed by the Faculty of Theology at Paris to the Bishops and Chapters of France, March 12th, 1445, quoted by E. K. Chambers, *The Mediaeval Stage*.   Oxford, 1903.

Ciszewski, Stanislaus, *Künstliche Verwandtschaft bei den Südslaven*.   Leipsic, 1897.

Clark, J. V. H., quoted by W. M. Beauchamp, "The Iroquois White Dog Feast," in *American Antiquarian*, vii. (1885).

Clark, M. S., "An Old South Pembrokeshire Harvest Custom," in *Folk-lore*, xv. (1904).

Clark, W. G., *Peloponnesus*.   London, 1858.

Clarke, E. D., *Travels in Various Countries of Europe, Asia, and Africa*. London, 1810.
   Second Edition.   London, 1813.
   Third Edition.   London, 1814.
   Fourth (octavo) Edition.   London, 1816.

Classical Review, The.

Clavel, Charles, *Les Marquisiens.* Paris, 1885.

Clavigero, F. S., *History of Mexico.* Translated by Charles Cullen. Second Edition. London, 1807.

Clearchus of Soli, quoted by Athenaeus. Greek historian. Fragments in *Fragmenta Historicorum Graecorum*, ed. C. Müller, vol. ii.

Clement, E., "Ethnographical Notes on the Western Australian Aborigines," in *Internationales Archiv für Ethnographie*, xvi. (1904).

Clément, Madame, *Histoire des fêtes civiles et religieuses*, etc., *de la Belgique Méridionale*, etc. Avesnes, 1846.

Histoire des fêtes civiles et religieuses, etc., *du Département du Nord.* Second Edition. Cambrai, 1836.

Clement of Alexandria, *Opera.* Ed. R. Klotz. Leipsic, 1831–1834.
Paedagogus.
Protrepticus.
Stromateis.

Clercq, F. S. A. de, *Bijdragen tot de Kennis der Residentie Ternate.* Leyden, 1890.
"De West- en Noordkust van Nederlandsch Nieuw-Guinea," in *Tijdschrift van het koninklijke Nederlandsch Aardrijkskundig Genootschap*, Tweede Serie, x. (1893).

Clicteur, in *Annales de l'Association de la Propagation de la Foi*, iv. (1830).

Clinton, H. F., *Fasti Hellenici.* Oxford, 1834–1851.

Clitarchus, cited by Suidas.
cited by the Scholiast on Plato, *Republic.*

Clodd, E., in *Folk-lore*, vi. (1895).
Myths and Dreams. London, 1885.
"The Philosophy of Punchkin," in *Folk-lore Journal*, ii. (1884).
Tom-tit-tot. London, 1898.

Clouston, W. A., *A Group of Eastern Romances and Stories.* Privately printed, 1889.
Popular Tales and Fictions. Edinburgh and London, 1887.

Cluverius, Ph., *Italia Antiqua.* Leyden, 1624.

Cochinchine française : Excursions et Reconnaissances. Saigon.

Cochran, W., *Pen and Pencil Sketches in Asia Minor.* London, 1887.

Code of Hammurabi, translated by C. H. W. Johns, *Babylonian and Assyrian Laws, Contracts and Letters.* Edinburgh, 1894.

Codex Theodosianus.

Codrington, R. H., D.D., "Notes on the Customs of Mota, Banks Islands," in *Transactions and Proceedings of the Royal Society of Victoria*, xvi. (1880).
"Religious Beliefs and Practices in Melanesia," in *Journal of the Anthropological Institute*, x. (1881).
The Melanesians. Oxford, 1891.

Coillard, "Voyage au pays des Banyais et au Zambèse," in *Bulletin de la Société de Géographie* (Paris), VIme Série, xx. (1880).

Cole, Fay-Cooper, *The Wild Tribes of Davao District, Minandao.* Chicago, 1913. (Field Museum of Natural History, Publication 170.)

Cole, Rev. H., "Notes on the Wagogo of German East Africa," in *Journal of the Anthropological Institute*, xxxii. (1902).

Cole, Lieutenant-Colonel H. W. G., "The Lushais," in *Census of India, 1911*, vol. iii. *Assam*, Part I. *Report.* Shillong, 1912.

Cole, W. E. R., "African Rain-making Chiefs, the Gondokoro District, White Nile," in *Man*, x. (1910).

Coleman, Ch., *Mythology of the Hindus.* London, 1832.

Colenso, W., "The Maori Races of New Zealand," in *Transactions and Proceedings of the New Zealand Institute* (1868), vol. i.

Collections of the Georgia Historical Society. Savannah, 1848.

Collections of the Minnesota Historical Society for the Year 1867. Saint Paul, 1867.

Collins, Lieut.-Colonel D., *An Account of the English Colony in New South Wales.* London, 1798.
  Second Edition. London, 1804.

Collitz, H., *Sammlung der griechischen Dialekt-Inschriften.* Göttingen, 1884–1914.

Colombia, being a geographical, etc., account of that country. London, 1822.

Colshorn, Carl und Theodor, *Märchen und Sagen.* Hanover, 1854.

Columella, *De re rustica.* In *Scriptores Rei Rusticae Veteres Latini.* Ed. J. G. Schneider. Leipsic, 1794–1796.

Colvin, Sir Auckland, *The Making of Modern Egypt.* London, 1906.

*Comical Pilgrim's Pilgrimage into Ireland (1723), quoted by J. Brand, *Popular Antiquities of Great Britain.* London, 1882–1883.

Comparetti, D., *Vergil in the Middle Ages.* London, 1895.

Compte-rendu de la Commission Impériale Archéologique. St. Petersburg, 1863, 1870, 1877.

Comptes rendus de l'Académie des Inscriptions et Belles-Lettres. Paris.

Concradt, L., "Die Ngumbu in Südkamerun," in *Globus,* lxxxi. (1902).

Conder, C. R., *Heth and Moab.* London, 1883.
  in *Journal of the Anthropological Institute,* xvi. (1887).
  Tent-work in Palestine. London, 1878.

Conférences faites au Musée Guimet, Bibliothèque de Vulgarisation.

Conon, *Narrationes,* in *Scriptores Poeticae Historiae Graeci.* Ed. A. Westermann. Brunswick, 1843.
  in Photius, *Bibliotheca.* Ed. Im. Bekker. Berlin, 1824.

Conradt, L., "Das Hinterland der deutschen Kolonie Togo," in *Petermanns Mittheilungen,* xlii. (1896).

Contemporary Review, The.

Conti, Nicolo, in *India in the Fifteenth Century.* Ed. R. H. Major. Hakluyt Society. London, 1857.

Contributions to North American Ethnology.

Conway, Professor R. S., in letters to the Author.

Conybeare, F. C. Private communications (i. 407 $n.^3$, iv. 5 $n.^3$).
  The Apology and Acts of Apollonius and other Monuments of Early Christianity. London, 1894.
  "The History of Christmas," in *American Journal of Theology,* iii. (1899).

Cook, A. B., in *The Classical Review,* xvi. (1902).
  "Oak and Rock," in *The Classical Review,* xv. (1901).
  "The European Sky-God," in *Folklore,* xv. (1904), xvi. (1905), xvii. (1906).
  "The Gong at Dodona," in *Journal of Hellenic Studies,* xxii. (1902).
  "Who was the Wife of Hercules?" in *The Classical Review,* xx. (1906).
  "Zeus, Jupiter, and the Oak," in *The Classical Review,* xvii. (1903), xviii. (1904).

Cook, Captain James, *Voyages.* London, 1809.

Cook, S. A., *The Laws of Moses and the Code of Hammurabi.* London, 1903.

Cooke, G. A., *Text-book of North-Semitic Inscriptions.* Oxford, 1903.

Cooper, Rev. Sydney, in letter to the Author.

Cooper, T. T., *Travels of a Pioneer of Commerce.* London, 1871.

"Coorg Folk-lore," in *Folk-lore Journal,* vii. (1889).

Coreal, Fr., *Voyages aux Indes Occidentales.* Amsterdam, 1722.

1 Corinthians.

Cornaby, Rev. W. A., in letter to Rev. Dr. W. T. A. Barber (iv. 275 *sq.*).

Cornelius Nepos. Ed. C. Halm. Leipsic, 1871.
  Atticus.
  Cimon.
  Hannibal.

Cornford, F. M., in Lecture delivered before the Classical Society of Cambridge, 28th February 1911.

Cornutus, *Theologiae Graecae Compendium.* Ed. C. Lang. Leipsic, 1881.

Corpus Inscriptionum Atticarum. Berlin, 1873–

Corpus Inscriptionum Graecarum. Ed. Aug. Boeckh, etc. Berlin, 1828–1877.

Corpus Inscriptionum Graecarum Graeciae Septentrionalis, vol. i. Berlin, 1892.

Corpus Inscriptionum Latinarum. Berlin, 1862–

Corpus Inscriptionum Semiticarum. Paris, 1881–

Cortet, Eugène, *Essai sur les Fêtes religieuses.* Paris, 1867.

Cosmas Hierosolymitanus, *Commentarii in Sancti Gregorii Nazianzeni Carmina,* in Migne's *Patrologia Graeca,* xxxviii.

Cosquin, Emmanuel, *Contes populaires de Lorraine.* Paris, N.D.

    Le Prologue-cadre des Mille et Une Nuits, les légendes Perses, et le Livre d'Esther. Paris, 1909. (Extract from the **Revue Biblique Internationale,* Janvier et Avril, 1909, published by the Dominicans of Jerusalem.)

Cottrell, C. H., *Recollections of Siberia.* London, 1842.

Coudreau, H. A., *Chez nos Indiens : quatre années dans la Guayane Française.* Paris, 1895.

    La France équinoxiale. Paris, 1887.

Coulbeaux, "Au pays de Menelik : à travers l'Abyssinie," in *Les Missions Catholiques,* xxx. (1898).

County Folk-lore :

    East Riding of Yorkshire. Collected and edited by Mrs. Gutch. London, 1912.

    Leicestershire and Rutlandshire. Collected and edited by C. J. Billson. London, 1895.

    Lincolnshire. Collected by Mrs. Gutch and Mabel Peacock. London, 1908.

    North Riding of Yorkshire, York and the Ainsty. Collected and edited by Mrs. Gutch. London, 1901.

    Northumberland. Collected by M. C. Balfour and edited by Northcote W. Thomas. London, 1904.

    Orkney and Shetland Islands. Collected by G. F. Black and edited by Northcote W. Thomas. London, 1903.

    Suffolk. Collected and edited by Lady Eveline Camilla Gurdon. London, 1893.

Couppé, Mgr., "En Nouvelle-Poméranie," in *Les Missions Catholiques,* xxiii. (1891).

Courtois, Father, "À travers le haut Zambèze," in *Les Missions Catholiques,* xvi. (1884).

    "Scènes de la vie Cafre," in *Les Missions Catholiques,* xv. (1883).

    "Coutumes étranges des indigènes du Djebel-Nouba (Afrique centrale), notes communiqués par les missionnaires de Vérone," in *Les Missions Catholiques,* xiv. (1882).

Cowie, Robert, M.A., M.D., *Shetland, Descriptive and Historical.* Aberdeen, 1871.

Cowley Evangelist, The.

Cox, Miss M. Roalfe, *Introduction to Folklore.* London, 1895.

Cox, Ross, *The Columbia River.* Second Edition. London, 1832.

Crabouillet, "Les Lolos," in *Les Missions Catholiques,* v. (1873).

Crane, T. F., *Italian Popular Tales.* London, 1885.

*"Crannoges," in *Chambers's Encyclopaedia,* quoted by R. Munro, *Ancient Scottish Lake Dwellings.* Edinburgh, 1882.

Crantz, D., *History of Greenland.* London, 1767.

Crauford, L., in *Journal of the Anthropological Institute,* xxiv. (1895).

Crawford, Dr. T. W. W., cited by Mr. A. C. Hollis in letter to the Author (xi. 262 $n.^2$).

Crawley, E., *The Mystic Rose*. London, 1902.

Credner, C. A., "De natalitiorum Christi origine," in *Zeitschrift für die historische Theologie*, iii. (1833).

*Cregeen, *Manx Dictionary*, referred to by Joseph Train, *Historical and Statistical Account of the Isle of Man*. Douglas, Isle of Man, 1845.

Creighton, C., *s.v.* "Leprosy," in *Encyclopaedia Biblica*, iii.

Cremat, "Der Anadyrbezirk Sibiriens und seine Bevölkerung," in *Globus*, lxvi. (1894).

Crevaux, J., *Voyages dans l'Amérique du Sud*. Paris, 1883.

Crofts, W. C., in letter to the Author (ii. 92 $n.^4$).

Crombie, J. E., "The Saliva Superstition," in *International Folk-lore Congress, 1891, Papers and Transactions*. London, 1892.

Cromer, Martin, *De origine et rebus gestis Polonorum*. Bâle, 1568.

Crooke, W., in *Indian Antiquary*, xix. (1890).

in *Journal of the Anthropological Institute*, xxviii. (1899).

in *North Indian Notes and Queries*, i. (July, 1891).

Natives of Northern India. London, 1907.

Notes sent to the Author (i. 406 $n.^1$, iv. 53 $n.^1$, 157 $n.^5$, 159 $n.^1$, v. 65 $n.^1$, vii. 234 $n.^2$, viii. 56 $n.^3$).

"The Legends of Krishna," in *Folk-lore*, xi. (1900).

The Popular Religion and Folk-lore of Northern India. Westminster, 1896.

The Tribes and Castes of the North-Western Provinces and Oudh. Calcutta, 1896.

Things Indian. London, 1906.

Croonenberghs, Father, in *Annales de la Propagation de la Foi*, liii. (1881).

"La Fête de la Grande Danse dans le haut Zambèze," in *Les Missions Catholiques*, xiv. (1882).

"La Mission du Zambèze," in *Les Missions Catholiques*, xiv. (1882).

Cross, Rev. E. B., "On the Karens," in *Journal of the American Oriental Society*, iv. (1854).

Crossland, quoted by H. Ling Roth. *The Natives of Sarawak and British North Borneo*.

Crowther, S., and Taylor, J. C., *The Gospel on the Banks of the Niger*. London, 1859.

Cruise, R. A., *Journal of a Ten Months' Residence in New Zealand*. London, 1823.

Crusius, O., *s.vv.* "Kadmos" and "Lityerses," in W. H. Roscher's *Ausführliches Lexikon der griechischen und römischen Mythologie*.

Cruz, D. Luis de la, "Descripcion de la Naturaleza de los Terrenos que se comprenden en los Andes, poseidos por los Peguenches y los demas espacios hasta el rio de Chadileuba," in Pedro de Angelis's *Coleccion de Obras y Documentos relativos a la Historia antigua y moderna de las Provincias del Rio de la Plata*, vol. i. Buenos-Ayres, 1836.

Ctesias, in the second book of his Persian history (Athenaeus, xiv.).

cited by John of Antioch, in C. Müller's *Fragmenta Historicorum Graecorum*, vol. iv.

Cuénot, Mgr., in *Annales de la Propagation de la Foi*, xiii. (1841).

Cuissard, Ch., *Les Feux de la Saint-Jean*. Orléans, 1884.

Culin, Stewart, *Korean Games*. Philadelphia, 1895.

Cullen, Dr., "The Darien Indians," in *Transactions of the Ethnological Society of London*, N.S., iv. (1866).

Cumming, Miss C. F. Gordon, *In the Hebrides*. London, 1883.

Cummins, S. L., "Sub-tribes of the Bahr-el-Ghazal Dinkas," in *Journal of the Anthropological Institute*, xxxiv. (1904).

BIBLIOGRAPHY

29

Cumont, Franz, *s.vv.* " Anaitis," " Atargatis," " Attepata," " Caelestis," " Dea Syria," " Dendrophori," and " Dolichenus," in Pauly-Wissowa's *Real-Encyclopädie der classischen Altertumswissenschaft.*
" L'Aigle funéraire des Syriens et l'Apothéose des Empereurs," in *Revue de l'Histoire des Religions,* lxii. (1910).
" La Polémique de l'Ambrosiaster contre les Païens," in *Revue d'Histoire et de Littérature religieuses,* viii. (1903).
" Le Natalis Invicti," in *Comptes Rendus de l'Académie des Inscriptions et Belles-Lettres,* 1911. Paris, 1911.
" Le roi des Saturnales," in *Revue de Philologie,* xxi. (1897).
" Le Tombeau de S. Dasius de Durostorum," in *Analecta Bollandiana,* xxvii. Brussels, 1908.
" Les Actes de S. Dasius," in *Analecta Bollandiana,* xvi. (1897).
Les Religions Orientales dans le Paganisme Romain. Second Edition. Paris, 1909.
s.v. " Mithras," in W. H. Roscher's *Lexikon der griechischen und römischen Mythologie,* ii.
Textes et Monuments Figurés relatifs aux Mystères de Mithra. Brussels, 1896–1899.
" Une formule grecque de renonciation au judaïsme," in *Wiener Studien,* xxiv. (1902).
Cumont, F., et Cumont, E., *Voyage d'Exploration archéologique dans le Pont de la Petite Arménie.* Brussels, 1906.
Cunningham, J. F., *Uganda and its Peoples.* London, 1905.
Cuny, C., " De Libreville au Cameroun," in *Bulletin de la Société de Géographie* (Paris), vii. Série, xvii. (1896).
Cupet, Le Capitaine, " Chez les populations sauvages du Sud de l'Annam," in *Tour du Monde,* No. 1682, April 1, 1893.
in *Mission Pavie, Indo-Chine 1879–95, Géographie et Voyages,* iii. Paris, 1900.
Cureton, W., *Spicilegium Syriacum.* London, 1855.
Curr, Edward M., *The Australian Race.* Melbourne and London, 1886–1887.
Curtin, Jeremiah, *Myths and Folk-lore of Ireland.* London, N.D.
Myths and Folk-tales of the Russians, Western Slavs, and Magyars. London, 1891.
Curtiss, S. I., *Primitive Semitic Religion To-day.* Chicago, New York, and Toronto, 1902.
Curtius, E., in *Archäologischer Anzeiger,* 1895.
Curtius, G., *Grundzüge der griechischen Etymologie.* Fifth Edition. Leipsic, 1879.
Curtius, L., " Christi Himmelfahrt," in *Archiv für Religionswissenschaft,* xiv. (1911).
Curzon, G. N., *Problems of the Far East.* Westminster, 1896.
Cushing, Frank H., " My Adventures in Zuñi," in *The Century Illustrated Monthly Magazine,* May 1833.
Cyril of Alexandria, *Commentary on Hosea,* in Migne's *Patrologia Graeca,* lxxi.
In Isaiam, in Migne's *Patrologia Graeca,* lxx.

Dahle, L., " Sikidy and Vintana," in *Antananarivo Annual and Madagascar Magazine,* xi. (1887).
Daily Graphic, The.
Dale, Rev. G., " An Account of the Principal Customs and Habits of the Natives inhabiting the Bondei Country," in *Journal of the Anthropological Institute,* xxv. (1896).
Dall, W. H., *Alaska and its Resources.* London, 1870.
in *American Naturalist,* xii.

Dall, W. H.—*continued.*
    in *The Yukon Territory.* London, 1898.
    "On Masks, Labrets, and certain Aboriginal Customs," in *Third Annual Report of the Bureau of Ethnology.* Washington, 1884.
Dallet, Ch., *Histoire de l'Église de Corée.* Paris, 1874.
Dalton, Colonel E. T., *Descriptive Ethnology of Bengal.* Calcutta, 1872.
    "The Kols of Chota-Nagpore," in *Transactions of the Ethnological Society,* N.S., vi. (1868).
Dalyell, John Graham, *The Darker Superstitions of Scotland.* Edinburgh, 1834.
Dalzel, A., *History of Dahomy.* London, 1793.
Damascius, "Vita Isodori," in Photius, *Bibliotheca.* Ed. Im. Bekker. Berlin, 1824.
Dames, M. Longworth, and Seemann, Mrs. E., "Folk-lore of the Azores," in *Folk-lore,* xiv. (1903).
Dana, Richard H., *Two Years before the Mast.*
Dania, i. No. 1. Copenhagen, 1890.
Danicourt, Mgr., "Rapport sur l'origine, les progrès et la décadence de la secte des *Tao-sse,* en Chine," in *Annales de la Propagation de la Foi,* xxx. (1858).
Danks, Rev. B., "Marriage Customs of the New Britain Group," in *Journal of the Anthropological Institute,* xviii. (1889).
Dannert, Rev. E., "Customs of the Ovaherero at the Birth of a Child," in *(South African) Folk-lore Journal,* ii. (1880).
Dannert, E., *Zum Rechte der Herero.* Berlin, 1906.
Dapper, O., *Description de l'Afrique.* Amsterdam, 1686.
Daremberg, Ch., et Saglio, Edm., *Dictionnaire des antiquités grecques et romaines.* Paris, 1877–
Dareste, R., in *Recueil d'Inscriptions Juridiques Grecques.* Deuxième Série. Paris, 1898.
Dargun, L., *Mutterrecht und Raubehe und ihre Reste im germanischen Recht und Leben.* Breslau, 1883.
Darmesteter, James, *Ormazd et Ahriman.* Paris, 1877.
    The Zend-Avesta. Oxford, 1880, 1883. (*Sacred Books of the East,* vols. iv. and xxiii.)
Darwin, Charles, *The Origin of Species.* Sixth Edition. London, 1878.
Darwin, Sir Francis, in letters to the Author.
Darwin, (Sir) George Howard, Presidential Address to the British Association, in *Report of the 75th Meeting of the British Association for the Advancement of Science.* South Africa, 1905.
Darwin and Modern Science. Cambridge, 1909.
Das, Sarat Chandra, *Journey to Lhasa and Central Tibet.* London, 1902.
Das Gilgamesch-Epos, neu übersetzt von Arthur Ungnad *und gemeinverständlich erklärt von* Hugo Gressmann. Göttingen, 1911.
"Das Volk der Tanala," in *Globus,* lxxxix. (1906).
Dasent, G. W., *Popular Tales from the Norse.* Edinburgh, 1859.
    Tales from the Fjeld. London, 1874.
Dass, Baboo Ishuree, *Domestic Manners and Customs of the Hindoos of Northern India.* Benares, 1860.
David, Abbé Armand, "Voyage en Mongolie," in *Bulletin de la Société de Géographie* (Paris), VIme Série, ix. (1875).
*David of Antioch, *Tazyin,* in the story "Orwa," cited by W. Robertson Smith.
Davidson, A. B., *The Book of Job.* Cambridge, 1893. (*The Cambridge Bible for Schools and Colleges.*)
Davies, Johathan Ceredig, *Folk-lore of West and Mid-Wales.* Aberystwyth, 1911.

Davis, E. J., *Anatolica*. London, 1874.
   Life in Asiatic Turkey. London, 1879.
   "On a New Hamathite Inscription at Ibreez," in *Transactions of the Society of Biblical Archaeology*, iv. (1876).
Davis, R. F., in a letter to the Author.
Dawkins, R. M., "The Modern Carnival in Thrace and the Cult of Dionysus," in *Journal of Hellenic Studies*, xxvi. (1906).
Dawson, G. M., "Notes and Observations on the Kwakiool People of the Northern Part of Vancouver Island and adjacent Coasts," in *Proceedings and Transactions of the Royal Society of Canada for the Year 1887*. Montreal, 1888.
   "Notes on the Shuswap People of British Columbia," in *Proceedings and Transactions of the Royal Society of Canada*, ix. Montreal, 1892. *Transactions*, section ii.
   "On the Haida Indians of the Queen Charlotte Islands," in *Geological Survey of Canada, Report of Progress for 1878-1879*. Montreal, 1880.
   Report on the Queen Charlotte Islands, 1878. Montreal, 1880.
Dawson, James, *Australian Aborigines*. Melbourne, Sydney, and Adelaide, 1881.
Day, Lal Behari, *Folk-tales of Bengal*. London, 1883.
D'Abbadie, A., *Douze ans dans la Haute Éthiopie*. Paris, 1868.
D'Almeida, W. B., *Life in Java*. London, 1864.
De Barros, *Da Asia, dos feitos, que os Portuguezes fizeram no descubrimento e conquista dos mares e terras do Oriente*. Decada Terceira. Lisbon, 1777.
"De Dajaks op Borneo," in *Mededeelingen van wege het Nederlandsche Zendelinggenootschap*, xiii. (1869).
De Gids.
"De godsdienst en godsdienst-plegtigheden der Alfoeren in de Menhassa op het eiland Celebes," in *Tijdschrift van Nederlandsch Indië* (1849).
De Indische Gids.
De Marchi, A., *Il Culto privato di Roma antica*. Milan, 1896.
D'Orbigny, Alcide, *L'Homme américain (de l'Amérique Méridionale)*. Paris (1839).
   Voyage dans l'Amérique Méridionale. Paris and Strasburg, 1839-1844.
D'Penha, G. F., "A Collection of Notes on Marriage Customs in the Madras Presidency," in *Indian Antiquary*, xxv. (1896).
   in *Indian Antiquary*, xxxi. (1902).
   "Superstitions and Customs in Salsette," in *Indian Antiquary*, xxviii. (1899).
De Russorum Muscovitarum et Tartarorum religione, sacrificiis, nuptiarum, funerum ritu. Spires, 1582.
*De Thuy, *Étude historique, géographique et ethnographique sur la province de Tuléar*, Notes, Rec., Expl., 1899, quoted by A. van Gennep, *Tabou et totémisme à Madagascar*.
D'Unienville, Baron, *Statistique de l'Île Maurice*. Paris, 1838.
D'Urville, J. Dumont, *Voyage autour du monde et à la recherche de La Pérouse, exécuté sous son commandement sur la corvette " Austrolabe " : histoire du voyage*. Paris, 1832-1833.
De Vogüé, *Mélanges d'Archéologie Orientale*. Paris, 1868.
"Death from Lockjaw at Norwich," in *The People's Weekly Journal for Norfolk*, July 19, 1902.
Decken, Baron C. C. von der, *Reisen in Ost-Afrika*. Leipsic and Heidelberg, 1869-71.
Decle, L., *Three Years in Savage Africa*. London, 1898.
Defoe, Daniel, *History of the Plague in London*. Edinburgh, 1810.

Degrandpré, L., *Voyage à la côte occidentale d'Afrique.* Paris, 1801.
Dehon, Rev. P., S.J., "Religion and Customs of the Uraons," in *Memoirs of the Asiatic Society of Bengal*, vol. i. No. 9. Calcutta, 1906.
Delafosse, Maurice, *Haut-Sénégal-Niger, Le Pays, les Peuples, les Langues, l'Histoire, les Civilisations.* Paris, 1912.
    in *L'Anthropologie*, xi. (1895).
    in *La Nature*, No. 1086, March 24th, 1894.
    "Le peuple Siéna ou Sénoufo," in *Revue des Études Ethnographiques et Sociologiques*, i. (1908).
Delamare, in *Annales de la Propagation de la Foi*, xii. (1840).
Delaporte, H., "Une Visite chez les Araucaniens," in *Bulletin de la Société de Géographie* (Paris), Quatrième Série, x. (1855).
Delbrück, Prof. B., "Das Mutterrecht bei den Indogermanen," in *Preussische Jahrbücher*, lxxix. (1895).
Delegorgue, A., *Voyage dans l'Afrique Australe.* Paris, 1847.
Demelić, F., *Le Droit Coutumier des Slaves Méridionaux.* Paris, 1876.
Demosthenes, *Orationes.* Ed. G. Dindorf. Leipsic, 1864–1872.
    Contra Androtionem.
    Contra Aristocratem.
    Contra Neaeram.
    De corona.
Dena, Dom Daniel Sour Dharim, in *Annales de la Propagation de la Foi*, lx. (1888).
Denham Tracts, The: a Collection of Folk-lore by Michael Aislabie Denham. Edited by Dr. James Hardy. London, 1892–1895.
Denian, Father A., "Croyances religieuses et mœurs des indigènes de l'île Malo (Nouvelles-Hébrides)," in *Les Missions Catholiques*, xxxiii. (1901).
Deniker, J., "Les Ghiliaks d'après les derniers renseignements," in *Revue d'Ethnographie*, ii. (1883).
    The Races of Man. London, 1900.
Denjoy, P., "An-nam, Médecins et Sorciers, Remèdes et Superstitions," etc., in *Bulletins de la Société d'Anthropologie de Paris*, v. (1894).
    "Du droit successoral en Annam," etc., in *Bulletins de la Société d'Anthropologie de Paris*, Ve Série, iv. (1903).
Denkschriften der kaiserlichen Akademie der Wissenschaften in Wien.
Dennis, G., *Cities and Cemeteries of Etruria.* Third Edition. London, 1883.
"Departure of my Lady Mary from this World," in *Journal of Sacred Literature and Biblical Record*, New Series, vii. London, 1865.
"Der Anadyr-Bezirk nach A. W. Olssufjew," in *Petermanns Mittheilungen*, xlv. (1899).
"Der Muata Cazembe und die Völkerstämme der Maravis, Chevas, Muembas, Lundas und andere von Süd-Afrika," in *Zeitschrift für allgemeine Erdkunde*, vi. Berlin, 1856.
Der Pentamerone, aus dem Neapolitanischen übertragen von Felix Liebrecht. Breslau, 1846.
Der Urquell. Monatsschrift für Volkkunde. N.F.
Dercylus, quoted by a Scholiast on Euripides, *Phoenissae.*
Des Marchais, *Voyage en Guinée et à Cayenne.* Amsterdam, 1731.
Deschamps, G., and Cousin, G., in *Bulletin de Correspondance hellénique*, xi. (1887), xii. (1888).
"Description of the Natives of King George's Sound (Swan River) and adjoining Country," in *Journal of the Royal Geographical Society*, i. (1832).
Desgranges, M., "Usages du Canton de Bonneval," in *Mémoires de la Société Royale des Antiquaires de France*, i. Paris, 1817.
Desjardins, E., *Essai sur la Topographie du Latium.* Paris, 1854.

Dessau, H., in *Corpus Inscriptionum Latinarum*, xiv.
Inscriptiones Latinae selectae. Berlin, 1892–1914.
Deubner, L., *De incubatione.* Leipsic, 1900.
Deuteronomy, The Book of.
Deutsche geographische Blätter.
Deutsches Kolonialblatt.
Dezobry, L. Ch., *Rome au siècle d'Auguste.* Third Edition. Paris, 1870.
Dhorme, P., *La Religion Assyro-Babylonienne.* Paris, 1910.
[Dicaearchus], " Descriptio Graeciae," in *Geographi Graeci Minores*, ed. C.
    Müller, vol. i. Paris, 1882.
Dickens, Charles, *David Copperfield.*
    Martin Chuzzlewit.
Dictys Cretensis, *Bellum Trojanum.* Ed. F. Meister. Leipsic, 1872.
Die Edda. Übersetzt von K. Simrock. Eighth Edition. Stuttgart, 1882.
" Die Ethnographie Russlands nach A. F. Rittich," in *Petermanns Mit-
    theilungen, Ergänzungsheft*, No. 54. Gotha, 1878.
Die gestriegelte Rockenphilosophie. Fifth Edition. Chemnitz, 1759.
" Die Pschawen und Chewsuren im Kaukasus," in *Zeitschrift für allgemeine
    Erdkunde*, ii. (1857).
" Die Sommerwendfeier im St. Amarinthale," in *Der Urquell*, N.F., i. (1897).
Die Woche.
Dieffenbach, E., *Travels in New Zealand.* London, 1843.
Diels, H., *Die Fragmente der Vorsokratiker.* Second Edition. Berlin, 1906–
    1910.
    Herakleitos von Ephesos. Second Edition. Berlin, 1909.
    in Lecture on Greek Religion, heard by the Author at Berlin.
Dieterich, Albrecht, *Eine Mithrasliturgie.* Leipsic, 1903.
    "Sommertag," in *Beiheft* to *Archiv für Religionswissenschaft*, viii. (1905).
Dieterich, Anton, *Russian Popular Tales.* London, 1857.
Digest, in *Corpus Juris Civilis*, vol. i. Berlin, 1877. (*Institutiones*, recog-
    novit P. Krueger. *Digesta*, recognovit Th. Mommsen.)
Diguet, Colonel E., *Les Annamites, Société, Coutumes, Religions.* Paris, 1906.
Dijk, P. A. L. E. van, "Eenige aanteekeningen omtrent de verschillenden stam-
    men (*Margas*) en de stamverdeling bij de Battaks," in *Tijdschrift voor
    Indische Taal- Land- en Volkenkunde*, xxxviii. (1895).
Dill, S., *Roman Society from Nero to Marcus Aurelius.* London, 1904.
    Roman Society in the Last Century of the Western Empire. Second
    Edition. London, 1899.
Dillmann, Aug., *Die Bücher Exodus und Leviticus.* Leipsic, 1880 (in *Kurz-
    gefasstes exegetisches Commentar zum Alten Testament*).
Dinkard, a Pahlavi work.
Dinnschenchas, or *Dinnsenchus.*
Dinter, B. C. A. J. van, " Eenige geographische en ethnographische aanteeken-
    ingen betreffende het eiland Siaoe," in *Tijdschrift voor Indische Taal-
    Land- en Volkenkunde*, xli. (1899).
Dio Cassius. Ed. L. Dindorf. Leipsic, 1863–1865.
Dio Chrysostom, *Orationes.* Ed. L. Dindorf. Leipsic, 1857.
Diodorus, quoted by Photius, *Bibliotheca.* Ed. Im. Bekker. Berlin, 1824.
Diodorus Siculus, *Bibliotheca.* Ed. L. Dindorf. Leipsic, 1866–1868.
    in Eusebius, *Chronica.* Ed. A. Schoene. Berlin, 1866–1875.
Diogenes Laertius, *Vitae Philosophorum.* Ed. C. G. Cobet. Paris (Didot), 1878.
Diogenianus, in *Paroemiographi Graeci.* Ed. E. L. Leutsch et F. G. Schneide-
    win. Göttingen, 1839–1851.
Dionysius, *Periegetes, Descriptio orbis terrarum*, in *Geographi Graeci Minores*,
    ed. C. Müller, vol. ii. Paris, 1882.
Dionysius Halicarnasensis, *Opera.* Ed. J. J. Reiske. Leipsic, 1774–1777.
    Antiquitates Romanae. Ed. C. Jacoby. Leipsic, 1885–1905.

Dioscorides. Ed. C. Sprengel. Leipsic, 1829–1830.
  De arte medica.
  De materia medica.
Dittenberger, G. (W.), *Sylloge Inscriptionum Graecarum.* Second Edition. Leipsic, 1898–1901.
  Orientis Graeci Inscriptiones Selectae. Leipsic, 1903–1905.
Dittmar, C. von, "Über die Koräken und die ihnen sehr nahe verwandten Tschuktschen," in *Bulletin de la Classe historico-philologique de l'Académie Impériale de Sciences de St-Pétersbourg,* xiii. (1856).
Dixon, Roland B., "The Northern Maidu," in *Bulletin of the American Museum of Natural History,* vol. xvii. part iii. New York, 1905.
Dixon, Dr. W. E. Private communication (ii. 139 *n.*[1]).
Dobell, P., *Travels in Kamtchatka and Siberia.* London, 1830.
Dobrizhoffer, M., *Historia de Abiponibus.* Vienna, 1784.
Dodge, Colonel R. I., *Our Wild Indians.* Hartford, Connecticut, 1886.
Dodwell, E., *A Classical and Topographical Tour through Greece.* London, 1819.
Domaszewski, A. von, "Briefe der Attaliden an der Priester von Pessinus," in *Archaeologische-epigraphische Mittheilungen aus Oesterreich-Ungarn,* viii. (1884).
  Die Religion des Römischen Heeres. Treves, 1895.
  "Magna Mater in Latin Inscriptions," in *The Journal of Roman Studies,* i. (1911).
Donaldson, T. L., *Architectura Numismatica.* London, 1859.
Dongen, G. J. van, "De Koeboe in de Onderafdeeling Koeboe-streken der Residentie Palembang," in *Bijdragen tot de Taal- Land- en Volkenkunde van Nederlandsch-Indië,* lxiii. (1910).
Donselaar, W. M., "Aanteekeningen over het eiland Saleijer," in *Mededeelingen van wege het Nederlandsche Zendelinggenootschap,* i. (1857).
Doolittle, Rev. J., *Social Life of the Chinese.* Edited and revised by the Rev. Paxton Hood. London, 1868.
Dorsa, Vincenzo, *La Tradizione Greco-Latina negli usi e nelle credenze popolari della Calabria Citeriore.* Cosenza, 1884.
Dorsey, J. Owen, "An Account of the War Customs of the Osages," in *American Naturalist,* xviii. (1884).
  "A Study of Siouan Cults," in *Eleventh Annual Report of the Bureau of Ethnology.* Washington, 1894.
  "Omaha Sociology," in *Third Annual Report of the Bureau of Ethnology.* Washington, 1884.
  "Osage Traditions," in *Sixth Annual Report of the Bureau of Ethnology.* Washington, 1888.
  "Teton Folk-lore," in *American Anthropologist,* ii. (1889).
  "Teton Folk-lore Notes," in *Journal of American Folk-lore,* ii. (1889).
Dos Santos, J., "Eastern Ethiopia," in G. McCall Theal's *Records of South-Eastern Africa,* vii. (1901).
Doughty, Ch. M., *Travels in Arabia Deserta.* Cambridge, 1888.
Doutté, Edmond, "Figuig," in *La Géographie, Bulletin de la Société de Géographie* (Paris), vii. (1893).
  Les Aissâoua à Tlemcen. Châlons-sur-Marne, 1900.
  Magie et Religion dans l'Afrique du Nord. Algiers, 1908.
Dove, quoted by James Bonwick, *Daily Life and Origin of the Tasmanians.*
Dozon, Aug., *Contes albanais.* Paris, 1881.
Drechsler, P., *Sitte, Brauch und Volksglaube in Schlesien.* Leipsic, 1903–1906.
Drexler, W., *s.vv.* "Gaia," "Isis," "Men," and "Meridianus daemon," in W. H. Roscher's *Lexikon der griechischen und römischen Mythologie.*

Driver, S. R., *Critical and Exegetical Commentary on Deuteronomy.* Third Edition. Edinburgh, 1902. (In *The International Critical Commentary.*)

— in *Authority and Archaeology Sacred and Profane.* Edited by D. G. Hogarth. London, 1899.

— *Introduction to the Literature of the Old Testament.* Eighth Edition. Edinburgh, 1909.

— *Notes on the Hebrew Text and the Topography of the Books of Samuel.* Second Edition. Oxford, 1913.

— *s.v.* "Mesha," in *Encyclopaedia Biblica*, vol. iii.

— *The Book of Genesis.* Fourth Edition. London, 1905.

— *The Books of Joel and Amos.* Cambridge, 1901. (In *The Cambridge Bible for Schools and Colleges.*)

— *The Minor Prophets.* Edinburgh, 1906. (In *The Century Bible.*)

Drosinis, G., *Land und Leute in Nord-Eubōa.* Leipsic, 1884.

Dryden, John, *Works.* Ed. Walter Scott. London, 1808.

— *The Tempest.*

Du Pratz, Le Page, *History of Louisiana, or of the western parts of Virginia and Carolina.* Translated from the French. New Edition. London, 1774.

Dubois, J. A., *Mœurs, institutions, et cérémonies des peuples de l'Inde.* Paris, 1825.

Duchesne, Mgr. L., *Origines du Culte Chrétien.* Third Edition. Paris, 1903.

Duloup, G., "Huit jours chez les M'Bengas," *Revue d'Ethnographie*, ii. (1883).

Dümichen, J., "Die dem Osiris im Denderatempel geweiten Räume," in *Zeitschrift für ägyptische Sprache und Altertumskunde* (1882).

Duncan, John, *Travels in Western Africa.* London, 1847.

Duncan, Leland L., "Fairy Beliefs and other Folk-lore Notes from County Leitrim," in *Folk-lore*, vii. (1896).

— "Folk-lore Gleanings from County Leitrim," in *Folk-lore*, iv. (1893).

— "Further Notes from County Leitrim," in *Folk-lore*, v. (1894).

Duncan, Mr., quoted by Commander R. C. Mayne, *Four Years in British Columbia and Vancouver Island.* London, 1862.

Duncker, M., *Geschichte des Alterthums.* Fifth Edition. Leipsic, 1878–1886.

Dundas, Hon. K. R., "Notes on the Tribes inhabiting the Baringo District, East Africa Protectorate," in *Journal of the Royal Anthropological Institute*, xl. (1910).

Dunn, J., *History of the Oregon Territory.* London, 1844.

Dupin, Baron, "Notice sur quelques fêtes et divertissemens populaires du département des Deux-Sèvres," in *Mémoires et dissertations publiées par la Société Royale des Antiquaires de France*, iv. (1823).

Dupont, É., *Lettres sur le Congo.* Paris, 1889.

Duran, Diego, *Historia de las Indias de Nueva España.* MS. edited by J. F. Ramirez. Mexico, 1867–1880.

Durand, J. B. L., *Voyage au Sénégal.* Paris, 1802.

Durand, L'Abbé, "Le Rio Negro du Nord et son bassin," in *Bulletin de la Société de Géographie* (Paris), 6ème Série, iii. (1872).

Durandus, G. (Wilh. Durantis), *Rationale Divinorum Officiorum.* Lyons, 1584.

Durham, Miss M. Edith, *High Albania.* London, 1909.

Düringsfeld, Ida von, und Reinsberg-Düringsfeld, Otto Freiherr von. *Hochzeitsbuch.* Leipsic, 1871.

Dusburg, P. de, *Chronicon Preussiae.* Ed. Chr. Hartknoch. Frankfort and Leipsic, 1679.

Dussaud, René, "La matérialisation de la prière en Orient," in *Bulletins et Mémoires de la Société d'Anthropologie de Paris*, 5ème Série, vii. (1906).

— *Notes de Mythologie Syrienne.* Paris, 1903.

Dutreuil de Rhins, J. L., *Mission scientifique dans la Haute Asie, 1890–1895.* Paris, 1897.

Duveyrier, H., *Exploration du Sahara* : *les Touareg du Nord*. Paris, 1864.

Dwight, Timothy, *Travels in New England and New York*. London, 1823.

*Dybeck, *Runa*, 1844 and 1845, quoted by J. Grimm, *Deutsche Mythologie* (Fourth Edition), and A. Kuhn, *Die Herabkunft des Feuers und des Göttertranks* (Second Edition, Gütersloh, 1886).

Dyer, T. F. Thiselton, *British Popular Customs*. London, 1876.

— *English Folk-lore*. London, 1884.

— *Folk-lore of Plants*. London, 1889.

Ebeling, H., *Lexicon Homericum*. Leipsic, 1880–1885.

Ebn-el-Dyn el-Eghouâthy, " Relation d'un voyage dans l'intérieur de l'Afrique septentrionale," in *Bulletin de la Société de Géographie* (Paris), 2ème Série, i. (1834).

Eck, R. van, " Schetsen van het eiland Bali," in *Tijdschrift voor Nederlandsch Indië*, N.S., viii. (1879), ix. (August 1880).

Eckstein, Miss L., *Comparative Studies in Nursery Rhymes*. London, 1906.

Edda Rhythmica seu Antiquior, vulgo Saemundina dicta. Copenhagen, 1828.

*Edgar, Major, *Litafi na Tatsuniyoyi na Hausa*, referred to by Major A. J. N. Treamearne, *Hausa Superstitions and Customs*. London, 1913.

Edkins, J., *Religion in China*. Second Edition. London, 1878.

Edmonds, Richard, *The Land's End District*. London, 1862.

Edmonston, A., *Zetland Islands*. Edinburgh, 1809.

Edmonston, Rev. Biot, and Saxby, Jessie M. E., *The Home of a Naturalist*. London, 1888.

Eels, Rev. Myron, " The Twana, Chemakum, and Klallam Indians of Washington Territory," in *Annual Report of the Smithsonian Institution for 1887*.

" Eenige bijzonderheden betreffende de Papoeas van de Geelvinksbaai van Niew-Guinea," in *Bijdragen tot de Taal- Land- en Volkenkunde van Neêrlandsch-Indië*, ii. (1854).

" Eenige mededeelingen betreffende Rote door een inlandischen School-meester," in *Tijdschrift voor Indische Taal- Land- en Volkenkunde*, xxvii. (1882).

Eerde, J. C. van, " Een huwelijk bij de Minangkabausche Maliers," in *Tijdschrift voor Indische Taal- Land- en Volkenkunde*, xliv. (1901).

" Gebruiken bij den rijstbouw en rijstoogst op Lombok," in *Tijdschrift voor Indische Taal- Land- en Volkenkunde*, xlv. (1902).

Egede, Hans, *A Description of Greenland*. Second Edition. London, 1818.

Egyptian Exploration Fund Archaeological Reports.

Ehrenreich, P., " Materialen zur Sprachenkunde Brasiliens," in *Zeitschrift für Ethnologie*, xxvi. (1894).

Einhorn, P., " Historia Lettica," in *Scriptores Rerum Livonicarum*, ii. Riga and Leipsic, 1848.

— *Reformatio gentis Letticae in Ducatu Curlandiae*. Preface dated 17th July 1636. Reprinted in *Scriptores rerum Livonicarum*, ii. Riga and Leipsic, 1848.

— "Wiederlegunge der Abgötterey : der ander (*sic*) Theil." Printed at Riga in 1627, and reprinted in *Scriptores rerum Livonicarum*, ii. Riga and Leipsic, 1848.

" Einige Notizen aus einem alten Kräuterbuche," in *Zeitschrift für deutsche Mythologie und Sittenkunde*, iv. Göttingen, 1859.

Eisel, Robert, *Sagenbuch des Voigtlandes*. Gera, 1871.

Eitel, " Les Hak-ka," in *L'Anthropologie*, iv. (1893).

Ekris, A. van, " Het Ceramsche Kakianverbond," in *Mededeelingen van wege het Nederlandsche Zendelinggenootschap*, ix. (1865). Repeated with slight changes in *Tijdschrift voor Indische Taal- Land- en Volkenkunde*, xvi. (1867).

Eliot, J., " Observations on the Inhabitants of the Garrow Hills," in *Asiatick Researches*, iii.

*Elizabeth, Charlotte, *Personal Recollections*, quoted by Rev. Alexander Hislop, *The Two Babylons.* Edinburgh, 1853.
*Elliot, C. A., *Hoshangábád Settlement Report*, quoted in *Panjab Notes and Queries*, iii. (October and December 1885).
Elliot, Sir Henry M., *Memoirs on the History, Folk-lore, and Distribution of the Races of the North-Western Provinces of India.* Edited, revised, and re-arranged by John Beames. London, 1869.
The History of India as told by its own Historians. London, 1867–1877.
Elliot, R. H., *Experiences of a Planter in the Jungles of Mysore.* London, 1871.
Ellis, A. B., *The Ewe-speaking Peoples of the Slave Coast of West Africa.* London, 1890.
The Tshi-speaking Peoples of the Gold Coast of West Africa. London, 1887.
The Yoruba-speaking Peoples of the Slave Coast of West Africa. London, 1894.
Ellis, Robinson, *Commentary on Catullus.* Oxford, 1876.
Ellis, Rev. William, *History of Madagascar.* London, N.D., preface dated 1838.
Polynesian Researches. Second Edition. London, 1832–1836.
*Elmslie, Dr., MS. notes used by J. Macdonald in *Myth and Religion.* London, 1893.
Elmslie, W. A., *Among the Wild Ngoni.* Edinburgh and London, 1899.
Elton, Charles, *Origins of English History.* London, 1882.
El-Tounsy, Mohammed Ibn-Omar, *Voyage au Darfour.* Traduite de l'Arabe par le Dr. Perron. Paris, 1845.
Voyage au Ouadây. Paris, 1851.
Emery, Lieutenant, in *Journal of the Royal Geographical Society*, iii.
Emin Pasha, quoted by Fr. Stuhlmann, *Mit Emin Pascha ins Herz von Afrika.* Berlin, 1894.
Emin Pasha in Central Africa, being a Collection of his Letters and Journals. London, 1888.
Empedocles, in *Fragmenta Philosophorum Graecorum*, ed. F. G. A. Mullach, Paris, 1885 ; also in H. Diels, *Die Fragmente der Vorsokratiker*, i.
Empire Review.
Emslie, J. P., in *Folklore*, xi. (1900).
Encyclopaedia Biblica. Edited by T. K. Cheyne and J. S. Black. London, 1899–1903.
Encyclopaedia Britannica. Ninth Edition. Edinburgh, 1875–1889.
Encyclopaedia of Religion and Ethics. Edited by J. Hastings, D.D. Edinburgh, 1908–
Ende, L. von, " Die Baduwis auf Java," in *Mittheilungen der Anthropologischen Gesellschaft in Wien*, xix. (1889).
Enderli, J., " Zwei Jahre bei den Tchuktschen und Korjaken," in *Petermanns Mitteilungen*, xlix. (1903).
Endle, Rev. S., *The Kacharis.* London, 1911.
Engel, W. H., *Kypros.* Berlin, 1841.
Engelhaard, H. E. D., " Aanteekeningen betreffende de Kindjin Dajaks in het Landschap Baloengan," in *Tijdschrift voor Indische Taal- Land- en Volkenkunde*, xxxix. (1897).
" Mededeelingen over het eiland Saleijer," in *Bijdragen tot de Taal- Land- en Volkenkunde van Neêrlandsch-Indië*, Vierde Volgreeks, viii. (1884).
Engler, A., in V. Hehn's *Kulturpflanzen und Hausthiere.* Seventh Edition. Berlin, 1902.
English Historical Review.
Ennius, cited by Festus, *s.v.* " Puelli." Ed. C. O. Müller.
quoted by Cicero, *De natura deorum.*
Ἐφημερὶς ἀρχαιολογική. Athens, 1883, 1884, 1898.
Ephippus, cited by Athenaeus, xii.
Epictetus, *Dissertationes.* Ed. H. Schenkl. Leipsic, 1894.
Epigrammata Graeca ex lapidibus conlecta. Ed. G. Kaibel. Berlin, 1878.

Epiphanius, *Adversus Haereses*, in Migne's *Patrologia Graeca*, xlii.

Eratosthenes, *Catasterismi*, in *Mythographi Graeci*, ed. A. Westerman. Brunswick, 1843.

Erdweg, M. J., " Die Bewohner der Insel Tumleo, Berlinhafen, Deutsch-Neu-Guinea," in *Mittheilungen der Anthropologischen Gesellschaft in Wien*, xxxii. (1902).

Ergänzungshefte zu Petermanns Geographischen Mittheilungen.

Ergebnisse der Südsee-Expedition 1908–1910. Herausgegeben von G. Thilenius. Hamburg, 1913.

Erhard, Professor A., of Strasburg. Verbal communication (ii. 310 *n.*[1]).

Eriston, Prince, " Die Pschawen und Chewsurier im Kaukasus," in *Zeitschrift für allgemeine Erdkunde*, Neue Folge, ii. (1857).

Ériu, the Journal of the School of Irish Learning, Dublin.

Erman, A., *Archiv für wissenschaftliche Kunde von Russland*, vol. i. Berlin, 1841.

Travels in Siberia. London, 1848.

" Ethnographische Wahrnehmungen und Erfahrungen an den Küsten der Berings-Meeres," in *Zeitschrift für Ethnologie*, ii. (1870).

Erman, Adolf, *Ägypten und ägyptisches Leben im Altertum.* Tübingen, N.D.

Die ägyptische Religion. Berlin, 1905.
Second Edition. Berlin, 1909.

" Eine Reise nach Phönizien im 11. Jahrhundert v. Chr.," in *Zeitschrift für ägyptische Sprache und Altertumskunde*, xxxviii. (1900).

"Zehn Vorträge aus dem mittleren Reich," in *Zeitschrift für ägyptische Sprache und Alterthumskunde*, xx. (1882).

Erskine, J. E., *Journal of a Cruise among the Islands of the Western Pacific.* London, 1853.

Essays and Studies presented to William Ridgeway. Cambridge, 1913.

Esther, The Book of.

Etheridge, R., jun., " The ' Widow's Cap' of the Australian Aborigines," in *Proceedings of the Linnaean Society of New South Wales for the Year 1899*, xxiv. Sydney, 1900.

Ethnological Survey Publications, Department of the Interior. Manilla.

Ethnologisches Notizblatt herausgegeben von der Direktion des Königlichen Museums für Völkerkunde in Berlin. Berlin, 1894–

Etymologicum Magnum. Ed. F. Syllburg. Editio Nova. Leipsic, 1816.

Eubulus, cited by Athenaeus.

Eudoxi ars astronomica, qualis in charta Aegyptiaca superest. Ed. F. Blass. Kiliae, 1887.

Eudoxus of Cnidus, quoted by Athenaeus.

Eumenes, Letter preserved in inscription at Sivrihissar.

Eunapius, *Vitae sophistarum.* Ed. J. F. Boissonade. Paris (Didot), 1878.

Euphorion of Chalcis, quoted by Athenaeus, iv. 40.

Euripides, in *Poetae Scenici Graeci.* Ed. G. Dindorf. London, 1869.
Ed. F. A. Paley. Second Edition. London, 1872–1880.

    Bacchae.
    Electra.
    Hercules Furens.
    Hippolytus.
    Ion.
    Iphigenia in Tauris.
    Medea, Argumentum.
    Orestes.
    Phoenissae.
    Supplices.

Eusebius, *Chronicorum liber prior.* Ed. A. Schoene. Berlin, 1866–1875.

Praeparatio Evangelii. Ed. F. A. Heinichen. Leipsic, 1842–1843.

Vita Constantini, in Migne's *Patrologia Graeca*, xx.

Eustathius, *Commentary on Dionysius Periegetes*, in *Geographi Graeci Minores*, ed. C. Müller, vol. ii. Paris, 1882.
on Homer, *Iliad.* Leipsic, 1827–1830.
on Homer, *Odyssey.* Leipsic, 1825–1826.
Eutropius. Ed. D. C. G. Baumgarten-Crusius et H. R. Dietsch. Leipsic, 1868.
Evangelion de Mepharreshe. Edited by F. C. Burkitt. Cambridge, 1904.
Evans, A. J., "Mycenaean Tree and Pillar Cult," in *Journal of Hellenic Studies,* xxi. (1901).
Evans, D. Jenkyn, "The Harvest Customs of Pembrokeshire," in *Pembroke County Guardian,* 7th December 1895.
Evans, D. Silvan, in *The Açademy,* 13th November 1875.
Evans, Ivor H. N., "Notes on the Religious Beliefs, Superstitions, Ceremonies and Tabus of the Dusuns of the Tuaran and Tempassuk Districts, British North Borneo," in *Journal of the Royal Anthropological Institute,* xlii. (1912).
Evelyn, John, *Memoirs.* New Edition. London, 1827.
Everybody's Magazine. New York.
"Excavations in Cyprus, 1887–1888," in *Journal of Hellenic Studies,* ix. (1888).
"Excursion de M. Brun-Rollet dans la région supérieure du Nil," in *Bulletin de la Société de Géographie* (Paris), 4ème Série, iv. (1852) ; viii. (1854).
Exodus, The Book of.
"Exorcism of the Pest Demon of Japan." From a series of notes on medical customs of the Japanese, contributed by Dr. C. H. H. Hall of the United States Navy, to the **Sei-I Kwai Medical Journal.*
Expositor, The.
"Extract from a Letter of Mr. Alexander Loudon," in *Journal of the Royal Geographical Society,* ii. (1832).
Extract from a Report by Captain Foulkes to the British Colonial Office.
"Extracts from Diary of the late Rev. John Martin, Wesleyan Missionary in West Africa, 1843–1848," in *Man,* xii. (1912).
"Extrait du journal des missions évangeliques," in *Bulletin de la Société de Géographie* (Paris), 2ème Série, ii. (1834).
Eyre, E. J., *Journals of Expeditions of Discovery into Central Australia.* London, 1845.
Ezekiel, The Book of.
Ezra, The Book of.
Ezra, Nehemiah and Esther. Edited by Rev. T. Witton Davies. Edinburgh and London, N.D. (*The Century Bible.*)

Fabbri, P., "Canti popolari raccolti sui monti della Romagna-Toscana," in *Archivio per lo Studio delle Tradizioni Popolari,* xxii. (1903).
Fabrega, H. Pittier de, "Die Sprache der Bribri-Indianer in Costa Rica," in *Sitzungsberichte der philosophischen-historischen Classe der Kaiserlichen Akademie der Wissenschaften* (Vienna), cxxxviii. (1898).
Fabricius, D., "De cultu, religione et moribus incolarum Livoniae," in *Scriptores rerum Livonicarum,* ii. Riga and Leipsic, 1848.
"Livonicae Historiae compendiosa series," in *Scriptores Rerum Livoni-carum,* ii. Riga and Leipsic, 1848.
Fabricius, J. A., *Bibliotheca Graeca.* Fourth Edition. Hamburg, 1780–1809.
Fage, Missionary, in *Annales de la Propagation de la Foi,* xxix. (1857).
Fairbairn, Rev. Dr. A. M., in *Contemporary Review,* June 1899.
Fairclough, T. J., "Notes on the Basutos," in *Journal of the African Society,* No. 14, January 1905.
Fairholt, F. W., *Gog and Magog, the Giants in Guildhall, their real and legendary History.* London, 1859.

Fairweather, in W. F. W. Owen's *Narrative of Voyages to explore the Shores of Africa, Arabia, and Madagascar*. London, 1833.

Fancourt, Charles St. John, *History of Yucatan*. London, 1854.

Fanggidaej, J., "Rottineesche Verhalen," in *Bijdragen tot de Taal- Land- en Volkenkunde van Nederlandsch-Indië*, lviii. (1905).

Farler, J. P., "The Usambara Country in East Africa," in *Proceedings of the Royal Geographical Society*, N.S. i. (1879).

Farnell, L. R., in *The Hibbert Journal*, iv. (1906), (April 1907).

"Sociological Hypotheses concerning the position of Women in Ancient Religion," in *Archiv für Religionswissenschaft*, vii. (1904).

The Cults of the Greek States. Oxford, 1896-1909.

Fasciculi Malayenses, Anthropology.

Fawcett, Fr., in *Madras Government Museum Bulletin*, iii. No. 1. Madras, 1900.

"Note on a Custom of the Mysore 'Gollaválu' or Shepherd Caste People," in *Journal of the Anthropological Society of Bombay*, i.

"On Basivis," in *Journal of the Anthropological Society of Bombay*, ii.

"On the Saoras (or Savaras), an Aboriginal Hill People of the Eastern Ghats," in *Journal of the Anthropological Society of Bombay*, i.

Fawckner, Captain James. *See s.v.* Narrative.

Feasey, H. J., *Ancient English Holy Week Ceremonial*. London, 1897.

Featherman, A., *Social History of the Races of Mankind, Fourth Division, Dravido-Turanians*, etc. London, 1891.

Fehr, A., *Der Niasser im Leben und Sterben*. Barmen, 1901.

Fehrle, E., *Die kultische Keuschheit im Altertum*. Giessen, 1910.

*Feilberg, H. F., *Bidrag til en Ordbog over Jyske Almuesmål*. Fjerde hefte. Copenhagen, 1888.

in *Folk-lore*, vi. (1895).

"Zwieselbäume nebst verwandtem Aberglauben in Skandinavien," in *Zeitschrift des Vereins für Volkskunde*, vii. (1897).

Felkin, Dr. R. W., "Notes on the For Tribe of Central Africa," in *Proceedings of the Royal Society of Edinburgh*, xiii. (1884-1886).

"Notes on the Madi or Moru Tribe of Central Africa," in *Proceedings of the Royal Society of Edinburgh*, xii. (1882-1884).

"Notes on the Waganda Tribe of Central Africa," in *Proceedings of the Royal Society of Edinburgh*, xiii. (1884-1886).

See also s.v. Wilson, C. T.

Fellows, Ch., *An Account of Discoveries in Lycia*. London, 1841.

Journal written during an Excursion in Asia Minor. London, 1839.

Fellows, Rev. S. B., quoted by George Brown, D.D., *Melanesians and Polynesians*. London, 1910.

Ferrand, G., *Les Musalmans à Madagascar*. Deuxième Partie. Paris, 1893.

Ferraro, Giuseppe, *Superstizioni, Usi e Proverbî Monferrini*. Palermo, 1886.

Ferrars, Max and Bertha, *Burma*. London, 1900.

Festgaben für Gustav Homeyer. Berlin, 1871.

Festschrift des Vereins für Erdkunde zu Dresden. Dresden, 1888.

Festschrift zum fünfzigjährigen Doctorjubiläum L. Friedlaender dargebracht von seinen Schülern. Leipsic, 1895.

Festus, *De verborum significatione*. Ed. C. O. Müller. Leipsic, 1839.

Feuillet, Madame Octave, *Quelques années de ma vie*. Fifth Edition. Paris, 1895.

Fewkes, Jesse Walter, "Hopi *Katcinas*," in *Twenty-first Annual Report of the Bureau of American Ethnology*. Washington, 1903.

"The Group of Tusayan Ceremonials called *Katcinas*," in *Fifteenth Annual Report of the Bureau of Ethnology*. Washington, 1897.

"The Lesser New-fire Ceremony at Walpi," in *American Anthropologist*, N.S. iii. (1901).

"The Tusayan New Fire Ceremony," in *Proceedings of the Boston Society of Natural History*, xxvi. (1895).

Fiedler, K. G., *Reise durch alle Theile des Königreichs Griechenland.* Leipsic, 1840–1841.

Field Museum of Natural History, Publication 170. Chicago.

Fielding, H., *The Soul of a People.* London, 1898.

Finamore, Gennaro, *Credenze, Usi e Costumi Abruzzesi.* Palermo, 1890.

Finaz, Father, S.J., in *Les Missions Catholiques,* vii. (1875).

Finlay, George, *Greece under the Romans.* Second Edition. Edinburgh and London, 1857.

Finsch, Otto, *Neu Guinea und seine Bewohner.* Bremen, 1865.

"Fire-Walking Ceremony at the Dharmaraja Festival," in *The Quarterly Journal of the Mythic Society,* vol. ii. No. 1 (October 1910).

"Fire-Walking in Ganjam," in *Madras Government Museum Bulletin,* vol. iv. No. 3. Madras, 1903.

Firmicus Maternus, *De errore profanarum religionum.* Ed. C. Halm. Vienna, 1867.

Fischer, Dr. Emil, "Paparuda und Scaloian," in *Globus,* xciii. (1908).

Fison, Rev. Lorimer, in letters to the Author (i. 316, 331 $n.^2$, 378, 389 $n.^3$, ii. 13 $n.^1$, iii. 30 $n.^1$, 40 $n.^1$, 92 $n.^3$, 131 $n.^2$, 264 $nn.^3$ and ^{4}, iv. 156 $n.^2$, v. 202 $n.$).

"Notes on Fijian Burial Customs," in *Journal of the Anthropological Institute,* x. (1881).

"The Nanga, or Sacred Stone Enclosure, of Wainimala, Fiji," in *Journal of the Anthropological Institute,* xiv. (1885).

Fison, L., and Howitt, A. W., *Kamilaroi and Kurnai.* Melbourne, Sydney, Adelaide, and Brisbane, 1880.

Fitzgerald, D., in *Revue Celtique,* iv. (1879–1880).

FitzGerald, Edward, quoted in *County Folk-lore, Suffolk.* London, 1893.

Fitzpatrick, J. F. J., "Some Notes on the Kwolla District and its Tribes," in *Journal of the African Society,* No. 37 (October 1910).

Fitz-roy, Captain R., *Narrative of the Surveying Voyages of His Majesty's Ships "Adventure" and "Beagle."* London, 1839.

Flacourt, E. de, *Histoire de la grande Isle Madagascar.* Paris, 1658.

Flad, Martin, *A Short Description of the Falasha and Kamants in Abyssinia.* Chrishona, near Basle, 1866.

Flaget, Mgr., in *Annales de la Propagation de la Foi,* vii. (1834).

Flavius Vopiscus, in *Scriptores Historiae Augustae.* Ed. H. Peter. Leipsic, 1884. *Aurelianus.* *Probus.*

Fleckeisen's Jahrbücher für classische Philologie.

Fleet, J. F., "A New System of the Sixty-Year Cycle of Jupiter," in *The Indian Antiquary,* xviii. (1889).

Fleming, Rev. Francis, *Kaffraria and its Inhabitants.* London, 1853. *Southern Africa.* London, 1856.

Fletcher, Miss Alice C., *The Import of the Totem, a Study from the Omaha Tribe.* Paper read before the American Association for the Advancement of Science, August 1897. Separate reprint.

Fletcher, Miss A. C., and Flesch, F. la, "The Omaha Tribe," in *Twenty-seventh Annual Report of the Bureau of American Ethnology.* Washington, 1911.

Floquet, A., *Histoire du privilège de Saint Romain.* Rouen, 1833.

Florus, *Epitoma.* Ed. C. Halm. Leipsic, 1854.

Foerster, R., *Der Raub und die Rückkehr der Persephone.* Stuttgart, 1874.

Folk-lore. London, 1890–

Folk-lore Journal. London, 1883–1889.

Folklore Journal, edited by the Working Committee of the South African Folklore Society. Cape Town, 1879–1880.

Folk-lore Record.

Fontana, N., "On the Nicobar Isles," in *Asiatick Researches*, iii. London, 1799.

Forbes, Captain C. J. F. S., *British Burma*. London, 1878.

Forbes, D., "On the Aymara Indians of Bolivia and Peru," in *Journal of the Ethnological Society of London*, ii. (October 1870).

Forbes, Fred. E., *Dahomey and the Dahomans*. London, 1851.

Forbes, H. O., "On some Tribes of the Island of Timor," in *Journal of the Anthropological Institute*, xiii. (1884).

Forbes, Major, *Eleven Years in Ceylon*. London, 1840.

*Fordun, *Scotichronicon*, quoted by J. Jamieson, *Etymological Dictionary of the Scottish Language*. New Edition. Paisley, 1879–1882.

Fortnightly Review, The.

Fossel, V., *Volksmedicin und medicinischer Aberglaube in Steiermark*. Second Edition. Graz, 1886.

Fossey, C., *La Magie assyrienne*. Paris, 1902.

Foucart, G., in Dr. J. Hastings's *Encyclopaedia of Religion and Ethics*, iii. (1910).

Foucart, P., *Des Associations Religieuses chez les Grecs*. Paris, 1873.
   Le Culte de Dionysos en Attique. Paris, 1904. (*Mémoires de l'Académie des Inscriptions et Belles-lettres*, xxxvii.)
   Les Grands Mystères d'Eleusis. Paris, 1900. (*Mémoires de l'Académie des Inscriptions*, xxxvii.)
   Recherches sur l'origine et la nature des mystères d'Eleusis. Paris, 1895. (*Mémoires de l'Académie des Inscriptions*, xxxv.)

Fouju, G., "Légendes et superstitions préhistoriques," in *Revue des Traditions populaires*, xiv. (1899).

Fouqué, F., *Santorin et ses éruptions*. Paris, 1879.

"Four Years' Journeying through Great Tibet, by one of the Trans-Himalayan Explorers," in *Proceedings of the Royal Geographical Society*, N.S., vii. (1885).

Fourdin, E., "La foire d'Ath," in *Annales du Cercle Archéologique de Mons*, ix. Mons, 1869.

Fournier, P., "De Zuidkust van Ceram," in *Tijdschrift voor Indische Taal-Land- en Volkenkunde*, xvi. (1867).

Fowler, W. Warde, in *The Classical Review*, vi. (1892).
   "Passing under the Yoke," in *The Classical Review* (March 1913).
   "The Oak and the Thunder-god," in *Archiv für Religionswissenschaft*, xvi. (1913).
   The Religious Experience of the Roman People. London, 1911.
   The Roman Festivals of the Period of the Republic. London, 1899.
   "Was the Flaminica Dialis priestess of Juno?" in *The Classical Review*, ix. (1895).

Foxwell, Ernest, of St. John's College, Cambridge. Private communication (xi. 10 n.[1]).

Foy, W., in *Archiv für Religionswissenschaft*, x. (1907).

Fraas, F., *Synopsis Plantarum Florae Classicae*. Munich, 1845.

Fragmenta historicorum Graecorum. Ed. C. Müller. Paris, 1868–1883.

Fragmenta Philosophorum Graecorum. Ed. F. G. A. Mullach. Paris, 1875.

France, Anatole, "Le roy boit," in *Annales Politiques et Littéraires*, 5 janvier, 1902.

France, H., "Customs of the Awuna Tribes," in *Journal of the African Society*, No. 17 (October 1905).

Francis, W., in *Census of India, 1901*, vol. xv. *Madras*, Part I. Madras, 1902.

Fränkel, Max, *Die Inschriften von Pergamon*. Berlin, 1890–1895.

Fraser, E. H., "The Fish-skin Tartars," in *Journal of the China Branch of the Royal Asiatic Society for the Year 1891–1892*, N.S. xxvi.

Fraser, J., "The Aborigines of New South Wales," in *Journal and Proceedings of the Royal Society of New South Wales*, xvi. (1882).

Fraser, W., in Sir John Sinclair's *Statistical Account of Scotland*. Edinburgh, 1793.

Fraser's Magazine.

Frazer, J. G., "A Suggestion as to the Origin of Gender in Language," in *The Fortnightly Review*, January 1900.

" Attis and Christ," in *The Athenaeum*, No. 4184, January 4th, 1908.

" Beliefs and Customs of the Australian Aborigines," in *Folk-lore*, xx. (1909).

" Folk-lore at Balquhidder," in *The Folk-lore Journal*, vi. (1888).

" Folk-lore in the Old Testament," in *Anthropological Essays presented to E. B. Tylor*. Oxford, 1907.

" Hide-measured Lands," in *The Classical Review*, ii. (1888).

" Howitt and Fison," in *Folk-lore*, xx. (1909).

in *The Athenaeum*, Nov. 21st, 1891.

in *Man*, vi. (1906).

Lectures on the Early History of the Kingship. London, 1905.

"Notes on Harvest Customs," in *The Folk-lore Journal*, vii. (1889).

" On certain Burial Customs as illustrative of the Primitive Theory of the Soul," in *Journal of the Anthropological Institute*, xv. (1886).

" On Some Ceremonies of the Central Australian Tribes," in the *Proceedings of the Australasian Association for the Advancement of Science for the Year 1900*. Melbourne, 1901.

Passages of the Bible chosen for their Literary Beauty and Interest. Second Edition. London, 1909.

Pausanias's Description of Greece, translated with a commentary. London, 1898.

Psyche's Task. Second Edition. London, 1913.

" Some Popular Superstitions of the Ancients," in *Folk-lore*, i. (1890).

" Statues of Three Kings of Dahomey," in *Man*, viii. (1908).

" Taboo" and "Thesmophoria," in *Encyclopaedia Britannica*, Ninth Edition, vol. xxiii.

The Belief in Immortality and the Worship of the Dead, vol. i. London, 1913.

"The Language of Animals," in *The Archaeological Review*, i. (April and May 1888).

" The Leafy Bust at Nemi," in *The Classical Review*, xxii. (1908).

" The Origin of Circumcision," in *The Independent Review*, November 1904.

"The Prytaneum, the Temple of Vesta, the Vestals, Perpetual Fires," in *The Journal of Philology*, xiv. (1885).

" The Youth of Achilles," in *The Classical Review*, vii. (1893).

Totemism. Edinburgh, 1887.

Totemism and Exogamy. London, 1910.

Frazer, Mrs. J. G. (Lady Frazer). Private communication (iii. 324 *n.*[4]). *See also* Grove, Mrs. Lilly.

Freeman, E. A., *History of the Norman Conquest of England*. Third Edition. Oxford, 1877.

Freeman, R. A., *Travels and Life in Ashanti and Jaman*. Westminster, 1898.

Frere, Mary, *Old Deccan Days*. Third Edition. London, 1881.

Freycinet, L. de, *Voyage autour du Monde*. Paris, 1829.

Frič, V., " Eine Pilcomayo-Reise in den Chaco Central," in *Globus*, lxxxix. (1906).

Frič, V., and Radin, P., "Contributions to the Study of the Bororo Indians," in *Journal of the Anthropological Institute*, xxxvi. (1906).

Friederich, R., "Voorloopig Verslag van het eiland Bali," in *Verhandelingen van het Bataviaasch Genootschap van Kunsten en Wetenschappen*, xxiii. (1849).

Friend, Rev. Hilderic, *Flowers and Flower Lore*. Third Edition. London, 1886.

Fries, C., " Das ' Koppensnellen ' auf Nias," in *Allgemeine Missions-Zeitschrift*, February 1908.

Fritsch, Gustav, *Die Eingeborenen Süd-Afrika's*.   Breslau, 1872.

Fritze, H. von, " Zum griechischen Opferritual," in *Jahrbuch des Kaiserlichen Deutschen Archäologischen Instituts*, xviii. (1903).

Frobenius, L., *Die Masken und Geheimbünde Afrikas*.   Halle, 1898.   (*Nova Acta, Abhandlungen der Kaiserlichen Leop.-Carol. Deutschen Akademie der Naturforscher*, vol. lxxiv. No. 1.)

Frodsham, Dr., Bishop of North Queensland, in letter to the Author (v. 103 *n.*[8]).

Froehner, W., *Musée Nationale du Louvre, Les Inscriptions Grecques*.   Paris, 1880.

Fulgentius, *Mythographiae*, in *Auctores Mythographi Latini*.   Ed. Aug. van Staveren.   Leyden and Amsterdam, 1742.

Fulton, R., " An Account of the Fiji Fire-walking Ceremony, or *Vilavilairevo*, with a probable explanation of the mystery," in *Transactions and Proceedings of the New Zealand Institute*, xxxv. (1902).

Furness, W. H., *Folk-lore in Borneo, a Sketch*.   Wallingford, Pennsylvania, 1899.   Privately printed.

" The Ethnography of the Nagas of Eastern Assam," in *Journal of the Anthropological Institute*, xxxii. (1902).

The Home-life of Borneo Head-hunters.   Philadelphia, 1902.

The Island of Stone Money, Uap of the Carolines.   Philadelphia and London, 1910.

Furnivall, J. S., in letter to the Author, dated Pegu Club, Rangoon, 6/6 (*sic*) (vii. 191 *n.*[1]).

Furtwängler, Adolf, *Die antiken Gemmen*.   Leipsic, 1900.

" Herakles," in W. H. Roscher's *Lexikon der griechischen und römischen Mythologie*, i.

Meisterwerke der griechischen Plastik.   Leipsic—Berlin, 1893.

" Futuna, or Horne Island and its People," in *Journal of the Polynesian Society*, vol. i. No. 1 (April 1892).

Fytche, Lieut.-General A., *Burma, Past and Present*.   London, 1878.

G * * *, Mathias, *Lettres sur les Îles Marquises*.   Paris, 1843.

Gabb, Wm. M., " On the Indian Tribes and Languages of Costa Rica," in *Proceedings of the American Philosophical Society held at Philadelphia*, xiv.   Philadelphia, 1876.

Gabet, Father, in *Annales de la Propagation de la Foi*, xx. (1848).

Gabriele, S., " Usi dei contadini della Sardegna," in *Archivio per lo Studio delle Tradizioni Popolari*, vii. (1880).

Gaertringen, F. Hiller von, in *Aus der Anomia*.   Berlin, 1890.

Gage, Thomas, *A New Survey of the West Indies*.   Third Edition.   London, 1677.

Gagnière, in *Annales de la Propagation de la Foi*, xxxii. (1860).

Gaidoz, H., " Bulletin critique de la Mythologie Gauloise," in *Revue de l'histoire des Religions*, ii.   Paris, 1880.

" Le dieu gaulois du soleil et le symbolisme de la roue," in *Revue Archéologique*, 3ème Série, iv. (1884).

" Les Langues coupées," in *Mélusine*, iii. (1886–1887).

Un Vieux Rite médical.   Paris, 1892.

Gait, E. A., in *Census of India, 1901*, vol. vi.   Calcutta, 1902.

in *Journal of the Asiatic Society of Bengal* (1898), quoted by Major P. R. T. Gurdon, *The Khasis*.   London, 1907.

Gaius, *Institutiones*.   Ed. P. E. Huschke.   Third Edition.   Leipsic, 1878.

Gallieni, " Missions dans le Haut Niger et à Ségou," in *Bulletin de la Société de Géographie* (Paris), 8ème Série, v. (1883).

Galton, (Sir) Francis, " Domestication of Animals," in *Transactions of the Ethnological Society of London*, N.S., iii. (1865).

Galton, (Sir) Francis—*continued.*
  Narrative of an Explorer in Tropical South Africa. Third Edition.
    London, 1890.
  In letter to the Author (v. 29 *n.*).
Gandavo, Pero de Magalhanes de, *Histoire de la province de Sancta-Cruz.*
    Paris, 1837. In H. Ternaux-Compans's *Voyages, relations, et mémoires
    originaux pour servir à l'histoire de la découverte de l'Amérique.*
    *Original published at Lisbon in 1586.
Garcilasso de la Vega, *Royal Commentaries of the Yncas.* Translated by (Sir)
    Clements R. Markham. Hakluyt Society. London, 1869–1871.
Gardiner, Professor J. Stanley. Private communication (ii. 154 *sq.*).
Gardner, E. A. Private communication (v. 232 *n.*).
Gardner, F., "Philippine (Tagalog) Superstitions," in *Journal of American
    Folk-lore,* xix. (1906).
Gardner, Percy, *Catalogue of Greek Coins, the Seleucid Kings of Syria.* London,
    1878.
  New Chapters in Greek History. London, 1892.
  Types of Greek Coins. Cambridge, 1883.
Garnett, Lucy M. J., *The Women of Turkey and their Folklore: The Christian
    Women.* London, 1890.
Garson, J. G., "On the Inhabitants of Tierra del Fuego," in *Journal of the
    Anthropological Institute,* xv. (1886).
Garstang, Professor J., MS. notes communicated to the Author (v. 135 *n.*).
  "Notes of a Journey through Asia Minor," in *Annals of Archaeology and
    Anthropology,* i. Liverpool and London, 1908.
  The Land of the Hittites. London, 1910.
  "The Sun God[dess] of Arenna," in *Annals of Archaeology and Anthro-
    pology,* vi. Liverpool, 1914.
  The Syrian Goddess. London, 1913.
Gason, Samuel, in E. M. Curr's *The Australian Race.* Melbourne, 1886–1887.
  in *Journal of the Anthropological Institute,* xxiv. (1895).
  "The Dieyerie Tribe," in *Native Tribes of South Australia.* Adelaide, 1879.
Gasquet, F. A., *Parish Life in Mediaeval England.* London, 1906.
Gathas, The, translated by L. H. Mills. *The Zend-Avesta,* part iii. Oxford,
    1887. (*The Sacred Books of the East,* vol. xxxi.)
Gatschet, A. S., in letter to the Author (xi. 276 *n.*[1]).
  A Migration Legend of the Creek Indians. Vol. I., Philadelphia, 1884.
    Vol. II., St. Louis, 1888.
  *The Karankawa Indians, the Coast People of Texas (Archaeological and
    Ethnological Papers of the Peabody Museum, Harvard University,* vol. i.
    No. 2).
  The Klamath Indians of South-Western Oregon. Washington, 1890. (*Con-
    tributions to North American Ethnology,* vol. ii. part i.)
Gay, C., "Fragment d'un voyage dans le Chili et au Cusco patrie des anciens
    Incas," in *Bulletin de la Société de Géographie* (Paris), Deuxième Série,
    xix. (1843).
Gazette archéologique.
Gazetteer of the Bombay Presidency. Bombay, 1877–1904.
Geddes, (Sir) W. D., in his edition of Plato's *Phaedo.* London and Edinburgh,
    1863.
Geiger, W., *Altiranische Kultur im Altertum.* Erlangen, 1882.
Geikie, J., *Prehistoric Europe.* Edinburgh, 1881.
Geiseler, *Die Oster-Insel.* Berlin, 1883.
Gell, Sir W., *The Topography of Rome and its Vicinity.* London, 1834.
Gellius, Aulus. *Noctes Atticae.* Ed. M. Hertz. Leipsic, 1861–1871.
Gellius, Cnaeus. Roman historian. Fragments in *Historicorum Romanorum
    Fragmenta,* ed. H. Peter. Leipsic, 1883.

Geminus, *Elementa Astronomiae.* Ed. C. Manitius. Leipsic, 1898.
Genesis, The Book of.
Gengler, Dr. J., "Der Kreuzschnabel als Hausarzt," in *Globus,* xci. (1907).
Gennep, A. van, "Janus Bifrons," in *Revue des traditions populaires,* xxii. (1907). *Tabou et Totémisme à Madagascar.* Paris, 1904.
Gennep, J. L. van, "Bijdrage tot de kennis van den Kangean-Archipel," in *Bijdragen tot de Taal- Land- en Volkenkunde van Nederlandsch-Indië,* xlvi. (1896).
Gentleman's Magazine, The.
Geographical Journal, The.
Geographi Graeci Minores. Ed. C. Müller. Paris, 1882.
Geological Survey of Canada, Report of Progress for 1878-1879.
Geoponica. Ed. J. N. Niclas. Leipsic, 1781.
Georgeakis, G., et Pineau, L., *Le Folk-lore de Lesbos.* Paris, 1894.
Georgi, J. G., *Beschreibung aller Nationen des russischen Reichs.* St. Petersburg, 1776.
Georgius Syncellus, *Chronographia.* Ed. G. Dindorf. Bonn, 1829.
Gerard, Miss E., *The Land beyond the Forest.* Edinburgh and London, 1888.
Gerhard, E., *Gesammelte akademische Abhandlungen.* Berlin, 1866-68.
Germain, Adrien, "Note zur Zanzibar et la Côte Orientale d'Afrique," in *Bulletin de la Société de Géographie* (Paris), 5ème Série, xvi. (1868).
Germania, N.R.
Gervasius von Tilbury, *Otia Imperialia.* Ed. F. Liebrecht. Hanover, 1856.
Geurtjens, H., "Le Cérémonial des voyages aux Îles Keij," in *Anthropos,* v. (1910).
Gibbon, Edward, *Decline and Fall of the Roman Empire.* Edinburgh, 1811.
Gibbs, George, in *Contributions to North American Ethnology.* Washington, 1877.
"Notes on the Tinneh or Chepewyan Indians of British and Russian America," in *Annual Report of the Smithsonian Institution* (1866).
Gilbert, G., *Handbuch der griechischen Staatsalterthümer.* Second Edition. Leipsic, 1893.
Gilbert, O., *Geschichte und Topographie der Stadt Rom im Altertum.* Leipsic, 1883-1890.
Giles, Professor H. A. Private communication (iv. 275).
Chinese Dictionary, quoted by W. G. Aston, *Shinto, the Way of the Gods.* London, 1905.
Giles, P., *Manual of Comparative Philology.* Second Edition. London, 1901.
Gilhodes, Ch., "La Culture matérielle des Katchins (Birmanie)," in *Anthropos,* v. (1910).
Gilij, F. S., *Saggio di Storia Americana.* Rome, 1781.
Gill, Captain W., *The River of Golden Sand.* London, 1880.
Gill, W. Wyatt, *Jottings from the Pacific.* London, 1885.
Life in the Southern Isles. London, N.D.
Myths and Songs of the South Pacific. London, 1876.
Gillen, F. J., "Notes on some Manners and Customs of the Aborigines of the McDonnel Ranges belonging to the Arunta Tribe," in *Report on the Work of the Horn Scientific Expedition to Central Australia,* Part iv. *Anthropology.* London and Melbourne, 1896. *See also s.v.* Spencer, Baldwin.
Ginzel, F. K., *Handbuch der mathematischen und technischen Chronologie,* vol. i. Leipsic, 1906.
Giornale della Società Asiatica Italiana.
Giovanni, G. di, *Usi, credenze e pregiudizî del Canavese.* Palermo, 1889.
Giraldus Cambrensis, *The Historical Works, containing The Topography of Ireland, etc.* Revised and edited by Thomas Wright. London, 1887. *See also s.v.* Hoare, Sir Richard Colt.

Giran, Paul, *Magie et Religion Annamites.* Paris, 1912.
Giraud-Teulon, A., *Les Origines du mariage et de la famille.* Geneva and Paris.
Girschner, Max, "Die Karolineninsel Namōluk und ihre Bewohner," in *Baessler-Archiv,* ii. (1912).
Gittée, A., *De hand en de vingeren in het volksgeloof.*
Glanvil, Joseph, *Saducismus Triumphatus or Full and Plain Evidence concerning Witches and Apparitions.* London, 1681.
Glaumont, "La culture de l'igname et du taro en Nouvelle-Calédonie," in *L'Anthropologie,* viii. (1897).
" Usages, mœurs et coutumes des Néo-Calédoniens," in *Revue d'Ethnographie,* vii. (1889).
Glave, E. J., *Six Years of Adventure in Congo Land.* London, 1893.
Globus. Illustrierte Zitschrift für Länder- und Völkerkunde.
*Glossarium Isidore Mart., cap. ii., cited by W. Mannhardt, *Antike Wald- und Feldkulte.*
Glover, T. R., in letter to the Author (ii. 231 *n.*[6]).
*Glükstad, Pastor Chr., *Sundalen og Oksendalens Beskrivelse.* Christiania.
Gmelin, J. G., *Reise durch Sibirien.* Göttingen, 1751–1752.
Gobin, C. le, *Histoire des Isles Marianes.* Paris, 1700.
Godden, Miss G. M., "Naga and other Frontier Tribes of North-Eastern India," in *Journal of the Anthropological Institute,* xxvii. (1898).
Goeje, Professor M. J. de, in *Internationales Archiv für Ethnographie,* xvi. (1904).
Goes, Damião de, "Chronicle of the Most Fortunate King Dom Emanuel," in *Records of South-Eastern Africa,* collected by G. McCall Theal, vol. iii. (1899).
Goldie, H., *Calabar and its Mission.* New Edition, with additional chapters by the Rev. John Taylor Dean. Edinburgh and London, 1901. Preface to original edition dated 1890.
Goldie, W. H., "Maori Medical Lore," in *Transactions and Proceedings of the New Zealand Institute,* xxxvii. (1904).
Goldmann, Dr. Emil, *Die Einführung der deutschen Herzogsgeschlechter Kärntens in den Slovenischen Stammesverband, ein Beitrag zur Rechts- und Kulturgeschichte.* Breslau, 1903.
Goldziher, Ignaz, "Der Dîwân des Garwal b. Aus Al-Hutej' a," in *Zeitschrift der Deutschen Morgenländischen Gesellschaft,* xlvi. (1892).
" Der Seelenvogel im islamischen Volksglauben," in *Globus,* lxxxiii. (1903).
Muhammedanische Studien. Halle a. S., 1888–1890.
Golther, W., *Handbuch der germanischen Mythologie.* Leipsic, 1895.
Gomes, Rev. E. H., *Seventeen Years among the Sea Dyaks of Borneo.* London, 1911.
" Two Sea Dyak Legends," in *Journal of the Straits Branch of the Royal Asiatic Society,* No. 41 (January 1904). Singapore.
Gomme, Mrs. A. B., "A Berwickshire Kirn-dolly," in *Folk-lore,* xii. (1901).
" Harvest Customs," in *Folk-lore,* xiii. (1902).
Gonzenbach, Laura, *Silicianische Märchen.* Leipsic, 1870.
Goodrich-Freer, Miss A., "More Folk-lore from the Hebrides," in *Folk-lore,* xiii. (1902).
" The Powers of Evil in the Outer Hebrides," in *Folk-lore,* x. (1899).
Googe, Barnabe, *The Popish Kingdom.* Reprinted London, 1880.
Gordon, Rev. E. M., in *Journal and Proceedings of the Asiatic Society of Bengal,* New Series, i. (1905).
Indian Folk Tales. London, 1908.
" Some Notes concerning the People of Mungēli Tahsīl, Bilaspur District," in *Journal of the Asiatic Society of Bengal,* lxxi. Part iii. Calcutta, 1903.
Gordon, W. R., "Words about Spirits," in (*South African*) *Folk-lore Journal,* ii. Cape Town, 1880.

Gore, Captain, cited by Capt. W. C. Robinson (iv. 139 *n.*[1]).
Gospel to the Hebrews (apocryphal), quoted by Origen.
Gottschling, Rev. E., "The Bawenda, a Sketch of their History and Customs," in *Journal of the Anthropological Institute*, xxxv. (1905).
Goudie, Gilbert, in letter to Sheriff-Substitute David J. Mackenzie (ix. 169 *n.*[2]).
Goudswaard, A., *De Papoewa's van de Geelvinksbaai*. Schiedam, 1863.
Gouldsbury, C., and Sheane, H., *The Great Plateau of Northern Rhodesia*. London, 1911.
Gover, Ch. E., *The Folk-songs of Southern India*. London, 1872.
"The Pongol Festival in Southern India," in *Journal of the Royal Asiatic Society*, N.S., v. (1870).
Gowing, L. F., *Five Thousand Miles in a Sledge*. London, 1889.
Gowland, W., "Dolmens and other Antiquities of Corea," in *Journal of the Anthropological Institute*, xxiv. (1895).
Graafland, N., *De Minahassa*. Rotterdam, 1869.
"Eenige aanteekeningen op ethnographisch gebied ten aanzien van het eiland Rote," in *Mededeelingen van wege het Nederlandsche Zendeling-genootschap*, xxxiii. (1889).
Grabowsky, F., "Der Bezirk von Hatzfeldthafen und seine Bewohner," in *Petermanns Mitteilungen*, xli. (1895).
"Der Distrikt Dusson Timor in Südost-Borneo und seine Bewohner," in *Das Ausland*, 1884, No. 24.
"Der Tod, das Begräbnis, etc., bei den Dajaken," in *Internationales Archiv für Ethnographie*, ii. (1889).
"Die Theogonie der Dajaken auf Borneo," in *Internationales Archiv für Ethnographie*, v. (1892).
"Über verschiedene weniger bekannte Opfer bei den Oloh Ngadju in Borneo," in *Internationales Archiv für Ethnographie*, i. (1888).
Graetz, H., *Geschichte der Juden*. Second Edition. Leipsic, 1866.
Graevius, J. G., *Thesaurus Antiquitatum Romanarum*. Leyden, 1694-1699.
Grainge, H. W., "Journal of a Visit to Mojanga on the North-West Coast," in *Antananarivo Annual and Madagascar Magazine*, No. 1 (Reprint of the First Four Numbers). Antananarivo and London, 1885.
Gramberg, J. S. G., "De Troeboekvisscherij," in *Tijdschrift voor Indische Taal- Land- en Volkenkunde*, xxiv. (1887).
"Eene maand in de Binnenlanden van Timor," in *Verhandelingen van het Bataviaasch Genootschap van Kunsten en Wetenschappen*, xxxvi. (1872).
Grandidier, A., "Des rites funéraires chez les Malgaches," in *Revue d'Ethnographie*, v. (1886).
"Madagascar," *Bulletin de la Société de Géographie* (Paris), Cinquième Série, xvii. (1869) ; also in Sixième Série, iii. (1872).
Grangeon, Damien, "Les Chams et leurs superstitions," in *Les Missions Catholiques*, xxviii. (1896).
Granger, Professor Frank, "A Portrait of the Rex Nemorensis," in *The Classical Review*, xxi. (1907), xxii. (1908).
"Early Man," in *The Victoria History of the County of Nottingham*, i. Edited by William Page. London, 1906.
The Worship of the Romans. London, 1895.
Grant, Rev. J., in Sir John Sinclair's *Statistical Account of Scotland*. Edinburgh, 1791-1799.
Grant, J. A., *A Walk across Africa*. Edinburgh and London, 1864.
Grant, W., "Magato and his Tribe," in *Journal of the Anthropological Institute*, xxxv. (1905).
Grant, W. Colquhoun, "Description of Vancouver's Island," in *Journal of the Royal Geographical Society*, xxvii. (1857).
Grant, W. M., in *Journal of American Folk-lore*, i. (1888).
Graphic, The.

Gratius Faliscus, *Cynegeticon*, in *Corpus Poetarum Latinorum*, ed. J. P. Postgate. London, 1894–1905.

Gray, G. B., *Studies in Hebrew Proper Names*. London, 1896.

Gray, Archdeacon J. H., *China*. London, 1878.

Gray, L. H., "The Double Nature of the Iranian Archangels," in *Archiv für Religionswissenschaft*, vii. (1904).

Gray, W., "Some Notes on the Tannese," in *Internationales Archiv für Ethnographie*, vii. (1894).

Greenidge, A. J. H., *Roman Public Life*. London, 1901.

Gregor, Rev. Walter, "Notes on Beltane Cakes," in *Folk-lore*, vi. (1895).
Notes on the Folk-lore of the North-East of Scotland. London, 1881.
"Preliminary Report on Folklore in Galloway, Scotland," in *Report of the British Association for 1896*.
"Quelques coutumes du Nord-est du Comté d'Aberdeen," in *Revue des Traditions populaires*, iii. (October 1888). Translated into French by M. Loys Brueyre.

Gregorius Cyprius, *Proverbia*, in *Paroemiographi Graeci*. Ed. E. L. Leutsch et F. Schneidewin. Göttingen, 1839–1851.

Gregorovius, F., *Corsica*. London, 1855.

Gregory, Professor J. W., "Is the Earth drying up?" in *The Geographical Journal*, xliii. (1914).

Gregory of Tours, *De gloria confessorum*, in Migne's *Patrologia Latina*, lxxi.
Historia Francorum, in Migne's *Patrologia Latina*, lxxi.
Histoire ecclésiastique des Francs. Traduction de M. Guizot. Nouvelle édition. Paris, 1874.

Greig, James S., in letter to the Author (xi. 187 n.[3]).

Grenfell, B. P., and Hunt, A. S., in *Egyptian Exploration Fund Archaeological Report*, 1902–1903.
New Classical and other Greek and Latin Papyri. Oxford, 1897.

*Grenier, Dom, *Histoire de la Province de Picardie*, quoted by Émile Hublard, *Fêtes du Temps Jadis, les Feux du Carême*. Mons, 1899.

Gressmann, H., *Altorientalische Texte und Bilder zum Alten Testamente*. Tübingen, 1909.

Greve, *s.vv.* "Hyakinthos" and "Linos," in W. H. Roscher's *Lexikon der griechischen und römischen Mythologie*.

Grey, (Sir) George, *Journals of Two Expeditions of Discovery in North-West and Western Australia*. London, 1841.

Grierson, G. A., *Bihār Peasant Life*. Calcutta, 1885.

Griffis, W. E., *Corea, the Hermit Nation*. London, 1882.

Grihya Sûtras, The. Translated by H. Oldenberg. Oxford, Part I., 1886, and Part II., 1892. (*Sacred Books of the East*, vols. xxix. and xxx.)

Grimm, Jacob, *Deutsche Mythologie*. Fourth Edition. Berlin, 1875–1878.
Deutsche Rechtsalterthümer. Third Edition. Göttingen, 1881.
Deutsche Sagen. Second Edition. Berlin, 1865–1866.
Deutsches Wörterbuch.
Household Tales. Translated by Margaret Hunt. London, 1884.
Kinder- und Hausmärchen. Seventeenth Edition. Berlin, 1880.
"Ueber die Marcellischen Formeln," in *Abhandlungen der Königlichen Akademie der Wissenschaft zu Berlin* (1855).
"Ueber Marcellus Burdigalensis," in *Abhandlungen der Königlichen Akademie der Wissenschaft zu Berlin* (1847).

Grimme, H., *Das israelitische Pfingstfest und der Plejadenkult*. Paderborn, 1907.

Grimshaw, Beatrice, *From Fiji to the Cannibal Islands*. London, 1907.

Grinnell, G. B., *Blackfoot Lodge Tales*. London, 1893.
"Cheyenne Woman Customs," in *American Anthropologist*, New Series, iv. New York, 1902.
Pawnee Hero-Stories and Folk-tales. New York, 1889.

Grohmann, Joseph Virgil, *Aberglauben und Gebräuche aus Böhmen und Mähren.* Prague and Leipsic, 1864.

Groome, F. H., *In Gipsy Tents.* Edinburgh, 1880.

Groome, W. Wollaston, "Suffolk Leechcraft," in *Folk-lore*, vi. (1895).

Groot, Professor J. J. M. de, "De Weertijger in onze Koloniën en op het oostaziatische Vasteland," in *Bijdragen tot de Taal- Land- en Volkenkunde van Nederlandsch-Indië*, xlix. (1898).

Les Fêtes annuellement célébrées à Emoui (Amoy). Paris, 1886.

Sectarianism and Religious Persecution in China. Amsterdam, 1903.

The Religion of the Chinese. New York, 1910.

The Religious System of China. Leyden, 1892–

Grose, Francis, *A Provincial Glossary.* New Edition. London, 1811.

Grossman, Captain, cited in *Ninth Annual Report of the Bureau of Ethnology.* Washington, 1892.

Grout, Rev. Lewis, *Zulu-land, or Life among the Zulu Kafirs.* Philadelphia, N.D.

Grove, Miss Florence, in letter to the Author (xi. 287 n.[1]).

Grove, Mrs. Lilly (Lady Frazer), *Dancing.* London, 1895.

Grubb, Rev. W. Barbrooke, *An Unknown People in an Unknown Land.* London, 1911.

Grunau, Simon, *Preussische Chronik.* Herausgegeben von Dr. M. Perlbach. Leipsic, 1876.

Grundtvig, Svend, *Dänische Volksmärchen.* Übersetzt von Willibald Leo. Leipsic, 1878.

Dänische Volksmärchen. Übersetzt von A. Strodtmann. Zweite Sammlung. Leipsic, 1879.

Grünwedel, A., "Sinhalesische Masken," in *Internationales Archiv für Ethnographie*, vi. (1893).

Gruppe, O., *s.v.* "Orpheus," in W. H. Roscher's *Lexikon der griechischen und römischen Mythologie*, iii.

Grützner, H., "Über die Gebräuche der Basutho," in *Verhandlungen der Berliner Gesellschaft für Anthropologie, Ethnologie und Urgeschichte* (1877).

Grynaeus, Simon, *Novus Orbis regionum ac insularum veteribus incognitarum.* Paris, 1532.

*Guagnini, *Sarmatiae Europaeae descriptio* (1578), quoted by L. Leger, *La Mythologie slave.* Paris, 1901.

Guagninus, Alexander, "De ducatu Samogitiae," in *Respublica sive status regni Poloniae, Lituaniae, Prussiae, Livoniae*, etc. Leyden (Elzevir), 1627.

Gubernatis, Angelo de, *La Mythologie des Plantes.* Paris, 1878–1882.

Usi Nuziali in Italia e presso gli altri Popoli Indo-Europei. Second Edition. Milan, 1878.

Güdemann, M., *Geschichte des Erziehungswesens und der Cultur der abendländischen Juden.* Vienna, 1880–1888.

Guerlach, "Chez les sauvages Ba-hnars," in *Les Missions Catholiques*, xvi. (1884), xix. (1887).

"Chez les sauvages de la Cochinchine Orientale, Bahnar, Reungao, Sédang," in *Les Missions Catholiques*, xxvi. (1894).

"Mœurs et superstitions des sauvages Ba-hnars," in *Les Missions Catholiques*, xix. (1887).

Guerry, "Sur les usages et traditions du Poitou," in *Mémoires et dissertations publiées par la Société Royale des Antiquaires de France*, viii. (1829).

Guevara, Jose, "Historia del Paraguay, Rio de la Plata, y Tucuman," in Pedro de Angelis's *Coleccion de Obras y Documentos relativos a la Historia antigua y moderna de las Provincias del Rio de la Plata*, vol. ii. Buenos-Ayres, 1836.

Guignes, De, *Voyages à Peking, Manille et l'Île de France.* Paris, 1808.

Guillain, *Documents sur l'histoire, la géographie, et le commerce de l'Afrique Orientale.* Paris, N.D.

Guillemé, Father, in *Annales de la Propagation de la Foi*, lx. (1888).
"Au Bengouéolo," in *Les Missions Catholiques*, xxxiv. (1902).
"Credenze religiose dei Negri di Kibanga nell' Alto Congo," in *Archivio per lo studio delle tradizioni popolari*, vii. (1888).
Guis, Le R. P., "Les Canaques, ce qu'ils font, ce qu'ils disent," in *Les Missions Catholiques*, xxx. (1898).
"Les Canaques, Mort-Deuil," in *Les Missions Catholiques*, xxxiv. (1902).
"Les *Nepu* ou Sorciers," in *Les Missions Catholiques*, xxxvi. (1904).
"Les Papous," in *Les Missions Catholiques*, xxxvi. (1904).
Guise, R. E., "On the Tribes inhabiting the Mouth of the Wanigela River, New Guinea," in *Journal of the Anthropological Institute*, xxviii. (1899).
Gumilla, J., *Histoire naturelle, civile et géographique de l'Orénoque*. Avignon, 1758.
Gunkel, H., *Genesis übersetzt und erklärt*. Göttingen, 1901.
Schöpfung und Chaos in Urzeit und Endzeit. Göttingen, 1895.
"Über die Beschneidung im alten Testament," in *Archiv für Papyrusforschung*, ii. (1903).
Gunthorpe, Lieut.-Colonel, "On the Ghosí or Gaddí Gaolís of the Deccan," in *Journal of the Anthropological Society of Bombay*, i.
Guppy, H. B., *The Solomon Islands and their Natives*. London, 1887.
Gupte, B. A., "Harvest Festivals in honour of Gauri and Ganesh," in *Indian Antiquary*, xxxv. (1906).
Gurdon, Major P. R. T., *The Khasis*. London, 1907.
Guthrie, Miss E. J., *Old Scottish Customs*. London and Glasgow, 1885.
Gutmann, Bruno, "Feldbausitten und Wachstumsbräuche der Wadschagga," in *Zeitschrift für Ethnologie*, xlv. (1913).
"Trauer und Begräbnissitten der Wadschagga," in *Globus*, lxxxix. (1906).
Gutschmid, A. von, *Kleine Schriften*. Leipsic, 1889–1894.

H. H., in *The Century Magazine*, May 1883.
Habakkuk, The Book of the Prophet.
Habbema, J., "Bijgeloof in de Praenger-Regentschappen," in *Bijdragen tot de Taal- Land- en Volkenkunde van Nederlandsch-Indië*, li. (1900).
Haddon, A. C., "A Batch of Irish Folk-lore," in *Folk-lore*, iv. (1893).
Head-hunters, Black, White, and Brown. London, 1901.
"Legends from Torres Straits," in *Folk-lore*, i. (1890).
in *Reports of the Cambridge Anthropological Expedition to Torres Straits*, v. Cambridge, 1904.
"The Ethnography of the Western Tribe of Torres Straits," in *Journal of the Anthropological Institute*, xix. (1890).
"The Religion of the Torres Straits Islanders," in *Anthropological Essays presented to E. B. Tylor*. Oxford, 1907.
The Study of Man. London and New York, 1898.
Haddon, A. C., and Browne, C. R., "The Ethnography of the Aran Islands," in *Proceedings of the Royal Irish Academy*, ii. (1893).
Haddon, Kathleen, *Cat's Cradles from Many Lands*. London, 1911.
Hagen, B., "Beiträge zur Kenntniss der Battareligion," in *Tijdschrift voor Indische Taal- Land- en Volkenkunde*, xxviii. (1883).
Unter den Papuas. Wiesbaden, 1899.
Hager, C., *Kaiser Wilhelms-Land und der Bismarck-Archipel*. Leipsic, N.D.
Haggard, Lieutenant Vernon H., in *Folk-lore*, xiv. (1903).
Hahl, A., "Das mittlere Neumecklenburg," in *Globus*, xci. (1907).
Hahl, Dr., "Mitteilungen über Sitten und rechtliche Verhältnisse auf Ponape," in *Ethnologisches Notizblatt*, ii. Heft 2. Berlin, 1901.
"Über die Rechtsanschauungen der Eingeborenen eines Teiles der Blanchebucht und des Innern der Gazelle Halbinsel," in *Nachrichten über Kaiser Wilhelms-Land und den Bismarck-Archipel* (1897).

Hahn, C. v., "Religiöse Anschauungen und Totengedächtnisfeier der Chewsuren," in *Globus*, lxxvi. (1899).

Hahn, Dr. C. H., in (*South African*) *Folklore Journal*, ii. (1880).

Hahn, Rev. F., "Some Notes on the Religion and Superstitions of the Orãos," in *Journal of the Asiatic Society of Bengal*, lxxii. part iii. Calcutta, 1904.

Hahn, J., "Das Land der Herero," in *Zeitschrift der Gesellschaft für Erdkunde zu Berlin*, iii. (1868).

Hahn, J. G. von, *Albanesische Studien*. Jena, 1854.
Griechische und albanesische Märchen. Leipsic, 1864.

Hahn, Josaphat, "Die Ovaherero," in *Zeitschrift der Gesellschaft für Erdkunde zu Berlin*, iv. (1869).

Hahn, Theophilus, "Die Buschmänner," in *Globus*, xviii.
Tsuni- || Goam, the Supreme Being of the Khoi-Khoi. London, 1881.

Haig, Captain Wolseley, "Notes on the Velamā Caste in Bārār," in *Journal of the Asiatic Society of Bengal*, lxx. part iii. (1901).

Haigh, A. E., *The Attic Theatre*. Oxford, 1889.

Halde, J. B. du, *The General History of China*. Third Edition. London, 1741.

Hale, A., "On the Sakais," in *Journal of the Anthropological Institute*, xv. (1886).

Hale, Horatio, "Iroquois Sacrifice of the White Dog," in *American Antiquarian*, vii. (1885).
The United States Exploring Expedition, Ethnography and Philology. Philadelphia, 1846.

Halévy, "Travels in Abyssinia," in *Publications of the Society of Hebrew Literature*, Second Series, vol. ii.

Halkin, J., *Quelques Peuplades du district de l' Uelé*. Liége, 1907.

Hall, Charles F., *Life with the Esquimaux*. London, 1864.
Narrative of the Second Arctic Expedition made by Charles F. Hall. Edited by Professor J. E. Nourse. Washington, 1879.

*Hall, Dr. C. H. H., in the *Sei-I Kwai Medical Journal*.

Hall, Rev. G. H., quoted in *The Denham Tracts*, edited by J. Hardy. London, 1892-1895.

Hallett, H. S., *A Thousand Miles on an Elephant in the Shan States*. Edinburgh and London, 1890.

Haltrich, Josef, *Deutsche Volksmärchen aus dem Sachsenlande in Siebenbürgen*. Fourth Edition. Vienna and Hermannstadt, 1885.
Zur Volkskunde der Siebenbürger Sachsen. Vienna, 1885.

Hamberger, P. Alois, in *Anthropos*, v. (1910).

Hamilton, Alexander, "A New Account of the East Indies," in J. Pinkerton's *Voyages and Travels*, viii.

Hamilton, Gavin, "Customs of the New Caledonian Women," in *Journal of the Anthropological Institute*, vii. (1878).

Hamilton, Professor G. L. Private communication (v. 57 *n.*[1]).

Hamilton, Mary, *Greek Saints and their Festivals*. Edinburgh and London, 1910.

Hamilton, Mr. (British Envoy at the Court of Naples), Letter in *Journal of the Royal Geographical Society*, ii. (1832).

Hamilton, W. J., *Researches in Asia Minor, Pontus, and Armenia*. London, 1842.

Hampson, R. T., *Medii Aevi Kalendarium*. London, 1841.

Handbook of American Indians north of Mexico. Edited by F. W. Hodge. Washington, 1907-1910 (*Bureau of American Ethnology*, Bulletin 30).

Hanway, Jonas, *An Historical Account of the British Trade over the Caspian Sea: with the Author's Journal of Travels*. Second Edition. London, 1754.

Hardisty, W. L., "The Loucheux Indians," in *Report of the Smithsonian Institution for 1866*.

Hardy, J., "Wart and Wen Cures," in *Folk-lòre Record*, i. (1878).
Hardy, Thomas, in *Folk-lore*, viii. (1897).
Harkness, Captain H., *Description of a Singular Aboriginal Race inhabiting the Summit of the Neilgherry Hills*. London, 1832.
Harland, John, and Wilkinson, T. T., *Lancashire Folk-lore*. Manchester and London, 1882.
Harmon, D. W., quoted by Rev. Jedidiah Morse, *Report to the Secretary of War of the United States on Indian Affairs*, Appendix. New-haven, 1822.
Harnack, A., *Lehrbuch der Dogmengeschichte*. Freiburg i. B., 1886–1890.
Harper, R. F., *Assyrian and Babylonian Literature*. New York, 1901.
Harpocration, *Lexicon*. Ed. G. Dindorf. Oxford, 1853.
Harrebomée, G. J., "Een ornamentenfeest van Gantarang (Zuid-Celebes)," in *Mededeelingen van wege het Nederlandsche Zendelinggenootschap*, xix. (1875).
Harris, John, *Complete Collection of Voyages and Travels*. London, 1744–1748.
Harris, J. Rendel, in letter to the Author (i. 15 *n*.).
  MS. notes of Folk-lore collected in the East.
  The Annotators of the Codex Bezae. London, 1901.
  The Cult of the Heavenly Twins. Cambridge, 1906.
  The Dioscuri in the Christian Legends. London, 1903.
Harris, W. B., "The Berbers of Morocco," in *Journal of the Anthropological Institute*, xxvii. (1898).
Harris, W. Cornwallis, *The Highlands of Aethiopia*. London, 1844.
Harrison, Rev. C., "Religion and Family among the Haidas," in *Journal of the Anthropological Institute*, xxi. (1892).
Harrison, Miss J. E., "Mystica Vannus Iacchi," in *Journal of Hellenic Studies*, xxiii. (1903).
  Mythology and Monuments of Ancient Athens. London, 1890.
  Prolegomena to the Study of Greek Religion. Second Edition. Cambridge, 1908.
Harte, Bret, *Complete Poetical Works*. London, 1886.
  "Friar Pedro's Ride."
  "Relieving Guard."
  "The Angelus, heard at the Mission Dolores, 1868."
Hartford Seminary Record.
Harthoorn, S. E., "De Zending op Java en meer bepaald die van Malang," in *Mededeelingen van wege het Nederlandsche Zendelinggenootschap*, iv. (1860).
Hartknoch, Chr., *Alt und neues Preussen*. Frankfort and Leipsic, 1684.
  Selectae dissertationes historicae de variis rebus Prussicis, bound up with his edition of P. de Düsburg's *Chronicon Prussiae*. Frankfort and Leipsic, 1679.
Hartland, E. S., in *Folk-lore*, i. (1890), iv. (1893), vii. (1896), viii. (1897).
  Primitive Paternity. London, 1909–1910.
  The Legend of Perseus. London, 1894–1896.
  "The Physicians of Myddfai," in *Archaeological Review*, i. (1888).
  "The Sin-eater," in *Folk-lore*, iii. (1892).
Härtter, G., "Der Fischfang im Evheland," in *Zeitschrift für Ethnologie*, xxxviii. (1906).
Hartung, O., "Zur Volkskunde aus Anhalt," in *Zeitschrift des Vereins für Volkskunde*, vii. (1897).
Harvard Studies in Classical Philology.
Hasselt, A. L. van, "Nota betreffende de rijstcultuur in de Residentie Tapanoeli," in *Tijdschrift voor Indische Taal- Land- en Volkenkunde*, xxxvi. (1893).
  Volksbeschrijving van Midden-Sumatra. Leyden, 1882.

Hasselt, J. L. van, " Aanteekeningen aangaande de gewoonten der Papoeas in de Dorebaai, ten opzichte van zwangerschap en geboorte," in *Tijdschrift voor Indische Taal- Land- en Volkenkunde,* xliii. (1901).

" Die Papuastämme an der Geelvinkbai, Neu-Guinea," in *Mitteilungen der Geographischen Gesellschaft zu Jena,* ix. (1891).

" Eenige Aanteekeningen aangaande de bewoners der N. Westkust van Nieuw Guinea, meer bepaaldelijk den Stam der Noefooreezen," in *Tijdschrift voor Indische Taal- Land- en Volkenkunde,* xxxi. (1886), xxxii. (1889).

Hasselt, Th. J. F. van, " Gebruik van vermomde Taal door de Nufooren," in *Tijdschrift voor Indische Taal- Land- en Volkenkunde,* xlv. (1902).

in *Tijdschrift voor Indische Taal- Land- en Volkenkunde,* xlvi. (1903).

Hastings, Dr. J., *Encyclopaedia of Religion and Ethics.* Edinburgh, 1908–

Hatton, Frank, *North Borneo.* 1886.

Haug, Martin, *Essays on the Sacred Language, Writings, and Religion of the Parsees.* Third Edition. London, 1884.

Haupt, Karl, *Sagenbuch der Lausitz.* Leipsic, 1862–1863.

Haupt, P., *Purim.* Leipsic, 1906.

Haussoulier, B., in *Recueil d'Inscriptions Juridiques Grecques.* Deuxième Série. Paris, 1898.

Havamal, in K. Simrock's *Die Edda* (Eighth Edition), and K. Müllenhoff's *Deutsche Altertumskunde,* v.

Havard, Mgr., in *Annales de la Propagation de la Foi,* vii. (1834).

Hawes, Mrs. (Miss Boyd). Private communication (v. 232 *n.*).

Hawkins, Benjamin, " A Sketch of the Creek Country," in *Collections of the Georgia Historical Society,* iii., part i. Savannah, 1848.

Haxthausen, August Freiherr von, *Studien über die inneren Zustände, das Volksleben und insbesondere die ländlichen Einrichtungen Russlands.* Hanover, 1847.

Transkaukasia. Leipsic, 1856.

*Hay, Sir John Drummond, *Western Barbary, its Wild Tribes and Savage Animals* (1844), quoted in *Folk-lore,* vii. (1896).

Hazeu, G. A. J., " Kleine bijdragen tot de ethnografie en folklore van Java," in *Tijdschrift voor Indische Taal- Land- en Volkenkunde,* xlvi. (1903).

Hazelwood, in J. E. Erskine's *Cruise among the Islands of the Western Pacific.* London, 1853.

Head, B. V., *Coins of Ephesus.* London, 1880.

Historia numorum. Oxford, 1887.

Headlam, W., in *Classical Review,* xv. (1901).

*Heanley, Rev. R. M., " The Vikings : traces of their Folklore in Marshland." A Paper read before the Viking Club, London, and printed in its *Saga-Book,* vol. iii. Part I., Jan. 1902.

Hearn, Captain G. R., " Passing through the Fire at Phalon," in *Man,* v. (1905).

Hearn, Lafcadio, *Glimpses of Unfamiliar Japan.* London, 1894.

Hearn, Dr. W. E., *The Aryan Household.* London, 1859.

Hearne, Samuel, *Journey from the Prince of Wales's Fort in Hudson's Bay to the Northern Ocean.* London, 1795.

*Hearne, Thomas, *Robert of Gloucester's Chronicles* (Oxford, 1724), quoted by (Sir) J. Rhys, *Celtic Heathendom.*

Heberdey, R., und Wilhelm, A., " Reisen in Kilikien," in *Denkschriften der Kaiserlichen Akademie der Wissenschaften, Philosophisch-historische Classe,* xliv. (Vienna, 1896), No. vi.

Hebrew and English Lexicon. Edited by F. Brown, S. R. Driver, and Ch. A. Briggs. Oxford, 1906.

Hebrews, The Epistle to the.

Heckewelder, Rev. John, " An Account of the History, Manners, and Customs of the Indian Nations who once inhabited Pennsylvania and the neighbouring States," in *Transactions of the Historical and Literary Committee of the American Philosophical Society*, vol. i. Philadelphia, 1819.

Hecquard, H., *Reise an die Küste und in das Innere von West-Afrika.* Leipsic, 1854.

Hegel, G. W. F., *Vorlesungen über die Philosophie der Religion.* (Vol. xi. of the first collected edition of Hegel's works. Berlin, 1832.) *Lectures on the Philosophy of Religion.* Translated by the Rev. E. B. Spiers, D.D., and J. Burdon Sanderson. London, 1895.

Hehn, V., *Kulturpflanzen und Haustiere in ihrem Übergang aus Asien.* Seventh Edition. Berlin, 1902.

Heiberg, Sigurd K., in letter to Miss Anderson of Barskimming (x. 171 *n*.[3]).

Heijmering, G., " Zeden en gewoonten op het eiland Rottie," in *Tijdschrift für Neêrlands Indië* (1843).

" Zeden en gewoonten op het eiland Timor," *Tijdschrift voor Neêrlands Indië* (1845).

" Heilige Haine und Bäume der Finnen," in *Globus*, lix. (1891).

Heimskringla. Done into English by W. Morris and E. Magnússon. *The Saga Library*, vol. iii.

Heimskringla, The, or Chronicle of the Kings of Norway. Translated from the Icelandic of Snorri Sturluson, by S. Laing. London, 1844.

Heine, H., *The Pilgrimage to Kevlaar* (*Die Wallfahrt nach Kevlaar*, in *Buch der Lieder*).

" *Ich hatte einst ein schönes Vaterland.*"

Heinrich, A., *Agrarische Sitten und Gebräuche unter den Sachsen Siebenbürgens.* Hermannstadt, 1880.

Helbig, W., in *Bulletino dell' Instituto di Corrispondenza Archeologica*, 1885. *Die Italiker in der Poebene.* Leipsic, 1879.

Führer durch die öffentlichen Sammlungen klassischer Altertümer in Rom. Second Edition. Leipsic, 1899.

in *Notizie degli Scavi*, 1885.

Helderman, W. D., " De tijger en het bijgeloof der Bataks," in *Tijdschrift voor Indische Taal- Land- en Volkenkunde*, xxxiv. (1891).

Heliodorus, *Aethiopica.* Ed. Im. Bekker. Leipsic, 1855.

Helladius, in Photius, *Bibliotheca.* Ed. Im. Bekker. Berlin, 1824.

Hellanicus, cited by the Scholiast on Apollonius Rhodius, *Argonautica.* Fragments in *Fragmenta Historicorum Graecorum*, ed. C. Müller, vol. i.

Hely, B. A., " Notes on Totemism, etc., among the Western Tribes," in *British New Guinea, Annual Report for 1894–1895.*

Hemingway, Mr., quoted by E. Thurston, *Castes and Tribes of Southern India.*

Henderson, J., " The Medicine and Medical Practice of the Chinese," in *Journal of the North China Branch of the Royal Asiatic Society*, New Series, i. Shanghai, 1865.

Henderson, William, *Notes on the Folk-lore of the Northern Counties of England and the Borders.* London, 1879.

Hennepin, L., *Description de la Louisiane.* Paris, 1683.

Nouvelle Découverte d'un très grand pays situé dans l'Amérique. Utrecht,1697.

Nouveau voyage d'un pais plus grand que l'Europe. Utrecht, 1698.

Henry, Travels among the Northern and Western Indians, quoted by the Rev. Jedediah Morse, in *Report to the Secretary of War of the United States on Indian Affairs.* Appendix. Newhaven, 1822.

Travels, quoted by J. Mooney, " Myths of the Cherokee," in *Nineteenth Annual Report of the Bureau of American Ethnology*, Part i. Washington, 1900.

Henry, A., " The Lolos and other Tribes of Western China," in *Journal of the Anthropological Institute*, xxxiii. (1903).

Henry, Miss Tenira, in *_Journal of the Polynesian Society_, vol. ii. No. 2, quoted by Andrew Lang, _Modern Mythology_.

Henry, W. A., "Bijdrage tot de Kennis der Bataklanden," in _Tijdschrift voor Indische Taal- Land- en Volkenkunde_, xvii.

Henshaw, Richard, Agent for Native Affairs at Calabar, quoted by Mr. John Parkinson, in _Man_, vi. 1906.

Henzen, in _Annali dell' Instituto_, 1856.

Henzen, G. [W.], _Acta Fratrum Arvalium_. Berlin, 1874.

Henzen, W., in _Hermes_, vi. (1872).

Hepding, H., _Attis, seine Mythen und sein Kult_. Giessen, 1903.

Heraclides Cumanus, in Athenaeus.

Heraclides Ponticus, in _Fragmenta Historicorum Graecorum_, ed. C. Müller, vol. ii.

Heraclitus, griechisch und deutsch, von H. Diels. Second Edition, Berlin, 1909 ; also in _Die Fragmente der Vorsokratiker_, ed. H. Diels, vol. i.

Héricourt, C. E. X. d', _Voyage sur la côte orientale de la Mer Rouge dans le pays d'Adel et le royaume de Choa_. Paris, 1841.

Hermann, K. F., _Lehrbuch der gottesdienstlichen Alterthümer der Griechen_. Second Edition. Heidelberg, 1858.

 Lehrbuch der griechischen Privatalterthümer. Ed. H. Blümner. Freiburg i. Baden und Tübingen, 1882.

 "Über griechische Monatskunde," in _Abhandlungen der historisch-philologischen Classe der Königlichen Gesellschaft der Wissenschaften zu Göttingen_, ii. (1843–44).

Hermann, P., _Nordische Mythologie_. Leipsic, 1903.

Hermes.

Herndon, W. Lewis, _Exploration of the Valley of the Amazon_. Washington, 1854.

Herodas, _Mimes_. Ed. J. Arbuthnot Nairn. Oxford, 1904.

Herodian. Ed. Im. Bekker. Leipsic, 1855.

Herodotus. Ed. J. C. F. Baehr. Editio Altera. Leipsic, 1856–1861.

 Erklärt von H. Stein. Berlin, 1877–1883.

 Zweites Buch mit sachlichen Erläuterungen herausgegeben von Alfred Wiedemann. Leipsic, 1890.

Herold, Lieutenant, "Bericht betreffend religiöse Anschauungen und Gebräuche der deutschen Ewe-Neger," in _Mittheilungen von Forschungsreisenden und Gelehrten aus den deutschen Schutzgebieten_, v. Berlin, 1892.

Herrera, Antonio de, quoted by A. Bastian, in _Die Culturländer des alten Amerika_. Berlin, 1878.

 The General History of the Vast Continent and Islands called America. Translated by Captain John Stevens. London, 1725–1726.

Herrick, Robert, _Works_. Edinburgh, 1823.

 "Hesperides."

 "The Hock-cart or Harvest Home."

 "Twelfth Night, or King and Queene."

Herrmann, E., "Über Lieder und Brauche bei Hochzeiten in Kärnten," in _Archiv für Anthropologie_, xix. (1891).

Herrmann, P., _Deutsche Mythologie_. Leipsic, 1906.

 Nordische Mythologie. Leipsic, 1903.

Hertz, W., _Der Werwolf_. Stuttgart, 1862.

 "Die Sage vom Giftmädchen," in _Gesammelte Abhandlungen_. Stuttgart and Berlin, 1905.

Herve, G., "Quelques superstitions de Morvan," in _Bulletins de la Société d'Anthropologie de Paris_, 4ème série, iii. (1892).

Hervey, D. F. A., in _Indian Notes and Queries_ (December, 1886).

 "The Mentra Traditions," in _Journal of the Straits Branch of the Royal Asiatic Society_, No. 10. Singapore, 1883.

Herzog, H., _Schweizerische Volksfeste, Sitten und Gebräuche_. Aarau, 1884.

Herzog, J. J., und Plitt, G. F., *Real-Encyclopädie für protestantische Theologie und Kirche*. Second Edition. Leipsic, 1877.
Hesiod. Ed. F. A. Paley. Second Edition. London, 1883.
    Theogony.
    Works and Days.
Hesychius, *Lexicon*. Ed. M. Schmidt. Editio Altera. Jena, 1867.
Hesychius Milesius, in *Fragmenta Historicorum Graecorum*, ed. C. Müller, vol. iv.
Hetherwick, Rev. A., "Some Animistic Beliefs among the Yaos of British Central Africa," in *Journal of the Anthropological Institute*, xxxii. (1902).
Heuzey, L., *Le Mont Olympe et l'Acarnanie*. Paris, 1860.
Hewitt, J. B. N., "New Fire among the Iroquois," in *The American Anthropologist*, ii. (1889).
Hewitt, Mrs., "Some Sea-Dyak Tabus," in *Man*, viii. (1908).
Heyting, Th. A. L., "Beschrijving der onderafdeeling Groot Mandeling en Batang-Natal," in *Tijdschrift van het Nederlandsch Aardrijkskundig Genootschap*, Tweede Serie, xiv. (1897).
Hibbert Journal, The.
Hibeh Papyri, Part I. Edited by B. P. Grenfell and A. S. Hunt. London, 1906.
*Hibernian Magazine, July 1817, quoted by T. F. Thiselton Dyer, *British Popular Customs*. London, 1876.
Hicks, E. L., "Inscriptions from Western Cilicia," in *Journal of Hellenic Studies*, xii. (1891).
Hickson, S. J., *A Naturalist in North Celebes*. London, 1889.
Higgins, Rev. J. C., Notes furnished to the Author (x. 207 *n.²*).
High History of the Holy Graal. Translated from the French by Sebastian Evans. London, 1898.
Hildebrandt, J. M., "Ethnographische Notizen über Wakamba und ihre Nachbarn," in *Zeitschrift für Ethnologie*, x. (1878).
Hill, G. F., *Catalogue of the Greek Coins of Cyprus*. London, 1904.
    Catalogue of the Greek Coins of Lycaonia, Isauria, and Cilicia. London, 1900.
    Catalogue of the Greek Coins of Lycia, Pamphylia, and Pisidia. London, 1897.
    in letters to the Author (v. 35 *n.²*, 126 *n.²*, 162 *n.¹*, 165 *n.⁶*).
Hill, Miss Nina, in letter to the Author (ii. 95 *n.*).
Hillebrandt, A., *Ritual-Litteratur, Vedische Opfer und Zauber*. Strasburg, 1897.
Hillner, Johann, *Volksthümlicher Brauch und Glaube bei Geburt und Taufe im Siebenbürger Sachsenlande*. Apparently a programme of the High School (*Gymnasium*) at Schässburg in Transylvania for the year 1876–1877.
Hill-Tout, C., "Ethnological Report on the Stseelis and Skaulits Tribes of the Halokmelem Division of the Salish of British Columbia," in *Journal of the Anthropological Institute*, xxxiv. (1904).
    in "Report of the Committee on the Ethnological Survey of Canada," *Report of the British Association for the Advancement of Science*. Bradford, 1900.
    "Report on the Ethnology of the Stlatlum Indians of British Columbia," in *Journal of the Anthropological Institute*, xxxv. (1905).
    The Far West, the Home of the Salish and Déné. London, 1907.
Himerius, *Orationes*. Ed. Fr. Dübner. Paris (Didot), 1878.
Hinde, S. L., and Hinde, H., *The Last of the Masai*. London, 1901.
Hippocrates, *Opera*. Ed. C. G. Kühn. Leipsic, 1825–1827.
    De aere, locis et aquis.
    De morbo sacro (quoted by E. Rohde, *Psyche*, Third Edition).

Hippolytus, *Commentary on Daniel.* Ed. G. N. Bonwetsch and H. Achelis. Leipsic, 1897.

Refutatio omnium haeresium. Ed. L. Duncker and F. G. Schneidewin. Göttingen, 1859.

Hipponax, cited by Strabo.

quoted by Athenaeus.

quoted by J. Tzetzes, *Chiliades.* Ed. Th. Kiesseling. Leipsic, 1826.

Hirn, Y., *Origins of Art.* London, 1900.

Hirt, H., *Die Indogermanen.* Strasburg, 1905–1907.

"Die Urheimat der Indogermanen," in *Indogermanische Forschungen*, i. (1892).

Hislop, Rev. Alexander, *The Two Babylons.* Edinburgh, 1853.

"Histoire des rois de l'Hindoustan après les Pandaras, traduite du texte hindoustani de Mîr Cher-i Alî Afsos, par M. l'abbé Bertrand," in *Journal Asiatique*, 4ème Série, iii. Paris, 1844.

History of the Sect of the Maharajas or Vallabhacharyas. Published by Trübner. London, 1865.

*Hitchin, *History of Cornwall*, quoted by William Hone, *Every-Day Book.* London, preface dated 1827.

Hoare, Sir Richard Colt, *The Itinerary of Archbishop Baldwin through Wales A.D. MCLXXXVIII.*, by Giraldus de Barri. London, 1806. *See also s.v.* Giraldus Cambrensis.

Hobley, C. W., "British East Africa, Anthropological Studies in Kavirondo and Nandi," in *Journal of the Anthropological Institute*, xxxiii. (1903).

Eastern Uganda. London, 1902.

"Further Researches into Kikuyu and Kamba Religious Beliefs and Customs," in *Journal of the Royal Anthropological Institute*, xli. (1911).

The Ethnology of A-Kamba and other East African Tribes. Cambridge, 1910. in letter to the Author (ii. 316 n.[3]).

Hocker, N., *Des Mosellandes Geschichten, Sagen und Legenden.* Trier, 1852. in *Zeitschrift für deutsche Mythologie und Sittenkunde*, i. (1853).

Hodgson, Adam, *Letters from North America.* London, 1824.

Hodson, T. C., "The *genna* amongst the Tribes of Assam," in *Journal of the Anthropological Institute*, xxxvi. (1906).

The Meitheis. London, 1908.

The Naga Tribes of Manipur. London, 1911.

"The Native Tribes of Manipur," in *Journal of the Anthropological Institute*, xxxi. (1901).

Hoeck, K., *Kreta.* Göttingen, 1828.

Hoensbroech, Graf von Paul, *14 Jahre Jesuit.* Leipsic, 1909–1910.

Hoëvell, G. W. W. C. Baron van, *Ambon en meer bepaaldelijk de Oeliasers.* Dordrecht, 1875.

"Iets over 't oorlogvoeren der Batta's," in *Tijdschrift voor Nederlandsch-Indië*, N.S., vii. (1878).

in *Internationales Archiv für Ethnographie*, viii. (1895).

"Leti-eilanden," in *Tijdschrift voor Indische Taal- Land- en Volkenkunde*, xxxiii. (1890).

Hoëvell, W. R. van, "Sjaïr Bidasari, een oorspronkelijk Maleisch Gedicht, uitgegeven en van eene Vertaling en Anteekeningen voorzien," in *Verhandelingen van het Bataviaasch Genootschap van Kunsten en Wetenschappen*, xix. Batavia, 1843.

Hoffman, G., *Auszüge aus Syrischen Akten persisischer Martyrer übersetzt.* Leipsic, 1880.

Hoffman, W. J., "The Menomini Indians," in *Fourteenth Annual Report of the Bureau of Ethnology.* Washington, 1896.

"The Midewiwin or Grand Medicine Society of the Ojibwa," in *Seventh Annual Report of the Bureau of Ethnology.* Washington, 1891.

Hoffmann, E., in *Rheinisches Museum für Philologie*, N.F., l. (1895).
Hoffmann, H., *Sale Catalogue*. Paris, 1888.
Hoffmann-Krayer, E., *Feste und Bräuche des Schweizervolkes*. Zürich, 1913.
"Fruchtbarkeitsriten im schweizerischen Volksbrauch," in *Schweizerisches Archiv für Volkskunde*, xi. (1907).
Hofmayr, P. W., "Religion der Schilluk," in *Anthropos*, vi. (1911).
Hogarth, D. G., *A Wandering Scholar in the Levant*. London, 1896.
Devia Cypria. London, 1889.
"Recent Hittite Research," in *Journal of the Royal Anthropological Institute*, xxxix. (1909).
Hogarth, D. G., and Munro, J. A. R., "Modern and Ancient Roads in Eastern Asia Minor," in *Royal Geographical Society Supplementary Papers*, vol. iii. part 5. London, 1893.
Hoggan, Frances, M.D., "The Neck Feast," in *Folk-lore*, iv. (1893).
Holland, Lieutenant S. C., "The Ainos," in *Journal of the Anthropological Institute*, iii. (1874).
Hollander, J. J. de, *Handleiding bij de Beoffening der Land- en Volkenkunde van Nederlandsch Oost-Indië*. Breda, 1882–1884.
Holle, K. F., "Snippers van den Regent van Galoeh," in *Tijdschrift voor Indische Taal- Land- en Volkenkunde*, xxvii. (1882).
Holley, Missionary, in *Annales de la Propagation de la Foi*, liv. (1882).
"Étude sur les Egbas," in *Les Missions Catholiques*, xiii. (1881).
Hollis, A. C., in letter to the Author (xi. 262 *n.*[2]).
MS. notes sent to the Author (v. 68 *n.*[1]).
The Masai. Oxford, 1905.
The Nandi, their Language and Folklore. Oxford, 1909.
Holm, A., *Geschichte Siciliens im Alterthum*. Leipsic, 1870–1874.
Holmberg, H. J., "Ethnographische Skizzen über die Völker des russischen Amerika," in *Acta Societatis Scientiarum Fennicae*, iv. Helsingfors, 1856.
Holmes, Rev. J., "Initiation Ceremonies of Natives of the Papuan Gulf," in *Journal of the Anthropological Institute*, xxxii. (1902).
Holtzmann, A., *Das Mahābharata und seine Theile*. Kiel, 1895.
Holub, E., *Sieben Jahre in Süd Afrika*. Vienna, 1881.
Holzmayer, J. B., "Osiliana," in *Verhandlungen der Gelehrten Estnischen Gesellschaft zu Dorpat*, vii. No. 2. Dorpat, 1872.
Homer, *Hymni*. Ed. Aug. Baumeister. Leipsic, 1860.
Homeric Hymns. Edited by T. W. Allen and E. E. Sikes. London, 1904.
Hymn to Aphrodite.
Hymn to Apollo.
Hymn to Demeter.
Hymn to Earth.
Hymn to Mercury (Hermes).
Odyssey. Ed. W. W. Merry. Oxford, 1870–1878.
Homeward Mail.
Hommel, Fritz, *Grundriss der Geographie und Geschichte des alten Orients*. Second Edition. Munich, 1904. In Iwan von Müller's *Handbuch der klassischen Altertumswissenschaft*, vol. iii.
Hone, William, *Every-Day Book*. London, N.D., preface dated 1827.
Year Book. London, N.D., preface dated January 1832.
Hope, R. C., *The Legendary Lore of the Holy Wells of England*. London, 1893.
Horace. Ed. A. J. Macleane. Second Edition. London, 1869.
Ars poetica.
Carmen Saeculare.
Epodes.

Horrack, P. J. de, " Lamentations of Isis and Nephthys," in *Records of the Past*. London, N.D.

Horst, D. W., "Rapport van eene reis naar de Noordkust van Nieuw Guinea," in *Tijdschrift voor Indische Taal- Land- en Volkenkunde*, xxxii. (1889).

Horton, J. Africanus B., *West African Countries and Peoples*. London, 1868.

Hose, Bishop, "The Contents of a Dyak Medicine Chest," in *Journal of the Straits Branch of the Royal Asiatic Society*, No. 39, June 1903.

Hose, Dr. Charles, "In the Heart of Borneo," in *The Geographical Journal*, xvi. (1900).

    Notes on the Natives of British Borneo. (In manuscript.)

    "The Natives of Borneo," in *Journal of the Anthropological Institute*, xxiii. (1894).

    "Various Modes of computing the Time for Planting among the Races of Borneo," in *Journal of the Straits Branch of the Royal Asiatic Society*, No. 42. Singapore, 1905.

Hose, Ch., and McDougall, W., *The Pagan Tribes of Borneo*. London, 1912.

    "The Relations between Men and Animals in Sarawak," in *Journal of the Anthropological Institute*, xxxi. (1901).

Hose, C., and Shelford, R., "Materials for a Study of Tatu in Borneo," in *Journal of the Anthropological Institute*, xxxvi. (1906).

Hosea, The Book of the Prophet.

Houghton, B., in *Indian Antiquary*, xxv. (1896).

Houghton, E. P., " On the Land Dayaks of Upper Sarawak," in *Memoirs of the Anthropological Society of London*, iii. (1870).

Housman, Professor A. E., in letter to the Author (x. 221).

Howitt, A. W., " Further Notes on the Australian Class Systems," in *Journal of the Anthropological Institute*, xviii. (1889).

    "On Australian Medicine-Men," in *Journal of the Anthropological Institute*, xvi. (1887).

    "On some Australian Beliefs," in *Journal of the Anthropological Institute*, xiii. (1884).

    "On some Australian Ceremonies of Initiation," in *Journal of the Anthropological Institute*, xiii. (1884).

    "On the Migration of the Kurnai Ancestors," in *Journal of the Anthropological Institute*, xv. (1886).

    "The Dieri and other Kindred Tribes of Central Australia," in *Journal of the Anthropological Institute*, xx. (1891).

    "The Jeraeil, or Initiation Ceremonies of the Kurnai Tribe," in *Journal of the Anthropological Institute*, xiv. (1885).

    The Native Tribes of South-East Australia. London, 1904.

Howitt, Mary E. B., *Folklore and Legends of some Victorian Tribes*. (In manuscript.)

Hubert, H., and Mauss, M., "Esquisse d'une théorie générale de la magie," in *L'Année Sociologique*, vii. Paris, 1904.

    "Essai sur le sacrifice," in *L'Année Sociologique*, ii. Paris, 1899.

Hublard, Émile, *Fêtes du Temps Jadis, les Feux du Carême*. Mons, 1899.

Hubner, quoted by W. H. Dall, "On Masks, Labrets, and certain Aboriginal Customs," in *Third Annual Report of the Bureau of Ethnology*. Washington, 1884.

Huc, *L'Empire chinois*. Fourth Edition. Paris, 1862.

    Fifth Edition. Paris, 1879.

    Souvenirs d'un voyage dans la Tartarie et le Thibet. Sixième Edition. Paris, 1878.

Hueber, "A travers l'Australie," in *Bulletin de la Société de Géographie* (Paris), 5ème Série, ix. (1865).

Huelsen, Ch., *Die Ausgrabungen auf dem Forum Romanum.* Second Edition. Rome, 1903.
Hügel, Baron Charles, *Travels in Kashmir and the Panjab.* London, 1845.
Hughes, Miss E. P. Private communication (xi. 10 *n*.[1]).
Humann, K., und Puchstein, O., *Reisen in Kleinasien und Nordsyrien.* Berlin, 1890.
Humbert, A., *Le Japon illustré.* Paris, 1870.
Humboldt, A. de, *Voyage aux régions équinoxiales du Nouveau Continent.* Paris, 1819.
Humboldt, Alex. von, *Researches concerning the Institutions and Monuments of the Ancient Inhabitants of America.* London, 1814.
    Kosmos. Stuttgart and Tübingen, 1845.
        English version. Edited by E. Sabine.
Hunt, Robert, *Popular Romances of the West of England.* Third Edition. London, 1881.
Hunter, W. W., *Annals of Rural Bengal.* Fifth Edition. London, 1872.
    Orissa. London, 1872.
Hupe, C., "Korte Verhandeling over de Godsdienst, Zeden enz. der Dajakkers," in *Tijdschrift voor Neêrlands Indië.* Batavia, 1846.
Hurgronje, C. Snouck, *De Atjéhers.* Batavia and Leyden, 1893-1894.
    Het Gajöland en zijne Bewoners. Batavia, 1903.
Hutchinson, Thomas J., *Impressions of Western Africa.* London, 1858.
    "On the Chaco and other Indians of South America," in *Transactions of the Ethnological Society of London,* N.S., iii. (1865).
*Hutchinson, W., *History of Northumberland,* quoted by J. Brand, *Popular Antiquities of Great Britain,* ii., Bohn's Edition.
    View of Northumberland. Newcastle, 1778.
Hyde, Douglas, *A Literary History of Ireland.* London, 1899.
    Beside the Fire, a Collection of Irish Gaelic Folk Stories. London, 1890.
Hyde, Thomas, *Historia religionis veterum Persarum.* Oxford, 1700.
Hyginus, *Astronomica.* Ed. Bern. Bunte. Leipsic, 1874.
    Fabulae. Ed. Bern. Bunte. Leipsic, N.D.
Hylten-Cavallius, quoted by F. Liebrecht, *Zur Volkskunde.*
Hymns of the Atharva-Veda. Translated by Maurice Bloomfield. Oxford, 1897. (*Sacred Books of the East,* vol. xlii.)
Hymns of the Rigveda. Translated by R. T. H. Griffith, Benares, 1889-1892.
Hyperides, *Orationes.* Ed. Fr. Blass. Second Edition. Leipsic, 1881.

Ibbetson, D. C. J., *Outlines of Panjáb Ethnography.* Calcutta, 1883.
    Report on the Revision of Settlement of the Panipat, Tahsil, and Karnal Parganah of the Karnal District. Allahabad, 1883.
Ibn Batoutah, *Voyages.* Texte Arabe, accompagné d'une traduction par C. Défrémery et B. R. Sanguinetti. Paris, 1853-1858.
Ideler, L., *Handbuch der mathematischen und technischen Chronologie.* Berlin, 1825-1826.
"Ieso-Ki, ou description de l'île d'Iesso, avec une notice sur la révolte de Samsay-in, composée par l'interprète Kannemon," printed in Malte-Brun's *Annales des Voyages,* xxiv. Paris, 1814.
"Iets over het bijgeloof in de Minahasa," in *Tijdschrift voor Nederlandsch-Indië,* 3eme Série, iv. (1870).
Ihering, R. von, *Vorgeschichte der Indoeuropäer.* Leipsic, 1894.
Ihm, *s.vv.* "Abnoba" and "Arduinna," in Pauly-Wissowa's *Real-Encyclopädie der classischen Altertumswissenschaft.*
Il Fetha Nagast o legislazione dei re, codice ecclesiastico e civile di Abissinia. Tradotto e annotato da Ignazio Guidi. Rome, 1899.
Illustrated Missionary News, The.
Im Thurn, (Sir) Everard F., *Among the Indians of Guiana.* London, 1883.

Imhoof-Blumer, F., " Coin-types of some Kilikian Cities," in *Journal of Hellenic Studies*, xviii. (1898).

Kleinasiatische Münzen. Vienna, 1901–1902.

s.v. "Kronos," in W. H. Roscher's *Lexikon der griechischen und römischen Mythologie*, ii.

Monnaies Grecques. Amsterdam, 1883. (*Verhandelingen der Koninklijke Akademie von Wetenschappen*, Afdeeling Letterkunde, xiv.)

"Zur Münzkunde Kilikiens," in *Zeitschrift für Numismatik*, x. (1883).

Imhoof-Blumer, F., and Gardner, P., *Numismatic Commentary on Pausanias.*

Imhoof-Blumer, F., und Keller, O., *Tier- und Pflanzenbilder auf Münzen und Gemmen des klassischen Altertums.* Leipsic, 1889.

Immerwahr, W., *Die Kulte und Mythen Arkadiens.* Leipsic, 1891.

Immisch, O., in W. H. Roscher's *Lexikon der griechischen und römischen Mythologie*, ii.

Independent Review, The.

India in the Fifteenth Century, being a Collection of Voyages to India in the Century preceding the Portuguese Discovery of the Cape of Good Hope. Edited by R. H. Major. Hakluyt Society. London, 1857.

Indian Antiquary, The.

Indian Museum Notes, issued by the Trustees, vol. i. No. 3. Calcutta, 1890.

Indian Notes and Queries.

Indiculus Superstitionum et Paganiarum. Published with a Commentary by H. A. Saupe. Leipsic, 1891.

Indogermanische Forschungen.

Ingulfus, *Historia*, quoted in G. H. Pertz's *Monumenta Germaniae historica*, i.

Inscriptiones Graecae Siliciae et Italiae. Ed. G. Kaibel. Berlin, 1890.

Internationales Archiv für Ethnographie.

International Folk-lore Congress, 1891, Papers and Transactions. Edited by J. Jacobs and A. Nutt. London, 1892.

Ipolyi, A. von, " Beiträge zur deutschen Mythologie aus Ungarn," in *Zeitschrift für deutsche Mythologie und Sittenkunde*, i. (1853).

Irby, C. L., and Mangles, J., *Travels in Egypt and Nubia, Syria and the Holy Land.* London, 1844.

Irenaeus, quoted by H. Usener, *Das Weinachtsfest.*

*Irish Times, The.

Irle, Missionar J., *Die Herero, ein Beitrag zur Landes- Volks- und Missionskunde.* Gütersloh, 1906.

Irving, Washington, *Sketch-Book.* Bohn's Edition.

Isaacs, Nathaniel, *Travels and Adventures in Eastern Africa.* London, 1836.

Isaeus, *Speeches.* Ed. William Wyse. Cambridge, 1904.

Isaiah, The Book of the Prophet.

Isocrates, *Orationes.* Ed. G. E. Benseler. Leipsic, 1867–1871.

Evagoras.

Panegyricus.

Iyer, L. K. Anantha Krishna, *The Cochin Tribes and Castes.* Madras, 1909–1912.

*J. W., in *The Gentleman's Magazine*, vol. lxi., February 1791, quoted by J. Brand, *Popular Antiquities of Great Britain*, i., and by (Mrs.) E. M. Leather, *The Folk-lore of Herefordshire.*

Jablonski, P. E., *Pantheon Aegyptiorum.* Frankfort, 1750–1752.

Jackson, A. V. Williams, " Notes from India, Second Series," in *Journal of the American Oriental Society*, xxiii. (1902).

Jackson, F. Arthur, " A Fijian Legend of the Origin of the *Vilavilairevo* or Fire Ceremony," in *Journal of the Polynesian Society*, vol. iii. No. 2 (June 1894).

Jackson, J., in J. E. Erskine's *Journal of a Cruise among the Islands of the Western Pacific.* London, 1853.

Jackson, Rev. Sheldon, "Alaska and its Inhabitants," in *The American Antiquarian,* ii. Chicago, 1879-1880.

*Jacob, *Mœurs et Coutumes du moyen âge,* quoted by L. J. B. Bérenger-Feraud, *Superstitions et Survivances,* iv. Paris, 1896.

Jacob, G., *Altarabisches Beduinenleben.* Second Edition. Berlin, 1897.

Jacob's von Edessa, *Canones,* übersetzt und erläutert von C. Kayser. Leipsic, 1886.

Jacobs, Julius, *Eenigen tijd onder de Baliërs.* Batavia, 1883.

Jacobsen, Captain, cited in *Internationales Archiv für Ethnologie,* i. (1888).

Jacobsen, J. Adrian, "Geheimbünde der Küstenbewohner Nordwest-America's," in *Verhandlungen der Berliner Gesellschaft für Anthropologie, Ethnologie und Urgeschichte* (1891).

Reisen in die Inselwelt des Banda-Meeres. Berlin, 1896.

Jacottet, É., *Études sur les Langues du Haut-Zambèze,* Troisième Partie. Paris, 1901.

Jagor, "Über die Badagas im Nilgiri-Gebirge," in *Verhandlungen der Berliner Gesellschaft für Anthropologie* (1876).

in *Verhandlungen der Berliner Gesellschaft für Anthropologie,* 1877 (bound with *Zeitschrift für Ethnologie,* ix.).

Jagor, F., "Bericht über verschiedene Volksstämme in Vorderindien," in *Zeitschrift für Ethnologie,* xxvi. (1894).

Jahn, Otto, *Archäologische Beiträge.* Berlin, 1847.

in *Archäologische Zeitung,* vii. (1849).

Jahn, Ulrich, *Die deutschen Opfergebräuche bei Ackerbau und Viehzucht.* Breslau, 1884.

Hexenwesen und Zauberei in Pommern. Breslau, 1886.

Volkssagen aus Pommern und Rügen. Stettin, 1886.

Jahrbuch des kaiserlichen deutschen Archäologischen Instituts.

Jahresbericht der geographischen Gesellschaft von Bern. Bern, 1900.

Jamblichus, *Adhortatio ad philosophiam.* Ed. M. Theophilus Kiessling. Leipsic, 1813.

De mysteriis. Ed. G. Parthey. Berlin, 1857.

De vita Pythagorae. Ed. Ant. Westermann. Paris (Didot), 1878.

James, Edwin, *Account of an Expedition from Pittsburgh to the Rocky Mountains.* London, 1823.

James, M. E., "The Tide," in *Folklore,* ix. (1898).

James, Dr. M. R., in *The Classical Review,* vi. (1892).

Jamieson, John, *Etymological Dictionary of the Scottish Language.* New Edition. Edited by J. Longmuir and D. Donaldson. Paisley, 1879-1882.

Jastrow, M., *Die Religion Babyloniens und Assyriens.* Giessen, 1905-1912.

s.v. "Hittites," in *Encyclopaedia Biblica,* ii.

The Religion of Babylonia and Assyria. Boston, U.S.A., 1898.

Jatakas, The, or Stories of the Buddha's former Births. Translated into English by the late Professor E. B. Cowell, Dr. W. H. D. Rouse, and other scholars. 6 vols. Cambridge, 1895-1907.

Jaussen, Antonin, *Coutumes des Arabes au pays de Moab.* Paris, 1908.

"Coutumes Arabes," in *Revue Biblique,* 1er avril 1903.

Jelínek, Br., "Materialien zur Vorgeschichte und Volkskunde Böhmens," in *Mittheilungen der anthropologischen Gesellschaft in Wien,* xxi. (1891).

Jenks, A. E., *The Bontoc Igorot.* Manila, 1905.

Jensen, P., *Assyrisch-Babylonische Mythen und Epen.* Berlin, 1900.

Die Kosmologie der Babylonier. Strasburg, 1890.

"Elamitische Eigennamen," in *Wiener Zeitschrift für die Kunde des Morgenlandes,* vi. (1892).

Jensen, P.—*continued.*
    Hittiter und Armenier.   Strasburg, 1898.
    quoted by Th. Nöldeke, in *Encyclopaedia Biblica, s.v.* "Esther," vol. ii.
        London, 1901.
Jeremiah, The Book of the Prophet.
Jeremias, A., *Das Alte Testament im Lichte des Alten Orients.*   Second Edition.
    Leipsic, 1906.
    Die babylonisch-assyrischen Vorstellungen vom Leben nach dem Tode.
    Leipsic, 1887.
    Izdubar-Nimrod.   Leipsic, 1891.
    s.vv. "Marduk" and "Nergal," in W. H. Roscher's *Lexikon der griechi-*
    schen und römischen Mythologie.
Jerome, *Commentarium in Epistolam ad Galatas,* in Migne's *Patrologia Latina,*
    vol. xxvi.
    Commentarium in Ezechielem, in Migne's *Patrologia Latina,* xxv.
    Epistolae, in Migne's *Patrologia Latina,* xxii.
    on Jeremiah vii. 31, quoted in Winer's *Biblisches Realwörterbuch, s.v.*
    "Thopeth."   Second Edition.
    quoted by E. Meyer, in *Zeitschrift der Deutschen Morgenländischen Gesell-*
    schaft, xxxi.
    quoted by F. C. Movers, in *Die Phoenizier.*   Bonn, 1841.
Jerome of Prague, quoted by Aeneas Sylvius, *Opera.*   Bâle, 1571.
Jessen, *s.v.* "Marsyas," in W. H. Roscher's *Lexikon der griechischen und*
    römischen Mythologie, ii.
Jessen, E. J., *De Finnorum Lapponumque Norvegicorum religione pagana*
    tractatus singularis.   (Bound up with C. Leemius's *De Lapponibus*
    Finmarchiae eorumque lingua, vita, et religione pristina commentatio.
    Copenhagen, 1767.)
Jessopp, A., and James, M. R., *Life and Miracles of St. William of Norwich.*
    Cambridge, 1896.
Jesup North Pacific Expedition, Memoir of the American Museum of Natural
    History.   New York.
Jetté, Fr. Julius, S. J., "On the Medicine-Men of the Ten'a," in *Journal of the*
    Royal Anthropological Institute, xxxvii. (1907).
    "On the Superstitions of the Ten'a Indians," in *Anthropos,* vi.
    (1911).
Jevons, Dr. F. B., "Greek Law and Folklore," in *The Classical Review,* ix.
    (1895).
    Introduction to the History of Religion.   London, 1896.
    Plutarch's Romane Questions.   London, 1892.
Jewitt, John R.   See *s.v.* Narrative.
Joannes Lydus.   Ed. I. Bekker.   Bonn, 1837.
    De magistratibus.
    De mensibus.
Job, The Book of.
Jochelson, W., "Die Jukagiren im äussersten Nordosten Asiens," in *Jahresbericht*
    der Geographischen Gesellschaft von Bern, xvii.   Bern, 1900.
    "The Koryak, Religion and Myths," in *Memoir of the American Museum*
    of Natural History, The Jesup North Pacific Expedition, vol. vi. part i.
    Leyden and New York, 1908.
Jochim, E. F., "Beschrijving van den Sapoedi Archipel," in *Tijdschrift voor*
    Indische Taal- Land- en Volkenkunde, xxxvi. (1893).
Joest, W., "Bei den Barolong," in *Das Ausland,* 16th June 1884.
    "Beiträge zur Kenntniss der Eingebornen der Insel Formosa und Ceram,"
    in *Verhandlungen der Berliner Gesellschaft für Anthropologie, Ethnologie,*
    und Urgeschichte (1882).
    in B. Scheube's *Die Ainos.*

Johanni Apostoli de transitu Beatae Mariae Virginis Liber: ex recensione et cum interpretatione Maximiliani Engeri. Elberfeldae, 1854.

John, Alois, *Sitte, Brauch und Volksglaube im deutschen Westböhmen.* Prague, 1905.

John of Antioch, in *Fragmenta Historicorum Graecorum,* ed. C. Müller, vol. iv.

Johns, Rev. C. H. W., *Babylonian and Assyrian Laws, Contracts, and Letters.* Edinburgh, 1904.

— in private communications to the Author (ix. 357 *n.*[2], 367 *nn.* [2 and 3]).

— "Notes on the Code of Hammurabi," in *The American Journal of Semitic Languages and Literatures,* xix. (January, 1903).

— "Purim," in *Encyclopaedia Biblica,* iii. London, 1902.

*Johnson, Bishop James, "Yoruba Heathenism," quoted by R. E. Dennett, *At the Back of the Black Man's Mind.* London, 1906.

Johnson, Dr. Samuel, *A Journey to the Western Islands of Scotland.* (*The Works of Samuel Johnson, LL.D.,* vol. vi. Edited by the Rev. R. Lynam. London, 1825).

— *Journey to the Western Islands of Scotland.* Baltimore, 1810.

Johnston, C., in *Journal of the American Oriental Society,* xviii., First Half (1897).

Johnston, (Sir) Harry H., "A Visit to Mr. Stanley's Stations on the River Congo," in *Proceedings of the Royal Geographical Society,* N.S., v. (1883).

— *British Central Africa.* London, 1897.

— *Liberia.* London, 1906.

— "On the Races of the Congo," in *Journal of the Anthropological Institute,* xiii. (1884).

— *The River Congo.* London, 1884.

— *The Uganda Protectorate.* Second Edition. London, 1904.

Johnston, R. F., *Lion and Dragon in Northern China.* London, 1910.

Johnstone, Rev. A., in Sir John Sinclair's *Statistical Account of Scotland,* xxi. Edinburgh, 1791–1799.

Johnstone, H. B., "Notes on the Customs of the Tribes occupying Mombasa Sub-district, British East Africa," in *Journal of the Anthropological Institute,* xxxii. (1902).

Jolly, J., *Recht und Sitte,* in G. Bühler's *Grundriss der indoarischen Philologie.*

Jones, Bryan J., in *Folk-lore,* vi. (1895).

Jones, Peter, *History of the Ojebway Indians.* London, N.D.

Jones, W., *Finger-ring Lore.* London, 1877.

Jones, W. H., and Kropf, L. L., *The Folk-tales of the Magyar.* London, 1889.

Jonghe, Ed. de, *Les Sociétés Secrètes au Bas-Congo.* Brussels, 1907. (Extract from the *Revue des Questions Scientifiques,* October 1907.)

Jordan, H., *Die Könige im alten Italien.* Berlin, 1884.

— *Topographie der Stadt Rom im Altertum.* Berlin, 1878–1907.

Jordanus, Friar, *The Wonders of the East.* Translated by Colonel Henry Yule. Hakluyt Society. London, 1863.

Jornandes, *Romana et Getica.* Ed. Th. Mommsen. Berlin, 1882.

Josephus, *Opera.* Ed. Im. Bekker. Leipsic, 1855–1856.

— *Antiquitates Judaicae.*

— *Bellum Judaicum.*

— *Contra Apionem.*

Joshi, Pandit Janardan, in *North Indian Notes and Queries,* iii. (September 1893).

Joshua, The Book of.

Joske, A. B., "The Nanga of Viti-levu," in *Internationales Archiv für Ethnographie,* ii. (1889).

Joubert, quoted by Matthew Arnold, *Essays in Criticism*. First Series,
London, 1898.
Journal and Proceedings of the Asiatic Society of Bengal.
Journal and Proceedings of the Royal Society of New South Wales.
Journal Asiatique.
Journal des Savants.
Journal of American Folk-lore.
Journal of Hellenic Studies.
Journal of Philology.
Journal of Roman Studies.
Journal of Sacred Literature and Biblical Record. New Series, London, 1865.
Journal of the African Society.
Journal of the American Oriental Society.
Journal of the Anthropological Society of Bombay.
Journal of the Asiatic Society of Bengal.
Journal of the China Branch of the Royal Asiatic Society for the Year 1891-92.
N.S.
Journal of the Eastern Archipelago and Eastern Asia.
Journal of the Ethnological Society of London.
Journal of the Indian Archipelago.
Journal of the North China Branch of the Royal Asiatic Society. New Series.
Journal of the Polynesian Society.
Journal of the (Royal) Anthropological Institute of Great Britain and Ireland.
Journal of the Royal Asiatic Society of Great Britain and Ireland.
Journal of the Royal Geographical Society.
Journal of the Straits Branch of the Royal Asiatic Society.
Joustra, M., "De Zending onder de Karo-Batak's," in *Mededeelingen van wege
het Nederlandsche Zendelinggenootschap*, xli. (1897).
"Het leven, de zeden en gewoonten der Bataks," in *Mededeelingen van
wege het Nederlandsche Zendelinggenootschap*, xlvi. (1902).
"Naar het landschap Goenoeng," in *Mededeelingen van wege het Neder-
landsche Zendelinggenootschap*, xlv. (1901).
Joyce, P. W., *A Social History of Ancient Ireland*. London, 1903.
Joyce, T. A., "The Weeping God," in *Essays and Studies presented to William
Ridgeway*. Cambridge, 1913. See also s.v. Torday, E.
Juan de la Concepcion, *Historia general de Philipinas*. Manilla, 1788-1792.
Jubainville, H. d'Arbois de, *Cours de la littérature celtique*. Paris, 1883-1902.
Les Druides et les Dieux Celtiques à forme d'animaux. Paris, 1906.
Judges, The Book of.
Jülg, B., *Kalmückische Märchen*. Leipsic, 1866.
Mongolische Märchen-Sammlung, die neun Märchen des Siddhi-Kür.
Innsbruck, 1868.
Julian, *Opera*. Ed. F. C. Hertlein. Leipsic, 1875-1876.
Convivium.
Epistola ad Themistium.
Julian, C., in Daremberg et Saglio's *Dictionnaire des antiquités grecques et
romaines*, ii.
Julien, Stanislas, *Le Livre des Récompenses et des Peines, traduit du Chinois*.
Paris, 1835.
Julius Capitolinus, *Gordiani tres*, in *Scriptores Historiae Augustae*. Ed.
H. Peter. Leipsic, 1884.
Junghuhn, Fr., *Die Battaländer auf Sumatra*. Berlin, 1847.
Junod, Henri A., *Les Ba-ronga*. Neuchâtel, 1898.
Les Chants et les Contes des Ba-ronga. Lausanne, N.D.
"Les Conceptions physiologiques des Bantou Sud-Africains et leurs tabous,"
in *Revue d'Ethnographie et de Sociologie*, i. (1910).
The Life of a South African Tribe. Neuchâtel, 1912-1913.

Justin, *Historiarum Philippicarum Epitoma.* Ed. J. Jeep. Leipsic, 1862.
Justin Martyr, *Apologiae.* Ed. G. Krüger. Tübingen and Leipsic, 1904.
  Cohortatio ad Graecos. Ed. P. Maran. The Hague and Paris, 1742.
  Dialogus cum Tryphone, in Migne's *Patrologia Graeca,* vi.
Juvenal, *Satires.* Ed. A. J. Macleane. London, 1867.
  Thirteen Satires. With a Commentary by John E. B. Mayor.
    Second Edition. London and Cambridge, 1869–1878.

Kaempfer, Engelbert, *History of Japan.* Translated from the original Dutch
    manuscript by J. G. Scheuchzer. London, 1728.
  "History of Japan," in John Pinkerton's *Voyages and Travels,* vii.
Kaindl, Dr. R. F., "Aus dem Volksglauben der Rutenen in Galizien," in
    Globus, lxiv. (1893).
  "Aus der Volksüberlieferung der Bojken," in *Globus,* lxxix. (1901).
  Die Huzulen. Vienna, 1894.
  "Neue Beiträge zur Ethnologie und Volkeskunde der Huzulen," in *Globus,*
    lxix. (1896).
  "Viehzucht und Viehzauber in den Ostkarpaten," in *Globus,* lxix. (1896).
  "Volksüberlieferungen der Pidhireane," in *Globus,* lxxiii. (1898).
  "Zauberglaube bei den Huzulen," in *Globus,* lxxvi. (1899).
  "Zauberglaube bei den Rutenen in der Bukowina und Galizien," in *Globus,*
    lxi. (1892).
  "Zur Volkskunde der Rumänen in der Bukowina," in *Globus,* xcii. (1907).
* Kamp, Jens, *Danske Folkeminder.* Odense, 1877. (Referred to in *Feilberg's
    Bidrag til en Ordbog over Jyske Almuesmål.* Ferdje hefte. Copenhagen,
    1888.)
Karadschitsch, W. S., *Volksmärchen der Serben.* Berlin, 1854.
Karaka, D. J., *History of the Modern Parsis.* London, 1884.
Karasek, A., "Beiträge zur Kenntnis der Waschambaa," in *Baessler-Archiv,* i.
    Leipsic and Berlin, 1911.
Karppe, referred to in *Encyclopaedia Biblica, s.v.* "Creation."
Kate, H. Ten, "Notes ethnographiques sur les Comanches," in *Revue d'Ethno-
    graphie,* iv. (1885).
Katha Sarit Ságara. Translated by C. H. Tawney. Calcutta, 1880.
Kauffmann, Fr., *Balder, Mythus und Sage.* Strasburg, 1902.
Kaul, Pandit Harikishan, *Report,* in *Census of India, 1911,* vol. xiv. *Punjab,*
    Part I. Lahore, 1912.
Kausika Sutra. (W. Caland, *Altindisches Zauberritual.* Amsterdam, 1900.)
Kay, Stephen, *Travels and Researches in Caffraria.* London, 1833.
Kazarow, G., "Karnevalbräuche in Bulgarien," in *Archiv für Religionswissen-
    schaft,* xi. (1908).
Keating, Geoffrey, D.D., *The History of Ireland.* Translated from the
    original Gaelic and copiously annotated, by John O'Mahony. New
    York, 1857.
Keating, William H., *Narrative of an Expedition to the Source of St. Peter's
    River.* London, 1825.
Keats, John. *Last Sonnet.*
Keller, Ferdinand, *The Lake Dwellings of Switzerland and other Parts of
    Europe.* Second Edition. London, 1878.
Keller, Franz, *The Amazon and Madeira Rivers.* London, 1874.
Keller, J., "Über das Land und Volk der Balong," in *Deutsches Kolonialblatt,*
    1 Oktober 1895.
Keller, O., *Thiere des classischen Alterthums.* Innsbruck, 1887.
* Kelly, John, LL.D., *English and Manx Dictionary.* Douglas, 1866. (Re-
    ferred to by J. A. MacCulloch, *s.v.* "Calendar," in Dr. James
    Hastings's *Encyclopaedia of Religion and Ethics,* iii. Edinburgh,
    1910.)

Kelly, Walter K., *Curiosities of Indo-European Tradition and Folk-lore.* London, 1863.

Kemble, John Mitchell, *The Saxons in England.* London, 1849. New Edition. London, 1876.

*Kennan, G., *Tent Life in Siberia* (1870). (Referred to by J. F. McLennan, *Studies in Ancient History.* London, 1886.)

Kennedy, A. R. S., *Leviticus and Numbers,* Edinburgh, N.D. (in the *Century Bible*).

Kennedy, Patrick, *Legendary Fictions of the Irish Celts.* London, 1866.

Kennett, R. H., *The Composition of the Book of Isaiah in the Light of History and Archaeology.* London, 1910.

K[ern], H., " Bijgeloof onder de inlanders in den Oosthoek van Java," in *Tijdschrift voor Indische Taal- Land- en Volkenkunde,* xxvi. (1880).

Kern, H., "Een Spanisch schrijver over den godsdienst der heidensche Bikollers," in *Bijdragen tot de Taal- Land- en Volkenkunde van Neder-landsch-Indië,* xlvii. (1897).

Kern, O., in *Aus der Anomia, Archäologische Beiträge Carl Robert zur Erinnerung an Berlin dargebracht.* Berlin, 1890. *Die Inschriften von Magnesia am Maeander.* Berlin, 1900. *s.v.* " Dionysus," in Pauly-Wissowa's *Real-Encyclopädie der classischen Altertumswissenschaft,* v.

*Keysler, *Antiquitates Septentrionales.* (Referred to by A. Kuhn, *Die Herabkunft des Feuers und des Göttertranks.* Second Edition. Gütersloh, 1886.)

Keysser, Ch., "Aus dem Leben der Kaileute," in R. Neuhauss's *Deutsch Neu-Guinea,* iii. Berlin, 1911.

Kidd, Dudley, *Savage Childhood, a Study of Kafir Children.* London, 1906. *The Essential Kafir.* London, 1904.

Kielhorn, Professor F., "The Sixty-Year Cycle of Jupiter," in *The Indian Antiquary,* xviii. (1889).

Kinahan, G. H., " Notes on Irish Folk-lore," in *Folk-lore Record,* iv. (1881).

King, C. W., *The Gnostics and their Remains.* Second Edition. London, 1887.

King, J. E., " Infant Burial," in *The Classical Review,* xvii. (1903).

King, Captain J. S., " Notes on the Folk-lore and some Social Customs of the Western Somali Tribes," in *The Folk-lore Journal,* vi. (1888).

King, L. W., *A History of Sumer and Akkad.* London, 1910. *Babylonian Religion and Mythology.* London, 1899.

Kinglake, A. W., *Eothen.* Temple Classics Edition.

Kings, The First Book of the.

Kings, The Second Book of the.

Kingsley, Mary H., in *Journal of the Anthropological Institute,* xxix. (1899). *Travels in West Africa.* London, 1897.

Kirchmeyer, Thomas, *Regnum Papisticum.* Translated into English by Barnabe Googe. *See above, s.v.* Googe.

Kirkland, Rev. Mr., quoted by W. M. Beauchamp, " The Iroquois White Dog Feast," in *American Antiquarian,* vii. (1885).

Kirkpatrick, A. F., *The First Book of Samuel,* Cambridge, 1891 ; *The Second Book of Samuel,* Cambridge, 1893 (in *Cambridge Bible for Schools and Colleges*).

Kitching, Rev. A. L., *On the Backwaters of the Nile.* London, 1912.

Kittel, R., *Biblia Hebraica.* Leipsic, 1905–1906.

Klausen, R. H., *Aeneas und die Penaten.* Hamburg and Gotha, 1839–1840.

Kleintitschen, P. A., *Die Küstenbewohner der Gazellehalbinsel.* Hiltrup bei Münster, N.D., preface dated Christmas, 1906.

Klerks, E. A., " Geographisch en ethnographisch opstal over de landschappen Korintje, Serampas en Soengai Tenang," in *Tijdschrift voor Indische Taal- Land- en Volkenkunde,* xxxix. (1897).

Klose, H., *Togo unter deutscher Flagge.* Berlin, 1899.
Klunzinger, C. B., *Bilder aus Oberägypten, der Wüste und dem Rothen Meere.* Stuttgart, 1877.
Upper Egypt, its People and Products. London, 1878.
Knaack, G., "Zur Meleagersage," in *Rheinisches Museum*, N.F., xlix. (1894).
Knebel, J., "Amulettes javanaises," in *Tijdschrift voor Indische Taal- Land- en Volkenkunde*, xl. (1898).
"De Weertijger op Midden-Java, der Javaan naverteld," in *Tijdschrift voor Indische Taal- Land- en Volkenkunde*, xli. (1899).
"Varia Javanica," in *Tijdschrift voor Indische Taal- Land- en Volkenkunde*, xliv. (1901).
Knight-Bruce, G. W. H., *Memories of Mashonaland.* London and New York, 1895.
in *Proceedings of the Royal Geographical Society*, 1890.
Knoop, O., *Volkssagen, Erzählungen, Aberglauben, Gebräuche und Märchen aus dem östlichen Hinterpommern.* Posen, 1885.
Knowles, J. H., *Folk-tales of Kashmir.* Second Edition. London, 1893.
Koch, Theodor, "Die Anthropophagie der südamerikanischen Indianer," in *Internationales Archiv für Ethnographie*, xii. (1899).
Koch-Grünberg, Th., "Frauenarbeit bei den Indianern Nordwest-Brasiliens," in *Mitteilungen der Anthropologischen Gesellschaft in Wien*, xxxviii. (1908).
Zwei Jahre unter den Indianern. Berlin, 1909–1910.
Ködding, W., "Die batakschen Götter und ihr Verhältniss zum Brahmanismus," in *Allgemeine Missions-Zeitschrift*, xii. (1885).
Kohl, J. G., *Die deutsch-russischen Ostseeprovinzen.* Dresden and Leipsic, 1841.
Kitschi-Gami. Bremen, 1859.
Kohlbrugge, J. H. F., "Die Těnggěresen, ein alter Javanischen Volksstamm," in *Bijdragen tot de Taal- Land- en Volkenkunde van Nederlandsch-Indië*, liii. (1901).
"Naamgeving in Insulinde," in *Bijdragen tot de Taal- Land- en Volkenkunde van Nederlandsch-Indië*, li. (1900), liii. (1901).
Kohler, J., "Das Banturecht in Ostafrika," in *Zeitschrift für vergleichende Rechtswissenschaft*, xv. (1902).
"Das Recht der Herero," in *Zeitschrift für vergleichende Rechtswissenschaft*, xiv. (1900).
Köhler, J. A. E., *Volksbrauch, Aberglauben, Sagen und andre alte Überlieferungen im Voigtlande.* Leipsic, 1867.
Köhler, Dr. Reinhold, *Kleinere Schriften.* Weimar, 1898.
in *Orient und Occident*, ii. Göttingen, 1864.
in L. Gonzenbach's *Sicilianische Märchen.* Leipsic, 1870.
"Sage von Landerwerbung durch zerschnittene Häute," in *Orient und Occident*, iii.
Koike, Masanao, "Zwei Jahren in Korea," in *Internationales Archiv für Ethnographie*, iv. (1891).
Kolbe, W., *Hessische Volks-Sitten und Gebräuche im Lichte der heidnischen Vorzeit.* Second Edition. Marburg, 1888.
Kolben, Peter, *The Present State of the Cape of Good Hope.* Second Edition. London, 1738.
*Kolberg, Oskar, in *Mazowsze*, vol. iv., quoted by F. S. Krauss, "Altslavische Feuergewinnung," in *Globus*, lix. (1891).
Koldewey, R., "Das sogenannte Grab des Sardanapal zu Tarsus," in *Aus der Anomia.* Berlin, 1890.
Die Hettitische Inschrift gefunden in der Königsburg von Babylon. Leipsic, 1900. (*Wissenschaftliche Veröffentlichung der Deutschen Orient-Gesellschaft*, Heft 1.)
Kollmann, P., *The Victoria Nyanza.* London, 1899.

Kostromitonow, "Bemerkungen über die Indianer in Ober-Kalifornien," in K. F. v. Baer and Gr. v. Helmersen's *Beiträge zur Kenntniss des russischen Reiches*, i. St. Petersburg, 1839.

Kotzebue, O. von, *Entdeckungs-Reise in die Süd-See und nach der Berings-Strasse.* Weimar, 1821.

Reise um die Welt. Weimar, 1830.

Kowalewsky, M., in *Folk-lore*, i. (1890).

Krahmer, "Der Anadyr-Bezirk nach A. W. Olssufjew," in *Petermann's Mittheilungen*, xlv. (1899).

Kramer, Fr., "Der Götzendienst der Niasser," in *Tijdschrift voor Indische Taal-Land- en Volkenkunde*, xxxiii. (1890).

Kranz, A., *Natur- und Kulturleben der Zulus.* Wiesbaden, 1880.

Krapf, J. L., *Travels, Researches, and Missionary Labours during an Eighteen Years' Residence in Eastern Africa.* London, 1860.

Krascheninnikow, S., *Beschreibung des Landes Kamtschatka.* Lemgo, 1766.

Krause, Aurel, *Die Tlinkit-Indianer.* Jena, 1885.

Krause, E., "Abergläubische Kuren und songstiger Aberglaube in Berlin und nächster Umgebung," in *Zeitschrift für Ethnologie*, xv. (1883).

"Das Sommertags-Fest in Heidelberg," in *Verhandlungen der Berliner Gesellschaft für Anthropologie*, 1895.

Krause, G. A., "Merkwürdige Sitten der Haussa," in *Globus*, lxix. (1896).

Krause, R., *Sitten, Gebräuche und Aberglauben in Westpreussen.* Berlin, preface dated March 1904.

Krauss, Friedrich S., "Altslavische Feuergewinnung," in *Globus*, lix. (1891).

"Der Bauopfer bei den Südslaven," in *Mittheilungen der Anthropologischen Gesellschaft in Wien*, xvii. (1887).

"Haarschurgodschaft bei den Südslaven," in *Internationales Archiv für Ethnographie*, vii. (1894).

Kroatien und Slavonien. Vienna, 1889.

Sagen und Märchen der Südslaven. Leipsic, 1883-1884.

Sitte und Brauch der Südslaven. Vienna, 1885.

"Slavische Feuerbohrer," in *Globus*, lix. (1891).

"Vampyre im südslavischen Volksglauben," in *Globus*, lxi. (1892).

Volksglaube und religiöser Brauch der Südslaven. Münster i. W., 1890.

Kreemer, J., "De Loeboes in Mandailing," in *Bijdragen tot de Taal- Land- en Volkenkunde van Nederlandsch-Indië*, lxvi. (1912).

"Hoe de Javaan zijne zieken verzorgt," in *Mededeelingen van wege het Nederlandsche Zendelinggenootschap*, xxxvi. (1892).

"Regenmaken, Oedjoeng, Tooverij onder de Javanen," in *Mededeelingen van wege het Nederlandsche Zendelinggenootschap*, xxx. (1886).

"Tiang-dèrès," in *Mededeelingen van wege het Nederlandsche Zendelinggenootschap*, xxvi. (1882).

Krefft, Gerard, "On the Manners and Customs of the Aborigines of the Lower Murray and Darling," in *Transactions of the Philosophical Society of New South Wales*, 1862-1865. Sydney, 1866.

Kretschmer, P., *Einleitung in die Geschichte der griechischen Sprache.* Göttingen, 1896.

Kreutzwald, Fr., und Neus, H., *Mythische und magische Lieder der Ehsten.* St. Petersburg, 1854.

Krick, Missionary, in *Annales de la Propagation de la Foi*, xxvi. (1854).

Krieger, Max, *Neu-Guinea.* Berlin, N.D., preface dated 1899.

*Kristensen, E. T., *Jydske Folkeminder.* (Referred to in *Feilberg's *Bidrag til en Ordbog over Jyske Almuesmål.* Fjerde hefte. Copenhagen, 1888.)

Kroeber, A. L., "The Religion of the Indians of California," in *University of California Publications in American Archaeology and Ethnology*, vol. iv. No. 6. Berkeley, September 1907.

*Krohn, J., *Suomen suvun pakanallinen jumalen palvelus.* Helsingfors, 1894.

Kropf, A., "Die religiösen Anschauungen der Kaffern," in *Verhandlungen der Berliner Gesellschaft für Anthropologie, Ethnologie und Urgeschichte* (1888).

Kruijt (Kruyt), A. C., "De Rijstmoeder in den Indischen Archipel," in *Verslagen en Mededeelingen der Koninklijke Akademie van Wetenschappen*, Afdeeling Letterkunde, Vierde Reeks, v. Amsterdam, 1903.

"De weerwolf bij de Toradja's van Midden-Celebes," in *Tijdschrift voor Indische Taal- Land- en Volkenkunde*, xli. (1899).

"Een en ander aangaande het geestelijk en maatschappelijk leven van den Poso-Alfoer," in *Mededeelingen van wege het Nederlandsche Zendelinggenootschap*, xxxix. (1895), xl. (1896), xli. (1897), xliv. (1900).

"Eenige ethnografische aanteekeningen omtrent de Toboengkoe en de Tomori," in *Mededeelingen van wege het Nederlandsche Zendelinggenootschap*, xliv. (1900).

"Gebruiken bij den rijstoogst in enkele streken op Oost-Java," in *Mededeelingen van wege het Nederlandsche Zendelinggenootschap*, xlvii. (1903).

Het Animisme in den Indischen Archipel. The Hague, 1906.

"Het ijzer in Midden-Celebes," in *Bijdragen tot de Taal- Land- en Volkenkunde van Nederlandsch-Indië*, liii. (1901).

"Het koppensnellen der Toradja's van Midden-Celebes, en zijne Beteekenis," in *Verslagen en Mededeelingen der Koninklijke Akademie van Wetenschappen*, Afdeeling Letterkunde, IV. Reeks, III. Deel. Amsterdam, 1899.

"Het rijk Mori," in *Tijdschrift van het Koninklijk Nederlandsch Aardrijkskundig Genootschap*, II. Serie, xvii. (1900).

"Het wezen van het Heidendom te Posso," in *Mededeelingen van wege het Nederlandsche Zendelinggenootschap*, xlvii. (1903).

"Mijne eerste ervaringen te Poso," in *Mededeelingen van wege het Nederlandsche Zendelinggenootschap*, xxxvi. (1892).

"Regen lokken en regen verdrijven bij de Toradja's van Midden Celebes," in *Tijdschrift voor Indische Taal- Land- en Volkenkunde*, xliv. (1901).

"Van Paloppo naar Posso," in *Mededeelingen van wege het Nederlandsche Zendelinggenootschap*, xlii. (1898).

See also s.v. Adriani, N.

Kubary, J. [S.], "Die Bewohner der Mortlock-Inseln," in *Mittheilungen der Geographischen Gesellschaft in Hamburg* (1878–1879).

"Die Religion der Pelauer," in A. Bastian's *Allerlei aus Volks- und Menschenkunde.* Berlin, 1888.

Die socialen Einrichtungen der Pelauer. Berlin, 1885.

"Die Todtenbestattung auf den Pelau-Inseln," in *Original-Mittheilungen aus der ethnologischen Abtheilung der königlichen Museen zu Berlin*, i. Berlin, 1885.

Ethnographische Beiträge zur Kenntniss des Karolinen Archipels. Leyden, 1895.

Kuhn, Adalbert, *Die Herabkunft des Feuers und des Göttertranks.* Second Edition. Gütersloh, 1886.

Märkische Sagen und Märchen. Berlin, 1843.

Mythologische Studien, vol. ii. Gütersloh, 1912.

Sagen, Gebräuche und Märchen aus Westfalen. Leipsic, 1859.

"Wodan," in *Zeitschrift für deutsches Alterthum*, v. (1845).

Kuhn, A., und Schwartz, W., *Norddeutsche Sagen, Märchen und Gebräuche.* Leipsic, 1848.

Kühnau, R., *Schlesische Sagen.* Berlin, 1910–1913.

Kühner-Blass, *Grammatik der griechischen Sprache.*

Kühr, E. L. M., in *Internationales Archiv für Ethnographie*, ii. (1889).

Kühr, E. L. M.—*continued.*
  "Schetsen uit Borneo's Westerafdeeling," in *Bijdragen tot de Taal- Land-en Volkenkunde van Nederlandsch-Indië,* xlvii. (1897).
Kükenthal, W., *Forschungsreise in den Molukken und in Borneo.* Frankfort, 1896.
Kunstmann, Fr., "Valentin Ferdinand's Beschreibung der Serra Leoa," in *Abhandlungen der historischen Classe der Königlichen Bayerischen Akademie der Wissenschaften,* ix. Munich, 1866.
Kurze, G., "Sitten und Gebräuche der Lengua-Indianer," in *Mitteilungen der Geographischen Gesellschaft zu Jena,* xxiii. (1905).

La Bresse Louhannaise, Bulletin Mensuel, Organe de la Société d'Agriculture et d'Horticulture de l'Arrondissement de Louhans. 1906.
La Mission lyonnaise d'exploration commerciale en Chine 1895–97. Lyons, 1898.
La Nature.
Labat, J. B., *Nouveau Voyage aux isles de l'Amerique.* Paris, 1713.
  Relation historique de l'Éthiopie Occidentale. Paris, 1732.
  Voyage du Chevalier des Marchais en Guinée, Isles voisines, et à Cayenne. Paris, 1730. Amsterdam, 1731.
Labbé, P., *Un Bagne Russe, l'Île de Sakhaline.* Paris, 1903.
Labuan, The Bishop of, "Wild Tribes of Borneo," in *Transactions of the Ethnological Society of London,* New Series, ii. (1863).
Lacombe, Father, in *Missions Catholiques,* ii. (1869).
*Lacombe, Leguével de, *Voyage à Madagascar* (Paris, 1840), quoted by A. van Gennep, *Tabou et Totémisme à Madagascar.* Paris, 1904.
Lactantius, *Opera.* Ed. J. G. Walchius. Leipsic, 1715.
  De mortibus persecutorum.
  Divinae Institutiones.
  Divinarum Institutionum Epitome.
Lactantius Placidus, *Commentatio in Statii Thebaida.* Ed. R. Jahnke. Leipsic, 1898.
  Narrationes Fabulae, in *Auctores Mythographi Latini,* ed. Aug. van Staveren. Leyden and Amsterdam, 1742.
Lafaye, G., *Histoire du culte des divinités d'Alexandrie.* Paris, 1884.
Lafitau, J. F., *Mœurs des sauvages Ameriquains.* Paris, 1724.
Lafond, G., in *Bulletin de la Société de Géographie* (Paris), 2ème série, ix. (1838).
Lagarde, P. A. de, "Purim," in *Abhandlungen der Königlichen Gesellschaft der Wissenschaften zu Göttingen,* xxxiv. (1887).
  *Reliquiae juris ecclesiastici antiquissimae.
Lagrange, M. J., *Études sur les Religions Sémitiques.* Second Edition. Paris, 1905.
Lake, H., and Kelsall, H. J., "The Camphor-tree and Camphor Language of Johore," in *Journal of the Straits Branch of the Royal Asiatic Society,* No. 26 (January 1894).
Lambert, Father, in *Les Missions Catholiques,* xi. (1879); xxv. (1893).
  "Mœurs et superstitions de la tribu Bélep," in *Les Missions Catholiques,* xii. (1880).
  Mœurs et superstitions des Néo-Calédoniens. Nouméa, 1900.
Lamberti, "Relation de la Colchide ou Mingrélie," in *Voyages au Nord,* vii. Amsterdam, 1725.
Lammert, G., *Volksmedizin und medizinischer Aberglaube aus Bayern.* Würz-burg, 1869.
Lampridius, in *Scriptores Historiae Augustae.* Ed. H. Peter. Leipsic, 1884.
  Alexander Severus.
  Commodus.
Lampson, M. W., in letter to Lord Avebury (iv. 273).

Lanciani, R., in the *Athenaeum*, Oct. 10, 1885.
New Tales of Old Rome. London, 1901.
Ruins and Excavations of Ancient Rome. London, 1897.
Landa, Diego de, *Relation des choses de Yucatan.* Texte espagnol et traduction française par l'Abbé Brasseur de Bourbourg. Paris, 1864.
Landes, A., "Contes et légendes annamites," in *Cochinchine française: excursions et reconnaissances*, Nos. 20, 23, and 25. Saigon, 1885–1886.
"Contes Tjames," in *Cochinchine française, excursions et reconnaissances*, No. 29. Saigon, 1887.
Lane, E. W., *Arabic-English Lexicon.* London and Edinburgh, 1863–1885.
Manners and Customs of the Modern Egyptians. Paisley and London, 1895.
Lang, Andrew, in *Athenaeum*, 26th August and 14th October 1899.
Custom and Myth. London, 1884.
in *Folk-lore*, xii. (1901), xiv. (1903).
Modern Mythology. London, 1897.
Myth, Ritual, and Religion. London, 1887.
Lang, J. D., *Queensland.* London, 1861.
Lange, R., "Bitten um Regen in Japan," in *Zeitschrift des Vereins für Volkskunde*, iii. (1893).
Langley, S. P., in *Folk-lore*, xiv. (1901).
"The Fire-walk Ceremony in Tahiti," in *Report of the Smithsonian Institution for 1901.* Washington, 1902.
Langsdorff, G. H. von, *Reise um die Welt.* Frankfort, 1812.
L'Année Sociologique.
L'Anthropologie.
Lanzone, R. V., *Dizionario di Mitologia Egizia.* Turin, 1881–1884.
Lasch, R., "Die Ursache und Bedeutung der Erdbeben im Volksglauben und Volksbrauch," in *Archiv für Religionswissenschaft*, v. (1902).
"Rache als Selbstmordmotiv," in *Globus*, lxxiv. (1898).
Lasicius (Lasiczki), Johan, "De diis Samagitarum caeterorumque Sarmatarum," in *Respublica sive Status regni Poloniae, Lituaniae, Prussiae, Livoniae, etc.* Leyden (Elzevir), 1627.
"De diis Samagitarum caeterorumque Sarmatarum," ed. W. Mannhardt, in *Magazin herausgegeben von der Lettisch-Literarischen Gesellschaft*, xiv. Mitau, 1868.
Lassen, Christian, *Indische Alterthumskunde.* First and Second Editions. Leipsic, 1858–1874.
Latcham, R. E., "Ethnology of the Araucanos," in *Journal of the Royal Anthropological Institute*, xxxix. (1909).
Latham, Charlotte, "Some West Sussex Superstitions lingering in 1868, collected at Fittleworth," in *Folklore Record*, i. (1878).
Latham, R. G., *Descriptive Ethnology.* London, 1859.
Lauth, "Über den ägyptischen Maneros," in *Sitzungsberichte der Königlichen Bayerischen Akademie der Wissenschaften zu München* (1869).
Lavallée, A., "Notes ethnographiques sur diverses tribus du Sud-Est de l'Inde-Chine," in *Bulletin de l'École Française d'Extrême-Orient*, i. Hanoi, 1901.
Lawes, W. G., "Ethnological Notes on the Motu, Koitapu, and Koiari Tribes of New Guinea," in *Journal of the Anthropological Institute*, viii. (1879).
"Notes on New Guinea and its Inhabitants," in *Proceedings of the Royal Geographical Society* (1880).
Lawrie, Rev. Dr. George, in Sir John Sinclair's *Statistical Account of Scotland*, iii. Edinburgh, 1792.
Laws of Manu. Translated by G. Bühler. Oxford, 1886. (*Sacred Books of the East*, vol. xxv.)

Lawson, J. C., *Modern Greek Folklore and Ancient Greek Religion.* Cambridge, 1910.
Lay of the Nibelungs. Translated by Alice Horton. London, 1898.
Le Braz, A., *La Légende de la Mort en Basse-Bretagne.* Paris, 1893.
Le Brun, *Histoire critique des pratiques superstitieuses.* Amsterdam, 1733.
Le Gentil, *Voyage dans les Mers de l'Inde.* Paris, 1781.
Le Mesurier, C. J. R., "Customs and Superstitions connected with the Cultivation of Rice in the Southern Province of Ceylon," in *Journal of the Royal Asiatic Society*, N.S., xvii. (1885).
Le Muséon, N.S.
Le Petit, "Relation des Natchez," in *Recueil de voyages au Nord*, ix.
Le Roy, Mgr., "Les Pygmées," in *Les Missions Catholiques*, xxix. (1897).
Le Temps.
Le Tour du Monde.
   Nouvelle Série.
Leake, W. M., *Journal of a Tour in Asia Minor.* London, 1824.
   Travels in Northern Greece. London, 1835.
Leared, A., *Morocco and the Moors.* London, 1876.
Leather, Mrs. Ella Mary, in *Folk-lore*, xxiv. (1913).
   The Folk-lore of Herefordshire. Hereford and London, 1912.
Lechaptois, Mgr., *Aux Rives du Tanganika.* Algiers, 1913.
Lecky, W. E. H., *History of England in the Eighteenth Century.* London, 1892.
   History of European Morals from Augustus to Charlemagne. Third Edition. London, 1877.
   History of the Rise and Influence of the Spirit of Rationalism in Europe. New Edition. London, 1882.
Leclère, A., *Le Buddhisme au Cambodge.* Paris, 1899.
Lecœur, Jules, *Esquisses du Bocage Normand.* Condé-sur-Noireau, 1883–1887.
Lederbogen, W., "Duala Märchen," in *Mitteilungen des Seminars für Orientalische Sprachen zu Berlin*, v. (1902), Dritte Abteilung.
Leemius, C., *De Lapponibus Finmarchiae eorumque lingua, vita et religione pristina commentatio.* Copenhagen, 1767.
Lefébure, E., "La Vertu et la vie du nom en Egypte," in *Mélusine*, viii. (1897).
   Le mythe Osirien. Paris, 1874–1875.
   "Le Paradis Égyptien," in *Sphinx*, iii. Upsala, 1900.
Lefebvre, Th., *Voyage en Abyssinie.* Paris, N.D. (preface dated June, 1845).
Leger, L., *La Mythologie slave.* Paris, 1901.
Leges Graecorum sacrae. Ed. J. de Prott et L. Ziehen. Leipsic, 1896–1906.
Leggat, F. W., quoted by H. Ling Roth, in *The Natives of Sarawak and British North Borneo.* London, 1896.
Legrand, Émile, *Contes populaires grecs.* Paris, 1881.
Lehmann-Haupt, Professor C. F. Private communications (ix. 415 *n.*[1]).
   Die historische Semiramis und ihre Zeit. Tübingen, 1910.
   in the *English Historical Review*, April 1913.
   Israel, seine Entwicklung im Rahmen der Weltgeschichte. Tübingen, 1911.
   Šamaššumukîn, König von Babylonien, 668–648 v. Chr. Leipsic, 1892.
   s.v. "Semiramis," in W. H. Roscher's *Lexikon der griechischen und römischen Mythologie*, iv.
Lehner, Stefan, "Bukaua," in R. Neuhauss's *Deutsch Neu-Guinea*, iii. Berlin, 1911.
Leipziger Studien für classischen Philologie. Leipsic, 1884.
Leitch, Archie. Private communication (vii. 158 *n.*[1]).
Leitner, G. W., *The Languages and Races of Dardistan.* Third Edition. Lahore, 1878.
Lejeune, Father, "Dans la forêt," in *Les Missions Catholiques*, xxvii. (1895).

Lekkerkerker, C., "Enkele opmerkingen over sporen van Shamanisme bij Madoereezen en Javanen," in *Tijdschrift voor Indische Taal- Land- en Volkenkunde*, xlv. (1902).

*Leland, *Collectanea*, Bagford's letter quoted by J. Brand, *Popular Antiquities*, ii. Bohn's Edition. London, 1882–1883.

Lemke, E., *Volksthümliches in Ostpreussen*. Mohrungen, 1884–1887.

Lenormant, François, *s.vv.* "Bacchus" and "Ceres," in Daremberg et Saglio, *Dictionnaire des Antiquités Grecques et Romaines*.

"Il mito di Adone-Tammuz nei documenti cuneiformi," in *Atti del IV. Congresso Internazionale degli Orientalisti*. Florence, 1880.

Lenormant, F., and Pottier, E., *s.v.* "Eleusinia," in Daremberg et Saglio, *Dictionnaire des Antiquités Grecques et Romaines*, ii.

Lentner and Dahn, in *Bavaria, Landes- und Volkskunde der Königreichs Bayern*, i. Munich, 1860.

Lenz, H. O., *Botanik der alten Griechen und Römer*. Gotha, 1859.

Lenz, O., *Skizzen aus Westafrika*. Berlin, 1878.

Leo the Great, *Sermones*, in Migne's *Patrologia Latina*, liv.

Leonard, Major A. G., *The Lower Niger and its Tribes*. London, 1906.

Leoprechting, Karl Freiherr von, *Aus dem Lechrain*. Munich, 1855.

Lepsius, R., *Die Chronologie der Aegypter*. Berlin, 1849.

Letters from Egypt, Ethiopia, and the Peninsula of Sinai. London, 1853.

"Über den ersten ägyptischen Götterkreis und seine geschichtlich-mythologische Entstehung," in *Abhandlungen der königlichen Akademie der Wissenschaften zu Berlin* (1851).

Lerius (Lery), J., *Historia Navigationis in Brasiliam, quae et America dicitur*. 1586.

Lerouze, in *Mémoires de l'Académie Celtique*, iii. (1809).

Leskien, A., und Brugmann, K., *Litauische Volkslieder und Märchen*. Strasburg, 1882.

Leslie, David, *Among the Zulus and Amatongas*. Second Edition. Edinburgh, 1875.

Leslie, Lieut.-Colonel Forbes, *The Early Races of Scotland and their Monuments*. Edinburgh, 1866.

Lett, H. W., "Winning the Churn (Ulster)," in *Folk-lore*, xvi. (1905).

Letteboer, J. H., "Eenige aanteekeningen omtrent de gebruiken bij zwangerschap en geboorte onder de Savuneezen," in *Mededeelingen van wege het Nederlandsche Zendelinggenootschap*, xlvi. (1902).

"Lettre de Mgr. Bruguière, évêque de Capse, à M. Bousquet, vicaire-général d'Aire," in *Annales de l'Association de la Propagation de la Foi*, v. Paris and Lyons, 1831.

"Lettre du curé de Santiago Tepehuacan à son évêque sur les mœurs et coutumes des Indiens soumis à ses soins," in *Bulletin de la Société de Géographie* (Paris), Deuxième Série, ii. (1834).

Lettres édifiantes et curieuses. Nouvelle Édition. Paris, 1780–1783.

Levchine, A. de, *Description des hommes et des steppes des Kirghiz-Kazaks ou Kirghiz-Kaisaks*. Paris, 1840.

Lévi, Sylvain, *La Doctrine du sacrifice dans les Brâhmanas*. Paris, 1898.

Leviticus, The Book of.

Levrault, "Rapport sur les provinces de Canélos et du Napo," in *Bulletin de la Société de Géographie* (Paris), Deuxième Série, xi. (1839).

Lew, H., "Der Tod und die Beerdigungs-gebräuche bei den polnischen Juden," in *Mittheilungen der Anthropologischen Gesellschaft in Wien*, xxxii. (1902).

Lewin, Captain T. H., *Wild Races of South-Eastern India*. London, 1870.

Lewis, E. W., in letter to the Author (iii. 106 *n.*[2]).

Lewis, Rev. Thomas, "The Ancient Kingdom of Kongo," in *The Geographical Journal*, xix. (1902).

Lewis and Clarke, Captains, *Expedition to the Sources of the Missouri,* etc. London, 1814.
    Reprinted at London, 1905.
    Travels to the Source of the Missouri River. London, 1815.
Lexer, M., "Volksüberlieferungen aus dem Lesachtal in Kärnten," in *Zeitschrift für deutsche Mythologie und Sittenkunde,* iii. (1855).
"Lexicon Mythologicum," appended to the *Edda Rhythmica seu Antiquior, vulgo Saemundina dicta,* Pars iii. Copenhagen, 1828.
L'Heureux, Jean, "Ethnological Notes on the Astronomical Customs and Religious Ideas of the Chokitapia or Blackfeet Indians," in *Journal of the Anthropological Institute,* xv. (1886).
Lhwyd, Edward, in a letter quoted by W. Borlase, in *Antiquities, Historical and Monumental, of the County of Cornwall.* London, 1769.
Libanius. Ed. J. J. Reiske. Altenburg, 1791–1797.
Lichtenstein, H., *Reisen im südlichen Afrika.* Berlin, 1811–1812.
Licinius Imbrex, quoted by Aulus Gellius, xiii. 23 (22). 16.
Liebrecht, F., *Des Gervasius von Tilbury Otia Imperialia.* Hanover, 1856.
    "Lappländische Märchen," in *Germania,* N.R., iii. (1870).
    in *Philologus,* xxii.
    Zur Volkskunde. Heilbronn, 1879.
*Liebstadt, Marcgrav de, *Historia rerum naturalium Brasiliensium.* Amsterdam, 1648. (Referred to by Th. Waitz, in *Anthropologie der Naturvölker,* iii. Leipsic, 1862.)
Liefrinck, F. A., "Bijdrage tot de Kennis van het eiland Bali," in *Tijdschrift voor Indische Taal- Land- en Volkenkunde,* xxxiii. (1890).
*Ligertwood, Miss J., MS. notes, quoted by Rev. J. Macdonald, *Religion and Myth.* London, 1893.
Lî-Kî. Translated by James Legge. Oxford, 1885. (*Sacred Books of the East,* vol. xxvii.)
Linde, S., *De Jano summo Romanorum deo.* Lund, 1891.
*Lindenbrog, Glossary on the Capitularies, quoted by J. Grimm, *Deutsche Mythologie,* Fourth Edition.
Lindley, J., and Moore, T., *The Treasury of Botany.* New Edition. London, 1874.
Lindsay, W. M., *The Latin Language.* Oxford, 1894.
Liorel, J., *Kabylie du Jurjura.* Paris, N.D.
Lisiansky, Ury, *A Voyage Round the World in the Years 1803, 4, 5, ana 6.* London, 1814.
Little, H. W., *Madagascar, its History and People.* London, 1884.
*Littmann, E., *Publications of the Princeton Expedition to Abyssinia.* Leyden, 1910. (Referred to by Th. Nöldeke, "Tigre-Texte," in *Zeitschrift für Assyriologie,* xxiv. 1910.)
Liverpool Mercury, of June 29th, 1867, quoted by T. F. Thiselton Dyer, *British Popular Customs.* London, 1876.
Livingstone, David, *Missionary Travels and Researches in South Africa.* London, 1857.
    Narrative of Expedition to the Zambesi. London, 1865.
    Last Journals in Central Africa. London, 1874.
Livinhac, Mgr., in *Annales de la Propagation de la Foi,* liii. (1881), lx. (1888).
Livy. Ed. J. N. Madvig et J. L. Ussing. Copenhagen, 1863–1880.
    Ed. W. Weissenborn. Berlin, 1873–1900.
*Ljibenov, P., *Baba Ega.* Trnovo, 1887. (Quoted by F. S. Krauss, "Altslavische Feuergewinnung," in *Globus,* lix., 1891.)
Lloyd, L., *Peasant Life in Sweden.* London, 1870.
"Lo Scoppio del Carro," in *Resurrezione, Numero Unico del Sabato Santo.* Florence, April 1906.
Lobeck, Chr. Aug., *Aglaophamus.* Königsberg, 1829.

Lockhart, J. G., *Memoirs of the Life of Sir Walter Scott.* First Edition.
Edinburgh, 1837–1838.
Second Edition. Edinburgh, 1839.
Loftus-Tottenham, A. R., quoted by E. Thurston in *Castes and Tribes of Southern India.* Madras, 1909.
Logan, James, *The Scottish Gael or Celtic Manners.* Edited by the Rev. Alex. Stewart. Inverness, N.D.
Logan, J. R., "The Orang Binua of Johore," in *Journal of the Eastern Archipelago and Eastern Asia*, i. (1847).
Logan, W., *Malabar.* Madras, 1887.
Longus, *Pastoralia de Daphnide et Chloë*, in *Erotici Scriptores*, ed. G. A. Hirschig. Paris (Didot), 1885.
Lord, John Keast, *The Naturalist in Vancouver Island and British Columbia.* London, 1866.
Loret, Victor, "L'Égypte au temps du totémisme," in *Conférences faites au Musée Guimet, Bibliothèque de Vulgarisation*, xix. Paris, 1906.
"Les fêtes d'Osiris au mois de Khoiak," in *Recueil de Travaux relatifs à la Philologie et à l'Archéologie Égyptiennes et Assyriennes*, iii. (1882), iv. (1883), v. (1884).
Loria, Dr. L., "Notes on the Ancient War Customs of the Natives of Logea and Neighbourhood," in *British New Guinea, Annual Report for 1894–1895.* London, 1896.
Loskiel, G. H., *History of the Mission of the United Brethren among the Indians in North America.* London, 1794.
Loth, J., "L'Année celtique," in *Revue Celtique*, xxv. (1904).
"Les douze jours supplémentaires (*gourdeziou*) des Bretons et les douze jours des Germains et des Indous," in *Revue Celtique*, xxiv. (1903).
Loubère, De la, *Du royaume de Siam.* Amsterdam, 1691.
Louis, J. A. H., *The Gates of Thibet, a Bird's Eye View of Independent Sikkhim, British Bhootan, and the Dooars.* Second Edition. Calcutta, 1894.
Louvet, L. E., *La Cochinchine religieuse.* Paris, 1885.
Louwerier, D., "Bijgeloovige gebruiken, die door de Javanen worden in acht genomen bij het bouwen hunner huizen," *Mededeelingen van wege het Nederlandsche Zendelinggenootschap*, xlviii. (1904).
"Bijgeloovige gebruiken, die door de Javanen worden in acht genomen bij de verzorging en opvoeding hunner kinderen," in *Mededeelingen van wege het Nederlandsche Zendelinggenootschap*, xlix. (1905).
Low, H., in *Journal of the Anthropological Institute*, xxv. (1896).
Low, Hugh, *Sarawak.* London, 1848.
Low, Lieut.-Colonel James, "On the Laws of Muung Thai or Siam," in *Journal of the Indian Archipelago*, i. Singapore, 1847.
Löw, L., *Die Lebensalter in der jüdischen Literatur.* Szedegin, 1875.
Lowell, P., *Chosön, the Land of the Morning Calm, a Sketch of Korea.* London, preface dated 1885.
Loyer, G., "Voyage to Issini on the Gold Coast," in T. Astley's *New General Collection of Voyages and Travels*, ii. London, 1745.
Lozano, Pedro, *Descripcion chorographica del terreno, rios, arboles, y animales de las dilatadissimas Provincias del Gran Chaco, Gualamba*, etc. Cordova, 1733.
Luard, Captain C. Eckford, in *Census of India, 1901*, vol. i., *Ethnographic Appendices.* Calcutta, 1903.
in *Census of India, 1901*, vol. xix. *Central India.* Lucknow, 1902.
Lucan, *Pharsalia.* Ed. C. E. Haskins. London, 1887.
Lucian, *Opera.* Ed. C. Jacobitz. Leipsic, 1866–1881.
Alexander.
Amores.
Anacharsis.

Lucian—*continued.*
    Bacchus.
    Bis accusatus.
    Calumniae non temere credendum.
    Charidemus.
    De astrologia.
    De dea Syria.
    De morte Peregrini.
    De saltatione.
    Dialogi deorum.
    Dialogi meretricii.
    Hermotimus.
    Jupiter Tragoedus.
    Lexiphanes.
    Muscae encomium.
    Necyomanteia.
    Philopatris.
    Philopseudes.
    Rhetorum praeceptor.
    Saturnalia.
    Somnium.
    Tragodopodagra.
Lucius, Prof. E., *Die Anfänge des Heiligenkultes in der christlichen Kirche.*
    Tübingen, 1904.
Lucretius, *De rerum natura.* Ed. H. A. J. Munro. Third Edition. Cam-
    bridge, 1873.
Luders, O., *Die dionysischen Künstler.* Berlin, 1873.
Lumholtz, C., *Among Cannibals.* London, 1889.
    "Symbolism of the Huichol Indians," in *Memoirs of the American Museum
    of Natural History,* vol. iii. May 1900.
    Unknown Mexico. London, 1903.
Luschan, F. von, "Einiges über Sitten und Gebräuche der Eingeborenen Neu-
    Guineas," in *Verhandlungen der Berliner Gesellschaft für Anthropologie,
    Ethnologie, und Urgeschichte* (1900).
Luzel, F. M., *Contes populaires de Basse-Bretagne.* Paris, 1887.
    Veillées Bretonnes. Morlaix, 1879.
Lyall, Sir Alfred C., *Asiatic Studies.* First Series. London, 1899.
Lyall, Sir Charles J., in his Introduction to *The Khasis,* by Major P. R. T.
    Gurdon.
Lycophron, *Alexandra (Cassandra).* Griechisch und deutsch von C. von
    Holzinger. Leipsic, 1895.
Lyell, Sir Charles, *Principles of Geology.* Twelfth Edition. London, 1875.
    The Geological Evidence of the Antiquity of Man. Fourth Edition.
    London, 1873.
Lynker, Karl, *Deutsche Sagen und Sitten in hessischen Gauen.* Second Edition.
    Cassel and Göttingen, 1860.
Lyon, G. F., *Private Journal.* London, 1824.
Lysias, *Orationes.* Ed. C. Scheibe. Leipsic, 1852.
    Contra Andocidem.
Lyttelton, Dr., Bishop of Carlisle, quoted by William Borlase, *Antiquities,
    Historical and Monumental, of the County of Cornwall.* London, 1769.

Maan, G., "Enige mededeelingen omtrent de zeden en gewoonten der Toerateya
    ten opzichte van den rijstbouw," in *Tijdschrift voor Indische Taal- Land-
    en Volkenkunde,* xlvi. (1903).
Maass, A., *Bei liebenswürdigen Wilden, ein Beitrag zur Kenntniss der Mentawai-
    Insulaner.* Berlin, 1902.

Maass, Ernst, *Die Tagesgötter.* Berlin, 1902.
    Orpheus. Munich, 1895.
Macalister, Mrs. Alexander. Private communication (vii. 157 *n.*[3]).
Macalister, Professor R. A. Stewart, *Bible Side-lights from the Mound of Gezer.*
    London, 1906.
    Reports on the Excavations of Gezer. London, N.D. Reprinted from the
    Quarterly Statement of the Palestine Exploration Fund.
    The Philistines, their History and Civilization. London, 1913.
M'Alpine, N., *Gaelic Dictionary.* Seventh Edition. Edinburgh and London,
    1877.
Macarius, *Proverbia,* in *Paroemiographi Graeci.* Ed. E. L. Leutsch et
    F. G. Schneidewin. Göttingen, 1839-1851.
Macaulay, T. B., *History of England.* First Edition. London, 1855.
Macbain, A., *Etymological Dictionary of the Gaelic Language.* Inverness, 1896.
Maccabees, The Second Book of.
MacCauley, C., "Seminole Indians of Florida," in *Fifth Annual Report of the
    Bureau of Ethnology.* Washington, 1887.
M'Caw, S. R., "Mortuary Customs of the Puyallups," in *The American Anti-
    quarian and Oriental Journal,* viii. (1886).
McClintock, Walter, *The Old North Trail.* London, 1910.
McCullagh, J. B., in *The Church Missionary Gleaner,* xiv. No. 164 (August
    1887).
MacCulloch, J. A., "Calendar," in Dr. James Hastings's *Encyclopaedia of
    Religion and Ethics,* iii. Edinburgh, 1910.
    The Religion of the Ancient Celts. Edinburgh, 1911.
M'Culloch, Colonel W. J., quoted by G. Watt, "The Aboriginal Tribes of
    Manipur," in *Journal of the Anthropological Institute,* xvi. (1887).
Macdonald, A., "Midsummer Bonfires," in *Folk-lore,* xv. (1904).
    "Some former Customs of the Royal Parish of Crathie, Scotland," in
    Folk-lore, xviii. (1907).
Macdonald, George, *Catalogue of Greek Coins in the Hunterian Collection.*
    Glasgow, 1899-1905.
Macdonald, Rev. James, "East Central African Customs," in *Journal of the
    Anthropological Institute,* xxii. (1893).
    Light in Africa. Second Edition. London, 1890.
    "Manners, Customs, Superstitions, and Religions of South African Tribes,"
    in *Journal of the Anthropological Institute,* xix. (1890), xx. (1891).
    MS. notes sent to the Author (iv. 183 *n.*[2]).
    Religion and Myth. London, 1893.
Macdonell, A. A., *Vedic Mythology.* Strasburg, 1897.
Macdonell, Lady Agnes, in letter to the Author (ix. 164 *n.*[1]).
    in *The Times,* May 3rd, 1913.
Macdougall, Rev. J., *Folk and Hero Tales.* London, 1891. (*Waifs and Strays
    of Celtic Tradition,* No. III.)
MacFarlane, Dr., quoted by A. C. Haddon, in *Journal of the Anthropological
    Institute,* xix. (1890).
Macfarlane, Mr., of Faslane, Gareloch. Private communication (viii. 158 *n.*[2]).
M'Gillivray, A. A., in H. R. Schoolcraft's *Indian Tribes of the United States.*
    Philadelphia, 1853-1856.
Macgillivray, J., *Narrative of the Voyage of H.M.S. Rattlesnake.* London, 1852.
Macgowan, D. S., M.D., "Self-immolation by Fire in China," in *The Chinese
    Recorder and Missionary Journal,* xix. (1888).
McGregor, A. W., quoted by W. S. Routledge and K. Routledge, *With a
    Prehistoric People, the Akikuyu of British East Africa.* London, 1910.
MacGregor, Sir William, *British New Guinea.* London, 1897.
    "Lagos, Abeokuta, and the Alake," in *Journal of the African Society,*
    No. 12 (July 1904).

MacInnes, Rev. D., *Folk and Hero Tales.* London, 1890.
Mackay, Alexander, quoted by Alexander Carmichael, *Carmina Gadelica.* Edinburgh, 1900.
McKellar, Mr., quoted by the Rev. W. Ridley, in "Report on Australian Languages and Traditions," in *Journal of the Anthropological Institute,* ii. (1873).
Mackenzie, A., "Descriptive Notes on Certain Implements, Weapons, etc., from Graham Island, Queen Charlotte Islands, B.C.," in *Transactions of the Royal Society of Canada,* ix. (1891).
Mackenzie, Alexander, *Voyages from Montreal through the Continent of North America.* London, 1801.
Mackenzie, Sheriff-Substitute David J. Private communications (ix. 169 *n.*²).
*Mackenzie, E., *An Historical, Topographical, and Descriptive View of the County of Northumberland.* Second Edition. Newcastle, 1825. (Quoted in *County Folk-lore,* vol. iv. *Northumberland.* Collected by M. C. Balfour. London, 1904.)
Mackenzie, Captain J. S. F., "The Village Feast," in *Indian Antiquary,* iii. (1874).
Mackenzie, John, *Ten Years North of the Orange River.* Edinburgh, 1871.
Mackinlay, J. M., *Folk-lore of Scottish Lochs and Springs.* Glasgow, 1893.
Maclagan, R. C., M.D., "Corn-maiden in Argyleshire," in *Folk-lore,* vii. (1896).
"Notes on Folk-lore Objects collected in Argyleshire," in *Folk-lore,* vi. (1895).
"Sacred Fire," in *Folk-lore,* ix. (1898).
Maclean, Colonel, *A Compendium of Kafir Laws and Customs.* Cape Town, 1866.
McLennan, J. F., *Studies in Ancient History.* London, 1886.
The Patriarchal Theory. Edited and completed by D. McLennan. London, 1885.
M'Mahon, A. R., *The Karens of the Golden Chersonese.* London, 1876.
MacPhail, Rev. M., "Folk-lore from the Hebrides," in *Folk-lore,* xi. (1900).
"Traditions, Customs, and Superstitions of the Lewis," in *Folk-lore,* vi. (1895).
Macpherson, Captain, in *North Indian Notes and Queries,* ii.
Macpherson, W., *Memorials of Service in India from the Correspondence of the late Major S. C. Macpherson.* London, 1865.
Macridy-Bey, Th., *La Porte des Sphinx à Eyuk.* (*Mitteilungen der Vorderasiatischen Gesellschaft,* 1908, No. 3, Berlin.)
Macrobius, *Opera.* Ed. L. Jan. Quedlinburg and Leipsic, 1848–1852.
Commentarium in Somnium Scipionis.
Saturnalia.
McTaggart, J. McT. Ellis, *Some Dogmas of Religion.* London, 1906.
Madras Government Museum Bulletin.
Maeletius (Maletius, Meletius, Menecius, Ian Malecki), Jo., "De religione et sacrificiis et idolatria veterum Borussorum, Livonum, aliarumque vicinarum gentium," in *De Russorum Muscovitarum et Tartarorum religione, sacrificiis, nuptiarum, funerum ritu.* Spires, 1582.
Reprinted in *Scriptores rerum Livonicarum,* vol. ii. (Riga and Leipsic, 1848), and in *Mitteilungen der Litterarischen Gesellschaft Masovia,* viii. (Lötzen, 1902).
Magazin herausgegeben von der Lettisch-Literarischen Gesellschaft. Mitau, 1868.
Magazin pittoresque. Paris, 1840.
Magoun, H. W., "The Asuri-Kalpa ; a Witchcraft Practice of the Atharva-Veda," in *American Journal of Philology,* x. (1889).
Magyar, Ladislaus, *Reisen in Süd-Afrika in den Jahren 1849–1857.* Buda-Pesth and Leipsic, 1859.

Mahabharata. Condensed into English by Romesch Dutt. London, 1898.

Mahaffy, J. P., *The Empire of the Ptolemies.* London, 1895.

Maimonides, quoted and translated by D. Chwolsohn, *Die Ssabier und der Ssabismus.* St. Petersburg, 1856.

Makrîzî, quoted by Lagarde, "Purim," in *Abhandlungen der Königlichen Gesellschaft der Wissenschaften zu Göttingen,* xxxiv. (1887).

Malalas, Joannes, *Chronographia.* Ed. L. Dindorf. Bonn, 1831.

Malcolm, Sir John, *History of Persia.* London, 1815.

Maler, T., "Mémoire sur l'état de Chiapa (Mexique)," in *Revue d'Ethnographie,* iii. (1885).

Mallat, J., *Les Philippines.* Paris, 1846.

Malte-Brun, *Annales des Voyages.* Paris, 1814.

Man, a Monthly Record of Anthropological Science.

Man, E. H., "Notes on the Nicobarese," in *Indian Antiquary,* xxviii. (1899).

On the Aboriginal Inhabitants of the Andaman Islands. London, N.D.

Mandlesloe, J. A. de, in J. Harris's *Voyages and Travels,* i. London, 1744.

Manilius, *Astronomica.* Ed. M. Bechert, in *Corpus Poetarum Latinorum,* ed. J. P. Postgate. London, 1894–1905.

Mann, J. F., "Notes on the Aborigines of Australia," in *Proceedings of the Geographical Society of Australasia,* i. (1885).

Manners and Customs of the Japanese in the Nineteenth Century. from recent Dutch Visitors to Japan, and the German of Dr. Ph. Fr. von Siebold. London, 1841.

Mannhardt, W., *Antike Wald- und Feldkulte.* Berlin, 1877.

"Das älteste Märchen," in *Zeitschrift für deutsche Mythologie und Sittenkunde,* iv. (1859).

Der Baumkultus der Germanen und ihrer Nachbarstämme. Berlin, 1875.

Die Götter der deutschen und nordischen Völker. Berlin, 1860.

Die Korndämonen. Berlin, 1868.

Germanische Mythen. Berlin, 1858.

in *Magazin herausgegeben von der Lettisch-Literarischen Gesellschaft,* xiv. (1868).

Mythologische Forschungen. Strasburg, 1884.

Roggenwolf und Roggenhund. Second Edition. Danzig, 1866.

Manning, J., "Notes on the Aborigines of New Holland," in *Journal and Proceedings of the Royal Society of New South Wales,* xvi. Sydney, 1883.

Manning, Percy, in *Folk-lore,* iv. (1893), viii. (1897).

Manning, Thomas. *See s.v.* Narratives.

Mansfeld, Alfred, *Urwald Dokumente, vier Jahre unter den Crossflussnegern Kameruns.* Berlin, 1908.

Mansveld, G. (Kontroleur van Nias), "Iets over de namen en Galars onder de Maleijers in de Padangsche Bovenlanden, bepaaldelijk in noordelijk Agam," in *Tijdschrift voor Indische Taal- Land- en Volkenkunde,* xxiii. (1876).

Manuscrit Ramirez: Histoire de l'origine des Indiens qui habitent la Nouvelle Espagne selon leurs traditions. Publié par D. Charnay. Paris, 1903.

Marcellinus on Hermogenes, in *Rhetores Graeci.* Ed. Chr. Walz. Stuttgart and Tübingen, 1832–1836.

Marcellus, *De medicamentis.* Ed. G. Helmreich. Leipsic, 1889.

Marchoux, "Ethnographie, Porto-Novo," in *Revue Scientifique,* Quatrième Série, iii. (1895).

Marcus Antoninus, *Commentarii.* Ed. J. Stich. Leipsic, 1882.

Marett, R. R., *The Threshold of Religion.* London, N.D.

Margoliouth, D. S., *Mohammed and the Rise of Islam.* New York, 1905.

Mariette-Bey (Pacha), A., *Dendérah.* Paris, 1873–1880.

*Marilaun, Anton Kerner von, *Pflanzenleben.* 1888.
The Natural History of Plants. Translated and edited by F. W. Oliver. London, 1894-1895.
Marindin, G. E. M., *s.v.* "Oscilla," in W. Smith's *Dictionary of Greek and Roman Antiquities.* Third Edition. London, 1890-1891.
Mariner, W., *An Account of the Natives of the Tonga Islands.* Edited by John Martin. Second Edition. London, 1818.
Tonga Islands, Vocabulary (appended to the preceding).
Marini, Gio. Filippo de, *Historia et relatione del Tunchino et del Giappone.* Rome, 1665.
Mariny, *Relation nouvelle et curieuse des royaumes de Tunquin et de Lao.* Traduite de l'Italien du P. Mariny (*sic*) Romain. Paris, 1666.
Marmor Parium, in *Fragmenta Historicorum Graecorum,* vol. i. Paris (Didot), 1874. Ed. C. Müller.
Marno, Ernst, *Reisen im Gebiete des blauen und weissen Nil.* Vienna, 1874.
Marquardt, Joachim, *Privatleben der Römer.* Second Edition. Leipsic, 1886.
Römische Staatsverwaltung. Second Edition. Leipsic, 1885.
Marriott, H. P. Fitzgerald, *The Secret Tribal Societies of West Africa.* Reprinted from *Ars quatuor Coronatorum,* the Transactions of a Masonic Lodge of London.
Marsden, W., *History of Sumatra.* Third Edition. London, 1811.
Marshall, A. S. F., in letter to Professor A. C. Seward (vi. 136 *n.*[3]).
Marshall, W. E., *Travels amongst the Todas.* London, 1873.
Marston, Major M., in Rev. Jedidiah Morse's *Report to the Secretary of War of the United States on Indian Affairs,* Appendix. Newhaven, 1822.
Marti, D. K., *Kurzer Hand-Commentar zum alten Testament.* Freiburg i. B.
Martial, *Epigrammata.* Ed. L. Friedlaender. Leipsic, 1886.
Martianus Capella. Ed. Franciscus Eyssenhardt. Leipsic, 1866.
Martin, C., "Über die Eingeborenen von Chiloe," in *Zeitschrift für Ethnologie,* ix. (1877).
Martin, Father, in *Lettres édifiantes et curieuses,* Nouvelle Edition, xi. Paris, 1781.
Martin, K., "Bericht über eine Reise ins Gebiet des Oberen-Surinam," in *Bijdragen tot de Taal- Land- en Volkenkunde van Nederlandsch-Indië,* xxxv. (1886).
Bericht über eine Reise nach Nederlandsch West-Indien, Erster Theil. Leyden, 1887.
Martin, M., "A Description of the Western Islands of Scotland," in John Pinkerton's *Voyages and Travels,* iii.
Description of the Western Islands of Scotland. London, 1673 [1703].
Martin, Th. Henry, in *Revue Archéologique,* N.S., xiii. (1866).
Martinengo-Cesaresco, E., in *The Academy,* No. 671, March 14, 1885.
Martius, C. F. Phil. von, *Beiträge zur Ethnographie und Sprachenkunde Amerika's, zumal Brasiliens.* Leipsic, 1867.
**Martyrologium Romanum Vetus,* quoted by W. Smith and S. Cheetham, *Dictionary of Christian Antiquities,* i.
Mason, Rev. F., D.D., "On Dwellings, Works of Art, Law, etc., of the Karens," in *Journal of the Asiatic Society of Bengal,* xxxvii. (1868).
"Physical Character of the Karens," in *Journal of the Asiatic Society of Bengal,* New Series, No. cxxxi. Calcutta, 1866.
Mason, quoted in A. Bastian's *Die Völker des östlichen Asien.*
Maspero, Sir Gaston, *Études de Mythologie et d'Archéologie Égyptiennes.* Paris, 1893-1912.
Histoire ancienne. Fourth Edition. Paris, 1886.
Histoire ancienne des peuples de l'Orient classique: les origines. Paris, 1895.
Histoire ancienne des peuples de l'Orient classique: les premières mêlées des peuples. Paris, 1897.

Maspero, Sir Gaston—*continued.*
Histoire ancienne des peuples de l'Orient classique : *les Empires.* Paris, 1899.
in *Journal des Savants,* année 1899.
" Le rituel du sacrifice funéraire," in *Études de Mythologie et d'Archéologie Égyptiennes,* i.
Les Contes populaires de l'Égypte ancienne. Third Edition. Paris, N.D.
quoted by Miss R. E. White, in *Journal of Hellenic Studies,* xviii. (1898).
Massaja, F. G., in *Bulletin de la Société de Géographie* (Paris), 5ème Série, i. (1861).
Massaja, G., *I miei trentacinque anni di missione nell' alta Etiopia.* Rome and Milan, 1885–1893.
Massaja, Mgr., in *Annales de la Propagation de la Foi,* xxx. (1858).
Masson, Bishop, in *Annales de la Propagation de la Foi,* xxiv. (1852).
Masui, Th., *Guide de la Section de l'État Indépendant du Congo à l'Exposition de Bruxelles-Tervueren en 1897.* Brussels, 1897.
Mateer, Rev. S., *Native Life in Travancore.* London, 1883.
The Land of Charity. London, 1871.
Matheson, R., in *The Folk-lore Journal,* vii. (1889).
Mathew, J., *Eaglehawk and Crow.* London and Melbourne, 1899.
Mattei, Le Commandant, *Bas-Niger, Bénoué, Dahomey.* Paris, 1895.
Matthes, Dr. B. F., *Beknopt Verslag miiner reizen in de Binnenlanden van Celebes, in de jaren 1857 en 1861.* (*Verzameling van Berigten betreffende de Bijbelverspreiding,* Nos. 96-99.)
Bijdragen tot de Ethnologie van Zuid-Celebes. The Hague, 1875.
Einige Eigenthümlichkeiten in den Festen und Gewohnheiten der Makassaren und Büginesen. Leyden, 1884. Separate reprint from *Travaux de la 6ème Session du Congrès Internationale des Orientalistes à Leide,* vol. ii.
Makassaarsch-Hollandsch Woordenboek. Amsterdam, 1859.
" Over de âdâ's of gewoonten der Makassaren en Boegineezen," in *Verslagen en Mededeelingen der Koninklijke Akademie van Wetenschappen,* Afdeeling Letterkunde, Derde Reeks, ii. Amsterdam, 1885.
Over de Bissoes of heidensche priesters en priesteressen der Boegineezen. Amsterdam, 1872. Reprinted from the *Verhandelingen der Koninklijke Akademie van Wetenschappen,* Afdeeling Letterkunde, Deel vii.
Matthews, John, *A Voyage to the River Sierra-Leone.* London, 1791.
Matthews, Washington, *Ethnography and Philology of the Hidatsa Indians.* Washington, 1877.
" Myths of Gestation and Parturition," in *American Anthropologist,* New Series, iv. New York, 1902.
" The Mountain Chant : a Navajo Ceremony," in *Fifth Annual Report of the Bureau of Ethnology.* Washington, 1887.
Mauch, C., *Reisen im Inneren von Süd-Afrika.* Gotha, 1874. (*Petermanns Mittheilungen,* Ergänzungsheft, No. 37.)
Maud, Captain Philip, " Exploration in the Southern Borderland of Abyssinia," in *The Geographical Journal,* xxiii. (1904).
Maund, E. A., " Zambesi, the new British Possession in Central South Africa," in *Proceedings of the Royal Geographical Society,* 1890.
Maundrell, Henry, *A Journey from Aleppo to Jerusalem at Easter,* A.D. *1697.* Fourth Edition. Perth, 1800.
" A Journey from Aleppo to Jerusalem at Easter, A.D. 1697," in Bohn's *Early Travellers in Palestine.* Edited by Thomas Wright. London, 1848.
Maurer, Konrad, *Isländische Volkssagen der Gegenwart.* Leipsic, 1860.
Vorlesungen über altnordische Rechtsgeschichte. Leipsic, 1907.
Maury, A., *Histoire des Religions de la Grèce Antique.* Paris, 1857–1859.
Maury, L. F. Alfred, " Les Populations primitives du nord de l'Hindoustan," in *Bulletin de la Société de Géographie* (Paris), 4ème Série, vii. (1854).

Maximilian, Prinz zu Wied, *Reise in das Innere Nord-America.* Coblenz, 1839–41.

Reise nach Brasilien. Frankfort, 1820–1821.

Maximus Tyrius, *Dissertationes.* Ed. Fr. Dübner. Paris (Didot), 1877.

Maxwell, W. E., "The Folk-lore of the Malays," in *Journal of the Straits Branch of the Royal Asiatic Society,* No. 7 (June 1881).

Mayer, M., *s.v.* "Kronos," in W. H. Roscher's *Lexikon der griechischen und römischen Mythologie,* ii. Leipsic, 1890–1897.

Mayne, J. D., *A Treatise on Hindu Law and Usage.* Third Edition. Madras and London, 1883.

Mayne, Commander R. C., *Four Years in British Columbia and Vancouver Island.* London, 1862.

Mazzuconi, Father, in *Annales de la Propagation de la Foi,* xxvii. (1855).

Meakin, Budgett, *The Moors.* London, 1902.

Mededeelingen van wege het Nederlandsche Zendelinggenootschap.

Meerburg, J. W., "Proeve einer beschrijving van land en volk van Midden-Manggarai (West-Flores), Afdeeling Bima," in *Tijdschrift voor Indische Taal- Land- en Volkenkunde,* xxxiv. (1891).

Meerwaldt, J. H., "Gebruiken der Bataks in het maatschappelijk leven," in *Mededeelingen van wege het Nederlandsche Zendelinggenootschap,* xlix. (1905), li. (1907).

Meier, Ernst, *Deutsche Sagen, Sitten und Gebräuche aus Schwaben.* Stuttgart, 1852.

"Über Pflanzen und Kräuter," in *Zeitschrift für deutsche Mythologie und Sittenkunde,* i. Göttingen, 1853.

Meier, Josef, "Mythen und Sagen der Admiralitäts-insulaner," in *Anthropos,* iii. (1908).

Meiners, C., *Geschichte der Religionen.* Hanover, 1806–1807.

Meissner, Bruno, "Zur Entstehungsgeschichte des Purimfestes," in *Zeitschrift der deutschen morgenländischen Gesellschaft,* l. (1896).

Mela, Pomponius, *Chorographia.* Ed. G. Parthey. Berlin, 1867.

Meldon, Major J. A., "Notes on the Bahima of Ankole," in *Journal of the African Society,* No. xxii. (January 1907).

Melito, "Oration to Antoninus Caesar," in W. Cureton's *Spicilegium Syriacum.* London, 1855.

Meltzer, *s.v.* "Dido," in W. H. Roscher's *Lexikon der griechischen und römischen Mythologie,* i.

Mélusine.

*Melville, H., *Van Diemen's Land* (Hobart Town, 1833), quoted by H. Ling Roth, *The Aborigines of Tasmania.* London, 1890.

Memoir of the American Museum of Natural History, The Jesup North Pacific Expedition.

Mémoires de l'Académie Celtique.

Mémoires de l'Académie des Inscriptions et Belles-Lettres.

Mémoires de la Société des Antiquaires de Picardie.

Mémoires de la Société de Linguistique de Paris.

Mémoires de la Société Finno-Ougrienne.

Mémoires et dissertations publiées par la Société Royale des Antiquaires de France.

Memoirs of the Anthropological Society of London.

Memoirs of the Asiatic Society of Bengal.

Memorials of the Empire of Japon in the XVI. and XVII. Centuries. Edited by T. Rundall. Hakluyt Society. London, 1850.

Menander of Ephesus, in *Fragmenta Historicorum Graecorum,* ed. C. Müller, vol. iv.

Quoted by Eusebius, *Chronicorum liber prior.* Ed. A. Schoene.

Quoted by Josephus, *Contra Apionem.*

Menander Protector, in *Fragmenta Historicorum Graecorum*, ed. C. Müller, vol. iv.

Menecius, J., in *Scriptores rerum Livonicarum*, ii. Riga and Leipsic, 1848. See above, *s.v.* Maeletius.

Mensignac, C. de, *Recherches ethnographiques sur la Salive et le Crachat*. Bordeaux, 1892.

Merensky, A., *Beiträge zur Kenntnis Süd-Afrikas*. Berlin, 1875.

"Das Konde-volk im deutschen Gebiet am Nyassa-See," in *Verhandlungen der Berliner Gesellschaft für Anthropologie, Ethnologie und Urgeschichte* (1893).

Mergel, J., *Die Medizin der Talmudisten*. Leipsic and Berlin, 1885.

Merker, Captain M., *Die Masai*. Berlin, 1904.

Rechtsverhältnisse und Sitten der Wadschagga. Gotha, 1902. (*Petermanns Mitteilungen*, Ergänzungsheft, No. 138.)

Merolla, G., *Relazione del viaggio nel regno di Congo*. Naples, 1726.

Merolla, J., "Voyage to Congo," in John Pinkerton's *Voyages and Travels*, xvi.

Merz, Dr., "Bericht über seine erste Reise von Amoy nach Kui-kiang," in *Zeitschrift der Gesellschaft für Erdkunde zu Berlin*, xxiii. (1888).

Messerschmidt, L., *Corpus Inscriptionum Hettiticarum*. Berlin, 1900.

The Hittites. London, 1903.

Metlahkatlah, quoted by Sir John Lubbock, *Origin of Civilisation*. Fourth Edition. London, 1882.

Metz, F., *The Tribes inhabiting the Neilgherry Hills*. Second Edition. Mangalore, 1864.

Meyer, C., *Der Aberglaube des Mittelalters*. Bâle, 1884.

Meyer, Eduard, "Ägyptische Chronologie," in *Abhandlungen der Königlichen Preussischen Akademie der Wissenschaften*, 1904.

s.vv. "Anaitis," "Astarte," "Dolichenus," "Isis," and "Melqart," in W. H. Roscher's *Lexicon der griechischen und römischen Mythologie*.

s.v. "Atys," in Pauly-Wissowa's *Real-Encyclopädie der classischen Altertumswissenschaft*, ii.

Geschichte des Altertums, vol. i. Stuttgart, 1884.

Vol. i. 2. Second Edition. Stuttgart and Berlin, 1909.

"Nachträge zur ägyptischen Chronologie," in *Abhandlungen der Königlichen Preussischen Akademie der Wissenschaften vom Jahre 1907*. Berlin, 1908.

quoted by J. Kohler, "Das Recht der Herero," in *Zeitschrift für vergleichende Rechtswissenschaft*, xiv. (1900).

"Über einige semitische Götter," in *Zeitschrift der Deutschen Morgenländischen Gesellschaft*, xxxi.

Meyer, Elard Hugo, *Badisches Volksleben im neunzehnten Jahrhundert*. Strasburg, 1900.

Indogermanische Mythen, ii. *Achilleis*. Berlin, 1877.

Mythologie der Germanen. Strasburg, 1903.

Meyer, H. E. A., "Manners and Customs of the Aborigines of the Encounter Bay Tribe, South Australia," in *The Native Tribes of South Australia*. Adelaide, 1879.

*Meyer, Kuno, *Hibernia Minora* and *Glossary*, referred to by P. W. Joyce, *A Social History of Ancient Ireland*. London, 1903.

Meyer, W., "Ein Labyrinth mit Versen," in *Sitzungsberichte der philosophischen philologischen und historischen Classe der Königlichen Bayerischen Akademie der Wissenschaften zu München* (1882).

Meyrac, Albert, *Traditions, coutumes, légendes et contes des Ardennes*. Charleville, 1890.

Micah, The Book of the Prophet.

Michel, Ch., *Recueil d'Inscriptions Grecques*. Brussels, 1900.

Supplément. Paris, 1912.

Michov, Matthias A., " De Sarmatia Asiana atque Europea," in Simon
Grynaeus's *Novis Orbis regionum ac insularum veteribus incognitarum.*
Paris, 1532.
  in J. Pistorius's *Polonicae historiae corpus.* Bâle, 1582.
Middleton, John Henry, in *Journal of Hellenic Studies,* ix. (1888).
  The Remains of Ancient Rome. London and Edinburgh, 1892.
Miesen, J. H. W. van der, " Een en ander over Boeroe," in *Mededeelingen van
  wege het Nederlandsche Zendelinggenootschap,* xlvi. (1902).
Migne, J. P., *Patrologia Graeca.* Paris, 1857–1866.
  Patrologia Latina. Paris, 1844–1864.
Mijatovich, Chedo, *Servia and the Servians.* London, 1908.
Mijatovies, Madam Csedomille, *Serbian Folk-lore.* Edited by the Rev. W.
  Denton. London, 1874.
Mikhailoviskij, Professor V. M., " Shamanism in Siberia and European Russia,"
  in *Journal of the Anthropological Institute,* xxiv. (1895).
Miklucho-Maclay, N. von, " Ethnologische Bemerkungen über die Papuas der
  Maclay-Küste in Neu-Guinea," in *Natuurkundig Tijdschrift voor Neder-
  landsch Indie,* xxxv. (1875), xxxvi. (1876).
  in *Verhandlungen der Berliner Gesellschaft für Anthropologie, Ethnologie
  und Urgeschichte,* 1880.
  in *Verhandlungen der Berliner Gesellschaft für Anthropologie,* 1882. Bound
  with *Zeitschrift für Ethnologie,* xiv.
Miller, Hugh, *My Schools and Schoolmasters.* Edinburgh, 1854.
  Scenes and Legends of the North of Scotland. Edinburgh, 1889.
Millin, Aubin-Louis, *Voyage dans les Départmens du Midi de la France.* Paris,
  1807–1811.
Milman, H. H., *History of Latin Christianity.* Fourth Edition. London,
  1883–1905.
Milne, J., *Earthquakes.* London, 1886.
Milne, Mrs. Leslie, *Shans at Home.* London, 1910.
Milner, Annie, in William Hone's *Year Book.* London, preface dated January,
  1832.
Milner, John, *The History, Civil and Ecclesiastical, and Survey of the Antiquities
  of Winchester.* Winchester, N.D.
Milton, John, " Apology for Smectymnuus," in *Complete Collection of the
  Historical, Political, and Miscellaneous Works of John Milton.* London,
  1738.
  Paradise Lost.
Mindeleff, C., in *Seventeenth Annual Report of the Bureau of American
  Ethnology,* part 2. Washington, 1898.
Minucius Felix, *Octavius.* Ed. C. Halm. Vienna, 1867.
Mirror, The.
Mission Evangelica al reyno de Congo por la serafica religion de los Capuchinos.
  Madrid, 1649.
Mission Pavie, Indo-Chine 1879-95, Géographie et Voyages. Paris, 1900.
Mission scientifique du Cap Horn, 1882-83. Paris, 1891.
" Mission Voulet-Chanoine," in *Bulletin de la Société de Géographie* (Paris),
  8ème Série, xx. (1899).
Missions Catholiques, Les.
Mitchell, (Sir) Arthur, A.M., M.D., *On various Superstitions in the North-West
  Highlands and Islands of Scotland.* Edinburgh, 1862. (Reprinted
  from the *Proceedings of the Society of Antiquaries of Scotland,* vol. iv.)
Mitchell, T. L., *Three Expeditions into the Interior of Eastern Australia.*
  London, 1838.
Mitra, Sarat Chandra, in *Journal of the Anthropological Society of Bombay,* iv.
  No. 7 (1898).
  in *North Indian Notes and Queries,* v.

Mitra, Sarat Chandra—*continued.*
" Notes on two Behari Pastimes," in *Journal of the Anthropological Society of Bombay,* iii.
" On some Ceremonies for producing Rain," in *Journal of the Anthropological Society of Bombay,* iii. (1893).
" On the Har Paraurī, or the Behari Women's Ceremony for producing Rain," in *Journal of the Royal Asiatic Society of Great Britain and Ireland,* N.S. xxix. (1897).
" On Vestiges of Moon-Worship in Behar and Bengal," in *Journal of the Anthropological Society of Bombay,* ii.
Mittheilungen der Afrikanischen Gesellschaft in Deutschland.
Mittheilungen der Anthropologischen Gesellschaft in Wien.
Mittheilungen der Deutschen Gesellschaft bei Sud und Sud-Ostasiens. Yokohama.
Mitteilungen der Deutschen Orient-Gesellschaft zu Berlin.
Mittheilungen der Geographischen Gesellschaft in Hamburg.
Mittheilungen der Geographischen Gesellschaft zu Jena.
Mittheilungen des Kaiserlich Deutschen Archaeologischen Instituts, Athenische Abtheilung.
Mittheilungen der Kaiserlichen Königlichen Geographischen Gesellschaft in Wien.
Mittheilungen der Litterarischen Gesellschaft Masovia. Lötzen, 1902.
Mitteilungen des Seminars für orientalische Sprachen zu Berlin.
Mitteilungen der Vorderasiatischen Gesellschaft.
Mittheilungen von Forschungsreisenden und Gelehrten aus den deutschen Schutzgebieten.
Mockler-Ferryman, A. F., *British Nigeria.* London, 1902.
Up the Niger. London, 1892.
Modi, Jivangi Jimshedji, B.A., " On the Chariot of the Goddess, a Supposed Remedy for driving out an Epidemic," in *Journal of the Anthropological Society of Bombay,* vol. iv. No. 8. Bombay, 1899.
Modigliani, E., *L' Isola delle Donne.* Milan, 1894.
Un Viaggio a Nías. Milan, 1890.
Moerenhout, J. A., *Voyages aux Îles du Grand Océan.* Paris, 1837.
Moffat, Dr. R., *Missionary Labours and Scenes in Southern Africa.* London, 1842.
Mofras, Duflos de, " Fragment d'un Voyage en Californie," in *Bulletin de la Société de Géographie* (Paris), 2ème Série, xix. (1843).
Moggridge, Mr., reported in *Archaeologia Cambrensis,* Second Series, iii., and in *Journal of the Anthropological Institute,* v. (1876).
Mogk, Eugen, " Mythologie," in H. Paul's *Grundriss der germanischen Philologie,* iii. Second Edition. Strasburg, 1900.
" Sitten und Gebräuche im Kreislauf des Jahres," in R. Wuttke's *Sächsische Volkskunde.* Second Edition. Dresden, 1901.
Molina, " Fables and Rites of the Yncas," in *Rites and Laws of the Yncas,* translated and edited by (Sir) Clements R. Markham. Hakluyt Society, London, 1873.
Molina, J. I., *Geographical, Natural, and Civil History of Chili.* London, 1809.
Mommsen, August, *Chronologie.* Leipsic, 1883.
Delphika. Leipsic, 1878.
Feste der Stadt Athen im Altertum. Leipsic, 1898.
Heortologie. Leipsic, 1864.
Über die Zeit der Olympien. Leipsic, 1891.
Mommsen, Theodor, in *Corpus Inscriptionum Latinarum,* vol. i. Pars prior. Editio Altera. Berlin, 1893.
History of Rome. New Edition. London, 1894.
Römisches Staatsrecht. Third Edition. Leipsic, 1887.
Römisches Strafrecht. Leipsic, 1899.

Monatsberichte der Königlichen Preussischen Akademie der Wissenschaften.

Moncelon, L., in *Bulletins de la Société d'Anthropologie de Paris*, 3ème Série, ix. (1886).

Monckton, W., "Some Recollections of New Guinea Customs," in *Journal of the Polynesian Society*, v. (1896).

Mone, F. J., *Geschichte des Heidenthums im nördlichen Europa.* Leipsic and Darmstadt, 1822–23.

Monk, James Henry, D.D., *Life of Bentley.* Second Edition. London, 1833.

Monnier, Désiré, *Traditions populaires comparées.* Paris, 1854.

Monseur, E., in *Bulletin de Folklore*, 1903.
  Le Folklore Wallon. Brussels, N.D.
  in *Revue de l'Histoire des Religions*, xxxj. (1895).

Montaigne, *Essais.* Paris (Charpentier), N.D.

Montanus, *Die deutschen Volksfeste, Volksbräuche und deutscher Volksglaube.* Iserlohn, N.D.

Monteiro, J. J., *Angola and the River Congo.* London, 1875.

Montet, E., "Religion et Superstition dans l'Amérique du Sud," in *Revue de l'Histoire des Religions*, xxxii. (1895).

Monumenti ed Annali pubblicati dall' Instituto di Corrispondenza Archeologica.

Monumenti inediti, pubblicati dall' Instituto di Corrispondenza Archeologica.

Mooney, James, "Calendar History of the Kiowa Indians," in *Seventeenth Annual Report of the Bureau of American Ethnology*, Part I. Washington, 1898.
  "Cherokee Theory and Practice of Medicine," in *American Journal of Folk-lore*, iii. (1890).
  "Myths of the Cherokee," in *Nineteenth Annual Report of the Bureau of American Ethnology*, Part I. Washington, 1900.
  "Sacred Formulas of the Cherokees," in *Seventh Annual Report of the Bureau of Ethnology.* Washington, 1891.
  "The Indian Navel Cord," in *Journal of American Folk-lore*, xvii. (1904).

Moor, Captain Edward, "Account of an Hereditary Living Deity," in *Asiatic Researches*, vii. London, 1803.

*Moorcroft and Trebeck, *Travels in the Himalayan Provinces of Hindustan and the Panjáb*, quoted in *North Indian Notes and Queries*, i. 57, No. 428.

*Moore, *Manx Surnames*, quoted by (Sir) John Rhys, "Manx Folk-lore and Superstitions," in *Folk-lore*, ii. (1891).

*Moore, Edward, *Hindu Infanticide*, cited by H. A. Rose, in *Indian Antiquary*, xxxi. (1902).

Moore, Dr. G. F., *s.vv.* "Asherah," "Massebah," and "Molech, Moloch," in *Encyclopaedia Biblica.*

Moore, George Fletcher, *Descriptive Vocabulary of the Language in Common Use amongst the Aborigines of Western Australia.* Published along with the Author's *Diary of Ten Years' Eventful Life of an Early Settler in Western Australia*, but paged separately. London, 1884.

Moore, Father H. S., in *The Cowley Evangelist*, May 1908.

Moore, Thomas, *Life of Lord Byron*, prefixed to the collected edition of Byron's works. London, 1832–1833.

"More about Fire-walking," in *Journal of the Polynesian Society*, vol. x. No. 1 (March 1901).

Moresby, Captain John, *Discoveries and Surveys in New Guinea.* London, 1876.

Moresinus, Thomas, *Papatus seu Depravatae Religionis Origo et Incrementum.* Edinburgh, 1594.

Moret, Alexandre, *Du Caractère religieux de la Royauté Pharaonique.* Paris, 1902.

Moret, Alexandre—*continued.*
"Du sacrifice en Égypte," in *Revue de l'Histoire des Religions*, lvii. (1908).
Kings and Gods of Egypt. New York and London, 1912.
Le Rituel du culte divin journalier en Égypte. Paris, 1902.
Mystères Égyptiens. Paris, 1913.
Morga, A. de, *The Philippine Islands, Moluccas, Siam, Cambodia, Japan, and China.* Hakluyt Society. London, 1868.
Morgan, A., in *Journal of American Folk-lore*, x. (1897).
Morgan, E. Delmar, "Notes on the Lower Congo," in *Proceedings of the Royal Geographical Society*, N.S., vi. (1884).
Morgan, L. H., *Ancient Society.* London, 1877.
League of the Iroquois. Rochester, U.S. America, 1851.
Morgan, Professor M. H., "De ignis eliciendi modis apud antiquos," in *Harvard Studies in Classical Philology*, i. (1890).
Morice, Rev. Father A. G., *Au pays de l'Ours Noir: chez les sauvages de la Colombie Britannique.* Paris and Lyons, 1897.
"Notes, archaeological, industrial, and sociological, on the Western Dénés," in *Transactions of the Canadian Institute*, iv. (1892–1893).
"The Canadian Dénés," in *Annual Archaeological Report, 1905.* Toronto, 1906.
"The Western Dénés, their Manners and Customs," in *Proceedings of the Canadian Institute, Toronto*, Third Series, vii. (1888–1889).
Morley, H., *Ireland under Elizabeth and James the First.* London, 1890.
Morning Post, The.
Morris, D. F. van Braam, in *Tijdschrift voor Indische Taal- Land- en Volkenkunde*, xxxiv. (1891).
Morris, M. C. F., *Yorkshire Folk-talk.* London, 1892.
Morrison, Rev. C. W., cited by Dr. Frodsham, in letter to the Author (v. 103 *n.*[3]).
Morritt, in Robert Walpole's *Memoirs relating to European and Asiatic Turkey.* Second Edition. London, 1818.
Morse, Rev. Jedidiah, *Report to the Secretary of War of the United States on Indian Affairs.* Newhaven, 1822.
Moschus, *Carmina.* Ed. Chr. Ziegler. Tübingen, 1868.
Mosheim, J. L., *Ecclesiastical History*, translated by Archibald Maclaine, D.D. London, 1819.
Mouhot, H., *Travels in the Central Parts of Indo-China.* London, 1864.
Moulton, Professor J. H., in letters to the Author (vii. 131 *n.*[4], ix. 373 *n.*[1]).
Early Religious Poetry of Persia. Cambridge, 1911.
Early Zoroastrianism. London, 1913.
Two Lectures on the Science of Language. Cambridge, 1903.
Moura, J., *Le Royaume du Cambodge.* Paris, 1883.
Mourenhout, J. A., *Voyages aux îles du Grand Océan.* Paris, 1837.
"Mourning for the Dead among the Digger Indians," in *Journal of the Anthropological Institute*, iii. (1874).
Movers, F. C., *Die Phoenizier.* Bonn, 1841–1856.
Much, M., *Die Heimat der Indogermanen.* Jena and Berlin, 1904.
Muir, John, *Original Sanscrit Texts.* London, 1858–1872.
Mullen, B. H., "Fetishes from Landana, South-West Africa," in *Man*, v. (1905).
Müllenhoff, Karl, *Deutsche Altertumskunde.* Berlin, 1870–1900.
Sagen, Märchen und Lieder der Herzogthümer Schleswig, Holstein und Lauenburg. Kiel, 1845.
"Über den Schwerttanz," in *Festgaben für Gustav Homeyer.* Berlin, 1871.
Müller, C., *Fragmenta Historicorum Graecorum.* Paris, 1868–1883.
Geographi Graeci Minores. Paris, 1882.

Müller, F. Max, *Lectures on the Science of Language.*   Sixth Edition.   London, 1871.
   Selected Essays on Language, Religion, and Mythology.   London, 1881.
Müller, Iwan von, *Handbuch der klassischen Altertumswissenschaft.*
Müller, J. B., " Les Mœurs et usages des Ostiackes," in *Recueil de voiages au Nord*, viii.   Amsterdam, 1727.
Müller, J. G., *Geschichte der amerikanischen Urreligionen.*   Bâle, 1867.
Müller, K. O., *Aeschylos Eumeniden.*   Göttingen, 1833.
   Denkmäler der alten Kunst.   Second Edition.   Ed. Fr. Wieseler.   Göttingen, 1854.
   Die Dorier.   Second Edition.   Breslau, 1844.
   Die Etrusker.   Ed. W. Deecke.   Stuttgart, 1877.
   Kunstarchaeologische Werke.   Berlin, 1873.
   Orchomenus und die Minyer.   Second Edition.   Breslau, 1844.
   Prolegomena zu einer wissenschaftlichen Mythologie.   Göttingen, 1825.
   " Sandon und Sardanapal," in *Kunstarchaeologische Werke*, iii.
Müller, P. E., on Saxo Grammaticus, *Historia Danica.*   Copenhagen, 1839–1858.
Müller, S., *Reizen en Onderzoekingen in den Indischen Archipel.*   Amsterdam, 1857.
Müller, W. " Über die Wildenstämme der Insel Formosa," in *Zeitschrift für Ethnologie*, xlii. (1910).
Müller, Willibald, *Beiträge zur Volkskunde der Deutschen in Mähren.*   Vienna and Olmütz, 1893.
Müller, W. Max, *Asien und Europa.*   Leipsic, 1893.
   " Der Bündnisvortrag Ramses' II. und des Chetitirkönigs," in *Mitteilungen der Vorderasiatischen Gesellschaft*, No. 5.   Berlin, 1902.
   in *Mitteilungen der Vorderasiatischen Gesellschaft*, 1900, No. 1.
Müller-Wieseler, *Denkmäler der alten Kunst.*   See Müller, K. O.
Münchener Neuesten Nachrichten, No. 235, May 21st, 1909, quoted by L. Curtius, " Christi Himmelfahrt," in *Archiv für Religionswissenschaft*, xiv. (1911).
Mundy, Captain Rodney, *Narrative of Events in Borneo and Celebes, from the Journal of James Brooke, Esq., Rajah of Sarawak.*   London, 1848.
Munro, R., *Ancient Scottish Lake Dwellings or Crannogs.*   Edinburgh, 1882.
   The Lake Dwellings of Europe.   London, Paris, and Melbourne, 1890.
Münzer, *s.v.* " Cincius," in Pauly-Wissowa's *Real-encyclopädie der classischen Altertumswissenschaft*, iii.
Munzinger, W., *Ostafrikanische Studien.*   Schaffhausen, 1864.
   Sitten und Recht der Bogos.   Winterthur, 1859.
Murdoch, J., " Ethnological Results of the Point Barrow Expedition," in *Ninth Annual Report of the Bureau of Ethnology.*   Washington, 1892.
Murr, J., *Die Pflanzenwelt in der griechischen Mythologie.*   Innsbruck, 1890.
Murray, *Handbook for Essex, Suffolk, etc.*
Murray, Sir James A. H.   Private communication (vii. 151 *n.*³).   *See also s.v.* New English Dictionary.
Murray, Margaret A., *The Osireion at Abydos.*   London, 1904.
Murray-Aynsley, H. G. M., in *Folk-lore*, iv. (1893).
Murray-Aynsley, Mrs. J. C., " Secular and Religious Dances," in *Folk-lore Journal*, v. (1887).
Museo Italiano di Antichità Classica.
Musters, G. C., in *Journal of the Royal Geographical Society*, xli. (1871).
   At Home with the Patagonians.   London, 1871.
   " Notes on Bolivia," in *Journal of the Royal Geographical Society*, xlvii. (1877).
   " On the Races of Patagonia," in *Journal of the Anthropological Institute*, i. (1872).

Mutch, Captain J. S., quoted by Fr. Boas, in *Bulletin of the American Museum of Natural History*, xv. (1901).
Myres, Professor J. L. Private communication (vii. 62 *n.*⁵).
Mythographi Graeci. Ed. A. Westermann. Brunswick, 1843. (The full title of this work is Μυθογράφοι. *Scriptores Poeticae Historiae Graeci*.)
Mythographi Vaticani. Ed. G. H. Bode. Cellis, 1834. See *s.v.* Scriptores rerum mythicarum.

Nachrichten über Kaiser-Wilhelmsland und den Bismarck-Archipel.
Nachtigal, G., "Die Tibbu," in *Zeitschrift für Erdkunde zu Berlin*, v. (1870). *Sahârâ und Sûdân*. Leipsic, 1879–1889.
Nadaillac, Marquis de, *L'Amérique Préhistorique*. Paris, 1883.
Nanjundayya, H. V., *The Ethnographical Survey of Mysore*, vi. *Komati Caste*. Bangalore, 1906.
Napier, James, *Folk Lore, or Superstitious Beliefs in the West of Scotland within this Century*. Paisley, 1879.
Narrative of Captain James Fawckner's Travels on the Coast of Benin, West Africa. London, 1837.
Narrative of the Adventures and Sufferings of John R. Jewitt. Middletown, 1820. Edinburgh, 1824.
"Narrative of the Adventures of Four Russian Sailors, who were cast in a storm upon the uncultivated island of East Spitzbergen." Translated from the German of P. L. Le Roy, in John Pinkerton's *Voyages and Travels*, vol. i.
Narrative of the Captivity and Adventures of John Tanner, during Thirty Years' Residence among the Indians. Prepared for the Press by Edwin James, M.D. London, 1830.
*Narrative of Travels in Europe, Asia, and Africa in the Seventeenth Century by Evliyâ Efendî. Translated from the Turkish by the Ritter Joseph von Hammer. Oriental Translation Fund.
Narratives of the Mission of George Bogle to Tibet and of the Journey of Thomas Manning to Lhasa. Edited by (Sir) Clements R. Markham. London, 1876.
Nassau, R. H., *Fetichism in West Africa*. London, 1904.
Nath, Rai Bahadur Lala Baij, B.A., *Hinduism Ancient and Modern*. Meerut, 1905.
"Native Stories from Santa Cruz and Reef Islands." Translated by the Rev. W. O'Ferrall, in *Journal of the Anthropological Institute*, xxxiv. (1904).
Native Tribes of South Australia, with an introductory chapter by J. D. Woods. Adelaide, 1879.
Natuurkundig Tijdschrift voor Nederlandsch Indie.
Naville, E., *La Religion des anciens Égyptiens*. Paris, 1906.
Negelein, J. von, "Die volksthümliche Bedeutung der weissen Farbe," in *Zeitschrift für Ethnologie*, xxxiii. (1901).
"Eine Quelle der indische Seelenwanderungvorstellung," in *Archiv für Religionswissenschaft*, vi. (1903).
"Seele als Vogel," in *Globus*, lxxix. (1901).
Neil, R. A., of Pembroke College, Cambridge. Private communications (viii. 22 *n.*⁴, xi. 82 *n.*⁵).
*Nelson, A. E., Central Provinces Gazetteer, Bilaspur District, 1910.
Nelson, E. W., "The Eskimo about Bering Strait," in *Eighteenth Annual Report of the Bureau of American Ethnology*, Part I. Washington, 1899.
Nery, F. J. de Santa-Anna, *Folklore Brésilien*. Paris, 1889.
Nesfield, J. C., in *Panjab Notes and Queries*, ii.
Neuhauss, R., *Deutsch Neu-Guinea*. Berlin, 1911.
Neumann, C., und Partsch, J., *Physikalische Geographie von Griechenland*. Breslau, 1885.

Neumann, J. B., " Het Pane- en Bila-Stroomgebied op het eiland Sumatra,"
    Tijdschrift van het Nederlandsch Aardrijkskundig Genootschap, Tweede
    Serie, deel iii. meer uitgebreide artikelen, No. 2 (Amsterdam, 1886);
    deel iv. No. 1 (1887).
Neumann, J. E., [? H.], "*Kemali, Pantang*, en *Rêboe* bij de Karo-Bataks," in
    Tijdschrift voor Indische Taal- Land- en Volkenkunde, xlviii. (1906).
Neumann, J. H., " De *begoe* in de godsdienstige begrippen der Karo-Bataks in
    de Doesoen," in *Mededeelingen van wege het Nederlandsche Zendeling-
    genootschap*, xlvi. (1902).
" De *tĕndi* in verband met Si Dajang," in *Mededeelingen van wege het
    Nederlandsche Zendelinggenootschap*, xlviii. (1904).
" Iets over den landbouw bij de Karo-Bataks," in *Mededeelingen van wege
    het Nederlandsche Zendelinggenootschap*, xlvi. (1902).
Neumann, K., *Die Hellenen im Skythenlande*. Berlin, 1855.
New, Charles, *Life, Wanderings, and Labours in Eastern Africa*. London,
    1873.
New English Dictionary. Edited by Sir James A. H. Murray, etc. Oxford,
    1888–
Newberry, Professor P. E., in letter to the Author (vi. 109 n.[1]).
Newbold, T. J., *Political and Statistical Account of the British Settlements in
    the Straits of Malacca*. London, 1839.
Newell, J. E., " Chief's Language in Samoa," in *Transactions of the Ninth
    International Congress of Orientalists*. London, 1893.
Newman, Ch. L. Norris, *Matabeleland and how we got it*. London, 1895.
Newman, J. H., *Sermons preached before the University of Oxford*. Third
    Edition. London, 1872.
Newman, W. L., in his edition of Aristotle, *Politics*. Oxford, 1887–1902.
Newton, Alfred, *Dictionary of Birds*. New Edition. London, 1893–1896.
Neyret, Mgr., Bishop of Vizagapatam, in *Annales de la Propagation de la Foi*,
    xxiii. (1851).
Nicander. Ed. F. S. Lehrs, in *Poetae Bucolici et Didactici*. Paris (Didot),
    1862.
    Alexipharmaca.
    Theriaca.
Nicholas, Francis C., " The Aborigines of Santa Maria, Colombia," in *American
    Anthropologist*, N.S., iii. New York, 1901.
Nicholson, Mrs. C., quoted by R. C. Maclagan, in " Notes on Folk-lore Objects
    collected in Argyleshire," *Folk-lore*, vi. (1895).
Nicholson, J., *Folk-lore of East Yorkshire*. London, Hull, and Driffield, 1890.
    Supplemented by a letter addressed to Mr. E. S. Hartland, and dated
    33 Leicester Street, Hull, 11th September 1890.
Nicolaus Damascenus, in *Fragmenta Historicorum Graecorum*, ed. C. Müller,
    vol. iii.
    quoted by Athenaeus, iv. 39.
    quoted by Stobaeus, *Florilegium*. Ed. Meineke.
Nicolson, Alexander, *A Collection of Gaelic Proverbs and Familiar Phrases*,
    based on Macintosh's Collection. London and Edinburgh, 1881.
Nicolson, F. W., " The Saliva Superstition in Classical Literature," in *Harvard
    Studies in Classical Philology*, viii. (1897).
Nicolson, J., in *The World's Work and Play* (February 1906).
Niebuhr, B. G., *History of Rome*. Third Edition. London, 1837–1838.
Niemann, G. K., " De Boegineezen en Makassaren," in *Bijdragen tot de Taal-
    Land- en Volkenkunde van Nederlandsch-Indië*, xxxviii. (1889).
Nietzold, J., *Die Ehe in Ägypten zur ptolemäisch-römischen Zeit*. Leipsic,
    1903.
Nieuw Guinea, ethnographisch en natuurkundig onderzocht en beschreven.
    Amsterdam, 1862.

Nieuwenhuis, Dr. A. W., *In Centraal Borneo.* Leyden, 1900.
  Quer durch Borneo. Leyden, 1904–1907.
  "Tweede Reis van Pontianak naar Samarinda," in *Tijdschrift van het Koninklijke Nederlandsch Aardrijkskundig Genootschap,* II. Serie, xvii. (1900).
Nieuwenhuisen, J. T., en Rosenberg, H. C. B. von, "Verslag omtrent het Eiland Nias en deszelfs Bewoners," in *Verhandelingen van het Bataviaasch Genootschap van Kunsten en Wetenschappen,* xxx. Batavia, 1863.
Nigmann, E., *Die Wahehe.* Berlin, 1908.
Nilles, N., *Kalendarium Manuale utriusque Ecclesiae Orientalis et Occidentalis.* Second Edition. Innsbruck, 1896–97.
Nilsson, Professor Martin P., *Griechische Feste von religiöser Bedeutung.* Leipsic, 1906.
  Studia de Dionysiis Atticis. Lund, 1900.
Nind, Scott, "Description of the Natives of King George's Sound (Swan River Colony)," in *Journal of the Royal Geographical Society,* i. (1832).
Nineteenth Century, The.
Nino, Antonio de, *Usi e Costumi Abruzzesi.* Florence, 1879–1883.
Nissen, H., *Italische Landeskunde.* Berlin, 1883–1902.
Noel, V., "Île de Madagascar : recherches sur les Sakkalava," in *Bulletin de la Société de Géographie* (Paris), Deuxième Série, xx. (1843).
Noguès, J. L. M., *Les Mœurs d'autrefois en Saintonge et en Aunis.* Saintes, 1891.
Nöldeke, Professor Theodor, in letter to the Author (ix. 373 *n.*[1]).
  "Die Selbstentmannung bei den Syrern," in *Archiv für Religionswissenschaft,* x. (1907).
  s.vv. "Esther," and "Names" in *Encyclopaedia Biblica.*
  Geschichte der Perser und Araber zur Zeit der Sassaniden, aus der arabischen Chronik des Tabari übersetzt. Leyden, 1879.
  "Tigre-Texte," in *Zeitschrift für Assyriologie,* xxiv. (1910).
Nonius Marcellus, *De compendiosa doctrina.* Ed. L. Quicherat. Paris, 1872.
Nonnus, *Les Dionysiaques.* Grec et Français par le Comte de Marcellus. Paris (Didot), 1856.
Nonnus Abbas, *Ad S. Gregorii orationes ii. contra Julianum,* in Migne's *Patrologia Graeca,* xxxvi.
Norden, E., *P. Vergilius Maro, Aeneis Buch VI.* Leipsic, 1903.
Nordenskiöld, Baron E., "Travels on the Boundaries of Bolivia and Argentina," in *The Geographical Journal,* xxi. (1903).
Nore, Alfred de, *Coutumes, Mythes et Traditions des provinces de France.* Paris and Lyons, 1846.
Norman, H., *The Peoples and Politics of the Far East.* London, 1905.
North China Herald.
North Indian Notes and Queries.
North Star (Sitka, Alaska, December 1888), quoted in *Journal of American Folk-lore,* ii. (1889).
Noskowÿj, P. B., *Maqrizii de valle Hadhramaut libellus arabice editus et illustratus.* Bonn, 1866.
Notes analytiques sur les collections ethnographiques du Musée du Congo. Brussels, 1902–1906.
Notes and Queries.
"Notes on the River Amur and the Adjacent Districts." Translated from the Russian, in *Journal of the Royal Geographical Society,* xxviii. (1858).
Notizie degli Scavi.
Nova Acta, Abhandlungen der kaiserlichen Leop.-Carol. Deutschen Akademie der Naturforscher.
Novus Orbis regionum ac insularum veteribus incognitarum. Paris, 1532.

Nowack, W., *Lehrbuch der hebräischen Archäologie.*   Freiburg i. B. and
      Leipsic, 1894.
Numbers, The Book of.
Numismatic Chronicle.
Nuova Antologia.
Nusselein, A. H. F. J., "Beschrijving van het landschap Pasir," in *Bijdragen
      tot de Taal- Land- en Volkenkunde van Nederlandsch-Indië*, lviii. (1905).
Nutt, D., *The Voyage of Bran.*   London, 1895–1897.
Nuttall, Zelia, "The Periodical Adjustments of the Ancient Mexican Calendar,"
      in *American Anthropologist*, N.S. vi. (1904).
* Nyrop, in *Dania*, i. No. 1 (Copenhagen, 1890), referred to by H. Gaidoz, *Un
      Vieux Rite médical.*   Paris, 1892.
Nyuak, Leo, "Religious Rites and Customs of the Iban or Dyaks of Sarawak."
      Translated from the Dyak by the Very Rev. Edm. Dunn, in *Anthropos*,
      i. (1906).

Oberhummer, E., *Die Insel Cypern.*   Munich, 1903.
Obsequens, Julius, *Prodigiorum liber*, appended to W. Weissenborn's edition of
      Livy, vol. x. 2.   (Berlin, 1881).
"Observations on the Creek and Cherokee Indians, by William Bartram, 1789,
      with prefatory and supplementary notes by E. G. Squier," in *Trans-
      actions of the American Ethnological Society*, iii. Part i. (1853).
O'Donovan, E., *The Merv Oasis.*   London, 1882.
O'Ferrall, Rev. W., "Native Stories from Santa Cruz and Reef Islands," in
      Journal of the Anthropological Institute, xxxiv. (1904).
Ogilby, J., *Africa.*   London, 1670.
O'Grady, Standish H., *Sylva Gadelica.*   Translation.   London, 1892.
Olaus Magnus, *Historia de gentium septentrionalium variis conditionibus.*
      Bâle, 1567.
"Old Harvest Customs in Devon and Cornwall," in *Folk-lore*, i. (1890).
Old New Zealand.   By a Pakeha Maori.   London, 1884.
Oldenberg, H., *Buddha.*   Fifth Edition.   Stuttgart and Berlin, 1906.
      Die Literatur des alten Indien.   Stuttgart and Berlin, 1903.
      Die Religion des Veda.   Berlin, 1894.
Oldfield, A., "On the Aborigines of Australia," in *Transactions of the Ethno-
      logical Society of London*, N.S. iii. (1865).
Oldfield, H. A., *Sketches from Nipal.*   London, 1880.
Oldham, C. F., "The Nagas," in *Journal of the Royal Asiatic Society for 1901.*
      London, 1901.
"Old-Time Survivals in Remote Norwegian Dales," in *Folk-lore*, xx. (1909).
      Translated from * Pastor Chr. Glükstad's *Sundalen og Öksendalens
      Beskrivelse*, published at Christiania.
Oman, J. C., *The Great Indian Epics.*   London, 1894.
"On a Far-off Island," in *Blackwood's Magazine*, February 1886.
On the Passing of the Blessed Virgin Mary.   Apocryphal work attributed to the
      Apostle John.   See *s.v.* Johanni Apostoli.
Opigez, O., "Aperçu général sur la Nouvelle-Calédonie," in *Bulletin de la
      Société de Géographie* (Paris), 7ème Série, vii. (1886).
Oppert, G., "Note sur les Sālagrāmas," in *Comptes rendus de l'Académie des
      Inscriptions et Belles-Lettres.*   Paris, 1900.
      On the Original Inhabitants of Bharatavarsa or India.   Westminster and
      Leipsic, 1893.
Oppianus, *Halieutica.*   Ed. F. S. Lehrs, in *Poetae Bucolici et Didactici.*   Paris
      (Didot), 1862.
Ordish, T. Fairman, "English Folk-Drama," in *Folk-lore*, iv. (1893).
Orelli, J. C., *Inscriptionum Latinarum selectarum amplissima collectio.*   Zürich,
      1828–1856.

Orient und Occident.

Origen, *Commentarium in Joannem II.*, in Migne's *Patrologia Graeca*, xiv.
  Contra Celsum, in Migne's *Patrologia Graeca*, xi.
  In Jeremiam Hom. XV. 4, in Migne's *Patrologia Graeca*, xiii.
  Selecta in Ezechielem, in Migne's *Patrologia Graeca*, xiii.

Original-Mittheilungen aus der ethnologischen Abtheilung der königlichen Museen zu Berlin.

Orphica. Ed. E. Abel. Leipsic and Prague, 1885.

Orphica. Ed. G. Hermann. Leipsic, 1805.

*Ortiz, Padre Tomas, *La Pratica del ministerio.* Manila, 1713.

Osculati, G., *Esplorazione delle regioni equatorali lungo il Napo ed il fiume delle Amazzoni.* Milan, 1850.

Ostasiatischer Lloyd, March 14, 1890, quoted by J. E. D. Schmeltz, "Das Pflugfest in China," in *Internationales Archiv für Ethnographie,* xi. (1898).

Otto, W., "Juno," in *Philologus,* lxiv. (1905).

Overbeck, J., *Griechische Kunstmythologie.* Leipsic, 1873–1878.

Ovid, *Opera,* in *Corpus Poetarum Latinorum,* ed. J. P. Postgate. London, 1894–1905.
  Amores.
  Ars amatoria.
  Ex Ponto.
  Fasti. Ed. R. Merkel. Berlin, 1841. Ed. F. A. Paley, London, N.D.
  Heroides.
  Ibis.
  Metamorphoses.
  Tristia.

Oviedo y Valdés, Fernandez de, *Historia General y Natural de las Indias.* Madrid, 1851–1855.

Oviedo y Valdes, G. F., *Histoire de Nicaragua.* Published in Ternaux-Compans's *Voyages, relations et mémoires originaux, pour servir à l'histoire de la découverte de l'Amérique.* Paris, 1840.

Owen, Rev. Elias, *Welsh Folk-lore.* Oswestry and Wrexham, N.D., preface dated 1896.

Owen, Mary Alicia, *Folk-lore of the Musquakie Indians of North America.* London, 1904.

Owen, Captain W. F. W., *Narrative of Voyages to explore the Shores of Africa, Arabia, and Madagascar.* London, 1833.

Oxyrhynchus Papyri. Ed. B. P. Grenfell and A. S. Hunt. Part iii. London, 1903.

"Padstow 'Hobby Hoss,'" in *Folk-lore,* xvi. (1905).

Pahlavi Texts. Translated by E. W. West. Oxford, 1892. (*The Sacred Books of the East,* vol. xxxvii.)

Pais, Ettore, *Ancient Legends of Roman History.* London, 1906.

Palaephatus, *De incredibilibus,* in *Mythographi Graeci,* ed. Ant. Westermann. Brunswick, 1843.

Palestine Exploration Fund Quarterly Statement for 1884.

Palladius, *De re rustica,* in *Scriptores Rei Rusticae Veteres Latini,* ed. J. G. Schneider, vol. iii.

Pallas, P. S., *Reise durch verschiedene Provinzen des russischen Reichs.* St. Petersburg, 1771–1776.

Pallegoix, Mgr., *Description du royaume Thai ou Siam.* Paris, 1854.

Palmer, E., "Notes on some Australian Tribes," in *Journal of the Anthropological Institute,* xiii. (1884).

"On Plants used by the Natives of North Queensland," in *Journal and Proceedings of the Royal Society of New South Wales for 1883,* xvii.

Palmer, J., quoted by R. H. Codrington, *The Melanesians.*

Palmer, L. Linton, "A Visit to Easter Island," in *Journal of the Royal Geographical Society*, xl. (1870).

Pander, Professor E., "Das lamaische Pantheon," in *Zeitschrift für Ethnologie*, xxi. (1889).

"Geschichte des Lamaismus," in *Verhandlungen der Berliner Gesellschaft für Anthropologie, Ethnologie und Urgeschichte*, 1889.

Panikkar, T. K. Gopal, *Malabar and its Folk.* Madras, N.D. Preface dated Chowghaut, 8th October 1900.

Panjab Notes and Queries.

Pantschatantra. Übersetzt von Th. Benfey. Leipsic, 1859.

Panyasis, cited by Apollodorus, *Bibliotheca.*

Panzer, Fr., *Beitrag zur deutschen Mythologie.* Munich, 1848–1855.

Papon, Histoire générale de la Provence, quoted by L. J. B. Bérenger-Feraud, *Superstitions et Survivances*, iv. Paris, 1896.

Park, Mungo, *Travels in the Interior Districts of Africa.* Fifth Edition. London, 1807.

Parker, E. H., *China Past and Present.* London, 1903.

Parker, Joseph, in Brough Smyth's *Aborigines of Victoria*, ii.

Parkinson, John, "Note on the Asaba People (Ibos) of the Niger," in *Journal of the Anthropological Institute*, xxxvi. (1906).

"Notes on the Efik Belief in ' Bush-soul,'" in *Man*, vi. (1906).

"Southern Nigeria, the Lagos Province," in *The Empire Review*, vol. xv. (May 1908).

Parkinson, R., "Beiträge zur Ethnologie der Gilbertinsulaner," in *Internationales Archiv für Ethnographie*, ii. (1889).

"Die Berlinhafen Section, ein Beitrag zur Ethnographie der Neu-Guinea Küste," in *Internationales Archiv für Ethnographie*, xiii. (1900).

Dreissig Jahre in der Südsee. Stuttgart, 1907.

Im Bismarck Archipel. Leipsic, 1887.

Zur Ethnographie der Nordwestlichen Salomo Inseln. Berlin, 1899.

"Zur Ethnographie der Ontong Java- und Tasman-Inseln," in *Internationales Archiv für Ethnographie*, x. (1897).

Parkinson, Th., *Yorkshire Legends and Traditions.* Second Series. London, 1889.

Parkyns, Mansfield, *Life in Abyssinia.* Second Edition. London, 1868.

Parmentier, L., and Cumont, Fr., "Le Roi des Saturnales," in *Revue de Philologie*, xxi. (1897).

Paroemiographi Graeci. Ed. E. L. Leutsch et F. G. Schneidewin. Göttingen, 1839–1851.

Parsons, Harold G., in letter to Mr. Theodore A. Cooke (iv. 203 *n.*[5]).

Parthenius, *Narrationes Amatoriae*, in *Mythographi Graeci*, ed. Ant. Westermann.

Partridge, Charles, *Cross River Natives.* London, 1905.

"The Burial of the Atta of Igaraland and the ' Coronation ' of his Successor," in *Blackwood's Magazine* (September 1904).

In letter to the Author (ii. 294 *n.*[2]).

Paschal Chronicle, in Migne's *Patrologia Graeca*, xcii.

Pasquier, E., *Recherches de la France.* Paris, 1633.

Passarini, L., "Il Comparatico e la Festa di S. Giovanni nelle Marche e in Roma," in *Archivio per lo Studio delle Tradizioni Popolari*, i. (1882).

"Passio Sancti Symphoriani," in Migne's *Patrologia Graeca*, v.

Paton, L. B., *s.v.* "Atargatis," in J. Hastings's *Encyclopaedia of Religion and Ethics*, ii.

Critical and Exegetical Commentary on the Book of Esther Edinburgh, 1908.

The Early History of Syria and Palestine. London, 1902.

Paton, W. R., " Die Kreuzigung Jesu," in *Zeitschrift für die neutestamentliche Wissenschaft*, ii. (1901).
    in *Folk-lore*, i. (1890), ii. (1891), vi. (1895), xii. (1901).
    in letters to the Author (vi. 78 *n.*[1], xi. 319).
    " The Holy Names of the Eleusinian Priests," in *International Folk-lore Congress, 1891, Papers and Transactions.*
    " The *Pharmakoi* and the Story of the Fall," in *Revue archéologique*, 4ème Série, ix. (1907).
Paton, W. R., and Hicks, E. L., *The Inscriptions of Cos.* Oxford, 1891.
Paul, H., *Grundriss der germanischen Philologie.* Second Edition, vol. iii. Strasburg, 1900.
Paulitschke, Ph., *Ethnographie Nordost-Afrikas : die geistige Cultur der Danâkil, Galla und Somâl.* Berlin, 1896.
    Ethnographie Nordost-Afrikas : die materielle Cultur der Danâkil, Galla und Somâl. Berlin, 1893.
Paulus Diaconus, *Historia Langobardorum.* Ed. G. Waitz. Hanover, 1878.
Paulus Fagius, quoted by J. Selden, *De dis Syris.* Leipsic, 1668.
Pauly, A., *Real-Encyclopädie der classischen Alterthumswissenschaft.* Stuttgart, 1842–1866 (vol. i. Second Edition ; vols. ii.-vi. First Edition).
Pauly, T. de, *Description ethnographique des Peuples de la Russie : Peuples de l'Amérique Russe.* St. Petersburg, 1862.
    Peuples ouralo-altaïques. St. Petersburg, 1862.
    Peuples de la Sibérie orientale. St. Petersburg, 1862.
Pauly-Wissowa, *Real-Encyclopädie der classischen Altertumswissenschaft.* Stuttgart, 1894–
Pausanias, *Graeciae Descriptio.* Ed. Fr. Spiro. Leipsic, 1903.
Payne, Bishop, quoted by Sir Harry Johnston, *Liberia.* London, 1906.
Payne, E. J., *History of the New World called America*, vol. i. Oxford, 1892.
Payne, J. H., quoted in " Observations on the Creek and Cherokee Indians, by William Bartram, 1789, with Prefatory and Supplementary Notes by E. G. Squier," in *Transactions of the American Ethnological Society*, vol. iii. part i. (1853).
Peacock, Miss Mabel, in letter to the Author (ii. 231 *n.*[3]).
    " The Folk-lore of Lincolnshire," in *Folk-lore*, xii. (1901).
Peake, Professor A. S., on Job xxxviii. 31, in *The Century Bible.*
Peale, Titian R., in *The American Naturalist*, xviii. (1884).
Pearse, J., " Customs connected with Death and Burial among the Sihanaka," in *The Antananarivo Annual and Madagascar Magazine*, vol. ii., *Reprint of the Second Four Numbers, 1881–1884.* Antananarivo, 1896.
Pechuel-Loesche, " Indiscretes aus Loango," in *Zeitschrift für Ethnologie*, x. (1878).
Pedlow, M. R., in *Indian Antiquary*, xxix. (1900).
Peet, T. E., *The Stone and Bronze Ages in Italy and Sicily.* Oxford, 1909.
*Peking Gazette, quoted in *Lettres édifiantes et curieuses*, xxi. Nouvelle Edition.
Pelleschi, G., *Eight Months on the Gran Chaco of the Argentine Republic.* London, 1886.
Pelleschi, J., *Los Indios Matacos.* Buenos Ayres, 1897.
Pembroke County Guardian.
*" Penitential of Theodore," quoted by J. M. Kemble, *Saxons in England*, i.
Pennant, Thomas, " A Tour in Scotland, 1769," in John Pinkerton's *Voyages and Travels*, iii.
    " A Tour in Scotland and Voyage to the Hebrides in 1772," in John Pinkerton's *Voyages and Travels*, iii.
    MS., quoted by J. Brand, *Popular Antiquities of Great Britain.* London, 1882–1883.
People of Turkey, The. By a Consul's Daughter and Wife. London, 1878.

People's Weekly Journal for Norfolk.

Pepys, Samuel, *Memoirs.* Edited by Lord Braybrooke. Second Edition. London, 1828.

Percival, Major C., "Tropical Africa, on the Border Line of Mohamedan Civilization," in *The Geographical Journal*, xlii. (1913).

Percival, R., *Account of the Island of Ceylon.* Second Edition. London, 1805.

Perdrizet, P., "Terres - cuites de Lycosoura, et mythologie arcadienne," in *Bulletin de Correspondance hellénique*, xxiii. (1899).

Perelaer, M. T. H., *Ethnographische Beschrijving der Dajaks.* Zalt-Bommel, 1870.

Perera, Arthur A., "Glimpses of Singhalese Social Life," in *Indian Antiquary*, xxxi. (1902), xxxii. (1903), xxxiii. (1904).

Perham, Rev. J., in H. Ling Roth's *Natives of Sarawak and British North Borneo.* London, 1896.

"Manangism in Borneo," in *Journal of the Straits Branch of the Royal Asiatic Society*, No. 19. Singapore, 1887.

"Mengap, the Song of the Dyak Sea Feast," in *Journal of the Straits Branch of the Royal Asiatic Society*, No. 2. Singapore, December 1878.

"Petara, or Sea Dyak Gods," in *Journal of the Straits Branch of the Royal Asiatic Society*, No. 8, December 1881.

"Sea Dyak Religion," in *Journal of the Straits Branch of the Royal Asiatic Society*, No. 10 (December 1882), No. 14 (December 1884).

Pérot, Francis, "Prières, Invocations, Formules Sacrées, Incantations en Bourbonnais," in *Revue des Traditions Populaires*, xviii. (1903).

Perregaux, E., *Chez les Achanti.* Neuchâtel, 1906.

Perrot, G., et Chipiez, Ch., *Histoire de l'Art dans l'Antiquité.* Paris, 1882– .

Persian Tales, quoted in *The Spectator*, No. 578. August 9, 1714.

Persius, *Satires.* Ed. J. Conington. Second Edition. Oxford, 1874.

Pertz, Georg Heinrich, *Monumenta Germaniae historica.*

Peschel, Oscar, *Völkerkunde.* Sixth Edition. Leipsic, 1885.

Peter, Anton, *Volksthümliches aus Österreichisch-Schlesien.* Troppau, 1865–1867.

Peter, R., *s.vv.* "Fortuna," "Mefitis," and "Orcus," in W. H. Roscher's *Lexikon der griechischen und römischen Mythologie.*

Peter of Dusburg, *Chronicon Prussiae.* Ed. Chr. Hartknoch. Frankfort and Leipsic, 1679.

Petermanns Mitteilungen.
        Ergänzungshefte.

Petersen, Ch., "Das Grab und die Todtenfeier des Dionysos," in *Philologus*, xv. 1860.

Petersen, E., *Vom alten Rom.* Leipsic, 1900.

Petit, Dr. Antoine, in Th. Lefebvre's *Voyage en Abyssinie.*

Petitot, Émile, *Monographie des Dènè-Dindjié.* Paris, 1876.
        Monographie des Esquimaux Tchiglit. Paris, 1876.
        Traditions indiennes du Canada Nord-ouest. Paris, 1886.

Petrarch, *Epistolae de rebus familiaribus.* Ed. J. Fracassetti. Florence, 1859–1862.

Petrie, Professor W. M. Flinders, in letters to the Author (v. 231 $n.^3$, vi. 216 $n.^1$).
        Egyptian Tales. Second Series. London, 1895.
        Researches in Sinai. London, 1906.
        The Religion of Ancient Egypt. London, 1906.
        The Royal Tombs of the Earliest Dynasties. London, 1901.

Petroff, Ivan, *Report on the Population, Industries, and Resources of Alaska.* Preface dated August 7, 1882.

Petronius, *Satyricon.* Ed. Fr. Buecheler. Third Edition. Berlin, 1882.

*Petrus, Martyr, *De nuper sub D. Carolo repertis insulis.* Basileae, 1521. (Referred to by E. Seler, in *Alt-Mexikanische Studien,* ii. Berlin, 1899.)

Pettazzoni, R., "Mythologie Australienne du Rhombe," in *Revue de l'histoire des Religions,* lxv. (1912).

Pettigrew, T. J., *On Superstitions connected with the History and Practice of Medicine and Surgery.* London, 1844.

Pettigrew, Rev. Wm., "Kathi Kasham, the 'Soul Departure' Feast as practised by the Tangkkul Nagas, Manipur, Assam," in *Journal and Proceedings of the Asiatic Society of Bengal,* N.S., vol. v. 1909. Calcutta, 1910.

Pfannenschmid, H., *Germanische Erntefeste.* Hanover, 1878.

Pfeil, Joachim Graf, in *Journal of the Anthropological Institute,* xxvii. (1898). *Studien und Beobachtungen aus der Südsee.* Brunswick, 1899.

Pfizmaier, A., "Nachrichten von den alten Bewohnern des heutigen Corea," in *Sitzungsberichte der philosophischen-historischen Classe der kaiserlichen Akademie der Wissenschaften,* lvii. Vienna, 1868.

Phaedrus, *Fabulae Aesopiae.* Ed. L. Müller. Leipsic, 1877.

Philippson, A., *Der Peloponnes.* Berlin, 1891.

Phillips, J. Thomas, *Account of the Religion, Manners, and Learning of the People of Malabar.* London, 1717.

Philo of Byblus, in *Fragmenta Historicorum Graecorum,* ed. C. Müller, vol. iii., quoted by Eusebius, *Praeparatio Evangelii,* i.

Philo Judaeus (Philo of Alexandria). Ed. Th. Mangey. London, 1742.
Adversus Flaccum.
De specialibus legibus.

Philo vom Walde, *Schlesien in Sage und Brauch.* Berlin, N.D., preface dated 1883.

Philocalus, *Calendarium,* in *Corpus Inscriptionum Latinarum,* vol. i. Pars prior, Editio Altera, with Th. Mommsen's commentary. Berlin, 1893.

Philochorus, cited by Athenaeus.
in *Fragmenta Historicorum Graecorum,* ed. C. Müller, vol. i.

Philologus.

Philostephanus, cited by Arnobius and Clement.

Philostratus, *Opera.* Ed. C. L. Kayser. Leipsic, 1870–1871.
Epistolae.
Heroica.
Imagines.
Vita Apollonii Tyanensis.
Vitae Sophistarum.

Philostratus Junior, *Imagines.* Ed. C. L. Kayser. Leipsic, 1871.

Photius, *Bibliotheca.* Ed. Im. Bekker. Berlin, 1824.
Lexicon. Ed. S. A. Naber. Leyden, 1864–1865.

Phylarchus, cited by Athenaeus.
in *Fragmenta Historicorum Graecorum,* ed. C. Müller, vol. i.

Picarda, Father, "Autour du Mandéra, Notes sur l'Ouzigoua, l'Oukwéré et l'Oudoé (Zanguebar)," in *Les Missions Catholiques,* xviii. (1886).

Pickering, Anna Maria Wilhelmina, *Memoirs.* Edited by her son, Spencer Pickering. London, 1903.

Pierret, P., *Le Livre des Morts.* Paris, 1882.

Piers, Sir Henry, *Description of the County of Westmeath,* written in 1682. Published by (General) Charles Vallancey, *Collectanea de Rebus Hibernicis,* i. Dublin, 1786.

Pietschmann, R., *Geschichte der Phoenizier.* Berlin, 1889.

Piggul, James, in report to Baron de Bogouschefsky, *Journal of the Anthropological Institute,* iii. (1874).

Pilsudski, B., "Schwangerschaft, Entbindung und Fehlgeburt bei den Bewohnern der Insel Sachalin," in *Anthropos*, v. (1910).

Pinabel, "Notes sur quelques peuplades dépendant du Tong-King," in *Bulletin de la Société de Géographie*, Septième Série, v.   Paris, 1884.

Pinart, A., "Les Indiens de l'État de Panama," in *Revue d'Ethnographie*, vi. (1887).

Pindar, *Opera*.   Ed. Aug. Boeckh.   Leipsic, 1811–1821.
   Isthmia.
   Olympia.
   Pythia.
   quoted by Clement of Alexandria, *Stromateis*, iii.
   quoted by Plutarch, *Isis et Osiris*.

Pineau, L., *Le Folk-lore du Poitou*.   Paris, 1892.

Pinkerton, John, *General Collection of Voyages and Travels*.   London, 1808–1814.

Piolet, J. B., *Madagascar et les Hovas*.   Paris, 1895.

Pioneer Mail of May 1890, extract quoted in *The Indian Antiquary*, xxxii. (1903).

Pischel, K. F., and Geldner, *Vedische Studien*.   Stuttgart, 1889.

*Piso, L., *Annals*, first book referred to, in Pliny, *Naturalis Historia*.

Pistorius, A. W. P. V., *Studien over de inlandsche huishouding in de Padangsche Bovenlanden*.   Zalt-Bommel, 1871.

Pistorius, J., *Polonicae historiae corpus*.   Bâle, 1582.

Pitrè, Giuseppe, *Feste patronali in Sicilia*.   Turin and Palermo, 1900.
   Fiabe, Novelle e Racconti popolari Siciliani.   Palermo, 1875.
   Spettacoli e Feste Popolari Siciliane.   Palermo, 1881.
   Usi e Costumi, Credenze e Pregiudizî del Popolo Siciliano.   Palermo, 1889.

Pittier de Fabrega, H., "Die Sprache der Bribri-Indianer in Costa Rica," in *Sitzungsberichte der philosophischen-historischen Classe der kaiserlichen Akademie der Wissenschaften*.   Vienna, 1898.

Placci, Signor Carlo, in letter to the Author (x. 127 *n.*[1]).

Placucci, M., *Usi e pregiudizj dei contadini della Romagna*.   Palermo, 1885.

Plan de Carpin (de Plano Carpini), *Relation des Mongols ou Tartares*.   Ed. D'Avezac.   Paris, 1838.

Plancy, Collin de, *Dictionnaire Infernal*.   Paris, 1825–1826.

Plassard, Dr. Louis, "Les Guaraunos et le delta de l'Orénoque," in *Bulletin de la Société de Géographie* (Paris), 5ème Série, xv. (1868).

Plate, L. M. F., "Bijdrage tot de kennis van de lykanthropie bij de Sasaksche bevolking in Oost-Lombok," in *Tijdschrift voor Indische Taal- Land- en Volkenkunde*, liv. (1912).

Plath, J. H., "Die Religion und der Cultus der alten Chinesen," in *Abhandlungen der Königlichen Bayerischen Akademie der Wissenschaften*, i. Cl. ix. (1863).

Plato, *Opera omnia*.   Ed. G. Stallbaum.   Leipsic, 1850.
   Cratylus.
   Gorgias.
   Laws.
   Meno.
   Minos.
   Phaedo.
   Phaedrus.
   Politicus.
   Republic.
   Sophist.
   Symposium.
   Theaetetus.
   Timaeus.

Plautus, *Comoediae.* Ed. G. Goetz et Fr. Schoell. Leipsic, 1898–1901.
    Casina.
    Cistellaria.
    Pseudolus.
Playfair, Major A., *The Garos.* London, 1909.
Plehn, Dr. A., " Beobachtungen in Kamerun, über die Anschauungen und
    Gebräuche einiger Negerstämme," in *Zeitschrift für Ethnologie*, xxxvi.
    (1904).
Pleyte, C. M., " Ethnographische Beschrijving der Kei-Eilanden," in *Tijdschrift
    van het Nederlandsch Aardrijkskundig Genootschap*, Tweede Serie, x.
    (1893).
    " Herinneringen uit Oost-Indië," in *Tijdschrift van het Koninklijk Neder-
    landsch Aardrijkskundig Genootschap*, II. Serie, xvii. (1900).
    " Plechtigheden en gebruiken uit den cyclus van het familienleven der
    volken van den Indischen Archipel," in *Bijdragen tot de Taal- Land-
    en Volkenkunde van Nederlandsch-Indië*, xli. (1892).
Pliny, *Naturalis Historia.* Ed. D. Detlefsen. Berlin, 1866–1882.
Pliny the Younger, *Epistolae.* Ed. H. Keil. Leipsic, 1868.
    Panegyricus. Ed. H. Keil. Leipsic, 1868.
Ploix, Ch., " Les Dieux qui proviennent de la racine *DIV*," in *Mémoires de la
    Société de Linguistique de Paris*, i. (1868).
Ploss, H., *Das Kind in Brauch und Sitte der Völker.* Second Edition. Leipsic,
    1884.
    Das Weib. Second Edition. Leipsic, 1887.
Plummer, C., " Cáin Eimíne Báin," in *Ériu, the Journal of the School of Irish
    Learning, Dublin*, vol. iv. part i. (1908).
Plutarch, *Moralia.* Ed. G. N. Bernardakis. Leipsic, 1888–1896.
            Ed. Fr. Dübner. Paris (Didot), 1868–1877.
    Vitae parallelae. Ed. C. Sintenis. Leipsic, 1867–1882.
    Adversus Coloten.
    Agesilaus.
    Agis.
    Alcibiades.
    Alexander.
    Antoninus.
    Aratus.
    Aristides.
    Artoxerxes.
    Caesar.
    Camillus.
    Cato.
    Cato the Younger.
    Cleomenes.
    Consolatio ad Apollonium.
    Consolatio ad uxorem.
    Coriolanus.
    De Alexandri Magni fortuna aut virtute.
    De audiendis poetis.
    De defectu oraculorum.
    De E Delphico (*De EI apud Delphos*).
    De educatione puerorum.
    De esu carnium.
    De exilio.
    De facie in orbe lunae.
    De fortuna Romanorum.
    De fraterno Amore.
    De genio Socratis.

Plutarch—*continued.*
  Demetrius.
  Demosthenes.
  De mulierum virtutibus.
  De musica.
  De Pythiae oraculis.
  De sera numinis vindicta.
  De Stoicorum repugnantiis.
  De superstitione.
  [*De vita et poesi Homeri.*]
  Fabius Maximus.
  Instituta Laconica.
  Isis et Osiris. Ed. G. Parthey. Berlin, 1850.
  Lucullus.
  Lycurgus.
  Lysander.
  Marcellus.
  Nicias.
  Numa.
  Otho.
  Parallela.
  Pompeius.
  Praecepta Conjugalia.
  Praecepta gerendae reipublicae.
  Proverbia.
  Proverbia Alexandrinorum.
  Publicola.
  Quaestiones conviviales.
  Quaestiones Graecae.
  Quaestiones Romanae.
  Regum et imperatorum apophthegmata, Gelon I.
  Romulus.
  Septem Sapientum Convivium.
  Solon.
  Sulla.
  Themistocles.
  Theseus.
  Timoleon.
  Vitae X. Oratorum.
Pöch, R., " Vierter Bericht über meine Reise nach Neu-Guinea," in *Sitzungs-berichte der mathematisch-naturwissenschaftlichen Klasse der Kaiser-lichen Akademie der Wissenschaften,* cxv. Vienna, 1906.
Poensen, C., " Iets over de Kleeding der Javanen," in *Mededeelingen van wege het Nederlandsche Zendelinggenootschap,* xx. (1876).
Poeppig, E., *Reise in Chile, Peru und auf dem Amazonenstrome.* Leipsic, 1835–36.
Poestion, J. C., *Fridthjofs Saga, aus dem Altisländischen.* Vienna, 1879.
  Isländische Märchen. Vienna, 1884.
  Lappländische Märchen. Vienna, 1886.
Poetae Lyrici Graeci. Ed. Th. Bergk. Third Edition. Leipsic, 1866–1867.
Pogge, Paul, " Bericht über die Station Mukenge," in *Mittheilungen der Afrika-nischen Gesellschaft in Deutschland,* iv. (1883–1885).
  Im Reiche des Muata Jamwo. Berlin, 1880.
Polack, J. S., *Manners and Customs of the New Zealanders.* London, 1840.
Polek, J., " Regenzauber in Ost-Europa," in *Zeitschrift des Vereins für Volkskunde,* iii. (1893).

Polemo, Periegeta, *Fragmenta.* Ed. L. Preller. Leipsic, 1838.
  cited by Athenaeus.
  cited by a scholiast on Homer, *Iliad.* Ed. Im. Bekker.
Pollini, quoted by H. O. Lenz, *Botanik der alten Griechen und Römer.* Gotha, 1859.
Pollux, Julius, *Onomasticon.* Ed. G. Dindorf. Leipsic, 1824.
  Ed. Im. Bekker. Berlin, 1846.
Polo, Marco, The Book of. Translated by Col. H. Yule. Second Edition. London, 1875.
Polyaenus, *Strategica.* Ed. E. Woelfflin. Leipsic, 1860.
Polybius. Ed. L. Dindorf. Leipsic, 1866–1868.
Pommerol, Dr., "La fête des Brandons et le dieu Gaulois Grannus," in *Bulletins et Mémoires de la Société d'Anthropologie de Paris,* 5ème Série, ii. (1901).
Pomtow, H., in *Rheinisches Museum,* N.F., li. (1896).
Poncy, quoted by Breuil, *Mémoires de la Société des Antiquaires de Picardie,* viii. (1845).
Pond, G. H., "Dakota Superstitions," in *Collections of the Minnesota Historical Society for the Year 1867.* Saint Paul, 1867.
Ponder, Stephen, letter quoted by Andrew Lang. *Modern Mythology.* London, 1897.
Pope-Hennessy, Lieut. H., "Notes on the Jukos and other Tribes of the Middle Benue," *Anthropological Reviews and Miscellanea,* appended to *Journal of the Anthropological Institute,* xxx. (1900).
Popish Kingdome, The, or Reigne of Antichrist, written in Latin verse by Thomas Naogeorgus and Englyshed by Barnabe Googe, 1570. Edited by R. C. Hope. London, 1880.
Porphyry, *De abstinentia.* Ed. R. Hercher. Paris (Didot), 1858.
  De antro nympharum. Ed. R. Hercher. Paris (Didot), 1858.
  De vita Plotini. Ed. Ant. Westermann. Paris (Didot), 1878.
  De vita Pythagorae. Ed. Ant. Westermann. Paris (Didot), 1878.
Porte, Father, "Les Reminiscences d'un missionnaire du Basutoland," in *Les Missions Catholiques,* xxviii. (1896).
Porter, David, *Journal of a Cruise made to the Pacific Ocean in the U.S. Frigate "Essex."* New York, 1822.
  Second Edition. New York, 1882.
Portman, M. V., "Disposal of the Dead among the Andamanese," in *Indian Antiquary,* xxv. (1896).
Posidonius, quoted by Athenaeus, iv. 40. Fragments in *Fragmenta Historicorum Graecorum,* ed. C. Müller, vol. iii.
Post, A. H., *Afrikanische Jurisprudenz.* Oldenburg and Leipsic, 1887.
Postans, Mrs., *Cutch.* London, 1839.
Potkanski, K., "Die Ceremonie der Haarschur bei den Slaven und Germanen," in *Anzeiger der Akademie der Wissenschaften in Krakau* (May 1896).
Potocki, J., *Voyages dans les Steps d'Astrakhan et du Caucase.* Paris, 1829.
Pottier, E., *Étude sur les lécythes blancs attiques.* Paris, 1883.
Powell, F. York, in O. Elton's translation of Saxo Grammaticus's *Danish History.* London, 1894.
Powell, Wilfred, *Wanderings in a Wild Country.* London, 1883.
Powers, Stephen, *Tribes of California.* Washington, 1877. (*Contributions to North American Ethnology,* vol. iii.)
Praelections delivered before the Senate of the University of Cambridge. Cambridge, 1906.
Prahn, H., "Glaube und Brauch in der Mark Brandenburg," in *Zeitschrift des Vereins für Volkskunde,* i. (1891).

Prätorius, Matthäus, *Deliciae Prussicae oder Preussische Schaubuhne, in wört-lichen Auszüge aus dem Manuscript herausgegeben,* von Dr. William Pierson. Berlin, 1871.

Pratt, A. E., "Two Journeys to Ta-tsien-lu on the Eastern Borders of Tibet," in *Proceedings of the Royal Geographical Society,* xiii. (1891).

Pratt, Rev. John B., *Buchan.* Second Edition. Aberdeen, Edinburgh, and London, 1859.

Preller, L., *Ausgewählte Aufsätze.* Berlin, 1864.

   Demeter und Persephone. Hamburg, 1837.

   Griechische Mythologie. Third Edition. Berlin, 1875.

      Fourth Edition, vol. i. Ed. C. Robert. Berlin, 1894.

   in Pauly's *Realencyclopädie der classischen Altertumswissenschaft.*

   Römische Mythologie. Third Edition. Berlin, 1881–1883.

Preuss, K. Th., "Die Feuergötter als Ausgangspunkt zum Verständnis der mexikanischen Religion," in *Mitteilungen der anthropologischen Gesell-schaft in Wien,* xxxiii. (1903).

   Die Nayarit-Expedition, I. *Die Religion der Cora-Indianer.* Leipsic, 1912.

   "Die religiösen Gesänge und Mythen einiger Stämme der mexikanischen Sierra Madre," in *Archiv für Religionswissenschaft,* xi. (1908).

   in *Verhandlungen der Berliner anthropologischen Gesellschaft,* November 15, 1902.

Preussischer Jahrbücher.

Priklonski, Vasilij, "Todtengebräuche der Jakuten," in *Globus,* lix. (1891).

Priklonski, W. L., "Über das Schamenthum bei den Jakuten," in A. Bastian's *Allerlei aus Volks- und Menschenkunde,* i. Berlin, 1888.

Priscian, *Institutiones.* Ed. M. Hertz. In *Grammatici Latini,* ed. H. Keil, vols. ii., iii. Leipsic, 1855–1860.

*Pritchard, Hesketh, *Through the Heart of Patagonia.* London, 1902. Referred to in *Journal of American Folk-lore,* xvii. (1904).

Pritchard, W. T., "Notes on Certain Anthropological Matters respecting the South Sea Islanders (the Samoans)," in *Memoirs of the Anthropological Society of London,* i. (1863–64).

Probus, *In Virgilium Commentarius,* appended to the editions of Servius by H. A. Lion (Göttingen, 1826), and G. Thilo and H. Hagen, vol. iii. Fasc. ii. (Leipsic, 1902).

Proceedings and Transactions of the Royal Society of Canada.

Proceedings of the American Academy of Arts and Sciences.

Proceedings of the American Folk-lore Society held at Philadelphia.

Proceedings of the American Philosophical Society held at Philadelphia.

Proceedings of the Australasian Association for the Advancement of Science for the Year 1900. Melbourne, 1901.

**Proceedings* of the Berwickshire Naturalists' Club, vi., quoted in *The Denham Tracts.* Edited by J. Hardy. London, 1892–1895.

Proceedings of the Boston Society of Natural History.

Proceedings of the British Academy.

Proceedings of the Canadian Institute, Toronto.

Proceedings of the Geographical Society of Australasia.

Proceedings of the Linnaean Society of New South Wales for the Year 1899. Sydney, 1900.

Proceedings of the Royal Geographical Society.

Proceedings of the Royal Irish Academy.

Proceedings of the Royal Society of Edinburgh.

Proceedings of the Society of Antiquaries of Scotland.

Proceedings of the Society of Biblical Archaeology.

Proclus, *Hymn to Minerva,* quoted by Ch. A. Lobeck, *Aglaophamus.*

   on Hesiod, *Works and Days,* appended to Ed. Vollbehr's edition of Hesiod (Kiel, 1844).

Proclus—*continued.*
  in Photius, *Bibliotheca.* Ed. I. Bekker. Berlin, 1824.
  on Plato, *Cratylus,* quoted by E. Abel, *Orphica.*
  on Plato, *Timaeus,* quoted by Ch. A. Lobeck, *Aglaophamus,* and by E. Abel, *Orphica.*
Procopius, *Opera Omnia.* Ed. J. Haury. Leipsic, 1905–
  De Bello Gothico.
  De Bello Persico.
Pröhle, Heinrich, *Harzbilder, Sitten und Gebräuche aus dem Harzgebirge.* Leipsic, 1855.
  Harzsagen. Leipsic, 1859.
  in *Zeitschrift für deutsche Mythologie und Sittenkunde,* i. (1853).
*Promathion, *History of Italy,* cited by Plutarch, *Romulus.*
Propertius. Ed. F. A. Paley. Second Edition. London, 1872.
Prothero, Dr. G. W., in letters to the Author (ii. 71 *n.*[1], xi. 190 *n.*[3]).
Proyart's "History of Loango, Kakongo, and other Kingdoms in Africa," in J. Pinkerton's *Voyages and Travels,* xvi.
Prudentius, *Peristephanon.* Ed. Th. Obbarius. Tübingen, 1845.
Prudentius Trecensis, "Annales," anno 858, in G. H. Pertz's *Monumenta Germaniae historica,* i.
Pruyssenaere, E. de, "Reisen und Forschungen im Gebiete des Weissen und Blauen Nil," in *Petermanns Mittheilungen,* Ergänzungsheft, No. 50. Gotha, 1877.
Prym, E., und Socin, A., *Syrische Sagen und Maerchen.* Göttingen, 1881.
Psalms, The Book of.
Psellus, *Quaenam sunt Graecorum opiniones de daemonibus.* Ed. J. F. Boissonade. Nuremberg, 1838.
Pseudo-Dicaearchus, in *Fragmenta Historicorum Graecorum,* ed. C. Müller, vol. ii.
  Descriptio Graeciae, in *Geographi Graeci Minores,* ed. C. Müller, vol. i.
Pseudo-Plato, *Axiochus.*
  Minos.
Ptolomaeus Hephaestionis, *Nova Historia,* in *Mythographi Graeci,* ed. A. Westermann. Brunswick, 1843.
  In Photius, *Bibliotheca,* ed. Im. Bekker.
Publications of the Society of Hebrew Literature. Second Series.
Puchstein, O., "Die Bauten von Boghaz-Köi," in *Mitteilungen der Deutschen Orient-Gesellschaft zu Berlin,* No. 35, December 1907.
Puini, C., "Il fuoco nella tradizione degli antichi Cinesi," in *Giornale della Società Asiatica Italiana,* i. (1887).
Pullan, R. P., in *Archaeologia: Miscellaneous Tracts relating to Antiquity,* l. (1887).
Punch, C., in H. Ling Roth's *Great Benin.* Halifax, England, 1903.
Purcell, B. H., "Rites and Customs of the Australian Aborigines," in *Verhandlungen der Berliner Gesellschaft für Anthropologie* (*Zeitschrift für Ethnologie,* xxv., 1893).
Purvis, J. B., *Through Uganda to Mount Elgon.* London, 1909.
Puttenham, George, *The Arte of English Poesie.* London, 1811. Reprint of *the Original Edition of London, 1589.
Pyrard, François, *Voyages to the East Indies, the Maldives, the Moluccas, and Brazil.* Translated by Albert Gray. Hakluyt Society. London, 1887.

Quarterly Journal of the Mythic Society.
Quarterly Review, The.
Quarterly Statement of the Palestine Exploration Fund.
Quedenfelt, M., "Aberglaube und halbreligiöse Bruderschaft bei den Marokkanern," in *Verhandlungen der Berliner Gesellschaft für Anthropologie,*

Ethnologie und Urgeschichte, 1886 (bound up with the *Zeitschrift für Ethnologie,* xviii., 1886).

Quellien, M., quoted by Alexandre Bertrand, *La Religion des Gaulois.* Paris, 1897.

Quintus Curtius, *De gestis Alexandri Magni.* Ed. H. E. Foss. Leipsic, 1869.

R. M. O. K., "A Horrible Rite in the Highlands," in the *Weekly Scotsman,* Saturday, August 24, 1889.

Radau, H., *Early Babylonian History.* New York and London, 1900.

Radde, G., *Die Chews'uren und ihr Land.* Cassel, 1878.

Radiguet, Max, *Les Derniers Sauvages.* Paris, 1882.

Radin, P., "Ritual and Significance of the Winnebago Medicine Dance," *Journal of American Folk-lore,* xxiv. (1911).

Radloff, W., *Aus Sibirien.* Leipsic, 1884.

Proben der Volkslitteratur der nördlichen türkischen Stämme. St. Petersburg, 1885–1886.

Proben der Volksliteratur der türkischen Stämme Süd-Sibiriens. St. Petersburg, 1866–1872.

Rae, E., *The White Sea Peninsula.* London, 1881.

Raff, H., "Aberglaube in Bayern," in *Zeitschrift des Vereins für Volkskunde,* viii. (1898).

*Raffenel, A., *Nouveau voyage dans le pays des nègres.* Paris, 1856. (Referred to by Th. Waitz, *Anthropologie der Naturvölker,* ii. Leipsic, 1860.)

Voyage dans l'Afrique occidentale. Paris, 1846.

Raffles, T. Stamford, *History of Java.* London, 1817.

Raffray, A., "Voyage à la côte nord de la Nouvelle Guinée," in *Bulletin de la Société de Géographie* (Paris), 6ème Série, xv. (1878).

Rajacsich, Baron, *Das Leben, die Sitten und Gebräuche der im Kaiserthume Österreich lebenden Südslaven.* Vienna, 1873.

Ralston, W. R. S., Introduction to F. A. von Schiefner's *Tibetan Tales.*

Russian Folk-tales. London, 1873.

Songs of the Russian People. Second Edition. London, 1872.

Ramsay, John, of Ochtertyre, *Scotland and Scotsmen in the Eighteenth Century.* Edited by Alex. Allardyce. Edinburgh and London, 1888.

Ramsay, Sir W. M., "A Study of Phrygian Art," in *Journal of Hellenic Studies,* ix. (1888), x. (1889).

Historical Geography of Asia Minor. London, 1890.

Luke the Physician, and other Studies in the History of Religion. London, 1908.

"On the Early Historical Relations between Phrygia and Cappadocia," in *Journal of the Royal Asiatic Society,* N.S., xv. (1883).

"Phrygia," in *Encyclopaedia Britannica.* Ninth Edition, xviii., 1885.

The Church in the Roman Empire. London, 1893.

The Cities and Bishoprics of Phrygia, vol. i. Oxford, 1895.

"The Permanence of Religion at Holy Places in the East," in *The Expositor* (November 1906).

"The Worship of the Virgin Mary at Ephesus," in *The Expositor,* June 1905.

"Unedited inscriptions of Asia Minor," in *Bulletin de Correspondance Hellénique,* vii. (1883).

Ramsay, W. M., and Hogarth, D. G., in *American Journal of Archaeology,* vi. (1890).

"Pre-Hellenic Monuments of Cappadocia," in *Recueil de Travaux relatifs à la Philologie et à l'Archéologie Égyptiennes et Assyriennes,* xiv. (1903).

Ramseyer and Kühne, *Four Years in Ashantee.* London, 1875.

Randolph, C. B., "The Mandragora of the Ancients in Folk-lore and Medicine," in *Proceedings of the American Academy of Arts and Sciences*, No. 12 (January 1905).

Raoul-Rochette, D., "Mémoire sur les jardins d'Adonis," in *Revue Archéologique*, viii. (1851).

"Sur l'Hercule Assyrien et Phénicien," in *Mémoires de l'Académie des Inscriptions et Belles-Lettres*, xvii. Deuxième Partie. Paris, 1848.

Rapp, *s.vv.* "Attis," "Kybele," in W. H. Roscher's *Lexikon der griechischen und römischen Mythologie.*

Rappard, Th. C., "Het eiland Nias en zijne bewoners," in *Bijdragen tot de Taal- Land- en Volkenkunde van Nederlandsch-Indië*, lxii. (1909).

Rascher, P., "Die Sulka, ein Beitrag zur Ethnographie Neu-Pommern," in *Archiv für Anthropologie*, xxix. (1904).

Rasmussen, J. L., *Additamenta ad historiam Arabum ante Islamismum.* Copenhagen, 1821.

Rat, J. N., "The Carib Language," in *Journal of the Anthropological Institute*, xxvii. (1898).

Rattray, R. Sutherland, *Some Folk-lore Stories and Songs in Chinyanja.* London, 1907.

Raum, J., "Blut und Speichelbünde bei den Wadschagga," in *Archiv für Religionswissenschaft*, x. (1907).

Ravenstein, E. G., *The Russians on the Amur.* London, 1861.

Ray, S. H. Private communication (ii. 209 *n.*[3]).

Read, D. H. Moutray, "Hampshire Folk-lore," in *Folk-lore*, xxii. (1911).

Reade, Major, in *Panjab Notes and Queries*, ii.

Reade, W. Winwood, *Savage Africa.* London, 1863.

Realencyclopädie für protestantische Theologie. See *s.v.* Herzog, J. J.

Reche, Otto, *Der Kaiserin-Augusta-Fluss.* Hamburg, 1913. (*Ergebnisse der Südsee-Expedition 1908-1910.* Herausgegeben von G. Thilenius.)

Reclus, Élisée, *Nouvelle Géographie Universelle.* Paris, 1876-1894.

Records of the Past. London, N.D.

Recueil de divers voyages faits en Afrique et en l'Amerique, qui n'ont point esté encore publiez. Paris, 1684.

Recueil de Travaux relatifs à la Philologie et à l'Archéologie Égyptiennes et Assyriennes.

Recueil de voyages au Nord. Nouvelle Edition. Amsterdam, 1731-1738.

Reed, W. A., *Negritos of Zambales.* Manilla, 1904. (*Department of the Interior, Ethnological Survey Publications*, vol. ii. part i.)

Rees, W. A. van, *Die Pionniers der Beschaving in Neêrlands Indië.* Arnheim, 1867.

Rehse, Hermann, *Kiziba, Land und Leute.* Stuttgart, 1910.

Reich, A., und Stegelmann, F., "Bei den Indianern des Urubamba und des Envira," in *Globus*, lxxxiii. (1903).

Reichard, P., *Deutsch-Ostafrika.* Leipsic, 1892.

"Die Wanjamuesi," in *Zeitschrift der Gesellschaft für Erdkunde zu Berlin*, xxiv. (1889).

Reichel, W., *Über homerische Waffen.* Vienna, 1894.

Reichenbach, J. C., "Étude sur le royaume d'Assinie," in *Bulletin de la Société de Géographie* (Paris), 7ème Série, xi. (1890).

Reid, A. P., "Religious Belief of the Ojibois or Sauteux Indians," in *Journal of the Anthropological Institute*, iii. (1874).

Reimann, F. A., *Deutsche Volksfeste im neunzehnten Jahrhundert.* Weimar, 1839.

Rein, J. J., *Japan.* Leipsic, 1881-1886.

Reina, Paul, "Über die Bewohner der Insel Rook," in *Zeitschrift für allgemeine Erdkunde*, N.F., iv. (1858).

Reinach, Salomon, *Cultes, Mythes, et Religions.* Paris, 1905-1912.

"Hippolyte," in *Archiv für Religionswissenschaft*, x. (1907).

Reinach, Salomon—*continued.*
"L'Art et la magie," in *L'Anthropologie*, xiv. (1903).
"Les Vierges de Sena," in *Revue Celtique*, xviii. (1897).
Répertoire de la Statuaire grecque et romaine. Paris, 1897–1910.
Traité d'Épigraphie Grecque. Paris, 1885.
Reinach, Th., in *Recueil d'Inscriptions Juridiques Grecques.* Deuxième Série. Paris, 1898.
Reinegg, J., *Beschreibung des Kaukasus.* Gotha, Hildesheim, and St. Petersburg, 1796–1797.
Reinsberg-Düringsfeld, O. Freiherr von, *Calendrier Belge.* Brussels, 1861–1862.
Das festliche Jahr. Leipsic, 1863.
Fest-Kalender aus Böhmen. Prague, N.D., Preface dated 1861.
Hochzeitsbuch. Leipsic, 1871. *See s.v.* Düringsfeld.
*Reiskius, Joh., *Untersuchung des Notfeuers.* Frankfort and Leipsic, 1696. (Quoted by J. Grimm, *Deutsche Mythologie.* Fourth Edition.)
"Relation de la Louïsianne," in *Recueil de voyages au Nord*, v. Amsterdam, 1734.
"Relation des Natchez," in *Recueil de Voyages au Nord*, ix. Amsterdam, 1737.
Relations des Jésuites, 1626–1672. Canadian reprint. Quebec, 1858.
Remy, Jules, *Ka Mooolelo Hawaii, Histoire de l'Archipel Havaiien.* Paris and Leipsic, 1862.
Renan, E., *Histoire du peuple d'Israel.* Paris, 1893.
Marc-Aurèle et la Fin du Monde Antique. Paris, 1882.
Mission de Phénicie. Paris, 1864.
quoted by Ch. Vellay, *Le culte et les fêtes d'Adonis-Thammouz.*
Saint Paul. Paris, 1869.
Renan, E., et Berthelot, M., *Correspondance.* Paris, 1898.
Renouf, Sir P. Le Page, *Lectures on the Origin and Growth of Religion.* Second Edition. London, 1884.
"The Priestly Character of the Earliest Egyptian Civilisation," in *Proceedings of the Society of Biblical Archaeology*, xii. (1890).
Rentsch, M., in R. Wuttke's *Sächsische Volkskunde.* Second Edition. Dresden, 1901.
"Report of a Route Survey by Pundit —— from Nepal to Lhasa," etc., in *Journal of the Royal Geographical Society*, xxxviii. (1868).
Reports of the British Association for the Advancement of Science.
Reports of the Cambridge Anthropological Expedition to Torres Straits. Cambridge, 1904–
Report of the International Polar Expedition to Point Barrow, Alaska. Washington, 1885.
Reports of the Smithsonian Institution. Washington.
Report of the United States National Museum for 1895.
Report (Fourth) of the Wellcome Tropical Research Laboratories, Gordon Memorial College, Khartoum.
Reports on the North-Western Tribes of Canada. In *Reports of the British Association for the Advancement of Science.*
Report on the Work of the Horn Scientific Expedition to Central Australia. London and Melbourne, 1896.
Report to the Secretary of War of the United States on Indian Affairs. Newhaven, 1822.
Respublica sive status regni Poloniae, Lituaniae, Prussiae, Livoniae, etc. Leyden (Elzevir), 1627.
Resurrezione, Numerico Unico del Sabato Santo. Florence, April 1906.
Retord, Mgr., in *Annales de la Propagation de la Foi*, xxviii. (1856).
Revelation of St. John the Divine.

Reville, J., *La Religion à Rome sous les Sévères.* Paris, 1886.
Revon, Michel, *Le Shintoïsme.* Paris, 1907.
Revue Archéologique.
Revue Biblique Internationale. Published by the Dominicans of Jerusalem.
Revue Celtique.
Revue Coloniale Internationale.
Revue d'Ethnographie.
Revue d'Ethnographie et de Sociologie.
Revue d'Histoire et de Littérature religieuses.
Revue de l'Histoire des Religions.
Revue de Philologie.
Revue des Études Ethnographiques et Sociologiques.
Revue des Études grecques.
Revue des Questions Scientifiques.
Revue des traditions populaires.
Revue Scientifique.
Reyes y Florentino, De los, "Die religiösen Anschauungen der Ilocanen
    (Luzon)," in *Mittheilungen der Kaiserlichen Königlichen Geographischen
    Gesellschaft in Wien*, xxxi. (1888).
Reynolds, H., "Notes on the Azandé Tribe of the Congo," in *Journal of the
    African Society*, No. xi. (April 1904).
Rhamm, K., "Der heidenische Gottesdienst des finnischen Stammes," in
    Globus, lxvii. (1895).
"Der Verkehr der Geschlechter unter den Slaven in seinen gegensätzlichen
    Erscheinungen," in *Globus*, lxxxii. (1902).
Rheinisches Museum für Philologie.
Rhetores Graeci. Ed. Chr. Walz. Stuttgart and Tübingen, 1832–1836.
Rhins, J. L. Dutreuil de, *Mission scientifique dans la Haute Asie 1890–1895 :
    Récit du Voyage.* Paris, 1897.
Rhys, Sir John, "Celtae and Galli," in *Proceedings of the British Academy*, ii.
    1905-1906. London, N.D.
Celtic Folk-lore, Welsh and Manx. Oxford, 1901.
Celtic Heathendom. London and Edinburgh, 1888.
    in *Transactions of the Third International Congress for the History of
    Religion.* Oxford, 1908.
"Manx Folk-lore and Superstitions," in *Folk-lore*, ii. (1891), iii. (1892).
"Notes on the Coligny Calendar," in *Proceedings of the British Academy,
    1909-1910*, vol. iv.
"The Coligny Calendar," in *Proceedings of the British Academy, 1909-1910.*
"Welsh Fairies," in *The Nineteenth Century*, xxx. (July–December 1891).
Ribadeneira, P., *Flos Sanctorum, cioè Vite de' Santi.* Venice, 1763.
Ribbe, C., "Die Aru-Inseln," in *Festschrift des Vereins für Erdkunde zu
    Dresden.* Dresden, 1888.
    Zwei Jahre unter den Kannibalen der Salomo-Inseln. Dresden-Blasewitz,
    1903.
Ricci, S. de, "Le calendrier Celtique de Coligny," in *Revue Celtique*, xxi.
    (1900).
"Le calendrier Gaulois de Coligny," in *Revue Celtique*, xix. (1898).
"Un passage remarquable du calendrier de Coligny," in *Revue Celtique*,
    xxiv. (1903).
Richard, Jerome, "History of Tonquin," in J. Pinkerton's *Voyages and Travels*,
    ix. London, 1811.
Richardson, J., *A Dictionary of Persian, Arabic, and English.* New Edition.
    London, 1829.
Richardson, James, *Travels in the Great Desert of the Sahara.* London,
    1848.
Richardson, Rev. J., "Tanala Customs, Superstitions and Beliefs," in *The*

Antananarivo Annual and Madagascar Magazine, Reprint of the First Four Numbers. Antananarivo, 1885.

Richardson, R., in *Panjab Notes and Queries,* i. May 1884.

Richter, O., *Topographie der Stadt Rom.* Second Edition. Munich, 1902.

Rickard, Rev. R. H., quoted by Dr. George Brown, *Melanesians and Polynesians.* London, 1910.

Ridgeway, Professor W., in *Academy,* 10th May 1884.
Private communications (ii. 103 $n.^3$, ix. 353 $n.^4$).
in *The Classical Review,* x. (1896).
Paper read at Cambridge in 1911.
"Supplices of Aeschylus," in *Praelections delivered before the Senate of the University of Cambridge.* Cambridge, 1906.
The Early Age of Greece. Cambridge, 1901.
The Origin and Influence of the Thoroughbred Horse. Cambridge, 1905.
"The Origin of Jewellery," in *Report of the British Association for 1903.*
The Origin of Tragedy. Cambridge, 1910.

Ridley, Rev. William, in J. D. Lang's *Queensland.* London, 1861.
Kamilaroi and other Australian Languages. Second Edition. Sydney, 1875.
"Report on Australian Languages and Traditions," in *Journal of the Anthropological Institute,* ii. (1873).

Riedel, J. G. F., "Alte Gebräuche bei Heirathen, Geburt und Sterbefällen bei dem Toumbuluh-Stamm in der Minahasa (Nord Selebes)," in *Internationales Archiv für Ethnographie,* viii. (1895).
"De landschappen Holontalo, Limoeto, Bone, Boalemo, en Kattinggola, of Andagile," in *Tijdschrift voor Indische Taal- Land- en Volkenkunde,* xix. (1869).
"De Minahasa in 1825," in *Tijdschrift voor Indische Taal- Land- en Volkenkunde,* xviii. (1872).
De sluik- en kroesharige rassen tusschen Selebes en Papua. The Hague, 1886.
"De Topantunuasu of oorspronkelijke Volksstammen van Central Selebes," in *Bijdragen tot de Taal- Land- en Volkenkunde van Nederlandsch-Indië,* xxxv. (1886).
"Die Landschaft Dawan oder West-Timor," in *Deutsche geographische Blätter,* x.
"Galela und Toboloresen," in *Zeitschrift für Ethnologie,* xvii. (1885).
The Island of Flores. Reprinted from the *Revue Coloniale Internationale.*

Riggs, S. R., *Dakota-English Dictionary.* Washington, 1890. (*Contributions to North American Ethnology,* vol. vii.)
Dakota Grammar, Texts, and Ethnography. Washington, 1893. (*Contributions to North American Ethnology,* vol. ix.)

Rig-veda. Uebersetzt von H. Grassmann. Leipsic, 1876–77.
Translated by R. T. H. Griffiths. Benares, 1889–1892.
Kuhn's translation, quoted by J. V. Grohmann, *Aberglauben und Gebräuche aus Böhmen und Mähren.* Prague and Leipsic, 1864.

Rink, Henry, *Tales and Traditions of the Eskimo.* Translated from the Danish. Edinburgh and London, 1875.

"Riots and Unrest in the Punjab, from a Correspondent," in *The Times Weekly Edition,* May 24, 1907.

Ris, H., "De onderafdeeling klein Mandailing Oeloe en Pahantan en hare Bevolking met uitzondering van de Oeloes," in *Bijdragen tot de Taal- Land- en Volkenkunde van Nederlandsch-Indië,* xlvi. (1896).

Risley, (Sir) H. H., *The Tribes and Castes of Bengal: Ethnographic Glossary.* Calcutta, 1891–1892.

Rites and Laws of the Yncas. Translated and edited by (Sir) Clements R. Markham. Hakluyt Society, London, 1873.

Ritter, C., *Vergleichende Erdkunde von Arabien*. Berlin, 1847.
Ritter, H., et Preller, L., *Historia Philosophiae Graecae et Latinae ex fontium locis contexta*. Editio Quinta. Gothae, 1875.
Rivers, Dr. W. H. R., *The Todas*. London, 1906.
" Totemism in Polynesia and Melanesia," in *Journal of the Royal Anthropological Institute*, xxxix. (1909).
Rivet, Dr., " Le Christianisme et les Indiens de la République de l'Équateur," in *L'Anthropologie*, xvii. (1906).
Rivière, J., *Contes populaires de la Kabylie du Djurdjura*. Paris, 1882.
Rizzolati, Mgr., in *Annales de la Propagation de la Foi*, xvi. (1844).
Robert, C., in *Hermes*, xxi. (1886).
Roberts, E. S., and Gardner, E. A., *An Introduction to Greek Epigraphy*. Cambridge, 1887-1905.
Robertson, Sir George Scott, *The Kafirs of the Hindu Kush*. London, 1896.
Robertson, Rev. James, in Sir John Sinclair's *Statistical Account of Scotland*, xi.
[Robinson, Alfred], *Life in California*. New York, 1846.
Robinson, C. H., *Hausaland*. London, 1896.
Robinson, Edward, *Biblical Researches in Palestine*. Third Edition. London, 1867.
Robinson, W., *Descriptive Account of Assam*. London and Calcutta, 1841.
Robinson, Captain W. C. Private communication (iv. 139 *n.*[1]).
Rochefort, De, *Histoire naturelle et morale des Iles Antilles de l'Amérique*. Seconde Edition. Rotterdam, 1665.
Rochholz, C. L., *Deutscher Glaube und Brauch*. Berlin, 1867.
   *Schweizersagen aus dem Aargau, referred to by A. Kuhn, *Die Herabkunft des Feuers und des Göttertranks*. Second Edition. Gütersloh, 1886.
Rochon, Abbé, *Voyage to Madagascar and the East Indies*. Translated from the French. London, 1792.
Rockhill, W. Woodville, " Notes on some of the Laws, Customs, and Superstitions of Korea," in *The American Anthropologist*, iv. Washington, 1891.
   The Land of the Lamas. London, 1891.
   " Tibet, a Geographical, Ethnographical, and Historical Sketch, derived from Chinese Sources," in *Journal of the Royal Asiatic Society for 1891*. London, 1891.
Roehl, H., *Inscriptiones Graecae antiquissimae*. Berlin, 1882.
Roepstorff, F. A. de, " Ein Geisterboot der Nicobaresen," in *Verhandlungen der Berliner Gesellschaft für Anthropologie, Ethnologie und Urgeschichte* (1881).
   " Tiomberombi, a Nicobar Tale," in *Journal of the Asiatic Society of Bengal*, liii. (1884).
Roest, J. L. D. van der, " Uit het leven der Bevolking van Windessi," in *Tijdschrift voor Indische Taal- Land- en Volkenkunde*, xl. (1898).
Roger, M. le Baron, " Notice sur le Gouvernement, les Mœurs, et les Superstitions des Nègres du pays de Walo," in *Bulletin de la Société de Géographie*, viii. Paris, 1827.
Rogers, Ch., *Social Life in Scotland*. Edinburgh, 1884-1886.
Rogers, R. W., *Cuneiform Parallels to the Old Testament*. Oxford, N.D. Preface dated 1911.
Rohde, Erwin, *Psyche*. Third Edition. Tübingen and Leipsic, 1903.
   " Unedirte Luciansscholien, die attischen Thesmophorien und Haloen betreffend," in *Rheinisches Museum*, N.F., xxv. (1870).
Rohlf, G., " Reise durch Nord-Afrika," in *Petermanns Mittheilungen*, Ergänzungsheft, No. 25. Gotha, 1868.
Rolland, Eugène, *Faune populaire de la France*. Paris, 1877-1883.
Römer, Dr. R., " Bijdrage tot de Geneeskunst der Karo-Batak's," in *Tijdschrift voor Indische Taal- Land- en Volkenkunde*, l. (1908).

Romilly, H. H., *From my Verandah in New Guinea.* London, 1889.
"The Islands of the New Britain Group," in *Proceedings of the Royal Geographical Society,* N.S., ix. (1887).
Romilly, H. H., and Brown, Rev. George, in *Proceedings of the Royal Geographical Society,* N.S., ix. (1887).
Roos, S., "Bijdrage tot de Kennis van Taal, Land en Volk op het Eiland Soemba," in *Verhandelingen van het Bataviaasch Genootschap van Kunsten en Wetenschappen,* xxxvi. (1872).
Rosa, P., in *Monumenti ed Annali pubblicati dall' Instituto di Corrispondenza Archeologica nel 1856.*
Roscher, W. H., *Apollon und Mars.* Leipsic, 1873.
Ausführliches Lexikon der griechischen und römischen Mythologie. Leipsic, 1884–
"Die enneadischen und hebdomadischen Fristen und Wochen der ältesten Griechen," in *Abhanalungen der philologisch-historischen Klasse der Königlichen Sächsischen Gesellschaft der Wissenschaften,* xxi. No. 4 (1903).
"Die Legende vom Tode des grossen Pan," in *Fleckeisen's Jahrbücher für classische Philologie,* xxxviii. (1892).
Juno und Hera. Leipsic, 1875.
Nachträge zu meiner Schrift über Selene. Leipsic, 1895.
Über Selene und Verwandtes. Leipsic, 1890.
Roscoe, Rev. John, "Kibuka, the War God of the Baganda," in *Man,* vii. (1907).
"Notes on the Manners and Customs of the Baganda," in *Journal of the Anthropological Institute,* xxxi. (1901).
"Further Notes on the Manners and Customs of the Baganda," in *Journal of the Anthropological Institute,* xxxii. (1902).
"Notes on the Bageshu," in *Journal of the Royal Anthropological Institute,* xxxix. (1909).
The Baganda. London, 1911.
"The Bahima, a Cow Tribe of Enkole in the Uganda Protectorate," in *Journal of the Anthropological Institute,* xxxvii. (1907).
Also in many private communications to the Author.
Roscoe, William, *Life and Pontificate of Leo the Tenth.* Third Edition. London, 1827.
Rose, Cowper, *Four Years in Southern Africa.* London, 1829.
Rose, H. A., in *Folk-lore,* xiii. (1902).
"Hindu Birth Observances in the Punjab," in *Journal of the Royal Anthropological Institute,* xxxvii. (1907).
"Note on Female Tattooing in the Panjâb," in *Indian Antiquary,* xxxi. (1902).
Report, in *Census of India, 1901,* vol. xvii. *Punjab,* Part I. Simla, 1902.
Rose, H. A. [J. A.], "Unlucky and Lucky Children, and some Birth Superstitions," in *Indian Antiquary,* xxxi. (1902).
Rosenberg, H. von, *Der Malayische Archipel.* Leipsic, 1878.
Ross, Alexander, *Adventures of the First Settlers on the Oregon or Columbia River.* London, 1849.
Ross, L., "Inschriften von Cypern," in *Rheinisches Museum,* N.F. vii. (1850).
Reisen nach Kos, Halikarnassos, Rhodes und der Insel Cypern. Halle, 1852.
Wanderungen in Griechenland. Halle, 1851.
Rossbach, O., in *Verhandlungen der vierzigsten Versammlung deutscher Philologen und Schulmänner in Görlitz.* Leipsic, 1890.
Rostowski, S., quoted by A. Brückner, *Archiv für slavische Philologie,* ix. (1886).
Roth, H. Ling, *Great Benin.* Halifax, England, 1903.
"Low's Natives of Borneo," in *Journal of the Anthropological Institute,* xxi. (1892), xxii. (1893).

Roth, H. Ling—*continued.*
　The Aborigines of Tasmania. London, 1890.
　The Natives of Sarawak and British North Borneo. London, 1896.
Roth, Walter E., *Ethnological Studies among the North-West-Central Queens-land Aborigines.* Brisbane and London, 1897.
North Queensland Ethnography, Bulletin No. 5, Superstition, Magic, and Medicine. Brisbane, 1903.
Rouffaer, G. P., "Matjan Gadoengan," in *Bijdragen tot de Taal- Land- en Volkenkunde van Nederlandsch-Indië,* l. (1899).
Rouse, Denham, in *Folk-lore,* vii. (1889).
Rouse, W. H. D., "Folk-lore from the Southern Sporades," in *Folk-lore,* x. (1899).
　Greek Votive Offerings. Cambridge, 1902.
　"May-Day in Cheltenham," in *Folk-lore,* iv. (1893).
　"Notes from Syria," in *Folk-lore,* vi. (1895).
　Private communications to the Author (i. 15 *n.*[3], vii. 208 *n.*[1]).
Routledge, W. Scoresby, and Routledge, Katherine, *With a Prehistoric People, the Akikuyu of British East Africa.* London, 1910.
*Roux, M. E., *Aux sources de l'Irraouaddi, d'Hanoi à Calcutta par terre,* Troisième partie, quoted in *Le Tour du Monde,* iii. Paris, 1897.
Rowley, Rev. Henry, *Twenty Years in Central Africa.* London, N.D.
Royal Geographical Society, Supplementary Papers.
Rubensohn, O., *Die Mysterienheiligtümer in Eleusis und Samothrake.* Berlin, 1892.
Rubruquis, William de, "Travels into Tartary and China," in J. Pinkerton's *Voyages and Travels,* vol. vii.
"Rudhirádhyāyă, The, or Sanguinary Chapter." Translated from the *Calica Puran* by W. C. Blaquiere, in *Asiatick Researches,* v. London, 1807.
Runge, H., "Volksglaube in der Schweiz," in *Zeitschrift für deutsche Mythologie und Sittenkunde,* iv. (1859).
Russeger, J., *Reisen in Europa, Asien, und Afrika.* Stuttgart, 1844.
Russell, F., "The Pima Indians," in *Twenty-Sixth Annual Report of the Bureau of American Ethnology.* Washington, 1908.
Russell, R. V., *Report,* in *Census of India, 1901,* vol. xiii. *Central Provinces,* Part I. Nagpur, 1902.
Russwurm, C., "Aberglaube aus Russland," in *Zeitschrift für deutsche Mythologie und Sittenkunde,* iv. (1859).
Rutherford, E., *Radio-active Substances and their Radiations.* Cambridge, 1913.
Ruys, Th. H., "Bezoek an den Kannibalenstam van Noord Nieuw-Guinea," in *Tijdschrift van het Koninklijk Nederlandsch Aardrijkskundig Genootschap,* Tweede Serie, xxiii. (1906).

Sabir, C. de, "Quelques notes sur les Manègres," in *Bulletin de la Société de Géographie* (Paris), 5ème Série, i. (1861).
Sacred Books of China. Translated by James Legge. Part iii. *The Lî-Kî.* (*Sacred Books of the East,* vol. xxvii. Oxford, 1885.)
Sacred Books of the East, The. Edited by F. Max Müller. Oxford, 1879–1910.
Saga-Book, of the Viking Club, London.
Sagas from the Far East, or Kalmouk and Mongolian Traditionary Tales. London, 1873.
Sagard, F. Gabriel, *Le Grand Voyage du pays des Hurons.* Nouvelle Édition. Librairie Tross, Paris, 1865.
Sahagun, Bernardino de, *Histoire générale des choses de la Nouvelle-Espagne.* Traduite par D. Jourdanet et R. Siméon. Paris, 1880.

Sahagun, Bernardino de—*continued.*
> Aztec text of Book II., translated by Professor E. Seler, "Altmexi-canische Studien, ii.," in *Veröffentlichungen aus dem Königlichen Museum für Völkerkunde*, vi. 2/4 Heft. Berlin, 1899.

St. Ambrose, *Sermones*, in Migne's *Patrologia Latina*, xvii.

St. Clair, Henry R., quoted by Andrew Lang, *Modern Mythology.*

[S. Clemens Romanus], *Recognitiones.* Ed. E. G. Gersdorf. Also in Migne's *Patrologia Graeca*, i.

St. Cricq, De, "Voyage du Pérou au Brésil par les fleuves Ucayali et Amazone, Indiens Conibos," in *Bulletin de la Société de Géographie* (Paris), 4ème Série, vi. (1853).

St. James, The Epistle of.

St. John, The Gospel of.

St. John, Bayle, *Travels of an Arab Merchant in Soudan.* Abridged from the French. London, 1854.

St. John, H. C., *Notes and Sketches from the Wild Coasts of Nipon.* Edinburgh, 1880.
> "The Ainos," in *Journal of the Anthropological Institute*, ii. (1873).

St. John, R. F. St. Andrew, "A Short Account of the Hill Tribes of North Aracan," in *Journal of the Anthropological Institute*, ii. (1873).

St. John, Spenser, *Life in the Forests of the Far East.* Second Edition. London, 1863.

St. Luke, The Gospel of.

St. Mark, The Gospel of.

S. Martinus Dumiensis, Bishop of Braga, *De Pascha*, in Migne's *Patrologia Latina*, lxxii.

St. Matthew, The Gospel of.

S. Sophronius, "SS. Cyri et Joannis Miracula," in Migne's *Patrologia Graeca*, lxxxvii. Pars Tertia.

Saintyves, P., "Le Renouvellement du Feu Sacré," in *Revue des Traditions Populaires*, xxvii. (1912).

Salle, Laisnel de la, *Croyances et légendes du centre de la France.* Paris, 1875.

Sallustius philosophus, "De diis et mundo," in *Fragmenta Philosophorum Graecorum.* Ed. F. G. A. Mullach.

Salvado, R., *Mémoires historiques sur l'Australie.* Paris, 1854.

Samter, E., *Familienfeste der Griechen und Römer.* Berlin, 1901.

Samuel, The first Book of.

Samuel, The second Book of.

San Marte (A. Schulz), *Die Arthur-Sage.* Quedlinburg and Leipsic, 1842.

Sandberg, G., *Tibet and the Tibetans.* London, 1906.

Sanderval, Olivier de, *De l'Atlantique au Niger par la Foutah-Djallon.* Paris, 1883.

Sangermano, Father, *Description of the Burmese Empire.* Reprinted at Rangoon, 1885.

Sapper, Dr. C., "Beiträge zur Ethnographie des südlichen Mittelamerika," in *Petermanns Mitteilungen*, xlvii. (1901).
> "Die Gebräuche und religiösen Anschauungen der Kekchí-Indianer," in *Internationales Archiv für Ethnographie*, viii. (1895).
> "Ein Besuch bei den Guatusos in Costarica," in *Globus*, lxxvi. (1899).
> "Mittelamericanische Caraiben," in *Internationales Archiv für Ethnographie*, x. (1897).

Sartori, P., "Glockensagen und Glockenaberglaube," in *Zeitschrift des Vereins für Volkskunde*, vii. (1897).
> "Über das Bauopfer," in *Zeitschrift für Ethnologie*, xxx. (1898).

Satapatha-Brâhmana, The. Translated by Julius Eggeling. Oxford, 1882-1900. (*Sacred Books of the East*, vols. xii., xxvi., xli., xliii., xliv.)

Sauvé, L. F., *Le Folk-lore des Hautes-Vosges.* Paris, 1889.

Sawyer, F. E., "S. Swithin and Rain-makers," in *The Folk-lore Journal*, i. (1883).

Saxo Grammaticus, *Historia Danica.* Ed. P. E. Müller. Copenhagen, 1839–1858.

Saxo Grammaticus, The First Nine Books of the Danish History of Translated by O. Elton. London, 1894.

Sayce, Professor A. H., *Lectures on the Religion of the Ancient Babylonians.* London and Edinburgh, 1887.

The Hittites. Third Edition. London, 1903.

"The Hittite Inscriptions," in *Recueil de Travaux relatifs à la Philologie et à l'Archéologie Égyptiennes et Assyriennes*, xiv. (1893).

in W. Wright's *Empire of the Hittites.* Second Edition. London, 1886.

Schabelski, A., "Voyage aux colonies russes de l'Amérique," in *Bulletin de la Société de Géographie* (Paris), 2ème Série, iv. (1835).

Schadee, M. C., "Bijdrage tot de kennis van den godsdienst der Dajaks van Landak en Tajan," in *Bijdragen tot de Taal- Land- en Volkenkunde van Nederlandsch-Indië*, lvi. (1904).

"Het familieleven en familierecht der Dajaks van Landak en Tajan," in *Bijdragen tot de Taal- Land- en Volkenkunde van Nederlandsch-Indië*, lxiii. (1910).

Schadenberg, A., "Beiträge zur Kenntniss der im Innern Nordluzons lebenden Stämme," in *Verhandlungen der Berliner Gesellschaft für Anthropologie, Ethnologie und Urgeschichte* (1888), bound with *Zeitschrift für Ethnologie*, xx. (1888); and in *Verhandlungen der Berliner Gesellschaft für Anthropologie, Ethnologie und Urgeschichte* (1889), bound with *Zeitschrift für Ethnologie*, xxi. (1889).

"Die Bewohner von Süd-Mindanao und der Insel Samal," in *Zeitschrift für Ethnologie*, xvii. (1885).

Schäfer, H., *Die Mysterien des Osiris in Abydos.* Leipsic, 1904.

Schandein, L., in *Bavaria, Landes- und Volkskunde des Königreichs Bayern.* Munich, 1860–1867.

Schanz, M., *Geschichte der römischen Literatur.* Second Edition. Munich, 1898.

Scheffer, J., *Lapponia.* Frankfort, 1673.

Upsalia. Upsala, 1666.

Schell, O., "Einige Bemerkungen über den Mond im heutigen Glauben des bergischen Volkes," in *Am Urquell*, v. (1894).

Schellong, O., "Das Barlum-fest der Gegend Finsch-hafens," in *Internationales Archiv für Ethnographie*, ii. (1889).

"Über Familienleben und Gebräuche der Papuas der Umgebung von Finschhafen," in *Zeitschrift für Ethnologie*, xxi. (1889).

Scherzer, K., "Die Indianer von Santa Catalina Istlávacana (Frauenfuss), ein Beitrag zur Culturgeschichte der Urbewohner Central-Amerikas," in *Sitzungsberichte der philosophischen-historischen Classe der kaiserlichen Akademie der Wissenschaften*, xviii. Vienna, 1856.

Scheube, B., "Der Baerencultus und die Baerenfeste der Ainos," in *Mittheilungen der Deutschen Gesellschaft bei Süd und Süd-Ostasiens*, Heft xxii. Yokohama.

Die Ainos. Reprinted from *Mittheilungen der Deutschen Gesellschaft bei Süd und Süd-Ostasiens.* Yokohama.

Schickard, quoted by Lagarde, "Purim," in *Abhandlungen der Königlichen Gesellschaft der Wissenschaften zu Göttingen*, xxxiv. (1887).

Schiefner, Anton, *Awarische Texte.* St. Petersburg, 1873.

Heldensagen der Minussinschen Tataren. St. Petersburg, 1859.

Schiefner, F. Anton von, *Tibetan Tales.* Done into English from the German, with an introduction by W. R. S. Ralston. London, 1882.

Schinz, H., *Deutsch-Südwest-Afrika.*   Oldenburg and Leipsic, N.D., preface dated 1891.

Schlegel, G., "La fête de fouler le feu célébrée en Chine et par les Chinois à Java," in *Internationales Archiv für Ethnographie,* ix. (1896).

Uranographie Chinoise.   The Hague and Leyden, 1875.

Schleicher, August, *Litauische Märchen, Sprichwörter, Rätsel und Lieder.* Weimar, 1857.

"Lituanica," in *Sitzungsberichte der philosophischen-historischen Classe der Kaiserlichen Akademie der Wissenschaften,* xi.   Vienna, 1853, published 1854.

Volkstümliches aus Sonnenberg.   Weimar, 1858.

Schleiden, M. J., *Das Salz.*   Leipsic, 1875.

Schlich, Dr. W., *Manual of Forestry,* vol. iv.   *Forest Protection,* by W. R. Fisher, M.A.   Second Edition.   London, 1907.

Schlömann, "Die Malepa in Transvaal," in *Verhandlungen der Berliner Gesellschaft für Anthropologie, Ethnologie und Urgeschichte* (1894).

Schloss, Francis S., in letter to the Author (vi. 136 *n.*[4]).

Schlossar, A., "Volksmeinung und Volksaberglaube aus der Deutschen Steiermark," in *Germania,* N.R., xxiv. (1891).

Schmeltz, J. D. E., "Das Pflugfest in China," in *Internationales Archiv für Ethnographie,* xi. (1898).

Das Schwirrholz.   Hamburg, 1896.

Schmid, Von, "Het Kakihansch Verbond op het eiland Ceram," in *Tijdschrift voor Neêrlands Indië,* deel ii.   Batavia, 1843.

Schmidt, A., *Handbuch der griechischen Chronologie.*   Jena, 1888.

Schmidt, Bernhard, *Das Volksleben der Neugriechen.*   Leipsic, 1871.

Griechische Märchen, Sagen und Volkslieder.   Leipsic, 1877.

Schmidt, George, Moravian Missionary in 1737, quoted by Theophilus Hahn, in *Tsuni-Goam, the Supreme Being of the Khoi-Khoi.*   London, 1881.

Schmidt, K., *Jus primae noctis.*   Freiburg im Breisgau, 1881.

Schmidt, P. W., "Ethnographisches von Berlinhafen, Deutsch-Neu-Guinea," in *Mittheilungen der Anthropologischen Gesellschaft in Wien,* xxx. (1899).

Schmidt, Van, "Aanteekeningen nopens de zeden, gewoonten en gebruiken, benevens de vooroordeelen en bijgelovigheden der bevolking van de eilanden Saparoea, Haroekoe, Noessa Laut, en van een gedeelte van de zuidkust van Ceram," in *Tijdschrift voor Neêrlands Indië.*   Batavia, 1843.

Schmidt, W., *Das Jahr und seine Tage in Meinung und Brauch der Romänen Siebenbürgens.*   Hermannstadt, 1866.

Schmiedel, Professor P., in notes sent to Dr. J. S. Black (iv. 261 *n.*[1]).

Schmitz, J. H., *Sitten und Sagen, Lieder, Sprüchwörter und Räthsel des Eifler Volkes.*   Trèves, 1856–1858.

*Schneider, Zacharias, *Leipziger Chronik,* cited by K. Schwenk, *Die Mythologie der Slaven,* and by Fr. Kauffmann, *Balder.*

Schneller, Christian, *Märchen und Sagen aus Wälschtirol.*   Innsbruck, 1867.

Scholia Graeca in Aristophanem.   Ed. Fr. Dübner.   Paris (Didot), 1877.

Scholia in Caesaris Germanici Aratea.   Ed. Fr. Eyssenhardt, in his edition of Martianus Capella.   Leipsic, 1866.

Scholia in Lucianum.   Ed. H. Rabe.   Leipsic, 1906.

Scholia in Euripidem.   Ed. Edvardus Schwartz.   Berlin, 1887–1891.

Scholia in Homeri Iliadem.   Ex recensione Immanuelis Bekkeri.   Berlin, 1825.

Scholia in Pindarum.   Ed. Aug. Boeckh.   Leipsic, 1819.

Scholia in Sophoclis Tragoedias vetera.   Ed. P. N. Papageorgius.   Leipsic, 1888.

Scholia in Theocritum, Nicandrum et Oppianum.   Ed. Fr. Dübner et U. Cats Bussemaker.   Paris (Didot), 1849.

Scholiast on—
    Apollonius Rhodius, *Argonautica*.   Ed. Aug. Wellauer.
    Aristides.   Ed. G. Dindorf.
        Panathenaicus.
    Aristophanes, *Acharnenses.*
        Birds.
        Clouds.
        Ecclesiazusae.
        Frogs.
        Knights.
        Peace.
        Plutus.
        Thesmophoriazusae.
    Callimachus. (*Callimachea*, vol. i. Edidit O. Schneider. Leipsic, 1870–
        1873.)
    Clement of Alexandria, quoted by Chr. Aug. Lobeck, *Aglaophamus.*
        Königsberg, 1829.
    Demosthenes.
    Euripides, *Hippolytus.*
        Medea.
        Orestes.
        Phoenissae.
    Hesiod, *Works and Days*. Ed. E. Vollbehr. Kiel, 1844.
    Homer, *Iliad.*
    Lucian, *Dialogi Meretricii.*
        Jupiter Tragoedus.
    Nicander, *Alexipharmaca.*
        Theriaca.
    Oppianus, *Halieutica.*
    Ovid, *Ibis.*
    Persius, *Satires*. Ed. O. Jahn.
    Pindar, *Isthmia.*
        Olympia.
        Pythia.
    Plato, *Gorgias.*
        Republic.
        Theaetetus.
    Sophocles, *Antigone.*
        Oedipus Coloneus.
    Theocritus.
    Thucydides. Ed. Didot.
*Scholiastes Veronensis, on Virgil.
Schömann, G. F., *Griechische Alterthümer*. Fourth Edition. Berlin, 1897–
    1902.
Schomburgk, Sir R., *Reisen in Britisch-Guiana*. Leipsic, 1847–1848.
    in *Verhandlungen der Berliner Gesellschaft für Anthropologie, Ethnologie
    und Urgeschichte*, 1879.
Schön, J. F., and Crowther, S., *Journals*. London, 1848.
*Schönwerth, F., *Aus der Oberpfalz*, cited by Adalbert Kuhn, in *Mythologische
    Studien*. Gütersloh, 1912.
Schoolcraft, Henry R., *Indian Tribes of the United States*. Philadelphia, 1853–
    1856.
    Notes on the Iroquois. Albany, 1847.
    Onéota, or Characteristics of the Red Race of America. New York and
    London, 1845.
    The American Indians, their History, Condition, and Prospects. Buffalo,
    1851.

Schott, " Ueber die Sage von Geser-Chan," in *Abhandlungen der Königlichen Akademie der Wissenschaften zu Berlin* (1851).

Schott, Arthur und Albert, *Walachische Maehrchen.* Stuttgart and Tübingen, 1845.

Schrader, E., *Die Keilinschriften und das Alte Testament.* Dritte Auflage, neu bearbeitet von H. Zimmern und H. Winckler. Berlin, 1902.

Schrader, Otto, *s.v.* "Aryan Religion," in Dr. J. Hastings's *Encyclopaedia of Religion and Ethics*, ii. Edinburgh, 1909.

Reallexikon der indogermanischen Altertumskunde. Strasburg, 1901.

Sprachvergleichung und Urgeschichte. Second Edition. Jena, 1890. Third Edition. Jena, 1905–1907.

Schreiber, Th., *Apollon Pythoktonos.* Leipsic, 1879.

Schrenck, L. von, *Reisen und Forschungen im Amur-lande*, vol. iii. Part i. *Die Völker des Amur-Landes.* St. Petersburg, 1891.

Schroeder, L. v., *Die Hochzeitsbräuche der Esten.* Berlin, 1888.

" Lihgo (Refrain der lettischen Sonnwendlieder)," in *Mitteilungen der Anthropologischen Gesellschaft in Wien*, xxxii. (1902).

Schuchhardt, C., *Schliemann's Ausgrabungen.* Second Edition. Leipsic, 1891.

Schudt, J. J., *Jüdische Merkwürdigkeiten.* Frankfort and Leipsic, 1714.

Schulenburg, Wilibald von, "Volkskundliche Mittheilungen aus der Mark," in *Verhandlungen der Berliner Gesellschaft für Anthropologie, Ethnologie und Urgeschichte* (1896).

Wendische Volkssagen und Gebräuche aus dem Spreewald. Leipsic, 1880.

Wendisches Volksthum. Berlin, 1882.

Schuller, J. K., *Das Todaustragen und der Muorlef, ein Beitrag zur Kunde sächsischer Sitte und Sage in Siebenbürgen.* Hermannstadt, 1861.

Schulze, " Ueber Ceram und seine Bewohner," in *Verhandlungen der Berliner Gesellschaft für Anthropologie, Ethnologie, und Urgeschichte* (1877).

Schürmann, C. W., " The Aboriginal Tribes of Port Lincoln," in *Native Tribes of South Australia.* Adelaide, 1879.

Schurtz, H., *Altersklassen und Männerbünde.* Berlin, 1902.

Schuyler, E., *Turkistan.* London, 1876.

Schwally, Fr., *Semitische Kriegsaltertümer.* Leipsic, 1901.

Schwaner, C. A. L. M., *Borneo, Beschrijving van het stroomgebied van den Barito.* Amsterdam, 1853–1854.

Schwarz, B., *Kamerun.* Leipsic, 1886.

Schwartz, F. L. W., *Der Ursprung der Mythologie.* Berlin, 1860.

Schwegler, A., *Römische Geschichte.* Tübingen, 1853–1858.

Schweinfurth, G., *The Heart of Africa.* Third Edition. London, 1878.

Schweizerisches Archiv für Volkskunde.

Scotsman, The.

Scott, Rev. David Clement, *A Cyclopaedic Dictionary of the Mang'anja Language spoken in British Central Africa.* Edinburgh, 1892.

Scott, (Sir) J. G., and Hardiman, J. P., *Gazetteer of Upper Burma and the Shan States.* Rangoon, 1900–1901.

Scott, Sir Walter, *Journal.* First Edition. Edinburgh, 1890.

Letters on Demonology and Witchcraft. London, 1884.

Peveril of the Peak.

The Pirate.

Scriptores Rei Rusticae Veteres Latini. Ed. J. G. Schneider. Leipsic, 1794–1796.

Scriptores rerum Livonicarum. Riga and Leipsic, 1848.

Scriptores rerum mirabilium Graeci. Ed. A. Westermann. Brunswick, 1839.

Scriptores rerum mythicarum Latini tres Romae nuper reperti (commonly referred to as *Mythographi Vaticani*). Ed. G. H. Bode. Cellis, 1834.

Scriviner, G., in E. M. Curr's *The Australian Race.*
Scymnus Chius, *Orbis descriptio*, in *Geographi Graeci Minores*, ed. C. Müller, vol. i.
Sébillot, Paul, *Contes populaires de la Haute-Bretagne.* Paris, 1885.
 Coutumes populaires de la Haute-Bretagne. Paris, 1886.
 " La Fête des Rois," in *Revue des Traditions populaires*, iii. (1888).
 Le Folk-lore de France. Paris, 1904–1907.
 Légendes, Croyances et Superstitions de la Mer. Paris, 1886.
 Traditions et superstitions de la Haute-Bretagne. Paris, 1882.
Sechefo, J., " The Twelve Lunar Months among the Basuto," in *Anthropos*, iv. (1909).
Seeman, B., *Viti, an Account of a Government Mission to the Vitian or Fijian Islands in the Years 1860–1862.* Cambridge, 1862.
*Ségonzac, De, *Voyage au Maroc*, quoted by E. Doutté, *Magie et Religion dans l'Afrique du Nord.*
Seidel, H., " Der Yew'e Dienst im Togolande," in *Zeitschrift für afrikanische und oceanischen Sprachen*, iii. (1897).
 " Ethnographisches aus Nordost Kamerun," in *Globus*, lxix. (1896).
 " Krankheit, Tod, und Begräbnis bei den Togonegern," in *Globus*, lxxii. (1897).
Seidlitz, N. von, " Die Abchasen," in *Globus*, lxvi. (1894).
Seidlitz, R. von, " Der Selbstmord bei den Tschuktschen," in *Globus*, lix. (1891).
Seifart, K., *Sagen, Märchen, Schwänke und Gebräuche aus Stadt und Stift Hildesheim.* Zweite Auflage. Hildesheim, 1889.
Sei-I Kwai Medical Journal. See s.v. Hall, Dr. C. H. H.
Seland or Seeland, Dr., abstract of a Russian work on the Gilyaks by, in *Archiv für Anthropologie*, xxvi. (1900).
Selden, J., *De dis Syris.* Leipsic, 1668.
Seler, Professor Eduard, " Altmexicanische Studien," in *Veröffentlichungen aus dem Königlichen Museum für Völkerkunde.* Berlin, 1890, 1899.
 " The Mexican Chronology," in *Bureau of American Ethnology, Bulletin No. 28.* Washington, 1904.
Seleucus, quoted by Athenaeus, iv. 42.
Seligmann, Dr. C. G., " Ancient Egyptian Beliefs in Modern Egypt," in *Essays and Studies presented to William Ridgeway.* Cambridge, 1913.
 s.v. " Dinka," in *Encyclopaedia of Religion and Ethics*, vol. iv. Edited by J. Hastings, D.D. Edinburgh, 1911.
 in *Journal of the Anthropological Institute*, xxix. (1899).
 in letters and manuscripts sent to the Author (iv. 17 *n.*[3], 21 *n.*[1], 22 *n.*[1], 23 *n.*[1], 30 *nn.* [1 and 2], vi. 161 *n.*[2]).
 in *Reports of the Cambridge Anthropological Expedition to Torres Straits*, v. Cambridge, 1904.
 The Cult of Nyakang and the Divine Kings of the Shilluk. Khartoum, 1911. Reprinted from the *Fourth Report of the Wellcome Tropical Research Laboratories, Gordon Memorial College, Khartoum.*
 " The Medicine, Surgery, and Midwifery of the Sinaugolo," in *Journal of the Anthropological Institute*, xxxii. (1902).
 The Melanesians of British New Guinea. Cambridge, 1910.
Seligmann, C. G., and Murray, Margaret A., " Note upon an Early Egyptian Standard," in *Man*, xi. (1911).
Sellin, Dr. E., " Tell Ta'annek," in *Denkschriften der kaiserlichen Akademie der Wissenschaften, Philosophisch-historische Klasse*, l. Vienna, 1904.
Semper, C., *Die Philippinen und ihre Bewohner.* Würzburg, 1869.
Semper, K., *Die Palau-Inseln im Stillen Ocean.* Leipsic, 1873.
Seneca, *Opera.* Ed. Fr. Haase. Leipsic, 1877–1881.
 Tragoediae. Ed. J. C. Schröder. Delft, 1728.

Seneca—*continued*.
  Agamemnon.
  De Ira.
  Epistulae.
  Hippolytus.
  Naturales Quaestiones.
  quoted by Augustine, *De civitate Dei.*
Senfft, A., "Die Rechtssitten der Jap-Eingeborenen," in *Globus*, xci. (1907).
  "Ethnographische Beiträge über die Karolineninsel Yap," in *Petermanns Mitteilungen*, xlix. (1903).
Sepp, Professor Dr., *Altbayerischer Sagenschatz.* Munich, 1876.
  Die Religion der alten Deutschen. Munich, 1890.
Servant, Father, "Notice sur la Nouvelle Zélande," in *Annales de la Propagation de la Foi*, xv. (1843).
Servius, *Commentarii in Virgilium.* Ed. H. A. Lion. Göttingen, 1826.
  Ed. G. Thilo and H. Hagen. Leipsic, 1881–
Sessions, F., "Some Syrian Folklore Notes," in *Folk-lore*, ix. (1898).
Sextus Empiricus. Ed. Im. Bekker. Berlin, 1842.
Shakespear, Lieut.-Colonel J., "The Kuki-Lushai Clans," in *Journal of the Royal Anthropological Institute*, xxxix. (1909).
  The Lushei Kuki Clans. London, 1912.
Shakespeare, *Henry V.*
  Macbeth.
"Shamanism in Siberia and European Russia," in *Journal of the Anthropological Institute*, xxiv. (1895).
Shaw, Barnabas, *Memorials of South Africa.* London, 1840.
Shaw, G. A., "The Betsileo," in *The Antananarivo Annual and Madagascar Magazine.* Reprint of the First Four Numbers. Antananarivo, 1885.
Shaw, Rev. Mr., quoted by Thomas Pennant in his "Tour in Scotland, 1769," printed in J. Pinkerton's *Voyages and Travels*, iii. London, 1909.
Shaw, Thomas, "On the Inhabitants of the Hills near Rajamahall," in *Asiatic Researches*, vol. iv. London, 1807.
Sheane, J. H. West, "Wemba Warpaths," in *Journal of the African Society*, No. xli. (October 1911).
Shelford, R., "Two Medicine-Baskets from Sarawak," in *Journal of the Anthropological Institute*, xxxiii. (1903).
*Sherring, M. A., *Hindu Tribes and Castes*, cited by H. A. Rose, in *Indian Antiquary*, xxxi. (1902).
Shetland News, February 1st, 1913.
Shooter, Rev. Joseph, *The Kafirs of Natal and the Zulu Country.* London, 1857.
Shortland, Edward, *Maori Religion and Mythology.* London, 1882.
  The Southern Districts of New Zealand. London, 1851.
  Traditions and Superstitions of the New Zealanders. Second Edition. London, 1856.
Shortt, J., "The Bayadère or Dancing-girls of Southern India," in *Memoirs of the Anthropological Society of London*, iii. (1867–1869).
Sibree, Rev. J., "Curiosities of Words connected with Royalty and Chieftainship," *Antananarivo Annual and Madagascar Magazine*, No. xi. (1887).
  "Divination among the Malagasy," in *Folk-lore*, iii. (1892).
  in *Journal of the Anthropological Institute*, xxi. (1892).
  Madagascar and its People. London, [1870].
  "Remarkable Ceremonial at the Decease and Burial of a Betsileo Prince," in *Antananarivo Annual*, No. xxii. (1898), quoted by A. van Gennep, *Tabou et totémisme à Madagascar.*
  The Great African Island. London, 1880.

Sibthorp, in R. Walpole's *Memoirs relating to European and Asiatic Turkey.* London, 1817.

Siebold, H. von, *Ethnologische Studien über die Aino auf der Insel Yesso.* Berlin, 1881.

Siebs, Th., "Das Saterland," in *Zeitschrift für Volkskunde,* iii. (1893).

Silius Italicus. *Punica.* Ed. J. C. T. Ernesti. Leipsic, 1791–1792.

Simmons, Rev. E. Z., "Idols and Spirits," in *Chinese Recorder and Missionary Journal,* xix. (1888).

Simons, F. A., "An Exploration of the Goajira Peninsula, U.S. of Colombia," in *Proceedings of the Royal Geographical Society,* N.S., vii. (1885).

Simpson, William, *The Buddhist Praying Wheel.* London, 1896.
    Also in a private communication to the Author (iii. 125 n.[3]).

Simrock, K., *Die Edda.* Eighth Edition. Stuttgart, 1882.
    Handbuch der deutschen Mythologie. Fifth Edition. Bonn, 1878.

Simson, Alfred, in *Journal of the Anthropological Institute,* vii. (1878).
    "Notes on the Jivaros and Canelos Indians," in *Journal of the Anthropological Institute,* ix. (1880).
    Travels in the Wilds of Ecuador. London, 1887.

Sinclair, Sir John, *Statistical Account of Scotland.* Edinburgh, 1791–1799.

Singleton, Miss A. H., in letters to the Author (viii. 320 n.[1], xi. 192 n.[1]).

"Sitten und Gebräuche in Duderstadt," in *Zeitschrift für deutsche Mythologie und Sittenkunde,* ii. (1855).

Sitzungsberichte der Königlichen Bayerischen Akademie der Wissenschaften zu München.

Sitzungsberichte der Königlichen Preussischen Akademie der Wissenschaften zu Berlin.

Sitzungsberichte der mathematischen-naturwissenschaftlichen Klasse der Kaiserlichen Akademie der Wissenschaften. Vienna.

Sitzungsberichte der philosophischen-historischen Classe der Kaiserlichen Akademie der Wissenschaften. Vienna.

Sitzungsberichte der philosophischen-philologischen und historischen Classe der Königlichen Bayerischen Akademie der Wissenschaften zu München.

Six, J., "Die Eriphyle des Polygnot," in *Mittheilungen des Kaiserlich Deutschen Archaeologischen Instituts, Athenische Abtheilung,* xix. (1894).

Skeat, W. W., *Etymological Dictionary of the English Language.* Oxford, 1910.

Skeat, W. W., *Malay Magic.* London, 1900.
    "Snakestones and Stone Thunderbolts," in *Folk-lore,* xxiii. (1912).

Skeat, W. W., and Blagden, C. O., *Pagan Races of the Malay Peninsula.* London, 1906.

Skene, W. F., *Celtic Scotland.* 1876–1880.

Skinner, Principal J., Introduction to Kings, in *The Century Bible.* on 1 Kings xiv. 23.

Sleeman, Major-General Sir W. H., *Rambles and Recollections of an Indian Official.* New Edition. Westminster, 1893.

Sleigh, Mr., of Lifu, quoted by Prof. E. B. Tylor, in *Journal of the Anthropological Institute,* xxviii. (1898).

Smet, J. de, in *Annales de la Propagation de la Foi,* xi. (1838), xiv. (1842), xv. (1843).
    Voyages aux Montagnes Rocheuses. Nouvelle Edition. Paris and Brussels, 1873.

Smet, P. J. de, *Western Missions and Missionaries.* New York, 1863.

Smith, A. H., "Illustrations to Bacchylides," in *Journal of Hellenic Studies,* xviii. (1898).

Smith, Mrs. E. A., "Myths of the Iroquois," in *Second Annual Report of the Bureau of Ethnology.* Washington, 1883.

Smith, E. R., *The Araucanians.* London, 1855.

Smith, George Adam, *s.v.* "Bethlehem," in *Encyclopaedia Biblica*, i. *Historical Geography of the Holy Land.* London, 1894.

Smith, Prof. G. C. Moore, in letter to the Author (viii. 329 *n.*[1]).

Smith, G. H., "Some Betsimisaraka Superstitions," in *The Antananarivo Annual and Madagascar Magazine*, No. 10 (Christmas, 1886).

Smith, (Sir) Henry Babington, in *Folk-lore*, v. (1894).

Smith, J., *Trade and Travels in the Gulph of Guinea.* London, 1851.

Smith, Mrs. James, *The Booandik Tribe.* Adelaide, 1880.

Smith, W., *Dictionary of Greek and Roman Antiquities.* Third Edition. London, 1890-1891.

Dictionary of Greek and Roman Geography. London, 1873.

Smith, W., and Cheetham, S., *Dictionary of Christian Antiquities.* London, 1875-1880.

Smith, W. Robertson, "Animal Worship and Animal Tribes," in *Journal of Philology*, ix. (1880).

"Ctesias and the Semiramis Legend," in *English Historical Review*, ii. (1887).

Kinship and Marriage in Early Arabia. Cambridge, 1885.

New Edition. London, 1903.

Lectures on the Religion of the Semites. Second Edition. London, 1894.

"Sacrifice," in *Encyclopaedia Britannica.* Ninth Edition, vol. xxi. 1886.

The Old Testament in the Jewish Church. Second Edition. London and Edinburgh, 1892.

The Prophets of Israel. Second Edition. London, 1902.

Also in private communications to the Author (i. 301 *n.*[2], iii. 77 *n.*[1], 96 *n.*[1], v. 10 *n.*[1], vii. 259 *n.*[1], viii. 27 *n.*[5], 251 *n.*[5], 280 *n.*).

Smyth, R. Brough, *The Aborigines of Victoria.* Melbourne and London, 1878.

Smyth, W., and Lowe, F., *Narrative of a Journey from Lima to Para.* London, 1836.

Socrates, *Historia Ecclesiastica*, in Migne's *Patrologia Graeca*, lxvii.

Soddy, F., *The Interpretation of Radium.* Third Edition. London, 1912.

Söderblom, N., *La Vie Future d'après le Mazdéisme.* Paris, 1901.

Les Fravashis. Paris, 1899.

Soleillet, Paul, *L'Afrique Occidentale.* Paris, 1877.

Solinus, *Collectanea.* Ed. Th. Mommsen. Berlin, 1864.

Solms-Laubach, Graf zu, "Die Herkunft, Domestication und Verbreitung des gewöhnlichen Feigenbaums (*Ficus Carica*, L.)," in *Abhandlungen der Königlichen Gesellschaft der Wissenschaften zu Göttingen*, xxviii. (1882).

Solomon, V., "Extracts from Diaries kept in Car Nicobar," in *Journal of the Anthropological Institute*, xxxii. (1902).

Somerville, B. T., "Notes on some Islands of the New Hebrides," in *Journal of the Anthropological Institute*, xxiii. (1894).

Somerville, Professor William, of Oxford. Private communications to the Author (ii. 328 *n.*[4], vii. 193 *n.*).

Sommer, E., *Sagen, Märchen und Gebräuche aus Sachsen und Thüringen.* Halle, 1846.

Sonnerat, *Voyage aux Indes orientales et à la Chine.* Paris, 1782.

Sonnini, C. S., *Travels in Upper and Lower Egypt.* Translated from the French. London, 1800.

Sopater, in *Rhetores Graeci.* Ed. Chr. Walz.

Sophocles, *Plays and Fragments*, in *Poetae Scenici Graeci*, ed. G. Dindorf, London, 1869. Ed. R. C. Jebb. Cambridge, 1892-1900.

Ajax.
Antigone.
Electra.
Oedipus Coloneus.
Oedipus Tyrannus.

quoted by Plutarch, *De audiendis poetis.*

Sophocles—*continued.*
  Root-cutters, quoted by Macrobius, *Saturnalia.*
  Trachiniae.
  Triptolemus.
Souché, B., *Croyances, présages et traditions diverses.* Niort, 1880.
(*South African*) *Folk-lore Journal.*
Southey, R., *History of Brazil.* London, 1817–1819.
  Second Edition. London, 1822.
Sowerby, James, *English Botany.* London, 1796–1805.
Sozomenus, *Historia Ecclesiastica,* in Migne's *Patrologia Graeca,* lxvii.
Spafford, Jacob E., "Around the Dead Sea by Motor Boat," in *The Geographical Journal,* xxxix. (1912).
Spartianus, Aelius, in *Scriptores Historiae Augustae,* ed. H. Peter, Leipsic, 1884.
  Caracallus.
  Pescennius Niger.
"Specimen Calendarii Gentilis," appended to the *Edda Rhythmica seu Antiquior, vulgo Saemundina dicta,* Pars iii. Copenhagen, 1828.
Speck, Frank G., *Ethnology of the Yuchi Indians.* Philadelphia, 1909.
Speckmann, F., *Die Hermannsburger Mission in Afrika.* Hermannsburg, 1876.
Spectator, The. London, 1711–1712, 1714.
Speight, Harry, *The Craven and North-West Yorkshire Highlands.* London, 1892.
  Tramps and Drives in the Craven Highlands. London, 1895.
Speijer, J. S., "Le Dieu romain Janus," in *Revue de l'Histoire des Religions,* xxvi. (1892).
Spencer, Edmund, *Travels in Circassia, Krim Tartary, etc.* London, 1836.
Spencer, Herbert, *First Principles.* Third Edition. London, 1875.
Spencer, J., *De legibus Hebraeorum.* The Hague, 1686.
Spencer, W. Baldwin, in letter to the Author (v. 101 *n.*).
  An Introduction to the Study of Certain Native Tribes of the Northern Territory. (*Bulletin of the Northern Territory,* No. 2. Melbourne, 1912).
Spencer, Baldwin, and Gillen, F. J., *Across Australia.* London, 1912.
  The Native Tribes of Central Australia. London, 1899.
  The Northern Tribes of Central Australia. London, 1904.
Spenser, Edmund, *View of the State of Ireland.* Reprinted in H. Morley's *Ireland under Elizabeth and James the First.* London, 1890.
Sphinx.
Spiess, C., "Einiges über die Bedeutung der Personennamen der Evheer in Togo-Gebiete," in *Mitteilungen des Seminars für orientalische Sprachen zu Berlin,* vi. (1903), Dritte Abteilung.
  "Religionsbegriffe der Evheer in West-Afrika," in *Mitteilungen des Seminars für orientalische Sprachen zu Berlin,* vi. (1903), Dritte Abteilung.
Spieth, H., "Jagdgebräuche in Avatime," in *Mitteilungen der Geographischen Gesellschaft zu Jena,* ix. (1890).
Spieth, Jakob, "Der Jehve Dienst der Evhe-Neger," in *Mitteilungen der Geographischen Gesellschaft zu Jena,* xii. (1893).
  Die Ewe-Stämme: Material zur Kunde des Ewe-Volkes in Deutsch-Togo. Berlin, 1906.
  Die Religion der Eweer in Süd-Togo. Leipsic, 1911.
Spire, F., "Rain-making in Equatorial Africa," in *Journal of the African Society,* No. 17 (October 1905).
Spitta-Bey, G., *Contes arabes modernes.* Leyden and Paris, 1883.
Spix, J. B. von, und Martius, C. F. Ph. von, *Reise in Brasilien.* Munich, 1823–1831.
Spoer, Mrs. H. H., "The Powers of Evil in Jerusalem," in *Folk-lore,* xviii. (1907).
Spratt, T. A. B., and Forbes, E., *Travels in Lycia.* London, 1847.

Spreeuwenberg, A. F. van, "Een blik op de Minahassa," in *Tijdschrift voor Neêrland's Indië*. Zevende Jaargang, Vierde deel, Batavia, 1845; Achtste Jaargang, Erste deel, Batavia, 1846.

Sproat, G. M., *Scenes and Studies of Savage Life*. London, 1868.

Stanbridge, W., "On the Aborigines of Victoria," in *Transactions of the Ethnological Society of London*, N.S., i. (1861).

"Some Particulars of the General Characteristics, Astronomy, and Mythology of the Tribes in the Central Part of Victoria, South Australia," in *Transactions of the Ethnological Society of London*, N.S., i. (1861).

Stanbridge, W. E., quoted by R. Brough Smyth in *Aborigines of Victoria*.

Standing, H. F., "Malagasy *fady*," in *Antananarivo Annual and Madagascar Magazine*, vol. ii. (Reprint of the Second Four Numbers, 1881-1884.) Antananarivo, 1896.

Stanley, A. P., *Sinai and Palestine*. Second Edition. London, 1856.

Stanley, H. M., *Through the Dark Continent*. London, 1878.

Stannus, H. S., "Notes on some Tribes of British Central Africa," in *Journal of the Royal Anthropological Institute*, xl. (1910).

Starr, Frederick, "Holy Week in Mexico," in *The Journal of American Folklore*, xii. (1899).

Statius, *Opera Omnia*. London (Valpy), 1824.
   Sylvae.
   Thebaïs.

*Status Scholae Etonensis (A.D. 1560), quoted by John Brand, *Popular Antiquities of Great Britain*, and T. F. Thiselton Dyer, *British Popular Customs*.

Stchoukine, Ivan, *Le Suicide collectif dans le Raskol russe*. Paris, 1903.

Stebbing, E. B., "The Loranthus Parasite of the Moru and Ban Oaks," in *Journal and Proceedings of the Asiatic Society of Bengal*. New Series, v. Calcutta, 1910.

Steedman, A., *Wanderings and Adventures in the Interior of Southern Africa*. London, 1835.

Steel, F. A., and Temple, R. C., *Wide-awake Stories*. Bombay and London, 1884.

Steele, Sir Richard, in *The Spectator*, Friday, 14th December 1711.

Steere, Edward, *Swahili Tales*. London, 1870.

Stehle, Bruno, "Volksglauben, Sitten und Gebräuche in Lothringen," *Globus*, lix. (1891).

Steinen, Karl von den, *Unter den Naturvölkern Zentral-Brasiliens*. Berlin, 1894.

Stella, Erasmus, "De Borussiae antiquitatibus," in Simon Grynaeus's *Novus Orbis regionum ac insularum veteribus incognitarum*. Paris, 1532.

Steller, G. W., *Beschreibung von dem Lande Kamtschatka*. Frankfort and Leipsic, 1774.

Stengel, P., "Die Opfer der Hellenen an die Winde," in *Hermes*, xvi. (1881).

in Pauly-Wissowa's *Real-Encyclopädie der classischen Altertumswissenschaft*, v.

"Zum griechischen Opferritual," in *Jahrbuch des Kaiserlichen Deutschen Archaeologischen Instituts*, xviii. (1903).

Stenin, N. von, "Die Permier," in *Globus*, lxxi. (1897).

Stenin, P. von, "Das Gewohnheitsrecht der Samojeden," in *Globus*, lx. (1891).

"Die Kirgisen des Kreises Saissanak im Gebiete von Ssemipalatinsk," in *Globus*, lxix. (1906).

"Ein neuer Beitrag zur Ethnographie der Tscheremissen," in *Globus*, lviii. (1890).

"Jochelson's Forschungen unter den Jukagiren," in *Globus*, lxxvi. (1899).

"Über den Geisterglauben in Russland," in *Globus*, lvii. (1890).

Stephan, E., und Graebner, F., *Neu-Mecklenburg.* Berlin, 1907.
Stephani, L., in *Compte-rendu de la Commission Impériale Archéologique.* St. Petersburg, 1863.
    in *Compte-rendu de la Commission Impériale Archéologique pour l'année 1869.* St. Petersburg, 1870.
Stephanus Byzantius, *Ethnica.* Ed. Ant. Westermann. Leipsic, 1839.
Sternberg, Leo, "Die Religion der Gilyaken," in *Archiv für Religionswissenschaft,* viii. (1905).
Steuding, in W. H. Roscher's *Lexicon der griechischen und römischen Mythologie,* ii.
Stevens, H. Vaughan, " Mitteilungen aus dem Frauenleben der Ôrang Belendas, der Ôrang Djâkun und der Ôrang Lâut," bearbeitet von Dr. Max Bartels, in *Zeitschrift für Ethnologie,* xxviii. (1896).
*Stevens, Captain John, *The History of Persia.* London, 1715.
Stevenson, M. C., " The Sia," *Eleventh Annual Report of the Bureau of Ethnology.* Washington, 1894.
Stevenson, Mrs. Matilda Coxe, " The Zuñi Indians," in *Twenty-Third Annual Report of the Bureau of American Ethnology.* Washington, 1904.
Stewart, Rev. Allan, in Sir John Sinclair's *Statistical Account of Scotland,* xv.
Stewart, Balfour, *The Conservation of Energy.* Fourth Edition. London, 1877.
Stewart, C. S., *A Visit to the South Seas.* London, 1832.
Stewart, D., in E. M. Curr's *Australian Race,* iii.
Stewart, Rev. J., D.D., *Lovedale, South Africa.* Edinburgh, 1894.
Stewart, Lieut. R., " Notes on the Northern Cachar," in *Journal of the Asiatic Society of Bengal,* xxiv. (1855).
Stewart, W. Grant, *The Popular Superstitions and Festive Amusements of the Highlanders of Scotland.* Edinburgh, 1823.
    New Edition. London, 1851.
Stigand, Captain C. H., *To Abyssinia through an Unknown Land.* London, 1910.
Stigand, J. A., " The Volcano of Smeroe, Java," in *The Geographical Journal,* xxviii. (1906).
Stobaeus, *Eclogae.* Ed. A. Meineke. Leipsic, 1860–1864.
    Florilegium. Ed. A. Meineke. Leipsic, 1855–1857.
Stokes, H. J., " Walking through Fire," in *Indian Antiquary,* ii. (1873).
Stokes, Maive, *Indian Fairy Tales.* London, 1880.
Stoll, *s.vv.* " Kinyras" and " Melikertes," in W. H. Roscher's *Lexikon der griechischen und römischen Mythologie.*
Stoll, Otto, *Die Ethnologie der Indianerstämme von Guatemala.* Leyden, 1889.
    Suggestion und Hypnotism. Second Edition. Leipsic, 1904.
Stone, R. H., *In Afric's Forest and Jungle.* Edinburgh and London, 1900.
Stories of the Kings of Norway (*Heimskringla*). Done into English by W. Morris and E. Magnússon. London, 1893–1905.
Stout, Professor G. F., of St. Andrews. Private communication (viii. 261 *n.*[1]).
Stow, G. W., *Native Races of South Africa.* London, 1905.
Stow, John, *A Survay of London.* Edited by Henry Morley. London, N.D.
    A Survey of London, written in the Year 1598. Edited by William J. Thoms. London, 1876.
Strabo. Ed. Aug. Meineke. Leipsic, 1866–1877.
    Ed. C. Müller et F. Dübner. Paris (Didot), 1853.
Strachey, W., *Historie of travaile into Virginia Britannia.* Hakluyt Society. London, 1849.
Strack, H. L., *Das Blut im Glauben und Aberglauben der Menschheit.* Munich, 1900.
Strackerjan, L., *Aberglaube und Sagen aus dem Herzogthum Oldenburg.* Oldenburg, 1867.

Strauss und Torney, Victor von, *Die altägyptischen Götter und Göttersagen.* Heidelberg, 1889–1891.
Strausz, Adolf, *Die Bulgaren.* Leipsic, 1898.
Streatfield, H. C., "Ranchi," in *Journal of the Asiatic Society of Bengal,* lxxii. Part iii. Calcutta, 1904.
Strong, Dr., in C. G. Seligmann's *The Melanesians of British New Guinea.* Cambridge, 1910.
Strube, C., *Studien über den Bilderkreis von Eleusis.* Leipsic, 1870.
Strutt, Joseph, *The Sports and Pastimes of the People of England.* New Edition, by W. Hone. London, 1834.
Struys, John, *Voiages and Travels.* London, 1684.
Stuart, Mrs. A., in letter to the Author (xi. 287 *n.*[1]).
Stubbes, Phillip, *The Anatomie of Abuses.* F. J. Furnivall's reprint. London, 1877–1882.
Stuhlmann, Fr., *Mit Emin Pascha ins Herz von Afrika.* Berlin, 1894.
Stukeley, W., *The Medallic History of Marcus Aurelius Valerius Carausius, Emperor in Britain.* London, 1757–1759.
Stumpf, J., and Campell, Ulr., quoted by Dr. F. J. Vonbun, *Beiträge zur deutschen Mythologie gesammelt in Churrhaetien.* Chur, 1862.
Sturluson, Snorri, *Chronicle of the Kings of Norway.* See *s.v.* Heimskringla.
Suetonius. Ed. C. L. Roth. Leipsic, 1871.
    Caligula.
    Divus Augustus.
    Divus Claudius.
    Divus Iulius.
    Divus Vespasianus.
    Nero.
    Otho.
    Tiberius.
Suidas, *Lexicon.* Ed. Im. Bekker. Berlin, 1854.
Sulpicius Severus, *Vita S. Martini.* Ed. C. Halm. Vienna, 1866.
Sunder, D., "Exorcism of Wild Animals in the Sundarbans," in *Journal of the Asiatic Society of Bengal,* lxxii. part iii. Calcutta, 1904.
Sundermann, H., "Die Insel Nias und die Mission daselbst," in *Allgemeine Missions-Zeitschrift,* xi. (August, September, October 1884).
    Die Insel Nias und die Mission daselbst. Barmen, 1905.
*Survey of the South of Ireland, quoted by J. Brand, *Popular Antiquities of Great Britain.* London, 1882–1883.
Sutton, J., quoted by Rev. J. Macdonald, *Religion and Myth.* London, 1893.
Svoboda, W., "Die Bewohner des Nikobaren-Archipels," in *Internationales Archiv für Ethnographie,* v. (1892), vi. (1893).
Swainson, Rev. C., *The Folk Lore and Provincial Names of British Birds.* London, 1886.
**Swan, James G., *The Indians of Cape Flattery,* quoted by Franz Boas, "The Social Organization and the Secret Societies of the Kwakiutl Indians," in *Report of the United States National Museum for 1895.* Washington, 1897.
Swanton, J. R., "Contributions to the Ethnology of the Haida," in *Memoir of the American Museum of Natural History, The Jesup North Pacific Expedition.* Leyden and New York, 1905.
    Haida Texts and Myths, in *Bureau of American Ethnology, Bulletin,* No. 29. Washington, 1905.
    Indian Tribes of the Lower Mississippi Valley. Washington, 1911.
    "Social Conditions, Beliefs and Linguistic Relationship of the Tlingit Indians," in *Twenty-sixth Annual Report of the Bureau of American Ethnology.* Washington, 1908.
Symmachus, *Epistolae,* in Migne's *Patrologia Latina,* xviii.

*Tabari, Arab chronicler.
Taberer, W. S., "Mashonaland Natives," in *Journal of the African Society*, No. 15 (April 1905).
Tache, Mgr., letter in *Annales de la Propagation de la Foi*, xxiv. (1852).
Tacitus. Ed. J. G. Baiter et J. G. Orelli. Second Edition. Zürich, 1859–Berlin, 1877.
　　Annals.
　　Germania.
　　Historiae.
Taillepied, F. N., *Recueil des Antiquitez et singularitez de la ville de Rouen.* Rouen, 1587.
Taittīrya Brāhmana, quoted by Denham Rouse, in *Folk-lore*, vii. (1889).
Talbot, P. Amaury, in letter to the Author (v. 271 *n.*).
　　In the Shadow of the Bush. London, 1912.
Tanner, John. See *s.v.* Narrative.
Taplin, Rev. G., in E. M. Curr's *The Australian Race.*
　　"Notes on the Mixed Races of Australia," in *Journal of the Anthropological Institute*, iv. (1875).
　　"The Narrinyeri," in *Native Tribes of South Australia.* Adelaide, 1879.
Targioni-Tozzetti, G., *Saggio di novelline, canti ed usanze popolari della Ciociaria.* Palermo, 1891.
Tate, H. R., "Further Notes on the Kikuyu Tribe of British East Africa," in *Journal of the Anthropological Institute*, xxxiv. (1904).
　　"The Native Law of the Southern Gikuyu of British East Africa," in *Journal of the African Society*, No. xxxv. (April 1910).
Tatian, *Oratio ad Graecos.* Ed. J. C. T. Otto. Jena, 1851.
Tauern, O. D., "Ceram," in *Zeitschrift für Ethnologie*, xlv. (1913).
Tausch, "Notices of the Circassians," in *Journal of the Royal Asiatic Society*, i. (1834).
Tautain, Dr., "Notes sur les croyances et pratiques religieuses des Banmanas," in *Revue d'Ethnographie*, iii. (1885).
Tavernier, J. B., in John Harris's *Collection of Voyages and Travels*, vol. i. London, 1744.
　　Voyages en Turquie, en Perse, et aux Indes. The Hague, 1718.
Taylor, C. Boyson, "Easter in Many Lands," in *Everybody's Magazine.* New York, 1903.
Taylor, Isaac, *The Origin of the Aryans.* London, N.D. Preface dated December, 1889.
Taylor, Rev. Richard, *Te Ika A Maui, or New Zealand and its Inhabitants.* Second Edition. London, 1870.
Tchéraz, Minas, "Notes sur la mythologie Arménienne," in *Transactions of the Ninth International Congress of Orientalists.* London, 1893.
Tegner, Swedish poet, cited by J. Grimm, *Deutsche Mythologie.* Fourth Edition.
Teit, J., *The Lillooet Indians.* Leyden and New York, 1906. (*Memoir of the American Museum of Natural History, The Jesup North Pacific Expedition*, vol. ii. part v. New York.)
　　The Shuswap. Leyden and New York, 1909. (*Memoir of the American Museum of Natural History, The Jesup North Pacific Expedition*, vol. ii. part vii. New York.)
　　The Thompson Indians of British Columbia. (*Memoir of the American Museum of Natural History, The Jesup North Pacific Expedition*, vol. i. part iv. New York, April 1900.)
Temesváry, R., *Volksbräuche und Aberglauben in der Geburtshilfe und der Pflege des Neugeborenen in Ungarn.* Leipsic, 1900.
Temme, J. D. H., *Die Volkssagen der Altmark.* Berlin, 1839.
Temple, Lieut.-Colonel Sir Richard C., in *Indian Antiquary*, xi. (1882).
　　"Opprobrious Names," in *Indian Antiquary*, x. (1881).

Temple, Lieut.-Colonel Sir Richard C.—*continued.*
    The Andaman and Nicobar Islands, in *The Census of India, 1901*, vol. iii.
        Calcutta, 1903.
Tendeloo, H. J., "Verklaring van het zoogenaamd Oud-Alfoersch Teeken-
        schrift," in *Mededeelingen van wege het Nederlandsche Zendelinggenoot-
        schap*, xxxvi. (1892).
Tennant, R., *Sardinia and its Resources.*   Rome and London, 1885.
Teofilo, "La notte di San Giovanni in Oriente," in *Archivio per lo Studio delle
        Tradizioni Popolari*, vii. (1888).
Ternaux-Compans, H., *Essai sur l'ancien Cundinamarca.*   Paris, N.D.
    *Voyages, relations et mémoires originaux, pour servir à l'histoire de la
        découverte de l'Amérique.*   Paris, 1837–1841.
Terrien, Missionary F., in *Annales de la Propagation de la Foi*, liv. (1882).
Tertre, Jean Baptiste du, *Histoire generale des Antilles.*   Paris, 1667–1671.
    *Histoire generale des Isles de S. Christophe, de la Guadeloupe, de la Mar-
        tinique et autres dans l'Amerique.*   Paris, 1654.
Tertullian, *Opera.*   Ed. F. Oehler.   Leipsic, 1851–1854.   Ed. E. F. Leopold,
        Pars i.   *Libri Apologetici.*   Leipsic, 1839.
    Ad martyres.
    Ad Nationes.
    Adversus Judaeos.
    Adversus Marcionem.
    Apologeticus.
    Contra Gnosticos Scorpiace.
    De corona militis.
    De jejunio.
    De praescriptione haereticorum.
    De spectaculis.
    De virginibus velandis, in Migne's *Patrologia Latina*, ii.
Teschauer, Carl, S.J., "Mythen und alte Volkssagen aus Brasilien," in *Anthropos*,
        i. (1906).
Tessier, "Sur la fête annuelle de la roue flamboyante de la Saint-Jean, à Basse-
        Kontz, arrondissement de Thionville," in *Mémoires et dissertations
        publiées par la Société Royale des Antiquaires de France*, v. (1823).
Testaments of the Twelve Patriarchs.   Translated and edited by R. H. Charles.
        London, 1908.
Tettau, W. J. A. von, und Temme, J. D. H., *Die Volkssagen Ostpreussens,
        Litthauens und Westpreussens.*   Berlin, 1837.
Tetzlaff, W., "Notes on the Laughlan Islands," in *Annual Report on British
        New Guinea, 1890–1891.*   Brisbane, 1892.
Tetzner, Dr. F., "Die Kuren in Ostpreussen," in *Globus*, lxxv. (1899).
    "Die Tschechen und Mährer in Schlesien," in *Globus*, lxxviii. (1900).
Teysmannia, No. 2.   1896.
Theal, G. McCall, *Kaffir Folk-lore.*   Second Edition.   London, 1886.
    Records of South-Eastern Africa.   1901.
Theocritus, *Idyllia.*   Iterum edidit A. T. A. Fritsche.   Leipsic, 1868–1869.
Theodoretus, *In Ezechielis cap. viii.*, in Migne's *Patrologia Graeca*, lxxxi.
*Theodorus, *Metamorphoses.*
Theognis, in *Poetae Lyrici Graeci*, ed. Th. Bergk, vol. ii.
Theophanes, *Chronographia.*   Ed. J. Classen.   Bonn, 1839–1841.
Theophrastus, *Opera quae supersunt omnia.*   Ed. Fr. Wimmer.   Paris (Didot), 1866.
    Characters, "The Superstitious Man."
    De causis plantarum.
    De igne.
    De signis tempestatum.
    De ventis.
    Historia Plantarum.

Theopompus, cited by Athenaeus. Fragments in *Fragmenta Historicorum Graecorum*, ed. C. Müller, vol. i.
Thesaurus Linguae Latinae. Leipsic, 1906–
Thevenot, *Relations des divers voyages*, 4ème Partie (Paris, 1672), "Voyage à la Chine des PP. I. Grueber et d'Orville."
Thevet, André, *La Cosmographie universelle.* Paris, 1575.
Les Singularitez de la France Antarctique, autrement nommée Amérique. Antwerp, 1558.
Thiers, J. B., *Traité des Superstitions.* Paris, 1679.
Fifth Edition. Paris, 1741.
Thilenius, G., *Ethnographische Ergebnisse aus Melanesien.* Halle, 1903.
Thomas, Cyrus, *The Maya Year.* Washington, 1894. (*Smithsonian Institution, Bureau of Ethnology.*)
Thomas, J. W., "De jacht op het eiland Nias," in *Tijdschrift voor Indische Taal- Land- en Volkenkunde*, xxvi. (1880).
Thomas, Northcote W., *Anthropological Report on the Ibo-speaking Peoples of Nigeria.* London, 1913.
Natives of Australia. London, 1906.
"The Scape-Goat in European Folk-lore," in *Folk-lore*, xvii. (1906).
Thomas-de-Saint-Mars, "Fête de Saint Estapin," in *Mémoires de la Société Royale des Antiquaires de France*, i. (1817).
Thomas the Rhymer, verses ascribed to, quoted by the Rev. John B. Pratt, *Buchan.* Second Edition. Aberdeen, Edinburgh, and London, 1859.
Thompson, G., *Travels and Adventures in Southern Africa.* London, 1827.
Thompson, R. Campbell, *Semitic Magic.* London, 1908.
Thomson, A. S., *The Story of New Zealand.* London, 1859.
Thomson, Basil C., *Savage Island.* London, 1902.
South Sea Yarns. Edinburgh and London, 1894.
The Fijians. London, 1908.
Thomson, Joseph, *Through Masai Land.* London, 1885.
Thomson, W. M., *The Land and the Book.* London, 1859.
The Land and the Book, Central Palestine and Phoenicia. London, 1883.
The Land and the Book, Lebanon, Damascus, and beyond Jordan. London, 1886.
Thorpe, B., *Northern Mythology.* London, 1851–1852.
Thouar, A., *Explorations dans l'Amérique du Sud.* Paris, 1891.
Thousand and One Nights, The, commonly called, in England, The Arabian Nights' Entertainment. Translated by E. W. Lane. London, 1839–1841.
Thraemer, E., *s.v.* "Dionysos," in W. H. Roscher's *Lexikon der griechischen und römischen Mythologie*, i.
Θρακικὴ 'Επετηρίς. Athens, 1897.
Thucydides. Ed. Thomas Arnold. Fourth Edition. Oxford, 1857.
Thunberg, C. P., *Voyages au Japon.* Paris, 1796.
Thurnwald, R., "Im Bismarck-archipel und auf den Salomo-inseln," in *Zeitschrift für Ethnologie*, xlii. (1910).
Thurston, Edgar, *Castes and Tribes of Southern India.* Madras, 1909.
"Deformity and Mutilation," in *Madras Government Museum, Bulletin*, vol. iv. No. 3. Madras, 1903.
Ethnographic Notes in Southern India. Madras, 1906.
Tibullus, *Carmina.* Ed. C. G. Heyne et E. C. F. Wunderlich. Leipsic, 1817.
Tiede, *Merkwürdigkeiten Schlesiens* (1804), quoted by P. Drechsler, *Sitte, Brauch und Volksglaube in Schlesien*, i. Leipsic, 1903.
Tiele, C. P., *Babylonisch-assyrische Geschichte.* Gotha, 1886–1888.
Geschichte der Religion im Altertum. Gotha, 1896–1903.
Geschiedenis van den Godsdienst in de Oudheid. Amsterdam, 1893–1902.
History of the Egyptian Religion. London, 1882.

Tijdschrift van het Koninklijk Nederlandsch Aardrijkskundig Genootschap.
Tijdschrift voor Indische Taal- Land- en Volkenkunde.
Tijdschrift voor Neêrlands Indië.
Tilak, Bâl Gangâdhar, *The Arctic Home in the Vedas.* Poona and Bombay, 1903.
Tille, A., *Die Geschichte der deutschen Weihnacht.* Leipsic, preface dated 1893.
Tilton, E. L., quoted in *Folk-lore,* vi. (1895).
Timaeus, cited by Tertullian, *De spectaculis,* 5.
  in *Fragmenta Historicorum Graecorum,* ed. C. Müller, vol. i.
Times, The.
  Weekly Edition.
Timkowski, G., *Travels of the Russian Mission through Mongolia to China.* London, 1827.
Tiraboschi, A., " Usi pasquali nel Bergamasco," in *Archivio per lo Studio delle Tradizioni Popolari,* i. (1892).
Titelbach, Prof. Vl., " Das heilige Feuer bei den Balkanslaven," in *Internationales Archiv für Ethnographie,* xiii. (1900).
Tod, Lieutenant-Colonel James, *Annals and Antiquities of Rajast'han.* London, 1829 and 1832.
Toepffer, J., *Attische Genealogie.* Berlin, 1889.
  Beiträge zur griechischen Altertumswissenschaft. Berlin, 1897.
Toeppen, M., *Aberglauben aus Masuren.* Second Edition. Danzig, 1867.
  Geschichte der preussischen Historiographie. Berlin, 1853.
Tomassetti, G., in *Museo Italiano di Antichità Classica,* ii. (1888).
Tönjes, Hermann, *Ovamboland, Land, Leute, Mission.* Berlin, 1911.
Tonti, De, " Relation de la Louisiane et du Mississippi," in *Recueil de Voyages au Nord,* v. Amsterdam, 1734.
Toorn, J. L. van der, " Het animisme bij den Minangkabauer in der Padangsche Bovenlanden," in *Bijdragen tot de Taal- Land- en Volkenkunde van Nederlandsch-Indië,* xxxix. (1890).
Torday, E., " Der Tofoke," in *Mitteilungen der Anthropologischen Gesellschaft in Wien,* xli. (1911).
Torday, E., et Joyce, T. A., *Les Bushongo.* Brussels, 1910.
  " Note on the Southern Ba-Mbala," in *Man,* vii. (1907).
  " Notes on the Ethnography of the Ba-Mbala," in *Journal of the Anthropological Institute,* xxxv. (1905).
  " Notes on the Ethnography of the Ba-Yaka," in *Journal of the Anthropological Institute,* xxxvi. (1906).
  " On the Ethnology of the South-Western Congo Free State," in *Journal of the Royal Anthropological Institute,* xxxvii. (1907).
Torquemada, J. de, *Monarquia Indiana.* Madrid, 1723.
" Totemismus auf den Marshall-Inseln (Südsee)," in *Anthropos,* viii. (1913).
Tour du Monde, Le.
Tournefort, P. de, *Relation d'un Voyage du Levant.* Amsterdam, 1718.
Tournier, Lieut.-Colonel, *Notice sur le Laos Français.* Hanoi, 1900.
Toutain, J., *Les Cultes païens dans l'Empire Romain.* Paris, 1907 and 1911.
Tozer, H. F., *Selections from Strabo.* Oxford, 1893.
  Turkish Armenia and Eastern Asia Minor. London, 1881.
" Traditions, Customs, and Superstitions of the Lewis," in *Folk-lore,* vi. (1895).
*Traill, G. W., *Statistical Sketch of Kumaun,* quoted in *North Indian Notes and Queries,* July and August 1891.
Train, Joseph, *An Historical and Statistical Account of the Isle of Man.* Douglas, Isle of Man, 1845.
Transactions and Proceedings of the New Zealand Institute.
Transactions and Proceedings of the Royal Society of Victoria.
Transactions of the American Ethnological Society.

Transactions of the Canadian Institute.

Transactions of the Ethnological Society of London, N. S.

Transactions of the Historical and Literary Committee of the American Philosophical Society.

Transactions of the (London) Philological Society.

Transactions of the Ninth International Congress of Orientalists.

Transactions of the Philosophical Society of Victoria.

Transactions of the Royal Society of Canada.

Transactions of the Royal Society of Victoria.

Transactions of the Society of Biblical Archaeology.

Transactions of the Third International Congress for the History of Religion. Oxford, 1908.

Transactions of the Wisconsin Academy of Sciences, Arts, and Letters.

Travaux de la 6ème Session du Congrès International des Orientalistes à Leide.

Travels of an Arab Merchant [Mohammed Ibn-Omar El-Tounsy] *in Soudan.* Abridged from the French (of Perron) by Bayle St. John. London, 1854.

Travels of the Jesuits in Ethiopia. Collected and historically digested by F. Balthazar Telles, of the Society of Jesus. London, 1710.

Travers, W. T. L., "Notes of the Traditions and Manners and Customs of the Mori-oris," in *Transactions and Proceedings of the New Zealand Institute*, ix. (1876).

Trebellius Pollio, *Claudius*, in *Scriptores Historiae Augustae*, ed. H. Peter, Leipsic, 1884.

Trede, Th., *Das Heidentum in der römischen Kirche.* Gotha, 1889–1891.

Tregear, E., *Maori-Polynesian Comparative Dictionary.* Wellington, N.Z., 1891.

"The Maoris of New Zealand," in *Journal of the Anthropological Institute*, xix. (1890).

Treichel, A., "Reisig- und Steinhäufung bei Ermordeten oder Selbstmördern," in *Verhandlungen der Berliner Gesellschaft für Anthropologie, Ethnologie und Urgeschichte, 1888* (bound up with *Zeitschrift für Ethnologie*, xx., 1888).

"Reisighäufung und Steinhäufung an Mordstellen," in *Am Ur-Quelle*, vi. (1896).

Tremearne, Major A. J. N., *Hausa Superstitions and Customs.* London, 1913.

The Tailed Head-hunters of Nigeria. London, 1912.

Trevelyan, Marie, *Folk-lore and Folk-stories of Wales.* London, 1909.

Trilles, Father H., "Chez les Fangs," in *Les Missions Catholiques*, xxx. (1898).

Le Totémisme chez les Fân. Münster i. W., 1912.

"Mille lieues dans l'inconnu," in *Les Missions Catholiques*, xxxiv. (1902).

Tristram, H. B., *The Fauna and Flora of Palestine.* London, 1884.

The Land of Israel. Fourth Edition. London, 1882.

The Land of Moab. London, 1873.

The Natural History of the Bible. Ninth Edition. London, 1898.

Trogus Pompeius, *Historiarum Philippicarum Epitoma.* Ed. J. Jeep. Leipsic, 1862.

Tromp, J. C. E., "De Rambai en Sebroeang Dajaks," in *Tijdschrift voor Indische Taal- Land- en Volkenkunde*, xxv.

Tromp, S. W., "Een Dajaksch Feest," in *Bijdragen tot de Taal- Land- en Volkenkunde van Nederlandsch-Indië*, xxxix. (1890).

"Uit de Salasila van Koetei," in *Bijdragen tot de Taal- Land- en Volkenkunde van Nederlandsch-Indië*, xxxvii. (1888).

Trumbull, H. C., *The Blood Covenant.* London, 1887.

The Threshold Covenant. New York, 1896.

Tsakni, N., *La Russie sectaire.* Paris, N.D.

Tschudi, J. J. von, *Peru, Reiseskizzen aus den Jahren 1838–1842.* St. Gallen, 1846.

Türk, in W. H. Roscher's *Lexikon der griechischen und römischen Mythologie.*

Turner, George, *Nineteen Years in Polynesia.* London, 1861.

    Samoa, a Hundred Years ago and long before. London, 1884.

Turner, L. M., " Ethnology of the Ungava District, Hudson Bay Territory," in *Eleventh Annual Report of the Bureau of Ethnology.* Washington, 1894.

Turpin, " History of Siam," in J. Pinkerton's *Voyages and Travels,* vol. ix.

Tusser, Thomas, *Five Hundred Points of Good Husbandry.* New Edition. London, 1812.

Tuuk, H. N. van der, "Notes on the Kawi Language and Literature," in *Journal of the Royal Asiatic Society,* N.S., xiii. (1881).

Tyerman, D., and Bennet, G., *Journal of Voyages and Travels in the South Sea Islands, China, India, etc.* London, 1831.

Tylor, Sir Edward B., *Anthropology.* London, 1881.

    in *International Folk-lore Congress, 1891, Papers and Transactions.*

    in *Journal of the Anthropological Institute,* xxviii. (1898).

    in *Proceedings of the Society of Biblical Archaeology,* xii. (1890).

    " On a Method of Investigating the Development of Institutions," in *Journal of the Anthropological Institute,* xviii. (1889).

    Primitive Culture. Second Edition. London, 1873.

    Researches into the Early History of Mankind. Third Edition. London, 1878.

Tyrtaeus, in *Poetae Lyrici Graeci,* ed. Th. Bergk, vol. ii.

Tzetzes, J., *Antehomerica.* Ed. F. S. Lehrs. Paris (Didot), 1878.

    Chiliades. Ed. Th. Kiesseling. Leipsic, 1826.

    Scholia on Lycophron. Ed. Chr. G. Müller. Leipsic, 1811.

" Über die Religion der heidnischen Tscheremissen im Gouvernement Kasan," in *Zeitschrift für allgemeine Erdkunde,* N.F., iii. (1857).

" Über den religiösen Glauben und die Ceremonien der heidnischen Samojeden im Kreise Mesen," in *Zeitschrift für allgemeine Erdkunde,* N.F., viii. (1860).

Ulrichs, H. N., *Reisen und Forschungen in Griechenland.* Bremen, 1840. Berlin, 1863.

Unger, G. F., " Der Isthmientag und die Hyakinthien," in *Philologus,* xxxvii. (1877).

    " Zeitrechnung der Griechen und Römer," in Iwan Müller's *Handbuch der klassischen Altertumswissenschaft,* i. Nördlingen, 1886.

Ungnad, Arthur, *Das Gilgamesch-Epos.* Göttingen, 1911.

University of California Publications in American Archaeology and Ethnology.

University Studies. Lincoln, Nebraska.

Urquhart, Sir Thomas, *The Discovery of a most Exquisite Jewel, more precious than Diamonds inchased in Gold.* Edinburgh, 1774.

Usener, H., *Das Weihnachtsfest.* Second Edition. Bonn, 1911.

    Dreiheit, ein Versuch mythologischer Zahlenlehre. Bonn, 1903.

    Götternamen. Bonn, 1896.

    " Italische Mythen," in *Rheinisches Museum,* N.F., xxx. (1875).

    Kleine Schriften, vol. iv. Leipzic and Berlin, 1913.

Utiešenović, Og. M., *Die Hauskommunionen der Südslaven.* Vienna, 1859.

Vahness, reported by F. von Luschan, in *Verhandlungen der Berliner Gesellschaft für Anthropologie, Ethnologie und Urgeschichte* (1900).

*Valdés, *Los Majos de Cadiz.*

Valdez, F. T., *Six Years of a Traveller's Life in Western Africa.* London, 1861.

Valentia, Viscount, *Voyages and Travels.* London, 1811.
Valentyn, François, *Oud en nieuw Oost-Indiën.* Dordrecht and Amsterdam, 1724–1726.
Valerius Flaccus, *Argonautica.* Ed. Aemil. Baehrens. Leipsic, 1875.
Valerius Maximus. Ed. C. Halm. Leipsic, 1865.
Vallancey, General Charles, *Collectanea de rebus Hibernicis.* Dublin, 1786.
Vambery, H., *Das Türkenvolk.* Leipsic, 1885.
Vancouver, Capt. George, *Voyage of Discovery to the North Pacific Ocean and round the World.* London, 1798.
Vaniček, A., *Griechisch-lateinisches etymologisches Wörterbuch.* Leipsic, 1877.
Varenius, B., *Descriptio regni Japoniae et Siam.* Cambridge, 1673.
    First Edition published by Elzevir at Amsterdam in 1649.
Varonen, reported by Hon. J. Abercromby in *Folk-lore*, ii. (1891).
Varro, cited by Servius, on Virgil, *Aeneid.*
    De agri cultura (*De re rustica*). Ed. H. Keil. Leipsic, 1884–1902.
    De lingua Latina. Ed. C. O. Müller. Leipsic, 1833. Ed. G. Goetz et Fr. Schoell. Leipsic, 1910.
    in Priscian (*Grammatici Latini*, ed. H. Keil).
    quoted by Nonius Marcellus, *De compendiosa doctrina*, s.v. "Lemures." Ed. L. Quicherat.
    Satirae Menippeae. Ed. F. Bücheler. Berlin, 1882.
Varthema, Ludovico di, *Travels in Egypt, Syria, etc.* Translated by J. W. Jones and edited by G. P. Badger. Hakluyt Society. London, 1863.
Veckenstedt, Edm., *Die Mythen, Sagen und Legenden der Zamaiten* (*Litauer*). Heidelberg, 1883.
    Wendische Sagen, Märchen und abergläubische Gebräuche. Graz, 1880.
Velasco, Juan de, "Histoire du royaume de Quito," in H. Ternaux-Compans's *Voyages, Relations et Mémoires originaux pour servir à l'Histoire de la Découverte de l'Amérique*, xviii. Paris, 1840.
Vellay, Ch., *Le culte et les fêtes d'Adonis-Thammouz dans l'Orient antique.* Paris, 1904.
    "Le dieu Thammuz," in *Revue de l'Histoire des Religions*, xlix. (1904).
Velleius Paterculus. Ed. C. Halm. Leipsic, 1876.
Velten, C., *Schilderungen der Suaheli.* Göttingen, 1901.
    Sitten und Gebräuche der Suaheli. Göttingen, 1903.
Venketswami, M. N., "Superstitions among Hindus in the Central Provinces," in *The Indian Antiquary*, xxviii. (1899).
    "Telugu Superstitions," in *The Indian Antiquary*, xxiv. (1895).
Verhandelingen der Koninklijke Akademie van Wetenschappen.
Verhandelingen van het Bataviaasch Genootschap van Kunsten en Wetenschappen.
Verhandlungen der Berliner Gesellschaft für Anthropologie, Ethnologie und Urgeschichte.
Verhandlungen der Gelehrten Estnischen Gesellschaft zu Dorpat. Dorpat, 1872.
Verhandlungen der vierzigsten Versammlung deutscher Philologen und Schulmänner in Görlitz.
Vernaleken, Theodor, *Mythen und Bräuche des Volkes in Österreich.* Vienna, 1859.
Veröffentlichungen aus dem Königlichen Museum für Völkerkunde. Berlin.
Verrall, A. W., "The Name Anthesteria," in *Journal of Hellenic Studies*, xx. (1900).
Verrall, Mrs., and Harrison, Miss J. E., *Mythology and Monuments of Ancient Athens.* London, 1890.
Verslagen en Mededeelingen der Koninklijke Akademie van Wetenschappen. Amsterdam.

Verzameling van Berigten betreffende de Bijbelverspreiding.

Veth, P. J., *Borneo's Wester-Afdeeling.* Zaltbommel, 1854–1856.

" De Leer der Signatuur, iii. De Mistel en de Riembloem," in *Internationales Archiv für Ethnographie,* vii. (1894).

" De Mandragora," in *Internationales Archiv für Ethnographie,* vii. (1894).

Het eiland Timor. Amsterdam, 1855.

Java. Haarlem, 1875–84.

Vetter, [K. ?], " Aberglaube unter dem Jabim-Stamme in Kaiser-Wilhelmsland," in *Mitteilungen der Geographischen Gesellschaft zu Jena,* xii. (1893).

Vetter, J. [K. ?], in *Mitteilungen der Geographischen Gesellschaft zu Jena,* xi. (1892).

Vetter, K., cited by M. Krieger, *Neu-Guinea.* Berlin, preface dated 1899.

in *Nachrichten über Kaiser-Wilhelmsland und den Bismarck-Archipel, 1897.* Berlin.

Komm herüber und hilf uns! oder die Arbeit der Neuen-Dettelsauer Mission. Barmen, 1898.

Vetustius Occidentalis Ecclesiae Martyrologium. Ed. Franciscus Maria Florentinus. Lucca, 1667.

Vial, P., " Les Gni ou Gnipa, tribu Lolote du Yun-Nan," in *Les Missions Catholiques,* xxv. (1893).

Victoria History of the County of Nottingham. Edited by William Page. London, 1906.

Viehe, Rev. G., " Some Customs of the Ovaherero," in (*South African) Folk-lore Journal,* i. Cape Town, 1879.

Vigfusson, Gudbrand, and Powell, F. York, *Corpus Poeticum Boreale.* Oxford, 1883.

Vikramânkadevacharita, The. Edited by G. Bühler. Bombay, 1875.

*Villagomez, Pedro de, *Carta pastorale de exortacion e instruccion contra las idolatrias de los Indios del arçobispado de Lima.* Lima, 1649. (Quoted by W. Mannhardt, *Mythologische Forschungen.*)

Villault, Le Sieur, *Relation des costes appellées Guinée.* Paris, 1669.

Vincendon-Dumoulin et Desgraz, C., *Îles Marquises ou Nouka-Hiva.* Paris, 1843.

Vinson, J., *Le folk-lore du pays Basque.* Paris, 1883.

Violette, L. Th., in *Les Missions Catholiques,* iii. (1870).

Virgil. Ed. J. Conington. London, 1863–1871.

Aeneid.

Bucolica (Eclogues).

Georgics.

Vitarum Scriptores Graeci. Ed. A. Westermann. Brunswick, 1845.

Vitruvius, *De architectura.* Ed. V. Rose and H. Müller-Strübing. Leipsic, 1867.

*Vizyenos, G. M., in Θρακικὴ 'Επετηρίς. Published at Athens in 1897.

Voeltzkow, A., " Vom Morondava zum Mangoky, Reiseskizzen aus West-Madagascar," in *Zeitschrift der Gesellschaft für Erdkunde zu Berlin,* xxxi. (1896).

Vogt, F., " Scheibentreiben und Frühlingsfeuer," in *Zeitschrift des Vereins für Volkskunde,* iii. (1893), iv. (1894).

Voigt and Thraemer, *s.v.* " Dionysus," in W. H. Roscher's *Lexikon der griechischen und römischen Mythologie,* i.

Vollers, K., " Calendar (Muslim)," in Dr. James Hastings's *Encyclopaedia of Religion and Ethics,* iii. Edinburgh, 1910.

Voltaire, *Essai sur les Mœurs.* (*Œuvres complètes de Voltaire,* vols. xi.-xiii. Paris, 1878.)

Vonbun, Dr. F. J., *Beiträge zur deutschen Mythologie gesammelt in Churrhaetien.* Chur, 1862.

Vonbun, J., *Volkssagen aus Vorarlberg.* Innsbruck, 1850.
Vopiscus, Flavius, in *Scriptores Historiae Augustae*, ed. H. Peter, vol. ii.
    Aurelianus.
    Numerianus.
Vorderman, A. G., "Planten-animisme op Java," in *Teysmannia*, No. 2, 1896.
Vormann, Franz, "Tänze und Tanzfestlichkeiten der Monumbo-Papua (Deutsch
    Neuguinea)," in *Anthropos*, vi. (1911).
"Zur Psychologie, Religion, Soziologie und Geschichte der Monumbo-
    Papua, Deutsch-Neuguinea," in *Anthropos*, v. (1910).
Vosmaer, J. N., *Korte beschrijving van het Zuid-oostelijk Schiereiland van Celebes.*
    Batavia, 1835.
Voyages au Nord. See *s.v.* Recueil de Voyages.
Vries, J. H. de, "Reis door enige eilandgroepen der Residentie Amboina," in
    *Tijdschrift van het Koninklijke Nederlandsch Aararijkskundig Genoot-
    schap*, Tweede Serie, xvii. (1900).
Vuillier, G., "Chez les magiciens et les sorciers de la Corrèze," in *Tour du
    Monde*, N.S., v. (1899).
"La Sicile, impressions du présentet du passé," in *Tour du Monde*, lxvii.
    (1894).

Wachsmuth, C., *Das alte Griechenland im neuem.* Bonn, 1864.
Waddell, A. L., "Frog-Worship among the Newars," in *The Indian Antiquary*,
    xxii. (1893).
Waddell, L. Austine, *Among the Himalayas.* Westminster, 1899.
"Demonolatry in Sikhim Lamaism," in *The Indian Antiquary*, xxiii.
    (1894).
    Lhasa and its Mysteries. London, 1905.
    The Buddhism of Tibet. London, 1895.
"The Tribes of the Brahmaputra Valley," in *Journal of the Asiatic Society
    of Bengal*, lxix., Part iii. Calcutta, 1901.
Wagler, P., *Die Eiche in alter und neuer Zeit.* In Two Parts. Würzen, N.D.,
    and Berlin, 1891.
Wagner, *s.v.* "Nana," in W. H. Roscher's *Lexikon der griechischen und
    römischen Mythologie.*
Wahlenberg, G., *Flora Suecica.* Upsala, 1824–1826.
Waifs and Strays of Celtic Tradition.
Waitz, Theodor, *Anthropologie der Naturvölker.* Leipsic, 1860–1877.
Waldau, A., *Böhmisches Märchenbuch.* Prague, 1860.
Waldfreund, J. E., "Volksgebräuche und Aberglaube in Tirol und dem
    Salzburger Gebirg," in *Zeitschrift für deutsche Mythologie und Sitten-
    kunde*, iii. (1855).
Waldron, G., *Description of the Isle of Man.* Reprinted for the Manx Society,
    Douglas, 1865.
Walen, A., "The Sakalava," in *Antananarivo Annual and Madagascar
    Magazine*, vol. ii., Reprint of the Second Four Numbers. Antananarivo,
    1896.
Walhouse, M. J., "Passing through the Fire," in *Indian Antiquary*, vii. (1878).
Wallace, A. R., *Narrative of Travels on the Amazon and Rio Negro.*
    Minerva Library Edition. London, 1889.
    The Malay Archipelago. Sixth Edition. London, 1877.
Wallace, Sir D. Mackenzie, *Russia.* London, Paris, and New York, N.D.
Wallis, G. H., *Illustrated Catalogue of Classical Antiquities from the Site of the
    Temple of Diana, Nemi, Italy.* Preface dated 1893.
Walpole, R., *Memoirs relating to European and Asiatic Turkey.* London, 1817.
Walter-Tornow, W., *De apium mellisque apud veteres significatione.* Berlin,
    1894.
Walton, Izaak, *Compleat Angler.*

Ward, Herbert, "Ethnographical Notes relating to the Congo Tribes," in *Journal of the Anthropological Institute*, xxiv. (1895).
Five Years with the Congo Cannibals. London, 1890.
Ward, the late Professor H. Marshall, of Cambridge.   Private communications (ii. 252, 315 *n.*[1]).
Warner, Mr., "Notes" in Colonel Maclean's *Compendium of Kaffir Laws and Customs.*   Cape Town, 1866.
Warren, W. W., "History of the Ojibways," in *Collections of the Minnesota Historical Society*, vol. v.   Saint Paul, Minnesota, 1885.
*Warton, *History of English Poetry*, referred to by R. Chambers, *The Book of Days.*   London and Edinburgh, 1886.
Wasiljev, J., *Übersicht über die heidnischen Gebräuche, Aberglauben und Religion der Wotjäken.*   Helsingfors, 1902.   (*Mémoires de la Société Finno-Ougrienne*, xviii.)
Watson, Miss A., quoted by A. C. Haddon, "A Batch of Irish Folk-lore," in *Folk-lore*, iv. (1893).
Watt, G., *Dictionary of the Economic Products of India.*   London and Calcutta, 1893.
"The Aboriginal Tribes of Manipur," in *Journal of the Anthropological Institute*, xvi. (1887).
Watters, T., "Some Corean Customs and Notions," in *Folk-lore*, vi. (1895).
Webb, F. N., in *Folk-lore*, xvi. (1905).
Webster, Hutton, *Rest Days, a Sociological Study* (*University Studies*, Lincoln, Nebraska, vol. xi. Nos. 1-2, January–April 1911).
Webster, W., *Basque Legends.*   London, 1877.
Weddell, H. A., *Voyage dans le Nord de la Bolivie et dans les parties voisines du Pérou.*   Paris and London, 1853.
Weekly Scotsman, The.
Weeks, Rev. John H., *Among Congo Cannibals.*   London, 1913.
"Anthropological Notes on the Bangala of the Upper Congo River," in *Journal of the Royal Anthropological Institute*, xxxix. (1909), xl. (1910).
"Notes on some Customs of the Lower Congo People," in *Folk-lore*, xix. (1908), xx. (1909).
Weil, H., in *Revue des Études grecques*, x. (1897).
Weinel, H., "נפש und seine Derivate," in *Zeitschrift für die alttestamentliche Wissenschaft*, xviii. (1898).
Weinhold, Karl, *Deutsche Frauen.*   Second Edition.   Vienna, 1882.
"Die mystische Neunzahl bei den Deutschen," in *Abhandlungen der Königlichen Akademie der Wissenschaften zu Berlin*, 1897.
Weinacht-Spiele und Lieder aus Süddeutschland und Schlesien.   Vienna, 1875.
Weir, T. S., "Note on Sacrifices in India as a Means of averting Epidemics," in *Journal of the Anthropological Society of Bombay*, i.
Weiss, M., *Die Völkerstämme im Norden Deutsch-Ostafrikas.*   Berlin, 1910.
Weissenberg, Dr. S., "Die Karäer der Krim," in *Globus*, lxxxiv. (1903).
"Kinderfreud und -leid bei den südrussischen Juden," in *Globus*, lxxxiii. (1903).
"Krankheit und Tod bei den südrussischen Juden," in *Globus*, xci. (1907).
Welcker, F. G., *Alte Denkmäler*   Göttingen, 1849–1864.
Griechische Götterlehre.   Göttingen, 1857–1862.
Wellhausen, J., *Prolegomena zur Geschichte Israels.*   Third Edition.   Berlin, 1886.
Reste arabischen Heidentums.   First Edition.   Berlin, 1887.
Second Edition.   Berlin, 1897.
"Zwei Rechtsriten bei den Hebräern," in *Archiv für Religionswissenschaft*, vii. (1904).
Welsh, Miss, formerly Principal of Girton College, Cambridge.   Private communication (vii. 155 *n.*[1]).

Wendland, P., "Jesus als Saturnalien-König," in *Hermes*, xxxiii. (1898).
Wendland, P., und Kern, O., *Beiträge zur Geschichte der griechischen Philosophie und Religion.* Berlin, 1895.
*Werenfels, *Dissertation upon Superstition.* London, 1748. (Quoted by J. Brand in *Popular Antiquities of Great Britain.* London, 1882–1883.)
Werner, Alice, in *Contemporary Review*, lxx. (July–December 1896).
   in letter to the Author (xi. 314 *n.*[1]).
   "The Custom of *Hlonipa* in its Influence on Language," in *Journal of the African Society*, No. 15 (April 1905).
   The Natives of British Central Africa. London, 1906.
   "Two Galla Legends," in *Man*, xiii. (1913).
Werner, Dr. E., "Im westlichen Finsterregebirge und an der Nordküste von Deutsch-Neuguinea," in *Petermanns Mitteilungen*, lv. (1909).
Wernicke, K., *s.v.* "Artemis," in Pauly-Wissowa's *Real-Encyclopädie der classischen Altertumswissenschaft*, ii.
   in W. H. Roscher's *Lexikon der griechischen und römischen Mythologie*, iii.
Westenberg, C. J., "Aanteekeningen omtrent de godsdienstige begrippen der Karo-Bataks," in *Bijdragen tot de Taal- Land- en Volkenkunde van Nederlandsch-Indië*, xli. (1892).
Westermann, Diedrich, *The Shilluk People, their Language and Folk-lore.* Berlin, preface dated 1912.
Westermarck, Dr. Edward, *Ceremonies and Beliefs connected with Agriculture, certain Dates of the Solar Year, and the Weather in Morocco.* Helsingfors, 1913.
   "Midsummer Customs in Morocco," in *Folk-lore*, xvi. (1905).
   "The Killing of the Divine King," in *Man*, viii. (1908).
   The Origin and Development of the Moral Ideas. London, 1906–1908.
   "The Popular Ritual of the Great Feast in Morocco," in *Folk-lore*, xxii. (1911).
Weston, Jessie L., "The *Scoppio del Carro* at Florence," in *Folk-lore*, xvi. (1905).
Weston, W., in *Journal of the Anthropological Institute*, xxvi. (1897).
   in *The Geographical Journal*, vii. (1896).
   Mountaineering and Exploration in the Japanese Alps. London, 1896.
Wheeler, G. C., "Sketch of the Totemism and Religion of the People of the Islands in the Bougainville Straits (Western Solomon Islands)," in *Archiv für Religionswissenschaft*, xv. (1912).
Wherry, Beatrix A., "Miscellaneous Notes from Monmouthshire," in *Folk-lore*, xvi. (1905).
Whetham, W. C. D., "The Evolution of Matter," in *Darwin and Modern Science.* Cambridge, 1909.
White, Rev. George E., in letter to the Author (v. 170 *n.*[2]).
   Present Day Sacrifices in Asia Minor. Reprinted from *The Hartford Seminary Record*, February 1906.
   Survivals of Primitive Religion among the People of Asia Minor. Paper read before the Victoria Institute or Philosophical Society of Great Britain, 6 Adelphi Terrace, Strand, London.
White, Gilbert, *The Natural History and Antiquities of Selborne.* Edinburgh, 1829.
White, Rachel Evelyn (Mrs. Wedd), "Women in Ptolemaic Egypt," in *Journal of Hellenic Studies*, xviii. (1898).
Whitehead, Rev. G., "Notes on the Chins of Burma," in *Indian Antiquary*, xxxvi. (1907).
Whitehouse, O. C., Introduction to Isaiah, in *The Century Bible.*
Whiteway, R. S. Private communication (iv. 51 *n.*[2]).
Whymper, F., in *Journal of the Royal Geographical Society*, xxxviii. (1868).
   "The Natives of the Youkon River," in *Transactions of the Ethnological Society of London*, N.S., vii. (1869).

Wickremasinghe, in *Am Urquell*, v. (1894).

Wide, S., *De sacris Troezeniorum, Hermionensium, Epidauriorum.* Upsala, 1898.

Lakonische Kulte. Leipsic, 1893.

Widenmann, A., *Die Kilimandscharo-Bevölkerung.* Gotha, 1899. (*Petermanns Mittheilungen*, Ergänzungsheft, No. 129.)

Widukind, *Res gestae Saxonicae*, i., in Migne's *Patrologia Latina*, cxxxvii.

Wiedemann, Professor Alfred, *Ägyptische Geschichte.* Gotha, 1884.

Altägyptische Sagen und Märchen. Leipsic, 1906.

Die Religion der alten Ägypter. Münster i. W., 1890.

"Ein altägyptischer Weltschöpfungsmythus," in *Am Urquell*, N.F., ii. (1898).

Herodots zweites Buch. Leipsic, 1890.

"L'Osiris végétant," in *Le Muséon*, N.S., iv. (1903).

"Menschenvergötterung im alten Ägypten," in *Am Urquell*, N.F., i. (1897).

Religion of the Ancient Egyptians. London, 1897.

The Ancient Egyptian Doctrine of the Immortality of the Soul. London, 1895.

Wiedemann, F. J., *Aus dem inneren und äusseren Leben der Ehsten.* St. Petersburg, 1876.

Wiener, Ch., *Pérou et Bolivie.* Paris, 1880.

Wiener Studien.

Wiener Zeitschrift für die Kunde des Morgenlandes.

Wiese, C., "Beiträge zur Geschichte der Zulu im Norden des Zambesi, namentlich der Angoni," in *Zeitschrift für Ethnologie*, xxxii. (1900).

Wieseler, Fr., in *Philologus*, ix. (1854).

Wilamowitz-Moellendorff, Prof. U. von, *Aristoteles und Athen.* Berlin, 1893.

Wilcken, U., "Arsinoitische Steuerprofessionen aus dem Jahre 189 n. Chr.," in *Sitzungsberichte der Königlichen Preussischen Akademie der Wissenschaften zu Berlin* (1883).

Wilde, Lady, *Ancient Cures, Charms, and Usages of Ireland.* London, 1890.

Ancient Legends, Mystic Charms, and Superstitions of Ireland. London, 1887.

Wildeboer, D. G., Commentary on Esther, in *Kurzer Hand-Commentar zum alten Testament*, Lieferung 6. Herausgegeben von D. K. Marti. Freiburg i. B., 1898.

Wilford, Captain F., "An Essay on the Sacred Isles in the West," in *Asiatic Researches*, ix. London, 1809.

"Vicramaditya and Salivahana," in *Asiatic Researches*, ix. London, 1809.

Wilken, G. A., "Bijdrage tot de Kennis der Alfoeren van het eiland Boeroe," in *Verhandelingen van het Bataviaasch Genootschap van Kunsten en Wetenschappen*, xxxviii. Batavia, 1875.

"De betrekking tusschen menschen- dieren- en plantenleven naar het volksgeloof," in *De Indische Gids*, November, 1884.

"De Simsonsage," in *De Gids*, 1888, No. 5. Separate reprint.

De verspreide Geschriften van Prof. Dr. G. A. Wilken, Verzameld door Mr. F. D. E. van Ossenbruggen. The Hague, 1912.

Handleiding voor de vergelijkende Volkenkunde van Nederlandsch-Indië. Leyden, 1893.

"Het animisme bij de volken van den Indischen Archipel," in *De Indische Gids*, June 1884.

Het animisme bij de volken van den Indischen Archipel. Tweede Stuk. Leyden, 1885.

"Het animisme bij de volken van den Indischen Archipel," in *Verspreide Geschriften.* The Hague, 1912.

"Het Shamanisme bij de Volken van de Indischen Archipel," in *Bijdragen tot de Taal- Land- en Volkenkunde van Nederlandsch-Indië*, xxxvi. (1887).

Wilken, G. A.—*continued.*
" Iets over de Papoewas van de Geelvinksbaai." Separate reprint from
Bijdragen tot de Taal- Land- en Volkenkunde van Nederlandsch-Indië,
5e Volgreeks ii.
" Iets over de schedelvereering," in *Bijdragen tot de Taal- Land- en Volken-
kunde van Nederlandsch-Indië,* xxxviii. (1889).
*" Over de primitieve vormen van het huwelijk," in *Indische Gids,*
1880, etc.
*Über das Haaropfer und einige andere Trauergebräuche bei den Völkern
Indonesiens.* Reprinted from the *Revue Coloniale Internationale.*
Amsterdam, 1886–1887.
Wilken, N. P., en Schwarz, J. A., " Allerlei over het land en volk van Bolaäng
Mongondou," in *Mededeelingen van wege het Nederlandsche Zendeling-
genootschap,* xi. (1867).
" Het heidendom en de Islam in Bolaäng Mongondou," in *Mededeelingen
van wege het Nederlandsche Zendelinggenootschap,* xi. (1867).
Wilken, P. N., " Bijdragen tot de kennis van de zeden en gewoonten der Alfoeren
in de Minahassa," in *Mededeelingen van wege het Nederlandsche Zendeling-
genootschap,* vii. (1863).
" De godsdienst en godsdienstplegtigheden der Alfoeren in de Menahassa
op het eiland Celebes," *Tijdschrift voor Neêrlands Indië* (December
1849). Reprinted in N. Graafland's *De Minahassa.* Rotterdam,
1869.
German translation in *Zeitschrift für allgemeine Erdkunde,* N.F., x.
(1861).
Wilkes, Ch., *Narrative of the United States Exploring Expedition.* London,
1845.
New Edition. New York, 1851.
Wilkinson, Sir J. Gardiner, *Manners and Customs of the Ancient Egyptians,*
Edited by S. Birch. London, 1878.
A Second Series of the Manners and Customs of the Ancient Egyptians,
London, 1841.
Wilkinson, R. J., *Malay Beliefs.* London and Leyden, 1906.
Willcock, Rev. Dr. J., of Lerwick, in letter to Sheriff-Substitute David J.
Mackenzie (ix. 169 n.[2]).
Willems, A., *Notes sur la Paix d'Aristophane.* Brussels, 1899.
Willer, " Verzameling der Battasche Wetten en Instellingen in Mandheling en
Pertibie," in *Tijdschrift voor Neêrlands Indië* (1846).
Williams, John, *Narrative of Missionary Enterprises in the South Sea Islands.*
London, 1838.
Williams, Meta E., " Hittite Archives from Boghaz-Keui." Translated from
the German transcripts of Dr. Winckler. (*Annals of Archaeology and
Anthropology,* iv. Liverpool and London, 1912.)
Williams, Monier, *Buddhism.* Second Edition. London, 1890.
Religious Thought and Life in India. London, 1883.
Williams, S. W., *The Middle Kingdom.* New York and London, 1848.
Williams, Thomas, *Fiji and the Fijians.* Second Edition. London, 1860.
Willibald, *Life of S. Boniface,* in Pertz's *Monumenta Germaniae Historica,* ii.
Willoughby, Rev. W. C., " Notes on the Totemism of the Becwana," in *Journal
of the Anthropological Institute,* xxxv. (1905).
Wilmanns, G., *Exempla Inscriptionum Latinarum.* Berlin, 1873.
Wilson, Captain, " Report on the Indian Tribes," in *Transactions of the
Ethnological Society of London,* N.S., iv. (1866).
Wilson, Sir Charles, *Picturesque Palestine.* London, N.D.
Wilson, Rev. C. T., *Peasant Life in the Holy Land.* London, 1906.
Wilson, C. T., and Felkin, R. W., *Uganda and the Egyptian Sudan.* London,
1882.

Wilson, Daniel, *The Archaeology and Prehistoric Annals of Scotland.* Edinburgh, 1851.
Wilson, Colonel Henry, in letter to the Author (vii. 226 *n.*[6]).
Wilson, H. H., "The Religious Festivals of the Hindus," in *Journal of the Royal Asiatic Society*, ix. (1848).
Wilson, Captain James, *Missionary Voyage to the Southern Pacific Ocean.* London, 1799.
Wilson, Rev. J. Leighton, *Western Africa.* London, 1856.
Winckler, H., *Altorientalische Forschungen.* Zweite Reihe. Leipsic, 1900.
　　Dritte Reihe. Leipsic, 1901.
Die Gesetze Hammurabi. Second Edition. Leipsic, 1903.
Die Thontafeln von Tell-el-Amarna. Berlin, 1889–1890.
Geschichte Babyloniens und Assyriens. Leipsic, 1902.
Geschichte Israels. Leipsic, 1895–1900.
　　in E. Schrader's *Die Keilinschriften und das Alte Testament.* Third Edition. Berlin, 1902.
"Vorläufige Nachrichten über die Ausgrabungen in Boghaz-Köi im Sommer 1907, I. Die Tontafelfunde," in *Mitteilungen der Deutschen Orient-Gesellschaft zu Berlin*, No. 35, December 1907.
Windt, H. de, *Through the Gold-fields of Alaska to Bering Straits.* London, 1898.
Winer, G. B., *Biblisches Realwörterbuch.* Second Edition. Leipsic, 1833–1838.
Winter, A. C., "Russische Volksbräuche bei Seuchen," in *Globus*, lxxix. (1901).
Winter, C. F., "Instellingen, gewoonten en gebruiken der Javanen te Soerakarta," in *Tijdschrift voor Neêrlands Indië*, Vijfde Jaargang, Eerste Deel (1843).
Winter, J. W., "Beknopte Beschrijving van het hof Soerokarta in 1824," in *Bijdragen tot de Taal- Land- en Volkenkunde van Nederlandsch-Indië*, liv. (1902).
Winterbottom, Thomas, *An Account of the Native Africans in the Neighbourhood of Sierra Leone.* London, 1803.
Winternitz, M., "Das altindische Hochzeitsrituell," in *Denkschriften der kaiserlichen Akademie der Wissenschaften in Wien*, xl. Vienna, 1892.
"Der Sarpabali, ein altindischer Schlangencult," in *Mittheilungen der Anthropologischen Gesellschaft in Wien*, xviii. (1888).
*Wisla, vol. iv.
Wissenschaftliche Mittheilungen aus Bosnien und der Hercegovina. Redigiert von Moriz Hoernes. Vienna, 1895.
Wissenschaftliche Veröffentlichungen der Deutschen Orient-Gesellschaft.
Wissmann, H. von, *My Second Journey through Equatorial Africa, from the Congo to the Zambesi.* London, 1891.
Wissowa, Professor G., *s.v.* "Cincius," in Pauly-Wissowa's *Real-encyclopädie der classischen Altertumswissenschaft.*
De feriis anni Romanorum vetustissimi observationes selectae. Reprinted in his *Gesammelte Abhandlungen zur römischen Religions- und Stadtgeschichte.* Munich, 1904.
s.vv. "Egeria," "Mater Matuta," and "Pales," in W. H. Roscher's *Ausführliches Lexikon der griechischen und römischen Mythologie.*
Gesammelte Abhandlungen zur römischen Religions- und Stadtgeschichte. Munich, 1904.
Religion und Kultus der Römer. Munich, 1902.
　　Second Edition. Munich, 1912.
Wit, Miss Augusta de, *Facts and Fancies about Java.* Singapore, 1898.
"Witch-burning at Clonmell," in *Folk-lore*, vi. (1895).
Witte, Anton, "Menstruation und Pubertätsfeier der Mädchen in Kpandugebiet Togo," in *Baessler-Archiv*, i. (1911).

Witzschel, August, *Sagen, Sitten und Gebräuche aus Thüringen.* Vienna, 1878.
Wlislocki, H. von, *Sitten und Brauch der Siebenbürger Sachsen.* Hamburg, 1888.
Volksglaube und religiöser Brauch der Magyar. Münster i. W., 1893.
Volksglaube und religiöser Brauch der Zigeuner. Münster i. W., 1891.
Volksglaube und Volksbrauch der Siebenbürger Sachsen. Berlin, 1893.
Woeste, J., in *Zeitschrift für deutsche Mythologie und Sittenkunde*, ii. (1855).
Woeste, J. F. L., *Volksüberlieferungen in der Grafschaft Mark.* Iserlohn, 1848.
Woldt, A., *Captain Jacobsen's Reise an der Nordwestküste Americas, 1881–1883.* Leipsic, 1884.
   "Die Kultus-Gegenstände der Golden und Giljaken," in *Internationales Archiv für Ethnographie*, i. (1888).
Wolf, J. W., *Beiträge zur deutschen Mythologie.* Göttingen and Leipsic, 1852–1857.
   Deutsche Hausmärchen. Göttingen and Leipsic, 1851.
   Deutsche Märchen und Sagen. Leipsic, 1845.
   Niederländische Sagen. Leipsic, 1843.
Wood, J. G., *Natural History of Man.* London, 1874–1880.
Wood, J. T., *Discoveries at Ephesus.* London, 1877.
   Inscriptions from the Augusteum.
   Inscriptions from the City and Suburbs.
   Inscriptions from the Great Theatre.
   Inscriptions from the Temple of Diana.
Wood, W. Martin, "The Hairy Men of Yesso," in *Transactions of the Ethnological Society of London*, N.S., iv. (1866).
Woodford, C. M., *A Naturalist among the Head-hunters, being an Account of Three Visits to the Solomon Islands.* London, 1890,
Woods, J. D. *See s.v.* Native Tribes of South Australia.
Woodthorpe, Colonel R. G., "Some Account of the Shans and Hill Tribes of the States on the Mekong," in *Journal of the Anthropological Institute*, xxvi. (1897).
"Words about Spirits," in (*South African*) *Folk-lore Journal*, ii. (1880).
Wordsworth, J., *Fragments and Specimens of Early Latin.* Oxford, 1874.
Wordsworth, W., *Ode on Intimations of Immortality.*
World's Work and Play, The.
Worrall, Rev. H., in report of a lecture delivered in Melbourne, December 9, 1898.
Worth, R. N., *History of Devonshire.* Second Edition. London, 1886.
Wrangell, De, *Le Nord de la Sibérie.* Paris, 1843.
Wratislaw, A. H., *Sixty Folk-tales from exclusively Slavonic Sources.* London, 1889.
Wright, Elizabeth Mary, *Rustic Speech and Folk-lore.* Oxford, 1913.
Wright, Joseph, *The English Dialect Dictionary.* London, 1898–1905.
Wright, Th., *Early Travels in Palestine.* London, 1848.
Wright, W., *The Empire of the Hittites.* Second Edition. London, 1886.
Wunenberger, Ch., "La Mission et le royaume de Humbé, sur les bords du Cunène," in *Les Missions Catholiques*, xx. (1888).
Wünsch, R., *Das Frühlingsfest der Insel Malta.* Leipsic, 1902.
   "Eine antike Rachepuppe," in *Philologus*, lxi. (1902).
Wüstenfeld, F., *Macrizi's Geschichte der Copten.* Göttingen, 1845.
Wuttke, A., *Der deutsche Volksaberglaube.* Second Edition. Berlin, 1869.
Wuttke, R., *Sächsische Volkskunde.* Second Edition. Dresden, 1901.
Wyatt, W., in *Native Tribes of South Australia.*
Wyse, Miss A. Private communication (ii. 88 *n.*[1]).
Wyse, William. Private communications (i. 101 *n.*[2], 105 *n.*[5], ii. 356 *n.*[3], iv. 144, vi. 35 *n.*[1], 51 *n.*[1]).
Wyttenbach, Daniel, *Animadversiones in Plutarchi Scripta Moralia.* Leipsic, 1820–1834.

Xanthus, in *Fragmenta Historicorum Graecorum*, ed. C. Müller, vol. i.
Xenophanes, in *Die Fragmente der Vorsokratiker*, ed. H. Diels, vol. i.
    quoted by Clement of Alexandria, *Stromateis*.
    quoted by Eusebius, *Praeparatio Evangelii*, xiii.
Xenophon. Ed. L. Dindorf. Leipsic, 1870–1871.
    Anabasis.
    Cynegeticus.
    Cyropaedia.
    Hellenica (*Historia Graeca*).
    Oeconomicus.
    Respublica Lacedaemoniorum, in *Xenophontis opuscula politica, equestria, et venatica*, ex recensione et cum annotationibus L. Dindorfii. Oxford, 1866.
Xeres, Fr., *Relation véridique de la conquête du Pérou et de la Province de Cuzco nommée Nouvelle-Castille*, in H. Ternaux-Compans's *Voyages, relations et mémoires, etc.* Paris, 1837.

Yarborough, Rev. J. J. C.. Private communication (viii. 51 *n.*[5]).
Yate, W., *An Account of New Zealand.* London, 1835.
"Ynglinga Saga," in *The Heimskringla or Chronicle of the Kings of Norway.* Translated from the Icelandic of Snorri Sturluson by S. Laing. London, 1844.
Yoe, Shway, *The Burman, his Life and Notions.* London, 1882.
Young, Arthur, "Tour in Ireland," in J. Pinkerton's *Voyages and Travels*, iii.
Young, Ernest, *The Kingdom of the Yellow Robe.* Westminster, 1898.
*Young, George, *A History of Whitby and Streoneshalth Abbey* (Whitby, 1817), quoted in *County Folk-lore*, vol. ii., *North Riding of Yorkshire, York, and the Ainsty.* London, 1901.
Young, Hugh W., F.S.A. Scot., *Notes on the Ramparts of Burghead as revealed by recent Excavations.* Edinburgh, 1892.
    Notes on further Excavations at Burghead. Edinburgh, 1893.
Younghusband, (Sir) F. E., "A Journey across Central Asia," in *Proceedings of the Royal Geographical Society*, x. (1888).
Yukon Territory, The. London, 1898.
Yule, Colonel H., in *Journal of the Anthropological Institute*, ix. (1880).
Yuzbashi, "Tribes on the Upper Nile," in *Journal of the African Society*, No. 14 (January 1905).

Zahler, H., *Die Krankheit im Volksglauben des Simmenthals.* Bern, 1898.
Zahn, H., "Die Jabim," in R. Neuhauss's *Deutsch Neu-Guinea*, iii. Berlin, 1911.
Zamachschar, cited by Graf zu Solms-Laubach, in *Abhandlungen der Königlichen Gesellschaft der Wissenschaften zu Göttingen*, xxviii. (1882).
Zanetti, Z., *La Medicina delle nostre donne.* Città di Castello, 1892.
Zechariah, The Book of the Prophet.
Zeitschrift der Deutschen Morgenländischen Gesellschaft.
Zeitschrift des Deutschen Palaestina-Vereins.
Zeitschrift der Gesellschaft für Erdkunde zu Berlin.
Zeitschrift der Savigny-Stiftung für Rechtsgeschichte.
Zeitschrift des Vereins für Volkskunde.
Zeitschrift für ägyptische Sprache und Altertumskunde.
Zeitschrift für afrikanischen und oceanischen Sprachen.
Zeitschrift für allgemeine Erdkunde.
Zeitschrift für Assyriologie.
Zeitschrift für deutsches Alterthum.
Zeitschrift für deutsche Mythologie und Sittenkunde.
Zeitschrift für die alttestamentliche Wissenschaft.

Zeitschrift für die historische Theologie.
Zeitschrift für die neutestamentliche Wissenschaft.
Zeitschrift für Ethnologie.
*Zeitschrift für Missionskunde und Religionswissenschaft, xv. (1900), referred to
 by A. Dieterich in *Archiv für Religionswissenschaft*, viii. (1904).
Zeitschrift für Numismatik.
Zeitschrift für vergleichende Rechtswissenschaft.
Zeitschrift für Volkskunde.
Zeller, E., *Die Philosophie der Griechen.* Third and Fourth Editions. Leipsic,
 1875–1881.
Zend-Avesta. Translated by James Darmesteter and L. H. Mills. Oxford,
 1880–1887. (*Sacred Books of the East*, vols. iv., xxiii., and xxxi.)
Zenobius. *Proverbia*, in *Paroemiographi Graeci*, vol. i., ed. E. L. Leutsch et
 F. G. Schneidewin. Göttingen, 1839–1851.
**Zeumer, J. K., *Laetare vulgo Todten Sonntag* (Jena, 1701), quoted by Fr. Kauff-
 mann, in *Balder* (Strasburg, 1902).
Ziebarth, E., " Der Fluch im griechischen Recht," in *Hermes*, xxx. (1895).
Zimmer, H., *Altindisches Leben.* Berlin, 1879.
 " Das Mutterrecht der Pikten," in *Zeitschrift der Savigny-Stiftung für
 Rechtsgeschichte*, xv. (1894), Romanistische Abtheilung.
Zimmermann, W. F. A., *Die Inseln des Indischen und Stillen Meeres.* Berlin,
 1864–1865.
Zimmern, H., *s.v.* " Creation," in *Encyclopaedia Biblica*, i.
 " Der babylonische Gott Tamūz," in *Abhandlungen der philologisch-
 historischen Klasse der Königlichen Sächsischen Gesellschaft der Wissen-
 schaften*, xxvii. No. xx. Leipsic, 1909.
 in E. Schrader's *Die Keilinschriften und das Alte Testament.* Third
 Edition. Berlin, 1902.
 " Sumerisch-babylonische Tamūzlieder," in *Berichte über die Verhandlungen
 der Königlich Sächsischen Gesellschaft der Wissenschaften zu Leipzig,
 philologisch-historische Klasse*, lix. (1907).
 " Zum Babylonischen Neujahrsfest," in *Berichte über die Verhandlungen
 der Königlich Sächsischen Gesellschaft der Wissenschaften zu Leipzig,
 philologisch-historische Klasse*, lviii. (1906).
 " Zur Frage nach dem Ursprunge des Purimfestes," in *Zeitschrift für die
 alttestamentliche Wissenschaft*, xi. (1891).
Zimmern, Helen, *The Epic of Kings, Stories retold from Firdusi.* London, 1883.
**Zincke, F. Barham, *Some Materials for the History of Wherstead.* Ipswich,
 1887. (Quoted in *County Folk-lore, Printed Extracts*, No. 2, *Suffolk.*
 Collected and edited by Lady Eveline Camilla Gurdon. London,
 1893.)
Zingerle, Ignaz V., " Der heilige Baum bei Nauders," in *Zeitschrift für deutsche
 Mythologie und Sittenkunde*, iv. Göttingen, 1859.
 Kinder- und Hausmärchen aus Tirol. Second Edition. Gera, 1870.
 " Perahta in Tirol," in *Zeitschrift für deutsche Mythologie und Sittenkunde*,
 iii. Göttingen, 1855.
 Sitten, Bräuche und Meinungen des Tiroler Volkes. Second Edition.
 Innsbruck, 1871.
 " Wald, Bäume, Kräuter," in *Zeitschrift für deutsche Mythologie und
 Sittenkunde*, i. Göttingen, 1853.
Zippel, G., " Das Taurobolium," in *Festschrift zum fünfzigjährigen Doctor-
 jubiläum L. Friedlaender dargebracht von seinen Schülern.* Leipsic,
 1895.
Zonaras, *Annales.* Ed. M. Pinder. Bonn, 1841–1844.
Zondervan, H., " Timor en de Timoreezen," in *Tijdschrift van het Nederlandsch
 Aardrijkskundig Genootschap*, Tweede Serie, v. 1888.
Zosimus, *Historia.* Ed. Im. Bekker. Bonn, 1837.

Zündel, G., "Land und Volk der Eweer auf der Sclavenküste in West-afrika," in *Zeitschrift der Gesellschaft für Erdkunde zu Berlin*, xii. (1877).

Zurita, Alonzo de, "Rapport sur les differentes classes de chefs de la Nouvelle-Espagne," in H. Ternaux-Compans's *Voyages, Relations et Mémoires originaux, pour servir à l'Histoire de la Découverte de l'Amérique*. Paris, 1840.

Zweifel et Moustier, "Voyage aux sources du Niger," in *Bulletin de la Société de Géographie* (Paris), 6ème Série, xv. (1878), xx. (1880).

GENERAL INDEX

GENERAL INDEX

The Roman numerals (i., ii., iii., etc.) refer to the volumes; the Arabic numbers (1, 2, 3, etc.) refer to the pages. The volumes of the work are cited by the following numerals:—

i. = *The Magic Art and the Evolution of Kings*, vol. i.
ii. =   ,,   ,,   ,,   vol. ii.
iii. = *Taboo and the Perils of the Soul*.
iv. = *The Dying God*.
v. = *Adonis, Attis, Osiris*, Third Edition, vol. i.
vi. =   ,,   ,,   ,,   vol. ii.
vii. = *Spirits of the Corn and of the Wild*, vol. i.
viii. =   ,,   ,,   ,,   vol. ii.
ix. = *The Scapegoat*.
x. = *Balder the Beautiful*, vol. i.
xi. =   ,,   ,,   vol. ii.

Aachen, effigy burnt on Ash Wednesday at, x. 120, xi. 25

Aargau, Swiss canton of, the Whitsuntide Basket in, ii. 83; Lenten fire-custom in, x. 119; superstition as to oak-mistletoe in, xi. 82; mistletoe called "thunder-besom" in, xi. 85, 301; birth-trees in, xi. 165

Ab, a Jewish month, equivalent to August, i. 14, vii. 259 *n.*[1]

Ababa, a tribe of the Congo region, believe that their souls transmigrate at death into animals, viii. 288 *sq.*

Ababua, the, of the Congo valley, their belief as to falling stars, iv. 65

Aban, a Persian month, vi. 68

Abbas Effendi, divine head of the Babites, i. 402

Abbas the Great, Shah of Persia, temporary substitute for, iv. 157

Abbehausen, fever transferred to dog and cat at, ix. 51

Abbeville, huge trunks of oak in the peat-bog near, ii. 351

Abbot of Folly in France, ix. 334

—— of Unreason in Scotland, ix. 312, 331

Abchases of the Caucasus, their ceremony of rain-making, i. 282 *n.*[4]; their worship of the thunder-god, ii. 370; their memorial feasts, iv. 98, 103; their use of effigies as substitutes to save the lives of people, viii. 105; their sacrament of shepherds, viii. 313; their sacrifice of white ox, viii. 313 *n.*[1]

Abd-Hadad, priestly king of Hierapolis, v. 163 *n.*[3]

Abdera, human scapegoats at, ix. 254

Abdication of kings in favour of their infant children, iii. 19, 20; during the reign of their substitutes, iv. 115; annual, of kings, iv. 148; of father when his son is grown up, iv. 181; of the king on the birth of a son, iv. 190; temporary, of chief, viii. 66, 68

Abduction of souls by demons, iii. 58 *sqq.*

Abeghian, Manuk, on the belief of the Armenians in demons, ix. 107 *sq.*; on creeping through cleft trees in Armenia, xi. 172

Abensberg in Bavaria, burning the Easter Man at, x. 144

Abeokuta, in West Africa, the Alake (king) of, iv. 203; his head kept and delivered to his successor, iv. 203; use of bull-roarers at, xi. 229 *n.*

Aber, the Lake of, in Upper Austria, xi. 189

Aberdeenshire, All Souls' Day in, vi. 79 *sq.*; harvest customs in, vii. 158 *sqq.*, 215 *sq.*, x. 12; need-fire in, x. 296; holed rock used by childless women in, xi. 187

Aberdour, parish of, in Aberdeenshire, the cutting of the *clyack* sheath in, vii. 158 *sqq.*

Aberfeldy, Hallowe'en fires near, x. 232

Abi-baal, "father of Baal," v. 51 *n.*[4]

Abi-el, "father of El," v. 51 *n.*[4]

147

Abi-jah, King, his family, v. 51 $n.^2$; "father of Jehovah," v. 51 $n.^4$

Abi-melech, "father of a king," v. 51 $n.^4$

Abi-milk (Abi-melech), king of Tyre, v. 16 $n.^5$

Abimelech massacres his seventy brothers, v. 51 $n.^2$

Abingdon in Berkshire, May carols and garlands at, ii. 60

Abipones, the, of South America thought it sinful to mention their own names, iii. 328; the dead not named among the, iii. 352; changes in their language caused by the fear of naming the dead, iii. 360; their belief as to meteors, iv. 63; their worship of the Pleiades, v. 258 $n.^2$, vii. 308; ate jaguars to become brave, viii. 140

Abjuration, form of, imposed on Jewish converts, ix. 393

Abnormal mental states accounted inspiration, iii. 248

Abolition of the kingship at Rome, ii. 289 sqq.

Abomey, the old capital of Dahomey, iv. 40

Abonsam, an evil spirit on the Gold Coast, ix. 132

Aborigines retained as priests of the local gods by conquering races, ii. 288; of Victoria, their custom as to emu fat, x. 13

Abortion, superstition as to woman who has procured, iii. 153

Abougit, Father X., S.J., on the ceremony of the new fire at Jerusalem, x. 130

Abraham, his attempted sacrifice of Isaac, iv. 177, vi. 219 $n.^1$

—— and Sarah, ii. 114

——, the Pool of, at Ourfa, i. 285

Abrahams, Israel, on the Purim bonfires, ix. 393 $n.^2$

Abruzzi, barren fruit-trees threatened in the, ii. 22; belief as to falling stars in the, iv. 66, 67; burning an effigy of the Carnival in the, iv. 224; seven-legged effigy of Lent in the, iv. 244 sq.; gossips of St. John in the, iv. 245 $n.^2$; marvellous properties attributed to water on St. John's Night in the, v. 246; Easter ceremonies in the, v. 256; the feast of All Souls in the, vi. 77 sq.; rules as to sowing seed and cutting timber in the, vi. 133 $n.^3$; Epiphany in the, ix. 167 $n.^2$; new Easter fire in the, x. 122; water consecrated at Easter in the, x. 122 sqq.; Midsummer rites of fire and water in the, x. 209 sq.

Absalom, his intercourse with his father's concubines, ix. 368

Absence and recall of the soul, iii. 30 sqq.

Absites, the, iii. 312

Absrot, village of Bohemia, precaution against witches on Walpurgis Night at, ix. 161

Abstinence, periods of, observed before sowing, ii. 98, 105; as a charm to promote the growth of the seed, ix. 347 sqq.

Abstract notions, the personification of, not primitive, iv. 253

Abu 'Ilberecat, a Berber, ii. 153 sq.

Abu Rabah, resort of childless wives in Palestine, v. 78, 79

Abuse (vituperation), beneficial virtue ascribed to, i. 279 sq.

Abydos, head of Osiris at, vi. 11; the favourite burial-place of the Egyptians, vi. 18 sq.; specially associated with Osiris, vi. 18, 197; tombs of the ancient Egyptian kings at, vi. 19; the ritual of, vi. 86; hall of the Osirian mysteries at, vi. 108; representations of the Sed festival at, vi. 151; inscriptions at, vi. 153; temple of Osiris at, vi. 198; ancient shrine of Osiris at, vii. 260 $n.^2$

Abyssinia, rain-making in, i. 258; rain-making priests among tribes on the borders of, ii. 2 sq.; Tigre-speaking tribes to the north of, ii. 19; fear of the evil eye in, iii. 116; severed hands and feet preserved against the resurrection in, iii. 281; personal names concealed in, iii. 322; the Kamants of, iv. 12; sacrifice of first-born children among tribes on the borders of, iv. 181 sq.; the Falashas of, viii. 266 $n.^1$

Abyssinian festival of Mascal or the Cross, ix. 133 sq.

Acacia, Osiris in the, vi. 111; the heart in the flower of the, xi. 135 sq.

—— -tree, worshipped in Patagonia, ii. 16; sacred in Arabia, ii. 42

Acacia albida, used in kindling fire by friction, ii. 210

—— catechu, used in kindling fire by friction, ii. 249

—— Suma, ii. 250 $n.$

Academy at Athens, funeral games held in the, iv. 96

Acagchemem tribe of California, their worship of the sacred buzzard, viii. 170 sq.

Acaill, Book of, on kings of Ireland, iv. 39

Acarnanian story of Prince Sunless, x. 21

Acatay mita, festival to make alligator pears ripen, ii. 98

Accession of a Shilluk king, ceremonies at the, iv. 23 sq.

Accoleian family, coins of the, ii. 185

Accusations of ritual murders brought against the Jews, ix. 394 sqq.

Achaia, subject to earthquakes, v. 202
Acharaca, cave of Pluto at, v. 205 *sq.*
Acharnae, Attic township, Dionysus Ivy at, vii. 4
Achelous and Dejanira, ii. 161 *sq.*
Achern, St. John's fires at, x. 168
Achilles at the court of Lycomedes, ii. 278 ; his hair devoted to the river Sperchius, iii. 261
Achinese, the, of northern Sumatra, their observation of the Pleiades, vii. 315
Achinese fishermen, special vocabulary employed by, at sea, iii. 409
Achterneed, in Ross-shire, Beltane cakes at, x. 153
Acilisena, in Armenia, temple and worship of Anaitis at, v. 38, ix. 369 *n.*[1]
Acireale, in Sicily, Midsummer fires at, x. 210
Acorns as an attribute of Artemis, i. 38 *n.*[1] ; shamans responsible for crop of edible, i. 358 ; found in the lake-dwellings of Europe, ii. 353 ; as food, ii. 353, 355 *sq.* ; as fodder for swine, ii. 354, 356
Acosta, J. de, early Spanish historian of Peru and Mexico, ix. 276 *n.*[1] ; on the Peruvian Mother of the Maize, vii. 171 *sq.* ; on the sacramental eating of bread among the ancient Mexicans, viii. 86 *sqq.* ; on the annual expulsion of evils in Peru, ix. 131 *n.* ; on Aztec custom of sacrificing human representatives of the gods, ix. 275 *sqq.* ; on the sacrifice of the human representative of Quetzalcoatl, ix. 281 *sqq.*
Acre, in Syria, residence of the head of the Babites, i. 402
Acropolis of Athens, the sacred serpent on the, iv. 86 *sq.* ; Sacred Ploughing at foot of the, vii. 108 *n.*[4], 109 *n.*[1] ; annual sacrifice of a goat on the, viii. 41
Actium, games celebrated at, vii. 80, 85
Acts, tabooed, iii. 101 *sqq.*
Açvina, an Indian month, iv. 124
Adad, Syrian king, v. 15 ; Babylonian and Assyrian god of thunder and lightning, v. 163
Adad-Nirari, king of Assyria, ix. 370 *n.*[1]
Adair, James, on the self-inflicted mortifications of the Creek Indians in war, iii. 161 *sqq.* ; on the refusal of American Indians to taste blood, iii. 240 ; on Indian belief in homoeopathic magic of animal flesh, viii. 139 ; on American Indian custom of cutting out the sinew of the thigh of deer, viii. 264 ; his discovery of the Ten Lost Tribes in America, viii. 264 *n.*[4]
Adaklu, Mount, in West Africa, evils sent away to, ix. 135 *sq.*, 206 *sq.*

Adam, man in Lent called, ix. 214
—— and Eve, suggested explanation of their aprons of fig-leaves, ix. 259 *n.*[3]
—— of Bremen, on the thunder-god Thor, ii. 364
Adams, J., on divinity of king of Benin, i. 396
Adana in Cilicia, v. 169 *n.*[3]
Adar, a Jewish month, vii. 259 *n.*[1], ix. 361, 394, 397, 398, 415
Adder stones among the Celts, x. 15
Addison, Joseph, on the Italian opera, ii. 299 ; on the grotto *dei cani* at Naples, v. 205 *n.*[1] ; on witchcraft in Switzerland, ix. 42 *n.*[2]
Adelaide tribe of South Australia, namesakes of the dead change their names in the, iii. 355
Adeli, the, of the Slave Coast, their festival of new yams, viii. 116
Adhar, a Persian month, vi. 68
Adivi or forest Gollas of Southern India, seclusion of women at childbirth among the, iii. 149 *sq.*
Adom-melech or Uri-melech, king of Byblus, v. 14, 17
Adon, a Semitic title, v. 6 *sq.*, 16 *sq.*, 20, 49 *n.*[7]
Adonai, title of Jehovah, v. 6 *sq.*
Adoni, "my lord," Semitic title, v. 7 ; names compounded with, v. 17
Adoni-bezek, king of Jerusalem, v. 17
Adoni-jah, elder brother of King Solomon, v. 51 *n.*[2]
Adoni-zedek, king of Jerusalem, v. 17
Adonis at Byblus, i. 30 ; myth of, v. 3 *sqq.* ; Greek worship of, v. 6 ; in Greek mythology, v. 10 *sqq.* ; in Syria, v. 13 *sqq.* ; monuments of, v. 29 ; in Cyprus, v. 31 *sqq.*, 49 ; identified with Osiris, v. 32 ; mourning for, at Byblus, v. 38 ; said to be the fruit of incest, v. 43 ; his mother Myrrha, v. 43 ; son of Theias, v. 43 *n.*[4], 55 *n.*[4] ; the son of Cinyras, v. 49 ; the title of the sons of Phoenician kings in Cyprus, v. 49 ; his violent death, v. 55 ; music in the worship of, v. 55 ; sacred prostitution in the worship of, v. 57 ; inspired prophets in worship of, v. 76 ; human representatives of, perhaps burnt, v. 110 ; doves burned in honour of, v. 147 ; personated by priestly kings, v. 223 ; the ritual of, v. 223 *sqq.* ; his death and resurrection represented in his rites, v. 224 *sq.*, ix. 398 ; festivals of, v. 224 *sqq.* ; flutes played in the laments for, v. 225 *n.*[3] ; the ascension of, v. 225 ; images of, thrown into the sea or springs, v. 225, 227 *n.*[3], 236 ; born from a myrrh-tree, v. 227, vi. 110 ; bewailed by Argive women, v. 227 *n.* ;

analogy of his rites to Indian and European ceremonies, v. 227 ; his death and resurrection interpreted as representations of the decay and revival of vegetation, v. 227 *sqq.* ; interpreted as the sun, v. 228 ; interpreted by the ancients as the god of the reaped and sprouting corn, v. 229 ; as a corn-spirit, v. 230 *sqq.* ; hunger the root of the worship of, v. 231 ; perhaps originally a personification of wild vegetation, especially grass and trees, v. 233 ; the gardens of, v. 236 *sqq.* ; rain - charm in the rites of, v. 237 ; resemblance of his rites to the festival of Easter, v. 254 *sqq.*, 306 ; worshipped at Bethlehem, v. 257 *sqq.* ; and the planet Venus as the Morning Star, v. 258 *sq.* ; sometimes identified with Attis, v. 263 ; swine not eaten by worshippers of, v. 265 ; rites of, among the Greeks, v. 298 ; lamented by women at Byblus, vi. 23 ; and Linus, vii. 216, 258 ; at Alexandria, vii. 263, ix. 390 ; and the boar, viii. 22 *sq.* ; his marriage with Ishtar (Aphrodite), ix. 401. *See also* Tammuz

Adonis and Aphrodite, v. 11 *sq.*, 29, 280, xi. 294 *sq.* ; their marriage celebrated at Alexandria, v. 224 ; perhaps personated by human couples, ix. 386

—— and Attis identified with Dionysus, vi. 127 *n.*

——, Attis, Osiris, their mythical similarity, v. 6, vi. 201

—— and Osiris, similarity between their rites, vi. 127

—— or Tammuz, ii. 346 ; the summer lamentations for, iv. 7

—— and Venus (Aphrodite), i. 21, 25, 40, 41

——, the river, its valley, v. 28 *sqq.* ; annual discoloration of the, v. 30, 225

Adoption, pretence of birth at, i. 74 *sq.*

Adrammelech, burnt sacrifice of children to, iv. 171

Adultery of wife thought to spoil the luck of her absent husband, i. 123, 124 *sq.*, 128 ; supposed to blight the fruits of the earth, ii. 107 *sq.*, 114

Aeacus, the son of Zeus by Aegina, ii. 278, 359 *n.*[1] ; king of Aegina, the dispersal of his descendants, ii. 278 ; obtains rain from his father Zeus, ii. 359

Aedepsus, hot springs of Hercules at, v. 211 *sq.*

Aedesius, Sextilius Agesilaus, dedicates altar to Attis, v. 275 *n.*[1]

Aegina, daughter of Asopus and mother of Aeacus, ii. 359 *n.*[8]

——, island, Panhellenian Zeus worshipped on the peak of, ii. 359

Aegipan and Hermes, v. 157

Aegira in Achaia, inspired priestess of Earth at, i. 381 *sq.*

Aegis, Athena and the, viii. 40, 41

Aegisthus, the murder of, i. 12 *n.* ; at Mycenae, his marriage with the widow of his predecessor, ii. 281

—— and Agamemnon, ix. 19

Aegosthena, annual kingship at, i. 46

Aelian, on impregnation of Judean maid by serpent, v. 81 ; on a Babylonian king Gilgamus, ix. 372 *n.*[1]

Aelst, Peter van, painter, xi. 36

Aenach, Irish fair, iv. 100 *n.*[1]

Aeneas and the Golden Bough, i. 11, ii. 379, xi. 285, 293 *sq.* ; his vision of the glories of Rome, ii. 178 ; his disappearance in a thunderstorm, ii. 181 ; worshipped after death as Jupiter Indiges, ii. 181 ; and the Game of Troy, iv. 76

—— and Dido, iii. 312, 313, v. 114 *n.*[1]

Aeolus, King of the Winds, i. 326

Aeschines, spurious epistles of, ii. 162 *n.*[2]

Aeschylus, on Typhon, v. 156

Aesculapius brings Hippolytus or Virbius to life, i. 20, iv. 214 ; horses dedicated by Hippolytus to, i. 21 *n.*[2], viii. 41 *n.*[5] ; at Cos, ii. 10 ; in relation to serpents, v. 80 *sq.* ; reputed father of Aratus, v. 80 *sq.* ; his shrines at Sicyon and Titane, v. 81 ; his dispute with Hercules, v. 209 *sq.* ; said to have raised Hippolytus from the dead, viii. 41 *n.*[5] ; at Pergamus, viii. 85 ; at Epidaurus, ix. 47

Aeson and Medea, v. 181 *n.*[1], viii. 143

Aetna, Latin poem, v. 221 *n.*[4]

Aetolians, the, shod only on one foot, iii. 311

Afars. *See* Danakils

Afghanistan, ceremony at the reception of strangers in, iii. 108

Africa, treatment of the navel - string and afterbirth in, i. 195 *sq.* ; rise of magicians, especially rain-makers, to chieftainship and kingship in, i. 342 *sqq.*, 352 ; human gods in, i. 392 *sqq.* ; belief in, that sexual crimes disturb the course of nature, ii. 111 *sq.* ; the diffusion of round huts in, ii. 227 *n.*[3] ; corpulence as a beauty in, ii. 297 ; rules of life or taboos observed by kings in, iii. 5 *sq.*, 8 *sqq.* ; detention of souls by sorcerers in, iii. 70 *sq.* ; fear of being photographed in, iii. 97 *sq.* ; cleanliness from superstitious motives in, iii. 158 *n.*[1] ; smith's craft regarded as uncanny in, iii. 236 *n.*[5] ; reluctance of people to tell their own names in, iii. 329 *sq.* ; the Bogos of, iii. 337 ; names of animals and things tabooed in, iii. 400 *sq.*; belief as to trans-migration of the dead into serpents in, iv. 84 ; succession to the soul in, iv. 200 *sq.*; serpents as reincarnations of the dead in, v. 82 *sqq.*; infant burial in, v. 91 *sq.*; reincarnation of the dead in, v. 91 *sq.*; annual festivals of the dead in, vi. 66 ; worship of dead kings and chiefs in, vi. 160 *sqq.*; supreme gods in, vi. 165, 173 *sq.*, 174, 186, with *n.*⁵, 187 *n.*¹, 188 *sq.*, 190; worship of ancestral spirits among the Bantu tribes of, vi. 174 *sqq.*; inheritance of the kingship under mother-kin in, vi. 211 ; cat's cradle in, vii. 103 *n.*¹; woman's share in agriculture among the tribes of, vii. 113 *sqq.*; observation of the Pleiades by agricultural tribes in, vii. 315 *sqq.*; sacrifice of first-fruits in, viii. 109 *sqq.*; belief as to the homoeopathic magic of a flesh diet in, viii. 140 *sqq.*; crocodiles respected in, viii. 213 *sq.*; sickness transferred to animals in, ix. 31 *sq.*; girls secluded at puberty in, x. 22 *sqq.*; dread and seclusion of women at menstruation in, x. 79 *sqq,*; birth-trees in, xi. 160 *sqq.*; use of bull-roarers in, xi. 229 *n.*, 232

Africa, British Central, the tribes of, their custom of carrying about fire, ii. 259 ; the Yaos of, iii. 97 *sq.*, viii. 111 ; customs observed after a death in, iii. 286 ; the Angoni of, iv. 156 *n.*², viii. 149; the Nyanja-speaking tribes of, viii. 26 ; crops guarded against baboons and wild pigs in, viii. 32 ; flesh and hearts of lions eaten to make eaters brave in, viii. 142 ; parts of brave enemies eaten to make the eaters brave in, viii. 149 ; the Anyanja of, x. 81

——, British East, the Akikuyu (Kikuyu) of, ii. 44, iii. 175, 214, vii. 317, ix. 32, x. 81, xi. 262 *sq.*; the Nandi of, ii. 112, iii. 141, 175, 423, vii. 117, 317, viii. 64, xi. 229 *n.*; the Ketosh of, iii. 176 ; the En-jemusi of, vii. 118 ; the Suk of, vii. 118, viii. 84, 142, x. 81; observation of the Pleiades by tribes in, vii. 317 ; the Akamba of, viii. 113, ix. 122 *n.*; ceremony of new fire in, x. 135 *sq.*

—— Central, the Banyoro of, i. 348 ; the Lendu of, i. 348 ; the Basoga of, ii. 19, 112 ; the Baganda of, ii. 246, 269, iii. 78, vii. 118 ; the pygmies of, ii. 255, iii. 282 ; the Monbuttu of, ii. 297, iii. 118, vii. 119 ; reception of strangers in, iii. 108 ; the Latuka of, iii. 245, 284 ; the Madi or Moru tribe of, iii. 277, viii. 314, ix. 217 ; the Wahoko of, iii. 278 ; the Wanyoro (Banyoro)

of, iii. 278 ; the Fors of, iii. 281 ; Unyoro in, iii. 291 *sq.*, iv. 34 ; the Akamba of, iii. 353 ; the Nandi of, iii. 353 ; the Bahima of, iii. 375, viii. 288, ix. 32 ; the Niam-Niam of, vii. 119 ; the Wanyamwesi of, viii. 227

Africa, East, the Wambugwe of, i. 290, 342, iv. 65 ; the Wataturu of, i. 342 *sq.*, viii. 84 ; the Wanika of, ii. 12, iii. 247 ; the Tanga coast of, ii. 34 ; the Wakamba of, ii. 46 ; the Wabondei of, ii. 47, iii. 272, viii. 142 ; the Masai of, ii. 210 ; the Winam-wanga of, ii. 256 *n.*¹; the Wiwa of, ii. 256 *n.*¹; the Jaggas of, ii. 259 ; the Bogos of, ii. 267 *n.*⁴; avoidance of parents-in-law in, iii. 85 ; the Wa-teita of, iii. 98 ; custom of elephant-hunters in, iii. 107 ; the Nubas of, iii. 132 ; the Bageshu of, iii. 174 ; the Akamba of, iii. 204 ; the Akikuyu of, iii. 204 ; the Warundi of, iii. 225 *n.*; the Wajagga of, iii. 286, 290 ; the Barea of, iii. 337 ; the Masai of, iii. 354 ; the Waziguas of, iii. 400 ; infanticide in, iv. 196 ; the Danakils or Afars of, iv. 200 ; the Arabs of, viii. 164 ; propitiation of dead lions in, viii. 228 ; ceremony of the new fire in, x. 135 ; the Swahili of, xi. 160

——, German East, viii. 142 ; the Wagogo of, i. 343, iii. 186 *n.*¹, viii. 26, 149, 276, ix. 6 ; the Wahehe of, iii. 86 *n.*, viii. 26 ; the Wageia of, iii. 177 ; continence of hunters in, iii. 196 *sq.*; the Wadowe of, vii. 118 ; the Waheia of, viii. 26 ; the Wajagga of, viii. 276, xi. 160 ; the Washamba of, ix. 29, xi. 183 ; the Bondeis of, xi. 263 ; the Wadoe of, xi. 312

——, German South-West, the Ovambo of, xi. 183

——, North, magical images in, i. 65 *sq.*; contagious magic of footprints in, i. 210 ; the Arabs of, i. 277 ; artificial fertilization of fig-trees in, ii. 314 ; charms to render bridegrooms impotent in, iii. 300 *sq.*; festivals of swinging in, iv. 284; custom of bathing at Mid-summer among the Mohammedan peoples of, v. 249 ; cairns in, ix. 21 ; Mohammedan reverence for living saints in, ix. 22 ; popular cure for toothache in, ix. 62 ; tribes of, their expulsion of demons, ix. 110 *sq.*; Mid-summer fires in, x. 213 *sqq.*

——, South, use of rat's hair as a charm in, i. 151 ; the Herero of, i. 209 ; stopping rain by means of a rabbit in, i. 295 ; the Bechuanas of, i. 313 ; way of retarding the sun in, i. 318 ; the

Caffres of, i. 321, iii. 87 ; frightening away a storm in, i. 327 ; the Chevas of, i. 331 *n.*[2] ; the Tumbucas of, i. 331 *n.*[2]; chiefs as rain-makers in, i. 350 *sqq.* ; the Mashona of, i. 393 ; the Maraves of, ii. 31, ix. 19 ; the Ovambo of, ii. 264, iii. 176 ; the Ba-Pedi of, iii. 141, 148, 163, 202 ; the Ba-Thonga of, iii. 141, 148, 163, 202 ; Bantu tribes of, iii. 152, viii. 111, ix. 77 *sq.* ; seclusion and purification of manslayers in, iii. 174 *sq.* ; disposal of cut hair and nails in, iii. 278 ; magic use of spittle in, iii. 288 ; the Makalaka of, iii. 369 ; belief as to stepping over persons or things among the tribes of, iii. 423 ; the Baronga of, iv. 61 ; crops devastated by wild pigs in, viii. 32 ; the Matabele of, viii. 70 ; Caffre remedy for caterpillars in, viii. 280 ; heaps of sticks or stones to which passers-by add, in, ix. 11 ; dread of demons in, ix. 77 *sq.*; sacrificial fire in, ix. 391 *n.*[4]; the Thonga of, xi. 297
Africa, South-East, the Hlubies and Swazies of, i. 249 ; the Baronga of, i. 267 ; many tribes of, will not cut down timber while the corn is green, ii. 49 ; the Bantu tribes of, ii. 210 ; the Barotse of, iii. 107 ; custom of infanticide in some tribes of, iv. 183 ; flesh of lions and leopards eaten by warriors in, viii. 142 ; rites of initiation in, viii. 148 ; inoculation of warriors in, viii. 159 ; hunters cut out right eye of game in, viii. 268 ; prayers at cairns in, ix. 29
——, South-West, the Herero of, i. 211 ; the Ovambo of, iii. 227, viii. 109
——, West, rain-making in, i. 249 *sq.* ; magical functions of chiefs in, i. 349 *sq.* ; the Banjars of, i. 353 ; the Yorubas of, i. 364, iv. 41, viii. 98 ; reverence for silk-cotton trees in, ii. 14 *sq.* ; kings forced to accept office in, iii. 17 *sq.* ; fetish kings in, iii. 22 *sqq.* ; traps set for souls by wizards in, iii. 70 *sq.* ; the Bavili of, iii. 78 ; purification after a journey in, iii. 112 ; custom as to blood shed on ground in, iii. 245, 246 ; hair, nails, and teeth as rain-charms in, iii. 271 ; shorn hair burnt or buried for fear of witchcraft in, iii. 281 ; the Kru negroes of, iii. 322 *sq.* ; Human Leopard Societies of, iv. 83 ; human sacrifices at king's funeral in, iv. 117 ; stories of the type of Beauty and the Beast in, iv. 128 *sq.*, 130 *n.*[1] ; sacrificial blood smeared on doorways in, iv. 176 *n.*[1] ; sacred men and women in, v. 65 *sqq.* ; human sacrifices in, vi. 99 *n.*[2] ; human sacrifices for the crops in, vii. 239 ; the Kimbunda of, viii. 152 ; the Beku of, viii. 163 ; propitiation of dead leopards in, viii. 228 *sqq.* ; bones of sacrificial victims not broken in, viii. 258 *n.*[2]; belief in demons among the negroes of, ix. 74 *sqq.* ; dances at sowing in, ix. 234 ; theory of an external soul embodied in an animal prevalent in, xi. 200 *sqq.* ; ritual of death and resurrection at initiation in, xi. 251 *sqq.*
African stories of the external soul, xi. 148 *sqq.* ; Balders, xi. 312 *sqq.*
—— hunters, ceremonies of purification observed by, iii. 220 *sq.*
—— kings forbidden to see their mothers, iii. 86 ; thought to render themselves immortal by their sorceries, iv. 9
—— tribes, household fires extinguished after a death in, ii. 267 *n.*[4]; descent of property and power to sister's children among, ii. 285 ; combination of the elective with the hereditary principle in regulating the descent of kingships or chiefships among, ii. 292 *sqq.* ; believe that their dead kings turn into lions, leopards, pythons, etc., iv. 84
Afterbirth (placenta), portion of a man's spirit supposed to reside in his, i. 100 ; contagious magic of, i. 182-201 ; part of child's spirit in, i. 184 ; buried under a tree, i. 186, 187, 188, 194, 195, xi. 160 *sq.*, 162, 163, 164, 165; hung on a tree, i. 186, 187, 189, 190, 191, 194, 198, 199 ; thrown into the sea, i. 187, 190 ; regarded as brother or sister of child, i. 189, 191, 192, 193, xi. 162 *n.*[2]; seat of external soul, i. 193 *sq.*, 200 *sq.* ; regarded as a second child, i. 195, xi. 162 *n.*[2]; of cows, treatment of the, i. 198 *sq.* ; regarded as a person's double or twin, vi. 169 *sq.*; of child animated by a ghost and sympathetically connected with a banana - tree, xi. 162 ; and navel-string regarded as guardian angels of the man, xi. 162 *n.*[2]; regarded as a guardian spirit, xi. 223 *n.*[2] *See also* Afterbirths *and* Placenta
Afterbirths buried in banana groves, v. 93 ; regarded as twins of the children, v. 93 ; Shilluk kings interred where their afterbirths are buried, vi. 162
Agamemnon, sceptre of, worshipped as a god, i. 365 ; said to have reigned in his wife's home, Lacedaemon, ii. 279
—— and Aegisthus, ix. 19
Agar Dinka, rain-makers killed among the, iv. 33
Agaric growing on birch-trees, superstitions as to, x. 148

Agariste, daughter of Clisthenes, the wooing of, ii. 307

Agathias, on the identification of Anaitis and Aphrodite, ix. 369 n.[1]; on Sandes, ix. 389

Agathocles, his siege of Carthage, iv. 167

Agbasia, West African god, sacred slaves of, v. 79 ; prayers to, viii. 59, 60

Agdestis, a man-monster in the myth of Attis, v. 269

Age of Magic, i. 235, 237

Agesipolis, king of Sparta, his conduct in an earthquake, v. 196

Aglu, New Year fires at, x. 217

Agni, Indian god, viii. 120, ix. 410, x. 99 n.[2]; the fire-god, ii. 230, 249, xi. 1, 296 ; addressed at marriage, ii. 230

Agnihotris, Brahman fire-priests, ii. 247 *sqq.*

Agnus castus strewed by married women under their beds at the Thesmophoria, vii. 116 n.[2]; used in ceremony of beating, ix. 252, 257

Agome, in Togoland, ceremonies observed by hunters at, viii. 229

Agraulus, daughter of Cecrops, worshipped at Salamis in Cyprus, v. 145, 146

Agricultural peoples worship the moon, vi. 138 *sq.*

—— stage of society, the, viii. 35, 37

—— year determined by observation of the Pleiades, vii. 313 *sqq.* ; expulsions of demons timed to coincide with seasons of the, ix. 225

Agriculture, religious objections to, v. 88 *sqq.*, vii. 93, 108 ; in the hands of women in the Pelew Islands, vi. 206 *sq.*; its tendency to produce a conservative character, vi. 217 *sq.*; magical significance of games in primitive, vii. 92 *sqq.*; origin of, vii. 128 *sq.*; woman's part in primitive, vii. 113 *sqq.*

Agriculture of the Nabataeans, ii. 100, 346 n.[3]

Agrigentum, Empedocles at, i. 390 ; Phalaris of, iv. 75

Agrionia, a festival at Orchomenus, iv. 163

Agrippa, king of Judea, his mockery at Alexandria, ix. 418

Agrippina, her marriage with Claudius, ii. 129 n.[1]

Agu, Mount, in Togo, wind-fetish on, i. 327 ; fetish priest on, iii. 5

Ague, transferred to trees, ix. 56, 57 *sq.*; Suffolk cure for, ix. 68 ; Midsummer bonfires deemed a cure for, x. 162 ; leaps across the Midsummer bonfires thought to be a preventive of, x. 174

Agutainos of the Philippines, customs observed by widows among the, iii. 144

Agweh on the Slave Coast, custom at end of mourning at, iii. 286 ; custom of widows at, xi. 18 *sq.*

Agylla, in Etruria, funeral games at, iv. 95

Ahasuerus, King, ix. 397, 401 ; the Hebrew equivalent of Xerxes, ix. 360

Ahaz, King, his sacrifice of his children, iv. 169 *sq.*

Ahlen, in Munsterland, the Yule log at, x. 247

Ahne-bergen, near Stade, thresher of last corn called Corn-pug at, vii. 273

Ahriman, the devil of the Persians, x. 95

Ahts or Nootka Indians of Vancouver Island regard the moon as the husband of the sun, vi. 139 n.[1] ; seclusion of girls at puberty among the, x. 43 *sq.*

Ahura Mazda, the supreme being of the Persians, x. 95

Ai San Bushmen, their fire-sticks, ii. 218 n.[1]

Aijaruc, a Tartar princess, ii. 306

Ain, de l', French department, leaf-clad mummer on May Day in, ii. 81 n.[3] ; Lenten fires in, x. 114

Aino fishermen, their ways of making rain, i. 288

—— hunters, their custom at killing a fox, viii. 267

—— type of animal sacrament, viii. 312 *sq.*

—— women may not mention their husbands' names, iii. 337

Ainos, their contagious magic of footprints, i. 212 ; their rain-making, i. 251, 253 ; their fear of whirlwinds, i. 331 n.[2]; their ceremony at eating new millet, viii. 52 ; their custom as to eating the heads of otters and the hearts of water-ousels, viii. 144 ; their worship of bears, viii. 180 *sqq.*; their worship of eagle-owls, eagles, and hawks, viii. 199 *sq.*; thank the sword-fish which they kill, viii. 251 ; their customs in regard to the first fish of the season, viii. 255 *sq.* ; their propitiation of mice, viii. 278 ; their ambiguous attitude towards the bear, viii. 310 *sq.*

—— of Japan, their use of magical images, i. 60 ; reluctant to name the dead, iii. 353 ; their custom of killing bears ceremonially, viii. 180 *sqq.* ; their mourning caps, x. 20 ; their use of mugwort in exorcism, xi. 60 ; their veneration for mistletoe, xi. 79

—— of Saghalien, pregnant women forbidden to spin among the, i. 114 ; bear-festivals, viii. 188 *sqq.*

Aiora, festival of swinging, at Athens, i. 46 n.[1]

Air, prohibition to be uncovered in the open, iii. 3, 14 ; thought to be poisoned at eclipses, x. 162 n.

Airi, a deity of North-West India, his worshippers inspired, v. 170

Airu, Assyrian month corresponding to May, ii. 130

Aïsawa or Isowa, order of saints in Morocco, devour live goats, vii. 21 *sq.*

Aisne, Midsummer fires in the department of, x. 187

Ait Sadden, a tribe of Morocco, their tug-of-war, ix. 182

—— Warain, a Berber tribe of Morocco, their tug-of-war, ix. 178 *sq.*

—— Yusi, a tribe of Morocco, their tug-of-war, ix. 182

Aitan, a Khasi goddess, ix. 173

Aivilik, the Esquimaux of, i. 121

Aix, squibs at Midsummer at, x. 193; Midsummer king at, x. 194, xi. 25

Aiyar, N. Subramhanya, on Indian dancing-girls, v. 63 *sqq.*

Ajax and Teucer, names of priestly kings of Olba, v. 144 *sq.*, 161

Ajumba hunter, his apologies to the hippopotamus which he had killed, viii. 235

Akamba of British East Africa, believe that every woman has a spiritual husband who fertilizes her, ii. 317; continence observed by them on journeys and while the cattle are at pasture, iii. 204; their offerings of first-fruits to the spirits of the dead, viii. 113; riddles asked at circumcision among the, ix. 122 *n.*; seclusion of girls at puberty among the, x. 23

—— of Central Africa, reluctant to name the dead, iii. 353

Akawés, a tribe of Garos, their harvest festival, viii. 337

Akhetaton (Tell-el-Amarna), the capital of Amenophis IV., vi. 123 *n.*[1]

Akikuyu, the, of British East Africa, ceremony of the new birth among the, i. 75 *sq.*, 96 *sq.*, xi. 262 *sq.*; worship fig-trees, ii. 44 *sq.*; worship a snake, and marry girls to the snake-god, ii. 150, v. 67 *sq.*; believe that barren women can be fertilized by the wild fig-tree, ii. 316; purification of manslayers among the, iii. 175 *sq.*; continence observed by them on journeys and while the cattle are at pasture, iii. 204; auricular confession among the, iii. 214; use of scapegoats among the, iii. 214 *sq.*; their women purified after a miscarriage in childbirth, iii. 286; their treatment of premature and unusual births, iii. 286, 287 *n.*[6]; their belief in serpents as reincarnations of the dead, v. 82, 85; transfer guilt to a goat, ix. 32; their dread of menstruous women, x. 81. *See also* Kikuyu

Akurwa, a village of the Shilluk, iv. 19, 23, 24

Alabama, harvest festival of the Indians of, viii. 72 *n.*[3]

Aladdin and the Wonderful Lamp, Roman version of, xi. 105

Alafin of Oyo, paramount king of Yoruba land, iv. 203

Alake, the, of Abeokuta, custom of cutting off the head of his corpse, iv. 203

Alaska, the Esquimaux of, i. 121, 328, iii. 145, vi. 51, ix. 124, xi. 155; the Aleuts of, iii. 207; the Kaniagmuts of, iii. 207; the Koniags of, i. 121, vi. 106; seclusion of girls at puberty among the Indians of, x. 45 *sq.*

Alaskan hunters, their respect for dead sables and beavers, viii. 238

—— islanders mistook the Russians for cuttle-fish, viii. 206

Alastir and the Bare-Stripping Hangman, Argyleshire story of, xi. 129 *sq.*

Alba, Vestal fire and Vestal virgins at, i. 13

—— Longa, the kings of, ii. 178 *sqq.*, 268 *sq.*; perhaps mimicked Latian Jupiter, ii. 187

Alban dynasty descended from a Vestal, ii. 197

—— Hills, i. 2, ii. 178

—— kings, iv. 76

—— Lake, i. 2; tradition of a submerged city in the, ii. 180, 181 *n.*

—— League, religious centre of the, ii. 187

—— Mountain, the, ii. 187 *sq.*, 202, 387

Albania, bloodstones in, i. 165; milk-stones in, i. 165; fear of portraiture in, iii. 100; expulsion of Kore on Easter Eve in, iv. 265, ix. 157; marriage custom in, vii. 246; mock lamentations for locusts and beetles in, viii. 279; Midsummer fires in, x. 212; the Yule log in, x. 264

Albanian custom of beating men and beasts in March, ix. 266

—— story of the external soul, xi. 104 *n.*[3]

Albanians of the Caucasus, did not mention the names of the dead, iii. 349; their worship of the moon, v. 73; their use of human scapegoats, ix. 218

Albano, ancient necropolis near, ii. 201

Albert, Lake, Lendu tribe of, i. 348

—— Nyanza, Lake, the Wahuma of the, i. 250; crocodiles in the, viii. 213; the Wakondyo of the, xi. 162 *sq.*

Alberti, L., on Caffre purification of lion-killer, iii. 220

Albigenses worshipped each other, i. 407

Albino sacrificed to river, ii. 158; head of secret society on the Lower Congo, xi. 251

Albinoes the offspring of the moon, v. 91
Albîrûnî, Arab geographer, on the Persian festival of the dead, vi. 68 ; on the burning of effigies of Haman at Purim, ix. 393
Alchemy leads up to chemistry, i. 374
Alcheringa, remote legendary time of the Arunta, i. 88, 98, 102
Alcibiades of Apamea, his vision of the Holy Ghost, iv. 5 n.[3]
Alcidamus wins Barce in a foot-race, ii. 300 *sq.*
Alcman on dew, vi. 137
Alcmena, her long travail with Hercules, iii. 298 *sq.*
Alcyonian Lake, Dionysus at the, vii. 15
Alder branches, sacrificial, viii. 232
Alders free from mistletoe,. xi. 315
Alectrona, daughter of the Sun, taboos observed at her sanctuary in Rhodes, viii. 45
Alençon, the Boy Bishop at, ix. 337 n.[1]
Aleutian Islands, Atkhans of the, ix. 3 ; cairns in the, ix. 16
—— hunter injured by unchastity of absent wife or sister, i. 123
Aleutians, effeminate sorcerers among the, vi. 254
Aleuts of Alaska, seclusion of successful whaler among the, iii. 207
Alexander the Great, his fiery cresset, ii. 264 ; cuts the Gordian knot, iii. 316 ; funeral games in his honour, iv. 95 ; expels a king of Paphos, v. 42 ; his fabulous birth, v. 81 ; assumes costumes of deities, v. 165 ; sacrifices to Megarsian Athena, v. 169 n.[3]
Alexander Severus, at festival of Attis, v. 273
Alexandria, festival of Adonis at, v. 224, ix. 390 ; the Serapeum at, vi. 119 n., 217 ; mockery of King Agrippa at, 418
Alexandrian calendar, used by Plutarch, vi. 84 ; used by Theophanes, ix. 395 n.[1]
—— year, the fixed, vi. 28, 92 ; Plutarch's use of the, vi. 49
Alfai, title of rain-making priest among the Barea and Kunama, ii. 3
Alfoors of Buru, names of relations tabooed among the, iii. 341
—— or Toradjas of Central Celebes, their custom at child-birth, iii. 33 ; taboos observed by their priest, iii. 129 ; priest with unshorn hair among the, iii. 260 ; riddles among the, ix. 122 n. ; their custom at the smelting of iron, xi. 154 ; their doctrine of the plurality of souls, xi. 222. *See also* Toradjas
—— of Ceram, their high-priest regarded as a demigod, i. 400

Alfoors of Halmahera, name of wife's father tabooed among the, iii. 341 ; their expulsion of the devil, ix. 112
—— of Minahassa, inspired priest among the, i. 382 *sq.* ; ceremony at housewarming among the, iii. 63 *sq.*; names of relations tabooed among the, iii. 340 *sq.* ; their custom as to the first rice sowed and reaped, viii. 54 ; attempt to deceive demons of sickness, viii. 100
—— of Poso, in Central Celebes, their belief as to demons of trees, ii. 35 ; abduction of souls by demons among the, iii. 62 *sq.* ; will not pronounce their own names, iii. 332 ; names of relations tabooed among the, iii. 340
Algeds, rain-maker among the, ii. 3
Algeria, rain-making in, i. 250 ; the Aisawa sect in, vii. 22 n.[1] ; fever transferred to tortoise in, ix. 31 ; popular cure by knocking nails in, ix. 60 ; Midsummer fires in, x. 213
——, the Arabs of, avoid using the proper name for lion, iii. 400 ; tale of, iv. 130 n.[1]
Algidus, Mount, its oak forests, ii. 187, 380 ; a haunt of Diana, ii. 380
Algiers, the Moors of, light no fires after a death, ii. 268 n.
Algonquin Indians caught souls in nets, iii. 69 *sq.*
Algonquins or Algonkins, the, their treatment of the navel-string, i. 197; marry their fishing-nets to girls, ii. 147 *sq.* ; their women seek to be impregnated by the souls of the dying, iv. 199
Alice Springs in Central Australia, i. 259, xi. 238 ; magical stones at, i. 162
Aline, Loch, fishing magic on, i. 110
All-healer, name applied to mistletoe, xi. 77, 79, 82
All Saints, Feast of, perhaps substituted for an old pagan festival of the dead, vi. 82 *sq.*
All Saints' Day, November 1st, old Celtic New Year's Day, x. 225 ; omens on, x. 240 ; bonfires on, x. 246 ; sheep passed through a hoop on, xi. 184
All Souls, Festival of, iv. 98, vi. 51 *sqq.*, vii. 30, x. 223 *sq.*, 225 n.[2] ; originally a pagan festival of the dead, vi. 81 ; instituted by Odilo, abbot of Clugny, vi. 82
All Souls' College, Oxford, the Boy Bishop at, ix. 337
Allallu bird beloved by Ishtar, ix. 371
Allan, John Hay, on the Hays of Errol, xi. 283
Allandur temple, at St. Thomas's Mount, Madras, fire-festival at, xi. 8 n.[1]
Allatu, Babylonian goddess, v. 9

Allerton, the Boy Bishop at, ix. 338
Allhallow Even, the thirty-first of October, Lords of Misrule on, ix. 332
All-Hallows (All Saints' Day), iii. 11, 12
Allifae in Samnium, baths of Hercules at, v. 213 *n.*²
Alligator pears, Peruvian ceremony to make them ripen, ii. 98
Alligators, souls of dead in, viii. 297
Allumba, in Central Australia, magic tree at, i. 145 *sq.*
Almagest, the, vii. 259 *n.*¹
Almo, procession to the river, in the rites of Attis, v. 273
Almond causes virgin to conceive, v. 263 ; the father of all things, v. 263 *sq.*
—— -trees, mistletoe on, xi. 316
Almora, in Kumaon, ix. 197
A-Louyi, seclusion of girls at puberty among the, x. 28 *n.*⁵
Alpach, valley in Tyrol, the Wheat-bride or Rye-bride at harvest in, vii. 163
Alpheus, the sacred, ii. 8
Alqamar, tribe of nomads in Hadramaut, their way of stopping rain, i. 252
Alsace, May-trees in, ii. 64 ; the Little May Rose in, ii. 74 ; stuffed goat or fox at threshing in, vii. 287, 297 ; Midsummer fires in, x. 169 ; cats burnt in Easter bonfires in, xi. 40
Alt Lest, in Silesia, the binder of the last sheaf called the Beggar-man at, vii. 231
—— -Pillau, in Samland, harvest custom at, vii. 139
Altars, bloodless, ix. 307
Altdorf and Weingarten, in Swabia, the Carnival Fool on Ash Wednesday at, iv. 232
Althenneberg, in Bavaria, Easter fires at, x. 143 *sq.*
Altisheim, in Swabia, the last sheaf called the Old Woman at, vii. 136
Altmark, custom with birch branches at Whitsuntide in the, ii. 64 ; the May Bride at Whitsuntide in the, ii. 95 ; the He-goat at reaping in the, vii. 287 ; Easter bonfires in the, x. 140, 142
Alum burnt at Midsummer, ix. 214
Alungu, seclusion of girls at puberty among the, x. 24 *sq.*
Alur, a tribe of the Upper Nile, bury their cut hair and nails, iii. 277 *sq.* ; their fear of crocodiles, viii. 214 ; their treatment of insanity, x. 64
Alus, sanctuary of Laphystian Zeus at, iv. 161, 164 ; custom of sacrificing princes at, vii. 25
Alvarado, Pedro de, Spanish general, kills a *nagual*, xi. 214
Alyattes, king of Lydia, v. 133 *n.*¹
Alynomus, king of Paphos, v. 43 *n.*¹

Amadhlozi, Zulu ancestral spirits in serpent form, xi. 211 *n.*²
Ama-terasu, Japanese goddess of the Sun, vii. 212
Amambwe, a Bantu tribe of Northern Rhodesia, believe that their head chief at death turns into a lion, vi. 193, viii. 287 ; seclusion of girls at puberty among the, x. 24 *sq.*
Amapondo country, cairn to which passers-by added stones in the, ix. 30 *n.*²
Amasis, king of Egypt, substitutes images for human victims, iv. 217 ; his body burnt by Cambyses, v. 176 *n.*²
Amata, "Beloved," title of Vestals, ii. 197
Amata, wife of King Latinus, ii. 197
Amathus, in Cyprus, Adonis and Melcarth at, v. 32, 117 ; statue of lion-slaying god found at, v. 117
Amatongo, ancestral spirits (Zulu term), v. 74 *n.*⁴, vi. 184, xi. 212 *n.*
Amaxosa Caffres propitiate the elephants which they kill, viii. 227
Amazon, Indians at the mouth of the, ix. 264 ; ordeals of young men among the Indians of the, x. 62 *sq.*
Amazons set up a statue of Artemis under an oak, i. 38 *n.*¹
—— of Dahomey ate the hearts of brave foes to make themselves brave, viii. 149
Amazulu, their observation of the Pleiades, vii. 316
Ambabai, an Indian goddess, v. 243
Ambala District, Punjaub, rebirth of children in the, v. 94
Ambamba, in West Africa, death, resurrection, and new birth in, xi. 256
Ambarvalia, cattle crowned at the, ii. 127 *n.*² ; an agricultural festival of ancient Italy, ix. 359
Amboin, in Angola, new fire at, ii. 262
Amboyna, custom as to children's cast teeth in, i. 179 ; rice in bloom treated like a pregnant woman in, ii. 28 ; ceremony to fertilize clove-trees in, ii. 100 ; recovery of lost souls in, iii. 66 *sq.* ; abduction of souls by doctors in, iii. 73 ; fear to lose the shadow at noon in, iii. 87 ; sick people sprinkled with pungent spices in, iii. 105 ; new fruits offered to the gods in, viii. 123 ; belief in spirits in, ix. 85 ; disease-transference in, ix. 187 ; hair of criminals cut in, xi. 158
Ambras, Midsummer customs at, x. 173
Amedzowe, the spirit land, viii. 105
Amei Awa, a Kayan god, vii. 93
Amélineau, E., discovers the tomb of Egyptian King Khent, vi. 21 *n.*¹

Amelioration in the character of the gods, iv. 136

Amenophis III., king of Egypt, birth of, ii. 131 *sqq.* ; his birth represented on the monuments, iii. 28

Amenophis IV., king of Egypt, his attempt to abolish all gods but the sun-god, vi. 123 *sqq.*

Ameretât, a Persian archangel, ix. 373 *n.*[1]

America, treatment of the navel-string and afterbirth in, i. 195 *sqq.* ; the breach of England with, i. 216 ; association of the frog with rain in, i. 292 *n.*[3] ; reincarnation of the dead in, v. 91 ; the moon worshipped by the agricultural Indians of tropical, vi. 138 ; cat's cradle in, vii. 103 *n.*[1] ; the Corn-mother in, vii. 171 *sqq.*

——, Central, the Pipiles of, ii. 98 ; the Indians of, practise continence for the sake of the crops, ii. 105 ; the Quiches of, viii. 134 ; the Mosquito Indians of, viii. 258 *n.*[2]; the Mosquito territory in, x. 86

——, North, the Natchez of, i. 249 ; the Omahas of, i. 249 ; power of medicine-men in, i. 356 *sqq.* ; the Hidatsa Indians of, ii. 12 ; Indians of, their dread and avoidance of menstruous women, iii. 145 *sq.*, x. 87 *sqq.* ; Indians of, will not eat blood, iii. 240 ; sticks or stones piled on scenes of violent death in, ix. 15 ; Indians of, not allowed to sit on bare ground in war, x. 5 ; Indians of, seclusion of girls at puberty among, x. 41 *sqq.* ; Indians of, stories of the external soul among, xi. 151 *sq.* ; Indians of, religious associations among, xi. 267 *sqq. See also* North American Indians

——, North-West, contagious magic of footprints in, i. 210 ; the Chilcotin Indians of, i. 312 ; the Loucheux of, i. 356 ; artificial elongation of the head among the Indian tribes of, ii. 298 ; the Carrier Indians of, iv. 199 ; the Salish Indians of, viii. 80 ; the Tinneh Indians of, viii. 80 ; Indian tribes of, their masked dances, ix. 375 *sqq.* ; Secret Societies among the Indians of, ix. 377 *sqq.*

——, South, the Guarani of, i. 145 ; the Payaguas of, i. 330 ; power of medicine-men in, i. 358 *sqq.* ; the Itonamas of, iii. 31 ; custom of swallowing ashes of dead kinsfolk in, viii. 156 *sq.* ; the Palenques of, viii. 221 ; seclusion of girls at puberty among the Indians of, x. 56 *sqq.* ; effigies of Judas burnt at Easter in, x. 128 ; Midsummer fires in, x. 212 *sq. See also* South America

American Indians, power of medicine-men among the, i. 355 *sqq.* ; drive away the ghosts of the slain, iii. 170 *sq.* ; confession of sins among the, iii. 215 *sq.*, 216 *n.*[2]; personal names kept secret among the, iii. 324 *sqq.*, 327 *sq.* ; their fear of naming the dead, iii. 351 *sqq.* ; relations of the dead change their names among the, iii. 357 ; changes in their languages caused by fear of naming the dead, iii. 360 *sq.* ; their Great Spirit, iv. 3 ; women's agricultural work among the, vii. 120 *sqq.* ; their personification of maize, vii. 171 *sqq.* ; do not sharply distinguish between animals and men, viii. 204 *sqq.* ; their ceremonies at hunting bears, viii. 224 *sqq.* ; treat elans, deer, and elks with ceremonious respect, viii. 240 ; cut out the sinew of the thigh of deer which they kill, viii. 264. *See also* North American Indians *and* South American Indians

American prairies, skulls of buffaloes awaiting resurrection on, viii. 256

Amestris, wife of Xerxes, her sacrifice of children, vi. 220 *sq.*

Amethysts thought to keep their wearers sober, i. 165 ; in rain-charms, i. 345

Amiens, "killing the Cat" at harvest near, vii. 281

Amisus, in Pontus, ix. 421 *n.*[1]

Ammerland, in Oldenburg, cart-wheel used as charm against witchcraft in, x. 345 *n.*[3]

Ammon, the god, married to the queen of Egypt, ii. 130 *sqq.* ; human wives of, ii. 130 *sqq.*, v. 72 ; regarded as the father of Egyptian gods, ii. 131 ; costume of, ii. 133 ; king of Egypt masqueraded as, ii. 133 ; high priests of, their usurpation of regal power, ii. 134 ; identified with the sun, vi. 123 ; rage of King Amenophis IV. against, vi. 124 ; at Thebes in Egypt, ram annually sacrificed to, viii. 41, 172 ; the Theban, represented with the body of a man and the head of a ram, viii. 172 *sq.*

—— -Ra, king of the gods, ii. 132

Ammon (country), Hanun, king of, iii. 273 ; conquered by King David, iii. 273

——, Milcom, the god of, v. 19

Ammonite, fossil, regarded as an embodiment of Vishnu, ii. 26, 27 *n.*[2]

Amoor River, the Manegres of the, iii. 323 ; the Gilyaks of the, v. 278 *n.*[2], viii. 103, 267, ix. 101 ; the Goldi of the, viii. 103 ; bears in the valley of the, viii. 191 ; the Orotchis of the, viii. 197

Amorgos, the month of Cronion in, ix. 351 *n.*[2]

Amorites, their law as to fornication, v. 37 *sq.*

Amoy, fear of tree-spirits in, ii. 14; spirits who draw away the souls of children at, iii. 59; euphemism for fever among the Chinese of, iii. 400; puppets as substitutes among the Chinese of, viii. 104

Ampasimene, in Madagascar, viii. 40 *n.*

Amphictyon, king of Athens, married the daughter of his predecessor, ii. 277

Amphipolis, death of Brasidas at, iv. 94

Amphitryo besieges Taphos, xi. 103

Amsanctus, the valley of, v. 204 *sq.*

Amshaspands, Persian archangels, ix. 373 *n.*[1]

Amsterdam, "dew-treading" at Whitsuntide at, ii. 104 *n.*[2]

Amulets, hair and teeth of sacred kings preserved as, ii. 6; knots used as, iii. 306 *sqq.*; rings and bracelets as, iii. 314 *sqq.*, x. 92; crowns and wreaths as, vi. 242 *sq.*; against demons, ix. 95; as soul-boxes, xi. 155; degenerate into ornaments, xi. 156 *n.*[2]. *See also* Talismans

Amulius Silvius, his rivalry with Jupiter, ii. 180

Amyclae, ancient capital of Lacedaemon, Agamemnon buried at, ii. 279; in the vale of Sparta, v. 313; tomb of Hyacinth at, v. 314; festival of Hyacinthia at, v. 315

Amyclas, father of Hyacinth, v. 313

Anabis, in Egypt, human god at, i. 390

Anacan, a month of the Gallic calendar, ix. 343

Anacreon, on Cinyras, v. 55

Anacyndaraxes, father of Sardanapalus, v. 172

Anadates, at Zela, ix. 373 *n.*[1]

Anaitis, Persian goddess, afterwards equivalent to Ishtar, i. 16 *sq.*, ix. 369, 389; identified with Artemis, i. 37 *n.*[2]; served by prostitutes at Acilisena, in Armenia, ii. 282 *n.*[3], v. 38, ix. 369 *n.*[1]; her sanctuary at Zela, ix. 370, 421 *n.*[1]; associated with the Sacaea, ix. 355, 368, 369, 402 *n.*[1]; identified with Aphrodite, ix. 369 *n.*[1], 389

Anammelech, burnt sacrifice of children to, iv. 171

Anansa, tutelary god of Old Calabar, ii. 42

Anassa, "Queen," title of goddess, v. 35 *n.*[2]

Anatomie of Abuses, ii. 66

Anazarba or Anazarbus, in Cilicia, the olives of, ii. 107; Zeus at, v. 167 *n.*[1]

Ancestor, wooden image of, xi. 155
—— -worship among the Bantu peoples, ii. 221, vi. 176 *sqq.*; in relation to fire-worship, ii. 221; among the Khasis

of Assam, vi. 203; combined with mother-kin tends to a predominance of goddesses over gods in religion, vi. 211 *sq.*; in Fiji, xi. 243 *sq.*

Ancestors, prayers to, i. 285, 286, 287, 345, 352, vii. 105; skulls of, in rain-charm, i. 285; sacrifices to, i. 290 *sq.*, 339; souls of, in trees, ii. 29, 30, 31, 32, 317; represented by sacred fire-sticks, ii. 214, 216, 222 *sqq.*; dead, regarded as mischievous beings, ii. 221; souls of, in the fire on the hearth, ii. 232; propitiation of, by rubbing their skulls, iii. 197; names of, bestowed on their reincarnations, iii. 368 *sq.*; reborn in their descendants, iii. 368 *sq.*; propitiation of deceased, v. 46; images of, viii. 53; offerings of first-fruits to spirits of, viii. 111, 112, 113, 116, 117, 119, 121, 123, 124, 125; worshipped as guardian spirits, viii. 121, 123; spirits of, take up their abode in their skulls or in images, viii. 123; images of, viii. 124; dead, worshipped as gods, viii. 125; fear of the spirits of, ix. 76 *sq.*

Ancestral Contest at the *Haloa*, vii. 61; at the Eleusinian Games, vii. 71, 74, 77; at the Festival of the Threshing-floor, vii. 75
—— skulls used in magic, i. 163
—— spirits worshipped at the hearth, ii. 216 *sq.*, 221 *sq.*; cause sickness, iii. 53; sacrifices to, iii. 104, vi. 175, 178 *sq.*, 180, 181 *sq.*, 183 *sq.*, 190; on shoulders of medicine-men, v. 74 *n.*[4]; incarnate in serpents, v. 82 *sqq.*, xi. 211; in the form of animals, v. 83; worshipped by the Bantu tribes of Africa, vi. 174 *sqq.*; prayers to, vi. 175 *sq.*, 178 *sq.*, 183 *sq.*; on the father's and on the mother's side, the two distinguished, vi. 180, 181; propitiation of, ix. 86. *See also* Ancestors *and* Dead
—— tree, fire kindled from, ii. 221, 223 *sq.*

Anchiale in Cilicia, v. 144; monument of Sardanapalus at, v. 172

Ancient deities of vegetation as animals, viii. 1 *sqq.*

Ancona, sarcophagus of St. Dasius at, ii. 310 *n.*[1], ix. 310

Ancus Martius, Roman king, said to have murdered his predecessor, ii. 181 *n.*[5]; his maternal descent, ii. 270 *n.*[4]; his death, ii. 320

Andalusia, guisers in, ix. 173

Andaman Islanders, said to be ignorant of the art of making fire, ii. 253; perhaps first got fire from volcano, ii. 256 *n.*[2]; regard their reflections as their souls, iii. 92; their ideas as to shooting stars, iv. 60; boar's fat poured on novice at initiation among the, viii. 164

Andaman Islands, mourning custom in the, iii. 183 *n.* ; cat's cradle in the, vii. 103 *n.*[1]

Andania in Messenia, grove of the Great Goddesses at, ii. 122 ; mysteries of, iii. 227 *n.* ; sacred men and women at, v. 76 *n.*[3]

Anderida, forest of, ii. 7

Anderson, J. D., on the winds of Assam, ix. 176 *n.*[3]

Anderson, Miss, of Barskimming, ix. 169 *n.*[2], x. 171 *n.*[3]

Andes, the Colombian, i. 416

—, the Peruvian, net to catch the sun in, i. 316 ; the Indians of, their thunder-god, ii. 370 ; Indians of, their fear of the sea, iii. 10 ; cairns in, to which passing Indians add stones, ix. 9, 10 ; effigies of Judas burnt at Easter in, x. 128

Andjra, a district of Morocco, magical virtue of rain-water in, x. 17 ; Midsummer fires in, x. 213 *sq.* ; Midsummer rites of water in, x. 216 ; animals bathed at Midsummer in, xi. 31

Andreas, parish of, in the Isle of Man, x. 224, 305, 307 *n.*[1]

Andree, Dr. Richard, ix. 246 *n.*[1] ; on the Pleiades in primitive calendars, vii. 307

— -Eysn, Mrs., on the processions and masquerades of the *Perchten,* ix. 245 *sq.,* 249

Andriamasinavalona, a Hova king, vicarious sacrifice for, vi. 221

Andromeda and Perseus, ii. 163

Anemone, the scarlet, sprung from the blood of Adonis, v. 226

Aung Teng, in Burma, sacred fish at, viii. 291

Angakok, Esquimaux wizard or sorcerer, iii. 211, 212

Angamis (Angami), a Naga tribe of Assam, death custom among the, iv. 13 ; their human sacrifices, vii. 244 ; spare butterflies, viii. 291

Angass, the, of Manipur, their rain-making, i. 252 ; a tribe of the Brahmapootra, their custom of stabbing those who die a natural death, iv. 13 ; believe that the souls of the dead are in butterflies, viii. 291

—, the, of Northern Nigeria, their belief in external human souls lodged in animals, xi. 210

Angel, need-fire revealed by an, x. 287

— dance, the, viii. 328

— of Death, iv. 177 *sq.*

Angel, the Destroying, over Jerusalem, v. 24

— -man, effigy of, burnt at Midsummer, x. 167

Angelus bell, the, x. 110, xi. 47

Angla, on the Slave Coast, prohibition to ride on horseback in, viii. 45

Angola, the Matiamvo of, iv. 35

—, the Ovakumbi of, i. 318 *n.*[6] ; the Mucelis of, ii. 262 ; the Bangalas of, ii. 293 ; Humbe in, iii. 6 ; the negroes of, speak respectfully of lions, iii. 400 ; Cassange in, iv. 56, 203

Angoni, the, of British Central Africa, their way of stopping rain, i. 263 ; their sacrifices for rain and fine weather, i. 291 ; drive away the ghosts of the slain, iii. 174 ; purification of manslayers among the, iii. 176 ; custom observed by manslayers among the, iii. 186 *n.*[1] ; ceremony of standing on one leg among the, iv. 156 *n.*[2] ; sham burial to deceive demons among the, viii. 99 ; eat parts of enemies to acquire their qualities, viii. 149

Angoniland, British Central Africa, rain-making in, i. 250 ; the Nyanja-speaking tribes of, viii. 26 ; customs as to girls at puberty in, x. 25 *sq.* ; customs as to salt in, x. 27

Angoulême, poplar burned on St. Peter's day in, ii. 141

Angoy, the king of, must have no bodily defect, iv. 39

Angus, belief as to the weaning of children in, vi. 148 ; superstitious remedy for the "quarter-ill" in, x. 296 *n.*[1]

Anhalt, custom at sowing in, i. 139, v. 239 ; harvest customs in, vii. 226, 233, 279 ; Easter bonfires in, x. 140

Anhouri, Egyptian god, the mummy of, iv. 4 *sq.*

Animal, corn-spirit as an, vii. 270 *sqq.* ; killing the divine, viii. 169 *sqq.* ; worshipful, killed once a year and promenaded from door to door, viii. 322 ; bewitched, or part of it, burnt to compel the witch to appear, x. 303, 305, 307 *sq.,* 321 *sq.* ; sickness transferred to, xi. 181 ; and man, sympathetic relation between, xi. 272 *sq.*

— embodiments of the corn-spirit, on the, vii. 303 *sqq.*

— enemy of god originally identical with god, vii. 23, viii. 16 *sq.,* 31

— familiars of wizards and witches, xi. 196 *sq.,* 201 *sq.*

— form, god killed in, vii. 22 *sq.*

— food, supposed acquisition of virtues or vices through, viii. 139

— god, two types of the custom of killing the, viii. 312 *sq.*

Animal masks worn by Egyptian kings and others, ii. 133, iv. 72, vii. 260 sq. ; worn by mummers at Carnival, viii. 333
—— sacrament, types of, viii. 310 sqq.
Animals, homoeopathic magic of, i. 150 sqq. ; association of ideas common to the, i. 234 ; rain-making by means of, i. 287 sqq. ; spirits of plants in shape of, ii. 14 ; injured through their shadows, iii. 81 sq. ; propitiation of spirits of slain, iii. 190, 204 sq. ; atonement for slain, iii. 207 ; blood of, not allowed to fall on ground, iii. 247 ; dangerous, not called by their proper names, iii. 396 sqq. ; thought to understand human speech, iii. 398 sq., 400 ; sacred to kings, iv. 82, 84 sqq. ; transformations into, iv. 82 sqq., xi. 207 ; sacrificed by being hanged, v. 289 sq., 292 ; and plants, edible, savage lamentations for, vi. 43 sq. ; dead kings and chiefs incarnate in, vi. 162, 163 sq., 173, 193 ; sacrificed to prolong the life of kings, vi. 222 ; torn to pieces and devoured raw in religious rites, vii. 17, 18, 19, 20 sqq.¡; regarded as unclean were originally sacred, viii. 24 ; belief in the descent of men from, viii. 25 ; spirits of ancestors in, viii. 123 ; language of, acquired by eating serpent's flesh, viii. 146 ; resurrection of viii. 200 sq., 256 sqq. ; and men, savages fail to distinguish accurately between, viii. 204 sqq. ; wild, propitiation of, by hunters, viii. 204 sqq. ; apologies offered by savages to animals for killing them, viii. 221 sqq. ; bones of, not to be broken, viii. 258 sq. ; bones of, not allowed to be gnawed by dogs, viii. 259 ; savage faith in the immortality of, viii. 260 sqq. ; transmigration of human souls into, viii. 285 sqq.; two forms of the worship of, viii. 311 ; processions with sacred, viii. 316 sqq. ; transference of evil to, ix. 31 sqq., 49 sqq. ; as scapegoats, ix. 31 sqq., 190 sqq., 208 sqq., 216 sq. ; guardian spirits of, ix. 98 ; prayed to, ix. 236 ; dances taught by, ix. 237 ; imitated in dances, ix. 376, 377, 381, 382 ; burnt alive as a sacrifice in England, Wales, and Scotland, x. 300 sqq. ; witches transformed into, x. 315 sqq., xi. 311 sq. ; bewitched, buried alive, x. 324 sqq. ; live, burnt at Spring and Midsummer festivals, xi. 38 sqq. ; the animals perhaps deemed embodiments of witches, xi. 41 sq., 43 sq. ; the language of, learned by means of fern-seed, xi. 66 n. ; external soul in, xi.

196 sqq. ; helpful, in fairy tales. See Helpful
Animism, the Buddhist, not a philosophical theory, ii. 13 sq. ; passing into polytheism, ii. 45 ; passing into religion, iii. 213
Aninga, aquatic plant in Brazil, ix. 264
Anitos, spirits of ancestors, in Luzon, ii. 30, viii. 124
Anjea, mythical being, who causes conception in women, i. 100, 184, v. 103
Ankenmilch bohren, to make the needfire, x. 270 n.
Anklets, as amulets, iii. 315 ; made of human sinews, worn by king of Uganda, vi. 224 sq.
Ankole, in Central Africa, the Bahima of, vi. 190, viii. 288, x. 80
Anna, sister of Dido, v. 114 n.¹
Anna Kuari, an Oraon goddess, human sacrifices to, vii. 244
Annals of Tigernach and Ulster, ii. 286
Annam, rain-making ceremonies in caves of, i. 301 sq. ; the Chams of, ii. 159 ; dangers apprehended from women in childbed in, iii. 155 ; ceremonies observed when a whale is washed ashore in, iii. 223 ; wild beasts spoken of respectfully in, iii. 403 ; natives of, their indifference to death, iv. 136 sq. ; offerings to the dead in spring in, v. 235 n.¹ ; annual festivals of the dead in, vi. 62 sqq. ; inauguration of spring by means of an effigy of an ox in, viii. 13 sq. ; mountaineers of, sacrifice to their nets, viii. 240 n.¹ ; demons of sickness transferred to fowls in, ix. 33 ; demon of cholera sent away on a raft from, ix. 190 ; explanation of human mortality in, ix. 303 ; dread of menstruous women in, x. 85 ; use of wormwood to avert demons in, xi. 61 n.¹
Annamite tale of a bleeding tree, ii. 33
Annamites, their belief as to demons, iii. 58 ; their way of protecting infants from demons, iii. 235
Annandale, Nelson, as to H. Vaughan Stevens, ii. 237 n.
Anne, Queen, touches for scrofula, i. 370
Anno, in West Africa, use of magical dolls at, i. 71
Annual abdication of kings, iv. 148
—— death and resurrection of gods, v. 6
—— renewal of king's power at Babylon, iv. 113
—— sacrifice of a sacred animal, viii. 31
—— tenure of the kingship, iv. 113 sqq.
Anodynes based on the principle of sympathetic magic, i. 93 sq.
Anointed, human scapegoat, ix. 218

Anointing a stone in a rain-charm, i. 305
—— stones in order to avert bullets from absent warriors, i. 130
Anointment, of weapon which caused wound, i. 202 *sqq.* ; of priests at installation, iii. 14 ; as a ceremony of consecration, v. 21 *n.*[2] and [3], 68, 74 ; of sacred stones, custom of, v. 36 ; of the body as a means of acquiring certain qualities, viii. 162 *sqq.*
Anpu and Bata, ancient Egyptian story of, xi. 134 *sqq.*
Ant-hill, insane people buried in an, x. 64
Antaeus, grave of the giant, i. 286
——, king of Libya, and his daughter Barce, ii. 300 *sq.*
Antagonism of religion to magic, i. 226
Antaimorona, the, of Madagascar, their chiefs held responsible for failure of the crops, i. 354
Antambahoaka, the, of Madagascar, confession of sins among the, iii. 216 *sq.*
Antandroy, the, of Madagascar, their custom at circumcision, iii. 227
Antankarana tribe of Madagascar believe that their souls at death pass into animals, viii. 290
Antelope (*Antilope leucoryx*), ceremony after killing a, viii. 244
Antelopes, soul of a dead king incarnate in, vi. 163
Anthemis nobilis, camomile, gathered at Midsummer, xi. 63
Anthesteria, dramatic death and resurrection of Dionysus perhaps acted at the, iv. 32 ; festival of the dead at Athens, v. 234 *sq.*, ix. 152 *sq.* ; an Athenian festival of Dionysus, compared with a modern Thracian celebration of the Carnival, vii. 30 *sqq.*
Anthesterion, Attic month, corresponding to February, iii. 137, ix. 143 *n.*, 352
Anthropomorphism of the spirits of nature, vii. 212
Antiaris toxicaria, poison tree, superstition of the Kayans as to the, ii. 17
Antibes, Holy Innocents' Day at, ix. 336 *sq.*
Antichrist, expected reign of, iv. 44 *sq.*
Antigone, the execution of, ii. 228 *n.*[5]
Antigonus, King, v. 212 ; deified by the Athenians, i. 390, 391 *n.*[1]
Antilope leucoryx, ceremony of Ewe hunter after killing a, viii. 244
Antimachia in Cos, priest of Hercules dressed as woman at, vi. 258
Antimores of Madagascar, their chiefs held responsible for the operation of the laws of nature, i. 354

Antinmas, the twenty-fourth day after Christmas, ix. 167
Antinous, games in honour of, at Mantinea, vii. 80, 85
Antioch, destroyed by an earthquake, v. 222 *n.*[1] ; festival of Adonis at, v. 227, 257 *sq.* ; how it was freed from scorpions, viii. 280 *sq.*
Antiochus, Greek calendar of, v. 303 *n.*[3]
Antiquity, of the cultivation of the cereals in Europe, vii. 79 ; human scapegoats in classical, ix. 229 *sqq.*
Antoninus Liberalis, on the birth of Hercules, iii. 299 *n.*[1]
—— Marcus, plague in his reign, ix. 64
Antonius Mountain, in Thuringia, Christmas bonfire on the, x. 265 *sq.*
Antrim, harvest customs concerning the last corn cut in, vii. 144, 154 *sq.* ; "Winning the Churn" in, vii. 154 *sq.*
Ants, bites of, used in purificatory ceremony, iii. 105 ; eaten to make the eater brave, viii. 147 ; superstitious precaution against the ravages of, viii. 276 ; jealousy transferred to, ix. 33 ; stinging people with, ix. 263, x. 61, 62 *sq.*
Antwerp, Feast of All Souls in, vi. 70 ; wicker giants at, xi. 35 *sq.*
Anu, Babylonian god, visit of Ishtar to, ix. 399 *n.*[1]
Anubis, Egyptian jackal-headed god, vi. 15, 18 *n.*[3], 22 *n.*[2] ; represented by a masked man, ii. 133 ; finds the body of Osiris, vi. 85 ; personated by a priest wearing the mask of a dog or a jackal, vi. 85 *n.*[3]
Anula tribe of Northern Australia, their disposal of foreskins at circumcision, i. 95 ; burial customs of the, i. 102 *sq.* ; their way of stopping rain, i. 253 ; their mode of making rain, i. 287 *sq.* ; their rites of initiation, xi. 235
Anyanja of British Central Africa, their dread of menstruous women, x. 81 *sq.*
Anzikos, the, of West Africa, iii. 271
Aola, village of Guadalcanar, viii. 126
Apaches, the, iii. 182, 183, x. 21 ; their way of procuring rain, i. 306 ; avoidance of wife's mother among the, iii. 85 ; custom observed by them on the war-path, iii. 160 ; purify themselves after the slaughter of foes, iii. 184 ; keep their names from strangers, iii. 325, 328 ; propitiated the animal gods before hunting deer, antelope, or elk, viii. 242 ; use of bull-roarers among the, xi. 230 *n.*
Apachitas, heaps of stones in Peru, ix. 9
Apala cured by Indra in the Rigveda, xi. 192
Apamea in Syria, Alcibiades of, iv. 5 *n.*[3] ; worship of Poseidon at, v. 195

Ape in homoeopathic magic, i. 156; a Batta totem, xi. 223. *See also* Apes

Apepi, Egyptian fiend, i. 67

Apes, thought to be related to twins, i. 265; voices of, imitated as a charm, ii. 23; ceremony of Yuracares after killing, viii. 235 *sq.*

Aphaca in Syria, sanctuary of Astarte at, v. 28, 259; meteor as signal for festival at, v. 259

Ap-hi, Abchase god of thunder and lightning, ii. 370

Aphrodite, represented as mother of Demetrius Poliorcetes, i. 391; the grave of, iv. 4; human sacrifices to, iv. 166 *n.*[1]; her sacred doves, v. 33, 147; sanctuary of, at Paphos, v. 33 *sqq.*; the month of, v. 145; her blood dyes white roses red, v. 226; name applied to summer, vi. 41

—— and Adonis, i. 25, v. 11 *sq.*, 29, 280, ix. 386, xi. 294 *sq.*; their marriage celebrated at Alexandria, v. 224

—— Askraia, i. 26

—— and Cinyras, v. 48 *sq.*

—— of the Lebanon, the mourning, v. 29 *sq.*

—— the Oriental, ix. 369 *n.*[1]

—— and Pygmalion, v. 49 *sq.*

Aphtha or thrush transferred to a frog, ix. 50

Api, female hippopotamus goddess of Egypt, ii. 133

Apinagos Indians of Brazil, their dances and presentation of children to the moon, vi. 145 *sqq.*

Apis, sacred Egyptian bull, vi. 11, 119 *n.*, viii. 34 *sqq.*, ix. 217; mourning for the death of, v. 225; held to be an image of the soul of Osiris, vi. 130; drowned in a holy spring, viii. 36; not suffered to outlive a certain term of years, viii. 173

Apodtho, the ancestor of all men, iii. 79

Apollo at Delos, i. 32, 34 *sq.*, ii. 135; prophetess of, inspired by laurel, i. 384, iv. 80; image of, in sacred cave at Hylae, i. 386; at Patara, ii. 135; purification of, iii. 223 *n.*[1]; servitude of, iv. 70 *n.*[1], 78; and the laurel, iv. 78 *sqq.*; at Thebes, iv. 79; purged of the dragon's blood in the Vale of Tempe, iv. 81; dedication of a tithe-offering to, iv. 187 *n.*[5]; the friend of Cinyras, v. 54; music in the worship of, v. 54 *sq.*; his musical contest with Marsyas, v. 55, 288; reputed father of Augustus, v. 81; purified at Tempe, vi. 240; temple of, at the Lover's Leap, ix. 254; temple of, at Cumae, x. 99; identified with the Celtic Grannus, x. 112

Apollo and Artemis, birthdays of, i. 32; the birth of, ii. 58; their priesthood at Ephesus, vi. 243 *sq.*; cake with twelve knobs offered to, ix. 351 *n.*[3]

—— at Delphi, hair offered by boys at puberty to, i. 28; first-fruits offered to, i. 32; grave of, at Delphi, i. 34, 35, iv. 4; seems to have usurped the place of an older god or hero at Delphi and Thebes, ii. 88; and the Dragon at Delphi, iv. 78, 79, 80 *sq.*, vi. 240; sacrifices of Croesus to, v. 180 *n.*[1]

——, the Cataonian, v. 147 *n.*[3]

——, the Clarian, iv. 80 *n.*[1]

—— Diradiotes, inspired priestess at temple of, i. 381

—— Erithasean, ii. 121

—— the Four-handed, vi. 250 *n.*[2]

—— of the Golden Sword, v. 176

—— surnamed Locust and Mildew, viii. 282

—— the Mouse, his temple in the Troad, viii. 283

——, Soranus, xi. 14, 15 *n.*[3]

——, the Wolf-slayer, viii. 283 *sq.*

Apollonia, festival at Delos, i. 32 *n.*[2]

——, a city in Macedonia, ix. 143 *n.*

Apollonius of Tyana, how he rid Antioch of scorpions, viii. 280 *sq.*; how he rid Constantinople of flies, viii. 281

Apologies offered to trees for cutting them down, ii. 18 *sq.*, 30, 36 *sq.*; for trespass on sacred groves, ii. 328; offered by savages to the animals they kill, viii. 215, 217, 218, 221, 222 *sqq.*, 235 *sqq.*, 243

Apotheosis by being burnt alive, v. 179 *sq.*

Apoyaos, tribe in Luzon, their human sacrifices, vii. 241

Appam, a town on the Gold Coast, family descended from a fish at, iv. 129

Appian, on the costume of a priest of Isis, vi. 85 *n.*[3]

Apple, offered instead of ram or ox to Hercules, viii. 95 *n.*[2]; divination by a sliced, at Hallowe'en, x. 238; and candle, biting at, x. 241, 242, 243, 245

—— -tree, afterbirth of cow hung in an, i. 198 *sq.*; straw-man placed on oldest, viii. 6; as life-index of boy, xi. 165

—— -trees, barren women roll under, to obtain offspring, ii. 57; torches thrown at, x. 108; mistletoe on, xi. 315, 316 *n.*[5]

Apples at festival of Diana, i. 14, 16; forbidden to worshippers of Cybele and Attis, v. 280 *n.*[7]; dipping for, at Hallowe'en, x. 237, 239, 241, 242, 243, 245

Apricot-trees, mistletoe on, xi. 316

April, religious rites performed by the

Vestals in, ii. 229 ; the first Sunday of, custom observed at Naples on, iv. 241 ; Siamese festival of the dead in, ix. 150 ; ceremony of the new fire in, x. 136 *sq.*, xi. 3 ; Chinese festival of fire in, xi. 3

April 2nd, annual sacrifice of wild boars in Cyprus on, viii. 23 *n.*[3]

—— 15th, sacrifice on, ii. 229, 326

—— 21st, date of the Parilia, ii. 325, 326 ; ceremony performed by the Vestals on, viii. 42

—— 23rd, St. George's Day, ii. 75, 76, 330 *sqq.*

—— 24th, in some places St. George's Day, ii. 337, 343 ; the great *mondard* made on, viii. 6

—— 27th, in popular superstitions of Morocco, x. 17 *sq.*

—— 30th, Walpurgis Day, ix. 163

Apuleius, as to the love-charm of a Thessalian witch, iii. 270 ; his story of Cupid and Psyche, iv. 131 *n.*[1] ; on the worship of Isis, vi. 119 *n.* ; on a cure for scorpion bite, ix. 50 *n.*[1]

Aquaelicium and Jupiter, ii. 184 *n.*

Aquilex, rain-maker, i. 310 *n.*[4]

Arab belief that a game of ball may cause rain, ix. 179

—— charm to forget sorrow, i. 150 ; to bring back a runaway slave, i. 152 ; to ensure birth of strong children, i. 153 ; to fertilize a barren woman, i. 157 ; of the setting sun, i. 165 *sq.* ; to get good teeth, i. 181 ; to make rain, i. 303

—— commentator as to the fig and the olive, ii. 316 ; on the Koran as to knots in magic, iii. 302

—— cure by means of knotted thread, iii. 304 ; cure for melancholy, ix. 4

—— legend of king bled to death, iii. 243 *n.*[7]

—— love-charm by means of knots, iii. 305

—— mode of cursing an enemy, iii. 312

—— name for the scarlet anemone, v. 226

—— sacrifice for rain, i. 289

—— women, their custom of muffling their faces, iii. 122 ; in North Africa give their male children the hearts of lions to eat, viii. 142 *sq.* ; in Morocco, their superstitions as to plants at Midsummer, xi. 51

—— writer on the death of the King of the Jinn, iv. 8 ; on talismans against locusts and murrain, viii. 281

Arabia, sacred acacia-tree in, ii. 42 ; sticks or stones piled on scenes of violent death in, ix. 15 ; use of camel as scapegoat for plague in, ix. 33

Arabia, ancient, taboos observed by incense-growers in, ii. 106 *sq.* ; belief as to shadows in, iii. 82 ; Sabaea or Sheba in, iii. 124 ; tree-spirits in snake form in, xi. 44 *n.*[1]

Arabian, modern, story of the external soul, xi. 137 *sq.*

Arabian Nights, story of the external soul in the, xi. 137

Arabic treatise on magic, i. 65 ; writer on the mourning for Tâ-uz (Tammuz) in Harran, v. 230

Arabs believe the soul to be in the blood, iii. 241 ; avoid using the proper names for lion, leprosy, etc., iii. 400 ; ancient, supposed to know the language of birds, viii. 146 ; their custom as to widows, ix. 35 ; their custom in regard to murder, ix. 63 ; beat camels to deliver them from jinn, ix. 260

—— of Algeria, their story of the type of Beauty and the Beast, iv. 130 *n.*[1]

—— of East Africa, their faith in an unguent of lion's fat, viii. 164

——, the heathen, their custom as to a boy's cast teeth, i. 181 ; their way of procuring rain, i. 303 ; their treatment of a man stung by a scorpion, iii. 95 *n.*[8]

—— of Moab, their charm against scorpions, i. 153 ; their charm to ensure the birth of children, i. 157 ; their rain-making ceremony, i. 276 ; their use of shorn hair as a hostage, iii. 273 ; preserve their nail-parings against the resurrection, iii. 280 ; resort to the springs of Callirrhoe, v. 215 *sq.* ; their custom at harvest, vi. 48, 96, vii. 138 ; their remedies for ailments, vi. 242

—— of Morocco, their custom at the Great Feast, ix. 265 ; their Midsummer customs, x. 214

—— of North Africa, their rain-charm, i. 277 ; jinn invoked by their names among the, iii. 390

Aracan, ix. 117 ; the Mrus of, ix. 12 *n.*[1] ; dances for the crops in, ix. 236

Arachnaeus, Mount, altars of Zeus and Hera on, ii. 360

Arad, in Hungary, thresher of last corn wrapt in a cow's hide at, 291

Araguaya River in Brazil, iii. 348

Aran, in the valley of the Garonne, Midsummer fires at, x. 193

Aran Islands, off Galway, St. Eany's well in the, ii. 161

Aratus of Sicyon, sacrifices to, i. 105 ; deemed a son of Aesculapius, v. 81

Araucanians of South America, the, ix. 12 ; their idea as to toads, i. 292 *n.*[3] ;

their belief that thunder-storms are caused by the spirits of the dead, ii. 183 ; afraid of having their portraits taken, iii. 97; keep their names secret, iii. 324 ; eat fruit of Araucanian pine, v. 278 $n.^2$ *See also* Aucas

Araunah, the threshing-floor of, v. 24

Arawak Indians of British Guiana, murderers taste the blood of their victims among the, viii. 154 *sq.*; their explanation of human mortality, ix. 302 *sq.*

Arcadia, the oak forests of, ii. 354 *sq.*

Arcadian boys offer their hair to a river, i. 31

—— custom of beating Pan's image, ix. 256

Arcadians ate and eat acorns, ii. 355, 356 ; sacrifice to thunder and lightning, v. 157

Arch to shut out plague, ix. 5 ; creeping through, as a cure, ix. 55 ; child after an illness passed under an, xi. 192 ; young men at initiation passed under a leafy, xi. 193 ; triumphal, suggested origin of the, xi. 195. *See also* Arches, Archways

Archangel, worship of Leschiy in the Government of, ii. 125

Archangels, Persian, ix. 373 $n.^1$

Archbishop of Innocents, ix. 334

Archer (*Tirant*), effigy of, xi. 36

Archery, contest of, for a bride, ii. 306

Arches made over paths at expulsion of demons, ix. 113, 120 *sq.* ; novices at initiation passed under arches in Australia, xi. 193 $n.^1$ *See also* Arch, Archways

Archigallus, high-priest of Attis, v. 268, 279 ; prophesies, v. 271 $n.$

Archways, passing under, as a means of escaping evil spirits or sickness, xi. 179 *sqq.* *See also* Arch, Arches

Arctic origin, alleged, of the Aryans, v. 229 $n.^1$

—— regions, ceremonies at the reappearance of the sun in the, ix. 124 *sq.*, 125 $n.^1$

Arcturus, Greek vintage timed by, vii. 47 $n.^2$; Greek festival before, 51, 52

Arden, Forest of, ii. 7

Ardennes, May Day custom in the, ii. 80 ; Arduinna, goddess of the, ii. 126 ; effigies of Carnival burned in the, iv. 226 *sq.*; precautions against rats in the, viii. 277 ; the King of the Bean in the, ix. 314 ; the Eve of Epiphany in the, ix. 317 ; bonfires on the first Sunday of Lent in the, x. 107 *sq.* ; the French, Lenten fires and customs in, x. 109 *sq.* ; Midsummer fires in the, x. 188 ; the Yule log in the, x. 253 ; cats burnt alive in Lenten bonfires in the, xi. 40

Ardrishaig, in Argyleshire, the harvest Maiden at, vii. 155 *sq.*

Arduinna, goddess of the Ardennes, ii. 126

Aren palm-tree, superstition as to, ii. 22

Arenna or Arinna, the Hittite sun-goddess of, v. 136, with $n.^1$

Arensdorf, custom at sowing in, v. 239

Ares, men sacred to, iii. 111 ; the grave of, iv. 4

Argaeus, Mount, in Cappadocia, v. 190 *sq.*

Argentina and Bolivia, passes of, ix. 9

Argenton, in Berry, Mid-Lenten custom at, iv. 241 *sq.*

Argive brides wore false beards, vi. 260

—— maidens sacrificed their hair to Athena, i. 28

—— tradition as to descent of Dionysus into Hades, vii. 15

—— women bewailed Adonis, v. 227 $n.$

Argo, tree of which the ship was made, xi. 94 $n.^1$

Argolis, Eastern, physical features of, ii. 360

Argos, titular kings at, i. 47 $n.$; Apollo Diradiotes at, i. 381 ; Flowery Hera at, ii. 143 $n.^2$; new fire after a death in, ii. 267 $n.^4$; altar of Rainy Zeus at, ii. 360 $n.^8$

Argus, Hermes tried for the murder of, ix. 24

Argyleshire, locks unlocked at childbirth in, iii. 296 ; use of knotted threads as a cure in, iii. 304 ; last corn cut at harvest called the Maiden in, vii. 155 *sq.* ; the last corn cut at harvest called the Old Wife (*Cailleach*) in, vii. 164 stories of the external soul, xi. 127 *sqq.*

Argyrus, temple of Hercules at, x. 99 $n.^3$

Ari or totem, mode of determining a young man's, i. 99

Ariadne, Cyprian worship of, vii. 209 $n.^2$

—— and Dionysus, ii. 138

—— and Theseus, iv. 75

Ariadne's crown, ii. 138

—— Dance, iv. 75, 77

Ariccia, the modern descendant of Aricia, i. 3, xi. 309

Aricia, sacred grove at, i. 3, viii. 95 ; the beggars of, i. 4 ; Orestes at, i. 10 ; "many Manii at," i. 22, viii. 94 *sqq.* ; its distance from the sanctuary, ii. 2 ; the priest of, ix. 273 ; King of the Wood at, ix. 409 ; the priest of, and the Golden Bough, x. 1 ; the priest of Diana at, perhaps a personified Jupiter, xi. 302 *sq.*

Arician grove, the sacred, i. 20, 22, ii. 115, ix. 274, 305 ; horses excluded from, i. 20, viii. 40 *sqq.* ; ritual of, iv. 213 ; perhaps the scene of a common harvest celebration, viii. 44 ; said to have been founded by Manius, viii. 95 ; the Midsummer festival of fire in, xi. 285 ; the priest of, a personification of an oak-spirit, xi. 285. *See also* Nemi

Arician priesthood, ix. 305
—— slope, the, i. 4 *n.*⁵

Aries, the constellation, the sun in, ix. 361 *n.*¹, 403

Arikara Indians, their rule as to breaking marrow bones, i. 115 *sq.* ; their preparation for war by fasting and lacerating themselves, iii. 161

Ariminum, triumphal arch of Augustus at, xi. 194 *n.*⁴

Aristeas of Proconnesus, his soul as a raven, iii. 34

Aristides, the rhetorician, on first-fruit offerings, vii. 56 ; on Eleusinian Games, vii. 71

Aristomenes, Messenian hero, his fabulous birth, v. 81

Aristophanes, Strepsiades in, i. 285 ; on the Spartan envoy, v. 196 *n.*⁴ ; on Hercules as patron of hot springs, v. 209

Aristotelian philosophy, revival of the, v. 301

Aristotle, on death at ebb-tide, i. 167 ; on the marriage of the Queen to Dionysus, ii. 137 ; his *Constitution of Athens*, ii. 137 *n.*¹, vii. 79 ; on the political institutions of Cyprus, v. 49 *n.*⁷; on earthquakes, v. 211 *n.*³; on the trial of lifeless objects by the King at Athens, viii. 5 *n.*¹; on men of genius, viii. 302 *n.*⁵; his statement of the principle of the survival of the fittest, viii. 306

Arizona, the aridity of, i. 306 ; the Moquis of, iii. 228 ; mock human sacrifices in, iv. 215 ; the Pueblo Indians of, vii. 312; and New Mexico, use of bull-roarers in, xi. 230 *n.*, 231

Arjun and Draupadi, ii. 306

Arkansas Indians, their offerings of first-fruits to the Master of Life, viii. 134

Arkon, in Rügen, sacred shrine at, ii. 241 *n.*⁴

Arks, sacred, of the Cherokees, x. 11 *sq.*

Armadillos not to be shot with poisoned arrows, i. 116

Armengols, in the Pelew Islands, vi. 265

Armenia, rain-making in, i. 275 *sq.*, 277, 282, 285 ; rain-charm by means of pebbles in, i. 305 ; rain-charms by means of rocks in, i. 306 ; the Paulicians of, i. 407 ; barren fruit-trees threatened in, ii. 22 ; new fire after a death in, ii. 267 *n.*⁴ ; worship of Anaitis in, ii. 282 *n.*³, ix. 369 *n.*¹; sacred prostitution of girls before mar-

riage in, v. 38, 58 ; sticks or stones piled on scenes of violent death in, ix. 15 ; were-wolves in, x. 316 ; sick people creep through cleft trees in, xi. 173

Armenian charms by means of knots and locks, iii. 308
—— church, the day of the Virgin in the, i. 16 ; bonfires at Candlemas in the, x. 131
—— custom as to extracted teeth, i. 182
—— idea of the sun as a wheel, x. 334 *n.*¹

Armenians, their belief that lightning is produced by means of flints, ii. 374 ; preserve their cut hair and nails and extracted teeth for use at the resurrection, iii. 280 ; their festivals of the dead, vi. 65 *sq.* ; their opinion of the baleful influence of the moon on children, vi. 148 ; their belief in demons, ix. 107 *sq.*

Arms of youths punctured to make them good hunters, x. 58

Army under arms, Flamen Dialis forbidden to see, iii. 13

Arnobius on the Roman custom of keeping perpetual fires, ii. 260

Arnold, Matthew, on the English middle class, iv. 146

Arnstadt, witches burnt at, x. 6

Arran, magical stone in, i. 161 ; the need-fire in, x. 293

Arrephoroi at Athens, the, ii. 199

Arriaga, J. de, on the Peruvian Maizemothers, Coca-mothers, and Potatomothers, vii. 173 *n.*

Arrian, on sacrifices to Artemis, ii. 125 *sq.* ; on Attis, v. 282

Arrows, poisoned, not to be used against certain animals, i. 116 ; in homoeopathic magic, i. 143 ; in contagious magic, i. 201, 202 ; fire-tipped, shot at sun during an eclipse, i. 311 ; shot as a rain-charm, i. 396; shot at sacred trees as mark of respect, ii. 11 ; to keep off death, iii. 31 ; invisible, of demons, ix. 101, 126 ; used as a love-charm, x. 14

Arsacid house, divinity of Parthian kings of the, i. 417 *sq.*

Art, sylvan deities in classical, ii. 45 ; Demeter and Persephone in, vii. 43 *sq.*

Artaxerxes II., his promotion of the worship of Anaitis, ix. 370

Artemis at Ephesus, i. 7 ; temple dedicated to her by Xenophon, i. 7 ; the Asiatic, i. 7 ; vineyards dedicated to, i. 15 ; at Delos, i. 28 ; hair of maidens sacrificed to, before marriage, i. 28 *sq.* ; birthday of, i. 32, ii. 125 ; a goddess of the wild life of nature, i. 35 *sq.* ; mated with a male consort, i. 35

sq., not originally a virgin goddess, i. 35 *sq.* ; the patroness of childbirth, i. 37 ; identified with lewd Asiatic goddesses of love and fertility, i. 37 ; the birth of, ii. 58 ; sacrifices to, ii. 125 ; the Huntress, first-fruits of the chase offered to, ii. 125 *sq.* ; worshipped by the Celts, ii. 125 *sq.* ; at Perga, v. 35 ; name given by Greeks to Asiatic Mother Goddesses, v. 169

Artemis, Aetolian, her sacred grove among the Veneti, i. 27

—— and Apollo, birthdays of, i. 32 ; the birth of, ii. 58 ; their priesthood at Ephesus, vi. 243

——, Brauronian, sacrifice of a goat to, viii. 41 *n.*[3]

—— of Ephesus, i. 7, 37 *sq.*, ii. 128, 136 ; her image, i. 37 *sq.* ; in relation to the Virgin Mary, i. 38 *n.*[1]; served by eunuch priests, v. 269

—— the Hanged, v. 291

—— and Hippolytus, i. 19 *sq.*, 24 *sqq.*

——, Laphrian, at Patrae, v. 126 *n.*[2]

——, Munychian, sacrifice to, iv. 166 *n.*[1] ; mock human sacrifice in the ritual of, iv. 215 *sq.*

—— *Parthenos*, i. 36

——, Perasian, at Castabala in Cappadocia, v. 115, 167 *sqq.*, xi. 14

——, Sarpedonian, in Cilicia, v. 167, 171

——, Savonian, i. 26

——, the Tauric, human sacrifices to, v. 115

—— Tauropolis, v. 275 *n.*[1]

——, Wolfish, i. 26 *sq.*

Artemisia founds Mausoleum, iv. 94 *sq.*; drinks ashes of her husband Mausolus, viii. 158

Artemisia absinthium, wormwood, xi. 58 *n.*[3], 61 *n.*[1]

—— *laciniata*, garlands of, ix. 284

—— *vulgaris*, mugwort, gathered at Midsummer, xi. 58 *sqq.*

Artemision, a Greek month, vi. 239 *n.*[1], viii. 8

Artictis, the bear-cat, associated with the spirits of the dead, viii. 294

Artificers, worship of the, viii. 60 *sq.*

Artocarpus integrifolia, jack wood burnt in exorcism, iv. 216

Artois, mugwort at Midsummer in, xi. 59

Arts and crafts, use of spells or incantations in, ix. 81

Aru Archipelago, riddles propounded while a corpse is uncoffined in the, ix. 121 *n.*[3]

—— Islands, custom of not sleeping after a death in the, iii. 37, 95 ; children's hair deposited on a banana-tree in the, iii. 276 ; dog's flesh eaten to make eater brave in the, viii. 145

Arum acaule, forbidden as food to the king of Fernando Po, iii. 291

Arunta of Central Australia, magical ceremonies among the, i. 85 *sqq.* ; custom observed by women during operation of subincision, i. 93 *sq.* ; the rain or water totem among the, i. 98 ; burial customs of the, i. 102 ; cannibalism among the, i. 106 ; their treatment of the navel-string, i. 183 ; their rain-making ceremonies, i. 259 *sqq.* ; their belief as to the ghosts of the slain, iii. 177 *sq.* ; their fear of women's blood, iii. 251 ; ceremonies at the end of mourning among the, iii. 373 *sq.* ; their belief in the reincarnation of the dead, v. 99, 100 ; their sacred pole, x. 7 ; their dread of women at menstruation, x. 77 ; legend that the ancestors kept their spirits in their *churinga*, xi. 218 *n.*[3]; rites of initiation among the, xi. 233 *sq.* ; initiation of medicine-men among the, xi. 238

Arval Brothers, their holy pots, ii. 203 *sq.* ; expiation for bringing an iron tool into the sacred grove of the, iii. 226 ; their wreaths of corn, v. 44 *n.*, ix. 232 ; a Roman college of priests charged with the performance of rites for the crops, vi. 239, ix. 230, 232 ; their song, ix. 238. See also *Fratres Arvales*

Aryan custom of leading a bride thrice round the hearth of her new home, ii. 230 ; of counting by nights instead of days, ix. 326 *n.*[2]

—— family, custom of putting the old and sick to death in several branches of the, iv. 14 *n.*[3]; marriage customs of the, vi. 235

—— god of the oak and thunder, ii. 356 *sqq.*, x. 265 ; god of the sky, ii. 374 *sq.*

—— languages, names for moon and month in, ix. 325

—— peoples, descent of kingship through women among, ii. 280 ; their correction of the lunar year, ix. 342 ; stories of the external soul among, xi. 97 *sqq.*

—— stock, tree-worship among all the great European families of the, ii. 9

—— tribes of Gilgit revere the *chili*, a species of cedar, ii. 49

Aryans, magical powers ascribed to kings among the, i. 366 *sqq.* ; perpetual fires among the, ii. 260 ; female kinship among the, ii. 283 *sqq.* ; importance of cattle and milk among the ancient, ii. 324 *n.*[1]; the primitive, their theory of personal names, iii. 319 ; their alleged Arctic origin, v. 229 *n.*[1]; annual festivals of the dead among the, vi. 67 *sqq.*

—— of Europe, their oak forests and use

of oak-wood, ii. 372, 378 ; agriculture among the early, vii. 129 *sq.* ; totemism not proved for the, viii. 4 ; importance of the Midsummer festival among the, xi. 40 ; the oak the chief sacred tree of the, xi. 89 *sq.*

Aryans of India, transubstantiation among the, viii. 89 *sq.*

—— of the Vedic age, ix. 324 ; their calendar, ix. 325, 342

Aryenis, daughter of Alyattes, v. 133 *n.*[1]

Asa, a branch of the Masai, how they dispose of their cut hair and nails, iii. 278

Asaba, on the Lower Niger, chiefs eat in privacy at, iii. 118

Asada, name of a month in Bali, vii. 315

Asakusa, in Tokio, expulsion of the devil on the last day of the year at, ix. 213

Ascalon, the goddess Derceto at, v. 34 *n.*[3], ix. 370 *n.*[1]

Ascanius, the son of Aeneas, ii. 197 ; and the Game of Troy, iv. 76

Ascension of Adonis, v. 225

—— Day, the May-tree in Saxony on, ii. 69 ; annual pardon of a criminal at Rouen on, ii. 165, 166, 168, 169, ix. 215 *sq.*; the "Carrying out of Death" on, at Braller, iv. 222 *n.*[1], 247 *sqq.* ; cures on Eve of, ix. 54 ; annual expulsion of the devil on, ix. 214 *sq.* ; bells rung to make flax grow on, ix. 247 *sq.* ; parasitic rowan should be cut on, xi. 281

Ascent of Persephone, viii. 17

Ascetic idealism of the East, ii. 117

Asceticism not primitive, x. 65

Aschbach, in Bavaria, the Old Man at reaping and threshing at, vii. 219 *sq.*

Asclepias gigantea, man married to, in Barar, ii. 57 *n.*[4]

Ash-tree, parings of nails buried under an, iii. 276 ; in popular cure, ix. 57

—— -trees, children passed through cleft ash-trees as a cure for rupture or rickets, xi. 168 *sqq.*

—— Wednesday, death of Caramantran on, iv. 220 ; burial of the Carnival on, iv. 221 ; effigies of Carnival or of Shrove Tuesday burnt or buried on, iv. 226, 228 *sqq.*, x. 120 ; effigy of the Queen of Lent fashioned on, iv. 244 ; pea-soup and pigs' bones eaten on, vii. 300

Ashantee, licence accorded to king's sisters in, ii. 274 *sq.* ; royal criminals drowned in, iii. 242 *sq.* ; precaution as to the spittle of the king of, iii. 289 ; kings of, addressed as "Elephant" and "Lion," iv. 86 ; kings of, take one of their titles from *borri*, a venomous snake, iv. 86 ; human sacrifices at

earthquakes in, v. 201 ; kings of, their human sacrifices, vi. 97 *n.*[7] ; annual period of licence in, ix. 226 *n.*[1]

Ashantees, the, sanctity of the king's throne among, i. 365 ; their festivals of new yams, viii. 62 *sq.*; ate Sir Charles McCarthy to acquire his bravery, viii. 149

Asherim (singular *asherah*), sacred poles, in Canaan, iv. 169, v. 18, 18 *n.*[2], 107, 108

Ashes from a pyre used to cause sleep, i. 148 ; of serpents in homoeopathic magic, i. 152 *sq.*; of spiders in homoeopathic magic, i. 152 ; of wasps in homoeopathic magic, i. 152 ; of a blind cat in homoeopathic magic, i. 153 ; of the dead turned into rain, i. 287 ; scattered as a rain-charm, i. 304 ; scattered to make sunshine, i. 314 ; of holy fire rubbed on foreheads of warriors, ii. 215 ; of unborn calves used in a fertility charm, ii. 229, 326 ; strewn on the head, iii. 112 ; as manure, vii. 117 ; of human victims scattered on fields, vii. 258 ; of the dead swallowed as a mode of communion with them, viii. 156 *sqq.* ; in divination, x. 243, 244, 245. *See also* Sticks, Charred

—— of bonfires put in fowls' nests, x. 112, 338 ; mixed with seed at sowing, x. 121 ; increase fertility of fields, x. 141, 337 ; make cattle thrive, x. 141, 338 ; placed in a person's shoes, x. 156 ; administered to cattle to make them fat, xi. 4

—— of dead smeared on mourner, viii. 164 ; disposal of the, x. 11

—— of Hallowe'en fires scattered, x. 233

—— of holy fires a protection against demons, xi. 8, 17

—— of human victim scattered with winnowing-fans, vi. 97, 106, vii. 260, 262 ; scattered on earth to fertilize it, vii. 240 ; scattered on fields, vii. 249, 250, 251

—— of Midsummer fires strewed on fields to fertilize them, x. 170, 190, 203 ; a protection against conflagration, x. 174, 196 ; a protection against lightning, x. 187, 188 ; a protection against thunder, x. 190 ; put by people in their shoes, x. 191 *sq.* ; a cure for consumption, x. 194 *sq.* ; rubbed by people on their hair or bodies, x. 213, 214, 215 ; good for the eyes, x. 214

—— of the need-fire strewn on fields to protect the crops against vermin, x. 274 ; used as a medicine, x. 286

—— of New Year's fire used to rub sore eyes, x. 218

Ashes of Yule log strewed on fields, x. 250 ; used to heal swollen glands, x. 251

Ashintilly, Spalding of, bewitched, iii. 299

Ashira, the, of West Africa, make fetishes out of clipped hair, iii. 271 *sq.* ; women the agricultural labourers among, vii. 120

Ashtaroth, Babylonian goddess, ix. 365*sq.*

Ashtoreth (Astarte), v. 18 *n.*[2] *See* Astarte

Ashur, Arab New Year's Day, x. 217, 218

Ashurbanipal, king of Assyria, marries daughter of Sanda-sarme, v. 144 ; confused with the legendary Sardanapalus, v. 173 *sq.*, ix. 387 *sq.* ; carries off the bones of the kings of Elam, vi. 103

Ashwin (Ashvin), Indian month, iv. 55, v. 243

Asia, North-Eastern, the Chuckchees of, ii. 225 ; the Koryaks of, ii. 225, iii. 32 *sq.*

——, Western, Saturnalia in, ix. 354 *sqq.*

Asia Minor, pontiffs in, i. 47 ; the Yourouks of, ii. 43 ; priestly dynasties of, v. 140 *sq.* ; subject to volcanic forces, v. 190 ; subject to earthquakes, v. 202 ; the Caunians of, ix. 116 ; use of human scapegoats by the Greeks of, ix. 255 ; rapid diffusion of Christianity in, ix. 420 *sq.* ; the Celts in, xi. 89 ; cure for possession by an evil spirit in, xi. 186 ; creeping through rifted rocks in, xi. 189

Asiatic goddesses of love and fertility, their lewd worship, i. 37 ; served by eunuch priests, v. 269 *sq.*

Asin, Indian month, iv. 279

Asongtata, an annual ceremony performed by the Garos of Assam, ix. 208

Asopus, the river, ii. 140, 141, v. 81

" A-souling," custom of, in England, vi. 79

Aspalis, a form of Artemis, v. 292

Aspens, fevers transferred to, ix. 57 ; mistletoe on, xi. 315

Aspidium filix mas, the male fern, superstitions as to, xi. 66 *sq.*

Ass in rain-making ceremony, i. 282 *n.*[4] ; son of a god in the form of an, iv. 124 *sq.* ; the crest or totem of a royal family, iv. 132, 133 ; in cure for scorpion's bite, ix. 49 *sq.* ; introduced into church at Festival of Fools, ix. 335 *sq.* ; triumphal ride of a buffoon on an, ix. 402 *sq.* ; child passed under an, as a cure for whooping-cough, xi. 192 *n.*[1] *See also* Asses

Assam, viii. 116 ; the hill tribes of,

taboos in respect of food observed by headmen and their wives among, iii. 11 ; taboos observed by warriors among, iii. 165 ; concealment of personal names among, iii. 323 ; *genna* in, vii. 109 *n.*[2] ; agriculture in, vii. 123 ; head-hunting in, vii. 256

Assam, the Khasis of, i. 194, ii. 114 *n.*[1], 294, v. 46, vi. 202 *sqq.*, ix. 173, xi. 146 ; the Garos of, i. 291, viii. 43 *n.*[1], 116, ix. 208 *sq.* ; the Miris of, ii. 39, 267 *n.*[4], vii. 123, viii. 145 ; the Padams of, ii. 39 ; the Mundaris of, ii. 46 ; the Bodos of, iii. 285 ; the Dhimals of, iii. 285 ; the Kacha Nagas of, iii. 333 ; the Kukis of, iii. 333 ; the Zemis of, iii. 333 ; the Tangkul Nagas of, vi. 57 *sqq.*, ix. 177 ; the Nagas of, viii. 100, 290, ix. 177 ; the Kochs of, viii. 116 ; the Kacharis of, ix. 93 ; the Lushais of, ix. 94, xi. 185 *sq.* ; the Tangkuls of, ix. 177

" Assegai, child of the," iv. 183

Assembly of the gods at the New Year in Babylon, ix. 356

Asses crowned at Vesta's festival in June, ii. 127 *n.*[2] ; excluded from sanctuary of Alectrona, viii. 45 ; transmigration of sinners into, viii. 299, 308. *See also* Ass

—— and men, redemption of firstling, among the Hebrews, iv. 173

Assiga, tribe of South Nigeria, xi. 204

Assimilation of rain-maker to water, i. 260 *sqq.* ; of Egyptian kings to gods, ii. 133 ; of victims to gods, vii. 261 *sq.* ; of men to their totems or guardian animals, viii. 207 *sq.* ; of human victims to trees, ix. 257, 259 *n.*[3]

Assiniboins, their propitiation of slain bears, viii. 225

Assinie, West African kingdom, custom as to eating the new yams in, viii. 63

Association of ideas, magic based on a misapplication of the, i. 53, 174, 221 *sq.* ; common to the animals, i. 234

Associations, religious, among the Indian tribes of North America, xi. 267 *sqq.*

Assumption of the Virgin in relation to the festival of Diana, i. 14-16, v. 308, 309

Assusa, king of Fazoql, iv. 16 *sq.*, 17 *n.*[1]

Assyria, kings of, their annual homage to Marduk, iv. 113 ; festival of Zagmuk in, iv. 116 ; Ashurbanipal, king of, ix. 387 *sq.*

Assyrian cavalry, v. 25 *n.*[3]

—— eponymate, iv. 116 *sq.*

—— kings took into their harem the daughters of the vanquished princes, ix. 368 *n.*[1]

Assyrian monarchs, conquerors of Babylonia, ix. 356
—— monuments, illustrative of the artificial fertilization of the date-palm, ii. 25 *n.*, ix. 273 *n.*[1]
—— ritual, use of golden axe in, xi. 80 *n.*[3]
—— settlers in Israel petition for an Israelitish priest, ii. 288 *n.*[1]
Assyrians, their use of knotted cords in magic, iii. 303 *sq.*; forbidden to mention the mystic names of their cities, iii. 391; in Cilicia, v. 173; the ancient, their belief in demons, ix. 102
Astarte or Ishtar, a great Babylonian goddess, ix. 365; the moon-goddess, iv. 92; at Byblus, hair offerings to, i. 30, v. 13 *sq.*; her temple at Hierapolis, iii. 286; and the *asherim*, v. 18; kings as priests of, v. 26; at Paphos, v. 33 *sqq.*; doves sacred to, v. 147; identified with the planet Venus, v. 258; of the Syrian Hierapolis served by eunuch priests, v. 269 *sq.*; called by Lucian the Assyrian Hera, v. 280 *n.*[5]; the Heavenly Goddess, v. 303; the planet Venus her star, vi. 35. *See also* Ishtar
—— Aphrodite, v. 304 *n.*
—— and Semiramis, ix. 369 *sqq.*
Asteria, mother of the Tyrian Hercules (Melcarth), v. 112
Asthma transferred to a mule, ix. 50
Asti, a Thracian tribe, vii. 26
Aston, W. G., on the Japanese word for god, iii. 2 *n.*[2]; on the annual expulsion of demons in Japan, ix. 212 *sq.*; on Japanese and Chinese ceremonies of purification, ix. 213 *n.*[1]; on Japanese ceremony for averting pestilence, x. 137 *sq.*; on the fire-walk in Japan, xi. 10 *n.*[1]
Astral spirit of a witch, x. 317
Astrolabe Bay, in New Guinea, ii. 255 *n.*[1]; precaution as to spittle in, iii. 289
Astronomical considerations determining the early Greek calendar, iv. 68 *sq.*
Astronomy, origin of, vii. 307
Astyages, king of the Medes, v. 133 *n.*[1]
Asuras, the rivals of the Indian gods, viii. 120
Asvattha tree, v. 82
Aswang, an evil spirit, exorcism of, ix. 260
Atai, external soul in the Mota language, xi. 197 *sq.*
Atalanta and her wooers, ii. 301
Atargatis, Syrian goddess, v. 34 *n.*[3], 137; worshipped at Hierapolis - Bambyce, v. 162 *sq.*; derivation of the name, v. 162; her husband-god, v. 162 *sq.*
Ates, a Phrygian, v. 286

Ath, in Hainaut, procession of giants at, xi. 36
Athamanes of Epirus, women tilled the ground among the, vii. 129
Athamas, king of Alus, vii. 24, 25; and his children, legend of, iv. 161 *sqq.*; sentenced to be sacrificed as expiatory offering for the country, iv. 162; said to have reigned at Orchomenus, iv. 164; the dynasty of, v. 287
Athanasius, on the mourning for Osiris, vi. 217
Athboy, in County Meath, rath near, x. 139
'Atheh, Cilician goddess, v. 162
Athena, hair offered by maidens before marriage to, i. 28; mother of Erichthonius, ii. 199; perpetual lamp of, in the Erechtheum, ii. 199; at Troy, Locrian maidens in the sanctuary of, ii. 284; served by maidens on the Acropolis at Athens, iii. 227 *n.*; sacrifices to, iv. 166 *n.*[1], viii. 56; temple of, at Salamis in Cyprus, v. 145; and hot springs, v. 209, 210; and the *aegis*, viii. 40, 41; priestess of, uses a white umbrella, x. 20 *n.*[1]
——, Magarsian, a Cilician goddess, v. 169 *n.*[3]
—— Sciras, sanctuary of, vi. 238
Athenaeus, on Celtic and Roman indifference to death, iv. 143
Athenian boys, race of, at the vintage, vi. 238; boy carrying an olive-branch in procession, vi. 238
—— custom of keeping a sacred serpent on the Acropolis, iv. 86
—— festival of swinging, iv. 281
—— sacrifice of the *bouphonia*, viii. 4 *sqq.*
—— sacrifices to the Seasons, i. 310
Athenians decree divine honours to Demetrius Poliorcetes and his father Antigonus, i. 390 *sq.*; prayed to Zeus for rain, ii. 359; their tribute of youths and maidens to Minos, iv. 74; their superstition as to an eclipse of the moon, vi. 141; sacrifice to Dionysus for the fruits of the land, vii. 4; the first to receive corn from Demeter, vii. 54; claimed to be the first to spread the knowledge of corn among mankind, vii. 54 *sqq.*; sacrifice an apple to Hercules, viii. 95 *n.*[2]; their festival of the dead at the Anthesteria, ix. 152 *sqq.*; their use of human scapegoats, ix. 253 *sq.*; their mode of reckoning a day, ix. 326 *n.*[2]; their religious dramas, ix. 384; offer cakes to Cronus, x. 153 *n.*[3]
Athens, barrow of Hippolytus at, i. 25; sacred new fire brought from Delphi to, i. 32 *sq.*; King and Queen at, i.

44 *sq.* ; stone of swearing at, i. 160 ; the Eudanemi at, i. 325 *n.*[1] ; titular king at, ii. 1 ; marriage of Dionysus at, ii. 136 *sq.* ; sacred marriage of Zeus and Hera at, ii. 143 *n.*[1] ; female kinship at, ii. 277 ; sacred spots struck by lightning at, ii. 361 ; sacrificial hearth of Lightning Zeus at, ii. 361 ; kings at, iii. 21 *sq.* ; ritual of cursing at, iii. 75 ; Athena served by maidens on the Acropolis at, iii. 227 *n.* ; Midsummer rites of Adonis at, iv. 7 ; the Laurel-bearing Apollo at, iv. 79 *n.*[3] ; funeral games at, iv. 96 ; hand of suicide cut off at, iv. 220 *n.* ; sacred serpent at, v. 87 ; the Commemoration of the Dead at, v. 234 ; sacrifice of an ox at, v. 296 *sq.* ; marriage custom at, vi. 245 ; Dionysus of the Black Goatskin at, vii. 17 ; Queen of, married to Dionysus, vii. 30 *sq.* ; sacred ceremony of ploughing at, vii. 31 ; the Prytaneum at, vii. 32 ; sanctuary of Green Demeter at, vii. 42, 89 *n.*[2] ; first-fruits of the corn sent to, vii. 51, 56, 71 ; called "the Metropolis of the Corn," vii. 58 ; Demeter worshipped as Fruit-bearer at, vii. 63 *n.*[14] ; sanctuary of Earth the Nursing-Mother at, vii. 89 *n.*[2] ; Sacred Ploughing at, vii. 108 *n.*[4], 109 *n.*[1] ; annual sacrifice of a goat at the Acropolis of, viii. 41 ; ceremony at killing a wolf at, viii. 221 ; the Lyceum at, viii. 283, 284 ; fever transferred to pillar at, ix. 53 ; Cronus and the Cronia at, ix. 351 *sq.* ; ceremony of the new fire at Easter in, x. 130

Athis, in Normandy, Christmas bonfires at, x. 266

Athletic competitions among harvesters, vii. 76 *sq.*

Athos, Mount, mistletoe at, xi. 319, 320 *n.*

Athribis, heart of Osiris at, vi. 11

Athyr, Egyptian month, vi. 8, 41, 49 *n.*[1] ; Osiris murdered on the seventeenth day of, vi. 8, 84 ; festival of Osiris in the month of, vi. 84 *sqq.*, 91

Atkhans, the, of the Aleutian Islands, transference of sin to weeds among, ix. 3

Atkinson, J. C., on the treatment of the placentas of mares, i. 199

Atlas, Berbers of the Great, ix. 178

Atlatatonan, Mexican goddess of lepers, ix. 292 ; woman annually sacrificed in the character of, ix. 292

Atomic disintegration, viii. 305

Atonement for slain animals, iii. 207 ; to animals for wrong done to them, viii. 310 *sq.* *See also* Expiation

Atonement, the Jewish day of, ix. 210

Atonga, the, of British Central Africa, their custom after a death, iii. 286 ; tribe of Lake Nyassa, their theory of earthquakes, v. 199

Atrae, city in Mesopotamia, x. 82

Atreus, king of Mycenae, ii. 279

—— and Thyestes, i. 365

Attacking the wind, i. 327 *sqq.*

Attacks on kings permitted, iv. 22, 48 *sqq.*

Attic months lunar, vii. 52

Attica, traces of female kinship in, ii. 284 ; tradition of sexual communism in, ii. 284 ; Sacred Ploughings in, iii. 108 ; summer festival of Adonis in, v. 226 ; Flowery Dionysus in, vii. 4 ; time of threshing in, viii. 4 ; the killing of an ox formerly a capital crime in, viii. 6 ; vintage custom in, viii. 133

Atticus, his villa on the Quirinal, ii. 182 *n.*[1]

Attis, vii. 2, 14, 214 ; priests of Cybele called, v. 140, 285, 287 ; sometimes identified with Adonis, v. 263 ; myth and ritual of, v. 263 *sqq.* ; beloved by Cybele, v. 263, 282 ; legends of his death, v. 264 ; his legend at Pessinus, v. 264 ; his self-mutilation, v. 264 *sq.* ; and the pine-tree, v. 264, 265, 267, 271, 277 *sqq.*, 285, vi. 98 *n.*[5] ; his eunuch priests, v. 265, 266 ; festival of his death and resurrection in March, v. 267 *sqq.*, 272 *sq.*, 307 *sq.* ; violets sprung from the blood of, v. 267 ; the mourning for, v. 272 ; bath of bull's blood in the rites of, v. 274 *sqq.* ; mysteries of, v. 274 *sq.* ; as a god of vegetation, v. 277 *sqq.*, 279 ; as the Father God, v. 281 *sqq.* ; identified with Zeus, v. 282 ; as a sky-god, v. 282 *sqq.* ; emasculation of, suggested explanation of myth, v. 283 ; his star-spangled cap, v. 284 ; identified with Phrygian moon-god Men Tyrannus, v. 284 ; human representatives of, v. 285 *sqq.* ; his relation to Lityerses, vii. 255 *sq.* ; killed by a boar, viii. 22

Attis, Adonis, Osiris, their mythical similarity, v. 6, vi. 201

—— and Cybele (Mother of the Gods), i. 18, 21, 40, 41 ; perhaps personated by human couples, ix. 386

Attiuoindarons, Indian tribe of Canada, their custom of resuscitating the dead in their namesakes, iii. 366 *sq.*

Attraction and repulsion in the physical universe, viii. 303 *sqq.*

Atua, Polynesian term for god or guardian-spirit, i. 387 *n.*[1], viii. 153, 156 ; ancestral spirit, iii. 134, 265

Atys, son of Croesus, his death, v. 286

Atys, early king of Lydia, v. 286
Aubrey, John, on soul-cakes, vi. 78 ; on sin-eating, ix. 43 *sq.* ; on the Midsummer fires, x. 197
Aucas (Araucanians), their custom of bleeding themselves to relieve fatigue, ix. 12. *See* Araucanians
Auch, the archbishop of, i. 232 *sq.*
Aufkirchen in Bavaria, burning the Easter Man at, x. 144
Augsburg, harvest custom near, vii. 298
Augur's staff at Rome, iii. 313
August, procession of wicker giants in, xi. 36
—— 1st, Festival of the Cross on the, x. 220
—— 6th, festival of St. Estapin, xi. 188
——, the Ides (13th) of, Diana's day, i. 12, 14-17
—— 15th, the day of the Assumption of the Virgin, i. 14-16
—— 18th, feast of Florus and Laurus, x. 220
Augustine, on the one God, i. 121 *n.*[1] ; on the effeminate priests of the Great Mother, v. 298 ; on the heathen origin of Christmas, v. 305 ; on the discovery of corn by Isis, vi. 116 ; on Salacia as the wife of Neptune, vi. 233 ; on the Eleusinian mysteries, vii. 88 ; on Roman deities of the corn, vii. 210 *n.*[3]
Augustodunum (Autun), worship of Cybele at, v. 279
Augustus as a ruler, i. 216 ; granted the oak crown, ii. 176 *sq.* ; reputed a son of Apollo, v. 81 ; celebrates games at Actium, vii. 80 ; triumphal arch of Augustus at Ariminum, xi. 195 *n.*[4]
Aulus Gellius on the influence of the moon, vi. 132. *See also* Gellius
Aun, or On, King of Sweden, sacrifices his sons to save his life, iv. 57, 160 *sq.*, 188, vi. 220
Aunis, Feast of All Souls in, vi. 69 *sq.* ; wonderful herbs gathered on St. John's Eve in, xi. 45 ; St. John's wort in, xi. 55 ; vervain gathered at Midsummer in, xi. 62 *n.*[4] ; four-leaved clover at Midsummer in, xi. 63
—— and Saintonge, Midsummer fires in, x. 192. *See* Saintonge
Aunts named after their nieces, iii. 332
Aunund, King, in Norse legend, viii. 146
Aurelia Aemilia, a sacred harlot, v. 38
Aurich, in East Friesland, "cutting the hare's tail off" at harvest at, vii. 268, 280
Auricular confession, iii. 214. *See* Confession
Aurohuaca Indians of Colombia, auricular confession among the, iii. 215 *sq.*, v. 23 *n.*[2]
Aurora, one of the New Hebrides, rain-making by means of a stone in, i. 308 ; magic practised on refuse of food in, iii. 127 ; *tamaniu* in, xi. 198
Aurora Australis, fear entertained by the Kurnai of the, iv. 267 *n.*[1]
Ausonius, on the Ides of August, i. 12 *n.*[2]
Aust, E., on the marriage of the Roman gods, vi. 236 *n.*[1]
Australia, use of magical images among the aborigines of, i. 62 ; cave-paintings in, i. 87 *n.*[1] ; rain-making in, i. 251 *sq.*, 254-261, 287 *sq.*, 304 ; dust-columns in, thought to be spirits, i. 331 *sq.* ; government of old men in aboriginal, i. 334 *sq.* ; influence of magicians in aboriginal, i. 334 *sqq.* ; ceremony observed at approaching the camp of another tribe in, iii. 109 ; custom of personal cleanliness observed from superstitious motives among the aborigines of, iii. 158 *n.*[1] ; names of relations tabooed among the aborigines of, iii. 345 *sq.* ; belief as to the reincarnation of the dead in, v. 99 *sqq.* ; totemism in, viii. 311 ; demons in, ix. 74 ; annual expulsion of ghosts in, ix. 123 *sq.* ; dread and seclusion of women at menstruation in, x. 76 *sqq.* ; passing under an arch as a rite of initiation in, xi. 193 *n.*[1] ; initiation of young men in, xi. 227, 233 *sqq.* ; use of bull-roarers in, xi. 289 *n.*[2] *See also* Australian aborigines, New South Wales, Queensland, Victoria
——, Central, ceremony to promote the growth of hair in, i. 83 ; magical ceremonies for the supply of food in, i. 85 *sqq.* ; charm to promote the growth of beards in, i. 153 *sq.* ; charm to ensure wakefulness in, i. 154 ; *churinga* (sacred sticks or stones) in, i. 199 ; contagious magic of wounds in, i. 204 ; the Arunta of, i. 259 ; headmen of the totem clans are public magicians in, i. 335 ; the Kaitish of, ii. 105, iii. 82, iv. 60 ; the Warramunga of, ii. 156, ix. 2 ; the Urabunna of, ii. 209 ; the tribes of, do not let women see men's blood, iii. 252 *n.* ; the aboriginal tribes of, make no magical use of shorn hair, iii. 268 *n.*[1] ; concealment of personal names among the aborigines of, iii. 321 *sq.* ; avoidance of the names of the dead among the tribes of, iii. 351 ; the Luritcha tribe of, iv. 180 *n.*[1], viii. 260 ; magical rites for the revival of nature in, iv. 270 ; the Dieri of, vii. 106, viii. 151, ix. 110 ; use of a species

of Claytonia as food in, vii. 128; the aborigines of, their ceremonies for the multiplication of kangaroos, viii. 165; the Tjingilli tribe of, ix. 2; pointing sticks or bones in, x. 14 *n.*[3]; its desert nature, xi. 230 *n.*[2]

Australia, Northern, the Anula of, i. 253, 287; the Tjingilli of, i. 288; homoeopathic magic of flesh diet in, viii. 145

——, North-West, fat about heart of great warrior eaten to acquire his courage in, viii. 150 *sq.*

——, South, custom as to the placenta in, i. 183; the Dieri of, ii. 29; the Narrinyeri of, iii. 126 *sq.*, 372, viii. 259 *n.*; the Encounter Bay tribe of, iii. 127, 251, 355, 359, 372, vii. 126; the Booandik tribe of, iii. 251, 346; the Adelaide tribe of, iii. 355; the Port Lincoln tribe of, iii. 365; firstborn children destroyed among some tribes of, iv. 180

——, South-Eastern, contagious magic of footprints in, i. 207 *sq.*; contagious magic of bodily impressions among the aborigines of, i. 213; belief as to the connexion of frogs with rain in, i. 292 *sq.*; the Theddora and Ngarigo tribes of, viii. 151; sex totems among the natives of, xi. 214 *sqq.*

——, South - Western, medicine - men (doctors) in, i. 336

——, Western, belief as to the placenta in, i. 183; belief as to water-serpents in, ii. 156; names of the dead not mentioned in, iii. 364; native women dig for yam roots in, vii. 126 *sq.*; the aborigines of, call certain flowering plants "Mothers," vii. 130

Australian aborigines, magical images among the, i. 62; ceremonies of initiation among the, i. 92 *sqq.*; contagious magic of teeth among the, i. 176; magic of navel-string and afterbirth among the, i. 183 *sy.*; magic universally practised but religion nearly unknown among the, i. 234; their custom of carrying fire with them, ii. 257; their conception of the soul, iii. 27; dread of a wife's mother among the, iii. 83 *sq.*; die from effects of imagination, iii. 136; their fear of menstruous women, iii. 145; of Queensland burn women's cut hair, iii. 282; burn women's hair after childbirth, iii. 284; personal names kept secret among the, iii. 320 *sqq.*; their fear of naming the dead, iii. 349 *sqq.*; namesakes of the dead change their names among the, iii. 355 *sq.*; changes in their languages caused by fear of naming the dead, iii. 358 *sqq.*;

their fear of a woman stepping over them, iii. 424; their beliefs as to shooting stars, iv. 60 *sq.*, 64; their custom of destroying first-born children, iv. 179 *sq.*; their custom of killing and eating children, iv. 180 *n.*[1]; infanticide among the, iv. 187 *n.*[6]; their preparation for marriage, v. 60; belief in conception without sexual intercourse, v. 99 *sqq.*; their cuttings for the dead, v. 268; division of labour between the sexes in regard to the collection of food among, viii. 126 *sqq.*; worshipped the Pleiades as the givers of rain, vii. 307; their belief that the Pleiades were once women, vii. 308 *n.*; anoint themselves with the fat of the dead in order to acquire their qualities, viii. 162 *sq.*; their objection to breaking the bones of the native bear, viii. 258 *n.*[2]; their custom of burning the bones of the animals which they eat, viii. 259 *n.*[1]; their mutilations of the dead, viii. 272; their totemism the most primitive known to us, viii. 311; said to propitiate the kangaroos which they have killed, viii. 312 *n.*; their cure for toothache, ix. 6; their belief in demons, ix. 74

Australian blacks afraid of passing under a leaning tree, iii. 250 *n.*[1]

—— custom of placing stones in trees, i. 318; as to blood shed at initiatory rites, rain-making, etc., iii. 244

—— funeral custom, iv. 92

—— languages, words for fire and wood in, xi. 296

—— magic wrought on cut hair, iii. 269

—— medicine-man, his recovery of a lost soul, iii. 54

—— mode of magically tying up the inside of an enemy, iii. 303

—— tribes, their custom of knocking out teeth of boys at initiation, i. 176

—— way of detaining the sun, i. 318; of hastening the descent of the sun, i. 318 *sq.*

Australians, the Central, their ceremony for multiplying kangaroos, viii. 165

Austria, dancing or leaping as a charm to make flax grow tall in, i. 138; gipsy mode of stopping rain in, i. 295 *sq.*; meal offered to the wind in, i. 329 *n.*[5]; peasants of, their belief in the sensitiveness of trees, ii. 18; belief as to stepping over a child in, iii. 424; leaping over Midsummer fires in, v. 251; children warned against the Corn-cock in, vii. 276; mythical Calf in corn in, vii. 292; cure for warts in, ix. 48; dances or leaps to make the crops grow high in, ix. 238; "Easter Smacks" in, ix. 268 *sq.*; custom of young people beating each other on Holy Innocents' Day in, ix. 270; weather of the twelve months thought to be determined by the weather of the Twelve Days in, ix. 322; weather forecasts in, ix. 323; the three mythical kings on Twelfth Day in, ix. 329; Midsummer fires in, x. 172 *sqq.*; the Yule log among the Servians of, x. 262 *sqq.*; fern-seed at Midsummer in, xi. 65; mistletoe used to prevent nightmare in, xi. 85

Austria, Lower, presages as to shadows on St. Sylvester's Day in, iii. 88

——, Upper, processions round fields on St. George's Day in, ii. 344; need-fire in, x. 279

Austrian charm to make fruit-trees bear, i. 140 *sq.*

Autumn, ceremony of the Esquimaux in late, ix. 125

—— fires, x. 220 *sqq.*

Autun, procession of goddess at, ii. 144; the Festival of Fools at, ix. 335

Auvergne, milk bewitched at Corrèze in, iii. 93; Lenten 'fires in, x. 111 *sq.*; story of a were-wolf in, x. 308 *sq.*

Auxerre, the last sheaf called the Corn-mother near, vii. 135; "killing the Bull" at threshing at, vii. 291

Auxesia and Damia, female powers of fertility at Troezen, i. 39

Ave Maria bell on Midsummer Eve, xi. 47

Avebury, Lord, on the distinction between religion and magic, i. 225 *n.*; on substitutes for capital punishment in China, iv. 146 *n.*, 273

Avengers of blood, ceremony performed by, before starting, i. 92

Aventine, Diana on the, ii. 128; oaks on the, ii. 185

Avernus, Lake, and the Golden Bough, xi. 285 *n.*[2]

Aversion of spirits and fairies to iron, iii. 229, 232 *sq.*; to innovation among savages, iii. 230 *sqq.*

Averting ill-luck at marrying a second, third, or fourth wife, ii. 57 *n.*[4]

Avestad, in Sweden, heaps of sticks and stones on graves at, ix. 20 *sq.*

Avoidance of the wife's mother, iii. 83 *sqq.*; of common words to deceive spirits or other beings, iii. 416 *sqq.*

"Awakening of Hercules," festival at Tyre, v. 111

Awa-nkonde, seclusion of girls at puberty among the, x. 28

"Awasungu, the house of the," x. 28

Awe, Loch, vii. 165; the Old Wife at harvest on, vii. 142

Awemba, Bantu tribe of Rhodesia, their belief in a supreme being, vi. 174; their worship of ancestral spirits, vi. 175; their prayers to dead kings before going to war, vi. 191 *sq.*; woman's part in agriculture among the, vii. 115; among them murderers mutilate their victims in order to disable their ghosts, viii. 272 *sq.*

Awka in South Nigeria, taboos observed by priest at, x. 4

Awujale, title of chief of the Ijebu tribe, in South Nigeria, iv. 112

Awuna tribes of the Gold Coast, their belief as to the sacredness of their heads, iii. 257

Axe, emblem of Hittite god of thundering sky, v. 134; as divine emblem, v. 163; symbol of Asiatic thunder-god, v. 183; that slew the ox, trial and condemnation of the, viii. 5

——, double-headed, symbol of Sandan, v. 127; carried by Lydian kings, v. 182; a palladium of the Heraclid sovereignty, v. 182; figured on coins, v. 183 *n.*

Axim, on the Gold Coast, annual expulsion of the devil at, ix. 131

Ayambori, in Dutch New Guinea, woman's share in agriculture among the Papuans of, vii. 123

Aymara Indians of Peru and Bolivia, their rain-charm by means of frogs, i. 292 *sqq.*; afraid of being photographed, iii. 97; their use of a black llama as a scapegoat in time of plague, ix. 193

Ayrshire, mode of cutting the last corn in, vii. 154; "cutting the Hare" at harvest in, vii. 279

Azadirachta Indica in a rain-charm, i. 293

Azazel, a bad angel, in connexion with the Jewish scapegoat, ix. 210 *n.*[4]

Azemmour, in Morocco, cairns reared by pilgrims near, ix. 21; Midsummer fires at, x. 214

Azores, bonfires and divination on Midsummer Eve in the, x. 208 *sq.*; fern-seed at Midsummer in the, xi. 66

Aztec mode of keeping sorcerers from houses, iii. 93

—— priests, their hair unshorn, iii. 259

Aztecs, their view of intoxication as inspiration, iii. 249 *sq.*; their priests, iii. 259; their festival at end of fifty-two years, vii. 310 *sq.*; their observation of the Pleiades, vii. 310 *sq.*; their sacred new fire, vii. 310 *sq.*; eating the god among the, viii. 86 *sqq.*; their custom of sacrificing human representatives of gods, ix. 275; their five supplementary days, ix. 339 ; their punishment of witches and wizards, xi. 159

Azur, the month of March, ix. 403

Azyingo, Lake, in West Africa, viii. 235

Ba-Bwende, a tribe of the Congo, v. 271 *n.*

Ba-Lua, in the Congo region, will not pronounce name of their tribe, iii. 330

—— -Mbala, a Bantu tribe, woman's share in agriculture among the, vii. 119

—— -Pedi, the, of South Africa, gravediggers not allowed to handle food among, iii. 141 ; women in childbed not allowed to handle food, iii. 148 *sq.*; their superstitions as to miscarriage in childbed, iii. 153 *sq.*; their continence in war, iii. 163 ; continence at building a new village among the, iii. 202 ; their belief as to a woman stepping over their legs, iii. 424

—— -Ronga, the, of South Africa, their women employ a child under puberty to light the potter's kiln, ii. 205. *See* Baronga

—— -Sundi, a tribe of the Congo, v. 271 *n.*

—— -Thonga, the, of South Africa, gravediggers not allowed to handle food among the, iii. 141 ; women in childbed not allowed to handle food, iii. 148 *sq.*; attribute drought to concealed miscarriage in childbed, iii. 154 ; their continence in war, iii. 163 ; continence at building a new village among the, iii. 202 ; their belief as to a woman stepping over their legs, iii. 424. *See also* Thonga

—— -Yaka, tribe of the Congo State, power of magicians among the, i. 348 ; custom observed by manslayers among the, iii. 186 *n.*[1] ; their use of nail-parings in making treaties, iii. 274

—— -Yanzi, tribe of the Congo State, the chief as a magician among the, i. 348 *sq.*

Baal, Semitic god, in relation to Minos and Minotaur, iv. 75 ; the prophets of, their cutting themselves with knives, i. 258 ; human sacrifices to, iv. 167 *sqq.*, 195, ix. 353, 354; kings claiming affinity with, v. 15 ; royal names compounded with, v. 16 ; as the god of fertility, v. 26 *sq.* ; conceived as god who fertilizes land by subterranean water, v. 159

—— and Beltane, x. 149 *n.*[1], 150 *n.*[1], 157

—— of the Lebanon, v. 32

—— and Sandan at Tarsus, v. 142 *sq.*, 161

Baal of Tarsus, v. 117 *sqq.*, 162 *sq.*

Baalath or Astarte, v. 26, 34

—— and Baal, v. 27

—— Gebal, v. 14

Baalbec (Heliopolis), in Syria, v. 28 ; the ruins at, i. 30 *n.*[8] ; sacred prostitution at, v. 37 ; image of Hadad at, v. 163

Baalim, the, lords of underground waters, ii. 159 ; firstlings and first-fruits offered to the, v. 27 ; called lovers, v. 75 *n.*

Baba or Boba, name given to last sheaf, vii. 144 *sq.* ; "the Old Woman," at the Carnival, viii. 332, 333

Babalawo, a Yoruba priest, ix. 212

Babar Archipelago, ceremony to obtain a child for a barren woman in the, i. 72 ; chastity and fasting of women during absence of warriors in the, i. 131 ; treatment of the afterbirth in the, i. 186 ; saturnalia at the marriage of the Sun and Earth in the, ii. 99 ; recovery of lost souls in the, iii. 67 ; souls as shadows in the, iii. 78 ; fatigue transferred to stones in the, ix. 8 *sq.* ; sickness expelled in a boat from the, ix. 187

Babaruda, girl as rain-maker in Roumania, i. 273

Babine Lake in British Columbia, x. 47

Babites, a Persian sect, their divine head, i. 402

Baboons, their depredations on crops, viii. 32 ; sent by evil spirits, ix. 110 *sq.*

Baby, effigy of, used to fertilize women, ix. 245, 249

Babylon, magical images in ancient, i. 66 *sq.*; theocratic despotism of ancient, i. 218 ; sanctuary of Bel at, ii. 129 *sq.* ; festival of Zagmuk at, iv. 110, 113, 115 *sqq.* ; festival of the Sacaea at, iv. 113 *sqq.*, ix. 354 *sqq.* ; early kings of, worshipped as gods, v. 15 ; worship of Mylitta at, v. 36 ; religious prostitution at, v. 58 ; human wives of Marduk at, v. 71 ; sanctuary of Serapis at, vi. 119*n.*

Babylonia, worship of Tammuz in, v. 6 *sqq.* ; the moon-god took precedence of the sun-god in ancient, vi. 138 *sq.* ; belief in demons in ancient, ix. 102 *sq.* ; the star-gazers of, ix. 326 ; conquered by Assyria, ix. 356 ; the feast of Purim in, ix. 393

Babylonian calendar, ix. 398 *n.*[2]

—— Genesis, ix. 410

—— gods, mortality of the, iv. 5 *sq.*

—— hymns to Tammuz, v. 9

—— kings, divinity of the early, i. 417

—— legend of creation, iv. 105 *sq.*, 110

—— myth of Marduk and Tiamat, iv. 105 *sq.*, 107 *sq.*

Babylonian witches and wizards, their use of knotted cords, iii. 302

Bacchanalia, Purim a Jewish, ix. 363

Bacchanals of Thrace chew ivy, i. 384 ; tore Pentheus in pieces, vi. 98, vii. 24, 25 ; wore horns, vii. 17

Bacchic frenzy, iv. 164 ; orgies suppressed by Roman Government, v. 301 *n.*²

Bacchus, his legendary connexion with the Athenian festival of swinging, iv. 281, 283

—— or Dionysus, vii. 2. *See* Dionysus

Bacchylides as to Croesus on the pyre, v. 175 *sq.*

Bachofen, J. J., on Roman kings and the Saturnalia, ii. 313 *n.*¹ ; on the *Nonae Caprotinae* and the Saturnalia, ii. 314 *n.*¹

Backache at reaping, leaps over the Midsummer bonfire thought to be a preventive of, x. 165, 168, 189, 344 *sq.* ; set down to witchcraft, x. 343 *n.*, 345 ; at harvest, mugwort a protection against, xi. 59 ; creeping through a holed stone to prevent backache at harvest, xi. 189

Backbone of Osiris represented by the *ded* pillar, vi. 108 *sq.*

Bacon, Francis, on anointing weapon that caused wound, i. 202

Bad Country, the, in Victoria, ceremonies observed at entering, iii. 109 *sq.*

Badache, double-axe, Midsummer King of the, x. 194

Badagas, the, of the Neilgherry Hills, their customs as to sowing and reaping the first grain, viii. 55 ; transfer the sins of the dead to a buffalo calf, ix. 36 ; their fire-walk, xi. 8 *sq.*

Baddeley, Mr. St. Clair, i. 5 *n.*²

Baden, homoeopathic magic at sowing in, i. 138 ; St. George's Day in, ii. 337 ; Feast of All Souls in, vi. 74 ; customs as to the last sheaf at harvest in, vii. 283, 292, 298 ; the Corn-goat at threshing in, vii. 286 ; Lenten fire-custom in, x. 117 ; Easter bonfires in, x. 145 ; Midsummer fires in, x. 167 *sqq.*

Badham, Rev. Charles, D.D., his proposed emendation of Euripides, iii. 156 *n.*

Badham Court oak, in Gloucestershire, xi. 316

Badi, performer at a tight-rope ceremony in India, ix. 197

Badnyak, Yule log, in Servia, x. 259, 263

Badnyi Dan, Christmas Eve, in Servia, x. 258, 263

Badonsachen, King of Burma, claims divinity, i. 400

Badumar, in West Africa, ii. 293

Baduwis, an aboriginal race in the mountains of Java, seclusion of their heredi-

tary ruler, iii. 115 *sq.* ; use no iron in husbandry, iii. 232

Baethgen, F., on goddess 'Hatheh, v. 162 *n.*²

Baffin Land, the Esquimaux of, i. 113, iii. 32 *n.*², 152, 207, 399, viii. 257, ix. 125

Bag, souls of persons deposited in a, iii. 63 *sq.*, xi. 142, 153, 155 ; soul of dying chief caught in a, iv. 199

Baganda, the, of Central Africa, their belief as to the sterilizing influence of barren women, i. 142, ii. 102 ; their treatment of the afterbirth and navel-string, i. 195 *sq.*, xi. 162 ; spirits of their dead kings preserved in the navel-strings and jawbones, i. 196 ; their notion as to whirlwinds, i. 331 *n.*² ; their incarnate human god of the Lake Nyanza, i. 395 ; their belief in the influence of the sexes on vegetation, ii. 101 *sq.* ; their customs in regard to twins, ii. 102 *sq.* ; their fire-drill, ii. 210 ; their Vestal Virgins, ii. 246 ; their list of kings, ii. 269 ; their mode of fertilizing women by means of a wild banana-tree, ii. 318 ; stabbed the shadows of enemies, iii. 78 ; their superstition as to shadows, iii. 87 ; their belief as to women stepping over a man's weapons, iii. 423 ; their belief as to the state of the spirits of the dead, iv. 11 ; their worship of the python, v. 86 ; rebirth of the dead among the, v. 92 *sq.* ; their belief in impregnation by the flower of the banana, v. 93 ; their theory of earthquakes, v. 199 ; their presentation of infants to the new moon, vi. 144, 145 ; ceremony observed by the king at new moon, vi. 147 ; their worship of dead kings, vi. 167 *sqq.* ; their veneration for the ghosts of dead relations, vi. 191 *n.*¹ ; their pantheon, vi. 196 ; human sacrifices offered to prolong the life of their kings, vi. 223 *sqq.* ; woman's share in agriculture among the, vii. 118 ; their ceremony at eating the new beans, viii. 64 ; significance of stepping over a woman among the, viii. 70 *n.*¹ ; their offerings of first-fruits, viii. 113 ; their precaution against the ghosts of the elephants which they kill, viii. 227 *sq.* ; dread the ghosts of sheep, viii. 231 ; propitiate the ghosts of slain buffaloes, viii. 231 ; treat ceremonially the first fish caught, viii. 252 *sq.* ; their custom of mutilating dead enemies, viii. 271 *sq.* ; their transference of plague to a plantain-tree, ix. 4 *sq.* ; transference of sickness to effigies, ix. 7 ; their precautions against the ghosts of suicides and other unfortunates, ix. 17 *sq.* ; throw sticks or grass on graves or places of execution of certain persons, ix. 18 ; their worship of the river Nakiza, ix. 27 ; transfer sickness to animals, ix. 32 ; human scapegoats among the, ix. 42 ; children live apart from their parents among the, x. 23 *n.*[2] ; seclusion of girls at puberty among the, x. 23 *sq.*; their superstition as to women who do not menstruate, x. 24 ; abstain from salt in certain cases, x. 27 *sq.* ; their dread of menstruous women, x. 80 *sq.* *See also* Uganda

Baganda fishermen, taboos observed by, iii. 194 *sq.*

Bagba, a wind-fetish, i. 327, iii. 5

Bagdad, death of the King of the Jinn reported at, iv. 8

Bageshu (Bagishu), the, of Mount Elgon, in East Africa, their belief in the re-incarnation of the dead, i. 103, v. 92 ; seclusion and purification of manslayers among, iii. 174

Bagobos of Mindanao, one of the Philippines, their human sacrifices at sowing, vii. 240 ; their way of detaining the soul in the body, iii. 31, 315 ; never utter their own names, iii. 323 *sq.* ; their theory of earthquakes, v. 200 ; their custom of hanging and spearing human victims, v. 290 *sq.* ; their pretence of feeding their agricultural implements at harvest, viii. 124

Baharutsis, a Bantu tribe of South Africa, their worship of ancestors, vi. 179

Bahaus. *See* Kayans

Bahima of Central Africa, ceremony of adoption among the, i. 75 ; custom of herdsmen at watering their cattle among the, iii. 183 *n.* ; names of their dead kings not mentioned, iii. 375 ; their belief as to dead kings and chiefs, v. 83 *n.*[1]; their worship of the dead, vi. 190 *sq.* ; their belief in a supreme god Lugaba, vi. 190 ; their belief in transmigration, viii. 288 ; believe that at death their kings turn into lions, and their queens into leopards, viii. 288 ; their transference of abscesses, ix. 6 ; their use of scapegoats to cure disease among their cattle, ix. 32 ; their dread of menstruous women, x. 80

—— of Kiziba, vi. 173

—— of the Uganda Protectorate, ix. 6, 32

Bahnars of Cochin-China, their recall of lost souls, iii. 52, 58 *sq.*

Bahr-el-Ghazal province, the Golos of the, i. 318 ; ceremony of the new fire in the, x. 134 *sq.*

Baiga, aboriginal priest in Mirzapur, ix. 27

Baigas, Dravidian tribe of India, their objection to agriculture, v. 89

Bailey, Mabel, on the May Queen, ii. 88 *n.*[1]

Bailly, J. S., French astronomer, on the Arctic origin of the rites of Adonis, v. 229

Bairu, the, of Kiziba, vi. 173

Baisâkh, Indian month (April), iv. 265

Bakairi, the, of Brazil, call bull-roarers "thunder and lightning," xi. 231 *sq.*

Bakara, a village of Sumatra, i. 398, 399

Baker, F. B., on relic of tree-worship at Magnesia, i. 386 *n.*[2]

Bakers, Roman, required to be chaste, ii. 115 *sq.*, 205

Baking, continence observed at, iii. 201

—— -forks, witches ride on, xi. 73, 74

Bakongs, the, of Borneo, associate the souls of the dead with bear-cats and other animals, viii. 294

Baku, on the Caspian, perpetual fires at, ii. 256, v. 192

Bakuba or Bushongo of the Congo, rule as to persons of royal blood among the, x. 4. *See* Bushongo

Bakundu of the Cameroons, burial custom of the, viii. 99

Balabulan, a person of the Batta Trinity, ix. 88 *n.*[1]

Bald-headed widow, transference of fever to a, ix. 38

Balder, the Norse god, and his lame foal, iii. 305 *n.*[1]; his body burnt, x. 102 ; worshipped in Norway, x. 104 ; camomile sacred to, xi. 63 ; burnt at Midsummer, xi. 87 ; Midsummer sacred to, xi. 87 ; a tree-spirit or deity of vegetation, xi. 88 *sq.* ; his invulnerability, xi. 94 ; why Balder was thought to shine, xi. 293 ; perhaps a real man deified, xi. 314 *sq.*

—— and the mistletoe, x. 101 *sq.*, xi. 76 *sqq.*, 302; interpreted as a mistletoe-bearing oak, xi. 93 *sq.* ; his life or death in the mistletoe, xi. 279, 283

——, the myth of, x. 101 *sqq.* ; reproduced in the Midsummer festival of Scandinavia, xi. 87 ; perhaps dramatized in ritual, xi. 88 ; Indian parallel to, xi. 280 ; African parallels to, xi. 312 *sqq.*

Balder's Balefires, name formerly given to Midsummer bonfires in Sweden, x. 172, xi. 87

—— Grove, x. 104, xi. 315

Balders-brå, Balder's eyelashes, a name for camomile, xi. 63

Baldness a supposed effect of breaking a taboo, iii. 140

Bâle, statuette of the Mexican god Xipe at, ix. 291 *n.*[1]; Lenten fire-custom in the canton of, x. 119

Balefires, Balder's, at Midsummer in Sweden, x. 172

Bali, inspired mediums in, i. 378 *sq.* ; special forms of speech used in addressing social superiors in, i. 402 *n.* ; the rice personified as husband and wife in, vii. 201 *sqq.* ; observation of the Pleiades in, vii. 314 *sq.* ; propitiation of mice to induce them to spare the fields in, viii. 278 ; belief in demons in, ix. 86 ; periodical expulsion of demons in, ix. 140 ; filing of teeth in, x. 68 *n.*[2]; birth-trees in, xi. 164

Balinese, their conduct in an earthquake, v. 198

Balkan Peninsula, the Slavs of the, ii. 237, 241 ; need-fire in the, x. 281

Ball, Valentine, on hook-swinging, iv. 279

Ball, game of, played as a rite, viii. 76, 79 ; played as a magical ceremony, ix. 179 *sq.*; in Normandy, ix. 183 *sq.*; played to determine the King of Summer, x. 195

—— -players, homoeopathic charms employed by, i. 144, 155

Balli Atap, the God of the Roof, among the Kenyahs, ii. 385

Ballinasloe, in County Galway, Candlemas custom at, ii. 95 *n.*

Balls, gold and silver, to imitate the sun and moon, ii. 63

Ballymagauran, in County Cavan, ancient idol near, iv. 183

Ballymote, the Book of, iv. 100

Ballyvadlea, in Tipperary, woman burnt as a witch at, x. 323 *sq.*

Balnagown Loch, in Lismore, witch-hare at, x. 316

Baloi, mythical beings of the Basutos, i. 177 ; witches and wizards, vi. 104

Balolo, a sea-slug, ix. 141. *See also Palolo veridis*

Balong of the Cameroons, their external souls in animals, xi. 203

Balquhidder, in Perthshire, the harvest Maiden at, vii. 157 ; hill of the fires at, x. 149 ; Hallowe'en bonfires at, x. 232

Balsam plants, wild, as representatives of the harvest-goddess, vii. 207

Balsamorrhiza sagittata, Nutt., the sunflower root, superstitions of Thompson Indians concerning the, viii. 81

Balthasar, one of the three mythical kings on Twelfth Day, ix. 329 *sqq.*

Balum, a mythical being of German New Guinea, iii. 306

Balum, spirits, vii. 104, ix. 83, xi. 242

Balwe in Westphalia, Burying the Carnival at, iv. 232

Bâm-Margi, Hindoo sect, their use of magical images, i. 65

Bambaras of the Niger, their sacred trees, ii. 42

Bamboo-rat sacrificed for riddance of evils, ix. 208 *sq.*

Bampton-in-the-Bush in Oxfordshire, May garlands at, ii. 62

Banana, women impregnated by the flower of the, v. 93 ; shoots beaten to make them grow, ix. 264

—— -tree, supposed to fertilize barren women, ii. 318 ; child's hair deposited on a, iii. 276 ; afterbirth of child buried under a, xi. 162, 163, 164

—— -trees, fruit-bearing, hair deposited under, iii. 286

Bananas, homoeopathic magic at sowing, i. 142 ; sown by young children, vii. 115 ; cultivated by women, vii. 115, 118 ; cultivated in South America, vii. 120, 121 ; cultivated in New Britain, vii. 123 ; cultivated in New Guinea, vii. 123 ; soul of dead man in, viii. 298 ; mode of fertilizing, ix. 264 ; the cause of human mortality, ix. 303

Banars of Cambodia, their prayers for the crops, viii. 33

Bancroft, H. H., on the external souls of the Zapotecs, xi. 212

Bandages to prevent the escape of the soul, iii. 32, 71

Bandiagara, Mount, in Nigeria, iii. 124

Bandicoot in rain-making, i. 288

Bangala, the, of the Upper Congo, continence observed by fishers and hunters among, iii. 195 *sq.* ; names of fishermen not mentioned among, iii. 330 *sq.*; rebirth of dead among, v. 92 ; women's share in agriculture among, vii. 119. *See also* Boloki

Bangalas of Angola, elective chieftainship among the, ii. 293

Bangerang, an Australian tribe, iii. 321

Bangkok, ix. 150 ; human foundation sacrifices at, iii. 90

Bangweolo, Lake, custom as to sowing on the islands of, vii. 115

Banished prince, charm to restore a, i. 145

Banishment of homicide, iv. 69 *sq.* ; of evil spirits, ix. 86

Banivas of the Orinoco, their scourging of girls at puberty, x. 66 *sqq.*

Banjars in West Africa punish their king for drought or excessive rain, i. 353

Banks' Islanders, their ways of making sunshine, i. 314 ; their observation of the Pleiades, vii. 313 ; their story of the origin of death, ix. 304

Banks' Islands, magical stones in the, i. 164 ; supernatural power of chiefs in the, i. 338 ; ghosts in stones in the, iii. 80 ; Vanua Lava in the, iii. 85 ; names of relations by marriage tabooed in the, iii. 344 *sq.* ; burial of women who have died in childbed in the, viii. 97 *sq.* ; fatigue transferred to stones, sticks, or leaves in the, ix. 9

Banksia, used as fuel by Australian aborigines, ii. 257

Banmanas of Senegambia, their custom at the death of an infant, ix. 261 *sq.*

Banna, a tribe accustomed to strangle their first-born children, iv. 181 *sq.*

Banner, Macleod's Fairy, i. 368

Banquets in honour of the spirits of disease, ix. 119

Bantiks of Celebes, their story of the type of Beauty and the Beast, iv. 130 *n.*[1]

Banting in Sarawak, rules observed by women during absence of warriors at, i. 127, 128

Bantu tribes, ancestor-worship among the, ii. 221, vi. 174 *sqq.* ; their small regard for the ghosts of women, ii. 224 *n.*[4] ; their belief in serpents as reincarnations of the dead, v. 82 *sqq.* ; their worship of dead chiefs or kings, vi. 175 *sqq.*, 191 *sqq.* ; cohabitation of husband and wife enjoined as a matter of ritual on certain occasions among the, viii. 70 *n.*[1]

—— tribes of Kavirondo, custom observed by manslayers among the, iii. 176 *sq.* ; their belief as to the effect of eating a totemic animal, viii. 26

—— tribes of South Africa, their ideas as to the virulent infection spread by a woman who has had a miscarriage, iii. 152 *sqq.* ; their rule as to eating the new corn, viii. 111 ; their fear of demons, ix. 77 *sq.*

—— tribes of South-East Africa, their fire-drill, ii. 210 *sq.*

—— tribes of West Africa, their belief in demons, ix. 74

Banyai, chieftainship among the, ii. 292

Banyan-trees revered by the Chinese, ii. 14

Banyoro, the, of Central Africa, foes of the Baganda, ix. 42, 194 ; the king as rain-maker among, i. 348 ; succession to the throne determined by mortal combat among, ii. 322 ; their worship of serpents, v. 86 *n.*[1] *See also* Unyoro

Baobab-trees thought to be inhabited by mischievous spirits, ii. 34 ; worshipped, ii. 46 ; goats sacrificed to, ii. 47

Baoules of the Ivory Coast, extraction of chief's soul among the, iii. 70

Baperis or Malekootoos, a Bechuana tribe, their customs as to their totem the porcupine, viii. 164 *sq.*

Baptism of bull's blood in the rites of Cybele, v. 274 *sqq.*

Baptist, St. John the, day of, i. 277. *See* St. John

Bar-rekub, king of Samal,, v. 15 *sq.*

Bar-tree (*Ficus Indica*), married to a mango in India, ii. 25 ; sacred in India, ii. 43

Bara, a tribe of Madagascar, names of dead kings not pronounced among the, iii. 380

—— country in Madagascar, fear of being photographed in the, iii. 98

Barabbas and Christ, ix. 417 *sqq.*

Baraka, blessed or magical virtue, in North Africa, ix. 23 *n.*, x. 216, 218, xi. 51 ; of saints, ix. 22 ; of skins of sacrificed sheep, ix. 265

Baram River, in Sarawak, tree-worship on the, ii. 38 *sq.* ; in Borneo, magical stones on the, iii. 30

Barar, third marriage deemed unlucky in, ii. 57 *n.*[4]

Barat, a ceremony performed in Kumaon, ix. 196

Barber, Rev. Dr. W. T. A., on substitutes for capital punishment in China, iv. 145 *n.*, 275

Barbosa, Duarte, on the suicide of the kings of Quilacare, iv. 46 *sq.*

Barce or Alceis, daughter of Antaeus, ii. 300 *sq.*

Barcelona, ceremony of " Sawing the Old Woman " at, iv. 242

Barclay, Sheriff, on Hallowe'en fires, x. 232

Bardney bumpkin, on witch as hare, x. 318

Bare-Stripping Hangman, Argyleshire story of the, xi. 129 *sq.*

Barea, of East Africa, rain-making priest among the, ii. 3 ; women will not name their husbands, iii. 337

—— and Kunama, their annual festival of the dead, vi. 66

Barenton, the fountain of, used in rain-making, i. 306, 307

Bari, the, of the Upper Nile, rain-makers as chiefs among, i. 345, 346 *sq.* ; Rain Kings among, ii. 2

Barito, the, of Borneo, sacrifice cattle instead of human victims, iv. 166 *n.*[1]

——, river in Borneo, worship of spirits on the, ix. 87

Bark of sacred tree used to make garments for pregnant women, ii. 58

Barker, W. G. M. Jones, on need-fire in Yorkshire, x. 286 *sq.*

Barking a tree, old German penalty for, ii. 9

Barley forced for festival, v. 240, 241, 242, 244, 251 *sq.* ; awarded as a prize in the Eleusinian games, vii. 73, 74, 75 ; oldest cereal cultivated by the Aryans, vii. 132

—— Bride among the Berbers, vii. 178 *sq.*

—— -cow at harvest, vii. 289, 290

—— -harvest, time of, in ancient Greece, vii. 48, 77

—— loaf eaten by human scapegoat before being put to death, ix. 255

—— -meal and water drunk as a form of communion with the Barley-Goddess at Eleusis, vii. 161

—— -mother, the, vii. 131 ; the last sheaf called the, vii. 135

—— plant, external soul of prince in a, xi. 102

—— seed used to strengthen weakly children, vii. 11

—— -sow at threshing, vii. 298

—— -water, draught of, as a form of communion in the Eleusinian mysteries, vii. 38

—— and wheat discovered by Isis, vi. 116

—— -wolf in the last sheaf, vii. 271, 273

Barolongs, a Bantu tribe of South Africa, their worship of ancestors, vi. 179 ; their custom of inoculation, viii. 159 *n.*[4]

Baron, R., on the reverence for dead kings in Madagascar, iii. 380

Baron, S., on annual expulsion of demons in Tonquin, ix. 147 *sq.*

Baronga, the, of South Africa, their charm against worms, i. 152 ; their charm against snake - bite, i. 153 ; their beliefs and customs as to twins, i. 267 *sq.* ; preserve the hair and nails of dead chiefs, iii. 272 ; their belief as to the state of the spirits of the dead, iv. 10 *sq.* ; their custom as to falling stars, iv. 61 ; women's part in agriculture among the, vii. 114 *sq.* ; their mode of freeing the fields from beetles, viii. 280 ; their story of a clan whose external souls were in a cat, xi. 150 *sq.* *See also* Ba-Ronga

Barotse or Marotse, a Bantu tribe of the Zambesi, rain-making among the, i. 310 *n.*[7] ; regard their chief as a demi-god, i. 392 *sq.* ; exorcism after a funeral among the, iii. 107 ; their belief in a supreme god Niambe, vi. 193 ; their worship of dead kings, vi. 194 *sq.* ; woman's part in agriculture among the, vii. 115 ; inoculation among the, viii. 159 ; seclusion of girls at puberty among the, x. 28, 29

Barren cattle driven through fire, x. 203, 338

—— fruit-trees threatened in order to make them bear fruit, ii. 20 *sqq.*

—— women, charms to procure offspring for, i. 70 *sqq.* ; sterilizing influence ascribed to, i. 142 ; embrace a tree to obtain offspring, i. 182 ; thought to conceive through eating nuts of a palm-tree, ii. 51 ; fertilized by trees, ii. 56 *sq.*, 316 *sq.* ; thought to blight the fruits of the earth, ii. 102 ; fertilized by water-spirits, ii. 159 *sqq.*, v. 213 *sq.*, 216 ; resort to graves in order to get children, v. 90 ; entice souls of dead children to them, v. 94 ; hope to conceive through fertilizing influence of vegetables, xi. 51. *See also* Childless

Barrenness of women cured by passing through holed stone, v. 36, with *n.*[4] ; removed by serpent, v. 86 ; children murdered as a remedy for, v. 95

Barricading the road against a ghostly pursuer, xi. 176

"Barring the fire," i. 231 *n.*[3]

Barringtonia, offerings made under a, in Guadalcanar, viii. 126

Barros, De, Portuguese historian, on custom of regicide at Passier, iv. 51 *sq.*

Barrows of Halfdan, vi. 100

Barsana, in North India, Holi bonfires at, xi. 2, 5

Barsom, bundle of twigs used by Parsee priests, v. 191 *n.*[2]

Barth, H., on sculptures at Boghaz-Keui, v. 133 *n.*[1]

Bartle Bay, in British New Guinea, power of magicians at, i. 338 ; festival of the wild mango tree at, x. 7 *sqq.*

Barwan, river in Australia, annual expulsion of ghosts on the, ix. 123

Bas Doda, in India, marriage of girls to the god at, ii. 149

Basagala, the, of Central Africa, changes in their language caused by their fear of naming the dead, iii. 361

Bashada, a tribe accustomed to strangle their first-born children, iv. 181 *sq.*

Bashilange, a tribe of the Congo Basin, reception of subject chiefs by head chief among the, iii. 114

Bashkirs, their horse-races at funerals, iv. 97

Basil, curses at sowing, i. 281 ; the Holy, plant worshipped in India, ii. 25 *sqq.* ; pots of, on St. John's Day in Sicily, v. 245. *See also* Tulasi

Basilai, officials at Olympia, i. 46 *n.*[4]

Basis, physical, of magic, i. 174 *sq.* ; for the theory of an external soul, i. 201

Basket, souls gathered into a, iii. 72

Basoga, the, of Central Africa, form blood-brotherhood with the trees which they fell, ii. 19 *sq.* ; their punishment of the seduction of a virgin, ii. 112 ; their abhorrence of incest in cattle, ii. 112 *sq.* ; their pretended human sacrifice, iv. 215

Basque hunter transformed into bear, xi. 226, 270

—— story of the external soul, xi. 139

Bassa tribe, of the Cameroons, reputed to be magicians, ix. 120

Bassareus, a title of Dionysus, viii. 282 *n.*[5]

Bassari, the, of Togoland, their superstition as to the mothers of twins, ii. 102 *n.*[1]; their offerings of new yams, viii. 116

Bassia latifolia worshipped, viii. 119

Bassus, Roman officer, ix. 309

Bastar, province of India, treatment of witches in, xi. 159

Bastard, traveller in Madagascar, iii. 103

——, name applied to the last sheaf in West Prussia, vii. 150

Bastian, Adolf, on extinguishing fires after a death, ii. 268 ; as to sanctity of head in Siam and Burma, iii. 252 *sq.* ; on animal sacraments among pastoral tribes, viii. 313 ; on the worship of nats in Burma, ix. 96 *n.*[3]; on rites of initiation in West Africa, xi. 256 *sq.*

Basutoland, attempts to regulate the calendar in, vii. 116 *sq.* ; inoculation in, viii. 158 *sq.*, 160

Basutos, use of magical dolls among the, i. 71 ; their custom as to extracted teeth, i. 177 ; their contagious magic of bodily impressions, i. 214 ; keep all defiled persons from the sight of corn, ii. 112 ; their belief as to the spirits of waterfalls, ii. 157 ; their custom of kindling a new fire after a birth, ii. 239 ; abhor the sea, iii. 10 ; avoidance of wife's mother among the, iii. 85 ; their superstition as to reflections in water, iii. 93 ; their burial custom, iii. 107 ; their purification of warriors, iii. 172 ; purification of cattle among the, iii. 177 ; their chiefs buried secretly, vi. 104 ; their worship of the dead, vi. 179 *sq.* ; their customs as to the new corn, viii. 110 ; their sacrifice of first-fruits, viii. 110 ; eat the hearts of brave men to make themselves brave, viii. 148 ; their custom of placing stones on cairns, ix. 30 *n.*[2]; their seclusion of girls at puberty, x. 31

Bata and Anpu, ancient Egyptian story of, xi. 134 *sqq.*

Bataks or Battas of Sumatra, their theory of earthquakes, v. 199 *sq.* ; their *tondi*, the soul of human beings and of rice, vii. 182. *See* Battas

Batang Lupar, in Borneo, the Dyaks of, their "lying heaps," ix. 14

—— -Lupars of Borneo, the foes of the Kayans, vii. 96

Bataraguru, a person of the Batta Trinity, v. 199 *sq.*, ix. 88 *n.*[1]

Batari Sri, a goddess in Lombok, vii. 202

Batavia, rain-making by means of a cat in, i. 289

Batchelor, Rev. J., on the Aino ceremony with the new millet, viii. 52 ; on the Aino *kamui*, viii. 180 *n.*[2]; on the bear as a totem or god of the Ainos, viii. 180, 198 ; on the suckling of bears by the Aino women, viii. 182 *n.*[2]; on the bear-festivals of the Ainos, viii. 183 *sq.*; on the *inao* of the Ainos, viii. 186 *n.*; on the Aino belief in the resurrection of animals, viii. 201 ; his purification after visiting an Aino grave, ix. 261

Bath before marriage, intention of, ii. 162 ; of ox blood, iv. 35, 201 ; in river at the rites of Cybele, v. 273, 274 *n.* ; of bull's blood in the rites of Attis, v. 274 *sqq.* ; of image of Cybele perhaps a rain-charm, v. 280

—— of Aphrodite, v. 280

—— of Demeter, v. 280

—— of Hera in the river Burrha, v. 280 ; in the spring of Canathus, v. 280

Bathing and washing forbidden to rain-doctor when he wishes to prevent rain from falling, i. 271, 272 ; bathing as a rain-charm, i. 277 *sq.* ; (washing) as a ceremonial purification, iii. 141, 142, 150, 153, 168, 169, 172, 173, 175, 179, 183, 192, 198, 219, 220, 222, 285, 286 ; forbidden, vii. 94

—— on St. John's Day or Eve (Midsummer Day or Eve), v. 246 *sqq.* ; pagan origin of the custom, v. 249

—— at Easter, x. 123 ; at Midsummer, x. 208, 210, 216, xi. 29 *sqq.* ; thought to be dangerous on Midsummer Day, xi. 26 *sq.*

Baths of Hercules, v. 212

—— of Solomon in Moab, v. 215

Baton of Sinope, on the Thessalian festival Peloria, ix. 350

Batoo Bedano, an earthquake god in Nias, v. 202

Bats, souls of dead in, viii. 287 ; the lives of men in, xi. 215 *sq.*, 217 ; called men's "brothers," xi. 215, 216, 218

Batta magicians exorcize demons by means of images, viii. 102

Battambang, a province of Siam, ceremony to procure rain in, i. 299

Battas or Bataks of Sumatra, magical images among the, i. 71 *sq.*; their belief as to the placenta, i. 193 ; fight the storm, i. 330 ; worship a prince as a deity, i. 398 *sq.* ; revere the Sultan of Minangkabau, i. 399 ; their sacred trees, ii. 41 ; think that fornication and incest injure the crops, ii. 108 ; their use of rice to prevent the soul from wandering, iii. 34 *sq.*; their recall of lost souls, iii. 45 *sqq.* ; their belief in the transmigration of souls, iii. 65 ; afraid of being photographed, iii. 99 ; ceremony at the reception of a traveller among the, iii. 104 ; their custom as to eating, iii. 116 ; untie things to facilitate childbirth, iii. 296 *sq.*; names of relations tabooed among the, iii. 338 *sq.*; use a special language in searching for camphor, iii. 405 *sq.* ; their personification of the rice, vii. 196 ; their observation of Orion and the Pleiades, vii. 315 ; their ceremonies at killing a tiger, viii. 216 *sq.* ; believe that the souls of the dead often transmigrate into tigers, viii. 293 ; their use of swallows as scapegoats, ix. 34 *sq.* ; their belief in demons, ix. 87 *sq.* ; their belief in a Trinity, ix. 88 *n.*[1] ; their use of human scapegoats, ix. 213 ; their doctrine of the plurality of souls, xi. 223 ; their totemic system, xi. 224 *sqq. See also* Bataks

Battel, Andrew, on the king of Loango, iii. 117 *sq.* ; on the colour of negro children at birth, xi. 251 *n.*[1]

Battle, purificatory ceremonies after a, iii. 165 *sqq.*, vi. 251 *sq.*; mock, viii. 75 ; annual, among boys in Tumleo, ix. 143

—— of the gods and giants, v. 157

—— of Summer and Winter, iv. 254 *sqq.*

Battle-axe, sacred golden, i. 365

Battus, king of Cyrene, i. 47

Baudissin, W. W. Graf von, on Tammuz and Adonis, v. 6 *n.*[1] ; on Adonis as the personification of the spring vegetation, v. 228 *n.*[6]; on summer festival of Adonis, v. 232 *n.*; on Linus song, vii. 216 *n.*[4]

Baumeister, A., on the date of the Homeric *Hymn to Demeter*, vii. 35 *n.*[1]

Bautz, Dr. Joseph, on hell fire, iv. 136 *n.*[1]

Bavaria, custom as to cast teeth in, i. 178 ; greasing the weapon instead of the wound which it inflicted, in, i. 204 ; green bushes placed at doors of newly-married pairs in, ii. 56 ; the May-pole renewed every few years in, ii. 70 ; the *Walber* in, ii. 75 ; drama of the Slaying of the Dragon at Furth in, ii. 163 *sq.*; Whitsuntide mummers in, iv. 206 *sq.* ; carrying out Death in, iv. 233 *sqq.* ; dramatic contests between Summer and Winter in, iv. 255 *sq.* ; gardens of Adonis in, v. 244 ; Dinkelsbühl in, vii. 133 ; Weiden in, vii. 139 ; harvest customs in, vii. 147, 148, 150, 219 *sq.*, 221 *sq.*, 223, 232, 282, 286, 287, 289, 296, 298, 299 ; the thresher of the last corn obliged to "carry the Pig" in, vii. 299 ; cure for fever in, ix. 49 ; annual expulsion of witches on Walpurgis Night in, ix. 159 *sq.* ; old Mrs. Perchta (a mythical old woman) in, ix. 240 *sq.* ; mode of reckoning the Twelve Days in, ix. 327 ; Easter bonfires in, x. 143 *sq.* ; belief as to eclipses in, x. 162 ; Midsummer fires in, x. 164 *sqq.* ; leaf-clad mummer at Midsummer in, xi. 26 ; the divining-rod in, xi. 67 *sq.* ; peasants' belief as to hazel in, xi. 69 *n.* ; creeping through a holed stone or narrow opening in, xi. 188 *sq.*

Bavaria, Rhenish, treatment of the navel-string in, i. 198 ; homoeopathic treatment of a broken leg in, i. 205 ; leaf-clad mummer at Whitsuntide in, ii. 81 ; gout transferred to willow-bush in, iv. 56

——, Upper, the bride-race in, ii. 304 ; ceremonies on Ascension Day in villages of, ix. 215 ; use of mistletoe in, xi. 85 *n.*[4]

Bavarian charm at sowing wheat, i. 137; to make fruit-trees bear, i. 140 *sq.*

—— farmers will not name the fox, iii. 396

—— peasants, their homoeopathic magic as to fruit-trees, i. 143

—— saying as to crossed legs, iii. 299

Bavili, the, of Loango, their belief that certain unlawful marriages are punished by God with drought, ii. 112 ; tampering with people's shadows among, iii. 78 ; seclusion of girls at puberty among, x. 31

Bawenda, tribe of the Transvaal, their chief a rain-maker, i. 351 ; special terms used with reference to persons of the blood royal among the, i. 401 *n.*[3] ; blood of princes not to be shed among the, iii. 243 ; their custom of placing stones in the forks of trees, ix. 30 *n.*[2] ; the positions of their villages hidden, vi. 251

Bayazid, the Sultan, and his soul, iii. 50

Bayfield, M. A., on the punishment of unfaithful Vestals, ii. 228 *n.*[5]

Beal-fires on Midsummer Eve in Yorkshire, x. 198

Bealltaine, May Day, iii. 11. *See* Beltane

Bean, sprouting of, in superstitious ceremony, i. 266 ; the budding of a, as an omen, ii. 344

——, King of the, ix. 313 *sq.*, x. 153 *n.*[1] ; Queen of the, ix. 313, 315

—— clan among the Baganda, ix. 27

—— -cock at harvest, vii. 276

—— -goat among the beans, vii. 282

Beans in ceremony performed by parents of twins in Peru, i. 266, ii. 102 *n.*[1] ; not to be touched or named by the Flamen Dialis, ii. 248, iii. 13 *sq.* ; in magical rite, vii. 9 *sq.* ; the Spirit of, conceived by the Iroquois as a woman, vii. 177 ; cultivated in Burma, vii. 242 ; ceremony at eating the new, viii. 64 ; forbidden as food by Empedocles, viii. 301 ; thrown about the house at the expulsion of demons, ix. 143 *sq.* ; thrown about the house at the expulsion of ghosts, ix. 155 ; divination by, on Midsummer Eve, x. 209

Bear, customs observed by Lapps after killing a, iii. 221 ; ambiguous attitude of the Ainos towards the, viii. 180 *sqq.*, 310 *sq.* ; importance of the, for people of Siberia, viii. 191 ; the corn-spirit as a, viii. 325 *sqq.* ; external soul of warrior in a, xi. 151 ; Basque hunter transformed into a, xi. 226, 270; simulated transformation of novice into a, xi. 274 *sq.* *See also* Bears

——, the Great, constellation, vii. 315 ; the soul of Typhon in, iv. 5

——, the polar, taboos concerning, iii. 209

—— -cats, souls of dead in, viii. 294

—— clan of the Moquis, descended from bears, viii. 178 ; of the Otawa Indians, their propitiation of slain bears, viii. 224 *sq.* ; of the Niska Indians, xi. 271, 272 *n.*[1]

—— -dance of man who pretends to be a bear, xi. 274

—— -dances, viii. 191, 195

—— -festivals of the Ainos, viii. 182 *sqq.* ; of the Gilyaks, viii. 190 *sqq.* ; of the Goldi, viii. 197 ; of the Orotchis, viii. 197

—— -hunting, continence before, iii. 197, 198

—— -skin worn by woman dancer, viii. 223

Bear's bile and heart eaten to make the eater brave, viii. 146

—— flesh, a person who has eaten of, obliged to abstain from fish for a year, viii. 251

Bear's heart eaten, viii. 146

—— "little tongue" removed by American Indian hunters, viii. 269

—— liver, as a medicine, viii. 187 *sq.*

—— skin, Lapp women shoot blindfold at a, xi. 280 *n.*

"Beard of Volos," vii. 233

Beard, the first, consecrated, i. 29

Bearded Venus, in Cyprus, v. 165, vi. 259 *n.*[3]

"Beardless One, the Ride of the," a Persian ceremony, ix. 402 *sq.*

Beards, homoeopathic magic to promote the growth of, i. 153 *sq.* ; not pulled out by chiefs and sorcerers, iii. 260

Bearers to carry royal personages, x. 3 *sq.*

Bears sacrificed by the Gilyaks of Saghalien, iii. 370 ; not to be called by their proper names, iii. 397 *sq.*, 399, 402; killed ceremonially by the Ainos, viii. 180 *sqq.* ; souls of dead in, viii. 286 *sq.* ; processions with, in Europe, viii. 326 *n.*[3]

——, slain, propitiated by Kamtchatkans, Ostiaks, Koryaks, Finns, and Lapps, viii. 222 *sqq.* ; by American Indians, viii. 224 *sqq.* *See also* Bear

Beast, the number of the, iv. 44

Beasts, sacred Egyptian, offerings to the, i. 29 *sq.*; sacred, held responsible for the course of nature in ancient Egypt, i. 354

Beathag, the lucky well of, i. 323

Beating as a mode of purification, ix. 262, x. 61, 64 *sqq.*

—— the air to drive away demons or ghosts, iii. 373, ix. 109, 111, 115, 122, 131, 152, 156, 234

—— boys with leg-bone of eagle-hawk, viii. 165 *n.*[2]

—— cattle to make them fat or fruitful, iv. 236

—— effigy of ox with rods in China, viii. 11 *sq.*

—— floors or walls of houses to drive away ghosts, iii. 168, 170

—— frogs as a rain-charm, i. 292

—— girls at puberty, x. 61, 66 *sq.*

—— human scapegoats, ix. 196, 252, 255, 256 *sq.*, 272 *sq.*

—— a man clad in a cow's hide on last day of year, viii. 322 *sqq.*

—— a man's garments instead of the man, i. 206 *sq.*

—— people for good luck, vii. 309 ; as a mode of conveying good qualities, ix. 262 *sqq.* ; with skins of sacrificial victims, ix. 265 ; with green boughs, ix. 270 *sqq.* ; to stimulate the reproductive powers, ix. 272

—— persons, animals, or things to

deliver them from demons and ghosts, ix. 259 *sqq.*

Beating with rods in rain-making, i. 257 *sq.*

—— the sea with rods as a rain-charm, i. 301

Beauce, the great *mondard* in, viii. 6 ; festival of torches in, x. 113 ; story of a were-wolf in, x. 309

Beauce and Perche, treatment of the navel-string in, i. 198 ; conflagrations supposed to be extinguished by priests in, i. 231 *n.*[3] ; belief as to falling stars in, iv. 67 ; fever transferred to an aspen in, ix. 57 ; cure for toothache in, ix. 62 ; Midsummer fires in, x. 188

Beaufort, F., on perpetual flame in Lycia, v. 222 *n.*

Beauty and the Beast type of tale, iv. 125 *sqq.*

Beauvais, the Festival of Fools at, ix. 335 *sq.*

Beaver asked to give a new tooth, i. 180; the Great, prayers offered by beaver-hunters to, viii. 240

—— clan of the Carrier Indians, xi. 273

Beavers, their bones not allowed to be gnawed by dogs, viii. 238 *sqq.* ; their blood not allowed to fall on ground, viii. 240

Bechuana charms, i. 150 *sq.*

—— king, cure of, ix. 31 *sq.*

Bechuanas, the, of South Africa, their homoeopathic charms made from animals, i. 150 *sq.* ; their sacrifice for rain, i. 291 ; their ceremony to cause the sun to shine, i. 313 ; the hack-thorn sacred among the, ii. 48 *sq.* ; their purification after a journey, iii. 112, 285 ; their purification of manslayers, iii. 172 *sq.*, 174 ; will not tell their stories before sunset, iii. 384 ; think it unlucky to speak of the lion by his proper name, iii. 400 ; their fear of meteors, iv. 61 ; their ritual at founding a new town, vi. 249 ; their sacrifice of a blind bull on various occasions, vi. 249, 250 *sq.* ; human sacrifices for the crops among the, vii. 240 ; their observation of the Pleiades, vii. 316 ; of the Crocodile clan, their fear of meeting or seeing a crocodile, viii. 28 ; their ceremonies before eating the new fruits, viii. 69 *sq.* ; the Baperis, a tribe of, viii. 164; their custom of mutilating an ox after a battle, viii. 271 ; their belief as to sympathetic relation of man to wounded crocodile, xi. 210 *sq.*

Bed of absent hunter or warrior not to be used, i. 123, 127, 128, 129 ; feet of, smeared with mud, iii. 14 ; prohibition to sleep in a, iii. 194. *See also* Beds

Bed-clothes, contagious magic of bodily impressions on, i. 213

Bedding at home not to be raised in the absence of hunters, i. 121

Bede, on the succession of Pictish kings, ii. 286 ; on the Feast of All Saints, vi. 83

Bedouins of East Africa attack whirlwinds, i. 331 ; regard an acacia-tree as sacred, ii. 42 ; fire-drill of the ancient, ii. 209 ; annual festival of the Sinaitic, iv. 97

Bedriacum, the battle of, iv. 140, ix. 416

Beds of absent hunters, children not to play on, i. 123

Bee, external soul of an ogre in a, xi. 101. *See also* Bees

Beech, M. W. H., on serpent-worship among the Suk, v. 85

Beech or fir used to make the Yule log, x. 249

—— -tree in sacred grove of Diana, i. 40 ; burnt in Lenten bonfire, x. 115 *sq.*

—— -woods of Denmark, ii. 351

Beeches of Latium, ii. 188 ; struck by lightning, proportion of, xi. 298 *sq.* ; free from mistletoe, xi. 315

Beef and milk not to be eaten at the same meal, iii. 292

Beena marriage, ii. 271 ; in Ceylon, vi. 215

Beer, continence observed at brewing, iii. 200 ; in relation to Dionysus, vii. 2 *n.*[1] ; drunk out of dead king's skull as means of inspiration, viii. 150

Bees on image of Artemis at Ephesus, i. 37; the King Bees (Essenes) at Ephesus, ii. 135 *sq.* ; the sting of, a popular cure for rheumatism, iii. 106 *n.*[2] ; transmigration of quiet people into, viii. 308 ; thought to be killed by menstruous women, x. 96 ; ashes of bonfires used to cure ailments of, x. 142

Beetle, in magic, i. 152 ; external soul in a, xi. 138, 140

Beetles, superstitious precautions against, viii. 279, 280

Befana at Rome and elsewhere, ix. 167

Begbie, General, v. 62 *n.*

Begetting novices anew at initiation, pretence of, xi. 248

Beggar, name given to last sheaf, vii. 231 *sq.*

—— -man, the binder of the last sheaf called the, vii. 231

Behanzin, king of Dahomey, represented with the head and body of a fish, iv. 85

Behar district of India, virtue ascribed to abuse in, i. 279 ; rain-charm by means of a stone in, i. 305 ; "wives of the snake" in, ii. 149 ; custom of swinging in, iv. 279 ; bullocks let loose on

eleventh day of mourning in, ix. 37 $n.$[4];
the fire-walk in, xi. 5
Beheading the King, a Whitsuntide
pageant in Bohemia, iv. 209 sq.
—— Whitsuntide mummers, pretence of,
iv. 206 sqq.
Beifuss, German name for mugwort, xi.
60 n.[6]
Bekes, in Hungary, mode of fertilizing
women in, ix. 264
Beku, dwarf tribe of West Africa, their
magical ointment for acquiring the
power of the dead, viii. 163 sq.
Bel or Marduk, a Babylonian deity, v.
71 ; his human wife, ii. 129 sq. ; identified with Zeus, ix. 389 ; created the
world by cleaving the monster Tiamat
in two, ix. 410 ; the fires of, x. 147,
157, 158 sq.
Belep, the, of New Caledonia, their
charm to disable an enemy, i. 150
Beleth, John, his Rationale Divinorum
Officiorum quoted, x. 161 n.[2]
Belethus, J., on " Easter Smacks," ix.
270 n.
Belfast, the last sheaf called Granny near,
vii. 136
Belford, in Northumberland, the Yule log
at, x. 256
Belgian cure for fever, ix. 56 n.[1]
Belgium, mirrors covered after a death
in, iii. 95 ; cut hair burnt in, iii. 283 ;
belief as to stepping over a child
in, iii. 424 ; belief as to meteors in,
iv. 67 ; Feast of All Souls in, vi. 70 ;
fox's tongue a remedy for erysipelas
in, viii. 270 ; the King of the Bean
in, ix. 313 ; the three mythical kings
on Twelfth Day in, ix. 329 ; Lenten
fires in, x. 107 sq. ; Midsummer fires
in, x. 194 sq. ; the Yule log in, x.
249 ; bathing on Midsummer Day in,
xi. 30 ; divination by flowers on Midsummer Eve in, xi. 53 ; mugwort
gathered on St. John's Day or Eve in,
xi. 59 sq.; vervain gathered on St.
John's Day in, xi. 62 ; four-leaved
clover at Midsummer in, xi. 63 ; the
witches' Sabbath in, xi. 73
Bell-ringing as a charm to dispel evil
influences, ii. 343 sq.   See Bells
Bella Coola (Bilqula) Indians of British
Columbia, their conception of the soul
as a bird, iii. 34 ; their cannibal rites,
vii. 20 ; their masked dances, ix. 376
n.[2]; seclusion of girls at puberty among
the, x. 46 ; custom of mourners among
the, xi. 174
Bellerophon and Pegasus, v. 302 n.[4]
Belli-Paaro society in West Africa, rites
of initiation in the, xi. 257 sqq.
Bellochroy, enchanter at, x. 290

Bellona and Mars, vi. 231
Bells, carried by leaf-clad mummers, ii.
83, 84 sq. ; worn by father of twins,
ii. 102 ; rung to drive away witches,
ii. 127 ; hung on cattle on St. George's
Day, ii. 332 ; used in exorcism, iii.
102 ; rung to conjure spirits, iii. 120 ;
worn as amulets, iii. 235 ; worn by
mummers, vii. 26, 28, viii. 332, 333,
ix. 242, 243, 244, 246 sqq., 250 sq. ;
attached to hobby-horse, viii. 337 sq.;
on animal used as scapegoat, ix. 37 ;
rung to expel demons, ix. 117, 118 ;
rung as a protection against witches, ix.
157, 158, 159, 161, 165, 166 ; used in
the expulsion of evils, ix. 196, 200 ;
used at the expulsion of demons, ix.
204, 214, 246 sq., 251 ; worn by
dancers, ix. 242, 243, 246 sqq.,
250 sq.; used to exorcize storm fiend,
ix. 246 ; rung to make grass and flax
grow, ix. 247 sq. ; golden, worn by
human representatives of gods in
Mexico, ix. 278, 280, 284 ; worn by
priest in exorcism, x. 5 ; on priest's
legs, xi. 8
——, church, silenced in Holy Week, x.
123, 125 n.[1]; rung on Midsummer
Eve, xi. 47 sq. ; rung to drive away
witches, xi. 73
Beltana, in South Australia, first-born
children destroyed among the tribes
about, iv. 180
Beltane, the Celtic May Day, x. 146
sqq.; popularly derived from Baal, x.
149 n.[1], 150 n.[1]; the need-fire at, x.
293 ; the Yellow Day of, x. 293 ; sheep
passed through a hoop at, xi. 184
—— cakes, x. 148 sq., 150, 152, 153,
154, 155
—— carline, x. 148, 153
—— Eve (the Eve of May Day), precautions against witchcraft on, ii. 53 ;
a witching time, x. 295
—— fire, pretence of throwing a man
into the, x. 148, xi. 25 ; kindled by the
friction of oak-wood, x. 148, 155, xi. 91
—— fires in Scotland, x. 146 sqq. ; in
Wales, x. 155 sq. ; in Ireland, x. 157
sq.; in Nottinghamshire, x. 157
—— and Hallowe'en the two chief fire-
festivals of the British Celts, xi. 40 sq.
Belty, the parish of, sacred trees in, ii.
44
Ben Cruachan on Loch Awe, vii. 142
Ben-hadad, king of Damascus, v. 15
Benametapa, the king of, in East Africa,
x. 135
Benares, the clod festival at, i. 279 ;
Hindoo gentleman worshipped as a
god at, i. 404 ; serpent in likeness of
Brahman at, iv. 132

Bendall, Professor C., v. 229 n.[1]
Beneficent powers of tree-spirits, ii. 45 *sqq.*
Benefit of clergy, v. 68
Benefits conferred by magic, i. 218 *sq.*
Benfey, Th., on Buddhist animism, ii. 13 ; on story of Pururavas and Urvasi, iv. 131
Bengal, rain-making in, i. 278, 283, 284 n. ; the Maghs of, ii. 38 ; marriage ceremony at the digging of wells in, ii. 146 ; the Oraons of, ii. 148, viii. 117 ; mourners touch a coral ring in, iii. 315 ; Bengalee women, their euphemisms for snakes and thieves, iii. 402 ; kings of, their rule of succession, iv. 51 ; the Oraons and Mundas of, v. 46, 240, xi. 311 ; the Korwas of, vii. 123 ; the Hos of, viii. 117 ; seclusion of girls at puberty in, x. 68 ; stories of the external soul in, xi. 101 *sq.*, 102
Bengkali, East Indian island, swinging as a religious rite in, iv. 277 *sq.*
Bengweolo, Lake, in Central Africa, state governed by a queen near, ii. 277
Beni Ahsen, a tribe in Morocco, their Midsummer fires, x. 215 *sq.* ; their precaution at bathing on Midsummer Day, xi. 31
—— -Chougran tribe of North Africa, their rain-charm by means of a black cow, i. 290
—— Mgild, a Berber tribe of Morocco, their Midsummer fires, x. 215
—— Snous, the, of Morocco, their Midsummer rites, x. 216
Benin, belief as to twins in, i. 265 ; rule as to the Queen-mother of, iii. 86 ; ceremony at the reception of strangers in, iii. 108 ; kings of, not allowed to quit their palace, iii. 123 ; kings of, put their brothers to death, iii. 243 ; human victims crucified at, v. 294 n.[3] ; human sacrifices for the crops at, vii. 240 ; festival of the new yams at, viii. 63 *sq.* ; time of the " grand devils " in, ix. 131 *sq.*
——, king of, worshipped as a god, i. 396, iii. 123 ; represented with panther's whiskers, iv. 85 *sq.* ; human sacrifices at the burial of a, iv. 139 *sq.*
Bennett, George, on the placenta in New Zealand, i. 182 *sq.*
Bennisch district of Silesia, custom at threshing in, vii. 148
Benomotapa, king of, his sacred fire, ii. 264
Benson, E. F., on May Day custom in Cornwall, ii. 52
Bent, J. Theodore, discovers ruins of Olba, v. 151 ; identifies site of Hiero-

polis-Castabala, v. 168 n.[1] ; on passing sick children through a cleft oak, xi. 172
Bentley, Richard, as to the soul on the lips, iii. 33 n.[3]
Benue River, tributary of the Niger, the Jukos of the, iv. 34, viii. 160 ; the Igbiras of the, viii. 115
Benvenuto Cellini, his alleged halo, ii. 197 n.[6]
Benzoni, G., Italian historian, on *Viracocchie*, i. 57 n.
Bera Pennu, Earth Goddess of the Khonds, human sacrifices to, vii. 245
Berar, sacred groves in, ii. 41 *sq.*
Berawans of Sarawak, ceremony of adoption among the, i. 74 *sq.*
Berber belief as to water at Midsummer, xi. 31
—— tale, milk-tie in a, xi. 138 n.[1]
Berbers of North Africa, the Barley Bride among the, vii. 178 *sq.* ; their Midsummer customs, x. 213 *sqq.*, 219
Berecynthia, title of Cybele, v. 279 n.[4]
Bérenger-Feraud, L. J. B., on the Festival of Fools, ix. 334 *sq.*
Berenice and Ptolemy, annual festival in their honour, vi. 35 n.[1]
Bergell, in the Grisons, bells rung to make the grass grow at, ix. 247
Bergen, Midsummer bonfires at, x. 171
Bergkirchen, horse-races after harvest at, vii. 76
Bergslagshärad, in Sweden, the Yule Goat at, viii. 327
Bering Strait, the Esquimaux of, i. 9, 70, iii. 96, 205, 206, 228, 328, 371, 399, viii. 150, 247
Berkhampstead, in Hertfordshire, ague transferred to oaks at, ix. 57 *sq.*
Berkshire, May garlands in, ii. 60
Berleburg in Westphalia, the Yule log at, x. 248
Berlin, fox's teeth as an amulet in, i. 180 ; treatment of the navel-string in, i. 198 ; curses for good luck in, i. 281 ; insignia of royal family of Hawaii at, i. 388 n.[3] ; the Ethnological Museum at, i. 388 n.[3], ix. 70 n.[1]; the divining-rod at, xi. 68
Bern, Midsummer fires in the canton of, x. 172 ; the Yule log in the canton of, x. 249 ; witches put to death in the canton of, xi. 42 n.[2]
Bernara, the harvest *Cailleach* in, vii. 166
Berneck, in Upper Franken, custom at threshing at, vii. 148
Bernera, on the west of Lewis, customs as to the last corn cut in, vii. 140 *sq.*
Bernkastel, on the Moselle, the harvest Goat at, vii. 285

Berosus, Babylonian historian, on the festival of the Sacaea, iv. 113 *sq.*, vii. 258 *sq.*, ix. 355, 358, 359

Berries, the first of the season, ceremonies before eating, viii. 80 *sqq.*

Berry, province of France, ceremony of "Sawing the Old Woman" in, iv. 241 *sq.* ; the calf at harvest in, vii. 292 ; "seeing the Horse" at harvest in, vii. 294 ; Lenten fire custom in, x. 115 ; Midsummer fires in, x. 189; the Yule log in, x. 251 *sq.* ; four-leaved clover at Midsummer in, xi. 63

Bertat, a people on the Blue Nile, their orgiastic annual festivals, iv. 16 *n.*[2]

Berwickshire, kirn-dollies of last corn at harvest in, vii. 153 *sq.*

Bes, grotesque Egyptian god, ii. 133, v. 118 *n.*[1]

Besbau, near Luckau, races after harvest at, vii. 76

Besisis of the Malay Peninsula, their dread of noon, iii. 87 ; their carnival at rice-harvest, ix. 226 *n.*[1]

Besoms placed crosswise at doors of cattle-stalls as a protection against witches, ii. 127

——, burning, hurled against witches, ix. 162 ; flung aloft to make the corn grow high, x. 340 ; used to drive away witches, xi. 74

Bessy, one of the mummers on Plough Monday, viii. 329, 331

Bethlehem, worship of Adonis at, v. 257 *sqq.*; fertility of the neighbourhood of, v. 257 *n.*[3]; the Star of, v. 259, ix. 330 ; new Easter fire carried to, x. 130 *n.*

Betimor, woman turned into crocodile, viii. 212

Betsileo, the, of Madagascar, attribute divine powers to their chiefs, i. 397 ; lickers of blood and eaters of nail-parings among the, iii. 246 ; their belief in serpents as reincarnations of the dead, v. 83 ; offer the first-fruits of all crops to their king, viii. 116 ; their belief in the transmigration of souls, viii. 289 *sq.*

" Between the two Beltane fires," x. 149

Beul, fire of, need-fire, x. 293

Bevan, Professor A. A., on the Arab fire-drill, ii. 210 *n.* ; on magical knots, iii. 302 *n.*[4]; on the change of *m* to *v* in Semitic, ix. 367 *n.*[2] ; on a passage of Tabari, xi. 83 *n.*[1]

Beveridge, P., on the suppression of the names of the dead among the aborigines of New South Wales, iii. 363 *sq.*

Beverley, the Boy Bishop at, ix. 338

Beverley, on the initiatory rites of the Virginian Indians, xi. 266 *sq.*

Bewitched animals burnt alive, x. 300 *sqq.* ; buried alive, x. 324 *sqq.*

—— cow, mugwort applied to, xi. 59

—— things burnt to compel the witch to appear, x. 322

Bezoar stone in rain-charms, i. 305

Bghais, a Karen tribe of Burma, their annual festival of the dead, vi. 60 *sq.*

Bhâdon, Indian month, i. 279, v. 243

Bhagats, mock human sacrifices among the, iv. 217 *sq.*

Bhagavati, goddess, her shrine at Cranganore, i. 280

Bhairava, Hindoo goddess, image of, i. 65 ; temple of, iv. 219

Bharbhunjas of the Central Provinces, India, marriage custom of the, vi. 262

Bharias of the Central Provinces, India, exchange of costume between men and women at marriage among the, vi. 260 *sq.*

Bhars of India, their use of a scapegoat in time of cholera, ix. 190

Bhils, the, of Central India, worship of the peacock among, viii. 29 ; their torture of witches, xi. 159

Bhîmsen or Bhîm Deo, an Indian deity, viii. 118

Bhootan, the Dhurma Rajah in, i. 410 ; heaps of stones or sticks in, ix. 12 ; offerings at cairns in, ix. 26

Bhotiyas of Juhar, their use of a scapegoat, ix. 209

Bhuiyars of Mirzapur will not speak of monkeys or bears by their proper names in the morning, iii. 403 ; their dread of menstrual pollution, x. 84

Bhuiyas, the, of North-Eastern India, ceremony at the installation of a rajah among the, iv. 56 ; fire-walk among the, xi. 5 *sq.*

Bhujariya, festival in the Central Provinces of India, v. 242

Bhumiya, Himalayan deity, viii. 117, 118 *n.*

Bhut, demon, xi. 312

Bhutan, demons diverted into images of animals in, viii. 103

Biajas of Borneo, their annual expulsion of evils in a little ship, ix. 200

Biak, island of, precautions against strangers in, iii. 104

Bibili, island off New Guinea, the natives reputed to make wind, i. 322

Bidasari and the golden fish, Malay story of, xi. 147 *sq.*, 220

Biddulph, J., on custom at wheat-sowing in Gilgit, ii. 50 *sq.*

Biennial cycle, vii. 87

—— festivals, vii. 14, 86

Biggar, "Burning out the Old Year" at ix. 165

Bikol, in Luzon, demon exorcized by beating in, ix. 260

Bilaspur or Bilaspore, twirling spindles forbidden in, while men are in council, i. 114; way of stopping rain in, i. 253 *sq.* ; iron as an amulet in, iii. 234 *sq.* ; women's hair unknotted at childbirth in, iii. 298; temporary rajah in, iv. 154; infant burial in, v. 94 *sq.* ; annual festival of the dead in, vi. 60; new-born children placed in winnowing-fans in, vii. 6 *sq.* ; cairns to which passers-by add stones in, ix. 27 *n.*[4]; the Rajah of, food eaten out of his dead hand by a Brahman, ix. 44 *sq.*

Bilda, in Algeria, nails knocked into olive-tree as a cure at, ix. 60

Bilqula. *See* Bella Coola

Bima, in Celebes, sacred horse at, i. 364

——, a district of Sambawa, human foundation-sacrifices in, iii. 90 *sq.*

Bin-Thuan, the Chams of, ii. 28, viii. 56

Binbinga tribe of Northern Australia, burial customs of the, i. 102 *sq.* ; cannibalism among the, i. 106 *sq.* ; their rites of initiation, xi. 234 *sq.* ; initiation of medicine-man in the, xi. 239

Binder of last sheaf represents the Corn-mother, vii. 150, 253; tied up in straw or corn-stalks, vii. 220, 221; called the Beggar-man, vii. 231; called the Wolf, vii. 273 *sq.* ; called Goat, vii. 283

Binders of corn, contests between, vii. 136, 137, 138, 218 *sq.*, 220, 221, 222, 253

Binding up a cleft stick or tree a mode of barricading the road against a ghostly pursuer, xi. 176

Bingfield, the Borewell near, ii. 161

Binsenschneider, vii. 230 *n.*[5]

Binuas of the Malay Peninsula use a special language in searching for camphor, iii. 405

Bion, the atheist, his attempts to avert death, ii. 191

Bion, Greek poet, on the scarlet anemone, v. 226 *n.*[1]

Bir, a tribal hero of the Bhuiyas, xi. 6

Birbhum district of Bengal, rain-making in the, i. 278

Birch, a protection against witches, ii. 54; crowns of, ii. 64; leaves of, girl clad in, ii. 80; used to kindle need-fire, x. 291

——, branches of, on Midsummer Day, x. 177, 196; a protection against witchcraft, xi. 185

—— and plane, fire made by the friction of, x. 220

Birch, sprigs of, a protection against witches, ix. 162; used to beat people with at Easter and Christmas, ix. 269, 270

—— -tree dressed in woman's clothes, ii. 64, 141

—— -trees used to keep off witches, ii. 54, 55, xi. 20 *n.* ; gout transferred to, ix. 56 *sq.*; set up at Midsummer, x. 177; mistletoe on, xi. 315

—— -wreath at Whitsuntide, girls kiss each other through a, ii. 93

Bird, Miss I. L., on the bear-festivals of the Ainos, viii. 184 *n.*[1]

Bird, soul conceived as a, iii. 33 *sqq.*, vii. 181, 182 *n.*[1]; soul of a tree in a, vi. 111 *n.*[1]; corn-spirit as a, vii. 295 *sq.* ; disease transferred to, xi. 187; brings first fire to earth, xi. 295

—— called "the soul of Osiris," vi. 110

—— -chief of the Sea Dyaks, ix. 383, 384

—— -lime made from mistletoe, xi. 317

—— of prey, inoculation with a, viii. 162

——, soul of the rice as a, vii. 182 *n.*[1]

—— -wife, Dyak story of the, iv. 127 *sq.* ; Indian story of, iv. 131

Birds, ghosts of slain as, iii. 177 *sq.*; cause headache through clipped hair, iii. 270 *sq.*, 282; absent warriors called, iii. 330; burnt in honour of Artemis, v. 126 *n.*[2]; ancestral spirits in, viii. 123; tongues of, eaten, viii. 147; souls of dead in, viii. 296; as scapegoats, ix. 35 *sq.*, 51 *sq.* ; external souls in, xi. 104, 111, 119, 142, 144, 150; carry seed of mistletoe, xi. 316

——, language of, learned by means of serpents, i. 158; known to Indian king, iv. 123; learned by eating serpent's flesh, viii. 146; learned by tasting dragon's blood, viii. 146

——, migratory, as representatives of a divinity, vii. 204 *sq.*

—— of omen, stories of their origin, iv. 126, 127 *sq.*

——, white, souls of dead kings incarnate in, vi. 162

Birk, in Transylvania, the harvest Hare at, vii. 280

Birks, Rev. E. B., on harvest custom at Orwell, v. 237 *n.*[4]

Birseck, Lenten fires at, x. 119

Birth of children, magical images to ensure the, i. 70 *sqq.* ; pretence of, at adoption, i. 74 *sq.*, at return of supposed dead man, i. 75, at circumcision, i. 75 *sq.* ; a man's fortune determined by the day or hour of his, i. 173; from the fire, ii. 195 *sqq.* ; new fire kindled by friction of wood after a, ii. 239 ; from a golden image, iii. 113 ; of child on harvest-field, vii. 150 *sq.*, 209. *See also* Births *and* Miscarriage

Birth, new i. 74 *sqq.* ; of Brahman sacrificer, simulation of, i. 380 *sq.* ; through blood in rites of Attis, v. 274 *sq.* ; of Egyptian kings at the Sed festival, vi. 153, 155 *sq.* ; of novices at initiation, xi. 247, 251, 256, 257, 261

——, premature, iii. 213. *See* Miscarriage

Birth-names of Central American Indians, xi. 214 *n.*[1]

—— -trees in Africa, xi. 160 *sqq.* ; in Europe, xi. 165

Birthday, Greek custom of sacrificing to a dead man on his, i. 105 ; celebration in China, i. 169

—— of the Sun at the winter solstice, v. 303 *sqq.*, x. 246

Birthdays of Apollo and Artemis, i. 32

"Birthplace of Rainy Zeus," ii. 360

Births, premature, how treated by the Akikuyu, iii. 286, 286 *n.*[6]

Bisa chiefs reincarnated in pythons, iv. 193

—— woman, her mode of sowing bananas, vii. 115

Bisaltae, a Thracian tribe, sanctuary of Dionysus among the, vii. 5

Bisection of the year, Celtic, x. 223

Bishnois of the Punjaub, infant burial among the, v. 94

Bishop, Mrs., on cairns in Corea, ix. 11 *n.*[5] ; on the belief in demons in Corea, ix. 99 *sq.*

Bishop, the Boy, on Holy Innocents' Day, ix. 336 *sqq.*

—— of Fools, ix. 312

—— of Innocents, ix. 333

Bismarck Archipelago, iv. 61 ; magical powers ascribed to chiefs in the, i. 340 ; magic practised on refuse of food in the, iii. 128 *sq.* ; reluctance to mention personal names in the, iii. 329 ; the Melanesians of the, their belief in demons, ix. 83

Bisons, the resurrection of, viii. 256

Bissagos Islands, natives of, their sacrifices to sacred trees, ii. 16

—— Archipelago, precaution as to spittle in the, iii. 289

Bistritz district of Transylvania, belief as to quail in last corn in the, vii. 295

Bitch, the last sheaf called the, vii. 272

Bites of ants used as purificatory ceremony, iii. 105. *See* Ants

Bithynia, Arrian of, ii. 126 ; mournful song of reapers in, vii. 216

—— and Pontus, rapid spread of Christianity in, ix. 420 *sq.*

Bithynians invoke Attis, v. 282

Biting bark of tree as mode of transferring a malady, ix. 54, 55

—— a sword as a charm, i. 160

Biyârs, the, of North-Western India, their ceremony of "burning the old year," ix. 230 *n.*[7]

Bizya (modern Viza), capital of old Thracian kings, vii. 26, 30

Black, Dr. J. Sutherland, on the burning of Winter at Zurich, iv. 260 *sq.*

Black animals in rain-charms, i. 250, 290 *sqq.*, ii. 367 ; as scapegoats, ix. 190, 192, 193

—— bull sacrificed to the dead, iv. 95

—— cats, witches turn into, ii. 334

—— colour in magic, i. 83 ; in rain-making ceremonies, i. 269 *sq.*, iii. 154

—— Corrie of Ben Breck, the giant of, in an Argyleshire tale, xi. 129 *sq.*

—— Demeter, vii. 263

—— drink, an emetic, viii. 76

—— Forest, Midsummer fires in the, x. 168

—— goat-skin, in relation to Dionysus, vii. 17

—— god and white god among the Slavs, ix. 92

—— hair, homoeopathic charm to restore, i. 154

—— Isle, Ross-shire, x. 301

—— Mountains, in France, ix. 166 ; story of sleeping witch in the, iii. 42

—— ox in magic, iii. 154 ; bath of blood of, iv. 201

—— poplars, mistletoe on, xi. 316, 318 *n.*[6]

—— ram sacrificed to Pelops, ii. 300, iv. 92, 104 ; in magic, iii. 154

—— -snake clan of the Warramunga, v. 100

—— spauld, a disease of cattle, cure for, x. 325

—— three-legged horse ridden by witches, xi. 74

—— victims in rain-making, iii. 154 ; sacrificed to the dead, iv. 92, 95

—— and white in relation to human scapegoats, ix. 220, 253, 257, 272

Blackened faces, vii. 287, 291, 299, viii. 321, 332, ix. 247, 314, 330 ; of actors, vii. 27

Blackening faces of warriors, iii. 163 ; of manslayers, iii. 169, 178, 181, 186 *n.*[1]; of girls at puberty, x. 41, 60

Blackfoot Indians, taboos observed by eagle-trappers among the, i. 116 ; taboos observed by the wives and children of eagle-hunters among the, i. 119 ; their use of skulls as charms, i. 149 *sq.* ; their way of bringing on a storm of rain, i. 288 ; their marriage of the Sun and Moon, ii. 146 *sq.* ;

taboos observed by man who kept the sacred pipe among the, iii. 159 n. ; unwilling to speak their names, iii. 326 ; their worship of the Pleiades, vii. 311 ; their propitiation of the eagles which they have killed, viii. 236

Bladders, annual festival of, among the Esquimaux, iii. 206 sq., 228 ; of sea-beasts returned by the Esquimaux to the sea, viii. 247 sqq.

Bland, J. O. P., on substitutes for capital punishment in China, iv. 274 sq.

Blankenfelde, in district of Potsdam, the Old Man at harvest at, vii. 221

Blankenheim in the Eifel, the King of the Bean at, ix. 313

Blay, men's clubhouse in the Pelew Islands, vi. 265

Bleeding trees, ii. 18, 20, 33

Blekinge, Swedish province, the Midsummer Bride and Bridegroom in, ii. 92, v. 251

Blemishes, bodily, a ground for putting kings to death, iv. 36 sqq. ; physical, transferred to witches, x. 160 n.¹

"Blessers" or sacred kings, iii. 125 n.

Blessing of maize, game, and fish by medicine-men among the Bororos, viii. 71 sq.

Blighting effect of illicit love on the fruits of the earth, ii. 107 sqq.

Blind bull sacrificed at the foundation of a town, vi. 249 ; sacrificed before an army going to war, vi. 250

—— cat in homoeopathic magic, i. 153

—— Tree, the, i. 147

Blindfolded reapers, vii. 144, 153 sq.

Blindness, charm to cause, i. 147

—— of Hother, x. 279 n.⁴

Block, the Yule, x. 247

Blocksberg, dance of the witches on the, ix. 163 n.¹ ; the resort of witches, x. 171 ; the Mount of the Witches, xi. 74

Blood shed at circumcision and sub-incision, uses of, i. 92, 94 sq. ; drawn from virgin bride, i. 94 ; the flow of, arrested by blood-stones, i. 165 ; sympathetic connexion between wounded person and his shed blood, i. 205 ; of contracting parties sprinkled on their footprints in making a treaty, i. 211 ; used to imitate rain, i. 256, 257 sq. ; smeared on regalia, i. 363 ; smeared on king's throne, i. 365 ; of sacrificial victim, inspiration by sucking the, i. 381 sq. ; offered to trees, ii. 13, 16, 19, 34, 44, 47, 367 ; smeared on wood-work of house to appease the tree-spirits, ii. 39 ; smeared on house as an expiatory rite, ii. 109 n.¹ ; of incestuous persons, blighting effects attributed to the, ii. 110 sq. ; smeared

on new fire-boards, ii. 225 ; smeared on sacred trees, ii. 367 ; put on doorposts, iii. 15 ; smeared on person as a purification, iii. 104, 115, 219 ; of slain, supposed effect of, it on the slayer, iii. 169 ; drawn from bodies of manslayers, iii. 176, 180 ; tabooed, iii. 239 sqq. ; not eaten, iii. 240 sq. ; soul in the, iii. 240, 241, 247, 250 ; of game poured out, iii. 241 ; spilt on ground, covered up, iii. 241, 245, 246 ; unwillingness to shed, iii. 243, 246 sq. ; received on bodies of kinsfolk, iii. 244 sq. ; drops of, effaced, iii. 245 sq. ; horror of, iii. 245 ; spilt, used by magicians for evil purposes, iii. 246 ; of chief sacred, iii. 248 ; of women, dread of, iii. 250 sq. ; fetish priests allowed to drink fresh blood, iii. 291 ; of sacrifice splashed on door-posts, house-posts, etc., iv. 97, 175, 176 n.¹ ; remission of sins through the shedding of, v. 299 ; used in expiation for homicide, v. 299 n.² ; not to be shed in certain sacrifices, vi. 222 n.² ; of sacrificial horse, use made of, viii. 42 ; drawn from men as a religious rite, viii. 75, 91 sq. ; of men drunk to acquire their qualities, viii. 148, 150, 151, 152 ; as a means of communion with a deity, viii. 316 ; fatigue let out with, ix. 12 ; of children used to knead a paste, ix. 129 ; drawn from ears as penance, ix. 292 ; girls at puberty forbidden to see, x. 46 ; drawn from women who do not menstruate, x. 81

Blood, bath of ox, iv. 35, 201 ; bath of bull's, in the rites of Attis, v. 274 sqq.

—— of bear drunk, viii. 146

—— of beavers not allowed to fall on ground, viii. 240 n.²

—— of childbirth, supposed dangerous infection of, iii. 152 sqq. ; received on heads of friends or slaves, iii. 245

——, the Day of, in the festival of Attis, v. 268, 285

—— of dragon imparts knowledge of language of birds, viii. 146

——, human, strengthening and fertilizing virtue attributed to, i. 85 sqq., 90 sqq., 105 ; offered at grave, i. 90 sq., 101 ; given to sick people, i. 91 ; used to knit men together, i. 92 ; used in rain-making ceremonies, i. 256, 257 sq., xi. 232 sq.; offered to the dead, iv. 92 sq., 104 ; libations of, poured on grave of Pelops, iv. 92 ; mixed with maize and eaten as a blessed food, viii. 91 sq.

—— of human victims in rain-making ceremonies, iv. 20 ; smeared on faces of idols, iv. 185 ; sprinkled on seed, vii. 239, 251 ; scattered on field, vii. 244, 251

Blood of lamb sprinkled on people, viii. 315

——, menstruous, dread of, x. 76 ; disastrous effect of seeing, x. 77 ; deemed fatal to cattle, x. 80 ; miraculous virtue attributed to, x. 82 sq. ; medicinal application of, x. 98 n.[1]

—— of pigs in purificatory rites, ii. 107, 108, 109, v. 299 n.[2], ix. 262

——, royal, reluctance to spill, ii. 228 ; not to be shed on the ground, iii. 241 sqq.

—— of St. John found on St. John's wort and other plants at Midsummer, xi. 56, 57

—— of sheep poured on image of god as a sin-offering, x. 82

—— of slain men tasted by their slayers, viii. 154 sqq.

Blood-brotherhood formed by woodman with the tree which he fells, ii. 19 sq.; between men and animals among the Fans, xi. 201, 226 n.[1] ; between men and animals among the Indians of Honduras, xi. 214, 226 n.[1]

—— -covenant, iii. 130, viii. 154 sqq. ; by mixture of blood between husband and wife, viii. 69. See also Blood-brotherhood

—— -lickers among the Betsileo, iii. 246

—— -stones thought to arrest the flow of blood, i. 81, 165

Bloodless altars, ix. 307

Bloomfield, Professor Maurice, on the magical nature of Vedic ritual, i. 229

—— River, Queensland, magical effigies on the, i. 62 ; namesakes of the dead change their names on the, iii. 355 sq.

Blowing on a fire, forbidden to sacred chiefs, iii. 136, 256 ; upon knots, as a charm, iii. 302, 304

—— of trumpets in the festival of Attis, v. 268

Blows to drive away ghosts, ix. 260 sqq.

Blue Spring, the, at Syracuse, v. 213 n.[1]

Bluk, the bull-frog, i. 292

Blu-u Kayans of Borneo, iii. 104 ; expiation for unchastity among the, ii. 109 sq.

Blydeuitzigt, in Cape Colony, ix. 16

Boa-constrictor, purification of man who has killed a, iii. 221 sq. ; need of appeasing the soul of a, viii. 296

Boa-constrictors, kings at death turn into, iv. 84, xi. 212 n. ; souls of dead in, viii. 289 sq.

Boanerges, "sons of thunder," i. 266 n.[1]

Boar, in homoeopathic magic, i. 151 ; grunting like a wild, a charm against sore feet, ii. 22 sq.; and Adonis, v. 11, viii. 22 sq. ; Attis killed by a, v. 264 ;

corn-spirit as, vii. 298 sqq.; the Yule, vii. 300 sqq., 302 sq. See also Boars

Boar's fat poured on novices at initiation in the Andaman Islands, viii. 164

—— head mask worn by actor at a sowing festival, vii. 95 sq.

—— skin, shoes of, worn by a king at inauguration, x. 4

Boars, evil spirits transferred to, ix. 31 ; familiar spirits of wizards in, xi. 196 sq. ; lives of persons bound up with those of, xi. 201, 203, 205 ; external human souls in, xi. 207

——, wild, hunted in Italy, i. 6 ; in ancient Greece, i. 6 n.[6] ; not to be called by their proper names, iii. 411, 415 ; annually sacrificed in Cyprus, viii. 23 n.[3] ; their ravages in the corn, viii. 31 sqq. ; eaten to make eater brave, viii. 140. See also Swine

Boas, Dr. Franz, on the taboos observed by Esquimaux hunters, iii. 210 sqq.; on the confession of sins, iii. 214 ; on the masked dances of the Indians of North-Western America, ix. 375 sq. ; on seclusion of Shuswap girls at puberty, x. 53 ; on customs observed by mourners among the Bella Coola Indians, xi. 174 ; on initiation into the wolf society of the Nootka Indians, xi. 270 sq. ; on the relation between clans and secret societies, xi. 273 n.[1]

Boba or Baba, "the Old Woman," name given to the last sheaf, vii. 144 sq., 223

Bocage of Normandy, rule as to the clipping of wool in the, vi. 134 n.[3] ; "catching the quail," at harvest in the, vii. 295 ; games of ball in the, ix. 183 sq. ; Eve of Twelfth Night in the, ix. 316 sq. ; weather of the twelve months predicted from the Twelve Days in the, ix. 323 ; Midsummer fires in the, x. 185 ; the Yule log in the, x. 252 ; torchlight processions on Christmas Eve in the, x. 266

Bock, C., on birth-ceremonies in Laos, vii. 8 ; on the fear of demons in Laos, ix. 97

Bodia or Bodio, a West African pontiff responsible for the fertility of the earth, i. 353 ; taboos observed by him, iii. 14 sq., 23

Bodies, souls transferred to other, iii. 49

—— of the dead, magical uses made of the, vi. 100 sqq. ; guarded against mutilation, vi. 103 ; thought to be endowed with magical powers, vi. 103, 104 sq.

Bodmin, in Cornwall, Lord of Misrule at, ii. 319 n.[1]

Bodos, the, of Assam, mourners shaved among the, iii. 285

Bodroum in Cilicia, ruins of, v. 167
Body-without-soul in a Ligurian story, xi. 107 ; in a German story, xi. 116 *sq.* ; in a Breton story, xi. 132 *sq.* ; in a Basque story, xi. 139
Boedromion, an Attic month, vii. 52, 77, viii. 6 *n.*
Boemus, Joannes, on the "carrying out of Death," iv. 234 ; on the King of the Bean, ix. 315 *n.*
Boeotian festival of the Great Daedala, xi. 77 *n.*[1]
—— sacrifice to Hercules, viii. 95 *n.*[2]
Bogadjim, in German New Guinea, belief in wind-making at, i. 322 ; charm to attract fish at, viii. 251
Boghaz-Keui, Hittite capital, excavations of H. Winckler at, v. 125 *n.* ; situation and remains of, v. 128 *sqq.* ; the gods of, v. 128 *sqq.* ; rock-hewn sculptures at, v. 129 *sqq.*
Bogle, George, envoy to Tibet, his account of a Tibetan New Year ceremony, ix. 203
Bogomiles, a Russian sect, worship each other as embodiments of Christ, i. 407 *sq.*
Bogos of East Africa allow no fire in a house after a death, ii. 267 *n.*[4] ; women of the, will not mention their husbands' names, iii. 337
Bogota, capital of the Chibchas, i. 416 ; rigorous training of the heir to the throne of, x. 19
Bohemia, customs as to children's cast teeth in, i. 180 ; contagious magic of footprints in, i. 210 *sq.* ; Midsummer-tree burned in, ii. 66 ; throwing Death into the water on the fourth Sunday in Lent in, ii. 73 *sq.* ; Whitsuntide King in, ii. 85 ; girl called Queen on fourth Sunday in Lent in, ii. 87 ; the soul as a white bird in, iii. 34 ; belief as to stepping over a child in, iii. 424 ; belief as to falling stars in, iv. 66 ; "burying the Carnival" in, iv. 209 ; Whitsuntide mummers in, iv. 209 *sqq.* ; "Carrying out Death" in, iv. 237 *sq.* ; bringing in Summer in, iv. 246 ; May-pole or Midsummer-tree in, v. 250 ; Feast of All Souls in, vi. 72 *sq.* ; harvest customs in, vii. 138, 145, 149, 150, 225 *sq.*, 232, 286, 289 ; fox's tongue as amulet in, viii. 270 ; snake's tongue cut on St. George's Eve confers eloquence in, viii. 270 ; custom as to mice in, viii. 279, 283 ; the Shrovetide or carnival Bear in, viii. 325 *sq.* ; sticks or stones piled on scenes of violent death in, ix. 15 ; precautions against witches on Walpurgis Night in, ix. 161 ; "Easter Smacks" in, ix.

268, 269 ; the Three Kings of Twelfth Day in, ix. 330 *sq.* ; the Festival of Fools in, ix. 336 *n.*[1] ; water and fire consecrated at Easter in, x. 123 *sq.* ; bonfires on May Day in, x. 159 ; Midsummer fires in, x. 173 *sqq.* ; need-fire in, x. 278 *sq.* ; charm to make corn grow high in, x. 340 ; offering to water-spirits on Midsummer Eve in, xi. 28 ; simples gathered on St. John's Night in, xi. 49 ; divination by means of flowers on Midsummer Eve in, xi. 52 *sq.* ; mugwort at Midsummer in, xi. 59 ; elder-flowers gathered at Midsummer in, xi. 64 ; wild thyme gathered on Midsummer Day in, xi. 64 ; magic bloom of fern-seed at Midsummer in, xi. 66 ; "thunder besoms" in, xi. 85 ; fern-seed on St. John's Day in, xi. 287, 288
Bohemia, the Germans of Western, their phrase for man who cuts last corn, vii. 138 ; their custom at Christmas, ix. 270 ; Twelfth Day among, ix. 331
Bohemian belief that serpents get their poison annually on St. George's Day, ii. 344 *n.*[4] ; cures for fever, ix. 49, 51, 55 *sq.*, 58, 59, 63 ; remedy for jaundice, ix. 52
—— charm to make fruit-trees bear, i. 141
—— custom of "Shooting the Witches" on St. Sylvester's Day, ix. 164
—— love-charms on St. George's Day, ii. 345 *sq.*
—— poachers, their use of vervain, xi. 62 ; their use of seeds of fir-cones, xi. 64
—— story of the external soul, xi. 110
—— superstition as to understanding the language of animals, viii. 146
Bohemians, their precautions against witches on Walpurgis Night, ii. 55
Bohlingen, in Baden, the last sheaf called the Oats-stallion at, vii. 292 ; the last sheaf called the Rye-sow or the Wheat-sow at, vii. 298
Böhmerwald Mountains, the Oats-goat at harvest in the, vii. 284 ; annual expulsion of witches on Walpurgis Night in the, ix. 159 *sq.*
Bohus, Midsummer fires in, x. 172
Bohuslän, in Sweden, prehistoric rock-carving at, vii. 129 *n.*[1]
Boidès, torches or bonfires on the first Sunday in Lent, x. 111 *n.*[1]
Boiled flesh tabooed to manslayers, iii. 185
—— meat offered to the Seasons, i. 310
Boiling bewitched animal or part of it to compel witch to appear, x. 321 *sq.*, 323
—— a thief's name, iii. 331

Boiling milk, omens drawn from, xi. 8
—— resin, ordeal of, x. 311
Boils caused by magical stones, i. 147;
  thought to be caused by eating or
  touching a totemic animal, viii. 25,
  29; crawling under a bramble as a
  cure for, xi. 180
Bolang Mongondo, a district of Celebes,
  recall of lost soul in, iii. 53 sq.; disposal
  of child's first hair, iii. 279; names of
  relations tabooed in, iii. 341; rajahs of,
  their names not to be mentioned, iii.
  376; custom as to eating the new rice
  in, viii. 54; belief in demons in, ix. 85
  sq.; riddles only asked when there is
  a corpse in the village in, ix. 121 n.³
Bolbe in Macedonia, lake of, ix. 142 n.¹
Bolivia, the Moxos Indians of, i. 123;
  Aymara Indians of, i. 292, iii. 97,
  ix. 193; the Chiriguanos Indians of,
  vi. 143 n.⁴, 145, viii. 140, 286, ix.
  26, 193, x. 56; Tarija in, vii. 173 n.;
  the Guarayos of, viii. 157; the Pechuyos of, viii. 157; the Retoroños of, viii.
  157; the Yuracares Indians of, viii.
  235 sq., 257, x. 57 sq.; heaps of stones
  or sticks in, ix. 12; sticks or stones
  piled on scenes of violent death in,
  ix. 15; Indians of, their offerings at
  cairns, ix. 26 sq.; fires on St. John's
  Eve in, x. 213; La Paz in, xi.
  50
Boloki, or Bangala, of the Upper Congo,
  their ceremonies at the new moon, vi.
  143; attempt to deceive spirit of disease, vi. 262; their fear of demons,
  ix. 76 sq.; birth-plants among the, xi.
  161 sq.; use of bull-roarers among the,
  xi. 229 n.
Bombay, belief as to absence of sleeper's
  soul in, iii. 41; the Suni Mohammedans of, their customs as to mirrors,
  iii. 95; burial custom in, viii. 100
Bomma, King of the Rain at, ii. 2
Bondeis of German East Africa, rites of
  initiation among the, xi. 263 sq.
Bonds, no man in bonds allowed in
  house of Flamen Dialis, iii. 14
Bone used to point with in sorcery, x.
  14; of bird (eagle or swan), women at
  menstruation obliged to drink out of,
  x. 45, 48, 49, 50, 73 n.³, 90, 92; inci-
  dent of, in folk-tales, x. 73 n.³
—— of old animals eaten to make the
  eater old, viii. 143
Bones, departing souls bottled up in
  hollow, iii. 31; burnt in the Easter
  bonfires, x. 142; burnt in Midsummer
  fires, x. 203
—— of animals not allowed to be gnawed
  by dogs, viii. 225, 238 sqq., 243, 259;
  preserved in order that the animals

may come to life again, viii. 256 sqq.;
  burned or thrown into water, viii. 257;
  not to be broken, viii. 258 sq.; that
  have been eaten as a sacrament treated
  with ceremonious respect, viii. 313
Bones of the dead, in magic, i. 148, 150;
  of dead shamans placed in trees, ii. 32;
  their treatment after the decay of the
  flesh, iii. 372 n.⁵; disinterred and
  scraped, iii. 373 n., iv. 96; used in
  rain-making ceremonies, v. 22; of
  dead kings carried off or destroyed by
  enemies, vi. 103 sq.; cakes baked in
  the shape of, and eaten as the bones
  of a god, viii. 87 sqq.; virtues acquired
  by contact with the, viii. 153 sq.; preserved to facilitate resurrection, viii.
  259; of dead enemies destroyed to
  prevent their resurrection, viii. 260;
  of dead husbands carried by their
  widows, x. 91 n.⁴
—— of deer not given to the dogs, viii.
  241, 242, 243
—— of fish not burned, viii. 250, 251;
  thrown into the sea or a river, viii. 250,
  254; not to be broken, viii. 255
——, fossil, source of myths about giants,
  v. 157 sq.
——, human, buried as rain-charm, i.
  287; burned as a charm against
  sorcery, iii. 330; of bodies which have
  been eaten, special treatment of, iii.
  189 sq.
——, marrow, not to be broken in a hut,
  i. 115 sq.
—— of sacrificial victim not broken, iv. 20
—— of salmon not to touch the ground,
  viii. 254
—— and skulls of enemies not destroyed,
  viii. 260
—— of white whale kept from dogs,
  iii. 206
Bonfire Day in County Leitrim, x. 203
Bonfires on St. John's Day (Midsummer
  Day) in Esthonia, iv. 280; leaping over,
  iv. 262, ix. 159; on St. John's Eve,
  dances round, v. 245; on Walpurgis
  Night to keep off witches, ix. 163; on
  the Eve of Twelfth Day, ix. 316 sqq.;
  supposed to protect against conflagrations, x. 107, 108; lit by the persons
  last married, x. 107, 109; a protection
  against witchcraft, x. 108, 109, 154; a
  protection against sickness, x. 108,
  109; a protection against sorcery, x.
  156; quickening and fertilizing influence of, x. 336 sqq.; omens of
  marriage drawn from, x. 338 sqq.; protect fields against hail, x. 344; protect
  houses against lightning and conflagration, x. 344; at festivals in India, xi.
  1 sqq. See also Fires

Bonfires, Midsummer, ii. 65; intended to drive away dragons, x. 161; protect cattle against witchcraft, x. 188; thought to ensure good crops, x. 188, 336

Bongo, the, of the Upper Nile, magical powers of chiefs among, i. 347

Boni, Commendatore G., on the Vestal fire, ii. 186 n.[1]

Boni, in Celebes, etiquette at the court of the king of, iv. 40

Boniface, Archbishop of Mainz, x. 270

Bonnach stone in a Celtic story, xi. 126

Bonnets, special, worn by women at menstruation, iii. 146

Bonny River, human sacrifices at mouth of the, ii. 157 sq.

Bontoc, in Luzon, sacred trees of the natives of, ii. 30; human sacrifices at planting and reaping rice in, vii. 240

Booandik tribe of South Australia, their fear of women's blood, iii. 251; special form of speech used between relations by marriage in the, iii. 346 sq.

Boobies, the aborigines of Fernando Po, their sacred king, iii. 8 sq.

Booginese. See Buginese

Book of Acaill, ancient Irish work, iv. 39

—— of the Dead, the ancient Egyptian, vi. 13, vii. 215, ix. 103

—— of Rewards and Penalties, Chinese work, i. 61

—— of Rights, ancient Irish work, iii. 12 n.[2]

Booth of Orestes, i. 26

Bor, the ancient Tyana, Hittite monument at, v. 122 n.[1]

Bor tribe of Dinka, their rain-maker, iv. 32

Borâna Gallas, custom observed by man-slayers among the, iii. 186 n.[1]

Borans, their custom of sacrificing their children to a sky-spirit, iv. 181

Bordeaux, May-poles at, ii. 69; magical use of knotted cords at, iii. 299; "killing the Bull" at threshing near, vii. 291

Bordes, torches carried on the first Sunday in Lent, x. 111 n.[1]

Borewell, the, in Northumberland, resorted to by barren women, ii. 161

Borlase, William, on the Cornish custom of the Maypole, ii. 67; on Midsummer fires in Cornwall, x. 199

Bormus, mournful song of Marian-dynian reapers, vii. 216, 264; compared to Lityerses, vii. 257

Born again, pretence of being, i. 74 sqq., iii. 113. See also Birth, new

—— "of an oak or a rock," i. 100 n.[1]

—— thrice, said of Brahmans, i. 381

Borneo, use of magical images in, i. 59 sq.; the Dyaks of, i. 73, iii. 52, ix. 14, 383, x. 5, xi. 222; rules observed by camphor hunters in, i. 115; telepathy in war in, i. 127; the Mahakam Dyaks of, i. 159; treatment of the afterbirth and navel-string in, i. 194; gongs beaten in storms in, i. 328; beliefs as to the blighting effect of sexual crime in, ii. 108 sqq.; the Kenyahs of, ii. 385, iii. 110, 415; hooks to catch souls in, iii. 30; rice used to prevent the soul, conceived as a bird, from wandering, in, iii. 35; recall of lost souls in, iii. 55 sq.; the Ot Danoms of, iii. 103; precautions against strangers in, iii. 103 sq.; the Blu-u Kayans of, iii. 104; exorcism of spirits by means of rice in, iii. 106; the Dusuns of, iii. 230, ix. 200; natives of, reluctant to name the dead, iii. 353; the Malanau tribes of, iii. 406; the Sakarang Dyaks of, iii. 416; the Barito of, iv. 166 n.[1]; custom of head-hunting in, v. 294 sqq.; effeminate sorcerers in, vi. 253, 256; division of agricultural work between the sexes in, vii. 124; use of puppets as substitutes for living persons in, viii. 100 sq.; custom in the search for camphor in, viii. 186 n.; the Kalamantans of, viii. 293 sq.; belief in demons in, ix. 87; sickness expelled in a ship from, ix. 187; the Biajas of, ix. 200; festivals in, x. 13; seclusion of girls at puberty in, x. 35 sq.; birth-custom in, xi. 154 sq.; trees and plants as life-indices in, xi. 164 sq.; the Madangs of, xi. 175; creeping through a cleft stick after a funeral in, xi. 175 sq.; giving the slip to an evil spirit in, xi. 179 sq.

Borneo, Central, the Kayans of, i. 330, ii. 17, 109, iii. 47, 99, 110, 113, 164, 239, 260, 286, 406, iv. 218, vii. 92, 184, viii. 54 sq., ix. 154 n., 236, 382 sq., x. 4 sq., xi. 175; agricultural communities of, vii. 92

——, Eastern, Tengaroeng in, iv. 280, 281

——, Northern, the Dyaks of, vii. 188

——, South-Eastern, the Dyaks of, iii. 72 n.[1]

——, Western, precautions against frightening the spirit of the rice in, ii. 28

Bornu, the Sultan of, hides himself from his people, iii. 120 sq.

Boroma, on the Zambesi, rain-maker with unshorn hair at, iii. 259 sq.

Bororos of Brazil, best singers chosen chiefs among the, ii. 298 sq.; their conception of the soul as a bird, iii. 34; their belief in dreams, iii. 36; their belief and custom as to meteors,

iv. 62 *sq.* ; consecration of maize, game, and fish by medicine - men among the, viii. 71 *sq.* ; their identification of themselves with parrots, viii. 207 *sq.* ; their use of bull-roarers, xi. 230 *n.*

Borrow, witches come to, x. 322, 323, xi. 73

Borsippa, temple of E-zida at, iv. 110

Bosanquet, Professor R. C., on the Four-handed Apollo, vi. 250 *n.*[2]

Boscana, Father Geronimo, on the customs and superstitions of the Californian Indians, vii. 125, viii. 169

Bosco Sacro, the grove of Egeria, i. 18 *n.*[4]

Bosman, W., on serpent - worship in Guinea, v. 67

Bosnia, hawthorn used as a protection against vampyres in, ix. 153 *n.*[1] ; need-fire in, x. 286 ; life-trees of children in, xi. 165

Bosnian Turks, ceremony of adoption among the, i. 74

Bossuet, Bishop, on the Midsummer bonfires, x. 182

Botocudos of Brazil, their reason for eating the flesh of their enemies, viii. 156

Bottesford, in Lincolnshire, mistletoe deemed a remedy for epilepsy at, xi. 83

Bottle, external soul of queen in a, xi. 138

Bouche, Abbé, on West African priestesses, v. 66 *n.*[3], 69

Bougainville Straits, the natives of, their observation of the Pleiades and Orion's belt, vii. 313 ; their expulsion of demons, ix. 116 ; use of bull-roarers in, xi. 229 *n.*

Bough, the Golden, xi. 279 *sqq.* ; plucked by Aeneas, i. 11, ii. 379 ; and the King of the Wood, i. 11, x. 1 ; the plucking of it not a piece of bravado, ii. 123 *sq.* ; grew on an evergreen oak, ii. 379 ; a branch of mistletoe, xi. 284 *sqq.*, 315 *sqq.* *See also* Golden Bough

Boughs, green, a charm against witches, ii. 52-55, 127. *See also* Branches

Boulia district of Queensland, magical pointing bones in the, x. 14

Bouphonia, "the murder of the ox," ritual flight at the, ii. 309 *n.*[2] ; an Athenian sacrifice, viii. 4 *sqq.*

Bouphonion, a Greek month, viii. 6 *n.*

Bourail, in New Caledonia, ceremony at eating the new yams at, viii. 53

Bourbonnais, the Fox in the corn in, vii. 296 ; mistletoe a remedy for epilepsy in, xi. 83

Bourbourg, Brasseur de, on Mexican human sacrifices in connexion with the crops, vii. 237

Bourdifailles, bonfires on first Sunday in Lent, x. 111 *n.*[1]

Bourges, ceremony of "Sawing the Old Woman" at Mid-Lent in, iv. 242

Bourgogne, in Ain, the Fox in the last sheaf at, vii. 297

Bourke, Captain J. G., on the Pimas, iii. 184 ; on mock human sacrifices in Arizona, iv. 215 ; on the totem clans of the Zuni, viii. 178 ; on the bull-roarer, xi. 231

Bourlet, A., on the belief of the Thay in spirits, ix. 97 *sqq.*

Bouzygai, "Ox-yokers," priestly family at Eleusis, curses uttered by the, vii. 108 *sq.*

Bouzygios, epithet applied to the Sacred Ploughing at Athens, vii. 109 *n*[1]

Bovillae, King of the Sacred Rites at, i. 44 *n.*[1] ; Vejovis at, ii. 179 ; the Julian family at, ii. 179, 180 *n.*

Bowels, novice at initiation supplied by spirits with a new set of, xi. 235 *sqq.*

Bowes, in Yorkshire, need-fire at, x. 287

Box, strayed soul caught in, iii. 45, 70, 76 ; external soul of king in a, xi. 102, 149 ; external soul of cannibal in a, xi. 117. *See also* Boxes

——- -tree, external soul of giant in a, xi. 133

Boxers at funerals, iv. 97

Boxes opened in house to facilitate childbirth, iii. 296 ; or arks, sacred, x. 11 *sq.* *See also* Box

Boxing, in the pancratium, vii. 71 *n.*[5], viii. 131

Boxwood blessed on Palm Sunday, x. 184, xi. 47

Boy and girl produce need-fire by friction of wood, xi. 281

——- Bishop on Holy Innocents' Day, ix. 336 *sqq.*

Boys of living parents in ritual, vi. 236 *sqq.* ; dressed as girls to avert the Evil Eye, vi. 260 ; marriage customs to ensure the birth of, vi. 262 ; at initiation thought to be swallowed by wizards, xi. 233 ; at initiation thought to be born again, xi. 246 *sqq.*

Brabant, Whitsuntide custom in, ii. 80 ; Midsummer fires in, x. 194 ; St. Peter's bonfires in, x. 195 ; wicker giants in, xi. 35

Bracelets as amulets, iii. 55, 315, x. 92

Bradbury, Professor J. B., on hemlock as an anaphrodisiac, ii. 139 *n.*[1]

Braemar Highlanders, their Hallowe'en fires, x. 233 *sq.*

Brahma, Vishnu, and Siva, the Hindoo Trinity, i. 225

Brahma, the Hindoo creator, x. 95

Brahman, priest, derivation of name, i. 229 ; not to blow a fire with his mouth, ii. 241 ; called "twice born," xi. 276. *See also* Brahmans

Brahman boys sacrificed, vii. 244 ; forbidden to see the sun, x. 68 n.[2]
—— charms by treading on a stone, i. 160
—— fire-priests, ii. 247 sqq.
—— householder supposed to become a deity through sacrifice, i. 380 ; new birth of the, i. 380 sq.
—— marriage ceremony, i. 160
—— marriage in Southern India, bride dressed as a boy at, vi. 260
—— student, his cut hair and nails, iii. 277 ; his observances at end of his studentship, x. 20
—— teachers, taboos observed by, iii. 239
—— theology, gods at first mortal in, i. 373 n.[1]
—— women in rain-making ceremonies, i. 283
Brâhmaṇas, the magical nature of the sacrifices prescribed in the, i. 228 sq.
Brahmanic ritual at inauguration of a king, x. 4
Brahmanism akin to shamanism, i. 229 ; vestiges of, under Mohammedanism, ix. 90 n.[1]
Brahmans deemed superior to the gods, i. 226 ; morning offerings of the, i. 314 ; thrice-born, i. 381 ; divinity of the, i. 403 sq. ; their common and secret names, iii. 322 ; the ceremonial swinging of, iv. 150, 156 sq. ; on transubstantiation, viii. 89 ; first-fruits of sugar-cane given to, viii. 119 ; sacrificial custom of the, ix. 25 ; as human scapegoats, ix. 42 sq., 44 sq. ; their theory of sacrifice, ix. 410 sq.
Brahmapootra, head-hunting tribes in the valley of the, iv. 13
Brain, drippings of, used to acquire wisdom of dead, viii. 163 sq.
Brains of enemies eaten to acquire their qualities, viii. 152
Braller in Transylvania, the hanging of Carnival at, iv. 230 sq. ; "Carrying out Death" at, iv. 247 sqq. ; the Harvest-cock at, vii. 276
Bramble, crawling under a, as a cure for whooping-cough, etc., xi. 180
Bran úa Faeláin, King of Leinster, saved by the voluntary death of fifty monks, iv. 159 n.[1]
Branch of sacred cedar cut and brought home at wheat-sowing, ii. 50 sq. ; of hawthorn in bloom on May Day, ii. 52 ; of oak dipped in a spring as a rain-charm, ii. 359 ; lost soul brought back in a, iii. 67
Branches dipped in water as a rain-charm, i. 248, 250, 309, ii. 46 sq. ; not to be broken or cut in sacred

groves, ii. 9, 10, 41 sqq. ; stuck in fields to ensure rain or an abundant crop, ii. 46, 47, 48 ; stuck in flax-fields to make the flax grow tall, ii. 86 ; used in exorcism, iii. 109 ; fatigue transferred to, ix. 8 ; sickness transferred to, ix. 186. See also Bough, Boughs
Brand, John, on the Harvest Queen, vii. 146 ; on the Yule log, x. 247, 255
Brandenburg, Mark of, fruit-trees girt with straw at Christmas in, ii. 17 ; race of bride and bridegroom in, ii. 303 ; race to a sheaf on harvest-field in, vii. 137 ; cure for headache and giddiness in, ix. 52, 53 ; cure for toothache in, ix. 60 ; simples culled at Midsummer in, xi. 48
Brandons, the Sunday of the, first Sunday in Lent, x. 110 ; torches carried about fields and streets, x. 111 n.[1]
Brands of Midsummer fires a protection against lightning, conflagration, and spells, x. 183 ; a protection against thunder, x. 191 ; lighted, carried round cattle, x. 341. See also Sticks, charred
Brandy, North American Indian theory of, viii. 147
Bras Basah, a village on the Perak river, ix. 199
Brasidas, funeral games in his honour at Amphipolis, iv. 94
Brass rings as amulets, iii. 31, 314 ; instruments sounded to frighten away demons, ix. 147
Braunrode in the Harz Mountains, Easter fires at, x. 142
Braunsberg, in East Prussia, the Corn-goat at harvest at, vii. 282
Brauronia, festival of Brauronian Artemis, viii. 41 n.[3]
Bray, Mrs., on Devonshire custom of "crying the neck," vii. 265 sq.
Brazen serpent, the, viii. 281
Brazier, walking through a lighted, xi. 3 sqq.
Brazil, the Tupinambas of, i. 142, vii. 122 ; contagious magic of footprints in, i. 210; the Guayana Indians of, iv. 12 ; the Apinagos of, vi. 145 ; the Kaua and Kobeua Indians of, vii. 111, ix. 236, 381 ; observation of the Pleiades by the Indians of, vii. 309 sq. ; the Bororos of, viii. 71, 207 sq., xi. 230 n.; the Botocudos of, viii. 156 ; the Passes of, viii. 157 ; the Xomanas of, viii. 157 ; the Chiambioa Indians of, viii. 208 n.[1]; the Tupi Indians of, viii. 272 ; the Guaranis of, x. 56 ; the Uaupes of, x. 61 ; effigies of Judas burnt at Easter in, x. 128 ; fires of St. John in, x. 213 ; the Caripunas of, xi. 230 ; the

Nahuqua of, xi. 230 ; the Bakairi of, xi. 231

Brazil, Indians of, their rule as to hamstringing deer, i. 115 ; their charm to strengthen a girl's teeth, i. 153; power of medicine-men among the, i. 358 *sq.* ; their explanation of headache, iii. 40 ; death from imagination among the, iii. 136; think that wind may be caused by reading, iii. 231 ; their indifference to death, iv. 138 ; their belief in the noxious influence of the moon on children, vi. 148 ; play various games of cat's cradle, vii. 103 *n.*[1]; women's agricultural labours among the, vii. 122 ; their belief in the homoeopathic magic of animal flesh, viii. 139 ; their apologies to the ounces which they have caught in traps, viii. 235 ; at mouth of Amazon, beat themselves with an aquatic plant to increase their generative force, ix. 264 ; seclusion of girls at puberty among the, x. 56, 59 *sq.* ; ordeals undergone by young men among the, x. 62 *sq.*

——, Indians of North-Western, their masked dances, vii. 111 *sq.*, ix. 236, 381

Bread, leavened, Flamen Dialis forbidden to touch, iii. 13 ; fast from, in mourning for Attis, v. 272 ; communion, baked from first corn cut, viii. 51 ; eaten sacramentally as the body of a god, viii. 86 *sqq.* ; unleavened, baked with new corn, viii. 136 ; the sacramental use of, viii. 167 ; reverence for, x. 13

Bread-fruit, magical stones to promote the growth of, i. 162. *sq.*, 164 ; ceremony at eating the new, viii. 52 *sq.* ; tree planted over navel-string of child, xi. 163

Breadalbane, use of a scapegoat in, ix. 209 ; "hill of the fires" in, x. 149 ; treatment of mad cow in, x. 326

Breasted, Professor J. H., on the eye of Horus, vi. 121 *n.*[3]; on Amenophis IV., vi. 123 *n.*[1]; on the Sed festival, vi. 156 *n.*[1]

Breath, holy fire not to be blown upon with the, ii. 241 ; of chief sacred, iii. 136, 256 ; of dying chief caught by his successor, iv. 198 ; not to defile sacred flame, v. 191

" ——, scoring above the," cutting a witch on the forehead, x. 315 *n.*[2]

Breathing on a person as a mode of purification, iii. 149

Breconshire, the sin-eater in, ix. 43

Breech-cloth worn by widow to keep off her husband's ghost, iii. 143

Breezes, magical means of securing, iv. 287

Breitenbrunn, the "Charcoal Man" at Midsummer at, xi. 26 *n.*[2]

Brekinjska, in Slavonia, need-fire at, x. 282

Brenner, J. von, on savage fear of being photographed, iii. 99

Bresse, the *Mariée* in May in, ii. 96 ; "cutting off the fox's tail" at harvest in, vii. 268 ; the King of the Bean in, ix. 315 *n.*[1]; Midsummer bonfires in, x. 189

Brest, Midsummer fire-custom at, x. 184

Bret Harte, *Relieving Guard*, iv. 66 *n.*[4]; on the Spanish missions in California, viii. 171 *n.*[1]

Breteuil, canton of, Midsummer fires in the, x. 187

Brethren of the Free Spirit, i. 408

—— of the Ploughed Fields (*Fratres Arvales*), a Roman college of priests, ii. 122, vi. 239, ix. 232. *See also* Arval Brothers

Breton belief that women can be impregnated by the moon, x. 76

—— peasants, their way of getting rain, i. 306 *sq.* ; throw knives at the wind, i. 329

—— stories of the external soul, xi. 132 *sq.*

—— superstitions as to the tides, i. 167

Bretons, their dread of noon, iii. 88

Brewing, continence observed at, iii. 200, 201 *sq.* ; water to be called by another name in, iii. 395

Brezina, in Slavonia, need-fire at, x. 282

Bṛhaspati, as a magician, i. 241

Briançon, in Dauphiné, the Bridegroom of the Month of May at, ii. 92 *sq.* ; "the Cat of the ball-skin" at harvest at, vii. 280 *sq.*

Briar-thorn, divination by, x. 242

Bribri Indians of Costa Rica, their ideas as to the uncleanness of women, iii. 147, 149 ; seclusion of women at menstruation among the, x. 86

Bricknell, J., on a custom of the Carolina Indians, iv. 184 *sq.*

Bridal pair, the, at Whitsuntide in Saxony, ii. 91 ; at rice-harvest in Java, vii. 200 *sq.*

Bride tied to tree at marriage, ii. 57 ; the Whitsuntide, ii. 89, 96 ; the May, ii. 95 ; led to or round the hearth at marriage, ii. 221, 230, 231 ; races for a, ii. 300 *sqq.* ; contests for a, ii. 305 *sqq.* ; fishing-net thrown over, iii. 307; dressed as a man, vi. 260 ; the last, privilege of, ix. 183 ; not allowed to tread the earth, x. 5 ; last married, made to leap over bonfire, xi. 32

—— and bridegroom, the Whitsuntide, ii. 91 *sq.* ; the Midsummer, in Sweden, ii. 92, v. 251 ; all knots on their garments unloosed, iii. 299 *sq.* ; carry locked locks at marriage, iii. 308 ; mock, at bonfires, x. 109 *sq.*

Bride of God, the, in a rain-making ceremony, i. 276

——, name given to last sheaf, vii. 162, 163

—— of the Nile, vi. 38

—— race among Teutonic peoples, ii. 303 *sqq.*

Bride, parish of, in the Isle of Man, x. 306, 307 *n.*[1]

Bridegroom, the Whitsuntide, ii. 91 ; girt with a net, iii. 307; dressed as a woman, vi. 260 *sq.* ; disfigured in order to avert the evil eye, vi. 261 ; not to touch the ground with his feet, x. 5

—— of May, ii. 91, 93, iv. 266

Bridget's bed on the night before Candlemas in the Highlands of Scotland and the Isle of Man, ii. 94 *sq.* *See also* St. Bridget

Bridlington, the Boy Bishop at, ix. 338

Brie (Isle de France), the May-tree and Father May at, ii. 74 *sq.* ; farmer tied up in first sheaf at, vii. 221 ; stranger tied up in sheaf at harvest at, vii. 226 ; effigy of giant burnt on Midsummer Eve at, xi. 38

Brigit, a Celtic goddess, ii. 95, 240 *sqq.* ; her Christian namesake and successor at Kildare, ii. 240 *sqq.* *See also* St. Brigit

Brihaspati, Hindoo deity, i. 166, x. 99 *n.*[2]

Brimo and Brimos, in the mysteries of Eleusis, ii. 139

Brincker, Dr. P. H., on the sacred sticks representing ancestors among the Herero, ii. 224 *n.*[4]

Bringing in Summer, iv. 233, 237, 238, 246 *sqq.*

Briony, wreaths of, at Midsummer, x. 210

Brisbane River in Queensland, use of bull-roarers on the, xi. 233 *sqq.*

British Columbia, Indians of, their dislike of telling their own names, iii. 328 ; respect the animals and plants which they eat, vi. 44 ; their address to the first fish of the season, viii. 253 ; seclusion of girls at puberty among the, x. 46 *sqq.* ; dread and seclusion of menstruous women among the, x. 89 *sq.* ; rites of initiation among the, xi. 270 *sqq.*

——, Koskimo Indians of, xi. 229

——, the Kwakiutl of, i. 263, iii. 53, 188, 386, viii. 220, 250, xi. 152, 186

——, the Shuswap Indians of, i. 265, iii. 83, 142, viii. 226, 238, x. 53, xi. 174 *n.*[2], 276 *n.*[1], 297 *n.*[3]

——, the Thompson Indians of, i. 132, ii. 208, viii. 81, 133, 140, 207, 226, 268, ix. 154 *n.*, x. 49, 89 *sq.*, 98 *n.*[1], xi. 275, 297

Britomartis and Minos, iv. 73

Brittany, belief as to death at ebb-tide in, i. 167 *sq.* ; the Veneti of, ii. 353 ; belief as to falling stars in, iv. 66 ; Burial of Shrove Tuesday or of the Carnival in, iv. 229 *sq.* ; Feast of All Souls in, vi. 69 ; belief as to warts and the moon in, vi. 149 ; Mothersheaf at harvest in, vii. 135, 209 ; custom of sticking pins into a saint's image in, ix. 70 ; riddles asked after a burial in, ix. 121 *sq.*, *n.* ; forecasting the weather for the year in, ix. 323 *sq.* ; Midsummer fires in, x. 183 *sqq.* ; stones thrown into the Midsummer fires in, x. 240 ; the Yule log in, x. 253 ; mistletoe hung over doors of stables and byres in, xi. 287 ; fern-seed used by treasure-seekers in, xi. 288

Broceliande, the wild woods of, i. 306

Brochs, prehistoric ruins, x. 291

Brockelmann, C., on the Assyrian eponymate, iv. 116

Brocken, in the Harz mountains, associated with witches, x. 160 *n.*[1], 171 *n.*[3]

Brodek, in Moravia, drama of Summer and Winter at, iv. 257

Bromios, epithet of Dionysus, vii. 2 *n.*[1]

Bromo, volcano in Java, worshipped, v. 220 *sq.*

Bronze employed in expiatory rites, iii. 226 *n.*[6] ; priests to be shaved with, iii. 226

—— Age, in Denmark, ii. 351 ; rock-carving of the, in Sweden, vii. 129 *n.*[1]

—— knife to cut priest's hair, iii. 14

—— ploughs used by Etruscans at founding cities, iii. 157

Brooke, Rajah, of Sarawak, viii. 211 ; supposed to fertilize the rice-crops, i. 361 *sq.*

Broom, a protective against witchcraft, x. 210

Brooms used to sweep misfortune out of house, ix. 5

Broomstick in rain-making, i. 275

Broomsticks, witches ride on, ix. 162, 163

Brother of a god, v. 51 ; dead elder, worshipped, vi. 175

—— and sister not allowed to mention each other's names, iii. 344

"Brother" and "sister," titles given by men and women to their sex totems, xi. 215, 216, 218

Brotherhood formed with trees by sucking their sap, ii. 19 *sq.* ; of the Green Wolf at Jumièges in Normandy, x. 185 *sq.* *See also* Blood-brotherhood

Brothers reviled by sisters for good luck, i. 279 ; of king put to death on his accession, iii. 243 ; childless persons named after their younger, iii. 332, 333; ancient Egyptian story of the Two, xi. 134 *sqq.*

Brothers and sisters, marriages of, in royal families, iv. 193 *sq.*, v. 44; in ancient Egypt, vi. 214 *sqq.*; their intention to keep the property in the family, vi. 215 *sq.*

—— -in-law, their names not to be pronounced, iii. 338, 342, 343, 344, 345

Brown, A. R., as to the Andaman Islanders, ii. 254 *n.*; on the beliefs of the West Australian aborigines as to the causes of childbirth, v. 104 *sqq.*

Brown, Dr. Burton, on a burial custom of the Nagas, viii. 100 *n.*[2]

Brown, Dr. George, on the magical powers ascribed to chiefs in New Britain, i. 340; on snakes as reincarnations of chiefs, v. 84; on the annual appearance of the *Palolo veridis* in the Samoan Sea, ix. 142 *n.*[1]; on the seclusion of girls at puberty in New Ireland, x. 32 *sqq.*; on external soul in Melanesia, xi. 199

Bruck in Styria, the last sheaf called the Corn-mother at, vii. 134

Bructeri, a German tribe, worship a woman, i. 391

Bruges, Feast of All Souls in, vi. 70

Brughe, John, his cure for bewitched cattle, x. 324 *sq.*

Brugsch, H., on Egyptian names for a year, vi. 26 *n.*[1]; on the Sothic period, vi. 37 *n.*; on the grave of Osiris at Philae, vi. 111; on Isis as a personified corn-field, vi. 117

Bruguière, Mgr., on the fear of demons in Siam, ix. 97; on the annual expulsion of the devil in Siam, ix. 150 *sq.*

Brund (or brand), the Christmas, the Yule log, x. 257

Brunhild, Queen of Iceland, the wooing of, ii. 306 *sq.*

Brunnen, Twelfth Night at, ix. 165

Brunshaupten, in Mecklenburg, the Wheat-wolf at harvest at, vii. 274

Brunswick, custom at Whitsuntide in, ii. 56 *n.*[3]; May King at Whitsuntide in, ii. 84, 85; the May Bride at Whitsuntide in, ii. 96; dramatic contest between Summer and Winter in, iv. 257; toothache nailed into a wall or a tree in, ix. 62; belief as to menstruous women in, x. 96; Easter bonfires in, x. 140; need-fire in, x. 277 *sq.*

Brushes used in magic, i. 132

Brutus, D. Junius, his mitigation of human sacrifices at graves, iv. 143 *n.*[4]

——, L. Junius, one of the first consuls, ii. 290; his feigned imbecility, ii. 291

Brutus, the assassin, his meeting with Cicero, i. 5

Bryant, Jacob, and Noah's ark, i. 334

Bubastis, shrine of, at Nemi, i. 5

Bubui River, in German New Guinea, viii. 295

Buch, Max, on a ceremony of the Wotyaks, ii. 146

Buchan, Hallowe'en fires in, x. 232 *sq.*

Buchanan, Francis, on Burmese *nats*, ix. 175 *sq.*

Bûche de Noël, the Yule log, x. 249

Buckie, names tabooed by fishermen in the village of, iii. 395

Buckthorn, a charm against witches on May Day, ii. 54; a protection against thunderbolts, ii. 191 *n.*[1]; torch of, at a Roman marriage, ii. 191 *n.*[1]; a protection against witches, ii. 191, ix. 153 *n.*[1], 163; used in making fire by friction, ii. 251; chewed to keep off ghosts, ix. 153; used to beat cattle, ix. 266

Buckwheat cultivated in Burma, vii. 242

Bucolium at Athens, vii. 30

Buddha appealed to for rain, i. 251, 299; image of, whipped in drought, i. 297 *n.*[7]; images of, drenched as a rain-charm, i. 308; imitated by a king of Burma, i. 400; thought to be incarnate in the Grand Lamas, i. 411; images of, iii. 253; transmigrations of, viii. 299, 301, ix. 41; date of his death, viii. 302 *n.*[7]; in relation to spirits, ix. 97; offerings to, ix. 150

—— and Buddhism, vi. 159

—— and the crocodile, Indian story, xi. 102 *n.*[4]

——, Footprint of, in Siam, iii. 275

Buddhas, living, i. 410 *sq.*

Buddhism, Tibetan form of, iii. 20; spiritual declension of, v. 310 *sq.*; in relation to lower religions, ix. 89, 90 *n.*[1], 94, 95 *sqq.*; in Burma, ix. 95 *sq.*; the pope of, ix. 223

Buddhist animism not a philosophical theory, ii. 13 *sq.*

—— Lent, the, ix. 349 *sq.*

—— monk, who sent his soul out of himself, ii. 49 *sq.*

—— monks, suicide of, iv. 42 *sq.*; ceremony at the funeral of, ix. 175

—— priests expel demons, ix. 116

Buddhists of Ceylon, their propitiation of demons, ix. 90 *n.*[1]; the Laosians of Siam nominal, ix. 97

Budding of a bean an omen, ii. 344

Budge, E. A. Wallis, on trinities of Egyptian gods, iv. 5 *n.*[3]; on goddess Net, v. 282 *n.*; on an Egyptian funeral rite, vi. 15 *n.*[2]; on Isis, vi. 115 *sq.*; on the nature of Osiris, vi. 126 *n.*[2]; on the solar theory of Osiris, vi. 131 *n.*³; on the historical reality of Osiris, vi. 160 *n.*¹; on Khenti-Amenti, vi. 198 *n.*²; on human sacrifices in ancient Egypt, vii. 259 *n.*³; on the shrines of Osiris, vii. 260 *n.*²; on the fear of demons among the ancient Egyptians, ix. 103 *sq.*

Buduna tribe of West Australia, their beliefs as to the birth of children, v. 104 *sq.*

Buecheler, F., his corruption of the text of Petronius, ix. 253 *n.*²

Buffalo sacrificed for human victim, vii. 249; external souls of a clan in a, xi. 151; a Batta totem, xi. 223

Buffalo-bull, name given to the last sheaf, vii. 289

—— calf, sins of dead transferred to a, ix. 36 *sq.*

—— clan in Uganda, x. 3

—— dance to ensure a supply of buffaloes, ix. 171

—— Society among the Omahas, i. 249

Buffaloes not to be mentioned by their proper name, iii. 407, 408, 412; sacrificed instead of young girls, iv. 124; propitiation of dead, viii. 229, 231; their death bewailed, viii. 242; the resurrection of, viii. 256; revered by the Todas, viii. 314; as scapegoats, ix. 190, 191; external human souls in, xi. 207, 208

Buffooneries at the Festival of Fools, ix. 335 *sq.*

Buginese of Celebes, their homoeopathic charm to ensure longevity, i. 158; their use of the regalia as a remedy for plague or dearth, i. 363; their belief as to the blighting effects of incestuous blood, ii. 110; their custom of swinging at harvest, iv. 277; ascribe a soul to rice, vii. 183

—— sailors, words tabooed to, iii. 413

Bugis of South Celebes, effeminate priests or sorcerers among the, vi. 253 *sq.*

Bühl, St. John's fires at, x. 168

Bühler, G., on the identity of the names Perkunas and Parjanya, ii. 367 *n.*³; on Parjanya, ii. 369

Building shadows into foundations, iii. 89 *sq.*

—— of a canoe, continence at the, iii. 202

—— a house, taboos observed after, ii. 40; Malay custom as to shadows in, iii. 81

—— houses, magic art resorted to in, ix. 81

—— a new village, continence at, iii. 202

Buir, in district of Cologne, last sheaf shaped like wolf at, vii. 274

Bukaua, the, of German New Guinea, tell stories to promote the growth of the crops, vii. 103 *sq.*, 105; their observation of the Pleiades, vii. 313; their offerings of first-fruits to the spirits of the dead, viii. 124 *sq.*; their belief in demons, ix. 83 *sq.*; girls at puberty secluded among the, x. 35; their rites of initiation, xi. 239 *sqq.*

Bukowina, the Ruthenians of, i. 198; witches on St. George's Day in, ii. 335

Bu-ku-rú, ceremonial uncleanness, in Costa Rica, iii. 147, x. 65 *n.*¹, 86

Bulaa, village in New Guinea, iii. 192 *n.*⁵

Bulawayo, capital of the Matabele, rain-making ceremony at, i. 351; ceremony of the first-fruits at, viii. 70

Bulebane, in Senegambia, precaution as to the spittle of chiefs at, iii. 289

Buléon, Mgr., on the rite of blood-brotherhood with an animal, quoted by Father H. Trilles, xi. 202 *n.*¹

Bulgaria, ceremony of adoption in, i. 74; rain-making in, i. 274; rolling in the dew on St. George's morning in, ii. 333; superstition as to milk and butter on St. George's Day in, ii. 339; building custom in, iii. 89; marriage customs in, vi. 246; masquerade at Carnival in, viii. 333 *sq.*; cure for fever in, ix. 55; the Yule log in, x. 264 *n.*¹; need-fire in, x. 281, 285; simples and flowers culled on St. John's Day in, xi. 50; creeping through an arch of vines as a cure in, xi. 180; creeping under the root of a willow as a cure for whooping-cough in, xi. 180 *sq. See also* Bulgarian *and* Bulgarians

——, Simeon, prince of, xi. 156 *sq.*

Bulgarian charm for guarding cattle from wolves, iii. 307

—— peasants threaten fruit-trees to make them bear fruit, ii. 21

—— superstition as to crossed legs, iii. 299

—— women, their charm to hoodwink their husbands, i. 149; their charm to procure offspring on St. George's Day, ii. 344

Bulgarians, their customs as to the last sheaf at harvest, vii. 146; the Carnival among the, viii. 331 *sqq.*; their way of keeping off ghosts, ix. 153 *n.*¹

Bull sacrificed to Poseidon, i. 46; blood of, drunk by priestess to procure inspiration, i. 381 *sq.*; as emblem of a thunder-god, ii. 368, v. 134 *sqq.*, 136; sacrificed to the dead, iii. 227; Pasiphae and the, iv. 71; as symbol of the sun, iv. 71 *sq.*; as type of reproductive energy, iv. 72; the brazen, of Phalaris, iv. 75; perhaps the king's crest at Cnossus, iv. 111 *sq.* ; said to have guided the Samnites, iv. 186 *n.*[4] ; as emblem of generative force, v. 123 ; worshipped by the Hittites, v. 123, 132 ; Hittite god standing on a, v. 135 ; as symbol of thunder and fertility, v. 163 *sq.* ; the emblem of the Father God, v. 164 ; worshipped at Euyuk, v. 164 ; testicles of, used in rites of Cybele and Attis, v. 276 ; in relation to Dionysus, vii. 16 *sq.*, 31 ; corn-spirit as, vii. 288 *sqq.*, viii. 8 ; sacrificed at Zulu festival of first-fruits, viii. 68 *n.*[3]; sacrificed to the dead, viii. 113. *See also* Bulls

Bull, black, sacrificed to the dead at Plataea, iv. 95

—— and cow, represented by masked actors, iv. 71

——, live, torn to pieces in rites of Dionysus, vii. 15, 17, viii. 16

——, sacrifice of, at Egyptian funeral, vi. 15 ; to prolong the life of a king, vi. 222 ; to Zeus, the Saviour of the City, vi. 238 ; at the foundation of a town, vi. 249 ; at Magnesia, viii. 7 *sq.* ; in Mithraic religion, viii. 10 ; at festival of new fruits, viii. 68 *n.*[3] ; at tomb of dead chief, viii. 113. *See also* Bulls

——, white, sacrificed, ii. 188 *sq.* ; soul of dead king incarnate in a, vi. 164

Bull-fights and athletic games at festival of new fruits, viii. 66

—— -headed image of the sun, iv. 75, 76, 78

—— -roarers, sacred, used in magical ceremonies to multiply totems, i. 88 ; used to make fine weather, i. 265, with note[4] ; sounded to make wind blow, i. 324, xi. 232 ; whirled at tearing dogs to pieces, vii. 19 *n.*[1] ; whirled to make the crops thrive and to multiply game, vii. 104, 106 *sq.*, 110, xi. 230 *sq.*, 232 ; fertilizing virtue attributed to, by savages, vii. 106, xi. 230 *sq.* ; called the "mother of yams," vii. 106 ; swung at Greek mysteries, vii. 110 ; sounded at initiation of lads, viii. 295, xi. 227, 228 *sqq.*, 233 *sqq.*, 240, 241 ; swung at kindling of sacred fire, x. 133 ; sound of, thought to resemble thunder, xi. 228 *sqq.* ; sounded at festivals of the dead, xi. 230 *n.* ; made from trees struck by lightning, xi. 231 ; called "thunder and lightning," xi. 232 ; magical instrument for causing thunder, wind, and rain, xi. 233 ; sound of, supposed to be the voice of a spirit, xi. 233, 234, 235 ; not to be seen by women, xi. 234, 235, 242 ; called by name which means a ghost or spirit of the dead, xi. 242 ; called by the same name as the monster who swallows lads at initiation, xi. 242 ; kept in men's clubhouse, xi. 242 ; named after dead men, xi. 242 *n.*[1]

Bull-shaped deities, vii. 3 *sqq.*

Bull's blood drunk as means of inspiration, i. 381 *sq.* ; as ordeal, i. 382 *n.*[1] ; bath of, in the rites of Attis, v. 274 *sq.*

—— hide, bride seated on a, vi. 246 ; cut in strips and pegged down round the site of a new town, vi. 249

—— skin, body of the dead placed in a, vi. 15 *n.*[2]

Bullets, magical treatment of, i. 110 ; magical modes of averting, i. 130 ; blessed by St. Hubert used to shoot witches with, x. 315 *sq.*

Bullock, bewitched, burnt to cause the witch to appear, x. 303

Bullocks as scapegoats, ix. 34, 35

Bulloms, the, of Sierra Leone, their observation of the Pleiades, vii. 318

Bulls sacrificed to water-spirits, ii. 157 ; husband-god at Hierapolis seated on, v. 163 ; sacrificed at caves of Pluto, v. 206 ; sacrificed to Persephone, v. 213 *n.*[1] ; sacrificed to dead chiefs, vi. 191 ; eaten to make eater brave, viii. 140 ; as scapegoats in Cashmeer, ix. 190 *n.*[5] ; as scapegoats in ancient Egypt, ix. 216 *sq.*

——, sacred, of ancient Egypt, viii. 34 *sqq.*

Bulmer, J., on concealment of personal names among the aborigines of Victoria, iii. 321

Bundelcund, stopping rain in, i. 296

Bundles of sticks representing ancestors, ii. 214, 216

Bunjil Kraura, a wind-maker of the Kurnai, i. 324

Bunsen, Baron C. C. J., on St. Hippolytus, i. 21 *n.*[2]

Bunyoro, in Central Africa, scapegoats sent to, ix. 195

Bunzlau, district of Silesia, last sheaf made up in shape of ox in, vii. 289 *sq.*

Burchard, Bishop of Worms, his condemnation of a heathen practice, xi. 191

Bures, bonfires on the first Sunday in Lent, x. 110 *n.*[1], 111 *n.*[1]

Burford, in Oxfordshire, Midsummer giant and dragon at, xi. 37

Burgebrach in Bavaria, straw-man burnt on Ash Wednesday at, iv. 232

Burghead, the burning of the Clavie at, iii. 229 *sq.*, x. 266 *sq.* ; the old rampart at, x. 267 *sq.*

Burghers or Badagas. *See* Badagas

Burglars, charms employed by, to cause sleep, i. 148 *sq.*

Burgundians deposed their kings for failure of the crops, i. 366

Burgundy, Firebrand Sunday in, x. 114 ; the Yule log in, x. 254

Burial at flood tide, i. 168 ; alive of unfaithful virgins in Rome and Peru, ii. 228, 244 ; alive, in other cases, ii. 228 *n.*⁵ ; at night, iii. 15 ; of the aged, iv. 11 *sq.* ; in jars, iv. 12 *sq.* ; of Shrove Tuesday, iv. 228

—— of infants, ix. 45 ; to ensure their rebirth, iv. 199 *sq.*, v. 91, 93 *sqq.*

—— under a running stream, iii. 15 ; at cross-roads, v. 93 *n.*¹; at Gezer, v. 108 *sq.* ; of Osiris in his rites, vi. 88

—— of the wren in the Isle of Man, viii. 318 *sq.*

Burial customs, certain, perhaps designed to ensure reincarnation, i. 101 *sqq.* ; to prevent the escape of the soul, iii. 51, 52

—— -grounds, magical stones kept in, i. 163 ; regarded as holy, ii. 31 ; deemed sacred, viii. 111

—— rites intended to deceive ghosts or demons, viii. 97 *sqq.*

Burials, customs as to shadows at, iii. 80 *sq.* ; fictitious, to divert the attention of demons from the real burials, viii. 98 *sqq.* ; passing through narrow openings after, xi. 175 *sq.*, 177 *sq.*, 178 *sq.*

Buring Une, a Kayan goddess, vii. 93

Burkitt, Professor F. C., on Jesus Barabbas, ix. 420 *n.*¹

Burlesques of ecclesiastical ritual, ix. 336 *sq.*

Burma, magical images in, i. 62 *sq.* ; the Shans of, i. 128, 308; the Karens or Karennis of, i. 209, ii. 69, 107, iii. 13, 43, 250, 252, 292, iv. 130 *n.*¹, vii. 10, 189, xi. 157 ; rain-making by means of fish in, i. 288 *sq.* ; king of, claims divinity, i. 400 *sq.* ; the En of, ii. 41 ; Sagaing district of, ii. 46 ; Kengtung in, ii. 150 ; the Kachins of, ii. 237, iii. 200, viii. 120 ; fire on hearth extinguished after a death in, ii. 267 *n.*⁴ ; kings of, screened from public gaze, iii. 125 *sq.* ; the Sotih of, iii. 237 ; royal princes executed without bloodshed in, iii. 242 ; the Sgaus of, iii. 337 ; names of the kings of, not to be pronounced by their subjects, iii. 375 ; the Bghais of, vi. 60 ; securing the rice - soul in, vii. 189 *sqq.* ; the Taungthu of, vii. 190 ; the Szis of Upper, vii. 203 *sq.* ; custom of threshing rice in, vii. 203 *sq.* ; head-hunting in, vii. 256 ; offering of first-fruits to the king of, viii. 116 ; the Chins of, viii. 121 ; ravages of rats in, viii. 282 *n.*⁸ ; sacred fish in, viii. 291 ; heaps of stones or sticks in, ix. 12 ; belief in demons in, ix. 95 *sq.* ; expulsion of demons in, ix. 116 *sq.* ; the tug-of-war in, ix. 175 *sq.*

Burmese, their conception of the soul as a butterfly, iii. 51 *sq.*; their belief as to ghosts of men who have died a violent death, iii. 90 ; their conduct during an earthquake, v. 201

—— cure by burying effigy of sick man, viii. 103

—— custom on return from a funeral, iii. 51

—— doctrine of *nats*, ix. 175

—— Lent, ix. 349 *sq.*

—— mode of rain-making, i. 284 ; of disposing of cut hair and nails, iii. 277

—— recall of lost soul, iii. 51 *sq.*

—— superstitions as to the head, iii. 253

Burne, Miss C. S., on Devonshire custom of "crying the neck," vii. 266

——, Miss C. S., and Miss G. F. Jackson, on "Souling Day" in Shropshire, vi. 78 *sq.* ; on the fear of witchcraft in Shropshire, x. 342 *n.*⁴

Burning refuse of food as a magical means of causing the eater to fall ill, i. 341 ; of sacred trees or poles, ii. 141 *sq.* ; of cut hair and nails to prevent them being used in sorcery, iii. 281 *sqq.*; of Melcarth, v. 110 *sqq.* ; of Sandan and Hercules, v. 117 *sqq.*, 388 *sqq.*; of Cilician gods, v. 170 *sq.* ; of Sardanapalus, v. 172 *sqq.* ; of Croesus, v. 174 *sqq.* ; of a god, v. 188 *sq.* ; of last sheaf of corn, vii. 146 ; of the Clavie at Burghead, x. 266 *sq.* ; of a bewitched animal or part of it to cause the witch to appear, x. 303, 305, 307 *sq.* ; of human beings in the fires, xi. 21 *sqq.* ; of live animals at spring and Midsummer festivals, xi. 38 *sq.* ; the animals perhaps deemed embodiments of witches, xi. 41 *sq.*, 43 *sq.* ; of human victims annually, xi. 286 *n.*²

—— alive as a mode of executing royal criminals, iii. 243 ; human victims to prolong king's life, vi. 226 ; human victims of Fire-god, ix. 301 ; animals to stay cattle-plague, x. 300 *sqq.*

—— effigies of the Carnival, iv. 223, 224, 228 *sq.*, 229 *sq.*, 232 *sq.* ; of Shrove Tuesday, iv. 227 *sqq.* ; of Winter at Zurich, iv. 260 *sq.*; in the Midsummer fires, x. 195

—— the Easter Man, x. 144

" —— the Old Wife (Old Woman)," x. 116, 120

Burning the Old Witch, vii. 224

"—— the Old Year," at Biggar, ix. 165 ; among the Biyars of North-Western India, ix. 230 n.[7]

—— the Witches (invisible or represented by effigies) on May Day in the Isle of Man, ii. 54, x. 157, in the Tyrol, ix. 158 sq. ; on Walpurgis Night in Bohemia, ix. 161, x. 159, in Silesia and Saxony, ix. 161, x. 160; on Twelfth Night in Herefordshire, ix. 319; on the first Sunday in Lent in Luxemburg, the Tyrol, and Swabia, x. 116, in Switzerland, x. 118 sq. ; on Beltane (May Day) in Scotland, x. 154; at Hallowe'en in Scotland, x. 232 sq. ; "Burning the Witches" name for fires of European festivals, xi. 43

—— witches (in flesh and blood) among the Baganda, ix. 19 ; at Leith, ix. 165; in Germany, x. 6 ; after shaving them, xi. 158

Burning discs thrown into the air, x. 116 sq., 119, 143, 165, 166, 168 sq., 172

—— -glass or mirror, fire kindled by, ii. 207 n.[1], 243, 244 n.[1]

—— wheels rolled down hill, x. 116, 117 sq., 119, 141, 143, 161, 162 sq., 163 sq., 166, 173, 174, 201, 328, 334, 337 sq. ; rolled over fields at Midsummer to fertilize them, x. 191, 340, sq. ; perhaps to burn witches, x. 345

Burnings for dead kings of Judah, v. 177 sq. ; for dead Jewish Rabbis at Meiron, v. 178

Burns, Robert, on John Barleycorn, v. 230 sq. ; "bonny woods and braes" of Loudon, x. 207 ; on Hallowe'en, x. 234

Burnt alive, apotheosis by being, v. 179 sq.

—— Land of Lydia, v. 193 sq.

—— sacrifices to stay cattle-plague in England, Wales, and Scotland, x. 300 sqq.

Burrha, river, Hera's bath in the, v. 280

Burs, homoeopathic magic of, i. 144 ; a preservative against witchcraft, x. 177

Buru, East Indian island, sacrifice of girl to crocodile in, ii. 152 ; oil made by unmarried girls in, iii. 201 ; natives of, forbidden to utter their own names, iii. 324 ; names of relations tabooed among the Alfoors of, iii. 341 ; unlawful to use words resembling the names of the dead in, iii. 361 ; use of oil as a charm in, v. 21 n.[2] ; the natives of, ascribe a soul to rice, vii. 183 ; "eating the soul of the rice" in, viii. 54 ; dog's flesh eaten to make eater brave in, viii. 145 ; demons of sickness expelled in a proa from, ix. 186

Buryat shaman, his mode of recovering lost souls, iii. 56 sq.

Buryats of Siberia place the bones of dead shamans in trees, ii. 32

"Burying the Carnival," iv. 209, 220 sqq.

—— bewitched animals alive, x. 324 sqq.

—— the evil spirit, ix. 110

—— girls at puberty in the ground, x. 38 sqq.

"—— the sheaf" in Ireland, i. 69

Bush negroes of Surinam set up two-headed idols at entrance of villages, ii. 385 ; their belief that leprosy is caused by eating a certain animal, viii. 26

Bushes, ailments transferred to, ix. 54, 56

Bushmen, magical telepathy among the, i. 123 ; of the Kalahari desert, their fire sticks, ii. 218 n.[1] ; custom as to their shadows, iii. 83 ; think it unlucky to speak of the lion by his proper name, iii. 400 ; their rules of diet based on sympathetic magic, viii. 140 sq. ; will not let their children eat a jackal's heart, viii. 141 ; unable to distinguish between animals and men, viii. 206 ; will not eat the sinew in the thigh of a hare, viii. 266 n.[1] ; throw stones on the devil's grave, ix. 16 ; their prayers at a cairn, ix. 30 ; their dread of menstruous women, x. 79 ; their way of warming up the star Sirius, x. 332 sq.

Bushongo, royal persons among the, not allowed to set foot on the ground, x. 4 ; their use of bull-roarers, xi. 229 ; their rites of initiation, xi. 264 sqq.

Busiris, an Egyptian city, "the house of Osiris," iii. 390, vii. 260 ; backbone of Osiris at, vi. 11, 18 ; ritual of Osiris at, vi. 86, 87 sq. ; festival of Osiris in the month of Khoiak at, vi. 108 ; temple of Usirniri at, vi. 151

——, king of Egypt, his human sacrifices, vii. 259 ; slain by Hercules, vii. 259

Busiro, district containing the graves and temples of the kings of Uganda, vi. 168, 169, 224

Busk, festival of first-fruits among the Creek Indians, viii. 72

Busoga, pretended human sacrifice in, iv. 215

Bust, double-headed, at Nemi, i. 41 sq.

Bustard totem of the Ingarda, v. 104

Butea frondosa worshipped, viii. 119 ; its flowers offered, ix. 136

Butlers, Roman, required to be chaste, ii. 115 sq., 205

Buto, city in Egypt, Horus and Isis at, vi. 10

Butter, time for making, i. 167; stolen by witches on May Day, ii. 53 ; stolen by witches on Walpurgis Night and Midsummer Eve, ii. 127 ; thought to

be improved by the Midsummer fires, x. 180 ; bewitched, burnt at a crossroad, x. 322
"Butter-churning," Swiss expression for kindling a need-fire, x. 279
Butterflies, souls of dead in, vi. 164, viii. 290, 291, 296 *sq.* ; annual expulsion of, ix. 159 *n.*[1]
Butterfly, the soul as a, iii. 29 *n.*[1], 41, 51 *sq.*
—— of the rice, vii. 190
Butterfly dance in Brazil, ix. 381
—— god in Samoa, viii. 29
Buttmann, Ph., on Virbius and the King of the Wood, i. 40 *n.*[2] ; on Janus as the god of doors, ii. 383 *n.*[3] ; on the derivation of *janua* from *Janus*, ii. 384 *n.*[2]
Büttner, C. G., on the firesticks of the Herero, ii. 218
Button-snake root used as a purgative, viii. 73, 75
Buzzard, the bald-headed, in homoeopathic magic, i. 155 ; killing the sacred, viii. 169 *sqq.*
Byblus, hair offerings to Astarte at, i. 30 ; Adonis at, v. 13 *sqq.* ; the kings of, v. 14 *sqq.* ; mourning for Adonis at, v. 38 ; religious prostitution at, v. 58 ; inspired prophets at, v. 75 *sq.* ; festival of Adonis at, v. 225 ; Osiris and Isis at, vi. 9 ; the queen of, vi. 9 ; Osiris associated with, vi. 22 *sq.*, 127 ; its relation to Egypt, vi. 127 *n.*[1]
Byrne, H. J., on Twelfth Night in Roscommon, ix. 321 *sq.*
Byron, Lord, and the oak, xi. 166
Byrsa, origin of the name, vi. 250

Cabag Head, witches at, i. 135
Cabbages, charm to make cabbages grow, i. 136 *sq.* ; divination by, at Hallowe'en, i. 242 ; threatened by Esthonian peasants to make them grow, ii. 22. *See also* Kail
Cabugatan, in the Philippine Islands, the Igorrots of, viii. 292
Cabunian, Mount, grave of the Creator on, iv. 3
Cachar, the Kookies of, i. 160 *n.*[3]
Cacongo, in West Africa, rules observed by the king of, iii. 115, 118
Cactus, taboos observed by the Huichol Indians during their search for the sacred, i. 123 *sq.* ; hung at door of house where there is a lying-in woman, iii. 155
Cadiz, death at low tide at, i. 167 ; custom of swinging at, iv. 284
Cadmea, the, at Thebes, named after Cadmus, iv. 79
Cadmus, servitude of, for the slaughter of the dragon, iv. 70 *n.*[1], 78 ; the slayer of the dragon at Thebes, iv. 78 *sq.* ; seeks Europa and founds Thebes, iv. 88 ; at Samothrace, iv. 89 *n.*[4] ; turned into a snake, v. 86 *sq.* ; perhaps personated by the Laurelbearer at Thebes, vi. 241
Cadmus and Harmonia, their transformation into serpents, iv. 84 ; marriage of, iv. 88, 89
——, Mount, v. 207
Cadys, king of Lydia, ii. 281 ; his son Sadyattes; v. 183
Caeculus born from the fire, ii. 197 ; son of the fire-god Vulcan, vi. 235
Caeles Vibenna, an Etruscan, ii. 196 *n.*
Caelian hill at Rome, ii. 185, 190
Caesar, Julius, robs Capitoline Jupiter, i. 4 ; his villa at Nemi, i. 5 ; his beneficent rule, i. 5 ; on the Hercynian forest, ii. 7 ; as to German observation of the moon, vi. 141 ; his regulation of the calendar, vi. 37, vii. 83 *sq.*, ix. 345 ; on the fortification walls of the Gauls, x. 267 ; on human sacrifices among the Celts of Gaul, xi. 32
Caesar, Lucius, his villa at Nemi, i. 5
Caesarea. *See* Everek
Caesars, their name derived from *caesaries*, ii. 180
Caffre boys at circumcision, customs observed by, iii. 156 *sq.*
—— girls, their remedy for a plague of caterpillars, viii. 280
—— hunters, their ceremonies after killing a lion, iii. 220 ; their propitiation of the elephants which they kill, viii. 227
—— kings turn at death into boa-constrictors, iv. 84
—— villages, women's tracks at, x. 80
Caffres, their rule as to eating mice, i. 118 ; corpulence a mark of rank among the, ii. 297 ; race for a bride among the, ii. 303 ; their superstitions as to their shadows, iii. 78 *sq.*, 83, 87 ; think that the shadows of trees are sensitive, iii. 82 ; expiation performed by man who had killed a boa-constrictor among the, iii. 221 *sq.* ; their horror of the pollution of blood, iii. 245 *sq.* ; their custom as to the blood of sacrifice, iii. 247 ; their disposal of their cut hair and nails, iii. 278 ; their use of knots as a charm on a journey, iii. 306 ; their custom of boiling a thief's name, iii. 331 ; call brides after their future children, iii. 333 ; "women's speech" among the, iii. 335 *sq.* ; their purificatory ceremonies after a battle, vi. 251 *sq.* ; their festival of new fruits, viii. 64

sqq. ; inoculation with powdered charcoal among the, viii. 159 *sq.* ; their custom of fumigating infants, viii. 166 *sq.* ; will not eat the sinew of the thigh, viii. 266 *n.*[1] ; their custom of adding stones to heaps, ix. 11 ; their prayers at cairns, ix. 30

Caffres of Natal, their rain-charm by means of a black sheep, i. 290 ; their festival of first-fruits, viii. 64 *sqq.*

—— of Sofala, their dread of hollow things, i. 157 *sq.*

—— of South Africa, ix. 11, 30 ; their way of stopping a high wind, i. 321 *sq.* ; their superstition as to shadows, iii. 87 ; purified after battle, iii. 172, 174 *sq.* ; their belief and custom as to falling stars, iv. 65 ; date their new year by observation of the Pleiades, vii. 116, 315 *sq.* ; woman's share in agriculture among the, vii. 116 ; transfer sickness from men to goats, ix. 31 ; seclusion of girls at puberty among the, x. 30 ; use of bull-roarers among the, xi. 229 *n.*, 232

—— of the Zambesi region believe that human souls transmigrate after death into animals, viii. 288 *sq.*

Cages, girls at puberty confined in, x. 32 *sqq.*, 44, 45

Caidu, a Tartar king, ii. 306

Caiem, the caliph, iv. 8

Cailleach (Old Wife), name given to last corn cut, vii. 140 *sqq.*, 164 *sqq.*

—— *beal-tine*, the Beltane carline, x. 148

Caingua Indians of Paraguay, their fire customs, ii. 258 *sq.* ; their belief in the transmigration of human souls into animals, viii. 285 *sq.*

Cairns, cut hair buried in, iii. 274 *sq.* ; to which every passer-by adds a stone, ix. 9 *sqq.* ; near shrines of saints, ix. 21 ; offerings at, ix. 26 *sqq.* See also Heaps

Cairnshee, in Kincardineshire, Midsummer fires on, x. 206

Cairo, ceremony of cutting the dams at, vi. 38, 39 *sq.* ; the old south gate of, ix. 63 ; cure for toothache and headache at, ix. 63

Caithness, the cutter of the last sheaf called Winter in, vii. 142 ; need-fire in, x. 290 *sqq.*

Cajaboneros Indians of Central America, their period of abstinence before sowing, ii. 105

Cajanus Indicus, pulse, cultivated by the Korwas, vii. 123

Cake called the Christmas Boar, vii. 302 *sq.* ; with coin in it at Carnival, omens drawn from, viii. 332 ; on

Twelfth Night used to determine the King, ix. 313 *sqq.* ; put on horn of ox, ix. 318 *sq.* ; St. Michael's, x. 149, 154 *n.*[3]; salt, divination by, x. 238 *sq.* ; the Yule or Christmas, x. 257, 259, 261

Cakes rolled as a mode of divination on St. George's Day, ii. 338 ; in obscene shapes, vii. 62 ; in human form, vii. 149 ; special, baked at threshing, vii. 150 ; of dough at the Thesmophoria, viii. 17 *sq.* ; as substitutes for animal victims, viii. 25 ; in the form of animals, viii. 95 *n.*[2]; sacrificial, baked of new barley or rice, viii. 120 ; made at Christmas out of last sheaf in form of goats, rams, or boars, viii. 328 ; special, at New Year, ix. 149 *sq.* ; with twelve knobs offered to Cronus and other deities, ix. 351, 351 *n.*[3]; Hallowe'en, x. 238, 241, 245 ; Beltane, x. 148 *sq.*, 150, 152, 153, 154, 155 ; divination by, x. 242, 243

Calabar, fetish king at, iii. 22 *sq.* ; soul of chief in sacred grove at, xi. 161 ; negroes of, their belief in external or bush souls lodged in animals, xi. 204 *sqq.*, 220, 222 *n.*[5]; the fattening-house for girls in, xi. 259

—— district, heads of chiefs buried secretly in the, vi. 104

——, Old, sacred grove of, ii. 42 ; annual expulsion of demons at, viii. 108 ; biennial expulsion of demons at, ix. 203 *sq.*

—— River, iv. 197, ix. 28

Calabash, ceremony of breaking the, at festival of new fruits, viii. 68 *n.*[3]

Calabashes, souls shut up in, iii. 72

Calabria, ceremony of " Sawing the Old Woman " in, iv. 241 ; custom of swinging in, iv. 284 ; Easter custom in, v. 254 ; murderers taste the blood of their victims in, viii. 156 ; annual expulsion of witches in, ix. 157 ; holy water at Easter in, x. 123

Calah, ancient capital of Assyria, annual marriage of the god Nabu at, ii. 130

Calamities, almost all, set down to witchcraft, xi. 19 *sq.*

Caland, Dr. W., on the magical nature of Vedic ritual, i. 229

Calauria, Poseidon worshipped in, v. 203 *n.*[2]

Calbe, in the Altmark, the He-goat at harvest near, vii. 287

Calchaquis Indians of Paraguay, their way of keeping off death, iii. 31

Calcutta, keys as amulets in, iii. 236

Caldwell, Bishop R., on devil-dancers in Southern India, i. 382

Calenberg, holy oak near, ii. 371

Calendar, regulation of the early, an

affair of religion, iv. 69, vii. 83 ; the natural, vi. 25 ; change in Chinese, x. 137 ; the reform of the, in relation to floral superstitions, xi. 55 *n.*[1]

Calendar, the Alexandrian, used by Plutarch, vi. 84 ; used by Theophanes, ix. 395 *n.*[1]
—— of the primitive Aryans, ix. 325
——, the Babylonian, ix. 398 *n.*[2]
—— of the Celts of Gaul, ix. 342 *sq.*
——, the Coligny, i. 17 *n.*[2], ix. 342 *sqq.*
——, the Coptic, vi. 6 *n.*[3]
——, the Egyptian, vi. 24 *sqq.* ; date of its introduction, vi. 36 *n.*[2]
—— of the Egyptian farmer, vi. 30 *sqq.*
—— of Esne, vi. 49 *sq.*
——, the ancient Greek, determined by astronomical considerations, iv. 68 *sq.* ; regulated by the moon and of little use to the husbandman, vii. 52 *sq.*, 80
—— of the Indians of San Juan Capistrano in California, vii. 125 *sq.*
——, the Julian, vi. 93 *n.*[1] ; used by Mohammedans, x. 218 *sq.*
—— of the Maya Indians of Yucatan, vi. 29 *n.*, ix. 171
—— of the ancient Mexicans, its mode of intercalation, vi. 28 *n.*[3]
——, the Mohammedan, x. 216 *sq.*, 218 *sq.*
—— of Philocalus, v. 303 *n.*[2], 304 *n.*[3], vi. 95 *n.*[1]
——, the Roman, vii. 83 *sq.*
——, the Syro-Macedonian, iv. 116

Calendars, the Roman Rustic, vi. 95 *n.*[1] ; the Pleiades in primitive, vii. 307 *sqq.* ; conflict of, x. 218

Calendeau, calignau, the Yule-log at Marseilles, x. 250

Calf shod in buskins sacrificed to Dionysus, vii. 33 ; the genitals of, served up to man who gave last stroke at threshing, vii. 148 ; killed at harvest, vii. 290 ; mythical, in the corn, vii. 292 ; name applied to bunch of corn on harvest-field, vii. 292 ; sacrifice of buffalo, viii. 314 ; burnt alive to stop a murrain, x. 300 *sq.* *See also* Calves

Calica Puran, an Indian law-book, i. 63, iv. 217

Calicut, rule of succession observed by the kings of, iv. 47 *sqq.*, 206 ; ceremonies at sowing in, ix. 235

California, the Digger Indians of, viii. 164
——, the Karok Indians of, vi. 47, viii. 255
——, the Maidu Indians of, i. 122, 357, xi. 295, 298
——, the Nishinam tribe of, iii. 338

California, the Pomos of, ix. 170 *sq.*
——, the Senal Indians of, xi. 295
——, the Yuki Indians of, i. 133

Californian Indians, their notion as to whirlwinds, i. 331 ; secrecy of personal names among the, iii. 326 ; names of the dead not mentioned among the, iii. 352 ; their custom as to meteors, iv. 62 ; eat pine nuts, v. 278 *n.*[2] ; their annual festivals of the dead, vi. 52 *sq.* ; their notion that the owl is the guardian of the " California big tree," vi. 111 *n.*[1] ; women's work among the Indians of San Juan Capistrano, vii. 125 ; their calendar, vii. 125 *sq.* ; their custom of killing the sacred buzzard, viii. 169 *sqq.* ; their belief in the transmigration of human souls into animals, viii. 286 *sq.* ; seclusion of girls at puberty among the, x. 41 *sqq.* ; ordeals among the, x. 64
—— missions, the Spanish, viii. 171 *n.*[1]

Caligula, his barges on the lake of Nemi, i. 5 ; and the priest of Nemi, i. 11 ; and King Agrippa, ix. 418

Callander, the parish of, Beltane fires in, x. 150 *sqq.* ; Hallowe'en fires in, x. 231

Callaway, Rev. Henry, on chiefs as medicine-men, i. 350 *n.*[2] ; on the worship of the dead among the Zulus, vi. 184 *sq.* ; on the observation of the Pleiades by the Amazulu, vii. 316

Callias, the Eleusinian Torch-bearer, vii. 54, 73 *n.*[3]

Callirrhoe, the springs of, in Moab, v. 214 *sqq.*

Callo, a holy spirit among the Gallas, i. 396

Calmucks, race for bride among the, ii. 301 *sq.* ; divine by shoulder-blades of sheep, iii. 229 *n.*[4] *See also* Kalmucks

Calotropis gigantea, man married to, in Southern India, ii. 57 *n.*[4]
—— *procera,* used in kindling fire by friction, ii. 209

Calpurnius Piso, L., on the wife of Vulcan, vi. 232 *sq.*

Caltanisetta, in Sicily, violence done to St. Michael at, i. 300

Calves, unborn, sacrifice of, viii. 42 ; burnt to stop disease in the herds, x. 301, 306. *See also* Calf

Calycadnus River, in Cilicia, v. 167 *n.*[2]

Calymnos, a Greek island, superstition as to menstruous women in, x. 96 *sq.* ; Midsummer fires in, x. 212

Camasene and Janus, vi. 235 *n.*[6]

Cambaita, custom of religious suicide at, iv. 54

Cambodia, mode of annulling evil omens in, i. 170 *sqq.* ; custom as to effacing impressions of pots in ashes in, i. 214 ;

the Chams of, i. 280 ; the regalia regarded as a palladium in, i. 365 ; human incarnations of gods in, i. 385 *sq.* ; special terms used with reference to persons of the blood royal in, i. 401 *n.*[3] ; Kings of Fire and Water in, ii. 3 *sqq.*, iii. 17, iv. 14 ; the King of, sends presents to the Kings of Fire and Water, ii. 5 ; sacred trees in, ii. 46 ; use of fire kindled by lightning in, ii. 256 *n.*[1] ; kings of, not to be touched, iii. 226 ; the king of, ceremony at cutting his hair, iii. 265 ; kings of, their names not to be mentioned, iii. 376 ; annual temporary king in, iv. 148 *sq.* ; annual festival of the dead in, vi. 61 *sq.* ; the Banars of, viii. 33 ; vicarious use of effigies to save sick people in, viii. 103 ; the Stiens of, viii. 237 ; annual expulsion of demons in, ix. 149 ; palace of the kings of, annually purged of devils, ix. 172 ; seclusion of girls at puberty in, x. 70 ; ritual at cutting a parasitic orchid in, xi. 81

Cambodian hunter, homoeopathic magic used by, i. 109 *sq.*

—— or Siamese story of the external soul, xi. 102

Cambodians, their superstitions as to the head, iii. 254

Cambridge, the May Lady at, ii. 62 ; Jack-in-the-Green at, ii. 83 *n.*[1] ; personal relics of Kibuka, the war-god of the Baganda, preserved at, vi. 197 ; ancient customs in, vii. 146 ; Plough Monday in, viii. 330 *n.*[1] ; Lord of Misrule at, ix. 330

Cambridgeshire, greasing the weapon instead of the wound in, i. 203 ; permanent May-pole in, ii. 71 *n.*[1] ; the Straw-bear in, viii. 329 ; Plough Monday in, viii. 330 *n.*[1] ; witch as cat in, x. 317

Cambulac (Peking), Marco Polo as to, iii. 243 *sq.*

Cambus o' May, near Ballater, holed stone at, xi. 187

Cambyses, king of Persia, his treatment of Amasis, v. 176 *n.*[2]

Camden, W., on Irish precautions against witches on May Day, ii. 53 ; on custom observed by the Irish when they fall, iii. 68

Camel, plague transferred to, ix. 33

Camel-races in honour of the dead, iv. 97

Camels not called by their proper name, iii. 402 ; infested by jinn, ix. 260

Cameron, Hugh E., on the harvest Maiden in Inverness-shire, vii. 162 *n.*[3]

Cameron, V. L., on divinity claimed by an African chief, i. 395

Cameroon negroes, expiation for homicide among the, v. 299 *n.*[2]

Cameroons, chiefs as fetish-men in the, i. 349 ; the Ngumbu of the, ii. 210 ; the Duala tribe of the, iv. 130 *n.*[1] ; the Bakundu of the, viii. 99 ; expulsion of the spirits of disease in the, ix. 120 *sq.* ; life of person bound up with tree in the, xi. 161 ; theory of the external soul in the, xi. 200, 202 *sq.*

Camillus, his triumph, ii. 174 *n.*[2]

Camomile (*Anthemis nobilis*) burnt in Midsummer fire, x. 213 ; sacred to Balder, xi. 63 ; gathered at Midsummer, xi. 63

Camp shifted after a death, iii. 353

Campbell, Rev. John, on Bechuana superstition as to trees and rain, ii. 49 ; on refusal of Bechuanas to tell stories before sunset, iii. 384 ; on Coranna treatment of the sick, xi. 192, 192 *n.*[1]

Campbell, Major-General John, on Khond human sacrifices, vii. 248, 250

Campbell, Rev. J. G., on the Harvest Old Wife in the Highlands of Scotland, vii. 140, 165 *sq.* ; on *deiseal*, x. 151 *n.*

Campe, near Stade, the Fox in the corn at, vii. 296

Camphor, taboos observed in search for, i. 114 *sq.* ; telepathy in search for, i. 124 *sq.* ; special language employed by searchers for, iii. 405 *sqq.* ; custom observed in the search for, viii. 186 *n.*

Camphor-trees, ceremonies at cutting down, iii. 406

Campo di Giove, in the Abruzzi, Easter candles at, x. 122

—— Santo at Pisa, contest between angels and devils in the, ix. 175

Camul, custom as to hospitality in, v. 39 *n.*[3]

Canaanite kings of Jerusalem, v. 17

Canaanites, their custom of burning their children in honour of Baal, iv. 168

Canada, Indians of, their belief that winds are caused by a fish, i. 320 ; capture of souls by wizards among the, iii. 73 ; kept their names secret, iii. 326 ; their ceremony for mitigating the cold of winter, iv. 259 *sq.* ; kept the bones of beavers from dogs, viii. 239 *sq.* ; would not eat the embryos of elks from fear of offending the mother-elks, viii. 243

Cañar (Cuenca), in Ecuador, human sacrifices at harvest in, vii. 236

Canarese of South India, their euphemisms for a tiger, iii. 402

Canarium nuts, first-fruits of, offered to ghosts in Solomon Islands, viii. 126

Canary Islands, rain-making in the, by beating the sea, i. 301

Canathus, Hera's annual bath in the spring of, v. 280

Cancer, Tropic of, vii. 125

Candaules, king of Lydia, murdered by Gyges, ii. 281 ; descended from Hercules, ii. 282 ; and the double-headed axe, v. 182, 183

Candle sent by Fire King to the King of Cambodia, ii. 5 *sq.* ; virginity tested by flame of, ii. 240, x. 139 *n.* ; the Easter or Paschal, x. 121, 122, 125 ; divination by the flame of a, at Hallowe'en, x. 229 ; the Yule or Christmas, x. 255, 256, 260 ; external soul in a, xi. 125 *sq.* See also Candles

—— and apple, biting at, a Hallowe'en sport, x. 241, 242, 243, 245

Candlemas (February 2nd), dances at, to make flax grow tall, i. 138 ; Bridget's bed on the night before, ii. 94, 242 ; pea-soup and pigs' bones eaten at, vii. 300; dances for the crops at, ix. 238 ; Lord of Misrule at, ix. 332, 333 ; in the Armenian church, bonfires at, x. 131 ; the Yule log at, x. 256 *n.*

—— candles, x. 264 *n.*[4]

Candles, Catholic practice of dedicating, i. 13 ; magical, used by burglars to cause sleep, i. 148, 149 ; made of human tallow and used by thieves, i. 236 ; lighted, tied to sacred oak, ii. 372 ; twelve, on Twelfth Night, ix. 321 *sq.*; burnt at the Feast of Purim, ix. 394 ; used to keep off witches, x. 245

Candy, sugar, in homoeopathic magic, i. 157

Canelos Indians of Ecuador, afraid of being photographed, iii. 97 ; their belief in the transmigration of human souls into jaguars, viii. 285

Canicular year, a Sothic period, vi. 36 *n.*[2]

Cannibal banquets of the ancient Mexicans, viii. 92, ix. 279 *n.*[1], 283, 298

—— feast, legendary, at the Boeotian Orchomenus, iv. 164

—— orgies among the Indians of North-West America, vii. 18 *sqq.*

—— societies in ancient Greece and Africa, iv. 83 ; among the Indians of North-West America, vii. 20 *sq.*

—— Spirit among the Haida Indians, vii. 21

Cannibalism, in Australia, perhaps intended to ensure the reincarnation of the dead, i. 106 *sq.* ; at hair-cutting in Fiji, iii. 264 ; in certain cases perhaps intended to form a blood-covenant with the dead, viii. 156

Cannibals, taboos imposed on, among the Kwakiutl Indians, iii. 188 *sqq.* ; a secret society of the Kwakiutl Indians, vii. 20

Cannons, toy, as regalia, i. 364

Canoe, fish offered to, iii. 195

Canoes, continence observed at building, iii. 202

Canopus, town in Egypt, the decree of, vi. 27, 34 *n.*[1], 37 *n.*, 88 *n.*[2]

Canopus, star, observed by the aborigines of Victoria, vii. 308

—— in Bushman lore, x. 333

Cantabrian coast of Spain, belief as to death at ebb-tide on the, i. 167

Cantabrians, mother-kin among the, ii. 285

Canton, the province of, the Hak-Ka in, ix. 144

——, violence done to the rain-god at, in time of drought or excessive rain, i. 299

Canute, King of England, his marriage with Emma, ii. 282 *sq.*

Capaneus and Evadne, v. 177 *n.*[3]

Capart, Jean, on palettes found in Egyptian tombs, xi. 155 *n.*[3]

Cape Bedford in Queensland, belief of the natives as to the birth of children, v. 102

—— Coast Castle, on the Gold Coast, annual expulsion of demons at, ix. 132 *sq.*

—— Padron, in Guinea, priestly king near, iii. 5

—— Vancouver, iii. 228, viii. 249 *n.*[1]

—— York Peninsula in Queensland, extraction of teeth among the natives of, i. 99, 100 ; the Gudangs of, iii. 346, 359 ; seclusion of girls at puberty among the natives of, x. 37, 38

Capena, the Porta, at Rome, i. 18

Caper-spurge (*Euphorbia lathyris*) burned on May Day as a protection against witches, ix. 158 *sq.* ; identified with mythical springwort, xi. 69

Capillary attraction in magic, i. 83

Capital of column, external soul in, xi. 156 *sq.*

Capital punishment among some peoples originally a sacrifice, v. 290 *n.*[2]

Capitol at Rome, temple of Jupiter on the, ii. 174, 176, 184 ; image of Jupiter on the, ii. 175 ; built by Romulus, ii. 176 ; Jupiter worshipped on the, ii. 361 ; ceremonies at the rebuilding of the, vi. 244 ; the oak of Jupiter on the, xi. 89

—— at Cirta, image of Jupiter on the, ii. 177

Capitoline hill, Jupiter on the, ii. 184 ; hut of Romulus on the, ii. 200

Cappadocia, volcanic region of, v. 189 *sqq.* ; fire-worship in, v. 191 *sq.* ; the fire-walk at Castabala in, xi. 14

Capri, feast of the Nativity of the Virgin in, x. 220 *sq.*

Capricorn, Tropic of, vii. 125 ; time when the sun enters the, xi. 1

Caprificatio, ii. 314 n.[2]

Caprification, the artificial fertilization of fig-trees, ix. 257. See Fig-tree

Caprificus, the wild fig-tree, ii. 314 sq., ix. 258

Caps of clay worn by Australian widows in mourning, iii. 182 n.[2] ; worn by Aino mourners, x. 20

Captives killed and eaten, iii. 179 sq. ; unbound in house of Flamen Dialis, iii. 316

Car Nicobar, charm to make sunshine in, i. 314 ; exorcism in, v. 299 n.[2] ; annual expulsion of devils in, ix. 201 sq.

Carabas and Barabbas, ix. 418 sq.

Caramantran, death of, on Ash Wednesday in Provence, iv. 226

Carayahis, tribe of Brazilian Indians, dialectical differences in the speech of men and women among the, iii. 348 sq.

Carberry Kinncat, king of Ireland, misfortunes of his reign, i. 367 sq.

Carcassone, hunting the wren at, viii. 320 sq.

Carceri, Father S., on the sacred king of the Nubas, iii. 132 n.[1]

Carchemish, Hittite capital on Euphrates, v. 123, 137 n.[2], 138 n.

Carchi, a province of Ecuador, All Souls' Day in, vi. 80

Cardiganshire, Hallowe'en in, x. 226

Carew, R., on a Cornish custom, iv. 154 n.[1]

Caria, Zeus Labrandeus in, v. 182 ; poisonous vapours in, v. 205 sq.

Carian Chersonese, viii. 85

Carians, their mournings for Osiris, vi. 86 n.[1]

Caribou, taboos concerning, iii. 208

Caribs, war custom of the, i. 134 ; difference of language between men and women among the, iii. 348 ; their worship of the moon in preference to the sun, vi. 138 ; woman's share in agriculture among the, vii. 120 ; their belief in the homoeopathic magic of animal flesh, viii. 139 sq. ; young warriors among the, ate the heart of a bird of prey to acquire courage, viii. 162 ; their theory of the plurality of souls, xi. 221

Carinthia, Green George in, ii. 75, 343 ; bride-race in, ii. 304 ; ceremony at the installation of a prince of, iv. 154 sq. ; harvest custom in, vii. 224 sq. ; new fire at Easter in, x. 124

Caripunas Indians of Brazil, use of bull-roarers among the, xi. 230 n.

Carley, the last bunch of corn at harvest in Antrim, vii. 144

Carlin or Carline, "the Old Woman," female figure formed out of the last corn cut at harvest, vii. 140

Carlyle, Thomas, on the execution of the astronomer Bailly, v. 229 n.[1]

Carman (Wexford), the fair of, iv. 100, 101

Carmichael, Alexander, on need-fire, x. 293 sqq. ; on snake-stones, xi. 311

Carmona, in Andalusia, annual ceremony observed by disguised boys at, ix. 173

Carn Brea, in Cornwall, Midsummer fires on, x. 199

Carna, nymph, won by Janus, ii. 190, vi. 235 n.[6]

Carnac, in Egypt, temples at, vi. 124 ; sculptures at, vi. 154. See also Karnak

Carnarvonshire, the cutty black sow at Hallowe'en in, x. 240

Carniola, "Sawing the Old Woman" at Mid-Lent in, iv. 242

Carnival, dances at the, to make hemp grow tall, i. 137 ; a sort of, at Fazoql on the Blue Nile, iv. 17 ; burying the, iv. 209, 220 sqq. ; the burial and resurrection of the, an expression of the death and revival of vegetation, iv. 252 ; swings taken down at, iv. 287 ; at Rome in the rites of Attis, v. 273 ; modern Thracian drama at the, vi. 99 sq., vii. 26 sqq., viii. 331 sqq. ; similar masquerade in Bulgaria at, viii. 333 sq. ; bell-ringing processions at the, ix. 247 ; Senseless Thursday in, ix. 248 ; in relation to the Saturnalia, ix. 312, 345 sqq. ; effigy burnt at end of, x. 120 ; wicker giants at the, xi. 35

—— and Purim, ix. 394

—— or Shrovetide Bear in Bohemia, viii. 325 sq.

"—— (Shrovetide) Fool," iv. 231

Carnmoor, in Mull, need-fire kindled on, x. 289 sq.

Carnwath, in Cornwall, Midsummer fires at, x. 199

Carolina, Indians of, king's son wounded among the, x. 184 sq. ; their fear of harming snakes, viii. 217

Caroline Islands, treatment of the navel-string in the, i. 184 sq.; Ponape in the, i. 401 n.[3], iii. 25, 259, 362 ; Uap (Yap) in the, iii. 193, 227, 282, 290, 293, vi. 265, x. 36 ; taboos on fishermen in the, iii. 193 ; wizards in the, iii. 290 ; traditional origin of fire in the, xi. 295

Caron's Account of Japan, iii. 4 n.[2]

Carp clan of the Otawa Indians, viii. 225 n.[1]

Carpathian Mountains, the Huzuls of the, i. 113, 137, 280, iii. 270, 314, 396, 397, viii. 43 n.[1], 275, ix. 32 sq., xi. 49 ;

Midsummer fires in the, x. 175 ; need-fire in the, x. 281

Carpathus, fear of having one's likeness taken in, iii. 100 ; laying out of corpses in, iii. 313 *sq.* See also Karpathos

Carpenter, son of, as a human god, i. 376

Carpentras in Provence, rain-making at, i. 307

Carpet-snakes, magical ceremony for the multiplication of, i. 90

Carpini, de Plano, on funeral customs of the Mongols, v. 293

Carrier Indians of North - Western America, their magic to snare martens, i. 110 ; their contagious magic of footprints, i. 210 ; their chastity before hunting, iii. 197 ; confession of sins among the, iii. 215 ; their belief in the reincarnation of the dead, iii. 367 *sq.* ; succession to the soul among the, iv. 199 ; their regard for the bones of martens and beavers, viii. 238 *sq.* ; funeral custom of the, x. 11 ; their dread and seclusion of menstruous women, x. 91 *sqq.* ; their honorific totems, xi. 273 *sqq.*

"Carrying out Death," iv. 221, 233 *sqq.*, 246 *sqq.*, ix. 227 *sq.*, 230, 252

Carthage, Christians worshipping each other at, i. 407 ; legend and worship of Dido at, v. 113 *sq.* ; Hamilcar worshipped at, v. 116 ; the *suffetes* of, v. 116 *n.*[1] ; rites of Cybele at, v. 274 *n.* ; the effeminate priests of the Great Mother at, v. 298 ; legend as to the foundation of, vi. 250

Carthaginian sacrifice of children to Moloch, iv. 75 ; to Baal, iv. 167 *sq.*

Carver, Captain Jonathan, on the rite of death and resurrection among the Naudowessies, xi. 267 *sq.*

Casablanca in Morocco, ix. 21 ; Midsummer fires at, x. 214

Casalis, E., on purification of Basuto warriors, iii. 172 ; on Zulu serpent-worship, v. 84 ; on the worship of the dead among the Basutos, vi. 179 *sq.*

Cashmeer, the Takhas of, i. 383 ; bulls as scapegoats in, ix. 190 *n.*[5]

Cashmeer stories of the external soul, ix. 100 *sq.*, 138 *n.*[1]

Caspar, Melchior, and Balthasar, the Three Kings of Twelfth Day, ix. 329 *sqq.*, xi. 68

Cassange Valley in Angola, the Bangalas of the, ii. 293 ; human sacrifice at installation of king of, iv. 56 *sq.* ; kings of, their teeth preserved after death, iv. 203

Cassava or manioc cultivated by South American Indians, vii. 120 *sq.*, 122

Cassel, in France, wicker giants on Shrove Tuesday at, xi. 35

Cassotis, oracular spring at Delphi, iv. 79

Cassowaries, souls of dead in, viii. 295 ; imitated by masked dancers, ix. 382 ; men disguised as, in Dukduk ceremonies, xi. 247

Cassowary totem in Mabuiag, viii. 207

Castabala in Cappadocia, the fire-walk at, v. 115, 168, xi. 14

—— in Cilicia, worship of Perasian Artemis at, v. 167 *sqq.*

Castabus, in the Carian Chersonese, sanctuary of Hemithea at, viii. 24 *n.*[5], 85

Castaly, the oracular spring of, at Delphi, iv. 79

Castel Gandolfo, on the Alban Lake, i. 2

Castellamare, seven-legged effigy of Lent at, iv. 245

Castelnau, F. de, on the reverence of the Apinagos for the moon, vi. 146 *sq.*

Castiglione a Casauria, in the Abruzzi, Midsummer customs at, v. 246, x. 210

Castilian peasants, their dances in May, ix. 280

Casting the skin supposed to be a mode of renewing youth, ix. 302 *sqq.*

Castle Ditches, in the Vale of Glamorgan, bonfires at, x. 156

Castor and Pollux thought to attend the Spartan kings, i. 49 *sq.* ; their appearance in battle, i. 50

Castor's tune, v. 196 *n.*[3]

Castration, religious, in honour of Cybele, ii. 144 *sq.* ; practised by a modern sect in Russia, ii. 145 ; of Cronus and Uranus, v. 283 ; of sky-god, suggested explanation of, v. 283 ; of priests, suggested explanation of, v. 283 *sq.*

Castres, in Southern France, xi. 187

Casuarina leptoclada in magic, i. 213

Cat, blind, in homoeopathic magic, i. 153 ; wetted as a rain-charm, i. 262, 289 ; black, in rain-charm, i. 291 ; stone resembling a, used in rain-making, i. 308 *sq.* ; corn-spirit as, vii. 280 *sq.* ; killed at harvest, vii. 281 ; fever transferred to a, ix. 51 ; a representative of the devil, xi. 40 ; story of a clan whose souls were all in one, xi. 150 *sq.* ; a Batta totem, xi. 223. See also Cats

Cat's cradle forbidden to boys among the Esquimaux, i. 113 ; as a charm to arrest the sun, i. 316 *sq.*, vii. 103 *n.*[1] ; as a charm to promote the growth of the crops, vii. 101, 103 ; played by savages, vii. 103 *n.*[1]

—— tail, name given to last standing corn, viii. 268

Catafalque burnt at funeral of king of Siam, v. 179

Catalangans of Luzon offer first-fruits to the souls of their ancestors, viii. 124

Catalonia, funeral of Carnival in, iv. 225

Catania in Sicily, the vineyards of, v. 194; gardens of Adonis at, v. 245

Catat, Dr., his difficulty in photographing in Madagascar, iii. 98

Caterpillars, superstitious precautions against, viii. 275 sq., 279, 280; bonfires as a protection against, x. 114

Catgut plant in homoeopathic magic, i. 144

Catholic Church, ritual of the, v. 54; ceremonies on Good Friday in the, v. 254, 255 sq.; institutes feasts of All Saints and All Souls, vi. 83; enjoins continence during Lent, ix. 348; consecrates the Midsummer festival to St. John the Baptist, x. 181

—— custom of dedicating candles, i. 13; as to partaking of the Eucharist, viii. 83; of eating effigies of the Madonna, viii. 94

—— Germany, St. Leonhard in, i. 7

—— times in Scandinavia, i. 16

Catlin, George, on the power of medicine-men in North America, i. 356; on the conciliation of the spirits of slain foes, iii. 182

Cato, the Elder, on dedication of Arician grove to Diana, i. 22, 23; on expiation for thinning a grove, ii. 122; on the fodder of cattle, ii. 328 n.[1]; on lucky and unlucky trees, iii. 275 n.[3]; on a Roman cure for dislocation, xi. 177

Cats worshipped in Egypt, i. 29 sq.; witches changed into, ii. 334, x. 315 n.[1], 317, 318, 319 sq., xi. 311 sq.; with stumpy tails, reason of, iii. 128 sq.; burnt in bonfires, x. 109, xi. 39 sq.; perhaps burnt as witches, xi. 41. See also Cat

Cattle, magical stones for the increase of, i. 162; Zulu charm to recover strayed, i. 212; fire tied to tails of, in rain-charm, i. 303; sacrificed in rain-making, i. 350; influence of tree-spirits on, ii. 50 sq., 55, 124 sq.; crowned, as a protection against witchcraft, ii. 75, 126 sq., 339, 341; under the protection of woodland spirits, ii. 124 sq.; crowned at the Ambarvalia, ii. 127 n.[2]; and milk, importance of, for the early Italians, ii. 324; Roman personal names derived from, ii. 324 n.[1]; driven to pasture for the first time on St. George's Day, ii. 331; bred by the people of the Italian pile villages, ii. 353 n.[3]; continence observed for sake of, iii. 204; protected against wolves by charms, iii. 307; sacrificed instead of human beings, iv. 166 n.[1];

driven out to pasture at Whitsuntide, iv. 207 n.[1]; last sheaf given to, vii. 134, 155, 158, 161, 170; (plough oxen) Yule or Christmas Boar given to the, vii. 301, 302, 303; worship of, viii. 35, 37 sqq.; first-fruits offered to, viii. 118; ceremony for recovering lost, ix. 14; disease of, transferred to scapegoats, ix. 32 sq.; exposed to attacks of witches, ix. 162; beaten to do them good, ix. 266 sq.; sacrificed at holy oak, x. 181; protected against sorcery by sprigs of mullein, x. 190; fire carried round, x. 201, 206; driven out to pasture in spring and back in autumn, x. 223; acquire the gift of speech on Christmas Eve, x. 254; driven through the need-fire, x. 270 sqq.; killed by fairy darts, x. 303; lighted brands carried round, x. 341; thought to benefit by festivals of fire, xi. 4, 7; fumigated with smoke of Midsummer herbs, xi. 53. See also Cows

Cattle and sheep driven through, round, or between bonfires, ii. 327, x. 108, 109, 141, 154, 157, 158, 159, 165, 175, 176, 179, 185, 188, 192, 202, 203, 204, 285, 301, xi. 8, 9, 11 sq., 13

Cattle disease, the Midsummer fires a protection against, x. 176; attributed to witchcraft, x. 302 sq., 343. See also Murrain

—— -plague, need-fire kindled as a remedy for, x. 270 sqq.; sacrifice of an animal to stay a, x. 300 sqq.

—— -rearing tribes of South Africa, their dread of menstruous women, x. 79 sq.

—— stall, the, at Athens, ii. 137

Catullus on Diana, i. 6, 16; on self-mutilation of a priest of Attis, v. 270

Caucasus, the Pshaws of the, i. 182; the Chewsurs of the, i. 282, vi. 65; the Abchases of the, i. 282 n.[4], ii. 370, viii. 105; the Albanians of the, iii. 349, v. 73, ix. 218; the Cheremiss of the, iii. 391; funeral games among the people of the, iv. 97 sq.; sacraments of pastoral tribes in the, viii. 313

Caul, children born with a, can see spirits and are counted lucky, i. 187 sq., 199; used to fertilize a rice-field, i. 190 sq.; guardian spirit of child thought to reside in its, i. 199 sq. See also Cauls

Caul-fat extracted by Australian enemies, iii. 303; human, rubbed on body as a magical ointment, viii. 162

"Cauld airn," a protective charm, iii. 233

Cauldron, the magical, which makes the old young again, v. 181

Cauls bought by advocates, i. 199

Caunians of Asia Minor, their expulsion of foreign gods, ix. 116

Causal sequences in nature, recognition of, i. 374

Cauxanas, Indian tribe of the Amazon, kill all their first-born children, iv. 185 *sq.*

Cava, preparation and drinking of, viii. 131

Cavan, County, legendary idol in, iv. 183

Cave, spirit of, worshipped, i. 302 ; human god in, i. 394 *sq.* ; of Apollo at Hylae, i. 386 ; spirit of reindeer in, viii. 245 ; initiation of medicine-men by spirits in, xi. 237 *sqq. See also* Caves

Cave of Cruachan, the " Hell-gate of Ireland," x. 226

Caverns of Demeter, v. 88

Caves, prehistoric paintings of animals in, i. 87 *n.*[1] ; in which ceremonies for producing rain are performed, i. 301 *sq.* ; limestone, v. 152 ; in Semitic religion, v. 169 *n.*[3] *See also* Cave

Cavo, Monte, in the Alban Hills, i. 2

Cawthorne, in Yorkshire, May garlands (hoops) at, ii. 62 *sq.*

Caxton, in Cambridgeshire, ii. 71 *n.*[1]

Cayeli, in Buru, sacrifice of girl to crocodile in, ii. 152

Cayenne, the Indians of, their belief in the transmigration of human souls into fish, viii. 285

Cayor, in Senegal, king of, not allowed to cross the river or the sea, iii. 9

Cayzac, P., on confession among the Akikuyu, iii. 214

Cazembe, the king of, not to be seen drinking, iii. 118

Cazembes, the, of Angola, their dread of contact with their king, iii. 132 *sq.*

Cecrops, first king of Attica, married the daughter of his predecessor, ii. 277 ; said to have instituted marriage, ii. 284 ; half-serpent, half-man, iv. 86 *sq.* ; father of Agraulus, v. 145 ; father of Pandion, vii. 70 ; institutes the festival of Cronus, ix. 351

Cedar, sacred, in Gilgit, ii. 49, 50 *sq.* ; smoke of, inhaled as mode of inspiration, i. 383 *sq.*

—— sprung from the body of Osiris, vi. 110

Cedar-bark, ornaments of, worn in dances, ix. 376 ; red, used in ceremonies of a secret society, xi. 271

—— forests of Cilicia, v. 149, 150 *n.*[1]

—— tree, girl annually sacrificed to, ii. 17 ; Osiris interpreted as a cedar-tree god, vi. 109 *n.*[1]

—— wood burned as a religious rite, ii. 130

Ceklinj, in Crnagora, divination on St. George's morning at, ii. 345

Celaenae in Phrygia, skin of Marsyas shown at, v. 288 ; home of Lityerses, vii. 217

Celebes, the Buginese of, i. 158, iv. 277 ; rain-making in, i. 277 ; magical virtue of regalia in, i. 362 *sqq.* ; Loowoo in, i. 364 ; fear of offending forest-spirits in, ii. 40 ; hooking souls in, iii. 30 ; the Alfoors of, iii. 33, 129, 260 ; Bolang Mongando in, iii. 53, viii. 54, ix. 121 *n.*[3] ; Minahassa in, iii. 63, 99, iv. 214, vii. 296, viii. 100, 123, 153 ; exorcism of spirits by means of rice in, iii. 106 ; propitiation of the souls of slain enemies in, iii. 166 ; the Toumbuluh tribe of, iii. 295, 298 ; Poso in, iii. 332, vii. 236, viii. 244 ; Boni in, iv. 40 ; the Bantiks of, iv. 130 *n.* ; sanctity of regalia in, iv. 202 ; the Macassars of, iv. 277 ; conduct of the inhabitants in an earthquake, v. 200 ; division of agricultural work between the sexes in, vii. 124 ; observation of the Pleiades in, vii. 313 ; customs as to eating the new rice in, viii. 54 ; harvest festivals in, viii. 122 *sq.* ; kinship of men with crocodiles in, viii. 212 ; precautions against mice in, viii. 277 *sq.* ; sticks or stones piled on scenes of violent death in, ix. 15 ; Macassar in, x. 14 ; souls of persons removed for safety from their bodies in, xi. 153 *sq.*

——, Central, ix. 122 *n.* ; the Toradjas of, i. 109, 114, 129, 159, 172, 253, 271, 286, 303, ii. 39, 113, iii. 62, 111, 263, 340, 373 *n.*, vi. 33, vii. 182 *n.*[1], 183, 228, 295, viii. 153, ix. 34, 112 *n.*[2], 265, x. 311 *sqq.* ; Parigi in, i. 188 ; the Tolalaki of, i. 188, ii. 111, viii. 152 ; the Toboongkoos of, i. 189, ii. 28, 35, iii. 48, 78, iv. 219 ; the Tomori of, i. 189, ii. 29, 35, 110, vii. 193, 288 ; Poso in, ii. 29, 35, iii. 411, vii. 194 ; rice strewn on heads of warriors after a raid in, iii. 36 ; the Tolindoos of, iii. 78 ; the Tolampoos of, iii. 319

——, Northern, Minahassa in, i. 382, viii. 54, ix. 111 *sq.*

——, Southern, treatment of the navel-string and afterbirth in, i. 189 *sq.* ; rain-charm by means of a cat in, i. 289 ; the Toorat-eyas of, i. 361 ; customs at childbirth in, ii. 32, iii. 32, 245 ; the Macassars and Bugineese of, ii. 110 ; rice strewn on heads of bridegrooms and victors in, iii. 35 *sq.* ; rule as to treatment of a prince's corpse in, iii. 238 ; marriage custom in, vi. 260 ; birth-trees in, xi. 164

——, West, Bolang Mongondo in, iii. 341, 376, ix. 85, 121

Celenderis in Cilicia, v. 41

Celestial power acquired by inoculation, viii. 160 *sq.*

Celeus, king of Eleusis, vii. 37; and Demeter, viii. 334
Celibacy of holy milkmen, iii. 15, 16; of the Vestal Virgins, x. 138 n.[5]
Celtic bisection of the year, x. 223
—— calendar of Coligny, i. 17 n.[2]
—— divinity akin to Artemis, ii. 126
—— festival of the dead, vi. 82
—— and Italian languages akin, ii. 189
—— population, their superstition as to Snake Stones, x. 15
—— stories of the external soul, xi. 126 sqq.
—— Vestals, ii. 241 n.[1]
—— year reckoned from November 1st, vi. 81
Celts, their worship of the oak, ii. 9, 362 sq., xi. 89; their worship of the Huntress Artemis, ii. 125 sq.; their worship of Arduinna, ii. 126; holy fires tended by virgins among the, ii. 240; in Asia, ii. 363; their theory of names, iii. 319; their festival of All Souls, vi. 81 sq.; their mode of forecasting the weather of the year, ix. 323 sq.; their two great fire-festivals on the Eve of May Day and Hallowe'en, x. 222, 224
——, the British, their chief fire-festivals, Beltane and Hallowe'en, xi. 40 sq.
—— of Brittany, their use of mistletoe, xi. 320
—— of Gaul, their harvest festival, i. 17; their indifference to death, iv. 142 sq.; their calendar, ix. 342 sqq.; their human sacrifices, xi. 32 sq.; the victims perhaps witches and wizards, xi. 41 sq.; W. Mannhardt's theory of the sacrifices, xi. 43
—— of Ireland, their belief in the blighting effect of incest, ii. 116; their new fire on Hallowe'en, x. 139
—— of northern Italy, xi. 320
Celts (prehistoric implements), called "thunderbolts," x. 14 sq.
Cemeteries, cut hair and nails buried in, iii. 274; fairs held at, iv. 101, 102
Cenaed, king of the Scots, ii. 286
Censorinus, on the date of the rising of Sirius, vi. 34 n.[1]; on the octennial cycle, vii. 81 n.[4], 82 n.[2], 86 sq.
Centipedes not to be called by their proper name, iii. 407, 411
Central Provinces of India, belief as to twins in, i. 269; use of frogs in rain-charms in, i. 293; ceremonies observed by rearers of silk-worms in the, iii. 194 n.[1]; gardens of Adonis in the, v. 242 sq.; custom as to cutting the last corn at harvest in the, vii. 222 n.[2]; the Parjas of the, viii. 27 sq., 28, 119; customs as to first-fruits in the, viii.

118 sq.; the Gadbas of the, viii. 118; the Mannewars of the, viii. 119; the Nahals of the, viii. 119; cholera expelled by means of chickens in the, ix. 190; cure for fever in the, xi. 190
Ceos, Greek island of, funeral customs in, i. 105; the rising of Sirius observed in, vi. 35 n.[1]; rule as to the pollution of death in, vi. 227; sick children passed through a cleft oak in, xi. 172
Ceram, i. 125; treatment of the navel-string in, i. 187; rain-making in, i. 248; Alfoors of, their veneration for their high-priest, i. 400; expiation for unchastity in, ii. 109 n.[1]; rule as to girl scratching herself in, iii. 146 n.[1]; fear of women's blood in, iii. 251; men do not crop their hair in, iii. 260; division of agricultural work between the sexes in, vii. 124; ceremony at eating the new rice in, viii. 54; offerings of first-fruits to ancestors in, viii. 123; kinship of men with crocodiles in, viii. 212; sicknesses expelled in a ship from, ix. 185; sickness transferred to branches in, ix. 186; seclusion of girls at puberty in, x. 36; belief that strength of young people is in their hair in, xi. 158; rites of initiation to the Kakian association in, xi. 249 sqq.
Ceramicus, the, at Athens, graves of warriors in, iv. 96
Cereal deity, viii. 52, 83
Cereals cultivated in ancient Egypt, vi. 30; in Europe, antiquity of the cultivation of, vii. 79; cultivated by the early Aryans, vii. 132
Ceremonial purity observed in war, iii. 157. See Purity, Chastity, Continence
Ceremonies at cutting down haunted trees, ii. 34 sqq.; at the reception of strangers, iii. 102 sqq.; at entering a strange land, iii. 109 sqq.; after slaughter of panthers, lions, bears, serpents, etc., iii. 219 sqq.; at haircutting, iii. 264 sqq.
——, initiatory, of Central Australian aborigines, i. 92 sqq.
——, magical, for the multiplication of totems, i. 85 sqq.; for the regulation of the seasons, v. 3 sqq.; to ensure fertility of women, x. 23 sq., 31
——, purificatory, on return from a journey, iii. 111 sqq.
Ceremony of the Horse at rice-harvest among the Garos, viii. 337 sqq.
Ceres, names of fathers and daughters tabooed during the rites of, iii. 337; married to Orcus, vi. 231; corn the gift of, vii. 42; the, in France, vii. 135; festival of, vii. 297 n[5]; Roman sacrifices to, viii. 133; first ears of corn sacrificed to, viii. 133

Cervulus muntjac, species of deer, supposed to house the soul of an ancestor, viii. 294

Cervus equinus, a species of deer, claimed as relations by Malanaus in Borneo, viii. 294

Cetchwayo, king of Zululand, iii. 377

Cetraro in Calabria, Easter custom at, x. 123

Ceylon, *deega* and *beena* marriage in, ii. 271 *n.*[1], vi. 215 ; custom of tying a knot on a threshing-floor in, iii. 308 *sq.* ; sanctity of the threshing-floor in, viii. 110 *n.*[4] ; fear of demons in, ix. 94 *sq.* ; the king of, and his external soul, xi. 102

Chaco, the Gran, Lengua Indians of, i. 313, 330, 359, iii. 38, 357, iv. 11, 63, viii. 245 ; the Guaycurus of, iii. 357, vii. 309 ; the Matacos of, x. 58, 59 ; the Tobas of, x. 59 ; marriage custom of Indians of, x. 75 ; Indians of, their treatment of a wound, x. 98 *n.*[1]

——, the Paraguayan, ix. 78, x. 56, 75 *n.*[2]

Chadwars of the Central Provinces, India, expiation for slaughter of totemic animal among the, viii. 28

Chadwick, Professor H. M., on female descent of kingship in Greece and Sweden, ii. 278 *n.*[1] ; on the story of Hamlet, ii. 281 *n.*[2] ; on the marriage of Canute and Emma, ii. 283 *n.*[1] ; on the festival of October 1st, vi. 81 *n.*[3] ; on the dismemberment of Halfdan the Black, vi. 100 *n.*[2] ; on a priest dressed as a woman, vi. 259 *n.*[2] ; on a passage in the *Voluspa*, x. 103 *n.*

Chaeronea, the sceptre of Agamemnon worshipped at, i. 365 ; the "expulsion of hunger" at, ix. 252

Chain used to expel demons, ix. 260

Chains, iron, worn as amulets, iii. 235 ; clanked as a protection against witches, ix. 163 ; clanked in masquerade, ix. 244

Chait, an Indian month, ii. 149, viii. 119

Chaka, the Zulu despot, iv. 36 *sq.*, viii. 67, xi. 212 *n.* ; as a diviner, i. 350

Chaldean priests as to the human wife of Bel, ii. 129 *sq.*

Chaldeans, magic of, ix. 64

Chalk, white, bodies of newly initiated lads coated with, xi. 241

Chalk mark on brow a protection against a ghost, iii. 186 *n.*[1]

Chalking up crosses as a protection against witches, ix. 160, 162, 165 ; on Twelfth Night, ix. 314, 315 *n.*, 331

Chama, town on the Gold Coast, Horse-mackerel people at, iv. 129

Chamar caste in the Punjaub, ix. 196

Chamba, in India, ceremony at the funeral of a Rani of, ix. 45

Chambers, E. K., on the Festival of Fools, ix. 336 *n.*[1] ; on the Celtic bisection of the year, x. 223

Chambéry, the harvest Wolf near, vii. 275 ; "the wound of the Ox" at harvest near, vii. 288 ; "killing the Ox" at threshing at, vii. 291

Chambezi river in Central Africa, ii. 277

Chameleon, ceremony at killing a, ix. 28

Champion at English coronation ceremony, ii. 322

Chams, the, of Indo-China, their taboos in search for eagle-wood, ·i. 120 ; their homoeopathic magic at sowing, i. 144 ; precautions against ghosts among the, i. 280 ; their fear of waking the rice at mid-day, ii. 28 *sq.* ; their traditions of human victims sacrificed by drowning, ii. 159 ; continence at the making of a dam among the, iii. 202 ; open cattle-stalls and unyoke ploughs to aid women in childbed, iii. 297 ; use an artificial jargon in searching for eagle-wood, iii. 404 ; their story of the type of Beauty and the Beast, iv. 130 *n.*[1] ; their ceremonies at ploughing, sowing, reaping and eating the new rice, viii. 56 *sqq.* ; their sacrifices to the "god rat," viii. 283 ; their belief in transmigration, viii. 291 *sq.*

Chang, the house of, ancient Chinese family, i. 413

Change in date of Egyptian festivals with the adoption of the fixed Alexandrian year, vi. 92 *sqq.*

—— of language caused by taboo on the names of the dead, iii. 358 *sqq.*, 375 ; caused by taboo on names of chiefs and kings, iii. 375, 376 *sqq.*

—— of name to deceive ghosts, iii. 354 *sqq.* ; as a cure for ill health, iv. 158

Changes of shape, magical, vii. 305

Chants, plaintive, of corn-reapers in antiquity, vi. 45 *sq.*

"Charcoal Man" at Midsummer, xi. 26 *n.*[2]

Charente Inférieure, department of, St. John's fires in the, x. 192

Chariot in rain-charm, i. 309 ; procession with god riding in a, ii. 130 ; patient drawn through the yoke of a, xi. 192

—— and horses dedicated to the sun, i. 315

Chariot-race at Olympia, iv. 91, 104 *sq.*, 287 ; annual, on the Field of Mars at Rome, viii. 42

—— -races in honour of the dead, iv. 93

Chariots, epidemics sent away in toy, ix. 193 *sq.* ; used by sacred persons, x. 4 *n.*[1]

Charlemagne, x. 270 ; compared to Osiris, vi. 199

Charles I. touches for scrofula, i. 368

Charles II. touches for scrofula, i. 368 *sq.* ; champion at his coronation, ii. 322

Charlotte Waters, in Central Australia, the Blind Tree at, i. 147

Charm to protect a town, vi. 249 *sqq.*

Charms to ensure long life, i. 168 *sq.* ; to prevent the sun from going down, i. 316 *sqq.* ; to facilitate childbirth, iii. 295 *sq.* *See also* Amulets, Magic, Talismans

Charon, places of, v. 204, 205

Charonia, places of Charon, v. 204

Chasas of Orissa believe that leprosy is caused by injuring a totemic animal, viii. 26 *sq.*

"Chasing the Wild Man out of the bush," a Whitsuntide custom, iv. 208 *sq.*

"Chasms of Demeter and Persephone," viii. 17

Chaste young men kindle need-fire, x. 273

Chastity observed for sake of absent persons, i. 123, 124, 125, 131 ; required of rain-doctor, i. 271 ; practised to make the crops grow, ii. 104 *sqq.* ; required of persons who handle dishes and food, ii. 115 *sq.*, 205 ; Milton on, ii. 118 *n.*[1] ; as a virtue not understood by savages, ii. 118 ; observed by sacred men, perhaps the husbands of a goddess, ii. 135, 136 ; observed by sacred women, ii. 137 ; observed by women in making pottery, ii. 204 ; required in those who make fire by friction, ii. 238 *sq.* ; observed by women at festival of the corn-goddess, v. 43 ; ordeal of, v. 115 *n.*[2] ; required in sower of seed, vii. 115 *sq.* ; observed by matrons at the Thesmophoria, vii. 116 ; required in service of sacred serpent, viii. 18 ; required of hunter before hunting bears, viii. 226 ; associated with abstinence from salt, x. 27 *sq.* *See also* Continence

Château-Thierry, Midsummer fires at, x. 187 *sq.*

Chateaubriand, his description of the Natchez festival, viii. 135 *sqq.*

Chatham Islands, birth-trees in the, xi. 165

Chatti, German tribe, their custom as to their hair, iii. 262

Chauci, a German tribe, on the North Sea, ii. 353

Chauta, Master, prayer for rain to, i. 250

Chavandes, bonfires on the first Sunday in Lent, x. 109 *n.*[2]

Chavantes, Indian tribe of the Tocantins River, iv. 12 *n.*[5]

Cheadle, in Staffordshire, the Yule log at, x. 256

Cheese, eaten by human scapegoat before being put to death, ix. 255 ; the Beltane, kept as a charm against the bewitching of milk-produce, x. 154

Cheese Monday, the Monday of the last week in Carnival, celebrated by Thracian and Bulgarian peasants, vii. 26, viii. 333

Chegilla, food taboos in Congo, iii. 137

Cheltenham, Jack-in-the-Green at, ii. 82 *sq.*

Chemakum tribe of Washington State, prohibition to mention the names of the dead in the, iii. 365

Chemistry, alchemy leads up to, i. 374

Chemmis in Egypt, temple of Perseus at, iii. 312 *n.*[2]

Chêne-Doré, "the gilded oak," in Perche, xi. 287 *n.*[1]

Chenourazah, king of the Maldive Islands, ii. 153

Chent-Ament (Khenti-Amenti), title of Osiris, vi. 87

Chephren, king of Egypt, his statue, vi. 21 *sq.*

Chepstow oak, in Gloucestershire, mistletoe on the, xi. 316

Cheremiss, the, of Russia, their sacred groves, ii. 44 ; will not fell trees while the corn is in bloom, ii. 49 ; keep the names of their villages secret, iii. 391 ; their custom at eating the new corn, viii. 51 ; offer cakes instead of horses, viii. 95 *n.*[2] ; their expulsion of Satan, ix. 156 ; their Midsummer festival, x. 181

Chero, the, of Mirzapur, their contagious magic of footprints, i. 209

Cherokee Indians, their myth of the Old Woman of the Corn, vi. 46 *sq.* ; their lamentations after "the first working of the corn," vi. 47 ; annual expulsion of evils among the, ix. 128. *See also* Cherokees

—— hunters pray to the eagles they have killed, viii. 236 ; ask pardon of the deer they kill, viii. 241

—— mythology, viii. 204 *sq.*

—— sorcery with spittle, iii. 287 *sq.*

Cherokees, homoeopathic magic of plants among the, i. 144, 146 *sq.* ; their charms to ensure success in ball-playing, i. 144, 155 ; foods avoided by the, on homoeopathic principles, i. 155 ; homoeopathic magic of animals among the, i. 155 *sq.* ; their charm to become good singers, i. 156 ; their charm to strengthen a child's grip, i. 156 ; their mode of averting an evil omen, i. 172 ;

their custom as to children's cast teeth, i. 180; their treatment of the navel-string, i. 198; their mode of averting a storm, i. 321; try to deceive the spirits of rattlesnakes and eagles, iii. 399; think that to step over a vine blasts it, iii. 424; personify maize as an Old Woman, vii. 177; their way of attracting the corn, vii. 190; their festival of first-fruits, viii. 72 *n.*[2]; their belief in the homoeopathic magic of the flesh of animals, viii. 139; no clear distinction between animals and men in their mythology, viii. 204 *sq.*; their respect for rattlesnakes, viii. 218 *sq.*; their ceremonies at killing a wolf, viii. 220 *sq.*; their propitiation of the eagles which they have killed, viii. 236; their custom of removing the hamstring of deer, viii. 266; their sacred arks, x. 11 *sq.*; their ideas as to trees struck by lightning, xi. 296 *sq.*

Cherrington, in Warwickshire, the Queen of May at, ii. 88

Cherry-tree, charm to make it bear fruit, i. 141; wood used for Yule log, x. 250

—— -trees, branches of, used to beat people with in the Christmas holidays, ix. 270; torches thrown at, x. 108

Chersonese, the Thracian, iv. 93

Chervil-seed burnt in Midsummer-fire, x. 213

Cheshire, May-poles in, ii. 70 *sq.*; popular cure for rheumatism in, iii. 106 *n.*[2]; All Souls' Day in, vi. 79; Plough Monday in, viii. 330 *n.*[1]; cure for thrush in, ix. 50; cure for warts in, ix. 57

Chesnitsa, Christmas cake in Servia, x. 261

Chester, Midsummer giants at, xi. 37

Chet, Indian month (March-April), iv. 265

Chetang, mountains of, in Tibet, ix. 220

Chetti worshipped in the Deccan, vii. 7

Chevannes, bonfires on the first Sunday in Lent, x. 111 *n.*[1]

Chevas of South Africa, their notion as to whirlwinds, i. 331 *n.*[2]

Chewsurs of the Caucasus, their rain-charm, i. 282; taboos observed by an annual official among the, iii. 292 *sq.*; their annual Festival of All Souls, iv. 98, vi. 65; their funeral games, iv. 98

Cheyenne Indians, seclusion of girls at puberty among the, x. 54 *sq.*

—— women secluded at menstruation, x. 89

Cheyne, Professor T. K., on the brazen serpent, iv. 86 *n.*[4]; on lament for kings of Judah, v. 20 *n.*[2]

Chhatarpur, in Bundelcund, ceremony for stopping rain at, i. 296 *sq.*

Chiambioa Indians of Brazil, their masked dances, viii. 208 *n.*[1]

Chiaromonte in Sicily, Midsummer custom at, x. 210

Chibchas (Muyscas or Mozcàs), the, of Colombia, their reverence for the pontiff of Sogamozo, i. 416

Chibisa, an African chief, killed by a sand-bullet, xi. 314

Chica or *chicha,* a native American intoxicant, ii. 105, iii. 250 *n.*[1], x. 57, 58

Chi-chi Mama, "the Drenched Mother," in rain-making, in Armenia, i. 276

Chicken bones, omens from, ii. 70

Chickens, sickness transferred to, ix. 31; as scapegoats, ix. 190

Chicomecohuatl, Mexican goddess of maize, vii. 176, ix. 286 *n.*[1], 291, 292; girl annually sacrificed in the character of, ix. 292 *sqq.*

Chicory, the white flower of, opens all locks, xi. 71

Chidley, Cape, spirit of reindeer in cave at, viii. 245

Chief, power of divination possessed by, i. 344; as priest, ii. 215 *sqq.*; ancestral, reincarnate in snakes, v. 84; the divinity of a, supposed to reside in his eyes, viii. 153. *See also* Chiefs

Chief's daughter, ceremonies observed by her at puberty, x. 30, 43

—— head not to be touched, i. 344

Chiefs, sorcerers regarded as, in New Guinea, i. 337 *sq.*; in Melanesia, supernatural power of, i. 338 *sq.*; evolved out of magicians, especially out of rain-makers, in Africa, i. 342 *sqq.*; magical powers ascribed to, i. 349; not allowed to leave their premises, i. 349; punished for drought and dearth, i. 352 *sqq.*; as priests, ii. 215 *sq.*, viii. 126; chosen from several families in rotation, ii. 292 *sqq.*; foods tabooed to, iii. 291, 292; names of, tabooed, iii. 376 *sq.*, 378 *sq.*, 381, 382

——, dead, worshipped, vi. 175, 176, 177, 179, 181 *sq.*, 187; thought to control the rain, vi. 188; sacrifices to, vi. 191, viii. 113; spirits of, prophesy through living men and women, vi. 192 *sq.*; spirits of, give rain, viii. 109; deified after death, viii. 125; souls of, in lions, viii. 287 *sq.*

—— and kings tabooed, iii. 131 *sqq.*

—— in the Pelew Islands, custom of slaying, vi. 266 *sqq.*

——, sacred, viii. 28; not allowed to leave their enclosures, iii. 124; regarded as dangerous, iii. 138

Chiefs' daughters entrusted with the sacred fire among the Herero, ii. 215, 228

Chieftainship and kingship in Africa fully developed, i. 342

Chikumbu, a Yao chief, xi. 314

Chilblains, the Yule log a preventive of, x. 250

Chilcotin Indians of North-West America, their ceremony at an eclipse of the sun, i. 312, iv. 77

Child, carried by sower to ensure fertility, i. 142 ; under puberty employed by Ba-Ronga women to light the potter's kiln, ii. 205 ; placed in bride's lap as a fertility charm, ii. 230 sq. ; born on harvest-field, pretence of, vii. 150 sq. See also Children

"—— of the assegai," iv. 183

—— and father, supposed danger of resemblance between, iii. 88 sq., iv. 287 (288, in Second Impression)

"Child-stones," where souls of dead await rebirth, v. 100

Child's life bound up with the tree with or under which its navel-string or after-birth was planted, i. 182, 184, 194

—— nails bitten off, iii. 262

—— Well at Oxford, ii. 161

Childbed, woman in, thought to control the wind, i. 324 ; souls of women dying in, live in trees, ii. 31 ; taboos on women in, iii. 147 sqq. ; precautions taken with women in, iii. 314 ; deceiving the ghosts of women who have died in, viii. 97 sq.

Childbirth, Diana as goddess of, i. 12, ii. 128 ; precautions taken with mothers at, iii. 32, 33, 233, 234, 239, 245 ; women tabooed at, iii. 145 ; supposed dangerous infection of, iii. 147 sqq. ; confessions of sins to expedite, iii. 216 sq. ; women after, their hair shaved and burnt, iii. 284 ; knots untied at, iii. 294, 296 sq., 297 sq. ; homoeopathic magic to facilitate, iii. 295 sqq. ; primitive ignorance of the causes of, v. 106 sq. ; customs of women after, x. 20

Childermas (Holy Innocents' Day), the 28th day of December, Boy Bishop on, ix. 336, 337

Childless couples leap over bonfires to procure offspring, x. 214, 338

—— persons named after their younger brothers, iii. 332, 333

—— women divorced, i. 142 ; their corpses thrown away, i. 142 ; homoeopathic charm employed by, to ensure the birth of children, i. 157 ; expect offspring from St. George, v. 78 ; resort to Baths of Solomon, v. 78 ; receive offspring from serpent, v. 86 ;

resort to graves in order to secure offspring, v. 96 ; resort to hot springs in Syria, v. 213 sqq. ; creep through a holed stone, xi. 187. See also Barren

Children thought to be reincarnations of the dead, i. 103 sqq. ; taboos observed by, in the absence of their fathers, i. 116, 119, 122, 123, 127, 131 ; homoeopathic charm to ensure the birth of, i. 157 ; born with a caul thought to be lucky and to see spirits, i. 187 sq., 199 ; buried to the neck as a rain-charm, i. 302 sq. ; dislike of parents to have children like themselves, iii. 88 sq., iv. 287 (288, in Second Impression) ; young, tabooed, iii. 262, 283 ; parents named after their, iii. 331 sqq., 339 ; called the fathers or mothers of their first cousins, iii. 332 sq. ; sacrificed to Moloch, iv. 75 ; sacrificed by the Semites, iv. 166 sqq. ; bestowed by saints, v. 78 sq. ; given by serpent, v. 86 ; murdered that their souls may be reborn in barren women, v. 95 ; sacrificed to volcano in Siao, v. 219 ; sacrificed at irrigation channels, vi. 38 ; sacrificed by the Mexicans for the maize, vi. 107 ; presented to the moon, vi. 144 sqq. ; guarded against evil spirits, vii. 6 sqq. ; employed to administer drugs and the poison ordeal, vii. 115 ; employed to sow seed, vii. 115 sq. ; sacrificed at harvest, vii. 236 ; blood of, used to knead a paste, ix. 129 ; personating spirits, ix. 139 ; live apart from their parents among the Baganda, x. 23 n.[2] ; passed across the Midsummer fires, x. 182, 189 sq., 192, 203 ; born feet foremost, curative power attributed to, x. 295 ; passed through holes in ground or turf to cure them, xi. 190 sq. See also Child

—— of God in Kikuyu, v. 68

—— of living parents in ritual, vi. 236 sqq. ; apparently thought to be endowed with more vitality than others, vi. 247 sq.

——, new-born, brought to the spirits of the ancestors, ii. 216, 221 ; passed through the smoke of a fire, ii. 232 ; brought to the hearth, ii. 232 ; placed in winnowing-fans, vii. 6 sqq.

Children's nails not pared, iii. 262 sq.

Chili, sacred cedar among the Aryan tribes of Gilgit, ii. 49, 50 sq.

Chili stone, ceremony of fertilizing goats at the, ii. 51

Chili, the Chilote Indians of, i. 168 ; the Araucanians of, i. 292 n.[3], iii. 97 ; disposal of shorn hair in, iii. 280 ; earthquakes in, v. 202

Chillingworth, Thomas, passed through a cleft ash-tree for rupture, xi. 168 sq.

Chiloe, the Indians of, keep their names secret, iii. 324

Chilote Indians of Chili, their belief as to death at ebb-tide, i. 168 ; their magical use of shorn hair, iii. 268 ; make magic with the spittle of an enemy, iii. 287

Chimaera, Mount, in Lycia, perpetual fire on, v. 221

Chimché-gelin, rain-bride, in Armenia, i. 276

Chimney, witches fly up the, xi. 74

Chimney-piece, divination by names on, x. 237

China, homoeopathic magic of city sites in, i. 169 sq. ; birthday celebration in, i. 169 ; trees planted on graves· in, ii. 31 ; new-born children passed through the smoke of fire in, ii. 232 n.[2] ; custom as to shadows at funerals in, iii. 80 ; custom at an execution in, iii. 171 ; geomancy in, iii. 239 ; suicide of Buddhist monks in, iv. 42 ; substitutes for corporal punishment in, iv. 275 sq. ; ceremony at beginning of spring in, viii. 10 sqq. ; belief in demons in, ix. 99 ; men possessed by spirits in, ix. 117 ; annual expulsion of demons in, ix. 145 sqq. ; annual ceremony of the new fire in, x. 136 sq., xi. 3 ; were-wolves in, x. 310 sq. ; use of fire to bar ghosts in, xi. 17 sq. ; spirits of plants in snake form in, xi. 44 n.[1] ; use of mugwort in, xi. 60. See also Chinese

——, aboriginal tribes of, their use of a human scapegoat, ix. 196 ; their annual destruction of evils, ix. 202

——, Emperor of, superior to the gods, i. 416 sq. ; seldom quitted his palace, iii. 125 ; his directions for averting the devil, iii. 239 ; his name not to be pronounced nor written by his subjects, iii. 375 sq. ; etiquette at his court, iv. 40 ; funeral of, v. 294 ; inaugurates the ploughing in spring, viii. 14 sq.

——, emperors of, as priests, i. 47 ; held responsible for drought, i. 355

——, the Miotse of, ix. 4

——, the Mossos of, ix. 139

——, South and West, the Miao-Kia of, ii. 31

——, Southern, expulsion of the demons of cholera in, ix. 117 sq. ; the Shans of, ix. 141

Chinchvad, human gods at, i. 405 sq.

Chinese, magical images among the, i. 60 sq. ; their charms to ensure long life, i. 168 sq. ; their superstition as to placenta (afterbirth), i. 194 ; their belief as to the influence of the dead on rain, i. 287 ; their modes of compelling the rain-god to give rain, i. 297 sqq. ; their emperor responsible for drought, i. 355 ; their belief in spirits of plants, ii. 14 ; their custom of marrying a girl to the Yellow River, ii. 152 ; kindle a sacred fire by means of a metal mirror or burning-glass, ii. 245 n. ; their story of a wandering human soul and its deserted body, iii. 49 sq. ; attribute convulsions to the action of demons, iii. 59 ; their use of mirrors to frighten demons, iii. 93 n.[3] ; use no knives nor needles after a death, iii. 238 ; their belief as to the intimate association of names with beings, iii. 390; their indifference to death, iv. 144 sqq., 273 sqq. ; report a custom of devouring first-born children, iv. 180 ; their character compared to that of the ancient Egyptians, vi. 218 ; their use of sieve or winnowing-fan in superstitious rites, vii. 6, 9 sq. ; their ceremony of ploughing, viii. 14 sq. ; their theory as to courage, viii. 145 sq., 152; their ceremonies of purification in spring and autumn, ix. 213 n.[1] ; their festival of fire, ix. 359, xi. 3 sqq. ; their story of the external soul, xi. 145 sq. ; their theories as to the human soul, xi. 221

Chinese of Amoy averse to call fever by its proper name, iii. 400 ; their use of effigies to divert ghostly and other evil influences from persons, viii. 104 sq.

Chinese author on disturbance of earth-spirits by agriculture, v. 89

—— books, bleeding trees in, ii. 18

—— comedies played as a rain-charm, i. 301 n.

—— empire, incarnate human gods in the, i. 412 sqq.

—— geomancy, i. 170

—— New Year, viii. 10

—— writers on kings of Corea, i. 355 ; as to injury to men and birds through their shadows, iii. 79 ; as to blood containing the soul, iii. 241 ; profess themselves unable to distinguish between men and animals, viii. 206

Chingilli, an Australian tribe, their custom of knocking out teeth, i. 99

Chinigchinich, a Californian god, viii. 170

Chinna Kimedy, in India, vii. 247, 249

Chinook Indians, prohibition to mention the names of the dead among the, iii. 365 ; seclusion of girls at puberty among the, x. 43

Chins, the, of Upper Burma, their offerings of first-fruits to their ancestors, viii. 121 ; their way of keeping off cholera, ix. 123

Chios, titular kings in, i. 45, 46 n.[4];
human beings torn in pieces at the
rites of Dionysus in, vi. 98 sq., vii. 24

Chippeway Indians, magical images
among the, i. 77 ; their dread and
seclusion of menstruous women, x.
90 sq.

Chiquites Indians of Paraguay, their
belief as to *chica*, iii. 250 n.[1]; their
fear of dead deer and turtles, viii. 241 ;
their theory of sickness, xi. 226 n.[1]

Chirbury, in Shropshire, the Yule log at,
x. 257

Chiriguanos, the, of South America, their
preference for a violent death, iv. 12 ;
their address to the sun, vi. 143 n.[4];
why they will not eat the vicuña, viii.
140 ; their belief in the transmigration
of human souls into animals, viii. 286 ;
their practice of bleeding themselves
to relieve fatigue, ix. 13 ; seclusion of
girls at puberty among the, x. 56

Chiriqui, volcano, v. 181

Chirol, (Sir) Valentine, on substitutes for
capital punishment in China, iv. 274

Chiron, the centaur, taught Hippolytus
venery, i. 19

Chirouba, festival in Manipur, ix. 40

Chirus of Manipur, their rain-making by
means of a crab, i. 289 ; their tug-of-
war, ix. 177 n.[3]

Chisaks, a tribe of Garos, their harvest
festival, viii. 337

Chissumpe, the spiritual head of the
Maraves, i. 393

Chitariah Gossaih, god of a hill-tribe in
India, viii. 118

Chitomé or Chitombé, a pontiff of Congo,
his perpetual fire, ii. 261 ; regarded as
a god on earth, iii. 5 sq., 7 ; slain by
his successor, iv. 14 sq., 206

Chitral, devil-driving in, ix. 137

Chittagong, opening everything in house
to facilitate childbirth in, iii. 297 ;
nail knocked into threshold at a burial
in, ix. 63 n.[4]

—— Hill Tracts, the Chukmas of the,
ix. 174

Chittim (Citium) in Cyprus, Phoenician
kings at, v. 31

Chnum of Elephantine, Egyptian god
identified with the sun, vi. 123

Choctaws, taboos observed by manslayers
among the, iii. 181 ; their annual festival of the dead, vi. 53 sq. ; their
women secluded at menstruation, x.
88

Chodoi, in Selangor, ceremony of bringing home the soul of the rice at, vii.
198

Choerilus, Greek historian, as to the
epitaph of Sardanapalus, ix. 388 n.[1]

Cholera sent away in animal scapegoats,
ix. 190, 191 sq.

——, demon of, expelled, ix. 116, 117,
172 ; threatened with swords, ix. 123 ;
conjured into an image, ix. 172 ; sent
away on a raft, ix. 190

——, goddess of, kept off by iron, iii.
234 ; sent away in a little chariot, ix. 194

Cholones, the, of eastern Peru, their
custom as to poisoned arrows, i. 116 ;
their charms against snake-bite, etc.,
i. 153

Cholula, a city of Mexico, worship of
Quetzalcoatl at, ix. 281

Chonga, on the Niger, the king of, keeps
himself concealed, iii. 121

Chopping-knife, soul of woman in childbirth transferred for safety to a, xi.
153 sq.

Chorinchen, custom at threshing at, vii.
148

Chorion or foetal membrane, Icelandic
belief as to, i. 199 sq.

Chota Nagpur in India, ceremonies observed by rearers of silkworms in, iii.
194 n.[1]; the Oraons of, vii. 244 ; stones
or leaves piled on places where persons
have been killed by wild beasts in, ix.
19 ; annual expulsion of disease in, ix.
139 ; the fire-walk in, xi. 5

Chouquet, in Normandy, the Green Wolf
at, x. 185

Chouville, Léon, on the King of the
Bean in France, ix. 315 n.[1]

Chréais or Jaray, tribe in the mountains
of Cambodia, their Kings of Fire and
Water, ii. 3

Christ, his Nativity, v. 304 sq. ; his
crucifixion, v. 306 sqq., ix. 412 sqq. ;
his resurrection, v. 306, 307 n., 308
sqq. ; doubts as to his historical reality
unfounded, v. 311 n.[2], ix. 412 n.[1];
and Osiris, vi. 59

Christbrand, the Yule log, x. 248

Christenburg Crags, in Northumberland,
Midsummer fires at, x. 198

Christian, Captain, his mode of execution, iii. 244

Christian, F. W., on the prostitution of
unmarried girls in Yap, vi. 265 sq.

Christian Church, its treatment of witches,
xi. 42. *See* Church

—— festivals displace heathen festivals,
i. 14 sqq., v. 308, vi. 81 sqq. ; the
great, timed by the Church to coincide
with old pagan festivals, ix. 328

Christianity, purifying influence of, v.
80 ; its conflict with the Mithraic religion, v. 302 sqq. ; its success due to
the personal influence of its founder,
vi. 159 sq. ; its rapid diffusion in Asia
Minor, ix. 420 sq.

Christianity, Latin, its tolerance of rustic paganism, ix. 346
—— and Buddhism, comparison between their history, v. 310 *sqq.*
—— and paganism, their resemblances explained as diabolical counterfeits, v. 302, 309 *sq.*
Christians, pretenders to divinity among, i. 407 *sqq.*
—— and pagans, their controversy as to Easter, v. 309 *sq.*
Christklotz, the Yule log, x. 248
Christmas, custom of swinging at, iv. 284 ; festival of, borrowed from the Mithraic religion, v. 302 *sqq.* ; the heathen origin of, v. 305 ; straw of Corn-mother placed in manger of cattle at, vii. 134 ; the last sheaf given to cattle at, vii. 155, 158, 160 *sq.* ; boar sacrificed at, vii. 302 ; pretence of human sacrifice at, vii. 302 ; dances to make the flax grow at, viii. 328 ; custom of young men and women beating each other at, ix. 270 ; an old midwinter festival of the sun-god, ix. 328, x. 246, 331 *sq.* ; new fire made by the friction of wood at, x. 264 ; mistletoe gathered at, xi. 291. *See also* Yule
Christmas Boar among the Esthonians, vii. 302 *sq.*
—— cake, x. 257, 259, 261
—— candle, the, x. 255, 256, 260
—— custom in Poland, vii. 275 ; in Sweden, vii. 301 *sq.*
—— Day, hunting the wren on, viii. 319, 320 ; Mexican festival on, ix. 287 ; divination on, ix. 316 *n.*[1] ; Old (Twelfth Night), ix. 321
—— drama in Sweden, viii. 327 *sq.*
—— Eve, fruit-trees girt or tied together with straw on, ii. 17, 27 *sq.* ; barren fruit-trees threatened on, ii. 21 ; presages as to shadows on, ii. 88 ; celebration of, in Oesel, vii. 302 ; hunting the wren on, viii. 318, 321 ; witches active on, ix. 160 ; cattle acquire the gift of speech on, x. 254 ; torchlight processions on, x. 266 ; trees fumigated with wild thyme on, xi. 64 ; the fern blooms on, xi. 66 ; witches dreaded on, xi. 73 ; sick children passed through cleft trees on, xi. 172
—— night, fern-seed blooms on, xi. 289
—— pig in Servia, x. 259
—— visitor, the, x. 261 *sq.*, 263, 264
Christs, Russian sect of the, i. 407 *sq.*
Chrudim in Bohemia, effigy of Death burnt at, iv. 239
Chu-en-aten, name assumed by King Amenophis IV. of Egypt, vi. 124

Chu-Tu-shi, a Chinese were-tiger, x. 310 *sq.*
Chua-hang or Troc, the caves of, in Annam, i. 301 *sq.*
Chuckchees or Chukchees of North-Eastern Asia, their chief sacrificed in time of pestilence, i. 367 *n.*[1] ; sacred fire-boards of the, ii. 225 *sq.* ; divine by the shoulder-blades of sheep, iii. 229 *n.*[4] ; change the name of the youngest son after his mother's death, iii. 358 ; voluntary deaths among the, iv. 13 ; effeminate sorcerers among the, vi. 256 *sq.* ; their ceremony at killing a wolf, viii. 221
Chukmas, a tribe of the Chittagong Hill Tracts, the tug-of-war among the, ix. 174
Chunar, in Bengal, rain-making ceremony at, i. 283
Church, the Christian, borrows the festival of Christmas from the worship of Mithra, v. 303 *sqq.* ; its compromise with paganism, v. 308 ; its treatment of witches, xi. 42. *See also* Catholic
Church bells a protection against witchcraft, ix. 157, 158 ; on Midsummer Eve, custom as to ringing, xi. 47 *sq.* ; rung to drive away witches, xi. 73
Churches used as places of divination at Hallowe'en, x. 229
Churinga, sacred stick and stones, resembling bull-roarers, of the Arunta and other Central Australian tribes, i. 88, 199, 335, xi. 218 *n.*[3], 234
Churn, last corn cut, vii. 151, 153, 154 *sq.*
Churn wreathed with rowan on May Day, ii. 53
Churn-dashers ridden by witches, ix. 160
—— -staff made of rowan as a protection against witchcraft, ii. 53, 54
Churning, precaution against witches in, ii. 53 *n.*[1]
Chuwash, their test of a sacrificial victim, i. 385
Chuzistan, rumour of the death of the King of the Jinn in, iv. 8
Chwolsohn, D., on the worship of Haman, ix. 366 *n.*[1]
Ciallos, intercalary month of Gallic calendar, ix. 343
Cicero invited to meet the assassin Brutus, i. 5 ; at Cybistra, v. 122 *n.*[3] ; corresponds with Cilician king, v. 145 *n.*[2] ; on the Attic origin of corn, vii. 58 ; on transubstantiation, viii. 167 ; on the custom of knocking in a nail annually, ix. 67 *n.*[2]
Cieza de Leon on the Peruvian Vestals, ii. 244 *n.*[1], 245 *n.*
Cilicia, male deity of, assimilated to Zeus, v. 118 *sq.*, 144 *sqq.*, 148, 152 ;

kings of, their affinity to Sandan, v. 144 ; names of priests in, v. 144 ; pirates in, v. 149 ; goddesses in, v. 161 *sqq.* ; the burning of gods in, v. 170 *sq.* ; the Assyrians in, v. 173 ; Tarsus in, ix. 388, 389, 391

Cilicia, Western or Rugged, described, v. 148 *sqq.* ; fossils of, v. 152 *sq.*

Cilician Gates, pass of the, v. 120

Cimbrians, the, take arms against the tide, i. 331 *n.*[3]

Ciminian forest, ii. 8

Cincius Alimentus, L., on Maia as the wife of Vulcan, vi. 232

Cinet or sinnet, iii. 69 *n.*[3]

Cingalese (Cinglese), their fear of demons, ix. 95 ; the tug-of-war among the, ix. 181. *See also* Singhalese

Cingalese remedy by means of devil-dancers, ix. 38

Cinteotl or Centeotl, Mexican goddess of maize, vii. 176, ix. 286 *n.*[1] ; personated by a priest, ix. 290

Cinyrads, dynasty of the, v. 41 *sqq.*

Cinyras, the father of Adonis, v. 13, 14, 49 ; king of Byblus, v. 27 ; founds sanctuary of Astarte, v. 28 ; said to have instituted religious prostitution, v. 41, 50 ; his daughters, v. 41, 50 ; his riches, v. 42 ; his incest, v. 43 ; wooed by Aphrodite, v. 48 *sq.* ; meaning of the name, v. 52 ; the friend of Apollo, v. 54 ; legends of his death, v. 55

Ciotat in Provence, bathing at Midsummer at, v. 248 ; Midsummer rites of fire and water at, x. 194

Circassia, custom as to pear-trees in, ii. 55 *sq.* ; games in honour of the dead in, iv. 98

Circe, the land of, ii. 188

Circensian games at Bovillae, ii. 180 *n.*

Circumambulating fields with lighted torches, x. 233 *sq.*

Circumcision, pretence of new birth at, i. 76, 96 *sq.* ; among the aborigines of Australia, i. 92 *sqq.* ; uses of blood shed at, i. 92, 94 *sq.*, iii. 244 ; among the dwarf tribes of the Gaboon, i. 95 *n.*[4] ; suggested origin of, i. 96 *sq.* ; in Central Australia, i. 204, 208, iii. 244, xi. 227 *sq.*, 233, 234, 235 ; among the Caffres, iii. 156 *sq.* ; performed with flints, not iron, iii. 227 ; of father as a mode of redeeming his offspring, iv. 181 ; story told by Israelites to explain the origin of, iv. 181 ; mimic rite of, iv. 219 *sq.* ; exchange of dress between men and women at, vi. 263 ; period of seclusion after, determined by the appearance of the Pleiades, vii. 316 ;

ceremonies at, in South-East Africa, viii. 148 ; custom at, in Celebes, viii. 153 ; riddles asked at, ix. 122 *n.* ; among the Washamba, xi. 183 ; in New Guinea, xi. 240 *sq.* ; in Fiji, xi. 243 *sq.* ; in Rook, xi. 246 ; on the Lower Congo, xi. 251, 255 *n.*[1]

Circumcision Day, the 1st of January, Pope of Fools on, ix. 334

Circumlocutions adopted to avoid naming the dead, iii. 350, 351, 355 ; caused by fear of the dead, iii. 354 ; employed by reapers, iii. 412

Circus, the games of the, ii. 174

Cirta, image of Jupiter at, ii. 177

Cithaeron, Mount, bonfire on the top of, ii. 140 *sq.* ; forest of oaks at, iv. 82 ; Pentheus torn to pieces on, vii. 25 *n.*[3]

Cities, guardian deities of, evoked by enemies, iii. 391 ; Etruscan ceremony at the founding of, iv. 157

Citium (Chittim), in Cyprus, Phoenician kings at, v. 31, 50

Citrus hystrix, the afterbirth hung on a, i. 186

Civilization advanced by great conquering races, i. 218 ; threatened by an underlying stratum of savagery, i. 236 ; ancient, undermined by Oriental religions and other causes, v. 299 *sqq.*

Clach-nathrach, serpent stone, xi. 311

Clam shell, sacred, of the Omahas, x. 11

Clan of the Cat, xi. 150 *sq.*

Clangour of metal used to dispel demons, ix. 233

Clanking chains as a protection against witches, ix. 163

Clans, paternal and maternal, of the Herero, ii. 217

Clappers, used instead of church bells in Holy Week, x. 125 ; wooden, used in China, x. 137

Clarian Apollo, the, iv. 80 *n.*[1]

Clark, J. V. H., on the New Year festival of the Iroquois, ix. 209

Clarke, E. D., on the bride-race among the Calmucks, ii. 301 *sq.* ; on image of Demeter at Eleusis, vii. 64 *n.*[2] ; on the Harvest Queen, vii. 146 *sq.* ; on heaps of sticks or stones on graves in Sweden, ix. 20 *sq.*

Clashing of metal instruments a protection against witchcraft, ix. 158 ; used to dispel demons, ix. 233

Clasping of hands forbidden, iii. 298

Classificatory system of relationship, xi. 234 *n.*[1], 314 *n.*[4]

Claudianus, Lucius Minius, on the goddess of Hieropolis-Castabala, v. 168

Claudius, the Emperor, shrine of, at Nemi, i. 13 ; trial for incest under, ii. 115 ; his marriage with Agrippina, ii. 129 *n.*[1] ;

statues of, crowned with oak, ii. 177 $n.$[2];
his history of Etruria, ii. 196 $n.$; on the
Etruscan origin of Servius Tullius, ii.
196 $n.$; on the foreign descent of the
Roman kings, ii. 270 $n.$[6]; and the
rites of Attis, v. 266 ; his execution of
a Gaulish knight, x. 15

Claudius Gothicus, the Emperor, v. 266 $n.$[2]

Clavie at Burghead, made without the
use of a hammer, iii. 229 *sq.* ; the
burning of the, x. 266 *sq.*

Clavigero, F. S., historian of Mexico,
on the Mexican calendar, vi. 29 $n.$;
on Cinteotl, the Mexican goddess of
maize, ix. 286 $n.$[1]

Claws of sea-eagle, charm made from, i.
152

Clay, people smeared with white, at
festival, viii. 75 ; plastered on girls at
puberty, x. 31 ; bodies of novices
at initiation smeared with white, xi.
255 $n.$[1], 259

Clayton, A. C., on a Badaga funeral, ix.
36

Claytonia, a species of, principal vegetable food of the aborigines of Central
Australia, vii. 128

Cleanliness promoted by contagious
magic, i. 175, 342 ; fostered by superstition, iii. 130; personal, observed
in war, iii. 157, 158 $n.$[1]

Cleansing streets from superstitious
motive, beneficial effect of, ix. 205 *sq.*

Clearing land for cultivation, ceremonies
to appease the tree spirits at, ii. 36,
38 *sq.*

Cleary, Bridget, burnt as a witch in
Tipperary, x. 323 *sq.*

Cleary, Michael, burns his wife as a witch,
x. 323 *sq.*

Clee, in Lincolnshire, the Yule log at,
x. 257

Clee Hills, in Shropshire, fear of witchcraft in the, x. 342 $n.$[4]

Cleft stick, passage through a, in connexion with puberty and circumcision,
xi. 183 *sq.*

Clement of Alexandria on the Eleusinian
mysteries, vii. 39

Cleomenes, king of Sparta, and serpents,
v. 87

Cleon of Magnesia at Gades, v. 113

Cleostratus of Tenedos, said to have
introduced the Greek octennial cycle,
vii. 81

Clergyman employed to cut first corn at
harvest, viii. 51

Cleveland in Yorkshire, treatment of the
placentas of mares at, i. 199

Climacteris scandens, women's "sister"
among the Kulin, xi. 216

Climatic and geographical conditions,

their effect on national character, vi.
217

Clippings of hair, magic wrought through
iii. 268 *sqq.*, 275, 277, 278 *sq.* See
also Hair

—— of nails in popular cures, ix. 57, 58.
See *also* Nails

Clisthenes and Hippoclides, ii. 307 *sq.*

Clitus and Dryas, their contest for a
bride, ii. 307

—— and Pallene, ii. 307

" Clod festival of the fourth " at Benares,
i. 279

Clodd, Edward, on the external soul, xi.
97 $n.$[1]

Clog, the Yule, x. 247

Clonmel, trial for witch-burning at, x. 324

Clotaire murders his nephews, iii. 259

Clothes, homoeopathic magic of, i. 157 ;
magic sympathy between a person and
his, i. 205-207 ; of sacred persons
tabooed, iii. 131. See *also* Grave-
clothes

Cloths used to catch souls, iii. 46, 47, 48
52, 53, 61, 64, 67, 75 *sq.*

Clotilde, Queen, the murder of her grand
children, iii. 259

Cloud-dragon, myth of the, iv. 107

Clouds imitated by smoke, i. 249 ; imitation of, in rain-making, i. 249, 256,
261, 262, 263, 275 ; imitated by stones,
i. 256 ; magicians painted in imitation
of, i. 323

Clove-trees in blossom treated like pregnant women, ii. 28. See *also* Cloves

Clover, time for sowing, i. 167 ; four-
leaved, a counter-charm for witchcraft,
x. 316 ; found at Midsummer, xi. 62 *sq.*

Cloves, sexual ceremony to make cloves
grow, ii. 100. See *also* Clove-trees

Clovis, gift of touching for the evil
derived from, i. 370

Clown in spring ceremonies, ii. 82, 89 ;
at Whitsuntide, ii. 89 ; in processions,
ix. 244 *sq.*

Clubhouses of men in New Guinea, i.
125, iii. 168, 169; in the Caroline
Islands, iii. 193 ; in the Pelew Islands,
iii. 193 $n.$[2]

Clucking like a hen to recall a truant
soul, iii. 34, 35, 55, 74, 75

Clucking-hen, the, at threshing, vii. 277

Clue of yarn, divination by a, at Hallow-
e'en, x. 235, 240, 241, 243

Cluis Dessus and Cluis-Dessous, custom
of " Sawing the Old Woman " at, iv.
241 *sq.*

Clyack sheaf, vii. 158 *sqq.*, 215 *sq.*, viii. 43

Clyack-kebback, a cheese at the harvest
supper in Aberdeenshire, vii. 160

Clymenus, king of Arcadia, his incest, v.
44 $n.$[1]

Clytaemnestra, a native of Lacedaemon, ii. 279

Cnossus in Crete, sacred marriage of Zeus and Hera at, ii. 143 n.[1]; Minos at, iv. 70 sqq.; the labyrinth at, iv. 75 sqq.; the bull perhaps the king's crest at, iv. 111 sq.; prehistoric palace at, v. 34; marriage of the Bull-god to the Queen at, vii. 31; octennial tenure of kingship at, vii. 82, 85

Coal, magical, that turns to gold at Midsummer, xi. 60 sq.

Coast Murring tribe of New South Wales, the drama of resurrection exhibited to novices at initiation in the, xi. 235 sqq.

Cobern, effigy burnt on Shrove Tuesday at, x. 120

Coblentz, the Yule log near, x. 248

Cobra worshipped, i. 383 n.[4]; ceremonies after killing a, iii. 222 sq.; the crest of the Maharajah of Nagpur, iv. 132 sq.

Cobra-capella, guardian-deity of Issapoo, viii. 174

Coca-mother, among the Peruvians, vii. 172, 173 n.

Coccus Polonica and St. John's blood, xi. 56

Cochin, Cranganore in, i. 280

Cochin China, the Chams of, i. 144, ii. 28, iii. 202, 297, iv. 130 n.[1]; the Bahnars of, iii. 52, 58; tigers respected in, iii. 403, viii. 217; annual festival of the dead in, vi. 65; mode of disposing of ghosts in, ix. 62

Cock killed in fight not to be eaten by soldiers, i. 117; king represented with the feathers of a, iv. 85; as emblem of a priest of Attis, v. 279; corn-spirit as, vii. 276 sqq.; killed on harvest field, vii. 277 sq., xi. 280 n.; effigy of, in bonfire, x. 111; external soul of ogre in a, xi. 100

——, black, buried on spot where epileptic patient fell down, ix. 68 n.[2]; used as counter-charm to witchcraft, x. 321

—— and hen sacrificed by the Lithuanians at harvest, viii. 49 sq.; or hen, striking blindfold at a, xi. 279 n.[4]

——, red, killed to cure person struck by lightning, xi. 298 n.[2]

——, white, buried at boundary, iii. 109; sacrificed, viii. 117, 118; disease transferred to a, ix. 187; as scapegoat, ix. 210 n.[4]; burnt in Midsummer bonfire, xi. 40. See also Cocks

Cock-sheaf, vii. 276

Cock's blood poured on divining-rod, xi. 282

Cockatoos, magical ceremony for the multiplication of, i. 89

Cockchafer, external soul in a golden, xi. 140

Cockchafers, witches as, x. 322

Cocks as scapegoats, ix. 191 sq.

Coco-nut, soul of child deposited in a, x. 154 sq.

—— -nuts, magical stones to produce a crop of, i. 162; sacred and regarded as emblems of fertility in Upper India, ii. 51; gathered by pure youths, iii. 201

Coco-nut oil made by chaste women, iii. 201; a charm against demons, iii. 201

—— -nut palm worshipped, ii. 16; planted over navel-string and afterbirth of child, xi. 161, 163, compare xi. 164; attracts lightning, xi. 299 n.[2]

—— -nut trees revered, ii. 12, 16

Codjour or Cogiour, a priestly king of the Nubas, iii. 132 n.[1], viii. 114

Codrington, Dr. R. H., on the confusion of religion and magic in Melanesia, i. 227 sq.; on the supernatural powers ascribed to chiefs in Melanesia, i. 338; on mother-kin in Melanesia, vi. 211; on the Melanesian conception of the external soul, xi. 197 sq.

Codrus, king of Athens, Ionian kings descended from, i. 47

Coel Coeth, Hallowe'en bonfire, x. 239

Coffin, nails from a, in magic, i. 210, 211

Cogiour. See Codjour

Cohabitation of husband and wife enjoined as a matter of ritual, viii. 69, 70 n.[1]. See also Intercourse

Cohen, S. S., x. 128 n.[1]

Coil, sick children passed through a, xi. 185 sq.

Coimbatore, dancing-girls at, v. 62

Coincidence between the Christian and the heathen festivals of the divine death and resurrection, v. 308 sq.

Coins from the eyes of corpses, their magical virtue, i. 149; placed on the eyes of corpses, i. 149 n.[5]; portraits of kings not stamped on, iii. 98 sq.

Colchis, Phrixus in, iv. 162

Cold food, festival of the, in China, x. 137

—— weather, charm to bring on, i. 319; ceremonies to procure, i. 329 n.[1]

Cole, Lieut.-Colonel H. W. G., on a custom of the Lushais, xi. 185 sq.

Colic, a Bahnar cure for, iii. 59; popular remedies for, x. 17; leaping over bonfires as a preventive of, x. 107, 195 sq., 344; attributed to witchcraft, x. 344

Coligny calendar of Gaul, i. 17 n.[2], ix. 342 sqq.

Coll, Dr. Samuel Johnson in the island of, viii. 322; the Hole Stone in the island of, xi. 187

Collatinus, L. Tarquinius, one of the first consuls, ii. 288, 290
Colleda, an old Servian goddess, x. 259
Collobrieres in Provence, rain-making at, i. 307
Colluinn, custom of beating a cow's hide in the Highlands, viii. 323, 324
Colocasia antiquorum, charm used at gathering, ii. 23
Cologne, Petrarch at, on St. John's Eve, v. 247 *sq.* ; St. John's fourteen Midsummer victims at, xi. 27
Colombia, the Goajiro Indians of, iii. 30 *sq.*, 325, 352, x. 34 *n.*[1] ; the Muysca Indians of, iii. 121 ; the Aurohuaca Indians of, iii. 215 ; rule as to the felling of timber in, vi. 136 ; the Popayan Indians of, their belief in the transmigration of human souls into deer, viii. 286 ; Guacheta in, x. 74
Colophon, the Clarian Apollo at, iv. 80 *n.*[1]
Columbia, British, the Indians of, their use of magical images to procure fish, i. 108 ; taboos imposed on the parents of twins among the, i. 262 *sqq.* ; pay compliments to the first fish of the season, viii. 253
——, British, the Thompson Indians of, i. 132, 181, 197, 253, 288, 293, ii. 13, 208, iii. 37, 65, 117, 142, 181, 278, 399, viii. 81, 133, 140, 207, 226, 268, ix. 154 ; the Kwakiutl Indians of, i. 197, 201, 263, 324, iii. 53, 76, 188, 386, viii. 250 ; the Tsimshian Indians of, i. 262, viii. 254 ; the Nootka Indians of, i. 263, iii. 27, 146 *n.*[1], viii. 225, 251 ; the Lillooet Indians of, i. 265 ; the Shuswap Indians of, i. 265, 319, iii. 83, 142, 146 *n.*[1], viii. 238 ; the Skungen Indians of, iii. 32 ; the Bella Coola Indians of, iii. 34, x. 46, xi. 174 ; the Nass River in, iii. 76 ; the Carrier Indians of, iii. 197, 367 ; the Tsetsaut Indians of, iii. 198, 260 ; the Tinneh or Déné Indians of, iii. 240 ; the Kutonaqa of, iv. 183 ; the coast tribes of, their ceremonial cannibalism, vii. 18 *sqq.* ; the Koskimo of, vii. 20 *n.* ; the Nishga Indians of, viii. 106 ; the Okanaken Indians of, viii. 134
Columbia River, the Indians of, their customs in regard to the first salmon caught in the season, viii. 255
Columella, on chastity to be observed by those who handle food, ii. 205 ; on the date for the fertilization of fig-trees, ii. 314 ; on the fodder of cattle, ii. 328 *n.*[1] ; on caprification, ix. 258
Comana in Cappadocia, v. 136 *n.*[1]
—— in Pontus, worship of goddess

Ma at, v. 39, ix. 421 *n.*[1] ; swine not allowed to enter, v. 265 *n.*[1] ; sacred harlots at, ix. 370 *n.*[1]
Comana, the two cities, v. 168 *n.*[6]
Comanches, the, their way of procuring rain or sunshine, i. 297 ; changes in their language caused by fear of naming the dead, iii. 360
Combat, mortal, for the kingdom, ii. 322
Combe, in Oxfordshire, May garlands at, ii. 62 *n.*[2]
Combe d'Ain, x. 114
Combing the hair forbidden, i. 157, iii. 14, 159 *n.*, 181, 187, 203, 208, 264 ; thought to cause storms, iii. 271
Combretum primigenum, the sacred tree of the Herero, ii. 213, 218
Combs not to be used by wives during absence of camphor hunters, i. 125 ; in homoeopathic magic, i. 125, 157 ; used by girls in their seclusion at puberty, iii. 146 *n.*[1] ; of sacred persons, iii. 256
Comedies played as a rain-charm, i. 301 *n.*
Comitium, dances of the Salii in the, ix. 232
Commagny, the priory of, i. 307
Commemoration of the Dead at Athens, v. 234
Comminges, Midsummer fires in, x. 192 *sq.*
Commodus, the Emperor, conspiracy against, v. 273 ; addicted to the worship of Isis, vi. 118
Common objects, names of, changed when they coincide more or less with those of relations, iii. 335, 336, 337, 339, 339 *sq.*, 340, 341, 345, 346 ; changed when they are the names of the dead, iii. 358 *sqq.*, 375, or the names of chiefs and kings, iii. 375, 376 *sqq.*
—— words tabooed, iii. 392 *sqq.*
Communal rights over women, v. 40, 61 *n.*
—— taboos, vii. 109 *n.*[2]
Communion with demons by drinking blood, i. 383 ; with deity in Eleusinian mysteries, vii. 38, 161 ; with deity by eating of new fruits, viii. 83 ; with the dead through food, viii. 154 ; with the dead by swallowing their ashes, viii. 156 *sqq.* ; with deity by eating his body and drinking his blood, viii. 325 ; with saints, alive or dead, by means of stones, ix. 21 *sq.*
Communion bread baked from the first corn cut, viii. 51
Communism, tradition of sexual, ii. 284
Community, welfare of, bound up with the life of the divine king, x. 1 *sq.* ;

purified in the persons of its representatives, xi. 24
Comorin, Cape, iv. 46
Compelling rain-gods to give rain, i. 296 *sqq.*
Compitalia, a Roman festival, effigies dedicated at, viii. 94, 96, 107
Complexity of social phenomena, i. 332 ; of religious phenomena, viii. 36
Compromise of Christianity with paganism, parallel with Buddhism, v. 310 *sqq.*
Comrie, well of St. Fillan at, ii. 161
Con or Cun, a thunder-god of the Indians of the Andes, ii. 370
Conca d'Oro at Palermo, i. 299
Concealment from superstitious motives at eating and drinking, iii. 116 *sqq.* ; of the face or person from superstitious motives, iii. 120 *sqq.* ; of miscarriage in childbed, supposed effects of, iii. 152 *sqq.*, 211, 213 ; of cut hair and nails to prevent them from falling into the hands of sorcerers, iii. 276 *sqq.*; of personal names from fear of magic, iii. 320 *sqq.*; of graves, vi. 103 *sqq.*, viii. 98 *sqq.*
Conception in women, supposed causes of, i. 100, v. 96, 102, 103, 104, 105 ; caused by trees, ii. 51, 56 *sq.*, 316-318 ; supposed, without sexual intercourse, v. 91, 93 *n.*[2], 96 *sqq.*, 264, ix. 18 ; animals and plants as causes of, in women, v. 97 *sq.*, 104 *sq. See also* Impregnation
Conchucos, the, of Peru, esteemed foxes sacred, viii. 258 *n.*[1]
Conciliating the spirits of the land, iii. 110 *sq.*
Conciliation involved in religion, i. 224 ; of slain enemies, iii. 182
Concord, temple of, at Rome, i. 11, 21 *n.*[2]
Concordia, nurse of St. Hippolytus, i. 21 *n.*[2]
Concubines, temporary king allowed to use the real king's, iv. 114 ; human, of the god Ammon, v. 72 ; of a king taken by his successor, ix. 368
Condé, in Normandy, ix. 183 ; bonfires on Christmas Eve near, x. 266
Conder, C. R., on "holy men" in Syria, v. 77 *n.*[4]; on turning money at the new moon, v. 149 *n.*[2]
Condor, the bird of the thunder-god, ii. 370
Conduct, standard of, shifted from natural to supernatural basis, iii. 213 *sq.*
Conductivity, electric, of various kinds of wood, xi. 299 *n.*[2]
Condylea in Arcadia, sacred grove of Artemis at, v. 291

Cone, image of Astarte, v. 14
Cones as emblems of a goddess, v. 34 *sqq.*, 165, 166 ; votive, found in Babylonia, v. 35 *n.*[5]
Confession of the dead, the Egyptian, vi. 13 *sq.*
—— of sins, i. 266, iii. 114, 191, 195, 211 *sq.*, 214 *sqq.*, viii. 69, ix. 31, 36, 127 ; enjoined as a religious duty among the Huichol Indians, i. 124 ; originally a magical ceremony, iii. 217; the Jewish, over the scapegoat, ix. 210
Conflagrations, bonfires supposed to protect against, x. 107, 108, 140, 142, 344 ; brands of Midsummer bonfires thought to be a protection against, x. 165, 174, 183, 188, 196 ; the Yule log a protection against, x. 248 *sq.*, 250, 255, 256, 258 ; Midsummer flowers a protection against, xi. 48 ; mountain arnica a protection against, xi. 58 ; oak-mistletoe a protection against, xi. 85
Conflict of calendars, solar and lunar, x. 218
Conflicts, sanguinary, as rain-charms, i. 258 ; annual, at the New Year, old intention of, ix. 184
Confucianism, its success due to the personal influence of its founder, vi. 159 *sq.*
Confusion between a man and his totem, i. 107
—— of magic and religion, i. 226 *sq.*; in Melanesia, i. 227 *sq.*; in ancient India, i. 228 *sq.*; in ancient Egypt, i. 230 *sq.*; in modern Europe, i. 231 *sqq.*; the confusion not primitive, i. 233 *sq.*
Congo Free State, the Ba-Yaka and Ba-Yanzi of the, i. 348, iii. 186 *n.*[1]; the Tofoke of the, vii. 119
Congo, the French, the Fans of the, xi. 161
——, kingdom or region of, palm-wine offered to trees in the, ii. 15 ; custom observed by pregnant women in the, ii. 58 ; the pontiff Chitomé in the, iii. 5, iv. 14 ; conjuring spirits at meals in the, iii. 120 ; food taboos in the, iii. 137 ; precaution as to the spittle of the king of the, iii. 289 *sq.*; priest dressed as a woman in, vi. 254 *sq.*; images stuck with nails in the, ix. 70 *n.*[1]; birth-trees in the, xi. 161 *sq.* ; theory of the external soul in the, xi. 200; the Bushongo of the, xi. 229 *n.*; use of bull-roarers in the, xi. 229 *n.*
——, the Lower, belief in the reincarnation of the dead among the natives of, i. 103 *sq.* ; superstition as to resemblance between parent and child among the tribes of, iii. 89 ; natives of, their belief as to stepping over a person,

iii. 423 *sq.* ; burial of infants on the, v. 91 ; taboos observed by women who plant seeds among the tribes of, vii. 115 *sq.* ; seclusion of girls at puberty on the, x. 31 ; rites of initiation on the, xi. 251 *sqq.*

Congo, the Upper, Kibanga on, iv. 34 ; the Bangala of, vii. 119 ; the Boloki of, xi. 161, 229 *n.*

——, King of Rain at mouth of the, ii. 2

Congo negroes, their belief in the abstraction of souls by sorcerers, iii. 70

—— tribes, recall of stray souls among the, iii. 44 *sq.*

Congrégation de Notre Dame at Paris, Childermas at the, ix. 337

Conibos Indians of the Ucayali River, regard thunder as the voice of the dead, ii. 183 *n.*[2] ; their theory of earthquakes, v. 198

Conical stone as divine emblem, v. 165, 166. *See also* Cones

Conitz, in West Prussia, saying as to wind in corn at, vii. 288

Conjunction of sun and moon, viii. 15 *n.*[1] ; a time for marriage, iv. 73 ; time chosen for ritual observances, viii. 15 *n.*[1]

Conjuring spirits at meals, iii. 120

Connaught, taboos observed by the ancient kings of, iii. 11 *sq.* ; Midsummer fires in, x. 203 ; cave of Cruachan in, x. 226 ; palace of the kings of, xi. 127

Connemara, Midsummer fires in, x. 203

Conquering races, great, have advanced civilization, i. 128

Conquerors sometimes leave a nominal kingship to the conquered, ii. 288 *sq.*

Consecration of the sacrificer of Soma in Vedic India, iii. 159 *n.*; of the first-born among the Hebrews, iv. 172 ; among the ancient Italians, iv. 187

Conservation of energy, viii. 262, 303

" Consort, the divine," ii. 131, 135

Constance, the Council of, forbade processions with bears and other animals, viii. 326 *n.*[3]

——, the Lake of, superstition as to St. John's Day on, xi. 26

Constantine destroys temple of Astarte, v. 28 ; suppresses sacred prostitution, v. 37 ; removes standard cubit from the Serapeum, vi. 216 *sq.*

Constantinople, accusation of binding the winds by magic at, i. 325 ; protected against flies and gnats, viii. 281 ; column at, xi. 157

Constellations observed by the aborigines of Victoria, vii. 308 ; observed by savages, vii. 313, 314 *sq.*, 315, 317

Constitution of Athens, Aristotle's, ii. 137 *n.*[1]

Consuls, the first Roman, ii. 290

Consulship at Rome, institution of, ii. 290 *sq.*

Consummation of marriage prevented by knots and locks, iii. 299 *sqq.*

Consumption transferred to bird, ix. 51, xi. 187 ; ashes of the Midsummer fires a cure for, x. 194 *sq.*

Consumptive patients passed through holes in stones or rocks, xi. 186 *sq.*

Consus and Ops, vi. 233 *n.*[6]

Contact with sacred things deemed dangerous, viii. 27 *sqq.* ; between certain foods in stomach of eater forbidden, viii. 83 *sqq.*, 90

—— or contagion in magic, law of, i. 52, 53

Contagion of death, banishment of the, ix. 37

Contagious magic, i. 52, 53 *sq.*, 174-214, iii. 246, 268, 272; of teeth, i. 176-182 ; of navel-string and afterbirth (placenta), i. 182-201 ; of wound and weapon, i. 201 *sqq.*; of footprints, i. 207-212 ; of other impressions, i. 213 *sq.* ; of the man-god, iii. 132

—— taboos, i. 117

Contempt of death, iv. 142 *sqq.*

Contest for the kingship at Whitsuntide, ii. 89 *sq.* ; for the throne of Egypt, traditions of a, vi. 17 *sq.*

——, Ancestral, at the Eleusinian Games, vii. 71, 74, 77

Contests for a bride, ii. 305 *sqq.*; for possession of the corn-spirit, vii. 74 *sq.*, 180 ; between reapers, vii. 74 *sq.*, 136, 140, 141, 142, 144, 152, 153 *sq.*, 155, 156, 164 *sq.*, 219, 253, 273 ; between binders of corn, vii. 136, 137, 138, 218 *sq.*, 220, 221, 222, 253, 273 ; between threshers, vii. 147 *sqq.*, 218, 219 *sq.*, 221 *sq.*, 223 *sq.*, 253

——, dramatic, between actors representing Summer and Winter, iv. 254 *sqq.*

Conti, Nicolo, on religious suicide, iv. 54

Continence in magical ceremonies, i. 88 ; required during the search for the sacred cactus, i. 124 ; at rain-making ceremonies, i. 257, 259 ; required of parents of twins, i. 266 ; practised before fertility ceremonies, ii. 98 ; practised in order to make the crops grow, ii. 104 *sqq.* ; enjoined on people during the rounds of sacred pontiff, iii. 5 ; of priests, iii. 6, 159 *n.* ; on eve of period of taboo, iii. 11 ; observed by those who have handled the dead, iii. 141, 142 ; during war, iii. 157, 158 *n.*[1], 161, 163, 164, 165 ; after victory, iii. 166 *sqq.*, 175, 178, 179, 181 ; by cannibals, iii. 188 ; by fishers and hunters, iii. 191,

192, 193, 194, 195, 196, 197, 198, 207; by workers in salt-pans, iii. 200; at brewing beer, wine, and poison, iii. 200 *sq.*, 201 *sq.*; at baking, iii. 201; at making coco-nut oil, iii. 201; at building canoes, iii. 202; at house-building, iii. 202; at making or repairing dams, iii. 202; on trading voyages, iii. 203; after festivals, iii. 204; on journeys, iii. 204; while cattle are at pasture, iii. 204; by lion-killers and bear-killers, iii. 220, 221; before handling holy relics, iii. 272; by tabooed men, iii. 293; at consulting an oracle, iii. 314; at sowing and reaping, vii. 109 *n.*[2]; and fasting observed before ploughing and sowing, viii. 14, 15; at festival of first-fruits, viii. 75; combined with abstinence from salt, viii. 75, 93, 93 *n.*; after eating of a god, viii. 93; at bladder festival of the Esquimaux, viii. 248; during Lent, ix. 348; as preparation for walking through fire, xi. 3. *See also* Chastity

Conty, in France, Lenten fires at, x. 113

Conway, Professor R. S., on the etymology of Virbius, ii. 379 *n.*[5]; on the etymology of Soranus, xi. 15 *n.*[1]

Conybeare, F. C., on Christians worshipping each other as Christs, i. 407 *n.*[3]; on the feminine sex of the Holy Ghost, iv. 5 *n.*[3]

Cook, A. B., i. 40 *n.*[3] and [4], ii. 307 *n.*[2], v. 49 *n.*[6]; on the slope of Virbius, i. 4 *n.*[5]; on circular basement at Nemi, i. 13 *n.*[5]; on Manius Egerius, i. 23 *n.*; on association of horse and wolf, i. 27 *n.*[5]; on double-headed bust at Nemi, i. 42 *n.*[1]; on the name Egeria, ii. 172 *n.*[3]; on parallelism between Rome and Aricia, ii. 173 *n.*[2]; on personification of Zeus by Greek kings, ii. 177 *n.*[6]; on the Alban kings, ii. 178 *n.*[3]; on the Alban sow, ii. 187 *n.*[4]; on substitution of poplar for oak, ii. 220 *n.*[3]; on the consulship, ii. 290 *n.*[3]; on the death of Servius Tullius, ii. 321 *n.*[1]; on gongs at Dodona, ii. 358 *n.*[4]; on the oak as the tree of Zeus, ii. 359 *n.*[3]; on connexion of the King of the Wood with the Silvii, ii. 379 *n.*[4]; on Plautus, *Casina*, ii. 379 *n.*[5]; on association of Diana with the oak, ii. 380 *n.*[4]; on Jupiter-Janus, Juno-Diana, ii. 383 *n.*[2]; on derivation of *janua* from *Janus*, ii. 384 *n.*[2]; on Minos and Pasiphae, iv. 71 *n.*[2]; on octennial tenure of Greek kingship, iv. 78 *n.*[2]; on festival of Laurel-bearing at Thebes, iv. 79 *n.*[1], vi. 241 *n.*[3]; on sacred oak at Delphi, iv. 80; on substitution of laurel for oak, iv. 81 *sq.*; as to a scene on the frieze of the Parthenon, iv. 89 *n.*[5]; on assimilation of Olympic victors to Zeus, iv. 90; on name of priest of Corycian Zeus, v. 155 *n.*[1]; on death of Romulus, vi. 98 *n.*[2]; on traces of mother-kin in myth and ritual of Hercules, vi. 259 *n.*[4]; on use of bells and gongs to ban demons in antiquity, ix. 246 *n.*[2]; on the oak of Errol, xi. 284 *n.*[1]

Cook, Captain James, on the Tahitian belief in spirits or gods, ix. 80 *sq.*

Cook, menstruous women not allowed to, x. 80, 82, 84, 90

Cooking, taboos as to, iii. 147 *sq.*, 156, 165, 169, 178, 185, 193, 194, 198, 209, 221, 256

Cooks, Roman, required to be chaste, ii. 115 *sq.*, 205

Coomassie, in Ashantee, human sacrifice for earthquake at, v. 201; the festival of the new yams at, viii. 62 *sqq.*; bones of Sir Charles M'Carthy kept as fetishes at, viii. 149

Cooper, Rev. Sydney, on the harvest "neck" in Cornwall, vii. 262 *n.*[3]

Coorgs, the, of Southern India, their ceremonies at reaping and eating the new rice, viii. 55 *sq.*

Cootchie, a demon of the Dieri, expelled by medicine-men, ix. 110

Copenhagen, the museum at, ii. 352; bathing on St. John's Eve at, v. 248; statue of Demeter at, vii. 43 *n.*[5]

Copper, unstamped, early Italian money, i. 23

Copper needle, story of man who could only be killed by a, xi. 314

—— rings as amulets, iii. 315

—— River, Esquimaux of the, iii. 184

Coptic calendar, vi. 6 *n.*[3]

—— church forbade use of iron in exorcism, iii. 235; forbade the tying of magic knots, iii. 310 *n.*[5]; enjoins continence during Lent, ix. 348

Cor-mass, procession of wicker giants at Dunkirk, xi. 34

Cora Indians of Mexico, their magical images, i. 55 *sq.*; their dance at sowing, ix. 238; their dramatic dances, ix. 381

Coral rings as amulets, iii. 315

Coran, the, in incantations, i. 64; verse of, recited as a charm, ix. 62. *See also* Koran

Corannas of South Africa, custom as to succession among the, iv. 191 *sq.*; their children after an illness passed under an arch, xii. 192 '

Corc, his purification, ii. 116

Cordia ovalis, used in kindling fire by friction, ii. 210

Cords, knotted, in magic, iii. 299, 302,

303 *sq.*, 309 ; tied tightly round the bodies of girls at puberty, x. 92 *n.*[1]
Corea, offerings to souls of the dead in trees in, ii. 31 ; the effigy of the king not struck on coins of, iii. 99 ; clipped hair burned in, iii. 283 ; custom of swinging in, iv. 284 *sq.* ; dance of eunuchs in, v. 270 *n.*[2] ; use of effigies to prolong life in, viii. 105 ; first-fruits of all crops formerly offered to king of, viii. 122 ; bones of tigers prized in, as means of inspiring courage, viii. 145 ; cairns to which each passer-by adds a stone in, ix. 11 ; offerings at cairns in, ix. 27 ; traps for demons in, ix. 61 *sq.* ; belief in demons in, ix. 99 *sq.*; spirit of disease expelled in, ix. 119 ; annual expulsion of demons in, ix. 147 ; the tug-of-war in, ix. 177 *sq.*; custom observed after childbirth by women in, x. 20 ; use of torches to ensure good crops in, x. 340
——, the kings of, held responsible for rain and the crops, i. 355 ; formerly confined to their palace, iii. 125 ; not to be touched with iron, iii. 226 ; their names not to be uttered by their subjects, iii. 376
Coreans, their belief as to absence of soul in sleep, iii. 41 ; their ceremony on the fifteenth day of the moon, vi. 143 ; their annual ceremonies for the riddance of evils, ix. 202 *sq.*
Corfu, May songs and trees in, ii. 63 *sq.*
Corinth, family supposed to control the winds at, i. 324
Corinthians make images of Dionysus out of a pine-tree, vii. 4
Cormac, on Beltane fires, x. 157
Cormac Mac Art, king of Ireland, iv. 39
Corn ground by pregnant women, i. 140 ; defiled persons kept from the, ii. 112 ; reaped ear of, displayed at mysteries of Eleusis, ii. 138 *sq.*, vii. 38; sheaf of, dressed up to represent Death, iv. 248 ; water thrown on the last corn cut, a rain-charm, v. 237 *sq.* ; sprouting from the dead body of Osiris, vi. 89 ; personified as Demeter, vii. 42 ; the various kinds of, called " Demeter's fruits," vii. 42 ; first-fruits of, offered to Demeter and Persephone at Eleusis, vii. 53 *sqq.* ; first bestowed on the Athenians by Demeter, vii. 54 ; personified as female, vii. 130 ; wreath of, made from last sheaf, vii. 134 ; double personification of, as mother and daughter, vii. 207 *sqq.*; the first corn cut, customs connected with, vii. 215 *sq.* ; patches of unreaped, left at harvest, vii. 233 ; identification of persons with, vii. 252 ; the

last left standing, the corn-spirit supposed to be in, vii. 254, 268 ; the new, eaten sacramentally, viii. 48 *sqq.*; the first cut, used to bake the communion bread, viii. 51 ; sanctity of the, viii. 110 ; the last cut, corn-spirit in, viii. 328 ; charm to make the corn grow tall, x. 18 ; thrown on the man who brings the Yule log, x. 260, 262, 264 ; blazing besoms flung aloft to make the corn grow high, x. 340
Corn and grapes, symbols of the god of Tarsus, v. 119, 143 ; of the god of Ibreez, v. 121 ; figured with double-headed axe on Lydian coin, v. 183
—— and poppies as symbols of Demeter, vii. 43 *sq.*
—— and vine, emblems of the gods of Tarsus and Ibreez, v. 160 *sq.*
Corn Baby at harvest, vii. 150 *sq.*, 152, 292
—— -bull at threshing, vii. 291
—— -cat in the corn, vii. 280
—— -cow at reaping, vii. 289
—— -dog at harvest, vii. 272
—— -ears, Queen of the, vii. 146 ; crown of, vii. 163, 221, 283 ; wreath of, as badge of priestly office, ix. 232
—— festivals of the Cora Indians, ix. 381
—— -flowers, the blue, supposed danger of plucking, vii. 272, 282
—— -foal, the corn-spirit as, vii. 294
—— -fool at threshing, vii. 148
—— -goat, vii. 282, 283, 286, 287
—— -god, Adonis as a, v. 230 *sqq.*; Attis as a, v. 279 ; mourned at midsummer, vi. 34 ; Osiris as a, vi. 89 *sqq.*, 96 *sqq.*
—— -harvest, the first-fruits of the, offered at Lammas, iv. 101 *sq.*
—— -horse, the corn-spirit as, vii. 294
—— -maiden at harvest, vii. 150, 230 ; in the Highlands of Scotland, vii. 155 *sqq.*, 164 *sqq.*
—— -mallet at threshing, vii. 148
—— -man at harvest, vii. 223 ; the goal of a women's race, vii. 76 *sq.*
—— -mother, the, vii. 150 ; at Eleusis, ii. 139 ; in Northern Europe, vii. 131 *sqq.*; makes the crops to grow, vii. 133 ; in last sheaf, vii. 133 *sqq.* ; personated by a woman, vii. 150, 261 ; primitive character of the European, vii. 170 ; in America, vii. 171 *sqq.*; in many lands, vii. 171 *sqq.* ; in canton of Zurich, vii. 232
—— -pug at threshing, vii. 273
—— queen made out of last sheaf, vii. 146
—— -reapers, songs of the, vii. 214 *sqq.*
—— -reaping in Egypt, Palestine, and Greece, date of the, i. 32, v. 231 *n.*[3]
—— -sheaf, image of Metsik made of a, ii. 55

Corn-sieve, severed limbs of Osiris placed on a, vi. 97 ; new-born infant placed in, vii. 7 ; beaten at ceremony of expulsion of poverty, ix. 145. *See also* Winnowing-fan

—— -sow at harvest, vii. 271, 298

—— -spirit called the Old Man or the Old Woman, iv. 253 *sq.* ; Tammuz or Adonis as a, v. 230 *sqq.* ; propitiation of the, perhaps fused with a worship of the dead, v. 233 *sqq.* ; represented as a dead old man, vi. 48, 96 ; represented by human victims, vi. 97, 106 *sq.*; contests for possession of the, vii. 74 *sq.*, 180 ; conceived as old, vii. 136 *sqq.* ; in last sheaf threshed, vii. 139, 147, 168, viii. 48 ; represented in duplicate, vii. 139 ; lurks among the corn in the barn till driven out by the threshing-flail, vii. 147, 274 *sq.*, 286 ; personal representative of, killed in mimicry, vii. 149 *sq.*, 224 *sq.* ; conceived as young, vii. 150 *sqq.* ; as Bride and Bridegroom, vii. 162 *sqq.* ; as male and female, vii. 164, viii. 9 ; as female, both old and young, vii. 164 *sqq.* ; represented by person who cuts, binds, or threshes the last corn, vii. 167 *sq.*, 220 *sqq.*, 236, 253 *sq.* ; fertilizing influence of, vii. 168 ; its influence on women, vii. 168 ; represented by human beings, vii. 168, 204 *sqq.*, viii. 333 ; preserved in last sheaf, vii. 171 ; conceived by the Iroquois as a woman, vii. 177 ; in form of an old man, vii. 206 *sq.* ; conceived either as immanent in the corn or as external to it, vii. 211 ; in first corn cut, vii. 215 ; personal representative of, killed in mimicry, vii. 216 ; killing the, vii. 216 *sqq.*, 223 *sqq.* ; represented by living man, vii. 224 ; represented by a puppet, vii. 224 ; represented by persons wrapt in corn, vii. 225 *sq.* ; represented by a stranger, vii. 225 *sqq.*, 230 *sq.*; conceived as poor and robbed by the reapers, vii. 231 *sqq.* ; slain in his human representatives, vii. 251 *sqq.* ; in last standing corn, vii. 254, 268 ; the neck of the, vii. 268 ; beheaded when last corn is cut, vii. 268 ; the tail of the, vii. 268, 272, 300, viii. 10, 43; as animal, vii. 270 *sqq.*, xi. 43 *sqq.* ; as wolf or dog, vii. 271 *sqq.*, viii. 327; as cock, vii. 276 *sqq.* ; killed in form of live cock, vii. 277 *sq.* ; as hare, vii. 279 *sq.* ; as cat, vii. 280 *sq.*; as goat, vii. 281 *sqq.*; killed as goat, vii. 284 *sq.*, 287, viii. 327 *sq.*; lame, vii. 284 ; as bull, cow, or ox, vii. 288 *sqq.*, viii. 6 *sqq.*, 8, 34; killed in form of bull, vii. 290, 291 *sq.* ; killed at threshing,

vii. 291 *sq.* ; in form of calf, vii. 292 ; as old and young in form of cow and calf, vii. 292 ; as horse or mare, vii. 292 *sqq.* ; as a bird, vii. 295; as a quail, vii. 295 ; as fox, vii. 296 *sq.* ; as pig (boar, sow), vii. 298 *sqq.*; in form of boar, vii. 301, viii. 328 ; immanent in the last sheaf, vii. 301 ; on the animal embodiments of the, vii. 303 *sqq.*; represented by an ox, viii. 9 *sqq.* ; killed in animal form and eaten sacramentally, viii. 20 ; reason for killing the, viii. 138 ; as a bear, viii. 325 *sqq.* ; represented dramatically, viii. 325 ; as ram, viii. 328 ; kept through the winter in the form of an animal, viii. 328 ; represented by a man called the Straw-bear, viii. 329 ; human representative of the, dragged over the fresh furrows, viii. 332, 333 ; in last standing corn, x. 12 ; human representatives of, put to death, xi. 25

Corn-spirits, male and female, a pair of, vii. 286

—— -stalks, harvesters wrapt up in, vii. 220 *sqq.*

—— -steer at reaping last ears of corn, vii. 289

—— -stuffed effigies of Osiris buried with the dead as a symbol of resurrection, vi. 90 *sq.*, 114

—— -wolf in corn, vii. 272, 273, 275

—— -woman, vii. 230, 233 ; at threshing, vii. 149 ; among the North American Indians, vii. 177

—— -wreaths as first-fruits, v. 43 ; worn by Arval Brethren, v. 44 *n.*

Cornaby, Rev. W. A., iv. 273 ; on reported substitutes for capital punishment in China, iv. 275 *sq.*

Corne, near Tusculum, sacred grove of Diana at, ii. 190 *n.*[3]

Cornel branches, men and beasts beaten with, for their health, ix. 266

—— -tree, sacred, in Rome, ii. 10 ; in popular remedy, ix. 55 ; laziness transferred to a, ix. 55 ; wood used to kindle need-fire, x. 286

Corners of fields not to be reaped, vii. 234 *sq.*

Cornford, F. M., on the Olympic victors as personifying the Sun and Moon, iv. 91 *n.*[7]

Cornish customs on May Day, ii. 52, 60, 67

Cornouaille, in Brittany, weather forecast for the year at, ix. 323 *sq.*

Cornstalks, festival of the, at Eleusis, vii. 63

Cornutus on the poppy as a symbol of Demeter, vii. 44 ; on Persephone as the seed sown, vii. 46 *n.*[2]

Cornwall, May Day custom as to hawthorn in bloom in, ii. 52 ; temporary king in, iv. 153 *sq.* ; custom of "crying the neck" in, vii. 266 *sq.* ; Snake Stones in, x. 15, 16 *n.*[1] ; Midsummer fires in, x. 199 *sq.* ; burnt sacrifices to stay cattle disease in, x. 300 *sq.* ; holed stone through which people used to creep in, xi. 187

Coro, province of Venezuela, custom of drinking powdered body of dead chief in, viii. 157

Coronation, human sacrifices to prolong a king's life at his, vi. 223

Coronation ceremony in England, challenge to mortal combat at, ii. 322

Corp chre, magical clay image in Scotland, i. 68 *sq.*

Corporal punishment, voluntary substitutes for, in China, iv. 275 *sq.*

Corporeal relics of dead kings confer right to throne, iv. 202 *sq.*

Corpse, priest of Earth forbidden to see a, x. 4

"Corpse-praying priest," ix. 45

Corpses, knots not allowed about, iii. 310 ; devoured by members of Secret Societies, ix. 377

Corpulence regarded as a distinction and beauty, ii. 297

Corpus Christi Day, the Slaying of the Dragon on the Sunday after, ii. 163 ; the Pleiades worshipped by the Peruvian Indians on, vii. 310 ; processions on, x. 165

Corrèze, district of the Auvergne, superstition as to reflections in, iii. 95

—— and Creuse, departments of, St. John's fires in the, x. 190

Corsica, blood-revenge in, ii. 321 ; Midsummer fires in, x. 209

Corsicans divine by the shoulder-blades of sheep, iii. 229 *n.*[4]

Corycian cave, priests of Zeus at the, v. 145 ; the god of the, v. 152 *sqq.* ; described, v. 153 *sq.* ; saffron at the, v. 187 ; name perhaps derived from crocus, v. 187

Corycus in Cilicia, ruins of, v. 153

Cos, king of, sacrifices to Hestia, i. 45 ; titular kings in, i. 46 *n.*[4] ; sanctuary of Aesculapius in, ii. 10 ; altar of Rainy Zeus in, ii. 360 ; traces of mother-kin in, vi. 259 ; Sacred Marriage in, vi. 259 *n.*[4] ; bridegroom dressed as woman in, vi. 260 ; harvest-home in, vii. 47 ; image of Demeter in, vii. 47, 61 ; Zeus Polieus in, viii. 5 *n.*[2] ; custom of beating cattle in March in, ix. 266 ; effigies of Judas burnt at Easter in, x. 130 ; Midsummer fires in, x. 212

Cosenza in Calabria, Easter custom at, v. 254

Cosmogonies, primitive, perhaps influenced by human sacrifices, ix. 409 *sqq.*

Cosquin, E., on the book of Esther, ix. 367 *n.*[3] ; on helpful animals and external souls in folk-tales, xi. 133 *n.*[1]

Cosse de Nau, the Yule log, x. 251

Costa Rica, the Bribri Indians of, iii. 147, x. 86 ; Indians of, their treatment of the bones of animals, viii. 259 *n.*[1] ; their customs in fasts, x. 20 ; ceremonial uncleanness among the, x. 65 *n.*[1] ; the Guatusos of, xi. 230 *n.*

Côte d'Or, the Fox at reaping in, vii. 296

Cotton, the Mother of, in the Punjaub, vii. 178 ; treatment of first cotton picked, viii. 119

Cotton-bleacher, human god the son of a, i. 376

Cottonwood trees, the shades or spirits of, ii. 12

Cotys, king of Lydia, v. 187

Coudreau, H., on the custom of stinging with ants among the Indians of French Guiana, x. 63 *sq.*

Coughs transferred to animals, ix. 51, 52

Couit-gil, the spirit of a dead person, among the aborigines of Victoria, iii. 350

Coulommiers, in France, notion as to mistletoe at, xi. 316 *n.*[1]

Counter-charm for witchcraft, "scoring above the breath," x. 316 *n.*[2]

Couples married within the year obliged to dance by torchlight, x. 115, 339

Coupling ewes and rams, the time for, ii. 328, 328 *n.*[4]

Couppé, Mgr., on the belief in demons in New Britain, ix. 82

Courage acquired by eating the flesh of fierce beasts, viii. 140, 141 *sqq.* ; seated in gall-bladder, viii. 145 *sq.* ; acquired by eating the flesh or drinking the blood of brave men, viii. 148 *sqq.*

Court etiquette, iv. 39 *sq.*

Courtiers required to imitate their sovereign, iv. 39 *sq.*

Cousins, male and female, not allowed to mention each other's names, iii. 344

Couteau or Knife Indians, viii. 227 *n.*

Covenant formed by eating together, iii. 130 ; formed by mixing the blood of the covenanting parties, iii. 130 ; spittle used in making a, iii. 290

Coventry, Midsummer giants at, xi. 37

Covering up mirrors at a death, iii. 94 *sq.*

Cow bewitched, iii. 93 ; ceremony of rebirth from a golden, iii. 113 ; as symbol of the moon, iv. 71 *sq.* ; image of, in the rites of Osiris, vi. 50, 84 ;

Isis represented with the head of a, vi. 50 ; thought to be impregnated by moonshine, vi. 130 *sq.* ; in calf treated like woman in childbed, vii. 33 ; corn-spirit as, vii. 288 *sqq.*

Cow, black, in rain-charm, i. 290

——, white, with red ears, used in expiation, ii. 116

Cow-goddess Shenty, vi. 88

—— -headed women, statuettes of, found at Lycosura, viii. 21 *n.*[4]

Cow's hide, thresher of last corn wrapt in, vii. 291 ; custom of beating the, on Hogmanay, viii. 322 *sqq.*

Cowboy of the king of Unyoro, taboos observed by the, iii. 159 *n.*

Cows, the afterbirths of, how treated, i. 198 *sq.* ; charm to increase the milk of, i. 198 *sq.* ; milked as a rain-charm, i. 284 ; washed in dew on Midsummer morning, ii. 127 ; pregnant, sacrificed to the Earth Goddess, ii. 229 ; milked through a ring as a precaution against witchcraft, iii. 314 *sq.* ; sacred to Isis, vi. 50 ; milked by women, vii. 118 ; the Hindoo worship of, viii. 37 ; and their milk, superstitions as to, viii. 84 *ns.*[1] and [2] ; bewitched on Walpurgis Night, ix. 162 ; as scapegoats, ix. 193, 216 ; witches steal milk from, x. 343 ; mistletoe given to, xi. 86 ; milked through a hole in a branch or a " witch's nest," xi. 185

Coyohuacan, city of Mexico, paste idol eaten by warriors in, viii. 91

Coyote not to be named by children in winter, iii. 399

Crab in rain-charm, i. 289

Crabs used to extract vicious propensity, ix. 34 ; change their skin, ix. 303

Crackers ignited to expel demons, ix. 117, 146 *sq.* ; burnt to frighten ghosts, xi. 17, 18

Crackling of grain in fire a sign that the dead are eating it, viii. 65

Cracow, customs as to the last sheaf in the district of, vii. 145 ; Midsummer fires in the district of, x. 175

Craig, Captain Wolsey, on unlucky marriages in Barar, ii. 57 *n.*[4]

Crane, emblem of longevity, i. 169 *n.*[1] ; dance called the, iv. 75

Cranes, trumpeting of the, signal for ploughing, vii. 45 ; their seasons of migration, vii. 45 *n.*[1]

Cranganore in Cochin, shrine of the goddess Bhagavati at, i. 280

Crannogs or lake-dwellings in the British Islands, ii. 352

Crannon, in Thessaly, rain-making by means of a chariot at, i. 309 ; coins of, i. 309 *n.*[6]

Crassus, Publicius Licinius, funeral games in his honour, iv. 96

Crawfish in homoeopathic magic, i. 156 ; worshipped by Indians of Peru, viii. 250

Crawley, E., on the external soul in the placenta and navel-string, i. 201 *n.*[1]

Cream, ceremony for thickening, x. 262

Cream-bowl wreathed with hawthorn in bloom on May morning, ii. 52

Creation, myths of, iv. 106 *sqq.* ; Babylonian legend of, iv. 106, 110

—— of the world thought to be annually repeated, v. 284 ; legends of, influenced by human sacrifices, ix. 409 *sqq.*

Creator, the grave of the, iv. 3 ; beheaded, ix. 410 ; sacrifices himself daily to create the world afresh, ix. 411

Creek Indians of North America, their tradition of the first fire, ii. 256 *n.*[2] ; taboos imposed on lads at initiation among the, iii. 156 ; their mortification of themselves in war, iii. 161 *sqq.* ; the *busk* or festival of first-fruits among the, viii. 72 *sqq.* ; their belief in the homoeopathic magic of the flesh of animals, viii. 139 ; their dread of menstruous women, x. 88

—— Town, in Guinea, periodic expulsion of demons at, ix. 204 *n.*[1]

Creepers, homoeopathic magic of, i. 145

Creeping through an arch as a cure, ix. 55 ; through a tunnel as a remedy for an epidemic, x. 283 *sq.* ; through cleft trees as cure for various maladies, xi. 170 *sqq.* ; through narrow openings in order to escape ghostly pursuers, xi. 177 *sqq.*

Crescent-shaped chest in the rites of Osiris, vi. 85, 130

Crests of the Cilician pirates, v. 149

Cretan festival of Dionysus, vii. 14 *sq.* ; of Hermes, ix. 350

—— myth of the murder of Dionysus, vii. 13

Crete, milk-stones in, i. 165 ; precinct of Dictaean Zeus in, ii. 122 ; sacrifices without the use of iron in, iii. 226 *sq.* ; grave of Zeus in, iii. 3 ; sacred trees and pillars in, v. 107 *n.*[2] ; ancient seat of worship of Demeter, vii. 131 ; pig not eaten in, viii. 21 *n.*[1]

Creuse and Corrèze, departments of, St. John's fires in the, x. 190

Crevaux, J., on stinging with ants as a ceremony, iii. 105

Crianlarich, in Strath Fillan, the harvest *Cailleach* at, vii. 166

Cricket, soul in form of, iii. 39 *n.*[1]

Crickets in homoeopathic magic, i. 156

Cries of reapers, vii. 263 *sqq.*

Crimea, the Karaits of the, iii. 95 ; the Taurians of the, v. 294

Crimes, sticks or stones piled on the scene of, ix. 13 *sqq.*

Criminals shaved as a mode of purification, iii. 287 ; sacrificed, iv. 195, ix. 354, 396 *sq.*, 408 ; shorn to make them confess, xi. 158 *sq.*

Cripple or Lame Goat at harvest in Skye, vii. 284

Crnagora, divination on St. George's morning in, ii. 345

Croatia, souls of witches said to pass into trees in, ii. 32 ; Good Friday custom in, ix. 268 ; Midsummer fires in, x. 178

Croats of Istria, "Sawing the Old Woman" among the, iv. 242 ; their belief as to the activity of witches on Midsummer Eve, xi. 75

Crocodile not to be met or seen by people of the crocodile clan, viii. 28 ; supposed to be born as the twin of a human child, viii. 212 ; clay image of, as a protection against mice, viii. 279 ; a Batta totem, xi. 223

Crocodile-catchers, rules observed by, viii. 209 *sq.*

—— clan of the Dinka, iv. 31

—— -shaped hero, in Yam, v. 139 *n.*[1]

Crocodiles, Malay magic to catch, i. 110 *sq.* ; girls sacrificed to, ii. 152 ; not called by their proper names, iii. 401, 403, 410, 411, 415 *sq.* ; ancestral spirits in, viii. 123 ; hunted by savages for their flesh, viii. 208 *n.*[2] ; often spared by savages out of respect, viii. 208 *sqq.* ; ceremonies observed at catching, viii. 209 *sqq.* ; kinship of men with, viii. 212 *sq.*, 214 *sq.* ; men sacrificed to, viii. 213 ; inspired human medium of, viii. 213 ; temple dedicated to, viii. 213 ; respected in Africa and Madagascar, viii. 213 *sqq.* ; sacred at Dix Cove, viii. 287 ; souls of the dead in, viii. 289, 290, 291, 295 ; fat of, x. 14 ; lives of persons bound up with those of, xi. 201, 202, 206, 209 ; external human souls in, xi. 207, 209

Croesus, king of Lydia, his war with the Persians, ii. 316 ; captures Pteria, v. 128 ; the burning of, v. 174 *sqq.*, 179, ix. 391 ; his burnt offerings to Apollo at Delphi, v. 180 *n.*[1] ; dedicates golden lion at Delphi, v. 184 ; his son Atys, v. 286

Crofts, W. C., on Whitsuntide Bride in Norway, ii. 92 *n.*[4]

Cromarty Firth, words tabooed by fishermen of the, iii. 394

Cromer, Martin, on the Lithuanian worship of fire, ii. 366 *n.*[2]

Cromm Cruach, a legendary Irish idol, iv. 183

Cronia, a Greek festival resembling the Saturnalia, ix. 351 ; at Olympia, ix. 352 *sq.*

Cronion, a Greek month, vi. 238, viii. 7, 8 *n.*[1], ix. 351 *n.*[2]

Cronius, Mount, at Olympia, sacrifice at the spring equinox on, i. 46 *n.*[4]

Cronus, an older god in Greece than Zeus, ii. 323 ; buried in Sicily, iv. 4 ; his sacrifice of his son, iv. 166, 179 ; his treatment of his father and children, iv. 192 ; his marriage with his sister Rhea, iv. 194 ; identified with the Phoenician El, v. 166 ; castrates his father Uranus and is castrated by his son Zeus, v. 283 ; name applied to winter, vi. 41 ; and the Cronia, ix. 351 *sq.* ; his sacred hill at Olympia, ix. 352 ; and the Golden Age, ix. 353 ; and human sacrifice, ix. 353 *sq.*, 397 ; cakes offered to, x. 153 *n.*[3]

Crook and scourge or flail, the emblems of Osiris, vi. 108, 153, compare 20

Crooke, Rev. Mr., missionary in Tahuata, i. 387 *n.*[1]

Crooke, W., i. 406 *n.*[1], iv. 53 *n.*[1], vii. 234 *n.*[2], viii. 56 *n.*[3] ; on marriage to trees in India, ii. 57 *n.*[4] ; on local gods served by aboriginal priests in India, ii. 288 *n.*[1] ; on temporary substitutes for the Shah of Persia, iv. 157 *n.*[5], 159 *n.*[1] ; on sacred dancing-girls, v. 65 *n.*[1] ; on Mohammedan saints, v. 78 *n.*[2] ; on infant burial, v. 93 *sq.* ; on the custom of the False Bride, vi. 262 *n.*[2] ; on Bhumiya, viii. 118 *n.* ; as to use of spindle in ritual, viii. 119 *n.*[5]

Crop supposed to be spoilt if a man were to name his father and mother, iii. 341

Crops, dancing and leaping as charms to promote the growth of the, i. 137 *sqq.*, ix. 232, 238 *sqq.*, x. 119, 165, 166, 166 *sq.*, 168, 173, 174, 337 ; intercourse of the sexes to promote the growth of the, ii. 98 *sqq.* ; thought to be blighted by sexual crime, ii. 107 *sqq.* ; swinging for the good of the, iv. 156 *sq.*, 277, 278, 283 ; dependent on serpent-god, v. 67 ; games to promote the growth of the, v. 92 *sqq.* ; tales as a charm to promote the growth of the, v. 102, 103 *sq.* ; human victims sacrificed for the, v. 290 *sq.*, vii. 236 *sqq.* ; charms and spells for growth of, vii. 100 ; bull-roarers sounded to promote the growth of the, vii. 104, 106, xi. 232 ; rotation of, vii. 117 ; vermin the enemies of the crops, superstitious devices for destroying, intimidating, or propitiating,

viii. 274 *sqq.*; supposed to be spoiled by menstruous women, x. 79, 96; leaping over bonfires to ensure good, x. 107; Midsummer fires thought to ensure good, x. 188, 336; torches swung by eunuchs to ensure good, x. 340

Cross, Days of the, in Esthonia, i. 325; wind of the, i. 325

—— of twisted corn on Candlemas, ii. 95 *n.*

"—— of the Horse," first sheaf called the, vii. 294. *See also* Crosses

Cross River of Southern Nigeria, Eatin on the, i. 349; the Indem tribe of the, ii. 32; sacred chiefs on the, confined to their compounds, iii. 124; natives of the, their offerings of new yams to the deities, viii. 115; natives of the, their lives bound up with those of certain animals, xi. 202 *sq.*, 204

Cross-road, trap for demon at, ix. 61; ague nailed down at, ix. 68 *sq.*

—— -roads, in magical rites, ii. 340, iii. 59; burial at, v. 93 *n.*[1], ix. 10; things used in purificatory rites deposited at, vii. 9; sacrifices at, viii. 284; disease deposited at, ix. 6, 7; bodies of suicides burnt at, ix. 18; bodies of parricides to be thrown away at, ix. 24; fever deposited at, ix. 49; offerings at, ix. 140; ceremonies at, ix. 144, 159, 196, x. 24; beaten as a precaution against witches, ix. 161; witches at, ix. 162, x. 160 *n.*[1]; Midsummer fires lighted at, x. 172, 191; divination at, x. 229; bewitched things burnt at, x. 322

Crossbills in magic, i. 81 *sq.*

Crosses cut on stumps of felled trees, ii. 38; of rowan-tree used to protect cows from witches, iii. 53, ix. 267; chalked on doors as a protection against witchcraft, ii. 54, 331, 335, 336, 339, ix. 160, 162 *sq.*, 165; made with tar on cattle to protect them against evil spirits, ii. 342; painted with tar as charms against ghosts and vampyres, ix. 153 *n.*[1]; white, made by the King of the Bean, ix. 314, 315 *n.*; chalked up on Twelfth Night, ix. 331; chalked up to protect houses and cattle-stalls against witches, x. 160 *n.*[1], xi. 74. *See also* Cross

Crossing of legs forbidden, iii. 295, 298 *sq.*

Crow asked to give a new tooth, i. 181; soul in form of, iii. 42 *n.*; head of, eaten to prolong life, viii. 143; transmigration of sinner into, viii. 299; as scapegoat, ix. 193. *See also* Crows

——, hooded, sacrifice to, x. 152

Crow Song, the Greek, viii. 322 *n.*

Crowdie, a dish of milk and meal, x. 237

Crown, Ariadne's, ii. 138

—— of corn-ears, vii. 163, 221, 283; worn by Demeter and Persephone, vii. 43; or garland of flowers in Midsummer bonfire, x. 184, 185, 188, 192. *See also* Flowers

——, imperial, as palladium, iii. 4

—— of laurel, ii. 175, 175 *n.*[1], iv. 78, 80 *sqq.*

—— of oak leaves, ii. 175, 176 *sq.*, 184, iv. 80 *sqq.*

—— of olive at Olympia, iv. 91

—— of Roses, festival of the, x. 195

——, the Whitsuntide, ii. 89 *sq.* *See also* Crowns

Crown-wearer, priest of Hercules at Tarsus, v. 143

Crowning, festival of the, at Delphi, iv. 78 *sqq.*

Crowning cattle, ii. 75, 339, 341; as a protection against witchcraft, ii. 126 *sq.*, 339

—— dogs, custom of, i. 14, ii. 125 *sq.*, 127 *sq.*

Crowns, the royal, in ancient Egypt, i. 364; magical virtue of royal, i. 364 *sq.*; of birch at Whitsuntide, ii. 64; or wreaths, custom of wearing, ii. 127 *n.*[2]; as amulets, vi. 242 *sq.*; laid aside in mourning, etc., vi. 243 *n.*[2]; of figs worn at sacrifice to Saturn (Cronus), ix. 253 *n.*[3]; of maize, ix. 280. *See also* Crown

—— of Egypt, the White and the Red, vi. 21 *n.*[1]

Crows in magic, i. 83; hearts of, eaten by diviners, viii. 143. *See also* Crow

Cruachan, the palace of the ancient kings of Connaught, iii. 12; pagan cemetery at, iv. 101; the fair of, iv. 101; in Connaught, the cave of, x. 226; the herdsman or king of, Argyleshire story of, xi. 127 *sqq.*

Crucifixion of Christ, ix. 412 *sqq.*; crossbills at the, i. 82; tradition as to the date of, v. 306 *sqq.*

—— of human victims at Benin, v. 294 *n.*[3]; gentile, at the spring equinox, v. 307 *n.*

Crux ansata, the Egyptian symbol of life, ii. 133, vi. 89

"Crying the Mare" at harvest in Hertfordshire, vii. 292 *sq.*; in Shropshire, vii. 293

"—— the neck," at harvest, vii. 264 *sqq.*

Cryptocerus atratus, F., stinging ants, used in ordeal by the Mauhes, x. 62

Crystals, magic of, i. 176 *sq.*; used in rain-making, i. 254, 255, 304, 345, 346; used in divination, iii. 56; superstitions as to, iv. 64 *n.*[6]

Ctesias, on the Sacaea, ix. 402 *n*.[1]
Cubit, the standard, kept in the temple of Serapis, vi. 217
Cublay-Khan, ii. 306
Cuissard, Ch., on Midsummer fires, x. 182 *sq.*
Cultivation of staple food in the hands of women (Pelew Islands), vi. 206 *sq.* ; shifting, vii. 99. *See* Agriculture
Cumae, the Sibyl at, x. 99
Cumanus, inquisitor, xi. 158
Cumberland, Midsummer fires in, x. 197
Cumberland inlet, the Esquimaux of, iii. 108
Cummin, curses at sowing, i. 281
Cumont, Professor Franz, on the Saturnalia of the Roman soldiers, iv. 310 ; on the *taurobolium*, v. 275 *n.*[1] ; on the Nativity of the Sun, v. 303 *n.*[3] ; as to the parallel between Easter and the rites of Attis, v. 310 *n.*[1] ; on the martyrdom of St. Dasius, ix. 308 *sq.* ; on a form of abjuration imposed on Jewish converts, ix. 393 *n.*[1]
"Cup of offering," viii. 184
——, sacred golden, i. 365
Cup-and-ball as a charm to hasten the return of the sun, i. 317
Cupid and Psyche, story of, iv. 131
Cups, special, used by girls at puberty, x. 50, 53
Cura, sacred grove of the Wotyaks at, ii. 145
Curative powers ascribed to persons born feet foremost, x. 295
Curcho, old Prussian god, viii. 133, 174 *n.*
Cures based on principles of homoeopathic magic, i. 78 *sqq.* ; effected by recalling the soul, iii. 42 *sqq.* ; by means of knotted cords and threads, iii. 303 *sqq.* ; by swinging, iv. 280 *sq.*, 282 ; by transferring the malady to things, animals, or persons, ix. 2 *sqq.* ; by the expulsion of demons, ix. 109 *sqq.* ; popular, prescribed by Marcellus of Bordeaux, x. 17
Curetes, their war-dance, vii. 13
Curland, Midsummer festival in, iv. 280
Curr, E. M., on the superstition as to personal names among the Australian aborigines, iii. 320 *sq.*
Curses, public, i. 45 ; supposed beneficial effects of, i. 279 *sqq.* ; uttered by Bouzygai, vii. 108
Cursing at Athens, ritual of, iii. 75
—— an enemy, Arab mode of, iii. 312
—— fishermen and hunters for good luck, i. 280 *sq.*
—— a mist in Switzerland, x. 280
—— at sowing, i. 281
Curtains to conceal kings, iii. 120 *sq.*
Curtiss, Professor S. I., on the head of the Babites, i. 402

Curtius, Quintus, on Alexander the Great's cresset, ii. 264 *n.*[7]
Curumbars, a tribe of the Neilgherry Hills, viii. 55
Cuscuses, souls of dead in, viii. 296, 298
Cushing, Frank H., on the killing of sacred turtles among the Zuñi, viii. 175 *sqq.*
Custom more constant than myth, viii. 40
Customs of the Pelew Islanders, vi. 253 *sqq.*, 266 *sqq.*
Cut hair and nails, disposal of, iii. 267 *sqq.*
Cuthar, father of Adonis, v. 13 *n.*[2]
Cuts made in the body as a mode of expelling demons or ghosts, iii. 106 *sq.* ; in bodies of manslayers, iii. 174, 176, 180 ; in bodies of slain, iii. 176. *See also* Incisions, Scarification
Cutting or lacerating the body in honour of the dead, iv. 92 *sq.*, 97
—— the hair a purificatory ceremony, iii. 283 *sqq.* *See also* Hair
Cutting weapons planted in ground to repel the demon of smallpox, ix. 122
Cuttings for the dead, v. 268
Cuttle-fish presented to Greek infants, i. 156 ; expiation for killing a, iv. 217
Cuzco, the temple of the Sun at, ii. 243, vii. 310 ; its scenery, ix. 128 *sq.* ; ceremony of the new fire in, x. 132
Cyaxares, king of the Medes, v. 133 *n.*, 174
Cybele, her image carted about at Autun, ii. 144 ; the image of, v. 35 *n.*[3] ; her cymbals and tambourines, v. 54 ; her lions and turreted crown, v. 137 ; priests of, called Attis, v. 140 ; the Mother of the Gods, v. 263 ; her love for Attis, v. 263, 282 ; her worship adopted by the Romans, v. 265 ; sacrifice of virility to image of, v. 268 ; subterranean chambers of, v. 268 ; orgiastic rites of, v. 278 ; a goddess of fertility, v. 279 ; worshipped in Gaul, v. 279 ; fasts observed by the worshippers of, v. 280 ; a friend of Marsyas, v. 288 ; effeminate priests of, vi. 257, 258
—— and Attis, i. 18, 21, 40, 41, v. 280, ix. 386
Cybistra in Cappadocia, v. 120, 122, 124
Cychreus, king of Salamis, bequeaths his kingdom to Telamon, ii. 278 *n.*[2] ; changed at death into a serpent, ix. 87
Cycle, the octennial, based on an attempt to reconcile solar and lunar time, iv. 68 *sq.*, vii. 80 *sq.* ; apparently the period of certain kings' reigns in ancient Greece, iv. 70 *sq.* ; octennial festivals connected with the, iv. 87 *sqq.* ; Olympiads originally based on the, iv. 89 *sq.*, vii. 80 ; antiquity of the octennial cycle in Greece, vii. 81 *sq.* ; the cycle

based on religious rather than practical considerations, vii. 82 sq.

Cycle of thirty years (Druidical), xi. 77

Cycles of sixty years (Boeotian, Indian, and Tibetan), xi. 77 n.[1]

Cyclopes, slaughter of the, iv. 78 n.[4]

Cymbal, drinking out of a, v. 274

Cymbals in religious music, v. 52, 54

—— and tambourines in worship of Cybele, v. 54

Cyme, titular kings at, i. 46 n.[4]

Cynaetha, in Arcadia, people of, massacre committed by the, iii. 188 ; winter festival of Dionysus at, vii. 16 sq.

Cynopolis, the cemetery of, vi. 90

Cypresses, sacred, in the sanctuary of Aesculapius at Cos, ii. 10 ; in the sanctuary of Aesculapius at Titane, v. 81

Cypriote syllabary, v. 49 n.[7]

Cyprus, grave of Aphrodite in, iv. 4 ; Salamis in, iv. 166 n.[1] ; natural riches of, v. 31 ; Phoenicians in, v. 31 · sq. ; Adonis in, v. 31 sqq. ; sacred prostitution in, v. 36, 50, 59 ; Melcarth worshipped in, v. 117 ; human sacrifices in, v. 145 sq. ; the bearded Venus in, vi. 259 n.[3] ; wild boars annually sacrificed in, viii. 23 n.[3]

Cyrene, kingship at, i. 47 ; the people of, their sacrifice to Saturn (Cronus), ix. 253 n.[3]

Cyril of Alexandria on the festival of Adonis at Alexandria, v. 224 n.[2]

Cyrus and Croesus, iv. 174 sqq., ix. 391

Cythnos, Greek island, sickly children pushed through a hole in a rock in, xi. 189

Cytisorus, son of Phrixus, iv. 162

Cyzicus, council chamber at, built without iron, iii. 230 ; worship of the Placianian Mother at, v. 274 n. ; bull-shaped image of Dionysus at, vii. 16 ; vicarious sacrifice at, viii. 95 n.[2]

Czech maidens, love charm practised by, on St. George's Eve, ii. 345 sq.

—— saying as to the dying, iii. 33 n.[3]

—— villages of Bohemia, the Shrove-tide Bear in the, viii. 326 ; the Three Kings of Twelfth Night in, ix. 330 sq.

Czechs of Bohemia, the Carrying out of Death among the, iv. 221 ; the Corn-mother among the, vii. 132 sq. ; cull simples at Midsummer, xi. 49

Dabelow, in Mecklenburg, precaution against witches on Walpurgis Night at, ix. 163 n.[1]

Daçaratha festival in India, iv. 124

Dacia, hot springs in, v. 213

Dacotas or Sioux, the, their fear of having their pictures taken, iii. 96 ; custom observed by manslayers among, iii. 181 ; avoidance of wife's mother among, iii. 338 ; their belief as to stepping over animals, iii. 423 ; their theory of the waning moon, vi. 130 ; ate the livers of dogs to make them brave, viii. 145 ; their belief in the resurrection of dogs, viii. 256 sq. ; ritual of death and resurrection among, xi. 268 sq.

Dad pillar. See Ded pillar

Daedala, Boeotian festival of the Great, ii. 140 sq., xi. 77 n.[1]

Daedalus, the artist, made a dance for Ariadne, iv. 71 ; made a hollow cow for Pasiphae, iv. 71

Dag, an early king of the Shilluk, iv. 28

Dageon, fire kept up during king's life in, ii. 261 sq.

Dagobert, King, privilege granted by him to St. Romulus or St. Ouen, ii. 165

Dah River, in Ashantee, royal criminals drowned in, iii. 243 ; annual ablutions in the, viii. 63

Dahomans, their annual festival of the dead, vi. 66

Dahomey, human wives of gods in, ii. 149 ; royal criminals drowned or strangled in, iii. 243 ; indifference to death in, iv. 138 ; religious massacres in, iv. 138 ; the Amazons of, viii. 149

——, the king of, iii. 374 ; human victims drowned by, ii. 158 ; not allowed to behold the sea, iii. 9 ; not to be seen eating, iii. 118

——, kings of, their true names kept secret, iii. 374 ; their "strong names," iii. 374 ; represented partly in human, partly in animal forms, iv. 85 ; their human sacrifices, vi. 97 n.[7]

——, Porto Novo in, annual expulsion of demons at, ix. 205

——, royal family of, iii. 243 ; related to leopards, iv. 85

Dainyal, diviner or Sibyl, in the Hindoo Koosh, i. 383

Daira or Mahadev Mohammedans in Mysore, mock rite of circumcision among the, iv. 220

Dairi, the, or Mikado of Japan, iii. 2, 4. See Mikado

Dairies, sacred, of the Todas, iii. 15 sqq.

Dairy, mistletoe used to make the dairy thrive, xi. 86

Dairyman, sacred, of the Todas, iii. 15 sqq. ; his custom as to the pollution of death, vi. 228 ; bound to live apart from his wife, vi. 229

Daizan, king of Atrae, his treacherous daughter, x. 83

Dajang, Miss, a personification of the rice among the Battas, vii. 196

Dalai Lama of Lhasa, regarded as a

living god, i. 411 *sq.* ; his palace, i. 412

Dalarne, the Yule-ram in, viii. 328

Dalecarlia, observances at turning out the cattle to the summer pastures in, ii. 342

Dalhousie Castle, the Edgewell Tree at, xi. 166

Dalisandos in Isauria, inscriptions at, vi. 213 *n.*[1]

Dallet, Ch., on the Corean objection to put the face of the king on coins, iii. 99

Dalmatia, rain-making in, i. 274 ; belief as to the souls of trees in, ii. 14 ; the Yule log in, x. 263

Dalsland, in Sweden, observances at turning out the cattle to graze in the forest in, ii. 341 *sq.*

Dalton, Colonel E. T., on mock human sacrifices among the Bhagats, iv. 217 *sq.* ; on the fear of demons among the Oraons, ix. 92 *sq.* ; on the annual expulsion of demons among the Hos of North-East India, ix. 136 *sq.*

Dalyell, J. G., on Beltane, x. 149 *n.*[1]

Dama, exorcism of demons of sickness in the island of, viii. 101 *sq.*

Damara hunters, ceremony observed by, iii. 220

Damaras or Herero, their fire-customs, ii. 211 *sqq.* ; their ceremony on return from a journey, iii. 112 ; their mode of killing their cattle, iii. 247. *See also* Herero

Damascus, Aramean kings of, v. 15

Damasen, a giant, in a Lydian story, slays a serpent, v. 186

Damatrius, a Greek month, vi. 49 *n.*[1], vii. 46

Damba, island in Lake Victoria Nyanza, crocodiles sacred in, viii. 213

Damia and Auxesia, female powers of fertility at Troezen, i. 39

Dams, continence at making or repairing, iii. 202 ; in Egypt, the cutting of the, vi. 31 *sq.*, 37 *sq.*, 39 *sq.*

Damun, in German New Guinea, ceremony of initiation at, xi. 193

Danae, the story of, her impregnation by Zeus, x. 73 *sq.*

Danakils or Afars of East Africa, their belief as to the rebirth of souls of magicians, iv. 200

Danaus and the suitors of his daughters, ii. 301

Dance at giving of oracles, i. 379 ; executed as tribute by a human god, i. 394 ; of milkmaids on May-day, ii. 52 ; to propitiate souls of slain foes, iii. 166 ; of women on return of warriors, iii. 170 ; at driving ghost into grave, iii. 373, 374 ; of youths and maidens at Cnossus, iv. 75 *sq.* ; of eunuchs in Corea, v. 270 *n.*[2]; of eunuchs at new moon, on the Congo, v. 271 *n.* ; of hermaphrodites in Pegu, v. 271 *n.* ; at harvest supper, vii. 134, 135, 145 ; of harvesters with or round the last sheaf, vii. 135, 141, 145, 160, 219, 220, 294, 297 ; of masked men before sowing, vii. 186 ; of Dyaks to secure soul of rice, vii. 188 *sq.* ; of old women as representatives of the corn-goddess, vii. 205 ; Pawnee, before human sacrifice, vii. 238 ; round skulls of human victims, vii. 241, 242 ; round oak and goat-skin at harvest, vii. 288 ; of executioners, viii. 63 ; of Zulu king, viii. 66, 68, 68 *n.*[3]; of Pondo chief at festival of new fruits, viii. 67 ; before the king at ceremony of first-fruits, viii. 70 *sq.* ; of medicine-man, viii. 72 ; at harvest festival of Indians of Alabama, viii. 72 *n.*[2]; of warriors at festival of first-fruits, viii. 74 *sq.*, 79 ; of men and women, by torchlight, at festival of first-fruits, viii. 79 ; of Dacota warriors, viii. 145 ; of Caffre girls after mock funeral of caterpillars, viii. 280 ; at the burial of the wren, viii. 319 ; on Twelfth Day, viii. 321 ; of mummers at Carnival, viii. 333, 334 ; of mummer wearing a horse-headed mask, viii. 338 ; at cairns, ix. 29 ; to ensure a supply of buffaloes, ix. 171 ; to cause the grass to grow, ix. 238 ; by men carrying a box and axes at Sipi in Northern India, x. 12 ; of young women at puberty, xi. 183 ; in the grave at initiation, xi. 237 ; in honour of the big or grey wolf, xi. 276 *n.*[2]. *See also* Dances

" Dance, the Angel," viii. 328

——, Ariadne's, iv. 77

——, the Green Corn, viii. 76

—— of King, iii. 123 ; before the ghosts of his ancestor, vi. 192

——, the rattle-snake, to ensure immunity from snake-bites, i. 358

——, sacred, at the Sed festival, vi. 154

Dancers personate spirits, ix. 375

Dances, for rain, i. 250, 255, 268, 273, 274, 284, 284 *n.*, iii. 154, iv. 32, 62, ix. 236 *sq.*, 238 ; for wind, i. 321 ; as means of inspiration, i. 408 *n.*[1] ; round sacred trees, ii. 47, 55 ; at harvest, ii. 48 ; round the May-pole, ii. 65, 67, 69, 74 *sq.* ; round bonfires on the Eve of St. John (Midsummer Eve), ii. 65 ; performed by parents of twins to fertilize gardens, ii. 102 ; for a good harvest, ii. 106 ; on graves, ii. 183 *n.*[2]; round an oak,

ii. 371; of manslayers, iii. 168; of victory, iii. 169, 170, 178, 182; at sowing, vii. 95, ix. 234 *sqq.*; at human sacrifices, vii. 246, 247; at the reappearance of the Pleiades, vii. 307, 309, 311, 312, 317; in imitation of totemic animals, viii. 76; and processions in connexion with offerings of first-fruits, viii. 111, 113, 115, 116, 126, 131, 134; of men personifying deities, viii. 179; round dead tigers, viii. 216; of the Koryak at the slaughter of bears or wolves, viii. 223; in honour of slain leopards, viii. 228; to amuse the souls of dead sea-beasts, viii. 248; of the Karoks for salmon, viii. 255; to make the crops thrive, viii. 326, 328, 330 *sq.*, ix. 232 *sqq.*, 347; of mummers on Plough Monday, viii. 329 *sqq.*; at cairns, ix. 26, 29; Etruscan, in time of plague at Rome, ix. 65; at harvest, ix. 134; at the expulsion of demons, ix. 139; of the witches, ix. 162; with burning besoms on fields to drive away witches, ix. 163; of women at expulsion of demons, ix. 200; of the Salii, ix. 232, 233; of the Tarahumare Indians of Mexico, ix. 236 *sqq.*; taught by animals, ix. 237; solemn Mexican, ix. 279, 285; of Castilian peasants in May, ix. 280; to make hemp grow tall, ix. 315; round bonfires on the Eve of Twelfth Night, ix. 317; in churches at the Festival of Fools, ix. 335, 336; accompanying the Boy Bishop, ix. 338; as dramatic performances of myths, ix. 375 *sqq.*; bestowed on men by spirits, ix. 375; in imitation of animals, ix. 376, 377, 381, 382; of fasting men and women at festival, x. 8 *sq.*; of Duk-duk society, x. 11; of girls at puberty, x. 28, 29, 30, 37, 42, 50, 58, 59; round bonfires, x. 108, 109, 110, 111, 114, 116, 120, 131, 142, 145, 148, 153 *sq.*, 159, 166, 172, 173, 175, 178, 182, 183, 185, 187, 188, 189, 191, 193, 194, 195, 198, 246, xi. 2, 39; of novices at initiation, xi. 258, 259. *See also* Dance

Dances, masked, of the Kayans at the festival of sowing, vii. 95 *sq.*, 111, 186; of the Kaua and Kobeua Indians of Brazil, vii. 111 *sq.*; of the Chambioa Indians of Brazil, viii. 208 *n.*[1]; at carnival, viii. 333, 334; in ritual, of Demeter and Persephone, viii. 339; of devil-dancers, ix. 38; to promote fertility, ix. 236; of savages, ix. 374 *sqq.*; supposed to be derived from guardian spirits, ix. 375 *sqq.*; to ensure good crops,

ix. 382; bull-roarers used at, xi. 230 *n.*

Dances, Mexican, viii. 88; solemn, ix. 280, 284, 286, 287, 288, 289; of saltmakers, ix. 284

——, religious, of dancing girls in India, v. 61, 65; of inspired novices on the Slave Coast, v. 68; at festivals of the dead, vi. 52, 53, 55, 58, 59; at the new moon, vi. 142

—— of Shrovetide Bear, viii. 325 *sq.*

—— of women while men are away fighting, i. 131-134; at bear-festival, viii. 185, 186 *sq.*, 191, 195; at catching a crocodile, viii. 211; at slaughter of whales, viii. 232 *sq.*

Dancing as a fertility charm, i. 137 *sqq.*, ii. 106; for salmon, viii. 255; to obtain the favour of the gods, ix. 65, 236; with the fairies at Hallowe'en, x. 227

—— -girls in India, harlots and wives of the gods, v. 61 *sqq.*

Dandaki, King, and the ascetic, story of, ix. 41 *sq.*

Dandelions gathered at Midsummer, xi. 49

Danes, female descent of the kingship among the, ii. 282 *sq.*

Danger of being overshadowed by certain birds or people, iii. 82 *sq.*; supposed, of portraits and photographs, iii. 96 *sqq.*; supposed to attend contact with divine or sacred persons, such as chiefs and kings, iii. 132 *sqq.*, 138; apprehended from women in childbed, iii. 150 *sqq.*; thought to attend women at menstruation, x. 94; apprehended from the sexual relation, xi. 277 *sq.*

Danger Island, snares set for souls by sorcerers in, iii. 69; the Pleiades worshipped in, vii. 312

Dañh-gbi, python-god, on the Slave Coast, v. 66

Danish magic of footprints, i. 211

—— story of a girl who was forbidden to see the sun, x. 70 *sqq.*; of the external soul, xi. 120 *sqq.*

Danserosse or *danseresse*, a stone in the wood of St. Antony near Épinal, x. 110

Danube, worship of Grannus on the, x. 112

Danzig, disposal of cut hair at, iii. 276 *sq.*; the siege of, iii. 279 *n.*[4]; the last sheaf at harvest at, vii. 133, 218 *sq.*; the immortal lady of, x. 100

Daphne gnidium gathered at Midsummer, xi. 51

Daphnephoria, Greek festival, ii. 63 *n.*[2]. *See* Laurel-bearing

Daphnis and the magic knots, in Virgil, iii. 305

Daphnis, play by Sositheus, vii. 217

Dapper, O., on ritual of death and resurrection at initiation in the Belli-Paaro society, xi. 257 *sqq.*

Daramulun, a mythical being who instituted and superintends the initiation of lads in Australia, xi. 228, 233, 237 ; his voice heard in the sound of the bull-roarer, xi. 228. *See also* Thrumalun *and* Thuremlin

'' Darding Knife,'' pretence of death and resurrection at initiation to the, xi. 274 *sq.*

Dardistan, custom of swinging in, iv. 279

Dards, their belief that a storm follows the troubling of a spring, i. 301

Darfur, power of extinguishing fire ascribed to chaste women in, ii. 240 *n.*[3] ; tampering with a man's shadow in, iii. 81 ; the sultan of, veils his face, iii. 120 ; etiquette at the court of the sultans of, iv. 39 ; the people of, believe the liver to be the seat of the soul, viii. 147 *sq.*

Dargle Vale, Whitsuntide custom at, ii. 103 *n.*[3]

Darien, the Indians of, concealment of personal names among, iii. 325

Darius, King, would not pass through a gate over which was a tomb, iii. 257

'' Dark '' moon and '' light '' moon, ix. 140, 141 *n.*[1]

Darling River, funeral custom of tribes on the, i. 90 ; custom as to extracted teeth among the tribes of the, i. 176 ; the Karamundi nation on the, i. 257 ; tributaries of the, iv. 180 ; the Ualaroi of the, xi. 233

Darma Rajah, Hindoo god, fire-festival in honour of, xi. 6

Darmesteter, James, on the Fravashis, vi. 67 *n.*[2] ; his theory as to the date of the *Gathas*, vi. 84 *n.*

Darowen, in Wales, Midsummer fires at, x. 201

Darwin, Charles, and Empedocles, viii. 306 ; on the cooling of the sun, xi. 307 *n.*[1]

Darwin, Sir Francis, on double-headed bust at Nemi, i. 42 *n.*[1] ; on *rhamnus* (buckthorn), ix. 153 *n.*[1]; on the Golden Bough, xi. 318, 319 *n.*[3]

Dashers of churns, witches ride on, xi. 73 *sq.*

Dâsî, dancing-girl in India, v. 63

Dasius, St., martyrdom of, ix. 308 *sqq.* *See* St. Dasius

Dassera festival in Nepaul, iii. 316, ix. 226 *n.*[1]; swings and kites at the, iv. 277

Dastarkon in Cappadocia, Cataonian Apollo at, v. 147 *n.*[3]

Date of Chinese festival changed, x. 137

Date month when date-palms are artificially fertilized, ii. 25

—— -palm, artificial fertilization of the, ii. 24 *sq.*, ix. 272 *sq.*

Dates forbidden to worshippers of Cybele and Attis, v. 280

Dathi, king of Ireland, and his Druid, x. 228 *sq.*

Daughter of a god, v. 51

—— of a king, succession to kingdom by marriage with a, ii. 271, 277 *sqq.*

—— -in-law, her name not to be pronounced, iii. 338 ; in ritual, viii. 121 *sq.*

Daughters of chiefs entrusted with the sacred fire among the Herero, ii. 215, 228

Dauphiné, the Bridegroom of the Month of May in, ii. 93 ; the harvest Cat in, vii. 280 *sq.*

Daura, a Hausa kingdom, sick or infirm kings killed in, iv. 35 ; custom of succession to the throne in, iv. 201

David, King, his conquest of Ammon, iii. 273, v. 19 ; and the brazen serpent, iv. 86 ; in relation to the old kings of Jerusalem, v. 18 *sq.* ; his taking of a census, v. 24 ; as a harper, v. 52, 53, 54

—— and Goliath, v. 19 *n.*[2]

—— and the King of Moab, iii. 273

—— and Saul, v. 21

Davies, J. Ceredig, as to witches in Wales, x. 321 *n.*[2]

Davies, Professor T. Witton, on the date of the Book of Esther, ix. 360 *n.*[2]

Davis, Mr. R. F., on harvest custom in Nottinghamshire, v. 238 *n.*

Dawkins, R. M., on a carnival custom in Thrace, vii. 25 *n.*[4], 29 *n.*[2]

Dawn of the Day, prayers of adolescent girls to the, i. 70, x. 50 *sq.*, 53, 98 *n.*[1]

——, the rosy, in mythology, i. 334

Dawson, James, on the difference of language between husbands and wives among the aborigines of Victoria, iii. 347 *sq.* ; on the constellations observed by the aborigines of Victoria, vii. 308 ; on sex totems in Victoria, xi. 216

Day of Blood in rites of Attis, v. 268, 285

—— of Stones, in Behar and Bengal, i. 279

Days of the Cross in Esthonia, i. 325

De Barros, Portuguese historian, on the custom of killing kings at Passier, iv. 51

De Goeje, M. J., on the rite of stone-throwing at Mecca, ix. 24 *n.*[1]

De Groot, J. J. M., on the authority of the Chinese emperors, i. 416 *sq.* ; on the Chinese belief in tree-spirits, ii. 14 ; on the Chinese theory of names, iii. 390

De Mortival, Roger, on the Boy Bishop at Salisbury, ix. 338

D'Orbigny, A., on the division of labour between the sexes among the South American Indians, vii. 120

De Plano Carpini, on the funeral customs of the Mongols, v. 293

De Ricci, S., on the Celtic month Equos, ix. 343 *n.*

De Smet, J., on the sacrifice of a Sioux girl, vii. 239 *n.*[1]

Dea Dia, a Roman goddess of fertility, vi. 239

Dead, hair offered to the, i. 31 ; pretence of new birth at return of supposed dead man, i. 75 ; belief of the Central Australian aborigines in the reincarnation of the, i. 96 ; homoeopathic magic of the, i. 147 *sqq.*; prayers and offerings to the, i. 163 ; magic blent with the worship of the, i. 164 ; making rain by means of the, i. 284 *sqq.* ; the illustrious, represented by masked men, ii. 178 ; thunder and lightning made by the, ii. 183 ; taboos on persons who have handled the, iii. 138 *sqq.* ; to name the dead a serious crime, iii. 352 ; relations of the, change their names from fear of the ghost, iii. 356 *sqq.* ; incarnate in their namesakes, iii. 365 *sqq.* ; appear to the living in dreams, iii. 368, 374 ; offerings of food to the, iii. 371, 372 *n.*[5], ix. 154 ; deposited on platforms of sticks, iii. 372 ; rebirth of the, iv. 70, vii. 85 ; human blood offered to the, iv. 92 *sq.*, 104 ; incarnate in serpents, v. 82 *sqq.*, xi. 211 *sq.* ; cuttings for the, v. 268 ; Osiris king and judge of the, vi. 13 *sq.* ; the Egyptian, identified with Osiris, vi. 16 ; magical uses made of their bodies, vi. 100 *sqq.* ; the worship of the, founded on the theory of the soul, vii. 181 ; the fear of the, one of the most powerful factors in religious evolution, viii. 36 *sq.* ; buried in the houses, viii. 115 ; bones of the, viii. 153 *sq.* ; mourners rub themselves with the fat or putrefying juices of the, viii. 162 *sq.*; food eaten out of the hand of the, ix. 44 *sq.* ; worship of the, based on fear, ix. 98 ; ghosts of the, periodically expelled, ix. 123 *sq.* ; annual sacrifices in honour of the, ix. 148 *n.*[1]. *See also* Ancestral spirits

——, communion with the, by means of food, viii. 154 ; by swallowing their ashes, viii. 156 *sqq.*

——, festivals of the, iii. 367, 371, v.

220, vi. 51 *sqq.*, x. 223 *sq.*, 225 *sq.* ; at end of harvest, viii. 110 ; bullroarers sounded at, xi. 230 *n.*

Dead, names of, tabooed, iii. 349 *sqq.* ; not borne by the living, iii. 354

——, reincarnation of the, iii. 365 *sqq.*, v. 82 *sqq.* ; in Central Australia, i. 196 ; in America, v. 91 ; in Africa, v. 91 *sq.*

——, sacrifices to the, i. 163, iii. 15, 88, 226 *sq*, iv. 92, 93, 94, 95, 97, xi. 178 ; on their birthdays, i. 105

——, souls of the, trees animated by, ii. 29 *sqq.* ; in certain fish, ii. 30 ; all malignant, iii. 145 ; associated with falling stars, iv. 64 *sqq.* ; lodged in serpents, iv. 84 ; received by their relations once a year, vi. 51 *sqq.*, ix. 150 *sqq.* ; invoked to make the crops thrive, vii. 104 ; supposed to partake of new grain, viii. 64 ; supposed to be in caterpillars, viii. 275 *sq.* ; supposed to be in animals, viii. 285 *sqq.* ; disembodied, dreaded, ix. 77 ; sit round the Midsummer fire, x. 183, 184 ; first-fruits offered to, xi. 243. *See also* Dead, spirits of the

——, spirits of the, the savage a slave to the, i. 217 ; personated by living men, ii. 178, iii. 371, vi. 52, 53, 58 ; in wild fig-trees, ii. 317, viii. 113 ; thought to be incarnate in their namesakes, iii. 365 *sqq.* ; supposed to influence the crops, vii. 104 ; offerings to, for the sake of the crops, vii. 228 ; give rain, viii. 109 *sq.* ; first-fruits offered to, viii. 109 *sq.*, 111 *sqq.*, 115, 116, 117, 119, 121, 123, 124 *sqq.* ; prayers to, viii. 112, 113, 124 *sq.* ; omnipresent, in the Philippine Islands, ix. 82 ; swarm in the air, in Timor, ix. 85 ; purification of mourners intended to protect them against, ix. 105 *n.*[1] *See also* Ancestral spirits

——, worship of the, ix. 97 ; perhaps fused with the propitiation of the cornspirit, v. 233 *sqq.* ; among the Bantu tribes of Africa, vi. 176 *sqq.*

Dead body, Flamen Dialis forbidden to touch, iii. 14 ; defilement caused by, vii. 74

—— kings and chiefs in Africa turn into lions, leopards, hyaenas, hippopotamuses, etc., iv. 84 ; dead kings in Africa worshipped, vi. 160 *sqq.*

—— kings of the Barotse worshipped, vi. 194 *sq.* ; consulted as oracles, vi. 195

—— kings of Egypt worshipped, i. 418, vi. 160

—— kings of the Shilluk worshipped, iv. 24 *sq.*, vi. 161 *sqq.* ; their spirits thought to possess sick people, iv. 25 *sq.* ; incarnate in animals, vi. 162, 163 *sq.* ; sacrifices offered to, vi. 162, 164, 166 *sq.*

Dead kings of Sofala, annual obsequies for, iv. 201 ; consulted as oracles, iv. 201

—— kings of Uganda consulted as oracles, i. 196, iv. 200 *sq.*, vi. 167, 171, 172 ; human sacrifices to, vi. 173

—— man's hand used in magical ceremony, iv. 267 *n.*[1]

—— men believed to beget children, v. 91, 264 ; mutilated in order to disable their ghosts, viii. 271 *sqq.*

—— One, the, name applied to the last sheaf, iv. 254

—— Sea, v. 23

—— Sunday, iv. 239 ; generally the fourth Sunday in Lent, iv. 221 ; also called Mid-Lent, iv. 222 *n.*[1]

Deane, Mrs. J. H., viii. 319 *n.*[2]

Dearth, chiefs and kings punished for, i. 352 *sqq.*

Death, pretence of, in magic, i. 84 ; infection of, i. 143 ; at ebb tide, i. 167 *sq.* ; puppet called, carried out of village, ii. 73 *sq.* ; kept off by arrows, iii. 31 ; mourners forbidden to sleep in house after a, iii. 37 ; custom of covering up mirrors at a, iii. 94 *sq.* ; from imagination, iii. 135 *sqq.* ; sharp instruments tabooed after a, iii. 237, 238 ; of the king of the Jinn, iv. 8 ; preference for a violent, iv. 9 *sqq.* ; European fear of, iv. 135 *sq.*, 146 ; indifference to, displayed by many races, iv. 136 *sqq.* ; the "carrying out" of, iv. 221, 233 *sqq.*, 246 *sqq.*, ix. 227 *sq.*, 230, 252, x. 119 ; conception of, in relation to vegetation, iv. 252, 253 *sq.* ; in the corn, iv. 254 ; represented at the maize harvest by a child covered with maize leaves, iv. 254 ; and revival of vegetation, iv. 263 *sq.* ; in the fire as an apotheosis, v. 179 *sq.* ; the pollution of, vi. 227 *sqq.*, viii. 85 *n.*[3] ; banishment of the contagion of, ix. 37 ; riddles propounded after a, ix. 121 *n.* ; the funeral of, ix. 205 ; savage tales of the origin of, ix. 302 *sqq.* ; "the burying of," x. 119 ; omens of, xi. 54, 64 ; customs observed by mourners after a death in order to escape from the ghost, xi. 174 *sqq.* ; identified with the sun, xi. 174 *n.*[1]

——, the Angel of, iv. 177 *sq.*

——, effigy of, feared and abhorred, iv. 239 *sq.* ; potency of life attributed to, iv. 247 *sqq.* ; burnt in spring fires, xi. 21 *sq.*

—— of the Great Pan, iv. 6 *sq.*

Death, the Lord of, viii. 103

——, natural, of sacred king or priest, supposed fatal consequences of, iii. 6, 7 ; regarded as a calamity, iv. 11 *sq.*

—— and resurrection, of Kostrubonko at Eastertide, iv. 261 ; annual, of gods, v. 6, vii. 1, 12 *sqq.*, 15 ; of Adonis represented in his rites, v. 224 *sq.* ; of Attis, v. 272 *sq.*, 306 ; of Dionysus, v. 302 *n.*[4], vii. 14 *sq.* ; coincidence between the pagan and the Christian festival of the divine, v. 308 *sq.* ; of Osiris dramatically represented in his rites, vi. 85 *sq.* ; of Osiris interpreted as the decay and growth of vegetation, vi. 126 *sqq.* ; drama of, at the Carnival, vii. 27 *sq.* ; of Eabani, ix. 398 *sq.* ; the ritual of, in initiatory ceremonies, xi. 225 *sqq.* ; in Australia, xi. 227 *sqq.* ; in New Guinea, xi. 239 *sqq.* ; in Fiji, xi. 243 *sqq.* ; in Rook, xi. 246 ; in New Britain, xi. 246 *sq.* ; in Ceram, xi. 249 *sqq.* ; in Africa, xi. 251 *sqq.* ; in North America, xi. 266 *sqq.* ; traces of it elsewhere, xi. 276 *sq.*

Debang monastery at Lhasa, ix. 218

Debden in Essex, May garlands at, ii. 60

Debregeasia velutina, used to kindle fire by friction, xi. 8

Debschwitz or Dobschwitz, near Gera, the custom of "driving out Death" at, iv. 235

Debt of civilization to savagery, iii. 421 *sq.*

Deccan, the Gaolis of the, vii. 7

Deceiving the spirits of plants and trees, ii. 22 *sqq.* ; demons and ghosts by substituting effigies for living persons, viii. 94 *sqq.*

December, the Saturnalia held in, ii. 311 *n.*[4], ix. 306, 307, 345 ; the twenty-fifth of, reckoned the winter solstice and the birthday of the Sun, v. 303 *sqq.* ; annual expulsion of demons in, ix. 145 ; custom of the heathen of Harran in, ix. 263 *sq.* ; the last day of, Hogmanay, x. 266 ; the twenty-first, St. Thomas's Day, x. 266

Decle, L., on heaps of sticks or stones to which passers-by add, ix. 11 *n.*[1] ; on a custom of the kings of Uganda, x. 4 *n.*[1]

Decline of magic with the growth of religion, i. 374

—— of the civic virtues under the influence of Oriental religions, v. 300 *sq.*

Ded or *tet* pillar, the backbone of Osiris, vi. 108 *sq.*

Dedication of girls to the service of a temple, v. 61 *sqq.* ; of men and women in Africa, v. 65 *sqq.* ; of children to gods, v. 79

Dee, river in Aberdeenshire, holed stone in the, used by childless women, v. 36 *n.*⁴, xi. 187

Deega marriage, ii. 271 *n.*¹

Deer, magic to attract, i. 109 ; rule as to hamstringing, i. 115 ; taboos observed during the hunting of, i. 122 ; imitation of, as a homoeopathic charm, i. 155 *sq.* ; descent of Kalamants from a, iv. 126 *sq.* ; sacrificed instead of human beings, iv. 166 *n.*¹; flesh of, eaten to prolong life or to avoid fever, viii. 143 ; not eaten by warriors, viii. 144 ; treated with respect by American Indians, viii. 240 *sqq.* ; their bones not given to dogs, viii. 241, 242, 243 ; Indian custom of cutting out the sinew of the thighs of, viii. 264 *sqq.* ; souls of dead in, viii. 286, 293 *sq.*

—— and the family of Lachlin, superstition concerning, xi. 284

Deer clan among the Moquis, viii. 178

—— -hoofs in homoeopathic magic, i. 155 ; used to keep out ghosts, ix. 154 *n.*

Deffingen, in Swabia, Midsummer bonfires at, x. 166 *sq.*

Defiled hands, iii. 174. *See* Hands

—— persons not allowed to look at corn, ii. 112

Defoe, Daniel, on the Angel of the Plague, v. 24 *n.*²

Dehon, P., on witches as cats among the Oraons, xi. 312

Deification of deceased mandarins, i. 415

Deified men, sacrifices of, ix. 409

Deir el Bahari, paintings at, ii. 131, 133

Deiseal, deiseil, deisheal, dessil, according to the course of the sun, viii. 323, 324 ; the right-hand turn, in the Highlands of Scotland, x. 150 *n.*¹, 154

Deities duplicated through dialectical differences in their names, ii. 380 *sq.* *See* Gods

—— of vegetation as animals, viii. 1 *sqq.*

Deity, savage conception of, different from ours, i. 375 *sq.* ; communion with, viii. 325

Dejanira wooed by the river Achelous, ii. 161 *sq.*

Delagoa Bay, the Baronga of, i. 152, 267 *sq.*, vii. 114, viii. 280 ; the Thonga of, x. 29

Delaware Indians, their respect for rattlesnakes, viii. 218 ; their remedies for sins, ix. 263 ; seclusion of girls at puberty among the, x. 54

Delbrück, B., on mother-kin among the Aryans, ii. 283 *n.*⁵

Delena, in British New Guinea, evil magic at, i. 213

Delia, festival at Delos, i. 32 *n.*²

Delian virgins and youths before marriage offer their hair on the grave of dead maidens, i. 28

Delirium, supposed cause of, iii. 83

Delivery, easy, granted to women by Diana, i. 12 ; by trees, ii. 57 *sq.* ; charms to ensure women an, x. 49, 50 *sq.*, 52 ; women creep through a rifted rock to obtain an, xi. 189

Delmenhorst, in Oldenburg, Easter fires at, x. 142

Delos, graves of Hyperborean maidens in, i. 28 *sqq.* ; Apollo and Artemis at, i. 28, 32-35 ; new fire brought from, i. 32, x. 138 ; the temple at, not to be entered after drinking wine, iii. 249 *n.*²; Theseus at, iv. 75 ; sacred embassy to, vi. 244 ; the calendar of, viii. 6 *n.* ; the Thesmophoria in, viii. 17 *n.*²

Delphi, Apollo at, i. 28 ; new fire sent from, i. 32 *sq.* ; gold and silver offerings at, i. 32 *n.*¹; the common hearth at, i. 33 ; grave of Apollo at, i. 34 ; ceremony performed by the king at, i. 45 *sq.* ; slaughter of the python by Apollo at, iii. 223 *n.*¹; tombs of Dionysus and Apollo at, iv. 3 *sq.*, vii. 14 ; festival of Crowning at, iv. 78 *sqq.* ; sacred oak at, iv. 80 *sq.* ; Apollo and the Dragon at, vi. 240 ; perpetual fire at, xi. 91 *n.*⁷; the picture of Orpheus at, xi. 294 ; Stheni, near, xi. 317

Delphic oracle, as to sacrifices to murdered Phocaeans, iv. 95 ; on the cause of dearth, iv. 162 ; as to first-fruits offered at Eleusis, vii. 55, 60 ; on Athens as "the Metropolis of the Corn," vii. 58

Delphinium Ajacis, the flower of Ajax, v. 314 *n.*¹

Delubrum, ancient explanation of the word, viii. 186 *n.*

Demeter, her sacred caverns, v. 88 ; sacred vaults of, v. 278 ; sorrowing for the descent of the Maiden, vi. 41 ; the month of, vi. 41 ; mysteries of, at Eleusis, vi. 90 ; at the well, vi. 111 *n.*⁶; identified with Isis, vi. 117 ; mother of Dionysus by Zeus, vii. 14, 66 ; Homeric Hymn to, vii. 35 *sqq.*, 70 ; her search for Persephone, vii. 36, 57 ; institutes the Eleusinian mysteries, vii. 37 ; a personification of the corn, vii. 39, 40 *sq.* ; etymology of her name, vii. 40 *n.*³, 131 ; distinguished from the Earth-goddess, vii. 41, 43, 89 ; associated with the threshing-floor, vii. 41 *sq.*, 43, 47, 61 *sq.*, 63, 64 *sq.* ; in art, vii. 43 *sq.*, 67 *sq.*, 88 *sq.* ; offerings of first-fruits to, vii. 46 *sqq.*; surnamed Proerosia, vii. 51 ; bestows corn on the Athenians and the Sicilians, vii. 54, 56 *sq.* ; worshipped in Sicily, vii. 56 *sqq.*; sacrifices to her at sowing, vii. 57; associated with seed-corn, vii. 58, 90; her epithets, vii. 63 *sq.*; her image at Eleusis, vii. 64; her intrigue with Zeus, vii. 66; her love-adventure in the furrows of a thrice-ploughed fallow-field, vii. 66, 69; her ancient worship in Crete, vii. 131; in relation to the pig, viii. 16 *sqq.*; horse-headed, of Phigalia, viii. 21, 338; said to have eaten the shoulder of Pelops, viii. 263; rustic prototype of, viii. 334; her mourning for Persephone, ix. 349; the torches of, x. 340 *n.*[1]; serpents in the worship of, xi. 44 *n.*

Demeter, Black, vii. 263; of Phigalia, viii. 21
—— the Corn Goddess, vii. 41 *sqq.*, 56 *sqq.*, 63 *sqq.*, 77 *sq.*
—— the Corn Mother, vii. 53, 58 *sq.*, 75, 131, 184, viii. 334
——, and ears of corn, v. 166
——, Eleusinian, at Ephesus, i. 47
——, Green, vii. 42, 63, 89 *n.*[2], 263
—— and Iasion, vii. 208
—— and the king's son at Eleusis, v. 180
—— and Persephone, vii. 35 *sqq.*; their myth acted in the mysteries of Eleusis, vii. 39, 187 *sq.*; resemblance of their artistic types, vii. 67 *sq.*; their essential identity, vii. 90; associated with death and immortality, vii. 90 *sq.*; double personification of the corn as, vii. 208 *sqq.*; masked dance in rites of, viii. 339; represented by maskers wearing the heads of animals, viii. 339
—— and Poseidon, v. 280
—— and the snake of Cychreus, iv. 87 *n.*[5]
—— Yellow, vii. 41 *sq.*
—— and Zeus, viii. 9; their marriage at Eleusis, ii. 138 *sq.*, vii. 65 *sqq.*

Demeter's corn, vii. 42
Demetrius Poliorcetes deified at Athens, i. 390 *sq.*
Demnat, in the Atlas, New Year rites at, x. 217, 218
Democracy to despotism, social revolution from, i. 371
Democritus, on the generation of serpents, viii. 146; on a cure for scorpion bite, ix. 50 *n.*[1]
Demon supposed to attack girls at puberty, x. 67 *sq.*; festival of fire instituted to ban a, xi. 3. *See* Demons
Demon-worship, ix. 94, 96. *See also* Propitiation
Demonophobia in India, ix. 91
Demons, communion with, by drinking blood, i. 383; of trees, ii. 33 *sq.*, 35, 42; abduction of souls by, iii. 58 *sqq.*; of disease expelled by pungent spices, pricks, and cuts, iii. 105 *sq.*;

coco-nut oil a protection against, iii. 201; infants exposed to the attacks of, iii. 235; deceived by substitution of effigies for living persons, viii. 96 *sq.*; of disease exorcized by masked devil-dancers, ix. 38; bunged up, ix. 61 *sq.*; omnipresence of, ix. 72 *sqq.*; thought to cause sickness and disease, famine, etc., ix. 92, 94, 95, 100, 102, 103, 109 *sqq.*; propitiation of, ix. 93, 94, 96, 100; religious purification intended to ward off, ix. 104; public expulsion of, ix. 109 *sqq.*; of cholera, ix. 116, 117, 123; men disguised as, ix. 170 *sq.*, 172, 173, 213, 214, 235; conjured into images, ix. 171, 172, 173, 203, 204, 205; decoyed by a pig, ix. 200, 201; put to flight by clangour of metal, ix. 233; banned by masks, ix. 246; exorcized by bells, ix. 246 *sq.*, 251; attack women at puberty and childbirth, x. 24 *n.*[2]; expelled at the New Year, x. 134 *sq.*; abroad on Midsummer Eve, x. 172; ashes of holy fires a protection against, xi. 8, 17; vervain a protection against, xi. 62; guard treasures, xi. 65. *See also* Devil, Devils, *and* Evil Spirits

Demons or ghosts averse to iron, iii. 232 *sqq.*; deceived by dummies, viii. 96 *sqq.*; repelled by gun-shots, viii. 99
Denderah or Dendereh, inscriptions at, vi. 11, 86 *sqq.*, 89, 91, 130 *n.*; the hall of Osiris at, vi. 110; sculptures at, vii. 260
Dendit or *Dengdit*, "Great Rain," the Supreme Being of the Dinkas, iv. 30, 32, viii. 40 *n.*, 114 *n.*[2]
Déné or Tinneh Indians, their dread and seclusion of menstruous women, x. 91 *sqq.*; the, Western, tattooing among the, x. 98 *n.*[1] *See also* Tinneh
Denham Tracts, on need-fire in Yorkshire, x. 287 *sq.*
Denmark, precautions against witchcraft on Walpurgis Night in, ii. 54; Whitsun bride in, ii. 91 *sq.*; oaks in the peat-bogs of, ii. 351; the beechwoods of, ii. 351; the Bronze Age in, ii. 351, 352; the Iron Age in, ii. 352; the Stone Age in, ii. 352; the last sheaf at harvest in, vii. 139 *sq.*, 231; the Yule Boar in, vii. 300 *sq.*; fires on St. John's Eve in, x. 171; passing sick children through a hole in the ground in, x. 190, 191; children passed through a cleft oak as a cure for rupture or rickets in, xi. 170, 172
Dennett, R. E., on prince-consorts in Loanga, ii. 277 *n.*[1]
Dedce, a divine spirit in the kingdom of Kaffa, i. 410

Departmental kings of nature, ii. 1 *sqq.*
Deputy, the expedient of dying by, iv. 56, 160
Derbyshire, Plough Monday in, viii. 330 *n.*[1]
Derceto, the fish goddess of Ascalon, v. 34 *n.*[3], ix. 370 *n.*[1]
Dercylus, on Cadmus and the dragon, iv. 84 *n.*[4]
Derry, the oaks of, ii. 242 *sq.* ; the church of, ii. 363
Dervishes, inspired, i. 386 ; the dancing, i. 408 *n.*[1] ; revered in Syria, v. 77 *n.*[4] ; of Asia Minor, v. 170
Descent of people from animals, viii. 25
—— of Persephone, vii. 46, viii. 17
Deslawen, village of Bohemia, expulsion of witches on Walpurgis Night at, ix. 161
Despotic governments, the first advances made to civilization under, i. 218
Dessil. See *Deiseal*
Deucalion at Hierapolis, v. 162 *n.*[2]
Deuteronomic redactor, v. 26 *n.*[1]
Deuteronomy (iv. 17 *sq.*), prohibition of images of animals, i. 87 *n.*[1]; (xxiii. 10, 11), as to custom in time of war, iii. 158 *n.*[1]; (xii. 31, xviii. 9-12), on the sacrifice of children by fire, iv. 168 ; (xv. 19 *sq.*), on the sanctification of the first-born, iv. 173 *n.*[1]
——, publication of, v. 18 *n.*[3]
Deutsch-Zepling in Transylvania, rule as to sowing in, vi. 133 *n.*[3]
Deux-Sèvres, department of, Midsummer fires in the, x. 191 ; fires on All Saints' Day in the, x. 245 *sq.*
Dêvadâsî or *Dêvaratiâl*, dancing-girl in Travancore, v. 63 *sq.*
Devil driven away by paper kites, ix. 4 ; seen on Midsummer Eve, x. 208 ; his partiality for mustard, x. 208 ; brings fern-seed on Christmas night, xi. 289
Devil-dancers, inspired, worshipped as deities in Southern India, i. 382 ; their exorcism of demons, iv. 216 ; conjure demons of disease into themselves, ix. 38
—— -driving in Chitral, ix. 137
Devil's bit, St. John's wort, xi. 55 *n.*[2]
—— Neck, the, ix. 16, 30
—— shoestring (*Tephrosia*) in homoeopathic magic, i. 144
Devils, abduction of souls by, iii. 58 *sqq.*; personated by men, ix. 235 ; ghosts, and hobgoblins abroad on Midsummer Eve, x. 202. *See* Demons
Devonshire, cries of reapers in, vii. 264 *sqq.*; cure for cough in, ix. 51 ; need-fire in, x. 288 ; animals burnt alive as a sacrifice in, x. 302 ; belief in witchcraft in, x. 302 ; crawling under a

bramble as a cure for whooping-cough in, xi. 180
Dew, washing in the, on May morning to ensure a fine complexion and guard against witchcraft, ii. 54, 67 ; gathered on Midsummer morning protects cattle against witchcraft, ii. 127, xi. 74 ; shepherds wash in the, on April 21st, ii. 327 ; rolling or washing in the, on St. George's morning, ii. 333, 339 ; protects cattle against witchcraft on St. George's morning, ii. 335; washing or rolling in, on Midsummer Eve or Day, as a remedy for diseases of the skin, v. 246 *sq.*, 248, x. 208, with *n.*[1]; a daughter of Zeus and the moon, vi. 137
"Dew-treading" in Holland, ii. 104 *n.*[2]
Dharmi or Dharmesh, the Supreme God of the Oraons, ix. 92 *sq.*
Dhimals, the, of Assam, mourners shaved among, iii. 285
Dhinwar class in North-West India, girls of the, married to a god, ii. 149
Dhurma Rajah, incarnate deity in Bhotan, i. 410
DI, Aryan root meaning "bright," ii. 381
Dia, Roman goddess, her grove on the Tiber, ii. 122
Diabolical counterfeits, resemblances of paganism to Christianity explained as, v. 302, 309 *sq.*
Diagora, elective monarchy in, ii. 293
Dialectical differences a cause of the duplication of deities, ii. 382 *sq.*
Diana, as patroness of cattle, i. 7, ii. 124 ; as a torch-bearer, i. 12 ; as goddess of childbirth, i. 12, 40, ii. 128, 378 ; her festival on the 13th of August, i. 12, 14 ; in relation to vines and fruits, i. 15 *sq.*, ii. 128 ; as a goddess of fertility, i. 40, 120 *sqq.*, ii. 115, 378 ; in relation to animals of the woods, ii. 121, 124, 125 *sqq.*; associated with Silvanus, ii. 121 ; groves sacred to, ii. 121 ; as the moon, ii. 128 ; on the Aventine, ii. 128 ; Mount Algidus a haunt of, ii. 380 ; her temple on Mount Tifata, ii. 380 ; a Mother Goddess, v. 45
—— and Dianus, ii. 376 *sqq.*, v. 27, 45
—— (Jana), a double of Juno, ii. 190 *sq.*, 381 *sq.*, xi. 302 *n.*[2]
—— at Nemi, her sanctuary, i. 2 *sqq.*, v. 45 ; as huntress, i. 6 ; priest of, i. 8 *sqq.*, xi. 315 ; as Vesta, i. 13, ii. 380 ; mate of the King of the Wood, i. 40, 41, ii. 121, 380 ; as a goddess of the oak, ii. 380
——, the Tauric, i. 10 *sq.*; her bloody ritual, i. 11, 24

Diana and Virbius, i. 19 *sqq.*, 40 *sq.* ; perhaps annually married at Nemi, ii. 129

Diana's day, 13th of August, iii. 253

—— Mirror, the Lake of Nemi, i. 1, xi. 303

Dianus (Janus), a double of Jupiter, ii. 190 *sq.*, 381 *sq.*

—— and Diana, ii. 376 *sqq.*, v. 27, 45

Diapina, in West Africa, ii. 293

Diascorea, a species of, eaten by the Australian aborigines, vii. 127 *n.*[2]

Diasia, an Athenian festival, cakes shaped like animals sacrificed at the, viii. 95 *n.*[2]

Dice used in divination, ix. 220 ; played at festivals, ix. 350

Dickens, Charles, *Martin Chuzzlewit* quoted, i. 149 *n.*[5] ; on death at ebb-tide, i. 168

Dictynna and Minos, iv. 73

Dido, her magical rites, iii. 312 ; flees from Tyre, v. 50 ; her traditional death in the fire, v. 114 ; worshipped at Carthage, v. 114 ; meaning of the name, v. 114 *n.*[1] ; an Avatar of Astarte, v. 177 ; how she procured the site of Carthage, vi. 250

Diels, Professor H., on human gods in ancient Greece, i. 390 *n.*[2]

Dieppe, fishermen of, their tabooed words, iii. 396

Dieri, the, tribe of Central Australia, their magic for the multiplication of carpet-snakes and iguanas, i. 90 ; their custom as to extracted teeth, i. 177 ; rain-making ceremonies of, i. 255 *sqq.*, xi. 232 ; principal headman of, a medicine-man, i. 336 ; believe certain trees to be their fathers transformed, ii. 29 ; use of bull-roarers among, vii. 106, xi. 229 *sq.*, 232 ; drank blood of slain men to make themselves brave, viii. 151 ; their expulsion of a demon, ix. 110 ; their dread of women at men-struation, x. 77

Diet regulated on the principle of homoeopathic magic, i. 135 ; of kings and priests regulated, iii. 291 *sqq.*

Dieterich, A., on rebirth, iii. 369 *n.*[3]

Difference of language between husbands and wives, iii. 347 *sq.* ; between men and women, iii. 348 *sq.*

Digger Indians of California, ashes of dead smeared on head of mourner among the, viii. 164

Digging the fields, homoeopathic magic at, i. 139

Digging-sticks used by women, vii. 118, 120, 122, 124, 126, 128

Dijon, ox killed at harvest near, vii. 290 ; Lenten fires at, x. 114

Diminution of shadow regarded with apprehension, iii. 86 *sq.*

Dinant, Feast of All Souls in, vi. 70

Dingelstedt, in district of Erfurt, harvest custom at, vii. 221

Dingle, church of St. Brandon near, xi. 190

Dinkas or Denkas, the, of the White Nile, iv. 28 *sqq.* ; magical powers of chiefs among, i. 347 ; worship a supreme being called Dengdit, iv. 30 ; totemism of, iv. 30 *sq.* ; their rain-makers, iv. 31 *sqq.* ; their rain-makers not allowed to die a natural death, iv. 33 ; their belief in serpents as reincarnations of the dead, v. 82 *sq.* ; pour milk on graves, v. 87 ; their reverence for their cattle, viii. 37 *sqq.* ; their offering of first-fruits, viii. 114 ; their use of cows as scapegoats, ix. 193

Dinkelsbühl in Bavaria, the Corn-mother at, vii. 133

Dinnschenchas or *Dinnsenchus*, early Irish document, iv. 183 *n.*[4]

Dio Chrysostom, as to the soul on the lips, iii. 33 ; on fame as a shadow, iii. 86 *sq.* ; on the people of Tarsus, v. 118 ; on pyre at Tarsus, v. 126 *n.*[1] ; on the Sacaea, ix. 368, 402 *n.*[1] ; on Sardanapalus, ix. 390 *n.*[1] ; his account of the treatment of the mock king of the Sacaea, ix. 414

Diocles, prince of Eleusis, vii. 37

Diodorus Siculus, on divine honours accorded to Hippolytus, i. 25 *n.*[1] ; on adoption of Hercules by Hera, i. 74 ; on the worship of Egyptian kings, i. 418 *n.*[2] ; on Amulius Silvius, king of Alba, ii. 180 ; on the origin of fire, ii. 256 *n.*[1] ; on Peleus in Phthia, ii. 278 *n.*[4] ; on the rules of life observed by Egyptian kings, iii. 12 *sq.* ; on the worship of Poseidon in Peloponnese, v. 203 ; on the burial of Osiris, vi. 10 *sq.* ; on the rise of the Nile, vi. 31 *n.*[1] ; on the date of harvest in Egypt, vi. 32 *n.*[2] ; on Osiris as a sun-god, vi. 120 ; on the predominance of women over men in ancient Egypt, vi. 214 ; on worship of Demeter and Persephone, vii. 56 *sqq.* ; on the laments of the Egyptian reapers, vii. 215 ; on the human sacrifices of the Celts, xi. 32

Diomede, at Troezen, i. 27 ; white horses sacrificed to, i. 27 ; sacred grove of, i. 27 ; marries the daughter of the king of Daunia, ii. 278 *sq.* ; human sacrifices to, iv. 166 *n.*[1], v. 145

Dionaea, Venus' fly-trap, homoeopathic magic of, i. 144

Dione, wife of Zeus at Dodona, ii. 189 ; the old consort of Zeus, ii. 381, 382

Dionysiac festival of the opening of the wine jars, ix. 351 *sq.*

Dionysius of Halicarnassus, on the simplicity of Roman worship, ii. 202 *sq.* ; on the Etruscans, ii. 287 *n.*⁴ ; on Tarquin the Proud, ii. 291 *n.*²

Dionysus, vii. 1 *sqq.*; mated with Artemis, i. 36 ; advises the Edonians to put their king Lycurgus to death, i. 366 ; the Lenaean festival of, ii. 44 ; marriage of, to the Queen of Athens, ii. 136 *sq.*, vii. 30 *sq.* ; in the Marshes, sanctuary of, ii. 137 ; as a bull, ii. 137 *n.*¹, v. 123, vii. 16 *sq.*, 31, viii. 3 *sqq.* ; and Ariadne, ii. 138 ; his face or body sometimes painted red, ii. 175 ; identified with ivy, ii. 251 ; in the city, festival of, iii. 316 ; the tomb of, at Delphi, iv. 3 ; human sacrifice consummated by a priest of, iv. 163 ; boys sacrificed to, iv. 166 *n.*¹ ; with vine and ploughman on a coin, v. 166 ; ancient interpretation of, v. 194, 213 ; death, resurrection, and ascension of, v. 302 *n.*⁴, vii. 12 *sqq.*, 32 ; torn in pieces, vi. 98, vii. 13, 14 ; and Lycurgus, vi. 98, vii. 24 ; and Pentheus, vi. 98, vii. 24 ; human sacrifices to, in Chios, vi. 98 *sq.*, vii. 24 ; his coarse symbolism, vi. 113 ; identified with Osiris, vi. 113, vii. 3 ; similarity of the rites of, to those of Osiris, vi. 113, 127 ; race of boys at vintage from his sanctuary, vi. 238 ; men dressed as women in the rites of, vi. 258 ; the effeminate, vi. 259 ; god of the vine, vii. 2 *sq.* ; god of trees, vii. 3 *sq.* ; the Flowery, vii. 4 ; a god of agriculture and corn, vii. 5, 29 ; and the winnowing-fan, vii. 5 *sqq.*, 27, 29 ; as Zagreus, vii. 12 ; horned, vii. 12, 16 ; son of Zeus by Persephone, Demeter, or Semele, vii. 12, 14 ; the sacred heart of, vii. 13, 14, 15 ; ritual of, vii. 14 *sq.* ; his grave at Delphi or at Thebes, vii. 14 ; torn to pieces at Thebes, vii. 14, 25 ; his descent into Hades, vii. 15 ; as god of the dead, vii. 16 ; live animals rent in rites of, vii. 17, 18, viii. 16 ; as a goat, vii. 17 *sq.*, viii. 1 *sqq.* ; human sacrifices in his rites, vii. 24 ; his death and resurrection perhaps acted at the Anthesteria, vii. 32 ; a barbarous deity, vii. 34 ; son of Zeus and Demeter, vii. 66 ; and the bull-roarer, vii. 110 *n.*⁴ ; his relations to Pan, Satyrs, and Silenuses, viii. 1 *sqq.* ; his resurrection perhaps enacted in his rites, viii. 16 ; the Foxy, viii. 282 ; and the drama, ix. 384

Dioscorides on mistletoe, xi. 318 *n.*¹

Diospolis Parva (How), monument of Osiris at, vi. 110

Diphilus, king of Cyprus, v. 146

Dipping for apples at Hallowe'en, x. 237, 239, 241, 242, 245

Dirk to be called by another name on meeting a goblin, iii. 396

Disappearance of early kings, iv. 28, 31

Disc, winged, as divine emblem, v. 132

Discoloration, annual, of the river Adonis, v. 30, 225

Discovery of fire, ii. 255 *sqq.* ; of the body of Osiris, vi. 85 *sq.*

Discs, burning, thrown into the air, x. 116 *sq.*, 119, 143, 165, 166, 168 *sq.*, 172, 328, 334 ; burning, perhaps directed at witches, x. 345

Disease, demons of, expelled by pungent spices, pricks, and cuts, iii. 105 *sq.* ; transferred to other people, ix. 6 *sq.* ; transferred to tree, ix. 7 ; transferred to effigies, ix. 7 ; demons of, exorcized by devil-dancers, ix. 38 ; caused by ghosts, ix. 85 ; annual expulsion of, ix. 139 ; sent away in little ships, ix. 185 *sqq.* ; walking through fire as a remedy for, xi. 7 ; conceived as something physical that can be stripped off the patient and left behind, xi. 172. *See also* Cures, Demons, Sickness

—— of language the supposed source of myths, vi. 42

Disease-makers in Tana, i. 341 *sq.*

Diseases thought to be caused by demons, ix. 92, 94, 95, 100, 102, 103

—— of cattle ascribed to witchcraft, x. 343

Disenchanting strangers, various modes of, iii. 102 *sqq.*

Disguises to avert the evil eye, vi. 262 ; to deceive dangerous spirits, vi. 262 *sq.*, 263 *sq.*

Dish, external soul of warlock in, xi. 141

Dishes, effect of eating out of sacred, iii. 4 ; of sacred persons tabooed, iii. 131 ; special, used by girls at puberty, x. 47, 49. *See* Vessels

Disintegration, atomic, viii. 305

Dislike of people to have children like themselves, iii. 88 *sq.*, iv. 287 (288 in Second Impression)

Dislocation, Roman cure for, xi. 177

Dismemberment of Osiris, suggested explanations of, vi. 97, vii. 262 ; of Halfdan the Black, king of Norway, vi. 100, 102 ; of Segera, a magician of Kiwai, vi. 101 ; of kings and magicians, and use of their severed limbs to fertilize the country, vi. 101 *sq.* ; of the bodies of the dead to prevent their souls from becoming dangerous ghosts, vi. 188

Displacement of heathen festivals by two days in the Christian calendar, i. 14

Disposal of cut hair and nails, iii. 267 *sqq.*

Ditino, deified dead kings of the Barotse, vi. 194

Dittenberger, W., on the Eleusinian games, vii. 77 *n.*[4]

Dittmar, C. von, on the fear of demons among the Koryaks, ix. 100 *sq.*

Diurnal tenure of the kingship, iv. 118 *sq.*

Dius, a Macedonian month, vii. 46 *n.*[2]

Divination from spittle, i. 99 ; by casting stones, inspection of entrails, and interpretation of dreams, i. 344 ; regalia employed as instruments of, i. 363 ; various modes of, on May morning to discover who should be married first, ii. 67 *sq.*; by flowers, ii. 345 ; by wells, ii. 345 ; as to love on St. George's Day among the Slavs, ii. 345 *sq.* ; by crystals, iii. 56 ; by shoulder-blades, iii. 229, viii. 234 ; by knotted threads, iii. 304 *n.*[5] ; to determine the ancestor who is reborn in a child, iii. 368 *sq.* ; by tree and water at Delphi, iv. 80 ; at Midsummer, v. 252 *sq.*, x. 208 *sq.* ; magic dwindles into, vii. 110 *n.*, x. 336 ; by crocodile - hunter, viii. 210 ; on Christmas Day, ix. 316 *n.*[1] ; on Twelfth Night, ix. 316 ; on St. John's Night (Midsummer Eve), x. 173, xi. 46 *n.*[3], 50, 52 *sqq.*, 61, 64, 67 *sqq.* ; at Hallowe'en, x. 225, 228 *sqq.* ; by stones at Hallowe'en fires, x. 230 *sq.*, 239, 240 ; by stolen kail, x. 234 *sq.*, 241 ; by clue of yarn, x. 235, 240, 241, 243 ; by hemp seed, x. 235, 241, 245 ; by winnowing-basket, x. 236 ; by thrown shoe, x. 236 ; by wet shirt, x. 236, 241 ; by white of eggs, x. 236 *sq.*, 238 ; by apples in water, x. 237 ; by a ring, x. 237 ; by names on chimney-piece, x. 237 ; by three plates or basins, x. 237 *sq.*, 240, 244 ; by nuts in fire, x. 237, 239, 241, 242, 245 ; by salt cake, or salt herring, x. 238 *sq.* ; by a sliced apple, x. 238 ; by eaves-dropping, x. 238, 243, 244 ; by knife, x. 241 ; by briar-thorn, x. 242 ; by melted lead, x. 242 ; by cabbages, x. 242 ; by cake at Hallowe'en, x. 242, 243 ; by ashes, x. 243, 244, 245 ; by salt, x. 244 ; by raking a rick, x. 247. *See also* Divining-rod

Divine animal, killing the, viii. 169 *sqq.*

—— animals as scapegoats, ix. 216 *sq.*, 226 *sq.*

" —— consort, the," ii. 131

—— king, the killing of the, iv. 9 *sqq.*

—— kings of the Shilluk, iv. 17 *sqq.*

—— men as scapegoats, ix. 217 *sqq.*, 226 *sq.*

Divine personages not allowed to touch the ground with their feet, x. 2 *sqq.* ; not allowed to see the sun, x. 18 *sqq.* ; suspended for safety between heaven and earth, x. 98 *sq.*

—— spirit incarnate in Shilluk kings, iv. 21, 26 *sq.*

Diviners, ancient, their rules of diet, viii. 143

Divining bones, vi. 180, 181

—— -rod cut on Midsummer Eve, xi. 67 *sqq.* ; made of hazel, xi. 67 *sq.*, 291 *n.*[3] ; made of mistletoe in Sweden, xi. 69, 291 ; made of four sorts of wood, xi. 69 ; made of willow, xi. 69 *n.* ; made out of a parasitic rowan, xi. 281 *sq.*

Divinities, human, bound by many rules, iii. 419 *sq.* ; of the volcano Kirauea, v. 217

Divinity of the Brahmans, i. 403 *sq.*

—— of chief supposed to reside in his eyes, viii. 153

—— claimed by Fijian chiefs, i. 389

—— of kings, i. 48 *sqq.*, 372 ; in the Pacific, i. 386 *sqq.*; in Africa, i. 392 *sq.*, 396 ; among the Hovas, i. 397 ; among the Sakkalava, i. 397 *sq.*; among the Malays, i. 398 ; in India, i. 403 ; in great historical empires, i. 415 *sqq.* ; growth of the conception of the, ii. 376 *sqq.* ; among the Semites, v. 15 *sqq.* ; among the Lydians, v. 182 *sqq.*

Divisibility of life, doctrine of the, xi. 221

Division of labour in relation to social progress, i. 420 ; between the sexes, vii. 129

Divorce of spiritual from temporal power, iii. 17 *sqq.*

Diwali, Hindoo feast of lamps, ii. 160, ix. 145

Dix Cove, in Guinea, crocodiles sacred at, viii. 287

Dixmude, in Belgium, feast of All Souls at, vi. 70

Dixon, Roland B., on the importance of shamans among the Maidu, i. 357

Dixon, Dr. W. E., on hemlock as an anaphrodisiac, ii. 139 *n.*[1]

Djakuns of the Malay Peninsula, their mode of making fire, ii. 236

Djuldjul, girl dressed in leaves and flowers at rain-making ceremony, i. 274

Dobischwald, in Silesia, custom at threshing at, vii. 148 ; need-fire at, x. 278

Dobrizhoffer, Father M., on the reluctance of the Abipones to utter their own names, iii. 328 ; on changes of language among the Abipones, iii. 360 ; on the respect of the Abipones for the Pleiades, v. 258 n.[2]

Doctrine of lunar sympathy, vi. 140 sqq.

Dôd, "beloved," v. 19 n.[2], 20 n.[2]

Dodge, Colonel R. I., on exorcism of strangers among North American Indians, iii. 105; on the death of the Great Spirit, iv. 3

Dodola, girl clad in grass and herbs at rain-making ceremony, i. 273

Dodona, oracular spring at, ii. 172; Zeus at, ii. 177; Zeus and Dione at, ii. 189; bronze gongs at, ii. 358 sq.; Zeus and his oracular oak at, ii. 358, xi. 89 sq.

Dodwell, E., on image of Demeter at Eleusis, vii. 64

Dog, sacrificed to war-god, i. 173; used in rain-making, i. 302; used in stopping rain, i. 303; sacrificed to tree-spirit, ii. 36; sacrificed on roof of new house, ii. 39; prohibition to touch or name, iii. 13; killed instead of king, iv. 17; corn-spirit as, vii. 271 sqq.; of the harvest, vii. 273; feast on flesh of, viii. 256; Iroquois sacrifice of white, viii. 258 n.[1], ix. 127, 209; transmigration of sinner into, viii. 299; sickness transferred to, ix. 33; cough transferred to, ix. 51; fever transferred to, ix. 51; sacrifice of, in time of smallpox, ix. 121; as scapegoat, ix. 209 sq.; not allowed to enter priest's house, x. 4; beaten to ensure woman's fertility, x. 69; charm against the bite of a mad, xi. 56; a Batta totem, xi. 223. See also Dogs

——, black, sacrificed for rain, i. 291; used to stop rain, i. 303

——, white, sacrifice of, viii. 258 n.[2], ix. 127, 209

Dog-demon of epilepsy, ix. 69 n.

—— -eating Spirit, vii. 21

Dog Star, red-haired puppies sacrificed to the, vii. 261; supposed to blight the crops, vii. 261; supposed by the ancients to cause the heat of summer, x. 332. See Sirius

Dog's ghost feared by women, viii. 232 n.[1]

Dogrib Indians will not taste blood, iii. 241; do not pare nails of female children, iii. 263

Dogs crowned, i. 14, ii. 125 sq., 127 sq.; sacrificed at the marriage of Sun and Earth, ii. 99; witches turn into, ii. 334; sacrificed and hung on trees of sacred grove, ii. 365; bones of game kept from, iii. 206; unclean, iii. 206; tigers called, iii. 402; devoured in religious rites, vii. 19, 20, 21, 22; their flesh or liver eaten to acquire

bravery, viii. 145; sacrificed at bear-feasts, viii. 196, 202; not allowed to gnaw bones of slain animals, viii. 225, 238 sqq., 243, 259; bones of deer not given to, viii. 241, 242, 243; the resurrection of, viii. 256 sq.; pairing, fertilizing virtue of stick which has been used to separate, ix. 264 sq.; imitated by dancers, ix. 382. See also Dog, Hounds

Dolac, need-fire at, x. 286

Doliche in Commagene, Jupiter Dolichenus at, v. 136

Doll made of last corn at harvest, vii. 140, 151, 153, 155, 157, 162. See also Dolls

Dollar-bird associated with rain, i. 287 sq.

Dolls or puppets employed for the restoration of souls to their bodies, iii. 53 sqq., 62 sq. See also Doll, Puppets

Dolmen, sick children passed through a hole in a, xi. 188

Domalde, a Swedish king, sacrificed for good seasons, i. 366 sq.

Domaszewski, Professor A., on the rites of Attis at Rome, v. 266 n.[2]

Dominica rosae, the fourth Sunday in Lent, iv. 222 n.[1]

Domitian and the oak crown, ii. 177 n.[2]

Dommartin, Lenten fires at, x. 109

Domovoy, Russian house-spirit, ii. 233 n.[1]

Doms of India, their primitive beliefs, ii. 288 n.[1]

Don Quixote, as to edible acorns, ii. 356

"Donald of the Ear," magic effigy of, i. 69

Donar or Thunar, the German thunder god, the oak of, ii. 364

Door, the words for, in Aryan languages, ii. 384; of house protected against fiends, viii. 96; certain fish and portions of animals not to be brought into house through the, viii. 189 sq., 193, 196, 242 sq., 256; separate, for girls at puberty, x. 43, 44. See also Doors

Doorie, hill of, at Burghead, x. 267

Doorposts, blood of sacrificial victims smeared on, iii. 15, iv. 97, 175, 176 n.[1]

Doors, Janus as a god of, ii. 383 sq.; opened to facilitate childbirth, iii. 296, 297; opened to facilitate death, iii. 309; separate, used by menstruous women, x. 84

Doorway, to stand or loiter in the, forbidden under certain circumstances, i. 114; creeping through narrow opening in, as a cure, xi. 181 sq.

Dorasques of Panama, their theory of earthquakes, v. 201

Dordrecht, "dew-treading" at Whitsuntide at, ii. 104 n.[2]

Doreh in Dutch New Guinea, ghosts of the murdered driven away at, iii. 170; the tug-of-war at, ix. 178

Doreh Bay in Dutch New Guinea, i. 125, iv. 288

Dorians, their superstition as to meteors, iv. 59

Dormice, charm against, viii. 281

Dorpat, rain-making at, i. 248

Dos Santos, J., on the divinity of African kings, i. 392; on the method adopted by a Caffre king to prolong his life, vi. 222 *sq.*

Dosadhs, an Indian caste, the fire-walk among the, xi. 5

Dosuma, king of, not allowed to touch the ground, x. 3

Douay, procession of the giants at, xi. 33 *sq.*

Double, the afterbirth or placenta, regarded as a person's double, vi. 169 *sq.*

Double-axe, Midsummer king of the, x. 194

—— -headed axe, symbol of Sandan, v. 127; carried by Lydian kings, v. 182; a palladium of the Heraclid sovereignty, v. 182; figured on coins, v. 183 *n.*

—— -headed bust at Nemi, i. 41 *sq.*

—— -headed eagle, Hittite emblem, v. 133 *n.*

—— -headed fetish among the Bush negroes of Surinam, ii. 385

—— -headed Janus, explanation of, ii. 384 *sq.*

—— personification of the corn as male and female, vii. 163 *sq.*; of the corn in female form as old and young, vii. 164 *sqq.*, 209 *sq.*; of the corn as mother and daughter, vii. 207 *sqq.*

Doubles, spiritual, of men and animals, in ancient Egypt, iii. 28 *sq.*

Doubs, Montagne de, bonfires on the Eve of Twelfth Night in the, ix. 316

Dough image of god eaten sacramentally, viii. 86 *sqq.*, 90 *sq.*

—— images of animals sacrificed instead of the animals, viii. 95 *n.*[2]

—— puppets as substitutes for live human beings, viii. 101 *sq.*

Douglas, Alexander, victim of witchcraft, ix. 39

Dourgne, in Southern France, crawling through holed stones near, xi. 187 *sq.*

Doutté, Edmond, on the invocation of jinn by their names, iii. 390; on sacred prostitution in Morocco, v. 39 *n.*[3]; on the blessed influence (*baraka*), of Mohammedan saints, ix. 22

Dove, the ceremony of the fiery, at Easter in Florence, x. 126; a Batta totem, xi. 223

Doves burnt in honour of Adonis, v. 126 *n.*[2], 147; external soul of magicians in, xi. 104; Aeneas led by doves to the Golden Bough, xi. 285, 316 *n.*[1]

Doves, sacred, of Aphrodite, v. 33; of Astarte, v. 147, ix. 370 *n.*[1]

Down, County, "Winning the Churn" at harvest in, vii. 154 *sq.*

Dowries earned by prostitution, v. 38, 59

Dracaena terminalis, in magic, i. 159; its leaves used to beat the sick, ix. 265

Dragon, rain-god represented as, i. 297, 298; or serpent of water, ii. 155 *sqq.*; the Slaying of the, at Furth, ii. 163 *sq.*; effigy of, carried at Ragusa on St. George's Day, ii. 164 *n.*[1]; drama of the slaughter of the, iv. 78 *sqq.*, 89; myth of the slaughter of the, iv. 105 *sqq.*; slain by Cadmus at Thebes, vi. 241; at Midsummer, effigy of, xi. 37; external soul of a queen in a, xi. 105; of the water-mill, Servian story of the, xi. 111 *sqq.*

—— and Apollo, at Delphi, iv. 78 *sqq.*, vi. 240

—— of Rouen, destroyed by St. Romain, ii. 164 *sqq.*, 167

—— of Tarascon, carried in procession on Whitsunday, ii. 170 *n.*[1]

—— and Tiger mountains, palace of the head of Taoism on the, i. 413 *sq.*

Dragon-crest of kings, iv. 105

—— divinity of stream prayed to for rain, i. 291 *sq.*

—— stone thought to confer sharpness of vision, i. 165 *n.*[6]

Dragon's blood, a protection against witchcraft, ii. 164; knowledge of the language of birds learnt through tasting, viii. 146

Dragons, artificial, in rain-making, i. 297; or serpents personated by kings, iv. 82; driven away by smoke of Midsummer bonfires, x. 161; St. Peter's fires lighted to drive away, x. 195

—— of water, folk-tales of virgins sacrificed to, ii. 155

Draguignan, in the department of Var, Midsummer fires at, x. 193

Drama, sacred, of the death and resurrection of Osiris, vi. 85 *sq.*; modern Thracian, at the Carnival, vii. 25 *sqq.*; magical, vii. 187 *sq.*

Dramas, magical, to promote vegetation, ii. 120; for the regulation of the seasons, v. 4 *sq.*; to ensure good crops, vii. 187 *sq.*

——, sacred, as magical rites, ix. 373 *sqq.*

Dramatic contests of actors representing Summer and Winter, iv. 254 *sqq.*

—— exhibitions sometimes originate in magical rites, ii. 142

Dramatic performance instituted in time of plague to appease the god, ix. 65
—— representation of the resurrection of Osiris in his rites, vi. 85 ; of the corn-spirit, viii. 325
—— rites practised with magical intention, vii. 1
—— weddings of gods and goddesses, ii. 121
Draupadi or Krishna, the wooing of the princess, ii. 306 ; the heroine of the *Mahabharata*, xi. 7
Dravidian tribes of Northern India forbid a menstruous woman to touch house-thatch, i. 179 n.[1] ; their cure for epilepsy, ix. 259 sq.
Drawing on wood or sand forbidden in absence of hunters, i. 122
Dread and seclusion of menstruous women, x. 76 sqq. ; dread of witchcraft in Europe, x. 342
Dream, guardian spirit or animal acquired in a, xi. 256 sq.
Dreaming on flowers on Midsummer Eve, x. 175. *See* Dreams
Dreams, modes of counteracting evil, i. 172 sq. ; the telling of, a charm to calm a storm, i. 321 ; the interpretation of, i. 344 ; absence of soul in, iii. 36 sqq. ; belief of savages in the reality of, iii. 36 sq. ; omens drawn from, iii. 161, 163, 404, 406 ; spirits of the dead appear to the living in, iii. 368, 374, vi. 162, 190 ; revelations in, iv. 25 ; women visited by a serpent in dreams in a sanctuary of Aesculapius, v. 80 ; revelations given to sick people by Pluto and Persephone in, v. 205 ; as causes of attempted transformation of men into women, vi. 255 sqq. ; as a source of belief in immortality, viii. 260 sq. ; and their fulfilment in time of sickness, ix. 121 ; festival of, among the Iroquois, ix. 127 ; oracular, x. 238, 242 ; of love on Midsummer Eve, xi. 52, 54 ; prophetic, on the bloom of the oak, xi. 292 ; prophetic, on mistletoe, xi. 293
Dreikönigstag, Twelfth Day in Germany and Austria, ix. 329
Drenching of people with water as a rain-charm, i. 250, 251, 269 sq., 272, 273, 274, 275, 277 sq., ii. 47 ; of leaf-clad mummer as a rain-charm, iv. 211 ; of last corn cut with water as a rain-charm, v. 237 sq.
Drinking, modes of, practised by tabooed persons, iii. 117 sqq., 120, 143, 146, 147, 148, 160, 182, 183, 185, 189, 197, 198, 256 ; juices of dead kinsfolk, viii. 163 n.[3]

Drinking out of a king's skull in order to be inspired by his spirit, vi. 171
—— and eating, taboos on, iii. 116 sqq.
Drischila, a threshing cake in West Bohemia, vii. 150
Driver, Professor S. R., on the prae-Israelitish inhabitants of Canaan, iv. 170 n.[5] ; on the consecration of the firstling males, iv. 173 n.[1]
"Driving out the Witches" on Walpurgis Night in Bohemia, ix. 162 ; on Walpurgis Night in Voigtland, x. 160 ; at Midsummer in Switzerland, x. 170, 171
Drobede (Draupadi), the heroine of the epic *Mahabharata*, xi. 7
Drömling, in Brunswick, dramatic contest between Summer and Winter at, iv. 257
Drömling district, in Hanover, need-fire in, x. 277
Drops of water in homoeopathic magic, i. 173
Dropsy, ancient Greek mode of preventing, i. 78 ; ceremony to prevent, in India, i. 79
Drought, funeral of, a rain-making ceremony, i. 274 ; supposed to be caused by unburied dead, i. 287 ; violence done to the rain-powers in time of, i. 296 sqq. ; magical ceremony for causing, i. 313 ; and dearth, chiefs and kings punished for, i. 352 sqq. ; rain-makers killed in time of, ii. 2, 3 ; supposed to be caused by sexual crime, ii. 110, 111, 113 ; supposed to be caused by a concealed miscarriage, iii. 153 sq. ; kings answerable for, v. 21 sq. ; attributed to misconduct of young girls, x. 31
Drowned, souls of the, thought to pass into trees, animals, or fish, ii. 30 ; in holy spring, the sacred bull Apis, viii. 36
Drowning as a punishment for sexual crimes, ii. 109, 110, 111 ; sacrifice by, ii. 364 ; as a mode of executing royal criminals, iii. 242, 243
Drowning girls in rivers as sacrifices, ii. 151 sq.
—— human victims as sacrifices to water-spirits, ii. 157 sqq.
Drowo, gods, in the language of the Ewe-speaking peoples of West Africa, ix. 74
Druid, purification performed by an Irish, ii. 116 ; etymology of the word, x. 76 n.[1]
Druid's Glass, certain beads called the, x. 16 ; prediction, the, x. 229
Druidical festivals, so-called, of the Scotch Highlanders, x. 147, 206 ; custom of

burning live animals, xi. 38; the animals perhaps deemed embodiments of witches, xi. 41 *sq.*, 43 *sq.*

Druidical sacrifices, W. Mannhardt's theory of the, xi. 43

Druidism, so-called, remains of, x. 233, 241 ; and the Christian Church in relation to witchcraft, xi. 42

Druids, Lucan on the, i. 2 *n.*[1] ; oak and mistletoe worshipped by the, ii. 9, 358, 362, xi. 76 *sq.*, 301 ; female, ii. 241 *n.*[1] ; derivation of the name, ii. 363 ; the Irish, ii. 363 ; their superstition as to "serpents' eggs," x. 15 ; their human sacrifices, xi. 32 *sq.* ; in relation to the Midsummer festival, xi. 33 *sqq.*, 45 ; their cycle of thirty years, xi. 77 ; catch the mistletoe in a white cloth, xi. 293

—— of Gaul, their sacrifices of white bulls, ii. 189

—— of Ireland, their custom of driving cattle between two fires at Beltane (May Day), x. 157

Druids' Hill, the, in County Sligo, x. 229

Drum, eating out of a, as a sacrament in the rites of Attis, v. 274

Drumconrath, near Abbeyleix, in Ireland, cut hair kept against the Day of Judgment at, iii. 280 *sq.*

Drums, homoeopathic magic at the making of, i. 134 *sq.* ; beaten as a charm against a storm, i. 325 ; human sacrifice for royal, vi. 223, 225 ; beaten to expel demons, ix. 111, 113, 116, 118, 120, 126, 146, 204

Drunkard, corpse of, in rain-charm, i. 285

Dry food eaten, on principle of homoeopathic magic, i. 114, 144 ; food to be eaten by rain-doctor when he wishes to avert rain, i. 271

Dryas, killed by his father King Lycurgus, vii. 24

—— and Clitus, their contest for a bride, ii. 307

Drynemetum, "the temple of the oak," in Galatia, ii. 363, xi. 89

Du Chaillu, P. B., the Ashira dispute for the clippings of his hair, iii. 271 *sq.*

Du Pratz, Le Page, on the fire-temples of the Natchez, ii. 263; on the festival of the new corn among the Natchez Indians, viii. 77 *sqq.*

Duala tribe of the Cameroons, their story of the type of Beauty and the Beast, iv. 130 *n.*[1]

Duals, a tribe of Garos, their harvest festival, viii. 337

Dublin, Whitsuntide custom near, ii. 103 ; custom on May Day at, ii. 141 *sq.*

Dubrajpur, in Bengal, rain-making at, i. 278

Dubrowitschi, a Russian village, expulsion of spirit of plague at, ix. 173

Duchesne, Mgr. L., on the origin of Christmas, v. 305 *n.*[4] ; on the date of the Crucifixion, v. 307

Duck, gripes transferred to a, ix. 50 ; baked alive as a sacrifice in Suffolk, x. 304

Duck's egg, external soul in a, xi. 109 *sq.*, 115 *sq.*, 116, 119 *sq.*, 120, 126, 130, 132

Ducks and frogs imitated in rain-making, i. 255

—— and ptarmigan, dramatic contest of the, iv. 259

Dudilaa, a spirit who lives in the sun, flesh of pig offered to, ix. 186

Dudulé, boy decked with ferns and flowers at rain-making ceremony, i. 274

Dugong, magical models of, i. 108 ; skulls and bones of, preserved, viii. 258 *n.*[2]

Dugong fishing, taboos in connexion with, iii. 192

Duk-duk, a disguised man representing a cassowary, xi. 247

Duk-duk, secret society of New Britain, New Ireland, and Duke of York Island, x. 11, xi. 246 *sq.*

Duke Town, on the Calabar River, crocodile animated by soul of chief at, xi. 209

—— Town, in Guinea, human sacrifices to the river at, ii. 158 ; periodic expulsion of demons at, ix. 204 *n.*[1]

Duke of York Island, xi. 199 *n.*[2] ; the natives of, pay the fish for those which they catch, viii. 252 ; Duk-duk society in, xi. 247 ; exogamous classes in, xi. 248 *n.*

Dukkala, in Morocco, New Year customs in, x. 218

Dulyn, the tarn of, on Snowdon, i. 307

Dumannos, a month of the Gallic calendar, ix. 343

Dumbartonshire, the harvest Maiden in, vii. 157 *sq.*, 218 *n.*[2] ; harvest custom in, vii. 268 ; Hallowe'en in, x. 237 *n.*[5]

Dumfriesshire, mode of cutting the last standing corn in, vii. 154

Dummies to avert attention of ghosts or demons, viii. 96 *sqq.*

"Dumping" people on harvest field, vii. 226 *sq.*

Dumplings in human form at threshing, vii. 148 ; in form of pigs at harvest supper, vii. 299

Dunbeath, in Caithness, need-fire at, x. 291

Duncan, Mr., on the ceremonial canni-
balism of the coast tribes of British
Columbia, vii. 18 *sq.*
Dung-beetle imitated by actor or dancer,
ix. 381
Dunkeld, Hallowe'en fires near, x. 232
Dunkirk, procession of giants on Mid-
summer Day at, xi. 34 *sq.*
Dunvegan, the laird of, supposed to
attract herring, i. 368
Duplication of deities, vii. 212 *sq.*, ix.
405 *sq.*; an effect of dialectical differences, ii. 382 *sq.*
Duran, Diego, Spanish historian of
Mexico, ix. 295 *n.*[1]; on the human
representative of Xipe, "the Flayed
God," ix. 297; on the date of the
festival of the flaying of men, ix.
300 *n.*[1]
Durandus, G. (W. Durantis), his *Rationale Divinorum Officiorum*, x. 161
Durga, image of, in a magical ceremony,
i. 65
Durham, Miss M. E., on Albanian superstition as to portraits, iii. 100
Durham, the *mell* or *kirn* at harvest in,
vii. 151; Easter candle in the cathedral
of, x. 122 *n.*
Durian-tree threatened in order to make
it bear fruit, ii. 20 *sq.*
Durostorum in Moesia, martyrdom of
St. Dasius at, ii. 310 *n.*[1]; celebration
of the Saturnalia at, ix. 309
Dürrenbüchig, in Baden, the last sheaf
called Goat at, vii. 283
Durris, parish of Kincardineshire, Mid-
summer fires in the, x. 206 *sq.*
Durrow, the oaks of, ii. 242
Dusk of the Evening, prayers of girl at
puberty to the, x. 53
Dussaud, Réné, on stones deposited at
shrines, ix. 22 *n.*[2]
Düsseldorf, Shrove Tuesday custom in
the district of, x. 120
Dussera festival in Behar, i. 279
Dusuns of Borneo, their suspicion of
novelties, iii. 230; their annual expulsion of evils, ix. 200 *sq.*
Dutch custom at the madder-harvest, vii.
231; names for mistletoe, xi. 319 *n.*[1]
Dux, in the Tyrol, "striking down the
dog" at harvest at, vii. 273
Dwandwes, a Zulu tribe, change of name
for the sun among the, iii. 376 *sq.*
Dwarf-elder at Midsummer detects witchcraft, xi. 64
Dwarf tribes of Central Africa, their custom at circumcision, i. 95 *n.*[4]; said
not to know how to make fire, ii. 255
Dyak medicine-men, homoeopathic cure
effected by, i. 84; their use of crystals
in divination, iii. 56

Dyak mode of fishing for a lost soul,
iii. 38
—— sorcerer, his use of effigies to heal
a child, viii. 102
—— stories of the type of Beauty and
the Beast, iv. 126 *sqq.*
—— taboos observed in absence of hunters, i. 120
—— warriors shear their hair on their
return, iii. 261
Dyaks, the, of Borneo, ceremony to aid
a woman in childbirth among, i.
73 *sq.*; telepathy in war among, i.
127; their way of strengthening their
souls, i. 159 *sq.*; their ascription of
souls to trees, ii. 13; believe that the
souls of those who die by accident or
drowning pass into trees, animals, or
fish, ii. 30 *sq.*; call on tree-spirit to
quit tree before it is felled, ii. 37;
their custom at felling a jungle, ii. 38;
their belief as to the blighting effects of
sexual crimes, ii. 108 *sq.*; their use of
effigies to heal the sick, iii. 63 *n.*[2], viii.
100 *sq.*, 102; their mode of securing the
souls of their enemies, iii. 71 *sq.*; extract
the souls of captured foes, iii. 72 *n.*[1];
taboos as to tying knots during
a woman's pregnancy among, iii.
294; children called the fathers or
mothers of their first cousins among,
iii. 332 *sq.*; names of relations tabooed
among, iii. 339 *sq.*; their belief as to
the spirit of gold, iii. 409 *sq.*; taboos
observed by, in digging for gold,
iii. 410; sacrifice cattle instead of
human victims, iv. 166 *n.*[1]; practice of
swinging among their medicine-men,
iv. 280 *sq.*; their whole life dominated
by religion, vii. 98; their ceremonies
to secure the rice-soul, vii. 188 *sq.*;
their sun-dial, vii. 314 *n.*[4]; their use
of images to deceive demons of plague,
viii. 100 *sq.*; their festival of first-fruits,
viii. 122; will not let warriors eat
venison lest it make them timid, viii.
144; their unwillingness to kill crocodiles, viii. 209; their ceremonies at
killing crocodiles, viii. 209 *sqq.*; their
priestesses, ix. 5; their transference of
evil, ix. 5; their "lying heaps," ix.
14; their mode of neutralizing bad
omens, ix. 39; their Head Feast, ix.
383; birth-trees among, xi. 164; trees
and plants as life indices among, xi.
164 *sq.*; their doctrine of the plurality
of souls, xi. 222. *See also* Sea Dyaks
—— of Landak and Tajan, marriage
custom of the, x. 5; birth-trees among
the, xi. 164
—— of Pinoeh, their custom at a birth,
xi. 154 *sq.*

Dyaks of Poelopetak, their words for soul, vii. 182 *sq.*

—— of Sarawak, their belief in the power of the Rajah to fertilize the rice-crops, i. 361 *sq.* ; their custom at rice harvest and sowing, ii. 48 ; story of their descent from a fish, iv. 126 ; their custom of swinging at harvest feast, iv. 277 ; their observation of the Pleiades, vii. 314 ; eat parts of slain foes, viii. 152

——, the Sea, or Ibans, of Sarawak, viii. 279 ; rules observed by women among, while the men are at war, i. 127 *sq.*; their sacred trees, ii. 40 *sq.*; their sorcerers supposed to hook departing souls, iii. 30 ; their modes of recalling the soul, iii. 47 *sq.*, 52 *sq.*, 55 *sq.*, 60, 67 ; taboos observed by head-hunters among, iii. 166 *sq.*; their propitiation of dead omen birds, iv. 126 ; their sacrifices during an epidemic, iv. 176 *n.*[1]; their custom of head-hunting, v. 295 *sq.* ; the idea of metampsychosis among, viii. 294 *sq.*; their modes of protecting their farms against mice, viii. 279 ; their festival of departed spirits, ix. 154

Dying at ebb tide, i. 167 *sq.*; custom of catching the souls of the, iv. 198 *sqq.*; by deputy, iv. 56, 160

Dying god as scapegoat, ix. 227

—— and Reviving God, vii. 1, 33

—— and risen god, the, in Western Asia, ix. 421 *sq.*

Dynder, in Herefordshire, sin-eater at, ix. 43

Dziewanna, puppet representing the goddess of spring in Polish districts of Silesia, iv. 246

Ea, Babylonian god, v. 9 ; the inventor of magic, i. 240

Eabani, Babylonian hero, his death and resurrection, ix. 398 *sq.*

Eagle, guardian spirit as, i. 200 ; tree on which an eagle has built its nest deemed holy, ii. 11 ; the bird of Jove, ii. 175 ; soul in form of, iii. 34 ; to carry soul to heaven, v. 126 *sq.* ; sacrifice to, x. 152

——, double-headed, Hittite emblem, v. 133 *n.*

Eagle bone, used to drink out of, x. 45

—— clan of the Niskas, xi. 271, 272 *n.*[1]

—— hawk totem, i. 162 ; legs of boys beaten with leg-bone of, to make them strong, viii. 165 *n.*[2]; external soul of medicine-man in, xi. 199

—— hunters, taboos observed by, i. 116, iii. 198 *sq.* ; taboos observed by the wives and children of, i. 119 ; charms employed by, i. 149 *sq.*

Eagle-owl worshipped by the Ainos, viii. 199 *sq.*

—— -spirits and buried treasures, x. 218

—— -wood, telepathy in search for, i. 120 ; special language employed by searchers for, iii. 404

Eagle's gall in homoeopathic magic, i. 154

—— tongue torn out and worn as talisman, viii. 270

Eagles not called by their proper names, iii. 399 ; worshipped by the Ainos, viii. 200 ; propitiation of dead, viii. 236

——, sacred among the Ostyaks, ii. 11

Eames, W., on voluntary substitutes for capital punishment in China, iv. 273

Ear of corn, reaped, displayed to the initiates at the Eleusinian mysteries, ii. 138 *sq.*, vii. 38 ; emblem of Demeter, v. 166

Ears cleansed by serpents, i. 158 ; stopped to prevent the escape of the soul, iii. 31 ; of sacrificial victims cut off, iv. 97 ; of seers licked by serpents, vii. 147 *n.*[1] ; regarded as the seat of intelligence, vii. 148 ; of brave men eaten, viii. 148 ; of dead enemies cut out, viii. 271 *sq.* ; blood drawn from, as penance, ix. 292

Earth, inspired priestess of, i. 381 *sq.* ; from a grave, magical uses of, i. 147 *sq.*, 150 ; spring festival of the marriage of, ii. 76 *sq.*, 94 ; conceived by the Greeks as the Mother of corn, cattle, and human beings, ii. 128 *n.*[4]; praying to Zeus for rain, image of, ii. 359 ; festival in honour of, iii. 247 ; subterranean, sacrifices to, vii. 66 ; Lithuanian prayers to the, viii. 49 ; the spirit of, worshipped before sowing, viii. 120 ; first berries of the season offered to the, viii. 133 *sq.* ; taboos observed by the priest of, in Southern Nigeria, x. 4 ; prayers to, x. 50

——, the goddess, mother of Typhon, v. 156

——, Grandmother, the cause of earthquakes, v. 198

—— and heaven, between, xi. 1 *sqq.*

——, the Mistress of the, ix. 85

——, Mother, v. 27 ; prayed to for rain, i. 283 ; festival of, v. 90 ; vicarious sacrifices offered to, viii. 105

——, the Nursing-Mother at Athens, vii. 89 *n.*[2]

—— and sky, myth of their violent separation, v. 283

——, the spirit of the, worshipped before sowing, viii. 120

—— and Sun, marriage of the, ii. 98 *sq.*, 148

Earth-demons dreaded by Tibetans, viii. 96
—— -god, vii. 69, ix. 28, 61 ; the Egyptian, ix. 341
—— -goddess, sacrifice for rain to, i. 291 ; pregnant cows sacrificed to, ii. 229 ; annually married to Sun-god, v. 47 sq. ; disturbed by the operations of husbandry, v. 88 sqq. ; married to Skygod, v. 282, with n.² ; distinguished from Demeter, vii. 41, 43, 89 ; in Greek art, vii. 89 ; human sacrifices offered to, vii. 245, 246, 249, 250 ; firstfruits of maize offered to the, viii. 115
—— -gods, slaves of the, viii. 61, 62 n.¹
—— -mothers, name given to maizespadices growing as twins, vii. 173 n.
—— -spirits possess the ore in mines, iii. 407 n.² ; disturbed by agriculture, v. 89
Earthman, the, representing the god of the earth, ix. 61
Earthquake god, v. 194 sqq.
Earthquakes supposed to be caused by indulgence in illicit love, ii. 111 n.³ ; attempts to stop, v. 196 sqq. ; Manichean theory of, v. 197
Earthworms eaten by dancing girls, viii. 147
Easing nature, a charm used by robbers, vii. 235
East, the ascetic idealism of the, ii. 117 ; mother-kin and Mother Goddesses in the ancient, vi. 212 sqq. ; the Wise Men of the, ix. 330 sq.
—— Indian evidence of the belief in the transmigration of human souls into animals, viii. 298 n.²
East Indian islands, epilepsy transferred to leaves in the, ix. 2 ; demons of sickness expelled in little ships in the, ix. 185
—— Indies, pregnant women forbidden to tie knots in the, iii. 294 ; everything in house opened to facilitate childbirth in the, iii. 297 ; reluctance of persons to tell their names in the, iii. 328 ; the Rice-mother in the, vii. 180 sqq. ; sacrifices of first-fruits in the, viii. 122 sqq. ; the tug-of-war in the, ix. 177
Easter, rolling down a slope at, ii. 103 ; first Sunday after, iv. 249 ; custom of swinging on the four Sundays before, iv. 284 ; gardens of Adonis at, in Sicily, v. 253 sq. ; resemblance of the festival of, to the rites of Adonis, v. 254 sqq., 306 ; the festival of, assimilated to the spring festival of Attis, v. 306 sqq. ; controversy between Christians and pagans as to the origin of, v. 309 sq. ; White Russian custom at, to preserve the corn from hail, vii. 300 ; an old vernal festival of the

vegetation - god, ix. 328 ; fern - seed blooms at, xi. 292 n.²
Easter candle, x. 121, 122, 125
—— ceremonies in the New World, x. 127 sq.
—— eggs, ix. 269, x. 108, 143, 144
—— Eve, in Albania, expulsion of Kore on, iv. 265, ix. 157 ; grain of Cornmother scattered among the young corn on, vii. 134 ; new fire on, x. 121, 124, 126, 158 ; the fern blooms at, xi. 66
—— fires, x. 120 sqq.
—— Islanders, their modes of killing animals, iii. 247 ; their offerings of first-fruits, viii. 133
—— Man, burning the, x. 144
—— Monday, festival of Green George on, ii. 76 ; "Easter Smacks" on, ix. 268 ; fire-custom on, x. 143
—— Mountains, bonfires at Easter on, x. 140, 141
—— Saturday, barren fruit-trees threatened on, ii. 22 ; new fire on, x. 121, 122, 124, 127, 128, 130 ; the diviningrod baptized on, xi. 69
"—— Smacks" in Germany and Austria, ix. 268 sq.
—— Sunday, vii. 33 ; ceremony observed by the gipsies of South-Eastern Europe on the evening of, ix. 207 sq. ; red eggs on, x. 122
—— Tuesday, swinging on, iv. 283 ; "Easter Smacks" on, ix. 268, 270 n.
Eastertide, death and resurrection of Kostrubonko at, iv. 261 ; expulsion of evils at, in Calabria, ix. 157
Eater of animals, as epithet of a god, vii. 23
"—— of the Dead," fabulous Egyptian monster, vi. 14
Eating out of sacred vessels, supposed effect of, iii. 4 ; together, covenant formed by, iii. 130 ; piece of slain man, custom obligatory on the slayer, iii. 174 ; the bodies of aged relations, custom of, iv. 14
—— and drinking, taboos on, iii. 116 sqq. ; fear of being seen in the act of, iii. 117 sqq.
—— the god, viii. 48 sqq. ; among the Aztecs, viii. 86 sqq. ; reasons for, viii. 138 sq., 167
—— the soul of the rice, viii. 54
Eaves, rain-drops from, in magic, i. 253
Eavesdropping, divination by, x. 238, 243, 244
Ebb tide, death at, i. 167 sq.
Echinadian Islands, death of the Great Pan announced at the, iv. 6
Echternach in Luxemburg, Lenten firecustom at, x. 116

Eck, R. van, on the belief in demons in Bali, ix. 86
Eckstein, Miss L., on hunting the wren, viii. 317 *n.*[2]
Eclipse, ceremonies at an, i. 311 *sq.*
—— of the moon, custom of the Indians of the Orinoco at an, i. 311 ; Athenian superstition as to an, vi. 141
—— of the sun, burning arrows shot into the air at an, i. 311 ; practice of the Kamtchatkans at an, i. 312 ; practice of the Chilcotin Indians at an, i. 312, iv. 77
—— of the sun and moon, belief of the Tahitians as to, iv. 73 *n.*[2]
Eclipses attributed to monster biting or attacking the sun or moon, i. 311 *n.*[1], x. 70, 162 *n.* ; air thought to be poisoned at, x. 162 *n.*
Ecliptic perhaps mimicked in dances, iv. 77
Economic history, the discovery of agriculture the greatest advance in, vii. 129
—— progress a condition of intellectual progress, i. 218
Ecstasy induced by smoking, viii. 72
Ecuador, the Canelos Indians of, iii. 97, viii. 285 ; the Saragacos Indians of, iii. 152 ; human sacrifices for the crops in, vii. 236 ; the Zaparo Indians of, viii. 139
Edbald, king of Kent, married his stepmother, ii. 283
Edda, the prose, story of Balder in, x. 101 ; the poetic, story of Balder in, x. 102
Eddesse, in Hanover, need-fire at, x. 275 *sq.*
Eden, the tree of life in, v. 186 *n.*[4]
Edersleben, Midsummer fire-custom at, x. 169
Edgewell Tree, oak at castle of Dalhousie, thought to be linked with the fate of the Dalhousie family, xi. 166, 284
Edom, blood royal apparently traced in the female line in, v. 16 *n.*
——, the kings of, take the name of a divinity, v. 15 ; their bones burned by the Moabites, v. 104
Edonians, a Thracian tribe, their king Lycurgus put to death to restore fertility to the land, i. 366, vi. 98, 99, vii. 24
Edward the Confessor, English kings said to derive their power of healing scrofula from, i. 370
Edward VI., his Lord of Misrule, ix. 332, 334
Eel-skins in homoeopathic magic, i. 155
Eels regarded as water-serpents, iv. 84 ; souls of dead in, viii. 289, 290, 292
Eesa, a Somali tribe, their custom of milk-drinking on the morning after a marriage, vi. 246
Effacing impressions from bed-clothes, ashes, etc., from superstitious motives, i. 213 *sq.*
Effect of geographical and climatic conditions on national character, vi. 217 ; supposed, of killing a totem animal, xi. 220
Effeminate sorcerers or priests, order of, vi. 253 *sqq.*
Effigies, substituted for human victims, iv. 215, 217 *sq.*, ix. 408 ; disease transferred to, ix. 7 ; demons conjured into, ix. 204, 205 ; burnt in bonfires, x. 106, 107, 116, 118 *sq.*, 119 *sq.*, 121, 122, 159 ; burnt in the Midsummer fires, x. 167, 172 *sq.*, 195 ; of witches burnt in the fires, x. 342, xi. 19, 43 ; of human beings burnt in the fires, xi. 21 *sqq.* ; of giants burnt in the summer fires, xi. 38. *See also* Effigy, Dolls, Images, Puppets
—— of Carnival destroyed, iv. 222 *sqq.*
—— of Death, iv. 233 *sq.*, 246 *sqq.*
—— of Judas burnt at Easter, x. 121, 127 *sq.*, 130 *sq.*
—— of Kupalo, Kostroma, and Yarilo drowned or buried in Russia, iv. 262 *sq.*
—— of Lent, seven-legged, in Spain and Italy, iv. 244 *sq.*
—— of men and women hung at doors of houses, viii. 94 ; buried with the dead to deceive their ghosts, viii. 97 *sq.* ; used to cure or prevent sickness, viii. 100 *sqq.*
—— of Osiris, stuffed with corn, buried with the dead as a symbol of resurrection, vi. 90 *sq.*, 114
—— of Shrove Tuesday destroyed, iv. 227 *sqq.*
—— of Winter burnt at Zurich, iv. 260 *sq.*
Effigy, human sacrifices carried out in, iv. 217 *sqq.* ; of an ox broken as a spring ceremony in China, viii. 10 *sqq.* ; of man used in exorcizing misfortune, ix. 8 ; of baby used to fertilize women, ix. 245, 249 ; of absent friend cut in a tree, xi. 159 *sq.*
Effiks or Agalwa, the, of West Africa, their custom of carrying fire, ii. 259 ; their belief in external or bush souls, xi. 206
Efiat, human sacrifices offered by the fishermen of, ii. 158
Efugaos, the, of the Philippine Islands, suck the brains of dead foes to acquire their courage, viii. 152
Egbas, the, of West Africa, their custom of putting their kings to death, iv. 41
Egede, Hans, on impregnation by the moon among the Greenlanders, x. 76

Egeria, water nymph at Nemi, i. 17-19, 41 ; and Numa, i. 18, ii. 172 *sqq.*, 193, 380; perhaps a local form of Diana, ii. 171 *sq.*, 267, 380; an oak-nymph, ii. 172, 267; the grove of, ii. 185

Egerius Baebius or Laevius, Latin dictator, dedicated the sacred grove at Nemi, i. 22

Egg broken in water, divination by means of, x. 208 *sq.*

—— -shells preserved lest chickens should die, viii. 258 *n.*[2]

Egghiou, a district of Abyssinia, rain-making in, i. 258

Eggs eaten by sower to make hemp grow tall, i. 138 ; of raven in homoeopathic magic, i. 154 ; or egg-shells, painted, in spring ceremonies, ii. 63, 65 ; collected on May Day, ii. 64, 65 ; yellow and red, fastened to Midsummer trees, ii. 65 ; collected at spring ceremonies, ii. 78 ; begged for by singers or maskers at Whitsuntide, ii. 81, 84, 85, 91 *sq.* ; in purificatory rite, ii. 109 ; offered at entering a strange land, iii. 110 ; reason for breaking shells of, iii. 129 *sq.* ; reason for not eating, viii. 140 ; charm to make hens lay, viii. 326 ; charm to ensure plenty of, x. 112, 338 ; begged for at Midsummer, x. 169 ; divination by white of, x. 236 *sq.*, 238 ; external souls of fairy beings in, xi. 106 *sqq.*, 110, 125, 132 *sq.*, 140 *sq.*

——, Easter, ix. 269, x. 108, 122, 143, 144

Egin, in Armenia, rain-making at, i. 276 ; rain-pebbles at, i. 305

Egypt, the hawk the symbol of the sun and of the king in, iv. 112 ; wives of Ammon in, v. 72 ; date of the corn-reaping in, v. 231 *n.*[3] ; the Nativity of the Sun at the winter solstice in, v. 303 ; in early June, vi. 31 ; the gods flee into, vii. 18 ; ghosts of murdered men nailed into the earth in, ix. 63 ; Isis and Osiris in, ix. 386

——, ancient, magical images in, i. 66, 67 *sq.* ; theocratic despotism of, i. 218 ; power of magicians in, i. 225 ; confusion of magic and religion in, i. 230 *sq.* ; ceremonies for the regulation of the sun in, i. 312 ; kings blamed for failure of the crops in, i. 354 ; the sacred beasts held responsible for the course of nature in, i. 354 ; the royal crowns in, i. 364 ; king of, masquerading as Ammon, ii. 133 ; sacrifice to the Sun in, iii. 227 *n.* ; mock human sacrifices in, iv. 217 ; mother-kin in, vi. 213 *sqq.* ; human

sacrifices in, vii. 259 *sqq.* ; stratification of religion in, viii. 35 ; story of the external soul in, xi. 134 *sqq.*

Egypt, the Flight into, xi. 69 *n.*

——, kings of, derive their titles from the sun-god, i. 418. *See* Egyptian

——, Lower, the Red Crown of, vi. 21 *n.*[1] ; Sais in, vi. 50

——, modern, magicians work enchantments through the name of God in, iii. 390 ; headache nailed into a door in, ix. 63 ; belief in the jinn in, ix. 104

——, Queen of, married to the god Ammon, ii. 131 *sq.*

——, Upper, temporary kings in, iv. 151 *sq.* ; the White Crown of, vi. 21 *n.*[1] ; new-born babes placed in corn-sieves in, vii. 7

Egyptian calendar, the official, vi. 24 *sqq.* ; date of its introduction, vi. 36 *n.*[2]

—— ceremony to help the sun-god against demons, i. 67 *sq.*

—— custom of drowning a girl as a sacrifice to the Nile, ii. 151

—— deities arranged in trinities, iv. 5 *n.*[3]

—— doctrine that a woman can conceive by a god, ii. 135

—— farmer, calendar of the, vi. 30 *sqq.* ; his festivals, vi. 32 *sqq.*

—— festivals, their dates shifting, vi. 24 *sq.*, 92 *sqq.* ; readjustment of, vi. 91 *sqq.*

—— gods, mortality of the ancient, iv. 4 *sqq.* ; trinities of gods, iv. 5 *n.*[3]

—— influence on Christian doctrine of the Trinity, iv. 5 *n.*[3]

—— kings deified in their lifetime, i. 418 *sqq.* ; rules of life observed by, iii. 12 *sq.* ; flesh diet of, iii. 13, 291 ; drank no wine, iii. 249 ; called bulls, iv. 72 ; worshipped as gods, v. 52 ; the most ancient, buried at Abydos, vi. 19 ; their oath not to correct the vague Egyptian year by intercalation, vi. 26 ; perhaps formerly slain in the character of Osiris, vi. 97 *sq.*, 102 ; as Osiris, vi. 151 *sqq.* ; renew their life by identifying themselves with the dead and risen Osiris, vi. 153 *sq.* ; born again at the Sed festival, vi. 153, 155 *sq.* ; perhaps formerly put to death to prevent their bodily and mental decay, vi. 154 *sq.*, 156 ; their animal masks, vii. 260 ; deified, their souls deposited during life in portrait statues, xi. 157

—— kings and queens, their begetting and birth depicted on the monuments, ii. 131 *sqq.*

—— magicians, their power of compelling the deities, iii. 389 *sq.*

Egyptian months, table of, vi. 37 *n*.
—— mothers glad when the holy crocodiles devoured their children, iv. 168 *n*.[1]
—— myth of the separation of earth and sky, v. 283 *n*.[3]
—— priests loathed the sea, iii. 10 ; abstained from swine's flesh, viii. 24 *n*.[2]
—— reapers, their lamentations and invocations of Isis, v. 232, vi. 45, 177, vii. 215, 261, 263 ; their song or cry, vii. 215, 263
—— religion, the development of, vi. 122 *sqq.*; dominated by Osiris, vi. 158 *sq.*
—— sacred beasts, offerings to the, i. 29 *sq.*
—— sovereigns masked as lions, bulls, and serpents, iv. 72 *n*.[7]
—— standard resembling a placenta, vi. 156 *n*.[1]
—— tombs, plaques or palettes of schist in, xi. 155
—— type of animal sacrament, viii. 312 *sq.*, 314
—— women plaster their heads with mud in mourning, iii. 182
—— year vague, not corrected by intercalation, vi. 24 *sq.*; the sacred, began with the rising of Sirius, vi. 35
Egyptians, their worship of sacred beasts, i. 29 *sq.* ; kept their hair unshorn on a journey, iii. 261 ; their funeral rites a copy of those performed over Osiris, vi. 15 ; their hope of immortality centred in Osiris, vi. 15 *sq.*, 114, 159 ; their dead identified with Osiris, vi. 16 ; their astronomers acquainted with the true length of the solar year, vi. 26, 27, 37 *n*. ; their ceremony at the winter solstice, vi. 50 ; their sacrifice of red-haired men, vi. 97, 106 ; their language akin to the Semitic, vi. 161 ; the conservatism of their character, vi. 217 *sq.* ; compared to the Chinese, vi. 218 ; worshipped crocodiles, viii. 209 *n.* ; their doctrine of the *ka* or external soul, xi. 157 *n*.[2]
——, the ancient, their festival, "the nativity of the sun's walking-stick," i. 312 ; worshipped men and animals, i. 389 *sq.* ; sycamores worshipped by, ii. 15 ; ritual flight at embalming among, ii. 309 *n*.[2] ; their conception of the soul, iii. 28 *sq.*; their practice as to souls of the dead, iii. 68 *sq.* ; personal names among, iii. 322; question of their ethnical affinity, vi. 161 ; human sacrifices offered by, vii. 259 *sq.*, xi. 286 *n*.[2] ; their religious attitude to pigs, viii. 24 *sqq.* ; their belief in spirits, ix. 103 *sq.* ; their use of

bulls as scapegoats, ix. 216 *sq.* ; the five supplementary days of their year, ix. 340 *sq.*
Eifel Mountains, the King of the Bean in the, ix. 313 ; Lenten fires in the, x. 115 *sq.*, 336 *sq.*; effigy burnt at Cobern in the, x. 120; St. John's fires in the, x. 169; the Yule log in the, x. 248 ; Midsummer flowers in the, xi. 48
Eight days, feast and license of, before expulsion of demons, ix. 131
—— years, reign of kings apparently limited in ancient Greece to, iv. 58, 70 *sqq.* ; cycle in ancient Greece, iv. 68 *sqq.*, vii. 80 *sqq.*
Eighty-one (nine times nine) men make need-fire, x. 289, 294, 295
Eimine Ban, an Irish abbot, legend of his self-sacrifice, iv. 159 *n*.[1]
Eiresione of ancient Greece, ii. 48, 71
Eisenach, effigy of Death burnt on the fourth Sunday of Lent at, iv. 247 ; harvest customs near, vii. 231
—— Oberland, the Corn-cat in the, vii. 280
Ekebergia sp., used in kindling fire by friction, ii. 210
Eket, in North Calabar, sacred lake near, xi. 209
Ekoi, the, of West Africa, their custom of mutilating men and women at festivals, v. 270 *n*.[2] ; ceremony observed by them at crossing a ford, ix. 28 ; throw leaves on dead chameleons, ix. 28 ; their belief in external or bush souls, xi. 206 *sqq.*
El, Phoenician god, v. 13, 16 *n*.[1] ; identified with Cronus, v. 166
—— -Bûgât, festival of mourning for Tammuz in Harran, v. 230
—— Kiboron, a Masai clan, may not pluck out their beards lest they lose their power of making rain, iii. 260 ; their respect for serpents as embodiments of the dead, viii. 288
—— Obeid, i. 122
Elam, the kings of, their bones carried off by Ashurbanipal, vi. 103 *sq.*
Elamite deities in opposition to Babylonian deities, ix. 366 ; inscriptions, ix. 367
Elamites, the hereditary foes of the Babylonians, ix. 366
Elangela, external soul in Fan language, xi. 201, 226 *n*.[1]
Elans treated with respect by American Indians, viii. 240
Elaphebolion, an Athenian month, ix. 143 *n*., 351
Elaphius, an Elean month, ix. 352
Elbe, the river, dangerous on Midsummer Day, xi. 26
Elder brother, his name not to be pro-

nounced, iii. 341 ; the sin of marrying before an, ix. 3

Elder, dwarf, in rain-making, i. 273

—— -bush cut hair buried under an, iii. 275 ; creeping under an, as a cure for fever, ix. 55

—— -flowers gathered at Midsummer, xi. 64

—— -tree, cut hair and nails inserted in an, iii. 275 *sq.* ; fever transferred to a twig of the, ix. 49

—— -trees sacred among the old Prussians, ii. 43

Elders, council of, in savage communities, i. 216 *sq.*

Eldest sons sacrificed for their fathers, iv. 161 *sqq.*

Elecampane in a popular remedy for worms, x. 17

Elective and hereditary monarchy, combination of the two, ii. 292 *sqq.*

—— kings and hereditary queens, ii. 295

Electric conductivity of various kinds of wood, xi. 299 *n.*^{2}

—— lights on mast-heads, spears, etc., ancient superstitions as to, i. 49 *sq.*

Electricity, spiritual, royal personages charged with, i. 371

Elephant-hunters, taboos observed by wives of absent, i. 120, x. 5 ; telepathy of, i. 123 ; scarify themselves after killing an elephant, iii. 107 ; continence of, iii. 196 *sq.* ; special language employed by, iii. 404 ; not to touch the earth with their feet, x. 5

—— -hunting, inoculation before, viii. 160

Elephant's flesh tabooed, i. 118 *sq.* ; thought to make eater strong, viii. 143

Elephants not to be called by their proper name, iii. 403, 407 ; souls of dead transmigrate into, iv. 85, viii. 289 ; ceremonies observed at the slaughter of, viii. 227 *sq.*, 237 ; lives of persons bound up with those of, xi. 202, 203 ; external human souls in, xi. 207

Eleusine grain, cultivated by the Nandi, vii. 117

Eleusinian Games, vii. 70 *sqq.*, 110, 180 ; held every four or two years, vii. 70, 77 ; victors in the, rewarded with measures of barley, vii. 73 ; primarily concerned with Demeter and Persephone as goddesses of the corn, vii. 74 ; less ancient than the Eleusinian mysteries, vii. 87 *sq.*

—— inscription dealing with first-fruits, vii. 55 *sq.*

—— mysteries, vii. 35 *sqq.* ; presided over by the king, i. 44 ; sacred marriage of

Zeus and Demeter in the, ii. 138 *sq.*, vii. 65, *sqq.*, viii. 9 ; origin of, told in the Homeric *Hymn to Demeter*, vii. 35 *sqq.* ; instituted by Demeter, vii. 37 ; the myth of Demeter and Persephone acted at the, vii. 39, 66, 187 *sq.* ; date of the celebration of the, vii. 69 *sq.* ; said to be instituted by Eumolpus, vii. 70 ; great antiquity of the, vii. 78 *sq.* ; hope of immortality associated with initiation into the, vii. 90 *sq.* ; designed to promote the growth of the corn, vii. 110 *sq.* ; sacrament of barley-meal and water at the, vii. 161 *sq.*

Eleusinian priests, their names sacred, iii. 382 *sq.*

Eleusis, mysteries of, ii. 138 *sq.*, vii. 35 *sqq.* ; Demeter and the king's son at, v. 180 ; sacrifice of oxen at, v. 292 *n.*^{3} ; mysteries of Demeter at, vi. 90 ; Demeter at, vii. 36 *sq.*, viii. 334 ; the Rarian plain at, vii. 36, 70, 74, 234, viii. 15 ; offerings of first-fruits at, vii. 53 *sqq.* ; festival of the threshing-floor at, vii. 60 *sqq.* ; the Green Festival and the Festival of Cornstalks at, vii. 63 ; image of Demeter at, vii. 64 ; prayer for rain at, vii. 69 ; the rites of, essentially concerned with the cultivation of the corn, vii. 88 ; Varro on the rites of, vii. 88

Eleutherian games at Plataea, vii. 80

Elfin race averse to iron, iii. 232 *sq.*

Elgin, medical use of mistletoe in, xi. 84

Elgon, Mount, ix. 246 ; the Bagishu of, i. 103

Eli, the sons of, their loose conduct, v. 76

Elijah as a rain-maker, i. 258 *n.*^{3} ; patch of rye left at harvest for, vii. 233

Elipandus of Toledo, on the divinity of Christians, i. 407

Elis, titular kings at, i. 46 *n.* ; Dionysus hailed as a bull by the women of, vii. 17 ; the ivory shoulder of Pelops at, viii. 263 *sq.*

——, law of, ix. 352 *n.*^{2}

Elisha prophesies to music, v. 53, 54 ; finds water in the desert, v. 53, 75

Elizabeth, Queen, touches for scrofula, i. 368

Elk, a totem of the Omahas, viii. 25 ; treated with respect, viii. 240 ; embryos of, not eaten, viii. 243

Elk clan of the Omaha Indians, their belief as to effect of touching an elk, viii. 29 ; their sacred clam shell, x. 11

Ellgoth, in Silesia, the King's Race at Whitsuntide at, ii. 84

Elliot, R. H., on Indian indifference to death, iv. 136

Ellis, A. B., on Ewe superstition as to eating, iii. 116 ; on the supposed material connexion between a man and his name, iii. 323; on sacred prostitution in West Africa, v. 65 *sq.*, 69 *sq.* ; on tattoo marks of priests, v. 74 *n.*[4]; on an ordeal of chastity, v. 115

Ellis, William, on the inspiration of priests in the Southern Pacific, i. 377 *sq.*; on the observation of the Pleiades in the Society Islands, vii. 312 ; on *faditras* in Madagascar, ix. 33 *sq.*; on Polynesian mythology, ix. 80

Ellwangen, in Würtemberg, the Goat at threshing at, vii. 287

Elm wood in the pile-dwellings of the Po, ii. 353 ; used to kindle need-fire, x. 299

Elopango, in Mexico, human sacrifices at, vii. 237

Eloquence, homoeopathic charms to ensure, i. 156

Elpenor, the grave of, on the headland of Circe, ii. 188

Elves, fear of, iii. 283

Elymais, Nanaea the goddess of, i. 37 *n.*[2]

Emain, in Ireland, annual fair at, iv. 100

—— Macha, in Ireland, pagan cemetery at, iv. 101

Embalming, flight and pursuit of man who opened body for purpose of, ii. 309 *n.*[2]; as a means of prolonging the life of the soul, iv. 4 ; dead bodies of kings of Uganda embalmed, vi. 168

Embers of bonfires planted in fields, x. 117, 121 ; stuck in cabbage gardens, x. 174, 175; promote growth of crops, x. 337. *See also* Ashes *and* Sticks, charred

—— of Midsummer fires a protection against conflagration, x. 188 ; a protection against lightning, x. 190

Emblica officinalis, a sacred tree in Northern India, ii. 51

Embodied evils, expulsion of, ix. 170 *sqq.*

Embodiment, human, of the corn-spirit, viii. 333

Emboq Sri, rice-bride in Java, vii. 200 *sq.*

Embryos of elk not eaten, viii. 243

Emesa, sun-god Heliogabalus at, v. 35

Emetic as mode of purification, iii. 175, 245 ; pretended, in auricular confession, iii. 214

Emetics used before eating new corn, viii. 73, 75 *sq.*, 76, 135 ; sacred, employed by the Creek Indians, viii. 74 ; as remedies for sins, ix. 263

Emily plain of Central Australia, xi. 238

Emin Pasha, on the Monbutto custom of lengthening the head, ii. 297 *n.*[7]; his reception in a village, iii. 108

Emma, widow of Ethelred and wife of Canute, ii. 282 *sq.*

Emmenthal, in Switzerland, superstition as to Midsummer Day in the, xi. 27 ; use of orpine at Midsummer in the, xi. 62 *n.*

Empedocles, his claim to divinity, i. 390 ; leaps into the crater of Etna, v. 181 ; his doctrine of transmigration, viii. 300 *sqq.* ; his resemblance to Buddha, viii. 302 ; his theory of the material universe like that of Herbert Spencer, viii. 303 *sqq.* ; as a forerunner of Darwin, viii. 306 ; his posing as a god, viii. 307

Emperor of China, funeral of an, v. 294

Emperors of China as priests, i. 47

Emu - wren, called men's " brother " among the Kurnai, xi. 215 *n.*[1], 216, 218

Emu's flesh eaten to make eater swift-footed, viii. 145 ; fat not allowed to touch the ground, x. 13

Emus, ceremony for the multiplication of, i. 85 *sq.*

En, the, of Burma, worship the spirits of hills and trees, ii. 41

En gidon, a Masai clan, i. 343

En-jemusi, the, of British East Africa, women's work among the, vii. 118

Ἐναγίζειν distinguished from θύειν, v. 316 *n.*[1]

Enchanters of crops, foods forbidden to, vii. 100

Encheleans or Eel-men in Illyria, iv. 84

Encounter Bay tribe of South Australia, magic practised on refuse of food by, iii. 127 ; their fear of women's blood, iii. 251 ; namesakes of the dead change their names in the, iii. 355 ; changes in their vocabulary caused by their fear of naming the dead, iii. 359; names of the recent dead not mentioned in the, iii. 372 ; division of work between the sexes in the, vii. 126 ; their dread of women at menstruation, x. 76

Endle, Rev. S., on the fear of demons among the Kacharis, ix. 93

Endymion and the Moon, i. 18 ; set his sons to race at Olympia, ii. 299 ; the sunken sun overtaken by the moon, iv. 90 ; his tomb at Olympia, iv. 287

Enemies, mutilation of dead, viii. 271 *sq.*

Enemy, animal, of god originally identical with god, vii. 23, viii. 16 *sq.*, 31

——, charms to disable an, vi. 252

Energy, the conservation of, viii. 226 ; sanctity and uncleanness, · different forms of the same mysterious, x. 97 *sq.*

Eneti, in Washington State, rain-charm at, i. 309

Englam-Mana, a tribe of New Guinea, their mode of making fire, ii. 254

England, belief as to death at ebb-tide in, i. 168 ; custom of anointing the weapon instead of the wound in the eastern counties of, i. 203 ; green branches and flowers on May Day in the north of, ii. 60 ; May garlands in, ii. 60 *sqq.* ; the May Queen in, ii. 87 ; rolling down a slope on May Day in, ii. 103 ; oak and fir in the sunken forests and peat-bogs of, ii. 351 ; acorns eaten in, ii. 356 ; mirrors covered after a death in, iii. 95 ; harvest custom in, v. 237 ; the Feast of All Souls in, vi. 78 *sq.* ; superstitions as to the wren in, viii. 317 *sq.* ; mummer called the Straw-bear in, viii. 328 *sq.* ; cure for warts in, ix. 48 ; the King of the Bean in, ix. 313 ; fires kindled on the Eve of Twelfth Day in, ix. 318 ; the Festival of Fools in, ix. 336 *n.*[1] ; the Boy Bishop in, ix. 337 *sq.* ; belief as to menstruous women in, x. 96 *n.*[1] ; Midsummer fires in, x. 196 *sqq.* ; the Yule log in, x. 255 *sqq.* ; the need-fire in, x. 286 *sqq.* ; Midsummer giants in, xi. 36 *sqq.* ; divination by orpine at Midsummer in, xi. 61 ; fern-seed at Midsummer in, xi. 65 ; the north of, mistletoe used to make the dairy thrive in, xi. 85 *sq.* ; birth-trees in, xi. 165 ; children passed through cleft ash-trees as a cure for rupture or rickets in, xi. 168 *sqq.* ; oak-mistletoe in, xi. 316

England, English cure for whooping-cough, rheumatism, and boils, xi. 180
—— custom of undoing locks and bolts at a death, iii. 307
—— kings touch for scrofula, i. 368 *sqq.*
—— middle class, their clinging to life, iv. 146
—— superstition as to water-fairies, iii. 94

Enigmas, ceremonial use of, ix. 121 *n.*[3]. *See* Riddles

'Εννέωρος βασιλεύς, iv. 70 *n.*[3]

Enniskerry, near Dublin, Whit-Monday custom observed near, ii. 103 *n.*[3]

Ennius, on Hora and Quirinus, vi. 233

Ensanzi, a forest of Central Africa, dead Bahima kings carried to, viii. 288

Ensival, in Belgium, bonfires on the first Sunday in Lent at, x. 108

Entellus monkey, sacrifice of an, ix. 208 *sq.*

Entlebuch in Switzerland, expulsion of Posterli at, ix. 214

Entraigues, hunting the wren at, viii. 321

Entrails of cattle tabooed as food, i. 119 ; divination by the inspection of, i. 344 ; external soul in, xi. 146 *sq.*, 152

"Entry of Osiris into the moon," vi. 130

Enylus, king of Byblus, v. 15 *n.*

Ephesus, Artemis of, i. 7, 37 *sq.*, ii. 128, v. 269 ; titular kings at, i. 47 ; the Essenes or King Bees at, ii. 135 *sq.* ; Hecate at, v. 291 ; the priesthood of Apollo and Artemis at, vi. 243 *sq.* ; Demeter worshipped at, vii. 63 *n.*[14]

Ephors, Spartan, bound to observe the sky for omens every eighth year, iv. 58 *sq.*

Epic of Kings, Firdusi's, x. 104

Epicurus, sacrifices offered to, i. 105

Epidaurus, Aesculapius at, v. 80, ix. 47 ; Demeter worshipped at, vii. 63 *n.*[14]

Epidemic, creeping through a tunnel as a remedy for an, x. 283 *sq.*

Epidemics thought to be caused by incest, ii. 108 ; attributed to evil spirits, iii. 30 ; sacrifices in times of, iv. 176 *n.*[1] ; attributed to demons, ix. 111 *sqq.* ; kept off by means of a plough, ix. 172 *sq.* ; sent away in toy chariots, ix. 193 *sq.*

Epilepsy, supposed cause of, iii. 83 ; attributed to possession by a demon, iii. 235 ; transferred to leaves, ix. 2 ; Highland treatment of, ix. 68 *n.*[2] ; Roman cure for, ix. 68 ; nails used in cure for, ix. 68, 330 ; Hindoo cure for, ix. 69 *n.* ; cured by beating, ix. 260 ; amulet a protection against, ix. 331 ; yellow mullein a protection against, xi. 63 ; mistletoe a cure for, xi. 78, 83, 84. *See also* Falling sickness

Epimenides, the Cretan seer, his rambling soul, iii. 50 *n.*[2]

Épinal, " killing the dog " at harvest at, vii. 272 *sq.* ; Lenten fires at, x. 109

Epiphany, the 6th of January, v. 305 ; part of Christmas Boar given to cattle on, vii. 302 ; annual expulsion of the powers of evil at, ix. 165 *sqq.* ; the King of the Bean on, ix. 313 *sqq.* *See also* Twelfth Night

Epirus, the kings of, their bones scattered by Lysimachus, vi. 104 ; the Athamanes of, vii. 129

Epitherses and the death of the Great Pan, iv. 6

Epithets applied to Demeter, vii. 63 *sq.*

Eponymate, the Assyrian, iv. 116 *sq.*

Eponymous magistrates, iv. 117 *n.*[1]

Eponyms, annual, as scapegoats, ix. 39 *sqq.*

Equinox, the autumnal, Egyptian festival of " the nativity of the sun's walking-stick " after the, i. 312
——, the spring (vernal), festival at Upsala at, ii. 364 ; Babylonian festival of the, iv. 110 ; drama of Summer and Winter at, iv. 257 ; custom of

swinging at, iv. 284 ; resurrection of Attis at, v. 273, 307 *sq.* ; date of the Crucifixion assigned to, v. 307 ; tradition that the world was created at, v. 307 ; human sacrifice offered soon after, vii. 239 ; festival of Cronus at, ix. 352 ; Persian marriages at, ix. 406 *n.*[3]

Equos, a Gallic month, ix. 343 *n.*

Erech, Babylonian city, Ishtar at, ix. 398, 399

Erechtheum, on the Acropolis of Athens, perpetual lamp of Athena in the, ii. 199 ; sacred serpent in, iv. 87, v. 87

Erechtheus or Erichthonius, and Minerva (Athena), i. 21 ; king of Athens, the Erechtheum his house, ii. 199 ; in relation to the sacred serpent on the Acropolis, iv. 86 *sq.*, v. 87 ; identified with Poseidon, iv. 87 ; daughters of the daughters of, iv. 192 *n.*[3] ; his incest with his daughter, v. 44 *n.*[1] ; the Eleusinian mysteries instituted in the reign of, vii. 70

Eregh (the ancient Cybistra) in Cappadocia, v. 120, 122

Eresh-Kigal, Babylonian goddess, v. 9

Erfurt, harvest customs in the district of, vii. 136, 221

Ergamenes, king of Meroe, slays the priests, iv. 15

Erhard, Professor A., on the martyrdom of St. Dasius, ii. 310 *n.*[1]

Erica-tree, Osiris in the, vi. 9, 108, 109

Erichthonius, son of the fire-god Hephaestus, ii. 199. *See* Erechtheus

Erigone, her suicide by hanging, iv. 281 *sq.*

—— and Icarius, first-fruits of vintage offered to, viii. 133

Erin, the king idol of, iv. 183

Eriphyle, the necklace of, v. 32 *n.*[2]

Eriskay, fairies at Hallowe'en in, x. 226 ; salt cake at Hallowe'en in, x. 238 *sq.*

Erithasean Apollo, sacred trees in the sanctuary of, ii. 121

Erlangen, the "carrying out of Death" in the villages near, iv. 234

Erman, Professor Adolf, on the confusion of magic and religion in ancient Egypt, i. 230 ; on Anubis at Abydos, vi. 18 *n.*[3] ; on corn-stuffed effigies of Osiris, vi. 91 ; on the development of Egyptian religion, vi. 122 *n.*[2]

Erme or *Nenneri*, gardens of Adonis in Sardinia, v. 244

Errephoroi or Arrephoroi at Athens, ii. 199

Errol, the Hays of, their fate bound up with oak-mistletoe, xi. 283 *sq.*

Error of judging savages by European standards, iv. 197 *sq.*

Ertingen, in Würtemberg, the Lazy Man on Midsummer Day at, ii. 83 ; festival of St. George at, ii. 337

Erukhan plant (*Calotropis gigantea*), man married to, in India, ii. 57 *n.*[4]

Eruptions of volcanoes supposed to be caused by incest, ii. 111

Erysipelas, fox's tongue a remedy for, viii. 270

Erzgebirge, Shrovetide custom in the, iv. 208 *sq.*; young men and women beat each other with something green at Christmas in the, ix. 271

Esagil or Esagila, temple of Marduk at Babylon, iv. 113, ix. 356

Esarhaddon, king of Assyria, his great inscription, iv. 116

Escouvion or *Scouvion*, the Great and the Little, in Belgium, x. 108

Eshmun, Phoenician deity, v. 111 *n.*[6]

Esne, the festal calendar of, vi. 49 *sq.*

Esquiline Hill at Rome, its name derived from oaks, ii. 185 ; the oak groves of the, ii. 320

Esquimaux, their belief as to the sculpin and rain, i. 288 ; play cat's cradle to detain the sun, i. 316 *sq.*, vii. 103 *n.*[1]; play cup-and-ball to hasten the return of the sun, i. 317 ; their ways of calming the wind, i. 327 *sq.* ; their conception of the soul, iii. 27 ; their dread of being photographed, iii. 96 ; ceremony at the reception of strangers among the, iii. 108 ; avoid dishes used by women in childbed, iii. 145 ; their ideas as to the dangerous vapour exhaled by lying-in women, iii. 152 ; taboos observed by hunters among the Esquimaux after killing sea-beasts, iii. 205 *sq.*; use of iron implements tabooed at certain times among the, iii. 228 ; taboos observed by them after a death, iii. 237 ; take new names when they are old, iii. 319 ; unwilling to tell their names, iii. 328 ; namesakes of the dead among the, iii. 371 ; their belief that animals understand human speech, iii. 399 ; suicide among the, iv. 43 ; their belief as to falling stars, iv. 65 ; their story of the type of Beauty and the Beast, iv. 131 *n.*; dramatic contest between Winter and Summer among the, iv. 259 ; their belief in the resurrection of seals, viii. 257 ; careful not to break bones of deer, viii. 258 *n.*[2]; their reluctance to let dogs gnaw the bones of animals, viii. 259 ; their superstition as to various meats, x. 13 *sq.*; seclusion of girls at puberty among the, x. 55 ; ceremony of the new fire among the,

x. 134 ; their custom at eclipses, x. 162 n.

Esquimaux of Aivilik and Iglulik, magical telepathy among the, i. 121 sq.

—— of Alaska, taboos observed by women in absence of whalers among the, i. 121 ; their annual festival of the dead, v. 51 sq. ; their custom at killing a fox, viii. 267 ; child's soul deposited in a bag among the, xi. 155

—— of Baffin Land, boys forbidden to play cat's cradle among the, i. 113 ; their use of a fox in homoeopathic magic, i. 151 ; their women in mourning may not mention the names of animals, iii. 399 ; their custom when a boy has killed his first seal, viii. 257 ; their expulsion of Sedna, ix. 125 sq.

—— or Inuit of Bering Strait, iii. 205 ; manslayers among the, i. 9 ; their use of magical images, i. 70 ; their annual festival of bladders, iii. 206 sq. ; drank blood of foes to acquire their bravery, viii. 150 ; their ceremony of restoring the bladders of dead sea-beasts to the sea, viii. 247 sqq. ; uncleanness of girl at puberty among the, viii. 268 n.[4] ; cut the sinews of bad dead men to prevent their ghosts from walking, viii. 272 ; their masquerades, ix. 379 sq. ; their belief as to menstruous women, x. 91

——, the Central, dietary rules of, viii. 84 ; their ceremonious treatment of dead sea-beasts, viii. 246 ; the tug-of-war among the, ix. 174

—— of Hudson Bay, propitiate the spirit who controls the reindeer, viii. 245 sq.

—— of Labrador, their fear of demons, ix. 79 sq.

—— of Point Barrow, Alaska, return the bones of seals to the sea, viii. 258 n.[2] ; their expulsion of the mischievous spirit Tuña, ix. 124 sq.

Esquimaux mourners plug their nostrils, iii. 32

Essenes or King Bees at Ephesus, i. 47 n.[2], ii. 135 sq.

Essex, greasing the weapon instead of the wound in, i. 204 ; May garlands in, ii. 60 ; hunting the wren in, viii. 320

Esther, the story of, acted as a comedy at Purim, ix. 364 ; her name equivalent to Ishtar, Astarte, ix. 365 ; fast of, ix. 397 sq.

——, the book of, its date and purpose, ix. 360 ; its Persian colouring, ix. 362, 401 ; based on a Babylonian myth, ix. 398 ; duplication of the personages in, ix. 400 sq. ; the personages unmasked, ix. 405 sqq.

—— and Mordecai equivalent to Ishtar and Marduk, ix. 405 ; the duplicates of Vashti and Haman, ix. 405 sq.

Esther and Vashti, ix. 365 ; temporary queens, ix. 401

Esthonia, the Christmas Boar in, vii. 302 ; bathing at Midsummer in, xi. 29 ; flowers gathered for divination and magic at Midsummer in, xi. 53 sq.

Esthonian belief as to the effect of seeing women's blood, iii. 251

—— celebration of St. John's Day by swings and bonfires, iv. 280

—— charm to make a wolf disgorge his prey, i. 135

—— charms to make cabbages thrive, i. 136 sq.

—— custom of throwing a knife, hat, stick, or stone at a whirlwind, i. 329, 330

—— fishermen, their use of curses for good luck, i. 280 sq.

—— mode of strengthening weakly children by means of hemp seed, vii. 11

—— peasants threaten cabbages to make them grow, ii. 22 ; loth to mention wild beasts by their proper names, iii. 398 ; regulate their sowing and planting by the moon, vi. 135 ; their treatment of weevils, viii. 274

—— reapers slash the wind with their sickles, i. 329 ; their belief as to pains in the back, vii. 285

Esthonians, their contagious magic of footprints, i. 211, 212 ; their ways of raising the wind, i. 323 ; their dread of Finnish witches and wizards, i. 325 ; their sacred trees, ii. 43 ; their worship of Metsik, a mischievous forest-spirit, ii. 55 ; their folk-tale of a tree-elf, ii. 71 sqq. ; their custom of leading a bride to the hearth, ii. 231 ; their custom of leading a bride thrice round a burning tree, ii. 234 ; St. George's Day among the, ii. 330 sqq. ; sacrifice under holy trees for the welfare of their horses, ii. 332 ; their thunder-god Taara, ii. 367 ; oak worshipped by the, ii. 367 ; their superstition as to a water-mill, iii. 232 ; refuse to taste blood, iii. 240 ; preserve their nail-parings against the day of judgment, iii. 280 ; their belief as to shooting stars, iv. 63, 66 sq. ; their custom on Shrove Tuesday, iv. 233, 252 sq. ; their celebration of St. John's Day, iv. 280 ; their ceremony at the new moon, vi. 143 ; their Christmas Boar, vii. 302 sq. ; their mode of transferring bad luck to trees, ix. 54 ; their expulsion of the devil, ix. 173 ; Midsummer fires among the, x. 179 sq.

—— of Oesel, their belief as to absence of souls from bodies, iii. 41 sq. ; call the last sheaf the Rye-boar, vii. 298, 300 ; their custom at eating new corn, viii. 51 ; cull St. John's herbs on St. John's Day, xi. 49

Estremadura, acorns as fodder for hogs in, ii. 356

Etatin, on the Cross River, in Southern Nigeria, the chief as fetish-man at, i. 349

Eteobutads as umbrella-bearers at the festival of Scira, x. 20 n.[1]

Eteocles and Polynices, their grave at Thebes, ii. 33

Eternal life, initiates born again to, in the rites of Cybele and Attis, v. 274 sq.

Etesian winds, v. 35 n.[1]

Ethelbald, king of the West Saxons, marries his stepmother, ii. 283

Ethelbert, king of Kent, ii. 283

Ethelwulf, king of the West Saxons, ii. 283

Ethical evolution, iii. 218 sq.

—— precepts developed out of savage taboos, iii. 214

Ethiopia, priestly kings in, iii. 13 ; shut up in their palace, iii. 124 ; chosen for their beauty, iv. 38 sq.

Ethiopian kings of Meroe put to death, iv. 15, 38

Ethiopians, succession to the kingdom among the, ii. 296 sq.

Etiquette at courts of barbarian kings, iv. 39 sq.

Etna, Mount, Typhon buried under, v. 156, 157 ; the death of Empedocles on, v. 181 ; the ashes of, v. 194 ; offerings thrown into the craters of, v. 221 ; Demeter said to have lit her torches at the craters of, vii. 57

Eton, Midsummer fires at, x. 197

Eton College, Boy Bishop at, ix. 338

Etruria, funeral games at Agylla in, iv. 95 ; actors fetched from, to Rome in time of plague, ix. 65

Etruscan crown, ii. 175 n.[1]

—— letters, ii. 186, 186 n.[4]

—— wizards, i. 310

Etruscans, female kinship among the, ii. 286 sq. ; their alleged Lydian descent, ii. 287 ; their ceremony at founding cities, iv. 157

Etymology, its uncertainty as a base for mythological theories, i. 41 n.

Euboea subject to earthquakes, v. 211 ; date of threshing in, v. 232 n. ; harvest custom in, v. 238

Eubuleus, legendary swineherd, brother of Triptolemus, viii. 19

Eubulus, sacrifices offered to, at Eleusis, vii. 56

Eucharist partaken of by Catholics fasting, viii. 83

Eudanemi at Athens, i. 325 n.[1]

Eudoxus of Cnidus, Greek astronomer, on the Egyptian festivals, vi. 35 n.[2] ; corrections of the Greek calendar perhaps due to, vii. 81 ; on the utility of the pig in ancient Egypt, viii. 30

Euhemerism, a theory of mythology, ix. 385

Euhemerists, ix. 385

Eukleia, epithet of Artemis, i. 37 n.[1]

Eumolpids direct the sacrifices of first-fruits, vii. 56

Eumolpus, prince of Eleusis, vii. 37 ; said to have founded the Eleusinian mysteries, vii. 70 ; founder of priestly Eleusinian family, vii. 73

Eunuch priests of Ephesian Artemis, i. 38 ; of the Mother Goddess, v. 206 ; in the service of Asiatic goddesses of fertility, v. 269 sq. ; in various lands, v. 270 n.[2] ; of Attis tattooed with pattern of ivy, v. 278 ; of Cybele, vi. 258

Eunuchs, dances of, v. 270 n.[2], 271 n. ; dedicated to a goddess in India, v. 271 n. ; sacred, at Hierapolis-Bambyce, their rule as to the pollution of death, vi. 272 ; perform a ceremony for the fertility of the fields, x. 340

Euphemisms employed for certain animals, iii. 397 sqq. ; for smallpox, iii. 400, 410, 411, 416

Euphorbia antiquorum, cactus, hung at door of house where there is a lying-in woman, iii. 155

—— lathyris, caper-spurge, sometimes identified with the mythical spring-wort, xi. 69

Euphorbus the Trojan, the soul of Pythagoras in, viii. 300

Euphorion of Chalcis, Greek writer, on Roman indifference to death, iv. 143, 144

Euripides, the Hippolytus of, i. 25 ; on Artemis as a midwife, i. 37 ; on the dragon at Delphi, iv. 79 ; on the death of Pentheus, vi. 98 n.[5] ; his account of Aegisthus pelting the tomb of Agamemnon with stones, ix. 19 ; his play on Meleager, xi. 103 n.[2]

Europa, a personification of the moon conceived as a cow, ii. 88 ; and Zeus, iv. 73 ; her wanderings, iv. 89

Europe, dancing or leaping high as a homoeopathic charm to make crops grow high in, i. 137 ; the Hand of Glory in, i. 148 sq. ; belief as to death at ebb-tide in, i. 167 ; treatment of the navel-string and afterbirth in, i. 198 sqq. ; contagious magic of footprints in, i. 210 sq. ; confusion of magic and religion in modern, i. 231-233 ; the belief in magic in modern, i. 235 sq. ; forests of ancient, ii. 7 sq. ; the May-tree or May-pole as an instrument of fertility in, ii. 51 *sq.* ; relics of tree-worship in modern, ii. 59 *sqq.* ; Midsummer festival in, ii. 272 *sq.* ; diffusion of the oak in, ii. 349 *sqq.* ; peat-bogs of, ii. 350 *sqq.* ; the lake-dwellings of, ii. 352 *sq.* ; fear of having one's likeness taken in, iii. 100 ; spitting as a charm in, iii. 279 ; belief as to consummation of marriage being impeded by knots and locks in, iii. 299 ; beliefs as to shooting stars in, iv. 66 *sqq.* ; fear of death in, iv. 135 *sq.*, 146 ; custom of showing money to the new moon in, vi. 148 *sq.* ; barley and wheat cultivated in prehistoric, vii. 79 ; transference of evil in, ix. 47 *sqq.* ; faith in magic and witchcraft in Christian, ix. 89 ; annual expulsion of demons and witches in, ix. 155 *sqq.* ; annual expulsion of evils in, ix. 207 *sq.* ; folk-custom of "carrying out Death" in, ix. 227 *sq.* ; masquerades in modern, ix. 251 *sq.* ; superstitions as to menstruous women in, x. 96 *sq.*; the fire-festivals of, x. 106 *sqq.* ; great dread of witchcraft in, xi. 342 ; birth-trees in, xi. 165 ; belief in, that strength of witches and wizards is in their hair, xi. 158

Europe, Eastern, great popular festival of herdsmen and shepherds on St. George's Day in, ii. 330
——, Eastern and Central, custom of beating people and cattle in spring in, ix. 266
——, mediaeval, belief in demons in, ix. 105 *sq.* ; human scapegoats in, ix. 214
——, Northern, human sacrifices in, iv. 214 ; Corn-mother and Corn-maiden in, vii. 131 *sqq.*
——, South-Eastern, rain-making ceremonies in, i. 272 *sqq.* ; superstitions as to shadows in, iii. 89 *sq.*
European custom as to green bushes on May Day, ii. 56
—— processions of animals or of men disguised as animals, viii. 325
—— rule that children's nails should not be paired, iii. 262 *sq.*
Euros, magical ceremony for the multiplication of, i. 89 ; homoeopathic charm to catch, i. 162
Eurydice, Orpheus and, xi. 294
Eurylochus rids Aegina of a snake, iv. 87 *n.*[5]
Eusebius on sacred prostitution, i. 30 *n.*[3], v. 37 *n.*[2], 73 *n.*[1]
Euyuk in Cappadocia, Hittite palace at, v. 123, 132, 133 *n.* ; bull worshipped at, v. 164
Evadne and Capaneus, v. 177 *n.*[3]

Evans, D. Silvan, on the sin-eater in Wales, ix. 44
Evans, Sebastian, as to a passage in the *History of the Holy Graal*, iv. 122 *n.*[1]
Eve and Adam, Mr. W. R. Paton's theory of, ix. 259 *n.*[3]
Eve, Christmas, the fern blooms on, xi. 66
——, Easter, in Albania, iv. 265 ; the fern blooms on, xi. 66
——, Fingan, in the Isle of Man, x. 266
—— of St. John (Midsummer Eve), Russian ceremony on, iv. 262
—— of Samhain (Hallowe'en) in Ireland, x. 139. *See also* Christmas Eve, Easter Eve, St. John's Eve, etc.
Evelyn, John, on Charles II. touching for scrofula, i. 369
Evening Star, Keats's sonnet to the, i. 166 ; the goddess of the, ix. 369 *n.*[1]
Everek (Caesarea), in Asia Minor, creeping through a rifted rock at, xi. 189
Evergreen oak, the Golden Bough grew on, ii. 379
—— trees in Italy, i. 8
Evessen, in Brunswick, toothache nailed into a tree at, ix. 59 *sq.*
Evil, the transference of, ix. 1 *sqq.* ; transferred to other people, ix. 5 *sqq.*, 47 *sqq.* ; transferred to sticks and stones, ix. 8 *sqq.* ; transferred to animals, ix. 31 *sqq.*, 49 *sqq.* ; transferred to men, ix. 38 *sqq.* ; transference of, in Europe, ix. 47 *sqq.* ; transferred to inanimate objects, ix. 53 *sq.* ; transferred to trees or bushes, ix. 54 *sqq.* *See also* Evils
Evil Eye, bad names a protection against the, i. 280 ; dreaded at eating, iii. 116 *sq.* ; boys dressed as girls to avert, vi. 260 ; bridegroom disfigured in order to avert the, vi. 261 ; disguises to avert the, vi. 262 ; preservatives against the, viii. 326 *n.*[3] ; rain-water mixed with tar, a protection against the, x. 17. *See also* Eye, the Evil
—— spirit, mode of cure for possession by an, xi. 186
—— spirits transferred from men to animals, ix. 31 ; banishment of, ix. 86 ; driven away at the New Year, x. 134 *sq.* ; kept off by fire, x. 282, 285 *sq.* ; St. John's herbs a protection against, xi. 49 ; kept off by flowers gathered at Midsummer, xi. 53 *sq.* ; creeping through cleft trees to escape the pursuit of, xi. 173 *sqq. See also* Demons
Evil-Merodach, Babylonian king, ix. 367 *n.*[2]
Evils transferred to trees, ix. 54 *sqq.* ; nailed into trees, walls, etc., ix. 59

sqq. ; public expulsion of, ix. 109 *sqq.*, 185 *sqq.* ; periodic expulsion of, ix. 123 *sqq.*, 198 *sqq.* ; expulsion of embodied, ix. 170 *sqq.* ; expulsion of, in a material vehicle, ix. 185 *sqq.* ; expulsion of, timed to coincide with some well-marked change of season, ix. 224 *sq.* *See also* Expulsion

Evolution of kings out of magicians or medicine-men, i. 420 *sq.* ; industrial, from uniformity to diversity of function, i. 421 ; political, from democracy to despotism, i. 421 ; ethical, iii. 218 *sq.* ; religious, powerful influence of the fear of the dead on the course of, viii. 36 *sq.*
—— and dissolution, viii. 305 *sq.*

Ewe, white - footed, as scapegoat, ix. 192 *sq.* *See also* Ewes

Ewe farmers fear to wound the Earth goddess, v. 90
—— hunters, their contagious magic of footprints, i. 212 ; of Togo-land, their ceremony after killing an antelope, viii. 244
—— negroes, their festival of new yams, viii. 58 *sqq.* ; their belief as to the spirit-land, viii. 105 *sq.* ; their ceremonies after killing leopards, viii. 228 *sqq.* ; feed their nets, viii. 240 *n.*[1] ; their dread of menstruous women, x. 82
—— negroes of Guinea worship falling stars, iv. 61 *sq.*
—— negroes of the Slave Coast, their charm to catch a runaway slave, i. 317; their reverence for silk - cotton trees, ii. 15 ; human wives of gods among the, ii. 149 ; taboos observed by their kings, iii. 9 ; their belief as to spirits entering the body through the mouth, iii. 116 ; their kings not to be seen eating or drinking, iii. 119 ; penance for killing a python among the, iii. 222 ; a mother's vow among the, iii. 263 ; their belief that a man can be injured through his name, iii. 323 ; rebirth of ancestors among the, iii. 369 ; sacred prostitution among the, v. 65 *sq.* ; worship pythons, v. 83 *n.*[1] ; their conception of the rain-god as a horseman, viii. 45 ; their belief in demons, ix. 74 *sqq.*
—— negroes of Togo-land, their festival in honour of Earth, iii. 247 ; reincarnation of the dead among the, iii. 369 ; their belief in the marriage of Sky with Earth, v. 282 *n.*[2] ; their use of clay images as substitutes to save the lives of people, viii. 105 *sq.* ; their worship of the Earth, viii. 115 ; their worship of goddess Mawu Sodza, viii. 115 ; their propitiation of slain leopards, wild buffaloes, etc., viii. 228 *sqq.*

Ewe-speaking negroes deem the heart the seat of courage and intellect, viii. 149
—— -speaking people of West Africa, their contagious magic of footprints, i. 210 ; eat elephant's flesh to become strong, viii. 143

Ewes and rams, the time for coupling, ii. 328, 328 *n.*[4]

Exaggerations of anthropological theories, i. 333

Exchange of wives at appearance of the Aurora Australis, iv. 267 *n.*[1] ; of dress between men and women in rites, vi. 259 *n.*[3] ; of dress at marriage, vi. 260 *sqq.* ; of dress at circumcision, vi. 263

Exclusion of strangers, iii. 108 *sq.*, vii. 94, 111

Excommunication of human scapegoat, ix. 254

Excuses offered by savages to the animals they kill, viii. 222 *sqq.*

Execution, peculiar modes of, for members of royal families, iii. 241 *sqq.* ; Roman mode of, iv. 144 ; by stoning, ix. 24 *n.*[2]

Executioners, their precautions against the ghosts of their victims, iii. 171 *sq.* ; seclusion and scarification of, iii. 180 *sq.*; taste the blood of their victims, viii. 155

Exeter, the Boy Bishop at, ix. 337

Exile of gods for perjury, iv. 70 *n.*[1]

Exodus (xiii. 1 *sq.*, 12, xxii. 29 *sq.*, xxxiv. 19), on the sanctification of the first-born, iv. 172

Exogamous clans in the Pelew Islands, vi. 204
—— classes in Duke of York Island, xi. 248 *n.*

Exogamy, ii. 271, iv. 130

Exorcising harmful influence of strangers, iii. 102 *sqq.*

Exorcism of demons of sickness, iii. 105 *sq.* ; of ghosts after a funeral, iii. 106 *sq.* ; of demons by devil dancers, iv. 216 ; by means of music, v. 54 *sq.* ; of devils in Morocco, ix. 63 ; of demons in China, ix. 99 ; annual, of the evil spirit in Japan, ix. 143 *sq.* ; of spirits at sowing the seed, ix. 235 ; Nicobarese ceremony of, ix. 262 ; of evil spirits at a funeral ceremony, x. 5 ; and ordeals, x. 66 ; at Easter, x. 123 ; of vermin with torches, x. 340 ; use of St. John's wort in, xi. 55 ; use of mugwort in, xi. 60 ; by vervain, xi. 62 *n.*[4]. *See also* Demons *and* Expulsion

Exorcists, ix. 2 *sq.*, 33

Expiation by means of blood for sexual crimes, ii. 107 *sqq.* ; for adultery or fornication, ii. 109 *sq.* ; for incest, ii.

110 *sq.*, 115, 116, 129 ; for violating the sanctity of a grove, ii. 122 ; for hearing thunder, iii. 14 ; for contact with a sacred chief, iii. 133 *sq.* ; for miscarriage in childbed, iii. 153 *sqq.* ; for bringing an iron tool into the grove of the Arval Brothers, iii. 226 ; for killing sacred animals, iv. 216 *sq.* ; for suicide by hanging, iv. 282 ; for homicide, v. 299 *n.*[2] ; Roman, for prodigies, vi. 244 ; for the defilement of the Eleusinian plain, vii. 74 ; for agricultural operations, vii. 228 ; for sin, ix. 39. *See also* Atonement *and* Purification

Expiatory sacrifices, Greek ritual of, viii. 27

Expulsion of evils, ix. 109 *sqq.* ; the direct or immediate and the indirect or mediate, ix. 109, 224 ; occasional, ix. 109 *sqq.*, 185 *sqq.* ; periodic, ix. 123 *sqq.*, 198 *sqq.*; annual, of demons and witches in Europe, ix. 155 *sqq.*, x. 135 ; of Trows in Shetland, ix. 168 *sq.* ; of embodied evils, ix. 170 *sqq.* ; of evils in a material vehicle, ix. 185 *sqq.* ; of evils timed to coincide with some well-marked change of season, ix. 224 *sq.* ; of devils timed to coincide with seasons of agricultural year, ix. 225 ; of hunger at Chaeronea, ix. 252 ; of winter, ceremony of the, ix. 404 *sq.*

External soul in afterbirth or navel-string, i. 200 *sq.* ; in folk-tales, xi. 95 *sqq.* ; in folk-custom, xi. 153 *sqq.* ; in inanimate things, xi. 153 *sqq.* ; in plants, xi. 159 *sqq.* ; in animals, xi. 196 *sqq.* ; kept in totem, xi. 220 *sqq. See also* Souls, external

Extinction of fires on chief's death, ii. 217 ; in village or parish before the making of "living fire" or need-fire, ii. 237, 238 ; at king's death, ii. 261 *sqq.*, 267 ; in houses after any death, ii. 267 *sq.* ; annual, of the sacred fire at Rome, ii. 267 ; of common fires before the kindling of the need-fire, x. 271, 272, 273, 274, 275, 276, 277 *sq.*, 279, 283, 285, 288, 289, 289 *sq.*, 291, 291 *sq.*, 292, 294, 297, 298 *sq.* ; of fires after tree has been kindled by lightning, xi. 297 *sq.*

Extinguishing fire, power of, ascribed to priests, i. 231, and to chaste women, ii. 240 *n.*[2]

Eye as a symbol of Osiris, vi. 121 ; of sacrificial ox cut out, vi. 251 *sq. See also* Eyes

——, the Evil, precautions against the, at meals, iii. 116 *sq.* ; boys dressed as girls to avert the, vi. 260 ; bridegroom disfigured in order to avert, vi.

261 ; cast on cattle, x. 302, 303 ; oleander a remedy for sickness caused by, xi. 51. *See also* Evil Eye

Eye of Horus, vi. 17, 121, with *n.*[3]

Eyelashes offered to the sun, i. 318

Eyeo, kings of, put to death, iv. 40 *sq.*

Eyeos, the, not allowed to behold the sea, iii. 9

Eyes smeared with eagle's gall to make them sharp-sighted, i. 154 ; shut at prayer, viii. 81 ; of owl eaten to make eater see in dark, viii. 144 *sq.* ; of men eaten, viii. 153 ; of falcon used to impart sharpness of sight, viii. 164 ; of slaughtered animals cut out, viii. 267 *sqq.*, 271 ; of dead enemies gouged out, viii. 271 *sq.* ; looking through flowers at the Midsummer fire thought to be good for the, x. 162, 163, 165 *sq.*, 171, 174 *sq.*, 344 ; ashes or smoke of Midsummer fire supposed to benefit the, x. 214 *sq.* ; sore, attributed to witchcraft, x. 344 ; mugwort a protection against sore, xi. 59 ; of newly initiated lads closed, xi. 241

—— of the dead, Egyptian ceremony of opening the, vi. 15

Eyre, E. J., on menstruous women in Australia, x. 77

Ezekiel (viii. 10-12), on idolatrous practices of the Israelites, i. 87 *n.*[1]; (xxxii. 18-32), H. Gunkel's interpretation of, i. 101 *n.*[2]; (xiii. 17 *sqq.*), the hunting of souls in, iii. 77 *n.*[1]; (xvi. 20 *sq.*, xx. 25, 26, 31), on the burnt sacrifice of children, iv. 169 *n.*[3]; (xx. 25, 26, 31), on the sacrifice of the first-born, iv. 171 *sq.* ; (viii. 14), on the mourning for Tammuz, v. 11, 17, 20 ; (xxiii. 5 *sq.*, 12), on the Assyrian cavalry, v. 25 *n.*[3]; (xxviii. 14, 16), on the king of Tyre, v. 114

E-zida, the temple of Nabu in Borsippa, iv. 110

Face of sleeper not to be painted or disfigured, lest his absent soul should not recognize his body, iii. 41 ; of human scapegoat painted half white half black, ix. 220

Faces veiled to avert evil influences, iii. 120 *sqq.* ; of warriors blackened, iii. 163 ; of manslayers blackened, iii. 169 ; of bear-hunters blackened, vii. 291, 299 ; blackened, vii. 302, viii. 321, 332, ix. 247, 314, 330 ; of bear-hunters painted red and black, viii. 226 ; of priests at exorcism reddened with paint and blood, ix. 189

Faditras among the Malagasy, ix. 33 *sq.*

Fàdy, taboo, iii. 327, viii. 46

"Faery dairts" thought to kill cattle, x. 303

Fafnir, the dragon, slain by Sigurd, iii. 324, viii. 146
Failles, bonfires on the first Sunday in Lent, x. 111 *n.*[1]
Fair, great, at Uisnech in County Meath, x. 158. *See also* Fairs
Fairies thought to be in eddies of wind, i. 329 ; averse to iron, iii. 229, 232 *sq.* ; let loose at Hallowe'en, x. 224 *sqq.* ; carry off men's wives, x. 227 ; at Hallowe'en, dancing with the, x. 227 ; thought to kill cattle by their darts, x. 303 ; active on Hallowe'en and May Day, xi. 184 *n.*[4], 185
Fairs of ancient Ireland, iv. 99 *sqq.*
Fairy Banner, Macleod's, i. 368
—— changelings, x. 151 *n.* ; mistletoe a protection against, xi. 283
Faiths of the world, the great, their little influence on common men, ix. 89
Falcon stone, at Errol, in Perthshire, xi. 283
Falcon's eyes used to impart sharpness of sight, viii. 164
Falerii, Juno at, ii. 190 *n.*[2]
Faleshas, a Jewish sect of Abyssinia, remove the vein from the thighs of slaughtered animals, viii. 266 *n.*[1]
Falkenauer district of Bohemia, custom at threshing in the, vii. 149
Falkenstein chapel of St. Wolfgang, creeping through a rifted rock near the, xi. 189
Fallacy of magic not easily detected, i. 242 *sq.* ; gradually detected, i. 372
Falling sickness transferred to fowl, ix. 52 *sq.* ; nails used in cure for, ix. 68, 330 ; mistletoe a remedy for, xi. 83, 84. *See also* Epilepsy
—— star as totem, iv. 61
—— stars, superstitions as to, iv. 58 *sqq.* ; associated with the souls of the dead, iv. 64 *sqq.*
Fallow, thrice-ploughed, vii. 66, 69 ; lands allowed to lie, vii. 117, 123
False Bride, custom of the, vi. 262 *n.*[2]
—— graves and corpses to deceive demons, viii. 98 *sqq.*
Falstaff, the death of, i. 168
Famenne in Namur, Lenten fires in, x. 108
Familiar spirits of wizards in boars, xi. 196 *sq.*
Families, royal, kings chosen from several, ii. 292 *sqq.*
Famine attributed to the anger of ghosts, iv. 103
Fan country, West Africa, custom of throwing branches on heaps in the, ix. 30 *n.*[2]
—— negro, his belief as to the effect of seeing women's blood, iii. 251

Fan tribe of West Africa, chiefs as medicine-men in the, i. 349. *See also* Fans
Fangola, a potent idol in Nias, viii. 102, 103
Fanning away ill luck, vii. 10
Fans of the French Congo, birth-trees among the, xi. 161
—— of the Gaboon, their theory of the external soul, xi. 200 *sqq.*, 226 *n.*[1] ; guardian spirits acquired in dreams among the, xi. 257
—— of West Africa, esteem the smith's craft sacred, i. 349 ; their rule as to eating tortoises, viii. 140 ; their custom of adding to heaps of leafy branches, ix. 30 *n.*[2] ; custom at end of mourning among the, xi. 18
Fans in homoeopathic magic, i. 130 *sq.*
Fantee country, succession of slaves to the kingship in the, ii. 275
Faosa, a Malagasy month, vii. 9
Farghana, rain-producing well in, i. 301
Farinaceous deities, viii. 169
Farmer, calendar of the Egyptian, vi. 30 *sqq.* ; saturnine temperament of the, vi. 218
Farmer's wife, ceremony performed by her to promote the rice-crop, ii. 104 ; pretence of threshing, vii. 149 *sq.*
Farmers, propitiation of vermin by, viii. 274 *sqq.*
Farnell, Dr. L. R., on Artemis as the patroness of childbirth, i. 36 *sq.* ; on Plautus, *Casina* (ii. 5, 23-29), ii. 379 *n.*[5] ; on Greek religious music, v. 55 *ns.*[1] and [3] ; on religious prostitution in Western Asia, v. 57 *n.*[1], 58 *n.*[2] ; on the position of women in ancient religion, vi. 212 *n.*[1] ; on the Flamen Dialis, vi. 227 ; on the children of living parents in ritual, vi. 236 *sq.* ; on the festival of Laurel-bearing at Thebes, vi. 242 *n.* ; on eunuch priests of Cybele, vi. 258 *n.*[1] ; on Thracian origin of Dionysus, vii. 3 *n.*[1] ; on the biennial period of certain Greek festivals, vii. 15 *n.* ; on the resemblance of the artistic types of Demeter and Persephone, vii. 68 *n.*[1] ; on Pan, viii. 2 *n.*[9]
Farwardajan, a Persian festival of the dead, vi. 68
Fashoda, the capital of the Shilluk kings, iv. 18, 19, 21, 24
Faslane, on the Gareloch, Dumbartonshire, last standing corn called the Head or Maidenhead at, vii. 158, 268
Fast from bread in mourning for Attis, v. 272 ; in the Eleusinian mysteries, vii. 38 ; before eating new fruits, viii. 73 *sq.*, 76 *sq.* ; before the festival of the

Mexican goddess of Maize, ix. 291 *sq.*; from flesh, eggs, and grease at sowing, ix. 347 *n.*[4]; at puberty, xi. 222 *n.*[5] *See also* Fasts *and* Fasting

"Fast of Esther" before Purim, ix. 397 *sq.*

Fasting obligatory on woman during absence of her husband at whale-fishery, i. 121 ; as a means of ensuring success in hunting, i. 121, 124 ; obligatory on women during the absence of warriors, i. 131 ; obligatory on all people left in camp during absence of warriors, iii. 157 *n.*[2]; rigorous, of warriors before going to war, iii. 161 ; of warriors as a preparation for attacking the enemy, iii. 162 ; of executioner after discharging his office, iii. 180 ; of warriors after killing enemies, iii. 182, 183 ; of eagle-hunters before trapping eagles, iii. 199 ; of Catholics before partaking of the Eucharist, viii. 83 ; of men and women at a dancing festival, x. 8 *sqq.* ; of girls at puberty, x. 56, 57, 58, 59, 60, 61, 66 ; of women at menstruation, x. 93, 94 ; as preparation for gathering magical plants, xi. 45, 55 *n.*[1], 58

—— and continence observed by parents of twins, i. 266; by Blackfoot priest, iii. 159 *n.*; as preparation for office among the Peruvian Indians, iii. 159 *n.*; of Indian warriors as preparation for war, iii. 163; of whalers before whaling, iii. 191 ; of hunters before hunting, iii. 198 ; before ploughing and sowing, viii. 14, 15

Fastnachtsbär, viii. 325

Fasts imposed on heirs to thrones in South America, x. 19 ; rules observed by Indians of Costa Rica during, x. 20

—— observed by the worshippers of Cybele and Attis, v. 280 ; of Isis and Cybele, v. 302 *n.*[4] *See also* Fast *and* Fasting

Fat, anointing the body with, from superstitious motives, viii. 162 *sq.*, 164, 165 ; of emu not allowed to touch the ground, x. 13; of crocodiles and snakes as unguent, x. 14

Fate of the king's life annually determined at a festival, ix. 356, 357

Father, reborn in his son, iv. 188 *sqq.*, 287 (288 in Second Impression); funeral rites performed for a, in the fifth month of his wife's pregnancy, iv. 189 ; named after his son, v. 51 *n.*[4]; of a god, v. 51, 52 ; dead, worshipped, vi. 175, 184 *sq.* ; the head of the family under a system of mother-kin, vi. 211

—— and child, supposed danger of resemblance between, iii. 88 *sq.*, iv. 287 (288 in Second Impression)

Father of Heaven, title of the Esthonian thunder-god, ii. 367

—— and mother, their names not to be mentioned, iii. 337, 341 ; names for, v. 281 ; as epithets of Roman gods and goddesses, vi. 233 *sqq.*

——, Mother, and Son divinities represented at Boghaz-Keui, v. 140 *sqq.*

Father-deity of the Hittites, the god of the thundering sky, v. 134 *sqq.*

—— God succeeded by his divine son, iv. 5 ; his emblem the bull, v. 164 ; Attis as the, v. 281 *sqq.* ; often less important than Mother Goddess, v. 282

—— -in-law, his name not to be pronounced by his daughter-in-law, iii. 335 *sqq.*, 343, 345, 346 ; by his son-in-law, iii. 338, 339, 340, 341, 342, 343, 344

—— Jove and Mother Vesta, ii. 227 *sqq.*

—— -kin at Rome, v. 41

—— May, leaf-clad mummer, ii. 75, 79

—— Sky fertilizes Mother Earth, v. 282

Fatherhood of God, the physical, v. 80 *sq.*

Fathers named after their children, iii. 331 *sqq.*, 339

Fatigue transferred to leaves, stones, or sticks, ix. 8 *sqq.* ; let out with blood, ix. 12

—— of the Horse, vii. 294. *See also* Weariness

Fattening-house for girls in Calabar, xi. 259

Fattest men chosen kings, ii. 297

Fauna, rustic Roman goddess, her relationship to Faunus, vi. 234

Fauns, rustic Italian gods, in relation to goats, viii. 1 *sqq.*

Faunus, old Roman god, consultation of, iii. 314 ; his relationship to Fauna or the Good Goddess, vi. 234

Fawckner, Captain James, on the annual expulsion of demons in Benin, ix. 131 *sq.*

Fazoql or Fazolglou, on the Blue Nile, kings of, put to death, iv. 16

Fear as a source of religion, ix. 93 ; the source of the worship of the dead, ix. 98

—— of having a likeness taken, iii. 96 *sqq.* ; of spirits, taboo on common words based on a, iii. 416 *sqq.* ; of death entertained by the European races, iv. 135 *sq.*, 146 ; of the dead one of the most powerful factors in religious evolution, viii. 36 *sq.*

Feast. *See also* Festival

—— of All Saints on November 1st, perhaps substituted for an old pagan festival of the dead, vi. 82 *sq.* ; instituted by Lewis the Pious, vi. 83

Feast of All Souls, vi. 51 *sqq.*, x. 223 *sq.*, 225 *n.*[8] ; the Christian, originally a pagan festival of the dead, vi. 81
—— of Fire at winter solstice,, iv. 215
—— of. Florus and Laurus on August 18th, x. 220
—— of the Golden Flower at Sardes, v. 187
——, the Great, in Morocco, ix. 180, 182, 265
—— of Lanterns in Japan, vi. 65, ix. 151 *sq.*
——· of the Nativity of the Virgin, x. 220 *sq.*
—— of Yams, iii. 123
Feathers worn by manslayers, iii. 180 ; red, of a parrot worn as a protection against a ghost, iii. 186 *n.*[1] ; of cock mixed with seed-corn, vii. 278 ; of wren, virtue attributed to, viii. 319
February, annual expulsion of demons in, ix. 148
—— the 1st, St. Bride's Day, ii. 94 *sq.*
—— the 2nd, Candlemas, ii. 94 *n.*[2]
—— the 22nd, St. Peter's Day, vii. 300
—— the 24th, the Flight of the King of the Sacred Rites on, ii. 308 *sq.*
—— and March, the season of the spring sowing in Italy, ix. 346
Fechenots, fechenottes, Valentines, x. 110
"Feeding the dead," iv. 102 ; in Ceram, viii. 123
Feet, homoeopathic charm to strengthen the, i. 151 ; washed, ceremony at reception of strangers, iii. 108 ; not to wet the, iii. 159 ; bare in certain magical and religious ceremonies, iii. 310 *sq.* *See also* Foot
—— of enemies eaten, viii. 151
—— first, children born, superstition as to, i. 266 ; custom observed at their graves, v. 93 ; sticks or grass piled on their graves, ix. 18 ; curative power attributed to children so born, x. 295
Fehrle, E., as to the chastity of the Vestals, ii. 199 *n.*[5]
Feilenhof, in East Prussia, wolf as corn-spirit at, vii. 272
Felkin, Dr. R. W., on the sacrament of a lamb among the Madi or Moru of Central Africa, viii. 314 *sq.*
——, Dr. R. W., and C. T. Wilson, on the worship of the dead kings of Uganda, vi. 173 *n.*[2]
Fellows, Ch., on flowers in Caria, v. 187 *n.*[6]
Feloupes of Senegambia, curse their fetishes in drought, i. 297
Female descent of the kingship in Rome, ii. 270 *sqq.*; in Africa, ii. 274 *sqq.*; in Greece, ii. 277 *sq.*; in Scandinavia, ii.

279 *sq.*; in Lydia, ii. 281 *sq.*; among Danes and Saxons, ii. 282 *sq.*
Female kinship or mother-kin defined, ii. 271 ; rule of descent of the throne under, ii. 271, vi. 18 ; indifference to paternity of kings under, ii. 274 *sqq.*; at Athens, ii. 277 ; indifference to paternity in general under, ii. 282 ; among the Aryans, ii. 283 *sqq.* *See also* Mother-kin
—— slaves, licence accorded to them on the *Nonae Caprotinae*, ii. 313 *sq.*
Femgericht in Westphalia, ii. 321
Feminine weakness, infection of, dreaded by savages, iii. 164 *sq.*, 202 *sq.*
Fen-hall, Frigga weeping in, x. 102
Feng, king of Denmark, married the widow of his predecessor, ii. 281
—— and Wiglet, ii. 281, 283
Fennel, fire carried in giant, ii. 260
Fenua, placenta, among the Maoris, i. 182
Ferghana, a province of Turkestan, combats between champions at the New Year in, ix. 184
Feriae Latinae, iv. 283
Ferintosh district, in Scotland, dancing with the fairies in, x. 227
Fern growing on a tree, in a popular remedy, x. 17 ; the male (*Aspidium filix mas*), a protection against witchcraft, xi. 66 ; blooms on Christmas Eve, Easter Eve, and St. John's Day, xi. 66 ; the root detects and foils sorcerers, xi. 66 *sq.*
—— owl or goatsucker, sex totem of women in Victoria, xi. 217
—— -seed gathered on Midsummer Eve, magical properties ascribed to, xi. 65 *sqq.*; blooms on Midsummer Eve, xi. 287 ; reveals treasures in the earth, xi. 287 *sqq.* ; blooms on Christmas Night, xi. 288 *sq.* ; brought by Satan on Christmas Night, xi. 289 ; gathered at the solstices, Midsummer Eve and Christmas, xi. 290 *sq.*; procured by shooting at the sun on Midsummer Day, xi. 291 ; blooms at Easter, xi. 292 *n.*[2]
Fernando Po, taboos observed by kings of, iii. 8 *sq.*, 115, 123, 291 ; the cobra-capella worshipped in, viii. 174
Feronia, Italian goddess, her sanctuary at Soracte, iv. 186 *n.*[4], xi. 14
Ferrara, synod of, denounces practice of gathering fern-seed, xi. 66 *n.*
Ferrers, George, a Lord of Misrule, ix. 332
Ferret, in homoeopathic magic, i. 150
Fertilization of women by a rattle, i. 347 ; of women by the wild fig-tree, ii. 316 ; of women by the wild banana-tree, ii. 318 ; of women by mummers,

ix. 249 ; of barren women by striking them with stick which has been used to separate pairing dogs, ix. 264 ; of mango trees, ceremony for the, x. 10 ; of fields with ashes of Midsummer fires, x. 170. *See also* Conception, Impregnation

Fertilization, artificial, of the date palm, ii. 24 *sq.*, ix. 272 *sq.* ; of fig-trees, ii. 314 *sq.*, vi. 98, ix. 257, 258, 259, 272 *sq.*

Fertilizing influence of the corn-spirit, vii. 168

—— power ascribed to the effigy of Death, iv. 250 *sq.*

—— virtue attributed to trees, ii. 49 *sqq.*, 316 *sqq.* ; attributed to sticks which have separated pairing dogs, ix. 264

Fertility, Artemis the embodiment of, i. 35 ; Asiatic goddesses of, i. 37 ; the coco-nut regarded as an emblem of, ii. 51 ; Diana as a goddess of, ii. 120 *sqq.* ; the thunder-god conceived as a deity of fertility, ii. 368 *sqq.* ; goddess of, served by eunuch priests, v. 269 *sq.* ; Osiris as god of, vi. 112 *sq.* ; supposed to be procured through masked dances, ix. 382

—— of the ground, thought to be promoted by prostitution, v. 39 ; promoted by marriage of women to serpent, v. 67 ; ceremonies to ensure the, viii. 332 *sqq.* ; magical ceremony to promote the, ix. 177 ; processions with lighted torches to ensure the, x. 233 *sq.* ; supposed to depend on the number of human beings sacrificed, xi. 32, 33, 42 *sq.*

—— of women, magical images designed to ensure the, i. 70 *sqq.* ; magical ceremonies to ensure the, x. 23 *sq.*, 31

Ferula communis, L., giant fennel, its stalks used to carry fire, ii. 260, 260 *n.*[1]

Festival. *See also* Feast

—— of All Souls, iv. 98

—— of the Assumption of the Virgin, August 15th, i. 14, 16

—— of " the awakening of Hercules " at Tyre, v. 111

—— of bladders among the Esquimaux, viii. 247 *sqq.*

—— of the cold food in China, shifted in the calendar, x. 137

—— of the Cornstalks at Eleusis, vii. 63

—— of the Cross on 1st August, x. 220

—— of the Crowning at Delphi, iv. 78 *sq.*, vi. 241

—— of the Dead, x. 223 *sq.*, 225 *sq.* ; among the Hurons, iii. 367 ; among the Esquimaux, iii. 371 ; in Java, v. 220. *See also* Dead

—— of Departed Spirits in Sarawak, ix. 154

" Festival of dreams " among the Iroquois, ix. 127

—— of the Flaying of Men, Mexican, ix. 296 *sqq.*

—— of Flowers (*Anthesteria*), v. 234 *sq.*

—— of Fools in France, ix. 334 *sqq.* ; in Germany, Bohemia, and England, ix. 336 *n.*[1]

—— of the Innocents, ix. 336 *sqq.*

—— of Joy (*Hilaria*) in the rites of Attis, v. 273

—— of lamps, Hindoo, ix. 145

—— of the Laurel-bearing at Thebes, iv. 78 *sq.*, 88 *sq.*

—— of Mascal or the Cross in Abyssinia, ix. 133 *sq.*

—— of the Matronalia, ix. 346

—— of New Fire, viii. 135

—— before Ploughing (*Proerosia*), at Eleusis, vii. 51 *sqq.*, 60, 108

—— of the Sacaea, at Babylon, iv. 113 *sqq.*, ix. 354 *sqq.*

—— of Sais, vi. 49 *sqq.*

—— of the Saturnalia, ix. 306 *sqq.*

—— of the Threshing-floor (*Haloa*) at Eleusis, vii. 60 *sqq.*, 75 ; obscenities in the, vii. 62

—— of the winter solstice, viii. 90

Festivals explained by myths, ii. 142 *sq.* ; of the Egyptian farmer, vi. 32 *sqq.* ; of Osiris, the official, vi. 49 *sqq.* ; Egyptian readjustment of, vi. 91 *sqq.* ; of new yams, viii. 58 *sqq.* ; the great Christian, timed by the Church to coincide with old pagan festivals, ix. 328 ; ancient Greek, resembling the Saturnalia, ix. 350 *sqq.* ; popular, primitive character of, ix. 404 ; of fire in Europe, xi. 106 *sqq.*

Festus, on a proposed etymology of Rome and Romulus, ii. 318 *n.*[3] ; on " the Sacred Spring," iv. 186 ; on the Roman custom of knocking a nail into a wall, ix. 67 *ns.*[1] and [2]

" Fetching the Wild Man out of the Wood," a Whitsuntide custom, iv. 208 *sq.*

Fête des Fous in France, ix. 334 *sqq.*

—— *des Rois*, Twelfth Day, ix. 329

Fetish or taboo rajah in Timor, iii. 24 ; the great, in West Africa, xi. 256

Fetish kings in West Africa, iii. 22 *sqq.*

Fetishes cursed in drought, i. 297

Fetishism early in human history, vi. 43

Feuillet, Madame Octave, on the burning of Shrove Tuesday at Saint-Lô, iv. 228 *sq.*

Fever cured by knotted thread, iii. 304 ; euphemism for, iii. 400 ; typhoid, transferred to tortoise, ix. 31 ; transferred to bald-headed widow, ix. 38 ; Roman cure for, ix. 47 ; transferred to a person by a scrap of paper or a twig, ix. 49 ; transferred to a dog, cat, or snipe, ix. 51 ; transferred to a pillar, ix. 53 ; transferred to a tree or bush, ix. 55 *sq.*, 56, 57, 58, 59 ; nailed into a wall, ix. 63 ; driven away by firing-guns, etc., ix. 121 ; leaping over the Midsummer bonfires as a preventive of, x. 166, 173, 194 ; Midsummer fires a protection against, x. 190 ; need-fire kindled to prevent, x. 297 ; cure for, in India, by walking through a narrow passage, xi. 190

Fewkes, J. Walter, on the observation of the Pleiades among the Pueblo Indians, vii. 312

Fey, devoted, x. 231

Fez, annual temporary sultan in, iv. 152 *sq.* ; orgiastic rites at, vii. 21 ; talisman against scorpions at, viii. 281 ; Midsummer custom of throwing water on people at, x. 216, xi. 31

Fictitious burials to divert the attention of demons from the real burials, viii. 98 *sqq.*

Fictores Vestalium, fictores Pontificum, ii. 204

Ficus Indica (the *bar* tree) sacred in India, ii. 43

——— *religiosa* (the *pipal* tree) sacred in India, ii. 43

——— *Ruminalis*, the fig-tree under which Romulus and Remus were suckled, ii. 318

——— *sycomorus*, used in kindling fire by friction, ii. 210

Fida. *See* Whydah

"Field of the giants," called so from great fossil bones, v. 158

" ——— of God," viii. 14, 15

——— of Mars at Rome, viii. 42, 43, 44

" ——— of secret tillage," viii. 57

Field-mice, burning torches as a protection against, x. 114, 115 ; and moles driven away by torches, xi. 340

" ——— speech," a special jargon employed by reapers, iii. 410 *sq.*, 411 *sq.*

Fielding, H., on the Buddhist Lent, ix. 349 *sq.*

Fields, miniature, dedicated to spirits, vii. 233 *sq.* ; cultivated, menstruous women not allowed to enter, x. 79 ; protected against insects by menstruous women, x. 98 *n.*[1] ; processions with torches through, x. 107 *sq.*, 110 *sqq.*, 113 *sqq.*, 179, 339 *sq.* ; protected against witches, x. 121 ; made fruitful by bonfires, x. 140 ; fertilized by ashes of Midsummer fires, x. 170 ; fertilized by burning wheel rolled over them, x. 191, 340 *sq.* ; protected against hail by bonfires, x. 344

Fiends burnt in fire, ix. 320

Fierte or shrine of St. Romain at Rouen, ii. 167, 168, 170 *n.*[1]

Fife, custom of "dumping" at harvest in, vii. 227

Fifeshire, the harvest Maiden in, vii. 162

Fifty-two years, Aztec cycle of, vii. 310 *sq.*

Fig, as an article of diet, ii. 315 *sq.* ; artificial fertilization of the, at Rome in July, vi. 98 ; Dionysus perhaps associated with the artificial fertilization of the, vi. 259 ; the wild, human scapegoats beaten with branches of, ix. 255.
See also Figs *and* Fig-tree

Fig Dionysus at Lacedaemon, vii. 4

——— -god perhaps personified by Roman kings, ii. 319, 322

——— -leaves, aprons of, worn by Adam and Eve, ix. 259 *n.*[3]

——— -tree of Romulus (*Ficus Ruminalis*), ii. 10, 318

——— -tree, sacred, ii. 44, 99, 249, 250, ix. 61 ; artificial fertilization (*caprificatio*) of the, ii. 314 *sq.*, ix. 257 *sqq.*, 272 *sq.*

——— -tree, the wild, its milky juice sacrificed to Juno Caprotina, ii. 313 ; a male, ii. 314 *sq.* ; supposed to fertilize women, ii. 316 *sq.* ; haunted by spirits of the dead, ii. 317 ; sacred all over Africa and India, ii. 317 *n.*[1]

——— -trees worshipped by the Akikuyu, ii. 44 ; associated with Dionysus, vii. 4 ; wild, held sacred as the abodes of the spirits of the dead, viii. 113 ; personated by human victims, ix. 257 ; charm to benefit, x. 18 ; sacred among the Fans, xi. 161

Fighting the wind, i. 327 *sqq.* ; the king, right of, iv. 22

Fights, sanguinary, as a ceremony to procure rain, i. 258 ; annual, at the New Year, old intention of, ix. 184 ; between men and women about their sex totems, xi. 215, 217

Figo, bonfire on the first Sunday in Lent, x. 111

Figs, soul-compelling virtue of, iii. 46 ; black and white, worn by human scapegoats, ix. 253, 257, 272 ; crowns of, worn at sacrifice to Saturn (Cronus), ix. 253 *n.*[3] ; eaten by human scapegoat before being put to death, ix. 255.
See also Fig

Fiji, treatment of the navel-string in, i. 184 ; catching the sun in, i. 316 ; temporary inspiration of priests in, i. 378 ; special vocabularies employed with reference to divine chiefs in, i. 402 *n.* ; War King and Sacred King in, iii. 21 ; catching away souls in, iii. 69 ; superstitions connected with eating in, iii. 117 ; tabooed persons not to handle food in, iii. 134 *n.*[1] ; taboo for handling dead chiefs in, iii. 141 ; manslayers tabooed in, iii. 178 *sq.* ; custom at cutting a chief's hair in, iii. 264 ; shorn hair hid in thatch of house in, iii. 277 ; voluntary deaths in, iv. 11 *sq.* ; custom of grave-diggers in, iv. 156 *n.*[2] ; abdication of father when his son is grown up in, iv. 191 ; circumcision practised in, iv. 220 ; chiefs buried secretly in, vi. 105 ; sacrifice of first-fruits in, viii. 125 ; leaves piled on spots where men were clubbed to death in, ix. 15 ; annual ceremony at appearance of sea-slug in, ix. 141 *sq.* ; brides tattooed in, x. 34 *n.*[1] ; the fire-walk in, xi. 10 *sq.* ; birth-trees in, xi. 163 ; the drama of death and resurrection exhibited to novices at initiation in, xi. 243 *sqq.*

Fijian belief as to a whirlwind, i. 331 *n.*[2]
—— chiefs claim divinity, i. 389 ; supposed effect of using their dishes or clothes, iii. 131
—— custom of personal cleanliness, iii. 158 *n.*[1]
—— god of fruit-trees, v. 90
—— Lent, v. 90

Fijians, gods of the, i. 389 ; their conception of the soul, iii. 29 *sq.*, 92 ; their notion of absence of the soul in dreams, iii. 39 *sq.* ; their custom of frightening away ghosts, iii. 170 ; their theory of earthquakes, v. 201

Filey, in Yorkshire, the Yule log and candle at, x. 256

Financial oppression, Roman, v. 301 *n.*[2]

Finchra, mountain in Rum, xi. 284

Fingan Eve (St. Thomas's Day) in the Isle of Man, x. 266

Finger bitten off as sacrifice, iii. 166 *n.*[2]

Finger-joints, custom of sacrificing, iv. 219 ; mock sacrifice of, iv. 219
—— -rings as amulets, iii. 315

Fingers cut off as a sacrifice, iii. 161

Finistère, effigy of Carnival at Pontaven in, iv. 230 ; the harvest Wolf in, vii. 275 ; bonfires on St. John's Day in, x. 183

Finland, sacred groves and trees in, ii. 11 ; cattle protected by the woodland spirits in, ii. 124 ; Midsummer fires in, x. 180 *sq.* ; fir-tree as life-index in, xi. 165 *sq.*
—— Gulf of, i. 325

Finlay, George, on Roman financial oppression, v. 301 *n.*[2]

Finnisch-Ugrian peoples, sacred groves of the, ii. 10 *sq.*

Finnish hunters do not call animals by their proper names, iii. 398

Finnish witches and wizards thought to cause winds, i. 325 *sq.*

Finns, feared as sorcerers, iii. 281 ; their propitiation of slain bears, viii. 223 *sq.*

Finow, a Tongan chief, iii. 140

Finsch Harbour in German New Guinea, Kolem on, i. 338 ; the Papuans of, iii. 329 ; the Kai tribe inland from, vii. 99, viii. 296, xi. 239

Fir used to beat people with at Christmas, ix. 270, 271
—— or beech used to make the Yule log, x. 249

Fir-branches, prayers of girl at puberty to, x. 51 ; at Midsummer, x. 177 ; Midsummer mummers clad in, xi. 25 *sq.*
—— -cones, seeds of, gathered on St. John's Day, xi. 64
—— -tree as life-index, xi. 165 *sq.*
—— -trees set up at Midsummer, ii. 65 ; gout transferred to, ix. 56 ; mistletoe on, xi. 315, 316
—— -wood used to kindle need-fire, x. 278, 282

Firdusi's *Epic of Kings*, x. 104

Fire in the worship of Diana, i. 12 *sq.* ; power of extinguishing, ascribed to priests, i. 231, and to chaste women, ii. 240 *n.*[2] ; used to stop rain, i. 252 *sq.* ; used in rain-making ceremonies, i. 303 *sq.* ; as a charm to rekindle the sun, i. 311, 313 ; the King of, in Cambodia, ii. 3 *sqq.* ; birth from the, ii. 195 *sqq.* ; the king's, ii. 195 *sqq.* ; impregnation of women by, ii. 195 *sqq.*, 230 *sqq.*, 234, vi. 235 ; kindled by the friction of wood, ii. 207 *sqq.*, 235 *sqq.*, 237 *sq.*, 243, 248 *sqq.*, 258 *sq.*, 262, 263, 336, 366, 372, viii. 127, 136, 314, x. 132, 133, 135, 136, 137, 138, 144 *sq.*, 148, 155, 169 *sq.*, 175, 177, 179, 220, 264, 270 *sqq.*, 335 *sq.*, xi. 8, 90, 295 ; taken from sacred hearth to found a new village, ii. 216 ; custom of extinguishing fire and rekindling it by the friction of wood, ii. 217, 237 ; kindled from ancestral tree, ii. 221, 233 *sq.* ; on the hearth, souls of ancestors in the, ii. 232 ; reasons for attributing a procreative virtue to, ii. 233 *sq.* ; made jointly by man and woman or boy and girl, ii. 235 *sqq.* ; need-fire made by married men, ii. 238 ; not to be blown upon with the breath, ii. 240, 241, iii. 136, viii. 254, x. 133 ; tribes reported to be ignorant of the art of kindling, ii. 253 *sqq.* ; people reported to be ignorant of the use of, ii. 254 *n.*[1] ; discovery of, by mankind, ii. 255 *sqq.* ;

kindled by natural causes, ii. 256; kindled by lightning, beliefs and customs concerning, ii. 256 *n.*[1], 263, xi. 297 *sq.* ; art of making fire by friction, how discovered, ii. 256 *sq.* ; carried about by savages, ii. 257 *sqq.* ; kept burning in houses of chiefs and kings, ii. 260 *sqq.* ; extinguished on the death of the king, ii. 261 *sqq.*; carried before king or chief, ii. 263 *sq.* ; a symbol of life, ii. 265 ; leaping over a, ii. 327, 329 ; sheep driven over, as a purification, ii. 327 ; rule as to removing fire from priest's house, iii. 13 ; purification by, iii. 108, 109, 111, 114, 168, 197, v. 115 *n.*[1], 179 *sqq.*, xi. 19 ; tabooed, iii. 178, 182, 256 *sq.* ; not to be blown upon by sacred chiefs, iii. 256 ; of a kiln called by a special name in the Outer Hebrides, iii. 395 ; not to be called by its proper name, iii. 411 ; voluntary death by, iv. 42 *sqq.*; Persian reverence for, v. 174 *sq.* ; death in the, as an apotheosis, v. 179 *sq.* ; not given out, vii. 249 ; leaping through, as a form of purification, viii. 249 ; girls at puberty forbidden to see or go near, x. 29, 45, 46 ; menstruous women not allowed to touch or see, x. 84, 85 ; extinguished at menstruation, x. 87 ; in fire-festivals, different possible explanations of its use, x. 112 *sq.* ; made by flints or flint and steel, x. 121, 124, 126, 127, 145, 146, 159 ; made by a burning-glass, x. 121, 127 ; made by a metal mirror, x. 132, 137, 138 *n.*[5] ; year called a fire, x. 137 ; thought to grow weak with age, x. 137 ; pretence of throwing a man into, x. 148, 186, xi. 25 ; carried round houses, corn, cattle, and women after child-bearing, x. 151 *n.*; used to drive away witches and demons at Midsummer, x. 170 ; as a protection against evil spirits, x. 282, 285 *sq.* ; made by means of a wheel, x. 335 *sq.*, xi. 91 ; as a destructive and purificatory agent, x. 341; used as a charm to produce sunshine, x. 341 *sq.* ; employed as a barrier against ghosts, xi. 17 *sqq.* ; used to burn or ban witches, xi. 19 *sq.* ; extinguished by mistletoe, xi. 78, 84 *sq.*, 293 ; of oak-wood used to detect a murderer, xi. 92 *n.*[4] ; life of man bound up with a, xi. 157 ; conceived by savages as a property stored like sap in trees, xi. 295 ; primitive ideas as to the origin of, xi. 295 *sq.* *See also* Bonfires, Extinction, Fires, Need-fire, *and* New Fire

Fire, Feast of, at winter solstice, among the Indians of Arizona, iv. 215

Fire, the god of, among the Huichol Indians, i. 124, viii. 93
'' —— of heaven," term applied to Midsummer bonfire, x. 334, 335
——, holy, not to be blown upon with the breath, ii. 240, 241
—— and lightning averted from houses by crossbills, i. 82
——, " living," made by friction of wood, ii. 237, x. 220 ; a charm against witchcraft, ii. 336
——, Mexican god of, ix. 300 ; human sacrifices to, ix. 300 *sqq.*
——, " new," sent from Delos and Delphi, i. 32 *sq.*, x. 138 ; made by friction in rain-charm, i. 290 ; at taking possession of new house, ii. 237 *sq.* ; made at Midsummer in Peru, ii. 243, x. 132 ; made at beginning of king's reign, ii. 262, 267 ; made by friction of wood, iii. 286, viii. 65, 74, 78 ; at eating new fruits, among the Caffres, viii. 65 ; among the Indians of Alabama, viii. 72 *n.*[2]; among the Creek Indians, viii. 74 ; among the Yuchi Indians, viii. 75 ; among the Natchez Indians, viii. 77, 135 *sqq.* ; at New Year, ix. 209, x. 134, 135, 138 ; Chinese festival of the, ix. 359, x. 136 *sq.* ; kindled on Easter Saturday, x. 121 *sqq.* ; at Candlemas, x. 131 ; festivals of, x. 131 *sqq.* ; among the Peruvians, x. 132 ; among the Mexicans, x. 132 ; among the Zuñi Indians, x. 132 *sq.*; among the Iroquois, x. 133 *sq.* ; among the Esquimaux, x. 134 ; in Wadai, x. 134 ; in the Egyptian Sudan, x. 134 ; among the Swahili, x. 135 ; in Benametapa, x. 135 ; among some tribes of British Central Africa, x. 135 *sq.*; among the Todas, x. 136 ; among the Nagas, x. 136 ; at Karma in Burma, x. 136 ; in Japan, x. 137 *sq.* ; in Lemnos, x. 138 ; at Rome, x. 138 ; among the Celts of Ireland, x. 139 ; near Moscow, x. 139 ; made by the friction of wood at Christmas, x. 264
——, perpetual, of oak wood at Novgorod, ii. 365 ; in front of holy oak in Prussia, iv. 42 ; in Zoroastrian religion, v. 191 ; worshipped, v. 191 *sqq.* ; in Cappadocia, v. 191 ; at Jualamukhi, v. 192 ; at Baku, v. 192 ; in the temples of dead king, vi. 174 ; of oak-bark, viii. 135 ; of oak-wood, xi. 285 *sq.*
——, sacred, annually extinguished at Rome and rekindled by friction of wood, ii. 186 *n.*[1], 267 ; in charge of a married pair, ii. 235 ; new, made by friction of wood at intervals of fifty-two years, vii. 311 ; new, made

by striking stones together, viii. 75; kindled by friction of wood, viii. 127, 314, ix. 391 *n.*⁴; in the sweating-house among the Karok Indians, viii. 255; of king of Uganda, ix. 195

Fire of St. Lawrence, viii. 318

—— of Vesta at Rome fed with oak-wood, ii. 186

——, Vestal, at Alba, i. 13; at Rome, rekindled by the friction of wood, ii. 207

—— and Water, Kings of, in Cambodia, ii. 3 *sqq.*, iv. 14; kingships of, iii. 17

Fire-bearer, the, at Delphi, i. 33; of Spartan king, ii. 264

—— -boards, sacred, of the Chuckchees and Koryaks, ii. 225 *sq.*

—— customs of the Herero or Damaras, ii. 211 *sqq.*; compared to those of the Romans, ii. 227 *sqq.*

—— -drill, the, ii. 207 *sqq.*, 248 *sqq.*, 258 *sq.*, 263; the kindling of fire by it regarded by savages as a form of sexual intercourse, ii. 208 *sqq.*, 218, 233, 235 *sq.*, 239, 249 *sq.*; of the Herero, ii. 217 *sq.*; used to kindle need-fire, x. 292

—— -festivals of Europe, x. 106 *sqq.*; interpretation of the, x. 328 *sqq.*, xi. 15 *sqq.*; at the solstices, x. 331 *sq.*; solar theory of the, x. 331 *sqq.*; purificatory theory of the, x. 341 *sqq.*; regarded as a protection against witchcraft, x. 342; the purificatory theory of the, more probable than the solar theory, xi. 346; elsewhere than in Europe, xi. 1 *sqq.*; in India, xi. 1 *sqq.*, 5 *sqq.*; in China, xi. 3 *sqq.*; in Japan, xi. 9 *sq.*; in Fiji, xi. 10 *sq.*; in Tahiti, the Marquesas Islands, and Trinidad, xi. 11; in Africa, xi. 11 *sqq.*; in classical antiquity in Cappadocia and Italy, xi. 14 *sq.*; their relation to Druidism, xi. 33 *sqq.*, 45

—— -god, married to a human virgin, ii. 195 *sqq.*; the Indian (Agni), ii. 249, xi. 1, 296; the father of Romulus, Servius Tullius, and Caeculus, vi. 235; Armenian, x. 131 *n.*⁸; of the Iroquois, prayers to the, x. 299 *sq.*

—— -priests in Roman religion, ii. 235; (*Agnihotris*) of the Brahmans, ii. 247 *sqq.*

—— -spirit, annual expulsion of the, ix. 141

—— -sticks of fire-drill regarded as male and female, ii. 208 *sqq.*, 235, 238, 239, 248 *sqq.*, ix. 391 *n.*⁴; called "husband and wife," viii. 65

—— -sticks, sacred, ii. 217 *sqq.*

Fire-walk, the, of king of Tyre, v. 114 *sq.*; of priestesses at Castabala, v. 168; in India, Japan, China, Fiji, etc., xi. 1 *sqq.*; a remedy for disease, xi. 7; the meaning of, xi. 15 *sqq.*

—— -worship a form of ancestor-worship, ii. 221; in Cappadocia, India, and on the Caspian, v. 191 *sq.*

Firebrand, external soul of Meleager in a, xi. 103

Firebrands, the Sunday of the, the first Sunday in Lent, x. 110, 114

Firefly, soul in form of, iii. 67

"Fireless and Homeless," a mythical giant, viii. 265, 266

Fires ceremonially extinguished, i. 33, viii. 73, 74, ix. 172; kept burning at home in absence of hunters, fishers, traders, and warriors, i. 120 *sq.*, 125, 128 *sq.*; lighted to warm absent warriors by telepathy, i. 127; leaping over, to make hemp grow tall, i. 138; extinguished at death of kings, ii. 261 *sqq.*, 267; extinguished at any death, ii. 267 *sq.*, 267 *n.*⁴; extinguished at driving herds out to pasture for the first time in spring, ii. 341; passing between two, as a purification, iii. 114; to burn the witches on the Eve of May Day (Walpurgis Night), ix. 163, x. 159 *sq.*; to burn witches on Twelfth Night, ix. 319; to burn fiends, ix. 320; extinguished as preliminary to obtaining new fire, x. 5; annually extinguished and relit, x. 132 *sqq.*; autumn, x. 220 *sqq.*; the need-fire, x. 269 *sqq.*; extinguished before the lighting of the need-fire, x. 270, 271, 272, 273, 274, 275, 276, 277 *sq.*, 279, 283, 285, 288, 289 *sq.*, 290, 291 *sq.*, 292, 294, 297, 298 *sq.*; cattle driven between two fires to rid them of vampyres, x. 285; of the fire-festivals explained as sun-charms, x. 329, 331 *sq.*; explained as purificatory, x. 329 *sq.*, 341 *sqq.*; the burning of human beings in the, xi. 21 *sqq.*; the solstitial, perhaps sun-charms, xi. 292; extinguished and relighted from a flame kindled by lightning, xi. 297 *sq.* *See also* Fire, Bonfires, Need-fire

——, the Beltane, x. 146 *sqq.*; cattle driven between, x. 157

——, ceremonial, kindled by the friction of oak-wood, ii. 372

——, the Easter, x. 120 *sqq.*

—— on the Eve of Twelfth Day, ix. 316 *sqq.*, x. 107

——, Hallowe'en, x. 222 *sq.*, 230 *sqq.*

——, the Lenten, x. 106 *sqq.*

——, Midsummer, x. 160 *sqq.*; a protection against witches, x. 180; supposed to stop rain, x. 188, 336; supposed to be a preventive of backache in reaping, x. 189, 344 *sq.* ; a protection against fever, x. 190

Fires, Midwinter, x. 246 *sqq.*

——, perpetual, of Vesta, i. 13 *sq.* ; in Ireland, ii. 240 *sqq.* ; in Peru and Mexico, ii. 243 *sqq.* ; origin of, ii. 253 *sqq.* ; associated with royal dignity, ii. 261 *sqq.* ; of oak-wood, ii. 365, 366, 372, xi. 91; fed with pine-wood, xi. 91 *n.*[7]

—— of St. John in France, x. 183, 188, 189, 190, 192, 193

Firing guns to repel demons, viii. 99. *See* Guns

Firmicus Maternus on the mourning for Osiris, vi. 86; on use of a pine-tree in the rites of Osiris, vi. 108; on the murder of Dionysus by the Titans, vii. 13; on Demeter and Persephone, vii. 40 *n.*[3]

Firs, sacred grove of, ii. 11, 32

——, Scotch, in the peat-bogs of Europe, ii. 351, 352

First-born, sacrifice of the, among the Hebrews, iv. 171 *sqq.* ; among various races, iv. 179 *sqq.* ; among the Semites, v. 110; at Jerusalem, vi. 219 *sq.*

—— -born killed and eaten, iv. 179 *sq.*

First-born lamb, wool of, used as cure for colic, x. 17

—— -born son never called by his parents by his name, iii. 337

—— -born sons make need-fire, x. 294; special magical virtue attributed to, x. 295

—— -fruits offered to Apollo at Delos, i. 32; of the chase dedicated to the Huntress Artemis, ii. 125 *sq.* ; offered to sacred pontiffs, iii. 5, 21; of the corn offered at Lammas, iv. 101 *sq.* ; offered to the dead, iv. 102; of the vintage offered to Icarius and Erigone, iv. 283; offered to the Baalim, v. 27; offered to the Mother of the Gods, v. 280 *n.*[1]; offered to dead chiefs, vi. 191; offered to Demeter, vi. 46 *sqq.* ; sent to Athens, vii. 51; offered to Demeter and Persephone at Eleusis, vii. 53 *sqq.* ; offered to gods or spirits, vii. 235; offered to the sun, vii. 237; primitive reluctance to taste, viii. 6; sacrament of, viii. 48 *sqq.* ; offered to goddess of agriculture, viii. 56, 58; why savages scruple to eat the, viii. 82 *sq.* ; sacrifice of, viii. 109 *sqq.* ; presented to the king, viii. 109, 116, 122; offered to the spirits or souls of the dead, viii. 109 *sq.*, 111 *sqq.*, 115, 116, 119, 121, 123, 124 *sqq.*, xi, 243

Firstlings, Hebrew sacrifice of, iv. 172

sq. ; Irish sacrifice of, iv. 183; offered to the Baalim, v. 27

Fish worshipped in Egypt, i. 30; magical ceremony for the multiplication of, i. 90; spirits of the dead thought to lodge in, i. 105; magical images to procure, i. 108; magical stones to ensure a catch of, i. 163; in raincharm, i. 288 *sq.* ; thought to cause winds, i. 320 *sq.* ; souls of dead in certain, ii. 30, v. 95 *sq.*, viii. 285, 291, 295; not to be eaten, iii. 10; offered by fisherman to his canoe, iii. 195; descent of the Dyaks from a, iv. 126; descent of a totem clan from a, iv. 129; sacred, viii. 26; the first caught, sacrificed, viii. 132; reason for not eating, viii. 140; treated with respect by fishing tribes, viii. 249 *sqq.* ; preachers to, viii. 250 *sq.* ; invited to come and be caught, viii. 250 *sq.*, 312 *n.* ; not to be eaten by persons who have eaten bear's flesh, viii. 251; compensated by fishermen, viii. 252; first of the season, treated ceremoniously, viii. 253 *sqq.* ; frightened or killed by proximity of menstruous women, x. 77, 93; external soul in a, xi. 99 *sq.*, 122 *sq.* ; lives of people bound up with, xi. 200, 202, 204, 209

——, bones of, not burned, viii. 250, 251; not to be broken, viii. 255

——, golden, external soul of girl in a, xi. 147 *sq.*

Fish-traps, magic of, i. 109; continence observed at making, iii. 196, 202

Fisheries supposed to be spoiled by menstruous women, x. 77, 78, 90 *sq.*, 93

Fishermen, their use of iron as a talisman, iii. 233; names of, not mentioned, iii. 330 *sq.* ; words tabooed by, iii. 394 *sq.*, 396, 408 *sq.*, 415; their superstitions as to herring, viii. 251 *sq.*

——, Shetland, their use of magical images, i. 69 *sq.*

Fishermen's magic in the East Indies, i. 109, 113

Fishers and hunters cursed for good luck, i. 280 *sq.* ; tabooed, iii. 190 *sqq.*

Fishing for a lost soul, iii. 38, 64

—— and hunting, homoeopathic magic in, i. 108 *sqq.* ; telepathy in, i. 120 *sqq.*

Fishing line, superstitious observances in connexion with, iii. 194 *sq.*

—— nets, taboos observed by sacred man at the making of, iii. 192

Fishtown, in Guinea, monkeys sacred at, viii. 287

Fison, Rev. Lorimer, i. 389 *n.*[3], ii. 13 *n.*[1]; on Fijian treatment of navel-string,

i. 184 ; on Fijian way of detaining the sun, i. 316; on Fijian belief as to whirlwinds, i. 331 *n.*[2]; on inspiration of priests in Fiji, i. 378 ; on the Sacred King and the War King of Fiji, iii. 21 ; on the Fijian conception of the soul as a mannikin, iii. 30 *n.*[1] ; on Fijian belief as to absence of soul in dreams, iii. 40 *n.*[1]; on the Fijian conception of the soul, iii. 92 *n.*[3] ; as to chief's dishes and clothes in Fiji, iii. 131 ; on Fijian custom of personal cleanliness, iii. 158 *n.*[1]; on the cutting of a chief's hair in Fiji, iii. 264; on custom of grave-diggers in Fiji, iv. 156 *n.*[2]; on Fijian god of earthquakes, v. 202 *n.* ; on secret burial of chiefs in Fiji, vi. 105 ; on offerings of first-fruits in Fiji, viii. 125; on Fijian religion, xi. 244 *ns.*[1,2,3], 246 *n.*[1]

Fits and convulsions set down to demons, iii. 59

Fittleworth, in Sussex, cleft ash-trees used for the cure of rupture at, xi. 169 *sq.*

Five days' reign of mock king at the Sacaea, iv. 114, ix. 355, 357 ; of Semiramis, ix. 369

—— days' duration of mock king's reign perhaps an intercalary period, ix. 407 *n.*[1]

—— knots in magic, iii. 306

—— years, despotic power for period of, iv. 53

Flacourt, De, on dances of women during war in Madagascar, i. 131

Fladda, island of, stone of swearing in, i. 161 ; the chapel of, wind-stone in the, i. 322 *sq.*

Fladdahuan, one of the Hebrides, i. 322

Flaget, Mgr., on a professed incarnation of the Son of God, i. 409 *n.*[3]

Flail, pretence of throttling persons with flail at threshing, vii. 149, 150, 230

—— or scourge, an emblem of Osiris, vi. 108, 153 ; for collecting incense, vi. 109 *n.*[1]

Flamen, derivation of the name, ii. 235, 247

Flamen Dialis, the, ii. 179, 235, 246, 247 ; an embodiment of Jupiter, ii. 191 *sq.* ; taboos observed by the, ii. 248, iii. 13 *sq.*, 239, 248, 257, 275, 291, 293, 315 *sq.* ; interpreted as a living image of Jupiter, iii. 13 ; the widowed, vi. 227 *sqq.* ; forbidden to touch a dead body, but allowed to attend a funeral, vi. 228 ; bound to be married, vi. 229 ; forbidden to divorce his wife, vi. 229 ; inaugurates the vintage at Rome, viii. 133

Flamen Dialis and Flaminica, v. 45 *sq.*, vi. 228 ; assisted by boy and girl of living parents, vi. 236

—— Virbialis, i. 20 *n.*[3]

—— of Vulcan, vi. 232

Flames of bonfires, omens drawn from, x. 159, 165, 336

Flamingoes, soul of a dead king incarnate in, vi. 163

Flaminica, the, ii. 191, 235 ; rules observed by the, iii. 14 ; and her husband the Flamen Dialis, v. 45 *sq.*, vi. 228, 236

Flanders, Midsummer fires in, x. 194 ; the Yule log in, x. 249 ; wicker giants in, xi. 35

Flannan Islands off the Lewis, iii. 392 *sq.*; certain words tabooed in the, iii. 393 *sq.*

Flathead Indians. *See* Salish

Flax, homoeopathic magic at sowing, i. 136 ; charms to make flax grow tall, i. 138 *sq.*, ii. 86, 164, x. 165, 166, 173, 174, 176, 180 ; omens from the growth of, v. 244 ; pigs' ribs used to make flax grow tall, vii. 300 ; dances to make the flax thrive, viii. 326, 328 ; giddiness transferred to, ix. 53 ; bells rung to make flax grow, ix. 247 *sq.* ; leaping over bonfires to make the flax grow tall, x. 119, 165, 166, 166 *sq.*, 173, 174

Flax crop, prayers and offerings of the old Prussians for the, iv. 156 ; omens of the, drawn from Midsummer bonfires, x. 165

—— -mother, near Magdeburg, vii. 133

—— -pulling, persons wrapt up in flax at, vii. 225

—— seed used to strengthen weakly children, vii. 11 ; sown in direction of flames of bonfire, x. 140, 337

Flaying of Men, Mexican festival of the, ix. 296 *sqq.*

Fleabane as a cure for headache, x. 17

Fleas, leaping over Midsummer fires to get rid of, x. 211, 212, 217

"Fleece of Zeus," Διὸς κῴδιον, iii. 312 *n.*[3]

Flemish cure for ague by transferring it to a willow, ix. 56

Flesh, boiled, not to be eaten by tabooed persons, iii. 185 ; of men eaten to acquire their qualities, viii. 148 *sqq.*

—— of human victim eaten, vii. 240, 244, 251 ; buried in field, vii. 248, 250

Flesh diet, restricted or forbidden, iii. 291 *sqq.* ; homoeopathic magic of a, viii. 138 *sqq.*

Fleuriers, in Switzerland, May-bridegroom at, ii. 91

Flies, in homoeopathic magic, i. 152;
mock burial of, by Russian girls, on
the first of September, viii. 279 *sq.*;
charms against, viii. 281; souls of
dead in, viii. 290 *sq.*
Flight of the priestly king (*Regifugium*)
at Rome, ii. 308 *sqq.*, 311 *n.*[4], iv.
213; in religious ritual, ii. 309 *n.*[2];
from the demons of disease, ix. 122 *sq.*
—— into Egypt, the, xi. 69 *n.*
—— of the People at Rome, ii. 319 *n.*[1]
Flint, holed, a protection against witches,
ix. 162
Flint implements supposed to be thunderbolts, ii. 374
Flints, not iron, cuts in manslayer or
lion-slayer to be made with, iii. 176;
sharp, circumcision performed with,
iii. 227; fire kindled by, x. 121, 124,
126, 127, 145, 146, 159
Flood, the great, ix. 399 *n.*[1]; early
account of, ix. 356
Floor, sitting on the, at Christmas, x.
261
Floquet, A., on the privilege of St.
Romain at Rouen, ii. 168, 169
Flora of Italy, change in the, i. 8
Florence, ceremony of "Sawing the Old
Woman" at, iv. 240 *sq.*; ceremony of
the new fire at Easter in, x. 126 *sq.*
Flores, island, treatment of the placenta
in, i. 191; spiritual ruler in, iii. 24;
the Manggarais of, iii. 324
Florida, American State, sacrifice of
first-born male children by the Indians
of, iv. 184; the Seminoles of, iv. 199,
viii. 76
Florida, one of the Solomon Islands, viii.
85, 126; ghosts that draw out men's
shadows in, iii. 80; magic practised on
refuse of food in, iii. 127; first-fruits
of canarium nuts offered to the dead
in, viii. 126; alligator-ghost in, viii.
297; cuscus-ghost in, viii. 297 *sq.*
Florus and Laurus, feast of, on August
18th, x. 220
Flower of the banana, women impregnated by the, v. 93
—— of plantain in fertility ceremony,
ii. 102
"—— of Zeus," v. 186, 187
Flower-bearers in the service of Hera,
ii. 143 *n.*[2]
Flowering plants called Mothers, vii. 130
Flowers, omens from, i. 128; divination
by, on St. George's Day, ii. 339, 345;
the goddess of, ix. 278; thrown on
bonfire among the Badagas, xi. 8;
external souls in, xi. 117 *sq. See also*
Crown *and* Garlands
—— and herbs cast into the Midsummer
bonfires, x. 162, 163, 172, 173

Flowers and leaves as talismans, vi. 242
sq., x. 183
—— at Midsummer thrown on roofs as
a protection against fire and lightning,
x. 169, xi. 48; Midsummer festival
of, in Riga, x. 177 *sq.*; magical virtue
attributed to flowers that have been
passed across the Midsummer fires, x.
183, 184, 190; crown of fresh, suspended over Midsummer fire, x. 188;
wreaths of, hung over doors and
windows at Midsummer, x. 201;
garlands or crowns of, placed on
mouths of wells at Midsummer, xi.
28; divination by, at Midsummer,
xi. 50 *sq.*
—— on Midsummer Eve, blessed by St.
John, x. 171; garlands of, thrown
into water on Midsummer Eve as an
offering to the water-spirits, xi. 28;
the magic flowers of Midsummer Eve,
xi. 45 *sqq.*; used in divination, xi. 52
sq.; used to dream upon, xi. 52, 54
Flowery Dionysus, vii. 4
Flute, magical, made from human leg-
bone, i. 148; skill of Marsyas on the,
v. 288
Flute music, its exciting influence, v.
54
—— players dressed as women at Rome,
vi. 259 *n.*[3]
Flutes played in the laments for Tammuz,
v. 9; for Adonis, v. 225 *n.*[3]
——, sacred, played at initiation, xi. 241
Fly, soul in form of, iii. 36, 39
Fly River, in British New Guinea, xi.
232
Fly-catcher Zeus, viii. 282
Flying-fish, the first of the season offered
to the dead, viii. 127
—— fox, transmigration of sinner into,
viii. 299
"——-rowan" (parasitic rowan), superstitions in regard to, xi. 281; used to
make a divining-rod, xi. 281 *sq.*
—— Spirits, the, at Lhasa, ix. 197 *sq.*
Fo-Kien, province of China, festival of
fire in, xi. 3 *sqq.*
Foam of the sea, the demon Namuci
killed by the, xi. 280; the totem of a
clan in India, xi. 281
Fog, charms to disperse, i. 314
Folgareit, in the Tyrol, Midsummer
custom at, xi. 47
Folk-custom, external soul in, xi. 153 *sqq.*
—— -tales, of virgins sacrificed to monsters, ii. 155; tongues of wild beasts
cut out in, viii. 269; reflect primitive
customs and beliefs, viii. 269; the external soul in, xi. 95 *sqq.*
Follies of Dunkirk, xi. 34 *sq.*
Foo-chow, the Chinese of, their use of a

winnowing-sieve in superstitious rites, vii. 6, 9

Food, homoeopathic magic for the supply of, i. 85 *sqq.* ; eaten dry on principle of homoeopathic magic, i. 114, 144 ; to be eaten dry by rain-doctor when he wishes to avert rain, i. 271 ; remnants of, buried as a precaution against sorcery, iii. 118, 119, 127 *sq.*, 129 ; magic wrought by means of refuse of, iii. 126 *sqq.* ; taboos on leaving food over, iii. 127 *sqq.* ; not to be touched with hands, iii. 133, 134 *n.*[1], 138 *sqq.*, 146 *sqq.*, 166, 167, 168, 169, 174, 203, 265 ; objection to have food over head, iii. 256, 257 ; as a cause of conception in women, v. 96, 102, 103, 104, 105 ; set out for ghosts, ix. 154 ; girls at puberty not allowed to handle, x. 23, 28, 36, 40 *sq.*, 42

——, sacred, not allowed to touch the ground, x. 13 *sq.*

Foods, forbidden, x. 4, 7, 19, 36 *sq.*, 38, 40, 41, 42, 43, 44, 45, 47, 48, 49, 54, 56, 57, 58, 68, 77, 78, 94 ; to enchanters of crops, vii. 100 ; to meet in stomach of eater, viii. 83 *sqq.*

—— tabooed, on homoeopathic principles, i. 117 *sqq.*, 135, 155, iii. 291 *sqq.*

Fool, the Carnival, burial of, iv. 231 *sq.* ; one of the mummers on Plough Monday, viii. 330

Fool-hen, reason for not eating the, viii. 140

"Fool's Stone" in ashes of Midsummer fire, x. 195

Fools, festival of, in France, ix. 334 *sqq.* ; in Germany, Bohemia, and England, ix. 336 *n.*[1]

—— in processions of maskers, ix. 243

Foot, custom of going with only one foot shod, iii. 311 *sqq.*, viii. 11 ; custom of standing on one, iv. 149, 150, 155, 156 ; limping on one, vii. 232, 284. *See also* Feet

Foot-race at Olympia, iv. 287 ; of boys at Lhasa, ix. 221 *n.*[1]

—— -races at Whitsuntide in Germany, ii. 69

Football, suggested origin of, ix. 184

Footprint of Buddha, iii. 275

Footprints of absent hunter not to be looked at by his sister, i. 122 ; contagious magic of, i. 207-212, iii. 74

Forbes, C. J. F. S., on the worship of demons in Burma, ix. 95 *sq.*

Forbidden thing of clan, xi. 313

"Forced fire" or need-fire, ii. 238. *See* Need-fire

Forchheim, in Bavaria, the burning of Judas at Easter at, x. 143

Fords, offerings and prayers at, ix. 27 *sq.*

Forefathers expected to give rain, i. 353. *See also* Ancestors

Forehead, skin of, regarded as the seat of perseverance, viii. 148 ; and eyebrow of enemy eaten, viii. 152

Foreigners marry princesses and receive the kingdom with them, ii. 270 *sqq.* ; as kings, v. 16 *n.*

Foreskins removed at circumcision, uses of, i. 92 *sq.*, 95 ; magical virtue attributed to, i. 95 ; used in rain-making, i. 256 *sq.* ; of young men offered to ancestral spirits in Fiji, xi. 243 *sq.*

Forespeaking men and cattle, x. 303

Forests of ancient Europe, ii. 7 *sq.*

——, demons of, abduct human souls, iii. 60 *sq.*, 67

Forgetfulness, pretence of, by men who have partaken of human flesh, iii. 189 ; of the past after initiation, xi. 238, 254, 256, 258, 259, 266 *sq.*

Forked shape of divining-rod, xi. 67 *n.*[3]

Forks used in eating by tabooed persons, iii. 148, 168, 169, 203

"Forlorn fire," need-fire, x. 292

Formosa, demon of smallpox transferred to sow in, ix. 33

Fornication thought to blight the fruits of the earth, ii. 107

Fors, the, of Central Africa, their superstition as to nail-parings, iii. 281

Fortuna and Servius Tullius, ii. 193 *n.*[1], 272

—— Primigenia, goddess of Praeneste, daughter of Jupiter, vi. 234

Fortune of the city on coins of Tarsus, v. 164 ; the guardian of cities, v. 164

——, a man's, determined by the day or hour of his birth, i. 173

Forty days, man treated as a god during, ix. 281 ; man personating god during, ix. 297 ; of Lent, possible pagan origin of the, ix. 348 *sq.*

—— nights of mourning for Persephone, ix. 348

Forum at Rome, temple of Vesta in the, i. 13, ii. 186, 200 ; sacred fig-tree of Romulus in the, ii. 10, 318 : funeral processions in the, ii. 178 ; prehistoric cemetery in the, ii. 186, 202 ; funeral games and gladiatorial fights in the, iv. 96

Fossil bones in limestone caves, v. 152 *sq.*, a source of myths about giants, v. 157 *sq.*

Foucart, G., on the legend of the origin of the supplementary Egyptian days, ix. 341 *n.*[1]

Foucart, P., on the Eleusinian mysteries, ii. 139 *n.*[1] ; identifies Dionysus with Osiris, vi. 113 *n.*[3] ; on the resurrection of Dionysus, vii. 32 *n.*[6]

Foul language at festival of Demeter, vii. 58

Foulahs of Senegambia, their fear of crocodiles, viii. 214

Foulères, bonfires on first Sunday in Lent, x. 111 *n.*[1]

Foulkes, Captain, on external souls among the Angass of Nigeria, xi. 210

Foundation sacrifices, iii. 89 *sqq.*

Founding cities, Etruscan ceremony at, iv. 157

Fountains Abbey, the Boy Bishop at, ix. 338

Four Comely Ones, church of the, ii. 161

—— -handed Apollo, vi. 250 *n.*[2]

—— -horse car of the sun-god, iv. 91

—— kinds of wood used to make the divining-rod, xi. 69, 291

—— -leaved clover, a counter-charm for witchcraft, x. 316 ; at Midsummer useful for magic, xi. 62 *sq.*

—— years, many Greek games held every, iv. 96, vii. 79 *sq.*

Fourdin, E., on the procession of the giants at Ath, xi. 36 *n.*[2]

Fowl in homoeopathic magic, i. 151 ; sacrificed on roof of new house, ii. 39 ; used in exorcism, iii. 106 ; in purificatory rite, iii. 177 ; used to divert evil spirits from pregnant woman, ix. 31. *See also* Fowls

Fowler, W. Warde, ii. 327 *n.*[2], 329 *n.*[6], ix. 67 *n.*[2]; on the derivation of June from Juno, ii. 190 *n.*[2]; on the date of the Saturnalia, ii. 311 *n.*[4]; on the death of Romulus, ii. 319 *n.*[1]; on Janus as the god of doors, ii. 383 *n.*[3]; on the celibacy of the Roman gods, vi. 230, 232 *n.*[1], 234 *n.*, 236 *n.*[1]; on Mamurius Veturius, ix. 229 *n.*[1]; on a Midsummer custom, x. 206 *n.*[2]; on *sexta luna*, xi. 77 *n.*[1]; on the ceremony of passing under the yoke, xi. 195 *n.*[4]; on the oak and the thunder-god, xi. 298, 299 *n.*[2], 300

Fowlers, words tabooed by, iii. 393, 407 *sq.*

Fowls, the ghosts of, dreaded by Baganda women, viii. 231 *sq.* ; as scapegoats, ix. 31, 33, 36, 52 *sq.* ; sacrificed, ix. 136. *See also* Fowl

Fowls' nests, ashes of bonfires put in, x. 112, 338

Fox, intestines of a, in homoeopathic magic, i. 151 ; imitation of, as a homoeopathic charm, i. 155 *sq.*; asked to give a new tooth, i. 180 ; guardian spirit as a, i. 200 ; stuffed, vii. 287, 297, viii. 258 *n.*[1]; corn-spirit as, vii. 296 *sq.* ; carried from house to house in spring, vii. 297 ; Koryak ceremony at killing a, viii. 223, 244 ; Esquimau

and Aino treatment of dead, viii. 267 ; soul of dead in a, viii. 286 ; prayed to spare lambs, x. 152. *See also* Foxes

Fox Indians, iii. 163 *n.*[2]

Fox's skin worn by mummer on Plough Monday, viii. 330

—— tail, name given to last standing corn, vii. 268

—— teeth as an amulet, i. 180

—— tongue as amulet, viii. 270

Foxes not to be mentioned by their proper names, iii. 396, 397, 398 ; with burning torches tied to their tails at a festival, vii. 297 *n.*[5]; skulls of, consulted as oracles, viii. 181 ; burnt in Midsummer fires, xi. 39, 41 ; witches turn into, xi. 41. *See also* Fox

Foxwell, Ernest, on the fire-walk in Japan, xi. 10 *n.*[1]

Foxy Dionysus, viii. 282

Fra Angelico, his influence on Catholicism, v. 54 *n.*[1]

Fraas, F., on the various sorts of mistletoe known to the ancients, xi. 318

Framin in West Africa, dance of women at, i. 132

Frampton-on-Severn in Gloucestershire, mistletoe on the oak at, xi. 316

France, prehistoric cave-paintings in, i. 87 *n.*[1]; contagious magic of footprints in, i. 210 ; images of saints dipped in water in, as a rain-charm, i. 307 ; kings of, touch for scrofula, i. 370 ; May customs in, ii. 63 ; leaf-encased mummer in, ii. 83 ; the May Queen in, ii. 87 ; acorns eaten in, ii. 356 ; belief as to stepping over a child in, iii. 424 ; belief as to meteors in, iv. 67 ; "Sawing the Old Woman" at Mid-Lent in, iv. 241 *sq.* ; harvest customs in, v. 237 ; timber felled in the wane of the moon in, vi. 136 ; the Corn-mother in, vii. 135 ; the corn-spirit as a dog or wolf in, vii. 271, 272, 275 ; "Killing the Hare" at harvest in, vii. 280 ; omens from the cry of the quail in, vii. 295 ; corn-spirit as fox in, vii. 296 ; superstitions as to the wren in, viii. 318 ; hunting the wren in, viii. 320 *sq.* ; sticks or stones piled on scenes of violent death in, ix. 15 ; cure for warts in, ix. 48 ; cure for toothache in, ix. 59 ; dances or leaps to make the crops grow high in, ix. 238 ; the King of the Bean in, ix. 313 *sqq.* ; divination on Christmas Day in, ix. 316 *n.*[1]; weather forecasts for the year in, ix. 323 *sq.* ; the three mythical kings on Twelfth Day in, ix. 329 ; Festival of Fools in, ix. 334 *sqq.* ; the Boy Bishop in, ix. 336 *sq.* ; Lenten fires in, x.

109 *sqq.* ; Midsummer fires in, x. 181 *sqq.* ; fires on All Saints' Day in, x. 245 *sq.* ; the Yule log in, x. 249 *sqq.* ; wonderful herbs gathered on St. John's Eve (Midsummer Eve) in, xi. 45 *sqq.* ; mugwort (herb of St. John) at Midsummer in, xi. 58 *sq.* ; fern-seed at Midsummer in, xi. 65 ; judicial treatment of sorcerers in, xi. 158 ; birth-trees in, xi. 165 ; children passed through a cleft oak as a cure for rupture or rickets in, xi. 170. *See also* French

Franche - Comté, dances in, to make hemp grow, i. 137 ; girl called "the spouse" on May Day in, ii. 88 *n.* ; effigies of Shrove Tuesday destroyed in, iv. 227 ; "catching or killing the cat" at harvest in, vii. 281 ; the goat at threshing in, vii. 286 *sq.* ; the King of the Bean in, ix. 313 ; bonfires on the Eve of Twelfth Night in, ix. 316 ; the Three Kings of Twelfth Day in, ix. 330 ; continence during Lent in, ix. 348 *n.*[1] ; Lenten fires in, x. 110 *sq.* ; fires of St. John in, x. 189 ; the Yule log in, x. 254

Franconia (Franken), the King of the Bean in, ix. 315 *n.*

Franken, Bavaria, customs at threshing in, vii. 148

——, Middle, the "Carrying out of Death" in, iv. 233 *sq.* ; fire custom at Easter in, x. 143

Frankenstein, precautions against witches in, xi. 20 *n.*

Frankenwald Mountains, ix. 160 ; the *Walber* on the 2nd of May in the, ii. 65 ; the Wood-woman at harvest in the, vii. 232

Frankfort, the feast of Purim at, ix. 363 *sq.*, 394

Frankish kings, their unshorn hair, iii. 258 *sq.*

Fraser Lake in British Columbia, x. 47

—— River, Indians of the, their conception of the soul, iii. 27 *sq.* ; their belief as to the shadow, iii. 80 ; asked pardon of the porcupines which they killed, viii. 243 ; their respectful treatment of the first sockeye-salmon of the season, viii. 253 *sq.*

Fratres Arvales, ii. 122, vi. 239, ix. 232. *See* Arval Brothers

Frauenkirche, the, at Munich, ix. 215

Fravashis, the souls of the dead in the Iranian religion, vi. 67 *n.*[2], 68

Frazer, Lady, on personal names among the Indians of Chiloe, iii. 324 *n.*[4] ; on Holy Innocents' Day, ix. 337 *n.*[2]

Free Spirit, Brethren of the, i. 408

Freiburg in Baden, St. George as the patron of horses in villages near, ii. 337

Freiburg in Switzerland, Lenten fires in, x. 119 ; fern and treasure on St. John's Night in, xi. 288

Freising, in Bavaria, creeping through a narrow opening in the cathedral of, xi. 189

"French and English" or the "Tug-of-war" as a religious or magical rite, ix. 174 *sqq.*

French cure for fever by tying patient to tree, ix. 55 ; for whooping-cough by passing patient under an ass, xi. 192 *n.*[1]

—— custom of crowning cattle on Midsummer Day, ii. 127

—— Islands, use of bull-roarers in the, xi. 229 *n.*

—— peasants ascribe magical powers to priests, i. 231-233 ; their superstition as to a virgin and a flame, ii. 240, x. 139 *n.* ; regulate their sowing and planting by the moon, vi. 133 *n.*[3], 135

—— reapers, their saying at reaping the last corn, vii. 268

Fresh and green, beating people, ix. 270 *sq.*

Fresh meat tabooed to persons who have handled a corpse, iii. 143

Frey, the Scandinavian god of fertility, vi. 100 *sq.* ; his human wife, ii. 143 *sq.* ; his image and festival at Upsala, ii. 364 *sq.*

Freycinet, L. de, on a Hawaiian festival, iv. 118 *n.*[1]

Frickthal, Switzerland, the Whitsuntide Lout in the, ii. 81 ; the Whitsuntide Basket in the, ii. 83

Friction of wood, fire kindled by, ii. 207 *sqq.*, 235 *sqq.*, 243, 248 *sqq.*, 258 *sq.*, 262, 263, 336, 366, 372, viii. 127, 136, x. 132, 133, 135, 136, 137, 138, 144 *sq.*, 148, 155, 169 *sq.*, 175, 177, 179, 220, 264, 270 *sqq.*, 335 *sq.*, xi. 8 ; new fire made by, vii. 311, viii. 74, 78 ; sacred fire made by, viii. 314 ; the most primitive mode of making fire, xi. 90, 295

Friedlingen, in Swabia, the thresher of the last corn called the Sow at, vii. 298

"Friendly Society of the Spirit" among the Naudowessies, xi. 267

Friesland, harvest custom in, vii. 268

——, East, the clucking-hen at threshing in, vii. 277

Frigento, Valley of Amsanctus near, v. 204

Frigg or Frigga, the Norse goddess, and Balder, x. 101, 102

Fringes to hide the eyes of girls at puberty, iii. 146, x. 47, 48

Fritsch, G., on Zulu festival of first-fruits, viii. 68 *n.*[3]

Frodsham, Dr., on aboriginal Australian belief in conception without sexual intercourse, v. 103 *n.*[3]

Frog, slipperiness of, in homoeopathic magic, i. 151 ; worshipped, i. 294 *sq.* ; love-charm made from the bone of a, ii. 345 ; transmigration of sinner into, viii. 299. *See also* Frogs

Frog-flayer, the, in Whitsuntide pageant, ii. 86

Frogs in homoeopathic magic, i. 155 ; and ducks imitated in rain-making, i. 255 ; in relation to rain, i. 292 *sqq.* ; worshipped by the Newars of Nepaul, i. 294 *sq.* ; hanged or beheaded by mummers at Whitsuntide, ii. 86 *sq.* ; maladies transferred to, ix. 50, 53

Frosinone in Latium, burning an effigy of the Carnival at, iv. 22 *sq.*

Froth from a mill-wheel as a charm against witches, ii. 340

Fruit-bearer, epithet of Demeter, vii. 63

—— -trees, grove of, round temple of Artemis, i. 7 ; Diana a patroness of, i. 15 *sq.*; homoeopathic magic in relation to, i. 140 *sq.*, 142, 143, 145 ; fertilized by fruitful women, i. 140 *sq.*; barren, clothed in woman's petticoat to make them bear, i. 142 ; barren women thought to make fruit-trees barren, i. 142 ; various superstitions as to, i. 143, 145 ; girt with ropes of straw on Christmas Eve in Germany, ii. 17 ; fear to fell, ii. 19 ; threatened to make them bear fruit, ii. 20-22, x. 114 ; barren women fertilized by, ii. 56 *sq.*, 344 ; worshippers of Osiris forbidden to injure, vi. 111 ; Dionysus a god of, vii. 3 *sq.* ; bound with Yule straw, vii. 301 ; presided over by dead chiefs, viii. 125 ; wrapt in straw during the Twelve Nights as a precaution against evil spirits, ix. 164 ; fire applied to, on Eve of Twelfth Night, ix. 317 ; Midsummer fires lit under, x. 215 ; shaken at Christmas to make them bear fruit, x. 248 ; fumigated with smoke of need-fire, x. 280 ; fertilized by burning torches, x. 340

Fruitful tree, use of stick cut from a, ix. 264

Fruits blessed on day of Assumption of the Virgin, i. 14 *sqq.* ; Artemis and Diana as patronesses of, i. 15 *sq.*

—— and roots, wild, ceremonies at gathering the first of the season, viii. 80 *sqq.*

Fuegian charm to make the wind drop, i. 320

Fuegians, their mode of kindling fire, ii. 258 ; their procedure at cutting hair, iii. 282

Fuga daemonum, St. John's wort, xi. 55

Fukhien, fear of tree-spirits in, ii. 14

Fulda, the Lord of the Wells at, xi. 28

Fulgora, a Roman goddess, vi. 231

Fumigating flocks and herds at the Parilia on April 21st, ii. 229, 326, 327

Fumigation with laurel, i. 384 ; of flocks and herds as a charm against witchcraft, ii. 327, 330, 335, 336, 339, 343 ; with incense a charm against witchcraft, ii. 336 ; as a mode of ceremonial purification, iii. 155, 177, 424 ; of flocks by shepherds, viii. 42 ; as a mode of cultivating moral virtues, viii. 166 *sq.* ; with juniper and rue as a precaution against witches, ix. 158 ; of pastures at Midsummer to drive away witches and demons, x. 170 ; of crops with smoke of bonfires, x. 201, 337 ; of fruit-trees, nets, and cattle with smoke of need-fire, x. 280 ; of byres with juniper, x. 296 ; of sheep and cattle in Africa, xi. 12, 13 ; of trees with wild thyme on Christmas Eve, xi. 64

Fünen, in Denmark, cure for childish ailments at, xi. 191

Funeral of Drought, a rain-making ceremony, i. 274 ; of Kostroma, iv. 261 *sqq.*; of caterpillars, viii. 279 ; of dead snake, viii. 317 ; of Death, ix. 205 ; relations whipped at a, ix. 260 *sq.*

Funeral customs in Ceos, i. 105 ; intended to save the souls of survivors, iii. 51 *sqq.*, xi. 18 ; of old Prussians and Lithuanians, iii. 238 ; of the Patagonians, v. 194 ; of the Mongols, v. 293 ; in Madagascar, vi. 247 ; in Tahiti, viii. 97 ; in Chamba, ix. 45 ; in Uganda, ix. 45 *n.*[2]; of the Michemis, x. 5 ; observed by mourners in order to escape from the ghost, xi. 174 *sqq.*

—— games, iv. 92 *sqq.*

—— pyre of Roman emperor, v. 126 *sq.*

—— rites, certain, perhaps intended to ensure reincarnation, i. 101 *sqq.*; performed for a father in fifth month of his wife's pregnancy, iv. 189 ; denied to those who have been hanged, iv. 282 ; of the Egyptians a copy of those performed over Osiris, vi. 15 ; of Osiris, described in inscription of Denderah, vi. 86 *sqq.*

Funerals, personation of the illustrious dead at Roman, ii. 178 ; in China, custom as to shadows at, iii. 80 ; exorcism of ghosts after, iii. 106 *sq.* ; mock human sacrifices at, iv. 216 ; bullocks as scapegoats at, ix. 37 ; the tug-of-war at, ix. 174 *sq. See also* Burial, Burials

Furfo, temple of Jupiter Liber at, iii. 230

Furies, invocation of the, by their names, iii. 390 ; their snakes, v. 88 *n.*[1]

Furnace, walking through a fiery, as a religious rite, xi. 3 *sqq.*

Furness, W. H., on prostitution of unmarried girls in Yap, vi. 266 ; on passing under an archway, xi. 179 *sq.*, 180 *n.*[1]

Furnivall, J. S., on the last sheaf at rice-harvest, vii. 190 *sq.*

Furrow drawn round village as protection against epidemic, ix. 172

Fürstenwald, athletic competition after harvest in villages near, vii. 76 ; the harvest Cock at, vii. 276

Furth in Bavaria, the Slaying of the Dragon at, ii. 163 *sqq.*

Furtwängler, A., on Diana at Nemi, i. 16 *n.*[2] ; on rain-making at Crannon, i. 309 *n.*[6]

Futuna, island in the South Pacific, inspired king in, i. 388 *sq.* ; boxing-matches in honour of the dead in, iv. 97

Fylgia, guardian spirit of child, i. 200

Fytche, A., on the execution of royal criminals in Burma, iii. 242

Gabb, W. M., on ceremonial uncleanness among the Indians of Costa Rica, x. 65 *n.*[1]

Gablingen, in Swabia, the Oats-goat at reaping at, vii. 282

Gablonz, in Bohemia, Midsummer bed of flowers at, xi. 57

Gaboon, circumcision among the dwarf tribes of the, i. 95 *n.*[4] ; Mpongwe kings of the, vi. 104; negroes of the, regulate their planting by the moon, vi. 134 ; the Mpongwe of the, their mode of agriculture, vii. 119 ; birth-trees in the, xi. 160 ; theory of the external soul in the, xi. 200 *sq.*

Gabriel, the archangel, iii. 302, 303 ; in a Malay charm, i. 58

Gacko, need-fire at, x. 286

Gad, Semitic god of fortune, v. 164, 165

Gadabursi, a Somali tribe, milk-drinking after marriage among the, vi. 246

Gadbas, the, of the Central Provinces in India, offer the first-fruits to the cattle, viii. 118 *sq.*

Gades (Cadiz), worship of Hercules (Melcarth) at, v. 112 *sq.* ; temple of Melcarth at, vi. 258 *n.*[5]

Gage, Thomas, on *naguals* among the Indians of Guatemala, xi. 213

Gaidoz, H., on the custom of passing sick people through cleft trees, xi. 171

Gaj, in Slavonia, need-fire at, x. 282

Gaktei, the, of New Britain, called "rotten tree-trunks" by their foes, iii. 331

Galatian senate met in Drynemetum, "the sacred oak grove" or "the temple of the oak," ii. 363, xi. 89

Galatians, their worship of the oak, ii. 126 ; their Celtic language, ii. 126 *n.*[2], xi. 89 *n.*[2]

Galela, dread of women at menstruation in, x. 79

Galelareese of Halmahera, hunter's magic among the, i. 110 ; fisherman's magic among the, i. 113 ; telepathy in war among the, i. 130 ; taboos on pregnant women among the, i. 141 *n.*[1]; their belief in the homoeopathic magic of fruits and vegetables, i. 143, 145 ; homoeopathic magic of the dead among the, i. 147 *sq.* ; their charm made from the ashes of spiders, i. 152 ; their superstition as to the sharpening of a knife, i. 158 ; their superstition as to the tide, i. 167 ; their treatment of the navel-string, i. 186 ; their contagious magic of footprints, i. 208 ; their way of deceiving the fruit of the *aren* palm, ii. 22 ; their superstition as to felling the last tree of a wood, ii. 38 ; their belief that incest causes heavy rain, earthquakes, and volcanic eruptions, ii. 111 ; abduction of souls among the, iii. 60 ; their superstition as to a child who resembles his father, iii. 88 ; their superstition as to mirrors, iii. 93 ; their taboos as to stepping over things, iii. 423 ; as to human sacrifices to volcanoes, v. 220 ; their belief as to a bird croaking among rice in ear, vii. 296 ; their custom of burying the stem of a banana-tree with the dead, viii. 97 ; their rites of initiation, xi. 248

Galelareese charm to make a fruit-tree bear, i. 142 ; to strengthen teeth, i. 157

—— sailors at sea, words tabooed to, iii. 414

Galicia, the Ruthenians of, their charm to increase a cow's milk, i. 198 ; witches on St. George's Day in, ii. 335 ; the Wheat-mother, Rye-mother, and Pea-mother in, vii. 135 ; the harvest Cock in, vii. 277

Galingale, flowers of, used to strike women or girls in Mexico, ix. 288

Gall of eagle in homoeopathic magic, i. 154 ; of sheep in rain-making, i. 290 ; of ox in rain-making, i. 291 ; of ox, man-slayers anointed with, iii. 172, 175 ; of sacrificial bull drunk by king and people, viii. 68 *n.*[3] ; of enemies drunk, viii. 152

Gall-bladders, the seat of courage, viii. 145 *sq.*

Gall, village in Yap, bananas tabooed as food at, iii. 293 *n.*[2]

Gallas, kings of the, i. 48 ; their magical use of tortoises, i. 151 ; their treatment of the navel-string, i. 195 ;

inspired women among the, i. 395
sq. ; sacred trees of the, ii. 34 ; dance round sacred trees, ii. 47 ; their perpetual fires, ii. 261 ; their king not allowed to fight, iii. 13 *n.*[5] ; sacrifice to the guardian spirits of their slain foes, iii. 166 *n.*[2] ; their worship of serpents, v. 86 *n.*[1] ; their communion with the dead through food, viii. 154 ; will not eat the flesh of the biceps, viii. 266 *n.*[1] ; cut out the tongues of animals, viii. 270 ; their mode of expelling fever, ix. 121 ; annual period of licence among the, ix. 226 *n.*[1] ; their story of the origin of death, ix. 304
Gallas, the Borâna, custom observed by manslayers among the, iii. 186 *n.*[1]
Galli, the emasculated priests of Attis, v. 266, 283
Gallic Councils, their prohibition of carrying torches, x. 199
—— recklessness of life, iv. 143
Galloway, " cutting the Hare " at harvest in, vii. 279
Gallows Hill, witches dance on the, on Walpurgis Night, ix. 162 ; magical plants gathered on the, xi. 57
—— -rope used to kindle need-fire, x. 277
Galton, Sir Francis, on European fear of death, iv. 146 *n.*[2] ; on the vale of the Adonis, v. 29
Galway, County, Candlemas custom in, ii. 95 *n.*
Gambling allowed during three days of the year in Siam, ix. 150
Game, dead, in certain cases not brought into house through door, viii. 256, 256 *n.*[1]. *See also* Door
Game law of the Njamus, vi. 39
Game of ball played as a rite, viii. 76, 79 ; played to produce rain or dry weather, ix. 179 *sq.*
—— with fruit-stones played by kings of Uganda, vi. 224
—— of Troy, iv. 76 *sq.*
Gamelion, Attic month, corresponding to January, ii. 137 *n.*[1]
Games, funeral, iv. 92 *sqq.* ; the great Greek, iv. 92 *sq.*, 103 *sqq.*; held by harvesters, vii. 75 *sqq.* ; magical significance of, in primitive agriculture, vii. 92 *sqq.* ; played at the sowing festival among the Kayans, vii. 94 *sqq.*, 97 *sq.* ; played by the Kai of New Guinea as charms for the good of the crops, vii. 101 *sq.*; many games probably originated in magical rites, vii. 103 *n.*[1]; athletic, viii. 66
——, the Eleusinian, vii. 70 *sqq.*, 87 *sq.*, 110, 180
——, the Eleutherian, vii. 80

Games, Greek, quadriennial period of, vii. 77 *sqq.*; octennial period of, vii. 80
——, the Isthmian, iv. 92, 93, 103, vii. 86
——, the Nemean, iv. 92, 93, vii. 86
——, the Olympic, iv. 90, 92, 98 *sq.*, 103, 105, vii. 80, 84, 86
——, the Panathenaic, vii. 80
——, the Pythian, iv. 80, 90, 92, 93, vii. 80, 84
Gamp, Mrs., as to coins on the eyes of a corpse, i. 149 *n.*[5]
Gander, the corn-spirit as a, vii. 268, 270
Gander's neck, name given to last standing corn, vii. 268
Gandersheim, in Brunswick, need-fire at, x. 277
Gandharva pice, iv. 132 *n.*[1]
—— -Sena, an ass by day and a man by night, iv. 124 *sq.*
Ganesa, new rice offered to image of, viii. 56
Gangas, fetish priests of the Loango coast, iii. 291
Ganges, first-born children sacrificed to the, iv. 180 *sq.*
Gaolis of the Deccan place new-born children on sieves, vii. 7 *sq.*
Gap, in the High Alps, cats roasted alive in the Midsummer fire at, xi. 39 *sq.*
Garcilasso de la Vega, on the reverence for the Incas, i. 415 *n.*[2] ; on the virgin Peruvian priestesses of fire, ii. 244 *n.*[1] ; on the fish-worship of the Peruvian Indians, viii. 249 *sq.* ; on the annual expulsion of evils in Peru, ix. 130 *n.*[1]
Garda, the Lake of, custom at Mid-Lent on, iv. 241
Gardelegen, in the Altmark, the He-goat at harvest near, vii. 287
Garden of Osiris, vi. 87 *sq.*
Gardens of Adonis, v. 236 *sqq.* ; charms to promote the growth of vegetation, v. 236 *sq.*, 239 ; in India, v. 239 *sqq.* ; in Bavaria, v. 244 ; in Sardinia, v. 244 *sq.* ; in Sicily, v. 245 ; at Easter, v. 253 *sq.*
—— of God, v. 123, 159
Gardiner, Professor J. Stanley, on the phosphorescence of the sea, ii. 154 *sq.*
Gardner, Professor Ernest A., on date of the corn-reaping in Greece, v. 232 *n.*
Gardner, Mrs. E. A., x. 131 *n.*[1]
Gardner, Professor Percy, on the representation of Persephone on a coin of Lampsacus, vii. 44
Gareloch, in Dumbartonshire, harvest customs on the, vii. 157 *sq.*, 218 *n.*[2], 268
Gargouille or dragon destroyed by St. Romain, ii. 167

Garlands of flowers (wreaths) placed on horns of cattle on St. George's Day to protect them against witchcraft, ii. 126, 339 ; cast into water as a form of divination on St. George's Day, ii. 339, and on Midsummer Eve, xi. 28 ; worn by young people jumping over the Midsummer fires, x. 165 ; thrown on roofs of houses at Midsummer to guard them against fire and lightning, x. 169, xi. 48 ; looking at Midsummer bonfires through, x. 174 ; placed on wells at Midsummer, xi. 28 ; twined of nine kinds of flowers used to dream on at Midsummer, xi. 52 ; thrown on trees, a form of divination, at Midsummer, xi. 53. See also Flowers and Wreaths

—— on May Day, ii. 60 sqq., 90 sq.

Garlic, soul-compelling virtue of, iii. 46 ; roasted at Midsummer fires, x. 193

Garman or Carman, the fair of, iv. 100

Garments, effect of wearing sacred, iii. 4

Garonne, Midsummer fires in the valley of the, x. 193

Garos of Assam, their rain-charm by means of a black goat, i. 291 ; ceremony of the Horse at rice - harvest among the, viii. 43 n.[1], 337 sqq. ; offer the first-fruits to the gods, viii. 116 sq. ; their annual use of a scapegoat, ix. 208 sq.

Garstang, Professor J., on Hittite sculptures at Ibreez, v. 122 n.[1], 123 n.[2]; on Hittite sculptures at Boghaz-Keui, v. 133 n., 135 n.; on Arenna, v. 136 n.[1]; on the Syrian god Hadad, v. 163 n.[3]

Gascon peasants, their belief in the magical power of priests, i. 232 sq.

Gashes cut in back, Australian initiatory rite, vii. 106

Gates of city opened or shut as charm for ensuring rain or sunshine, i. 298 sq. ; sacrifice of human beings at foundations of, iii. 98 sq.

Gateway, refusal of Marquesan chief to pass through, iii. 254

Gateways of villages, sacrificial blood smeared on, iv. 176 n.[1]

Gathas, a part of the Zend-Avesta, vi. 84 n.

Gatri, in Nigeria, kings of, formerly put to death, iv. 34 sq.

Gatschet, A. S., on absence of historic traditions caused by fear of naming the dead, iii. 363 ; on the absence of totemism in California and Oregon, viii. 175 n.[2]; on the Toukawe Indians, xi. 276 n.[2]

Gattanewa, a Marquesan chief, his regard for the sanctity of his head, iii. 254 sq.

Gatto, in Benin, annual expulsion of demons at, ix. 131 sq.

Gaul, the Druids of, ii. 189 ; Posidonius in, iv. 142 ; worship of Cybele in, v. 279 ; the Celts of, their calendar, ix. 342 sqq.; " serpents' eggs " in ancient, x. 15 ; human sacrifices in ancient, xi. 32 sq. See also Gallic

Gauls, their " sacred spring," iv. 187 n.[5]; their fortification walls, x. 267 sq.

Gauntlet, running the, penalty for killing a sacred python, iii. 222

Gauri, harvest - goddess, wife of Siva, represented by a girl and a bundle of plants, ii. 77 sq., vii. 207

Gavres, Persian fire-worshippers, iv. 158

Gayo, a district of Sumatra, rice fed like a pregnant woman and given water to drink in, ii. 29 ; the crops ravaged by wild swine and mice in, viii. 33

Gayos of Northern Sumatra, their offering to the Lord of the Wood before clearing a piece of forest, ii. 36 ; propitiate the Lord of the Wood before hunting in the forest, ii. 125 ; superstitions of gold-washers among the, iii. 409 n.[3]; their euphemism for smallpox, iii. 410

Gazelle Peninsula in New Britain, beneficial effect of contagious magic in the, i. 175; continence at the building of a canoe in the, iii. 202 ; the name of a brother-in-law not to be mentioned among the natives of the, iii. 344 ; the natives of the, their belief as to meteors, iv. 65 ; conduct of the natives in an earthquake, v. 201 ; the Melanesians of the, vi. 242 sq. ; woman's share in agriculture among the natives of the, vii. 123 ; the Livuans of the, their belief in demons, ix. 82 sq.; natives of the, their story of the origin of death, ix. 303 sq. ; the Ingniet society in the, xi. 156

Gazelles sacrificed at Egyptian funerals, vi. 15 ; souls of dead in, viii. 289

Ge-lug-pa, a Lamaist sect, ix. 94

Gebal, Semitic name of Byblus, v. 13 n.

Gebars of New Guinea, temporary seclusion of cannibals among the, iii. 190

Geelvink Bay in New Guinea, magical telepathy among the tribes of, i. 125 ; belief in a forest-spirit at, iii. 60 sq.

Geese sacrificed at Egyptian funerals, vi. 15 ; the straw of the Shrovetide Bear supposed to make geese lay eggs, viii. 326

Geismar, in Hesse, Jupiter's oak at, ii. 364

Gellius, Aulus, on the triumphal crowns, ii. 175 n.[1]; his list of old Roman deities, vi. 232. See also Aulus Gellius

Gellius, Cnaeus, on Mars and Nerio, vi. 232
Gelo, tyrant of Syracuse, iv. 167
Gem, external soul of magician in a, xi. 105 *sq.* ; external soul of giant in a, xi. 130
Geminus, Greek astronomer, on the vague Egyptian year, vi. 26 ; on the octennial cycle, vii. 81 ; on the supposed influence of the stars, vii. 318 *sq.*
Generalizations of science inadequate to cover all particular facts, viii. 37
Generation, male organ of, as emblem of Dionysus, vii. 12 ; effigy of, in Thracian ceremony, vii. 26, 29
Genesis, Sarah and Abraham in, ii. 114 ; account of the creation in, iv. 106 ; the Babylonian, ix. 410
Geneva, Midsummer fires in the canton of, x. 172
Genital organs of murdered people eaten, iii. 190 *n.*[2] ; of Osiris, tradition as to the, vi. 10, 102 ; of dead man used to fertilize the fields, vi. 102 *sq.*
Genius, the Roman guardian-spirit, symbolized by a serpent, v. 86, xi. 212 *n.*
Genius, Aristotle on men of, viii. 302 *n.*[5]
—— of Industry in China represented by a boy with one foot shod and one foot bare, viii. 11
—— or patron of animals, viii. 243
—— of Spring in Annam, viii. 14
Genna, taboo, among the hill tribes of Assam, iii. 11, vii. 109 *n.*[1]
Gennep, A. van, on the double-headed Janus, ii. 385 *n.*[1]
Gennesaret, the Lake of, viii. 32
Genzano, the village of, i. 5 *n.*[2]
Geographical and climatic conditions, their effect on national character, vi. 217
Geomancy in China, i. 170, iii. 239
George, Green, a leaf-clad mummer on St. George's Day, ii. 75, 76, 79
George the Third, i. 216
Georges d'Amboise, great bell at Rouen, ii. 168
Georgia, the Caucasian, rain-making in, i. 282
Geraestius, a Greek month, ix. 350
Geranium burnt in Midsummer fire, x. 213
Gerard, E., on the belief of the Roumanians in demons, ix. 106 *sq.*
Gerhausen, the Frauenberg near, x. 166
German belief as to the escape of the soul, iii. 37
—— cures for toothache by transferring it to trees, ix. 57, 58, 59
—— custom of throwing a knife or a hat at a whirlwind, i. 329 ; of crowning cattle on Midsummer Day, ii. 127 ;

of sowing seed over weakly children, vii. 11
German huntsmen call everything by special names, iii. 396
—— laws, old, their punishment for barking a tree, ii. 9
—— peasants, their treatment of the afterbirth of a cow, i. 198 *sq.* ; their homoeopathic treatment of a broken leg, i. 205
—— saying as to not leaving a knife edge upward, iii. 238
—— superstition as to largeness of last sheaf, vii. 139 *n.*[7]; as to understanding the language of animals, viii. 146
—— way of freeing gardens from caterpillars, viii. 275
—— women, their use of milk-stones, i. 165
—— woodmen, their ceremony at felling a tree, ii. 38
Germans, oldest sanctuaries of the, ii. 8 *sq.* ; evidence of mother-kin among the, ii. 285 ; the oak sacred among the, xi. 89
—— the ancient, their worship of women, i. 391 ; their tree-worship, ii. 8 *sq.* ; their worship of the oak, ii. 363 *sq.* ; their customs as to their hair, iii. 262 ; their regard for the phases of the moon, vi. 141 ; left the care of the fields to women and old men, vii. 129 ; their human sacrifices, xi. 28 *n.*[1]
—— of Moravia, their precautions against witchcraft on Walpurgis Night, ii. 55 ; their custom on *Laetare* Sunday, ii. 63
—— of Transylvania, their belief as to knots in a coffin, iii. 310
—— of West Bohemia call the last sheaf the Old Man, vii. 138 ; their custom of beating each other at Christmas, ix. 270 ; Twelfth Day among the, ix. 331
Germany, popular cures for jaundice, St. Anthony's fire, and bleeding in, i. 81 ; dancing or leaping as a charm to make flax grow tall in, i. 138 *sq.* ; custom as to cast teeth in, i. 178 ; treatment of weapons that have wounded in, i. 204 ; beating an absent man vicariously in, i. 207 ; contagious magic of footprints in, i. 210, 211 *sq.*; meal offered to the wind in, i. 329 *n.*[5]; fruit-trees girt or tied together with straw on Christmas Eve in, ii. 17, 27 *sq.*; the Harvest May in, ii. 47, 48 ; use of May-trees to make cows yield milk in, ii. 52 ; the rowan-tree a charm against witchcraft in, ii. 53 *n.*[5], ix. 267 ; precautions against witches on Walpurgis Night in, ii. 54 ; Midsummer trees in, ii. 65 *sq.*; races at Whitsuntide in, ii.

69 ; races at a marriage in, ii. 303 *sq.* ; acorns as fodder for swine in, ii. 356 ; custom of passing patients through a hole in an oak-tree as a cure in, ii. 371 ; presages as to shadows on St. Sylvester's Day and Christmas Eve in, iii. 88 ; mirrors covered after a death in, iii. 95 ; belief as to combing and cutting children's hair in, iii. 263 *sq.*; disposal of cut hair in, iii. 275 *sq.*; certain animals not to be called by their proper names between Christmas and Twelfth Night in, iii. 396 ; belief as to stepping over a child in, iii. 424 ; belief as to a man's star in, iv. 66 ; harvest custom in, v. 237 ; leaping over Midsummer fires in, v. 251 ; Feast of All Souls in, vi. 70 *sqq.* ; popular superstition as to the influence of the moon in, vi. 133, 140 *sq.*, 149 ; peasants regulate their sowing and planting by the moon in, vi. 135 ; the Corn-mother in, vii. 132 *sqq.* ; the last sheaf called the Old Woman in, vii. 136 ; the last sheaf called the Old Man in, vii. 137 ; the last sheaf at harvest called the Bride in, vii. 162 ; treatment of passing strangers by reapers and threshers in, vii. 225 ; cries of reapers in, vii. 269 ; the corn-spirit as a dog or wolf in, vii. 271, 273 ; the last corn as a cock in, vii. 276, 277 ; the last sheaf called the Hare in, vii. 279, 280 ; omens from the cry of the quail in, vii. 295 ; corn-spirit as fox in, vii. 296 ; pigs' bones in connexion with sowing in, vii. 300 ; the harvest-cock in, viii. 44 ; sticks or stones piled on scenes of violent death in, ix. 15 ; cure for warts in, ix. 54 ; cure for toothache in, by transplanting it to a tree, ix. 59 ; dances or leaps to make the crops grow high in, ix. 238 ; "Easter Smacks" in, ix. 268 *sq.*; custom of young people beating each other on Holy Innocents' Day in, ix. 270 ; the King of the Bean in, ix. 313 ; weather of the twelve months thought to be determined by the weather of the Twelve Days in, ix. 322 ; weather forecasts by means of a peeled onion in, ix. 323 ; the three mythical kings on Twelfth Night in, ix. 329 ; the festival of Fools in, ix. 336 *n.*[1]; Lenten fires in, x. 115 *sq.* ; Easter bonfires in, x. 140 *sqq.* ; custom at eclipses in, x. 162 *n.* ; the Midsummer fires in, x. 163 *sqq.* ; the Yule log in, x. 247 *sqq.* ; belief in the transformation of witches into animals in, x. 321 *n.*[2] ; colic, sore eyes, and stiffness of the back attributed to witchcraft in, x. 344 *sq.* ; mugwort at Midsummer in,

xi. 59 ; orpine gathered at Midsummer in, xi. 62 *n.* ; fern-seed at Midsummer thought to be endowed with marvellous properties in, xi. 65 ; mistletoe a remedy for epilepsy in, xi. 83 ; the need-fire kindled by the friction of oak in, xi. 91 ; oak-wood used to make up cottage fires on Midsummer Day in, xi. 91 *sq.* ; stories of the external soul in, xi. 116 *sqq.* ; birth-trees in, xi. 165 ; children passed through a cleft oak as a cure for rupture in, xi. 170 *sqq.*

Germany, ancient, the forests of, ii. 353

Gerontocracy, the rule of old men, in Australia, i. 335

Gervasius of Tilbury, on a rain-producing spring, i. 301

Gestr and the spae-wives, Icelandic story of, xi. 125 *sq.*

Getae, human god among the, i. 392 ; priestly kings of the, iii. 21

Gewar, king of Norway, his daughter Nanna wooed by Balder, x. 103

Gezer, Canaanitish city, excavations at, v. 108

Gezo, King, restricts the benefit of clergy on the Slave Coast, v. 68

Ghansyam Deo, a deity of the Gonds, protector of the crops, ix. 217

Ghats, the Eastern, use of scapegoats in the, ix. 191

Ghennabura, religious head of village in Manipur, iii. 292

Ghera, a Galla kingdom, birth names of kings not to be pronounced in, iii. 375

Ghineh, monument of Adonis at, v. 29

Ghost of afterbirth thought to adhere to navel-string, vi. 169 *sq.*

—— of husband kept from his widow, iii. 143 ; fear of evoking the ghost by mentioning his name, iii. 349 *sqq.* ; chased into the grave at the end of mourning, iii. 373 *sq.*

——, the Holy, regarded as female, iv. 5 *n.*[3]

——, oracular, in a cave, xi. 312 *sq.*

——, precaution against, i. 142, 154

Ghosts, supernatural power of chiefs in Melanesia thought to be derived from, i. 338 *sq.* ; draw away the souls of their kinsfolk, iii. 51 *sqq.* ; sacrifices to, iii. 56, 247 ; draw out men's shadows, iii. 80 ; as guardians of gates, iii. 90 *sq.* ; exorcized after funerals, iii. 106 *sq.* ; kept off by thorns, iii. 142 ; the purification of homicides and murderers designed to free them from the ghosts of their victims, iii. 186 *sq.* ; and demons averse to iron, iii. 232 *sqq.*; fear of wounding, iii. 237 *sq.* ; swept out of house, iii. 238 ; names changed in order to deceive ghosts or to avoid attracting their attention, iii. 354 *sqq.* ; easily duped, iii. 355 ; propitiated with blood, iv. 92 ; propitiated with games, iv. 96 ; dearth and famine attributed to the anger of, iv. 103 ; thought to impregnate women, v. 93, ix. 18 ; of the dead personated by living men, vi. 52, 53, 58 ; who preside over gardens, fear of offending the, viii. 85 ; deceived by the substitution of effigies for living persons, viii. 94 *sqq.*, 97 *sqq.* ; first-fruits offered to, viii. 126 *sq.* ; offerings to ancestral, viii. 127 ; disabled by the mutilation of their bodies, viii. 271 *sqq.* ; of suicides feared, ix. 17 *sq.* ; shut up in wood, ix. 60 *sq.* ; nailed into the ground, ix. 63 ; diseases caused by, ix. 85 ; epidemics thought to be caused by, ix. 116 ; periodically expelled, ix. 123 *sq.* ; driven off by blows, ix. 260 *sqq.* ; extracted from wooden posts, x. 8 ; fire used to get rid of, xi. 17 *sqq.* ; mugwort a protection against, xi. 59 ; kept off by thorn bushes, xi. 174 *sq.* ; creeping through cleft sticks to escape from, xi. 174 *sqq. See also* Ancestral Spirits *and* Dead

Ghosts of animals, dread of, iii. 223, viii. 216, 217, 218, 219, 220, 223, 224, 227 *sq.*, 229, 231 *sq.*, 235, 236, 237, 241, 245, 267 *sq.*, 269, 271

——, Roman festival of, in May, ix. 154 *sq.*

—— of the slain haunt their slayers, iii. 165 *sqq.* ; sacrifices to, iii. 166 ; scaring away the, iii. 168, 170, 171, 172, 174 *sq.* ; as birds, iii. 177 *sq.* ; precautions against, iii. 240

Giant who had no heart in his body, stories of the, xi. 96 *sqq.*, 119 *sq.* ; mythical, supposed to kill and resuscitate lads at initiation, xi. 243

Giant-fennel burnt in Midsummer fire, x. 213

Giants, myths of, based on discovery of fossil bones, v. 157 *sq.*

—— and gods, their battle, v. 157

—— of wicker-work at popular festivals in Europe, xi. 33 *sqq.* ; burnt in the summer bonfires, xi. 38

Giaour-Kalesi, Hittite sculptures at, v. 138 *n.*

Giddiness, transferred to flax, ix. 53

Giggenhausen, in Bavaria, burning the Easter Man at, x. 144

Gigha, island off Argyleshire, wind-charm in, i. 323

Gilbert, O., on the *lapis manalis* at Rome, i. 310 *n.*[3]

Gilbert Islands, treatment of the navel-string in the, i. 185 *sq.* ; sacred stones in the, v. 108 *n.*[1]

Giles, Professor H. A., on reported substitutes for capital punishment in China, iv. 275

Gilgamesh, the epic of, ix. 371, 398 *sq.* ; a Babylonian hero, beloved by the goddess Ishtar, ix. 371 *sq.*, 398 *sq.* ; his name formerly read as Izdubar, ix. 372 *n.*[1]

Gilgamus, a Babylonian king, ix. 372 *n.*[1]

Gilgenburg in Masuren, "Easter Smacks" at, ix. 269

Gilgit, custom at felling a tree in, ii. 44 ; the sacred *chili* (a kind of cedar) at, ii. 49, 50 ; in the Hindoo Koosh, custom at wheat harvest at, viii. 56

Gill, Captain W., on a tribe in China governed by a woman, vi. 211 *n.*[3]

Gill, W. W., on the observation of the Pleiades in the Hervey Islands, vii. 312

Gilolo. *See* Halmahera

Gilyak hunters, taboos observed in their absence by their children, i. 122

—— procession with bear, viii. 322, 325

—— shaman, his exorcism, viii. 103

Gilyaks, their ceremony at felling a tree, ii. 38 ; do not clearly distinguish animals from men, viii. 206 ; their respect for dead sables, viii. 238

—— of the Amoor, a Tunguzian people, viii. 190 ; eat nutlets of stone-pine, v. 278 *n.*[2] ; their exorcism by means of effigies, viii. 103 *sq.* ; their bear-festivals, viii. 190 *sqq.* ; why they put out the eyes of the seals they kill, viii. 267 ; their belief in demons, ix. 101 *sq.*

—— of Saghalien, their customs as to personal names, iii. 370

Ginger in purificatory rites, iii. 105, 151 ; cultivated, vii. 123

Gingiro, an Ethiopian kingdom, pretence of reluctance to accept the kingdom in, iii. 18 *sq.* ; wounded kings of, put to death, iv. 34 ; custom at accession of new king in, iv. 200

Ginzel, Professor F. K., on the rise of the Nile, vi. 31 *n.*[1]

Gion shrine in Japan, x. 138

Gippsland, in Victoria, the Kurnai of, i. 324, xi. 216 ; the natives of, concealed their personal names, iii. 331 *sq.*

Gipsies. *See* Gypsies

Giraffes, souls of dead kings incarnate in, vi. 162

Giraldus Cambrensis on transformation of witches into hares, x. 315 *n.*[1]

Girdle of wolf's hide worn by were-wolves, x. 310 *n.*[1]

——, sacred, of king of Tahiti, i. 388

Girdles of mugwort worn on St. John's Day or Eve as preservative against backache, sore eyes, ghosts, magic, and sickness, xi. 59

Girkshausen, in Westphalia, the Yule log at, x. 248

Girl annually sacrificed to cedar-tree, ii. 17

—— and boy produce need-fire by friction of wood, x. 281

Girlachsdorf, in Silesia, the last sheaf called the Old Man at, vii. 138

Girls or women dance to make crops grow tall, i. 139 *n.* ; married to nets, ii. 147 ; sacrificed to crocodiles, ii. 152 ; employed to sow seed, vii. 115 ; sacrificed for the crops, vii. 237, 239

—— at puberty obliged to touch everything in house, iii. 225 *n.* ; their hair torn out, iii. 284 ; ceremonial uncleanness of, viii. 268, 268 *n.*[4] ; secluded, x. 22 *sqq.* ; not allowed to touch the ground, x. 22, 33, 35, 36, 60 ; not allowed to see the sun, x. 22, 35, 36, 37, 41, 44, 46, 47, 68 ; not allowed to handle food, x. 23, 28, 36, 40 *sq.*, 42 ; half buried in ground, x. 38 *sqq.* ; not allowed to scratch themselves with their fingers, x. 38, 39, 41, 42, 44, 47, 50, 53, 92 ; not allowed to lie down, x. 44 ; said to be wounded by a snake, x. 56 ; said to be swallowed by a serpent, x. 57 ; gashed on back, breast, and belly, x. 60 ; stung by ants, x. 61 ; beaten severely, x. 61, 66 *sq.* ; supposed to be attacked by a demon, x. 67 *sq.* ; not to see the sky, x. 69 ; forbidden to break bones of hares, x. 73 *n.*[3]

—— under puberty used in rain-making, iii. 154

Girls' race at Olympia, iv. 91

Gisors, sickly children passed through a holed stone near, xi. 188

Givoy agon, living fire, in Russia, made by the friction of wood, x. 220

Gladiators at Roman funerals, iv. 96 ; at Roman banquets, iv. 143

Glamorganshire, cure for warts in, ix. 53; the Vale of, Beltane fires in, x. 154 ; Midsummer fires in, x. 154, 201, 338

Glands, ashes of Yule log used to cure swollen, x. 251

Glanvil, Joseph, on a witch in the form of a cat, x. 317

Glass, the Magician's or Druid's, name for certain beads, x. 16

Glatz, precautions against witches on Walpurgis Night in, xi. 20 *n.*

Glaucus, son of Minos, restored to life, v. 186 *n.*[4]

Glawi, in the Atlas, New Year fires at, x. 217

Gleiwitz, in Poland, sacrifice for horses near, ii. 336 *sq.*

Glen Farg, Perthshire, the harvest Maiden in, vii. 157, 157 *n.*[3]

—— Mor, in Islay, stone for the cure of toothache in, ix. 62

—— Moriston, Inverness-shire, vii. 162 *n.*[3]

Glencoe, the harvest Maiden and Old Wife in, vii. 165

Glencuaich, the hawk of, in a Celtic tale, xi. 127 *sqq.*

Glenorchy, the Beltane cake in, x. 149

Glory, the Hand of, a thief's talisman, i. 149

" ——, the Hand of," mandragora, xi. 316

Gloucester, the Boy Bishop at, ix. 337

Gloucestershire, fires kindled on the Eve of Twelfth Day in, ix. 318, 321 ; mistletoe growing on oaks in, xi. 316

Glover, T. R., on a fire-custom of the Telugus, ii. 231 *n.*[6]

Glue in homoeopathic magic, i. 157

Gnabaia, a spirit who swallows and disgorges lads at initiation, xi. 235

Gnats, charm against, viii. 280

Gnid-eld, need-fire, in Sweden, x. 280

Gniewkowo, in Prussian Lithuania, mummers on Twelfth Day near, viii. 327

Goajira peninsula in Colombia, personal names kept secret among the Indians of, iii. 325

Goajiras of Colombia, set hooks to catch demons, iii. 30 *sq.* ; the dead not named among the, iii. 352 ; their seclusion of girls at puberty, x. 34 *n.*[1]

Goat, blood of, drunk by devil-dancers and priests as means of inspiration, i. 382, 383 ; prohibition to touch or name, iii. 13 ; transference of guilt to, iii. 214 *sq.* ; sacrificed by being hanged, v. 292 ; in relation to Dionysus, vii. 17 *sq.*, viii. 1 *sqq.* ; torn to pieces in rites of Dionysus, vii. 18, viii. 16 ; sacrificed for human victim, vii. 249 ; corn-spirit as, vii. 281 *sqq.*, viii. 327 ; last sheaf made up in form of a, vii. 283 ; killed on harvest-field, vii. 285 ; stuffed, vii. 287 ; killed at sowing, vii. 288 ; the sacred animal of a Bushman tribe, viii. 28 *sq.* See also Goats

—— and Athena, viii. 40 *sq.*

——, black, in rain-making ceremonies, i. 250, 291

——, the Cripple or Lame, name given to the last sheaf, vii. 164, 284

Goat-formed deities and spirits of the woods, viii. 1 *sqq.*

Goat-skin, mask of, worn by mummers at Carnival, vii. 26 ; worn by farmer at harvest, vii. 285 ; hung on pole at sowing and danced round at harvest, vii. 288
—— -skins, mummers at Carnival clad in, vii. 26 *sqq.*
Goat's flesh, taboo as to entering a sanctuary after eating, viii. 85
—— Marsh at Rome, disappearance of Romulus at the, ii. 181, ix. 258
—— neck, name given to last standing corn, vii. 268
Goats fertilized at the Chili stone, ii. 51 ; sacrificed in ceremonies to fertilize barren women, ii. 316, 318 ; bred by the people of the Italian pile villages, ii. 353 *n.*³ ; not to be called by their proper name, iii. 415 ; sacrificed instead of human beings, iv. 166 *n.*¹ ; torn to pieces by fanatics in Morocco, vii. 21 *sq.* ; in relation to minor Greek and Roman deities (Satyrs, Fauns, etc.), viii. 1 *sqq.* ; the testicles of, eaten by lecherous persons, viii. 142 ; sacrificed to wolves, viii. 284 ; evil transferred to, ix. 31, 32 ; as scapegoats, ix. 190, 191, 192. *See also* Goat
Goats' horns used as a protection against witches, ix. 161, 162
Goatsucker or fern owl, shadow of the, iii. 82 ; sex totem of women, xi. 217
Gobar-bhacach (goabbir bhacagh), "the lame goat," name given to the last sheaf in Skye, vii. 164, 284
Gobi, the desert of, ix. 13
Gobir, a Hausa kingdom, infirm kings killed in, iv. 35
God, savage ideas of, different from those of civilized men, i. 375 *sq.* ; "the most great name" of, iii. 390 ; the killing and resurrection of a god in the hunting, pastoral, and agricultural stages of society, iv. 221, ix. 1 ; children of, v. 68 ; sons of, v. 78 *sqq.* ; the physical fatherhood of, v. 80 *sq.* ; gardens of, v. 123, 159 ; the burning of a, v. 188 *sq.* ; the hanged, v. 288 *sqq.* ; killed in animal form, vii. 22 *sq.* ; the animal enemy of a, originally identical with the god, vii. 23, viii. 16 *sq.*, 31 ; eating the, viii. 48 *sqq.* ; reasons for eating the, viii. 138 *sq.*, 167 ; dying, as scapegoat, ix. 1, 227 ; the black and the white, ix. 92 ; the killing of the, in Mexico, ix. 275 *sqq.* ; resurrection of the, ix. 400 ; the dying and risen, in Western Asia, ix. 421 *sq. See also* Gods
——, Aryan, of the thunder and the oak, ii. 356 *sqq.*, x. 265

God, Bride of, i. 276
——, the Dying and Reviving, vii. 1, 33
—— on Earth, title of supreme chief of the Bushongo, xi. 264
—— of earthquakes, v. 194 *sqq.*
"God - boxes," inspired priests called, i. 378
—— -man a source of danger, iii. 132 ; bound by many rules, iii. 419 *sq.*
God's Mouth (*Kirwaido*), supreme lord of the old Prussians, iv. 41 *sq.*
Godavari District, in Southern India, the Kois of, v. 95
Goddess, identified with priestess, v. 219 ; superiority of the, in the myths of Adonis, Attis, Osiris, vi. 201 *sq.*
Goddesses place infant sons of kings on fire to render them immortal, v. 180 ; of fertility served by eunuch priests, v. 269 *sq.* ; their superiority over gods in societies organized on mother-kin, vi. 202 *sqq.* ; the development of, favoured by mother-kin, vi. 259 ; personated by women, ix. 238
——, Cilician, v. 161 *sqq.*
Godiva, Lady, legend of, i. 284 *n.*
Godolphin, in Cornwall, Midsummer fires on, x. 199
Gods viewed as magicians, i. 240 *sqq.*, 375 ; ill-treated in times of drought or excessive rain, i. 296 *sqq.* ; appeal to the pity of the, as a rain-charm, i. 302 *sq.* ; sacrifice themselves by fire, i. 315 *n.*¹ ; conception of, slowly evolved, i. 373 *sq.* ; in Brahman theology held to have been at first mortal and to have dwelt on earth, i. 373 *n.*¹ ; gods and men, no sharp line of distinction between, in Fiji, i. 389 ; the marriage of the, ii. 129 *sqq.* ; married to women, ii. 129 *sqq.*, 143 *sq.*, 146 *sq.*, 149 *sqq.*, vi. 207 ; created by men in their own likeness, iii. 387, iv. 2 *sq.*, 194 ; their names tabooed, iii. 387 *sqq.* ; Xenophanes on the, iii. 387 ; morality of the, iv. 1 *sqq.* ; succeeded by their sons, iv. 5 ; exiled for perjury, iv. 70 *n.*¹ ; progressive amelioration in the character of the, iv. 136 ; death and resurrection of, v. 6, vii. 1, 12 *sqq.* ; personated by priests, v. 45, 46 *sqq.*, ix. 287 ; married to sisters, v. 316 ; made by men and worshipped by women, vi. 211 ; named the eaters of certain animals, vii. 23 ; distinguished from spirits, vii. 169 ; in the likeness of foreigners, vii. 236 ; shut up in wood, ix. 61 ; represented in masquerades, ix. 377. *See also* God *and* Myths
—— and giants, the battle of, v. 157
—— and goddesses, dramatic weddings

of, ii. 121 ; represented by living men and women, ix. 385 *sq.*

Gods and men not sharply distinguished by primitive peoples, i. 373, 374 *sq.* ; esteemed akin by the ancients, ii. 177

——, incarnate human, i. 373 *sqq.*, ii. 377 *sq.* ; bound by many rules, iii. 419 *sq.*

—— of the Maoris, ix. 81

——, Mexican, burn themselves to create the sun, ix. 410

——, Mother of the, in Mexico, ix. 289 ; woman annually sacrificed in the character of the, ix. 289 *sq.*

—— of the Pelew Islanders, ix. 81 *sq.*

Goepfritz, in Lower Austria, dramatic contest between Summer and Winter at, iv. 257

Goik, name of puppet carried out at Mid-Lent, iv. 237

Goitre transferred to a peach-tree, ix. 54

Gold as a cure for jaundice, i. 80 *sq.* ; excluded from some temples, iii. 226 *n.*[8] ; the flower of chicory to be cut with, xi. 71 ; root of marsh mallow to be dug with, xi. 80 *n.*[3] ; buried, revealed by mistletoe and fern-seed, xi. 287 *sqq.*, 291

—— and silver as totems, iii. 227 *n.*

Gold Coast of West Africa, the Tshi-speaking peoples of the, i. 132, ii. 274 *sq.*, iv. 128, v. 69 ; negroes of the, their sacrifices to trees, ii. 47 ; iron laid aside in consulting fetishes on the, iii. 228 *sq.* ; the Awuna tribes of the, iii. 257 ; expulsion of demons on the, ix. 120, 131, 132 *sq.*

—— coin, magic plant to be dug up with a, xi. 57

—— mines, spirits of the, treated with deference, iii. 409 *sq.*

Golden Age, the, ix. 306, 353, 386 ; the reign of Saturn, ix. 306, 344

—— apples, prize in race, ii. 301 ; of the Hesperides, iv. 80

—— axe, sacred tamarisk touched with, xi. 80 *n.*[3]

—— bells worn by human representatives of gods in Mexico, ix. 278, 280, 284

—— Bough, xi. 279 *sqq.* ; plucked by Aeneas, i. 11, ii. 379 ; the breaking of it not a piece of bravado, i. 123 *sq.* ; grew on an evergreen oak, ii. 379 ; and the priest of Aricia, x. 1 ; a branch of mistletoe, xi. 284 *sqq.*, 315 *sqq.* ; Virgil's account of the, xi. 284 *sq.*, 286, 293 *sq.*, 315 *sqq.* ; origin of the name, xi. 286 *sqq.*

" —— Disease," name for jaundice, i. 80

—— fish, girl's external soul in a, xi. 147 *sq.*, 220

—— fleece, ram with, iv. 162

Golden Flower, the Feast of the, v. 185

—— Garden of the Peruvian Vestals, ii. 244

—— keys to unlock the frozen earth in spring, ii. 333

—— knife, horse slain in sacrifice with a, xi. 80 *n.*[3]

—— lamb of Mycenae, i. 365

—— ornaments not to be worn in certain rites, iii. 227 *n.*

—— ring worn as a charm, i. 137 ; half a hero's strength in a, xi. 143

—— Sea, the, v. 150

—— sickle, mistletoe cut by Druids with a, xi. 77, 88 ; sacred olive at Olympia cut with a, xi. 80 *n.*[3]

—— or silver nails driven into a sacred tree, ii. 36

" —— summer," the, i. 32

—— sword and golden arrow, external soul of a hero in a, xi. 145

—— swords, youths dancing with, iv. 75

Goldfinch, consumption transferred to a, ix. 52

Goldfish worshipped by Indians of Peru, viii. 250

Goldi, the, of the Lower Amoor, their exorcism by means of effigies, viii. 103 *sq.* ; bear-festivals of the, viii. 197

Goldi shaman, his exorcism, viii. 103

Goldie, Rev. Hugh, on the fetish king of Calabar, iii. 22 *sq.* ; on the periodic expulsion of ghosts at Calabar, ix. 204 *n.*[1] ; on the *ukpong* or external soul in Calabar, xi. 206

Goldmann, Dr. Emil, on the installation of a prince of Carinthia, iv. 155 *n.*[1]

Goldsmith, transmigration of thief into, viii. 299

Goldziher, I., on a festival of the Bedouins of Sinai, iv. 97 *n.*[7]

Golgi in Cyprus, conical stones at, v. 35

Goliath, a straw-man stabbed at Whit-suntide, ii. 90 ; effigy of, carried in procession, xi. 36

—— and David, v. 19 *n.*[2]

Gollas, the, of Southern India, their treatment of a woman in childbed, iii. 149

Golos, on the Bahr-el-Ghazal, their way of detaining the sun, i. 318

Goluan, Midsummer, x. 199

Gomes, E. H., on sacrifices in time of epidemics, iv. 176 *n.*[1] ; on the head-feast of the Sea Dyaks, ix. 384 *n.*[1]

Gommern, near Magdeburg, reaper of last corn wrapt in corn-stalks at, vii. 221

Gonds of India, their belief in reincarnation, i. 104 *sq.* ; their custom at clearing away a jungle, ii. 39 ; mock human sacrifices among the, iv. 217 ; ceremony of bringing back souls of the dead among the, v. 95 *sq.* ; their human sacrifices at sowing and reaping, vii. 244 ; human scapegoats among the, ix. 217 *sq.*

Gongs beaten in a storm, i. 328 *sq.* ; at Dodona, ii. 358 ; beaten to expel demons, ix. 113, 117, 118, 147

Gontiyalamma, mud figure of, in a rain-making ceremony, i. 294

Good Friday, barren fruit-trees threatened on, ii. 22 ; Highland superstitions as to, iii. 229; effigies and sepulchres of Christ on, iv. 284, v. 254*sqq.*; of ancient Greece, vii. 33 ; expulsion of witches in Silesia on, ix. 157 ; absolution of man called Adam at Halberstadt on the day before, ix. 214 ; cattle beaten on, ix. 266 ; custom of beating each other with rods on, ix. 268 ; Judas driven out of church on, x. 146 ; the divining-rod cut on, xi. 68 *n.*[4] ; sick children passed through cleft trees on, xi. 172

—— Goddess (*Bona Dea*), at Rome, wine called milk in her ritual, iii. 249 *n.*[2] ; her relationship to Faunus, vi. 234

—— Spirit, the, vii. 206

Goodrich-Freer, A., on Beltane bannocks and fires in the Hebrides, x. 154 *n.*[3]

Googe, Barnabe, his translation of a Latin poem by Thomas Kirchmeyer, x. 124

Goomsur, Earth Goddess represented in peacock form in, vii. 248 *n.*[1]

Goorkhas, the, of Nepaul, their festival of Dassera, iii. 316

Goose, eaten by Egyptian kings, iii. 13, 291. *See also* Geese

" ——, to lose the," expression for overthrowing a load at harvest, vii. 277 *n.*[3]

Gooseberry-bushes, a protection against witches, ii. 55 ; wild, custom as to, xi. 48

Goowoong Awoo, volcano, children sacrificed to, v. 219

Gordian knot, iii. 316 *sq.*

Gordias and Midas, names of Phrygian kings, v. 286

Gordioi chose the fattest man king, ii. 297

Gordium, capital of the kings of Phrygia, iii. 316

Gordon, E. M., on iron as an amulet in Bilaspore, iii. 234 *sq.* ; on infant burial in Bilaspore, v. 94 *sq.* ; on the festival of the dead in Bilaspore, vi. 60 ; on cairns to which passers-by add stones in Bilaspore, ix. 27 *n.*[4]

Gore, Captain, on the behaviour of the Meriahs among the Khonds, iv. 139 *n.*[1]

Gorgon, Perseus and the, iii. 312

Gorillas, souls of dead in, viii. 289 ; lives of persons bound up with those of, xi. 202

Gorong archipelago, custom as to children's cast teeth in the, i. 179 ; rule as to gathering coco-nuts in the, iii. 201

Gorse burned on May Day to burn or drive away witches, ii. 54

Görz, belief as to witches at Midsummer about, xi. 75

Gospel to the Hebrews, the apocryphal, iv. 5 *n.*[3]

Goudie, Mr. Gilbert, on Up-helly-a' at Lerwick, ix. 169 *n.*[2]

Gour-deziou, "Supplementary Days," in Brittany, ix. 324

Gouri, an Indian goddess of fertility, v. 241 *sq.*

Gournia in Crete, prehistoric shrine at, v. 88 *n.*[1]

Gout, popular remedy for, in Java, iii. 106 ; transferred to trees, ix. 56 *sq.*

Government of old men in aboriginal Australia, i. 334 *sq.*

Govindji, an incarnation of Krishna, i. 284

Gowland, W., on cairns in Corea, ix. 11 *n.*[5]

Gowmditch-mara tribe of Victoria, difference of language between husbands and wives in the, iii. 348 *n.*[1]

Graal, History of the Holy, iv. 120, 134

Graetz, H., on death of a Christian child in the character of Haman, ix. 395 *n.*[1]

Grafting, superstitious ceremony at, ii. 100

Grain Coast of West Africa, the Bodio or fetish king of the, i. 353, iii. 23 ; initiation of girls on the, xi. 259

Grains of wheat, divination by, ix. 316 *n.*[1]

Grammont, in Belgium, festival of the "Crown of Roses" at, x. 195 ; the Yule log at, x. 249

Gran Chaco, the Lengua Indians of the, i. 313, 330, 359, iii. 37, 38, 357, iv. 11, 63, viii. 245, ix. 122, 262 ; the Indians of the, their belief in dreams, iii. 37 ; the Guaycurus of the, iii. 357, vii. 309 ; the Matacos Indians of the, iii. 37 *n.*

Granada (South America), youthful rulers secluded in, x. 19

Granary, ceremony at fetching rice from a, vii. 185

Grand Halleux, bonfires on first Sunday in Lent at, x. 107

Grandfather's corpse, custom of leaping over, iii. 424

Grandfathers, grandsons named after their deceased, iii. 370

Grandidier, A., on changes in the Malagasy language caused by taboo on names of the dead, iii. 380 *sq.*

Grandmother, title of an African priest, vi. 255 ; name given to last sheaf, vii. 136 ; or Mother of Ghosts at Rome, viii. 94, 96, 107

Grandmother Earth thought to cause earthquakes, v. 198

Grandmothers, grand-daughters named after their deceased, iii. 370

Grandparents, dead, worshipped, vi. 175

Granger, Professor F., on double-headed bust at Nemi, i. 42 *n.*[1]

Grannas-mias, torches, on the first Sunday in Lent, x. 111

Granno, invocation of, x. 111 *sq.*

Granno-mio, a torch, x. 111

Grannus, a Celtic deity, identified with Apollo, x. 111 *sq.*

Grant, the great laird of, not exempt from witchcraft, x. 342 *n.*[4]

Grape-cluster, Mother of the, iv. 8

Grapes as divine emblem, v. 165 ; the last, not to be stript, vii. 234 *sq.*

Grasausläuten, ringing bells to make grass grow, ii. 344

Grass, magical ceremonies to make grass grow, i. 87 *sq.*, x. 136 ; bell-ringing as a charm to make grass grow, ii. 343 *sq.*, ix. 247 ; knotted as a charm, iii. 305, 306, 310 ; thrown on heaps as ceremony, ix. 9, 10, 18, 20, 28 ; dances to cause the grass to grow, ix. 238

Grass King, the, at Whitsuntide, ii. 85 *sq.*

—— -ringers in the Tyrol and Switzerland, ix. 247

—— seed, magical ceremony for the multiplication of, i. 87 *sq.* ; continence at magical ceremony for growth of, ii. 105

Grasshoppers in homoeopathic magic, i. 173 *sq.*; charm against, viii. 281 ; sacrifice of, ix. 35

Gratz, puppet burned on St. John's Eve at, x. 173

Graubünden (the Grisons), Canton of Switzerland, capers of masked men to make corn grow in, ix. 239 ; "Sawing the Old Woman" in, iv. 242 *sq.*

Graudenz district of West Prussia, the harvest Bull in the, vii. 288

Grave, soul fetched from, iii. 54 ; annual festival at, iv. 97 ; human sacrifices at the, iv. 143, 143 *n.*[4]; dance at initiation in, xi. 237

—— of ancestor, milk poured on, ii. 223

—— of Apollo, i. 34 *sq.*, iv. 4

Grave of Dionysus, iv. 3, vii. 14

—— of Osiris, vi. 10 *sq.* ; human victims sacrificed at the, vi. 97

—— of Zeus, iv. 3

Grave-diggers, taboos observed by, iii. 141, 142; obliged to stand on one foot, iv. 156 *n.*[2]

—— -shrines of Shilluk kings, vi. 161 *sq.* ; of Barotse kings, vi. 194 *sq.*

Graveclothes, homoeopathic magic of, in China, i. 168 *sq.*; no knots in, iii. 310 ; no buttons in, iii. 313

Graves, human blood offered at, i. 90 *sq.*, i. 101, iv. 92 ; rain-charms at, i. 268, 286, 291, iii. 154 *sq.*; trees planted on, ii. 31 ; dances on, ii. 183 *n.*[2]; food offered on, iii. 53 ; puppets substituted for human victims sacrificed at, iv. 218; milk offered at, v. 87 ; childless women resort to, in order to ensure offspring, v. 96 ; illuminated on All Souls' Day, vi. 72 *sq.*, 74 ; the only places of sacrifice in the country of the Wahehe, vi. 190 ; false, to deceive demons, viii. 99 *sq.* ; offerings of first-fruits presented at, viii. 111, 113, 115 ; heaps of sticks or stones on, ix. 15 *sqq.*

—— of Heitsi-Eibib, iv. 3, x. 16

—— of Hermes, Aphrodite, and Ares, iv. 4

—— of Hyperborean maidens at Delos, i. 28, 33 *sqq.*

—— of kings, chiefs, and magicians kept secret, vi. 103 *sqq.*; human sacrifices at, vi. 168

—— of twins, water poured on, to procure rain, iii. 154 *sq.*

Gray, Archdeacon J. H., on reported human sacrifices in an aboriginal tribe of China, iv. 145

Grbalj, in Dalmatia, belief as to the souls of trees at, ii. 14

Greasing the weapon instead of the wound, i. 202 *sqq.*

Great Ardra in Guinea, the king of, not allowed to behold the sea, iii. 9

—— Bassam, in Guinea, annual sacrifice of oxen for the crops at, viii. 9 *sq.*; exorcism of evil spirit at, ix. 120

—— Bear observed by the Kamtchatkans, vii. 315

"—— burnings" for kings of Judah, v. 177 *sq.*

—— Eleusinian Games, vii. 71, 79

—— Feast, the, in Morocco, ix. 180, 182, 265

—— Goddesses, the grove of the, at Andania, ii. 122

—— Man, who created the world and comes down in the form of lightning, xi. 298

—— Marriage, annual festival of the

dead among the Oraons of Bengal, vi. 59

Great men, history not to be explained without the influence of, v. 311 *n.*² ; great religious systems founded by, vi. 159 *sq.* ; their influence on the popular imagination, vi. 199

—— Mother, popularity of her worship in the Roman empire, v. 298 *sq.* ; name given to the last sheaf, vii. 135 *sq.*

—— Mysteries of Eleusis, their date, vii. 51

—— Pan, death of the, iv. 6 *sq.*

" —— Purification," Japanese ceremony, ix. 213 *n.*¹

—— religious systems founded by individual great men, vi. 159 *sq.* ; religious ideals a product of the male imagination, vi. 211

—— Spirit, iv. 3 ; sacrifice of fingers to the, iii. 161 ; his gift of corn to men, vii. 177

—— Sun, title of Natchez chief, ii. 262, 263, viii. 77 *sqq.*

—— Vigil, an Aztec festival, vii. 176

—— year, the, a Greek cycle of eight or nine ordinary years, iv. 70

Grebo people of Sierra Leone, their pontiff, his magical functions and taboos, iii. 14 *sq.*

Greece, time of the corn-reaping in, i. 32, v. 232 *n.* ; priestly kings in, i. 44 *sqq.* ; homoeopathic cures for jaundice in, i. 80 ; rain-making in, i. 273 ; forests of, ii. 8 ; artificial fertilization of fig-trees in, ii. 314 *sq.* ; oaks in, ii. 355 ; acorns eaten in, ii. 355, 356 ; conception of the soul in, iii. 29 *n.*¹ ; customs as to foundations of new buildings in, iii. 89 ; customs as to manslayers, in, iii. 188 ; mode of reckoning intervals of time in, iv. 59 *n.*¹ ; sacred marriage of Zeus and Hera in, iv. 91 ; swinging as a festal rite in, iv. 283 *sq.* ; use of music in religion in, v. 54 *sq.* ; belief in serpents as reincarnations of the dead in, v. 86 *sq.* ; notion as to birth from trees and rocks in, v. 107 *n.*¹ ; purification for homicide in, v. 299 *n.*² ; notion of the noxious influence of moonshine on children in, vi. 148 ; marriage customs in, vi. 245 *sq.* ; summer rainless in, vii. 69 ; time of barley harvest in, vii. 77 ; use of swallows as scapegoats in, ix. 35 ; use of laurel in purification in, ix. 262 ; stories of girls who were forbidden to see the sun in, x. 72 *sqq.* ; belief as to menstruous women in, x. 98 *n.*¹ ; Midsummer fires in, x. 211 *sq.* ; stories of the external soul in, xi. 103 *sqq.* ; mistletoe in, xi. 316, 317

Greece, ancient, ceremon performed by persons supposed to have been dead in, i. 75 ; ceremony to prevent dropsy in, i. 78 ; contagious magic of footprints in, i. 211 ; curses at cutting hellebore in, i. 281 ; human gods in, i. 390 *sq.* ; tree-worship in, ii. 10 ; rule as to blowing on a fire in, ii. 240 ; female descent of kingship in, ii. 278 *sq.* ; maxim not to look at one's reflection in water in, iii. 94 ; names of the priests of the Eleusinian mysteries not to be mentioned in, iii. 382 ; the eight years' cycle in, iv. 68 *sqq.* ; custom of banishing homicides in, iv. 69 *sq.* ; human sacrifices in, iv. 161 *sqq.* ; time of the vintage in, vii. 47 *n.*² ; mode of ridding the fields of mice in, viii. 276 *sqq.* ; theory of the transmigration of souls in, viii. 300 ; custom of stone-throwing in, ix. 24 *sq.* ; belief in demons in, ix. 104 ; human scapegoats in, ix. 252 *sqq.* ; Saturnalia in, ix. 350 *sqq.*

—— Homeric, sancity of kings and chiefs in, i. 366

Greek armies before battle, custom observed by, iii. 111

—— art, the human soul represented sometimes as a mannikin and sometimes as a butterfly in, iii. 29 *n.*¹

—— belief as to impotence, i. 150 ; as to gods in the likeness of strangers, vii. 236

—— bride and bridegroom bathed before marriage, ii. 162

—— calendar, the early, iv. 68 ; in the Louvre, vii. 46 *n.*² ; based on the moon, of little use to the husbandman, vii. 53 ; regulated by the moon, vii. 80

—— charm to silence watchdogs, i. 149

—— charms to ensure wakefulness, clear sight, and black hair, i. 154

—— Church, ceremonies on Good Friday in the, v. 254 ; ritual of the new fire at Easter in the, x. 128 *sq.*

—— conception of Earth as the great Mother, ii. 128 *n.*⁴

—— custom of offering hair to rivers, i. 31 ; of ploughing the land thrice a year, vii. 53 *n.*⁴, 72 *sq.*

—— divinities who died and rose again, vii. 2

—— farmers, their seasons for ploughing and sowing, vii. 45, 50 ; their seasons for sowing and reaping determined by observation of the Pleiades, vii. 318

—— Feast of All Souls in May, vi. 78 *n.*¹

—— games, the great, iv. 92 *sq.*, 103 *sqq.* ; held every four years, vii. 79 *sq.*

—— gods, discrimination of their characters, v. 119 ; who took titles from vermin, viii. 282

Greek husbandmen, their maxim as to planting and gathering olives, ii. 107

—— infants, octopuses and cuttle-fish presented to, i. 156

—— kings, called Zeus, ii. 177, 361 ; ancient, their reign of eight years, iv. 58 *sq.*, 70 *sqq.*

—— lands, artificial fertilization of fig-trees in, ix. 272

—— maxim not to wear rings, iii. 314

—— mode of relighting a sacred fire by means of burning-glass, ii. 244 *n.*[1]

—— months lunar, vii. 52, 53, 80

—— mysteries, bull-roarers swung at, vii. 110

—— mythology, Adonis in, v. 10 *sqq.*

—— peasants used to carry fire in stalks of fennel, ii. 260

—— ploughman, his prayer to Zeus and Demeter, vii. 45, 50

—— practice of sacrificing to the dead on their birthdays, i. 105

—— purificatory rites, pigs sacrificed in, vii. 74

—— religion, rule of ancient, to exclude from temples all who had touched a corpse or a lying-in woman, iii. 155

—— ritual of purification, one shoe on and one shoe off in, iii. 312 ; of expiatory sacrifices, viii. 27

—— sacrifices, victims required to shake their heads in, i. 384, 384 *n.*[7]

—— sanctuaries, iron not to be brought into, iii. 226

—— sower of cummin, his use of curses, i. 281

—— story of Iphiclus and Melampus, i. 158 ; stories of the external soul, xi. 103 *sqq.*

—— superstitions as to certain woollen garments and certain stones, i. 157

—— use of winnowing-fans as cradles, vii. 6

—— women, their mourning for Persephone, ix. 349

——· writers on the worship of Adonis, v. 223 *sq.*

Greeks sacrifice pregnant victims to ensure fertility, i. 141 ; their belief in the homoeopathic magic of precious stones, i. 164 *sq.* ; rain-making ceremonies among, i. 272 *sq.* ; used branches of buckthorn to protect houses against sorcerers and spirits, ii. 191 ; their dread of noon, iii. 88 ; their use of magical wax figures, ix. 47

——, the ancient, their ceremonies for procuring rain, i. 309 *sq.* ; their belief that the sun rode in a chariot, i. 315 ; sacrificed to the winds, i. 330 *n.* ; their

notion as to the wasting effect of incest, ii. 115 ; ran round the hearth with new-born babes, ii. 232 ; fire-sticks, employed by the, ii. 251 ; prayed to Zeus for rain, ii. 359 ; dedicated locks of hair to rivers, iii. 261, 261 *n.*[5] ; vicarious sacrifices among, iv. ·166 *n.*[1] ; their modes of disposing of things used in purificatory rites, vii. 9 ; compared the begetting of children to the sowing of seed, vii. 11 ; their faith in Demeter as the corn-goddess, vii. 64 ; their cycle of eight years, vii. 80 *sqq.* ; their personification of the corn in double form as mother and daughter, vii. 209 *sqq.* ; their "swallow song" and "crow song," viii. 322 *n.* ; their cure for love, ix. 3 ; smeared pitch on their houses to keep off demons, ix. 153 *n.*[1] ; their use of laurel in purification, ix. 262 ; deemed sacred the places which were struck by lightning, xi. 299

Greeks of Asia Minor, their use of human scapegoats, ix. 255

——, the Homeric, their belief as to the effect of a good king's reign, i. 366, ii. 324 *sq.* ; cut out tongues of sacrificial victims, viii. 270

—— and Romans, rain-charms among the ancient, i. 309 *sq.*

Green boughs a charm against witches, ii. 52-55, 127, 342 *sq.* ; custom of beating young people with, at Christmas, ix. 270

—— Corn Dance of the Seminole Indians, viii. 76

—— Demeter, vii. 42, 63, 89 *n.*[2] ; sacrifices in spring to, vii. 263

—— Festival at Eleusis, vii. 63

—— George on St. George's Day, a leaf-clad mummer in Carinthia, Transylvania, Roumania, and Russia, ii. 75, 76, 79, 343

—— Thursday, the day before Good Friday, ii. 333

—— Wolf, Brotherhood of the, at Jumièges in Normandy, x. 185 *sq.*, xi. 15 *n.*, 25, 88

Greenidge, A. H. J., on the nomination of Roman kings, ii. 296 *n.*[3]

Greenland, woman in childbed thought to control the wind in, i. 324

Greenlanders, their belief in the mortality of the gods, iv. 3 ; careful not to offend the souls of dead seals, viii. 246 *sq.* ; their notion that women can conceive by the moon, x. 75 *sq.*

Greenwich-hill, custom of rolling down, at Easter and Whitsuntide, ii. 103

Gregor, Rev. Walter, of Pitsligo, on the cutting of the *clyack* sheaf in Aberdeenshire, vii. 158 *sqq.* ; on virtue of children born feet foremost, x. 295 *n.*[3]; on the "quarter-ill," x. 296 *n.*[1] ; on the bewitching of cattle, x. 303 ; on the oak and mistletoe of the Hays, xi. 284 *n.*[1]

Grégory IV. and the Feast of All Saints, vi. 83

Gregory of Tours, on image of goddess carted about at Autun, ii. 144 ; on a talisman against dormice and serpents, viii. 281

Greig, James S., on a holed stone in the Aberdeenshire river Dee, xi. 187 *n.*[3]

Grenfell, B. P., and A. S. Hunt on corn-stuffed effigies of Osiris, vi. 90 *sq.*

Grenoble, King and Queen of May at, ii. 90 ; the harvest goat at, vii. 285

Greta, river in Yorkshire, need-fire on the, x. 287

Grevia spec., a sacred tree of the Herero, ii. 214, 219

Grey, Sir George, on the prohibition to name the dead among the natives of Western Australia, iii. 364 *sq.* ; on the digging for yams by women in Western Australia, vii. 126 *sq.* ; on the *kobong* or totem in Western Australia, xi. 219 *sq.*

Grey hair a signal of death, iv. 36 *sq.*

—— hairs of kings, iv. 100, 102, 103

Grihya - Sûtras on the pole - star at marriage, i. 166 *n.*[2] ; on the burial of a child's hair, iii. 277

Grimm, J., on the oldest sanctuaries of the Germans, ii. 8 *sq.*; on the bride-race, ii. 303 *n.*[3]; on a passage of Maximus Tyrius, ii. 362 *n.*[6] ; on the oak as the principal sacred tree of the ancient Germans, ii. 363 *sq.* ; on old spell to cure a lame horse, iii. 305 *n.*[1]; on the installation of a prince of Carinthia, iv. 155 *n.*[1] ; on the "carrying out of Death," iv. 221 *sq.* ; on the custom of "Sawing the Old Woman," iv. 240, 244 ; on hide-measured lands, vi. 250 ; on need-fire, x. 270 *n.*, 272 *sq.* ; on the relation of the Midsummer fires to Balder, xi. 87 *n.*[6] ; on the sanctity of the oak, xi. 89 ; on the oak and lightning, xi. 300

Grinnell, G. B., on human sacrifices among the Pawnees, vii. 239 *n.*[1]

Gripes transferred to a duck, ix. 50

Grisons, masquerades to benefit the crops in the, ix. 239 ; threatening a mist in the, x. 280. *See also* Graubünden

Grizzly Bear clan of the Carrier Indians, xi. 274

—— bears supposed to be related to human twins, i. 264 *sq.*

Groot, Professor J. J. M. de, on the divinity of the emperors of China, i. 416 *sq.* ; on reported custom of eating first-born children, iv. 180 *n.*[7] ; on substitutes for capital punishment in China, iv. 275 ; on the belief in demons in China, ix. 99 ; on the annual expulsion of devils in China, ix. 145 *sq.* ; on mugwort in China, xi. 60

Gros Ventres, Indian tribe, prepare for war by fasting and lacerating themselves, iii. 161

Gross-Strehlitz, in Silesia, the custom of "carrying out Death" at, iv. 237

Grossvargula, the Grass King at Whitsuntide at, ii. 85 *sq.*

Grottkau, precautions against witches in, xi. 20 *n.*

Grotto of the Sibyl, at Marsala, v. 247

Ground, custom of sleeping on the, ii. 248 ; sacred persons not allowed to set foot on the, iii. 3, 4, 6, x. 2 *sqq.* ; prohibition to sleep on the, iii. 110 ; warriors not to sit on the, iii. 159, 162, 163, x. 5, 12 ; executioner not to set foot on the, iii. 180 ; royal blood not to be shed on the, iii. 241 *sqq.* ; priestesses not to touch the, vii. 97 ; last sheaf not to touch the, vii. 158, 159, 161 ; the bones of salmon not to touch the, viii. 254 ; priest of Earth not to sit on the, x. 4 ; girls at puberty not to touch the, x. 22, 33, 35, 36, 60 ; magical plants not to touch the, xi. 51 ; mistletoe not to touch the, xi. 280

Grouse, the ruffed, in homoeopathic magic, i. 155 ; the first, blinded by hunter, viii. 268 ; clan of the Carrier Indians, xi. 273

Grout, L., on sacrifice of bull at Zulu festival of first-fruits, viii. 68 *n.*[3]

Grove, Miss Florence, on withered mistletoe, xi. 287 *n.*[1]

Grove, sacred, of Nemi, i. 2, 17, xi. 315 ; of Egeria, i. 18 ; the Arician, i. 20, 22, ii. 115, 378, iv. 213, ix. 3 ; sacred, protected by curses, i. 45 ; Balder's, x. 104, xi. 315 ; soul of chief in sacred, xi. 161. *See also* Arician

Groves, sacred, ii. 9, 10 *sq.*, 20, 32, 39, 42, 43 *sqq.*; in Chios, i. 45 ; to Diana, ii. 121 ; in ancient Greece and Rome, ii. 121 *sqq.* ; expiation for violating, ii. 122 ; in West Africa, ii. 322 *n.*[1] ; apologies for trespass on, ii. 328

Growth and decay of all things associated with the waxing and waning of the moon, vi. 132 *sqq.*, 140 *sqq.*

Grub in the Grisons, masquerade to benefit the crops at, ix. 239

Grubb, Rev. W. Barbrooke, on the fear

of demons among the Lengua Indians, ix. 78 *sq.* ; on the seclusion of girls at puberty among the Lengua Indians, x. 57 *n.*[1]

Grueber and d'Orville, Fathers, on the Dalai Lama of Lhasai, i. 412

Gruel of barley-meal and water, drunk as a form of communion with the Barley - goddess at the Eleusinian mysteries, vii. 161 *n.*[4]

Grün, in Bohemia, mountain arnica gathered at Midsummer at, xi. 58 *n.*[1]

Grunau, Simon, early Prussian chronicler, his account of Romove and its sacred oak, ii. 366 *n.*[2]

Grünberg, in Silesia, the harvest Cat at, vii. 281 ; witches driven away on Walpurgis Night in the district of, ix. 163

Grunting like a wild boar or pig as a charm, ii. 22 *sq.*

Guacheta in Colombia, virgin impregnated by the sun at, x. 74

Guadalcanar, one of the Solomon Islands, sacrifice of first-fruits in, viii. 126 *sq.*

Guadeloupe, precaution as to spittle in, iii. 289

Guagnini, Alex., on the sacred oak of Romove, ii. 366 *n.*[2]

Guami Indians of Panama, concealment of personal names among the, iii. 325

Guanches of Teneriffe, their mode of procuring rain, i. 303

Guarani Indians of South America, their belief as to homoeopathic magic of millet, i. 145

Guaranis of Brazil, their seclusion of girls at puberty, x. 56

—— of Paraguay, revered the Pleiades, vii. 309

Guaraunos of the Orinoco, uncleanness of menstruous women among the, x. 85 *sq.*

Guarayo Indians, their magic to clear the sky, i. 314

—— Indians of Bolivia, their presentation of children to the moon, vi. 145 ; ate the powdered bones of their dead, viii. 157

Guardian angels, afterbirth and navel-string regarded as a man's, xi. 162 *n.*[2]

—— deities of cities, iii. 391

" —— gods " of the Hos, vii. 234, viii. 61

—— spirit of child thought to reside in its caul, i. 199 *sq.* ; as bear, boar, eagle, fox, ox, swan or wolf, i. 200 ; of family, vii. 121; among the Hos, viii. 60 ; afterbirth and seed regarded as, xi. 223 *n.*[2] ; acquired in a dream, xi. 256 *sq.*

—— spirits in the form of animals, i.

200, v. 83 ; of villages in Tonquin, i. 401 *sq.*; supposed to reside in people's heads, iii. 252 *sq.* ; in serpents, v. 83, 86 ; dead ancestors worshipped as, viii. 121, 123 ; among the American Indians, viii. 207 ; of wild animals exorcized by hunters, ix. 98 ; masked dances supposed to be derived from, ix. 375 *sqq.*

Guardian trees in Sweden, ii. 58

Guatemala, catching the soul of the dying in, iv. 199

—— the Indians of, confession of sins among the, iii. 216 ; their transference of fatigue to heaps of stones, ix. 10 ; their offerings at cairns, ix. 26 ; the *nagual* or external soul among the, xi. 212 *sq.*

——, the Kekchi Indians of, viii. 219, 241

Guatusos of Costa Rica, use of bull-roarers among the, xi. 230 *n.*

Guayana Indians of Brazil, voluntary deaths by being buried alive among the, iv. 12

Guayaquil, in Ecuador, the Indians of, their human sacrifices at sowing, vii. 236

Guaycurus, try to frighten the demon of the storm, i. 330

—— of Brazil, precaution as to chief's spittle among the, iii. 290; men dressed as women among the, vi. 254 *n.*[2]

—— of the Gran Chaco used to change their names after a death, iii. 357; their festival at the reappearance of the Pleiades, vii. 309, ix. 262

Guayquiries of the Orinoco, their beliefs as to menstruous women, x. 85

Guazacualco, in Mexico, bones of the dead preserved for the resurrection in, viii. 259

Gudangs, the, of Queensland, avoidance of parents-in-law among, iii. 346 ; changes of vocabulary among the, caused by fear of naming the dead, iii. 359

Gudea, king of Southern Babylonia, festival of the New Year known to, ix. 356

Guelelé, king of Dahomey, represented partly in lion, partly in human form, iv. 85

Guelphs, the oak of the, xi. 166

Guessing dreams at New Year festival of the Iroquois, ix. 127

Guevo Upas, the Valley of Poison, in Java, v. 203 *sq.*

Guezo, king of Dahomey, represented with the feathers of a cock, iv. 85

Guhrau, district of Silesia, custom of " Carrying out Death " in, iv. 237

Guiana, the Indians of, their precaution against heavy rain, i. 253 ; power of medicine-men among, i. 359 sq. ; their fire customs, ii. 259 ; their belief in dreams, iii. 36 sq. ; keep their names secret, iii. 324 sq. ; their offerings of food to the dead, iii. 372 n.⁵ ; do not sharply distinguish between animals and men, viii. 204 ; their custom after killing a tapir, viii. 236 ; their fear of demons, ix. 78

——, British, the Macusis of, iii. 159 n., x. 60 ; woman's share in agriculture among the Indians of, vii. 120 sq. ; the Arawaks of, viii. 154, ix. 302

——, French, difference of language between husbands and wives in the tribes of, iii. 348 ; the Roocooyen Indians of, ix. 181, 263 ; the Wayanas of, x. 63 ; ordeals undergone by young men among the Indians of, x. 63 sq.

Guinea, priestly kings in, iii. 5 ; negroes of, their belief in dreams, iii. 37 ; belief in the transmigration of human souls into animals in, viii. 287 ; transference of sickness to chickens in, ix. 31 ; annual expulsion of the devil in, ix. 131

——, French, the wild fig-tree regarded as a fetish-tree in, ii. 317 n.¹ ; dances at sowing in, ix. 235

——, North, disposal of cut hair and nails in, iii. 278

——, Southern, the negroes of, use drippings of dead men's brains to increase their wisdom, viii. 163

Guinea negroes, their transference of sickness to chickens, ix. 31

Guinea-fowl gives signal for planting, vii. 117

Guizing at Christmas in Lerwick, x. 268 sq.

Gujarat, rings as amulets in, iii. 315

Gujrat District, Punjaub, belief as to bodies of infants dug up by jackals or dogs in the, v. 94

Guleesh and the fairies at Hallowe'en, x. 277 sq.

Gull clan of the Otawa Indians, viii. 225 n.¹

Gunkel, H., on the circumcised and the uncircumcised, i. 101 n.²

Gunn, David, kindles need-fire, x. 291

Gunnar Helming disguises himself as the god Frey, ii. 144

Gunputty, elephant-headed god, human incarnation of, i. 405 sq.

Guns fired to expel demons, viii. 99, ix. 116 sq., 119, 120, 121, 125, 132, 133, 137, 147, 148, 149, 150, 203, 204, 221 n.¹ ; against witches, ix. 160, 161, 164, xi. 74

Gunther, king of the Burgundians, woos and wins Queen Brunhild, ii. 306

Gunthram, King, and his vagrant soul, iii. 39 n.¹

Gurdon, Major P. R. T., on the Khasis of Assam, vi. 202 ; on mother-kin among the Khasis, vi. 203 n.¹ ; on descent of the kingship among the Khasis, vi. 210 n.¹

Guré, a hobby-horse, at harvest festival of the Garos, viii. 337 sq.

Gurgaon, district of North-West India, fair at Bas Doda in, ii. 149

Guyana Indians of Brazil, their voluntary deaths, iv. 12 sq.

Guyenne, "the Wolf of the Field" at harvest in, vii. 275

Gwalior, Holi fires in, xi. 2

Gwanya, a worshipful dead chief, vi. 177

Gyges, king of Lydia, married the widow of his predecessor, ii. 281 ; his monument to his queen, ii. 282 ; dedicates double-headed axe to Zeus, v. 182

Gynaecocracy a dream, vi. 211

Gypsies, their way of stopping rain by means of a serpent, i. 295 sq. ; Green George among the, ii. 75 sq. ; their superstition about portraits, iii. 100 ; ceremony of "Sawing the Old Woman" among the, iv. 243 ; annual ceremony performed by the, ix. 207 sq.

Habes de Tornas, a tribe of Nigeria, revere a fetish doctor, iii. 124

Hack-thorn sacred, ii. 48

Hadad, chief male deity of the Syrians, v. 15, 16 n.¹ ; Syrian god of thunder and fertility, v. 163

Hadadrimmon, v. 164 n.¹ ; the mourning of or for, v. 15 n.⁴

Haddon, Dr. A. C., on rain-making in Mabuiag, i. 262 ; on magicians in the Torres Straits Islands, i. 420 n.² ; on worship of animal-shaped heroes, v. 139 n.¹ ; on bull-roarers, vii. 106 n.³

Hadeln, in Hanover, the Corn-mother at reaping last corn in, vii. 133

Hades, descent of Dionysus into, vii. 15

Hadji Mohammad shoots a were-wolf, x. 312 sq.

Hadramaut, mode of stopping rain in, i. 252

Hadrian builds at Nemi, i. 6 ; monument of, at Nemi, i. 6 n.¹ ; human sacrifice suppressed in reign of, v. 146 ; institutes games at Mantinea, vii. 80

Hag (wrach), name given to last corn cut in Wales, vii. 142 sqq.

Hagen, B., on the belief in demons among the Battas, ix. 87 sq.

Hagios Gheorgios, village in Thrace, mummery at Carnival at, vii. 26

Hahn, Dr. C. H., on the chief's hut among the Herero, ii. 213 *n.*[2]

Hahn, Theophilus, on the worship of the Pleiades among the Hottentots, vii. 317

Haida Indians of Queen Charlotte Islands, ceremony performed by pregnant women among the, i. 70 ; warlike pantomime of women while the men are at war, i. 133 ; their belief as to death at ebb-tide, i. 168 ; their charm to obtain a fair wind, i. 320 ; medicine-men among the, iii. 31 ; their recovery of lost souls, iii. 67 *n.* ; attempt to kill the souls of their enemies in war, iii. 72 *n.*[1] ; their story of the type of Beauty and the Beast, iv. 131 *n.*[1]; their religions of cannibalism and of dog-eating, vii. 20 *sq.* ; girls at puberty secluded among the, x. 44 *sq.*

—— medicine-men bottle up departing souls, iii. 31 ; their unshorn hair, iii. 259

—— shamans, their use of the tongues of otters and eagles, viii. 270

Hail, charm to protect corn from, vii. 300 ; ceremonies to avert, x. 144, 145; Midsummer fires a protection against, x. 176 ; bonfires thought to protect fields against, x. 344; mountain arnica a protection against, xi. 57 *sq.*

—— and thunderstorms caused by witches, x. 344

Hainan, island, the inhabitants of, call a year " a fire," x. 137

Hainaut, province of Belgium, fire customs in, x. 108 ; procession of giants in, xi. 36

Hair offered to gods and goddesses, heroes and heroines, i. 28 *sq.* ; offered to the dead, i. 31, 102 ; offered to rivers, i. 31, iii. 261 ; clippings of, used in magic, i. 57, 64, 65, 66, iii. 268 *sqq.*, 275, 277, 278 *sq.* ; charms to make hair grow, i. 83, 145, 153 *sq.*, 154 ; supposed to be the seat of strength, i. 102 ; of elephant hunter's wife not to be cut, i. 120 ; of warriors not to be cut, i. 127 ; of wife and children of absent warrior not to be cut, i. 127 ; loose as a charm, i. 136; homoeopathic charm to strengthen, i. 144 ; homoeopathic charm to turn white hair black, i. 154 ; human, used in rain-making, i. 251 *sq.* ; supernatural power of chief dependent on his, i. 344 ; of father of twins not to be cut for a time, ii. 102 ; long, a symbol of royalty, ii. 180 ; mode of cutting the Mikado's, iii. 3 ; cut with bronze knife, iii. 14 ; not to be combed, iii. 14, 159 *n.*, 181, 187, 203, 208,

264 ; pulled to give omens, iii. 55 ; of those who have handled the dead not cut, iii. 141 ; of man-slayers shaved, iii. 175, 177 ; of slain enemy, fetish made from, iii. 183 ; tabooed, iii. 258 *sqq.* ; of kings, priests, and wizards unshorn, iii. 258 *sqq.* ; regarded as the seat of a god or spirit, iii. 258, 259, 263 ; kept unshorn at certain times, iii. 260 *sqq.* ; unshorn during a vow, iii. 261 *sq.* ; of children unshorn, iii. 263 ; cut or combed out may cause rain and thunderstorms, iii. 271, 272, 282 ; clippings of, used as hostages, iii. 272 *sq.* ; infected by virus of taboo, iii. 283 *sq.* ; cut as a purificatory ceremony, iii. 283 *sqq.* ; of women after childbirth shaved and burnt, iii. 284 ; loosened at childbirth, iii. 297 *sq.* ; loosened in magical and religious ceremonies, iii. 310 *sq.* ; sacrifice of women's, v. 38 ; offered to goddess of volcano, v. 218 ; of head shaved in mourning for dead gods, v. 225 ; to be cut when the moon is waxing, vi. 133 *sq.* ; pulling each other's, a Lithuanian sacrificial custom, viii. 50 *sq.* ; of slain foes used to impart courage, viii. 153 ; of patient inserted in oak, ix. 57 *sq.* ; lock of, in cure for epilepsy, ix. 68 *n.*[2]; unguent for, x. 14 ; girl at puberty not to cut her, x. 28 ; of girls at puberty shaved, x. 31, 56, 57, 59 ; Hindoo ritual of cutting a child's, x. 99 *n.*[2] ; external soul in, xi. 103 *sq.*, 148 ; strength of people bound up with their, xi. 158 *sq.* ; of criminals, witches, and wizards shorn to make them confess, xi. 158 *sq.* ; of children tied to trees, xi. 165 ; of novices cut at initiation, xi. 245, 251

Hair, grey, a signal of death, iv. 36 *sq.*

—— and nails of sacred persons not cut, iii. 3, 4, 16

—— and nails, cut, of a chief guarded against evil magic, i. 350 *n.*[1]; deposited on or under trees, iii. 14, 275 *sq.*, 286 ; disposal of, iii. 267 *sqq.* ; as rain-charms, iii. 271, 272 ; deposited in sacred places, iii. 274 *sqq.* ; stowed away in any secret place, iii. 276 *sqq.*; kept for use at the resurrection, iii. 279 *sqq.* ; burnt to prevent them from falling into the hands of sorcerers, iii. 281 *sqq.* ; of child buried under a tree, xi. 161

—— of the Virgin or St. John looked for in ashes of Midsummer fire, x. 182 *sq.*, 190, 191

Hair-cutting, ceremonies at, iii. 264 *sqq.* ; thought to cause thunder and lightning, iii. 265

Hair-pins as instruments of longevity, i. 169

Hairy Stone, the, at Midsummer, x. 212

Hak-Ka, the, a native race in the province of Canton, their annual expulsion of the devil of poverty, ix. 144

Hakea flowers, ceremony for the multiplication of, i. 86

Hakim Singh claims to be Jesus Christ incarnate, i. 409 sq.

Halae in Attica, mock human sacrifice at, iv. 215 sq.

Halasarna in Cos, rites of Apollo and Hercules at, vi. 259

Halberstadt in Thüringen, need-fire in, ii. 238 sq., x. 273 ; annual ceremony on day before Good Friday at, ix. 214

Hale, Horatio, on voluntary deaths in Fiji, iv. 11 sq.

Half-sister by the same father, marriage with, legal in Attica, ii. 284

Halfdan the Black, king of Norway, dismembered after death, vi. 100, 102

Halford in Warwickshire, May Day customs at, ii. 88 sq.

Hali-Bonar, village in Sumatra, iii. 104

Halibut, the first of the season, treatment of, viii. 253

Halicarnassus, the Mausoleum at, iv. 94 sq. ; worship of Pergaean Artemis at, v. 35 n.[2]

Haliphloios, a species of oak, ii. 373 n.[1]

Hall, C. F., on the treatment of venison among the Esquimaux, x. 13 ; on new fire at New Year among the Esquimaux, x. 134

Hall, Dr. C. H. H., on the expulsion of the demon of plague in Japan, ix. 119 n.[1]

Hall, Rev. G. R., on Midsummer fires at Christenburg Crags, iv. 198

Hall, in the Tyrol, ceremony of whipping people on Senseless Thursday at, ix. 248 sq.

Hall of the Two Truths, the judgment hall in the other world, vi. 13

Hallowe'en, new fire at, in Ireland, x. 139, 225 ; an old Celtic festival of New Year, x. 224 sqq. ; divination at, x. 225, 228 sq., 231, 234 sqq. ; witches, hobgoblins, and fairies let loose at, x. 226 sqq., 245, xi. 184 n.[4], 185

—— and Beltane, the two chief fire festivals of the British Celts, xi. 40 sq.

Hallowe'en cakes, x. 238, 241, 245

—— fires, x. 222 sq. ; in Wales, x. 156, 239 ; in the Highlands of Scotland, x. 230 sqq.; in the Isle of Man, x. 243 ; in Lancashire, x. 244 sq.; in France, x. 245 sq.

Hallowmas in Scotland, last corn cut before or after, vii. 140

Halmahera, or Gilolo, rain-making in, i. 248 ; rain-charm by means of the dead in, i. 285 sq. ; ceremony at felling a tree in, ii. 38 ; the natives of, their words for soul, vii. 183 ; ceremonies at a funeral in, ix. 260 sq. ; rites of initiation in, xi. 248

——, the Alfoors of, a man may not address his father-in-law by name among, iii. 341 ; their expulsion of demons, ix. 112

—— the Galelareese of, i. 110, v. 220, vii. 296 ; their belief as to incest, ii. 111. See Galelareese

Haloa, Attic festival, vii. 60 sqq.

Haltwhistle, in Northumberland, burnt sacrifice at, x. 301

Haman, a god worshipped by the heathen of Harran, ix. 366 n.[1]

Haman, the Biblical, derivation of the name, ix. 366 ; effigies of, burnt at Purim, ix. 392 sqq.

—— and Mordecai, ix. 364 sqq. ; as temporary kings, ix. 400 sq.

—— and Vashti the duplicates of Mordecai and Esther, ix. 406

Hâmân-Sûr, a name for Purim, ix. 393

Hamaspathmaedaya, old Iranian festival of the dead, vi. 67

Hamatsas, cannibals among the Kwakiutl, vii. 20

Hametzes, Cannibals or Biters, a Secret Society among the Indians of North-Western America, ix. 378

Hamilcar, his self-sacrifice by fire at the battle of Himera, v. 115 sq., 176 ; worshipped by the Carthaginians after death, v. 116, 180

Hamilton, Alexander, his account of the Samorins or kings of Calicut, iv. 47 sq.; on hook-swinging in India, iv. 278 ; on dance of hermaphrodites in Pegu, v. 271 n.

Hamilton, Gavin, on the seclusion of girls at puberty among the Tinneh Indians, x. 47 sq.

Hamilton, Professor G. L., v. 57 n.[1]

Hamlet, his story half-historical, ii. 281 n.[2]; his feigned imbecility, ii. 291

Hammedatha, father of Haman, ix. 373 n.[1]

Hammer, used to make mock thunder, i. 248 ; iron, revered by the Lithuanians, i. 317 sq. ; sick people struck with a, ix. 259 n.[4]

Hammers, Thor's, i. 248 n.[1]

Hammocks, girls at puberty hung up in, x. 56, 59, 60, 61, 66

Hammurabi, king of Babylon, iv. 110 ; code of, ii. 130, v. 71 n.[3], 72 n.[1]

Hampstead in reign of Henry II., ii. 7

Hamstring of deer, custom of removing, viii. 266

Hamstringing dead animals, viii. 267, 271, 273
—— deer, rule as to, i. 115
—— men to disable their ghosts, viii. 272, 273
Hand of Glory, the, a thief's talisman, i. 149
" —— of Glory," mandragora, xi. 316
—— of suicide cut off, iv. 220 $n.$; of dead man in magical ceremony, iv. 267 $n.$[1] See also Hands
Hand-marks, white, viii. 338
Handel, the harmonies of, v. 54
Hands tabooed, iii. 133 $sq.$, 138, 140 $sqq.$, 146 $sqq.$, 158, 159 $n.$, 174, 265 ; food not to be touched with, iii. 138 $sqq.$, 146 $sqq.$, 166, 167, 168, 169, 174, 265 ; defiled, iii. 174 ; not to be clasped, iii. 298 ; of enemies eaten, viii. 151, 152 ; of deity, ceremony of grasping the, ix. 356. See also Hand
Hanged god, the, v. 288 $sqq.$
Hanging as a mode of capital punishment, iv. 114 $n.$[1] ; of an effigy of the Carnival, iv. 230 $sq.$; as a mode of sacrifice, v. 289 $sqq.$
Hannah's vow, iii. 263, v. 79
Hannibal, his prayers to Melcarth, v. 113 ; his retirement from Italy, v. 265 ; despoils the shrine on Soracte, xi. 15 ; within sight of Rome, xi. 15
Hanover, Hildesheim in, ii. 85 ; harvest customs in, vii. 133, 283 ; the Harvest-mother in, vii. 135 ; Easter bonfires in, x. 140 ; the need-fire in, x. 275 ; custom on St. John's Day about, xi. 56
Hantoes, spirits, in Borneo, ix. 87
Hanun, king of Moab, his treatment of David's messengers, iii. 273
Hanway, J., on worship of perpetual fires at Baku, v. 192
Happah tribe in Marquesas Islands, evil magic practised on hair by the, iii. 268
Hardanger, Norway, Whitsuntide Bride and Bridegroom at, ii. 92
Hardisty, W. L., on the power of medicine-men among the Loucheux Indians, i. 356 $sq.$
Hardy, Thomas, on the disastrous effect of looking at trees on an empty stomach, i. 136
Hare, name of, tabooed in the morning, iii. 402 $sq.$; as scapegoat, ix. 50 $sq.$; pastern bone of a, in a popular remedy, x. 17. See also Hares
——, corn-spirit as, vii. 279 $sq.$
Hare clan of the Moquis, viii. 178 ; of the Otawas, viii. 225 $n.$[1]
—— Indians will not taste blood, iii. 241 ; do not pare nails of female children, iii. 263

Hare-lips, superstition as to persons with, i. 266
—— -skin Indians, viii. 265. See Loucheux
" Hare's blood " at harvest, vii. 280
—— tail, name given to last standing corn, vii. 268
Hares thought to bewitch people, i. 212 ; witches in the form of, ii. 53, x. 157 ; killed on May Day as embodiments of witches, ii. 53, 54 ; not eaten lest they make the eaters timid, viii. 141 ; witches changed into, x. 315 $n.$[1], 316 $sqq.$, xi. 41, 197
Hareskin Tinneh, seclusion of girls at puberty among the, x. 48
Harlot's Tomb, the, in Lydia, ii. 282
Harlots, sacred, ix. 370, 371, 372 ; at Comana, ix. 370 $n.$[4], 421 $n.$[1]
Harma on Mount Parnes, lightning seen over, i. 33
Harmattan wind, in West Africa, iii. 5
Harmonia, the necklace of, v. 32 $n.$[2] ; turned into a snake, v. 86 $sq.$
—— and Cadmus, iv. 84 ; marriage of, iv. 88, 89
Haroekoe, East Indian island, fishermen's magic in, i. 109 ; hunter's magic in, i. 114 ; treatment of the afterbirth in, i. 187
Harold the Fair-haired, king of Norway, ii. 279, vi. 100 $n.$[2]
Harp, the music of the, in religion, v. 52 $sqq.$
Harpalyce, her incest with her father, v. 44 $n.$[1]
Harpocrates, the younger Horus, vi. 8, 9 $n.$; Osiris represented in the form of, vii. 260
Harpocration, on the human scapegoats at the Thargelia, ix. 254 $n.$[1]
Harpooning a spirit, ix. 126
Harran, mourning of women for Tammuz in, v. 230 ; legend of Tammuz in, vii. 258.
—— the heathen of, drank blood to enter into communion with demons, i. 383 ; their marriage festival of the gods in the Date Month, ii. 25 ; their custom at grafting, ii. 100 $n.$[2] ; human sacrifices offered by, vii. 261 $sq.$; sacrifices offered by, viii. 23 $n.$[3] ; their custom in December, ix. 263 $sq.$; their marriage festival of all the gods, ix. 273 $n.$[1] ; worship a god Haman, ix. 366 $n.$[1]
Harris, island of, witches of the, i. 135 ; Slope of Big Stones in, x. 227
Harris, J. Rendel, on borrowed Greek and Roman festivals in Syrian calendars, i. 15 $n.$; on the pedigree of St. Hippolytus, 21 $n.$[2]

Harrison, Miss J. E., on the Sacred Marriage of Dionysus, ii. 137 *n.*[1] ; on the Eleusinian mysteries, ii. 139 *n.*[1] ; on the hyacinth (*Delphinium Ajacis*), v. 314 *n.*[1] ; on the winnowing-fan in the myth and ritual of Dionysus, vii. 5 *n.*[4] ; on the offering of first-fruits at Eleusis, vii. 60 *n.*[1] ; on the date of the Festival of the Threshing-floor, vii. 62 *n.*[6] ; on buckthorn, ix. 153 *n.*[1]

Harrow used in rain-charm, i. 282, 284

Harte, Bret, on the old Spanish missions in California, viii. 171 *n.*[1]

Harthoorn, S. E., on belief in demons in Java, ix. 86 *sq.*

Hartland, E. S., as to Mimetic Magic, i. 52 *n.*[1] ; on the Godiva legend, i. 283 *n.*[3] ; on legends of the Perseus type, ii. 156 *n.* ; on the reincarnation of the dead, v. 91 *n.*[3] ; on primitive paternity, v. 106 *n.*[1] ; on the Hag at harvest in Wales, vii. 143 *n.*[1] ; on " burning the Old Witch " in Yorkshire, vii. 224 *n.*[4] ; on throwing sticks and stones on cairns, ix. 22 *n.*[2] ; on sin-eating, ix. 46 *n.*[2] ; on custom of knocking in nails as a magical rite, ix. 69 *n.*[1] ; on the life-token, xi. 119 *n.*

Hartlieb, in Silesia, dramatic contest between Summer and Winter at, iv. 256 *n.*[1]

Haruvarus, degenerate Brahmans, their fire-walk, xi. 9

Harvest, rain-charms at, ii. 47 ; custom of throwing water on the last corn cut as a rain-charm at, v. 237 *sq.* ; rites of, vi. 45 *sqq.* ; custom of the Arabs of Moab at, vi. 48, 96 ; annual festival of the dead after, vi. 61, viii. 110 ; new corn offered to dead kings or chiefs at, vi. 162, 166, 188 ; prayers to the spirits of ancestors at, vi. 175 *sq.* ; sacrifices to dead chiefs at, vi. 191 ; riddles propounded at, ix. 122 *n.* ; annual expulsion of demons at or after, ix. 134 *sq.*, 137 *sq.*, 225
—— in Egypt, date of, v. 231 *n.*[3], vi. 32
—— in Greece, the date of, i. 32, v. 232 *n.*, vii. 48
—— in Palestine, date of, v. 232 *n.*

Harvest ceremonies among the Shilluk, iv. 20, 25
—— -child, last sheaf called the, vii. 151
—— -cock, last sheaf called the, vii. 276 ; harvest-supper called the, vii. 277
—— -crown, vii. 221, 277 ; of wheat-ears and flowers, vii. 163
—— -customs, the Corn-mother in, vii. 133 *sqq.* ; and spring customs compared, vii. 167 *sqq.*
—— -goat, vii. 282, 283
—— Gosling, name for the harvest-supper, vii. 277 *n.*[3]

Harvest-man, a woman tied up in the last sheaf, vii. 221
—— May, the, ii. 47 *sq.*
—— -mother, last sheaf called the, vii. 135
—— -Queen, vii. 146 *sq.*, 152
—— -supper, vii. 134, 138, 156, 157, 159 *sq.*, 161 *sq.*, 289, 297, 299 ; sacramental character of, vii. 303, viii. 48
—— -woman, made of last sheaf, vii. 145
—— -wreath, vii. 283

Harvesters, athletic competitions among, vii. 76 *sq.* ; wrapt up in corn-stalks, vii. 220 *sqq.*

Harz Mountains, greasing the weapon instead of the wound in the, i. 204 ; fir-trees set up at Midsummer in the, ii. 65 *sq.* ; ceremony at Carnival in the, iv. 233 ; saying as to the dance of witches in the, ix. 163 *n.*[1] ; Easter fires in the, x. 140, 142 ; Midsummer fires in the, x. 169 ; need-fire in the, x. 276 ; springwort in the, xi. 69 *sqq.*

Haselberg in Bohemia, farmer swathed in the last corn to be threshed at, vii. 225 *sq.* ; the Oats-goat at threshing at, vii. 286

Hasselt, J. L. van, on the belief in demons among the Papuans, ix. 83

Hastings, Warren, his embassy to Tibet, ix. 203

Hatfield Moss, in Yorkshire, huge trunks of oak found in, ii. 351

Hathor, Egyptian goddess, ii. 133, vi. 9 *n.*

Hats, special, worn by girls at puberty, x. 45, 46, 47, 92. *See also* Hoods

Hatshopsitou, birth of Queen, represented in Egyptian paintings, ii. 131 *sqq.*

Hattusil, king of the Hittites, his treaty with Rameses II., v. 135

Haua, a god in Easter Island, viii. 133

Haupt, Professor P., on the principal personages in the Book of Esther, ix. 406 *n.*[2]

Hausa kings put to death, iv. 35
—— story of the external soul, xi. 148 *sq.*

Haussas, taboos on the names of relations among the, iii. 337

Havamal, how Odin learned the magic runes in the, v. 290

Hawaii, feather robes of royal family of, i. 388 *n.*[3] ; king of, not to be seen by day, iii. 24 ; capture of souls by sorcerers in, iii. 72 *sq.* ; exorcism of demons in, iii. 106 ; tabooed priest in, iii. 138 *n.*[1] ; customs as to chiefs and shadows in, iii. 255 ; annual festival in, iv. 117 *sq.* ; the volcano of Kirauea in, v. 216 *sqq.*

Hawaiian taboo, iii. 262
Hawaiians, the New Year of the, xi. 244
Hawes, Mrs., on date of the corn-reaping in Crete, v. 232 *n.*
Hawk, belief as to the shadow of a brown, iii. 82 ; symbol of the sun and of the king in Egypt, iv. 112 ; Isis in the form of a, vi. 8 ; the sacred bird of the earliest Egyptian dynasties, vi. 21 *sq.* ; epithet regularly applied to the king of Egypt, vi. 22 ; omens from, ix. 384 *n.*[1] *See also* Hawks
Hawk-town (Hieraconpolis) in Egypt, vi. 21 *sq.*
Hawk's head and wings, man represented wearing a, vii. 260
Hawkie, the harvest home, vii. 146, 147 *n.*[1]
Hawks worshipped in Egypt, i. 29 ; carved on the bier of Osiris, vi. 20 ; hearts of, eaten by diviners to acquire prophetic power, viii. 143 ; revered by the Ainos, viii. 200. *See also* Hawk
Hawkweed gathered at Midsummer, xi. 57
Hawthorn, Merlin under the, i. 306 ; in bloom on May Day, ii. 52 ; a protection against witches, ii. 55, 127 ; at doors on May Day, ii. 60 ; a charm against ghosts, ix. 153 *n.*[1] ; mistletoe on, xi. 315, 316
Haxthausen, A. von, on the Midsummer festival of the Cheremiss, x. 181
Hay, Sir John Drummond, on the Corn-woman among the Berbers, vii. 179
Hays of Errol, their fate bound up with an oak-tree and the mistletoe growing on it, xi. 283 *sq.*
Hazael, king of Syria, worshipped as a god by the people of Damascus, v. 15
Hazebrouck, in France, wicker giants on Shrove Tuesday at, xi. 35
Hazel, the divining-rod made of, xi. 67 *sq.* ; never struck by lightning, xi. 69 *n.*
Hazel leaves in rain ceremony, i. 295
—— rod used to beat an absent man vicariously, i. 207 ; used in rain-making, i. 301 ; to drive cattle with, x. 204
Head, sacrificial victim required to shake its, i. 384 ; strayed souls restored to, iii. 47, 48, 52, 53 *sq.*, 64, 67 ; prohibition to touch the, iii. 142, 183, 189, 252 *sq.* 254, 255 *sq.* ; plastered with mud, iii. 182 ; sacred in Polynesia, iii. 245 ; the human, regarded as sacred, iii. 252 *sqq.* ; tabooed, iii. 252 *sqq.* ; supposed to be the residence of spirits, iii. 252 ; objection to have any one overhead, iii. 253 *sqq.* ; washing the, iii. 253. *See also* Heads
—— of chief not to be touched, i. 344

Head of horse, in Roman sacrifice, viii. 42 ; used to protect garden from caterpillars, viii. 43 *n.*[1]; in effigy, at harvest festival, viii. 43 *n.*[1], 337
Head-dress, special, worn by girls at first menstruation, x. 92
" —— Feast" among the Dyaks of Borneo, v. 295 *sq.* ; of the Sea Dyaks, ix. 383, 384 *n.*[1]
—— -hunters, rules observed by people at home in absence of, i. 129 ; customs of, iii. 30, 36, 71 *sq.*, 111, 166 *sq.*, 169 *sq.*, 261
—— -hunting in Borneo, v. 294 *sqq.* ; in the Philippines, vii. 240 *sq.* ; among the Wild Wa of Burma, vii. 241 *sqq.* ; among the Nagas, vii. 243 *sq.* ; as a means of promoting the growth of the crops, vii. 256
Headache caused by fatigue of soul, iii. 40 ; caused by clipped hair, iii. 270 *sq.*, 282 ; cures for, ix. 2, 52, 58, 63, 64, x. 17 ; transferred to head-rings, ix. 2 ; transferred to animal, ix. 31 ; mugwort a protection against, xi. 59
Headington, in Oxfordshire, May garlands at, ii. 62 *n.*[2]; Lord and Lady of the May at, ii. 90 *sq.*
Headlam, Walter, on Dionysus as a god of beer, vii. 2 *n.*[1]
Headless Hugh, Highland story of, xi. 130 *sq.*
—— horsemen in India, xi. 131 *n.*[1]
Headman, sacred, ix. 177 *n.*[3]
Headmen of totem clans in Central Australia as public magicians, i. 335 ; headmen often magicians in South-East Australia, i. 335 *sq.*
Heads of lac gatherers not to be washed, i. 115 ; custom of moulding heads artificially, ii. 297 *sq.* ; of manslayers shaved, iii. 177 ; of dead kings removed and kept, iv. 202 *sq.* ; severed human, thought to promote the fertility of the ground and of women, v. 294 *sqq.* ; used as guardians by Taurians and tribes of Borneo, v. 294 *sqq.* ; of dead chiefs cut off and buried secretly, vi. 104 ; shaved after lightning has struck a kraal, viii. 161 ; or faces of menstruous women covered, x. 22, 24, 25, 29, 31, 44 *sq.*, 48 *sq.*, 55, 90. *See also* Head
Heaps of stones, sticks, or leaves, to which every passer-by adds, ix. 9 *sqq.* ; on the scene of crimes, ix. 13 *sqq.* ; "lying heaps," ix. 14 ; on graves, ix. 15 *sqq.*
Hearn, Lafcadio, on the exorcism of demons in Japan, ix. 144
Hearne, S., on taboos observed by manslayers among North American Indians,

iii. 184 *sqq.* ; on the seclusion of menstruous women among the Chippeway Indians, x. 90 *sq.*
Hearn, Dr. W. E., on mother-kin among the Aryans, ii. 283 *n.*[5]
Heart of Dionysus, the sacred, vii. 13, 14, 15 ; of human victim torn out, viii. 92 ; of jackal not eaten lest it make the eater timid, viii. 141 ; of hen not eaten lest it make the eater timid, viii. 142 ; of lion or leopard eaten to make the eater brave, viii. 142 *sq.* ; of water-ousel eaten in order to acquire wisdom and eloquence, viii. 144 ; of bear eaten to acquire courage, viii. 146 ; of serpent eaten to acquire language of animals, viii. 146 ; of wolf eaten to make eater brave, viii. 146 ; regarded as the seat of intellect, viii. 149 ; of bird of prey eaten to acquire courage, viii. 162 ; of salmon not to be eaten by a dog, viii. 255 *n.*[4] ; of bewitched animal burnt or boiled to compel the witch to appear, x. 321 *sq.* *See also* Hearts
—— of the Earth, a Mexican goddess, ix. 289
Hearth, bride at marriage conducted to the, ii. 221 ; custom of leading a bride round the, ii. 230, 231 ; new-born children brought to the, ii. 232
——, the common, at Delphi, i. 33 ; in Greek cities, i. 45
——, the king's, at Rome, ii. 195, 200, 206 ; oath by, ii. 265
——, the sacred, of the Herero, ii. 213, 214 ; seat of the ancestral spirits, ii. 216, 221
Hearts of men and animals offered to the sun, i. 315 ; of dead kings eaten by their successors, iv. 203 ; of men sacrificed, vii. 236 ; of crows, moles, or hawks eaten by diviners to acquire prophetic power, viii. 143 ; of men eaten to acquire their qualities, viii. 148 *sqq.* ; of human victims offered to the sun, ix. 279 *sq.*, 298 ; of human victims offered to the moon, ix. 282 ; of diseased cattle cut out and hung up as a remedy, x. 269 *n.*[1], 325. *See also* Heart
Heathen festivals displaced by Christian, v. 308
—— origin of Midsummer festival (festival of St. John), v. 249 *sq.* ; of Christmas, v. 302 *sqq.*
Heaven, vault of, imitated in rain-charm, i. 261, 262 ; threatened with conflagration as a rain-charm, i. 303 ; festivals of, i. 399 *sq.* ; slave treated as the representative of, i. 399 *sq.* ; temple and image of, i. 414 ; the Chinese

emperor a son of, i. 416 *sq.* ; eaten by heaven-herds among the Zulus, viii. 160 *sq.*
Heaven and earth, between, x. 1 *sqq.*, 98 *sq.*
——, the Queen of, xi. 303
" Heaven bird " in rain-making, i. 302
—— -herds among the Zulus, viii. 160
Heavenly Master, the head of Taoism, i. 413 *sqq.*
—— Virgin or Goddess, mother of the Sun, v. 303
Hebesio, god of thunder, on the Gold Coast, iii. 257
Hebrew kings, traces of their divinity, v. 20 *sqq.*
—— names ending in -*el* or -*iah*, v. 79 *n.*[3]
—— prohibition of images of animals, i. 87 *n.*[1]
—— prophecy, the distinctive character of, v. 75
—— prophets, their ethical religion, i. 223 ; their resemblance to those of Africa, v. 74 *sq.*
Hebrews, their notion of the blighting effect of sexual crime, ii. 114 *sq.* ; apocryphal Gospel to the, iv. 5 *n.*[3] ; sacrifice their children to Baal, iv. 168 *sqq.* ; their sacrifice of the first-born, iv. 171 *sqq.* ; forbidden to reap corners of fields and glean last grapes, vii. 234 *sq.* ; sacrificed and burned incense to nets, viii. 240 *n.*[1] ; the importance they ascribed to blessings and cursings, ix. 23 *n.* ; their use of birds as scapegoats for leprosy, ix. 35
Hebrides, wind-charms in the, i. 322 *sq.*; St. Bride's bed on St. Bride's Day in the, ii. 94 ; the Outer, the fire of a kiln called by a special name in the, iii. 395 ; peats cut in the wane of the moon in the, vi. 137 *sq.*
Hebron, practice of Moslem pilgrims at, ix. 21
Hecaerge, an epithet of Artemis, v. 292
Hecate at Ephesus, v. 291 ; sometimes identified with Artemis, v. 292 *n.*
—— and Zeus worshipped at Stratonicea, vi. 227
Hecatombaeon, an Athenian month, ix. 351
Hecatombeus, a Greek month, v. 314
Heckewelder, Rev. John, on attitude of North American Indians to the lower animals, viii. 205 *sq.*
Hecquard, H., on exorcism of evil spirit in Guinea, ix. 120
Hector, first chief of Lochbuy, xi. 131 *n.*[1]
Hedgehog not to be eaten by soldiers, i. 117 ; transmigration of sinner into, viii. 299

Hegel on magic and religion, i. 235 n.[1], 423 sqq.

Hegemone, epithet of Artemis, i. 37 n.[1]

Hehn, V., on evergreens in Italy, i. 8 n.[4]; on derivation of name Corycian, v. 187 n.[6]

Heiberg, Sigurd K., on Midsummer fires in Norway, x. 171 n.[3]

Heifer sacrificed at kindling need-fire, x. 290

Heimskringla or Sagas of the Norwegian Kings, ii. 280

Heine, H., Pilgrimage to Kevlaar, i. 77; on the oak woods of Germany, ii. 243

Heitsi-eibib, Hottentot god or hero, his graves, iv. 3, x. 16

Hekaerge and Hekaergos, i. 33, 34, 35

Helaga, holy or taboo, ii. 106 n.[2]

Helbig, W., on bronze statuettes at Nemi, i. 20 n.[5]

Helen and Menelaus, ii. 279

—— of the Tree, worshipped in Rhodes, v. 292

Helensburgh, in Dumbartonshire, Hallowe'en at, x. 237 n.[5]

Helernus, grove of, ii. 190 sq.

Heliacal rising of Sirius, vi. 152

Helice, in Achaia, destroyed by earthquake, v. 203; Poseidon worshipped at, v. 203 n.[2]

Heligoland, disappearance of herring about, viii. 251

Heliodorus, on the priesthood of Apollo and Artemis at Ephesus, vi. 243 sq.

Heliogabalus, the Emperor, his marriage of the Sun-god and Moon-goddess, iv. 92; his sacrifice of children of living parents, vi. 248

——, sun-god at Emesa, v. 35

Heliopolis (the Egyptian), Tum the god of, i. 419; the gods of, ii. 131; wine not to be taken into the temple at, iii. 249 n.[2]; the mummy of Toumou at, iv. 5; Mnevis the sacred bull of, iv. 72, viii. 34; trial of the dead Osiris before the gods at, vi. 17

—— (Baalbec), in Syria, v. 163 n.[2]; sacred prostitution at, i. 30 n.[3], v. 37, 58

Hell-broth in rain-charm, i. 352

—— fire in Catholic and Protestant theology, iv. 136

" —— -gate of Ireland," x. 226

Helle and Phrixus, the children of King Athamas, iv. 161 sqq.

Hellebore, curses at cutting, i. 281

Helmsdale, in Sutherland, need-fire at, x. 295

Helpful animals in fairy tales, xi. 107, 117, 120, 127 sqq., 130, 132, 133, 139 n.[2], 140 sq., 149

Hemingway, Mr., on unlucky marriages in India, ii. 57 n.[4]

Hemithea, her sanctuary at Castabus, viii. 24 n.[5], 85

Hemlock as an anaphrodisiac, ii. 138, 139 n.[1]; burned on May Day as a protection against witches, ix. 158 sq.

Hemlock branch, external soul of ogress in a, xi. 152

—— branches, passing through a ring of, in time of sickness, xi. 186

—— stone in Nottinghamshire, x. 157

Hemorrhoids, root of orpine a cure for, xi. 62 n.

Hemp, homoeopathic magic to promote the growth of, i. 137 sq.; augury as to the height of the, ix. 315; dances to make hemp grow tall, ix. 315; intoxication of women to make hemp grow tall, x. 109; leaping over the Midsummer bonfire to make the hemp grow tall, x. 166, 168

Hemp dance on Shrove Tuesday, i. 138

—— seed, divination by, at Hallowe'en, x. 235, 241, 245

Hen sacrificed by woodman after felling tree, ii. 14; soul in form of, iii. 42 n.; heart of, not eaten, viii. 142, 147. See also Hens

—— and chickens imitated by a woman and her children at Christmas, x. 260

Hen's egg, external soul of giant in a, xi. 140 sq.

Henderson, William, on need-fire, x. 288 sq.; on a remedy for cattle-disease, x. 296 n.[1]; on burnt sacrifice of ox, x. 301

Henna, image of Demeter at, vii. 65

Hennepin, L., on the New Year festival of the Iroquois, ix. 128 n.

Heno, the thunder-spirit of the Iroquois, ii. 369 sq.

Henry II., Hampstead in the reign of, ii. 7; at Rouen, ii. 164, 165

Hens not eaten lest they make the eaters timid, viii. 140, 142, 147; the straw of the Shrovetide Bear supposed to make the hens lay eggs, viii. 326. See also Hen

Henshaw, Richard, on external or bush souls in Calabar, xi. 205 sq.

Hepding, H., on Attis, v. 263 n.[1]; on Catullus's poem Attis, v. 270 n.[2]; on the bath of Cybele's image, v. 280

Hephaestion, funeral games in honour of, iv. 95

Hephaestius, a Greek month, vii. 46 n.[2]

Hephaestus, the Greek fire-god, reputed father of Erichthonius, ii. 199; (Ptah), temple of, at Memphis, iv. 259 n.[1]; and hot springs, v. 209; said to have killed Adonis, viii. 23 ; worshipped in Lemnos, x. 138

Hephaestus and Talos, iv. 74

Heqet, Egyptian frog-goddess, vi. 9 *n.*

Hera, her adoption of Hercules, i. 74 ; the love of Zeus for, i. 161 ; as an oak-goddess, ii. 142, 142 *n.*²; race of girls in honour of, at Olympia, iv. 91 ; the sister of her husband Zeus, iv. 194 ; represented wearing a goat's skin, vii. 23 *n.*⁴

——, Argive, her sacred grove among the Veneti, i. 27

—— the Flowery at Argos, ii. 143 *n.*²

—— and Hercules, i. 74

—— and Zeus, their sacred marriage, ii. 137 *n.*¹, 140 *sq.*, 142 *sq.*, v. 280

Heraclids, Lydian destiny of the, v. 182, 184 ; perhaps Hittite, v. 185

Heraclitus, on the souls of the dead, iv. 12

Heraean mountains in Sicily, the oaks of the, ii. 354

Heraeon, a Greek month, viii. 7

Heralds, tongues of sacrificial victims assigned to Greek, viii. 270 *sq.*

Herb, a magic, gathered at Hallowe'en, x. 228

—— of St. John, mugwort, gathered on St. John's Eve or Day, xi. 58 *sqq.*; wonderful virtues ascribed to, xi. 46, 58 *sqq. See also* Herbs

Herbert River in Queensland, personal names avoided for fear of magic on the, iii. 320

Herbrechtingen, in Thüringen, the cow at threshing at, vii. 291

Herbs thrown across the Midsummer fires, x. 182, 201 ; wonderful, gathered on St. John's Eve or Day, xi. 45 *sqq.*

—— and flowers cast into the Midsummer bonfires, x. 162, 163, 172, 173

Hercules adopted by Hera, i. 74 ; sacrifice with curses to, i. 281 *sq.*; his birth delayed by Lucina, iii. 298 *sq.* ; in the garden of the Hesperides, iv. 80 ; identified with Melcarth, v. 16, 111 ; slain by Typhon and revived by Iolaus, v. 111 ; burnt on Mount Oeta, v. 111, 116, 211 ; worshipped at Gades, v. 112 *sq.*; women excluded from sacrifices to, v. 113 *n.*¹; identified with Sandan, v. 125, 143, 161, ix. 388 ; burns himself, v. 176 ; the itch of, v. 209 ; his dispute with Aesculapius, v. 209 *sq.*; the patron of hot springs, v. 209 *sqq.*; altar of, at Thermopylae, v. 210 ; the effeminate, vii. 257, 258, 259 ; priest of, dressed as a woman, vi. 258 ; vernal mysteries of, at Rome, vi. 258 ; sacrifices to, at Rome, vi.

258 *n.*⁵; apple offered instead of ram to, viii. 95 *n.*²; surnamed Worm-killing, viii. 282 ; cake with twelve knobs offered to, ix. 351 *n.*³; his death on a pyre, ix. 389, 391

Hercules and Achelous, ii. 162

—— and Alcmena, iii. 298 *sq.*

—— at Argyrus, temple of, x. 99 *n.*³

—— and Busiris, vii. 259

—— and the lion, v. 184

—— with the lion's scalp, Greek type of, v. 117 *sq.*

—— and Lityerses, vii. 217

—— surnamed Locust, viii. 282

——, the Lydian, identical with the Cilician Hercules, v. 182, 184, 185

—— and Omphale, ii. 281 *sq.*, v. 182, vi. 258, ix. 389

—— and Sardanapalus, v. 172 *sqq.*

—— and Syleus, vii. 258

—— and Zeus, viii. 172

Hercynian forest, the, ii. 7, 354 ; etymology of the name, ii. 354 *n.*², 367 *n.*³

Herd-boys, taboos observed by Esthonian, ii. 331

Herdsmen dread witches and wolves, x. 343

Hereditary and elective monarchy, combination of the two, ii. 292 *sqq.*

—— deities, v. 51

—— queens and elective kings, ii. 295

Hereford, the Boy Bishop at, ix. 337

Herefordshire, soul-cakes in, vi. 79 ; the sin-eater in, ix. 43 ; fires kindled on the Eve of Twelfth Day in, ix. 318 *sqq* ; Midsummer fires in, x. 199 ; the Yule log in, x. 257 *sq.*

Herero or Damaras, a Bantu tribe of German South-West Africa, their contagious magic of footprints, i. 209 ; their prayers and sacrifices for rain, i. 287 ; their fire-customs, ii. 211 *sqq.*; their huts and villages, ii. 212 *sq.* ; their worship of ancestors, ii. 221 ; seclusion of women at childbirth among the, iii. 151 ; purification of warriors after battle among the, iii. 176 ; holiness of women in childbed among the, iii. 225 *n.* ; the worship of the dead among the, vi. 185 *sqq.*

Hermaphrodite son of Sky and Earth, v. 282 *n.*

Hermaphrodites, dance of, v. 271 *n.*

Hermegisclus, king of the Varini, enjoined his son to wed his stepmother, ii. 283

Hermes at Athens, the mutilation of the, iii. 75 ; the grave of, iv. 4 ; tongues of victims assigned to, viii. 270 ; tried for the murder of Argus, ix. 24 ; wayside images of, ix. 24 ; Cretan festival of, ix. 350

—— and Aegipan, v. 157

Hermes and Argus, ix. 24

Hermesianax, on the death of Attis, v. 264 *n.*[4]

Hermion, Dionysus of the Black Goat-skin at, vii. 17

Hermopolis, grave of Hermes at, iv. 4

Hermotimus of Clazomenae and his rambling soul, iii. 50

Hermsdorf, in Silesia, harvest custom at, vii. 139

Hermus, river, in Asia Minor, v. 185, 186

Hermutrude, legendary queen of Scotland, ii. 281

Herndon, W. L., on the ordeal of stinging with ants among the Indians of Brazil, x. 62 *n.*[3]

Hernia, cured by prayer of girl at puberty, x. 98 *n.*[1]

Herod *resorts* to the springs of Callirrhoe, v. 214 ; his slaughter of the young children, ix. 337 ; his soldiers' treatment of Christ, ix. 416

Herodas, as to the soul on the lips, iii. 33 *n.*[3]

Herodes Atticus, his benefaction at Thermopylae, v. 210

Herodias, cursed by Slavonian peasants, v. 345

Herodotus on the Hyperborean maidens, i. 34 *ns.* ; on the divinity of Spartan kings, i. 48 *sq.* ; on the destruction of the Psylli, i. 331 ; on descent of the Lydian crown, ii. 282 ; on sanctuary of Aphrodite at Paphos, v. 34 ; on religious prostitution, v. 58 ; on wife of Bel, v. 71 ; on Cyrus and Croesus, v. 174 ; on the sacrifices of Croesus to Apollo, v. 180 *n.*[1] ; on so-called monument of Sesostris, v. 185 ; on the festival of Osiris at Sais, vi. 50 ; on the mourning for Osiris, vi. 86 ; identifies Osiris with Dionysus, vi. 113 *n.*[2] ; on the similarity between the rites of Osiris and Dionysus, vi. 127 ; on human sacrifices offered by the wife of Xerxes, vi. 221 ; on the Linus song, vii. 258 ; on human sacrifices in ancient Egypt, vii. 259 *n.*[3] ; on the Egyptian sacrifice of pigs to Osiris and the moon, viii. 25 *n.*[1] ; on the worship of Ishtar (Astarte), ix. 372

Heroes worshipped in form of animals, v. 139 *n.*[1]

Herrera, A. de, on *naguals* among the Indians of Honduras, xi. 213 *sq.*

Herrick, Robert, *The Hock-cart or the Harvest Home*, vii. 147 *n.*[1] ; on the Yule log, x. 225

Herring thought to be attracted by the laird of Dunvegan, i. 368 ; superstitions as to, viii. 251 *sq.* ; salt, divination by, at Hallowe'en, x. 239

Herrings and dumplings to be eaten on Twelfth Night, ix. 241

Hersilia, a Sabine goddess, ii. 193 *n.*[1]

Hertfordshire, May garlands and carols in, ii. 61, 61 *n.*[1] ; " Crying the Mare " in, vii. 292 *sq.* ; ague transferred to oaks in, ix. 57 *sq.*

Hertz, W., on religious prostitution, v. 57 *n.*[1], 59 *n.*[4]

Heruli, a Teutonic tribe, their custom of killing the sick and old, iv. 14

Hervey Islands, South Pacific, legend of the origin of the Pleiades in the, vii. 312

Herzegovina, marriage custom at Mostar in, ii. 230 *sq.* ; the Yule log in, x. 263 ; need-fire in, x. 286

Hesiod, on acorns as food, ii. 355 ; on Demeter as goddess of the corn, vii. 42 ; on time for ploughing, vii. 45 ; on time of vintage, vii. 47 *n.*[2] ; on the farmer's calendar, vii. 53

Hesperides, garden of the, iv. 80

Hesse, homoeopathic treatment of a broken leg in, i. 205 ; race on horseback at a marriage in, ii. 303 *sq.* ; custom at ploughing in, v. 239 ; pigs' ribs used at sowing in, vii. 300 ; Lenten fire-custom in, x. 118 ; Easter fires in, x. 140 ; wells decked with flowers on Midsummer Day in, xi. 28

Hest, the Egyptian name for Isis, vi. 50 *n.*[4], 115 *n.*[1]

Hestia, the Greek equivalent of Vesta, i. 45 ; sacrifices offered by the king to, i. 45

Hettingen in Baden, custom at sowing at, v. 239

Heudanemi at Athens, i. 325 *n.*[1]

Hewitt, J. N. B., on need-fire of the Iroquois, x. 299 *sq.*

Heyne, C. G., on the Parilia, ii. 329 *n.*[1]

Hezekiah, King, and the brazen serpent, iv. 86 ; his reformation, v. 25, 107 ; date of his reign, v. 25 *n.*[4]

Hiaina district of Morocco, Midsummer custom of Arab women in, xi. 51

Hialto, how he became brave, viii. 146

Hibeh papyri, vi. 35 *n.*[1], 51 *n.*[1]

Hibiscus tree used in making fire-drill, iii. 227

Hidatsa Indians of North America, on the shades or spirits of cottonwood trees, ii. 12 ; taboos observed by eagle-hunters among the, iii. 198 *sq.* ; their theory of the plurality of souls, xi. 221 *sq.*

Hide, cow's, beaten with staves on the last day of the year in the Highlands of Scotland, viii. 322 *sqq.* ; beaten by the Salii with rods, ix. 231

Hide-measured lands, legends as to, vi. 249 *sq.*

Hiera Sykaminos, furthest point of Roman empire in southern Egypt, iv. 144 *n.*²

Hieracium pilosella, mouse-ear hawkweed, gathered at Midsummer, xi. 57

Hieraconpolis or Hawk-town, the oldest royal capital in Egypt, iv. 112; hawks worshipped at, vi. 22 *n.*¹; representations of the Sed festival at, vi. 151

Hierapolis on the Euphrates, biennial ceremony of pouring water at, i. 251 *n.*⁴; sacred pigs at, viii. 23

——, the Syrian, offerings of hair at, i. 29; rule as to mourners entering the temple of Astarte at, iii. 286; high priest of the Syrian goddess at, v. 143 *n.*⁴; festival of the Pyre or Torch at, v. 146, ix. 392; sacred doves at, v. 147; eunuch priests of Astarte at, v. 269 *sq.*

—— and *Hieropolis*, distinction between, v. 168 *n.*²

——, in the valley of the Maeander, cave of Pluto at, v. 206; hot springs at, v. 206 *sqq.*

Hierapolis-Bambyce, Atargatis the goddess of, v. 137, 162; mysterious golden image at, v. 162 *n.*²; rules as to the pollution of death at, vi. 227

Hieroglyphics, Hittite, v. 124, 125 *n.*

Hieroglyphs perhaps magical in origin, i. 87 *n.*¹

Hieron, Greek vase of, vii. 68 *n.*¹

Hierophant at Eleusis, temporarily deprived of his virility, ii. 138; his marriage, ii. 139 *n.*¹; his exhortation to offer the first-fruits, vii. 55, 59 *sq.*; unlawful sacrifice offered by a, vii. 61 *n.*⁴; perhaps represented Zeus in a sacred marriage, vii. 65

Higgins, Rev. J. C., on bonfires at Tarbolton, x. 207 *n.*²

High Alps, department of the, Midsummer fires in the, xi. 39 *sq.*

High History of the Holy Graal, iv. 120, 134

High Priest in Timor, rules observed by, during absence of warriors, i. 128 *sq.*; of the Kafirs of the Hindoo Koosh, taboos observed by the, iii. 14 *n.*²; of Syrian goddess at Hierapolis, v. 143 *n*⁴; the Jewish, viii. 27, ix. 210; the Fijian, xi. 245

—— Priestess, head of the State in Khyrim, vi. 203

Highland sorcerers use knotted cords, iii. 305 *n.*³

—— sportsmen, their guns or fishing-rods not to be stepped over, iii. 423

—— story of absence of soul in sleep, iii. 40 *sq.*; of Headless Hugh, xi. 130 *sq.*

Highland witches, how they sink ships, i. 135

Highlanders of Scotland, their notion as to whirlwinds, i. 329; their precautions against witchcraft on Beltane Eve, ii. 53; forced fire (need-fire) among the, ii. 238; their superstitions as to Good Friday, iii. 229; their belief as to cut hair, iii. 271; loose or cut all knots on a corpse, iii. 310; certain words tabooed to them at sea, iii. 394; on the influence of the moon, vi. 132, 134, 140; their medicinal applications of menstruous blood, x. 98 *n.*¹; their belief in the power of witches to destroy cattle, x. 343 *n.*¹; their belief concerning snake stones, xi. 311

Highlands of Scotland, magic to catch fish in the, i. 110; magical virtues ascribed to chiefs in the, i. 368; faith in the healing touch of a Macdonald in the, i. 370 *n.*³; St. Bride's day in the, ii. 94; fires put out in house of death in the, ii. 267 *n.*⁴; divination by the shoulder-blades of sheep in the, iii. 229; iron as a charm against fairies in the, iii. 232 *sq.*; saying about combing hair at night in the, iii. 271; knots untied and buckles removed at marriage in the, iii. 299 *sq.*; the last corn cut at harvest called the Old Wife (*Cailleach*) in the, vii. 140 *sqq.*; the last corn cut at harvest called the Maiden in the, vii. 155 *sqq.*; beating the cow's hide on the last day of the year in the, viii. 322 *sqq.*; custom of throwing stones on cairns in the, ix. 20 *sq.*; cock buried alive on spot where epileptic patient fell down in the, ix. 68 *n.*²; the Twelve Days in the, ix. 324; snake stones in the, x. 16; Beltane fires in the, x. 146 *sqq.*; Hallowe'en fires in the, x. 230 *sqq.*; divination at Hallowe'en in the, x. 229, 234 *sqq.*; need-fire in the, x. 289 *sqq.*; need-fire and Beltane fire kindled by the friction of oak in the, xi. 91

Hilaria, Festival of Joy in the rites of Attis, v. 273

Hildesheim, the Leaf King at Whitsuntide at, ii. 85; bell-ringing at, on Ascension Day, ix. 247 *sq.*; Easter rites of fire and water at, x. 124; Easter bonfires at, x. 141; the need-fire at, x. 272 *sq.*; hawk-weed gathered on Midsummer Day at, xi. 57

Hill, G. F., on image of Artemis at Perga, v. 35 *n.*²; on legend of coins at Tarsus, v. 126 *n.*²; on goddess 'Atheh, v. 162 *n.*¹; on coins of Mallus, v. 165 *n.*⁶

Hill, Miss Nina, on a Candlemas custom in County Galway, ii. 95 *n.*

Hill of the Fires in the Highlands of Scotland, x. 149

—— of Lloyd, near Kells, iv. 99

—— of Ward, in County Meath, x. 139

Hill Tout, C., on respect shown by the Indians of British Columbia for the animals and plants which they eat, vi. 44 ; on Indian ceremonies before eating the first wild berries or roots of the season, viii. 80 *sq.*, 134

Hills, spirits of, worshipped in Burma, ii. 41

Himalayan districts of the North-Western Provinces of India, gardens of Adonis in the, v. 242 ; sacrifices at sowing and harvest in the, viii. 117 ; prayers at cairns in the, ix. 29 ; mistletoe in the, xi. 316

Himalayas, cairns or heaps of sticks in the, ix. 12

Himera, the battle of, iv. 167, v. 115 ; hot springs of, v. 213 *n.*[1]

Himerius, on the gift of the corn, vii. 58

Hindoo bride led round the fire, ii. 230

—— ceremony of rebirth from a golden cow, iii. 113

—— charm to cause sleep, i. 148 ; ancient, by means of knots, iii. 306

—— expiation for killing sacred animals, iv. 216

—— marriage, the pole-star at, i. 166

—— marriages of trees and shrubs, ii. 25 *sq.*

—— places of pilgrimage, hair of criminals shaved at, iii. 287

—— ritual, confession of sins in, iii. 217 ; ancient, for the transference of thirst, ix. 38 ; abstinence from salt in, x. 27 ; as to cutting a child's hair, x. 99 *n.*[2]

—— story of the absence of the soul in a dream, iii. 38 *n.*[4]

—— Trinity, i. 225, 404

—— women will not name their husbands, iii. 333 ; their restrictions at menstruation, x. 84

—— worship of cows, viii. 37

Hindoo Koosh, sacred cedar of the, i. 383 ; diviners among the tribes of the, i. 383 *sq.* ; the Kafirs of the, i. 385 ; expulsion of demons after harvest in the, ix. 137, 225

Hindoos, magical images among the, i. 63 *sqq.* ; their contagious magic of footprints, i. 209 ; their test of a sacrificial victim, i. 384 *sq.* ; worship the Holy Basil (*tulasi*) plant, ii. 26 *sq.* ; their custom as to yawning, iii. 31 ; their custom as to paring children's nails, iii. 262 *sq.* ; their belief as to shooting stars, iv. 67 ; their indifference to death, iv. 136 ; sacredness of the first-born among the, iv. 181 ; their belief in the rebirth of a father in his son, iv. 188 ; burial of infants among the, v. 94 ; their worship of perpetual fire, v. 192 ; their marriage customs, vi. 246, x. 75 ; transference of evil among the, ix. 38 ; their fear of demons, ix. 91 *sq.* ; maidens secluded at puberty among the, x. 68 ; their use of menstruous fluid, x. 98 *n.*[1] ; stories of the external soul among the, xi. 97 *sqq.* *See also* India

Hindoos, ancient, magical images among the, i. 77 ; their treatment of jaundice, i. 79 ; barley in the religious ritual of the, vii. 132 ; sacrifice of first-fruits among the, viii. 119 *sq.* ; their cure for epilepsy, ix. 69 *n.*

—— of the Central Provinces, their belief that a twin can ward off hail and heavy rain, i. 269

—— of Northern India, their mode of drinking moonshine, vi. 144

—— of the Punjaub, their belief as to the length of a soul's residence in heaven, iv. 67 ; annual ceremony of the expulsion of poverty among the, ix. 144 *sq.* ; their custom of passing unlucky children through narrow openings, xi. 190

—— of Southern India, their ceremony at eating the new rice, viii. 56 ; their Pongol festival, xi. 1

Hinnom, the Valley of, sacrifice of first-born children in, iv. 169, 170, v. 178, vi. 219

Hippasus, torn to pieces by Bacchanals, iv. 164

Hippoclides and Clisthenes, ii. 307 *sq.*

Hippocrates, sacrifices offered to, ii. 105 ; on a Sarmatian custom of moulding the heads of children artificially, ii. 297

Hippodamia, her marriage with Pelops, iv. 91 ; institutes the girls' race at Olympia, iv. 91 ; grave of the suitors of, iv. 104 ; her incest with her father, v. 44 *n.*[1]

—— and Pelops, ii. 279, 299 *sq.*

Hippolytus killed by horses, i. 20, iv. 214, viii. 40 ; restored to life by Aesculapius, i. 20, iv. 214 ; dedicated horses to Aesculapius, i. 21 *n.*[2], viii. 41 *n.*[5] ; hair dedicated by youths and maidens to, i. 28, 39

—— and Artemis, i. 19 *sq.*, 24 *sqq.*

—— and Phaedra, i. 19

—— or Virbius, the first King of the Wood at Nemi, i. 19 *sq.*, iv. 214, viii. 40

Hippolytus, Christian Father, on the

exhibition of corn to the initiates at Eleusis, vii. 38

Hippolytus, Saint, martyrdom of, i. 21

Hippomenes wins Atalante in a race, ii. 301

Hippopotamus, ceremony after killing a, viii. 235 ; external soul of chief in a, xi. 200

Hippopotamuses, souls of dead in, viii. 289 ; lives of persons bound up with those of, xi. 201, 202, 205, 209

Hiqit, frog-headed Egyptian goddess, ii. 132, 133

Hirn, Y., as to homoeopathic magic, i. 52 n.[1] ; on magic by similarity and magic by contact, i. 54 n.[1]

Hiro, Polynesian thief-god, iii. 69

Hirpi Sorani, their fire-walk, xi. 14 sq.

Hirpini, the, traced their origin to a "sacred spring," iv. 186 ; guided by a wolf (hirpus), iv. 186 n.[4] ; valley of Amsanctus in the land of, v. 204

Hirschfeld, G., on Hittite hieroglyphs, i. 87 n.[1]

Hirt, Professor H., on the derivation of the name Perkunas, ii. 367 n.[3] ; on the Twelve Days, ix. 325 n.[3]

Hissar District, Punjaub, burial of dead infants at the threshold in the, v. 94

Historical tradition hampered by the taboo on the names of the dead, iii. 363 sqq.

History not to be explained without the influence of great men, v. 311 n.[2] ; of mankind not to be summed up in a few simple formulas, viii. 37 ; of religion a long attempt to reconcile old custom with new reason, viii. 40

Hitchin, in Hertfordshire, May carols at, ii. 61 n.[1]

Hittite, correct form of the national name Chatti or Hatti, v. 133 n.

Hittite god of thunder, v. 134, 163

—— gods at Tarsus and Sardes, v. 185

—— hieroglyphics, i. 87 n.[1], v. 124, 125 n.

—— inscription on Mount Argaeus, v. 190 n.[1]

—— priest or king, his costume, v. 131 sq., 133 n.

—— sculptures at Carchemish, v. 38 n., 123 ; at Ibreez, v. 121 sqq. ; at Bor (Tyana), v. 122 n.[1] ; at Euyuk, v. 123 ; at Boghaz-Keui, v. 128 sqq. ; at Babylon, v. 134 ; at Zenjirli, v. 134 ; at Giaour-Kalesi, v. 138 n. ; at Kara-Bel, v. 138 n. ; at Marash, v. 173 ; in Lydia, v. 185

—— Sun-goddess, v. 133 n.

—— treaty with Egypt, v. 135 sq.

Hittites worship the bull, v. 123, 132 ; their empire, language, etc., v. 124 sq. ;

their costume, v. 129 sq., 131 ; their seals of treaty, v. 136, 142 n.[1], 145 n.[2] ; traces of mother-kin among the, v. 141 sq. ; their deity named Tark or Tarku, v. 147

Hkamies of North Aracan, their annual festival of the dead, vi. 61

Hkön, race of Upper Burma, virgins of the, married to the spirit of a lake, ii. 150 sq.

Hlubi chief, his external soul in a pair of ox-horns, xi. 156

Hlubies, the, of South-Eastern Africa, their rain-making, i. 249

Ho tribe of Togoland, their kings buried secretly, vi. 104. See Hos

Hoare, Sir Richard Colt, on Hallowe'en in Wales, x. 239

Hobby-horse at Padstow, ii. 68 ; to carry away spirit of smallpox, ix. 119

Hobley, C. W., on the belief of the Akikuyu in the fertilization of women by wild fig-trees, ii. 316 ; on spiritual husbands among the Akamba, ii. 316 sq.

Hochofen, village of Bohemia, annual expulsion of witches on Walpurgis Night at, ix. 161 sq.

Hockey played as a ceremony, ix. 174

Hockey cart, the waggon on which the last corn is brought from the harvest vii. 147 n.[1]

Hodgson, Adam, on Indian parallel to Jacob wrestling with the angel, viii. field, 264

Hodson, T. C., on mode of keeping count of years in Manipur, iv. 117 n.[1] ; on taboos among the hill tribes of Assam, vii. 109 n.[2] ; on annual eponyms in Manipur, ix. 39 sq.

Hodum Deo, images of, i. 284 n.

Hoeck, K., on the pursuit of Britomartis by Zeus, iv. 73 n.[1]

Hoeing, rites at, vii. 96 ; done by women, vii. 113 sq.

Hoensbroech, Count von, his mode of communion with the Deity, viii. 94

Hoes used by women in agriculture, vii. 114, 115, 116, 118, 119

Hofmayr, P. W., on the Supreme Being of the Shilluks, iv. 18 n.[1] ; on the worship of Nyakang among the Shilluks, iv. 19 n.[3], vi. 164, 166

Hog-sucker in homoeopathic magic, i. 155

Hog's blood, purifying virtue of, i. 107. See Pig

Hog's wort (Peucedanum leiocarpum, Nutt.) burnt as an offering to salmon, viii. 254

Hogarth, D. G., on relics of paganism at Paphos, v. 36 ; on the Corycian cave, v. 155 *n.* ; on Roman remains at Tarsus, v. 172 *n.*[1]

Hogg, Alexander, and Midsummer bonfires, x. 206 *sq.*

Hoggan, Frances, on cutting "the neck" at harvest in Pembrokeshire, vii. 267

Hogmanay, the last day of the year, Highland custom of beating a cow's hide on, viii. 323 ; song in the Isle of Man, x. 224 ; the "Burning of the Clavie" at Burghead on, x. 266

Hogs sacrificed to goddess of volcano, v. 218 *sq.* *See* Pigs

Hohenstaufen Mountains in Wurtemberg, Midsummer fires in the, x. 166

Hole in tongue of medicine-man, xi. 238, 239

Holed flint a protection against witches, ix. 162

—— stone in magic, i. 313. *See also* Holes

Holes in rocks or stones which sick people creep through as a cure, xi. 186 *sqq.*

Holi, a festival of Northern India, bonfires at, xi. 2 *sq.*

Holiness conceived as a dangerous virus, viii. 29 ; or taboo conceived as a dangerous physical substance which needs to be insulated, x. 6 *sq.*

—— and pollution not differentiated by savages, iii. 224

Holland, belief as to cauls in, i. 199 ; Whitsuntide customs in, ii. 80, 104 ; story as to absence of soul from body in, iii. 39 *n.*[1] ; "Killing the Hare" at harvest in, vii. 280 ; Easter fires in, x. 145

Hollantide Eve (Hallowe'en) in the Isle of Man, x. 244

Hollertau, Bavaria, Easter fires in the, x. 122

Hollis, A. C., on a Masai custom as to the brewing of honey-wine, iii. 200 *n.*[3] ; on serpent-worship among the Akikuyu, v. 67 *sq.* ; on serpent-worship among the Masai, v. 84 ; on serpent-worship among the Nandi, v. 84 *sq.* ; on custom of manslayers among the Nandi, viii. 155 ; on pretence of being born again at circumcision among the Akikuyu, xi. 262

Hollow things, homoeopathic magic of, i. 157 *sq.*

Holly-oaks in sacred grove of Dia, ii. 122

Holly-tree, children passed through a cleft, xi. 169 *n.*[2]

Holm-oak or ilex, resemblance of its leaf to the laurel, iv. 81 *sq.* ; the Golden Bough growing on a, xi. 285

Holstein, the last sheaf called the Corn-

mother in, vii. 133 *sq.* ; fox carried from house to house in spring in, vii. 297

Holy Apostles, church of the, at Florence, x. 126

—— Basil, worshipped in India, ii. 26

—— candles, i. 13

—— Ghost, alleged incarnation of the, i. 409 ; regarded as female, iv. 5 *n.*[3]

—— of Holies, the Fijian, xi. 244, 245

—— Innocents' Day, young people beat each other on, ix. 270, 271 ; mock pope or bishop on, ix. 334, 336, 337, 338

—— Land, fire flints brought from the, x. 126

" —— men " in Syria, v. 77 *sq.*

—— Saturday, effigy of Queen of Lent beheaded on, iv. 244

—— Sepulchre, church of the, at Jerusalem, ceremony of the new fire in the, x. 128 *sq.*

—— water a charm against witchcraft, ii. 340 ; sprinkling with, iii. 285 *sq.* ; a protection against witches, ix. 158, 164 *sq.*

Holyrood, Charles the First at, i. 368

Homer on the loves of Zeus and Hera, ii. 143 ; kings called divine in, ii. 177 ; on Demeter as goddess of the corn, vii. 41 *sq.* ; on loves of Zeus and Demeter, vii. 66 ; on gods in likeness of foreigners, vii. 236

Homeric age, funeral games in the, iv. 93

—— Greeks cut out tongues of sacrificial victims, viii. 270

—— *Hymn to Demeter*, vii. 35 *sqq.*, 70, 161 *n.*[4], 211 *n.*[3]

Homesteads protected by bonfires against lightning and conflagration, x. 344

Homicide, banishment of, iv. 69 *sq.* *See* Manslayers

Hommel, Professor F., on the Hittite deity Tarku, v. 147 *n.*[3]

Homoeopathic or imitative magic, i. 52 *sqq.*, iii. 151, 152, 207, 295, 298, iv. 283, 285, vii. 10, 62, 262, viii. 267, 272, 331, 333, 334, ix. 177, 232, 257, 404, x. 49, 133, xi. 177, 287 ; for the making of rain, i. 247 *sqq.* ; of a flesh diet, viii. 138 *sqq.* *See also* Magic

—— taboos, i. 116

Homogeneity of civilization in prehistoric times in Southern Europe and Western Asia, ix. 409

Homolje mountains in Servia, "living fire" in time of epidemic at the, ii. 237, x. 282

Honduras, Indians of, their superstition as to the bones of deer, viii. 241 ; the *nagual* or external soul among the, xi. 213 *sq.*, 226 *n.*[1]

Hone, W., on May-poles, ii. 70 *sq.*; on "crying the neck," vii. 264 *sq.*

Honey offered to the sun-god, i. 311

—— and milk offered to snakes, v. 85, viii. 288

Honey-cakes, sacred serpent fed with, iv. 86, v. 87

—— -wine, continence observed at brewing, iii. 200

Honorific totems of the Carrier Indians, xi. 273 *sqq.*

Honorius and Theodosius, decree of, ix. 392

Honour and good faith, the bonds of, strengthened by superstition, iii. 130

Hood Bay in New Guinea, custom observed after a death at, ix. 84

Hood, Thomas, on the water-fairy, iii. 94

Hoods worn by women after childbirth, x. 20; worn by girls at puberty, x. 44 *sq.*, 48 *sq.*, 55; worn by women at menstruation, x. 90. *See also* Hats

Hook-thorn not to be cut while the corn is in the ground, ii. 49

Hooks used in magic, i. 132, 347; to catch souls, iii. 30 *sq.*, 51; Indian custom of swinging on, iv. 278 *sq.*

Hoop, crawling through a, as a cure or preventive of disease, xi. 184; of rowan-tree, sheep forced through a, xi. 184

Hoopoe brings the mythical springwort, xi. 70 *n.*[2]

Hop-picking, treatment of strangers at, vii. 226

Hope of immortality, the Egyptian, centred in Osiris, vi. 15 *sq.*, 90 *sq.*, 114, 159

Hopi Indians, their fire-drill, ii. 208 *sq.*

Hopladamus, a giant, v. 157 *n.*[2]

Hora and Quirinus, vi. 233

Horatius purified for the murder of his sister, xi. 194

Horkos, the Greek god of oaths, vi. 231 *n.*[5]

Hornbeam, mistletoe on, xi. 315

Horne Island, South Pacific, blood of wounded friends smeared on their relatives in, iii. 245

Horned cap worn by priest or god, v. 123; of Hittite god, v. 134

—— Dionysus, vii. 12, 16

—— god, Hittite and Greek, v. 123

—— lion on coins of Tarsus, v. 127

Hornkampe in Prussia, the last sheaf called the Old Woman at, vii. 137

Hornless ox in homoeopathic magic, i. 151

Horns, of goat hung on a sacred tree, ii. 42; of sacrificial oxen, iv. 32, 33; as a religious emblem, v. 34; worn by gods, v. 163 *sq.*; of a cow worn by Isis, vi. 50; of straw worn to keep off demons, ix. 118; of goat a protection against witches, ix. 162

Horns blown to expel demons, ix. 111, 117, 204, 214; to ban witches, ix. 160, 161, 165, 166; at Penzance on eve of May Day, ix. 163 *sq.*; by maskers, ix. 243, 244

Horse, prohibition to see a, iii. 9; prohibition to ride, iii. 13; "seeing the Horse," vii. 294; "Cross of the Horse," vii. 294; "fatigue of the Horse," vii. 294; sacrificed to Mars in October for the sake of the crops, viii. 42 *sqq.*, ix. 230; ceremony of the, at rice-harvest among the Garos, viii. 337 *sqq.*; sacrifice of, in Vedic times, ix. 122 *n.*; beloved by Ishtar, ix. 371, 407 *n.*[2]; beloved by Semiramis, ix. 407 *n.*[2]; witch in the shape of a, x. 319. *See also* Horses

—— black, in rain-charm, i. 290

—— or mare, last sheaf given to, vii. 141, 156, 158, 160, 161, 162, 294; corn spirit as, vii. 202 *sqq.*

——, red, sacrificed as a purification of the land, ix. 213

——, sacred, in Celebes, i. 364; sacrificed at Rome in October, ii. 229, 326

—— and Virbius, viii. 40 *sqq.*

——, the White, effigy carried through Midsummer fire, ix. 203 *sq.*

Horse-chestnut, mistletoe on, xi. 315

Horse-headed Demeter of Phigalia, viii. 21, 338

—— -mackerel, descent of a totemic clan from a, iv. 129

—— -race of boys at Lhasa, ix. 221 *n.*[1]

—— -races, at Whitsuntide in Germany, ii. 69; in honour of the dead, iv. 97, 98, 99, 101, 103; at fairs, iv. 99 *sqq.*; at Eleusis, vii. 71; at harvest, vii. 76, viii. 114

—— sacrifice in ancient India, xi. 80 *n.*[3]

—— -shoes a protection against witches, ix. 162

Horse's flesh tabooed, among Zulus, i. 118

—— Fount at Troezen, i. 26, 27

—— head, in Roman sacrifice, viii. 42; used to protect garden from caterpillars, viii. 43 *n.*[1]; in effigy at harvest festival, viii. 43 *n.*[1], 337 *sq.*; thrown into Midsummer fire, xi. 40

—— tail cut off in sacrifice, viii. 42, 43

Horseman, charm to make a good, i. 152

Horses, Hippolytus killed by, i. 19 *sq.*, iv. 214; excluded from Arician grove, i. 20, viii. 40 *sqq.*; dedicated by Hippolytus to Aesculapius, i. 21 *n.*[2], 27; branded with mark of wolf, i. 27; in relation to Diomede, i. 27; sacrifice of white, i. 27 ; sacrificed to the sun, i. 315 *sq.* ; Lycurgus, king of the Edonians, torn to pieces by, i. 366, vi. 98, vii. 24 ; sacrificed to trees, ii. 16 ; sacrificed to rivers, ii. 16 *sq.* ; sacrificed to water-spirits, ii. 157 ; sanctity of white, ii. 174 *n.*[2] ; sacrifices for, on St. George's Day, ii. 332, 336 *sq.* ; sacrificed and hung on trees of sacred grove, ii. 365 ; left unclipped for a year after a king's consecration, iii. 260 ; not to be called by their proper names, iii. 408, 413 ; sacrificed for the use of the dead, v. 293 *sq.* ; excluded from sanctuaries viii. 45 *sq.* ; used by sacred persons, x. 4 *n.*[1] ; not to be touched or ridden by! menstruous women, x. 88 *sq.*, 96 ; driven through the need-fire, x. 276, 297.   *See also* Horse

Horus, the eye of, i. 364, vi. 17, 121 with *n.*[3], viii. 30 ; the soul of, in Orion, iv. 5 ; the four sons of, in the likeness of hawks, vi. 22 ; decapitates his mother Isis, vi. 88 ; represented sacrificing a human victim to Osiris, vii. 260 ; his eye injured by Typhon, viii. 30 ; institutes the sacrifice of a pig, viii. 30 ; the birth of, ix. 341

—— of Edfu identified with the sun, vi. 123

—— the elder, vi. 6

——, the golden, i. 418

—— the younger, son of Isis and the dead Osiris, vi. 8, 15 ; accused by Set of being a bastard, vi. 17 ; his combat with Set, vi. 17 ; his eye destroyed by Set and restored by Thoth, vi. 17 ; reigns over the Delta, vi. 17

Hos of Bengal offer first-fruits of rice to the sun-god, viii. 117 ; their annual expulsion of demons at harvest, ix. 136 *sq.*

—— of Togoland (West Africa), a tribe of Ewe negroes, their customs as to twins, i. 265 ; sanctity of the king's throne among the, i. 365 ; their human gods, i. 396 *sq.* ; their ceremony at felling a palm for wine, ii. 19 ; their god and goddess of lightning, ii. 370 ; their priests with unshorn hair, iii. 259 ; their magical use of knots to facilitate childbirth, iii. 295 *sq.*; their use of knots in cursing, iii. 301 *sq.*; tie strings round the sick as a cure, iii. 304 ; their comparison of maize to a mother, vii. 130 ; their miniature gardens dedicated to "guardian gods," vii. 234 ; their festival of the new yams, viii. 58 *sqq.*; their offerings of new yams, viii. 115 *sq.*; their annual expulsion of evils, ix. 134 *sqq.*, 206 *sq.* ; their dread of menstruous women, x. 82

Hose, Dr. Charles, on ceremony of adoption in Sarawak, i. 75 *n.*[1] ; on creeping through a cleft stick after a funeral, xi. 175 *sq.*

——, Dr. Charles and W. McDougall, on head-hunting in Borneo, v. 295 *n.*[1] ; on the *ngarong* or secret helper of the Ibans, xi. 224 *n.*[1]

Hosea on religious prostitution, v. 58 ; on the Baalim, v. 75 *n.* ; on the prophet as a madman, v. 77

Hoshangábád, in Central India, custom as to the last corn cut at, vii. 222

Hospitality, bonds of, strengthened through superstition, iii. 130

Hosskirch, in Swabia, mode of predicting the weather for the year at, ix. 323

Hostages, clipped hair used as, iii. 272 *sq.*

Hostility of religion to magic in history, i. 226

Hot springs resorted to by women in order to obtain offspring, ii. 161 ; worship of, v. 206 *sqq.* ; Hercules the patron of, v. 209 *sqq.* ; resorted to by childless women in Syria, v. 213 *sqq.*

—— water drunk as a charm, i. 129

Hother, Hodr, or Hod, the blind god, and Balder, x. 101 *sqq.*, xi. 279 *n.*[4]

Hottentot charm to make the wind drop, i. 320

—— hunters, their contagious magic of footprints, i. 212

—— prayers for cattle at cairns, ix. 29 *sq.*

—— priest never uses an iron knife, iii. 227

—— women, rules observed by, in the absence of their husbands, i. 120 *sq.*

Hottentots, seclusion and purification of hunters among the, iii. 220 *sq.* ; the mortal god of the, iv. 3 ; their observation of the Pleiades, vii. 316 *sq.* ; throw stones or sticks on the graves of Heitsi-eibib, ix. 16 ; drive their sheep through fire, xi. 11 *sq.*

Hounds protected against spirits of wild beasts killed in the chase, ii. 128. *See also* Dogs

House, taboos observed after building a new, ii. 40 ; ceremony at entering a new, iii. 63 *sq.* ; taboos on quitting the, iii. 122 *sqq.*; destroyed after a death, iii. 286

House-building, homoeopathic magic of woods used in, i. 146 ; custom as to shadows at, iii. 81, 89 *sq.* ; continence observed at, iii. 202

—— -communities of the Servians, x. 259 *n.*[1]

—— -timber, homoeopathic magic of, i. 146 ; tree-spirits propitiated in, ii. 39 *sq.*

Housebreakers, charms employed by, to cause sleep, i. 148 *sq.*

Houses built with one story, reason for, iii. 253, 254 ; fumigated as a protection against witches, ix. 158 ; protected by bonfires against lightning and conflagration, x. 344 ; made fast against witches on Midsummer Eve, xi. 73

" —— of the soul" in Isaiah, xi. 155 *n.*[3]

Housman, Professor A. E., on the feast of the Nativity of the Virgin, x. 220 *sq.*

Houstry, in Caithness, need-fire at, x. 291 *sq.*

Hovas, the, of Madagascar, divinity of kings among, i. 397; offer the first-fruits of the crop to the king, viii. 116

How, the civil king of Tonga, iii. 21

Howitt, A. W., as to extracted teeth of Australian aborigines, i. 176 ; on contagious magic of footprints in Australia, i. 207 *sq.* ; on Australian magic, iii. 269; on superstitions as to personal names among the Australian aborigines, iii. 320; on Australian belief as to falling stars, iv. 64; on seclusion of menstruous women in Australia, x. 78; on killing a totem animal, xi. 220 *n.*[2]; on secrecy of totem names in Australia, xi. 225 *n.* ; on the drama of resurrection at initiation in Australia, xi. 235 *sqq.*

Howitt, Miss Mary E. B., her *Folklore and Legends of some Victorian Tribes*, xi. 226 *n.*[1]

Howth, the western promontory of, Midsummer fire on, x. 204

Howth Castle, life-tree of the St. Lawrence family at, xi. 166

Hoyerswerda, district of Silesia, the "Old Man" at threshing in, vii. 149; Walpurgis bonfires to keep off witches in the, ix. 163

Hsa Möng Hkam, a native state of Upper Burma, care for the butterfly spirit of the rice in, vii. 190

Huaca, Peruvian word for god, ii. 146

Huahine, one of the Tahitian Islands, xi. 11 *n.*[3]; offering of first-fruits in, viii. 132 *sq.*

Hubert, H., and M. Mauss, Messrs., on taboo as a negative magic, i. 111 *n.*[2]

Huckle-bone of hare in cure, ix. 50 *sq.*

Huddler or *Huttler*, mummers at Carnival to promote the flax crop in the Tyrol, ix. 248

Hudel-running in the Tyrol, ix. 248

Hudson Bay, the Esquimaux of, iii. 207, 228, viii. 257; the Chippeways of, x. 90

Hughes, Miss E. P., on the fire-walk in Japan, xi. 10 *n.*[1]

Huichol Indians of Mexico, their use of magical images, i. 71 ; taboos observed by them during the search for

the sacred cactus, i. 123 *sq.* ; their homoeopathic charm to ensure skill in weaving, i. 154 *sq.* ; their rain-making by carrying water, i. 302 ; their worship of water, ii. 156 ; their chastity before hunting, iii. 197 ; personify maize as a little girl, vii. 177 ; their communion with a god by partaking of his effigy, viii. 93 ; their transference of fatigue to heaps of stones, ix. 10

Huichol superstition as to the growth of corn, ix. 347 *n.*[3]

Huilla,. African kingdom, the king of, thought to make rain, i. 348

Huitzilopochtli, or Vitzilopochtli, a great Mexican god, viii. 95, ix. 300 ; dough image of him made and eaten sacramentally, viii. 86 *sqq.*, 90 *sq.* ; young man sacrificed in the character of, ix. 280 *sq.* ; temple of, ix. 287, 290, 297; hall of, ix. 294

Huixtocihuatl, Mexican goddess of Salt, ix. 283 ; woman annually sacrificed in the character of, ix. 283 *sq.*

Huligamma, Indian goddess, eunuchs dedicated to her, v. 271 *n.*

Human beings permanently possessed by deities, i. 386 *sqq.* ; torn to pieces in rites of Dionysus, vii. 24 ; burnt in the fires, xi. 21 *sqq.*

—— divinities put to death, x. i. *sq.*

—— flesh, transformation into animal shape through eating, iv. 83 *sq.*

—— god and goddess, their enforced union, ix. 386 *sq.*

—— gods, i. 373 *sqq.*, ii. 377 *sqq.* ; bound by many rules, iii. 419 *sq.*

—— immortality in relation to the immortality of animals, viii. 260 *sqq.*

—— Leopard Societies of West Africa, iv. 83

—— representatives of Attis, v. 285 *sqq.* ; of gods sacrificed in Mexico, ix. 275 *sqq.*

—— sacrifice, substitutes for, iv. 124, 214 *sqq.*, v. 146 *sq.*, 285, 289, vi. 99, 221, vii. 33 *sq.*, 249; successive mitigations of, ix. 396 *sq.*, 408

—— sacrifices offered to man-gods, i. 386, 387 ; to trees, ii. 15, 17 ; offered on roofs of new houses, iii. 39 ; at foundation of buildings, iii. 90 *sq.* ; at the cutting of a chief's hair, iii. 264 ; at Upsala, iv. 58 ; to renew the sun's fire, iv. 74 *sq.*; in ancient Greece, iv. 161 *sqq.*; mock, iv. 214 *sqq.*; offered by ancestors of the European races, iv. 214; in worship of the moon, v. 73 ; to the Tauric Artemis, v. 115 ; to Diomede at Salamis, v. 145 ; offered at earthquakes, v. 201 ; offered at irrigation channels, vi. 38 ; of the kings of Ashantee and

Dahomey, vi. 97 *n.*[7]; offered to Dionysus, vi. 98 *sq.* ; offered by the Mexicans for the maize, vi. 107 ; at the graves of the kings of Uganda, vi. 168 ; to dead kings, vi. 173 ; to dead chiefs, vi. 191 ; to prolong the life of kings, vi. 220 *sq.*, 223 *sqq.* ; for crops, vii. 236 *sqq.* ; offered by ancient Egyptians, vii. 259 *sq.* ; at festival of new yams in Ashantee, viii. 62, 63 ; in Mexico, viii. 88, ix. 275 *sqq.* ; at fire-festivals, ix. 300 *sqq.*, x. 106 ; in connexion with Cronus, ix. 353 *sq.* ; their influence on cosmogonical theories, ix. 409 *sqq.* ; traces of, x. 146, 148, 150 *sqq.*, 186, xi. 31 ; offered by the ancient Germans, xi. 28 *n.*[1] ; among the Celts of Gaul, xi. 32 *sq.* ; the victims in the Celtic sacrifices perhaps witches and wizards, xi. 41 *sqq.* ; W. Mannhardt's theory of the Celtic sacrifices, xi. 43. *See also* Human victims

Human scapegoats, ix. 38 *sqq.*, 194 *sqq.*, 210 *sqq.* ; in ancient Rome, ix. 229 *sqq.* ; in classical antiquity, ix. 229 *sqq.* ; in ancient Greece, ix. 252 *sqq.* ; reason for beating the, ix. 256 *sq.*

—— souls transmigrate into animals, viii. 285 *sqq.*

—— victims sacrificed to water-spirits, ii. 157 *sqq.* ; substitutes for, iv. 124, 214 *sqq.*, v. 146 *sq.*, 285, 289, vi. 99, 221, vii. 33 *sq.*, 249 ; thrown into volcanoes, v. 219 *sq.* ; uses made of their skins, v. 293 ; as representatives of the corn-spirit, vi. 97, 106 *sq.* ; killed with hoes, spades, and rakes, vi. 99 *n.*[2] ; treated as divine, vii. 250 ; men clad in the skins of, ix. 265 *sq.*, 294 *sq.*, 296 *sqq.* ; sacrificed as representatives of gods, ix. 275 *sqq.* ; annually burnt, xi. 286 *n.*[2]

Humbé, African kingdom, the king of, thought to make rain, i. 348 ; incontinence of young people under puberty thought to entail the death of the king of, iii. 6

Humboldt, A. von, on the theocracy of the Chibchas or Muyscas, i. 416

Humman or Hommon, national god of the Elamites, ix. 366

Humphrey's Island. *See* Manahiki

Hundred and eight girls and cows in rain-making, i. 284

Hungarian story of the external soul, xi. 140

Hungary, continence at sowing in, ii. 105 ; " Sawing the Old Woman " among the gypsies of, iv. 243 ; the harvest cock in, vii. 277 ; custom at threshing in, vii. 291 ; woman fertilized by being struck with certain sticks in, ix. 264 ; Midsummer fires in, x. 178 *sq.*

Hungary, German, Whitsuntide Queen in, ii. 87

Hunger the root of the worship of Adonis, v. 231 ; expulsion of, at Chaeronea, ix. 252

Hunt, Holman, his picture of the new fire at Jerusalem, x. 130 *n.*

Hunt, Robert, on burnt sacrifices in the West of England, x. 303

Hunter, the primitive, believes himself exposed to the vengeance of the ghosts of the animals which he has killed, viii. 208

Hunter River tribes of New South Wales, avoidance of the wife's mother among the, iii. 84

Hunters employ homoeopathic magic to ensure a catch, i. 109 *sqq.* ; homoeopathic taboos observed by hunters, their relations, and friends, i. 110 *sq.*, 113, 114 *sqq.* ; absent, thought to be affected by the conduct of their families at home, i. 120 *sqq.* ; absent, injured by the infidelity of wives at home, i. 123 ; employ contagious magic of footprints, i. 211 *sq.* ; chastity of, iii. 191 *sqq.* ; use knots as charms, iii. 306 ; words tabooed by, iii. 396, 398, 399, 400, 402, 404, 405 ; propitiation of wild animals by, viii. 204 *sqq.* ; of grisly bears, chastity observed by, viii. 226 ; exorcize the guardian spirits of wild animals, ix. 98 ; avoid girls at puberty, x. 44, 46 ; luck of, spoiled by menstruous women, x. 87, 89, 90, 91, 94

—— and fishers tabooed, iii. 190 *sqq.*

Huntin, a tree-god of the Ewe people of the Slave Coast, ii. 15

Hunting and fishing, homoeopathic magic in, i. 108 *sqq.* ; telepathy in, i. 120 *sqq.*

—— the wren, viii. 317 *sqq.*

Hunting dogs crowned at Diana's festival, i. 14, ii. 125, 126

—— stage of society, the, viii. 35, 37

Huntingdonshire, Plough Monday in, viii. 330 *n.*[1]

Huntsman, the Spectral, iv. 178

Huon Gulf in German New Guinea, the Bukaua of, vii. 103, xi. 239

Hupa Indians of California, seclusion of girls among the, x. 42

Hurling-matches for brides in Ireland, ii. 305 *sq.*

Huron, Lake, Ojibway Indians in a storm on, viii. 219

Hurons, reincarnation among the, i. 105, iv. 199 *sq.*, v. 91 ; their burial of infants, i. 105, iv. 199, v. 91 ; their way of annulling an ominous dream, i. 172 *sq.* ; marry their fishing-nets to girls, ii. 147 *sq.* ; their conception of the soul, iii. 27; their custom of reviving the dead by bestowing their names on the living, iii. 366 *sq.* ; their Festival of the Dead, iii. 367 ; their reason for not burning fish bones, viii. 250 ; preachers to the fish among the, viii. 250 *sq.* ; their way of expelling sickness, ix. 121 ; custom of their women at menstruation, x. 88 *n.*[1]

Husband, absent, thought to be injured by wife's infidelity, i. 123, 124 *sq.* ; charm to bring home a, i. 166. *See also* Husbands

—— and wife, the rice-spirit conceived as, vii. 201 *sqq.* ; name given to two fire-sticks, viii. 65

Husband's ghost kept from his widow, iii. 143

—— name not to be pronounced by his wife, iii. 333, 335, 336, 337, 338, 339

Husbandman, the Roman, his prayers to Mars, ix. 229

Husbands, spiritual, among the Akamba, fertility of wives thought to depend on, ii. 316 *sq.*

——, taboos observed by wives in the absence of their, i. 116, 119, 120, 121, 122 *sqq.*, 127 *sqq.* ; not to pronounce the names of their wives, iii. 337, 338, 339

—— and wives, difference of language between, iii. 347 *sq.*

Huskanaw, initiatory ceremony of the Virginian Indians, xi. 266

Huss, John, his participation in the Festival of Fools, ix. 336 *n.*[1]

Hut burnt at Midsummer, x. 215 *sq.* *See also* Huts

Hut-urns of ancient Latins, ii. 201 *sq.*

Hutchinson, W., his *History of Northumberland* on the Harvest Queen, vii. 146 ; on Midsummer fires, x. 197 *n.*[4]

Huts, round, of the ancient Latins, ii. 200 *sqq.* ; round, in Africa, ii. 227 *n.*[3] ; miniature, at foot of trees which are haunted by spirits of the dead, ii. 317 ; special, occupied by tabooed persons, iii. 142, 144, 156, 165, 166, 169, 171, 175, 179, 190, 199, 202, 207, 220, 221, 225 *n.* ; special, for menstruous women, iii. 146, x. 79, 82, 85 *sqq.* ; special, occupied by women in childbed, iii. 147, 148, 149 *sq.*, 150, 151 *sq.* ; miniature, for ghosts, viii. 113

Huttler or *Huddler* in the Tyrol, ix. 248. *See Huddler*

Huzuls, the, of the Carpathians, hunter's wife forbidden to spin among, i. 113 ; their homoeopathic magic at planting and sowing, i. 137 ; their precaution against the evil eye, i. 280; their precautions against witches on St. George's

Eve, ii. 335 *sq.* ; their belief as to shorn hair, iii. 270 ; their use of wedding-rings as amulets, iii. 314 *sq.* ; will not call bears, wolves, and serpents by their proper names, iii. 397 *sq.*; their theory of the waning moon, vi. 130 ; their cure for water-brash, vi. 149 *sq.* ; ascribe a special virtue to a horse's head, viii. 43 *n.*[1] ; their respect for weasels, viii. 275 ; transfer cattle disease to black dog, ix. 32 *sq.* ; kindle new fire at Christmas, x. 264 ; gather simples on St. John's Night, xi. 49

Hyacinth, son of Amyclas, killed by Apollo, v. 313 ; his flower, v. 313 *sq.* ; his tomb and festival, v. 314 *sq.* ; an aboriginal deity, v. 315 *sq.* ; his sister Polyboea, v. 316 ; perhaps a deified king of Amyclae, v. 316 *sq.*

Hyacinthia, the festival of Hyacinth, v. 314 *sq.*

Hyacinthius, a Greek month, v. 315 *n.*

Hyaenas, their supposed power over men's shadows, iii. 82 ; souls of the dead in, viii. 289 ; mén turned into, x. 313

Hyampolis in Phocis, worship of Artemis at, i. 7

Hybristica, an Argive festival, vi. 259 *n.*[3]

Hyes Attes, cry of the worshippers of Attis, viii. 22

Hygieia, the goddess, v. 88 *n.*[1]

Hyginus, on the death of Semiramis, ix. 407 *n.*[2]

Hylae, near Magnesia, image of Apollo in sacred cave at, i. 386

Hymettus, Mount, altar of Showery Zeus on, ii. 360

Hymn of the Arval Brothers, ix. 230 *n.*[2], 238 ; of the Cora Indians at sowing, ix. 238

Hymn to Demeter, Homeric, vii. 35 *sqq.*, 70

Hymns to the deified Demetrius Poliorcetes, i. 390 *sq.* ; to Parjanya, ii. 368 *sq.* ; to Tammuz, v. 9 ; to the sun-god, vi. 123 *sq.*

Hyperboreans, offerings of the, at Delos, i. 33

Hypericum perforatum, St. John's wort, gathered at Midsummer, xi. 54 *sqq.* *See also* St. John's Wort

Hyperoche, a Hyperborean maiden, i. 34 *n.*

Hyphear, a kind of mistletoe, xi. 317, 318

Hyria in Cilicia, Megassares king of, v. 41

Hyrrockin, a giantess in the legend of Balder, x. 102

Hysteria cured by beating, ix. 260

Ialysus in Rhodes, taboos observed at the sanctuary of Alectrona at, viii. 45

Iasion and Demeter, vii. 208
Ibadan in West Africa, the hearts of dead kings of, eaten by their successors, iv. 203
Ibani of the Niger delta, their sacrifices to prolong the lives of kings and others, vi. 222
Ibans of Borneo, their *ngarong* or secret helper, xi. 224 *n.*[1]
—— or Sea Dyaks of Borneo, their worship of serpents, v. 83 ; of Sarawak, their ways of getting rid of birds or vermin, viii. 279. *See* Sea Dyaks
Iberians of Spain, women tilled the ground among the, vii. 129
Ibn Batutah, Arab traveller, on a custom observed in the Maldive Islands, ii. 153, 154 ; on hereditary custom of suicide in Java, iii. 53 *sq.* ; on funeral of emperor of China, v. 293 *sq.*
Ibos of the lower Niger, their maintenance of fire, ii. 259 ; think that a manslayer must taste his victim's blood, viii. 155 ; their belief in external human souls lodged in animals, xi. 203 *sq.*
Ibrahim Pasha, at Jerusalem, x. 129
Ibreez in Southern Cappadocia, v. 119 *sqq.* ; village of, v. 120 *sq.* ; Hittite sculptures at, v. 121 *sqq.*
——, the god of, v. 119 *sqq.* ; his horned cap, v. 164
Icarus or Icarius, father of Penelope, ii. 300
—— and his daughter Erigone, iv. 281 *sq.* ; first-fruits of vintage offered to, iv. 283, viii. 133
Iceland, beliefs as to cauls in, i. 199 *sq.* ; Brunhild, Queen of, ii. 306 *sq.* ; stories of the external soul in, xi. 123 *sqq.*
Ichneumon, transmigration of sinner into, viii. 299
Ichneumons worshipped in Egypt, i. 29 *sq.*
Icolmkill, the hill of the fires in, x. 149
Ida, oracular cave of Zeus on Mount, iv. 70
Ida Batara, a god (Vishnu), vii. 202
Idah or Iddah, on the lower Niger, divinity claimed by the king of, i. 396 ; custom as to royal family at, ii. 294 ; treatment of dead leopard at, viii. 228
Idalium in Cyprus, Pygmalion, king of, v. 50 ; bilingual inscription of, v. 49 *n.*[7] ; Melcarth worshipped at, v. 117
Ideals of humanity, two different, the heroic and the saintly, v. 300 ; great religious, a product of the male imagination, vi. 211
Ideler, L., on the date of the introduction of the fixed Alexandrian year, vi. 28 *n.*[1] ; on the Sothic period, vi. 37 *n.* ;

on the quadriennial and biennial festivals, vii. 86 ; on the Arab year before Mohammed, x. 217 *n.*[1]
Identification with an animal as a homoeopathic charm, i. 155 *sq.* ; of woman with corn, vii. 149 *sq.* ; of persons with corn, vii. 252 ; of girl with Maize Goddess, ix. 295
Ides of August, Diana's day, i. 12 *n.*[2]
Idhlozi, ancestral spirit in serpent form, among the Zulus, xi. 211
Idolatry of the Hebrews, iv. 168 *sqq.*
Idols, nails knocked into, ix. 69 *sq.*
Ife, in West Africa, the king of, sacrifices to his crown, i. 365
Igague, Lake of, in New Granada, mythical serpents in, ii. 156
Igaras of the Niger, succession to the kingship among the, ii. 294 ; their propitiation of dead leopards, viii. 228
Igbiras, the, of the Niger, their offerings of first-fruits to the dead, viii. 115
Igbodu, a sacred oracular grove of the Yourbas, ix. 212 *n.*[1]
Igliwa, a Berber people of the Atlas, their tug-of-war, ix. 178
Iglulik, Esquimaux of, i. 121, 316, x. 134
Ignorance of paternity, primitive, v. 106 *sq.*
Ignorrotes of Lepanto, in the Philippines their sacred trees, ii. 30
Igorrots of the Philippines believe that the souls of the dead are in eels, viii. 292
Ihering, R. von, as to the "sacred spring" of the ancient Italians, iv. 187 *n.*[4]
Ijebu tribe of Southern Nigeria, iv. 112
Il Mayek clan of the Njamus, their supposed power over irrigation water and the crops, vi. 39
Ilamatecutli, Mexican goddess, ix. 287 ; woman sacrificed in the character of, ix. 287 *sq.*
Ilex or holm-oak, iv. 81 *sq.* *See* Holm-oak
Ilium, animals sacrificed by hanging at, v. 292
Ill Luck embodied in an ascetic, ix. 41 ; the casting away of, ix. 144
Illi, river in China, i. 298
Illicit love supposed to blight the fruits of the earth, ii. 107 *sqq.*
Illumination, nocturnal, at festival of Osiris, vi. 50 *sq.* ; of graves on All Souls' Day, vi. 72 *sq.*, 74
Illyria, the Encheleans of, iv. 84
Ilmenau, witches burnt at, x. 6
Ilocans or Ilocanes of Luzon, their homoeopathic magic at sowing, i. 142 ; their custom as to children's cast teeth, i. 179 ; their fear of tree-spirits, ii. 18 ; their recall of the soul, iii. 44

Ilpirra of Central Australia, their belief in the reincarnation of the dead, v. 99

Iluvans of Malabar, marriage custom of the, x. 5

Im Thurn, Sir E. F., on the secrecy of personal names among the Indians of Guiana, iii. 324 *sq.* ; on the belief in spirits among the Indians of Guiana, ix. 78

Image of god made of dough and eaten sacramentally, viii. 86 *sqq.*, 90 *sq.*, 93 *sq.* ; carried through fire, xi. 4 ; reason for carrying over a fire, xi. 24

—— of snake carried about, viii. 316 *sq.*

Images, Hebrew prohibition of, i. 87 *n.*[1] ; of saints dipped in water as a rain-charm, i. 307 ; used in recovery of lost souls, iii. 55, 59 ; of gods masked and veiled during the king's sickness, iii. 95 *n.*[8] ; made to represent dead chiefs and supposed to be animated by their souls, iv. 199 ; of Osiris made of vege-table mould, vi. 85, 87, 90 *sq.*, 91 ; of ancestors, viii. 53 ; of animals sacri-ficed instead of the animals, viii. 95 *n.*[2] ; vicarious use of, viii. 96 *sqq.* ; spirits of ancestors take up their abode in, viii. 123 ; of gods, suggested origin of, viii. 173 *sq.* ; of vermin made as a protection against them, viii. 280 *sq.* ; stuck with nails, ix. 70 *n.*[1] ; demons conjured into, ix. 171, 172, 173, 203 ; colossal, filled with human victims and burnt, xi. 32 *sq.* *See also* Effigies, Idols, Puppets

—— magical, to injure people, i. 55 *sqq.* ; to procure offspring, i. 70-74 ; to win love, i. 77

Imagination, death from, iii. 135 *sqq.*

Imerina, in Madagascar, taboo on name of crocodile in, iii. 378

Imitation the basis of homoeopathic magic, i. 52

——, magical, of rain, i. 248 *sqq.* ; of thunder and lightning in rain-making ceremonies, i. 248, 258, 309 *sq.* ; of clouds in rain-making, i. 249, 256, 262, 275 ; of ducks and frogs in rain-making, i. 255 ; of rainbow in rain-charm, i. 288 ; of spirits by maskers in Borneo, vii. 186

Imitative or homoeopathic magic, i. 52 *sqq.*, iii. 295, vii. 262, viii. 267, 331, 334, ix. 177, 232, 248, 257, 404, x. 329, xi. 231

Immestar in Syria, alleged Jewish mockery of Christ at, ix. 394

Immortality attained by sacrifice, i. 373 *n.*[1] ; belief of savages in their natural, iv. 1 ; firm belief of the North American Indians in, iv. 137 ; Egyptian hope of, centred in Osiris,

vi. 15 *sq.*, 90 *sq.*, 114, 159 ; hope of, associated with Eleusinian mysteries, vii. 90 *sq.* ; human, in relation to the immortality of animals, viii. 260 *sqq.* ; how men lost the boon of, ix. 302 *sqq.* ; the burdensome gift of, x. 99 *sq.*

Immortality of animals, savage faith in the, viii. 260 *sqq.*

—— of the soul revealed in mysteries of Dionysus, vii. 15 ; attempted ex-perimental demonstration of the, xi. 276

Immortelles, wreaths of, on Midsummer Day, x. 177

Immutability of natural laws, i. 224

Impalement inflicted by the Assyrians, iv. 114 *n.*[1] ; as form of sacrifice, vii. 239

Impatiens sp., touch-me-not, bundle of, representative of the Indian goddess Gauri, ii. 77

Impersonal forces, idea of the world as a system of, not primitive, i. 374

Implements, magical, not allowed to touch the ground, x. 14 *sq.*

Impotence caused by magic of the dead, i. 150 ; homoeopathic cure of, i. 158 *sq.*

Impregnation by the souls of the dying iv. 199 ; without sexual intercourse belief in, v. 96 *sqq.*

—— of Isis by the dead Osiris, vi. 8, 20

"—— rite" at Hindoo marriages, x. 75

—— of women by fire, ii. 195 *sqq.*, 230 *sqq.*, 234, vi. 235 ; by serpents, v. 80 *sqq.* ; by the dead, v. 91 ; by ghosts, v. 93, ix. 18 ; by the flower of the banana, v. 93 ; through eating food, v. 96, 102, 103, 104, 105 ; by the sun, x. 74 *sq.* ; by the moon, x. 75 *sq.* *See also* Conception

Impressions effaced from superstitious motives, i. 213 *sq.* ; on the senses re-garded by savages as the work of spirits, ix. 72

——, bodily, contagious magic of, i. 213 *sq.*

Impurity of manslayers, iii. 167. *See* Uncleanness

Inachi, an offering of first-fruits, in Tonga, viii. 128, 131

Inanimate things, homoeopathic magic of, i. 157 *sqq.* ; transference of evil to, ix. 1 *sqq.*

Inao, sacred whittled sticks of the Aino, viii. 185, 186 *n.*, 189, ix. 261

Inari, Japanese rice-god, vii. 297

Inauguration of a king in ancient India, ix. 263 ; in Brahmanic ritual, x. 4

Inca, fast of the future, x. 19

Incantation recited at kindling need-fire, x. 290

Incantations for growth of crops, vii. 100 ; employed in arts and crafts, ix. 81. *See* Spells

Incarnate human gods, i. 373 *sqq.*, ii. 377 *sqq.*

Incarnation of gods in human form temporary or permanent, i. 376 ; examples of temporary incarnation, i. 376 *sqq.* ; examples of permanent incarnation, i. 386 *sqq.* ; mystery of, i. 396 *n.*[5] ; of divine spirit in Shilluk kings, iv. 21, 26 *sq.*

Incarnations of Buddha in the Grand Lamas, i. 410 *sq.*

Incas of Peru, their treatment of the navel-string, i. 196 ; claim kindred with the sun, i. 313 *n.*[3] ; the children of the Sun, i. 415, ii. 243, iii. 279 ; venerated the Pleiades, vii. 310 ; their annual expulsion of evils, ix. 128 *sqq.* ; their ceremony of the new fire, x. 132

Incense, fumes of, inhaled to produce inspiration, i. 379, 384 ; offered to sacred oak, ii. 16 ; fumigation with, a protection against witchcraft, ii. 336 ; used in exorcism, iii. 102 ; burnt at the rites of Adonis, v. 228 ; burnt in honour of the Queen of Heaven, v. 228 ; collected by a flail, vi. 109 *n.*[1] ; burnt as a protection against witches, ix. 158, 159

Incense-gatherers, chastity of, ii. 106 *sq.*

—— -tree thought to be protected by a spirit, ii. 112

Incest, blighting effects attributed to, ii. 108, 110 *sq.*, 113, 115 *sqq.* ; expiation for, ii. 110 *sq.*, 115, 116, 129 ; punished with death, ii. 110 *sq.* ; of domestic animals abhorred by the Basoga, ii. 112 *sq.* ; of animals employed as a rain-charm, ii. 113 ; with a daughter in royal families, reported cases of, v. 43 *sq.*

Incisions made in bodies of warriors as a preparation for war, iii. 161 ; in bodies of manslayers, iii. 174, 176, 180 ; in bodies of slain, iii. 176. *See also* Cuts, Scarification

Inconsistency of common thought, v. 4

—— and vagueness of primitive thought, xi. 301 *sq.*

Incontinence of young people supposed to be fatal to the king, iii. 6

Increase of the moon the time for increasing money, vi. 148 *sq.*

Indecencies in the Eleusinian mysteries, the Festival of the Threshing-floor, and the Thesmophoria, vii. 62 *sq.*

Indem tribe, on the Cross River, believe that the souls of the dead pass into trees, ii. 32

" Index of Superstitions," x. 270

India, use of magical images in modern, i. 64 *sq.* ; treatment of the placenta in, i. 194 ; contagious magic of footprints in, i. 209 ; ascendency of sorcerers over gods in modern, i. 225 ; rain-charm in, i. 282 ; rain-charms by means of frogs in, i. 293 *sqq.* ; whirlwinds regarded as *bhuts* in, i. 331 *n.*[2] ; incarnate human gods in, i. 376, 402 *sqq.* ; human gods of humble origin in, i. 376 ; marriages of trees and shrubs in, ii. 25 *sq.* ; marriage of human beings to trees in, ii. 57 ; unlucky marriages in, ii. 57 *n.*[4] ; certain wells thought to cure sterility of women in, ii. 160 ; gold and silver as totems in, iii. 227 *n.* ; iron as an amulet in, iii. 235 *sq.* ; rings as amulets in, iii. 315 ; names of animals tabooed in, iii. 401 *sqq.* ; belief and custom as to meteors in, iv. 63 ; natives of, comparatively indifferent to death, iv. 136 ; sacrifice of first-born children in, iv. 180 *sq.* ; images of Siva and Pârvatî married in, iv. 265 *sq.* ; hook-swinging in, iv. 278 *sq.* ; swinging as a religious or magical rite in, iv. 278 *sqq.* ; sacred women (dancing-girls) in, v. 61 *sqq.* ; impregnation of women by stone serpents in, v. 81 *sq.* ; burial of infants in, v. 93 *sq.* ; gardens of Adonis in, v. 239 *sqq.* ; eunuchs dedicated to a goddess in, v. 271 *n.* ; drinking moonlight as a medicine in, vi. 142 ; the last sheaf of corn at harvest in, vii. 222, 234 *n.*[2] ; human sacrifices for the crops in, vii. 243 *sqq.* ; ceremonies at eating the new rice in, viii. 55 *sq.* ; offerings of first-fruits in, viii. 116 *sqq.*; sticks or stones piled on scenes of violent death in, ix. 15 ; fear of demons in, ix. 89 *sqq.* ; the use of animals as scapegoats in, ix. 190 *sqq.* ; epidemics sent away in toy chariots in, ix. 193 *sq.* ; origin of the drama in, ix. 384 *sq.* ; seclusion of girls at puberty in, x. 68 *sqq.* ; fire-festivals in, xi. 1 *sqq.* ; sixty years' cycle in, xi. 77 *n.*[1] ; torture of suspected witches in, xi. 159 ; *Loranthus* in, xi. 317

India, ancient, ceremony performed by persons supposed to have been dead in, i. 75 ; the magical nature of ritual in, i. 228 ; rain-charms in, i. 289, 290; fighting the wind in, i. 328 ; magical power of kings in, i. 366 ; maxim not to look at one's reflection in water in, iii. 94 ; magic practised on refuse of food in, iii. 129 ; sacrificial victims strangled in, iii. 247 ; new king not allowed to shave his hair for a year in, iii. 260 ; mourners cut their hair and nails in, iii. 285 ; knots loosed at childbirth in, iii. 294 ; doctrine of the transmigration of human

souls into animals in, viii. 298 *sq.* ;
king beaten at his inauguration in, ix.
263 ; the Twelve Days in, ix. 324 *sq.* ;
the horse-sacrifice in, xi. 80 *n.*[3]; traditional cure of skin disease in, xi. 192
India, the Central Provinces of, sacred
trees in, ii. 43 ; belief as to man's
shadow in the, iii. 82 *sq.* ; peacock
worshipped among the Bhils of, viii.
29 ; transference of sickness among
the Korkus of, ix. 7 ; expulsion of
disease in the, ix. 190
——, the North-Western Provinces of,
belief as to shadow of goat-sucker in,
iii. 82 ; harvest custom in, vii. 222
sq. ; arrest and imprisonment of deities
in, ix. 61 ; the tug-of-war in, ix. 181
——, Northern, coco-nuts sacred in, ii.
51 ; the *emblica officinalis* sacred in,
ii. 51 ; eyes of owl eaten in, viii.
144 *sq.* ; Dravidian tribes of, ix. 259
——, South-Eastern, the Lhoosai of, ii.
48, vii. 122
——, Southern, the Kapu of, i. 284
n. ; the Malas of, i. 294, viii. 93 ;
inspired devil - dancers in, i. 382 ;
the Kuruvikkarans of, i. 382 ; the
Vellalas of, ii. 57 *n.*[4] ; the Todas of,
iii. 15, 271 ; the Adivi or forest Gollas
of, iii. 149 ; the Maravars of, iii. 234;
names of relations tabooed in, iii. 338;
the Canarese of, iii. 402 ; kings formerly killed after a twelve years' reign
in, iv. 46 *sqq.*; law of retaliation among
a robber caste of, iv. 141 *sq.* ; the
Malayans of, iv. 216 ; sacrifice of
finger-joints in, iv. 219 ; the Coorgs
of, viii. 55
——, Upper, transference of smallpox in,
ix. 6
——, Vedic, consecration of the sacrificer
of soma in, iii. 159 *n.*
Indian Archipelago, division of agricultural work between men and women in
the, vii. 124 ; head-hunting in the,
vii. 256 ; kinship of men with crocodiles in the, viii. 212 ; expulsion of
diseases in the, ix. 199 ; birth-custom
in the, xi. 155
—— ceremonies analogous to the rites
of Adonis, v. 227
—— legend parallel to Balder myth,
xi. 280
—— prophet, his objections to agriculture, v. 88 *sq.*
—— rain-charm by means of an otter, i.
289
—— ritual, ancient, at felling a tree, ii. 20
—— stories of the transference of human
souls, iii. 49
—— tribes of North-Western America,
their masked dances, ix. 375 *sqq.*

Indians of Arizona, mock human sacrifice
among the, iv. 215
—— of Brazil, their attention to the moon
more than to the sun, vi. 138 *n.* *See
also* Brazil
—— of British Columbia, their cannibal
orgies, vii. 18 *sq.* *See also* Columbia,
British
—— of California, their annual festivals
of the dead, vi. 52 *sq.* *See also* California *and* Californian Indians
—— of Canada, their ceremony of mitigating the cold of winter, iv. 259 *sq.*
—— of Costa Rica, their customs in
fasts, x. 20
—— of Granada seclude their future
rulers, x. 19
—— of North America, their customs on
the war-path, iii. 158 *sqq.* ; their fear
of naming the dead, iii. 351 *sqq.* ;
effeminate sorcerers among the, vi.
254, 255 *sq.* ; not allowed to sit on
bare ground in war, x. 5 ; seclusion
of girls among the, x. 41 *sqq.* ; imitate
lightning by torches, x. 340 *n.*[1] ; rites
of initiation into religious associations
among the, xi. 267 *sqq.* *See also* North
American Indians
—— of San Juan Capistrano, vii. 125 ;
their ceremony at the new moon, vi. 142 ;
sacrifice the great buzzard, viii. 169
sqq. ; their ordeal by stings of ants, x. 64
—— of South America, women's agricultural work among the, vii. 119 *sqq.* ;
mutual scourgings among the, ix. 262.
See also South American Indians
—— of tropical America represent the
rain-god weeping, vi. 33 *n.*[8]
—— of the Ucayali River in Peru, their
greeting to the new moon, vi. 142. *See
also* America *and* American Indians
Indifference to death displayed by many
races, iv. 136 *sqq.*
—— to paternity of kings under female
kinship, ii. 274 *sqq.*
Indo-China, conventional names for common objects on certain occasions in, iii.
404, 404 *n.*[8] ; the Thay of, viii. 121 ;
worship of spirits in, ix. 97 *sq.*
Indonesian ideas of rice-soul, vii. 181 *sq.* ;
treatment of the growing rice as a
breeding woman, vii. 183 *sq.*
Indra, great Indian god, viii. 120 ; thunderbolt of, i. 269 ; figure of, painted in ceremony for stopping rain, i. 296 ; father
of Gandharva-Sena, iv. 124 ; sacrificial
cake of first-fruits offered to, viii. 120 ;
creation of, ix. 410
—— and Apala, in the Rigveda, xi. 192
—— and the demon Namuci, Indian
legend of, xi. 280
—— and the dragon Vṛtra, iv. 106 *sq.*

Indrapoera, the rajah of, related to crocodiles, viii. 211

Indrapoora, story of the daughter of a merchant of, xi. 147

Industrial evolution from uniformity to diversity of function, i. 421

—— progress essential to intellectual progress, i. 218

Inersdorf, in Upper Bavaria, the Goat at threshing at, vii. 287

Infant, children whipt at death of an, ix. 261 *sq.*

Infant sons of kings placed by goddesses on fire, v. 180. *See also* Infants, Child, *and* Children

Infanticide among the Australian aborigines, iv. 187 *n.* [6]; sometimes suggested by a doctrine of transmigration or reincarnation of human souls, iv. 188 *sq.*; prevalent in Polynesia, iv. 191, 196 ; among savages, iv. 196 *sq.*

Infants, burial of, so as to ensure their rebirth, i. 103 *sqq.*, iv. 199, v. 91, 93 *sqq.*; at Gezer, v. 108 *sq.*; burial of murdered, in the room where they were born, ix. 45

—— exposed to the attacks of demons, iii. 235, 323

—— tabooed, iii. 255, x. 5, 20

Infection, supposed dangerous, of lying-in women, iii. 147 *sqq.*, 150 *sqq.*

—— of death, i. 143

—— of feminine weakness, iii. 202 *sq.*; dreaded by savages, iii. 164 *sq.*

Infectiousness of personal acts or states on principles of homoeopathic magic, i. 142 *sq.*, 147

Infertility, evil spirits of, ix. 250

Infidelity of wife thought to injure absent husband, i. 123, 124 *sq.*, 128, 131, iii. 197

Influence of the sexes on vegetation, ii. 97 *sqq.*; of great men on the popular imagination, vi. 199 ; of mother-kin on religion, vi. 202 *sq.*

Influenza expelled by scapegoat, ix. 191, 193

Ingarda tribe of West Australia, their belief as to the birth of children, v. 104

Ingiald, son of King Aunund, ate wolf's heart, viii. 146

Ingleborough in Yorkshire, underground streams near, v. 152 ; the need-fire near, x. 288

Ingleton in Yorkshire, need-fire at, x. 288

Ingniet or Ingiet, a secret society of New Britain, xi. 156

Inhaling smoke as means of inspiration, i. 383

Inheritance of property under mother-kin, rules of, vi. 203 *n.* [1]

Inishmurray, perpetual fire in the monastery of, ii. 241 *sq.*

Initiation, teeth knocked out at, in Australia, i. 176 ; custom of covering the mouth after, iii. 122 ; taboos observed by novices at, iii. 141 *sq.*, 156 *sq.*; new names given at, iii. 320, 383 ; in the Eleusinian mysteries associated with the hope of immortality, vii. 90 *sqq.*; by spirits, ix. 375 ; at puberty, pretence o killing the novice and bringing him to life again during, xi. 225 *sqq.*; of young men, bull-roarers sounded at the, xi. 227 *sqq.*, 233 *sqq.*. *See also* Initiatory Ceremonies

—— in Africa, xi. 251 *sqq.*

—— in Australia, xi. 227, 233 *sq.*; of a medicine-man in Australia, xi. 237 *sqq.*

—— in Ceram, xi. 249 *sqq.*

—— in Fiji, xi. 243 *sqq.*; apparently intended to introduce the novices to the worshipful spirits of the dead, xi. 246

—— in German New Guinea, xi. 193

—— in Halmahera, xi. 248

—— in New Britain, xi. 246 *sq.*

—— in New Guinea, xi. 239 *sqq.*

—— in North America, xi. 266 *sqq.*

—— in Rook, xi. 246

Initiatory ceremonies of Central Australian aborigines, i. 92 *sqq.*; of the Australian aborigines perhaps intended to ensure reincarnation after death, i. 101, 106

—— rite, gashes cut in back of novice, vii. 106

Injibandi tribe of West Australia, their belief as to the birth of children, v. 105

Injury to a man's shadow conceived as an injury to the man, iii. 78 *sqq.*

Inn, the lower valley of the river, the "Grass-ringers" in, ix. 247 ; effigies burnt at Midsummer in, x. 172 *sq.*

Innerste river of Central Germany, x. 124

Inning Goose, name for the harvest-supper, vii. 277 *n.* [3]

Innocents, Bishop of, in France, ix. 334 ; Festival of the, ix. 336 *sqq.*

Innocents' Day, young people beat each other on, ix. 270, 271 ; mock pope or bishop on, ix. 336, 337, 338

Innovations, the savage distrust of, iii. 230 *sqq.*

Innuits (Esquimaux), their belief as to venison and walrus, x. 13 *sq.* *See* Esquimaux

Ino and Melicertes, iv. 161, 162

Inoculation as a mode of exorcizing demons and ghosts, iii. 106 *sq.*; with moral and other virtues, viii. 158 *sqq.*

Inquisition, the, i. 407; commits the Brethren of the Free Spirit to the flames, i. 408 *sq.*

Insanity, supposed cause of, iii. 83; burying in an ant-hill as a cure for, x. 64

Inscription, in Etruscan letters, ii. 186; in Phoenician and Greek, at Malta, v. 16; bilingual, in Hittite and cuneiform, on a seal, v. 145 *n.*[2]

——, Greek, in sanctuary of the Mistress at Lycosura, iii. 227 *n.*, 314 *n.*[3]; of Aurelia Aemilia at Tralles, v. 38; at Paphos relating to Paphian Aphrodite, v. 43 *n.*[1]; relating to Olbian Zeus, v. 159; relating to Megarsian Athena, v. 169 *n.*[3]; relating to first-fruits at Eleusis, vii. 55 *sq.*; great Eleusinian, of 329 B.C., vii. 61 *n.*[4]; relating to worship of Zeus at Magnesia, viii. 7

——, the Moabite stone, v. 15 *n.*[3], 20 *n.*[2], 163 *n.*[3]

—— of Nebuchadnezzar, ix. 357 *n.*[3]

—— Palmyrene, v. 162 *n.*[2]

——, Phoenician, of King Yehaw-melech, v. 14; of King Panammu, v. 16 *n.*[1]; of King Uri-milk or Adon-milk, v. 17 *n.*[1]

——, the Rosetta stone, vi. 27, 151 *n.*[3]

Inscriptions, Arabic, found in Sheba, iii. 125 *n.*

——, Assyrian, relating to King Shamash-shumukin, v. 174 *n.*[1]; relating to Queen Shammuramat, v. 177 *n.*[1], ix. 370 *n.*[1]

——, Attic (Athenian), relating to the Eleusinian games, vii. 71, 71 *n.*[5], 79 *n.*[2]

——, Egyptian, treaty with Hittites, v. 136; Pyramid Texts, vi. 4

——, Elamite, ix. 367

——, Greek, relating to Zeus at Panamara in Caria, i. 29; relating to kings of Mytilene, i. 45 *n.*[4]; relating to kings of Paphos, v. 42 *n.*[5]; at Olba with names of Teucer, v. 144 *n.*[3], 151; relating to Corycian Zeus, v. 155; relating to Kanyteldeis, v. 158; relating to Hieropolis-Castabala, v. 168 *n.*[1]; at Mantinea, relating to Demeter and Persephone, vii. 46 *n.*[2]; relating to festivals at Eleusis, vii. 51, 51 *n.*[1], 52, 61, 63 *n.*[2], 72 *n.*

——, Hittite, v. 134, 135 *n.*, 136, 185 *n.*[3]

——, Latin, at Nemi and Aricia, i. 4 *n.*, 19 *n.*[2]; relating to Flamens, i. 20 *n.*[3]; relating to Kings of the Sacred Rites, i. 44 *n.*[1]; relating to *fictores Vestalium* and *fictores Pontificum*, i. 204; relating to Dianus, i. 381 *n.*[1]; relating to Jupiter Dolichenus, v. 136 *n.*[2]; relating to *Dendrophori*, v. 266 *n.*[2];

relating to the *taurobolium* or *tauropolium*, v. 275 *sq.*, 275 *n.*[1]; relating to the paternity of Jupiter, vi. 234

Insects, spirits of the dead thought to lodge in, i. 105, v. 95 *sq.*, vi. 162, viii. 290; homoeopathic magic of, i. 152; charms to protect the fields against, viii. 275 *sq.*, 279 *sq.*, 281; transmigration of sinners into, viii. 299

Insensibility to pain as a sign of inspiration, v. 169 *sq.*

Inspiration, i. 376 *sqq.*; shiverings and shakings as signs of, i. 377; produced by intoxication, i. 378; by incense, i. 379; by blood, i. 381 *sqq.*; by sacred plant or tree, i. 383 *sqq.*; by smoke, i. 383 *sq.*; by snuffing up the savour of sacrifice, i. 383 *n.*[3]; of victims, i. 384 *sqq.*; primitive theory of, iii. 248; insensibility to pain as sign of, v. 169 *sq.*; savage theory of, v. 299

——, prophetic, through the spirits of dead kings and chiefs, iv. 201, vi. 171, 172, 192 *sq.*; under the influence of music, v. 52 *sq.*, 54 *sq.*, 74

Inspired or religious type of man-god, i. 244

—— men, in China, ix. 117; walk through fire unharmed, xi. 5 *sq.*

—— men and women in the Pelew Islands, vi. 207 *sq.*

—— priests and priestesses, i. 377 *sqq.*

Insulation of women at menstruation, x. 97

Intellectual progress dependent on economic progress, i. 218

Intercalary month in the Celtic calendar of Gaul, ix. 342 *sqq.*

—— periods, customs and superstitions attaching to, ix. 328 *sq.*; deemed unlucky, ix. 339 *sqq.*

—— periods of five days, ix. 339 *sqq.*, 407 *n.*[1]

Intercalation introduced to correct the vague Egyptian year, vi. 26, 27, 28, ix. 340 *sq.*; in the ancient Mexican calendar, vi. 28 *n.*[3], ix. 339 *sq.*; in Greek calendar, vii. 81, 83; rudimentary, to equate lunar and solar years, ix. 325 *sqq.*

Intercourse of the sexes practised to make the crops and fruits grow, ii. 98 *sqq.*; with wives enjoined before war, iii. 164 *n.*[1]; enjoined on manslayers, iii. 176; between husbands and wives enjoined on various occasions among Bantu tribes, viii. 70 *n.*[1] *See also* Continence

Interlunar day, celebration of Sacred Marriages on the, iv. 73

Interpretation of the fire-festivals, x. 328 *sqq.*, xi. 15 *sqq.*

Interregnum on intercalary days, ix. 328 *sq.*
Interrex, ii. 296
Intervals of time, Greek and Latin modes of reckoning, iv. 59 *n.*[1]
Intichiuma, magical totemic ceremonies in Central Australia, i. 85, viii. 165 *n.*[2]
Intoxicating liquors drunk to produce inspiration, i. 378
Intoxication accounted inspiration, iii. 248, 249, 250
Inua, a person's shade, among the Esquimaux, iii. 96
Inuas, manlike shades or spirits of animals, among the Esquimaux, ix. 380, 381
Inuit.   *See* Esquimaux
Inuus, epithet applied to Faunus, vi. 234 *n.*[3]
Inverness, the *corp chre* in, i. 69
Inverness-shire, the harvest Maiden in, vii. 162 ; Beltane cakes in, x. 153
Inversion of social ranks at the Saturnalia and kindred festivals, ix. 308, 337, 339, 350, 407
Invisibility acquired by magical ointment made out of a mouldering corpse, viii. 163 *sq.*
Invisible, charm to make an army, vi. 251
Invocation of the dead, iii. 172
Invocavit Sunday, "Sawing the Old Woman" on, iv. 243
Invulnerability, charm to produce, i. 146 *sq.* ; acquired by inoculation, viii. 160 ; conferred by a species of mistletoe, xi. 79 *sq.* ; conferred by decoction of a parasitic orchid, xi. 81 ; of Balder, xi. 94 ; attained through blood-brotherhood with animal, xi. 201 ; thought to be attained through initiation, xi. 275 *sq.*, 276 *n.*[1]
Invulnerable warlock or giant, stories of the, xi. 97 *sqq.*
Inzia River, in Africa, vii. 119
Iolaus, friend of Hercules, v. 111
Iolcus, Jason at, iii. 311
Iona, St. Columba's tomb in, i. 160
Ionian women would not name their husbands, iii. 337
Iowa Indians, their respect for rattlesnakes, viii. 217 *sq.*
Iphiclus and Melampus, i. 158
Iphinoe, libations and offerings of hair on tomb of the maiden, i. 28
Ipswich witches, x. 304 *sq.*
Irac, province of, report of death of King of the Jinn in, iv. 8
Iraca, or Sogamozo, the pontiff of, i. 416
Iran, marriage custom in, x. 75
Iranian year, the old, vi. 67
Iranians, the old, their annual festival of the dead (Fravashis), vi. 67 *sq.*

Irawadi River, royal criminals sunk in the, iii. 242
Irayas of Luzon offer first-fruits to the souls of their ancestors, viii. 124
Ireland, "burying the sheaf" in, i. 69 ; woman burnt as a witch in, i. 236, x. 323 *sq.* ; hoops wreathed with rowan and marigolds carried on May Day in, ii. 63 ; the May Queen in, ii. 87 ; perpetual fires in, ii. 240 *sqq.* ; oaks and yews in the peat-bogs of, ii. 351 ; Druidism and Christianity in, ii. 363 ; cut hair preserved against the day of judgment by old women in, iii. 280 *sq.* ; divination by knotted threads in, iii. 304 *n.*[5] ; the old kings of, might not have any personal blemish, iv. 39 ; sacred oaks in, v. 37 *n.*[2] ; cutting the last corn (the *churn*) at harvest in, vii. 154 *sq.* ; hunting the wren in, viii. 319 *sq.* ; sticks or stones piled on scenes of violent death in, ix. 15 ; candles on Twelfth Night in, ix. 321 *sq.* ; the Druid's Glass in, x. 16 ; new fire at Hallowe'en in, x. 139, 225 ; Beltane fires in, x. 157 *sq.* ; Midsummer fires in, x. 201 *sqq.* ; fairies at Hallowe'en in, x. 226 *sq.* ; Hallowe'en customs in, x. 241 *sq.* ; witches as hares in, x. 315 *n.*[1] ; bathing at Midsummer in, xi. 29 ; cure for whooping-cough in, xi. 192 *n.*[1]
——, ancient, the Celts of, ii. 116 ; sacred oak groves in, ii. 242 *sq.*, 363 ; taboos observed by the kings of, iii. 11 *sq.* ; the great fairs of, iv. 99 *sq.*
Irish belief as to green boughs on May Day, ii. 52
—— crannogs, oak timber in the, ii. 352
—— custom as to a fall, iii. 68 ; as to friends' blood, iii. 244 *sq.*
—— kings, magical virtues attributed to, i. 367
—— legend of the self-sacrifice of monks to stay a plague, iv. 159 *n.*[1]
—— precautions against witches on May Day, ii. 53
—— sacrifice of firstlings, iv. 183
—— story of the external soul, xi. 132
Irle, J., on the sacred sticks representing ancestors of the Herero, ii. 223 *n.*[2] ; on the religion of the Herero, vi. 186 *sq.*
Iron, homoeopathic magic of, i. 159 *sq.* ; not to be touched, iii. 167 ; tabooed, iii. 176, 225 *sqq.* ; used as a charm against spirits, iii. 232 *sqq.*, viii. 51 ; not allowed to touch Atys, v. 286 *n.*[5] ; not to be used in digging fern root, xi. 65 ; mistletoe gathered without the use of, xi. 78 ; not to be used in cutting certain plants, xi. 81 *n.* ; customs observed by the Toradjas at the working of, xi. 154

Iron Age in Denmark, ii. 352
—— axe, use of, forbidden, viii. 248
—— Beard, Dr., a Whitsuntide mummer, iv. 208, 212, 233
—— instruments, use of, tabooed, iii. 205, 206
—— rings as talismans, iii. 235, 315
—— -wort, bunches of, held in the smoke of the Midsummer fires, x. 179
Ironwood trees, spirits of, propitiated, ii. 40
Iroquois, their belief in the spirits of trees and plants, ii. 12 ; their thunder-god, ii. 369 sq. ; names of the dead not mentioned among the, iii. 352 ; tell their tales of wonder only in winter, iii. 385 ; their myth of the Spirits of Corn, Beans, and Squashes, vii. 177 ; their sacrifice of white dogs, viii. 258 n.[1], ix. 127, 209 sq. ; their "festival of dreams," ix. 127 ; their New Year festival, ix. 127, 209 sq. ; their use of scapegoats, ix. 209 sq., 233 ; ceremony of the new fire among the, x. 133 sq. ; need-fire among the, x. 299 sq.
Irrigation in ancient Egypt, vi. 31 sq. ; rites of, in Egypt, vi. 33 sqq. ; sacrifices offered in connexion with, vi. 38 sq.
Isa or Parvati, an Indian goddess, wife of Mahadeva, v. 241
Isaac, Abraham's attempted sacrifice of, iv. 177, vi. 219 n.[1]
Isaacs, Nathaniel, on custom of putting Zulu kings to death, iv. 36 sq.
Isaiah (vii. 14), on the virgin who shall bear a son, i. 36 n.[2] ; (xxx. 33), on the king's pyre in Tophet, v. 177, 178 ; possible allusion to gardens of Adonis in (xvii. 10), v. 236 n.[1] ; (xxvi. 19), on dew, v. 247 n.[1] ; " houses of the soul " in (iii. 20), xi. 155 n.[3]
Iser Mountains in Silesia, Walpurgis bonfires to keep off witches in the, ix. 163
Iserlohn in Westphalia, custom of " quickening " cattle on May morning at, ix. 266 sq.
Isfendiyar and Rustem, x. 104 sq., 314
Ishtar, great Babylonian goddess, her love for Tammuz, v. 8 sq. ; her descent into the world of the dead, v. 8 sq., ix. 406 ; her title Dodah, v. 20 n.[2] ; associated with Sirius, ix. 359 n.[1] ; Esther equivalent to, ix. 365 ; served by harlots, ix. 372 ; at Erech, ix. 398 ; her visit to Anu, ix. 399 n.[1] ; goddess of fertility in animals, ix. 406 n.[1] See also Astarte
—— (Astarte) and Mylitta, v. 36, 37 n.[1]
—— and Gilgamesh, ix. 371 sq., 398 sq.
—— and Semiramis, ix. 369 sqq.
—— and Tammuz, ix. 399, 406

Isilimela, the Pleiades, among the Amazulu, vii. 316
Isis, shrine of, at Nemi, i. 5 ; watches over childbirth, ii. 133 ; how she discovered the name of Ra, iii. 387 sqq. ; in Sirius, iv. 5, vi. 34 sq., 152 ; and the king's son at Byblus, v, 180 ; invoked by Egyptian reapers, v. 232, vi. 45, 117 ; sister and wife of Osiris, vi. 6 sq., 116 ; and the scorpions, vi. 8 ; in the form of a hawk, vi. 8, 20 ; in the papyrus swamps, vi. 8 ; in the form of a swallow, vi. 9 ; at Byblus, vi. 9 sq. ; at the well, vi. 9, 111 n.[6] ; her search for the body of Osiris, vi. 10, 50, 85 ; recovers and buries the body of Osiris, vi. 10 sq., vii. 262 ; mourns Osiris, vi. 12 ; restores Osiris to life, vi. 13 ; date of the festival of, vi. 26 n.[2], 33 ; her tears supposed to swell the Nile, vi. 33 ; as a cow or a woman with the head of a cow, vi. 50, 85, 88 n.[1], 91 ; her priest wears a jackal's mask, vi. 85 n.[3] ; decapitated by her son Horus, vi. 88 n.[1] ; her temple at Philae, vi. 89, 111 ; her many names, vi. 115 ; a corn-goddess, vi. 116 sq. ; her discovery of wheat and barley, vi. 116 ; identified with Ceres, vi. 117 ; identified with Demeter, vi. 117 ; as the ideal wife and mother, vi. 117 sq. ; refinement and spiritualization of, vi. 117 sq. ; popularity of her worship in the Roman empire, vi. 118 ; her resemblance to the Virgin Mary, vi. 118 sq. ; dirge of, vi. 215 ; at Tithorea, festivals of, viii. 18 n.[1] ; in relation to cows, viii. 35 ; etymology of her name, viii. 35 n.[4] ; collects the scattered limbs of Osiris, viii. 264 ; the birth of, ix. 341
—— -Hathor, worship of, perhaps derived from reverence of pastoral peoples for their cattle, viii. 35 n.[2]
—— and Osiris perhaps personated by human couples, ix. 386
Isistines Indians of Paraguay, mourners refrain from scratching their heads among the, iii. 159 n.
Island, need-fire kindled in an, x. 290 sq., 291 sq.
Islay, the corp chre in, i. 68 ; the Old Wife at harvest in, vii. 141 sq. ; the harvest Cailleach in, vii. 166 ; cures for toothache in, ix. 62
Isle de France, the May-tree and Father May in, ii. 74 sq. ; harvest customs in, vii. 221, 226 ; Midsummer giant burnt in, xi. 38
—— of Man, St. Bridget in the, ii. 94 sq. ; May Day in the, iv. 258 ; Queen of May and Queen of Winter in the,

iv. 258 ; hunting the wren in the, viii. 318 *sq.* ; Beltane fires in the, x. 157. *See* Man, Isle of

Isle of May, St. Mary's well in, ii. 161
—— of St. Mary, inhabitants of, apologize to mother-whale for destroying her offspring, viii. 235

Islip, in Oxfordshire, May garlands at, ii. 62 *n.*[2]

Isocrates on Aeacus, ii. 360 *n.*; a competitor for prize of eloquence at Halicarnassus, iv. 95 ; on Demeter's gift of the corn, vii. 54 *sq.*

Isolation of the man-god, iii. 132

Isowa or Aïsawa, a religious order in Morocco, vii. 21. *See* Aïsawa

Israelites covet the foreskins of the Philistines, i. 101 *n.*[2]; their rules of ceremonial purity observed in war, iii. 157 *sq.*, 177 ; their custom of burning their children in honour of Baal, iv. 168 *sqq.* ; their brazen serpent, viii. 281. *See also* Jews

Issapoo, in Fernando Po, the cobra-capella worshipped at, viii. 174

Issini on the Gold Coast, custom observed by executioners at, iii. 171 *sq.*

Isthmian games held every two years, vii. 86 ; instituted in honour of Melicertes, iv. 93, 103

Istria, the Croats of, xi. 75

Iswara or Mahadeva, an Indian god, v. 241, 242

Italian and Celtic languages akin, ii. 189
—— money, the oldest, i. 23
—— peoples, ancient, their custom of the "sacred spring," iv. 186
—— women, their disposal of their loose hair, iii. 281

Italians, their myths of kings or heroes begotten by the fire-god, vi. 235 ; their cure for fever, ix. 55 ; their season for sowing in spring, ix. 346 ; the oak the chief sacred tree among the ancient, xi. 89 ; their stories of the external soul, xi. 105 *sqq.* ; their ancient practice of passing conquered enemies under a yoke, xi. 193 *sq.*
—— the early, a pastoral as well as an agricultural people, ii. 324

Italmens of Kamtchatka, their effigy of a wolf, 173 *n.*[4]

Italones, the, of the Philippine Islands, drink the blood of slain foes to acquire their courage, viii. 152

Italy, change in the flora of, i. 8 ; "Sawing the Old Woman " at Mid-Lent in, iv. 240 *sq.*; seven-legged effigies of Lent in, iv. 244 *sq.* ; swinging as a festal rite in modern, iv. 283, 284 ; hot springs in, v. 213 ; divination at Midsummer in, v. 254 ; "killing the Hare "

at harvest in, vii. 280 ; cure of warts in, ix. 48; birth-trees in, xi. 165 ; mistletoe in, xi. 316, 317

Italy, ancient, spinning on highroads forbidden to women in, i. 113, viii. 119 *n.*[5]; forests of, ii. 8 ; tree-worship in, ii. 10 ; sacred groves in, ii. 122 ; oaks sacred to Jupiter in, ii. 361 ; vintage inaugurated by priests in, viii. 133 ; colleges of the Salii in, ix. 232 ; the Ambarvalia in, ix. 359

Itasy, Lake, in Madagascar, proclamation to crocodiles at, viii. 214

Itch of Hercules, v. 209

Itonamas of South America, their way of detaining the soul in the body, iii. 31

Itongo, an ancestral spirit (Zulu term, singular of Amatongo), iii. 88 *n.*, vi. 184 *n.*[2], 185, viii. 166, xi. 202 *n.*

Itzgrund, in Saxe-Coburg, the last sheaf called the Old Woman at, vii. 139

Ivory Coast, the Baoules of the, iii. 70 ; human souls in bats on the, viii. 287 ; totemism among the -Siena of the, xi. 220 *n.*[2]

Ivy chewed by Bacchanals, i. 384 ; identified or associated with Dionysus, ii. 251, vii. 4 ; used in kindling fire by friction, ii. 251, 252 ; prohibition to touch or name, iii. 13 *sq.* ; sacred to Attis, v. 278 ; sacred to Osiris, vi. 112 ; to dream on, x. 242

Ivy Girl in Kent, vii. 153

Ixia, a kind of mistletoe, xi. 317, 318

Iyyar, Assyrian month, corresponding to May, ii. 130

Izdubar. *See* Gilgamesh

Ja-Luo tribes of Kavirondo, spearing a man's shadow among the, iii. 79 ; purification of manslayers among the, iii. 177 ; eat leopard's flesh to become brave, viii. 142

Jablanica, need-fire at, x. 286

Jabim. *See* Yabim

Jablonski, P. E., on Osiris as a sun-god, vi. 120

Jabme-Aimo, the abode of the dead, among the Lapps, viii. 257

Jack-in-the-Green, ii. 82, xi. 37
—— o' Lent, iv. 230
—— wood burnt in exorcism, iv. 216

Jackal, transmigration of sinner into, viii. 299
—— -god Up-uat, in ancient Egypt, vi. 154

Jackal's head, Egyptian priest represented wearing a, vii. 260
—— heart not eaten lest it make the eater timid, viii. 141
—— mask worn by priest of Isis, vi. 85 *n.*[3]

Jackals, tigers called, iii. 402, 403
Jackson, Professor Henry, on the Pole-
march at Athens, iii. 22 *n.*[1]; on the use
of swallows as scapegoats in ancient
Greece, ix. 35 *n.*[3]
Jacob wrestling with the angel, American
Indian parallel to the story of, viii.
264 *sqq.*
Jacob of Edessa, viii. 280 *n.*
Jacob, G., on the fire-drill of the ancient
Bedouins, ii. 209
Jacobsen, J. Adrian, on the Secret
Societies of North-Western America,
ix. 377 *sqq.*
Jaffa, new Easter fire carried to, x.
130 *n.*
Jaga, title of the king of Cassange, iv.
56, 203
Jagas, a tribe of Angola, their custom of
infanticide, iv. 196 *sq.*
Jaggas of East Africa, their fire customs,
ii. 259
Jagor, as to ignorance of the art of
making fire, ii. 254 *n.*
Jaguar imitated by actor or dancer, ix.
381
Jaguars eaten in order to acquire courage,
viii. 140; souls of dead in, viii. 285, 286
Jahn, U., on girding fruit-trees with straw
at Christmas, ii. 17 *n.*[5]
Jaintias or Syntengs, a Khasi tribe of
Assam, custom of religious suicide
among the, iv. 55
Jakkaneri, in the Neilgherry Hills, the
fire-walk at, xi. 9
Jakun, the, of the Malay Peninsula,
power of medicine-men among the, i.
360; use a special language in searching for camphor, iii. 405
Jalina piramurana, a headman of the
Dieri, i. 336
Jalno, temporary ruler at Lhasa, ix. 218
sqq.
Jamadwitiya Day in Behar, brothers reviled by sisters on, i. 279
Jambi in Sumatra, temporary kings in,
iv. 154
Jamblichus on insensibility to pain as
sign of inspiration, v. 169; on the
purifying virtue of fire, v. 181
James, M. R., on the charges of ritual
murder brought against the Jews, ix.
395 *ns.*[2] and [3]; on the Sibyl's Wish,
x. 100 *n.*
James and Philip, the Apostles, feast of,
x. 158
James II. touches for scrofula, i. 370
Jamieson, John, on the fairies and Trows,
ix. 168 *n.*[1], 169 *n.*[2]; on the ''quarter-
ill,'' x. 296 *n.*[1]
Jana, another form of Diana, ii. 381,
382, 383. *See* Diana

Jangam, priest of the Lingayats, worshipped as a god, i. 404 *sq.*
Janiculum hill, the, secession of the
plebeians to, ii. 186; and the grove
of Helernus, ii. 190 *n.*[3]; the oak-
woods of the, ii. 382; Janus as a king
resident on, ii. 382
Jankari, a god, human sacrifices for the
crops offered to, vii. 244
Janua, derived from Janus, ii. 384
January, the 6th of, reckoned in the East
the Nativity of Christ, v. 304, x. 246;
the Holi festival in, xi. 1; the fire-
walk in, xi. 8
Janus, two-faced images like those of,
set up by mothers of still-born twins, i.
269 *n.*[1]; a god of the sky, ii. 381 *sq.*;
called Junonian, ii. 382; as a god of
doors, ii. 383 *sq.*; explanation of the
two-headed, ii. 384 *sq.*; double-headed
images of, with stick and key, ii. 385;
in Roman mythology, vi. 235 *n.*[6]
—— and Carna, ii. 190
—— (Dianus) and Diana, doubles of
Jupiter and Juno, ii. 190 *sq.*, 381 *sq.*
—— and Jupiter, xi. 302 *n.*[2]
Janus-like deity on coins, v. 165
Japan, contagious magic of footprints in,
i. 208 *sq.*; black dog sacrificed for rain
in the mountains of, i. 291 *sq.*; rain-
making by means of a stone in, i. 305;
the Mikado of, i. 417, iii. 2 *sqq.*; fruit-
trees threatened in, to make them bear
fruit, ii. 21; Kaempfer's history of,
iii. 3 *n.*[2]; Caron's account of, iii. 4
n.[2]; mock human sacrifices in, iv.
218; annual festival of the dead in, vi.
65; superstitious practice of robbers
in, vii. 235 *n.*[3]; the fox associated with
the rice-god in, vii. 297; the Ainos of,
viii. 52, x. 20, xi. 60; cure for toothache in, ix. 71; expulsion of demons
in, ix. 118 *sq.*, 143 *sq.*; Feast of
Lanterns in, ix. 151 *sq.*; annual expulsion of evil in, ix. 212 *sq.*; ceremony of new fire in, x. 137 *sq.*; the
fire-walk in, xi. 9 *sq.*
Japanese, their use of magical images, i.
60, 71; treatment of the placenta
among the, i. 195; use ropes to keep
off demons, ix. 154 *n.*
Japanese account of the Aino bear-
festival, viii. 187 *sq.*
—— alps, rain-making in the, i. 251
—— deities of the Sun, vii. 212
—— mode of procuring rain by an artificial dragon, i. 297; by doing violence
to deity, i. 297
Japura River in Brazil, viii. 157
Jar, the evils of a whole year shut up in
a, ix. 202. *See also* Jars
Jaray. *See* Chréais

Jargon, artificial, used by searchers for eagle-wood, iii. 404. *See also* Language, special

Järischau, in Silesia, athletic sports at harvest at, vii. 76

Jarkino, trees respected in, ii. 18

Jars, winds kept by priest in, iii. 5 ; souls conjured into, iii. 70 ; burial in, iv. 12 *sq.*, v. 109 *n.*[1]. *See also* Jar

Jasmine married to a tamarind in India, ii. 25

Jason and Medea, v. 181 *n.*[1]

—— and Pelias, iii. 311 *sq.*

Jassnitz, in Moravia, custom of "Carrying out Death" at, iv. 238 *sq.*

Jastrow, Professor M., on the festival of Tammuz, v. 10 *n.*[1] ; on the character of Tammuz, v. 230 *n.*; on the epic of Gilgamesh, ix. 399 *n.*[1]

Jatakas, collection of Buddhist tales, viii. 299 *n.*[5], ix. 41, 45

Jaundice treated by homoeopathic magic, i. 79 *sqq.*; called the royal disease, i. 371 *n.*[4] ; transferred to a tench, ix. 52

Java, magical images in, i. 58 ; ceremonies to procure offspring in, i. 73 ; belief as to the homoeopathic magic of house timber in, i. 146 ; charm to produce sleep in, i. 148 ; treatment of the afterbirth in, i. 192 ; rain-making in, i. 257 *sq.*; ceremonies for preventing rain in, i. 270 *sq.* ; rain-charm by means of cats in, i. 289 ; special forms of speech used in addressing social superiors in, i. 402 *n.* ; modes of deceiving the spirits of plants in, ii. 23 ; sexual intercourse practised to promote the growth of rice in, ii. 98 ; ceremony at tapping a palm-tree for wine in, ii. 100 *sq.*; custom observed in, when a child is first set on the ground, iii. 34 ; rice placed on heads of persons after a great danger in, iii. 35 ; remedy for gout or rheumatism in, iii. 106 ; the Baduwis of, iii. 115 ; superstitions as to the head in, iii. 254 ; everything opened in house to facilitate childbirth in, iii. 297 ; tabooed words in, iii. 409, 411 ; the Sultans of, hereditary custom of suicide practised for their benefit, iv. 53 *sq.* ; the Tenggeres (Tenggerese) of, iv. 130 *n.*[1], ix. 184 ; conduct of natives in an earthquake, v. 202 *n.*[1]; Valley of Poison in, v. 203 *sq.*; worship of volcanoes in, v. 220 *sq.* ; use of winnowing-basket as cradle in, vii. 6 ; Rice-bride and Rice-bridegroom in, vii. 199 *sqq.* ; earthworms eaten by dancing girls in, viii. 147 ; kinship of men with crocodiles in, viii. 212 ; belief in demons in, ix. 86 *sq.* ; birth-trees in, xi. 161 *n.*[1]

Javanese, their mode of rain-making i. 248 ; shadow-plays as a rain-charm among the, i. 301 *n.*; treat rice in bloom like a pregnant woman, ii. 28 ; ascribe a soul to rice, vii. 183

Jawbone of ancestor in magical ceremony, i. 312 ; the ghost of the dead thought to adhere to the, vi. 167 *sq.*

—— and navel-string of Kibuka, the war-god of the Baganda, vi. 197

Jawbones of deer and pigs, magical use of, i. 109 ; of executed persons a protective against their ghosts, iii. 171 ; of dead kings of Uganda preserved and worshipped, i. 196, iv. 200 *sq.*, vi. 167 *sq.*, 169 *sq.*, 171 *sq.*; the ghosts of the kings supposed to attach to their jaw-bones, vi. 169 ; of slain beasts propitiated by hunters, viii. 244 *sq.*

Jaws of corpse tied up to prevent the escape of the soul, iii. 31

Jay, blue, as scapegoat, ix. 51

Jâyi or Jawâra, festival in Upper India, v. 242

Jealousy, transferred to ants, ix. 33

Jebel Bela mountain, in the Sudan, wizard in form of hyaena on the, x. 313

—— *Hissar*, Olba, v. 151

—— Nuba, district of the Eastern Sudan, a species of birds respected in, viii. 221

Jebu, on the Slave Coast, the king of, not to be seen by anybody, iii. 121

Jehovah, savage taboos disguised as the will of, iii. 219 ; in relation to thunder, v. 22 *n.*[3] ; in relation to rain, v. 23 *n.*[1]

Jensen, P., on rock-hewn sculptures at Boghaz-Keui, v. 137 *n.*[4] ; on Hittite inscription, v. 145 *n.*[2] ; on Syrian god Hadad, v. 163 *n.*[3]; on etymology of Purim, ix. 362 *n.*[1]; his theory of Haman and Vashti as Elamite deities, ix. 366 *sq.* ; on Anaitis, ix. 369 *n.*[1]; on the fast of Esther, ix. 398 *sq.*

Jeoud, the only-begotten son of Cronus, sacrificed by his father, iv. 166

Jepur in India, use of scapegoat at, ix. 191

Jeremiah (vii. 31, xix. 5, xxxii. 35), on the burnt sacrifice of children, iv. 169 *n.*[3] ; (xxix. 26), on the prophet as a madman, v. 77 ; (ii. 27), on birth from stocks and stones, v. 107

Jericho, death of Herod at, v. 214 ; wild boars at, viii. 32

Jerome, on the Celtic language of the Galatians, ii. 126 *n.*[2], xi. 89 *n.*[2] ; on Tophet, iv. 170 ; on the date of the month Tammuz, v. 10 *n.*[1] ; on the worship of Adonis at Bethlehem, v. 257

Jerome of Prague, missionary to the heathen Lithuanians, on their worship of trees, ii. 46 ; on Lithuanian worship of the sun, i. 317 *sq.*

Jerusalem, the temple at, built without iron, iii. 230 ; the sacrifice of children at, iv. 169, vi. 219 ; mourning for Tammuz at, v. 11, 17, 20, ix. 400 ; the Canaanite kings of, v. 17 ; "sacred men" in the temple at, v. 17 ; the returned captives at, v. 23 ; the Destroying Angel over, v. 24 ; besieged by Sennacherib, v. 25 ; religious music at, v. 52 ; "great burnings" for the kings at, v. 177 *sq.* ; the king's pyre at, v. 177 *sq.* ; Church of the Holy Sepulchre at, Good Friday ceremonies in the, v. 255 *n.* ; ceremony of the new fire at Easter in, x. 128 *sq.*

" ——, the Road of," iv. 76

Jesus Christ, crossbills at the crucifixion of, i. 82 ; the historical reality of, ix. 412 *n.²*

Jetté, J., on the power of medicine-men among the Tinneh Indians, i. 357

Jeugny, the forest of, xi. 316

Jevons, F. B., on burial customs in Ceos, i. 105 ; on the opposition between religion and magic, i. 225 *n.* ; on the Roman *genius*, xi. 212 *n.*

Jewish calendar, New Year's Day of the, ix. 359

—— children, their custom as to cast teeth, i. 178

—— converts, form of abjuration used by, ix. 393

—— Day of Atonement, ix. 210

—— festival of Purim, ix. 360 *sqq.* ; the great deliverance of Jews at the, ix. 398

—— high priest, viii. 27, ix. 210

—— hunters pour out blood of game, iii. 241

—— priests, their rule as to the pollution of death, vi. 230

—— remedy for jaundice, i. 81

Jewitt, J. R., on the father of twins among the Nootkas, i. 264 ; on ritual of mimic death among the Nootka Indians, xi. 270

Jews, their attitude to the pig, viii. 23 *sq.* ; their ablutions, viii. 27 ; their use of scapegoats, ix. 210 ; accused of ritual murders, ix. 394 *sqq.*

—— of Egypt, costume of bride and bridegroom among the, vi. 260

——, Polish, their belief as to falling stars, iv. 66

—— of Roumania, mode of facilitating childbirth among the, iii. 298

Jeyt, Indian month, iv. 279

Jharkhandi, an Indian forest god, viii. 119

Jinn, haunt certain trees, ii. 34 ; the servants of their magical names, iii. 390 ; death of the King of the, iv. 8 ; falling stars thought to be, iv. 63 ; transferred from human beings to animals, ix. 31 ; belief in the, in modern Egypt, ix. 104 ; infesting camels, ix. 260

Jinnee of the sea, virgins married to a ii. 153 *sq.*

Joannes Lydus, on Phrygian rites at Rome, v. 266 *n.²* ; on Mamurius Veturius, ix. 229 *n.¹*

Job (xxxviii. 13), "the sweet influences of the Pleiades," vii. 319 *n.¹*

Job's protest, ii. 114

Jochelson, W., on the whale-festivals of the Koryaks, viii. 232 ; on the belief of the Koryaks in demons, ix. 101

Johanniswurzel, the male fern, xi. 66

John Barleycorn, Burns on, v. 230 *sq.*

Johns, Rev. Dr. C. H. W., on Babylonian votaries, v. 71 *ns.*³ and ⁵ ; on the name Zagmuku, ix. 357 *n.²* ; on the change of *m* into *w* or *v* in Semitic, ix. 367 *n.²* ; on the reading of an Elamite inscription, ix. 367 *n.³*

Johnson, Bishop James, on human scapegoats among the Yorubas, ix. 211 *sq.*

Johnson, Dr. Samuel, in the Highlands, i. 368 ; touched for scrofula by Queen Anne, i. 370 ; on Highland custom of beating a man in a cow's hide, viii. 322

Johnston, Sir H. H., on the diffusion of round huts in Africa, ii. 227 *n.³* ; on eunuch priests on the Congo, v. 271 *n.*

Johnstone, Rev. A., on Hallowe'en fires in Buchan, x. 233

Jokumara, a rain-god in Southern India, his effigy used in a rain-making ceremony, i. 284 *n.*

Jônee, joanne, jouanne, the Midsummer fire (the fire of St. John), x. 189

Jonendake, Mount, in Japan, rain-making ceremonies on, i. 251

Jordan, H., on the ordeal of battle in ancient Italy, ii. 321

Jordan, banks of the, infested by wild boars, viii. 32

Jordanus, Friar, on voluntary suicide in honour of idols in India, iv. 54

Josephus, on worship of kings of Damascus, v. 15 ; on the Tyropoeon, v. 178 ; on the Egyptian abstinence from swine's flesh, viii. 24 *n.²*

Josiah, King, his religious reform, v. 17 *n.⁵*, 18 *n.³*, 25, 107

Jotham, the fable of, ii. 315

Joubert, on religion, quoted, i. 223 *n.²*

Journey, conduct of women in absence of men on a, i. 125 ; purificatory ceremonies on return from a, iii. 111 *sqq.* ; continence observed on a, iii. 204 ; hair kept unshorn on a, iii. 261 ; knots as a charm on a, iii. 306, 310

Journeys, conventional names for common objects on long and perilous journeys, iii. 404 *n.*[3]

Joustra, M., on the fear of evil spirits among the Bataks, ix. 88

Jove (Father) and Mother Vesta, ii. 227 *sqq. See* Jupiter

Joyce, P. W., on Irish fairs, iv. 100 *n.*[1], 101 ; on driving cattle through fires, x. 159 *n.*[2]; on the bisection of the Celtic year, x. 223 *n.*[2]

Jualamukhi in the Himalayas, perpetual fires, v. 192

Jubainville, H. d'Arbois de, on a passage of Maximus Tyrius, ii. 362 *n.*[6] ; on Irish fairs, iv. 101

Judah, idolatrous kings of, their sacrifice of chariots and horses to the sun, i. 315 ; kings of, their custom of burning their children, iv. 169 ; laments for dead kings of, v. 20 ; the purple hills of, v. 215

Judas, effigies of, burnt in Easter fires, x. 121, 127 *sq.*, 130 *sq.*, 143, 146, xi. 23 ; driven out of church on Good Friday, x. 146

Judas candle, x. 122 *n.*

—— fire at Easter, x. 123, 144

Judean landscape, the austerity of the, v. 23 ; maid impregnated by serpent, v. 81

Judith, widow of Ethelwulf, ii. 283

Juggernaut, pilgrimage to, iv. 132

Jugra, in Selangor, durian-trees threatened at, ii. 21

Juhar, the Bhotiyas of, ix. 209

Juice of grapes conceived as blood, iii. 248

Jujube, arrows of the thorny, used to shoot at demons, ix. 146

Jujus, fetishes, i. 349

Jukagirs of Siberia, taboos observed by the sisters of hunters among the, i. 122

Jukos, the, of Nigeria, kings of, put to death, iv. 34 ; inoculate themselves before hunting elephants, viii. 160

Julbuck, the Yule goat, in Scandinavia, viii. 327

Julian, the Emperor, on the Hercynian forest, ii. 7 ; his entrance into Antioch, v. 227, 258 ; on the Mother of the Gods, v. 299 *n.*[3] ; restores the standard cubit to the Serapeum, vi. 217 *n.*[1]

Julian calendar introduced by Caesar, vi. 37, 93 *n.*[1] ; used by Mohammedans, x. 218 *sq.*

—— year, vi. 28

Julii, the, descended from Julus, ii. 179 ; rivals of the Silvii, ii. 182 ; as Little Jupiters, ii. 192

Julus, the Little Jupiter, ancestor of the Julii, ii. 179

Julus or Ascanius, the son of Aeneas, ii. 197

July, procession of giants at Douay in, xi. 33

—— the 5th, the Flight of the People at Rome on, ii. 319 *n.*[1]

—— the 7th, death of Romulus on, ii. 181 ; the festival of the *Nonae Caprotinae* at Rome, ii. 313 *sq.*, ix. 258 ; Lord of Misrule at Bodmin on, ii. 319 *n.*[1]

—— the 25th, St. James's Day, flower of chicory cut on, xi. 71

Jumièges, in Normandy, Brotherhood of the Green Wolf at, x. 185 *sq.*, xi. 25

Jumping over wife or children as a ceremony, iii. 112 ; over wife as a ceremony, iii. 164 *n.*[1], viii. 64, 253, x. 23 ; over a bonfire, iv. 262 ; over a woman, significance of, viii. 70 *n.*[1], x. 23. *See also* Leaping

Juncus tenuis in homoeopathic magic, i. 144

June, named after Juno, ii. 190, 190 *n.*[2]; Khasi ceremony of " driving away the plague " in, ix. 173 ; Mexican human sacrifice in, ix. 283 ; the fire-walk in, xi. 6

—— the 1st, a Roman festival, ii. 190

—— the 9th, Vesta's festival on, ii. 127 *n.*[2]

—— the 15th, St. Vitus's Day, x. 335

—— the 29th, St. Peter's Day, iv. 262

Juneh, magical pool at, where childless couples bathe, ii. 160

Jungle Mother, in Northern India, her shrines consist of piles of stones and branches, ix. 27

Juniper worn by mourners, iii. 143 ; burned to keep out ghosts, ix. 154 *n.* ; used to beat people with, ix. 271 ; burnt in need-fire, x. 288 ; used to fumigate byres, x. 296

Juniper berries, houses fumigated with, as a protection against witches, ix. 158

Juniperus excelsa, the *chili*-tree, a kind of cedar, sacred in Gilgit, ii. 49, 50

Juno on the Capitol, ii. 184, 189 ; her oak crown, ii. 184, 189 ; at Falerii, ii. 190 *n.*[2] ; a duplicate of Diana, ii. 381 *sq.* ; the Flaminica Dialis sacred to, vi. 230 *n.*[2] ; the wife of Jupiter, vi. 231 ; serpent in sacred grove of, at Lanuvium, viii. 18

—— and Diana, xi. 302 *n.*[2]

Juno Caprotina, the milky juice of the wild fig-tree (*caprificus*) offered to, ii. 313, 317, ix. 258 ; on a Roman coin, viii. 18 *n.*[2]

—— Lucina, no knots on garments of women in rites of, iii. 294

—— Moneta, ii. 189

Junod, Henri A., on twins regarded as children of the sky, i. 268 ; on superstitions as to miscarriage in childbirth, iii. 152 *sqq.* ; on the profundity of savage ritual, iii. 420 *n.*[1]; on the worship of the dead among the Thonga, vi. 180 *sq.*; on woman's part in agriculture among the Baronga, vii. 114 *sq.*

Juok, the supreme god and creator of the Shilluks, iv. 18, vi. 165

Jupiter, ox sacrificed to, as expiation, ii. 122 ; costume of, ii. 174 *sq.* ; the Roman kings in the character of, ii. 174 *sqq.*, ii. 266 *sq.*; oaks sacred to, ii. 175, 176 ; as god of the oak, the thunder, the rain, and the sky, ii. 178, 358, 361 *sq.* ; worshipped on the Capitol, ii. 361 ; as sky-god, ii. 374 ; a duplicate of Janus (Dianus), ii. 381 *sq.*, xi. 302 *n.*[2]; the husband of Juno, vi. 231 ; the father of Fortuna Primigenia, vi. 234 ; (Zeus) said to have transferred the sceptre to the young Dionysus, vii. 13 ; lamb sacrificed by Flamen Dialis to, viii. 133 ; perhaps personified by the King of the Wood, the priest of Diana at Nemi, xi. 302 *sq.*

—— the Fruitful One, ii. 362

—— and Juno, doubles of Janus (Dianus) and Diana, ii. 190 *sq.*, 381 *sq.*, xi. 302 *n.*[2]; sacred marriage of, ii. 190

—— and Juturna, vi. 235 *n.*[6]

——, Latian, on the Alban Mount, ii. 187, 379 ; human sacrifices in honour of, ix. 312 *n.*[1]

——, the Little, ii. 179, 192

——, the Rainy, ii. 362 *n.*[1]

—— and Saturn, ii. 323

——, the Serene, ii. 362

——, the Showery, ii. 362 *n.*[1]

Jupiter Capitoline, ii. 176, 187; robbed by Julius Caesar, i. 4; custom of annually knocking a nail in temple of, ix. 66, 67 *n.*[1]; represented by an oak-tree, xi. 89

—— Dianus, ii. 382

—— Dolichenus, v. 136

—— Elicius, ii. 183

—— Indiges, ii. 181

—— Liber, temple of, at Furfo, iii. 230

Jupiter, the planet, period of revolution of, iv. 49, xi. 77 *n.*[1]

Jupiters, probably many local, in Latium, ii. 184

Jura, fire-custom at Lent, in the, x. 114

Jura Mountains, Midsummer bonfires in the, x. 188 *sq.* ; the Yule log in the, x. 249

Jurby, parish of, in the Isle of Man, x. 305

Justice and Injustice in Aristophanes, v. 209

Justin, on the "sacred spring" among the Gauls, iv. 187 *n.*[5]

Justin II., Emperor of the East, his embassy to the Turks, iii. 102

Justin Martyr on the resemblances of paganism to Christianity, v. 302 *n.*[4]

Jutland, belief as to eating white snake in, viii. 146 ; sick children and cattle passed through holes in turf in, xi. 191 ; superstitions about a parasitic rowan in, xi. 281

Juturna, a water-nymph, the wife of Janus, ii. 382 ; beloved by Jupiter, ii. 382 ; in Roman mythology, vi. 235 *n.*[6]

Ka, spiritual double or external soul in ancient Egypt, ii. 134 *n.*[1], iii. 28, xi. 157 *n.*[2]

Kabadi, a district of British New Guinea, seclusion of girls at puberty in, x. 35

Kabenau river, in German New Guinea, ceremony of initiation on the, xi. 193

Kabuis, the, of Assam, their taboos at sowing and reaping, vii. 109 *n.*[2]

—— of Manipur, chastity before sowing among the, ii. 106

Kabyle tale, milk-tie in a, xi. 138 *n.*[1]; the external soul in a, xi. 139

Kabyles, marriage custom of the, to ensure the birth of a boy, vi. 262 ; their cure for jealousy, ix. 33

Kacha Nagas of Assam, parents named after their children among the, iii. 333

Kacharis, the, of Assam, their fear of demons, ix. 93

Kachh, the Rao of, i. 385 *n.*[1]

Kachins of Burma, their custom of making a new fire on taking possession of a new house, ii. 237 *sq.* ; continence of women at brewing beer among the, iii. 200 ; their offerings at sowing and reaping, viii. 121 *sq.*; their belief in demons, ix. 96

Kadesh, a Semitic goddess, v. 137 *n.*[2]

Kadiak, island off Alaska, uncleanness of women at childbirth in, iii. 148 ; customs as to whalers in, iii. 191 *sq.*

Kadombookoo, in Celebes, prayers for rain at a chief's grave in, i. 286

Kadouma, near the Victoria Nyanza, drums beat to still a storm at, i. 328

Kaempfer's *History of Japan*, iii. 3 *sq.*

Kafa, custom as to eating in, iii. 119 *n.*[6]

Kaffa, in East Africa, divine pope at, i. 410

Kafirs of the Hindoo Koosh, dances of their women while men are away fighting, i. 133 *sq.*; their test of a sacrificial victim, i. 385 ; sacred persons among them defiled by contact with a dog, iii. 13 *n.*[6]

Kahma, in Burma, annual extinction of fires in, x. 136

Kai of German New Guinea, their belief in conception without sexual intercourse, v. 96 sq. ; their superstitious practices to procure good crops, vii. 100 ; their games played to promote the growth of the crops, vii. 101 sq. ; their stories told to promote the growth of the crops, vii. 102 ; their observation of the Pleiades, vii. 313 ; why field labourers among them will not eat pork, viii. 33 ; eat the brains of slain foes, viii. 152 ; their belief in transmigration, viii. 296 ; beat their banana shoots to make them grow, ix. 264 ; their seclusion of women at menstruation, x. 79 ; their use of a cleft stick as a cure, xi. 182 ; their rites of initiation, xi. 239 sqq.

Kaiabara, Australian tribe, avoidance of names of the dead among the, iii. 351

Kaikolans, a Tamil caste, their dedication of girls to temple service, v. 62

Kail, divination by stolen, at Hallowe'en, x. 234 sq.

Kaimani Bay, in Dutch New Guinea, division of labour between the sexes among the natives of, vii. 123

Kaitish tribe of Central Australia, their ceremony to make grass grow, i. 87 sq. ; burial customs of the, i. 102 ; their treatment of the navel-string, i. 183 ; their rain-making, i. 258 sq. ; their continence at ceremonies to make grass grow, ii. 105 ; their belief as to the shadow of a hawk, iii. 82 ; custom of father after childbirth among the, iii. 295 ; their belief as to falling stars, iv. 60 ; their belief in the reincarnation of the dead, v. 99

Kakian association in Ceram, rites of initiation in the, xi. 249 sqq.

Kalahari desert, the Bushmen of the, ii. 218 n.[1]

Kalamantans, the, of Borneo, their descent from a deer, iv. 126 sq. ; their belief in the transmigration of human souls into animals, viii. 293 sq.

Kalamba, the, a chief in the Congo region, ceremony observed by subject chiefs on visiting, iii. 114

Kalanga Mountain, in Rhodesia, sacrifice at chief's grave on the, viii. 113

Kalat el Hosn, in Syria, shrine of St. George at, resorted to by childless women, ii. 346, v. 78

Kalau, demons, among the Koryaks, ix. 101

Kali, bloodthirsty Indian goddess, inspired priest of, i. 382 ; used to devour a king a day, iv. 123

Kalids, kaliths, deities in the Pelew Islands, vi. 204 n.[4], 207, ix. 81 sq. ; sacred animals of the Pelew Islanders, viii. 293 n.[2]

Kalingooa, village of Celebes, rain-making at, i. 286

Kalmucks, their consecration of a white ram, viii. 313 sq. ; story of the external soul among the, xi. 142, See also Calmucks

Kalotaszeg in Hungary, continence at sowing at, ii. 105

Kalunga, the supreme god of the Ovambo, vi. 188

Kalw, saying as to wind in corn near, vii. 292

Kamants, a Jewish tribe in Abyssinia, their custom of killing the dying, iv. 12

Kamenagora in Croatia, Midsummer fires at, x. 178

Kami, the Japanese word for god, iii. 2 n.[2]

Kamilaroi, the, of New South Wales, tribute of teeth exacted by, i. 101 ; burial custom of the, viii. 99 sq. ; ate livers and hearts of brave men to make themselves brave, viii. 151 ; anointed themselves with the fat of the dead, viii. 162 sq.

Kampot, in Cambodia, i. 170

Kamtchatka, the Italmens of, viii. 173 n.[4] ; bear-dance of the women of, viii. 195 ; the tug-of-war in, ix. 178

Kamtchatkans, their ceremony at an eclipse of the sun, i. 312 ; will not mention whales, bears, and wolves by their proper names, iii. 398 ; their attempts to deceive mice, iii. 399 ; their observation of the Great Bear, Pleiades, and Orion, vii. 315 ; offer excuses to bears and other animals which they kill, viii. 222 ; their belief in the resurrection of all creatures, viii. 257 ; stab the eyes of slain bears, viii. 268 sq. ; their fear of demons, ix. 89 ; their purification after a death, xi. 178

Kamui, the Aino equivalent of the Dacotan wakan, viii. 180 n.[2] ; Aino name for god, viii. 198

Kanagra, district of India, marriage of images of Siva and Pârvatî in, iv. 265 sq.

Kandhs or Khonds. See Khonds

Kangaroo, tooth of, in sympathetic magic, i. 180

Kangaroo fat, men of kangaroo totem anoint themselves with, viii. 165

—— flesh eaten to make eater swift-footed, viii. 145 ; eaten sacramentally by men of kangaroo totem, viii. 165

Kangaroo totem in Central Australia, viii. 165

Kangaroos, ceremony for the multiplication of, i. 87 *sq.* ; imitated by dancers, ix. 382

Kangean Archipelago, propitiation of mice to induce them to spare the fields in the, viii. 278 *sq.*

Kangra district, Punjaub, temporary rajahs in hill states about, iv. 154 ; special burials of infants in the, v. 94 ; "outcaste" Brahmans in the hill states about, ix. 45

—— mountains in the Punjaub, human sacrifices to cedar-tree in the, ii. 17

Kanhar river, in Mirzapur, ix. 60

Kaniagmuts of Alaska, uncleanness of whalers among the, iii. 207

Kanna district, Northern Nigeria, the Angass of the, xi. 210

Kanodrs, dairy-temple of the Todas at, iii. 16

Kansas Indians, eat dog's flesh to make them brave, viii. 145

Kantavu, a Fijian island, belief as to earthquakes in, v. 201

Kanytelideis, in Cilicia, v. 158

Kappiliyans of Madura, their seclusion of girls at puberty, x. 69

Kapu women of Southern India, their rain-charm by means of a figure of the rain-god, i. 284 *n.* ; their rain-charm by means of frogs, i. 294

Kapus or Reddis, in Madras Presidency, i. 294

Kara-Bel, in Lydia, Hittite sculpture at, v. 138 *n.*, 185

—— -Kirghiz, barren women fertilized by apple-trees among the, ii. 57

Karaits, a Jewish sect, cover mirrors after a death, iii. 95 ; lock all cupboards at a death, iii. 309

Karamundi nation of Australia, their rain-making, i. 257

Karels of Finland, sacrifice a lamb on St. Olaf's Day, viii. 258 *n.*[2]

Karen-nis of Burma, the, iii. 13. *See* Karens

Karens or Karennis of Burma, their contagious magic of footprints, i. 209 ; their custom of setting up a village pole every April, ii. 69 *sq.* ; their custom in regard to fornication and adultery, ii. 107 *sq.* ; rules observed by chiefs and their mothers among the, iii. 13 ; their recall of the soul, iii. 43 ; their customs at funerals, iii. 51 ; wizards among the, capture wandering souls of sleepers, iii. 73 ; afraid of passing under a house or a fallen tree, iii. 250 ; their belief as to a spirit in the head, iii. 252 ; foods tabooed to chiefs among

the, iii. 292 ; their story of the type of Beauty and the Beast, iv. 130 *n.*[1] ; their way of fanning away ill-luck from children, vii. 10 ; their ceremonies to secure the rice-soul, vii. 189 *sq.* ; their belief in demons, ix. 96 ; their custom at childbirth, xi. 157

Kariera tribe of West Australia, their beliefs as to birth of children, v. 105

Karkantzari, fiends or monsters in Macedonia, ix. 320

Karma-tree, ceremony of the Mundas over a, v. 240

Karnak, in Egypt, Ammon-Ra, the lord of, ii. 132 ; sculpture at, vii. 260. *See also* Carnac

Karneios, a Peloponnesian god mated with Artemis, i. 36

Karo-Battas (Bataks) of Sumatra, their belief as to the afterbirth, i. 193 *sq.* ; their rain-making ceremony, i. 277 *sq.* ; apologize to trees for cutting them down, ii. 19 ; their custom at a funeral, iii. 52 ; their custom at cutting a child's hair, iii. 263 ; names of relations tabooed among the, iii. 339 ; their euphemisms for the tiger, iii. 410 ; their custom as to the first sheaf of rice at harvest, vi. 239 ; their custom as to the largest sheaf at rice-harvest, vii. 196. *See also* Battas

Karok Indians of California, avoid the names of the dead, iii. 352 ; their lamentations at hewing sacred wood, vi. 47 *sq.* ; their ceremonies at catching the first salmon of the season, viii. 255

Karpathos, Greek island, custom of swinging in, iv. 284 ; transference of sickness to a tree in, ix. 55. *See also* Carpathus

Kartik, an Indian month, equivalent to October, i. 294

Karunga, the supreme god of the Herero, vi. 186, 187 *n.*[1]

Karwar, in Western India, hook-swinging at, iv. 278

Kasai district of the Congo Free State, the Ba-Yaka and Ba-Yanzi of the, i. 348

—— River, xi. 264

Kasan Government of Russia, the Wotyaks of the, ix. 156

Kashgar, effigy of ox beaten in spring at, viii. 13

Kashim, assembly-room or dancing-house of the Esquimaux of Bering Strait, viii. 247

'Katajalina, an Australian spirit who eats up boys at initiation and restores them to life, xi. 234 *sq.*

Katikiro, the, of Uganda, iii. 145 *n.*[4]

——, Baganda term for prime minister, vi. 168

Katodis, their ceremony at felling a tree, ii. 38

Katoemanggoengan, a lawgiver, born again in a crocodile, viii. 211

Katrine, Loch, x. 231

Katsina, a Hausa kingdom, custom of killing infirm kings in, iv. 35

Katzenthal in Baden, charm to make the hemp grow tall in, i. 138

Kaua Indians of North-Western Brazil, their masked dances, vii. 111, ix. 236, 381

Kauffmann, Professor F., on the Balder myth, x. 102 *n*.[1], 103 *n*. ; on the external soul, xi. 97 *n*.

Kaumpuli, the Baganda god of plague, ix. 4

Kaupole, a Midsummer pole in Eastern Prussia, xi. 49

Kausika Sutra, ancient Hindoo book of sorcery, i. 209, 229, ix. 192

Kavirondo, the Bantu tribes of, purification of manslayers among, iii. 176 *sq.* ; division of agricultural labour between the sexes among, vii. 117 *n*.[2] ; believe that skin disease is caused by eating a totemic animal, viii. 26 *sq.*

——, the Ja-Luo tribes of, iii. 79

Kawars of India, their cure for fever, xi. 190

Kaya-Kaya or Tugeri of Dutch New Guinea, their use of bull-roarers, xi. 242 *sq.*

Kayan family not allowed to cut their hair, iii. 260

Kayans or Bahaus of Central Borneo, vii. 107, 109, 111, 234 ; beat gongs in a storm, i. 328 ; threaten the demons of the storm, i. 330 ; ascribe souls to poison-trees, ii. 17 ; observe a period of penance after building a house, ii. 40 ; sacrifice to the spirits of ironwood trees, ii. 40 ; believe that adultery blights the crops, ii. 109 ; their expiation for adultery, ii. 109 ; threaten the demon of thunder, ii. 183 *n*.[2] ; try to prevent the departure of their souls from their bodies, iii. 32 ; their recall of lost souls, iii. 47 ; afraid of being photographed, iii. 99 *sq.* ; their ceremonies at entering a strange land, iii. 110 ; their custom of seclusion after a journey, iii. 113 ; their belief as to ill-luck of man who touches a loom or women's clothes, iii. 164 *sq.* ; their custom after killing a panther, iii. 219 ; regard smiths as inspired, iii. 237 ; remove sharp weapons from room at childbirth, iii. 239 ; cut their hair at end of mourning, iii. 286 ; use a special language in searching for camphor, iii. 406 ; mock human sacrifices

among the, iv. 218 ; their reasons for taking human heads, v. 294 *sq.* ; their New Year festival, vii. 93, 96 *sq.* ; their sowing festival, vii. 93 *sqq.*, 111, 186 *sq.* ; their ceremonies in connexion with rice, vii. 93 *sqq.*, 186 *sqq.*, viii. 54 *sq.*, 184 *sqq.* ; their games played at sowing festival, vii. 94 *sqq.*, 187 ; their observation of the sun, vii. 314 ; their observation of the Pleiades, vii. 314 *n*.[4] ; their custom as to eating venison, viii. 144 ; their belief in transmigration, viii. 293 ; throw sticks or stones at evil spirits, ix. 19 ; stretch ropes round their houses to keep off demons, ix. 154 *n*. ; their masked dances, ix. 236, 382 *sq.* ; their priestesses not allowed to step on the ground at certain rites, x. 4 *sq.* ; custom observed by them after a funeral, xi. 175 *sq.*; their way of giving the slip to a demon, xi. 179 *sq.*

Kayans of the Mahakam river, vii. 186

—— of the Mendalam river, vii. 97, 98

Keadrol, a Toda clan, vi. 228

Keating, Geoffrey, Irish historian, on the Hallowe'en fire-festival of the Irish Druids, x. 139 ; on the Beltane fires, x. 158 *sq.*

Keating, W. H., on the seclusion of menstruous women among the Potawatomis, x. 89

Keats, John, his sonnet to the Evening Star, i. 166

Keb (Geb or Seb), Egyptian earth-god, father of Osiris, v. 6, 283 *n*.[3], ix. 341

Kedeshim, sacred men, at Jerusalem, v. 17 *sq.* ; among the Western Semites, v. 38 *n*., 59, 72, 107 ; in relation to prophets, v. 76

Kedeshoth, sacred women, among the Western Semites, v. 59, 72, 107

Kei Islanders, their belief in the homoeopathic magic of creepers, i. 145 ; their charm to ensure trading profits, i. 152 ; their treatment of the navelstring, i. 186 ; dance for wind, i. 321 ; their offerings at graves, iii. 53

—— Islands, magical telepathy in the, i. 126 ; telepathy in war in the, i. 130 ; custom as to children's cast teeth in the, i. 179 ; fire maintained during absence of voyagers in the, ii. 265 ; offerings of first-fruits in the, vii. 123 ; expulsion of demons in the, ix. 112 *sq.* ; birth-custom in the, xi. 155

—— river, in South Africa, heaps of stones on the banks of the, ix. 11

Keisar, an East Indian island, avoidance of graves at night in, iii. 53

Keitele, Lake, in Finland, first-fruits of

harvest offered to an old fir-tree on, xi. 165

Kekchi Indians of Guatemala, their period of abstinence before sowing, ii. 105 ; their respect for serpents, viii. 219 ; their propitiation of dead deer, viii. 241

Kelah, Karen word for soul, vii. 189 *sq.*

Kells in Ireland, iv. 99 ; St. Columba at, ii. 243 *n.*[1]

Kemble, J. M., on need-fire, x. 288

Kemosh, god of Moab, v. 15

Kemping, contest between reapers in Scotland, vii. 152

Kĕna daulat, killed by the sanctity (*daulat*) of a Malay king, i. 398

Kengtung, a Shan state of Upper Burma, worship of a lake-spirit in, ii. 150 *sq.* ; expulsion of the demons of sickness in, ix. 116 *sq.*

Kennedy, Prof. A. R. S., on Azazel and the scapegoat, ix. 210 *n.*[4]

Kennett, Professor R. H., on David and Goliath, v. 19 *n.*[2] ; on Elisha in the wilderness, v. 53 *n.*[1] ; on *kedeshim*, v. 73 *n.*[1] ; on the sacrifice of first-born children at Jerusalem, vi. 219 ; on the eating of mice by the Jews, viii. 24 *n.*[1]

Kent, belief as to death at ebb-tide in, i. 168 ; the Weald of, ii. 7 ; May garlands in, ii. 62 ; the Ivy Girl in, vii. 153

Kent's Hole, near Torquay, fossil bones in, v. 153

Kenyahs of Borneo, their use of magical images, i. 59 *sq.* ; set up images of a god at the doors of houses, ii. 385 ; their recall of the soul, iii. 43 *sq.* ; their ceremony at entering a strange land, iii. 110 *sq.* ; their tabooed words, iii. 415 *sq.*

—— of Sarawak, their observation of the sun, vii. 314

Keonjhur, ceremony at installation of Rajah of, iv. 56

Kerak in Palestine, rain-making at, i. 276

Keramin tribe of New South Wales, their rain-making by means of a stone, i. 304

Keremet, a god of the Wotyaks, ceremony to propitiate, ii. 145 *sq.*

Kerr, Miss, of Port Charlotte, Islay, on the harvest *Cailleach*, vii. 166

Kerre, a tribe to the south of Abyssinia, accustomed to strangle their first-born children, iv. 181 *sq.*

Kerry, Midsummer fires in, x. 203

Kers, Robert, healed by witchcraft, ix. 38 *sq.*

Kersavondblok, the Yule log, in Flanders, x. 249

Kersmismot, the Yule log, at Grammont, x. 249

Ketane, river in Basutoland, mythical snake at waterfall on the, ii. 157

Ketosh warriors of British East Africa, their custom after battle, iii. 176

Kettles used to mimic thunder, i. 310

Kevlaar, Virgin Mary of, i. 77

Key as symbol of delivery in childbed, iii. 296

—— of the field, vii. 226

"Key-race" at a marriage in Bavaria, ii. 304

Keys as charms against devils and ghosts, iii. 234, 235, 236 ; as amulets, iii. 308. *See also* Locks

—— the golden, used by St. George to open the earth in spring, ii. 333

Keysser, Ch., on belief in conception without sexual intercourse, v. 96 *sq.* ; on games and stories as means of promoting the crops among the Kai, vii. 101 *sq.*

Khai-muh, kingdom to the west of Tonquin, first-born sons said to be devoured in, iv. 180

Khalij, old canal at Cairo, vi. 38

Khambu caste in Sikkhim, their custom after a funeral, xi. 18

Khan, ceremony at visiting a Tartar, iii. 114

—— the Great, his blood not to be spilt on ground, iii. 242

Khandh priest, his charm to bestow offspring on a barren woman, ii. 160

Khangars of the Central Provinces, India, bridegroom and his father dressed as women at a marriage among the, vi. 261

Kharwars of Northern India, will not name certain animals in the morning, iii. 402 *sq.* ; their use of scapegoats, ix. 192 ; their dread of menstruous women, x. 84

Khasis of Assam, their treatment of the placenta, i. 194 ; their belief as to the disastrous effects of marrying a woman of the same clan, ii. 114 *n.*[1] ; their system of mother-kin, ii. 294, v. 46, vi. 202 *sq.* ; succession to the kingdom among the, ii. 294 *sq.*, vi. 210 *n.*[1] ; goddesses predominate over gods in their religion, vi. 203 *sq.* ; their tribes governed by kings, not queens, vi. 210 ; their annual expulsion of demon of plague, ix. 173 *sq.* ; story of the external soul told by the, x. 146 *sq.*

Khasiyas, the, of India, their worship of village deities, ii. 288 *n.*[1]

Khatris, a caste in the Punjaub, perform funeral rites for a father in the fifth month of his wife's pregnancy, iv. 189

Khent, early king of the first dynasty in Egypt, vi. 154 ; his reign, vi. 19 *sq.*; his tomb at Abydos, vi. 19 *sqq.*; his tomb identified with that of Osiris, vi. 20, 197

Khenti-Amenti, title of Osiris, vi. 87, 198 *n.*[2], vii. 260

Khlysti, the, a Russian sect, abhor marriage, iv. 196 *n.*[3]

Khnoumou or Khnumu, Egyptian god, with his potter's wheel, ii. 132, 133 ; fashions a wife for Bata, xi. 135

Khoiak, festival of Osiris in the month of, vi. 86 *sqq.*, 108 *sq.*

Khön-ma, a Tibetan goddess, mistress of foul fiends, viii. 96

Khonds or Khands of India, their sacred groves, ii. 41 ; rebirth of ancestors among the, iii. 368 *sq.*; their human sacrifices for the crops, iv. 139, vii. 245 *sqq.*, xi. 286 *n.*[2] ; their annual expulsion of demons at seed-time, ix. 138, 234 ; their treatment of human victims, ix. 259

Khor-Adar Dinka, the, their custom of strangling their rain-makers, iv. 33

Khyrim State, in Assam, importance of the priestess in, v. 46 ; governed by a High Priestess, vi. 203

Kia blacks of Queensland, their treatment of girls at puberty, x. 39

Kia-King, Chinese emperor, his punishment of the rain-dragon, i. 297 *sq.*

Kiang-si, Chinese province, Dragon and Tiger Mountains in, i. 413 *sq.*

Kibanga, on the Upper Congo, kings of, put to death, iv. 34

Kibuka, the war-god of the Baganda, a dead man, vi. 197 ; his personal relics preserved at Cambridge, vi. 197

Kič tribe, of the Upper Nile, ventriloquist as chief of the, i. 347

Kickapoo Indians, iii. 171 ; their customs before going to war, iii. 163 *n.*[2]

Kid, surname of Dionysus, vii. 17

Kidd, Dudley, on use made of twins by Zulus in war, i. 49 *n.*[3] ; on chiefs as rain-makers in South Africa, i. 350 ; on the fire-drill of the Caffres, ii. 210 *sq.* ; on female ghosts among the Bantu peoples, ii. 224 *n.*[4] ; as to Caffre belief about the shadows of trees, iii. 82 ; on Caffre belief as to shadows, iii. 88 *n.*; on the worship of ancestral spirits among the Bantus of South Africa, vi. 177 *sqq.*; on external souls of chiefs, xi. 156 *n.*[2]

Kidneys tabooed to Malagasy soldiers, i. 117 *sq.*

Kiel, the corn-spirit as a cat at, vii. 280

Kigelia africana, used in kindling fire by friction, ii. 210

Kikuyu, the, of British East Africa, their observation of the Pleiades, vii. 317. *See* Akikuyu

Kilchrennan, on Loch Awe, vii. 165, 166

Kildare, fire and nuns of St. Brigit in, ii. 240 *sq.*; the church of, ii. 363 ; Midsummer fires in, x. 203

Kilema, in East Africa, strangers doctored before being admitted to see the king at, iii. 114 *sq.*

Kilimanjaro, the Wajaggas of, i. 250

——, Mount, attempted ascent of, iii. 103

Kilkenny, Midsummer fires in, x. 203

Killer of the Elephant, official who throttles sick kings, iv. 35

" —— of the Rye-woman," name given to the cutter of the last rye, vii. 223, 224

Killin, in Perthshire, the hill of the fires at, x. 149

Killing the spirit of the wind, i. 328 ; the divine king, iv. 8 *sqq.* ; the corn-spirit, vii. 216 *sqq.*; the divine animal, viii. 169 *sqq.*; a totem animal, xi. 220 ; the novice and bringing him to life again at initiation, pretence of, xi. 225 *sqq.*

—— a god, ix. 1 ; in the hunting, pastoral, and agricultural stages of society, iv. 221 ; in the form of an animal, vii. 22 *sq.*; two types of the custom of, viii. 312 *sq.*; in Mexico, ix. 275 *sqq.*

—— the tree-spirit, iv. 205 *sqq.*; a means to promote the growth of vegetation, iv. 211 *sq.*

Kilmainham, perpetual fire in the monastery of, ii. 241 *sq.*

Kilmarnock, mode of cutting the last corn near, vii. 279

Kilmartin, in Argyleshire, the harvest Maiden at, vii. 156

Kiln, the fire of a, called by special name, iii. 395

Kimbugwe, minister in charge of the king of Uganda's navel-string, i. 196

Kimbunda, the, of West Africa, their cannibalism at accession of new king, viii. 152

Kincardineshire, Midsummer fires in, x. 206

King, J. E., on infant burial, i. 105 *n.*[4], v. 91 *n.*[3]

King, torn to pieces by horses, i. 366 ; gives oracles, i. 377 ; not to be overshadowed, iii. 83 ; his life sympathetically bound up with the prosperity of the country, iv. 21, 27, xi. 1 *sq.*; slaying of the, in legend, iv. 120 *sqq.*; responsible for the weather and crops, iv. 165 ;

abdicates on the birth of a son, iv. 190;
at Whitsuntide, pretence of beheading
the, iv. 209 *sq.*; a masker at Carnival
called the, vi. 99, vii. 28 *sq.*; eats of new
fruits before his people, viii. 63, 70;
first-fruits presented to the, viii. 109,
116, 122; so called, at Carcassone, viii.
320 *sq.*; mock or temporary, ix. 151,
403 *sq.*; beaten at his inauguration in
ancient India, ix. 263; assembly for
determining the fate of the, ix. 356;
nominal, chosen at Midsummer, x.
194, xi. 25; presides at summer bonfire, xi. 38. *See also* Kings
King and Queen at Athens, i. 44 *sq.*; on
Whit - Monday near Königgrätz, ii.
89; at Whitsuntide in Silesia, ii. 89 *sq.*
—— and Queen of May, ix. 406; at
Halford, in Warwickshire, ii. 88; at
Grenoble, ii. 90; marriage of, iv. 266
—— and Queen of Roses at Grammont,
x. 195
King, the Grass, at Whitsuntide, ii.
85 *sq.*
——, the Leaf, on Whit-Monday, ii. 85
——, the Roman, as Jupiter, ii. 174 *sqq.*
King of the Bean, ix. 313 *sqq.*, x. 153 *n.*[3];
at Merton College, Oxford, ix. 332
—— of the Calf, vii. 290
—— of Fire in Cambodia, ii. 3 *sqq.*, iii.
17, iv. 14
—— of the harvesters, vii. 294
—— of the Jinn, death of the, iv. 8
—— of the Night at Porto Novo, iii. 23
—— of Rain at Poona in India, i. 275;
on the Upper Nile, ii. 2
—— of Rain and Storm at mouth of the
Congo, ii. 2
—— of the Rice in Sumatra, vii. 197
—— of Sacred Rites at Rome, i. 44, ii.
179, 201; exhorted to be watchful,
ii. 265; the successor of the old
Roman king, ii. 266; nominated by
the chief pontiff, ii. 296; his flight, ii.
309; of the Sacred Rites in other
Latin towns, i. 44, 44 *n.*[1], ii. 266
—— of the Saturnalia, ii. 311, ix. 308,
311, 312
—— of Summer chosen on St. Peter's
Day, x. 195
—— of Tyre, his walk on stones of fire,
v. 114 *sq.*
—— of Uganda, his navel-string preserved and inspected every new moon,
vi. 147 *sq. See* Baganda *and* Uganda
—— of Water in Cambodia, ii. 3 *sqq.*,
iii. 17, iv. 14
—— of the Wood at Nemi, i. 1 *sqq.*,
ii. 1, 378 *sqq.*, iv. 28, 205 *sq.*, 212 *sqq.*;
put to death, i. 11, x. 2; a mate of
Diana, i. 40, 41, ii. 380; representative
of Virbius, i. 40 *sq.*, ii. 129; a personi-

fication of the oak-god Jupiter, ii. 378
sqq., xi. 302 *sq.*; perhaps a successor
of the Alban dynasty of the Sylvii, ii.
379; compared to the Whitsuntide
mummers, iv. 212 *sqq.*; in the Arician
grove a personification of an oak-
spirit, xi. 285. *See also* Priest of Nemi
King of the Years at Lhasa, ix. 220, 221
King Bees (Essenes) at Ephesus, i. 47 *n.*[2],
ii. 135 *sq.*
—— Hop in Siam, iv. 149, 151
King George's Sound, influence of medicine-men among the tribes of, i. 336;
namesakes of the dead change their
names among the tribes of, iii. 355
King's brothers put to death on his
accession, iii. 243
—— College, Cambridge, Boy Bishop
at, ix. 338
—— County, Ireland, hurling-matches
for brides in, ii. 305 *sq.*
—— daughter offered as prize in a race,
iv. 104
—— disease, palsy called the, i. 371
—— Evil (scrofula), iii. 134; touching
for the, i. 368 *sqq.*
—— hearth, oath by the, ii. 265
—— jawbone preserved, i. 196, iv. 200
sq., vi. 167 *sq.*, 169 *sq.*, 171 *sq.*
—— name changed in time of drought,
i. 355
—— Race at Whitsuntide, ii. 84
—— skull, priest drinks beer out of, as
means of inspiration, in Uganda, iv.
200, viii. 150
—— son, sacrifice of the, iv. 160 *sqq.*,
vii. 13, 24 *sq.*
—— widow, succession to the throne
through marriage with, iv. 193
Kingaru, clan of the Wadoe in German
East Africa, xi. 313
Kingdom, in ancient Latium, succession
to, ii. 266 *sqq.*; the prize of a race,
ii. 299 *sqq.*, iv. 103; mortal combat
for the, ii. 322. *See also* Kingship
and Succession
Kinglake, A. W., on the great Servian
forest, ii. 237 *n.*[1]
Kings, magicians as, i. 332 *sqq.*; expected to give rain, i. 348, 350, 351
sq., 353, 356, 392 *sq.*, 396; punished
for drought and dearth, i. 353 *sqq.*;
among the Aryans, magical powers
attributed to, i. 366 *sqq.*; often
the lineal successors of magicians or
medicine-men, i. 371; the divinity of,
i. 372; worshipped and consulted as
oracles, i. 388; as gods in India, i.
403; sacrifices offered to, i. 417;
temples built in honour of, i. 417; of
nature, ii. 1 *sqq.*; of rain, ii. 2; expected to make thunder, ii. 180 *sq.*;

perpetual fire in houses of, ii. 261 *sq.*; paternity of, a matter of indifference under female kinship, ii. 274 *sqq.*; sometimes of a different race from their subjects, ii. 288 *sq.*; chosen from several royal families in rotation, ii. 292 *sqq.*; fat, ii. 297; handsomest men, ii. 297; long-headed, ii. 297; supernatural powers attributed to, iii. 1; their lives regulated by exact rules, iii. 1 *sqq.*, 101 *sq.*; taboos observed by, iii. 8 *sqq.*; beaten before their coronation, iii. 18; forbidden to see their mothers, iii. 86; portraits of, not stamped on coins, iii. 98 *sq.*; guarded against the magic of strangers, iii. 114 *sq.*; forbidden to use foreign goods, iii. 115; not to be seen eating and drinking, iii. 117 *sqq.*; concealed by curtains, iii. 120 *sq.*; forbidden to leave their palaces, iii. 122 *sqq.*; compelled to dance, iii. 123; punished or put to death, iii. 124; not to be touched, iii. 132, 225 *sq.*; their hair unshorn, iii. 258 *sq.*; foods tabooed to, iii. 291 *sq.*; names of, tabooed, iii. 374 *sqq.*; taboos observed by, identical with those observed by commoners, iii. 419 *sq.*; killed when their strength fails, iv. 14 *sqq.*; regarded as incarnations of a divine spirit, iv. 21, 26 *sq.*; attacks on, permitted, iv. 22, 48 *sqq.*; killed at the end of a fixed term, iv. 46 *sqq.*; related to sacred animals, iv. 82, 84 *sqq.*; personating dragons or serpents, iv. 82; addressed by names of animals, iv. 86; with a dragon or serpent crest, iv. 105; legends of. the custom of slaying, iv. 120 *sqq.*; the supply of, iv. 134 *sqq.*; abdicate annually, iv. 148; as lovers of a goddess, v. 49 *sq.*; held responsible for the weather and the crops, v. 183; marry their sisters, v. 316; slaughter human victims with their own hands, vi. 97 *n.*[7]; torn in pieces, traditions of, vi. 97 *sq.*; human sacrifices to prolong the life of, vi. 220 *sq.*, 223 *sqq.*; trace of custom of slaying them annually, vii. 254 *sq.*; eat of new fruits before their subjects, viii. 63, 70; magistrates at Olympia called, ix. 352; marry the wives and concubines of their predecessors, ix. 368

Kings and chiefs tabooed, iii. 131 *sqq.*; their spittle guarded against sorcerers, iii. 289 *sq.*

—— and magicians dismembered and their bodies buried in different parts of the country to fertilize it, vi. 101 *sq.*

—— and priests, their sanctity analogous to the uncleanness of women at menstruation, x. 97 *sq.*

Kings, dead, worshipped in Africa, iv. 24 *sq.*, vi. 160 *sqq.*, 191 *sqq.*; turn into lions, leopards, pythons, etc., iv. 84; reincarnate in lions, v. 83 *n.*[1], viii. 288; sacrifices offered to, vi. 162, 166 *sq.*; incarnate in animals, vi. 162, 163 *sq.*, 173; consulted as oracles, vi. 167, 171, 172, 195; human sacrifices to, vi. 173

——, divinity of Babylonian, i. 417 *sq.*; of Egyptian, i. 418 *sq.* See also Divinity

——, English, touch for scrofula, i. 368 *sqq.*

—— fetish or religious, in West Africa, iii. 22 *sqq.*

——, Hebrew, traces of divinity ascribed to, v. 20 *sqq.*

——, the Latin, thought to be the sons of the fire-god by mortal mothers, ii. 195 *sqq.* See also Latin

——, priestly, i. 44 *sqq.*, v. 42; of Sheba, iii. 125 *n.*; of the Nubas, iii. 132

——, Roman, as deities in a Sacred Marriage, ii. 172 *sq.*, 192, 193 *sq.*; costumed like Jupiter, ii. 174 *sqq.*; as public rain-makers, ii. 183; as personifications of Jupiter, ii. 266 *sq.*; as personifications of Saturn, ii. 311, 322. See also Roman

——, sacred or divine, in great historical empires, i. 415 *sqq.*; development of, ii. 376 *sqq.*; of the Shilluk, iv. 17 *sqq.*; Semitic, v. 15 *sqq.*; Lydian, v. 182 *sqq.*; put to death, x. 1 *sq.*; subject to taboos, x. 2

——, Shilluk, divine, iv. 17 *sqq.*; put to death before their strength fails, iv. 21 *sq.*, vi. 163

——, temporary, iv. 148 *sqq.*; their divine or magical functions, iv. 155 *sqq.*

——, Teutonic, i. 47

——, the Three, on Twelfth Day, ix. 329 *sqq.*

Kings of the Barotse worshipped after death, vi. 193 *sqq.*

—— of Dahomey and Benin represented partly in animal shapes, iv. 85 *sq.*

—— of Egypt worshipped as gods, v. 52; buried at Abydos, vi. 19; perhaps formerly slain in the character of Osiris, vi. 97 *sq.*, 102; as Osiris, vi. 151 *sqq.*; renew their life by identifying themselves with the dead and risen Osiris, vi. 153 *sq.*; born again at the Sed festival, vi. 153, 156 *sq.*; perhaps formerly put to death to prevent their bodily and mental decay, vi. 154 *sq.*, 156

—— of Fire and Water in Cambodia, ii. 3 *sqq.*, iii. 17, iv. 14

—— of France touch for scrofula, i. 370

Kings in Greece, titular or sacred, i. 44 *sqq.* ; called Zeus, ii. 177, 361
—— of Sweden answerable for the fertility of the ground, i. 366 *sq.*, vi. 220 ; sons of Swedish king sacrificed, iv. 160 *sq.*, vi. 220
—— of Uganda, dead, consulted as oracles, i. 196, iv. 200 *sq.*, vi. 171 *sq.* ; their life bound up with barkcloth trees, xi. 160. *See* Baganda *and* Uganda
Kings, The Epic of, Firdusi's, x. 104
Kings' fire, the, ii. 195 *sqq.*
—— Race, the, ii. 84
—— sisters, licence accorded to, ii. 274 *sqq.*
—— wives turned at death into leopards, viii. 288
Kingship, an annual office in some Greek states, i. 46 ; evolution of the sacred, i. 420 *sq.* ; contest for the, at Whitsuntide, ii. 89 ; burdens and restrictions attaching to the early, iii. 1 *sqq.*, 17 *sqq.*, iv. 135 ; octennial tenure of the, iv. 58 *sqq.* ; triennial tenure of the, iv. 112 *sq.* ; annual tenure of the, iv. 113 *sqq.* ; diurnal tenure of the, iv. 118 *sq.* ; modern type of, different from the ancient, iv. 135 ; under mother-kin, rules as to succession to the, vi. 210 *n.*[1]; mock, at the Saturnalia, ix. 308
—— in Africa under mother-kin inherited by men, not women, vi. 211
——, descent of the, in the female line, at Rome, ii. 270 *sqq.* ; in Africa, ii. 274 *sqq.* ; in Greece, ii. 277 *sq.* ; in Scandinavia, ii. 279 *sq.* ; in Lydia, ii. 281 *sq.* ; among the Danes and Saxons, ii. 282 *sq.*
——, double, at Sparta, ii. 290 ; traces of, at Rome, ii. 290
——, nominal, left by conquerors to indigenous race, ii. 288 *sq.*
——, Roman, abolition of the, ii. 289 *sqq.* ; a religious office, ii. 289 ; a plebeian institution, v. 45
Kingsley, Miss Mary H., on reincarnation of the dead in Nigeria, i. 411 *n.*[1]; on fetish kings in West Africa, iii. 22 ; on soul-traps in West Africa, iii. 71 ; on the confinement of the king of Benin to his palace, iii. 123 *n.*[2]; on negro notions as to blood, iii. 251 ; on custom of killing chief, iv. 119 *n.*[1]; on secret burial of chief's head, vi. 104 ; on West African belief in demons, ix. 74 ; on the periodic expulsion of demons at Calabar, ix. 204 *n.*[1]; on external or bush souls, xi. 204 *sq.* ; on rites of initiation in West Africa, xi. 259
Kingsmill Islanders, their belief as to falling stars, iv. 64

Kingsmill Islands, first-fruits offered to a god in the, viii. 127 *sq.*
Kingussie, in Inverness-shire, Beltane cakes at, x. 153
Kinnor, a lyre, v. 52
Kinross, custom of "dumping" at harvest in, vii. 227
Kinship of men with crocodiles, viii. 212 *sq.*, 214 *sq.* ; of men with tigers, viii. 216 ; created by the milk-tie, xi. 138 *n.*[1]
Kintu, the first man in Uganda, ii. 261
Kintyre, the last corn cut called the Old Wife in, vii. 142
Kioga Lake in Central Africa, ix. 246
Kiowa Indians, their treatment of the navel-string, i. 198 ; relations of the dead change their names among the, iii. 357 ; changes in their language caused by fear of naming the dead, iii. 360 *sq.*
Kirauea, volcano in Hawaii, v. 216 *sq.* ; divinities of, v. 217 ; offerings to, v. 217 *sqq.*
Kirchmeyer, Thomas, author of *Regnum Papisticum,* x. 124, 125 *n.*[1]; his account of Easter customs, x. 124 *sq.*, of Midsummer customs, x. 162 *sq.*
Kirghiz, "Love Chase" among the, ii. 301 ; divine by the shoulder-blades of sheep, iii. 229 *n.*[4]; games in honour of the dead among the, iv. 97 ; their story of girl who might not see the sun, x. 74
—— women will not pronounce names of their husbands' older relations, iii. 337
Kiriwina, one of the Trobriand Islands, annual festival of the dead in, v. 56 ; snakes as reincarnations of the dead in, v. 84 ; presentation of children to the full moon in, vi. 144 ; annual expulsion of spirits in, ix. 134
Kirk Andreas, in the Isle of Man, x. 306
Kirkland, Rev. Mr., on Iroquois sacrifice of white dogs, ix. 210
Kirkmichael, in Perthshire, Beltane fires and cakes at, x. 153
Kirn or *kern,* last corn cut, vii. 151, 152 *sqq.* ; name of the harvest-supper, vii. 158, 162 *n.*[3]
—— -baby, vii. 151, 153
—— -doll, vii. 151, 153, 154
—— -supper, vii. 154
Kirton Lindsey, in Lincolnshire, witch as cat at, x. 318 ; medical use of mistletoe at, xi. 84
Kirwaido, ruler of the old Prussians, iv. 41
Kisavaccha, an Indian ascetic, ix. 41
Kisser, East Indian island, worship of a measuring-tape in, iii. 91 *sq.*

Kit-fox skin in rain-making, i. 288

Kitching, Rev. A. L., on the use of bells to exorcize the storm fiend, ix. 246 *sq.*; on cure for lightning stroke, xi. 298 *n.*[2]

Kites, artificial, used to drive away the devil, ix. 4; paper, flown as scape-goats, ix. 203

Kiwai or Kiwaii, an island off New Guinea, vii. 106; intercourse of men with their wives before going to war in, iii. 164 *n.*[1]; magic for the growth of sago in, vi. 101; use of bull-roarers in, vii. 106, xi. 232

Kiziba, district of Central Africa, dead kings worshipped in, vi. 173 *sq.*; totemism in, vi. 173; women's agri-cultural work in, viii. 118 *sq.*; purifi-cation for the slaughter of a serpent in, viii. 219 *sq.*; theory of the after-birth in, xi. 162 *n.*[2]

Klallam Indians of Washington State not allowed to bear names of deceased paternal ancestors, iii. 354; prohibi-tion to name the dead in the, iii. 365

Klamath Indians of Oregon, their theory of the waning moon, vi. 130

—— River, in California, viii. 255

Klausenburg, in Transylvania, cock killed on harvest-field at, vii. 278

Kleintitschen, A., on the fear of demons in New Britain, ix. 82 *sq.*

Kleptomania, cure for, by means of spiders and crabs, ix. 34

Kling or Klieng, a mythical hero of the Dyaks, ix. 383, 384 *n.*[1]

Kloo, in the Queen Charlotte Islands, restrictions imposed on girls at puberty at, x. 45

Klöppel (mallet), at threshing, vii. 148

Kloxin, near Stettin, the last sheaf called the Old Man at, vii. 220

Knawel, St. John's blood on root of, xi. 56

Knife as charm against spirits, iii. 232, 233, 234, 235; adapted for religious suicide, iv. 55 *n.*[1]; divination by, x. 241; soul of child bound up with, xi. 157. *See also* Knives

" ——, Darding," honorific totem of the Carrier Indians, xi. 273, 274 *sq.*

Knives in homoeopathic magic, i. 158; thrown at the wind, i. 329; not to be left edge upwards, iii. 238; not used at funeral banquets, iii. 238; of special pattern used in reaping rice, vii. 184; under the threshold, a protection against witches, ix. 162. *See also* Knife

Knocking out of teeth as initiatory cere-mony in Australia, i. 97 *sqq.*

Knot, the Gôrdian, iii. 316 *sq.*

Knots, tying up the wind in, i. 326; prohibition to wear, iii. 13; untied at childbirth, iii. 294, 296 *sq.*, 297 *sq.*;

thought to prevent the consummation of marriage, iii. 299 *sqq.*; thought to cause sickness, disease, and all kinds of misfortune, iii. 301 *sqq.*; used to cure disease, iii. 303 *sqq.*; used to win a lover or capture a runaway slave, iii. 305 *sq.*; used as protective amulets, iii. 306 *sqq.*; used as charms by hunters and travellers, iii. 306; as a charm to protect corn from devils, iii. 308 *sq.*; magical virtue of, iii. 309 *sq.*, 312; on corpses untied, iii. 310; in a string as a cure for warts, ix. 48; tied in branches of trees as remedies, ix. 56 *sq.*

Knots and locks, magical virtue of, iii. 310, 313

—— and rings tabooed, iii. 293 *sqq.*

Knotted thread in magic, ix. 48

Knowledge, the disinterested pursuit of, i. 218

Kobeua Indians of North-Western Brazil, their masked dances, vii. 111, ix. 236; their way of sharpening their sight, viii. 164

Kobi, village in Ceram, first-fruits of rice offered to the dead at, viii. 123

Kobong, totem, in Western Australia, xi. 219 *sq.*

Koch-Grünberg, Th., on observation of the Pleiades among the Brazilian In-dians, vii. 122 *n.*[1]; on the masked dances of the Indians of North-Western Brazil, ix. 382

Kochs or Kocchs of North-Eastern India, succession to husband's property among the, vi. 215 *n.*[2]; offer first-fruits to their ancestors, viii. 116

Koepang, in Timor, sacrifice to croco-diles in, ii. 152

Kôhen and *Kâhin*, soothsayer rather than priest in ancient Arabia, i. 230 *n.*

Köhler, Joh., lights need-fire and burnt as a witch, x. 270 *sq.*

Köhler, Reinhold, on the external soul in folk-tales, xi. 97 *n.*

Kohlerwinkel, near Augsburg, the last standing corn called the Sow at, vii. 298

Kois of Southern India, infant burial among the, v. 95

Koita, the, of British New Guinea, seclusion of manslayers among, iii. 168 *sq.*

Kolelo, in East Africa, ghost of sorcerer at, xi. 313

Kolem, in German New Guinea, magical powers ascribed to a chief of, i. 338

Kolkodoons of Queensland, their custom at circumcision, i. 93

Kollmann, P., on sultans responsible for rain, i. 353

Kols of North India will not speak of

beasts of prey by their proper names, iii. 403

Kolvagat, village in New Britain, magioal stone figures supposed to control the plantations at, ii. 148

Komatis of Mysore, their worship of serpents, v. 81 sq.

Kon-Meney in Cochin China, transformation of man into toad at, viii. 291

Kondes, of Lake Nyassa, avoidance of husband's father among the, iii. 336 sq.

Kondhs, their belief in reincarnation, i. 104

Koniags of Alaska, magical telepathy among the, i. 121 ; their magical uses of the bodies of the dead, vi. 106

Königgrätz district of Bohemia, King and Queen on Whit-Monday in village of the, ii. 89 ; beheading the Whitsuntide king on Whit-Monday in the, iv. 209 sq.

Königshain, in Silesia, custom of "Driving out Death" at, iv. 264 sq.

Konkan, Southern, mode of getting rid of cholera in, ix. 191 sq.

Konkaus of California, their dance of the dead, vi. 53

Konz on the Moselle, custom of rolling a burning wheel down hill at, x. 118, 163 sq., 337 sq.

Kooboos of Sumatra, their theory of the afterbirth and navel-string, xi. 162 n.[2]

Koochee, a demon in Australia, i. 331

Kookies of Cachar, in India, marriage custom of the, i. 160 n.[3]

Koossa Caffres, customs observed by manslayers among the, iii. 186 n.[1]

Koppenwal, church of St. Corona at, xi. 188 sq.

Koragia at Mantinea, vii. 46 n.[2]

Koran on magical knots, iii. 302 ; passages of, used as charms, iii. 305 sq., x. 18. See also Coran

Kore, Maiden, title of Persephone, vii. 208

Kore expelled on Easter Eve in Albania, iv. 265, ix. 157

Korkus, the, of the Central Provinces, India, transfer sickness by means of a loin-cloth, ix. 7

Korong, human god, in the Pelew Islands, i. 389

Korwas, of Bengal, division of labour between men and women among the, vii. 123 ; of Mirzapur, their use of scapegoats, ix. 192

Koryaks, of North-Eastern Asia, sacred fire-boards of the, ii. 225 ; race for a bride among the, ii. 302 ; their mode of detaining the souls of the dying, iii. 32 sq. ; voluntary deaths among the, iv. 13 ; their ceremonies at killing bears, wolves, and foxes, viii. 223 ; their ceremonies at the slaughter of whales, viii. 232 sqq. ; propitiate the foxes which they kill, viii. 244 ; their belief in demons, ix. 100 sq. ; expulsion of demons among the, ix. 126 sq. ; their festivals of the dead and subsequent purification, xi. 178 ; their custom in time of pestilence, xi. 179

Koshchei the Deathless, Russian story of, xi. 108 sqq.

Kosio, a dedicated person among the Ewe-speaking peoples of the Slave Coast, v. 65, 66, 68

Koskimo Indians of British Columbia, mourning customs of the, iii. 144 ; their cannibal rites, vii. 20 n. ; use of bull-roarers among the, xi. 229 n.

Kosti, in Thrace, carnival customs at, vi. 99 sq., vii. 28 sq.

Kostroma, funeral of, in Russia, iv. 261 sqq.

Kostroma, district of Russia, the burial of Yarilo in, iv. 262 sq.

Kostrubonko, funeral of, at Easter in Russia, iv. 261

Kot, a mythical being of New Britain, iii. 384

Kota Gadang, in Sumatra, rain-charm at, i. 308 sq.

Kotas, a tribe of Southern India, their priests not allowed to be widowers, vi. 230

Kotchène, a Chukchee chief, sacrificed in time of pestilence, i. 367 n.[1]

Kotedougou, in West Africa, annual dances of disguised men at, ix. 136 n.[1]

Kothluwalawa, a sacred lake of the Zuni, viii. 179

Kou or Koo, Esthonian thunder-god, ii. 367 n.[4]

Koui hunters in Laos, why they hamstring game, viii. 267

Koukoura, in Elis, swinging on St. George's Day at, iv. 283

Kowraregas, the, of the Prince of Wales Islands, avoidance of parents-in-law among, iii. 346 ; changes of vocabulary among, caused by fear of naming the dead, iii. 358 sq.

Krajina, in Servia, divination on St. George's Day at, ii. 345

Krapf, Dr. J. L., on a reported custom of sacrificing first-born sons in East Africa, iv. 183 n.[1]

Krautweihe, the blessing of the herbs, on August 15th in Germany, i. 15 n.[2]

Kreemer, J., on the fear of the dead among the Looboos of Sumatra, xi. 182 sq.

Kretschmer, Professor P., on native

population of Cyprus, v. 145 $n.^3$; on Cybele and Attis, v. 287 $n.^2$

Kreutzburg, in East Prussia, the harvest Goat at, vii. 282

Kriml, in the Tyrol, custom of throwing stones into the waterfall of, ix. 26 $n.^1$

Krishna, Hindoo god, his incarnation Govindji, i. 284 ; his images swung in swings, i. 406 ; thought to be incarnate in the Maharajas, i. 406 ; annually married to the Holy Basil (*tulasi*), ii. 26 ; his wife Rukmini, ii. 26 ; festival of swinging in honour of, iv. 279 ; worshipped by men who assimilate themselves to women, vi. 254

Kroeber, A. L., on the seclusion of girls at puberty among the Indians of California, x. 41 *sq.*

Krooben, a malevolent spirit among the Kamilaroi, viii. 100

Kruijt, A. C., on superstition as to written names, iii. 319 ; on the custom of naming parents after their children, iii. 333 $n.^5$; on head-hunting, v. 296 $n.^1$; on the Indonesian conception of the rice-soul, vii. 182 *sq.* ; on Toradja custom as to the working of iron, xi. 154 $n.^3$

Kruman, his anxiety about his dream-soul, iii. 71

Kru-men of West Africa die from imagination, iii. 136 *sq.* ; personal names concealed among the, iii. 322 *sq.*

Kshetrpal, a Himalayan deity, viii. 117

Kshira, a village of Bengal, knife for religious suicide at, iv. 55 $n.^1$

Kü-yung, city in China, precautions against an evil spirit in, iii. 239

Kuar, an Indian month, vi. 144, ix. 181

Kubary, J., on the system of mother-kin among the Pelew Islanders, vi. 204 *sqq.* ; on the gods of the Pelew Islanders, ix. 81 *sq.*

Kublai Khan, his mode of executing a royal criminal, iii. 242

Kudulu, a hill tribe of India, their human sacrifices for the crops, vii. 244

Kuei-Ki, in China, i. 414

Kuel, whale-festival of the Koryaks at, viii. 232

Kuga, an evil spirit in Slavonia, expelled by fire, x. 282

Kuhn, Adalbert, on need-fire, x. 273 ; on Midsummer fire, x. 335 ; on the divining-rod, xi. 67

Kühnau, R., on precautions against witches in Silesia, xi. 20 $n.$

Kuinda, Cilician fortress, v. 144 $n.^1$

Κυκέων, the communion cup in the Eleusinian mysteries, vii. 161 $n.^4$

Kuker and *Kukerica*, carnival mummers

in Thrace and Bulgaria, viii. 332, 333, 334

Kŭki-Lushai, men dressed as women to deceive dangerous ghosts or spirits among the, vi. 263

Kukis of Assam, parents named after their children among the, iii. 333 ; their custom after killing a tiger, viii. 155 $n.^5$

Kuklia, Old Paphos, v. 33, 36

Kukulu, a priestly king in Lower Guinea, iii. 5

Kukunjevac, in Slavonia, need-fire at, x. 282

Kulin nation of South-Eastern Australia, sex totems in the, xi. 216

—— tribe of Victoria, avoidance of the wife's mother in the, iii. 84 ; man endowed with bear's spirit in the, xi. 226 $n.^1$

Kull Gossaih, goddess of a hill tribe in India, viii. 118

Kumaon, in North-Western India, custom observed by men who have been supposed dead, in, i. 75 $n.^3$; rain-making in, i. 278 ; use of frogs in rain-charms in, i. 293 ; way of stopping rain in, i. 303 ; bullocks as scapegoats at funerals in, ix. 37 ; ceremony of sliding down a rope in, ix. 196 *sq.* ; the Holi festival in, xi. 2

Kumis, the, of South-Eastern India, their precautions against the demon of smallpox, ix. 117

Kunama, tribe on the borders of Abyssinia, consult a rain-maker, ii. 3

Kundi in Cilicia, v. 144

Kunnui, in Yezo, bear-festival of the Ainos at, viii. 185 *sqq.*

Kuopio, in Finland, sacred grove at, ii. 11

Kupalo, mythical being in Russia, funeral of, iv. 261, 262 ; figure of, passed across fire at Midsummer, v. 250 *sq.* ; a deity of vegetation, v. 253 ; image of, burnt or thrown into stream on St. John's Night, x. 176 ; effigy of, carried across fire and thrown into water, xi. 5, 23

Kupalo's Night, Midsummer Eve, x. 175, 176

Kupferberg, in Bavaria, harvest custom at, vii. 232

Kupole's festival at Midsummer in Prussia, v. 253

Kuria, in Thrace, masquerade at carnival at, viii. 332

Kurile Islands, the Ainos of the, viii. 180

Kurmis of India, marriage to trees among the, ii. 57 $n.^3$; their use of a scapegoat in time of cholera, ix. 190

Kurnai, a tribe of Gippsland, wind-maker among the, i. 324 ; their belief as to women's shadows, iii. 83 ; avoidance of the wife's mother among the, iii. 84 ; their fear of naming the dead, iii. 350 *sq.* ; their fear of the Aurora Australis, iv. 267 *n.*[1] ; sex totems and fights concerning them among the, xi. 215 *n.*[1], 216

Kurs of East Prussia, their homoeopathic magic at sowing, i. 137

Kursk, in Russia, rain-making at, i. 277 ; harvest custom near, vii. 233

Kururumany, the Arawak creator, ix. 302

Kuruvikkarans of Southern India, inspired priest of Kali among the, i. 382

Kurze, G., on the power of medicine-men among the Lengua Indians, i. 359

Kusavans, potters of Southern India, their votive images, i. 56 *n.*[3]

Kushunuk, near Cape Vancouver, Esquimau festival at, viii. 249 *n.*[1]

Kuskokwim River, in Alaska, ix. 380

Küstendil, in Bulgaria, need-fire at, x. 281

Kutonaqa Indians of British Columbia, their sacrifice of their first-born children to the sun, iv. 183 *sq.*

Kvasir, in Norse mythology, the wisest of beings, his blood and wisdom absorbed by Odin, i. 241

Kwa River, in West Africa, propitiation of goddess who dwells in the, ix. 28

Kwakiutl Indians of British Columbia, their treatment of the afterbirth, i. 197 *sq.* ; their contagious magic of wounds, i. 201 *sq.* ; their beliefs and customs concerning twins, i. 263, 324 ; their custom as to coffining the dead, iii. 53 ; the swallowing of souls by shamans among the, iii. 76*sq.*; customs observed by cannibals among the, iii. 159 *n.*, 188 *sqq.* ; change of names in summer and winter among the, iii. 386 ; their story of the type of Beauty and the Beast, iv. 130 *n.*[1]; cannibals among the, vii. 20 ; their ceremonies at killing a wolf, viii. 220 ; their belief in the resurrection of salmon, viii. 250; their masked dances, ix. 376 *n.*[2], 378 ; their story of an ogress whose life was in a hemlock branch, xi. 152 ; pass through a hemlock ring in time of epidemic, xi. 186

—— medicine-men capture stray souls, iii. 67 *n.*

Kwilu River, in the Congo State, vii. 119

Kwun, the spirit of the head, in Siam, iii. 252 ; supposed to reside in the hair, iii. 266 *sq.*

Kylenagranagh, the hill of, in Ireland, the fairies on, x. 324

La Ciotat, near Marseilles, hunting the wren at, viii. 321

L'Étoile, Lenten fires at, x. 113

La Manche, in Normandy, Lenten fire-custom in, x. 115

La Palisse, in France, dough man eaten at close of harvest at, viii. 48 *sq.*

La Paz, in Bolivia, Midsummer fires at, x. 213 ; Midsummer flowers at, xi. 50 *sq.*

La Rochelle, effigy of Shrove Tuesday burnt on Ash Wednesday at, iv. 230

La Trobe River in Victoria, iii. 109

Labbé, P., on the *inao* of the Ainos, viii. 186 *n.*

Labour, division of, between the sexes, vii. 129

Labrador, fear of demons in, ix. 79 *sq.*

Labraunda in Caria, Zeus Labraundeus worshipped at, v. 182 *n.*[4]

Labruguière, in Southern France, expulsion of evil spirits on Twelfth Night at, ix. 166

Labrys, Lydian word for axe, v. 182

Labyrinth, the Cretan, iv. 71, 74, 75, 76, 77

Labyrinths in churches, iv. 76 ; in the north of Europe, iv. 76 *sq.*

Lac, taboos observed in gathering, i. 115

Lac gatherers not allowed to wash, i. 115

Lacaune, belief as to mistletoe at, xi. 83

Lacedaemon, Fig Dionysus at, vii. 4

Lachlan River, in Australia, novices thought to be slain and resuscitated on the, xi. 233

Lachlins of Rum and deer, superstition concerning, xi. 284

Laconia, stone associated with Orestes in, i. 161 ; subject to earthquakes, v. 203 *n.*[2]

Lactantius, on the grove of Egeria, i. 18 *n.*[4] ; on Hippolytus as the lover of Artemis, i. 39 *n.*[1] ; on sacrifice to Hercules, i. 282 *n.*[1] ; on the rites of Osiris, vi. 85

Lacueva, Father, missionary to the Yuracares, ii. 205 *n.*

Lada, mythical being in Russia, the funeral of, iv. 261, 262

Ladakh, offerings of wheat-harvest to spirit of agriculture in, viii. 117

Ladder for the use of a tree-spirit, ii. 35 ; to facilitate the descent of the sun, ii. 99 ; for use of soul, iii. 47

Ladders of paper pinned to shoulders of women at Mid-Lent, iv. 241

Ladon, in Arcadia, the wooded gorge of the river, ii. 8

Ladyday, divining rod to be secured in the twilight between the third day and the night after, xi. 282

Laetare, the fourth Sunday in Lent, iv.

222 n.[1]; custom observed by the Germans of Moravia on, ii. 63

Laevinus, M. Valerius, funeral games in his honour, iv. 96

Lafitau, J. F., on namesakes of the dead regarded as their reincarnation, iii. 365 sq.

Lagarde, P. A. de, on the " Ride of the Beardless One," ix. 402, 405

Lagash in Babylonia, votive cones of clay found at, v. 35 n.[5]

Lago di Naftia in Sicily, v. 221 n.[4]

Lagos, in West Africa, i. 365, iv. 112 ; Ibadan in the interior of, iv. 203 ; human sacrifices for the crops at, vii. 239 sq.

Lagrange, Father M. J., on the mourning for Adonis as a harvest rite, v. 231

Laguna, Pueblo village of New Mexico, festival of the dead at, vi. 54 n.[2]

Lahn, the Yule log in the valley of the, x. 248

Laibon, medicine-men among the Masai, i. 343

Laius and Oedipus, iv. 193

Lake inhabited by mythical serpents, i. 156 ; by a dragon, xi. 112 sq.

Lake-dwellers of Europe, barley cultivated by the, vii. 132

—— -dwellings of prehistoric Europe, ii. 352 sq.

Lakes, gods of lakes married to women, ii. 150 sq. ; human victims thrown into, as offerings to water spirits, ii. 158 sq.

Lakhubai, an Indian goddess, gardens of Adonis in her worship, v. 243

Lakomba, an island of Fiji, reeds tied together to prevent the sun from going down in, i. 316

Lakor, island of, taboos observed by women and children during war in, i. 131 ; treatment of the navel-string in, i. 187 ; theory of earthquakes in, v. 198 ; annual expulsion of diseases in a proa in, ix. 199

Lakshmi, wife of Vishnu, supposed to pervade the Holy Basil (tulasi) plant, ii. 26

Laluba, the, of the Upper Nile, rainmakers as chiefs among, i. 345

Lama of Tibet, the Grand, i. 411 sq., ix. 197, 220, 221, 222 ; mode of determining a new, i. 411 ; his palace at Lhasa, i. 412 ; worshipped as a true and living god, i. 412 ; and Sankara, iii. 78. See also Lamas

——, the Teshu, embassy of George Bogle to, ix. 203

Lamaist sects, ix. 94

Lamas, Grand, Buddha supposed to be incarnate in the, i. 410 sq.

Lamas River in Cilicia, v. 149, 150

Lamb, blood of, drunk by priestess to procure inspiration, i. 381 ; thrown into lake as offering to Hades, vii. 15 ; killed sacramentally, viii. 314 sq. ; burnt alive to save the rest of the flock, x. 301

—— and pig as expiatory victims, iii. 226

—— of Mycenae, the golden, i. 365

Lambing, time of, ii. 328 n.[4]

Lame, woman who throws fish-bones into sea, pretends to be, viii. 254

Lame Goat, the, at harvest in Skye, vii. 284

" —— reign," Sparta warned against a, iv. 38

Lamentations of Egyptian reapers, v. 232, vi. 45 ; of the savage for the animals and plants which he eats, vi. 43 sq. ; of Cherokee Indians " after the first working of the crop," vi. 47 ; of the Karok Indians at cutting sacred wood, vi. 47 sq. ; pretended, for insects which destroy the crops, viii. 279 sq.

Laments for Tammuz, v. 9 sq. ; for dead kings of Judah, v. 20 ; for Osiris, vi. 12

Lammas, the 1st of August, great fairs in Ireland at, iv. 99, 100, 101 ; a harvest festival, iv. 105 ; superstitious practice of Highlanders at, x. 98 n.[1]

Lamoa, gods in Poso, xi. 154

Lampblack used to avert the evil eye, vi. 261

Lampong in Sumatra, the natives of, adore the sea, iii. 10

Lamps, dedication of burning, i. 12 sq. ; in the grove at Nemi, i. 13 ; to light the ghosts to their old homes, iii. 371, vi. 51 sq. ; for the use of ghosts at the Feast of All Souls, vi. 72, 73. See also Lanterns

Lampsacus, citizens of, excluded from games in honour of Miltiades, iv. 94 ; Persephone as corn-goddess on a coin of, vii. 44

Lampson, M. W., on substitutes for capital punishment in China, iv. 146, 273

Lanarkshire, " burning out the Old Year " at Biggar in, ix. 165

Lancashire, custom of catching the breath and soul of the dying in, iv. 200 ; All Souls' Day in, vi. 79 ; Hallowe'en customs in, x. 244 sq.

Lancelot constrained to be king, iv. 120 sq., 135

Lanchang, a Malay craft, ix. 187

Land cleared for cultivation by men, vii. 113 sq., 117 sqq.

Landak, district of Dutch Borneo, the Dyaks of, names of parents and grandparents not to be mentioned among, iii. 340 ; bride and bridegroom not to tread the earth among, x. 5 ; birth-trees for children among, xi. 164

Lande-Patry in Normandy, game of ball on Shrove Tuesday at, ix. 183

Landen, the battlefield of, outcrop of poppies on, v. 234

Landowners, sacrifices offered to spirits of former, vii. 228

Lane, E. W., on the fire-drill of the ancient Bedouins, ii. 209 $n.^4$; on the rise of the Nile, vi. 31 $n.^1$; on the omnipresence of jinn in Egypt, ix. 104

Lanercost, Chronicle of, need-fire noticed in the, x. 286

Lanfine, in Ayrshire, mode of cutting the last corn at, vii. 154

Lang, Andrew, on stories of the type of Cupid and Psyche, iv. 130 $n.^1$; on the bull-formed Dionysus, viii. 4 ; on the fire-walk, xi. 2 $n.^1$; on the bull-roarer, xi. 228 $n.^2$

Langenbielau, in Silesia, custom at threshing at, vii. 148 sq.

Langensalza, Grass King at Whitsuntide near, ii. 85

Langrim, a Khasi state, king elected by all adult males in, ii. 295

Language of animals acquired by eating serpent's flesh, viii. 146 ; learned by means of fern-seed, xi. 66 n.

—— of birds, learned by means of serpents, i. 158 ; learned by tasting dragon's blood, viii. 146

—— of birds and beasts, knowledge of the, possessed by Indian king, iv. 123

——, change of, caused by taboo on the names of the dead, iii. 358 sqq., 375, 380 ; caused by taboo on the names of chiefs and kings, iii. 375, 376 sqq.

—— of husbands and wives, difference between, iii. 347 sq.

—— of men and women, difference between, iii. 348 sq.

——, special, devoted to the person and attributes of the king of Siam, i. 401 ; employed by hunters, iii. 396, 398, 399, 400, 402, 404, 410 ; employed by searchers for eagle-wood and lignum aloes, iii. 404 ; employed by searchers for camphor, iii. 405 sqq. ; employed by miners, iii. 407, 409 ; employed by reapers at harvest, iii. 410 sq., 411 sq. ; employed by sailors at sea, iii. 413 sqq.

—— See also Speech and Words

Lanquineros, Indians of Central America, their period of abstinence before sowing, ii. 105

L 'ánṣára (El Anṣarah), Midsummer Day in North Africa, x. 213, 214 n.

Lantana salvifolia, burnt by Nandi women in cornfields, vi. 47

Lanterns, the Feast of, in Japan, vi. 65, ix. 151 sq. See also Lamps

Lanuvium, King of the Sacred Rites at, i. 44 $n.^1$; sacred serpent at, viii. 18

Lanyon, in Cornwall, holed stone near, xi. 187

Lanzone, R. V., on the rites of Osiris, vi. 87 $n.^5$

Laodice, a Hyperborean maiden, at Delos, i. 34 n.

Laodicea in Syria, human sacrifices at, iv. 166 $n.^1$

Laon, Midsummer fires near, x. 187

Laos, a province of Siam, taboos observed by rhinoceros hunters and gatherers of lac in, i. 115 ; taboos observed by wives of absent elephant-hunters in, i. 120 ; rain-making at New Year in, i. 251 ; fire on hearth extinguished after a death in, ii. 267 $n.^4$; precautions against strangers in, iii. 104 ; knotted grass a charm used by hunters in, iii. 306 ; special language used by elephant-hunters in, iii. 404 ; hunters never step over their weapons in, iii. 424 ; boxers at funerals in, iv, 97 ; infants at birth placed in rice-sieves in, vii. 8 ; Koui hunters hamstring game in, viii. 267 ; ravages of rats in, viii. 282 $n.^8$; prayers at cairns in, ix. 29 ; beginning of year in, ix. 149 $n.^2$; elephant-hunters not allowed to touch the ground in, x. 5 ; the natives of, their doctrine of the plurality of souls, xi. 222

Laosian village, divinity of salt-pans at a, i. 410

Laosians of Siam, their belief in demons, ix. 97

Laphystian Zeus, his sanctuary at Alus, iv. 161 ; ram with golden fleece sacrificed to, iv. 162 ; sacrifices offered to, by the house of Athamas, iv. 163 ; sanctuary of, on Mount Laphystius, iv. 164 ; king's eldest son liable to be sacrificed to, iv. 164 sq., vii. 25

Laphystius, Mount, in the land of Orchomenus, iv. 164

Lapis manalis used in rain-making ceremony at Rome, i. 310

Lappland, tying up the wind in knots in, i. 326

Lapps will not extinguish fire in absence of fishers, i. 121 ; the forest-god of the, ii. 125 ; their customs after killing a bear, iii. 221, viii. 224, xi. 280 n. ; loose knots on lying-in women, iii. 294 ; brass ring worn as an amulet among the, iii. 314 ; reincarnation of ancestors among the, iii. 368 ; fear to call bears by their true name, iii. 398 ; arranged the bones of the animals they ate in anatomical order for the purpose of facilitating their resurrection, viii. 257 ; their rule as to menstruous women, x. 91 ; their story of the external soul, xi. 149 *sq.*

Larch-tree, sacred, in the Tyrol, ii. 20

Lares, images of the, beside the hearth, ii. 206

Larka Kols of India, their belief in tree-spirits, ii. 42

Larkspur, looking at Midsummer bonfires through bunches of, x. 163, 165 *sq.*

Larnax Lapethus in Cyprus, Melcarth worshipped at, v. 117

Laro, a Nuba spirit, viii. 114

Larrakeeyah or Larrekiya, Australian tribe, their belief in conception without cohabitation, v. 103 ; their treatment of girls at puberty, x. 38

Larvae or *lares*, viii. 94 *n.*[5]

Last day of the year, annual expulsion of demons on the, ix. 145 *sqq.* See also Hogmanay

—— sheaf called "the Dead One," iv. 254. See Sheaf

Lateran Museum, statue of Attis in the, v. 279

—— statue of Ephesian Artemis, i. 38 *n.*[1]

Latham, R. G., on succession to husband's property among the Kocchs, vi. 215 *n.*[2]

Latin Christianity, its tolerance of rustic paganism, ix. 346

—— confederacy, the, in relation to sacred Arician grove, i. 22 *sq.*

—— festival, the great (*Feriae Latinae*), iv. 283

—— kings thought to be the sons of the fire-god by mortal mothers, ii. 195 *sqq.* ; lists of, ii. 268 *sqq.* ; stories of their miraculous birth, ii. 272

—— League, the, ii. 386

—— mode of reckoning intervals of time, iv. 59 *n.*[1]

Latins, sanctity of the woodpecker among the, iv. 186 *n.*[4]

Latinus, King, changed into Latian Jupiter, ii. 187 ; founder of the Alban dynasty, ii. 197 ; his wife a Vestal, ii. 235 ; his disappearance, iv. 283

Latium, many local Jupiters in, ii. 184 ; in antiquity, the woods of, ii. 188 ; succession to the kingdom in ancient, ii. 266 *sqq.* ; female descent of the kingship in, ii. 271 ; the rustic militia of, shod only on one foot, iii. 311

Latuka, Lion-chief in, viii. 228

Latukas of the Upper Nile, rain-makers as chiefs among the, i. 346 ; punish their chiefs for drought and failure of the crops, i. 354 ; custom at childbirth among the, iii. 245 ; burn women's hair after childbirth, iii. 284

Laughing forbidden to hunters, iii. 196

Laughlan Islanders, their belief and custom as to shooting stars, iv. 63

Launceston, in Cornwall, Midsummer bonfire near, ii. 141

Laurel grown in place of purification, i. 26 ; eaten by Apollo's prophetess, i. 384 ; Apollo's prophetess fumigated with, i. 384 ; branch of, carried by Roman general in his triumph, ii. 175 ; wreath of, worn by Roman general in his triumph, ii. 175 ; used in kindling fire by friction, ii. 251, 252 ; Cadmus crowned with, iv. 78 *sq.*, vi. 241 ; crown of, substituted for crown of oak leaves as prize in the Pythian games, iv. 80 ; reason for substitution of laurel for oak, iv. 81 *sq.* ; Apollo crowned with wreath of laurel at Tempe, iv. 81, vi. 240 ; gold wreath of, worn by priest of Hercules, v. 143 ; in purificatory rites, vi. 240 *sq.*, ix. 262

——, sacred, used to form the victor's crown at Delphi and Thebes, iv. 79 *sqq.* ; guarded by a dragon, iv. 79 *sq.* ; chewed by priestess of Apollo, iv. 80

Laurel-Bearer at Thebes, iv. 88 *sq.*, vi. 241

—— bearing, festival of the, at Thebes, iv. 78 *sq.*, 88 *sq.*, vi. 241

—— -Bearing Apollo, iv. 79 *n.*[3]

Laurels, in sacred grove of Dia, ii. 122 ; in Latium, ii. 188 ; Roman ceremony of renewing the, ix. 346 *n.*[1]

Laurus and Florus, feast of, on August 18th, x. 220

Lausitz, Midsummer fires in, x. 170 ; marriage oaks in, xi. 165. See also Lusatia

Lavinia, daughter of Amata, ancestress of the Alban kings, ii. 197, 197 *n.*[4]

Lavinium, worship of Vesta at, i. 14, ii. 197 *n.*[4]

Lawes, W. G., on the belief in ghosts among the natives of British New Guinea, ix. 84 *sq.*

Lawgivers, ancient, on the uncleanness of women at menstruation, x. 95 *sq.*

Laws of Manu, on the effects of a good king's reign, i. 366 ; on the divinity of kings and Brahmans, i. 403 ; on a father as born again in his own son, iv. 188 ; on the transmigration of evil-doers into animals, viii. 298 *sq.*

Laws of nature, the conception of, not primitive, i. 374

Laying hands on children to bless them, i. 367

Laziness transferred to a cornel-tree, ix. 55

Lazy Man, a Midsummer masker enclosed in a leafy framework, ii. 83
Le Mole, on the Lake of Nemi, i. 17
Lead, melted, in Arab cure for melancholy or madness, ix. 4; divination by melted lead at Hallowe'en, x. 242
Leaf, lost soul brought back in a, iii. 67. *See also* Leaves
Leaf-clad dancers, vii. 95
—— -clad mummer on Midsummer Day, xi. 25 *sq.*
—— -clad mummers, ii. 74 *sqq.*, 78 *sqq.*; mock marriage of, ii. 97; represent the powers of vegetation, ii. 97; at Whitsuntide, iv. 207 *sqq.*
—— King, the, at Hildesheim on Whit-Monday, ii. 85
—— Man representative of tree-god in India, ix. 61; the Little, in spring at Ruhla in Thüringen, ii. 80 *sq.*
Leafy bust at Nemi, portrait of the King of the Wood, i. 41 *sq.*
Leake, W. M., on flowers in Asia Minor, v. 187 *n.*[6]
Leaning against a tree prohibited to warriors, iii. 162, 163
Leaping, a contest at the Eleusinian games, vii. 110
—— over fire at the Parilia, ii. 327; as a Roman purification, ii. 329; as a form of purification among the Esquimaux, viii. 249; after a burial to escape the ghost, xi. 18
—— over bonfires to make the flax or hemp grow tall, v. 251, x. 119, 165, 166 *sq.*, 168, 173, 174, 337; to get rid of the devil, ix. 156; to ensure good crops, x. 107; as a preventive of colic, x. 107, 195 *sq.*, 344; to ensure a happy marriage, x. 107, 108; to ensure a plentiful harvest, x. 155, 156; to be free from backache at reaping, x. 165, 168; as a preventive of fever, x. 166, 173, 194; for luck, x. 171, 189; in order to be free from ague, x. 174; in order to marry and have many children, x. 204, 338 *sq.*; as cure of sickness, x. 214; to procure offspring, x. 214, 338; over ashes of fire as remedy for skin diseases, xi. 2; a panacea for almost all ills, xi. 20; as a protection against witchcraft, xi. 40
—— and dancing to make the crops grow high, i. 137 *sqq.*, vii. 110, viii. 330 *sq.*, ix. 232, 238 *sqq.*
—— of women over the Midsummer bonfires to ensure an easy delivery, x. 194, 339. *See also* Jumping
Leaps, high and long, at New Year festival of the Kayans, vii. 98; of the Salii at Rome, ix. 232; of lovers over the Mid-summer bonfires, x. 165, 166, 168, 174. *See* Leaping
Learchus, son of King Athamas, iv. 161; killed by his father, iv. 162, vii. 24
Leared, A., on the Isowa or Aïsawa sect in Morocco, vii. 21 *sq.*
Leather, Mrs. Ella Mary, on the Yule log in Herefordshire, x. 257 *sq.*
Leather of priestess's shoes not to be made from hide of beast that died a natural death, iii. 14
Leavened bread, Flamen Dialis not allowed to touch, iii. 13
Leaves, disease transferred to, ix. 2, 259; fatigue transferred to, ix. 8 *sqq.*; thrown on dead chameleons, ix. 28; thrown on heap at ford, ix. 28; used to expel demons, ix. 201, 206, 262. *See also* Leaf
—— and flowers as talismans, vi. 242 *sq.*
—— and twigs of trees as fodder of cattle in Southern Europe, ii. 328
Leaving food over, taboos on, iii. 126 *sqq.*
Leavings of food, magic wrought by means of, iii. 118, 119, 126 *sqq.*
Lebadea, altar of Rainy Zeus at, ii. 360 *n.*[8]; Trophonius at, iv. 166 *n.*[1]
Lebanon, peasants of the, their custom as to children's cast teeth, i. 181 *sq.*; the forests of Mount, v. 14; the charm of the, v. 235; peasants of the, their dread of menstruous women, x. 83 *sq.*
——, Aphrodite of the, v. 30
——, Baal of the, v. 32
Lech, a tributary of the Danube, vi. 70; Midsummer fires in the valley of the, x. 166
Lechrain, milk-stones in, i. 165; Burial of the Carnival in, iv. 231; Feast of All Souls in, vi. 70 *sq.*; the divining rod in, xi. 68
Lecky, W. E. H., on the influence of great men on the popular imagination, vi. 199; on the treatment of magic and witchcraft by the Christian Church, xi. 42 *n.*[2]
Lecœur, J., on weather forecasts for the year in the Bocage of Normandy, ix. 323
Lee, the laird of, his "cureing stane," x. 325
Leeches, charm against, viii. 281
Leeds, the Boy Bishop at, ix. 338
Leeting the witches, x. 245
Lefébure, E., on Typhon in the form of a boar, viii. 30 *n.*[4]
Left shoe of bridegroom to be without buckle or latchet, iii. 300
Legend of the foundation of Carthage and similar tales, vi. 249 *sq.*
Legends of the custom of slaying kings, iv. 120 *sqq.*; told as charms, vii. 102

sq. ; of persons who could not die, x. 99 *sq.*

Legs not to be crossed, iii. 295, 298 *sq.*
—— and thighs of diseased cattle cut off and hung up as a remedy, x. 296 *n.*[1], 325

Lehmann-Haupt, Professor C. F., on the historical Semiramis, v. 177 *n.*[1]; on the historical reality of Christ, ix. 412 *n.*[2] ; on the date of the crucifixion, ix. 415 *n.*[1]

Lehner, Stefan, on stories told to promote the growth of the crops, vii. 104; on the fear of demons in German New Guinea, ix. 83 *sq.*

Leicestershire, Plough Monday in, viii. 330 *n.*[1]

Leine, river of Central Germany, water drawn from it silently on Easter night, x. 124

Leinster, taboos observed by the ancient kings of, iii. 11 ; the fair of Carman in, iv. 100 ; legend of the voluntary death of monks to stay a pestilence in, iv. 159 *n.*[1]; Midsummer fires in, x. 203

Leipsic, "Carrying out Death" at, iv. 236

Leitch, Archie, as to the harvest Maiden on the Gareloch, vii. 158 *n.*[1]

Leith Links, witches burnt on, ix. 165

Leitmeritz district of Bohemia, the Shrovetide Bear in, viii. 326

Leitrim, County, Midsummer fires in, x. 203 ; divination at Hallowe'en in, x. 242 ; need-fire in, x. 297 ; witch as hare in, x. 318

Leleen, the, a priest in Celebes, iii. 129

Leme, the river, at Ludlow, ix. 182

Lemnos, new fire brought annually from Delos to, i. 32, x. 138 ; worship of Hephaestus in, x. 138

Lemon, external souls of ogres in a, xi. 102

Lemons distasteful to the spirits of tin, iii. 407

Lenaean festival of Dionysus at Athens presided over by the King, i. 44

Lenaeon, a Greek month, vii. 66

Lendu tribe of Central Africa, rainmakers as chiefs among the, i. 348

Lengua Indians of the Gran Chaco, their ceremony to make the sun shine, i. 313 ; fling sticks at a whirlwind, i. 330 ; power of magicians among the, i. 359 ; their belief as to dreams, iii. 38 ; after a death the survivors change their names among the, iii. 357 ; their belief as to the state of the spirits of the dead, iv. 11 ; their fear of meteors, iv. 63 ; their practice of killing first - born girls, iv. 186 ; their custom of infanticide, iv. 197 ;

their festivals at the rising of the Pleiades, vii. 309 ; their way of bilking the ghosts of ostriches, viii. 245 ; their fear of demons, ix. 78 *sq.*; seclusion of girls at puberty among the, x. 56 ; masquerade of boys among the, x. 57 *n.*[1]; marriage feast extinct among the, x. 75 *n.*[2]

Lenormant, François, on the Eleusinian mysteries, vii. 39 *n.*[1] ; on Demeter as an Earth-goddess, vii. 40 *n.*[3]

Lent, personified by an actor or effigy, iv. 226, 230 ; symbolized by a seven-legged effigy, iv. 244 *sq.* ; ceremony at Halberstadt in, ix. 214 ; perhaps derived from an old pagan period of abstinence observed for the growth of the seed, ix. 347 *sqq.* ; rule of continence during, ix. 348
——, the Buddhist, ix. 349 *sq.*
——, the Indian and Fijian, v. 90
——, Queen of, iv. 244
—— and the Saturnalia, ix. 345 *sqq.*
——, the first Sunday in, bonfires and torches on, x. 107 *sqq.*
——, the third Sunday in, Death carried out on, iv. 238
——, the fourth Sunday in, Death carried out on, ii. 73 *sq.*, iv. 233 *sq.*, 235, 236 ; girl called the Queen on, ii. 87 ; called Dead Sunday, or Mid-Lent, iv. 221, 222 *n.*[1], 233 *sqq.*, 250, 255
——, the fifth Sunday in, Death carried out on, iv. 234 *sq.*, 239

Lenten fast, its origin, ix. 348
—— fires, x. 106 *sqq.*

Lenz, H. O., on ancient names for mistletoe, xi. 318

Leo the Great, as to the celebration of Christmas, v. 305
—— the Tenth, pope, his boar-hunting, i. 6 *sq.*

Leobschütz, district of Silesia, "Easter Smacks" in, ix. 268 ; Midsummer fires in, x. 170

Leonard, Major A. G., on death from imagination in Africa, iii. 136 *sq.* ; on sacrifices to prolong the lives of kings and others, vi. 222 ; on the custom of licking the blood from a sword with which a man has been killed, viii. 155 ; on the periodic expulsion of demons at Calabar, ix. 204 *n.*[1] ; on souls of people in animals, xi. 206 *n.*[2]

Leonidas, funeral games in his honour, iv. 94

Leopard, supposed transformation of a man into a, in West Africa, iv. 83 *sq.* ; the commonest familiar of Fan wizards, xi. 202. *See also* Leopards

Leopard Societies of Western Africa, iv. 83

Leopard's blood drunk, or its flesh or

heart eaten to make the eater brave, viii. 141 *sq.*
Leopard's whiskers in a charm, viii. 167
Leopards, dead kings turn into, iv. 84 ; related to royal family of Dahomey, iv. 85 ; inspired human mediums of, viii. 213 ; revered by the Igaras of the Niger, viii. 228 ; ceremonies observed by the Ewe negroes after the slaughter of, viii. 228 *sqq.* ; souls of dead in, viii. 288, 289 ; lives of persons bound up with those of, xi. 201, 202, 203, 204, 205, 206 ; external human souls in, xi. 207. *See also* Leopard
Lepanto, the Ignorrotes of, ii. 30
Leper disinterred as rain-charm, i. 285
Lepers sacrificed to the Mexican goddess of the White Maize, vii. 261 ; Mexican goddess of, ix. 292
Lepers' Island, the soul as an eagle in, iii. 34 ; child's soul brought back in, iii. 65
Lepidus, Marcus Aemilius, funeral games in his honour, iv. 96
Leprosy, king of Israel expected to heal, v. 23 *sq.* ; thought to be caused by drinking pig's milk, viii. 24, 25 ; caused by eating a sacred animal, viii. 25 *sqq.* ; thought to be caused by injuring a totemic animal, viii. 26 *sq.* ; in the Old Testament, viii. 27 ; Hebrew custom as to, ix. 35 ; Mexican goddess of, ix. 292
Lepsius, R., on a sort of carnival in Fazoql, iv. 17 *n.* [2] ; his identification of Osiris with the sun, vi. 121 *sq.*
Lerbach, in the Harz Mountains, custom on Midsummer Day at, ii. 66
Lerida in Catalonia, funeral of the Carnival at, iv. 225 *sq.*
Lerons of Borneo, use of magical images among the, i. 59
Lerotse leaves used in purification, viii. 69
Lerpiu, a powerful spirit revered by the Dinka and embodied in the rain-maker, iv. 32
Lerwick, winds sold at, i. 326 ; ceremony of Up-helly-a' at, ix. 169, x. 269 *n.* [1] ; Christmas *guizing* at, x. 268 *sq.* ; procession with lighted tar-barrels on Christmas Eve at, x. 268
Lesachthal (Carinthia), new fire at Easter in the, x. 124
Lesbos, barren fruit-trees threatened in, ii. 22 ; superstition as to shadows in, iii. 89 ; building custom in, iii. 89 ; charm to prevent the consummation of marriage in, iii. 300 ; the harvest Hare in, vii. 280 ; sticks or stones piled on scenes of violent death in, ix. 15 ; fires on St. John's Eve in, x. 211 *sq.*

Leschiy, a woodland spirit in Russia, ii. 124 *sq.*
Leslie, David, on Caffre belief as to spirits of the dead incarnate in serpents, xi. 211 *n.* [2], 212 *n.*
Lesneven, in Brittany, burning of an effigy (of Carnival) on Ash Wednesday at, iv. 229 *sq.*
Leti, island of, taboos observed by women and children during war in, i. 131 ; treatment of the navel-string in, i. 187 ; marriage of the Sun and Earth in, ii. 98 *sq.* ; theory of earthquakes in, v. 198 ; annual expulsion of diseases in a proa in, ix. 199
Leto said to have clasped a tree before bearing Apollo and Artemis, ii. 58
Letopolis, neck of Osiris at, vi. 11
Lettermore Island, Midsummer fires in, x. 203
Letts of Russia, swing to make the flax grow high, iv. 157, 277, vii. 107 ; their celebration of the summer solstice, iv. 280 ; their annual festival of the dead, vi. 74 *sq.* ; their sacrifices to wolves, viii. 284 ; Midsummer fires among the, x. 177 *sq.* ; gather aromatic plants on Midsummer Day, xi. 50
Leucadia, magical rock in, i. 161
Leucadians, their use of human scape-goats, ix. 254
Leucippe, daughter of Minyas, her Bacchic fury, iv. 164
Lévi, Professor Sylvain, on the magical nature of sacrifice in ancient India, i. 228 *sq.*
Leviathan or Rahab, a dragon of the sea, iv. 106 *n.* [2]
Leviticus (xviii. 24 *sq.*) on sexual crime as a defilement of the land, ii. 114 *sq.*
Lewin, Captain T. H., on the tug-of-war among the Chukmas, ix. 174 *sq.*
Lewis, E. W., on the sting of bees as a cure for rheumatism, iii. 106 *n.* [2]
Lewis, Rev. Thomas, on the mind of the savage, iii. 420 *n.* [1]
Lewis, Professor W. J., x. 127 *n.* [1]
Lewis the Pious, institutes the Feast of All Saints, vi. 83
Lewis, the island of, tying up the wind in knots in, i. 326 ; need-fire in, ii. 238, x. 293 ; the Old Wife at harvest in, vii. 140 *sq.* ; custom of fiery circle in the, x. 151 *n.*
Lexicon Mythologicum, author of, on the Golden Bough, xi. 284 *n.* [3]
Leza, supreme being recognized by the Bantu tribes of Northern Rhodesia, vi. 174
Lezayre parish, in the Isle of Man, custom on May Day in, ii. 54
Lhasa, the Dalai Lama of, i. 411 *sq.* ;

ceremony of the Tibetan New Year at, ix. 197 *sq.*, 218 *sqq.*

Lhoosai, the, of South-Eastern India, their harvest festival, ii. 48 ; woman's share in agriculture among, vii. 122

Lhota Naga, tribe of the Brahmapootra valley, their human sacrifices for the crops, vii. 243 *sq.*

Lhwyd, Edward, on snake stones, x. 16 *n.*[1]

" Liar's mound, the," in Borneo, ix. 14

Libanius, on human life before Demeter, vii. 43 *n.*[1]

Libations offered by maidens to the dead maiden Iphinoe, i. 28 ; in honour of tree-spirits, ii. 46, 51 ; Roman rule as to wine offered in, iii. 249 *n.*[2]; of beer to dead bears, viii. 181, 186 ; of beer to the fire-god and house-god, viii. 185

Libchowic, in Bohemia, girl called the Queen on the fourth Sunday in Lent at, ii. 87

Libebé, African kingdom, kings as rain-makers in, i. 348

Liber, Father, the Italian counterpart of Dionysus, vii. 12 ; Roman sacrifice of new wine to, viii. 133

Liberty, despotism more favourable than savagery to, i. 218

Libyans, the Alitemnian, awarded the kingdom to the fleetest runner, ii. 299. *See also* Panebian

Licata, in Sicily, St. Angelo ill-treated at, i. 300

Licence accorded to slaves at the Saturnalia, ii. 312, ix. 307 *sq.*, 350 *sq.*, 351 *sq.*; accorded to female slaves at the *Nonae Caprotinae*, ii. 313 *sq.*; periods of, viii. 62, 63, 66 *sqq.*, ix. 225 *sq.*, 306, 328 *sq.*, 343, 344, x. 135 ; annual periods of general, ix. 127, 131, 226 *n.*[1]; month of general, ix. 148 ; periods of, preceding or following the annual expulsion of demons, ix. 251 ; at Midsummer festival, x. 180, 339

Licentious rites for the fertilization of the ground, ix. 177

Lichfield, the Boy Bishop at, ix. 337

Licinius Imbrex, on Mars and Nerio, vi. 232

Licorice root used to beat people with at Easter, ix. 269

Lie down, manslayers forbidden to, iii. 179

Liebrecht, F., on the death of the Great Pan, iv. 7 *n.*[2]; on the Sacaea, ix. 392 *n.*[1]

Liège, Lenten fires near, x. 108

Lienz in the Tyrol, masquerade on Shrove Tuesday at, ix. 242, 245

Lierre, in Belgium, the witches' Sabbath at, xi. 73

Life, the Egyptian symbol of, ii. 133 ; in the blood, iii. 241, 250 ; human, valued more highly by Europeans than by many other races, iv. 135 *sq.*; of community bound up with life of divine king, x. 1 *sq.*; the water of, xi. 114 *sq.*; of woman bound up with ornament, xi. 156 ; of a man bound up with the capital of a column, xi. 156 *sq.*; of a man bound up with fire in hut, xi. 157 ; of child bound up with knife, xi. 157 ; of children bound up with trees, xi. 160 *sqq.*; the divisibility of, xi. 221. *See also* Soul

Life-indices, trees and plants as, xi. 160 *sqq.*

—— -tokens in fairy tales, xi. 118 *n.*[1]

—— -tree of the Manchu dynasty at Peking, xi. 167 *sq.*

—— trees of kings of Uganda, xi. 160

Ligho, a heathen deity of the Letts, x. 177, 178 *n.*[1]; compare iv. 280

Light, girls at puberty not allowed to see the, x. 57 ; external soul of witch in a, xi. 116. *See also* Lights

Lightning averted from houses by cross-bills, i. 82; magical imitation of, in rain-making, i. 248, 258, 303 ; one of twins regarded as a son of, i. 266 ; the lord and creator of rain, i. 266 ; imitation of, by kings, i. 310, ii. 180; wood of tree that has been struck by, i. 319 ; expiation for trees struck by, ii. 122 ; the art of drawing down, ii. 181 ; fire perhaps first procured from a tree struck by, ii. 256 ; fire kindled by, ii. 263 ; African deities of, ii. 370 ; supposed to be produced by means of flints, ii. 374 ; trees struck by, used in magic, iii. 287 ; not to be called by its proper name, iii. 401 ; thought by Caffres to be caused by the ghost of a powerful chief, vi. 177 with *n.*[1]; no lamentations allowed for persons killed by, vi. 177 *n.*[1]; eating flesh of bullock that has been struck by, viii. 161 ; treatment of men, animals, and houses that have been struck by, viii. 161, xi. 298 *n.*[2]; feet of men who have been killed by lightning slit to prevent their ghosts from walking, viii. 272 ; charred sticks of Easter fire used as a talisman against, x. 121, 124, 140 *sq.*, 145, 146 ; the Easter candle a talisman against, x. 122 ; brands of the Midsummer fire a protection against, x. 166 *n.*[1], 183 ; flowers thrown on roofs at Midsummer as a protection against, x. 169 ; charred sticks of Midsummer bonfires a protection against, x. 174, 187, 188, 190 ; ashes of Midsummer fires a protection against, x. 187, 188, 190 ; torches interpreted as imitations of, x. 340 *n.*[1]; bonfires a protection against, x. 344 ; a magical coal a protection against, xi. 61 ; pine-tree struck by, used to make bull-roarer, xi. 231 ; superstitions about trees struck by, xi. 296 *sqq.* ; thought to be caused by a great bird, xi. 297 ; strikes oaks oftener than any other tree of the European forests, xi. 298 *sq.* ; regarded as a god descending out of heaven, xi. 298 ; places struck by lightning enclosed and deemed sacred, xi. 299. *See also* Thunder

Lightning and thunder, the Yule log a protection against, x. 248, 249, 250, 252, 253, 254, 258, 264 ; mountain arnica a protection against, xi. 57 *sq.*

Lightning god of the Slavs, ii. 365

—— Zeus, i. 33, ii. 361

" Lights of the dead," to enable the ghosts to enter houses, vi. 65

Lights, three hundred and sixty-five, in the rites of Osiris, vi. 88

Lignum aloes, taboos observed in the search for, iii. 404

Liknites, epithet of Dionysus, vii. 5, 27

Lille, the corn-spirit in the shape of a horse near, vii. 294

Lillooet Indians of British Columbia, their belief concerning twins, i. 265 *n.*[1]; their propitiation of slain bears, viii. 226 *sq.* ; their regard for the bones of deer and beavers, viii. 243 ; seclusion of girls at puberty among the, x. 52 *sq.*

Limbs, amputated, kept by the owners against the resurrection, iii. 281

Limburg, processions with torches on the first Sunday in Lent in, x. 107 *sq.* ; Midsummer fires in, x. 194 ; the Yule log in, x. 249

Lime-kiln in divination at Hallowe'en, x. 235, 243

—— -tree, used in kindling fire by friction, ii. 251 ; toothache nailed into a, ix. 59 *sq.* ; the bloom of the, gathered at Midsummer, xi. 49 ; mistletoe on limes, xi. 315, 316

—— -trees sacred, ii. 366, 367

—— -wood used at expulsion of demons, ix. 156 ; used to kindle need-fire, x. 281, 283, 286

Limerick, execution of traitor at, iii. 244

Limping on one foot at carrying home the last sheaf, vii. 232, 284

Limu, the Assyrian eponymate, iv. 117

Lincoln, the Boy Bishop at, ix. 337

Lincolnshire, saying as to a woman's apron burnt by a spark in, ii. 231 ; Plough Monday in, viii. 330 *n.*[1]; the Yule log in, x. 257 ; witches as cats

and hares in, x. 318 ; calf buried to stop a murrain in, x. 326 ; mistletoe a remedy for epilepsy and St. Vitus's dance in, xi. 83 *sq.*

Lindau in Anhalt, the Corn-woman at harvest at, vii. 233

Lindenbrog, on need-fire, x. 335 *n.*[1]

Lindus in Rhodes, sacrifice to Hercules at, i. 281 ; taboos as to entering a sanctuary at, viii. 85

Lingayats, Hindoo sect, worship their priest as a god, i. 404 *sq.*

Lint seed, divination by, at Hallowe'en, x. 235

Linus, identified with Adonis, vii. 258

—— or Ailinus, Phoenician vintage song, vii. 216, 257 *sq.*, 263, 264

Lion, footprints of a, in magic, i. 209 ; king represented with the body of a, iv. 85 ; deity standing on a, v. 123 *n.*[2], 127 ; the emblem of Mother Goddess, v. 164 ; as emblem of Hercules and the Heraclids, v. 182, 184 ; carried round acropolis of Sardes, v. 184, vi. 249 ; beloved by Ishtar, ix. 371. *See also* Lions

" —— with the Sheepskins," among the Arabs of Morocco, ix. 265

——, the sun in the sign of the, xi. 66 *sq.*

Lion-chief, viii. 228

—— -god at Boghaz-Keui, the mystery of the, v. 139 *sq.* ; of Lydia, v. 184

—— -killer, purification of, iii. 176, 220

—— -slaying god, statue of, v. 117

—— -tamer as chief of his tribe, i. 347 *sq.*

Lion's claws in a charm, viii. 167

—— fat, unguent of, viii. 164

—— flesh or heart eaten to make eater brave, viii. 141, 142 *sq.*, 147

Liongo, an African Samson, xi. 314

Lions not called by their proper names, iii. 400 ; called foxes for euphemism, iii. 400 ; dead kings reincarnate in, iv. 84, v. 83 *n.*[1], vi. 163 ; carved, at gate, v. 128 ; as emblems of the great Asiatic Mother-goddess, v. 137 ; deities seated on, v. 162 ; spirits of dead chiefs reincarnated in, vi. 193 ; inspired human mediums of, viii. 213 ; propitiation of dead, viii. 228 ; souls of the dead in, viii. 287 *sqq.*

Lip, under, of bullock tabooed as food, i. 119

Lippe, the river, a tributary of the Rhine, i. 391

Lir majoran, a god of husbandry in the Kei Islands, viii. 123

Lisiansky, U., on annual festival in Hawaii, iv. 117 *sq.*

Lismore, witch as hare in, x. 316 *sq.*

Lithuania, the May Queen in, ii. 74; customs at driving the herds out to pasture for the first time in, ii. 340 *sq.*; wolves not to be called by their proper names during December in, ii. 396; the last sheaf called Boba (Old Woman) in, vii. 145; customs at threshing in, vii. 148, 223 *sq.*; custom at cutting the last corn in, vii. 223; old Lithuanian ceremonies at eating the new corn, viii. 49 *sq.*; mummers and dances on Twelfth Day in Prussian Lithuania, viii. 327; "Easter Smacks" in, ix. 269; Midsummer fires in, x. 176; sanctuary at Romove in, xi. 91. *See also* Lithuanians

Lithuanian mythology, ii. 348

Lithuanians, their contagious magic of footprints, i. 211; tree-worship among the, ii. 9, xi. 89; the thunder-god Perkunas of the, ii. 365 *sqq.*; their reverence for oaks, ii. 366, 371; the old, their funeral banquets, iii. 238; the Old Rye-Woman among the, vii. 133; their custom before first ploughing in spring, x. 18; their story of the external soul, xi. 113 *sqq. See also* Lithuania

——, the heathen, their worship of the sun, i. 317 *sq.*; their sacred groves, ii. 46; sacrificed to Pergrubius on St. George's Day, ii. 347

Little Deer, chief of the deer tribe, viii. 241

"—— Easter Sunday" (Low Sunday), in Cornwall, iv. 153, 154 *n.*[1]

—— Jupiter, the, ii. 179, 192

—— Leaf Man, ii. 80 *sq.*

—— Whitsuntide Man, ii. 81

—— Wood-woman, vii. 232

Lityerses, song of Phrygian reapers and threshers, vii. 216; son of Midas, king of Phrygia, vii. 217; his reaping-matches, vii. 217; his treatment of strangers on the harvest field, vii. 217; slain by Hercules, vii. 217; story of, its coincidences with harvest-customs of modern Europe, vii. 218 *sqq.*, 236, 252 *sqq.*; his relation to Attis, vii. 255 *sq.*; compared to Bormus, vii. 257

Liver, indurated, thought to be healed by touch of chief's feet, i. 371; induration of the, attributed to touching sacred chief, iii. 133; of kangaroo rubbed on back of man-slayer, iii. 167 *sq.*; of pig, omens drawn from, vii. 97; of deer eaten to make eater long-lived like deer, viii. 143; of dog eaten to acquire bravery, viii. 145; of serpent eaten to acquire language of animals, viii. 146; regarded as the seat of the soul, viii. 147 *sq.*; re-

garded as the seat of valour, viii. 148; of brave men eaten, viii. 148, 151 *sq.*; of bear, used as medicine, viii. 187 *sq.*

Lives of a family bound up with a fish, xi. 200; with a cat, xi. 150 *sq.*

"Living fire" made by the friction of wood, ii. 237, x. 220; as a charm against witchcraft, ii. 336; the needfire, x. 281, 286

—— parents, children of, in ritual, vi. 236 *sqq.*

Livingstone, David, on the government of the Banyai, ii. 292

Livinhac, Mgr., on chiefs as rain-makers in the Nyanza region, i. 353

Livonia, sacred grove in, ii. 43; belief as to were-wolves in, iii. 42; Midsummer festival in, iv. 280; story of a were-wolf in, x. 308

Livonians cull simples on Midsummer Day, xi. 49 *sq.*

Livuans, the, of New Britain, their belief in demons, ix. 82 *sq.*

Livy on the Ciminian forest, ii. 8; on the annual Roman custom of knocking a nail, ix. 66; on the Saturnalia, ix. 345 *n.*[1]

Lizard, soul in form of, iii. 38; external soul in, xi. 199 *n.*[1]; sex totem in the Port Lincoln tribe of South Australia, xi. 216; said to have divided the sexes in the human species, xi. 216

—— or snake in annual ceremony for the riddance of evils, ix. 208

Lizards and serpents supposed to renew their youth by casting their skins, ix. 302 *sqq.*

Ljeschie, Russian wood-spirits, viii. 2

Lkuñgen Indians, their charm to make hair grow long, i. 145; their magic uses of wasps, i. 152; their contagious magic of wounds, i. 202; believe trees to be men transformed, ii. 30

Llama, blood of, sprinkled on doorway, iv. 176 *n.*[1]; black, as scapegoat, ix. 193

Llandebie, sin-eater reported near, ix. 44

Llandegla in Wales, church of St. Tecla at, ix. 52

Llangors, in Breconshire, the sin-eater at, ix. 43

Lo Bengula, king of the Matabeles, i. 394; as a rain-maker, i. 351 *sq.*; treatment of strangers before admission to, iii. 114

Loaf made of corn of last sheaf, vii. 148 *sq.*; thrown into river Neckar on St. John's Day, xi. 28. *See also* Loaves

Loango, palsy called the king's disease in, i. 371; the negroes of, their belief that sexual crime entails drought and famine, ii. 111 *sq.*; the Bavili of, ii. 112; licence of princesses in, ii. 276

sq. ; taboos observed by kings of, iii. 8, 9 ; foods tabooed to priests and heirs to the throne in, iii. 291 ; practice of knocking nails into idols in, ix. 69 *sq.*, 70 *n.*[1] ; new-born infants not allowed to touch the earth in, x. 5 ; girls secluded at puberty in, x. 22

Loango, king of, deposed for failure of harvest or of fishing, i. 353 ; revered as a god, i. 396 ; fights all rivals for his crown, ii. 322 ; forbidden to see a white man's house, iii. 115 ; not to be seen eating or drinking, iii. 117 *sq.* ; confined to his palace, iii. 123 ; refuse of his food buried, iii. 129

Loaves in shape of a boar, vii. 300 ; hung on head of sacrificed horse, viii. 42, 43 ; in human shape, viii. 48 *sq.*, 94, 95. *See also* Loaf

Lobeck, Chr. A., on the Thesmophoria, viii. 17 *n.*[5] ; his emendation of Pausanias, viii. 18 *n.*[1] ; his emendation of Clement of Alexandria (*Protrept.* ii. 17), viii. 20 *n.*[7]

Lobo, spirit-house, among the Toradjas of Celebes, i. 129, ii. 39

Local totem centres in Central Australia, i. 96

Loch Katrine, x. 231

—— Tay, Hallowe'en fires on the banks of, x. 232

Lochaber, the harvest Maiden in, vii. 157

Lock and key in a charm, x. 283

Locks unlocked at childbirth, iii. 294, 296 ; thought to prevent the consummation of marriage, iii. 299 ; as amulets, iii. 308 ; unlocked to facilitate death, iii. 309 ; magical virtue of, iii. 310 ; opened by springwort, xi. 70 ; opened by the white flower of chicory, xi. 71 ; mistletoe a master-key to open all, xi. 85

—— and knots, magical virtue of, iii. 309 *sq.* *See also* Keys

Locrians, the Epizephyrians, female kinship among the, ii. 284 ; their sacrifice of maidens to the Trojan goddess, ii. 284 ; the prostitution of their daughters before marriage, ii. 285 ; vicarious sacrifice offered by the, viii. 95 *n.*[2]

Locust, a Batta totem, xi. 223

—— Apollo, viii. 282

—— Hercules, viii. 282

Locusts, sultans expected to drive away, i. 353 ; chiefs held responsible for the ravages of, i. 354 ; superstitious precautions against, viii. 276, 279, 281

Loeboes (Looboos), a tribe of Sumatra, exchange of costume between boys and girls among the, vi. 264. *See also* Looboos

Log, the Yule, x. 247 *sqq.*

Logan, W., on the custom of attacking the kings of Calicut, iv. 49

Logea, island off New Guinea, taboos observed by manslayers in, iii. 167 ; the dead not named in, iii. 354

Logic of the savage, viii. 202

Logierait, parish of, in Perthshire, knots unloosed at marriage in, iii. 299 *sq.* ; Beltane festival in, x. 152 *sq.* ; Hallowe'en fires in, x. 231 *sq.*

Loire, the Lower, the Fox at reaping in, vii. 296

Loiret, Lenten fires in the department of, x. 114

Loitering in the doorway forbidden under certain circumstances, i. 114

Loki and Balder, x. 101 *sq.*

Lokoala, initiation by spirits among the Indians of North-Western America, ix. 376

Lokoiya, the, of the Upper Nile, rainmakers as chiefs among, i. 345

Lokoja on the Niger, external human souls in crocodiles and hippopotamuses near, xi. 209

Lolos, of Western China, their recall of the soul in sickness, iii. 43 ; divine by shoulder-blades of sheep, iii. 229 *n.*[4] ; their belief as to the stars, iv. 65 *sq.*

Lombardy, oak forests of, in antiquity, ii. 354 ; the Day of the Old Wives in, iv. 241 ; belief as to the "oil of St. John" on St. John's Morning in, xi. 82 *sq.*

Lombok, East Indian island, the rice personified as husband and wife in, vii. 201 *sqq.*

London, the immortal girl of, x. 99 ; Midsummer fires in, x. 196 *sq.*

Long Man, a river-god, i. 144

" —— -haired mother," title of the Goddess of Maize in Mexico, i. 136

—— -headed men chosen kings, ii. 297

Longevity, homoeopathic charms to ensure, i. 158, 169

" Longevity garments," in China, i. 169

Longforgan, parish of, in Perthshire, the Maiden Feast at harvest in, vii. 156 *sq.*

Longnor, near Leebotwood, in Shropshire, the Mare at harvest at, vii. 294

Longridge Fell, *leeting* the witches at Hallowe'en at, x. 245

Lons-le-Saulnier, in the Jura, last sheaf called the Bitch at, vii. 272

Looboos (Loeboes) of Sumatra creep through a cleft rattan to escape a demon, xi. 182 *sq.* *See also* Loeboes

Look back, not to, in ritual, iii. 157

Looking at bonfires through mugwort a protection against headache and sore eyes, xi. 59

Loom, not to be touched by a man, iii. 164

Loon, the cry of the, associated with rain, i. 288

Loop in ceremony to detain the sun, i. 317

Loowoo, a kingdom in Celebes, regalia of, i. 364 ; superstitious belief as to the king of, i. 399

Loranthus europaeus, a species of mistletoe, xi. 315, 317 *sqq.* ; called "oak mistletoe" (*visco quercino*) in Italy, xi. 317

—— *vestitus*, in India, xi. 317

Lord of the Diamond, prayed to at cairns in Laos, ix. 29

" —— of the Heavenly Hosts," a temporary king in Siam, iv. 149, 150, 155, 156

—— and Lady of the May, ii. 62, 90 *sq.*

—— of Misrule, ix. 251, 312 ; at Bodmin, ii. 319 *n.*[1] ; in England, ix. 331 *sqq.*

—— of the Rice, in Siam, iv. 150 *n.*

—— of the Wells at Midsummer in Fulda, xi. 28

—— of the Wood among the Gayos of Sumatra, offerings to the, ii. 36, 125

Lorne, the Beltane cake in, x. 149

Lorraine, "killing the dog of the harvest" in, vii. 273 ; King and Queen of the Bean in, ix. 315 ; Midsummer fires in, x. 169 ; the Yule log in, x. 253 ; Midsummer customs in, xi. 47. *See also* Lothringen

Loryma in Caria, Adonis worshipped at, v. 227 *n.*

Losengrad, the district of, in Thrace, masquerade at Carnival in, viii. 332

Loss of the shadow regarded as ominous, iii. 88

Lostwithiel in Cornwall, temporary king at, iv. 153 *sq.*

Lot, the Fox at threshing in, vii. 297

Loth, J., on the Twelve Days, ix. 325 *n.*[3]

Lothringen (Lorraine), "Killing the Old Woman" at threshing in, vii. 223 ; the harvest Dog in, vii. 273 ; the harvest Bull in, vii. 288. *See also* Lorraine

Lots, Greek custom as to the drawing of, vi. 248 ; cast at Purim, ix. 361 *sq.*

Lottin, the island of, ix. 109

Lotus-tree, shorn tresses of Vestal virgins hung on a, iii. 275

Loucheux, the, of North-West America, the power of medicine-men among, i. 356 ; and Hare-skin Indians forbidden to eat the sinew of the leg of animals, viii. 265

Loudoun, in Ayrshire, fires on St. Peter's Day in the parish of, x. 207

Louhans, in Saône-et-Loire, the Fox at harvest at, vii. 296 *sq.*

Louis XIV. as King of the Bean, ix. 313 ; at Midsummer bonfire in Paris, xi. 39

Louisiade Islands, sacred trees in the, ii. 17

Louisiana, festival of new corn in, viii. 77 *sqq.*

——, the Indians of, kept bones of beavers and otters from dogs, viii. 239; lamented the death of the buffaloes which they were about to kill, viii. 242

Lous, a month of the Syro-Macedonian calendar, iv. 113, 116, vii. 258, 259, ix. 355, 358

Love, magical images to procure, i. 77 ; cures for, i. 161, ix. 3 ; illicit, thought to blight the fruits of the earth, ii. 107 *sqq.*

Love charm, footprints and marigolds in a, i. 211 ; of arrows, x. 14

—— -charms practised on St. George's Day, ii. 345 *sq.* ; by means of hair, iii. 270

" —— Chase" among the Kirghiz, ii. 301

Lover's Leap, a cape in the island of Leucas, human scapegoats at the, ix. 254

Lovers won by knots, iii. 305 ; term applied to the Baalim, v. 75 *n.* ; leap over the Midsummer bonfires, x. 165, 166, 168, 174

—— of goddesses, their unhappy ends, i. 39 *sq.*, vi. 158 *sq.*

—— of Semiramis and Ishtar, their sad fate, ix. 371 *sq.*

Low, Sir Hugh, on Dyak belief as to souls of dead in trees, ii. 30 *sq.* ; on Dyak treatment of heads of slain enemies, v. 295

Low Countries, the Yule log in the, x. 249

Lowell, Percival, his fire-walk, xi. 10 *n.*[1]

Loyalty Islands, recall of a lost soul in the, iii. 54

Lua and Saturn, vi. 233

Luang-Sermata Islands, belief as to cauls in the, i. 188

Luangwa, district of Northern Rhodesia, prayers to dead ancestors in, vi. 175 *sq.*

Luba, in Busoga, pretended human sacrifice at, iv. 215

Lubare, god, in the language of the Baganda, i. 395

Lübeck, church of St. Mary at, immortal lady in the, x. 100

Lucan, on the Druids, i. 2 *n.*[1]

——, the Thessalian witch in, iii. 390

Lucerne, Lenten fire-custom in the canton

of, x. 118 *sq.* ; bathing at Midsummer in, xi. 30

Luchon, in the Pyrenees, serpents burnt alive at the Midsummer festival in, xi. 38 *sq.*, 43

Lucian, on hair offerings, i. 28 ; on the procedure of a Syrian witch, iii. 270 ; on the names of the Eleusinian priests, iii. 382 ; on the death of Peregrinus, iv. 42, v. 181 ; on religious prostitution, v. 58 ; on image of goddess at Hierapolis-Bambyce, v. 137 *n.*[2] ; on dispute between Hercules and Aesculapius, v. 209 *sq.* ; on the ascension of Adonis, v. 225 *n.*[3] ; old scholium on, viii. 17 ; as to the rites of Hierapolis, ix. 392 ; on the Platonic doctrine of the soul, xi. 221 *n.*[1]

Lucina, how she delayed the birth of Hercules, iii. 298 *sq.* *See also* Juno Lucina

Lucius, E., on the Assumption of the Virgin, i. 15 *n.*[1]

Luck, bad, transferred to trees, ix. 54 ; leaping over the Midsummer fires for good, x. 171, 189

Luckau, races at harvest-festival near, vii. 76

Luckiness of the right hand, x. 151

Lucky names, men with, chosen by Romans to open enterprises of moment, iii. 391 *n.*[1]

Lucretius, on the origin of fire among men, ii. 257 *n.*

Ludhaura, marriage of the *tulasi* to the *Salagrama* at, ii. 27

Ludlow in Shropshire, the tug-of-war at, ix. 182

Lug, Celtic god, i. 17 *n.*[2] ; legendary Irish hero, iv. 99, 101

Lugaba, the supreme god of the Bahima, vi. 190

Lugg, river, in Radnorshire, ix. 183

Lugnasad, the 1st of August, in Ireland, iv. 101

Lules or Tonocotes of the Gran Chaco, their behaviour in an epidemic, ix. 122 *sq.*

Lumholtz, C., on agricultural ceremonies of the Tarahumare Indians of Mexico, vii. 227 *sq.* ; on the transference of fatigue to sticks or stones, ix. 10 ; on the dances of the Tarahumares of Mexico, ix. 236 *sqq.* ; on Huichol superstition as to the growth of corn, ix. 347 *n.*[3]

Lumi lali, consecrated rice-field, among the Kayans of Borneo, vii. 93, 108

Lunar calendar corrected by observation of the Pleiades, vii. 314 *sq.*, 315 *sq.* ; of Mohammedans, x. 216 *sq.*, 218 *sq.*

—— months of Greek calendar, vii.

52 *sq.*, 82 ; observed by savages, vii. 117, 125

Lunar and solar years, attempts to harmonize, iv. 68 *sq.*, vii. 80 *sq.*, ix. 325 *sq.*, 339, 341 *sqq.*

—— sympathy, the doctrine of, vi. 140 *sqq.*

—— year equated to solar year by intercalation, ix. 325, 342 *sq.*

Lüneburg, district of, harvest custom in the, vii. 230 ; the Harvest-goat at, vii. 283

Lunéville, calf killed at harvest at, vii. 290

Lung-fish clan among the Baganda, vi. 224

Lung-wong, Chinese rain-god, i. 299

Lungs or liver of bewitched animal burnt or boiled to compel the witch to appear, x. 321 *sq.*

Luritcha tribe of Central Australia, their custom of killing and eating children, iv. 180 *n.*[1] ; their belief in the reincarnation of the dead, v. 99 ; destroy the bones of their enemies to prevent them from coming to life again, viii. 260

Lusatia (Lausitz), custom of "Carrying out Death" in, iv. 239, 247, 249 ; the "Witch-burning" in, ix. 163. *See also* Lausitz

Luschan, Professor F. von, on kings of Dahomey and Benin in animal forms, iv. 85 *n.*[3], 86 *n.*[1] ; on images stuck with nails, ix. 70 *n.*[1]

Lushais of Assam, men dressed as women, women dressed as men, among the, vi. 255 *n.*[1] ; their belief in demons, ix. 94 ; sick children passed through a coil among the, xi. 185 *sq.*

Lussac, in Vienne, death of the Carnival on Ash Wednesday at, iv. 226 ; Midsummer fires at, x. 191

Lute-playing, charm for, i. 152

Luther, Martin, burnt in effigy at Midsummer, x. 167, 172 *sq.*, xi. 23

Luxembourg, "Burning the Witch" in, xi. 116

Luxor, paintings at, ii. 131, 133 ; reliefs in temple at, iii. 28 ; temples at, vi. 124

Luzon, in the Philippine Archipelago, the Ilocans of, i. 142, 179, ii. 18, iii. 44 ; Bontoc in, ii. 30, vii. 240 ; the Apoyaos of, vii. 241 ; rice-fields guarded against wild hogs in, viii. 33 ; the Catalangans of, viii. 124 ; the Irayas of, viii. 124 ; exorcism in, ix. 260

Lyall, Sir Alfred C., on the opposition between religion and magic, i. 224 *n.*[1]

Lyall, Sir Charles J., on the system of

mother-kin among the Khasis, vi. 202 *sq.*

Lycaeus, Mount, rain-making spring on, i. 309 ; rain-charm practised by the priest of Zeus on, ii. 359 ; sanctuary of Zeus on, iii. 88 ; festival of Zeus on, iv. 70 *n.*[1] ; human sacrifices on, iv. 163, ix. 353

Lycaonian plain, v. 123

Lyceum or Place of Wolves at Athens, viii. 283, 284

Lycia, Patara in, ii. 135 ; flowers in, v. 187 *n.*[6] ; Mount Chimaera in, v. 221 ; mother-kin in, vi. 212 *sq.*

Lycian language, question of its affinity, vi. 213 *n.*[1]

—— men dressed as women in mourning, vi. 264

Lycium europaeum, L., ix. 153 *n.*[1]

Lycomedes, king of Scyros, Achilles at the court of, ii. 278

Lycopolis, in Egypt, the wolf, the beast-god of, viii. 172

Lycosura, in Arcadia, taboos observed in the sanctuary of the Mistress at, iii. 227 *n.*, 314, viii. 46 ; statue of Demeter or Persephone in the sanctuary of the two goddesses at, viii. 339

Lycurgus, king of the Edonians in Thrace, put to death to restore fertility to land, i. 366 ; torn in pieces by horses, vi. 98, 99, vii. 241 ; slew his son Dryas, vii. 24, 25

Lycus, valley of the, at Hierapolis, v. 207

Lydia, female descent of kingship in, ii. 281 *sq.* ; prostitution of girls before marriage in, v. 38, 58 ; the lion-god of, v. 184 ; the Burnt Land of, v. 193 *sq.* ; traces of mother-kin in, vi. 259 ; the burning of kings in, ix. 391

Lydian kings held responsible for the weather and the crops, i. 366, v. 183 ; their divinity, v. 182 *sqq.* ; traced their descent from Ninus and Hercules, ix. 391

Lydians celebrate a festival of Dionysus in spring, vii. 15

Lydus, Joannes, on Phrygian rites at Rome, v. 266 *n.*[2] ; on the expulsion of Mamurius Veturius, ix. 229 *n.*[1]

Lyell, Sir Charles, on hot springs, v. 213 *n.*[4] ; on volcanic phenomena in Syria and Palestine, v. 222 *n.*[1]

Lying-in women, widespread fear of, iii. 150 *sqq.* ; sacred, iii. 151

Lynxes not called by their proper name, iii. 398

Lyons, the harvest Cat in the neighbourhood of, vii. 280

Lyre as instrument of religious music, v. 52 *sq.*, 54 *sq.* ; the instrument of Apollo, v. 288

Lysimachus scatters the bones of the kings of Epirus, vi. 104

Lythrum salicaria, purple loosestrife, gathered at Midsummer, xi. 65

Ma, goddess of Comana in Pontus, v. 39, 265 *n.*[1], ix. 421 *n.*[1]

Ma-hlaing, district of Burma, rain-making in, i. 288

Maass, E., on the identification of Donar with Jupiter, iii. 364 *n.*[3]

Mablaan, chief of the Bawenda, revered as rain-maker, i. 351

Mabuiag, island in Torres Straits, use of magical images in, i. 59 ; rain-making in, i. 262 ; charms to raise the wind in, i. 323 *sq.* ; the fire-drill in, ii. 209 ; seclusion of girls at puberty in, iii. 147, x. 36 *sq.* ; continence observed during turtle-season and before hunting dugong in, iii. 192 ; bull-roarers thought to promote the growth of garden produce in, vii. 106 ; the Sam or Cassowary totem in, viii. 207 ; dread and seclusion of women at menstruation in, x. 78 *sq.* ; girls at puberty in, x. 92 *n.*[1] ; belief as to a species of mistletoe in, xi. 79

Macahity, an annual festival in Hawaii, iv. 117

Macalister, Mrs. Alexander, on the harvest Maiden in Perthshire, vii. 157 *n.*[3]

Macalister, Professor R. A. Stewart, on infant burial at Gezer, v. 109 *n.*[1]

Macassar in Celebes, words tabooed to sailors in, iii. 413 ; magical unguent in, x. 14

Macassars of Celebes, their belief as to the blighting effect of the blood of incestuous persons, ii. 110 ; their custom of swinging, iv. 277 ; ascribe a soul to rice, vii. 183

Maccabees, the Second Book of, its date, ix. 360

M'Carthy, Sir Charles, eaten by the Ashantees to make them brave, viii. 149

McClintock, Walter, on a legend of the Blackfoot Indians concerning the Pleiades, vii. 311

MacCorquodale, John, on the harvest Maiden and Old Wife in Glencoe, vii. 165 ; on the harvest *Cailleach* at Crianlarich, vii. 166

Mac Crauford, the great arch witch, x. 293

MacCulloch, J. A., on the Twelve Days, ix. 326 *n.*

Macdonald, Rev. James, on magic to catch fish in the Highlands, i. 110 ; on Bride's bed in the Highlands, ii.

94 $n.^2$; on the fire-drill in South-East Africa, ii. 210 *sq.*; on a custom of infanticide in South Africa, iv. 183 $n.^2$; on the worship of ancestors among the Bantus, vi. 176; on the correction of the Caffre lunar calendar by observation of the Pleiades, vii. 315 *sq.*; on the Pondo festival of new fruits, viii. 66 *sq.*; on the expulsion of demons in some South African tribes, ix. 111 $n.^1$; on the story of Headless Hugh, xi. 131 $n.^1$; on external soul in South Africa, xi. 156

Macdonald, King of the Isles, i. 160, 161

Macdonalds, the, supposed to heal a certain disease by their touch, i. 370 $n.^3$

Macdonell, Professor A. A., on Agni, xi. 296

Macdonell, Lady Agnes, on the custom of horn-blowing at Penzance on May Day, ix. 164 $n.^1$

McDougall, W., and C. Hose, on creeping through a cleft stick after a funeral, among the Kayans of Borneo, xi. 176 $n.^1$ *See also* Hose, Dr. Charles

Mace of Narmer, representation of the Sed festival on the, vi. 154

Maceboard, the, a procession of Summer in the Isle of Man, iv. 258

Macedonia, custom as to children's cast teeth in, i. 180 *sq.*; rain-making among the Greeks of, i. 272 *sq.*, 274; wooden effigies of swallows carried about the streets on the 1st of March in, viii. 322 *n.*; demons and ghosts hammered into walls in, ix. 63 $n.^4$; Midsummer fires among the Greeks of, x. 212; bonfires on August 1st in, x. 220; need-fire among the Serbs of Western, x. 281; St. John's flower at Midsummer in, xi. 50

Macedonian calendar, vii. 258 *sq.*

—— farmers, their homoeopathic magic at digging their fields, i. 139

—— peasantry burn effigies of Judas at Easter, x. 131

—— superstitions as to the Twelve Days, ix. 320

Macedonians preserve their nail-parings for the resurrection, iii. 280

Macfarlane, Mr., of Faslane, as to the last corn at harvest, vii. 158 $n.^2$

McGregor, A. W., on the rite of new birth among the Akikuyu, xi. 263

MacGregor, Sir William, on the political power of magicians in British New Guinea, i. 337; and the Alake of Abeokuta, iv. 203 $n.^2$

Macha, Queen, Irish fair said to have been instituted in her honour, iv. 100

Machindranath temple at Lhasa, ix. 219

MacIntyre, Duncan, on the harvest *Cailleach*, vii. 166

Mack, a usurper in Tonquin, iii. 19

Mackay, Alexander, on need-fire, x. 294 *sq.*

Mackays, sept of the "descendants of the seal," xi. 131 *sq.*

Mackenzie, Sheriff-Substitute David J., on Up-helly-a' at Lerwick, ix. 169 $n.^2$, x. 268 $n.^1$

Mackenzie, E., on need-fire, x. 288

Maclagan, Dr. R. C., on the harvest Maiden and Old Wife in the Highlands of Scotland, vii. 165 *sq.*

Maclay coast of Northern New Guinea, ii. 254, iii. 109

McLennan, J. F., on *deega* and *beena* marriage, ii. 271 $n.^1$; on the bride-race, ii. 301 $n.^4$; on custom of chiefs marrying their sisters, iv. 194 $n.^1$; on brother and sister marriages, v. 44 $n.^2$, vi. 216 $n.^1$

"Macleod's Fairy Banner," i. 368

Macphail, John, on need-fire, x. 293 *sq.*

Macpherson, Major S. C., on human sacrifices among the Khonds, vii. 250

Macrobius, on Janus, ii. 385 $n.^2$; on the mourning Aphrodite, v. 30; on the Egyptian year, vi. 28 $n.^3$; on Osiris as a sun-god, vi. 121; his solar theory of the gods, vi. 121, 128; on the influence of the moon, vi. 132; on institution of the Saturnalia, ix. 345 $n.^1$

McTaggart, Dr. J. McT. Ellis, on transmigration, viii. 309 $n.^1$

Macusis of British Guiana, their belief in dreams, iii. 36 *sq.*; custom observed by parents after childbirth among the, iii. 159 *n.*; seclusion of girls at puberty among the, x. 60

Madagascar, kings of, as high-priests, i. 47 *sq.*; foods tabooed in, i. 117 *sq.*; custom of women in Madagascar while men are at war, i. 131; magical use of stones in, i. 160; modes of counteracting evil omens in, i. 173 *sq.*; chiefs held responsible for the operation of the laws of nature in, i. 354; the Antaimorona of, i. 354; the Antimores of, i. 354; the Betsileo of, i. 397, iii. 246, viii. 116, 289; the Hovas of, i. 397, viii. 116; special terms used with reference to persons of the blood royal in, i. 401 $n.^3$; custom of passing newborn children through the fire in, ii. 232 $n.^3$; recall of lost souls in, iii. 54; mirrors covered after a death in, iii. 95; the Mahafaly country in, iii. 103; the Zafimanelo of, iii. 116; the Antambahoaka of, iii. 216; the Antandroy of, iii. 227; the Tanala of, iii. 227, vii. 9, viii. 290; blood of nobles not to be shed in, iii. 243 ; taboo on mentioning personal names in, iii. 327 ; the Sakalavas of, iii. 327, iv. 202, viii. 40 *n.* ; natives of, reluctant to name the dead, iii. 353 ; names of chiefs and kings tabooed in, iii. 378 *sqq.* ; tabooed words in, iii. 401 ; belief as to the transmigration of the dead into serpents in, iv. 84 ; vicarious sacrifice for a king in, vi. 221 ; men dressed as women in, vi. 254 ; first - fruits offered to kings in, viii. 116 ; mourners rub themselves with the juices of the dead in, viii. 163 ; crocodiles respected in, viii. 214 *sq.* ; belief in the transmigration of human souls into animals in, viii. 289 *sq.* ; the Antankarana of, viii. 290 ; the Sihanaka of, ix. 2 *sq.* ; stones or clods thrown on solitary graves in, ix. 19 ; transference of evils in, ix. 33 *sq. See also* Malagasy

Madangs of Borneo, custom observed by them after a funeral, xi. 175 *sq.*

Madder-harvest, Dutch custom at, vii. 231, 235 *sq.*

Madenassana Bushmen, their reluctance to look on their sacred animal the goat, viii. 28 *sq.*

Madern, parish of, Cornwall, holed stone in, xi. 187

Madi or Moru tribe of Central Africa bury their nail - parings, iii. 277 ; their sacrament of a lamb, viii. 314 *sq.* ; their annual sacrifice of a lamb, ix. 217

Madium district in Java, deceiving the spirit of a plant in the, ii. 23

Madness of Orestes, cured by sitting on a stone, i. 161. *See also* Insanity

Madonie Mountains, in Sicily, Midsummer fires on the, x. 210

Madonna, effigies of, sold and eaten, viii. 94

—— and Isis, their resemblance, vi. 119

Madras, ceremonies after the killing of a cobra in, iii. 222 *sq.*

Madras Presidency, the fire-walk in the, xi. 6

Madura, island off Java, inspired mediums in, i. 384 ; the Kappiliyans of, x. 69 ; the Parivarams of, x. 69

Maeander, the river, supposed to take the virginity of brides, ii. 162 ; the valley of, subject to earthquakes, v. 194 ; sanctuaries of Pluto in the valley of, v. 205, 206 ; Lityerses thrown by Hercules into, vii. 217

Maera, the dog of Icarus, iv. 281

Maeseyck, in Belgium, processions with torches on first Sunday in Lent at, x. 107 *sq.*

Mafuie, the Samoan god of earthquakes, v. 200

Magarsus in Cilicia, v. 169 *n.*[3]

Magdalen College, Oxford, the Boy Bishop at, ix. 337

Magdeburg, the Flax-mother near, vii. 133 ; the last sheaf called Grandmother near, vii. 136 ; reaper who cut the last corn wrapt in corn-stalls near, vii. 221

Maggots eaten at an initiatory rite, viii. 141

Maghs of Bengal, their ceremony at felling a tree, ii. 38

Magian priests, ii. 241 *n.*[4]

Magic, principles of, i. 52 *sqq.* ; based on misapplications of the association of ideas, i. 53 *sq.*, 221 *sq.* ; in ancient India, i. 63 *sq.*, 228 *sq.*, ix. 91 ; in modern India, i. 64 *sq.* ; in ancient Egypt, i. 66, 67 *sq.*, 225, 230 *sq.* ; in ancient Babylonia, i. 66 *sq.* ; positive and negative, i. 111 *sq.*, 117 ; blent with the worship of the dead, i. 164 ; physical basis of, i. 174 *sq.* ; public and private, i. 214 *sq.*, 245 ; benefits conferred by, i. 218 *sq.* ; has paved the way for science, i. 219 ; attraction of, i. 221 ; fatal flaw of, i. 221 *sq.* ; opposed in principle to religion, i. 224 ; older than religion, i. 233 *sqq.* ; universality of belief in, i. 234 - 236 ; transition from magic to religion, i. 237 *sqq.*, ii. 376 *sq.* ; the fallacy of, not easy to detect, i. 242 *sq.* ; combined with religion, i. 347 ; the fallacy of, gradually detected, i. 372 ; declines with the growth of religion, i. 374 ; strangers suspected of practising, iii. 102 ; wrought by means of refuse of food, iii. 126 *sqq.* ; wrought through clippings of hair, iii. 268 *sqq.*, 275, 277, 278 *sq.* ; wrought on a man through his name, iii. 318, 320 *sqq.* ; degenerates into games, vii. 110 *n.* ; dwindles into divination, vii. 110 *n.*, x. 336 ; of a flesh diet, vii. 138 *sqq.* ; the belief in, persists under the higher religions, ix. 89 *sq.* ; movement of thought from magic through religion to science, xi. 304 *sq.*

——, the Age of, i. 235, 237, iv. 2

——, contagious, i. 52 - 54, 174 - 214, iii. 246, 268, 272 ; based on a mistaken association of ideas, i. 53 *sq.*, 174 ; of teeth, i. 176-182 ; of navel-string and afterbirth (placenta), i. 182-201 ; of wound and weapon, i. 201 *sqq.* ; of footprints, i. 207 - 212 ; of other impressions, i. 213 *sq.*

—— and ghosts, mugwort a protection against, xi. 59

——, homoeopathic or imitative, i. 52 *sqq.*, iii. 151, 152, 207, 295, 298, iv.

283, 285, vii. 10, 62, 262, 267, 331, 333, 334, viii. 272, ix. 177, 232, 248, 257, 404, x. 49, 133, 329, xi. 231, 287 ; based on a mistaken association of ideas, i. 53; in medicine, i. 78 *sqq.* ; for the supply of food, i. 85 *sqq.*; in fishing and hunting, i. 108 *sqq.* ; to make plants grow, i. 136 *sqq.* ; of the dead, i. 147 *sqq.* ; of animals, i. 150 *sqq.* ; of inanimate things, i. 157 *sqq.* ; of iron, i. 159 *sq.*; of stones, i. 160 *sqq.* ; of the heavenly bodies, i. 165 *sq.*; of the tides, i. 166 *sqq.* ; to annul evil omens, i. 170-174 ; for the making of rain, i. 247 *sqq.*
Magic, negative, equivalent to taboo, i. 111 *sqq.* ; examples of, i. 143
—— and religion, i. 220-243, 250, 285, 286, 347, 352, ii. 376 *sq.* ; confused together, i. 226 *sqq.* ; their historical antagonism comparatively late, i. 226 ; Hegel on, i. 423 *sqq.* ; combination of, v. 4
—— and science, their analogy, i. 220 *sq.* ; different views of natural order postulated by the two, xi. 305 *sq.*
—— sympathetic, i. 51 *sqq.*, iii. 126, 130, 164, 201, 204, 258, 268, 287, iv. 77, vii. 1, 11, 102, 139, viii. 33, 271, 311 *sq.*, ix. 399 ; the two branches of, Homoeopathic and Contagious, i. 54 ; examples of, i. 55 *sqq.*
—— and witchcraft, permanence of the belief in, ix. 89. *See also* Sorcery *and* Witchcraft
Magic flowers of Midsummer Eve, xi. 45 *sqq.*
Magical bone in sorcery, x. 14
—— ceremonies for the multiplication of totemic animals, plants, etc., in Central Australia, i. 85 *sqq.* ; for the revival of nature in spring, iv. 266 *sqq.*; for the revival of nature in Central Australia, iv. 270 ; for the regulation of the seasons, v. 3 *sqq.*
—— changes of shape, vii. 305
—— control of the weather, i. 244 *sqq.* ; of rain, i. 247 *sqq.* ; of the sun, i. 311 *sqq.* ; of the wind, i. 319 *sqq.*
—— dramas to promote vegetation, ii. 120, vii. 187 *sq.* ; for the regulation of the seasons, v. 4 *sq.*
—— implements not allowed to touch the ground, x. 14 *sq.*
—— influence of medicine-bag, xi. 268
—— origin of certain religious dramas, ii. 142 *sq.*, v. 4, vii. 187 *sq.*, ix. 373 *sq.*
—— significance of games in primitive agriculture, vii. 92 *sqq.*
—— type of man-god, i. 244
—— uses made of the bodies of the dead, vi. 100 *sqq.*

Magical virtues of plants at Midsummer apparently derived from the sun, xi. 71 *sq.*
Magician, public, his rise to power, i. 215 *sqq.*
—— and priest, their antagonism, i. 226
Magician's apprentice, Danish story of the, xi. 121 *sqq.*
—— Glass, the, x, 16
—— progress, the, i. 214 *sqq.*, 335 *sqq.*
Magicians claim to compel the gods, i. 225 ; gods viewed as, *in* 240 *sqq.* ; importance of rise of professional magicians, i. 245 *sqq.* ; as kings, i. 332 *sqq.* ; political power of, i. 335 *sqq.*; develop into gods and kings, i. 375 ; the oldest professional class in the evolution of society, i. 420 ; develop into kings, i. 420 *sq.*; make evil use of spilt blood, iii. 246. *See also* Magic, Medicine-men, Shamans, *and* Sorcerers
——, Egyptian, their power of compelling the deities, i. 225, iii. 389 *sq.*
Magnesia on the Maeander, sacred cave near, i. 386 ; device on coins of, i. 386 *n.*[2]; worship of Zeus at, vi. 238 ; image of Dionysus in a plane-tree at, vii. 3 ; sacrifice of bull at, viii. 7 *sq.* ; the month of Cronion in, viii. 7, 8 *n.*[1], ix. 351 *n.*[2]
Magnets thought to keep brothers at unity, i. 165
Magondi, a Mashona chief, i. 393 *sq.*
Magpies' nests, custom of robbing the, viii. 321 *n.*[3]
Magyar tale, resurrection of hero in a, viii. 263
Magyars, Midsummer fires among the, x. 178 *sq.* ; stories of the external soul among the, xi. 139 *sq.*
Maha Makham, the Great Sacrifice, celebrated every twelfth year at Calicut, iv. 49
Mahabharata, the, the Indian epic, the Nagas in, i. 383 *n.*[4]; Draupadi and her five husbands in, ii. 306, xi. 7
Mahadeo, mock human sacrifices offered by the Bhagats to a, iv. 217 *sq.*
—— and Parvati, married Indian deities, their images worshipped, v. 242, 251
Mahadeva, Indian god, husband of Parvati, v. 241 ; propitiation of, ix. 197
Mahafaly country, in Madagascar, formerly tabooed to strangers, iii. 103
Mahafalys of Madagascar, their chiefs not allowed to sail the sea or cross rivers, iii. 10
Mahakam Dyaks of Borneo, i. 159
—— River in Borneo, iii. 104, vii. 98,

99 n.[1], 186, 187, 314 ; the Kayans of the, vii. 314

Maharajas, a Hindoo sect, worship their spiritual chiefs as incarnations of Krishna, i. 406 ; believe that bathing in a sacred well is a remedy for barrenness in women, ii. 160 sq.

Mahdi, an ancient, v. 74

Mahratta, dancing-girls in, v. 62

Mahrattas, their belief in human incarnations of the elephant-headed god Gunputty, i. 405

Mahua tree (*Bassia latifolia*) worshipped by the Mannewars in India, viii. 119

Mahwá-tree, bride tied to, at a Munda marriage, ii. 57

Mai Darat, a Sakai tribe of the Malay Peninsula, their exorcism of demons by means of effigies, viii. 102

Maia or Majestas, the wife of Vulcan, vi. 232 sq.

Maiau, hero in form of crocodile, v. 139 n.[1]

Maiden, the (Persephone), the descent of, vi. 41 ; name given to last corn cut in the Highlands of Scotland, vii. 140, 153, 155 sqq., 164 sqq. ; or Cornmaiden, name given to puppet made of rye at end of reaping near Wolfenbuttel, vii. 150

Maiden Feast at end of harvest in Perthshire, vii. 156

" —— -flax " at Midsummer, xi. 48

Maiden's Well at Eleusis, vii. 36

Maidenhead, name of last standing corn on the Gareloch, vii. 158

Maidhdeanbuain or *Maighdean-Bhuana*, " the shorn Maiden " at harvest in the Highlands of Scotland, vii. 155 sq., 164, 165

Maidu Indians of California, taboos observed by women and children in absence of hunters among the, i. 122 ; the importance of shamans among the, i. 357 sq. ; seclusion of girls at puberty among the, x. 42 ; their notion as to fire in trees, xi. 295 ; their idea of lightning, xi. 298

Maillotins on May Day, in the department of Mayenne, ii. 63

Maimonides, on loading a fruit-tree with stones, i. 140 ; on a custom observed at grafting by the heathen of Harran, ii. 100 n.[2] ; on the seclusion of menstruous women, x. 83

Maine, French department, oaks worshipped in, ii. 371

Mairs, in India, their custom of sacrificing their first-born sons to the small-pox goddess, iv. 181

Maize, Mexican goddesses of, i. 136, vii. 176, ix. 285 sq., 286 n.[1], 290, 291, 292, 294, 295 ; homoeopathic magic to promote the growth of, i. 136, 137 ; magical stones for the increase of, i. 162 ; continence at sowing, ii. 105 ; custom at maize harvest in Transylvania, iv. 254 ; time of the maize-harvest in modern Greece, vii. 114, 115, 119, 130 ; cultivated in South America, vii. 122, 124 ; cultivated in Assam, vii. 123 ; compared to a mother, vii. 130 ; American personification of, vii. 171 sqq. ; personified as an Old Woman who Never Dies, vii. 204 sq. ; cultivated in Burma, vii. 242 ; Mexican goddess of the White, lepers sacrificed to her, vii. 261 ; thought to be dependent on the Pleiades, vii. 310 ; red, a totem of the Omahas, viii. 25 sq. ; the Mexican goddess of the Young, ix. 278

Maize-mother, vii. 172 sqq.

Majhwars, Dravidian race of Mirzapur, their use of iron as a talisman, iii. 234 ; their use of chickens as scapegoats, ix. 36 ; their imprisonment of ghosts in trees, ix. 60 sq.

Makalaka hills, to the west of Matabeleland, i. 394

Makalakas, their human god, i. 394 sq. ; ceremony at the naming of a child among the, iii. 369 sq. ; their offerings of first-fruits, viii. 110 sq.

Makalanga, a Bantu tribe near Sofala, x. 135 n.[2]

Makanga, African tribe, their belief that the souls of dead chiefs are in lions, viii. 287 sq.

Makaram, an Indian month, iv. 49

Makatissas of South Africa, their use of magical dolls, i. 71

Make-Make, a god in Easter Island, viii. 133

Makololo, the, of South Africa, burn or bury their shorn hair for fear of witchcraft, iii. 281

Makral, "the witch," on first Sunday in Lent, at Grand Halleux, x. 107

Makrizi, Arab historian, on mode of stopping rain, i. 252 ; on the custom of throwing a virgin into the Nile, ii. 151 n.[2] ; on the burning of effigies of Haman at Purim, ix. 393 sq.

Malabar, use of magical images in, i. 64 ; iron as an amulet in, iii. 234 ; custom of suicide observed by kings in, iv. 47 ; custom of *Thalavettiparothiam* in, iv. 53 ; religious suicide in, iv. 54 sq. ; use of cows as scapegoats in, ix. 216 ; the Iluvans of, x. 5 ; the Tiyans of, x. 68

Malacca, the Mentras of, iii. 404

Malagasy, their homoeopathic magic at planting maize, i. 137 ; their use of children of living parents in ritual, vi. 247 ; venerate crocodiles, viii. 215 ; *faditras* among the, ix. 33 *sq.*

Malagasy language, dialectical variations of, caused by taboos on the names of chiefs and kings, living or dead, iii. 378 *sq.*, 380

—— porters, their belief as to a woman stepping over their poles, iii. 424

—— soldiers, foods tabooed to, i. 117 *sq.*; male animals not to be killed in the houses of absent, i. 119

—— whalers, rules observed by, iii. 191. *See also* Madagascar

Malanau tribes of Borneo, their use of a special language in searching for camphor, iii. 406 *sq.*; their belief in the transmigration of human souls into animals, viii. 294

Malas, the, of Southern India, their treatment of the placenta, i. 194 ; their custom in drought, i. 284 *n.* ; their rain-charm by means of frogs, i. 294 ; talismans of Mala women at childbirth, iii. 235 ; their communion with a goddess by eating her edible image, viii. 93 *sq.*

Malassi, a fetish in West Africa, xi. 256

Malay charms by means of magical images, i. 57 *sq.* ; at reaping rice, i. 139 *sq.*

—— conception of the soul of rice, vii. 180 *sqq.*

—— life, prevalence of magic in, iii. 416 *n.*[4]

—— magic, to catch crocodiles, i. 110 *sq.* ; tinctured with a belief in spirits, i. 220 *n.*[1]

—— maxim at planting maize, i. 136

—— miners, fowlers, and fishermen, special forms of speech employed by, iii. 407 *sqq.*

—— mode of rain-making, i. 262

—— Peninsula, power of medicine-men among the wild tribes of the, i. 360 *sq.* ; special terms used with reference to persons of the blood royal in the, i. 401 *n.*[3] ; the Djakuns of the, ii. 236 ; race for a bride among the indigenous tribes of the, ii. 302 *sq.* ; art of abducting human souls in the, iii. 73 *sqq.* ; the Besisis of the, iii. 87, ix. 226 *n.*[1] ; the Mentras or Mantras of the, vi. 140 ; the Rice-mother in the, vii. 197 *sqq.* ; the Mai Darat of the, viii. 102 ; the Mantras of the, ix. 88

—— region, divinity of kings in, i. 398

—— society, parents named after their children in, iii. 332

Malay story of the absence of the soul in a dream, iii. 38 *n.*[4] ; of the transference of souls, iii. 49

—— superstitions in regard to tin, iii. 407

Malayalies of the Shervaray Hills, their euphemism for a tiger, iii. 402

Malayans, devil-dancers in Southern India, practise a mock human sacrifice, iv. 216

Malayo-Siamese families of the Patani States, their custom as to the after-birth, xi. 163 *sq.*

Malays, taboos observed by the, in the search for camphor, i. 114 *sq.*; telepathy in war among the, i. 127 ; their belief as to the sunset glow, i. 319 ; their superstitious veneration for their rajahs, i. 361 ; regalia regarded as talismans among the, i. 362 ; their ceremony for making the durian-tree bear fruit, ii. 21 ; their ways of deceiving the spirits of trees and plants, ii. 22 *sqq.* ; their superstition as to *toallong* trees, ii. 41 ; their conception of the soul as a mannikin, iii. 28 ; their conception of the soul as a bird, iii. 34 *sqq.* ; their custom as to shadows in building a house, iii. 81 ; their superstitions as to the head, iii. 254 ; taboos on cutting the hair among the, iii. 261 ; their belief in the Spectral Huntsman, iv. 178 ; their lunar years, vii. 314 ; their use of birds as scapegoats, ix. 35 ; stratification of religious beliefs among the, ix. 90 *n.*[1] ; their story of the external soul, xi. 147 *sq.* ; their belief as to sympathetic relation between man and animal, xi. 197 ; their doctrine of the plurality of souls, xi. 222

—— of Patani Bay, their ways of referring to tigers, iii. 404; special language used by them in fishing, iii. 408 *sq.*; a family of them related to crocodiles, viii. 212

Maldive Islands, special terms used with reference to persons of the blood royal in the, i. 401 *n.*[3] ; virgin sacrificed as bride to a jinnee of the sea in the, ii. 152 *sqq.*; disposal of cut hair and nails in the, iii. 274

Male and female, the sticks of the fire-drill regarded by savages as, ii. 208 *sqq.*, 218, 218 *n.*[1], 223, 224, 226, 238, 249 *sq.* ;. souls in Chinese philosophy, xi. 221

Male animals not to be killed in houses of absent Malagasy soldiers, i. 119

—— organ, effigy of, in rites of Dionysus, vii. 12 ; effigy of, in Thracian ceremony, vii. 26, 29

Malecki (Maeletius, Menecius), J., on the

heathen religion of the Lithuanians, ii. 366 *n.*[2]

Malekootoos, a Bechuana tribe. *See* Baperis

Malemut Esquimaux unwilling to tell their names, iii. 328

Malepa, Bantu tribe of the Transvaal, will not taste blood, iii. 241

Maletsunyane, river in Basutoland, ii. 157

Malikolo, in the New Hebrides, heads of infants moulded artificially in, ii. 298 *n.*[2]

Malkin Tower, witches at the, x. 245

Malko - Tirnovsko, in the district of Adrianople, masquerade at Carnival at, viii. 331

Mallans of India, their use of a scapegoat in time of cholera, ix. 190

Mallows, riddles asked by old men seated on, after a burial, ix. 122 *n.*

Mallus in Cilicia, deities on coins of, v. 165 *sq.*

Malmyz district of Russia, the Wotyaks of, ii. 145, ix. 156

Malo, one of the New Hebrides, title to nobility in, founded on sacrifice of pigs to ancestors, i. 339

Malta, death of the Carnival in, iv. 224 *sq.* ; bilingual inscription of, v. 16 ; Phoenician temples of, v. 35 ; fires on St. John's Eve in, x. 210 *sq.*

Maluango, the king of Loango, ii. 322

Malurus cyaneus, superb warbler, women's "sister," among the Kurnai, xi. 216

Malwa, in Western India, iv. 122

Mamilian tower at Rome, viii. 42, 44

Mamre, sacred oak or terebinth at, v. 37 *n.*[2]

Mamurius Veturius, annual expulsion of, in ancient Rome, ix. 229 *sqq.*, 252, 257

Man, E. H., on the ignorance of the Andaman Islanders of the art of making fire, ii. 253 ; on the first fire of the Andaman Islanders, ii. 256 *n.*[2]

Man and animal, sympathetic relation between, xi. 272 *sq.*

——, the Isle of, tying up the wind in knots in, i. 326 ; precautions against witches on May Day in, ii. 53 *sq.* ; hunting the wren in, viii. 318 *sq.* ; Midsummer fires in, x. 201, 337 ; old New Year's Day in, x. 224 *sq.* ; Hallowe'en customs in, x. 243 *sq.* ; bonfires on St. Thomas's Day in, x. 266 ; cattle burnt alive to stop a murrain in, x. 325 *sqq.* ; mugwort gathered on Midsummer Eve in, xi. 59. *See also* Isle of Man

"Man, the True," official title of the head of Taoism in China, i. 413

Man-god, the two types of, i. 244 *sq.* ; notion of a man-god belongs to early period of religious history, i. 374 *sq.* ; contagious magical virtue of the, iii. 132 ; necessity for the isolation of the, iii. 132 ; reason for killing the, iv. 9 *sq.* ; in China, ix. 117 *sq.*

Mana, supernatural or magical power in Melanesia, i. 111 *n.*[2], 227, 228 *n.*[1], 339

Manahiki, South Pacific, women after childbirth not allowed to handle food in, iii. 147 ; rejoicings at the appearance of the Pleiades in, vii. 312 *sq.*

Manasseh, King of Judah, his sacrifice of his children, iv. 170

Manchu dynasty, the life-tree of the, xi. 167 *sq.*

Mandai river, the Dyaks of the, ii. 40

Mandalay, human sacrifices at gateways of, iii. 90 ; kings of Burma screened from public gaze at, iii. 125 *sq.* ; the ceremony of head-washing at, iii. 253

Mandan Indians, afraid of having their portraits taken, iii. 97 ; their belief as to the stars, iv. 67 *sq.* ; their personification of maize as an Old Woman, vii. 204 *sq.* ; their annual expulsion of the devil, ix. 171

Mandarins, deceased, deification of, i. 415

Mandeling, a district of Sumatra, treatment of the afterbirth in, i. 192 *sq.* ; the King of the Rice in, vii. 197 ; respect for tigers in, viii. 216

Mandelings of Sumatra, their excuses to tree-spirits for cutting down trees, ii. 36 ; open boxes, pans, etc., to help childbirth, iii. 296

Mandingoes of Senegambia, their attention to the phases of the moon, vi. 141

—— of Sierra Leone, kingship an honour desired by few among the, iii. 18

Mandragora called "the hand of glory" in France, xi. 316

Manegres of the Amoor, concealment of personal names among the, iii. 323

Maneros, chant of Egyptian reapers, vi. 45, 46, vii. 215, 258, 259, 261, 263, 264

Manes, first king of Lydia, v. 186 *n.*[5]

Manetho, on the Egyptian burnt-sacrifice of red-haired men, vi. 97 ; on Isis as the discoverer of corn, vi. 116 ; on Osiris and Isis as the sun and moon, vi. 120 ; on human sacrifices in ancient Egypt, vi. 259 *n.*[3]

Mang-bettou. *See* Monbuttu

—— -Shen, Chinese god of agriculture, viii. 11, 12

—— Than, the Warder of the Ox, in Annam, viii. 13 *sq.*

Mangaia, Pacific island, priests inspired by gods in, i. 378 ; separation of religious and civil authority in, iii. 20

Mangaians, their story of a man whose strength varied with the length of his shadow, iii. 87 ; their preference for a violent death, iv. 10

Mang'anje woman, her external soul in an ivory ornament, xi. 156

Manggarais, the, of Flores, forbidden to utter their own names, iii. 324

Mango married to a tamarind or a jasmine in India, ii. 25

Mango crop, feast of the new, viii. 119

—— -tree, bridegroom tied to, at a Munda marriage, ii. 57 ; worshipped by the Nahals, viii. 119 ; festival of wild, x. 7 *sqq.* ; ceremony for the fertilization of the, x. 10

Mani of Chitombe or Jumba, potentate in West Africa, his hair, teeth, and nails kept after death as a rain-charm, iii. 271

Mania, an ancient Roman bogey, i. 22 ; the Mother or Grandmother of Ghosts, viii. 94, 96

Maniae, a kind of loaf, viii. 94

Manichaeans, their theory of earthquakes, v. 197

Manichaeus, the heretic, his death, v. 294 *n.*[3]

Manii, many, at Aricia, a proverb, i. 22, viii. 94 *sqq.*

Manioc or cassava cultivated in Africa, vii. 119 ; cultivated in South America, vii. 120 *sq.*, 122

Manipur, rain-making in, i. 252, 283 *sq.* ; the Chirus of, i. 289 ; rain-making by means of a stone in, i. 304 *sq.* ; the Tangkhuls of, ii. 100 ; the Kabuis of, ii. 106 ; the hill tribes of, diet of religious chiefs among, iii. 292 ; the Murrams of, iii. 292 ; the Naga tribes of, iii. 292, iv. 11, vi. 57 *sq.* ; mode of counting the years in, iv. 117 *n.*[1]; rajahs of, descended from a .snake, iv. 133 ; the Rajah of, his sins transferred to a substitute, ix. 39 ; annual eponyms in, ix. 39 *sq.*

Manitoo, personal totem, xi. 273 *n.*[1]

Manius Egerius, said to have founded the sacred grove at Aricia, i. 22, viii. 95

Manna, ceremony for the magical multiplication of, i. 88 *sq.*

Mannewars, the, a forest tribe of the Central Provinces in India, their worship of the *Bassia latifolia*, viii. 119

Mannhardt, W., iv. 249 *n.*[4], vii. 258, viii. 337 ; on loading trees with stones, i. 140 *n.*[6] ; on rain-making by drenching trees, ii. 47 ; on the Harvest-May, ii. 48 ; on the representation of the spirit of vegetation at the spring festivals of Europe, ii. 78 *sq.* ; on the May King, Queen of May, etc., ii. 84; on the pinching and beheading of frogs as a rain-charm, ii. 87 ; on a French custom at May Day, ii. 93 *n.*[1]; on the ''carrying out of Death,'' iv. 253 ; on the European ceremonies for the revival of vegetation in spring, iv. 267 *sq.* ; on placing children in winnowing-fans, vii. 11 ; on the etymology of Demeter, vii. 131 ; on the Corn-mother or Barley-mother in modern Europe, vii. 132 ; on corn-puppet called Ceres, vii. 135 ; on the identification of the harvester with the corn-spirit, vii. 138 *sq.*; on the Peruvian Maize-mother, Quino-mother, etc., vii. 172 ; on the corn-spirit in human form, vii. 204 ; on Lityerses, vii. 217 *n.*[1], 218 *n.*[1] ; on the corn-spirit in the corn last cut or threshed, vii. 222 ; on the mythical calf of the corn, vii. 292 ; on corn-spirit as horse, vii. 294; on goat-formed woodland deities, viii. 2 *sq.*; on the sacrifice of the October horse at Rome, viii. 42 *n.*[1] ; on the golden leg of Pythagoras, viii. 263 ; on processions of animals or of men disguised as animals, viii. 325 ; on processions of maskers representing the spirits of vegetation, ix. 250 ; on beating human scapegoats, ix. 255, 272 ; on the human victims at the Thargelia, ix. 257 *n.*[4]; on fire-customs, x. 106 *n.*[3] ; his theory that the fires of the fire-festivals are charms to secure sunshine, x. 329, 331 *sqq.* ; on torches as imitations of lightning, x. 340 *n.*[1] ; on the Hirpi Sorani, xi. 15 *n.* ; on burning leaf-clad representative of spirit of vegetation, xi. 25 ; on the human victims sacrificed by the Celts, xi. 33 ; his theory of the Druidical sacrifices, xi. 43 ; his solar theory of the bonfires at the European fire-festivals, xi. 72 ; on killing a cock on the harvest-field, xi. 280 *n.*

Mannikin, the soul conceived as a, iii. 26 *sqq.*

Manning, Percy, on May garlands in Hertfordshire, ii. 61 *sq.*

Man-slayers, purification of, iii. 165 *sqq.*; secluded, iii. 165 *sqq.* ; tabooed, iii. 165 *sqq.* ; haunted by ghosts of slain, iii. 165 *sqq.* ; their faces blackened, iii. 169 ; their bodies painted, iii. 175, 178, 179, 180, 186 *n.*[1]; their hair shaved, iii. 175, 177 ; taste the blood of their victims, viii. 154 *sq. See also* Homicide

Mantinea, Poseidon worshipped at, v.

203 *n.*[2] ; sanctuary of Demeter at, vii. 46 *n.*[2] ; games in honour of Antinous at, vii. 80, 85

Mantineans purify their city by sacrificial victims, iii. 189

Mantis religiosus, a totem in the Duke of York Island, xi. 248 *n.*

Mantras, the, of the Malay Peninsula, their fear of demons, xi. 88 *sq.*

Mantras, sacred texts recited as spells by the Brahmans, i. 403 *sq.*

Manu, Hindoo lawgiver, on the uncleanness of women at menstruation, x. 95 ; on the three births of the Aryan, xi. 276 *sq.* See also *Manu, the Laws of*

Manu, the Laws of, on the effects of a good king's reign, i. 366 ; on the divinity of kings and Brahmans, i. 403 ; on the rebirth of a father in his son, iv. 188 *sq.*; on the transmigration of evildoers into animals, viii. 298 *sq.*

Manure, ashes used as, vii. 117

Manx fishermen, tabooed words of, iii. 396
—— mummers at Hallowe'en, x. 224

Many Manii at Aricia, a proverb, i. 22, viii. 94 *sqq.*

Maori. *See also* New Zealand

Maori chiefs, their sanctity or taboo, iii. 134 *sqq.* ; their heads sacred, iii. 256 *sq.* ; their hair sacred, iii. 265
—— gods, ix. 81
—— language, synonyms in the, iii. 381
—— priest catches the soul of a tree, vi. 111 *n.*[1]
—— sorcerers, their use of clipped hair, nails, etc., iii. 269

Maoris, magical images among the, i. 71 ; magic of navel-string and afterbirth among the, i. 182 *sq.*; their contagious magic of footprints, i. 208 ; acquainted with the sexes of trees, ii. 24 ; their belief as to fertilizing virtue of trees, ii. 56 ; their ceremonies on entering a strange land, iii. 109 ; persons who have handled the dead tabooed among the, iii. 138 *sq.*; tabooed on the war-path, iii. 157 ; will not lean against the wall of a house, iii. 251 ; their spells at hair-cutting, iii. 264 *sq.* ; their belief as to falling stars, iv. 64 ; determined the beginning of their year by the rising of the Pleiades, vii. 313 ; their offering of first-fruits of sweet potatoes, viii. 133 ; warriors taste the blood of their slain foes among the, viii. 156 ; put the first fish caught back into the sea, viii. 252 ; birth-trees among the, xi. 163

Mar-na, a Philistine deity, ix. 418 *n.*[1]

Mara tribe of Northern Australia, burial rites of the, i. 102 *sq.* ; their rain-making, i. 251 ; their belief as to

falling stars, iv. 60 *sq.* ; initiation of medicine-men in the, xi. 239

Marake, an ordeal of being stung by ants and wasps among the Indians of French Guiana, x. 63 *sq.*

Marash, Hittite monuments at, v. 173

Maravars, the, of Southern India, their use of iron as a talisman, iii. 234

Maraves, the, of South Africa, revere a spiritual head called Chissumpe, i. 393 ; sanctity of burial-grounds among the, ii. 31 *sq.*; their offering of first-fruits to the dead, viii. 111 ; pile stones on places where witches were burnt, ix. 19

Marburg, in Steiermark, the thresher of last corn disguised as a wolf at, viii. 327

Marcellus of Bordeaux, homoeopathic remedies prescribed by, i. 84 ; his cure for warts, ix. 48 ; on transference of toothache to a frog, ix. 50 ; on transference of asthma to a mule, ix. 50 ; on transference of an intestinal disorder to a hare, ix. 50 *sq.* ; on medicines which may not touch the ground, x. 17

March, the old Slavs began the year with, iv. 221 *sq.* ; festival of Attis in, v. 267 ; annual expulsion of demons in, ix. 149 ; annual expulsion of witches in, ix. 157 ; annual expulsion of evils in, ix. 199 ; expulsion of Mamurius Veturius in, ix. 229, 231 ; old Roman year began in, ix. 231, 345 ; dances of the Salii in, ix. 232 ; custom of beating people and cattle in, ix. 266 ; festival of the Matronalia in, ix. 346 ; marriage festival of all the gods in, ix. 373 *n.*[1] ; the first month of the year in the oldest Persian calendar, ix. 402 ; the fire-walk in, xi. 6 ; mistletoe cut at the full moon of, xi. 84, 86
——, the 1st, sacred fire at Rome annually extinguished on, ii. 267 ; custom of "Driving out Death" on, iv. 235 ; wooden effigies of swallows carried about the streets on, viii. 322 *n.*; bells rung to make the grass grow on, ix. 247 ; Roman festival of the Matronalia on, ix. 346
——, the 25th, tradition that Christ was crucified on, v. 306

March moon, woodbine cut in the increase of the, xi. 184

Marco Polo, on beating as a punishment in China, iii. 243 *sq.*

Mardi Gras, Shrove Tuesday, iv. 227. *See* Shrove Tuesday

Marduk or Merodach, chief Babylonian god, ix. 356, 357, 399 ; as a magician, i. 240 *sq.* ; his wives, ii. 130, v. 71 ; New Year festival of, iv. 110, ix. 356 ; his image at Babylon, iv. 113 ; as a deliverer from demons, ix. 103 ; the votaries of, ix. 372 *n.*[2]

Marduk and Mordecai, ix. 365, 405

—— and Tiamat, iv. 105 *sq.*, 107 *sq.*

Mare, treatment of the placenta of a, i. 199

—— in foal, last sheaf of corn given to, vii. 160, 162, 168

—— or horse, corn-spirit as, vii. 292 *sqq.* ; "crying the Mare" at end of reaping in Hertfordshire and Shropshire, vii. 292 *sqq.* *See also* Mares

Mareielis, girls carrying May-trees or wreaths of flowers, at Zurich, iv. 260

Marena, Winter or Death, on Midsummer Eve in Russia, iv. 262

Mares in homoeopathic magic, i. 152, 153

Marett, R. R., on taboo as negative magic, i. 111 *n.*[2]

Margas, exogamous totemic clans of the Battas of Sumatra, xi. 222 *sq.*

Mariandynian reapers, mournful song of, vii. 216

Marianne Islands, precautions as to spittle in the, iii. 288

Mariette-Pacha, A., on the burial of Osiris, vi. 89 *n.*

Marigolds, magic of, i. 211 ; used to adorn tombstones on All Souls' Day, vi. 71. *See also* Marsh-marigolds

Marilaun, A. Kerner von, on mistletoe, xi. 318 *n.*[6]

Marimos, a Bechuana tribe, their human sacrifices for the crops, vii. 240, 251

Mariner, W., on taboo in Tonga, iii. 140 ; on the sacrifice of first-fruits in the Tonga Islands, viii. 128 *sqq.*

Mariners at sea, special language employed by, iii. 413 *sqq.*

Marjoram a protection against witchcraft, ix. 160, xi. 74 ; burnt at Midsummer, x. 214 ; gathered at Midsummer, xi. 51

Mark of Brandenburg, fruit-trees girt with straw at Christmas in the, ii. 17 ; race of bride and bridegroom in the, ii. 303 ; name of mice tabooed between Christmas and Twelfth Night in the, iii. 397 ; need-fire in the, x. 273 ; simples culled at Midsummer in the, xi. 48 ; St. John's blood in the, xi. 56 ; the divining-rod in the, xi. 67

Marketa, the holy, prayed to for good crops in Bohemia, iv. 238

Marks, bodily, of prophets, v. 74

Marksuhl, near Eisenach, harvest custom at, vii. 231

Marktl, in Bavaria, the Straw-goat at threshing at, vii. 286

Marno, Ernst, on the reverence of the Nuehr for their cattle, viii. 39

Maroni river in Guiana, i. 156

Marotse. *See* Barotse

Marquesans, their way of detaining the soul in the body, iii. 31 ; their regard for the sanctity of the head, iii. 254 *sq.* ; their customs as to the hair, iii. 261 *sq.* ; their dread of sorcery, iii. 268

Marquesas or Washington Islands, human gods in the, i. 386 *sq.* ; extinction of fires after a death in the, ii. 268 *n.* ; seclusion of manslayers in the, iii. 178 ; continence at making coco-nut oil and at baking in the, iii. 201 ; custom at childbirth in the, iii. 245 ; the fire-walk in the, xi. 11

Marriage of trees to each other, i. 24 *sqq.* ; of men and women to trees, i. 40 *sq.*, ii. 57 ; treading on a stone at, i. 160 ; bath before, i. 162 ; the pole-star at, i. 166 ; second, third, or fourth, regarded as unlucky, ii. 57 *n.*[4] ; of Earth in spring, ii. 76, 94 ; to a palm-tree before tapping it, ii. 101 ; of near kin, the prohibition of, perhaps based historically on superstition, ii. 117 ; of girls to spirits of lakes, ii. 150 *sq.* ; of girls to rivers, ii. 151 *sq.* ; with king's widow constitutes a claim to the kingdom, ii. 281 *sqq.*, iv. 193 ; with half-sister legal in Attica, ii. 284 ; rice strewn on bridegroom's head at, iii. 35 ; the consummation of, prevented by knots and locks, iii. 299 *sqq.* ; of brothers and sisters in royal families, iv. 193 *sq.* ; as an infringement of old communal rights, v. 40 ; of women to serpent-god, v. 66 *sqq.* ; exchange of dress between men and women at, vi. 260 *sqq.* ; of mice, viii. 278 ; of younger before elder brother deemed a sin, ix. 3 ; leaping over bonfires to ensure a happy, x. 107, 108, 110 ; omens of, drawn from Midsummer bonfires, x. 168, 174, 178, 185, 189, 338 *sq.* ; omens of, from flowers, xi. 52 *sq.*, 61 ; oak-trees planted at, xi. 165

—— of Adonis and Aphrodite celebrated at Alexandria, v. 224

—— of the god Marduk, ix. 356

——, mock, of leaf-clad mummers, i. 97 ; at Carnival masquerade, vii. 27 ; or real, of human victims, ix. 257 *sq.*

—— of the Roman gods, vi. 230 *sqq.*

——, Sacred, ii. 120 *sqq.* ; of Dionysus with the Queen of Athens, ii. 136 *sq.*, vii. 30 *sq.* ; of Zeus and Demeter in Eleusinian mysteries, ii. 138, vii. 65 *sqq.*, viii. 9 ; of Zeus and Hera, ii. 140 *sqq.*, iv. 91 ; of Frey and his wife, ii. 143 *sq.*, iv. 91 ; of Roman kings, ii. 172 *sq.*, 192, 193 *sq.*, 318 *sq.* ; of king and queen, iv. 71 ; of gods and goddesses, iv. 73 ; of actors disguised as animals, iv. 83 ; of priest and priestess as representatives of deities, v. 46 *sqq.* ; represented in the rock-hewn sculptures at Boghaz-Keui, v. 140 ; of Hercules and Hera perhaps celebrated in Cos, vi. 259 *n.*[4]

Marriage of Sky and Earth, v. 282 with *n.*[2]

—— of the Sun and Moon, mythical and dramatic, ii. 146 *sq.*, iv. 71, 73 *sq.*, 78, 87 *sq.*, 90, 92, 105 ; of the Sun and Earth, ii. 98 *sq.*, 148, v. 47 *sq.*

Marriage customs of the Aryan family, vi. 235 ; use of children of living parents in, vi. 245 *sqq.* ; to ensure the birth of boys, vi. 262

—— festival of the gods, i. 129 *sqq.*, ix. 273 *n.*[1] ; festival of all the gods and goddesses in the Date Month, ii. 25

'' —— Hollow " at Teltown, iv. 99

Marriages of brothers with sisters in ancient Egypt, vi. 214 *sqq.* ; their intention to keep the property in the family, vi. 215 *sq.*

Married, the person last, lights the bonfire, x. 107, 109, 111, 119, 339 ; young man last married provides wheel to be burnt, x. 116 ; the person last married officiates at Midsummer fire, x. 192 ; men married within the year collect fuel for Midsummer fire, x. 192 *sq.* ; last married bride made to leap over bonfire, xi. 22

Married men make fire by the friction of wood, ii. 238, 239 ; kindle need-fire, x. 289

—— pair of priestly functionaries in charge of the sacred fire, ii. 235

Marriott, Fitzgerald, on dance of women during war, i. 132

Marrow bones not to be broken in a hut, i. 115 *sq.*

Mars, the reputed father of Romulus and Remus, ii. 196 *sq.*, vi. 235 ; horse sacrificed to, in October, at Rome, viii. 42, ix. 230 ; a god of vegetation, ix. 229 *sq.*; the Old, at Rome, ix. 229, 231, 252 ; represented by Mamurius Veturius, ix. 229

—— and Bellona, vi. 231

——, Field of, at Rome, annual chariot-race on the, viii. 42

—— and his wife Nerio, vi. 232

——, the planet, red-haired men sacrificed to, vii. 261 *sq.*

—— and Silvia, xi. 105

——, temple of, at Rome, i. 310 ; nails knocked into the, ix. 67 *n.*[1]

Mars Silvanus, ix. 230

Marsaba, a devil in the island of Rook,

his expulsion, ix. 109 ; swallows lads at initiation, xi. 246

Marsala in Sicily, Midsummer customs at, v. 247

Marsden, W., on the confusion of the agricultural year in Sumatra caused by the introduction of the lunar Mohammedan calendar, vii. 315

Marseilles, drenching people with water at Midsummer in, v. 248 *sq.*, x. 193 ; human scapegoats at, ix. 253 ; Midsummer king of the double-axe at, x. 194 ; the Yule log at, x. 250; Midsummer flowers at, xi. 46

Marsh-marigolds, a protection against witchcraft, ii. 54, ix. 163 ; hoops wreathed with, carried on May Day, ii. 63, 88. *See also* Marigolds

Marshall, A. S. F., on the felling of timber in Mexico, vi. 136 *n.*[3]

Marshall Islands, belief in the external soul in the, xi. 200

Marshall Bennet Islands, magical powers of chiefs in the, i. 339

Marsi, Midsummer fires in the land of the ancient, x. 209

Marsyas, his musical contest with Apollo and his death, v. 55, 288 *sq.*; perhaps a double of Attis, v. 289

——, the river, v. 289

Martens, magic to snare, i. 110 ; bones of, kept from dogs, viii. 239

Martial on the Ides of August as Diana's day, i. 12 *n.*[2]

Martin, Father, on the indifference to human life of a robber caste in Southern India, iv. 141 *sq.*

Martin, Rev. John, on annual expulsion of the devil on the Gold Coast, ix. 132 *sq.*

Martin, M., on St. Bride's Day in the Hebrides, ii. 94 *n.*[2] ; on forced fire (need-fire) in Scotland, ii. 238, x. 289; on the cutting of peat in the Hebrides, vi. 138 ; on *dessil (deiseal)*, x. 151 *n.*

Martin of Urzedow, Polish priest, denounced heathen practices of women on St. John's Eve, x. 177

Martinique, precaution as to spittle in, iii. 289

Martius, C. F. Phil. von, on the political power of medicine-men among the Indians of Brazil, i. 359

Martyrdom of St. Dasius, ix. 308 *sqq.*

—— of St. Hippolytus, i. 21

Marwaris of India, Holi festival among the, ix. 2 *sq.*

Marxberg, the, on the Moselle, fiery wheel rolled down, in Lent, x. 118

Maryborough, in Queensland, custom of the tribes about, as to women stepping over things, iii. 424 ; exposure of first-born children among the tribes about, iv. 180; ate men to acquire their virtues, viii. 151

Marzana, goddess of Death, effigy of, in Polish parts of Silesia, iv. 237

Masai of East Africa, power of medicine-men among the, i. 343 *sq.*; their reverence for the *subugo* tree, ii. 16; their fire-drill, ii. 210; custom observed by manslayers among the, iii. 186 *n.*[1]; continence of man and woman at brewing honey-wine among the, iii. 200; beards not pulled out by chiefs and sorcerers among the, iii. 260; head chief of the, foods tabooed to him, iii. 291; their use of magic knots, iii. 309; their use of rings as amulets, iii. 315; unwilling to tell their own names, iii. 329 *sq.*; said to change the names of the dead, iii. 354 *sq.*; namesakes of the dead change their names among the, iii. 356; changes in their vocabulary caused by fear of naming the dead, iii. 361; their customs as to falling stars, iv. 61, 65; their custom as to the skulls of dead chiefs, iv. 202 *sq.*; their belief in serpents as reincarnations of the dead, v. 82, 84; their ceremonies at the new moon, vi. 142 *sq.*; their rule as to the choice of a chief, vi. 248; boys wear female costume at circumcision among the, vi. 263; their observation of the Pleiades, vii. 317; their rules as to partaking of meat and milk, viii. 83 *sq.*; the El Kiboron clan of the, viii. 288; their custom of throwing stones or grass on graves, ix. 20; peace-making ceremony among the, x. 139 *n.*

Masai pope, the, i. 343 *sq.*

Mascal or Festival of the Cross in Abyssinia, ix. 133 *sq.*

Mashona, the, of South Africa, revered human gods, i. 393

Mashonaland, chiefs of, not allowed to cross rivers, iii. 9 *sq.*

Mashti, supposed name of Elamite goddess, ix. 366 *sq.*

Mask of dog or jackal worn by priest who personated Anubis, vi. 85 *n.*[3]; two-faced, worn by image of goddess, ix. 287; priest of Earth not to wear a, x. 4. *See also* Masks

Masked dances, vii. 95 *sq.*, 111, 186, viii. 208 *n.*[1], 339, ix. 236; at Carnival, viii. 333, 334; in ritual of Demeter, viii. 339; to promote fertility, ix. 236; and ceremonies of savages, ix. 374 *sqq.*; bull-roarers used at, xi. 230 *n.* *See also* Dances

Maskers, representing the dead, ii. 178; in Thrace at Carnival, vii. 26 *sqq.*;

representing demons, vii. 95, 186 *sq.*; in the Grisons, ix. 239; in the Tyrol and Salzburg, ix. 242 *sqq.*; as representatives of the spirits of fertility, both vegetable and animal, ix. 249 *sq.*; supposed to be inspired by the spirits whom they represent, ix. 380, 382, 383

Masks worn by shamans in pursuit of lost souls, iii. 57 *sq.*; hung on trees at time of sowing, iv. 283; worn by actors who represent demons or spirits, vii. 95, 186; worn by Egyptian kings, vii. 260 *sq.*; worn in masked dances, not to be seen by women on pain of death, viii. 208 *n.*[1]; worn by women, viii. 232 *sq.*, 234; worn by mummers at Carnival, viii. 333; worn by Cingalese devil-dancers, ix. 38; worn at expulsion of demons, ix. 111, 127, 145, 213; worn at ceremonies to promote the growth of the crops, ix. 236, 240, 242 *sqq.*, 247, 248 *sq.*; worn by the *Perchten*, ix. 242, 243, 245, 247; intended to ban demons, ix. 246; worn by priests who personate gods, ix. 287; worn in religious dances and performances, ix. 375, 376 *n.*[2], 378, 379, 380, 382; representing mythical personages, ix. 375, 376 *n.*[2], 378, 379, 382 *sq.*; representing totemic animals, ix. 380; burned at end of masquerade, ix. 382; thought to be animated by demons, ix. 382; worn by girls at puberty, x. 31, 52; worn at Duk-duk ceremonies in New Britain, xi. 247; worn by members of a secret Wolf society among the Nootka Indians, xi. 270, 271. *See also* Mask, Maskers, *and* Masquerade

Masnes, a giant, in a legend of Sardes, v. 186

Masoka, the spirits of the dead, worshipped by the Wahehe of German East Africa, vi. 188 *sq.*

Maspéro, Sir Gaston, on the confusion of magic and religion in ancient Egypt, i. 230; on the assimilation of Egyptian kings to gods, ii. 133 *sq.*; edits the Pyramid Texts, vi. 4 *n.*[1]; on the nature of Osiris, vi. 126 *n.*[2], vii. 260 *n.*[2]

Masquerade at the Carnival in Thrace, vi. 99 *sq.*; at sowing festival in Borneo, vii. 95 *sq.*, 98, 186 *sq.*; of boys among the Lengua Indians, x. 57 *n.*[1]

Masquerades, Roman, of men personating the dead, ii. 178; of kings and queens, iv. 71 *sq.*, 78, 88, 89; Californian, of men personating the dead, vi. 53; in modern Europe, intention of certain, ix. 251 *sq.* *See also* Masks *and* Maskers

"Mass of the Holy Spirit," i. 231 *sq.*

Mass of Saint Sécaire, i. 232 *sq.*

Massacres for sick kings of Uganda, vi. 226

Massagetae sacrifice horses to the sun, i. 315

Massaya, volcano in Nicaragua, human victims sacrificed to, v. 219

Massebah (plural *masseboth*), sacred stone or pillar in ancient Israel, v. 107, 108

Masset, in Queen Charlotte Islands, dances of Haida women at, while their husbands were away at war, i. 133

Massim, the, of British New Guinea, seclusion of manslayers among, iii. 169

Masson, Bishop, on Annamite indifference to death, iv. 136 *sq.*

Mastarna, an Etruscan, ii. 196 *n.*

Master of the Fish, sacrifices offered by the Tarahumares to the, viii. 252

——, the Heavenly, the head of Taoism in China, i. 413

—— of Life, first-fruits offered by the Arkansas Indians to the, viii. 134

—— of the Revels, ix. 333 *sq.*

—— of Sorrows at corpse-burning among the Chams, i. 280

Master craftsman regarded as a magician, ix. 81

Masur, in Dutch New Guinea, belief in the transmigration of human souls into cassowaries at, viii. 295

Masuren, a district of Eastern Prussia, "Easter Smacks" in, ix. 269; Midsummer fire kindled by the revolution of a wheel in, x. 177, 335 *sq.*; divination by flowers on Midsummer Eve in, xi. 52, 53; divination by orpine at Midsummer in, xi. 61; camomile gathered at Midsummer in, xi. 63; fire kindled by friction of oak at Midsummer in, xi. 91

Mata, the smallpox goddess, sacrifice of first-born sons to, iv. 181

Matabele, magical effigies among the, i. 63; their rain-charm, i. 291; the power of witch-doctors among the, i. 351; their relation to the human god of the Mashona, i. 393 *sq.*; woman's part in agriculture among the, viii. 115; their festival of new fruits, viii. 70 *sq.*; their way of getting rid of caterpillars, viii. 275; fumigate their gardens, x. 337

——, kings of the, as priests, i. 48; as rain-makers, i. 351 *sq.*

——, Lobengula, king of the, iii. 114

Matabeleland, i. 394

Mataboole, rank next below chiefs in Tonga, viii. 130 *n.*[2], 131

Matacos, Indian tribe of the Gran Chaco, their belief as to the souls of the dead, iii. 373 *n.*; their custom of secluding girls at puberty, x. 58

Mataguayos, Indian tribe of the Gran Chaco, their custom of secluding girls at puberty, x. 58

Mateer, Rev. S., on the worship of demons in Travancore, ix. 94

Mater Dolorosa, the ancient and the modern, ix. 349

Materbert, off New Britain, natives of, carried fire about with them, ii. 258

Material vehicles of immaterial things (fear, misfortune, disease, etc.), ix. 1 *sqq.*, 22 *n.*[2], 23 *sqq.*

Materialization of prayer, ix. 22 *n.*[2]

Maternal uncle preferred to father, mark of mother-kin, ii. 285; in marriage ceremonies in India, v. 62 *n.*[1]

Maternity and paternity of the Roman deities, vi. 233 *sqq.*

Matiamvo, a potentate in Angola, the manner of his death, iv. 35 *sq.*

Matlalcuéyé, wife of Tlaloc, the Mexican thunder-god, human sacrifices offered to, vii. 237

"Matriarchate," v. 46; inappropriateness of the term, ii. 271 *n.*[2]

Matronalia, Roman festival on the 1st of March, ix. 346

Matse tribe of Togoland, two royal families in the, ii. 293; their sacrifice of new corn to the Earth Goddess, viii. 115; their transference of sorrow to leaves, ix. 3

Matthes, Dr. B. F., on harvest festival in Celebes, viii. 122 *sq.*; on sympathetic relation between man and animal among the Malays, xi. 197

Matthews, Dr. Washington, on unwillingness of Indians to speak of their gods at certain times, iii. 385

Mattogrosso, contagious magic of footprints in, i. 210; the Pleiades worshipped by some tribes of, vii. 309

Matuana, Zulu chief, drank gall of foes, viii. 152

Matuku, in Fiji, iii. 39, 40

Mauhes, Indians of Brazil, seclusion of girls at puberty among the, x. 59; ordeal of young men among the, x. 62

Maui, Fijian god of earthquakes, v. 202 *n.*

Maundrell, H., on the discoloration of the river Adonis, v. 225 *n.*[4]

Maundy Thursday, church bells silent on, x. 125 *n.*[1]

Maurer, Konrad, on succession to the kingdom in Scandinavia, ii. 280 *n.*[1]; on Icelandic story of the external soul, xi. 125 *n.*[1]

Mauretanians, rain-charm of the, i. 286

Maury, A., on the Easter ceremonies compared with those of Adonis, v. 257 *n.*[1]

Mausoleum at Halicarnassus, iv. 94 *sq.*
Mausolus, contests of eloquence in his honour, v. 95 ; his ashes swallowed by his widow Artemisia, viii. 158
Mauss, M., and H. Hubert, Messrs., on taboo as negative magic, i. 111 *n.*[2]
Mawu, god, in the language of the Hos of Togoland, i. 396 *sq.* ; Supreme Being of Ewe negroes, ix. 74 *sq.*, 76 *n.*[1]
Mawu Sodza, a Ewe goddess, viii. 115
Maximian and Diocletian, reign of, ix. 308
Maxims of Pythagoras, their superstitious nature, i. 213 *sq.*
Maximus, Tyrius, on conical image at Paphos, v. 35 *n.* ; on the rites of Demeter at the threshing-floor, vii. 62 *n.*[1]
Maxwell, W. E., on the stratification of religious beliefs among the Malays, ix. 90 *n.*[1]
May, J. D., viii. 281 *n.*[2]
May, modern Greek Feast of All Souls in, vi. 78 *n.*[1] ; puppets thrown into the Tiber at Rome in, viii. 107 ; Roman festival of ghosts in, ix. 154 *sq.* ; Mexican human sacrifices in, ix. 276, 280 ; dances of Castilian peasants in, ix. 280
——, the 2nd of, called Walburgis Day in Bavaria, ii. 75 *n.*[2]
——, King of, ii. 84, 85 *sq.* ; King and Queen of, iv. 266, ix. 406
——, Queen of, ii. 84, 87 *sq.* ; in the Isle of Man, iv. 258
May Bride, the, ii. 95, iv. 266 ; the, at Whitsuntide, in Brunswick, ii. 96
—— bridegroom, ii. 91, 93
—— -bushes, ii. 84, 85, 89, 90, 142 ; placed at doors of stables and byres, ii. 52
—— Day, the first of May, dance of milkmaids on, ii. 52 ; witches rob cows of milk on, ii. 52 *sqq.*, ix. 267 ; precautions against witchcraft on, ii. 52 *sqq.* ; green bushes placed at doors of loved maidens on, ii. 56 ; celebration of, ii. 59 *sqq.* ; licence of, ii. 67, 103 *sq.* ; a festival of flowers in Peloponnese, ii. 143 *n.*[2] ; in Sweden, iv. 254 ; in the Isle of Man, iv. 258, x. 157 ; magpies' eggs and young carried from house to house on, viii. 321 *n.*[3] ; in the Tyrol, "Burning out of the Witches" on, ix. 158 *sq.* ; dance of witches on the Blocksberg on, ix. 163 *n.*[1] ; ceremonies concerned with vegetation on, ix. 359 ; bonfires on, x. 146 *sqq.* ; bonfires on, a precaution against witchcraft, x. 295 ; sheep burnt as a sacrifice on, x. 306 ; witches active on, xi. 19, 184 *n.*[4], 185

May Day, the Eve of (Walpurgis Night), witches steal milk from cattle on, ii. 52 ; ceremony at Meiron in Galilee on, v. 178 ; Snake Stones thought to be formed on, x. 15 ; witches active on, ix. 158 *sqq.*, xi. 73 ; a witching time, x. 295. *See* Walpurgis
—— -flowers over the door a protection against elves and witches, ii. 53
—— Fools, ii. 91
—— garlands, ii. 60 *sqq.*, 90 *sq.*
—— Lady in Cambridge, ii. 62 ; representative of the spirit of vegetation, ii. 79
—— morning, custom of herdsmen on, ix. 266
—— -pole, apparently thought to fertilize women and cattle, ii. 52 ; at Midsummer in Sweden, ii. 65 ; carried on May Day in Warwickshire, ii. 88 *sq.* ; or Midsummer-tree in Sweden and Bohemia, v. 250 ; set up in front of house of mayor or burgomaster, viii. 44
—— -poles, ii. 59, 65 *sqq.* ; village, in England, ii. 66 *sqq.* ; permanent, ii. 70 *sq.*
—— Rose, the Little, ii. 74
—— -tree, apparently thought to fertilize women and cattle, ii. 52 ; burned at the end of the year, ii. 71 ; horse-race to, iv. 208 ; brought into village and called summer, iv. 246 ; carried about, x. 120, xi. 22
—— -trees, ii. 59 *sq.*, 64, 68 *sq.*, iv. 251 *sq.* ; at Whitsuntide, iv. 208, 210, 211
Mayas of Yucatan, their annual expulsion of the demon of evil, ix. 171 ; their calendar, ix. 171 ; their five supplementary days, ix. 171, 340
Mayenne, French department of, May carols and trees in, ii. 63
Mayo, County, story of Guleesh in, x. 228
Mayos or Mayes, on May Day in Provence, ii. 80
Mbaya Indians of South America, self-sacrifice of old woman among the, iv. 140 ; their custom of infanticide, iv. 197
M'Bengas of the Gaboon, birth-trees among the, xi. 160
Mbengga, in Fiji, the fire-walk in, xi. 10 *sq.*
Mbete, priest, in Fiji, i. 378
Me Bau, a Thay goddess, ix. 98
Méac (February), a Cambodian month, iv. 148
Meakin, Budgett, on Midsummer fires in Morocco, x. 214 *n.*
Meal offered to the wind, i. 329 *n.*[5] ; sprinkled to keep off evil spirits, iii.

112 ; rubbed on man as a purificatory rite, iii. 113

"Meal and ale," standing dish at harvest supper, vii. 160, 161

Measuring shadows at laying foundations, iii. 89 *sq.*

Measuring-tape deified, iii. 91 *sq.*

Meat and milk, dietary rules as to, viii. 83 *sq.*

Meath, County, hunting the wren in, viii. 320 *n.* ; Hill of Ward in, x. 139 ; Uisnech in, x. 158

Meaux, Midsummer bonfires in the diocese of, x. 182

Mecca, pilgrims to, not allowed to wear knots and rings, iii. 293 *sq.* ; stone-throwing at, ix. 24

Mechanisms, primitive, for determining the time of year by observation of the sun, vii. 314

Mecklenburg, contagious magic of footprints in, i. 210, 211 ; locks unlocked at childbirth in, iii. 296 ; wolves and other animals not to be called by their proper names between Christmas and Twelfth Night in, iii. 396 *sq.* ; harvest customs in, vii. 229, 274 ; the Corn-wolf in, vii. 273 ; the Harvest-goat in, vii. 283 ; cure for fever in, ix. 56 ; precaution against witches on Walpurgis Night in, ix. 163 *n.*[1] ; cattle beaten on Good Friday in, ix. 266 ; mode of reckoning the Twelve Days in, ix. 327 ; need - fire in, x. 274 *sq.* ; simples gathered at Midsummer in, xi. 48 ; mugwort at Midsummer in, xi. 60; the divining-rod in, xi. 67 ; treatment of the afterbirth in, xi. 165 ; children passed through a cleft oak as a cure in, xi. 171 *sq.* ; custom of striking blindfold at a half-buried cock in, xi. 279 *n.*[4]

Medea and her magic cauldron, v. 180 *sq.*

—— and Aeson, viii. 143

Medes, the king of, not to be seen by anybody, iii. 121 ; law of the, iii. 121

Medicine differentiated from magic, i. 421 *n.*[1]; in Bolang Mongondo nothing but sacrifice, magic, and talismans, ix. 86

Medicine-bag, instrument of pretended death and resurrection at initiation, xi. 268 *sq.*

—— -man bleeds a man, i. 91 ; bottles up departing souls, iii. 31 ; dance of, at blessing maize or dead game, viii. 71 *sq.* ; propitiates rattlesnake, viii. 217 ; atones for slaughter of wolf, viii. 220 ; conjures soul of infant into coconut, xi. 154 *sq.* ; his mode of cure in Uganda, xi. 181 *sq.* ; in Australia,

initiation of, xi. 237 *sqq.* *See also* Medicine-men

Medicine-men (magicians, sorcerers), drive away rain, i. 253 ; their political power in South-east Australia, i. 336 ; power of, among African tribes, i. 342 *sqq.* ; power of, among the American Indians, i. 355 *sqq.* ; develop into gods and kings, i. 375, 420 *sq.* ; progressive differentiation of, i. 420 *sq.* ; the oldest professional class, i. 420 ; employed to recover lost souls, iii. 42 *sq.*, 45, 47 *sq.*, 54, 56, 58, 66 ; swinging of, as a mode of cure, iv. 280 *sq.* ; of Zulus, feel ancestral spirits in their shoulders, v. 74 *n.*[4] ; of Wiimbaio, extract disease in shape of crystals, v. 75 *n.*[4]; assimilated to women or thought to be transformed into women, vi. 256 ; need of, to circumvent evil spirits, ix. 76 ; whirl bull-roarers, xi. 231 ; in initiatory rites, xi. 237. *See also* Magicians, Shamans, Sorcerers, *and* Wizards

Medium inspired by dead king of Uganda, vi. 171

Mediums, inspired, in Bali, i. 378 *sq.* ; human, inspired by the spirits of crocodiles, lions, leopards, and serpents, viii. 213

Medontids at Athens, changed from kings to magistrates, ii. 290 ; reduction in their tenure of office, vii. 86

Mefitis, Italian goddess of mephitic vapours, v. 204, 205

Megalopolis, battle of gods and giants in plain of, v. 157

Megara, annual kingship at, i. 46 ; besieged by Minos, xi. 103

Megara, sacred caverns or vaults, viii. 17 *n.*[6]

Megarian girls offer their hair to Iphinoe, i. 28

Megassares, king of Hyria, v. 41

Megha Raja, the lord of rain, his figure painted in a rain-charm, i. 296

Meilichios, epithet of Dionysus, vii. 4

Meiners, C., on purification by blood, v. 299 *n.*[2]

Meinersen, in Hanover, need-fire at a village near, x. 275

Meiningen, use of pigs' bones at sowing in, vii. 300

Meiron, in Galilee, burnings for dead Jewish Rabbis at, v. 178 *sq.*

Meissen or Thuringia, horse's head thrown into Midsummer fire in, xi. 40

Mekeo, district of British New Guinea, homoeopathic magic of drums in, i. 134 *sq.* ; taboos observed for the sake of the crops in, ii. 106 ; double chieftainship in, iii. 24 *sq.* ; customs observed by widowers in, iii. 144

sq. ; women after childbirth tabooed in, iii. 148
Mela's description of the Corycian cave, v. 155 *n.*, 156
Melampus and Iphiclus, i. 158
Melancholy, characteristic of men of genius, viii. 302 *n.*[5]
Melanesia, homoeopathic magic of stones in, i. 164 ; contagious magic of wounds in, i. 201 ; confusion of religion and magic in, i. 227 *sq.* ; wizards in, the variety of their functions, i. 227 *sq.* ; weather doctors in, i. 321 ; wind-charms in, i. 321 ; supernatural power of chiefs in, i. 338 *sqq.* ; continence observed while the yam vines are training in, ii. 105 ; close relation of mother's brother to his nephews in, ii. 285 ; practice of lengthening the head artificially in, ii. 298 *n.*[2] ; attempt to recover a lost soul in, iii. 65 ; ghost-haunted stones in, iii. 80 ; magic practised on refuse of food in, iii. 127 *sq.* ; tabooed persons not allowed to handle food in, iii. 141 ; cleanliness from superstitious motives in, iii. 158 *n.*[1] ; story of the type of Beauty and the Beast in, iv. 130 *n.*[1] ; belief in conception without sexual intercourse in, v. 97 *sq.* ; magicians buried secretly in, vi. 105 ; conception of the external soul in, xi. 197 *sqq.* *See also* Melanesians
Melanesian and Papuan stocks in New Guinea, xi. 239
—— wizard, his soul as an eagle, iii. 34
Melanesians of the Bismarck Archipelago, unwilling to tell their names, iii. 329 ; mother-kin among the, vi. 211 ; of New Britain, their use of flowers and leaves as talismans, vi. 242 *sq.* ; their observation of the Pleiades, vii. 313 ; their belief in demons, ix. 82 *sq.* ; their stories of the origin of death, ix. 303 *sq.*
—— of Florida, one of the Solomon Islands, their fear of offending ghosts after eating of certain foods, viii. 85
Melawie River, the Dyaks of the, iii. 71
Melcarth, the god of Tyre, identified with Hercules, v. 16, 111 ; worshipped at Amathus in Cyprus, v. 32, 117 ; the burning of, v. 110 *sqq.* ; worshipped at Gades, v. 112 *sq.*, vi. 258 *n.*[5]
Melchior, one of the three mythical kings on Twelfth Day, ix. 329 *sqq.*
Melchizedek, king of Salem, v. 17
Meleager, his life bound up with a fire-brand, ii. 265, xi. 103 ; and the olive-leaf, xi. 103 *n.*[2]
Melech and Moloch, vi. 219 *sq.*
Melenik, in Macedonia, rain-making at,

i. 274 ; fiends scalded to death on New Year's Eve at, ix. 320
Meles, king of Lydia, banished because of a dearth, v. 183 ; causes lion to be carried round acropolis, v. 184
Melicertes, Isthmian games at Corinth celebrated in his honour, iv. 93, 103 ; son of Athamas and Ino, iv. 161 ; changed with his mother into marine divinities, iv. 162 ; in Tenedos, human sacrifices to, iv. 162 ; a form of Melcarth, v. 113
Melite in Phthia, Aspalis, a form of the Hanged Artemis, at, v. 291 *sq.*
Melito on the father of Adonis, v. 13 *n.*[2]
Mell, last corn cut, vii. 151 *sq.*
Mell-doll, vii. 151
—— -sheaf, vii. 151 *sq.*
—— -supper, vii. 151
Melos, milk-stones in, i. 165
Melur, in the Neilgherry Hills, the fire-walk at, xi. 8 *sq.*
Memnonium at Thebes, vi. 35 *n.*
Memorial stones, flat and standing, in honour of women and men respectively, among the Khasis, vi. 203
Memphis, statues of Summer and Winter at, iv. 259 *n.*[1] ; head of Osiris at, vi. 11 ; oath of the kings of Egypt at, vi. 24 ; festival of Osiris in the month of Khoiak at, vi. 108 ; Apis the sacred bull of, vi. 119 *n.*, viii. 34 ; the sanctuary of Serapis at, vi. 119 *n.*
Men, masked, personating the dead, ii. 178, vi. 53 ; injured through their shadows, iii. 78 *sqq.* ; create gods in their own likeness, iv. 194 ; make gods, vi. 211 ; dressed as women, vi. 253 *sqq.* ; dressed as women at marriage, vi. 261 *sq.* ; dressed as women to deceive dangerous spirits, vi. 262 *sq.* ; dressed as women at circumcision, vi. 263 ; parts of, eaten to acquire their qualities, viii. 148 *sqq.* ; disguised as animals, processions of, viii. 325 *sqq.* ; evil transferred to, ix. 38 *sqq.* ; possessed by spirits in China, ix. 117 ; disguised as demons, ix. 170 *sq.*, 172, 173, 213, 214 *sq.*, 235 ; as scapegoats, ix. 194 *sqq.* ; divine, as scapegoats, ix. 217 *sqq.* ; masked, as representatives of the spirits of fertility, both vegetable and animal, ix. 249 *sq.* ; sacrifices of deified, ix. 409 ; disguised as women, x. 107
—— and asses, redemption of firstling, iv. 173
"—— of God," prophets, v. 76
—— and women, difference of language between, iii. 348 *sq.* ; inspired by the spirits of dead kings and chiefs, vi. 171, 172, 192 *sq.* ; forbidden by

Mosaic law to interchange dress, ix. 363; eat apart, x. 81

Men's blood not to be seen by women, iii. 252 *n.*

Men Tyrannus, Phrygian moon-god, v. 284 ; custom as to pollution of death at his shrine, vi. 227

Mên-an-tol, "holed stone" in Cornwall, xi. 187

Mendalam River in Borneo, vii. 97, 98, 187

Mendes, in Egypt, mummy of Osiris at, iv. 4 ; the ram-god of, iv. 7 *n.*² ; the goat the beast-god of, viii. 172

Menedemus, sacrifices without the use of iron to, iii. 226 *sq.*

Menelaus, husband of Helen and king of Sparta, ii. 279

Menelik, Emperor of Abyssinia, forbids sanguinary fights for purpose of procuring rain, i. 258

Mengap, a Dyak liturgy, ix. 383

Menoeceus, his voluntary death, iv. 192 *n.*³

Menomini Indians, ritual of death and resurrection among the, xi. 268 *n.*¹

Menstruation, women tabooed at, iii. 145 *sqq.*; seclusion of girls at the first, x. 22 *sqq.*; the first, attributed to defloration by a spirit, x. 24 ; reasons for secluding women at, x. 97

Menstruous blood, the dread of, x. 76. *See also* Blood

—— fluid, medicinal applications of the, x. 98 *n.*¹

—— woman forbidden to touch roof-thatch, i. 179 *n.*¹

—— women, avoidance of, by hunters, iii. 211 ; disability of, viii. 253 *sq.* ; keep their heads or faces covered, x. 22, 24, 25, 29, 31, 44 *sq.*, 48 *sq.*, 55, 90, 92 ; not allowed to cross or bathe in rivers, x. 77 ; not allowed to go near water, x. 77 ; supposed to spoil fisheries, x. 77, 78, 90 *sq.*, 93 ; painted red, or red and white, x. 78 ; not allowed to use the ordinary paths, x. 78, 80, 84, 89, 90 ; not allowed to approach the sea, x. 79 ; not allowed to enter cultivated fields, x. 79 ; obliged to occupy special huts, x. 79, 82, 85 *sqq.* ; supposed to spoil crops, x. 79, 96 ; not allowed to cook, x. 80, 82, 84, 90 ; not allowed to drink milk, x. 80, 84 ; not allowed to handle salt, x. 81 *sq.*, 84 ; kept from wells, x. 81, 82, 97 ; obliged to use separate doors, x. 84 ; not allowed to lie on high beds, x. 84 ; not allowed to touch or see fire, x. 84, 85 ; not allowed to cross the tracks of animals, x. 84, 91, 93 ; excluded from religious ceremonies, x. 85 ; not allowed to eat with men, x. 85, 90 ; thought to spoil the luck of hunters, x. 87, 89, 90, 91, 94 ; not allowed to ride horses, x. 88 *sq.*, 96 ; not allowed to walk on ice of rivers and lakes, x. 90 ; dangers to which they are thought to be exposed, x. 94 ; not allowed to touch beer, wine or vinegar, x. 96 ; not allowed to salt or pickle meat, x. 96 *n.*² ; not allowed to cross running streams, x. 97 ; not allowed to draw water at wells, x. 97 ; used to protect fields against insects, x. 98 *n.*¹

Menstruous women dreaded and secluded, iii. 145 *sqq.*, 206 ; in Australia, iii. 145, x. 76 *sqq.* ; in America, iii. 145 *sqq.*, x. 85 *sqq.*; in the Torres Straits Islands, x. 78 *sq.* ; in New Guinea, x. 79 ; in Galela, x. 79 ; in Sumatra, x. 79 ; in Africa, x. 79 *sqq.* ; among the Jews and in Syria, x. 83 *sq.* ; in India, x. 84 *sq.* ; in Annam, x. 85

Mentawei Islands, ceremony at reception of strangers in the, iii. 104

Mentras of Malacca use a special language in searching for *lignum aloes*, iii. 404 ; their tradition as to primitive man, vi. 140

Mephitic vapours, worship of, v. 203 *sqq.*

Mequinez in Morocco, custom of throwing water on each other at Midsummer at, x. 216

Mercato Nuovo at Florence, the Old Woman sawn through at Mid-Lent in the, iv. 241

Mercurial temperament of merchants and sailors, vi. 218

Merenra, king of Egypt, worshipped in his lifetime, i. 418

Meriahs, human victims sacrificed for good crops among the Khonds, iv. 139, vii. 245, 246, 249, 250

Merkel, R., on the grove of Helernus, ii. 190 *n.*²

Merker, Captain M., on the power of medicine-men among the Masai, i. 343 *sq.*

Merlin, the wizard, his magic sleep, i. 306

Merodach or Marduk, Babylonian deity, ix. 356. *See* Marduk

Meroe, Ethiopian kings of, put to death, iv. 15

Merolla, G., da Sorrento, on food taboos in Congo, iii. 137 ; on the custom of putting the Chitomé to death, iv. 14 *sq.* ; on seclusion of girls at puberty on the Congo, x. 31 *n.*³

Merovingian kings may have touched for scrofula, i. 370

Merrakech, in Morocco, custom of throwing water on each other at Midsummer at, x. 216 ; New Year fires at, x. 217

Merseburg, binder of last sheaf called the Oatsman near, vii. 221

Merton College, Oxford, King of the Bean at, ix. 332 *sq.*

Mesha, king of Moab, his god Kemosh, v. 15 ; sacrifices his first-born, v. 110

Mesopotamia, artificial fertilization of the date-palm in, ix. 272 *sq.* ; Atrae in, x. 82

Mespelaer, in Belgium, St. Peter's fires at, x. 195

Messaria, in Cythnos, children passed through holed rock near, xi. 189

Messenia, Andania in, ii. 122

Messiah, pretended new, in America, i. 409 ; pretended Jewish, at Smyrna, iv. 46 ; "the Anointed One," v. 21

Metageitnion, an Attic month, vii. 77, viii. 17 *n.*², ix. 354

Metal instruments, the clash of, a protection against witches, ix. 158

Metapontum, head of Demeter on a coin of, vii. 68 *n.*¹

Meteor as signal for festival, v. 259

Meteorite, powdered, in a charm, viii. 166 *sq.*

Meteors, superstitions as to, iv. 58 *sqq.* *See also* Falling Stars

Metharme, daughter of Pygmalion, v. 41

Methide plant growing over grave of Osiris, vi. 111

Metis, swallowed by her husband Zeus, iv. 192

Meton, his cycle of nineteen years, vii. 81 *n.*³

"Metropolis of the Corn," Athens called the, by Delphic oracle, vii. 58

Metsik, a forest-spirit, the patron of cattle, ii. 55 ; his effigy carried out of the village by the Esthonians on Shrove Tuesday, iv. 233, 252 *sq.*

Metz, F., on the fire-walk among the Badagas, xi. 9

Metz, cats burnt alive in Midsummer fire at, xi. 39

Mexican calendar, its mode of intercalation, vi. 28 *n.*³

—— custom of veiling the images of the gods during the king's sickness, iii. 95 *n.*⁸ ; of making images of gods out of dough and eating them sacramentally, viii. 86 *sqq.*

—— human sacrifices in connexion with the maize crop, vii. 236 *sqq.*, 251 ; assimilation of the victims to the gods in, vii. 261, ix. 275 *sqq.*

—— Indians, confession of sins among the, iii. 216 *n.*²

—— kings, oath taken by them at their accession, i. 356, 416

—— sacraments, viii. 86 *sqq.*

—— temples, their form, ix. 279

Mexicans, their custom of eating a man as an embodiment of a god, viii. 92 *sq.*

——, the ancient, their human sacrifices to the sun, i. 314 *sq.* ; human sacrifices of, vi. 107, vii. 236 *sqq.* ; their customs at maize-harvest, vii. 174 *sqq.*

Mexico, the Huichol Indians of, i. 123, 154 *sq.*, 302, iii. 197, vii. 177, viii. 93 ; Indians of, their charm to cause sleep, i. 148 ; the Tarahumare Indians of, i. 150, 155, 249, 284, ii. 156 *sq.*, vii. 227 *sq.*, viii. 252, ix. 10, 236 ; the Tepehuanes of, iii. 325, 424, ix. 10 ; rule as to the felling of timber in, vi. 136 ; the Zapotecs of, vii. 174, xi. 212 ; the Tzentales of, viii. 241 ; heaps of stones and sticks to which passers-by add, in, ix. 10 ; the Cora Indians of, ix. 238, 381 ; effigies of Judas burnt at Easter in, x. 127 *sq.*

——, ancient, custom as to children's cast teeth in, i. 179 ; treatment of the navel-string in, i. 196 *sq.* ; custom of passing new-born children through the smoke of fire in, ii. 232 *n.*³ ; virgin-priestesses of fire in, ii. 245 ; continence at brewing *pulque* in, iii. 201 *sq.* ; tears of human victims a sign of rain in, vii. 248 *n.*² ; magic ointment in, viii. 165 ; use of skins of human victims in, ix. 265 *sq.*, 297, 298 *sq.* ; killing the god in, ix. 275 *sqq.* ; story of the creation of the sun in, ix. 410 ; ceremony of new fire in, x. 132 ; representation of the sun as a wheel in, x. 334 *n.*¹

Meyer, Professor Eduard, on prophecy in Canaan, v. 75 *n.*⁵ ; on the Hittite language, v. 125 *n.* ; on costume of Hittite priest or king, v. 133 *n.*, 141 *n.*¹ ; on the rock-hewn sculptures of Boghaz-Keui, v. 133 *n.* ; on Anubis at Abydos, vi. 18 *n.*³ ; on the hawk as an Egyptian emblem, vi. 22 *n.*¹ ; on the date of the introduction of the Egyptian calendar, vi. 36 *n.*² ; on the nature of Osiris, vi. 126 *n.*², vii. 260 *n.*² ; on the relation of Byblus to Egypt, vi. 127 *n.*¹ ; on the Lycian language, vi. 213 *n.*¹ ; on the age of the Egyptian calendar, ix. 340 *n.*⁴

Meyer, Professor Kuno, on an Irish legend, iv. 159 *n.*¹

Mezentius, king of Caere, his battle with Latinus, iv. 283

Mhaighdean-Bhuana (or *Maighdean-Buana*), the Corn-maiden in the Highlands of Scotland, vii. 156, 164 *sq.*

Miamis, Indian tribe of North America, their myth of the Corn-spirit, vii. 206 *sq.*

Miao-Kia, aborigines of China, their sacred trees and groves, ii. 31

Micah, the prophet, on man's duty, i. 223, iv. 174 ; on sacrifice, iv. 171

Mice asked to give new teeth, i. 178, 179 ; and shorn hair, superstition as to, iii. 270 ; not to be called by their proper names, iii. 397, 399, 415 ; thought to understand human speech, iii. 399 ; eaten by the Jews as a religious rite, viii. 24 ; their ravages on the crops, viii. 33, 282 ; the genius of, viii. 243 ; superstitious precautions taken by farmers against, viii. 276 *sqq.*, 281 ; superstition as to white, viii. 279, 283 ; white, under the altar of Apollo, viii. 283. *See also* Mouse

―― and rats, teeth of, in magic, i. 178 *sqq.*

―― and twins, supposed connexion between, i. 118

Michael, in the Isle of Man, x. 307

Michael Angelo, the Pietà of, v. 257

Michaelmas, 29th September, festival of the dead among the Letts at, vi. 74 ; cakes baked at, x. 149. *See also* St. Michael

Michemis, a Tibetan tribe, a funeral ceremony among the, x. 5

Micksy, rivulet, holy oak on the, ii. 371 *sq.*

Microseris Forsteri, roots of, dug and eaten by Australian aborigines, vii. 127

Mid-Lent, the fourth Sunday in Lent, iv. 222 *n.*[1] ; also called Dead Sunday, iv. 221 ; custom of "Carrying out Death" at, iv. 234, 236 *sq.* ; ceremony of "Sawing the Old Woman" at, iv. 240 *sqq.*

Midas and his ass's ears, iii. 258 *n.*[1]

――― and Gordias, names of Phrygian kings, v. 286

―――, King of Gordium, iii. 316

―――, King of Phrygia, father of Lityerses, vii. 217 ; the tomb of, v. 286

Middle Ages, belief as to consummation of marriage being prevented by knots and locks in the, iii. 299 ; the Yule log in the, x. 252 ; the need-fire in the, x. 270

Middleton, J. H., on the temple of Apollo at Delphi, vii. 14 *n.*[3] ; on "crying the neck" in Cornwall, vii. 266

Midianites, the slaughter of the, iii. 177

Midsummer, precautions against witches at, ii. 127 ; new fire made at, ii. 242 ; reason for celebrating the death of the spirit of vegetation at, iv. 263 *sq.* ; gardens of Adonis at, v. 244 *sqq.* ; old heathen festival of, in Europe and the East, v. 249 *sq.* ; divination at, v. 252 *sq.* ; wells crowned with flowers at, xi. 28 ; processions of giants at, xi. 33 *sqq.* ; sacred to Balder, xi. 87

Midsummer bonfire called "fire of heaven," x. 334

―― bonfires in Sweden, ii. 65 ; intended to drive away dragons, x. 161. *See* Midsummer fires

―― Bride and Bridegroom in Sweden and Norway, ii. 92, v. 251

" ―― Brooms" in Sweden, xi. 54

―― Day (St. John's Day), cattle crowned on, ii. 127 ; ancient Roman festival of, ii. 272, x. 178 ; ceremonies concerned with vegetation on, ix. 359 ; charm for fig-trees on, x. 18 ; water claims human victims on, x. 26 *sqq.* ; regarded as unlucky, xi. 29. *See also* St. John's Day

―― Day or Eve, custom of bathing on, v. 246 *sqq.*, xi. 29 *sq.* ; pagan origin of the custom, v. 249

―― Eve (St. John's Eve), May-poles and bonfires in Sweden on, ii. 65 ; trees burned on, ii. 66, 141, v. 250 ; activity of witches and warlocks on, ii. 127, ix. 158, 160, x. 176 *sq.*, xi. 19, 73 *sqq.* ; bonfires in Cornwall on, ii. 141 ; figures of Kupalo carried over bonfires in Russia on, iv. 262, v. 250 *sq.* ; Snake Stones thought to be formed on, x. 15 ; trolls and evil spirits abroad on, x. 172 ; the season for gathering wonderful herbs and flowers, xi. 45 *sqq.* ; the magic flowers of, xi. 45 *sqq.* ; divination on, xi. 46 *n.*[3], 50, 52 *sqq.*, 61, 64, 67 *sqq.* ; dreams of love on, xi. 52, 54 ; fern-seed blooms on, xi. 65, 287 ; the divining-rod cut on, xi. 67 *sqq.* ; treasures bloom in the earth on, xi. 288 *n.*[5] ; the oak thought to bloom on, xi. 292, 293. *See also* St. John's Eve

―― festival, in Europe, ii. 272 *sq.*, x. 161 *sqq.* ; named after St. John, v. 244 ; the bonfires, processions with torches, and rolling wheels of the, x. 161 ; Kirchmeyer's account of the, x. 162 *sq.* ; of fire and water among the Mohammedan peoples of North Africa, x. 213 *sqq.* ; common to peoples on both sides of the Mediterranean, x. 219, xi. 31 ; the most important of the year among the primitive Aryans of Europe, xi. 40 ; its relation to Druidism, xi. 45

―― fires, x. 160 *sqq.* ; and couples in relation to vegetation, v. 250 *sq.* ; leaping over the fires to make flax or hemp grow tall, v. 251 ; in Germany, x. 163 *sqq.* ; in Denmark, Norway, and Sweden, x. 171 *sq.* ; in Austria, x. 173 *sqq.* ; cows driven through, to guard them against witchcraft, x. 175, 176, 185, 188 ; regarded as a protection against witchcraft, x. 176, 180 ; in Russia and Lithuania, x.

176 *sqq.* ; among the Magyars, x. 178 *sq.* ; among the Esthonians, x. 179 *sq.* ; in Finland and among the Cheremiss, x. 180 *sq.* ; in France, x. 181 *sqq.* ; in Belgium, x. 194 *sqq.* ; in England, x. 196 *sqq.* ; in Wales, x. 156, 200 *sq.* ; in Ireland, x. 201 *sqq.* ; in Scotland, x. 206 *sq.* ; in Spain and the Azores, x. 208 *sq.* ; in Italy, x. 209 *sq.* ; in Malta, x. 210 *sq.* ; in Greece, the Greek islands, and Macedonia, x. 211 *sq.* ; in America, x. 212 *sq.* ; among the Mohammedans of North Africa, x. 213 *sqq.* ; animals burnt in the, xi. 38 *sqq.* *See also* Cattle *and* Leaping

Midsummer flowers and plants used as talismans against witchcraft, xi. 72

—— Men, orpine, xi. 61

—— morning, church bells rung on, to drive away witches, ii. 127

—— mummers clad in green fir branches, xi. 25 *sq.*

—— solstice, rain-making ceremony performed at the, viii. 179. *See also* Solstice

—— tree burned in Bohemia, ii. 66

Midwinter fires, x. 246 *sqq.*

Migrations of princes in ancient Greece a trace of female descent of the kingship, ii. 278 *sq.*

Mijatovich, Chedo, on the *Zadrooga* or Servian house-community, x. 259 *n.*[1]

Mikado, the, an incarnation of the sun goddess, i. 417, iii. 2 ; rules of life of, iii. 3 *sqq.* ; not allowed to set foot on ground, iii. 3, x. 2 *sq.* ; the sun not allowed to shine on him, iii. 3, x. 18 *sq.* ; supposed effect of using his dishes or clothes, iii. 131 ; custom as to cutting his hair and nails, iii. 265 ; his absolution and remission of sins, ix. 213 *n.*[1]

Mikados, their relations to the Tycoons, iii. 19 ; human sacrifices formerly offered at the graves of the, iv. 218

Miklucho-Maclay, Baron, on the ignorance of the art of making fire on the Maclay coast of New Guinea, ii. 253 *sq.* ; on protective ceremony in New Guinea, iii. 109

Milan, alleged incarnation of the Holy Ghost at, i. 409 ; festival of the Three Kings of Twelfth Day at, ix. 331

Milcom, the god of Ammon, v. 19

Mildew worshipped by the Romans, viii. 282

Mildew Apollo, viii. 282

Milk, offered at graves, i. 287, v. 87 ; stolen by witches from cows on Walpurgis Night or May Day (Beltane), ii. 52 *sqq.*, ix. 267, x. 154 ; stolen by witches from cows on Midsummer Eve, ii. 127, x. 176 *sq.*, 185, xi. 74 ; poured on grave of ancestor, ii. 223 ; offered to the fig-tree of Romulus, ii. 318 ; stolen by witches on Eve of St. George, ii. 334 *sqq.*; not given away on St. George's Eve, ii. 339 ; customs observed when the king of Unyoro drinks, iii. 119 ; not drunk by those who have handled a corpse, iii. 141 ; not to be drunk by wounded men, iii. 174 *sq.* ; consecrated by lying-in woman, iii. 225 *n.*; wine called, iii. 249 *n.*[2] ; serpents fed with, v. 84 *sqq.*, 87 ; omens from boiling, viii. 56, xi. 8 ; taboos referring to, viii. 83 *sq.* ; temporary abstinence from, viii. 161 ; offered to snakes, viii. 288 ; heifers beaten to make them yield, ix. 266 *sq.*; girls at puberty forbidden to drink, x. 22, 30, 38 ; poured on fire-place, x. 30 ; not to be drunk by menstruous women, x. 80, 84 ; stolen by witches from cows, x. 343 ; libations of, poured on fire, xi. 8, 9 ; libations of, poured into a stream, xi. 9 ; poured on sick cattle, xi. 13

Milk and butter stolen from cows by witches at Midsummer, ii. 127, x. 185 ; thought to be improved by the Midsummer fires, x. 180 ; witchcraft fatal to, xi. 86

—— and cattle, importance of, for the early Italians, ii. 324

—— of cows, charm to increase the, i. 198 *sq.* ; chiefs held responsible for the, i. 354 ; thought to be promoted by green boughs on May Day, ii. 52

—— and meat (flesh), dietary rules as to, iii. 292, viii. 83 *sq.*

—— of pig thought to cause leprosy, viii. 24, 25

——, women's, promoted by milk-stones, i. 165

Milk pails wreathed with garlands on May Day, ii. 52 ; wreathed with rowan on May Day, ii. 53 ; wreathed with flowers on St. George's Day, ii. 338, 339

—— -stones, magical, produce milk, i. 165

—— -tie as a bond of kinship, xi. 138 *n.*[1]

—— -tree not to be cut while the corn is in the ground, ii. 49

—— -vessels not to be touched by menstruous women, x. 80

Milking cows as a rain-charm, i. 284 ; through a hole in a branch or a "witch's nest," xi. 185

Milkmaids on May Day, dance of, ii. 52

Milkmen of the Todas sacred or divine, i. 402 *sq.* ; taboos observed by, iii. 15 *sqq.*

Milky juice of wild fig-tree in religious rite, ii. 313, ix. 258

Mill, women mourning for Tammuz eat nothing ground in a, v. 230 ; Tammuz ground in a, vii. 258

Mill-stones crowned at Vesta's festival in June, ii. 127 *n.*³

Millaeus on judicial torture, xi. 158

Miller, Hugh, on absence of soul in sleep, iii. 40 *sq.*

Miller's wife a witch, story of the, x. 319 *sq.*

Millet, homoeopathic magic of, i. 145 ; cultivated in Africa, vii. 115, 117 ; cultivated in Assam, vii. 123 ; cultivated in New Guinea, vii. 123 ; the deity of, worshipped by the Ainos, viii. 52 ; first-fruits of, offered to the dead, viii. 111, 112

Millingtonia, the sacred tree of the Todas, viii. 314

Milne, Mrs. Leslie, on Shan custom as to cutting bamboos, vi. 136

Miltiades, funeral games celebrated in his honour in the Thracian Chersonese, iv. 93 *sq.*

Milton on chastity, ii. 118 *n.*¹; on the laments for Tammuz, v. 226 *n.*; on the Harvest Queen, vii. 147

Mimicry the principle of religious or magical dramas, ix. 374

Miming, a satyr of the woods, in the Balder legend, x. 103

Minahassa, a district of Celebes, rain-making in, i. 277 ; inspired priests among the Alfoors of, i. 382 *sq.* ; ceremony at house-warming among the Alfoors of, iii. 63 *sq.*, xi. 153 ; reluctance to be photographed in, iii. 99 ; Alfoors of, forbidden to pronounce the names of parents-in-law, iii. 340 *sq.* ; special language at rice-harvest in, iii. 412 ; mock human sacrifices in, iv. 214 *sq.* ; quail associated with rice in, vii. 296 ; customs as to sowing and plucking the new rice in, viii. 54 ; dummies to deceive demons in, viii. 100 ; festival of " eating the new rice " in, viii. 123 ; hair of slain foe used to impart courage in, viii. 153 ; expulsion of demons in, ix. 111 *sq.*

Minangkabau, the Sultan of, revered by the Battas, i. 399

Minangkabauers of Sumatra, their use of magical images, i. 58 ; their homoeopathic magic at building a rice barn, i. 140 ; their treatment of the navel-string, i. 193 ; their treatment of women in childbirth, iii. 32 ; their conception of the soul as a bird or a fly, iii. 36 ; their belief as to absence of soul in sleep, iii. 41 ; their customs as to the Mother of Rice, vii. 191 *sq.* ;

their respect for crocodiles, viii. 211 *sq.* ; their respect for tigers, viii. 215 *sq.* ; their belief as to menstruous women, x. 79 ; use of bull-roarers among the, xi. 229 *n.*

Mindanao, one of the Philippines, the Bogabos of, iii. 323, vii. 240

Minden, dances round an oak in the principality of, ii. 371

Miners, special language employed by, iii. 407, 409

Mingoli, spirits of the dead, among the Boloki, ix. 77

Mingrelia, holy image ducked as a rain-charm in, i. 308

Miniature fields dedicated to spirits in Nias, vii. 233 *sq.*

Minnetarees, Indian tribe of North America, their personification of maize as an Old Woman, vii. 204 *sq.* ; ceremony for securing good crop of maize among the, vii. 209 *n.*² ; their belief in the resurrection of bisons, viii. 256

Minnigaff, parish in Galloway, " cutting the Hare " at harvest in, vii. 279

Minoan age of Greece, v. 34

Minorca, seven-legged images of Lent in, iv. 244 *n.*¹

Minos, king of Cnossus, his reign of eight years, iv. 70 *sqq.*; tribute of youths and maidens sent to, iv. 74 *sqq.*

——, king of Crete, besieges Megara, xi. 103

—— and Britomartis, iv. 73

Minotaur, the, legend of, iv. 71, 74 ; perhaps an image of the sun, iv. 75, 77

—— and the labyrinth, iv. 71, 74, 77

—— and Pasiphae, iv. 71, vii. 31

Mint, flowers of, gathered on St. John's Day, xi. 51

Minucius Felix on the Ephesian Artemis, i. 38 *n.*¹ ; on the rites of Osiris, vi. 85 *n.*³ ; on the Salii, ix. 231 *n.*³

Minyas, king of Orchomenus, his treasury, iv. 164

Miotse, the, of China, drive away the devil by means of a kite, ix. 4

Mirabeau, hunting the wren at, viii. 321

Miracles, god-man expected to work, i. 376 ; not conceived by early man as breaches of natural law, i. 376 *sq.*

Miraculous births of gods and heroes, v. 107

Mirasans, the, of the Punjaub, their worship of snakes, viii. 316 *sq.*

Miris of Assam, fear to offend woodland spirits, ii. 39 ; new fire made after a death among the, ii. 267 *n.*⁴ ; woman's share in agriculture among the, vii. 123 ; eat tiger's flesh to make them brave, viii. 145

Mirror or burning-glass, fire made by means of, ii. 243, 245 *n.*

Mirrors, superstitions as to, iii. 92 *sq.*, 94 *sqq.* ; covered after a death, iii. 94 *sq.*

Mirzapur, the Chero of, i. 209 ; taboos and ceremonies connected with the rearing of silk-worms in, iii. 193 *sq.* ; the Majhwârs of, iii. 234, ix. 36, 60 ; the Pankas of, iii. 402 ; remedy for locusts in, viii. 276 ; transference of disease in, ix. 6 ; sacrifices at cairns in, ix. 27 ; the Korwas and Pataris of, their use of scapegoats, ix. 192 ; the Bhuiyars of, x. 84

Miscarriage in childbed, dread of, iii. 149, 152 *sqq.*; supposed danger of concealing a, iii. 211, 213

Misfortune swept out of house with brooms, ix. 5 ; burnt in Midsummer fires, x. 215 ; got rid of by leaping over Midsummer fires, x. 215

Misrule, the Lord of, ix. 251, 312 ; at Bodmin in Cornwall, ii. 319 *n.*[1] ; in England, ix. 331 *sqq.*

Missel-thrush and mistletoe, xi. 316

Missiles hurled at dangerous ghosts or spirits, ix. 17 *sqq.*

Mississippi, lighted torch carried before chiefs among the Indians of the, ii. 263 *sq.*

Missouri, the, cottonwood trees in the valley of, ii. 12

"Mist - healing," Swiss expression for kindling a need-fire, x. 279

Mistletoe, worshipped by the Druids, ii. 358, 362, xi. 76 *sq.*, 301 ; wreath of, on pole to which a wren is fastened, viii. 321 ; the divining-rod made of, xi. 69, 291 ; cut on the sixth day of the moon, xi. 77 ; makes barren animals and women to bring forth, xi. 77, 78, 79 ; cut with a golden sickle, xi. 77, 80 ; thought to have fallen from the sky, xi. 77, 80 ; called the "all-healer," xi. 77, 79, 82 ; an antidote to all poison, xi. 77, 83 ; gathered on the first day of the moon, xi. 78 ; not to touch the earth, xi. 78, 80, 280 ; a cure for epilepsy, xi. 78, 83, 84 ; extinguishes fire, xi. 78, 84, *sq.*, 293 ; venerated by the Ainos of Japan, xi. 79 ; growing on willow specially efficacious, xi. 79 ; confers invulnerability, xi. 79 *sq.*; its position as a parasite on a tree the source of superstitions about it, xi. 80, 81, 84 ; not to be cut but shot or knocked down with stones, xi. 81 *sq.*; in the folk-lore of modern European peasants, xi. 81 *sqq.*; medical virtues ascribed to, xi. 82 *sqq.*; cut when the sun is in Sagittarius, xi. 82, 86 ; growing on oak a panacea for green wounds, xi. 83 ; mystic qualities ascribed to mistletoe at Midsummer (St. John's Day or Eve), xi. 83, 86 ; these virtues a pure superstition, xi. 84 ; cut at the full moon of March, xi. 84, 86 ; called "thunder-besom" in Aargau, xi. 85, 301 ; a master-key to open all locks, xi. 85 ; a protection against witchcraft, xi. 85 *sq.*; given to first cow that calves after New Year, xi. 86 ; gathered especially at Midsummer, xi. 86 *sq.*; grows on oaks in Sweden, xi. 87 ; ancient Italian belief that mistletoe could be destroyed neither by fire nor water, xi. 94 ; life of oak in, xi. 280, 292 ; a protection against witchcraft and Trolls, xi. 282, 283, 294 ; a protection against fairy changelings, xi. 283 ; hung over doors of stables and byres in Brittany, xi. 287 ; thought to disclose treasures in the earth, xi. 287, 291 *sq.*; gathered at the solstices, Midsummer and Christmas, xi. 291 *sqq.*; traditional privilege of, xi. 291 *n.*[2] ; growing on a hazel, xi. 291 *n.*[3] ; growing on a thorn, xi. 291 *n.*[3] ; perhaps conceived as a germ or seed of fire, xi. 292 ; sanctity of mistletoe perhaps explained by the belief that the plant has fallen on the tree in a flash of lightning, xi. 301 ; two species of, *Viscum album* and *Loranthus europaeus*, xi. 315 *sqq.* ; found most commonly on apple-trees, xi. 315, xi. 316 *n.*[5]; growing on oaks in England, xi. 316 ; seeds of, deposited by missel - thrush, xi. 316 ; ancient names of, xi. 317 *sq.*; Virgil on, xi. 318 *sqq.*; Dutch names for, xi. 319 *n.*[1]

Mistletoe and Balder, x. 101 *sq.*, xi. 76 *sqq.*, 302 ; his life or death in the mistletoe, xi. 279, 283

—— and the Golden Bough, xi. 315 *sqq.*

Mistress, sanctuary of the, at Lycosura, in Arcadia, taboos observed at the, iii. 227 *n.*, 314, viii. 46 ; cow-headed or sheep-headed statuettes of women found at the, viii. 21 *n.*[4]

—— of the Earth, worshipped in Timor, ix. 85

" —— of Turquoise," goddess at Sinai, v. 35

Mitani, ancient people of Northern Mesopotamia, v. 135 *n.*

Mitchell, Sir Arthur, on a barbarous cure for murrain in Scotland, x. 326

Mithr, Armenian fire-god, x. 131 *n.*[3]

Mithra, Persian deity, popularity of his worship in the Roman Empire, v. 301 *sq.* ; identified with the Unconquered Sun, v. 304 ; his nativity on December 25th, v. 304

Mithraic mysteries, initiation into the, xi. 277
—— religion a rival to Christianity, v. 302 ; festival of Christmas borrowed from the, v. 302 *sqq.*
—— sacrifice of bull, viii. 10
Mithridates, his siege of Cyzicus, viii. 95 *n.*[2]
Mitigations of human sacrifices, vii. 33, ix. 396 *sq.*, 408
Mittelmark, district of Prussia, the last sheaf called the Old Man in, vii. 219
Mizimu, spirits of the dead, among the Wadowe of East Africa, xi. 312
Miztecs of Mexico, their annual festival of the dead, vi. 54 *sq.*
Mlanje, in British Central Africa, xi. 314 *n.*[1]
Mnasara tribe of Morocco kindle fires at Midsummer, x. 214
Mnevis, sacred Egyptian bull of Helio-polis, iv. 72, vi. 11, viii. 34 *sq.*, ix. 217
Moa, island of, taboos observed by women and children during war in, i. 131 ; treatment of the navel-string in, i. 187 ; theory of earthquakes in, v. 198 ; annual expulsion of diseases in a proa in, ix. 199
Moab, Arabs of, i. 153, 157, 276, iii. 280, vii. 138 ; their custom of shaving prisoners, iii. 273 ; their custom at harvest, vi. 48, 96 ; their remedies for ailments, vi. 242. *See also* Arabs
——, king of, and his god Kemosh, v. 15 ; sacrifices his son on the wall, iv. 166, 179
——, the wilderness of, v. 52 *sq.* ; the springs of Callirrhoe in, v. 214 *sqq.*
Moabite stone, the inscription on the, v. 15 *n.*[3], 20 *n.*[2], 163 *n.*[3]
Moabites, King David's treatment of the, iii. 273 *sq.* ; burn the bones of the kings of Edom, vi. 104
Mock battle at festival of new fruits among the Creek Indians, viii. 75. *See* Sham fight
—— executions, iv. 148, 158
—— human sacrifices, iv. 214 *sqq.* ; sacrifices of finger-joints, iv. 219
—— kings, iv. 148 *sqq.*, ix. 403 *sq.*
—— marriage of human victims, ix. 257 *sq.*
—— sultan in Morocco, iv. 152 *sq.*
—— sun in charm to secure sunshine, i. 314
Mockery of Christ, ix. 412 *sqq.*
Mocobis, the, of Paraguay, their rever-ence for the Pleiades, vii. 309
Modai, invisible spirits, among the Ka-charis, ix. 93
Models in cardboard offered to the dead

instead of the things themselves, vi. 63 *sq.*
Moesia, Durostorum in Lower, ix. 309
Moffat, Dr. R., on the power of rain-makers in South African tribes, i. 351 ; on the observation of the Pleiades by the Bechuanas, vii. 316
Mogador, in Morocco, devils nailed into a wall at, ix. 63
Moggridge, Mr., on sin-eating in Wales, ix. 44 *n.*[2]
Mogk, Professor Eugen, on May-trees and Whitsuntide-trees in Saxony, ii. 68 *sq.* ; as to the purificatory intention ·of the European fire-festivals, x. 330
Mohammed forbade the artificial fertiliza-tion of the palm, ii. 25 *n.*[1] ; on the fig, ii. 316 ; bewitched by a Jew, iii. 302 *sq.* ; said to have stoned the devil, ix. 24
Mohammed ben Isa or Aïsa, of Mequi-nex, founder of the order called Isowa or Aïsawa, vii. 21
Mohammedan belief as to falling stars, iv. 63 *sq.*
—— calendar lunar, x. 216 *sq.*, 218 *sq.*
—— custom of raising cairns near sacred places, ix. 21
—— New Year festival in North Africa, x. 217 *sq.*
—— peoples of North Africa, their custom of bathing at Midsummer, v. 249 ; Midsummer fires among the, x. 213 *sqq.*
—— popular belief, traces of the bird-soul in, iii. 36 *n.*[3]
—— saints as givers of children, v. 78 *n.*[2] ; reverence for, in North Africa, ix. 21, 22
—— students of Fez, their annual mock sultan, iv. 152 *sq.*
Mohammedanism, its success due to its founder, vi. 160 *sq.*
Mohammedans of India, no fire in their houses after a death, ii. 268 *n.* ; the Suni, of Bombay, cover mirrors after a death, iii. 95 ; of Oude, their mode of drinking moonshine, vi. 144
Moharram, first Mohammedan month, x. 217
Moire, sister of Tylon, v. 186
Mole-cricket in homoeopathic magic, i. 156
—— -hill, earth from a, thrown at fairies, i. 329
Moles, hearts of, eaten by diviners to acquire prophetic power, viii. 143
" —— and Field-mice," fire ceremony on Eve of Twelfth Night in Normandy, ix. 317
—— and field mice driven away by torches, x. 115, xi. 340

Molina, J. I., on Araucanian belief as to toads, i. 292 *n.*[3]; on the annual expulsion of evils in Peru, ix. 130 *n.*

Moloch, sacrifice of children to, iv. 75, 168 *sqq.*, v. 178; meaning of the name, v. 15; the king, vi. 219 *sqq.*

—— and *Melech*, vi. 219 *sq.*

Molonga, a demon of Queensland personified by a man, ix. 172

Molsheim in Baden, bonfires and burning discs on the first Sunday in Lent near, x. 117

Molucca Islanders, their festival of heaven, i. 399 *sq.*

Moluccas, clove-trees in blossom treated like pregnant women in the, ii. 28; fear of offending forest-spirits in the, ii. 40; abduction of human souls in the, iii. 61 *sq.*; ceremony on return from a journey in the, iii. 113

Mombasa, in British East Africa, king of, expected to give rain, i. 396; preceded on the march by fire, ii. 264; avoidance of the word smallpox at, iii. 400

Mommsen, August, on a Delphic ceremony, i. 46 *n.*[1]; on the Sacred Marriage, ii. 137 *n.*[1]; on the Eleusinian games, vii. 77 *n.*[4]; on the Anthesteria, ix. 153 *n.*[1]; on the Cronia at Athens, ix. 352 *n.*[1]

Mommsen, Theodor, on dictatorship of Tusculum, i. 23 *n.*[3]; on the costume of a Roman king, ii. 174 *n.*[1]; on the triumphal golden crown, ii. 175 *n.*[1]; on the election of the Roman kings, ii. 296; on the date of the festival of Osiris at Rome, vi. 95 *n.*[1]; on the Roman custom of knocking in a nail annually, ix. 67 *n.*[2]

Mon, island of, belief of Esthonian reapers in, as to cutting the first corn, vii. 285

Monarchy in ancient Greece and Rome, tradition of its abolition, i. 46; rise of, i. 216 *sqq.*; essential to emergence of mankind from savagery, i. 217; hereditary and elective, combination of the two, ii. 292 *sqq.*

Monbuttu (Monbutto) or Mangbettou of Central Africa, their custom of lengthening the heads of chiefs' children, ii. 297; their king takes his meals in private, iii. 118 *sq.*; women the agricultural labourers among the, vii. 119

Mondard, the great, a straw-man placed on oldest apple-tree while apples are ripening, viii. 6

Mondays, witches dreaded on, xi. 73

Money, the oldest Italian, i. 23; magical stones to bring, i. 164

Mongol transference of evil, ix. 7 *sq.*

Mongolia, rain-making in, i. 305; incarnate human gods in, i. 413

Mongolian peoples, their custom of stuffing skins of sacrificed animals or stretching them on a framework, viii. 257 *sq.*

—— story, milk-tie in a, x. 138 *n.*[1]; the external soul in a, xi. 143 *sq.*

Mongols feared by the Chinese government, i. 413; their recall of the soul, iii. 44; their recovery of souls from demons, iii. 63; reluctant to name the dead, iii. 353; sacred books of the, only to be read in spring or summer, iii. 384; funeral customs of the, v. 293

Monkey sacrificed for riddance of evils, ix. 208 *sq.*

Monkeys (apes) not to be called by their proper name, iii. 402, 403, 408, 413; sacred at Fishtown, viii. 287

Monmouthshire, All Souls' Day in, vi. 79

Monomotapa, in East Africa, the king of, his sacred fire, ii. 264; forbidden to wear foreign stuffs, iii. 115; his way of prolonging his life, vi. 222 *sq.*

Monster supposed to swallow and disgorge novices at initiation, xi. 240 *sq.*, 242

Mont des Fourches, in the Vosges, witch-hare at, x. 318

Montagne du Doubs, in Franche-Comté, bonfires on the Eve of Twelfth Night in the, ix. 316

Montaigne on ceremonial extinction of fires, x. 135 *n.*[2]

Montalto, in Calabria, custom of "Sawing the Old Woman" at, iv. 241

Montanists, their view that the Creation took place at the spring equinox, v. 307 *n.*[2]

Montanus, on the Yule log, x. 248

Montanus the Phrygian, claimed to be the incarnate Trinity, i. 407

Monteiro, Major, his expedition in South Africa, i. 393 *n.*[2]

Montenegro, the Yule log in, x. 263

Montezuma, King of Mexico, worshipped as a god, i. 416; not to be looked on by his subjects, iii. 121; not allowed to set foot on ground, x. 2

Month during which men disguised as devils go about, ix. 132; of general licence before expulsion of demons, ix. 148; intercalary, ix. 342 *sqq.*

—— and moon, names for, in Aryan languages, ix. 325

Months, the Egyptian, table of, vi. 37 *n.*; ancient Greek, lunar and therefore shifting in the solar year, vii. 52 *sq.*, 82; lunar, observed by savages, vii. 117, 125

Montols of Northern Nigeria, their belief

in their sympathetic relation to snakes, xi. 209 *sq.*

Monumbos, the, of German New Guinea, uncleanness of man-slayers among the, iii. 169 ; pregnant women do not use sharp instruments among, iii. 238 ; their masked dances, ix. 382

Monyo, village of Burma, tamarind-tree worshipped at, ii. 46

Moon, Esquimau custom at the new, i. 121 *sq.* ; wives sing to the, in the absence of their husbands, i. 125 ; ceremony at an eclipse of the, i. 311 ; charm to hasten the, i. 319 ; Diana conceived as the, ii. 128 ; women pray to the moon for an easy delivery, ii. 128 *n.*[2] ; woman chosen to represent the, ii. 146 ; ceremonies at new, iii. 15 ; represented by a cow, iv. 71 *sq.* ; myth of the setting and rising, iv. 73 ; married to Endymion, iv. 90 ; human victims sacrificed to the, v. 73, vii. 261 ; albinoes thought to be the offspring of the, v. 91 ; Osiris and the, vi. 129 *sqq.* ; popularly regarded as the cause of growth and decay, vi. 132, 138 ; practical rules based on a theory of the influence of the, vi. 132 *sqq.*, 140 *sqq.* ; popularly regarded as the source of dew and moisture, vi. 137 *sq.* ; worshipped by the agricultural Indians of tropical America, vi. 138 *sq.* ; viewed as the husband of the sun, vi. 139 *n.*; Athenian superstition as to an eclipse of the, vi. 141 ; children presented to the, vi. 144 *sqq.* ; thought to have a harmful influence on children, vi. 148 ; the Greek calendar regulated by the, vii. 80 ; Basutos attempt to reckon by the, vii. 117 ; pigs sacrificed to the, viii. 25 ; bodily ailments transferred to the, ix. 53 *sq.* ; the "dark" and the "light," ix. 140, 141 *n.*[1] ; temple of the, ix. 218 ; hearts of human victims offered to the, ix. 282 ; the goddess of the, personated by an actor or dancer, ix. 381 ; impregnation of women by the, x. 75 *sq.*; the sixth day of the, mistletoe cut on, x. 77 ; the first day of the, mistletoe gathered on, x. 78 ; the full, transformation of were-wolves at, x. 314 *n.*[1] ; reflected in Diana's Mirror, xi. 303

—— and Endymion, i. 18

——, the goddess of the, ix. 341, 381

——, the infant god, vi. 131, 153

—— and month, names for, in Aryan languages, ix. 325

——, the new, ceremonies at, vi. 141 *sqq.* ; dances at, vi. 142 ; custom of

showing money to, or turning it in the pocket, vi. 148 *sq.*

Moon and Sun, their marriage celebrated by the Blackfoot Indians, ii. 146 *sq.* ; mythical and dramatic marriage of the, iv. 71, 73 *sq.*, 78, 87 *sq.*, 90, 92, 105

——, the waning, theories to explain, vi. 130 ; thought to be broken or eaten up, vi. 130 ; rule that things should be cut or gathered at, vi. 133 ; rule that timber should be felled at, vi. 133, 135 *sq.* ; cure for toothache at, ix. 60

Moon Being of the Omahas, vi. 256

—— -god conceived as masculine, v. 73 ; inspiration by the, v. 73 ; in ancient Babylonia, vi. 138 *sq.*

Mooney, James, on the belief of the North American Indians that their names are parts of themselves, iii. 318 *sq.*; on want of discrimination between animals and men in Cherokee mythology, viii. 204 *sq.* ; on Cherokee ideas as to trees struck by lightning, xi. 29

Moonshine drunk as a medicine in India, vi. 144 ; thought to be beneficial to children, vi. 144

Móooi, Tongan god who causes earthquakes, v. 201

Mooraba Gosseyn, a Brahman, incarnation of the elephant-headed god Gunputty, i. 405

Moore, G. F., on the burnt sacrifice of children, vi. 219 *n.*[1]

Moore, *Manx Surnames*, quoted by Sir John Rhys, x. 306

Moors obliterate marks in sand from superstitious motives, i. 214

—— of Algiers, no fire in their houses after a death, ii. 268 *n.*

—— of Morocco, use boars to divert evil spirits, ix. 31 ; their superstition as to the "sultan of the oleander," x. 18

Moorunde tribe of Australia, the dead not named in the, iii. 358

Moosheim, in Wurtemberg, leaf-clad mummer at Midsummer festival at, xi. 26

Mopane country, South Africa, souls of dead chiefs supposed to transmigrate into lions in the, viii. 287

Moquis of Arizona, their use of stone implements in religious ritual, iii. 228; their theory of transmigration into their totemic animals, viii. 178 ; their totem clans, viii. 178

Moral evolution, iii. 218 *sq.*

—— guilt regarded as a corporeal pollution, iii. 217 *sq.*

Morality developed out of taboo, iii. 213 *sq.*; shifted from a natural to a supernatural basis, iii. 213 *sq.*; survival of savage taboos in civilized, iii. 218 *sq.*

Morasas, the, of South India, sacrifice of finger-joints among the, iv. 219

Moravia, precautions against witches on Walpurgis Night among the Germans of, ii. 55, ix. 162; custom observed by the Germans of, on *Laetare* Sunday, ii. 63; "Meeting the Spring" in, ii. 333; "Carrying out Death" in, iv. 238 *sq.*, 249; drama of Summer and Winter in, iv. 257 *sq.*; the Feast of All Souls in, vi. 73; harvest custom in, vii. 162; the Wheat-Bride in, vii. 162; the Shrovetide bear in, viii. 326 *n.*[1]; "Easter Smacks" in, ix. 268, 269; fires to burn the witches in, x. 160; Midsummer fires in, x. 175; the divining-rod in, xi. 67

Moravian belief that serpents get their poison annually on St. George's Day, ii. 344 *n.*[4]

Moravians cull simples at Midsummer, xi. 49, 54

—— of Silesia, their custom of "Carrying out Death," iv. 237

Moray Firth, disappearance of herring in the, viii. 251

Morayshire, remedy for a murrain in, x. 326; medical use of mistletoe in, xi. 84

Morbihan in Brittany, mistletoe hung over the doors of stables and byres at, xi. 287

Morbus regius, jaundice, i. 371 *n.*[4]

Mordecai, his name equivalent to Marduk or Merodach, ix. 365; his triumphal ride in Susa, ix. 403

—— and Esther equivalent to Marduk and Ishtar, ix. 405; the duplicates of Haman and Vashti, ix. 405 *sq.*

—— and Haman, ix. 364 *sqq.*; as temporary kings, ix. 400 *sq.*

Moresby, Captain John, his reception in Shepherd's Isle, iii. 104 *sq.*

Moresin, Thomas, on St. Peter's fires in Scotland, x. 207

Moret, Alexandre, on the divinity of Egyptian kings, i. 418 *sq.*; on assimilation of Egyptian kings to gods, ii. 134 *n.*[1]; on Amenophis IV., vi. 123 *n.*[1]; on the Sed festival, vi. 155 *sq.*

Morgan, L. H., as to Otawa totems, viii. 225 *n.*[1]

Morgan, Professor M. H., on an ancient Greek mode of making fire, ii. 207 *n.*[1]

Mori, a district of Central Celebes, belief of the natives as to a spirit in the moon, vi. 139 *n.*

Mori clan of the Bhils in Central India, their totem the peacock, viii. 29

Moriah, Mount, traditionally identified with Mount Zion, vi. 219 *n.*[1]

Morice, Father A. G., on the seclusion of menstruous women among the Tinneh Indians, iii. 146 *sq.*; on customs and beliefs of the Carrier Indians as to menstruous women, x. 91 *sqq.*; on the honorific totems of the Carrier Indians, xi. 273 *sqq.*

Morlaks, the Yule log among the, x. 264

Morlanwelz, in Belgium, bonfires on the first Sunday in Lent at, x. 107

Morning, certain notes not to be named in the, iii. 402

Morning Star, the, appearance of, perhaps the signal for the festival of Adonis, v. 258 *sq.*; human sacrifice at sowing enjoined by the, vii. 238; named in Nias, vii. 315; personated by a man in a dance or dramatic ceremony, ix. 238, 381; the god of the, ix. 381; girl at puberty bathes at the rising of the, x. 40; the rising of the, the signal for kindling new fire at the winter solstice, x. 133

Morocco, magic use of a fowl or pigeon in, i. 151; artificial fertilization of fig-trees in, ii. 314; iron used as a protection against demons in, iii. 233; disposal of cut hair in, iii. 275; nail-parings preserved for the resurrection in, iii. 280; annual temporary king in, iv. 152 *sq.*; custom of prostitution in an Arab tribe in, v. 39 *n.*[3]; live goats torn to pieces and devoured by a religious sect in, vii. 21; the Barley Bride in, vii. 178 *sq.*; homoeopathic magic of flesh diet in, viii. 147; sticks or stones piled on scenes of violent death in, ix. 15; cairns near Azemmour in, ix. 21; boars used to divert evil spirits in, ix. 31; devils nailed into a wall in, ix. 63; the tug-of-war in, ix. 178 *sq.*, 182; games of ball played in, to procure rain or sunshine, ix. 179 *sq.*; custom of beating people for their good in, ix. 265, 266; magical virtue ascribed to rain-water in, x. 17 *sq.*; Midsummer fires in, x. 213 *sqq.*; water thought to acquire marvellous virtue at Midsummer in, xi. 30 *sq.*; magical plants gathered at Midsummer in, xi. 51

Morris-dancers, ix. 250 *sq.*

Morrison, Rev. C. W., on belief of Australian aborigines as to childbirth, v. 103 *n.*[3]

Mortality, savage explanations of human, ix. 302 *sqq.*

—— of the gods, iv. 1 *sqq.*

Mortlock Islanders, their belief in spirits, ix. 82

Moru tribe of Central Africa, viii. 314. *See* Madi

Morven, x. 290; consumptive people

passed through rifted rocks in, xi. 186 *sq.*

Mosaic law forbids interchange of dress between men and women, ix. 363

—— laws, their similarity to savage customs, iii. 219 *n.*[1]

Mosbach, in Bavaria, the last sheaf called Goat at, vii. 283

Moschus on Europa and the bull, iv. 73 *n.*[1]

Moscow, annual new fire in villages near, x. 139

Moselle, the Treveri on the, ii. 126 *n.*[2] ; the Fox in the corn in the department of the, vii. 296 ; bonfires on the, x. 109 ; Konz on the, x. 118, 163 *sq.*

Moses, the tomb of, ix. 21 ; on the uncleanness of women at menstruation, x. 95 *sq.*

Moslem custom of raising cairns, ix. 21

Mosquito Indians of Central America preserve bones of deer and shells of eggs, viii. 258 *n.*[2]

—— -makers, magicians in Tana, i. 341

—— territory, Central America, seclusion of menstruous women in the, x. 86

Moss, W., iv. 284 *n.*[4]

Mossos of China, their annual expulsion of demons, ix. 139

Mostar, in Herzegovina, custom observed by bride at, ii. 230 *sq.*

Mostene in Lydia, double-headed axe at, v. 183 *n.*

Mosul, the "Mother of the Grapecluster" at, iv. 8 ; cure for headache at, ix. 64

Mosyni or Mosynoeci, in Pontus, kept their king in close custody, iii. 124

Mota, in the New Hebrides, belief as to conception in women in, v. 97 *sq.* ; conception of the external soul in, xi. 197 *sq.*

"Mother" and "Father" as epithets applied to Roman goddesses and gods, vi. 233 *sqq.*

"Mother of the Clan" in the Pelew Islands, vi. 205, 206

Mother, dead, worshipped, vi. 175, 185

—— of a god, v. 51, 52

—— of the gods, Attis associated with the, i. 21, v. 266 ; the Phrygian, her worship adopted by the Romans, v. 265 ; first-fruits offered in Thera to the, v. 280 *n.*[1] ; popularity of her worship in the Roman Empire, v. 298 *sq.* ; Mexican goddess, ix. 289 ; woman annually sacrificed in the character of the, ix. 289 *sq.*

—— or Grandmother of Ghosts at Rome, viii. 94, 96, 107

Mother of the Grape-cluster, iv. 8

——, the Great, Cybele, at Rome, v. 280 ; name given to the last sheaf, vii. 135 *sq.*

" —— of Kings," in Central African kingdom, ii. 277

—— of the Maize, among the Indians of Peru, vii. 172 *sqq.*

—— of the Rain, at a rain-making ceremony among the Arabs of Moab, i. 276

—— of the Rice, in Sumatra and Celebes, vii. 191 *sqq.*

Mother-corn, name given to last sheaf threshed, vii. 147

—— -cotton in the Punjaub, vii. 178

—— Earth prayed to for rain, i. 283 ; festival in her honour in Bengal, v. 90 ; fertilized by Father Sky, myth of, v. 282 ; sickness caused by, viii. 105

—— Goddess of Western Asia, sacred prostitution in the worship of the, v. 36 ; lions as her emblems, v. 137, 164 ; her eunuch priests, v. 206 ; of Phrygia conceived as a Virgin Mother, v. 281

—— -kin, the system of tracing relationship through women, ii. 271, iii. 333 ; in succession to Roman kingship, ii. 271 ; among the Aryans, ii. 283 *sqq.* ; superiority of maternal uncle to father under mother-kin, ii. 285 ; succession in royal houses with, v. 44 ; trace of, at Rome and Nemi, v. 45 ; among the Khasis of Assam, v. 46, vi. 202 *sqq.* ; among the Hittites, traces of, vi. 141 *sq.* ; and Mother Goddesses, vi. 201 *sqq.*, 212 *sqq.* ; and father-kin, vi. 202, 261 *n.*[3] ; favours the superiority of goddesses over gods in religion, vi. 202 *sqq.*, 211 *sq.* ; among the Pelew Islanders, vi. 204 *sqq.* ; does not imply that government is in the hands of women, vi. 208 *sqq.* ; among the Melanesians, vi. 211 ; in Africa, vi. 211 ; in Lycia, vi. 212 *sq.* ; in ancient Egypt, vi. 213 *sqq.* ; traces of, in Lydia and Cos, vi. 259 ; favours the development of goddesses, vi. 259 ; in royal families, ix. 368 *n.*[1]

See also Female kinship

—— -in-law, the savage's dread of his, iii. 83 *sqq.* ; her name not to be mentioned by her son-in-law, iii. 338, 339, 340, 341, 342, 343, 344, 345, 346

—— Plastene on Mount Sipylus, v. 185

—— -seed, among the Malays, vii. 198

—— -sheaf, in Brittany, vii. 135, 209

"Mother's Air," a tune on the flute, v. 288

Mother's brother preferred to father, mark of mother-kin, ii. 285

Mothers, African kings forbidden to see

their, iii. 86 ; named after their children, iii. 332, 333, 339

Motherwort, garlands of, at Midsummer, x. 162

Motlav, recall of lost souls in, iii. 56 ; belief as to conception in women in, v. 98

Motu of New Guinea, their way of detaining the sun, i. 317 ; taboos observed for the sake of the crops among the, ii. 106 ; tabooed persons not allowed to handle food among the, iii. 141 ; chastity of hunters and fishers among the, iii. 192 ; hunters and fishers regarded as holy among the, iii. 196 ; continence observed by them before and during a trading voyage, iii. 203 sq. ; unwilling to tell their names, iii. 329

Motumotu or Toaripi of New Guinea, magical telepathy among the, i. 125 ; their way of detaining the sun, i. 317 ; think that storms are sent by a sorcerer, i. 326 sq. ; sorcerers as chiefs among the, i. 337 ; their belief as to reflections in a mirror, iii. 92 ; taboos observed by manslayers among the, iii. 167 ; continence before fishing or hunting among the, iii. 196 ; unwilling to tell their names, iii. 329 ; homoeopathic magic of a flesh diet among the, viii. 145. See also Toaripi

Moulin, parish of, in Perthshire, Hallowe'en fires in, x. 230

Moulins-Engilbert, spring of St. Gervais near, i. 307

Moulton, Professor J. H., iv. 124 n.[1] ; on the etymology of Quirinus, ii. 182 n.[2] ; on the relation of the Italian and Celtic languages, ii. 189 n.[3] ; on the etymology of Flamen, ii. 247 n.[5] ; on proposed etymologies of Demeter, vii. 41 n., 131 n.[4] ; on the Twelve Days, ix. 325 n.[3] ; on the proposed identification of Haman and Hammedatha with two Persian archangels, ix. 373 n.[1] ; on the etymology of Soranus, xi. 15 n.[1]

Mounds of Semiramis, ix. 370, 371, 373

——, sepulchral, iv. 93, 96, 100, 104

Mountain of Parting, in Mexico, ix. 279

Mountain arnica gathered at Midsummer, xi. 57 sq. ; a protection against thunder, lightning, hail, and conflagration, xi. 58

—— -ash, a protection against witches, ii. 53 ; pastoral crook cut from a, ii. 331 ; parasitic, used to make the divining rod, xi. 69 ; mistletoe on, xi. 315. See also Rowan

—— scaur, external soul in, xi. 156

Mountains, first berries of the season offered to the, viii. 133 sq.

Mourne Mountains, x. 159

Mourners, customs observed by, iii. 31 sq., 159 n., 315 ; plug their nostrils, iii. 32 ; tabooed, iii. 138 sqq., x. 20 ; refrain from scratching their heads with their fingers, iii. 159 n.; heads of, smeared with mud or clay, iii. 182 n.[2] ; taboos observed by, in India, iii. 235 sq. ; hair and nails of, cut at end of mourning, iii. 285 sq. ; touch coral rings as a form of purification, iii. 315 ; shave their heads in order to escape recognition by the ghost, iii. 357 sq. ; rub themselves with the juices of the dead, viii. 163 ; drink the juices of the dead, viii. 163 n.[3]; the purification of, intended to protect them against the spirits of the dead, ix. 105 n.[1] ; whip themselves at a funeral to keep off evil spirits, ix. 260 sq. ; wear special caps, x. 20 ; pass over fire as a purification after a funeral, xi. 17, 18 ; customs observed by, among the Bella Coola Indians, xi. 174

Mournful character of the rites of sowing, vi. 40 sqq.

Mourning of slayers for the slain, iii. 181 ; for a dead whale, iii. 223 ; for Tammuz, v. 9 sqq., 230 ; for Adonis, v. 224 sq., 226 sq. ; of Egyptian reapers, v. 232, vi. 45, 117 ; for Attis, v. 272 ; for Osiris, vi. 12 ; for the corn-god at Midsummer, vi. 34 ; for the Old Woman of the Corn, vi. 47 ; at cutting wood of sacred tree, vi. 47 sq.; of Demeter for the descent of Persephone at the time of the autumn sowing, vii. 46 ; pretended, for insects that destroy the crops, viii. 279 sq. ; the great, for Isfendiyar, x. 105. See also Lamentations and Laments

Mourning costume of men in Lycia, vi. 264 ; perhaps a mode of deceiving the ghost, vi. 264

Mouse, soul in form of, iii. 37, 39 n.[1]. See also Mice

Mouse Apollo, viii. 282 sq.

Mouse-ear hawkweed (Hieracium pilosella) gathered at Midsummer, xi. 57

Mouse's head hung round child's neck at teething, i. 180

Mouth closed to prevent escape of soul, iii. 31, 33, 71 ; soul in the, iii. 33 ; spirits supposed to enter the body through the, iii. 116 ; covered to prevent entrance of demons, etc., iii. 122 ; of the dead, Egyptian ceremony of opening the, vi. 15 ; of dead fox tied up, viii. 267

Movement of thought from magic through religion to science, xi. 304 sq.

Movers, F. C., on the Sacaea, ix. 368, 387, 388, 391, 401

Mowat, in British New Guinea, magical powers of chief at, i. 338 ; continence observed during the turtle season at, iii. 192 ; boys beaten at, to make them strong, ix. 265

Moxos Indians of Bolivia, magical telepathy among the, i. 123

Moylar, male children of sacred prostitutes in Southern India, v. 63

Mozcas. See Chibchas

Mpongwe of the Gaboon, woman's share in agriculture among the, vii. 119

Mpongwe kings of the Gaboon, buried secretly, vi. 104

Mrus, the, of Aracan, their custom of placing grass on a pile, ix. 12 n.[1]

Muata Jamwo, a potentate of Angola, lights a new fire on his accession, ii. 262 ; not to be seen eating or drinking, iii. 118 ; precaution as to his spittle, iii. 290

Mucelis of Angola, all fires among them extinguished on king's death, ii. 262

Mud, rain-makers smear themselves with, i. 350 ; smeared on feet of bed of Flamen Dialis, iii. 14 ; plastered on heads of man-slayers, iii. 182 ; on heads of women in mourning, iii. 182 n.[2]

Muganda (singular of Baganda, plural), viii. 231

Mugema, the earl of Busiro, vi. 168

Müglitz, in Moravia, the Wheat Bride at reaping at, vii. 162

Mugumu or Mugomo, a species of fig-tree revered by the Akikuyu, ii. 42

Mugwort (Artemisia vulgaris), in magic, i. 209 ; wreaths of, at Midsummer, x. 163, 165, 174 ; a preventive of sore eyes, x. 174 ; a preservative against witchcraft, x. 177; gathered on Midsummer Day or Eve, xi. 58 sqq. ; a protection against thunder, ghosts, magic, and witchcraft, xi. 59 sq. ; thrown into the Midsummer fires, xi. 59 ; used in exorcism, xi. 60

Mühlbach, in Transylvania, trial of witch at, iii. 39

Mukasa, god of the Victoria Nyanza Lake, worshipped by the Baganda, ii. 150 ; provided with human wives, ii. 150 ; probably a dead man, vi. 196 sq. ; gives oracles through a woman, vi. 257 ; fish offered to, viii. 253

Mukuru, an ancestor (plural Ovakuru, ancestors), among the Herero, vi. 185 sq.

Mukylćin, the Earth - wife, among the Wotyaks, ii. 146

Mulai Rasheed II., Sultan of Morocco, iv. 153

Mule, asthma transferred to a, ix. 50

Mules excluded from sanctuary of Alectrona, viii. 45

Mulgarradocks, medicine-men in Southwestern Australia, i. 336

Mull, the island of, the harvest Maiden in, vii. 155, 166 ; the need-fire in, x. 148, 289 sq. ; the Beltane cake in, x. 149 ; remedy for cattle-disease in, x. 325 ; consumptive people passed through rifted rocks in, xi. 186 sq.

Mullein, sprigs of, passed across Midsummer fires protect cattle against sickness and sorcery, x. 190 ; bunches of, passed across Midsummer fires and fastened on cattle-shed, x. 191 ; yellow (Verbascum), gathered at Midsummer, xi. 63 sq. ; yellow hoary (Verbascum pulverulentum), its golden pyramid of blooms, xi. 64 ; great (Verbascum thapsus), called King's Candle or High Taper, xi. 64

Müller, K. O., on a custom of the Spartan kingship, iv. 59; on the eight years' cycle in ancient Greece, iv. 69 n.[1]; on octennial celebration of Olympic festival, iv. 90 ; on mitigation of human sacrifice, iv. 165 n.[1], 166 n.[1] ; on Sandan, ix. 389 sq.

Müller, F. Max, and the Rosy Dawn, i. 333 sq.

Müller, Professor W. Max, on Hittite name for god, v. 148 n.

Mulongo, "twin," term applied by the Baganda to the navel-string, i. 195, 196

Mulungu, spirits of the dead, among the Yaos, viii. 111 sq.

Mumbo Jumbos, iv. 178

Mummers dressed in leaves, branches, and flowers, ii. 74 sqq., 78 sqq. ; the Whitsuntide, iv. 205 sqq. ; at Hallowe'en in the Isle of Man, x. 224. See also Maskers

Mundaris of Assam, their sacred groves, ii. 39, 46, 47 ; their annual saturnalia at harvest, ix. 137

Mundas of Bengal, marriage to trees among the, ii. 57 ; gardens of Adonis among the, v. 240

Mungarai, Australian tribe, their belief in the reincarnation of the dead, v. 101

Muni, or Rishi Agastya, figure of, in ceremony to stop rain, i. 296

Munich, annual expulsion of the devil at, ix. 214 sq.

Munro, Dr. R., on crannogs, ii. 352

Munster, rain-producing fountain in, i. 301 ; dearth in, attributed to king's incest, ii. 116; taboos observed by the ancient kings of, iii. 11 ; tax on fires paid to the king of, x. 139; Midsummer fires in, x. 203

Münsterberg, precautions against witches in, xi. 20 n.

Münsterland, Easter fires in, x. 141; the Yule log in, x. 247

Munychian Artemis, iv. 166 n.[1] See Artemis

Munzerabad, district of South India, expulsion of the demon of cholera or smallpox in, ix. 172

Münzesheim, in Baden, the Corn-goat at harvest at, vii. 283

Muota Valley in Switzerland, custom observed on Twelfth Night in the, ix. 166

Mura-muras, the remote predecessors of the Dieri, appealed to for rain, i. 255 sq.

Muralug, dread of women at menstruation in, x. 78

Murder, heaps of sticks or stones on scenes of, ix. 15

—— of children to secure their rebirth in barren women, v. 95

Murderer, fire of oak-wood used to detect a, xi. 92 n.[4]

Murderers, taboos imposed on, iii. 187 sq. ; their bodies destroyed, iv. 11

Murli, female devotee, in Mahratta, v. 62

Murom, district of Russia, the " Funeral of Kostroma " in, iv. 262

Murrain, brazen oxen, a talisman against, viii. 281; need-fire kindled as a remedy for, x. 278, 282, 290 sqq. ; burnt sacrifices to stay a, in England, Wales, and Scotland, x. 300 sqq. ; calf burnt alive to stop a, x. 300 sq.; cattle buried to stop a, x. 326. See also Cattle disease

Murrams, the, of Manipur, foods tabooed to chief of, iii. 292

Murray, Sir James, on kern or kirn, vii. 151 n.[3]

Murray, Miss Margaret A., on human sacrifices to Osiris, vii. 260 sq.

Murray, the country of, Beltane fires in, x. 154 n.[1]

Murray Island, in Torres Straits, ceremony to raise the wind in, i. 322

—— Islands, in Torres Straits, the firedrill in the, ii. 209

—— River, in Australia, tribes of the Lower, avoid mentioning the names of the dead, iii. 351 ; namesakes of the dead change their names among the tribes of the Lower, iii. 355 ; wild yams on the, vii. 127 ; natives of the, their dread of menstruous women, x.

77 ; novices slain and resuscitated by Thrumalun on the, xi. 233

Murring tribe of New South Wales, their custom as to extracted teeth, i. 176

Muses at the marriage of Cadmus and Harmonia, iv. 89

Music as a means of prophetic inspiration, v. 52 sq., 54 sq., 74 ; and religion, v. 53 sq. ; in exorcism, v. 54 sq.

Muskau, in Lausitz, marriage oaks at, xi. 165

Muskoghees eat the hearts of foes to make themselves brave, viii. 150

Musquakie Indians, infant burial among the, v. 91 n.[3]

Mutch, Captain J. S., on the dramatic contest between Summer and Winter among the Esquimaux, iv. 259 n.[1]

Mutilation of the images of Hermes at Athens, iii. 75 ; of dead bodies of kings, chiefs, and magicians, vi. 103 sqq.; of dead magicians to prevent their souls from becoming dangerous ghosts, vi. 188 ; of dead men intended to disable their ghosts, viii. 271 sqq. ; of ox, magical equivalent to mutilation of enemy, viii. 271

Muysca Indians of Colombia not allowed to look at their chiefs, iii. 121

Muyscas, the, of New Granada, their way of procuring rain, i. 303 sq. See Chibchas

Muzaffarpur, district in India, rain-charm by means of frogs in, i. 293 sq.

Muzimbas or Zimbas, of South-East Africa, worship their king as a god, i. 392

Muzimos, spirits of the dead, among the Maraves, viii. 111

Muzimu, the human spirit or soul, among the Winamwanga, viii. 112 n.[3]

Muzzaffarnagar, in the Punjaub, ceremony for stopping rain at, i. 296

Mwamba, chief of the Wemba, swallowed the ashes of his victims to avert their furies, viii. 158

Mwanga, king of the Baganda, converted to Christianity, ii. 150

Mycenae, golden lamb of, i. 365 ; royal graves at, v. 33, 34 ; shield of Euphorbus at, viii. 300

Mycenaean age of Greece, v. 34

Myconus, sacrifices to Subterranean Zeus and Subterranean Earth at, vii. 66

Mylasa in Caria, v. 182 n.[4]

Mylitta, Babylonian goddess, ix. 372 n.[2], 390 ; sacred prostitution in her worship, v. 36, 37 n.[1]

Myndus, in Asia Minor, rain - making pebbles at, i. 305

Myres, Professor J. L., on the season of threshing in Greece, vii. 62 n.[5]

Myrrh or Myrrha, the mother of Adonis, v. 43, 227 *sq.*

Myrrh-tree, Adonis born of a, v. 227, vi. 110

Myrtle-tree with pierced leaves at Troezen, i. 25

—— -trees of the Patricians and Plebeians at Rome, xi. 168

Myrtles of Latium, ii. 188

Mysore in Southern India, rain-making in, i. 285 ; mimic rite of circumcision in, iv. 220 ; sacred women in, v. 62 *n.* ; the Komatis of, v. 81 *sq.* ; Munzerabad in, ix. 172

Mysteries as magical ceremonies, ix. 374

—— of Attis, v. 274 *sq.*

—— of Dionysus, vii. 15

——, Eleusinian, ii. 138 *sq.*, vii. 35, 37 *sqq.*, 65 *sqq.*, 69 *sq.*, 78 *sq.*, 111, 161 *sq.*, 188 ; founded by Demeter, vii. 37 ; the myth of Demeter and Persephone acted at the, vii. 39, 66 ; the Great, their date, vii. 51 *sqq.* ; instituted by Eumolpus, vii. 70 ; associated with belief in immortality, vii. 90 *sq.* ; designed to promote the growth of the corn, vii. 110 *sq.* *See also* Eleusinian Mysteries

——, Greek, bull-roarers swung at, vii. 110

—— at Mantinea, vii. 46 *n.*[2]

—— of Sabazius, v. 90 *n.*[4]

Myth of Adonis, v. 1 *sqq.* ; and ritual of Attis, v. 263 *sqq.* ; myth of Demeter and Persephone, vii. 35 *sqq.* ; myth less constant than custom, viii. 40

Mythical beings represented by men and women, ix. 385 *sq.*

Mythologists, two rival schools of, their views not necessarily exclusive of each other, ix. 385 *sq.*

Mythology, Roman, vi. 235

Myths explanatory of festivals, ii. 142 *sq.* ; supposed to originate in verbal misapprehensions or a disease of language, vi. 42 ; in relation to magic, ix. 374 ; performed dramatically in dances, ix. 375 *sqq.* ; dramatized in ritual, x. 105

—— of creation, iv. 106 *sqq.*

—— of gods and spirits to be told only in spring and summer, iii. 384 ; not to be told by day, iii. 384 *sq.* ; to be told only in winter, iii. 385 *sq.*

——, Italian, of kings or heroes begotten by the fire-god, vi. 235

—— of the origin of death, ix. 302 *sqq.*

Mytilene, titular kings at, i. 45, 46 *n.*[4]

Na Ivilankata, a Fijian clan, members of, walk over oven of hot stones, xi. 10

Naaburg, in Bavaria, custom at sowing at, v. 239

"Naaman, wounds of the," Arab name for the scarlet anemone, v. 226

Nabataeans, Agriculture of the, ii. 100

Nabopolassar, king of Babylon, v. 174

Nabu, a Babylonian god, ix. 358 *n.* ; marriage of, ii. 130 ; his temple in Borsippa, iv. 110

Nâga, serpent god, v. 81

Naga-padoha, the agent of earthquakes, among the Battas, v. 200

—— tribes of Manipur, their belief as to the state of the spirits of the dead, iv. 11

Nagas, demi-gods, concerned in the production of rain, i. 294

—— of Assam, their burial custom, viii. 100 ; believe that the dead are reborn as butterflies or flies, viii. 290 *sq.* ; the tug-of-war among the, ix. 177 ; their ceremony of the new fire, x. 136

—— of the *Mahabharata,* i. 383 *n.*[4]

Nagin, "wives of the snake," in Behar, ii. 149

Nagir, island of Torres Straits, mode of imparting courage in, viii. 153

Nagpur, the cobra the crest of the Maharajah of, iv. 132 *sq.* ; story of the type of Beauty and the Beast told in, iv. 132 *sq.*

Nagual, external soul, among the Indians of Guatemala and Honduras, xi. 212 *sqq.*, 220, 226 *n.*[1]

Nahak, rubbish used in magic, in Tana, i. 341

Nahals, the, a forest tribe of the Central Provinces in India, their worship of trees, viii. 119

Nahanarvals, German tribe, priest dressed as a woman among the, vi. 259

Nahr Ibrahim, the river Adonis, v. 14, 28

Nahum, the prophet, on Nineveh, ix. 390

Nahuntí, an Elamite goddess, ix. 369 *n.*[1]

Nahuqua Indians of Brazil, their use of bull-roarers, xi. 230

Nail of coffin in magic, i. 210, 211

Nail-parings swallowed, iii. 246. *See also* Nails

Nails, golden or silver, driven into a sacred tree, ii. 36 ; knocked into trees, walls, etc., ii. 42, 76, ix. 56 *sqq.* ; knocked into doors to keep out witches, ii. 339 *sq.* ; used as charms against fairies, demons, and ghosts, iii. 233, 234, 236 ; knocked as a solemn ceremony by the highest magistrate at Rome, ix. 64 *sqq.* ; annually knocked into walls to record the years, ix. 67, 67 *n.*[2] ; knocked into ground as cure for epilepsy, ix. 68, 330; knocked into idols or fetishes, ix. 69 *sq.*

Nails, pegs, or pins knocked into images, i. 61, 64, 65, 68, 69

Nails, parings of, used in magic, i. 57, 64, 65, 66; of father of twins not to be cut for a time, ii. 102; of owners of silk-worms not to be cut for a time, iii. 194; parings of, swallowed by attendants, iii. 246; of children not pared, iii. 262 *sq.*; parings of, swallowed by treaty-makers, iii. 274; clippings of, in popular cures, ix. 68 *n.*[2]
—— and hair, cut, disposal of, iii. 267 *sqq.*; as rain-charms, iii. 271, 272; deposited in sacred places, iii. 274 *sqq.*; stowed away in any secret place, iii. 276 *sqq.*; kept for use at the resurrection, iii. 279 *sqq.*; burnt to prevent them from falling into the hands of sorcerers, iii. 281 *sqq.*; in popular cures, ix. 57, 58
—— and teeth of sacred kings preserved as amulets, ii. 6

Nakedness of women in rain-charms, i. 248, 282, 283

Nakelo tribe in Fiji, custom at burial of chief in the, iii. 29

Nakiza, the river, worshipped by the Baganda, ix. 27

Namal tribe of West Australia, their belief as to birth of children, v. 105

Namaquas, their fear of falling stars, iv. 61; their belief in the homoeopathic magic of a flesh diet, viii. 141

Nambutiris of Malabar, their use of magical images, i. 64

Name, the personal, regarded as a vital part of the man, iii. 318 *sqq.*; identified with the soul, iii. 319; the same, not to be borne by two living persons, iii. 370; changed as a cure for ill health, iv. 158

Names of kings changed in time of drought, i. 355; of common objects changed when they coincide more or less with the names of relations, iii. 335, 336, 337, 339, 339 *sq.*, 340, 341, 345, 346; of relations tabooed, iii. 335 *sqq.*; changed to deceive ghosts, iii. 354 *sqq.*; of common objects changed when they are the names of the dead, iii. 358 *sqq.*, 375, or the names of chiefs and kings, iii. 375, 376 *sqq.*; of ancestors bestowed on their reincarnations, iii. 368 *sq.*; of kings and chiefs tabooed, iii. 374 *sqq.*; of supernatural beings tabooed, iii. 384 *sqq.*; of gods tabooed, iii. 387 *sqq.*; of spirits and gods, magical virtue of, iii. 389 *sqq.*; of Roman gods not to be mentioned, iii. 391 *n.*[1]; lucky, iii. 391

n.[1]; of dangerous animals not to be mentioned, iii. 396 *sqq.*; conventional, for common objects on long and perilous journeys, iii. 404 *n.*[3]; royal, signifying relation to deity, v. 15 *sqq.*; Semitic personal, indicating relationship to a deity, v. 51; Hebrew, ending in *-el* or *-iah*, v. 79 *n.*[3]; on chimney-piece, divination by, x. 237; of savages kept secret, xi. 224 *n.*[2]

Names of the dead tabooed, iii. 349 *sqq.*; not borne by the living, iii. 354; revived after a time, iii. 365 *sqq.*
——, new, given to the sick and old, iii. 319; taken by novices at initiation, iii. 320, 383, xi. 259
——, personal, tabooed, iii. 318 *sqq.*; kept secret from fear of magic, iii. 320 *sqq.*; different in summer and winter, iii. 386

Namesakes of the dead change their names to avoid attracting the attention of the ghost, iii. 355 *sqq.*; of deceased persons regarded as their reincarnations, iii. 365 *sqq.*

Naming the dead a serious crime, iii. 352, 354; of children, solemnities at the, connected with belief in the reincarnation of ancestors in their namesakes, iii. 372

Namoluk, one of the Caroline Islands, traditionary origin of fire in, xi. 295

Namosi, in Fiji, human sacrifice at cutting a chief's hair in, iii. 264

Namuci and Indra, legend of, xi. 280

Namur, Lenten fires in, x. 108

Nana, mother of Attis, v. 263, 269, 281

Nana or Nanaea, goddess of Elymais, i. 37 *n.*[2]

Nandi of British East Africa, power of medicine-men among the, i. 344; their custom as to an unchaste girl, ii. 112; their fire-drill, ii. 210; taboos observed by those who have handled the dead among the, iii. 141; purification of man-slayers among the, iii. 175; their use of shorn hair as hostage for a prisoner, iii. 273; their use of magic knots on a journey, iii. 310; names of absent warriors not mentioned among the, iii. 330; reluctant to name the dead, iii. 353; certain words tabooed to warriors among the, iii. 401; their belief as to stepping over things, iii. 423; their belief in serpents as reincarnations of the dead, v. 82, 85; their ceremony at the ripening of the eleusine grain, vi. 47; boys dressed as women and girls dressed as men at circumcision among the, vi. 263; woman's share in agriculture among the, vii. 117 ; their observation of the Pleiades, vii. 317 ; their ceremonies at eating the new eleusine grain, viii. 64 ; warriors eat hearts of foes to become brave among the, viii. 149 ; man-slayers drink the blood of their enemies among the, viii. 155 ; their custom of driving sick cattle round a fire, xi. 13 ; use of bull-roarers among the, xi. 229 n.

Nanga, sacred enclosure in Fiji, viii. 125, xi. 243, 244

Nanja spots, local totem centres in Central Australia, i. 96, 97 ; trees, haunted by disembodied spirits, i. 96

Nanjundayya, H. V., on serpent worship in Mysore, v. 81 sq.

Nanna, the wife of Balder, x. 102, 103

Nanny, a Yorkshire witch, x. 317

Nanumea, island of, precautions against strangers in, iii. 102 sq.

Naples, custom observed by boys on the first Sunday of April at, iv. 241 ; grotto *del cani* at, v. 205 n.[1] ; custom of bathing on St. John's Eve at, v. 246 ; protected against flies and grasshoppers, viii. 281 ; feast of the Nativity of the Virgin at, x. 220 sq.

Náráyan-chakra, a rain-making stone, i. 305

Narbrooi, a spirit or god of the forest, in New Guinea, iii. 60 sq.

Narcissus and his reflection, iii. 94

Narmer, the mace of, king of Egypt represented as Osiris on, vi. 154

Narrative spells, vii. 104 sqq.

Narrinyeri, the, of South Australia, take great care of the refuse of their food, iii. 126 sq. ; names of the recent dead not mentioned among, iii. 372 ; their custom at breaking bones of animals, viii. 259 n.

Narrow openings, creeping through, in order to escape ghostly pursuers, xi. 177 sqq.

Nass River in British Columbia, the Indians of the, believe that a physician may swallow his patient's soul, iii. 76

Nat, spirit, in Burma, ii. 46

Nat superstition in Burma, ix. 90 n.[1]

Natal, the Caffres of, their rain-charm by means of a black sheep, i. 290

Natchez Indians of North America, their rain-making, i. 249 ; claim kindred with the sun, i. 313 n.[3] ; special terms used with reference to persons of the blood royal among the, i. 401 n.[3] ; their perpetual fires, ii. 262 sq. ; customs of man-slayers among the, iii. 181 ; their festival of new corn, viii. 77 sqq. ; their festival of New Fire, viii. 135 sqq.

Nathuram, image supposed to make women fruitful, xi. 3

National character partly an effect of geographical and climatic conditions, vi. 217

Nativity of the Sun at the winter solstice, v. 303 sqq.

"—— of the sun's walking-stick," ancient Egyptian festival, i. 312

—— of the Virgin, feast of the, x. 220 sq.

Nats, spirits in Burma, iii. 90, ix. 175 sq.; propitiation of, ix. 96

Natural calendar of the husbandman, shepherd, and sailor, vi. 25

—— death of sacred king or priest, supposed fatal consequences of, iii. 6, 7 ; regarded as a calamity, iv. 11 sq.

—— law, the conception of, gradually evolved, i. 374 ; not grasped by primitive man, i. 376

—— timekeepers, vii. 53

Nature, conception of immutable laws of, not primitive, i. 374 ; the order and uniformity of, i. 376 ; of Osiris, vi. 96 sqq.

Nauders in the Tyrol, sacred larch-tree at, ii. 20

Naudowessies, Indian tribe of North America, ritual of death and resurrection among the, xi. 267

Naueld, need-fire, in Norway, x. 280

Nauras Indians of New Granada ate the hearts of Spaniards to make themselves brave, viii. 150

Nauroz and Eed festivals in Dardistan, women swing at the, iv. 279

Nauru, in the Marshall Islands, lives of people bound up with a fish in, xi. 200

Navajoes of New Mexico, their ceremony at the return of a man from captivity, iii. 112 sq.; keep their names secret, iii. 325 ; tell their stories only in winter, iii. 385 ; their story of the external soul, xi. 151 sq.; use of bull-roarers among the, xi. 230 n., 231

Navarre, rain-making, by means of images of St. Peter in, i. 307

Navel-string, contagious magic of, i. 182-201 ; planted with or under a tree, i. 182, 184, 186, 196 ; worn as an amulet, i. 183, 187, 197, 198 ; thrown into the sea, i. 184, 185, 190, 191 ; hung on a tree, i. 185, 186, 190, 198, ii. 56 ; regarded as brother or sister of child, i. 186, 189, xi. 162 n.[2]; called the "twin," i. 195 ; worn as amulet by camels, i. 195 ; used in divination, i. 196 ; of the living king of Uganda preserved and inspected every new moon, i. 196, vi. 147 sq.; seat of external soul, i. 200 sq.; used to recall the soul, iii. 48 ; term applied to last handful of corn, vii. 150; buried under a plant or tree, xi. 160 *sq.*, 161, 163

Navel-strings of dead kings of Uganda preserved, vi. 167, 168, 171; preserved by the Baganda as their twins and as containing the ghosts of their afterbirths, vi. 169 *sq.*

Navona, Piazza, at Rome, ceremony of Befana on the, ix. 166 *sq.*

Nawng Tung Lake, in Burma, virgins dedicated in marriage to the spirit of the lake, ii. 150 *sq.*

Naxos, Dionysus Meilichios in, vii. 4

Nayan, a rebel against Kublai Khan, iii. 242

Nazarite, vow of the, iii. 262

Ndem Efik, tutelary deity of Calabar, iii. 22

Ndembo, secret society on the Lower Congo, xi. 251 *sqq.*

Ndjambi, Njambi, Njame, Zambi, Nyambe, etc., name of the supreme god among various tribes of Africa, vi. 186, with note [5]

—— Karunga, the supreme god of the Herero, vi. 186

Ndok, biennial expulsion of spirits at Calabar, ix. 204

Ndolo, on the Moeko River, West Africa, chief with external soul in hippopotamus at, xi. 200

Nebseni, the papyrus of, vi. 112

Nebuchadnezzar, his record of the festival of Marduk, ix. 357

Neck, crying the, at harvest in Devonshire, vii. 264 *sqq.*

—— of the corn-spirit, vii. 268

Neckar, the river, requires three human victims at Midsummer, xi. 26; loaf thrown into the river, xi. 28

Necklace, girl's soul in a, xi. 99 *sq.*

Necropolis, ancient, in the Roman forum, ii. 186; near Albano, ii. 201 *sq.*

Neda, River, at Phigalia, cave of Demeter in the ravine of the, viii. 21

Need-fire, x. 269-300; made without metal, iii. 229; John Ramsay's account of, x. 147 *sq.*; kindled as a remedy for cattle-plague, x. 270 *sqq.*, 343; cattle driven through the, x. 270 *sqq.*; derivation of the name, x. 270 *n.*; kindled by the friction of a wheel, x. 270, 273, 289 *sq.*, 292; kindled with oak-wood, x. 271, 272, 275, 276, 278, 281, 289 *sq.*, 294; called "wild-fire," x. 272, 273, 277; kindled by nine kinds of wood, x. 278, 280; kindled by fir-wood, x. 278, 282; kindled as a remedy for witchcraft, x. 280, 292 *sq.*, 293, 295; called "living fire," x. 281, 286; healing virtue ascribed to, x. 281, 286; kindled by lime-wood, x. 281, 283, 286; kindled by poplar-wood, x. 282; regarded as a barrier interposed between cattle and an evil spirit, x. 282, 285 *sq.*; kindled by cornel-tree wood, x. 286; revealed by an angel from heaven, x. 287; used to heat water, x. 289; kindled on an island, x. 290 *sq.*, 291 *sq.*; kindled by birch-wood, x. 291; kindled between two running streams, x. 292; kindled to prevent fever, x. 297; probable antiquity of the, x. 297 *sq.*; kindled by elm-wood, x. 299; the parent of the periodic fire-festivals, x. 299, 343; Lindenbrog on, x. 335 *n.*[1]; used by Slavonic peoples to combat vampyres, x. 344; sometimes kindled by the friction of fir, plane, birch, lime, poplar, cornel-wood, xi. 91 *n.*[1]

Neftenbach, in Canton of Zurich, the Corn-mother at harvest, vii. 232

Negative magic or taboo, i. 111 *sqq.*, 143

Negritos of the Philippine Islands, their religion a fear of the dead, ix. 82

Negro children pale at birth, xi. 251 *n.*[1], 259 *n.*[2]; gods black and snub-nosed, iii. 387

Negroes of Guiana, their homoeopathic cure for stammering, i. 156

—— of Surinam. *See* Bush negroes

Nehrung, in East Prussia, custom at sowing among the Kurs of, i. 137

Neil, R. A., on Hyes Attes, viii. 22 *n.*[4]; on Gaelic name for mistletoe, xi. 82 *n.*

Neilgherry Hills, the Todas of the, i. 402, ix. 37, x. 136; the Burghers or Badagas of the, viii. 55, ix. 36, 37, xi. 8 *sq.*

Neisse, in Silesia, Oats-king and Oats-queen about, vii. 164; precautions against witches in the district of, xi. 20 *n.*

Neit, Neith or Net, Egyptian goddess, patroness of matrimony, ii. 131, v. 282 *n.*, vi. 51 *n.*[1]

Nekht, the papyrus of, vi. 112

Nel Gwynne, ii. 52

Nellingen in Lorraine, simples gathered on Midsummer Day at, xi. 47

Nelson, A. E., on custom as to cutting the last corn at harvest in India, vii. 234 *n.*[2]

Nelson, E. W., on the supposed effect of a breach of taboo among the Esquimaux, iii. 206; on the bladder festival of the Esquimaux, iii. 228, viii. 249 *n.*[1]; on taboos observed by Esquimaux after a death, iii. 237; on the masquerades of the Esquimaux, ix. 379 *sqq.*

Nemean games, celebrated in honour of Opheltes, iv. 93; held every two years, vii. 86

Nemi, sanctuary of Diana at, i. 2 *sqq.*; the priest of Diana at, i. 8 *sqq*, 40, 41, ii. 376, 386, 387, iv. 28, 212 *sq.*, 220, xi. 315; the King of the Wood at, i. 11, 40 *sqq.*, ii. 378 *sqq.*, iv. 205 *sq.*, 212 *sqq.*, x. 2; Virbius at, i. 20, 40, 41, ii. 378, 379; derivation of the name, ii. 9; sacred marriage of Diana and Virbius perhaps annually celebrated at, ii. 129; Dianus and Diana at, ii. 376 *sqq.*, v. 45; sacramental bread at, xi. 286 *n.*[2]; at evening, xi. 308 *sq.*

———, the Lake of, i. 1 *sqq.*; annual tragedy perhaps formerly enacted at, xi. 286

———, the sacred grove of, i. 2, 8, 12, 17, 40, 41, ii. 378, xi. 315; perhaps composed of oaks, ii. 379, 386

Nemontemi, the five supplementary days of the Aztec calendar, ix. 339

Nemus, meaning of the word, i. 2 *n.*[1]; supposed town of, i. 3 *n.*[1]; a grove or woodland glade, ii. 9

Neolithic implements found in the peat-bogs of Denmark and Scandinavia, ii. 352

Neoptolemus, son of Achilles, in Epirus, ii. 278

Nepaul, the Newars of, i. 294 *sq.*; fossil ammonites found in, ii. 27 *n.*[2]; the Dassera festival of, iv. 277, ix. 226 *n.*[1]

Nephele, wife of King Athamas, iv. 161

Nephews, uncles named after their, iii. 332

Nephthys watches over childbirth, ii. 133; Egyptian goddess, sister of Osiris and Isis, vi. 6; mourns Osiris, vi. 12; the birth of, ix. 341

Neptune and Salacia, vi. 231, 233

Nepu, sorcerers, in New Guinea, i. 337

Nerechta, district of Russia, Whitsuntide custom in, ii. 93

Nerio, wife of Mars, vi. 232

Nero consecrates his first beard, i. 29

Nerthus, old German goddess, xi. 28 *n.*[1]; procession of, ii. 144 *n.*[1]

Nestelknüpfen, spell laid on man and wife, x. 346 *n.*[2]

Net to catch the sun, i. 316; the soul or genius of a, ii. 147

Nets, marriage of girls to, ii. 147; to catch souls, iii. 38, 69 *sq.*; taboos observed at the making of fishing nets, iii. 192; as amulets, iii. 300, 307; treated as living beings, viii. 240 *n.*[1]; fumigated with smoke of need-fire, x. 280

Nettles, whipping with, ix. 263; Indians beaten with, as an ordeal, x. 64

Neuautz, in Courland, pig's tail at sowing barley at, vii. 300

Neuchatel, Midsummer fires in the canton of, x. 172

Neuenkirchen, in Oldenburg, plague hammered into a doorpost at, ix. 64

Neuerburg, in the Eifel, King and Queen of the Bean near, ix. 313

Neugramatin, in Bohemia, custom of beating young women with green boughs in the Christmas holidays at, ix. 270

Neuhausen, near Merseburg, binder of last sheaf wrapt in ears of oats at, vii. 221

Neuhof, near Marburg, remedy for gout at, ix. 56

Neumann, J. B., on the belief in demons among the Battas, ix. 87; on the Batta doctrine of souls, xi. 223 *n.*[2]

Neumark, "Easter Smacks" in, ix. 269

Neusass, in West Prussia, the last sheaf called the Old Woman at, vii. 137

Neustadt, in Silesia, Midsummer fires at, x. 170; near Marburg, the need-fire at, x. 270

Neuwied, Prince of, on a Minnetaree ceremony, vii. 209 *n.*[2]

New, Charles, on the exorcism of strangers in East Africa, iii. 103

New birth, simulation of, among the Akikuyu, i. 75 *sq.*, 96 *sq.*; of Brahman sacrificer, i. 380 *sq.*; through blood in the rites of Attis, v. 274 *sq.*; savage theory of, v. 299; of Egyptian kings at the Sed festival, vi. 153, 155 *sq.*; of novices at initiation, xi. 247, 251, 256, 257, 261, 262 *sq. See also* Birth

——— body obtained at initiation, xi. 252

——— -born children brought to the hearth, ii. 232

——— Britain, Gazelle Peninsula in, i. 175, iii. 202, iv. 65, vii. 123, ix. 303; contagious magic by means of personal relics in, i. 175; contagious magic of footprints in, i. 208; rain-making in, i. 248 *sq.*; the Sulka of, i. 252, 304, ii. 148, 155 *n.*[1], iii. 151, 331, 384, iv. 65; charm to make the wind blow in, i. 320; magical powers ascribed to chiefs in, i. 340; new-born children passed through the smoke of fire in, ii. 232 *n.*[3]; artificial deformation of heads in, ii. 298 *n.*[2]; avoidance of wife's mother in, iii. 85; magic practised on refuse of food in, iii. 128; names of relations by marriage tabooed in, iii. 344; theory of earthquakes in, v. 201; the Melanesians of, their belief in demons in, ix. 82 *sq.*; expulsion of devils in, ix. 109 *sq.*; the Duk-duk society of, x. 11, xi. 246 *sq.*

New Calabar River, human victims thrown into the, ii. 158
—— Caledonia, magical effigies in, i. 78 ; the Belep of, i. 150 ; homoeopathic magic of stones in, i. 162 *sqq.* ; magic blent with the worship of the dead in, i. 164 ; rain-making by means of a human skeleton in, i. 284 *sq.*, 314, ii. 47 ; ceremonies for making sunshine and drought in, i. 312 *sq.*, 314 ; ideas as to reflections among the natives of, iii. 92 *sq.*; taboos observed by men who bury corpses in, iii. 141 ; continence at the building of a canoe in, iii. 202 ; names of relations tabooed in, iii. 344 ; belief as to woman stepping over a cable in, iii. 424 ; ceremony at eating first yams in, viii. 53 ; bodies of slain foes eaten to acquire their bravery in, viii. 151 ; burying the evil spirit in, ix. 110 ; taro plants beaten to make them grow in, ix. 264

—— Caledonians, the, their ways of making rain and sunshine, i. 314 ; their way of detaining the soul in the body, iii. 31

—— College, Oxford, Boy Bishop at, ix. 338

—— corn, eaten sacramentally, viii. 48 *sqq.*

——, everything, excites awe of savages, iii. 230 *sqq.*

—— fire, made by friction in rain-charm, i. 290 ; made by the friction of sticks at Rome, ii. 207, 227 ; made by the friction of sticks at rebuilding a village, ii. 217, 222 ; made by friction at taking possession of a new house, ii. 237 *sq.* ; made by the friction of wood after a birth, ii. 239 ; made at Midsummer, ii. 243 ; made at beginning of a king's reign, ii. 262, 267 ; made by friction of wood, iii. 286, vii. 310 *sq.*, x. 264 ; made at festivals of new fruits, viii. 65, 74, 75, 78 ; festival of, among the Natchez, viii. 135 ; kindled on Easter Saturday, x. 121 *sqq.* ; made at the New Year, x. 134 *sq.*, 138, 140. *See also* Fire, new

—— fruits, ceremonies at eating, viii. 52 *sqq.*

—— Granada, the Muyscas of, i. 303 ; their belief as to water-serpents, ii. 156 ; the Nauras Indians of, viii. 150

—— Guinea, the Toaripi or Motumotu of i. 125, 317, 327, iii. 92 ; the Motu of, i. 317, ii. 106, iii. 141, 192, 203 ; taboos on pregnant women in, i. 141 *n.*[1]; charms to detain the sun in, i. 317 ; some of the natives of, reported to be

ignorant of the art of making fire, ii. 253 *sq.* ; Geelvink Bay in, iii. 60 ; use of effigies as substitutes for souls in, iii. 63 *n.*[2] ; the Maclay Coast of, iii. 109 ; seclusion and purification of man-slayers in, iii. 167 *sqq.* ; the Gebars of, iii. 190 ; Mowat in, iii. 192 ; the Wanigela River of, iii. 192 ; dread of sorcery in, iii. 246 ; cut hair destroyed for fear of witchcraft in, iii. 282 *n.* ; names of relations tabooed in, iii. 342 *sq.* ; bull-roarers used to ensure good crops in, vii. 110 ; division of agricultural work between the sexes in, vii. 124 ; mourners rub themselves with the juices of the dead in, viii. 163 ; belief in the transmigration of human souls into animals in, viii. 295 *sq.*

New Guinea, British, charms used by hunters in, i. 109 ; the Mekeo district of, i. 134, iii. 144, 148 ; charm against snake-bite in, i. 152 *sq.* ; contagious magic of bodily impressions in, i. 213 ; influence of magicians in, i. 337 *sq.* ; belief as to demons of trees in, ii. 42 ; the Sinaugolo tribe of, iii. 147 ; the Roro district of, iii. 148 ; the Motumotu tribe of, iii. 167, 196, 329, 145 ; the Koita of, iii. 168 ; the Roro-speaking tribes, iii. 168, 193 ; the Massim of, iii. 169 ; the Motu of, iii. 329 ; changes in the languages of, caused by fear of naming the dead, iii. 361 *sq.*; belief in ghosts in, ix. 84 *sq.* ; Mowat in, ix. 265 ; festival of wild mango in, x. 7 ; custom observed after childbirth in, x. 20 ; seclusion of girls at puberty in, x. 35 ; dread and seclusion of women at menstruation in, x. 79 ; the Toaripi of, x. 84 ; use of bull-roarers in, xi. 228 *n.*[2]

—— Guinea, Dutch, Windessi in, iii. 169 ; Doreh in, iii. 170, ix. 178 ; the Nufoors of, iii. 329, 332, 415 ; the Papuans of Doreh Bay in, iv. 287 (288, in Second Impression); Kaimani Bay in, vii. 123 ; the Papuans of Ayambori in, vii. 123 ; the Papuans of, their belief in demons, ix. 83

—— Guinea, German, the Yabim of, i. 182, iii. 151, 170, 186 *n.*[1], 306, 342, 354, 386, vii. 228, viii. 275, 295 *sq.*, ix. 188, 232 ; contagious magic of personal remains in, i. 213 ; charm to hasten the moon in, i. 319 ; magic practised on refuse of food in, iii. 128 ; the Monumbos of, iii. 169, xi. 382 ; precaution as to spittle in, iii. 289 ; the Kai of, v. 96, vii. 99 *sqq.*, 313, viii. 33, 152, ix. 264, xi. 182 ; the Tami of, v. 198 ; the Bukaua of, vii. 103 *sq.*, 313, viii. 124, ix. 83 *sq.*; rites of initiation in, xi. 193, 239 *sqq.*

New Guinea, North-West, spirits of ancestors thought to live on trees in, ii. 32

—— Guinea, South-Eastern, annual expulsion of demons in, ix. 134

—— Hebrideans, their story of the origin of death, ix. 304

—— Hebrides, Tana (Tanna) in the, i. 206, viii. 125 ; rain-making in the, i. 308; supernatural powers of chiefs in the, i. 339 ; artificial deformation of heads in the, ii. 298 *n.*[2]; ghosts impound souls in the, iii. 56 ; Lepers' Island in the, iii. 65 ; magic of refuse of food in the, iii. 127 ; Vaté in the, iv. 12 ; burial alive in the, iv. 12 ; the natives of the, their observation of the Pleiades, vii. 313 ; conception of the external soul in the, xi. 197 *sqq.*

—— Ireland, names of relations by marriage tabooed in, iii. 344 ; seclusion of girls at puberty in, x. 32 *sqq.*; Duk-duk society in, xi. 247

—— Mexico, the aridity of, i. 306 ; the Navajoes of, iii. 325 ; the Pueblo Indians of, vi. 54 ; the Zuni Indians of, viii. 175, x. 132 ; the Indians of, their attempts to escape the pursuit of smallpox, ix. 123 ; and Arizona, use of bull-roarers in, xi. 230 *n.*, 231

—— moon, ceremonies at the, vi. 141 *sqq.* *See also* Moon

—— names given to the sick and old, iii. 319 ; at initiation, iii. 320, 383, xi. 259

—— potatoes, how eaten, viii. 51

—— rice, ceremonies at eating the, viii. 54 *sqq.*

—— South Wales, custom observed at nose-boring in, i. 94 ; the Kamilaroi of, i. 101, viii. 151, 162 ; natives of, bury their dead at flood tide, i. 168 ; the Murring tribe of, i. 176 ; tribes of, their custom as to extracted teeth, i. 176 ; way of stopping rain in, i. 253 ; the Keramin tribe in, i. 304 ; the Ta-ta-thi of, i. 304 ; natives of, their charm for raising a wind, i. 321 *n.*[1] ; the Hunter River tribes of, iii. 84 ; the Yuin tribes of, iii. 84, 320 ; rule as to covering the mouth observed by newly initiated men in, iii. 122 ; the Ngarigo tribe of, iii. 141, iv. 60 ; aboriginal tribes of, mourning custom among the, iii. 182 ; namesakes of the dead change their names in, iii. 355 ; sacrifice of first-born children among the aborigines of, iv. 179 *sq.* ; the aborigines of, their ideas

as to the Pleiades, vii. 308 ; the Wollaroi of, viii. 163 ; fish invited to come and be caught among the aborigines of, viii. 312 *n.*; dread of women at menstruation in, x. 78 ; the Wongh tribe of, xi. 227 ; the drama of resurrection at initiation in, xi. 235 *sqq.*

New vessels used for new fruits, viii. 81, 83

—— water at Easter, x. 123

—— World, bathing on St. John's Day in the, v. 249 ; All Souls' Day in the, vi. 80 ; Easter ceremonies in the, x. 127 *sq.* ; magical virtue of plants at Midsummer in the, xi. 50 *sq.*

—— yams, ceremonies at eating, viii. 53, 58 *sqq.*, ix. 134 *sqq.* ; festival of the, in West Africa, viii. 115 *sq.* ; festival of the, in Tonga, viii. 128 *sqq*

—— Year, dated by the Pleiades, vii. 116, 310, 312, 315 ; the Chinese, viii. 10 ; expulsion of evils at the, ix. 127, 133, 149 *sq.*, 155 ; in Siam, ix. 149 *sq.*; not reckoned from first month, ix. 149 *n.*[2] ; in Japan, ix. 154 *n.* ; sham fight at the, ix. 184 ; the Tibetan, ix. 197, 203, 218 ; ceremony at the Tibetan, ix. 197 *sq.* ; new fire made at the, x. 134 *sq.*, 138, 140 ; the Celtic, on November first, x. 224 *sq.* ; the Fijian, Tahitian, and Hawaiian, xi. 244

—— Year festival in Laos, i. 251 ; at Babylon, iv. 110, 115, ix. 356 *sqq.*; of the Kayans at the end of harvest, vii. 93, 96 *sq.*, 98, 99 ; among the Iroquois, ix. 127, 209 *sq.* ; among the Tenggerese of Java, ix. 184; among the Mohammedans in North Africa, x. 217 *sq.*

—— Year's Day, festival of the dead on, vi. 53, 55, 62, 65 ; part of Christmas Boar given to cattle on, vii. 302 ; festival of new yams among the Igbiras on, viii. 115 ; at Onitsha, on the Niger, ix. 133 ; among the Wotyaks, ix. 155 ; in Corea, annual riddance of evil on, ix. 202 ; in Tibet, ceremony on, ix. 203 ; in Breadalbane, ix. 209 ; among the Swahili, ix. 226 *n.*[1] ; young women beat young men on, ix. 271 ; of the Jewish calendar, ix. 359

—— Year's Eve, divination by shadows on, iii. 88 ; Highland custom of beating a man in a cow's hide on, viii. 322 ; in Corea, ix. 147 ; "Shooting the Witches," on, ix. 164 ; in Macedonia, ix. 320. *See also* St. Sylvester's Day

—— Year's Night, omens on, iv. 66 *sq.*

—— Zealand, customs as to the navelstring in, i. 182 ; fires in the forests of, ii. 256 ; sanctity of chiefs in, iii.

134 *sqq.* ; customs as to eating observed by chiefs in, iii. 138 ; sacredness of chiefs' blood in, iii. 248 ; sacredness of chiefs' heads in, iii. 256 *sq.* ; customs at hair-cutting in, iii. 264 *sq.* ; disposal of cut hair in, iii. 274 ; magic use of spittle in, iii. 288 ; names of chiefs not to be pronounced in, iii. 381 ; Rotomahana in, v. 207, 209 *n.* ; effect of contact with a sacred chief in, viii. 28 ; eyes of slain chiefs swallowed by warriors in, viii. 153 ; sticks or stones piled on scenes of violent death in, ix. 15 ; human scapegoats in, ix. 39. *See also* Maori

Newars of Nepaul, their worship of frogs, i. 294 *sq.*

Newberry, Professor P. E., on Osiris as a cedar-tree god, vi. 109 *n.*[1]

Newman, Ch. L., on the human god of the Makalakas, i. 394 *n.*[3]

Newman, J. H., on music, v. 53 *sq.*

Newstead, Byron's oak at, xi. 166

Ngai, Masai god, festivals of prayer in honour of, i. 344 *sqq.* ; of the Akikuyu, sheep and goats sacrificed to, ii. 44, iii. 204 *n.*[3] ; children of, ii. 150, v. 68

Nganga, medicine-man, among the Boloki, ix. 76 ; "the Knowing Ones," initiates, on the Congo, xi. 251

Ngarigo tribe of New South Wales, novices not allowed to touch food with their hands in the, iii. 141 *sq.* ; their belief as to falling stars, iv. 60 ; ate the hands and feet of their foes, viii. 151

Ngarong, secret helper, of the Ibans of Borneo, xi. 224 *n.*[1]

Ngoc hoang, in Annam, his message of immortality to men, ix. 303

Ngoio, a province of Congo, rule of succession to the chiefship in, iv. 118 *sq.*

Ngoni, the, of British Central Africa, their fear of being photographed, iii. 98 ; their belief in serpents as reincarnations of the dead, v. 82. *See also* Angoni

Ngumbu, of South Cameroons, their fire-drill, ii. 210

Nguôn So'n valley in Annam, iii. 155

Nguruhi, the supreme god of the Wahehe, vi. 188 *sq.*

Nguu, district of German East Africa, ghost consulted as oracle in, xi. 312

Niam-Niam, the, of Central Africa, women the agricultural labourers among, vii. 119

Niambe, the supreme god of the Barotse, vi. 193

Nias, island of, magical ceremony to catch wild pigs in, i. 109 ; homoeopathic magic at planting rice in, i. 143 ; conception of the soul in, iii. 29 ; recovery of lost souls in, iii. 64, 67 ; taboos observed by hunters in, iii. 196 ; superstition as to personal names among the natives of, iii. 323 ; taboos observed during the hunting season in, iii. 410 ; special language of hunters in, iii. 410 ; special language employed by reapers in, iii. 410 *sq.* ; custom of succession to the chieftainship in, iv. 198 *sq.* ; mock human sacrifices at funerals in, iv. 216 ; conduct of the natives of, in an earthquake, v. 201 *sq.* ; head-hunting in, v. 296 *n.*[1] ; division of agricultural work between the sexes in, vii. 124 ; harvest custom in, vii. 233 *sq.*; the Pleiades observed in, vii. 315 ; crops guarded against wild pigs in, viii. 32 ; mode of diverting dangerous spirits from pregnant women in, viii. 102 *sq.*; first-fruits offered to ancestors in, viii. 124 ; polite treatment of destructive ants in, viii. 276 ; expulsion of demons in, ix. 113 *sqq.* ; explanation of human mortality in, ix. 303 ; story of the external soul told in, xi. 148 ; ceremonies performed by candidates for the priesthood in, xi. 173 *sq.*

Nias, the natives of, believe in demons of trees, ii. 33 *sq.* ; their custom of bunging up the nose and mouth of corpses, iii. 31 ; their fear of a rainbow, iii. 79 ; their custom of scrubbing the things they buy, iii. 107

Nibelungenlied, the, Brunhild and Gunther in, ii. 306

Nicaragua, maize mixed with human blood eaten at festivals in, viii. 91 *sq.*

——, Indians of, rules observed by them between sowing and harvest, ii. 105 ; sacrifice human victims to volcanoes, v. 219 ; their transference of weariness to heaps of stones, ix. 9

Niceros and the were-wolf, story of, x. 313 *sq.*

Nicholas Bishop, the Boy Bishop elected on St. Nicholas's Day, ix. 338

Nicholson, General, worshipped as a god in his life, i. 404

Nicholson, R. A., iii. 51 *n.*

Nicknames used in order to avoid the use of the real names, iii. 321, 331

Nicobar Islanders reluctant to name the dead, iii. 353 ; their annual expulsion of demons in little ships, ix. 201 *sq.*

—— Islands, homoeopathic magic at sowing in the, i. 141 ; pregnant woman used to fertilize the gardens in the, ii. 101 ; customs as to shadows at burials in the, iii. 80 *sq.* ; rain attributed to wrath of spirits in the, iii. 231 ; changes in the language of the, caused by fear of naming the dead, iii. 362 *sq.* ; assumption of the names of dead grandparents in the, iii. 370 ; demon of disease sent away in a boat from the, ix. 189 *sq.*

Nicobarese mourners change their names and shave themselves for fear of the ghost, iii. 357 *sq.* ; their sham fights in honour of the dead, ix. 96 *sq.* ; their belief in demons, ix. 88 ; their ceremony of exorcism by means of pig's blood and leaves, ix. 262

Nicolaus Damascenus on a bad king of Lydia, i. 366

Nicolson, Sheriff Alexander, on the last sheaf in the Highlands of Scotland, vii. 164 *sq.*

Nicosia, in Sicily, ceremonies to procure rain at, i. 300

Nidugala, in the Neilgherry Hills, the fire-walk at, xi. 8

Niebuhr, B. G., on Servius Tullius, ii. 196 *n.* ; on the list of Alban kings, ii. 269

Nieces, aunts named after their, iii. 332

Nieder-Lausitz, the Midsummer log in, xi. 92 *n.*[1]

Niederehe, in the Eifel Mountains, Midsummer flowers at, xi. 48

Niederpöring in Bavaria, pretence of beheading Whitsuntide mummer at, iv. 206 *sq.*

Nietzold, J., on the marriage of brothers with sisters in ancient Egypt, vi. 216 *n.*[1]

Nieuwenhuis, Dr. A. W., on the Kayan fear of being photographed, iii. 99 ; on the fear of strangers among the Kayans of Borneo, iii. 104 ; on the association of agriculture with religion among the Kayans, vii. 93 ; on the Kayan fear of strangers at religious rites, vii. 94 *n.*[2] ; on a Kayan masquerade, vii. 95 ; on the New Year festival of the Kayans, vii. 96 *sqq.* ; on games as religious rites among the Kayans, vii. 97 *sqq.*, 107 ; on the masked dances of the Kayans, ix. 382 *sq.*

Niger, the Bambaras of the, ii. 42 ; Onitsha on the, ix. 133, 210 ; use of human scapegoats on the, ix. 210 *sq.* ; belief as to external human souls lodged in animals on the, xi. 209

——, the Lower, customs observed by executioners among tribes of, iii. 172 *n.*[1], viii. 155

Niger Delta, tests of the reincarnation of the dead in the, i. 411 *n.*[1] ; deceiving the

ghosts of women who died in childbed in the, viii. 98 ; burial custom in the, viii. 98

Nigeria, the Tomas or Habes of, iii. 124 ; natives of, loth to mention the owl by its proper name, iii. 401 ; custom of putting kings to death in, iv. 34 *sq.*

——, Northern, the Jukos of, viii. 160

——, Southern, chief as fetishman in, i. 349 *sq.* ; trees inhabited by the spirits of the dead in, iii. 32 ; disposal of cut hair and nails in, iii. 278 ; the Ijebu tribe of, iv. 112 ; the Ibo of, x. 4 ; theory of the external soul in, xi. 150, 200, 203 *sqq.*

Night, burial at, iii. 15 ; King of the, at Porto Novo, iii. 23. *See also* Twelfth Night

Night-jars, the lives of women in, among the Wotjobaluk, xi. 215 ; called women's " sisters " among the Kulin, xi. 216

Nightingale, the flesh of, in homoeopathic magic, i. 154

Nights, custom of reckoning by, ix. 326 *n.*[2] *See also* Twelve Nights

Nigmann, E., on the religion of the Wahehe, vi. 188 *sq.*

Nihongi, a Japanese work, ix. 213

Nijegorod Government in Russia, smouldering faggots in stove not to be broken up in the, ii. 232

Nikclerith, Neane, buries cow alive, x. 324 *sq.*

Nikunau, one of the Gilbert Islands, sacred stones in, v. 108 *n.*[1]

Nile, young virgin drowned as a sacrifice to the, ii. 151 ; the rise and fall of the, vi. 30 *sqq.* ; rises at the summer solstice in June, vi. 31 *n.*[1], 33 ; commanded by the king of Egypt to rise, vi. 33 ; thought to be swollen by the tears of Isis, vi. 33 ; gold and silver thrown into the river at its rising, vi. 40 ; the rise of, attributed to Serapis, vi. 216 *sq.*

——, the Blue, custom as to kings of Fazoql on, iv. 16

——, the " Bride " of the, ii. 151, vi. 38

——, the Upper, medicine-men as chiefs among the tribes of, i. 345 ; rainmakers on, i. 345 *sqq.* ; Kings of the Rain on, ii. 2 ; the Alur of, x. 64

——, the White, the Shilluk of, iv. 17 ; tribes of, never shed human blood in their villages, iii. 246 *sq.* ; the Dinka of, viii. 37, 114, ix. 193

Nilles, N., on the blessing of the herbs on August 15th, i. 15 *n.*[2]

Nilsson, Professor M. P., on custom of sacred prostitution, v. 37 *n.*[2], 57 *n.*[1], 58 *n.*[2] ; on the sacrifice of a bull to Zeus Sosipolis at Magnesia, vi. 239 *n.*[1],

viii. 8 *n.*[2]; on "Bringing home the Maiden," vii. 58 *n.*[1]; on the festival of the Threshing-floor at Eleusis, vii. 62 *n.*[6]

Nīm tree, leaves of, as an amulet, iii. 234

Nimm, a river goddess of the Ekoi, ix. 28

Nine, ruptured child passed nine times on nine successive mornings through a left ash-tree and attended by nine persons, xi. 170

—— bonfires on Midsummer Eve an omen of marriage, x. 174, 185, 189, 339

—— cows milked for king, iii. 292

—— different kinds of wood burnt in the Beltane fires, x. 155; used for the Midsummer bonfires, x. 172, 201; used to kindle need-fire, x. 271, 278, 280; burnt in the need-fire, x. 278

—— fallen leaves in magic, i. 109

—— grains of oats in divination, x. 243

—— handfuls of each kind of grain at autumnal festival, viii. 49

—— knots in magic, iii. 302, 303, 304

—— leaps over Midsummer fire, x. 193

—— male animals of all sorts sacrificed at a festival held in Upsala every nine years and lasting nine days, ii. 364 *sq.*

—— men in purification of Orestes, i. 26; employed to make fire by the friction of wood, x. 148, 155

—— ridges of earth brought from nine mountains in a magical ceremony performed nine times, ix. 8; ridges of ploughed land in divination, x. 235

—— skeins of red wool in magic, iii. 307

—— sorts of flowers on Midsummer Eve, to dream on, x. 175, xi. 52; gathered for purposes of divination or medicine on Midsummer Eve, xi. 52 *sq.*

—— stalks of rice in bunches to make up the Rice Mother, vii. 195

—— times to crawl under a bramble as a cure, xi. 180

—— times nine men make need-fire, x. 289, 294, 295

—— (thrice three) times passed through a girth of woodbine, xi. 184; passed through a holed stone, xi. 187

—— turns round a rick, x. 243

—— waves, tops of, thrown on patient's head, xi. 186 *sq.*

Nineteen years' cycle of Meton, vii. 81 *n.*[3]

Nineveh, capital of Assyria, ii. 130; the end of, v. 174; tomb of Sardanapalus at, ix. 388 *n.*[1]; the burning of Sandan at, ix. 390

Ningu, the paramour of Tiamat, tablets of destiny wrested from, iv. 110

Ninus, Assyrian hero, ix. 391

Nirriti, goddess of evil, in Brahman ritual, ix. 25

Nirvana, Buddhist monks seek to attain, through voluntary death by fire, iv. 42

Nisan, a Jewish month, vii. 259 *n.*[1], ix. 356, 361, 415

Nishga Indians of British Columbia, their use of effigies as substitutes to save the lives of people, viii. 106 *sq.*

Nishinam Indians of California, ceremony performed by childless women among the, i. 70 *sq.*; secrecy of personal names among the, iii. 326; husbands never call their wives by name among the, iii. 338

Niska Indians of British Columbia, their cannibal rites, vii. 20; rites of initiation among the, xi. 271 *sq.*

Nisus and his purple or golden hair, story of, xi. 103

Niué or Savage Island, iv. 219. *See* Savage Island

Njamus, the, of British East Africa, their sacrifices of sheep at irrigation channels, vi. 38 *sq.*

Nkimba, secret society on the Lower Congo, xi. 255 *n.*[1]

No, annual expulsion of demons in China, ix. 145 *sq.*

Noa, common, opposed to *tapu*, sacred, iii. 109

Noah's ark, i. 334

Nobosohpoh, a Khasi state, two royal families in, ii. 295

Nocturnal creatures the sex totems of men and women, xi. 217 *n.*[4]

Noessa Laut, East Indian island, fishermen's magic in, i. 109; hunter's magic in, i. 114; treatment of the afterbirth in, i. 187

Nograd-Ludany, in Hungary, Midsummer fires at, x. 179

Noguès, J. L. M., on the wonderful herbs of St. John's Eve, xi. 45

Noises made to expel demons, ix. 109 *sqq.*, 147

Nöldeke, Professor Th., on the sacrifice of the first-born, iv. 179 *n.*[4]; on Purim and Esther, ix. 366 *sq.*, 367 *n.*[1], 368 *n.*; on proposed derivation of some names in the Book of Esther, ix. 368 *n.*; on Omanos and Anadates, ix. 373 *n.*[1]

Nomarchs in Egypt originally worshipped as gods, i. 390 *n.*[1]

Nonae Caprotinae, Roman celebration of the, ii. 313 *sq.*, ix. 258

Nonnus, on death of Dionysus, vii. 12 *sq.*

Noon, fear to lose the shadow at, iii. 87; sacrifices to the dead at, iii. 88; superstitious dread of, iii. 88

Noose, sun caught in a, i. 316

Nootka Indians of British Columbia,

superstitions as to twins among the, i. 263 *sq.* ; their idea of the soul, iii. 27 ; their recovery of lost souls, iii. 67 *n.*; seclusion of girls at puberty among the, iii. 146 *n.*[1], x. 43 *sq.* ; their preparation for war, iii. 160 *sq.* ; their custom of devouring dogs, vii. 20 ; their propitiation of slain bears, viii. 225 ; their fear of offending fish, viii. 251 ; ritual of death and resurrection among the, xi. 270 *sq.*

Nootka Sound, the Indians of, their preparation for whaling, iii. 191
—— wizard, his magic to procure fish, i. 108

Nord, the department of, giants at Shrove Tuesday in, xi. 35

Norden, E., on the Golden Bough, xi. 284 *n.*[3]

Nördlingen, in Bavaria, last thresher wrapt in straw at, vii. 221 *sq.*; strangers tied up in sheaves at harvest at, vii. 225 ; saying as to wind in corn at, vii. 296

Nore, A. de, on the Yule log in France, x. 250 *sq.*, 253

Norfolk, Plough Monday in, viii. 330 *n.*[1]; use of orpine for divination in, xi. 61 *n.*[4]

Norman peasants gather seven kinds of plants on St. John's Day, xi. 51 *sq.*

Normandy, rain-producing spring in, i. 301 ; Burial of Shrove Tuesday in, iv. 228 ; rolling in dew on St. John's Day in, v. 248 ; pretence of tying up landowner in last sheaf at harvest in, vii. 226 ; the quail at harvest in, vii. 295 ; the Bocage of, vii. 295, ix. 183 *sq.*, 316, 323 ; Midsummer fires in, x. 185 *sq.* ; the Yule log in, x. 252 ; torchlight processions on Christmas Eve in, x. 266 ; processions with torches on the Eve of Twelfth Day in, x. 340 ; wonderful herbs and flowers gathered at Midsummer in, xi. 46 ; wreaths of mugwort a protection against thunder and thieves in, xi. 59 ; vervain gathered at Midsummer in, xi. 62

Norrland, Midsummer bonfires in, x. 172

Norse legends as to eating hearts of wolf, bear, and dragon, viii. 146
—— stories of the external soul, xi. 119 *sq.*
—— trinities, ii. 364

Norsemen, their custom of wounding the dying, iv. 13 *sq.*

North Africa, festivals of swinging in, iv. 284 ; Midsummer festival of fire and water among the Mohammedans of, v. 249, x. 213 *sqq.*

North American Indian theory of brandy, viii. 147
—— American Indians, their exorcism of strangers, iii. 105 ; their dread of menstruous women, iii. 145 ; their customs on the war-path, iii. 158 *sqq.*; ceremonies observed by man-slayers among the, iii. 181 *sqq.* ; their chastity before hunting, iii. 197 *sqq.* ; their theory of names, iii. 318 *sq.* ; personal names kept secret among the, iii. 325 *sq.* ; namesakes of the dead change their names among the, iii. 356 ; tell their mythic tales only in winter, iii. 385 *sq.*; their funeral celebrations, iv. 97 ; their firm belief in immortality, iv. 137 ; the Corn Woman among the, vii. 177 ; their theory of the lower animals, viii. 205 *sq.* ; their respect for rattlesnakes, viii. 217 *sqq.*; their ceremonies at killing a wolf, viii. 220 *sq.*; their propitiation of slain bears, viii. 224 *sqq.*; their ceremonious treatment of dangerous animals, viii. 237 ; their belief that each species of animals has its patron or genius, viii. 243 *sq.*; may not break the bones of the animals they eat at feasts, viii. 258 *n.*[2]; their reluctance to let dogs gnaw the bones of animals, viii. 259 ; revere their totem animals, viii. 311 ; their personal totems, xi. 222 *n.*[5], 226 *n.*[1] *See also* America *and* American Indians
—— Berwick, Satan preaches at, xi. 158
—— -West America, Indians of, do not speak of a person till his bones are finally disposed of, iii. 372
—— -Western Provinces of India, gods shut up in wood in the, ix. 61 ; the tug-of-war in the, ix. 181. *See also* India

Northampton, May garlands in, ii. 60 *sq.*

Northamptonshire, May-trees in, ii. 59 *sq.*; May carols in, ii. 61 *n.*[1]; Plough Monday in, viii. 330 *n.*[1] ; cure for cough in, ix. 51 ; sacrifice of a calf in, x. 300

Northern Territory, Australia, beliefs as to the birth of children in the, v. 103 *sq.*

Northumberland, belief as to death at ebb-tide in, i. 168 ; the Borewell, near Bingfield in, ii. 161 ; child's first nail-parings buried under an ash-tree in, iii. 276 ; the *mell* sheaf in, vii. 151 ; Midsummer fires in, x. 197 *sq.*; divination at Hallowe'en in, x. 245 ; the Yule log in, x. 256 ; need-fire in, x. 288 *sq.* ; ox burnt alive in, to stop a murrain, x. 301

Nortia, Etruscan goddess, ix. 67

Norton Sound, the small sculpin of, i. 288

Norway, precautions against witches on Walpurgis Night in, ii. 54 ; the Whitsuntide Bride and Bridegroom in, ii. 92 ; buried timber in the peat-bogs of, ii. 352 ; nail-parings burnt or buried for fear of elves in, iii. 283 ; the Peamother in, vii. 132 ; the Old Hayman killed at haymaking in, vii. 223 ; harvest customs in, vii. 225, 282 ; "Killing the Hare " at harvest in, vii. 280 ; belief as to eating flesh of white snake in, viii. 146 ; cairns in, ix. 14 ; bonfires on Midsummer Eve in, x. 171 ; the need-fire in, x. 280 ; superstitions about a parasitic rowan in, xi. 281

Norwegian sailors, their use of rowan, ix. 267

——— witch sinks ship, i. 326

Norwich, greasing the weapon instead of the wound at, i. 203

——— Cathedral, the Boy Bishop at, ix. 337 ; Easter candle in, x. 122 n.

Nose stopped to prevent the escape of the soul, iii. 31, 71

Nose-boring, custom observed by medicine-men at, in New South Wales, i. 94

Nostrils, soul supposed to escape by the, iii. 30, 32, 33, 122

Nosy Be, an island of Madagascar, worshipful black bull kept in, viii. 40 n.

Nottinghamshire, harvesters drenched with water in, v. 238 n. ; Plough Monday in, viii. 330 n.[1] ; the Hemlock Stone in, x. 157

Nouer l'aiguilette, spells cast on man and wife, x. 346 n.[2]

Nouzon, in the Ardennes, the Yule log at, x. 253

Novelties, the savage distrust of, iii. 230 *sqq.*

November, festivals of the dead in, vi. 51, 54, 69 *sqq.* ; the month of sowing in Egypt, vi. 94 ; annual ceremony at catching sea-slug in, ix. 143 ; expulsion of demons in, ix. 204

——— the 1st, All Saints' Day, vi. 70 *sq.*, 77, 82, 83, x. 225 ; old New Year's Day in the Isle of Man, x. 224 *sq.*

——— the 2nd, All Souls' Day, vi. 69, 70 *sq.*, 81

Novgorod, image of Perun at, ii. 365 ; perpetual fire of oak-wood at, ii. 365

Novices at initiation, taboos observed by, iii. 141 *sq.*, 156 *sq.* ; supposed to be swallowed and disgorged by a spirit or monster, xi. 235, 240 *sq.*, 242, 246 ; supposed to be newly born, xi. 247, 251, 256, 257, 261, 262 *sq.* ; begotten anew, xi. 248 ; at initiation

killed as men and brought to life as animals, xi. 272

Novitiate of priests and priestesses, v. 66, 68

Nuba negroes, office of rain-maker among the, ii. 3

Nubas, the, of Jebel-Nuba, taboos observed by women in the absence of their husbands among, i. 122 ; will not cut a certain thorn-tree during the rainy season, ii. 49 n.[3] ; their priestly king, iii. 132 ; their customs at millet-harvest, viii. 114

Nuehr, a pastoral tribe of the Upper Nile, their reverence for their cattle, viii. 39

Nufoors of Dutch New Guinea unwilling to mention their names, iii. 329, and the names of their relations by marriage, iii. 332, 341 *sq.* ; taboo observed by them at sea, iii. 415

Nulit language in Victoria, iii. 110

Nullakun tribe of Australia, their belief as to the birth of children, v. 101

Numa, an adept in drawing down lightning, ii. 181 ; as Flamen Dialis, ii. 192 ; builds the temple of Vesta, ii. 200 *sq.* ; his sons, ii. 270 n.[3] ; a Sabine of Cures, ii. 270 n.[6] ; a priestly king, ii. 289 ; born on the day of the Parilia, April 21st, ii. 325, 329

——— and Egeria, i. 18, ii. 172 *sq.*, 193, 380

Numa's birthday, ii. 325, 348 ; " Numa's crockery," ii. 202

Numbering the herds on St. George's Day, ii. 338

Numicius, the river, ii. 181

Nuns of St. Brigit, at Kildare, ii. 240 *sq.*

Nuremberg, the "Carrying out of Death" at, iv. 234

Nurin, a mythical maiden in a rain-making ceremony, i. 275 *sq.*

Nurtunjas, sacred poles among the Arunta, xi. 219

Nusku, Egyptian fire-god, i. 67

Nut, Egyptian sky-goddess, mother of Osiris, v. 283 n.[3], vi. 6, 16, ix. 341 ; in a sycamore tree, vi. 110

Nut-trees, foreskins placed in, i. 95 n.[3]

——— -water brewed at Midsummer, xi. 47

Nutlets of pines used as food, v. 278 n.[2]

Nutritive and vicarious types of sacrifice, vi. 226

Nuts passed across Midsummer fires, x. 190 ; in fire, divination by, at Hallowe'en, x. 237, 239, 241, 242, 245

Nyadiri, river in Mashonaland, iii. 9

Nyakang, the first of the Shilluk kings, iv. 18 *sqq.* ; the' shrines of, iv. 19 ; as rain-giver, iv. 19, 20 ; worshipped as the god of his people, vi. 162 *sqq.* ; incarnate in various animals, vi. 163 *sq.* ; his mysterious disappearance, vi. 163 ; his graves, vi. 163, 166 ; historical reality of, vi. 164, 166 sq. ; his relation to the creator Juok, vi. 164 sq. ; compared to Osiris, vi. 167

Nyalich, synonym for Dengdit, the name of the Supreme Being of the Dinka, viii. 40 n.

Nyanja chief vulnerable by a sand-bullet, xi. 314

—— -speaking tribes of British Central Africa, their belief that skin-disease is caused by eating the totem, viii. 26 ; of Angoniland, their customs as to girls at puberty, x. 25 sq.

Nyanza, Lake, incarnate human god of, i. 395

——, Lake Victoria, vii. 118

Nyanza region, kings banished for drought in the, i. 353

Nyassa, Lake, iii. 97, viii. 99, 112, ix. 10, x. 28, 81 ; people to the east of, crawl through an arch as a precaution against sickness, evil spirits, etc., xi. 181

Nyassa-Tanganyika plateau, custom of carriers to deposit stones on heaps in the, ix. 10 sq.

Nyassaland, women will not name their husbands in, iii. 336

Nyeledit, the Supreme Being of the Nuehr, viii. 39

Nyikpla or Nyigbla, a negro divinity, associated with falling stars, iv. 61, viii. 45

Nymphs of oaks at Rome, ii. 172,185 ; of the Fair Crowns at Olympia, vi. 240

Nysa, in the valley of the Maeander, v. 205, 206 n.1 ; sacrifice of bull at, v. 292 n.3

Nyuak, L., on guardian spirits of Sea Dyaks, v. 83

Oak, statue of Artemis under an, i. 38 n.1 ; worshipped by the Galatians, ii. 126 ; sanctuary of the, at Dodona, ii. 176 ; its diffusion in Europe, ii. 349 sqq. ; worship of the, ii. 349 sqq. ; the British (Quercus robur), in France, Germany, Russia, and England, ii. 355 ; oracular, at Dodona, ii. 358 ; sacred to Jupiter, ii. 361 ; sacred to the ancient Celts, ii. 362 sq. ; worshipped by the ancient Teutons, ii. 363 sqq. ; worshipped by the ancient Slavs, ii. 365 ; worshipped by the ancient Lithuanians, ii. 365 sqq. ; revered by the Esthonians, ii. 367 sq. ; worshipped in modern Europe, ii. 370 sqq. ; effigy of Death buried under an, iv. 236 ; dance round, at harvest, vii. 288 ; sacred, of old Prussians, ix. 391 ;

associated with thunder, x. 145 ; the principal sacred tree of the Aryans, xi. 89 sq. ; human representatives of the oak perhaps originally burnt at the fire-festivals, xi. 90, 92 sq. ; children passed through a cleft oak as a cure for rupture or rickets, xi. 170 sqq. ; life of, in mistletoe, xi. 280, 292 ; supposed to bloom on Midsummer Eve, xi. 292, 293 ; struck by lightning oftener than any other tree of the European forest, xi. 298 sqq. See also Oak-tree and Oaks

Oak of Errol, fate of the Hays bound up with the, xi. 283 sq.

——, evergreen, in making fire, ii. 251 ; the Golden Bough grew on an, ii. 379

—— of the Guelphs, xi. 166 sq.

——, holy, of the old Prussians, iv. 42

—— planted by Byron, xi. 166

—— of Romove, xi. 286

" —— or rock, born of an," i. 100 n.1

——, sacred, in a Greek story, i. 158 ; on the Capitol, ii. 176, 184 ; at Delphi, iv. 80 sq.

—— or terebinth, sacred at Mamre, v. 37 n.2

—— and thunder, the Aryan god of the, ii. 356 sqq., x. 265 ; oak, sky, rain, and thunder, god of the, ii. 349 sq.

—— of the Vespasian family at Rome, xi. 168

—— and wild olive, pyre of Hercules made of, ix. 391

Oak branch in rain-charm, i. 309

—— branches, Whitsuntide mummer swathed in, iv. 207

—— crown sacred to Jupiter, ii. 176, 184, 189 ; sacred to Juno, ii. 184, 189

—— -god married to the oak-goddess, ii. 142, 189 sq. ; how he became a god of lightning, thunder, and rain, ii. 372 sqq.

—— Grove, Chapel of the, at Rome, ii. 185 ; Gate of the, at Rome, ii. 185 ; Street of the, at Rome, ii. 186

—— groves in ancient Ireland, ii. 242 sq., 363

—— leaves, crown of, ii. 175, 176 sq., 184, iv. 80 sqq. ; " oil of St. John " found on St. John's Morning upon, xi. 82 sq.

—— log a protection against witchcraft, xi. 92

—— -mistletoe an " all - healer " or panacea, xi. 77, 79, 82 ; a remedy for epilepsy, xi. 78, 83 ; to be shot down with an arrow, xi. 82 ; a panacea for green wounds, xi. 83 ; a protection against conflagration, xi. 85, 293

—— -nymphs at Rome, ii. 172, 185

—— -spirit, the priest of the Arician grove a personification of an, xi. 285

Oak-tree guarded by the King of the Wood at Nemi, i. 42 ; worshipped in Syria, ii. 16 ; pain pegged into an, ix. 58 ; worshipped by the Cheremiss, x. 181

—— -trees revered by the Wends, ii. 55 ; sacrifices to, ii. 366 ; ague transferred to, ix. 57 *sq.* ; rupture nailed into, ix. 60 ; toothache nailed into, ix. 60 ; planted at marriage, xi. 165

—— twigs and leaves used to keep off witches, xi. 20

—— -wood, Vesta's fire at Rome fed with, ii. 186 ; perpetual fire of, ii. 262, 365, 366, xi. 285 *sq.* ; ceremonial fires kindled by the friction of, ii. 372 ; used to kindle the need-fire, x. 148, 271, 272, 275, 276, 278, 281, 289 *sq.*, xi. 90 *sq.* ; used to kindle the Beltane fires, x. 148, 155 ; used to kindle Midsummer fire, x. 169, 177, xi.* 91 *sq.* ; used for the Yule log, x. 248, 250, 251, 257, 258, 259, 260, 263, 264 *sq.*, xi. 92 ; fire of, used to detect a murderer, xi. 92 *n.*[4]

—— -woods on the site of ancient Rome, ii. 184 *sqq.*

—— -worship of the Druids, ii. 9, xi. 76 *sq.*, 301

Oaken image dressed as a bride, ii. 140 *sq.* ; leaves in medicine, ix. 58

Oaks at Troezen, i. 26 ; revered by heathen Lithuanians, ii. 9 ; oracular, ii. 43 ; sacred among the old Prussians, ii. 43 ; sacred to Jupiter, ii. 175, 176 ; in peat-bogs of Europe, ii. 350 *sqq.* ; in peat-bogs of Ireland, ii. 351 ; in pile villages of Europe, ii. 352 *sq.* ; of Ireland, ii. 363 ; sick people passed through holes in, ii. 371 ; often struck by lightning, ii. 373 ; mistletoe growing on, in Sweden, xi. 87 ; planted by Sir Walter Scott, xi. 166 ; mistletoe growing on, in England and France, xi. 316

Oath by passing between the pieces of a sacrificial victim, i. 289 *n.*[4] ; taken by Mexican kings at their accession, i. 356, 416 ; by the Styx, iv. 70 *n.*[1] ; of Egyptian kings not to correct the vague Egyptian year by intercalation, vi. 26 ; of women by the Pleiades, vii. 311 ; not to hurt Balder, x. 101

Oaths on stones, i. 160 *sq.* ; by the king of Egypt, i. 419 ; accompanied by eating a sacred substance, viii. 313

Oats, nine grains of, in divination, x. 243

Oats-bride, vii. 162, 163, 164

—— -bridegroom, vii. 163

—— -cow, reaper of last oats, vii. 289 ; thresher of last oats, vii. 290

Oats-fool, vii. 148

—— -goat, at harvest, vii. 270, 282, 283, 284 ; at threshing, vii. 286, 287 ; mummer called the, viii. 327

—— -king, in Silesia, vii. 164

—— -man, at harvest, vii. 163, 221 ; at threshing, vii. 223

—— -mother, the last sheaf, vii. 135

—— -queen, in Silesia, vii. 164

—— -sow, at making last sheaf, vii. 298

—— -stallion, the last sheaf, vii. 292

—— -wolf, in the last sheaf, vii. 271, 273 ; woman who binds the last sheaf called, vii. 274

—— -woman, at harvest feast, vii. 163

Oban district, Southern Nigeria, belief as to external human souls lodged in animals in the, xi. 206 *sqq.*

Obassi Nsi, earth-god of the Ekoi, ix. 28

Obelisk, image of Astarte, v. 14

Obelisks, sacred, at Gezer, v. 108

Oberinntal, in Tyrol, the last thresher called Goat at, vii. 286

Oberkrain, the Slovenes of, their customs on Shrove Tuesday, ii. 93

Oberland, in Central Germany, the Yule log in the, x. 248 *sq.*

Obermedlingen, in Swabia, the Cow at threshing at, vii. 290 *sq.* ; fire kindled on St. Vitus's Day at, x. 335 *sq.*

Oberpfalz, Bavaria, the Old Man at threshing in some parts of, vii. 222

Objects, souls ascribed to inanimate, ix. 90

O'Brien, Murragh, executed for treason, iii. 244

Obscene images of Osiris, vi. 112

—— language in ritual, iii. 154, 155

—— songs sung by women on special occasions, viii. 280

Obscenities in the Eleusinian mysteries, the Festival of the Threshing-floor, and the Thesmophoria, vii. 62 *sq.*

Obscenity in rain-making, i. 267 *sq.*, 269, 278, 284 *n.*

Observational power of savages, ix. 326

Obubura district of Southern Nigeria, human souls in fish in, xi. 204

Ocrisia, mother of Servius Tullius, conceives by the fire-god, ii. 195 ; a slave-woman of Corniculum, ii. 270 *n.*[6]

Octavian plunders the sanctuary at Nemi, i. 4 ; his provision for knocking a nail into the temple of Mars, ix. 67 *n.*[1]

Octennial cycle based on an attempt to harmonize lunar and solar time, iv. 68 *sq.* ; old, in Greece, vi. 242 *n.*, vii. 80 *sqq.*

—— period of Greek games, vii. 80

—— tenure of the kingship, iv. 58 *sqq.*, vii. 82, 85

October, horse sacrificed at Rome in, ii. 229, 326, ix. 230 ; the 1st of, a great Saxon festival, vi. 81 n.[3] ; the vintage month in modern Greece, vii. 47 ; the month of ploughing and sowing in Greece, vii. 50 ; the 15th, annual sacrifice of horse at Rome on, viii. 42 sqq. ; annual expulsion of demons in, ix. 226 n.[1] ; ceremony of the new fire in, x. 136 ; the last day of (Hallowe'en), x. 139

Octopuses presented to Greek infants, i. 156

Ocymum sanctum, Holy Basil, worshipped in India, ii. 26 sq.

Ode branch of Ijebu tribe in Southern Nigeria, mysterious chief of the, iv. 112

Oder, the river, Whitsuntide custom on, ii. 84

Odessa, New Easter fire carried to, x. 130 n.

Odilo, abbot of Clugny, institutes Feast of All Souls, vi. 82

Odin, as a magician, i. 241 sq. ; King Olaf sacrificed to, for the crops, i. 367 ; the Norse god of war, ii. 364 ; thought to receive in Valhalla only the dead in war, iv. 13 ; legend of the deposition of, iv. 56 ; sacrifice of king's sons to, iv. 57, 160 sq., vi. 220 ; human sacrifices to, iv. 160 sq., 188 ; hanged on a tree, v. 290 ; human victims dedicated by hanging to, v. 290

——, Othin, or Woden, the father of Balder, x. 101, 102, 103 n.

Ododop tribe of Southern Nigeria, chiefs of the, keep their external souls in buffaloes, xi. 208

O'Donovan, E., on a Turcoman remedy for fever by means of knotted threads, iii. 304

Oedipus, supposed effects of his incest with his mother, ii. 115; his exposure, parricide, and incest, iv. 193

Oefoten, in Norway, laggards in reaping called goats at, vii. 282

Oels, in Silesia, expulsion of witches on Good Friday at, ix. 157 ; Midsummer fires at, x. 170

Oeneus, king of Calydon in Aetolia, father of Tydeus, ii. 278

Oeniadae, the ancient, Prince Sunless at, x. 21

Oenomaus, king of Pisa, father of Hippodamia, ii. 300 ; his chariot-race at Olympia, ii. 300, iv. 91 ; his incest with his daughter, v. 44 n.[1]

Oesel, the island of, the Esthonians of, i. 211, iii. 41 sq., vii. 298, viii. 51 ; contagious magic of footprints in, i. 211 ; custom of reapers in, i. 329 ; belief as to whirlwinds in, iii. 41 sq. ; belief as to falling stars in, iv. 66 ; the last sheaf called the Rye-boar in,

vii. 298 ; the Christmas Boar in, vii. 302 ; custom at eating the new corn in, viii. 51 ; heaps of sticks or stones in, ix. 14 ; Midsummer fires in, x. 180 ; St. John's herbs in, xi. 49

Oeta, Mount, Hercules burnt on, v. 111, 116, 211

Offenburg, in the Black Forest, Midsummer fires at, x. 168

Offerings to dead kings, vi. 194 ; at cairns, ix. 26 sqq. ; to demons, ix. 96. See also Sacrifices

"Offscouring" (περίψημα), term applied to a human scapegoat, ix. 255 n.[1]

Offspring, charms to procure, i. 70 sqq.

Ogboni, a secret society on the Slave Coast, xi. 229 n.

Ogginn, a white ox and a holy cave in the Caucasus, viii. 313 n.[1]

Ogom, a fetish doctor of Nigeria, not allowed to quit his house, iii. 124

Ogre whose soul was in a bird, story of the, xi. 98 sq.

Ogres in stories of the external soul, xi. 100 sqq.

Ogress whose life was in a spinning-wheel, xi. 100

Ogun, war-god of the Yorubas, viii. 149 sq.

Oho-harahi, "Great Purification," a Japanese ceremony performed on the last day of the year, ix. 213, 213 n.[1]

Oijo, the Alafin of, paramount king of Yoruba-land, iv. 203

Oil not to be touched by people at home in absence of hunters, i. 120 ; poured on stones as a means of averting bullets from absent warriors, i. 130 ; to be made when the tide is high, i. 167 ; poured on stone as a rain-charm, i. 305, 346 ; and wine poured on sacred tree, ii. 50 ; made by pure youths and maidens, iii. 201 ; made by chaste women, iii. 201 ; to be called water at evening and night, iii. 411 ; human victim anointed with, vii. 246, 247

——, holy, poured on king's head, v. 21 ; poured on sacred stones, v. 36 ; as vehicle of inspiration, v. 74 ; smeared on sick people, viii. 123

"—— of St. John," found on oaks on St. John's (Midsummer) morning, xi. 82 sq., 293

Oiling the body forbidden for magical reasons to wives in the absence of their husbands, i. 120, 122 ; as a protection against demons, iii. 201

—— the hair forbidden to women while their husbands are away at war, i. 127

Ointment, magical, applied to weapon instead of to wound, i. 202 ; extracted from dead bodies, the fat of animals, etc., viii. 163 sqq.

Oise, French department of, dolmen in, xi. 188

Ojebways, or Ojibways, the, magical images among, i. 55 ; their contagious magic of footprints, i. 212 ; their ceremony at an eclipse of the sun, i. 311 ; their belief in tree-spirits, ii. 18 ; custom observed by them on the war-path, iii. 160 ; their reluctance to tell their names, iii. 326 ; husbands and wives will not mention each other's names among the, iii. 338 ; their story of the type of Beauty and the Beast, iv. 130 *n.*[1] ; their respect for rattle-snakes, viii. 219 ; their propitiation of slain bears, viii. 225 *sq.* ; ritual of death and resurrection among, xi. 268

Okanaken Indians of British Columbia, their first-fruit ceremonies, viii. 134

Okhotsk Sea, whales in the, viii. 232

Oklahoma, the Yuchi Indians of, viii. 75

Okunomura, Japanese village, rain-making at, i. 297

Olachen fish, ceremonies at catching the first of the season, viii. 254 *sq.*

Olaf, king of Sweden, sacrificed to Odin for the crops, i. 367

Olala, secret society of the Niska Indians, xi. 271 *sq.*

Olaus Magnus, on were-wolves, x. 308

Olba, priestly kings of, v. 143 *sqq.*, 161 ; the name of, v. 148 ; the ruins of, v. 151 *sq.*

Old animal, bone of, eaten to make eater old, viii. 143

—— Barley-woman, last sheaf at harvest called the, vii. 139

—— Calabar, viii. 108

—— Christmas Day (Twelfth Night), ix. 321

—— Corn-woman at threshing, vii. 147

—— Hay-man at haymaking, vii. 223

—— Man, name of the corn-spirit, iv. 253 *sq.* ; name given to the last sheaf, vii. 136 *sqq.*, 148 *sq.*, 218 *sqq.*, 289 ; at threshing, vii. 148 *sq.*, 224

—— men, savage communities ruled by an oligarchy of, i. 216 *sq.* ; government by, in aboriginal Australia, i. 334 *sq.*

—— people killed, iv. 11 *sqq.*

—— Potato Woman, at digging potatoes, vii. 145

—— Rye-woman, the last sheaf called the, vii. 139 ; binder of the last sheaf called the, vii. 140, 145 ; killed in the last stalks cut, vii. 223 ; killed in the last corn threshed, vii. 224 ; last sheaf left for the, vii. 232

—— Testament, leprosy in the, viii. 27

—— Wheat-woman, vii. 139

—— Wife (*Cailleach*), name given to last corn cut, vii. 140 *sqq.*, 164 *sqq.* ;

("Old Woman"), effigy burnt on the first Sunday of Lent, x. 116 ; effigy burnt on the last day of Carnival, x. 120

Old Witch, burning the, at harvest, vii. 224

—— Wives, the Day of the, Thursday of Mid-Lent, iv. 241

—— Woman, Sawing the, a ceremony at Mid-Lent, iv. 240 *sqq.* ; name applied to the corn-spirit, iv. 253 *sq.* ; of the corn, mythical being of the Cherokee Indians, vi. 46 *sq.*, vii. 177 ; name given to the last corn cut or threshed, vii. 136 *sq.*, 147, 223 ; name given to the thresher of the last corn, vii. 147

—— Woman (*Baba*), a mummer at Carnival, viii. 332, 333, 334 ; perhaps a rustic prototype of Demeter, viii. 334

—— Woman who Never Dies, North American Indian personification of maize, vii. 204 *sqq.*

—— women as representatives of the Corn-goddess, vii. 205 *sq.*

Oldenberg, Professor H., on the distinction between religion and magic, i. 225 *n.* ; on the magical nature of ancient Indian ritual, i. 228 ; on the priority of magic to religion, i. 235 *n.*[1] ; on the ritual observed by a Brahman in learning the Sakvari song, i. 269 *sq.* ; on foundation-sacrifices, iii. 91 *n.* ; on King Vikramaditya, iv. 122 *n.*[2] ; on the belief in ghosts and demons among the Hindoos of the Vedic ages, ix. 90 *sq.* ; on the Indian drama, ix. 385 *n.*[1]

Oldenburg, mirrors covered after a death in, iii. 95 ; disposal of cut hair and nails in, iii. 275 *sq.* ; fox's tongue a remedy for erysipelas in, viii. 270 ; popular cures in, ix. 49, 51, 52, 53, 58 ; plague hammered into a wall in, ix. 64 ; the immortal dame of, x. 100 ; Shrove Tuesday customs in, x. 120 ; Easter bonfires in, x. 140 ; burning or boiling portions of animals or things to force witch to appear in, x. 321 *sq.* ; witch as toad in, x. 323 ; children passed through a cleft oak as a cure in, xi. 171 *sq.* ; custom as to milking cows in, xi. 185 ; sick children passed through a ring of yarn in, xi. 185

Oldfield, A., on the avoidance of the names of the dead among the Australian aborigines, iii. 350

Oldfield, H. A., on the Dassera festival in Nepaul, ix. 226 *n.*[1]

Olea chrysophilla, used as fuel for bonfire, xi. 11

Oleae, the, at Orchomenus, iv. 163, 164

"Oleander, the Sultan of the," x. 18, xi. 51 ; gathered at Midsummer, xi. 51

Oligarchy of old men, savage communities ruled by an, i. 216 *sq.* ; of old men the ruling body among the Australian aborigines, i. 335

Olive of the Fair Crown at Olympia, vi. 240

——, the sacred, at Olympia, vi. 240, xi. 80 *n.*[3]

——, wild, and oak, pyre of Hercules made of, ix. 391

Olive-branches carried in procession and hung over doors at Athens, vi. 238

—— crown of victor in chariot-race at Olympia, iv. 91, vi. 240 ; of Zeus at Olympia, iv. 91

—— -tree of Pallas, ii. 142 *n.*[2] ; nails knocked into an, as a cure, ix. 60

—— wood, sacred images carved of, i. 39

Olives planted and gathered by pure boys and virgins, ii. 107

Olmütz, district of, the last sheaf called the Beggar in, vii. 232

Olo Ngadjoe (Oloh Ngadju), the, of Borneo, their belief as to albinoes, v. 91 ; their use of puppets as substitutes for living persons, viii. 100 *sq.*

Olofaet, a fire-god, in Namoluk, xi. 295

Olonetz, the Government of, in Russia, collective suicide in, iv. 45 *n.*[1] ; festival of the dead in, vi. 75

Olori, a guardian spirit of the Yorubas, iii. 252

Oltscha (Orotchis?), their bear-feast, viii. 197 *n.*[2]

Olympia, home of Xenophon near, i. 7 ; Mount Cronius at, i. 46 *n.*[4] ; the sacred white poplar of Zeus at, ii. 220, xi. 90 *n.*[1], 91 *n.*[7] ; Endymion at, ii. 299, iv. 90 ; tomb of Endymion at, ii. 299, iv. 287 ; Pelops and Hippodamia at, ii. 299 *sq.*, iv. 91 ; races for the kingdom at, ii. 299 *sq.*, iv. 90, 90 *sq.* ; ram annually sacrificed to Pelops at, ii. 300, viii. 85 ; sacred precinct of Pelops at, ii. 300, iv. 287 ; Oenomaus at, ii. 300, iv. 91 ; chariot-races at, ii. 300, iv. 90 *sq.* ; worship of Thunderbolt Zeus at, ii. 361 ; girls' race at, iv. 91 ; image of Zeus at, iv. 91 ; victor's wreath of olive at, iv. 91, vi. 240 ; the sacred olive at, iv. 91, vi. 240, xi. 80 *n.*[3] ; the quack Peregrinus burns himself at, v. 181 ; rule as to cutting olive branches to form the victors' crowns at, vi. 240, xi. 80 *n.*[3] ; festival of Cronus at, ix. 352 *sq.*

Olympiads based on the octennial cycle, iv. 90 ; mode of calculating the, vii. 80 ; beginning of reckoning by, vii. 82

Olympic cycle of four or eight years, vii. 80

—— festival, death of Peregrinus by fire at the, iv. 42 ; based on the octennial cycle, iv. 89 *sq.*, vi. 242 *n.*[1] ; based on astronomical, not agricultural considerations, iv. 105

—— games, iv. 105, vii. 80, 86 ; said to have been founded in honour of Pelops, iv. 92

—— stadium, the, iv. 287

—— victors regarded as embodiments of Zeus, iv. 90 *sq.*, or of the Sun and Moon, iv. 91, 105

Olympus, Mount, in Cyprus, iv. 81, v. 32

—— Mount, at Tempe, iv. 81, vi. 240

Olynthiac, river in Macedonia, fish in the, ix. 142 *n.*[1]

Olynthus, tomb of, ix. 143 *n.*

Omagua Indians of Brazil, their belief in the influence of the Pleiades on human destiny, vii. 309

Omaha hunters cut out tongues of slain buffaloes, viii. 269

—— Indians, of North America, their rain-making, i. 249 ; their charm to start a breeze, i. 320 ; customs as to murderers among the, iii. 187 ; names of relations by marriage tabooed among the, iii. 338 ; effeminate men among the, vi. 255 *sq.* ; their belief as to boils caused by eating a totem animal, viii. 25 ; the Elk clan among the, viii. 29, x. 11 ; the Reptile clan among the, viii. 29 ; their belief in the assimilation of men to their guardian animals, viii. 207 ; their mutilation of men killed by lightning, viii. 272 ; their women secluded at menstruation, x. 88 *sq.*

Omanos at Zela, ix. 373 *n.*[1]

Omen, beasts and birds of, viii. 143

—— birds in Borneo, iii. 110 ; stories of their origin, iv. 126, 127 *sq.*

Omens, homoeopathic magic to annul evil omens, i. 170-174 ; from chicken bones, ii. 70 ; reliance on, iii. 110 ; from observation of the sky, iv. 58 ; drawn from pig's liver, vii. 97 ; from boiling milk, viii. 56, xi. 8 ; mode of neutralizing bad, xi. 39 ; from birds and beasts, x. 56 ; from the smoke of bonfires, x. 116, 131, 337 ; from flames of bonfires, x. 140, 142, 159, 165, 336, 337 ; from cakes rolled down hill, x. 153 ; from intestines of sheep, xi. 13

—— of death, xi. 54, 64

—— of marriage drawn from Midsummer bonfires, x. 168, 174, 178, 185, 189, 338 *sq.* ; from flowers, xi. 52 *sq.*, 61

Omnipresence of dèmons, ix. 72 *sqq.*

Omo River, custom of strangling firstborn children among tribes on the, iv. 181, 182

Omonga, a rice-spirit who lives in the moon, vi. 139 *n.*

Omphale and Hercules, ii. 281 *sq.*, v. 182, vi. 258, ix. 389

Omumborombonga (*Combretum primigenum*), the sacred tree of the Herero, ii. 213 *sq.*, 218, 219 *sq.*, 233

Omuongo tree, ceremony performed by the Ovambo before partaking of its fruit, viii. 71

Omuwapu tree (*Grevia spec.*), used by the Herero as a substitute for their sacred tree, ii. 219

On or Aun, King of Sweden, iv. 57, 160 *sq.*, 188. *See also* Aun

Onaght, in the Aran Islands, the rag well at, ii. 161

One shoe on and one shoe off, iii. 311 *sqq.*

One-eyed buffoon in New Year ceremony, ix. 402

Ongtong Java Islands, ceremony at the reception of strangers in the, iii. 107 *sq.*

Oni, the king of Ife, in West Africa, i. 365, iv. 204 *n.*

Onions used to foretell weather of the year, ix. 323

Onitsha, on the Niger, the king of, confined to his house, iii. 123 ; ceremony at eating the new yams at, viii. 58 ; sham funeral at, viii. 98 *sq.* ; annual expulsion of evils at, ix. 133 ; use of human scapegoats at, ix. 210 *sq.*

Onktehi, the great spirit of the waters among the Dacotas, xi. 268, 269

Onstmettingen, in Swabia, the Sow at threshing at, vii. 299

Oodeypoor, in Rajputana, gardens of Adonis at, v. 241 *sq.*

Ooloo-Ayar Dyaks observe taboos after building a new house, ii. 40

Opening, special, made to carry out the corpses of childless women, i. 142

Opening everything in house to facilitate childbirth, iii. 296 *sq.*

—— the eyes and mouth of the dead, Egyptian funeral rite, vi. 15

—— of the Wine-jars, Díonysiac festival of the, ix. 3 *s*2

Operations of husbandry regulated by observation of the moon, vi. 133 *sqq.*

Opheltes, Nemean games celebrated in honour of, iv. 91 ; his grave at Nemea, iv. 93

Ophites, the, on the Holy Ghost as feminine, iv. 5 *n.*[3]

Opis, a Hyperborean maiden, i. 33 ; a name of Artemis, i. 34 *n.*

Opium made by the Wild Wa of Burma, vii. 242

Opossum, imitation of, as a homoeopathic charm, i. 155 *sq.*

Opprobrious language levelled at goddess to please her, i. 280

Ops, the wife of Saturn, vi. 233 ; in relation to Consus, vi. 233 *n.*[6]

Oracles given by king as representative of the god, i. 377 ; given by inspired priests, i. 377 *sqq.* ; given by the spirits of dead kings, vi. 167, 171, 172 ; given by men who are inspired by the spirits of crocodiles, lions, leopards, and serpents, viii. 213

Oracular oaks in ancient Prussia, ii. 43 ; oak at Dodona, ii. 358, xi. 89 *sq.*

—— spring at Dodona, ii. 172

—— springs, iv. 79 *sq.*

—— trees among the Lithuanians, ii. 9

Oran, bathing at Midsummer in, x. 216

Orang-glai, the, of Indo-China, use a special language in searching for eaglewood, iii. 404

Orange River, the Corannas of the, xi. 192

Oraons or Uraons of Bengal, their spring festival of sál flowers at the marriage of the Sun and Earth, ii. 76 *sq.*, 94, 148, v. 46 *sqq.* ; gardens of Adonis among the, v. 240 ; their annual festival of the dead, vi. 59 ; human sacrifices for the crops among the, vii. 244 *sq.* ; their offerings of firstfruits to the Sun, viii. 117 ; their belief in demons, ix. 92 *sq.* ; their use of a human scapegoat, ix. 196 ; their belief as to the transformation of witches into cats, xi. 311 *sq.*

Orbigny, A. d', on the superstitions of the Yuracares as to the making of pottery, ii. 204 ; on division of labour between men and women among the American Indians, vii. 120 ; on the American Indian practice of bleeding themselves to relieve fatigue, ix. 12 *sq.*

Orchard, mock marriage before partaking of the fruits of a new, ii. 26, 101

Orchards, fire applied to, on Eve of Twelfth Day, ix. 317, 319, 320

Orchha, the Rajah of, celebrates annually the marriage of the *Salagrama* to the holy basil, ii. 27

Orchomenus in Arcadia, kingly government at. i. 47

—— in Boeotia, human sacrifice at, iv. 163 *sq.*

Orcus, Roman god of the lower world, his marriage celebrated by the pontiffs, vi. 231

Ordeal of battle among the Umbrians, ii. 321; by poison, fatal effects of, iv. 197 ; of chastity, v. 115 *n.*[2] ; the poison, administered by young children, vii. 115 ; of stinging ants undergone by girls at puberty, x. 61, and by young men, x. 62 *sqq.* ; of boiling resin, x. 311

Ordeals as an exorcism, x. 66 ; undergone by novices at initiation among the Bushongo, xi. 264 *sqq.*

Order of nature, different views of the, postulated by magic and science, xi. 305 *sq.*

Oregon, the Salish Indians of, recovery of lost souls among, iii. 66 ; avoidance of the names of the dead among the Indians of, iii. 352

Orestes at Nemi, i. 10 *sq.*, 21 *n.*², 24; the matricide, cleansed of his mother's murder at Troezen, i. 26 ; cured of his madness in Laconia, i. 161 ; appeases his mother's Furies by biting off his finger, iii. 166 *n.*² ; pursued by his mother's Furies, iii. 188 ; polled his hair, iii. 287 ; flight of, iv. 213 ; at Castabala, v. 115 ; his purification by laurel and pig's blood, ix. 262

Organs of generation, effigies of male, vii. 12, 26, 29 ; male and female, cakes in shape of, vi. 62

——, internal, of medicine-man, replaced by a new set at initiation, xi. 237, 238 *sq.*

Orgiastic rites of Cybele, v. 278

Orgies, sexual, as fertility charms, ii. 98 *sqq.*

Oriental mind untrammelled by logic, v. 4 *n.*¹

—— religions in the West, v. 298 *sqq.* ; their influence in undermining ancient civilization, v. 299 *sqq.* ; importance attached to the salvation of the individual soul in, v. 300

Origen, on the Holy Spirit, iv. 5 *n.*³ ; on the refusal of Christians to fight, v. 301 *n.*¹; on Jesus Barabbas, ix. 420 *n.*¹

Origin of Osiris, vi. 158 *sqq.* ; of agriculture, vii. 128 *sq.* ; of astronomy, vii. 307 ; of death, savage tales of the, ix. 302 *sqq.* ; of fire, primitive ideas as to the, xi. 295 *sq.*

Orinoco, Banivas of the, x. 66

——, Caribs of the, i. 134

——, Guaraunos of the, x. 85

——, Guayquiries of the, x. 85

——, Indians of the, employ women to sow the seed, i. 141 *sq.* ; their way of procuring rain by means of the dead, i. 287 ; their use of frogs in a rain-charm, i. 292 ; their ceremony at an eclipse of the moon, i. 311 *sq.* ; blow sacred trumpets to make palmtrees bear fruit, ii. 24 ; their belief in the superior fertility of seeds sown by women, vii. 124 ; their observation of the Pleiades, vii. 310 ; eat the hearts of their enemies to make them brave,

viii. 150 ; their treatment of the wild beasts which the hunters have killed, viii. 236

Orinoco, Piaroas Indians of the, viii. 285

——, Tamanachiers of the, ix. 303

——, Tamanaks of the, x. 61 *n.*³

Orion, the constellation, the soul of Horus in, iv. 5 ; appearance of, a signal for sowing, v. 290 *sq.* ; observed in Bali, vii. 314 *sq.* ; observed by the Battas of Sumatra, vii. 315 ; observed by the Kamtchatkans, vii. 315

Orion's belt, the constellation, observed by the natives of Bougainville Straits, vii. 313 ; observed by the Kamchatkans, vii. 315, 315 *n.*⁵

—— sword and belt, the constellations, observed by the Masai, vii. 317

Orissa, absence of gardens and fruittrees on the Khurda estate in, i. 279 ; Queen Victoria worshipped as a deity in, i. 404 ; rice treated as a pregnant woman in, ii. 29 ; well where women obtain offspring in, ii. 160 ; the Chasas of, viii. 26

Orkney Islands, magic knots in the, iii. 302 ; chapel of St. Tredwells in the, ix. 29 ; transference of sickness by means of water in the, ix. 49

Orlagau, in Thüringen, "whipping with fresh green" in the Christmas holidays at, ix. 271

Ornament, external soul of woman in an ivory, xi. 156

Ornaments, amulets degenerate into, xi. 156 *n.*²

Orne, Midsummer fires in the valley of the, x. 185

Oro, Polynesian war god, iii. 69

——, West African bogey, xi. 229

Orontes, Syrian women bathe in the, to procure offspring, ii. 160

Ororo, families of royal descent among the Shilluks, iv. 24

Orotchis, of Siberia, their theory of thunder, iii. 232 ; bear-festivals of the, viii. 197

Orpheus, prophet and musician, v. 55 ; the legend of his death, vi. 99

—— and the willow, xi. 294

Orpine (*Sedum telephium*) at Midsummer, x. 196 ; used in divination at Midsummer, xi. 61

Orvieto, Midsummer fires at, x. 210

Orwell in Cambridgeshire, harvest custom at, v. 237 *n.*⁴

Osages, their mourning for their foes, iii. 181

Oscans, the enemies of Rome, ix. 231

Oschophoria, vintage festival at Athens, vi. 258 *n.*⁶

Osculati, G., on American Indian belief in transmigration, viii. 285

Osirian mysteries, the hall of the, at Abydos, vi. 108

Osiris threatened by magicians, i. 225; threat of a magician that he will name Osiris aloud, iii. 390; the mummy of, iv. 4; his body broken into fourteen pieces, iv. 32, vi. 129; identified with Adonis and Attis, v. 32, vi. 127 n.; myth of, vi. 3 sqq.; his birth, vi. 6, ix. 341; introduces the cultivation of corn and the vine, vi. 7, 97, 112; his violent death, vi. 7 sq.; at Byblus, vi. 9 sq., 22 sq., 127; his body rent in pieces, vi. 10; the graves of, vi. 10 sq.; his dead body sought and found by Isis, vi. 10, 50, 85; tradition as to his genital organs, vi. 10, 102; mourned by Isis and Nephthys, vi. 12; invited to come to his house, vi. 12, 47; restored to life by Isis, vi. 13; king and judge of the dead, vi. 13 sq.; his body the first mummy, vi. 15; the funeral rites performed over his body the model of all funeral rites in Egypt, vi. 15; all the Egyptian dead identified with, vi. 16; his trial and acquittal in the court of the gods, vi. 17; represented in art as a royal mummy, vi. 18; specially associated with Busiris and Abydos, vi. 18; his tomb at Abydos, vi. 18 sq., 197 sq.; his emblems the sceptre or crook and the scourge or flail, vi. 20, 108, 153; official festivals of, vi. 49 sqq.; his sufferings displayed in a mystery at night, vi. 50; his festival in the month of Athyr, vi. 84 sqq.; dramatic representation of his resurrection in his rites, vi. 85; his images made of vegetable mould, vi. 85, 87, 90 sq., 91; the funeral rites of, described in the inscription of Denderah, vi. 86 sqq.; his festival in the month of Khoiak, vi. 86 sqq., 108 sq.; his "garden," vi. 87 sq.; ploughing and sowing in the rites of, vi. 87, 90, 96; the burial of, in his rites, vi. 88; the holy sepulchre of, under Persea-trees, vi. 88; represented with corn sprouting from his dead body, vi. 89, vii. 263; his resurrection depicted on the monuments, vi. 89 sq.; as a corn-god, vi. 89 sqq., 96 sqq.; corn-stuffed effigies of, buried with the dead as a symbol of resurrection, vi. 90 sq., 114; date of the celebration of his resurrection at Rome, vi. 95 n.[1]; the nature of, vi. 96 sqq.; his severed limbs placed on a corn-sieve, vi. 97; human sacrifices at the grave of, vi. 97, vii. 260; suggested explanations of his dismember-

ment, vi. 97, vii. 262; sometimes explained by the ancients as a personification of the corn, vi. 107; as a tree-spirit, vi. 107 sqq.; his image made out of a pine-tree, vi. 108; his backbone represented by the ded pillar, vi. 108 sq.; interpreted as a cedar-tree god, vi. 109 n.[1]; his soul in a bird, vi. 110; represented as a mummy enclosed in a tree, vi. 110, 111; obscene images of, vi. 112; as a god of fertility, vi. 112 sq.; identified with Dionysus, vi. 113, 126 n.[3], vii. 3, 32; a god of the dead, vi. 113 sq.; universal popularity of his worship, vi. 114; interpreted by some as the sun, vi. 120 sqq., reasons for rejecting this interpretation, vi. 122 sqq.; his death and resurrection interpreted as the decay and growth of vegetation, vi. 126 sqq.; interpreted as the moon by some of the ancients, vi. 129; reigned twenty-eight years, vi. 129; his soul thought to be imaged in the sacred bull Apis, vi. 130; identified with the moon in hymns, vi. 131; represented wearing on his head a full moon within a crescent, vi. 131; distinction of his myth and worship from those of Adonis and Attis, vi. 158 sq.; his dominant position in Egyptian religion, vi. 158 sq.; the origin of, vi. 158 sqq.; his historical reality asserted in recent years, vi. 160 n.[1]; his temple at Abydos, vi. 198; his title Khenti-Amenti, vi. 198 n.[2]; compared to Charlemagne, vi. 199; the question of his historical reality left open, vi. 199 sq.; his death still mourned in the time of Athanasius, vi. 217; his old type better preserved than those of Adonis and Attis, vi. 218; the cults of Adonis, Attis, Dionysus, and, vii. 214; perhaps the dead corn-spirit represented by human victims slain on the harvest-field, vii. 259 sqq.; represented in the form of Harpocrates, vii. 260; image of him perhaps annually thrown into the Nile as a rain-charm, vii. 262 sq.; black and green, vii. 263; key to mysteries of, vii. 263; and the pig, viii. 24 sqq.; his body mangled by Typhon, viii. 30; perhaps originally identified with the pig, viii. 31, 33 sq.; in relation to sacred bulls, viii. 34 sqq.; false graves of, viii. 100; one of his members eaten by a fish, viii. 264

Osiris, Adonis, Attis, their mythical similarity, v. 6, vi. 201

—— and Adonis, similarity between their rites, vi. 127

—— and Dionysus, similarity between their rites, vi. 127

Osiris and Isis perhaps personated by human couples, ix. 386
—— and Maneros, vii. 215
—— and the moon, vi. 129 sqq.
" —— of the mysteries," vi. 89
Osiris-Sep, title of Osiris, vi. 87
Osnabrück, in *Hanover, the Harvest-mother in, vii. 135
Ossa, Mount, and Olympus, iv. 81, vi. 240
Ossidinge district of the Cameroons, the chief as fetish-priest in the, i. 349
Oster-Kappeln, in Hanover, the oak of the Guelphs at, xi. 166 sq.
Osterode, Easter bonfires at, x. 142
Ostia, fresco at, i. 16
Ostiaks or Ostyaks, sacred groves and trees of the, ii. 11 ; their ceremonies at killing bears, viii. 222 sq.
Ostrich, ghost of, deceived, viii. 245
Ostrich-feather, king of Egypt supposed to ascend to heaven on an, vi. 154, 155
Ostroppa, a Polish village, sacrifice for horses at, ii. 336 sq.
Ostyaks. See Ostiaks
Ot Danoms of Borneo, their precautions against strangers, iii. 103 ; killing demon in effigy among the, viii. 101 ; seclusion of girls at puberty among the, x. 35 sq.
Otati tribe of Queensland, their treatment of girls at puberty, x. 38
Otho, the Emperor, suicide of, iv. 140 ; addicted to the worship of Isis, vi. 118 n.[1]
Ottawa or Otawa Indians, their way of calming a tempest, i. 321 ; tampering with a man's shadow among the, iii. 78 ; drive away the ghosts of the slain, iii. 171 ; their totem clans, viii. 224, 225 n.[1] ; their reason for not burning fish bones, viii. 250
—— medicine-man, his mode of catching stray souls, iii. 45
Otter in rain-charm, i. 289
Otter's head, Aino custom as to eating, viii. 144
Otters, their bones not allowed to be gnawed by dogs, viii. 239
Otters' tongues torn out and worn as talismans, viii. 670
Ottery St. Mary's, the Boy Bishop at, ix. 337
Oude, burial of infants in, ix. 45
Oulad Abdi, Arab tribe of Morocco, prostitution practised by their women for the sake of the crops, v. 39 n.[3]
Ounce, tooth of, a charm against toothache, i. 153 ; ceremony at killing an, viii. 235
" Our Ancestress," a Mexican goddess, ix. 289

" Our Mother among the Water," Mexican goddess, ix. 278
Oura, ancient name of Olba, in Cilicia, v. 148, 152
Ourfa, in Armenia, rain-making at, i. 276, 285
Ouwira, theory of earthquakes in, v. 199
Ovaherero, ii. 212 n.[1], 213 n.[2]. See Herero
Ovakuanjama, the, of South-West Africa, viii. 109. See Ovambo
Ovakumbi of Angola, their custom of placing stones in trees, i. 318 n.[6]
Ovakuru (singular omukuru) ancestors, among the Herero, ii. 221, 223
Ovambo or Ovakuanjama of German South - West Africa, use of magical images among the, i. 63 ; their contagious magic of footprints, i. 209 sq. ; pass new-born children through the smoke of fire, ii. 232 n.[3] ; fire carried before an army to battle among the, ii. 264 ; purification of man-slayers among the, iii. 176 ; custom as to circumcision among the, iii. 227 ; their ceremony at the new moon, vi. 142 ; worship of the dead among the, vi. 188, viii. 109 sq. ; their ceremony before partaking of the fruits of a certain tree, viii. 71 ; eat the hearts of foes to make them brave, viii. 149 ; custom observed by young women at puberty among the, xi. 183
—— women, their custom at sowing corn, ii. 46
Ovamboland, importance of rain in, viii. 110 sq.
Overshadowed, danger of being, iii. 82 sq.
Ovid, on the spring at Nemi, i. 4, 17 ; on the oak crown, ii. 176 sq. ; on the Roman use of whitethorn or buckthorn, ii. 191 ; on the Parilia, ii. 327 n.[1] ; on loosening the hair, iii. 311 ; on the story of Pygmalion, v. 49 n.[4] ; on the distinction between Ceres and the Earth Goddess, vii. 89 n.[4] ; on the Roman festival of the dead in May, ix. 155 n.[1]
Owl in homoeopathic magic, i. 156 ; bird of Pallas, ii. 142 n.[2] ; regarded as the guardian spirit of a tree, vi. 111 n.[1] ; eyes of, eaten, to make eater see in dark, viii. 144 sq. ; represented dramatically as a mystery, ix. 377 ; imitated by actor or dancer, ix. 381
Owls not mentioned by their proper name, iii. 401 ; lives of persons bound up with those of, xi. 202 ; sex totem of women, xi. 217 ; called women's " sisters," xi. 218
Ox, man-slayers anointed with gall of,

iii. 172, 175; purification by passing through the body of an, iii. 173; substituted for human victim in sacrifice, v. 146; embodying corn-spirit, sacrificed at Athens, v. 296 *sq.*; corn-spirit as, vii. 288 *sqq.*; killed on harvest field, vii. 290; slaughtered at threshing, vii. 291 *sq.*; sacrificed at the *Bouphonia*, viii. 5; as representative of the corn-spirit, viii. 9 *sqq.*, 34; effigy of, broken as a spring ceremony in China, viii. 10 *sqq.*; sacrificed to boa-constrictor, viii. 290; disease transferred to, ix. 31 *sq.*; burnt alive to stop a murrain, x. 301

Ox, black, in rain-making, i. 291, iii. 154; used in purificatory ceremonies after a battle, vi. 251 *sq.*; Bechuana sacrifice of a, viii. 271

——, hornless, in homoeopathic magic, i. 151

——, white, sacrament of a, viii. 313 *n.*[1]

Ox-blood, bath of, iv. 201

—— -horns, external soul of chief in pair of, xi. 156

—— -stall (Bucolium) at Athens, vii. 30 *sq.*

—— -yoked Ploughing at Athens, vii. 31

Ox's knee not to be eaten by soldiers, i. 117

Oxen sacrificed for rain, i. 350, 352; sacrificed instead of human beings, iv. 166 *n.*[1]; used in ploughing, vii. 129 *n.*[1]; pledged on Eve of Twelfth Day, ix. 319

Oxford, Child's Well at, ii. 161; Lords of Misrule at, ix. 332

Oxfordshire, May garlands in, ii. 62, 62 *n.*[2]

Oyampis, the, of French Guiana, their belief as to water-snakes, ii. 156

Oyo, kings of, among the Yorubas, put to death, iv. 41

Ozieri, in Sardinia, St. John's festival at, v. 244; bonfires on St. John's Eve at, x. 209

Pacasmayu, in Peru, the temple of the moon at, vi. 138

Pachamamas, Earth-mothers, among the Peruvian Indians, vii. 173 *n.*

Pacific, oracular inspiration of priests in the Southern, i. 377 *sq.*; human gods in the, i. 386 *sqq.*

Pacific Coast of North America, first salmon of the season treated with deference by the Indians of the, viii. 253

Padams of Assam, their mode of recovering a child lost in the forest, ii. 39

Paddy (unhusked rice), the Father and Mother of the, vii. 203 *sq.*

Paderborn, holy oak near, ii. 371

Padlocks as amulets, iii. 307

Padmavati, an Indian goddess, gardens of Adonis in her temple, v. 243

Padstow, in Cornwall, celebration of May Day, May-pole and Hobby Horse at, ii. 68

Padua, story of a were-wolf in, x. 309

Paestum, the ruins of, i. 236 *n.*[1]

Pagae, in ancient Greece, annual kingship at, i. 46

Pagan origin of the Midsummer festival (festival of St. John), v. 249 *sq.*

Paganism and Christianity, their resemblances explained as diabolic counterfeits, v. 302, 309 *sq.*

Pages, medicine-men, among the Indians of Brazil, i. 358

Paha, on the Gold Coast, sacred crocodiles at, xi. 210

Pains in back at reaping, goat-skin used as cure for, vii. 285

Paint-house, in which girls are secluded at puberty, ii. 111

Painting bodies of manslayers, iii. 175, 178, 179, 180, 186 *n.*[1]; body of lion-killer, iii. 220

Paintings, prehistoric, of animals in caves, i. 87 *n.*[1]

Pairing dogs, stick that has beaten, thought to make women fruitful, ix. 264

Pais, E., on Manius Egerius, i. 23 *n.*

Παῖς ἀμφιθαλής, a boy whose parents are both alive, vi. 236 *n.*[2]

Pakambia, a rainy district of Celebes, the word for rain not to be mentioned in, iii. 413

Palaces, kings not allowed to leave their, iii. 122 *sqq.*

Palatinate, mimic contest between Summer and Winter in the, iv. 254 *sq.*

——, the Upper, trees asked for pardon on being felled in, ii. 18; the Feast of All Souls in, vi. 72

Palatine Hill at Rome, sacred cornel-tree on the, ii. 10; the emperor's palace on the, ii. 176; grove of Vesta at foot of the, ii. 185; hut of Romulus on the, ii. 200

Palazzo degli Conservatori at Rome, ii. 142 *n.*[2]

Pale colour of negro children at birth, xi. 251 *n.*[1], 259 *n.*[2]

Palenque in Central America, ruins of, i. 48

Palenques, the, of South America, spare harmless animals which are not good for food, viii. 221

Palermo, drought at, i. 299 *sq.*; ceremony of "Sawing the Old Woman" at Mid-Lent at, iv. 240

Pales, a pastoral Roman deity, ii. 326, 327, 328, 329, 348

Palestine, rain-making in, i. 276; figs in, ii. 315; religious prostitution in, v. 58; date of the corn-reaping in, v. 232 *n.*; wild boars in, viii. 31 *sq.*; sticks or stones piled on scenes of violent death in, ix. 15

Palestinian Aphrodite, v. 304 *n.*

Palestrina, the harmonies of, v. 54

Palettes or plaques of schist in Egyptian tombs, xi. 155 *n.*[3]

Paley, F. A., on the fodder of cattle in Southern Europe, ii. 328 *n.*[1]

Pallades, female consorts of Ammon, ii. 135

Palladius on the date of the artificial fertilization of fig-trees, ii. 314

Pallas, her olive-tree and owl, ii. 142 *n.*[2]

Pallas, P. S., on the slaughter of sheep and cattle among the Kalmucks, viii. 314 *n.*[1]

Pallegoix, Mgr., on the Siamese year, ix. 149 *n.*[2]

Pallene, daughter of Sithon, the wooing of, ii. 307

Palm-branches, blessed on Palm Sunday, in ceremonies to procure rain, i. 300; waved to drive off demons, ix. 260 *n.*[3]; children beaten with, on Palm Sunday, ix. 268; ashes of, mixed with seed at sowing, x. 121; stuck in fields to protect them against hail, x. 144; (twigs of boxwood) burnt to avert a thunderstorm, xi. 30, 85 *n.*[4]

—— Sunday, churches swept on, i. 300; custom in Würtemberg on, ii. 71; the branches consecrated on, used as a protection against witches, ii. 336; "Sawing the Old Woman" on, iv. 243; Russian custom on, ix. 268; palm-branches consecrated on, used to protect fields against hail, x. 144; boxwood blessed on, x. 184, xi. 30, 47; fern-seed used on, xi. 288

—— -tree, thought to ensure fertility to barren women, ii. 51; ceremony at tapping a palm-tree for wine, ii. 100 *sq.*; child's hair fastened to, iii. 276. *See also* Date-palm

—— -trees as life-indices, xi. 161, 163, 164`

—— wine offered to trees, ii. 15; ceremony at felling a palm for, ii. 19

Palodes, announcement of the death of the Great Pan at, iv. 6

Palol, sacred milkman of the Todas, i. 403 *n.*[1]; taboos observed by him, iii. 15 *sq.*

Palolo veridis, a sea-slug, its annual appearance in the Samoan sea, ix. 142 *n.*

Paloo, in Celebes, propitiation of the souls of slain enemies at, iii. 166

Paloppo, in Celebes, the regalia at, i. 363 *sq.*

Palsy called the king's disease in Loango, i. 371

Pampa del Sacramento, Peru, earthquakes in, v. 198

Pampas, bones of extinct animals in the, v. 158

Pamyles, an Egyptian, announcement of the birth of Osiris to, vi. 6

Pan, dedication of Greek hunters to, i. 6 *n.*[4]; death of the Great, iv. 6 *sq.* *See also* Pans

Pan's image beaten by the Arcadians, ix. 256

Panaghia Aphroditessa at Paphos, v. 36

Panama, the Guami Indians of, iii. 325

Panamara in Caria, worship of Zeus and Hera at, i. 29

Panathenaic festival, iv. 89 *n.*[5]

—— games at Athens, vii. 80

Pancakes in homoeopathic magic, i. 137; to be eaten on the eve of Twelfth Night, ix. 241; to scald fiends on New Year's Eve, ix. 320

Panchalas, the king of the, father of Draupadi in the *Mahabharata*, ii. 306

Panda, king of Zululand, iii. 377; liberties taken with him by his subjects at the festival of first-fruits, viii. 67, 68

Pandarus, tattoo marks of, in the sanctuary of Aesculapius at Epidaurus, ix. 47 *sq.*

Pandharpur, in the Bombay Presidency, gardens of Adonis in temples at, v. 243

Pandion, king of Athens, son of Cecrops, the Eleusinian games founded in his reign, vii. 70

Panebian Libyans, their custom of cutting off the heads of their dead kings, iv. 202

Panes, annual bird-feast in the Acagchemem tribe of California, viii. 170

Pangaeum, Mount, in Thrace, King Lycurgus torn to pieces at, i. 366

Pango, title signifying god, bestowed on the king of Loango, i. 396

Pani, son of Rengo, the Maori god of sweet potatoes, viii. 133

Panionian festival, temporary king appointed for the, i. 46

Pankas of South Mirzapur will not call certain animals by their proper names, iii. 402

Panku, a being who causes earthquakes, in New Guinea, v. 198

Panoi, the land of the dead, in Melanesia, viii. 97

Panopeus, in Phocis, the ruins of, vii. 48

Pans, rustic Greek deities, in relation to goats, viii. 1 *sqq.*

Pantang, taboo among the Jakuns and Binuas of the Malay Peninsula and the Dyaks of Borneo, iii. 405

Panther, ceremonies at the slaughter of a, among the Kayans of Borneo, iii. 219 ; king of Benin represented with whiskers of a, iv. 86

Panua, tribe of Khonds, vii. 245

Papa Westray, one of the Orkney Islands, cairn to which people add stones in, ix. 29

Paparuda, gipsy girl employed in rain-making ceremony, i. 273 *sq.*

Papas, a name for Attis, v. 281, 282

Paphlagonian belief that the god is bound fast in winter, vi. 41

Paphos in Cyprus, v. 32 *sqq.* ; sanctuary of Aphrodite at, v. 32 *sqq.* ; founded by Cinyras, v. 41

Papirius Cursor, L., dedicates temple of Quirinus, ii. 182 *n.*[1]

Papuan and Melanesian stocks in New Guinea, xi. 239

Papuans, the, of Tumleo, their treatment of spilt blood and rags, i. 205 ; of Geelvink Bay, their belief in the abduction of souls by a forest spirit, iii. 60 *sq.* ; of New Guinea believe the soul to be in the blood, iii. 241 ; of Finsch Haven unwilling to tell their names, iii. 329 ; of Doreh Bay in New Guinea, their fear in regard to children who resemble their parents, iv. 287 (288 in Second Impression) ; of Ayambori in Dutch New Guinea, division of agricultural work between men and women among the, vii. 123 ; of Port Moresby and Motumotu districts, strong food to strengthen young lads among the, viii. 145 ; of the northern coast of New Guinea believe in the transmigration of human souls into animals, viii. 295 ; their belief in demons, ix. 83 ; life-trees among the, xi. 163

Papyrus of Nebseni, vi. 112 ; of Nekht, vi. 112

Papyrus swamps, Isis in the, vi. 8

Paracelsus, a forerunner of science, viii. 307

Paradoxurus, souls of dead in various species of, viii. 294

Paraguay, the Caingua Indians of, ii. 258 ; the Calchaquis Indians of, iii. 31 ; the Isistines Indians of, iii. 159 *n.*; the Chiquites Indians of, iii. 250 *n.*[1], viii. 241, xi. 226 *n.*[1] ; the Abipones of, iii. 352, 360, vii. 308, viii. 140 ; the Payagua Indians of, iv. 12 *sq.* ; the Guaranis of, vii. 309 ; the Lengua Indians of, vii. 309 ; the Mocobis of, vii. 309 ; the Canelos Indians of, viii. 285

Parahiya, a tribe of Mirzapur, sacrifice to the evil spirits of trees, ii. 42

Paraka, in India, the people of, supposed to know the language of animals, viii. 146

Parallelism between witches and werewolves, x. 315, 321

Paramatta, island, magical powers of chief in, i. 339

Parasitic mountain-ash (rowan) used to make the divining-rod, xi. 69 ; superstitions about a, xi. 281 *sq.*

——— orchid growing on a tamarind, ritual at cutting, xi. 81

——— plants, superstitions as to, ii. 250, 251 *sq.*

Pardon asked of tree at cutting it down, ii. 18, 19 ; of animal asked before killing it, viii. 183

Paremêsvara Bhûminâtha (title of frog), prayer for rain to, i. 295, 295 *n.*[1]

Parents of twins believed to possess power of fertilizing plantain-trees, ii. 102 ; named after their children, iii. 331 *sqq.*, 339

Parents-in-law, their names not to be pronounced, iii. 338, 339, 340, 341, 342

Parian chronicler, on the antiquity of the Eleusinian mysteries and games, vii. 70

Parigi, in Central Celebes, treatment of the afterbirth in, i. 188

Parilia, the, Roman festival of shepherds, ii. 123, 229, 273, 325 *sqq.* ; the shepherd's prayer at, ii. 123, 327 ; flocks fumigated at, ii. 229, 327 ; Numa born on the, ii. 273, 325 ; shepherds leap over bonfires at, ii. 273, 327 ; sheep driven over fires at, ii. 327 ; offerings of milk and millet to Pales at, ii. 327 ; compared to the festival of St. George, ii. 330 *sqq.*, v. 308

Parinarium, a sacred tree in Busoga, iv. 215

Paris protected against dormice and serpents, viii. 281 ; effigy of giant burnt in summer fire at, x. 38 ; cats burnt alive at Midsummer in, x. 39

Parivarams of Madura, their seclusion of girls at puberty, x. 69

Parjanya, the ancient Hindoo god of thunder and rain, i. 270, ii. 368 *sq.* ; derivation of the name, ii. 367 *n.*[3]

Parjas, a tribe of the Central Provinces, India, their ceremonial purification for killing a sacred animal, viii. 27 *sq.* ; their offerings of first-fruits to their ancestors, viii. 119

Parker, Professor E. H., on substitutes for capital punishment in China, iv. 146 *n.*[1]

Parkinson, John, on custom of killing chief after rule of three years among the Yorubas, iv. 112 *sq.*

Parkinson, R., on contagious magic in New Britain, i. 175 ; on the fear of demons in New Britain, ix. 83

Parkyns, Mansfield, on the Abyssinian festival of Mascal, ix. 133 *sq.*

Parnes, Mount, in Attica, lightning over, i. 33, ii. 361 ; altar of sign-giving Zeus on, ii. 360

Parr, Thomas, his great age, v. 55 *sq.*

Parricide, Roman punishment of, ii. 110 *n.*[2] ; of Oedipus, ii. 115

Parrot, external soul of warlock in a, xi. 97 *sq.*

—— and Punchkin, story of the, xi. 97 *sq.*

Parrot Island, in Guinea, human sacrifices to river at, ii. 158

Parrot's feathers worn as a protection against a ghost, iii. 186 *n.*[1] ; eggs, a signal of death, iv. 40 *sq.*

Parrots, assimilation of men to, viii. 208

Parsee priests wear a veil over their mouth, ii. 241

Parsees ascribe sanctity to fire kindled by lightning, ii. 256 ; their customs as to menstruous women, x. 85

Parsons, Harold G., on custom of king eating the heart of his predecessor, iv. 203 *n.*[5]

Parthe, the River, at Leipsic, effigy of Death thrown into the, iv. 236

Partheniai, offspring of unmarried women at Sparta, i. 36 *n.*[2]

Parthenon, sculptures in the frieze of the, iv. 89 *n.*[5] ; sculptures in the eastern gable of the, iv. 89 *n.*[5]

Parthenos as applied to Artemis, i. 36

Parthia, prince of, his structure at Nemi, i. 6

Parthian monarchs brothers of the Sun, i. 417 *sq.* ; worshipped as deities, i. 418

Parti, name of an Elamite deity, ix. 367

Partition of spiritual and temporal power between religious and civil kings, iii. 17 *sqq.*

Partridge, C., as to the election of a king of Idah, ii. 294 *n.*[2] ; as to sacred chief on the Cross River, iii. 124 ; as to human souls in fish, xi. 204

Partridge, transmigration of sinner into a, viii. 299

Parvati or Isa, an Indian goddess, wife of Mahadeva, v. 241 ; gardens of Adonis in her worship, v. 242

—— and Siva, marriage of the images of, iv. 265 *sq.*

Paschal candle, x. 121, 122 *n.*, 125

—— Mountains, in Münsterland, Easter fires on the, ix. 141

Pasicyprus, king of Citium, v. 50 *n.*[2]

Pasiphae identified with the moon, iv. 72

—— and the bull, iv. 71

—— and the Minotaur, vii. 31

Pasir, a district of eastern Borneo, treatment of the afterbirth in, i. 194

" Pass through the fire," meaning of the phrase as applied to the sacrifice of children, iv. 165 *n.*[3], 172

Passage of flocks and herds over or between fires, ii. 327, x. 157, 285 (*see further* Cattle) ; over or through fire a stringent form of purification, xi. 24 ; through cleft trees as a cure, xi. 168 *sqq.* ; through cleft trees to get rid of spirits or ghosts, xi. 173 *sqq.* ; through a cleft stick after a funeral, xi. 175 *sq.* ; through narrow openings after a death, xi. 177 *sqq.* ; through an archway to escape from demons, xi. 179 ; through an archway as a cure or preventive of maladies, xi. 180 *sq.* ; through a cleft stick to get rid of sickness or ghosts, xi. 182 *sq.* ; through a cleft stick in connexion with puberty and circumcision, xi. 183 *sq.* ; through hoops or rings as a cure or preventive of disease, xi. 184 *sqq.* ; through holed stones as a cure, xi. 186 *sqq.* ; through narrow openings as a cure or preventive, xi. 190 ; through holes in the ground as a cure, xi. 190 *sqq.* ; through a yoke as a cure, xi. 192 ; under a yoke or arch as a rite of initiation, xi. 193 ; passage of Roman enemies under a yoke, xi. 193 *sqq.* ; passage of victorious Roman army under a triumphal arch, xi. 195. *See also* Passing

Passes, Indian tribe of Brazil, drink the ashes of their dead as a mode of communion, viii. 157 ; seclusion of girls at puberty among the, x. 59

Passes of mountains, cairns and heaps of sticks or leaves on, ix. 9 *sqq.*, 29

Passier, in Sumatra, kings of, put to death, iv. 51 *sq.*

Passing between the pieces of a sacrificial victim, i. 289, 289 *n.*[4] ; between two fires as a purification, iii. 114 ; over fire to get rid of ghosts, xi. 17 *sq.* ; through cleft trees and other narrow openings to get rid of ghosts, etc., xi. 173 *sqq.* ; under a yoke as a purification, xi. 193 *sqq.* *See also* Passage

—— children through cleft trees, xi. 168 *sqq.* ; children, sheep, and cattle through holes in the ground, xi. 190 *sq.*

Passover, tradition of the origin of the, iv. 174 *sqq.* ; accusations of murders at the, ix. 395 *sq.* ; the crucifixion of Christ at the, ix. 414 *sqq.* ; sacrifice of the first-born at, ix. 419

Paste kneaded with the blood of children in Peru, ix. 129

Pastern-bone of a hare in a popular remedy, x. 17

Pastoral peoples, their reverence for their cattle, viii. 35, 37 *sqq.*
—— stage of society, the, viii. 35, 37
—— tribes, animal sacraments among, viii. 313
Pastures fumigated at Midsummer to drive away witches and demons, x. 170
Patagonia, acacia-tree worshipped in, ii. 16 ; funeral customs of Indians of, v. 294
Patagonian Indians, their charm to make a child a horseman, i. 152
Patagonians burn their loose hair for fear of witchcraft, iii. 281 ; effeminate priests or sorcerers among the, vi. 254 ; their remedy for smallpox, ix. 122
Patani Bay, in Siam, the Malays of, their belief as to absence of soul in sleep, iii. 41 ; speak respectfully of tigers, iii. 404 ; Malay fishermen of, will not mention certain words at sea, iii. 408 ; Malay family of, will not kill crocodiles, viii. 212
—— States, treatment of the afterbirth in the, i. 194, xi. 164
Patara, in Lycia, Apollo at, ii. 135
Pataris of Mirzapur call bears by a special title in the morning, iii. 403 ; their use of scapegoats, ix. 192
Patches of unreaped corn left at harvest, vii. 233
Paternity, uncertainty of, a ground for a theological distinction, ii. 135; of kings a matter of indifference under female kinship, ii. 274 *sqq.*, 282 ; primitive ignorance of, v. 106 *sq.* ; unknown in certain state of savagery, v. 282
—— and maternity of the Roman deities, vi. 233 *sqq.*
Pathian, a beneficent spirit, among the Lushais, ix. 94
Paths used by men forbidden to menstruous women, iii. 145 ; separate, for men and women, x. 78, 80, 89
Patiala, in the Punjaub, professed incarnation of Jesus Christ at, i. 409 *sq.*
Patiko, in the Uganda Protectorate, dread of lightning at, xi. 298 *n.*[2]
Patiné, a Cingalese goddess, ix. 181
Patmos, the month of Cronion in, ix. 351 *n.*[2]
Paton, L. B., on the origin of Purim, ix. 360 *n.*[1]
Paton, W. R., on the names of Eleusinian priests, iii. 382 *n.*[4], 383 *n.*[1]; on modern Greek Feast of All Souls in May, vi. 78 *n.*[1]; on human scapegoats in ancient Greece, ix. 257 *sq.*, 259, 272 ; on Adam and Eve, ix. 259 *n.*[3]; on the crucifixion, ix. 413 *n.*[2]; on the Golden Bough, xi. 319
Patrae, Laphrian Artemis at, v. 126 *n.*[2];

Flowery Dionysus at, vii. 4 ; sanctuary of Demeter at, vii. 89
Patriarch of Jerusalem kindles the new fire at Easter, x. 129
Patriarchal family at Rome, ii. 283
Patrician myrtle-tree at Rome, xi. 168
Patronymics not in use among the Tuaregs, iii. 353
Patschkau, precautions against witches near, xi. 20 *n.*
Pâturages, processions with torches on the first Sunday in Lent at, ix. 108
Pau Pi, an effigy of the Carnival, at Lerida in Catalonia, iv. 225
Paulicians of Armenia worship each other as embodiments of Christ, i. 407
Paunch of bullock tabooed as food, i. 119
Pauntley, parish of, in Gloucestershire, Eve of Twelfth Day in, ix. 318
Pausanias, Greek antiquary, on the priest of Nemi, i. 11 ; on Hippolytus at Troezen, i. 26 *sq.* ; on the offerings of the Hyperboreans, i. 33 *n.*[4]; his identification of Pasiphae and the moon, iv. 72 ; on the necklace of Harmonia, v. 32 *n.*[2]; on bones of superhuman size, v. 157 *n.*[2]; on offerings to Etna, v. 221 *n.*[4]; on the Hanged Artemis, v. 291 *n.*[2]; on the *bouphonia*, viii. 5 *n.*[1]
Pausanias, king of Sparta, funeral games in his honour, iv. 94
Pawnee story of the external soul, xi. 151
Pawnees, their notion as to whirlwinds, i. 331 *n.*[2]; ritual flight of sacrificers among the, ii. 309 *n.*[2]; their use of stone arrow-heads in sacrifices, iii. 228; human sacrifices offered by the, at sowing their fields, vii. 238 *sq.*, ix. 296, xi. 286 *n.*[2]
Paxos, Greek island, death of the Great Pan announced at, iv. 6
Payaguas of South America, fight the wind, i. 330 ; of Brazil, precaution as to chief's spittle among the, iii. 290 ; of Paraguay, their voluntary deaths, iv. 12 *sq.*
Payne, Bishop, on the Bodia of Sierra Leone, iii. 15 *n.*[1]
Payne, E. J., on the worship of the frog in America, i. 292 *n.*[3]; on the Incas of Peru, i. 415 *n.*[2]; on the religious aspect of early calendars, iv. 69 *n.*[2]; on the origin of moon-worship, vi. 138 *n.*[2]; on Cinteotl, the Mexican goddess of maize, ix. 286 *n.*[1]
Payne, J. H., on the purification festival of the Cherokees, ix. 128
Pazzi family at Florence, fire-flints brought by one of them from the Holy Land, x. 126
Pea-mother, thought to be among the

peas, vii. 132 ; name given to wreath made out of the last pea-stalks, vii. 135

Pea wolf, supposed to be caught in the last peas of the crop, vii. 271

Peace, ceremony at making, among the Ba-Yaka, iii. 274

Peace-making ceremony among the Masai, ix. 139 *n.*

Peach, Chinese emblem of longevity, i. 169 *n.*[1]

Peach-tree, goitre transferred to a, ix. 54
—— wood, bows of, used to shoot at demons, ix. 146, 213 ; staves of, used at the expulsion of demons, ix. 213

Peacock, Miss Mabel, on a Lincolnshire saying, ii. 231

Peacock, the bird of Hera, ii. 142 *n.*[2] ; Earth Goddess represented in the form of a, vii. 248 *n.*[1] ; a totem of the Bhils, viii. 29 ; transmigration of sinner into, viii. 299

Peacock's feather in a charm, viii. 167

Peaiman, sorcerer, among the Indians of Guiana, ix. 78

Peale, Titian R., as to the natives of Bowdich Island, ii. 254 *n.*[1]

Pear-tree as protector of cattle, ii. 55 ; as life-index of girl, xi. 165
—— -trees, torches thrown at, on first Sunday in Lent, x. 108 ; rarely attacked by mistletoe, xi. 315

Pearls not to be worn by wives in the absence of their husbands, i. 122 *sq.* ; in homoeopathic magic, i. 174

Peas, boiled, distributed by young married couples on first Sunday in Lent, x. 111 *n.*[1]

Peas-cow, name given to thresher of last peas, vii. 290
—— -pudding, taboo as to entering a sanctuary after eating, viii. 85
—— -pug, name given to cutter or binder of last peas, vii. 272

Pease-bear, name given to the man who gave the last stroke at threshing, viii. 327

Peat-bogs of Europe, ii. 350 *sqq.*

Pebbles in rain-making, i. 305 ; thrown into Midsummer fires, x. 183

Pechuyos, the, of Bolivia, ate the powdered bones of their dead, viii. 157

Peg used to transfer disease to tree, ix. 7

Pegasus and Bellerophon, v. 302 *n.*[4]

Pegging ailments into trees, ix. 58 *sqq.*

Pegu, dance of hermaphrodites in, v. 271 *n.* ; worship of *nats* in, ix. 96

Peguenches, Indian tribe of South America, seclusion of girls at puberty among the, x. 59

Peitho, epithet of Artemis, i. 37 *n.*[1]

Peking, the High Court of, i. 298 ; the Colonial Office at, i. 412 *sq.* ; Ibn

Batuta at, v. 289 ; life-tree of the Manchu dynasty at, xi. 167 *sq.*

Peking Gazette, i. 355, iv. 274, 275

Pélé, goddess of the volcano Kirauea in Hawaii, v. 217 *sqq.*

Peleus, son of Aeacus, reigned in Phthia, ii. 278

Pelew Islanders, pray tree-spirit to leave tree which is to be felled, ii. 35 ; their system of mother-kin, vi. 204 *sqq.* ; predominance of goddesses over gods among the, vi. 204 *sqq.* ; customs of the, vi. 253 *sqq.* ; their belief in the transmigration of human souls into animals, viii. 293 ; their gods, ix. 81 *sq.*
—— Islands, human gods in the, i. 389 ; special terms used with reference to persons of the blood-royal in the, i. 401 *n.*[3] ; removal of fire from a house after a death in the, ii. 267 *n.*[4] ; seclusion and purification of man-slayers in the, iii. 179 ; continence of fishermen in the, iii. 193 ; taboos observed by relations of murdered man in the, iii. 240 ; story of the type of Beauty and the Beast in the, iv. 130 *n.*[1] ; and the ancient East, parallel between, vi. 208 ; prostitution of unmarried girls in the, vi. 264 *sq.* ; custom of slaying chiefs in the, vi. 266 *sqq.* ; deceiving the ghost of woman who has died in childbed in the, viii. 98

Pelias and Jason, iii. 311

Pelion, Mount, sacrifices offered on the top of, at the rising of Sirius, vi. 36 *n.*

Pellene, Artemis at, i. 15 *n.*[4]

Pelopidae, the, migrations of, ii. 279

Peloponnese, May Day in, ii. 143 *n.*[2] ; worship of Poseidon in, v. 203

Pelops succeeded his father-in-law on the throne, ii. 279 ; Olympic games founded in his honour, iv. 92 ; restored to life, v. 181, viii. 263 ; his ivory shoulder, viii. 263 *sq.*
—— at Olympia, ii. 300, iv. 104, xi. 90 *n.*[1] ; sacred precinct of, ii. 300, iv. 104, 287 ; black ram sacrificed to, iv. 92, 104, viii. 85
—— and Hippodamia, at Olympia, ii. 299 *sq.*, iv. 91

Peloria, a Thessalian festival resembling the Saturnalia, ix. 350

Pelorian Zeus, ix. 350

Peltophorum africanum, Sond., branches of the tree used at sowing corn, ii. 46

Pemali, taboo, among the Dyaks, vii. 39

Pemba, island off German East Africa, xi. 263

Pembrokeshire, the last sheaf called the Hag in, vii. 142 *sqq.* ; "cutting the neck" at harvest in, vii. 267 ; hunting the wren in, viii. 320 ; cure for warts in, ix. 53

Penance observed after building a new house, ii. 40; for killing a boa-constrictor, iii. 222; for the slaughter of the dragon, iv. 78; by drawing blood from ears, ix. 292

Penates, the, Roman gods of the storeroom (*penus*), ii. 205 *sq.*

Pendle, gathering of witches at Hallowe'en in the forest of, x. 245

Penelope won by Ulysses in a race, ii. 300

Peneus, the river, at Tempe, iv. 81, vi. 240

"Penitential of Theodore" on the custom of wearing cows' hides on New Year's Day, viii. 323 *n.*[1]

Pennant, Thomas, on knots at marriage in the Highlands of Scotland, iii. 300 *nn.*[1] and [2]; on the custom of kindling twelve fires on Twelfth Day in Gloucestershire, ix. 321; on weather forecasts for the year in the Highlands of Scotland, ix. 324; on Beltane fires and cakes in Perthshire, x. 152; on Hallowe'en fires in Perthshire, x. 230

Pennefather River in Queensland, belief as to reincarnation among the natives of the, i. 99 *sq.*; beliefs as to the afterbirth among the natives of the, i. 183 *sq.*; belief of the natives as to the birth of children, v. 103; treatment of girls at puberty on the, x. 38; effigies of strangers among the natives of the, xi. 159

Pennyroyal, the communion cup in the Eleusinian mysteries flavoured with, vii. 161 *n.*[4]; burnt in Midsummer fire, x. 213, 214; gathered at Midsummer, xi. 51

Pentamerone, the, story of dragon twin in, xi. 105

Pentateuch, evidence of moral evolution in the, iii. 219

Pentheus, king of Thebes, torn to pieces by the Bacchanals, vi. 98, vii. 24, 25

Penza, Government of, in Russia, the "Funeral of Kostroma" in, iv. 262

Penzance, horn-blowing at, on the eve of May Day, ix. 163 *sq.*; Midsummer fires at, x. 199 *sq.*

Peoples said to be ignorant of the art of kindling fire, ii. 253 *sqq.*

—— of the Aryan stock, annual festivals of the dead among the, vi. 67 *sqq.*

Peperuga, girl dressed in greenery at rainmaking ceremony in Bulgaria, i. 274

Pepi the First, king of Egypt, vi. 5; his pyramid, vi. 4 *n.*[1]

Pepper rubbed into bodies of sufferers as a cure or exorcism, iii. 106; rubbed into eyes of strangers, iii. 114

—— and salt, abstinence from, during fasts, i. 266, ii. 98

Pepys, Samuel, on Charles II. touching

for scrofula, i. 369; on the milkmaids' dance on May Day, ii. 52; on the coronation ceremony of Charles the Second, ii. 322

Perak, Malay superstition as to *toallong* trees in, ii. 41; superstition as to bloodsucking snail in, iii. 81 *sq.*; belief as to the Spectral Huntsman in, iv. 178; periodic expulsion of evils in, ix. 198 *sqq.*; the rajah of, ix. 198 *sq.*

Perasia, Artemis, at Castabala, v. 115, 167 *sqq.*; walk of her priestesses over fire, v. 115, 168

Perche, in France, homoeopathic cure for vomiting in, i. 83 *sq.*; Midsummer fires in, x. 188; St. John's herb gathered on Midsummer Eve in, xi. 46; the *Chêne-Doré* in, xi. 287 *n.*[1]

—— and Beauce, treatment of the navelstring in, i. 198. *See* Beauce

Perchta, Frau, a mythical old woman in Germany, Austria, and Switzerland, ix. 240 *sq.*

Perchta's Day, Twelfth Night or the Eve of Twelfth Night, ix. 240, 242, 244

Perchten, maskers in Salzburg and the Tyrol, ix. 240, 242 *sqq.*

Percival, R., on the fear of demons in Ceylon, ix. 94 *sq.*

Perdoytus, the Lithuanian wind-god (reported), i. 326 *n.*[5]

Peregrinus, his death by fire at Olympia, iv. 42, v. 181

Perforating arms and legs of young men, girls, and dogs as a ceremony, x. 58

Perga in Pamphylia, Artemis at, v. 35

Pergamus, Aesculapius and Telephus at, viii. 85

Pergine, in the Tyrol, fern-seed on St. John's Night at, xi. 288 *n.*[6]

Pergrubius, a Lithuanian god of the spring, ii. 347 *sq.*

Perham, Rev. J., on the blighting effect which the Dyaks ascribe to adultery, ii. 109 *n.*[1]; on the Head-feast of the Sea Dyaks, ix. 383 *sq.*

Periander, tyrant of Corinth, his burnt sacrifice to his dead wife, v. 179

Periepetam in Southern India, devildancer at, i. 382 *n.*[2]

Perigord, rolling in dew on St. John's Day in, v. 248; the Yule log in, x. 250 *sq.*, 253; magic herbs gathered at Midsummer in, xi. 46; crawling under a bramble as a cure for boils in, xi. 180

Perils of the soul, iii. 26 *sqq.*

Perinthus, the month of Cronion in, ix. 351 *n.*[3]

Periodic expulsion of evils in a material vehicle, ix. 198 *sqq.*

Periods of licence preceding or following

the annual expulsion of demons, ix. 225 *sq.*

Periphas, king of Athens, called Zeus by his people, ii. 177

Περίψημα, " offscouring," applied to human scapegoat, ix. 255 *n.*[1]

Peritius, month of, festival of "the awakening of Hercules" in the, v. 111

Perkunas or Perkuns, the Lithuanian god of thunder and lightning, ii. 365 *sqq.*; derivation of his name, ii. 367 *n.*[3]; his perpetual fire, xi. 91 *n.*[5]

Permanence of simpler forms of religion, viii. 335; of the belief in magic and witchcraft, in ghosts and demons, under the higher forms of religion, ix. 89 *sq.*

Permanent possession of human beings by deities, i. 386 *sq.*

Péronne, mugwort at Midsummer near, xi. 58

Perperia, appealed to for rain by the Greeks of Thessaly and Macedonia, i. 273

Perpetual holy fire in temples of dead kings, vi. 174

—— fires worshipped, v. 191 *sqq.*; origin of the custom of maintaining, ii. 253 *sqq.*; associated with royal dignity, ii. 261 *sqq. See also* Fires

Perros-Guirec, in Brittany, Renan's home near, ix. 70

Perrot, G., on rock-hewn sculptures at Boghaz-Keui, v. 138 *n.*

Persea-trees in the rites of Osiris, vi. 87 *n.*[5]; growing over the tomb of Osiris, vi. 88

Persephone, mother of Zagreus by Zeus, vii. 12 ; carried off by Pluto, vii. 36, viii. 19 ; a personification of the corn, vii. 39 *sq.* ; in Greek art, vii. 43 *sq.*, 67 *sq.*, viii. 88 *sq.* ; the descent of, vii. 46, viii. 17 ; the Corn Maiden or Corn Daughter, vii. 53, 58 *sq.*, 75, 184 ; associated with the ripe ears of corn, viii. 58 ; forty days of mourning for, ix. 348 *sq.*

——, name applied to spring, vi. 41

—— and Aphrodite, their contest for Adonis, v. 11 *sq.*

—— and Demeter, vii. 35 *sqq.* ; their myth acted in the mysteries of Eleusis, vii. 39, 187 *sq.* ; as a double personification of the corn, vii. 209 *sqq.*

—— and Pluto, viii. 9 ; temple of, v. 205 ; rustic prototypes of, viii. 334

Perseus in Egypt, iii. 312 *n.*[2] ; the virgin birth of, v. 302 *n.*[4]

—— and Andromeda, ii. 163

—— and the Gorgon, iii. 312

Persia, temporary kings in, iv. 157 *sqq.* ; cure for toothache in, ix. 59 ; the feast of Purim in, ix. 393

Persian calendar, the oldest, March the first month of the year in, ix. 402

—— ceremony, " Ride of the Beardless One," ix. 402

—— charm to make the wind blow, i. 320

—— fire-worship and priests, v. 191

—— framework of the book of Esther, ix. 362, 401

—— kings, sacred fire carried before, ii. 264 ; their custom at meals, iii. 119 ; their heads cleaned once a year, iii. 253 ; married the wives of their predecessors, ix. 368 *n.*[1]

Persians sacrifice horses to the sun, i. 315 ; their reverence for fire, v. 174 *sq.* ; their festival of the dead, vi. 68 ; annually expel demons, ix. 145 ; the Sacaea celebrated by the, ix. 402 ; their marriages at the vernal equinox, ix. 406 *n.*[3]; celebrate a festival of fire at the winter solstice, x. 269

Personation of gods by priests, v. 45, 46 *sqq.*; by human victims, ix. 275 *sqq.*

Personification of abstract ideas not primitive, iv. 253 ; of corn as mother and daughter, vii. 130, 207 *sqq.*

Person's destiny bound up with his navel-string or afterbirth, i. 198

Persons thought to influence and to be influenced by plants homoeopathically, i. 139 *sqq.*, 144 *sqq.* ; tabooed, iii. 131 *sqq.* ; wrapt in corn as representatives of the corn-spirit, vii. 225 *sq.*

Perthshire, custom of unloosing knots at marriage in, iii. 299 *sq.* ; the harvest Maiden in, vii. 156 *sq.* ; Beltane fires and cakes in, x. 152 *sq.* ; traces of Midsummer fires in, x. 206 ; Hallowe'en bonfires in, x. 230 *sqq.* ; need-fire in, x. 296 *sq.*

Peru, theocratic despotism of ancient, i. 218 ; sacred new fire at the summer solstice in, ii. 243, x. 132 ; earthquakes in, v. 202 ; sacrifice of sons in, vi. 220 *n.*[4]; autumn festival in, ix. 262

——, the Aymara Indians of, i. 292, iii. 97, ix. 193

——, the Cholones of, i. 116

——, the Conchucos of, viii. 258 *n.*[1]

——, the Conibos of, ii. 183 *n.*[2]

——, the Incas of, i. 196, ii. 243 *sq.*, ix. 128 ; claim to be descended from the sun, i. 415. *See also* Incas

——, Indians of, ceremony to obtain offspring among the, i. 71 ; their charm to cause sleep, i. 148 ; their magical stones for the increase of maize, potatoes, and cattle, i. 162 ; their belief as to the relation of twins to rain and the weather, i. 265 *sqq.*; their way of making sunshine, i. 314 ; their festival to make alligator pears ripen, ii. 98 ; their women pray to the moon for an easy delivery, ii. 128 *n.*[2] ; their custom of marrying a girl to a sacred stone, ii. 146 ; no fire in their houses after a death, ii. 268 *n.* ; their belief as to washing their heads, iii. 253 ; preserved their cut hair and nails against the resurrection, iii.' 279 *sq.* ; their custom of sprinkling blood on doorways, iv. 176 *n.*[1] ; sacrifice of children among the, iv. 185 ; cultivation of fields left to women among the, vii. 122 ; their worship of the Pleiades, vii. 310 ; worshipped whales and fish of several kinds, viii. 249 *sq.* ; washed their sins away in a river, ix. 3 *sq.* *See also* Peruvian *and* Peruvians

Peru, the Piros Indians of, viii. 286
——, the Sencis of, i. 311
——, the Yuracares of, ii. 183 *n.*[2]

Perun, the thunder-god of the Slavs, ii. 365, vii. 233 ; sacrifice of first-born children to, iv. 183 ; the oak sacred to, xi. 89

Peruvian Andes, i. 316
—— Indians, their use of magical images, i. 56 ; their rain-charm by means of a black sheep, i. 290 ; their preparation for office, iii. 159 *n.* ; confession of sins among the, iii. 216 *n.*[2] ; their custom as to shooting stars, iv. 63 *n.*[1] ; their theory of earthquakes, v. 201 ; transfer weariness to heaps of stones, ix. 9 ; their offerings at cairns, ix. 27
—— Vestals, ii. 243 *sqq.*

Peruvians, division of agricultural labours between the sexes among the, vii. 120 ; their customs as to Mother of Maize, the Quinoa-mother, the Coca-mother, and the Potato-mother, vii. 171 *sqq.*

Pescara River, in the Abruzzi, washing in the, on St. John's Day, v. 246

Pescina, in the Abruzzi, Midsummer custom at, v. 246

Pessinus, priestly kings at, i. 47 ; image of Cybele at, v. 35 *n.*[3] ; priests called Attis at, v. 140 ; local legend of Attis at, v. 264 ; image of the Mother of the Gods at, v. 265 ; people of, abstain from swine, v. 265 ; high-priest of Cybele at, v. 285 ; high-priest perhaps slain in the character of Attis at, vii. 255

Pessnitz, in the district of Dresden, thresher of last corn called the Bull at, vii. 291

Peter of Dusburg, his *Chronicle of Prussia*, ii. 366 *n.*[2]

Petrarch at Cologne on St. John's Eve, v. 247 *sq.*

Petrie, Professor W. M. Flinders, on the date of the corn-reaping in Egypt and Palestine, v. 231 *n.*[3] ; on the Sed festival, vi. 151 *n.*[3], 152 *n.*[3], 154 *sq.* ; on the marriage of brothers with sisters in Egypt, vi. 216 *n.*[1]

Petrified cascades of Hierapolis, v. 207

Petroff, Ivan, on a custom of the Koniags of Alaska, vi. 106

Petronius on prayers to Jupiter for rain, ii. 362 ; as to the soul in the nose, iii. 33 *n.*[3] ; on human scapegoats at Marseilles, ix. 253 *n.*[2] ; his story of the were-wolf, x. 313 *sq.*

Pett, Grace, a Suffolk witch, x. 304

Petworth, in Sussex, cleft ash-trees used for the cure of rupture at, xi. 170

Peucedanum leiocarpum, hog's wort, burnt as an offering to salmon, viii. 254

Pfeiffer, Madame, her reception among the Battas, iii. 104

Pfingstl, a Whitsuntide mummer, iv. 206 *sq.*, 211

Phaedra and Hippolytus, i. 19, 25

Phalaris, the brazen bull of, iv. 75

Phalgun, an Indian month, equivalent to February, ii. 51, xi. 2

Phamenoth, an Egyptian month, vi. 49 *n.*[1], 130

Phaophi, an Egyptian month, vi. 49 *n.*[1], 94

Pharmacus, mythical personage, said to have been stoned to death, ix. 254 *n.*[1]

Pharnace, daughter of Megassares, v. 41

Phatrabot, a Cambodian month, vi. 61

Phaya Phollathep, "Lord of the Heavenly Hosts," temporary king in Siam, iv. 149

Phees (*phi*), evil spirits, in Siam, ix. 97, 98

Pheneus, lake of, ii. 8

Pherecydes, on the marriage of Zeus and Hera, ii. 143 *n.*[1] ; on the voluntary self-sacrifice of Phrixus, iv. 163 *n.*[1]

Phi, Siamese genii, iii. 90. *See also* Phees

Phidias, his influence on Greek religion, v. 54 *n.*[1]

Phigalia in Arcadia, sacrifice of hair at, i. 31 ; the cave of Demeter at, viii. 21, 22 *n.* ; horse-headed Demeter of, viii. 21, 338

Philadelphia, in Lydia, subject to earthquakes, v. 194 *sq.* ; coin of, ix. 389

Philae, Egyptian relief at, vi. 50 *n.*[5] ; sculptures illustrating the mystic history of Osiris in the temple of Isis at, vi. 89, 111 ; the grave of Osiris at, vi. 111 ; the dead Osiris in the sculptures at, vi. 112

Philip and James, the Apostles, feast of, x. 158

Philip Augustus, king of France, and the privilege of St. Romain at Rouen, ii. 165

Philippine Islanders believe the souls of their ancestors to be in certain trees, ii. 29 *sq.*

—— Islands, the Tagalogs of the, ii. 18 *sq.* ; the Tagales of the, ii. 36 ; the Bagobos of the, iii. 31, 315, vii. 240, viii. 124 ; the Agutainos of the, iii. 144 ; verbal taboos observed by natives of the, iii. 416 ; grave of the Creator in the, iv. 3 ; human sacrifices before sowing in the, vii. 240 ; head-hunting in the, vii. 240 *sq.*, 256 ; the Efugaos of the, viii. 152 ; the Italones of the, viii. 152 ; the Igorrots of the, viii. 292 ; the Negritos of the, ix. 82 ; spirits of the dead in the, ix. 82 ; the Tagbanuas of the, ix. 189

Philistines, the foreskins of the, coveted by the Israelites, i. 101 *n.*[2] ; their corn burnt by Samson, viii. 298 *n.* ; their charm against mice, viii. 281, 283

Philo of Alexandria (Judaeus), his doctrine of the Trinity, iv. 6 *n.*; on the date of the corn-reaping, v. 231 *n.*[3] ; on the mockery of King Agrippa, ix. 418

Philo of Byblus, on the sacrifice of kings' sons among the Semites, iv. 166, 179

Philocalus, ancient Roman calendar of, v. 303 *n.*[2], 304 *n.*[3], 307 *n.*, vi. 95 *n.*[1]

Philochorus, Athenian antiquary, on the date of the Festival of the Threshing-floor, vii. 62

Philosophy as a solvent of religion, ii. 377 ; primitive, iii. 420 *sq.*

——, school of, at Tarsus, v. 118

Philostephanus, Greek historian, on Pygmalion and Aphrodite, v. 49 *n.*[4]

Philostratus, on death at low tide, i. 167 ; on sacrifice to Hercules, i. 282 *n.*[1]

Phlius, gilt image of goat at, vii. 17 *sq.*

Phocaeans, dead, propitiated with games, iv. 95

Phocylides, the poet, on Nineveh, ix. 390

Phoenicia, song of Linus in, vii. 216

Phoenician kings in Cyprus, v. 49

—— temples in Malta, v. 35 ; sacred prostitution in, v. 37

—— vintage song, vii. 216, 257

Phoenicians, their custom of human sacrifice, iv. 166 *sq.*, 178, 179

—— in Cyprus, v. 31 *sq.*

Phong long, ill luck caused by childbirth in Annam, iii. 155

Phosphorescence of the sea, superstitions as to the, ii. 154 *sq.*

Photius, on Lityerses, vii. 217 *n.*[1]

Photographed or painted, supposed danger of being, iii. 96 *sqq.*

Phrixus and Helle, the children of King Athamas, iv. 161 *sqq.*

Phrygia, Attis a deity of, v. 263 ; festival of Cybele in, v. 274 *n.* ; indigenous race of, v. 287 ; Lityerses in, vii. 216 *sq.* ; Cybele and Attis in, ix. 386

Phrygian belief that the god sleeps in winter, vi. 41

—— cap of Attis, v. 279

—— cosmogony, v. 263 *sq.*

—— kings named Midas and Gordias, v. 286

—— moon-god, v. 73

—— priests named Attis, v. 285, 287

Phrygians, invaders from Europe, v. 287

Phyllanthus emblica worshipped by a forest tribe in India, viii. 119

Physical basis of magic, i. 174 *sq.* ; for the theory of an external soul, i. 201

Piaroas Indians of the Orinoco, their belief in the transmigration of human souls into tapirs, viii. 285

Piazza del Limbo at Florence, church of the Holy Apostles on the, x. 126

—— Navona at Rome, Befana on the, ix. 166 *sq.*

Picardy, the harvest cock in, vii. 277 ; Lenten fire-customs in, x. 113 ; Midsummer fires in, x. 187

Piceni, guided by a woodpecker (*picus*), iv. 106 *n.*[4] ; traced their origin to a "sacred spring," iv. 186

Picts, female descent of kingship among the, ii. 280 *sq.*, 286

Pictures, supposed danger of, iii. 96 *sqq.*

Pidhireanes, a Ruthenian people, custom as to knots on grave-clothes among the, iii. 310

Piedmont, effigy of Carnival burnt on Shrove Tuesday in, iv. 224 *n.*[1] ; belief as to the "oil of St. John" on St. John's morning in, xi. 82 *sq.*

Piers, Sir Henry, as to green bushes on the Eve of May Day, ii. 59 ; his *Description of Westmeath,* ii. 59 ; on candles on Twelfth Night in Ireland, ix. 321

Pietà of Michael Angelo, v. 257

Pietro in Guarano (Calabria), Easter custom at, x. 123

Pig, grunting like a, as a charm, ii. 23 ; Roman expiatory sacrifice of, ii. 122 ; the word unlucky, iii. 233 ; a tabooed word to fishermen, iii. 395 ; Greek expiatory sacrifice of, vii. 74 ; corn-spirit as, vii. 298 *sqq.* ;

in relation to Demeter, viii. 16 *sqq.* ; not eaten in Crete, viii. 21 *n.*[1]; attitude of the Jews to the, viii. 23 *sq.* ; in ancient Egypt, viii. 24 *sqq.* ; used to decoy demons, ix. 113, 200, 201 ; roast, at Christmas, x. 259 ; sacrificed to stay disease in the herd, x. 302. *See also* Pigs

Pig and Attis, viii. 22

——, black, sacrificed for rain, i. 291

—— and lamb as expiatory victims in the grove of the Arval Brothers at Rome, iii. 226

——, white or red, sacrificed for sunshine, i. 291

Pig's blood drunk by priests and priestesses as a means of inspiration, i. 382, 382 *n.*[2]; used to purge the earth from taint of sexual crime, ii. 107, 108, 109 ; used in exorcism and purification for homicide, v. 299 *n.*[2], ix. 262

—— bones inserted in the sown field or in the seed-bag among the flax-seed, to make the flax grow tall, vii. 300

—— flesh not eaten by Zulu girls, i. 118 ; forbidden to women at sowing seed, vii. 115 ; sown with seed-corn, viii. 18 ; not eaten by field labourers, viii. 33, 139 ; reasons for not eating, viii. 139 *sq. See also* Pork *and* Swine's flesh

—— liver, omens drawn from, vii. 97

—— milk thought to cause leprosy, viii. 24, 25

—— tail stuck in field at sowing to make the ears grow long, vii. 300

Pigeon in homoeopathic magic, i. 151 ; used in a love-charm, ii. 345 *sq.* ; family of Wild, in Samoa, viii. 29 ; external soul of ogre in a, xi. 100 ; external soul of dragon in a, xi. 112 *sq.*

Pigeon's egg, external soul of fairy being in, xi. 132 *sq.*, 139

Pigeons, special language employed by Malays in snaring, iii. 407 *sq.* ; souls of dead in, viii. 293 ; deposit seed of mistletoe, xi. 316 *n.*[1]

Pigs, magical ceremonies to catch wild pigs, i. 109 ; magical stones to breed, i. 164 ; sacrificed to souls of ancestors, i. 339 ; sacrificed at the marriage of Sun and Earth, ii. 99 ; bred by the people of the Italian pile villages, ii. 353 *n.*[3]; sacrificed once a year by the Egyptians to Osiris and the Moon, vi. 131, viii. 25 ; sacrificed by Kayans at New Year's festival, vii. 97 ; not to be eaten by enchanters of crops, vii. 100 *sq.*; the enemies of the crops, vii. 100 ; thrown into "chasms of Demeter and Persephone" at the Thesmophoria, viii. 17, 19, 34 ; ancestral spirits in, viii.

123 ; souls of dead in, viii. 286, 295, 296 ; sacrificed at festival of wild mango tree in New Guinea, x. 9 ; driven through Midsummer fire, x. 179 ; driven through the need-fire, x. 272, 273, 274 *sq.*, 275 *sq.*, 276 *sq.*, 277, 278, 279, 297 ; offered to monster who swallows novices in initiation, xi. 240, 246. *See also* Boar, Boars, Pig, *and* Swine

Piker or Pikere, Esthonian thunder-god, ii. 367 *n.*[4]

Pilae, human effigies, hung up at the Compitalia, viii. 95 *n.*[1]

Pilate, Pontius, crucifixion of Christ under, ix. 412 *n.*[1]

—— and Christ, ix. 416 *sq.*

Pilcomayo River, the Chiriguanos on the, iv. 12

Pile-villages in the valley of the Po, ii. 8 ; of Europe, ii. 352 *sq.*

Piles of sticks or stones. *See* Heaps

Pilgrimages on Yule Night in Sweden, x. 20 *sq.*

Pilgrims to Mecca not allowed to wear knots and rings, iii. 293 *sq.*

Pillar, fever transferred to a, ix. 53 ; external soul of ogre in a, xi. 100 *sq.*

Pillars as a religious emblem, v. 34, 108, 108 *n.*[1]; sacred, in Crete, v. 107 *n.*[2]

Pilsen, in Bohemia, Whitsuntide King at, ii. 86 ; beheading the Whitsuntide King at, iv. 210 *sq.*

Pima Indians, the purification of manslayers among the, iii. 182 *sqq.*, x. 21

Pindar on the rebirth of the dead, iv. 70, vii. 84 ; on the music of the lyre, v. 55 ; on Typhon, v. 156 ; old scholiast on, as to the Eleusinian games, vii. 71, 74, 77, 78

Pine-cones, symbols of fertility, v. 278 ; thrown into vaults of Demeter, v. 278 ; on the monuments of Osiris, vi. 110

—— -resin burnt as a protection against witches, ix. 164

—— seeds or nutlets used as food, v. 278

—— -tree in the myth and ritual of Attis, v. 264, 265, 267, 271, 277 *sq.*, 285, vi. 98 *n.*[5]; Marsyas hung on a, v. 288 ; in relation to human sacrifices, vi. 98 *n.*[5]; Pentheus on the, vi. 98 *n.*[5]; in the rites of Osiris, vi. 108 ; sacred to Dionysus, vii. 4

—— -trees in the peat-bogs of Europe, ii. 350, 351, 352

Pines, Scotch, struck by lightning, proportion of, xi. 298

Pinewood, fire of, at Soracte, xi. 14, 91 *n.*[1]

Pinoeh, district of South-Eastern Borneo,

treatment of infant's soul among the Dyaks of, xi. 154 *sq.*

Pins stuck into saint's image, ix. 70 *sq.*

Pinsk, district of Russia, custom observed on Whit-Monday in, ii. 80

Pinxterbloem, a kind of iris, at Whitsuntide, ii. 80

Pinzgau district of Salzburg, the *Perchten* maskers in, ix. 244

Pipal tree (*Ficus religiosa*), sacrifices to the spirits of the, ii. 42 ; sacred in India, ii. 43

Pipe, sacred, of the Blackfoot Indians, iii. 159 *n.*

Pipiles of Central America practise sexual intercourse at the time of sowing, ii. 98 ; expose their seeds to moonlight, vi. 135

Pippin, king of the Franks, need-fires in the reign of, x. 270

Pips of water-melon in homoeopathic magic, i. 143

Piraeus, processions in honour of Adonis at, v. 227 *n.*

Pirates, the Cilician, v. 149 *sq.*

Piros Indians of Peru, their belief in the transmigration of a human soul into a jaguar, viii. 386

Pirua, granary of maize, among the Indians of Peru, vii. 171 *sqq.*

Pisa, in Greece, Pelops at, ii. 279

Pit, sacrifices to the dead offered in a, iv. 96. *See also* Pits

Pitch smeared on doors to keep out ghosts, ix. 153 ; smeared on houses to keep off demons, ix. 153 *n.*[1]. *See also* Tar

Pitchforks ridden by witches, ix. 160, 162
—— and harrows a protection against witchcraft, ii. 54

Pithoria, in India, use of scapegoats at, ix. 191

Pitlochrie, in Perthshire, Hallowe'en fires near, x. 230

Pitr Pāk, the Fortnight of the Manes, in Bilaspore, vi. 60

Pitrè, Giuseppe, on the personification of the Carnival, iv. 224 *n.*[1] ; on Good Friday ceremonies in Sicily, v. 255 *sq.* ; on St. John's Day in Sicily, xi. 29

Pits to catch wild pigs, i. 109

Pitsligo, parish of, in Aberdeenshire, the cutting of the clyack sheaf in, vii. 158 *sqq.*

Pitt Rivers Museum at Oxford, i. 69

Pitteri Pennu, the Khond god of increase, ix. 138

Pity of rain-gods, appeal to, i. 302 *sq.*

Placci, Carlo, on the new Easter fire at Florence, x. 127 *n.*[1]

Place de Noailles at Marseilles, Midsummer flowers in the, xi. 46

Placenta (afterbirth) and navel-string, contagious magic of, i. 182-201 ; Egyptian standard resembling a, vi. 156 *n.*[1] *See also* Afterbirth

Placianian Mother, a form of Cybele, worshipped at Cyzicus, v. 274 *n.*

Plague transferred to plantain-tree, ix. 4 *sq.* ; the Baganda god of, battened down in a hole, ix. 4 ; transferred to camel, ix. 33 ; blocked up in holes of buildings, ix. 64 ; at Rome, attempted remedies for, ix. 65 ; demon of, expelled, ix. 173 ; sent away in scapegoat, ix. 193. *See also* Disease *and* Epidemics

Plaiting the last standing corn before cutting it, vii. 142, 144, 153, 154, 157, 158

Plane and birch, fire made by the friction of, x. 220

Plane-tree, Dionysus in, vii. 3

Planer district of Bohemia, custom at threshing in the, vii. 149

Planets, human victims sacrificed to, among the heathen of Harran, vii. 261 *sq.*

Plantagenets, royal forests under the, ii. 7

Plantain-tree, the afterbirth and navel-string buried under a, i. 195, 196 ; plague transferred to, ix. 4 *sq.* ; creeping through a cleft, as a cure, xi. 181
—— -trees, navel-strings of Baganda buried at foot of, i. 195 ; fertilized by parents of twins, ii. 102. *See also* Banana, Bananas

Planting, homoeopathic magic at, i. 136, 137, 143

Plants, homoeopathic magic to make plants grow, i. 136 *sqq.* ; influenced homoeopathically by a person's act or state, i. 139 *sqq.* ; influence persons homoeopathically, i. 144 *sqq.* ; spirits of, in shape of animals, ii. 14 ; sexes of, ii. 24 ; marriage of, ii. 26 *sqq.* ; thought to be animated by spirits, viii. 82 *sq.* ; spirits of, in the form of snakes ; xi. 44 *n.* ; external soul in, xi. 159 *sqq.* ; and trees as life-indices, xi. 160 *sqq.*

Plaques or palettes of schist in Egyptian tombs, xi. 155 *n.*[3]

Plastene, Mother, on Mount Sipylus, v. 185

Plataea, ceremonial extinction of fires at, i. 33 ; festival of the Daedala at, ii. 140 *sq.* ; Archon of, forbidden to touch iron, iii. 227 ; bull annually sacrificed to men who fell at the battle of, iii. 227 ; escape of besieged from, iii. 311 ; sacrifices and funeral games in honour of the slain at, iv. 95 *sq.* ; Eleutherian games at, vii. 80, 85

Plates or basins, divination by three, at Hallowe'en, x. 237 *sq.*, 240, 244

Plato on the magistrate called the King at Athens, i. 45 ; on the pre-existence of the human soul, i. 104 ; on human sacrifices, iv. 163 ; on gardens of Adonis, v. 236 *n.*[1] ; on the doctrine of transmigration, viii. 308 ; on purification for murder, ix. 24 *sq.* ; on poets, ix. 35 *n.*[3] ; on sorcery, ix. 47 ; on the distribution of the soul in the body, xi. 221 *n.*[1]

Plautus on Mars and his wife Nerio, vi. 232

Playfair, Major A., on the ceremony of the horse at rice-harvest among the Garos, viii. 337 *sq.* ; on the use of scapegoats among the Garos of Assam, ix. 208 *sq.*

Plebeian myrtle-tree at Rome, xi. 168

Plebeians, the Roman kings, ii. 289

Pleiades, the, morning rising of, time of the corn-reaping in Greece, i. 32, vii. 48 *sq.* ; worshipped by the Abipones, v. 258 *n.*[2] ; the setting of, the time of sowing, vi. 41; autumnal setting of, the signal for ploughing in Greece, vii. 45 ; in primitive calendars, vii. 116, 122 *n.*[1], 307 *sqq.*; associated with the rainy season, vii. 307, 309, 317, 318 ; supposed to cause the rain to fall, vii. 307, 317 ; worshipped, vii. 307, 308 *sq.*, 310, 311, 312, 317 ; legends of their origin, vii. 308 *n.*, 311, 312 ; the beginning of the year marked by the appearance of, vii. 309, 310, 312, 313, 314, 315, xi. 244, 245 *n.* ; the time for sowing and planting determined by observation of, vii. 309, 311, 313 *sqq.*; supposed to cause the maize to grow, vii. 310 ; women swear by, vii. 311 ; festival of the Guaycurus at the appearance of, ix. 262 ; observed by savages, ix. 326

Pliny the Elder, on electric lights, i. 49 *sq.* ; on a cure for jaundice, i. 80 ; on a tree-stone, i. 165 *n.*[1]; on death at ebb-tide, i. 167 ; on contagious magic of wounds, i. 201 ; on the sexes of trees, ii. 25 *n.* ; on the sacredness of woods, ii. 123 ; on the forests of Germany, ii. 353 *sq.*; on the use of acorns as food, ii. 355 ; on the derivation of the name Druid, ii. 363 *n.*[2] ; on lucky and unlucky trees, iii. 275 *n.*[3]; on the magical effect of clasping hands and crossing legs, iii. 298 ; on knotted threads, iii. 303 ; on the date of harvest in Egypt, vi. 32 *n.*[2] ; on the influence of the moon, vi. 132 ; on the grafting of trees, vi. 133 *n.*[3] ; on the time for

felling timber, vi. 136 *n.*; on the time for sowing cereals in Greece and Asia, vii. 45 *n.*[2] ; on the setting of the Pleiades, vii. 318 ; on cure of warts, ix. 48 *n.*[2] ; on cure for a stomachic complaint, ix. 50 ; on cure for gripes, ix. 50 ; on cure for epilepsy, ix. 68 ; on "serpents' eggs," x. 15 ; on medicinal plants, x. 17 ; on the touch of menstruous women, x. 196 ; on the fire-walk of the Hirpi Sorani, xi. 14 ; on the mythical springwort, xi. 71 ; on the Druidical worship of mistletoe, xi. 76 *sq.* ; on the virtues of mistletoe, xi. 78 ; on the birds which deposit seeds of mistletoe, xi. 316 *n.*[1]; on the different kinds of mistletoe, xi. 317

Pliny the Younger, on boar-hunting, i. 6 ; as to the historical reality of Christ, ix. 412 *n.*[1] ; his letter to Trajan on the spread of Christianity in Asia Minor, ix. 420 *sq.*; his government of Bithynia and Pontus, ix. 421

Ploska (in Wallachia?), rain-making at, i. 248

Plotinus, the death of, v. 87

Plough watered as a rain-charm, i. 282, 284 ; sacred golden, i. 365 ; in relation to Dionysus, vii. 5 ; in primitive agriculture, vii. 113 ; drawn round village to keep off epidemic, ix. 172 *sq.*; piece of Yule log inserted in the, x. 251, 337

Plough-horses, part of the Yule Boar eaten by the, vii. 301

—— Monday, vii. 33 ; rites of, viii. 325 *sqq.*, ix. 250 *sq.*; English celebration of, viii. 329 *sqq.*

—— -oxen, the first, vii. 5

Ploughing, by women as a rain-charm, i. 282 *sq.*; Prussian custom at, v. 238 ; in Greece, season of, vii. 45, 50 ; the land thrice a year, Greek custom of, vii. 53 *n.*[1], 72 *sq.*; with oxen, vii. 129 *n.*[1] ; annually inaugurated by the Chinese emperor, viii. 14 *sq.* ; in spring, custom at the first, x. 18

——, ceremonies at, among the Chams of Indo-China, viii. 57 ; at Calicut in India, ix. 235

——, ceremony of, performed by temporary King, iv. 149, 155 *sq.*, 157 ; in the rites of Osiris, vi. 87; at Carnival, vii. 28, 29, viii. 331, 332, 334 ; sacred at Athens, vii. 31

—— and sowing, rite of, at the Carnival, vii. 28

Ploughings, Sacred, in Attica, vii. 108

Ploughman worships the ploughshare, ix. 90

Ploughmen and sowers drenched with water as a rain-charm, v. 238 *sq.*; and

plough-horses, part of the Yule Boar given to, to eat, vii. 301, 303
Ploughs, bronze, used by Etruscans at founding of cities, iv. 157
Ploughshare worshipped by ploughman, ix. 90 ; crawling under a, as a cure, xi. 180
Plover in connexion with rain, i. 259, 261
Plugging or bunging up maladies in trees, ix. 58
Plum-tree wood used for Yule log, x. 250
Plurality of souls, doctrine of the, xi. 221 *sq.*
Plutarch on Numa and Egeria, i. 18 ; on hair offerings of boys at puberty, i. 28 ; on the stone-curlew as a cure for jaundice, i. 80 ; on Egeria, ii. 172 ; on the birth of Romulus, ii. 196 ; on the Roman Vestals, ii. 244 *n.*[1] ; on the violent deaths of the Roman kings, ii. 320; on the death of Tullus Hostilius, ii. 320 *n.*[3] ; on the Parilia, ii. 325 *n.*[3], 329 ; on the exclusion of gold from sanctuaries, iii. 226 *n.*[8] ; on the abstinence from wine of the Egyptian kings, iii. 249 ; on the death of the Great Pan, iv. 6 ; human sacrifice at Orchomenus in the lifetime of, iv. 163 ; on human sacrifices among the Carthaginians, iv. 167 ; on the double-headed axe of Zeus Labrandeus, v. 182 ; on the myth of Osiris, vi. 3, 5 *sqq.* ; on Harpocrates, vi. 9 *n.* ; on Osiris at Byblus, vi. 22 *sq.* ; on the rise of the Nile, vi. 31 *n.*[1] ; on the mournful character of the rites of sowing, vi. 40 *sqq.*; his use of the Alexandrian year, vi. 49, 84 ; on an Egyptian ceremony at the winter solstice, vi. 50 *n.*[4] ; on the date of the death of Osiris, vi. 84 ; on the festival of Osiris in the month of Athyr, vi. 91 *sq.*; on the dating of Egyptian festivals, vi. 94 *sq.*; on the rites of Osiris, vi. 108 ; on the grave of Osiris, vi. 111 ; on the similarity between the rites of Osiris and Dionysus, vi. 127 ; on the Flamen Dialis, vi. 229 *sq.*; on the Flaminica Dialis, vi. 230 *n.*[2] ; on immortality, vii. 15 ; on the myth of Osiris, vii. 32 *n.*[6]; on mourning festival of Demeter, vii. 46 ; on sacrifice, viii. 31 ; on Apis, viii. 36 ; on the custom of throwing puppets into the Tiber, viii. 108; on " the expulsion of hunger " at Chaeronea, ix. 252 ; on the Cronia and the rural Dionysiac festival, ix. 352 *n.*[1]; on oak-mistletoe, xi. 318 *n.*[1]
Pluto, the breath of, v. 204, 205 ; places or sanctuaries of, v. 204 *sqq.*; cave and temple of, at Acharaca, v. 205 ; carries

off Persephone, vii. 36, viii. 19 ; at Eleusis, sacrifices to, vii. 56
Pluto and Persephone, viii. 9 ; rustic prototypes of, viii. 334
—— called Subterranean Zeus, vii. 66
Plutonia, places of Pluto, v. 204
Plutus, begotten by Iasion on Demeter in a thrice-ploughed field, vii. 208
Po, pile-villages in the valley of the, ii. 8, 353 ; herds of swine in antiquity in the valley of the, ii. 354
Po Then, a great spirit, among the Thay of Indo-China, ix. 97
Po-nagar, the Cham goddess of agriculture, viii. 56, 57, 58
Pocahontas, an assumed name, iii. 318
Poelopetak, the Dyaks of, their names for soul-stuffs, vii. 182
Pogdanzig, in Prussia, witches' Sabbath at, xi. 74
Point Barrow, Alaska, the Esquimaux of, i. 328, viii. 258 *n.*[2], ix. 124
Pointing sticks or bones in magic among the Australian aborigines, iv. 60, x. 14
Poison, sympathetic magic of, in hunting and fishing, i. 116 *sq.*, 125 *sq.* ; continence observed at brewing, iii. 200
Poison ordeal in Sierra Leone, iii. 15 ; fatal effects of the use of the, iv. 197 ; ordeal administered by young children, vii. 115
—— tooth of a serpent a charm against snake-bite, i. 153
Poisoning the fish of a river, common words tabooed in, iii. 415
Poitou, the Fox in the last standing corn in, vii. 297 ; Midsummer fires in, x. 182, 190 *sq.*, 340 *sq.* ; fires on All Saints' Day in, x. 246 ; the Yule log in, x. 251 *n.*[1] ; mugwort at Midsummer in, xi. 59
Poix, Lenten fires at, x. 113
Pok Klai, a Chin goddess, viii. 121
Poland, objection to iron ploughshares in, iii. 232; "Carrying out Death" in, iv. 240 ; the last sheaf called the Baba (Old Woman) in, vii. 144 *sq.*; custom at threshing in, vii. 148 ; Christmas custom in, vii. 275 ; the harvest cock in, vii. 277 ; need-fire in, x. 281 *sq.* *See also* Poles *and* Polish
Polar bear, taboos concerning the, iii. 209
Polaznik, polazenik, polažaynik, Christmas visiter, among the Servians, x. 261, 263, 264
Pole, sacred, of the Arunta, x. 7
Pole-star, homoeopathic magic of the, i. 166
Polebrook in Northamptonshire, May carols at, ii. 61 *n.*[1]
Polemarch, the, at Athens, iii. 22

Poles, passing between two poles after a death, xi. 178 *sq.*; passing between two poles in order to escape sickness or evil spirit, xi. 179 *sqq.*

Poles, the Corn-mother among the, vii. 132 *sq.*

Polish custom at cutting last corn, vii. 150

—— Jews, their belief as to falling stars, iv. 66

Political evolution from democracy to despotism, i. 421

Polkwitz, in Silesia, custom of "Carrying out Death" at, iv. 237

Pollution caused by murder, ix. 25

——, ceremonial, of girl at puberty, viii. 268

—— of death, vi. 227 *sqq.*, viii. 85 *n.*[3]

—— and holiness not differentiated by savages, iii. 224

——, menstrual, widespread fear of, x. 76 *sqq.*

—— or sanctity, their equivalence in primitive religion, iii. 145, 158, 224. *See also* Uncleanness

Polo, Marco, on custom of people of Camul, v. 39 *n.*[3]

Polybius on the butchery of pigs in ancient Italy, ii. 354

Polyboea, sister of Hyacinth, v. 314, 316; identified with Artemis or Persephone, v. 315

Polydorus, in Virgil, ii. 33

Polygnotus, his picture of Orpheus under the willow, xi. 294

Polyidus, a seer, restored Glaucus to life, v. 186 *n.*[4]

Polynesia, sacred kings and priests not allowed to touch food with their hands in, iii. 138; persons who have handled the dead not allowed to touch food with their hands in, iii. 140; sacredness of the head in, iii. 245; sanctity of the heads of chiefs and others in, iii. 254 *sqq.*; names of chiefs tabooed in, iii. 381; belief as to falling stars in, iv. 67; remarkable rule of succession in, iv. 190; prevalence of infanticide in, iv. 191, 196; the beginning of the year marked by the rising of the Pleiades throughout, vii. 313; fear of demons among the natives of, ix. 80 *sq.*

Polynesian chiefs sacred, iii. 136

—— mothers, their way of infusing a divine spirit into their unborn babes, iii. 69

—— myth of the separation of earth and sky, v. 283

Polynesians, oracular inspiration of priests among the, i. 377; their mode of kindling fire, ii. 258; their way of ridding themselves of sacred contagion, viii. 28

Polynices and Eteocles, their grave at Thebes, ii. 33

Polytheism evolved out of animism, ii. 45

Pomegranate, growing on the grave of fratricides, ii. 33; causes virgin to conceive, v. 263, 269

Pomegranates forbidden to worshippers of Cybele and Attis, v. 280 *n.*[7]; sprung from blood of Dionysus, vii. 14; seeds of, not eaten at the Thesmophoria, vii. 14; not to be brought into the sanctuary of the Mistress at Lycosura, viii. 46

Pomerania, cut hair burnt in, iii. 282 *sq.*; treatment of passers-by at harvest in, vii. 229 *sq.*; sticks or stones piled on graves of suicides in, ix. 17; hills called the Blocksberg in, x. 171 *n.*[3]

Pometia sacked by the Romans, i. 22

Pommerol, Dr., on Granno and Grannus, x. 112

Pomona and Vertumnus, vi. 235 *n.*[6]

Pomos of California, their expulsion of devils, ix. 170 *sq.*

Pompeii, plan of labyrinth at, iv. 76

Pompey the Great beheads the last king Cinyras of Byblus, v. 27

Pompilia, mother of Ancus Martius, ii. 270 *n.*[4]

Ponape, one of the Caroline Islands, treatment of the navel-string in, i. 184 *sq.*; special terms used with reference to persons of the blood royal in, i. 401 *n.*[8]; kings and viziers in, iii. 25; the king of, his long hair, iii. 259; changes of vocabulary caused by fear of naming the dead in, iii. 362

Pond, G. H., on ritual of death and resurrection among the Dacotas, xi. 269

Pondomisi, a Bantu tribe of South Africa, attribute drought to wrath of dead chief, vi. 177

Pondos, of South Africa, their festival of new fruits, viii. 66 *sq.*

Pongal feast, in the Madras Presidency, vii. 244. *See* Pongol

Pongau district of Salzburg, the *Perchten* maskers in, ix. 244

Pongol, a family festival among the Hindoos of Southern India, viii. 56; Feast of Ingathering in Southern India, fires kindled at, xi. 1, 16

Ponnani River, near Calicut, iv. 49

Pons Sublicius at Rome built without iron, iii. 230

Pont à Mousson, calf killed at harvest at, vii. 290

Pontarlier, Eve of Twelfth Day in, ix. 316

Pontaven in Finistère, effigy (of Carnival)

thrown into the sea on Ash Wednesday at, iv. 230

Pontesbury, in Shropshire, the Yule log at, x. 257

Pontifex Maximus at Rome, his relation to the Vestals, ii. 228

Pontiff of Zela in Pontus, ix. 370, 372

Pontiffs, the Roman, their mismanagement of the Julian calendar, vi. 93 *n*.[1] ; celebrated the marriage of Orcus, vi. 231 ; regulate Roman calendar, vii. 83

—— and Vestals threw puppets into the Tiber at Rome, viii. 107

Pontifical law at Rome, iii. 391 *n*.[1]

Pontus, the Mosyni or Mosynoeci of, iii. 124 ; sacred prostitution in, v. 39, 58 ; rapid spread of Christianity in, ix. 420 *sq.*

Poona, rain-making at, i. 275 ; incarnation of elephant-headed god at, i. 405

Poor Man, name applied to the corn-spirit after harvest, vii. 231

—— Old Woman, corn left on field for, vii. 231 *sq.*

—— Woman, name applied to the corn-spirit after harvest, vii. 231

Popayan, district of Colombia, the Indians of, will not kill deer, viii. 286

Pope or Patriarch of Fools, elected on St. Stephen's Day, ix. 334

Popinjay, shooting at a, x. 194

Popish Kingdome, The, of Thomas Kirchmeyer, x. 125 *sq.*, 162

Poplar in magic, i. 145 ; burned on St. Peter's Day, ii. 141

——, black, mistletoe on, xi. 318 *n*.[6]

——, the silver, used to ban fiends, ii. 336

——, the white, at Olympia, a substitute for the oak, ii. 220 ; used in sacrificing to Zeus at Olympia, xi. 90 *n*.[1], 91 *n*.[7]

Poplar-wood used to kindle need-fire, x. 282

Poplars burnt on Shrove Tuesday, iv. 224 *n*.[1]

Poppies as symbols of Demeter, vii. 43 *sq.*

Poppy, the, cultivated for opium, vii. 242

Populonia, an unmarried Roman goddess, vi. 231

Populus trichocarpa in homoeopathic magic, i. 145

Porcupine, a Bechuana totem, viii. 164 *sq.* ; respected by some Indians, viii. 243 ; transmigration of sinner into, viii. 299 ; as charm to ensure women an easy delivery, x. 49

Pork forbidden to enchanters of crops, vii. 100 *sq.* ; not eaten by field labourers, viii. 33 ; taboo as to entering a sanctuary after eating, viii. 85 ;

reason for not eating, viii. 296. *See also* Pig's flesh *and* Swine's flesh

Porphyry, on a human god in Egypt, i. 390 ; on the souls of trees, ii. 12 ; on Phoenician sacrifices of children, iv. 167, 179 ; on the *Bouphonia,* viii. 5 *n*.[1] ; on the homoeopathic diet of diviners, viii. 143 *n*.[7] ; on demons, ix. 104

Porridge smeared on body as a purification, iii. 176

Port Charlotte in Islay, vii. 166 ; stone used in cure for toothache near, ix. 62

—— Darwin, in Australia, conception in women not regarded as a direct result of cohabitation among the tribes about, v. 103

—— Lincoln tribe of South Australia, prohibition to mention the names of the dead in, iii. 365 ; their superstition as to lizards, xi. 216 *sq.*

—— Moresby, in British New Guinea, ix. 84 ; taboos as to trading voyages at, iii. 203 ; homoeopathic magic of a flesh diet at, viii. 145

—— Stephens (Stevens), in New South Wales, burial at flood tide among the natives at, i. 168 ; medicine-men drive away rain at, i. 253

Porta Capena at Rome, i. 18, ii. 185, v. 273

Porta Querquetulana at Rome, ii. 185 *n*.[3]

—— *Triumphalis* at Rome, xi. 195

Porto Novo, the negroes of, their beliefs and customs concerning twins, i. 265 ; the King of Night at, ii. 23 *sq.* ; in Guinea, precaution taken by executioner against the ghosts of his victims at, iii. 171 ; on the Slave Coast, vicarious human sacrifices at, iv. 117 ; annual expulsion of demons at, ix. 205

Portrait statues, external souls of Egyptian kings deposited in, xi. 157

Portraits, souls in, iii. 96 *sqq.* ; supposed dangers of, iii. 96 *sqq.*

Portreath, sacrifice of a calf near, to cure disease of cows and horses, x. 301

Portugal, belief as to death at ebb-tide in, i. 167 *sq.*

Poseideon, an Attic month, vii. 62

Poseidon, sanctuary of, at Troezen, i. 27 ; mated with Artemis, i. 36 ; bull sacrificed to, i. 46 ; represented as father of Demetrius Poliorcetes, i. 391 ; identified with Erechtheus, iv. 87 ; the Establisher or Securer, v. 195 *sq.* ; the earthquake god, v. 195, 202 *sq.* ; his intrigue with Demeter, v. 280, viii. 21 ; first-fruits sacrificed to, viii. 133 ; cake with twelve knobs offered to, ix. 351 ; priest of, uses a white umbrella, x. 20 *n.*[1] ; makes Pterelaus immortal, xi. 103

Posidonius, ancient Greek traveller in Gaul, on indifference of Celts to death, iv. 142 ; on human sacrifices among the Celts, xi. 32

Poso, a district of Central Celebes, inspired priestesses in, i. 379 *sq.* ; ears of rice fed like children in, ii. 29 ; belief as to tree-demons in, ii. 35 ; ceremony performed by farmer's wife in, when the rice crop is not thriving, ii. 104 ; stranger taken for a spirit in, vii. 236 ; jawbones of deer and wild pigs propitiated by hunters in, viii. 244 *sq.* ; custom at the working of iron in, xi. 154

——, the Alfoors of, offer puppets to demons, iii. 62 ; will not pronounce their own names, iii. 332 ; may not pronounce the names of their fathers, mothers, grandparents, and parents-in-law, iii. 340 ; forbidden to use ordinary language in harvest-field, iii. 411 ; ask riddles while watching the crops, vii. 194 ; think that every man has three souls, xi. 222

Possession by the spirits of dead kings or chiefs, iv. 25 *sq.*, vi. 192 *sq.* ; of priest or priestess by a divine spirit, v. 66, 68 *sq.*, 72 *sqq.* ; by an evil spirit, cured by passing through a red-hot chain, xi. 186

Posterli, annual expulsion of, at Entlebuch in Switzerland, ix. 214

Pot in ashes, imprint of, effaced from superstitious motives, i. 214

Potala Hill at Lhasa, ix. 197

——, palace of the Dalai Lama at Lhasa, i. 412 *n.*[1]

Potato-dog, said to be killed at end of digging the potatoes, vii. 272 *sq.*

—— -mother, among the Indians of Peru, vii. 172, 173 *n.*

—— -wolf, said to be caught in the last potatoes, vii. 271 ; name given to woman who gathers the last potatoes, vii. 274

Potatoes, magical stones for the increase of, i. 162 ; fertilized by a fairy banner, i. 368 ; customs at eating new, viii. 50, 51

Potawatomi Indians, their respect for rattlesnakes, viii. 218 ; their women secluded at menstruation, x. 89

Potlatch, distribution of property, among the Carrier Indians, xi. 274

Potniae in Boeotia, goat substituted for child as victim in rites of Dionysus at, iv. 166 *n.*[1], vii. 24 ; priest of Dionysus killed at, vi. 99 *n.*[1]

Potrimpo, old Prussian god, his priest bound to sleep on bare earth for three nights before sacrificing, ii. 248

Pots of basil on St. John's Day in Sicily, v. 245

—— used by girls at puberty broken, x. 61, 69. *See also* Vessels

Potter in Southern India, custom observed by a, v. 191 *n.*[2]

Potters in Uganda bake their pots when the moon is waxing, vi. 135

Pottery, primitive, employed in Roman ritual, ii. 202 *sqq.* ; superstitions as to the making of, among the Yuracares of Bolivia and the Ba-Ronga of South Africa, ii. 204 *sq.*

Pouilly, near Dijon, ox killed on harvest-field at, vii. 290

Poverty, annual expulsion of, ix. 144 *sq.*

Powder, magic, rubbed into wounds for purpose of inoculation, viii. 159

Powers, Stephen, on the secrecy of personal names among the Californian Indians, iii. 326 ; on the expulsion of devils among the Pomos of California, ix. 170 *sq.*

Powers, extraordinary, ascribed to first-born children, x. 295

Powhatan, an assumed Indian name, iii. 318

Požega district of Slavonia, need-fire in, x. 282

Prabat, in Siam, Footprint of Buddha at, iii. 275

Practical man, the plain, i. 243

Praeneste, Fortuna Primigenia, goddess of, vi. 234 ; founded by Caeculus, ii. 197, vi. 235

Praetorius, Matthaeus, on the old Lithuanian god Pergrubius, ii. 347 *n.*[1] ; his work on old Lithuanian customs, viii. 50 *n.*[1]

Praetors, the consuls at first called, ii. 291 *n.*[1]

Prague, pieces of the May-tree burned in the district of, ii. 71 ; the Feast of All Souls in, vi. 73

Prajapati, the creator, his mystic sacrifice in the daily ritual of the Brahmans, ix. 411

Pramantha, the upper part of the Brahman fire-drill, ii. 249

Prättigau in Switzerland, Lenten fire-custom at, x. 119

Pratz, Le Page du, on the festival of new corn among the Natchez Indians, viii. 77 *sqq.*

Prauss, in Silesia, race of girls at harvest at, vii. 76

Prayer to the *tulasi* plant, ii. 26 ; the Roman shepherd's, ii. 327 ; to Per-

grubius, ii. 347; the materialization of, ix. 22 *n.*[2]; at sowing, ix. 138
Prayer, the Place of, viii. 113
—— and spell, vii. 105
Prayers to the sun, i. 72, 312; for rain to ancestors, i. 285, 286, 287, 346; for rain to skulls of racoons, i. 288; for rain to dragon, i. 291 *sq.*; to king's ancestors, i. 352; to sunflower roots, ii. 13; for rain to the spirit who controls the rain, ii. 46; to Zeus for rain, ii. 359; to Jupiter for rain, ii. 362; to Thunder, ii. 367 *sq.*; to an oak, ii. 372; for rain to Nyakang, iv. 20; to dead ancestors, vi. 175 *sq.*, 178 *sq.*, 183 *sq.*; to dead kings, vi. 192; for rain at Eleusis, vii. 69; to the spirits of the dead, viii. 112, 113, 124 *sq.*; to dead animals, viii. 184, 197, 224, 225, 226, 235, 236, 243, 253, 293; to crocodile goddess, viii. 212; to shark-idol, viii. 292; at cairns or heaps of sticks or leaves, ix. 26, 28, 29 *sq.*; of adolescent girls to the Dawn of Day, x. 50 *sq.*, 53, 98 *n.*[1]; to the Rain-makers up aloft, x. 133; to ancestral spirits, xi. 243
Preachers to fish, viii. 250 *sq.*
Precautions against witches on May Day, ii. 52 *sqq.*, ix. 267; against witches on St. George's Day, ii. 354 *sqq.*; against witches on Walpurgis Night (Eve of May Day), ix. 158 *sqq.*; against witches during the Twelve Days, ix. 164 *sq.*; against witches on Midsummer Eve, xi. 73 *sqq.*
Precious stones, homoeopathic magic of, i. 164 *sq.*
Pre-existence of the human soul, belief in the, i. 104
Preference for a violent death, iv. 9 *sqq.*
Pregnancy, ceremony in seventh month of, i. 72 *sq.*; husband's hair kept unshorn during wife's, iii. 261; conduct of husband during wife's, iii. 294, 295; superstitions as to knots during wife's, iii. 294 *sq.*; funeral rites performed for a father in the fifth month of his wife's, iv. 189; causes of, unknown, v. 92 *sq.*, 106 *sq.*; Australian beliefs as to the causes of, v. 99 *sqq.*
Pregnant cows sacrificed to ensure fertility, i. 141; sacrificed to the Earth goddess, ii. 229
—— women, forbidden to spin or twist ropes, i. 114; not to loiter in the doorways of houses where there are, i. 114; employed to fertilize crops and fruit-trees, i. 140 *sq.*, ii. 101; taboos on, i. 141 *n.*[1]; their superstitions about shadows, iii. 82 *sq.*; carry *nim* leaves or iron to scare evil spirits,

iii. 234; may not sew or use sharp instruments, iii. 238; loosen their hair, iii. 311; mode of protecting them against dangerous spirits, viii. 102 *sq.*; fowls used to divert evil spirits from, ix. 31
Preller, L., on the marriage of Dionysus and Ariadne, ii. 138
Premature birth, Esquimau ideas as to, iii. 152; to be announced publicly, iii. 213. *See* Miscarriage
Presages as to shadows on St. Sylvester's day, iii. 88
Presteign in Radnorshire, the tug-of-war at, ix. 182 *sq.*
Pretence made by reapers of mowing down visiters to the harvest-field, vii. 229 *sq.*; of throwing people into fire, x. 110, 148, 186, xi. 25
—— of human sacrifices substituted for the reality, iv. 214 *sqq.*; at Christmas, vii. 302
Pretenders to divinity among Christians, i. 407 *sqq.*
Priapus, image of, at need-fire, x. 286
Pricking patient with needles to expel demons of disease, iii. 106
Priene, Panionian festival at, i. 46
Priest drenched with water as a rain-charm, i. 277, ii. 77; rolled on fields as fertility charm, ii. 103; chief acting as, ii. 215 *sqq.*, viii. 126; brings back lost soul in a cloth, iii. 48, 64; recovers lost souls from the sun-god, iii. 64; conjures lost soul into a cup, iii. 67; catches the spirit of a god in a snare, iii. 69; inspired by spirit of dead king and giving oracles in his name, iv. 200 *sq.*; sows and plucks the first rice, viii. 54; the corpse-praying, ix. 45. *See also* Priests *and* High priest
—— of Aricia and the Golden Bough, x. i.
—— of Diana at Nemi, i. 8 *sqq.*; at Aricia, the King of the Wood, perhaps personified Jupiter, xi. 302 *sq.*
—— of Dionysus at the Agrionia, iv. 163
—— of Earth, taboos observed by the, x. 4
—— and magician, their antagonism, i. 226
—— of Nemi, i. 8 *sqq.*, 40, 41, ii. 376, 378, 386, 387, xi. 315. *See also* King of the Wood
—— of Poseidon, x. 20 *n.*[1]
—— of the Sun, x. 20 *n.*[1]
—— of Zeus on Mount Lycaeus, ii. 359
Priestess of the holy fire among the Herero, ii. 215; identified with goddess, v. 219; head of the State under a system of mother-kin, vi. 203; of Athena, x. 20 *n.*[1]
Priestesses, inspired, i. 379 *sq.*, 381 *sq.*; as physicians, bring back lost souls, iii. 53 *sq.*; more important than priests,

v. 45, 46 ; of Perasian Artemis walk over fire, v. 115, 168 ; beat corpse to exorcize a demon, ix. 260 ; not allowed to step on ground, x. 5

Priestesses, virgin, in the island of Sena, ii. 241 *n.*[1]; of fire in Peru, ii. 243 *sq.* ; of fire in Mexico, ii. 245 ; of fire in Yucatan, ii. 245 *sq.*

Priesthood of Aphrodite at Paphos, v. 43 ; vacated on death of priest's wife, v. 45 ; of Hercules at Tarsus, v. 143

Priestly dynasties of Asia Minor, v. 140 *sq.*

—— functions exercised by chiefs in New Britain, i. 340 ; gradually acquired by kings, i. 372

—— king and queen personating god and goddess, v. 45

—— kings, i. 44 *sqq.*, v. 42, 43 ; of Sheba, iii. 125 ; of the Nubas, iii. 132 ; of Olba, v. 143 *sqq.*, 161 ; Adonis personated by, v. 223 *sqq.*

Priests, magical powers attributed to priests by French peasants, i. 231-233 ; inspired by gods in the Southern Pacific, i. 377 *sq.* ; ancient Egyptian, recover lost souls, iii. 68 ; influence wielded by, iii. 107 ; to be shaved with bronze, iii. 226 ; their hair unshorn, iii. 259, 260 ; foods tabooed to, iii. 291 ; personate gods, v. 45, 46 *sqq.*, ix. 287 ; tattoo-marks of, v. 74 *n.*[4]; not allowed to be widowers, vi. 227 *sqq.* ; dressed as women, v. 253 *sqq.* ; firstfruits belong to, viii. 125 ; of sharks cover their bodies with the appearance of scales, viii. 292 ; sacrifice human victims, ix. 279, 280 *sq.*, 284, 286, 287, 290, 292, 294, 298, 301 ; expected to pass through fire, xi. 2, 5, 8, 9, 14

—— of Astarte, kings as, v. 26

—— of Attis, the emasculated, v. 265, 266

——, Jewish, their rule as to the pollution of death, vi. 230

—— of Tetzcatlipoca, viii. 165

—— of Zeus at the Corycian cave, v. 145, 155

Primitive ritual, marks of, vii. 169

—— thought, its vagueness and inconsistency, xi. 301 *sq.*

Primroses on threshold as a charm against witches, ii. 52

Prince Sunless, x. 21

Prince of Wales Islands, Torres Strait, the Kowraregas of, iii. 346, 358 *sq.* ; natives of, their belief as to falling stars, iv. 64 *sq.* ; their treatment of girls at puberty in, x. 40

Princess royal, ceremonies at the puberty of a, x. 29, 30 *sq.*

Princesses married to foreigners or men of low birth, ii. 274 *sqq.*; licence accorded to, in Loango, ii. 276 *sq.*

Prisoner condemned to death, treated as king for five days, iv. 113 *sq.*, ix. 355

Prisoners shaved and their shorn hair kept as security for their good behaviour, iii. 273 ; released at festivals, iii. 316

Private magic, i. 214 *sq.*

Privilege of the chapter of Rouen Cathedral to pardon a criminal once a year, ii. 165

Proa, demons of sickness expelled in a, ix. 185 *sqq.* ; diseases sent away in a, ix. 199 *sq. See also* Ship

Proarcturia, a Greek festival, vii. 51

Procession to the Almo in the rites of Attis, v. 273 ; with lighted tar-barrels on Christmas Eve at Lerwick, x. 268

Processions with ships perhaps raincharms, i. 251 *n.*[3]; for rain in Sicily, i. 300 ; carved on rocks at Boghaz-Keui, v. 129 *sqq.* ; in honour of Adonis, v. 224 *sq.*, 227 *n.*, 236 *n.*[1] ; with bears from house to house, viii. 192 ; with sacred animals, viii. 316 *sqq.* ; of men disguised as animals, viii. 325 *sqq.* ; for the expulsion of demons, ix. 117, 233 ; of monks and maskers at the Tibetan New Year, ix. 203 ; of mummers in Salzburg and the Tyrol, ix. 240, 242 *sqq.*; to drive away demons of infertility, ix. 245 ; bell-ringing, at the Carnival, ix. 247 ; of maskers, W. Mannhardt on, ix. 250 ; with lighted torches through fields, gardens, orchards, etc., x. 107 *sq.*, 110 *sqq.*, 113 *sqq.*, 141, 179, 233 *sq.*, 266, 339 *sq.* ; on Corpus Christi Day, x. 165 ; to the Midsummer bonfires, x. 184, 185, 187, 188, 191, 192, 193 ; across fiery furnaces, xi. 4 *sqq.* ; of giants (effigies) at popular festivals in Europe, xi. 33 *sqq.*

—— and dances in honour of the dead, viii. 111

Proclus on Dionysus, vii. 13

Procopius, on the custom of putting the sick and old to death among the Heruli, iv. 14 ; on the god of lightning of the Slavs, ii. 365 ; on the annual disappearance of the sun for forty days in Thule, ix. 125 *n.*[1]

Procreation, savage ignorance of the causes of, v. 106 *sq.*

Procreative virtue attributed to fire, ii. 233

Procris, her incest with her father Erechtheus, v. 44

Proculus, Julius, bids the Romans worship Romulus as a god, ii. 182

Proerosia, "Before the Ploughing," a Greek festival of Demeter, vii. 50 *sqq.*, 60, 108

Profligacy at rites designed to promote the fertility of trees and plants, ii. 97, 104 ; of human sexes supposed to quicken the earth, v. 48 ; at Holi festival in India, xi. 2

Progress, the magician's, i. 214 *sqq.*; intellectual, dependent on economic progress, i. 218; industrial and political, i. 421

Prohibited degrees of kinship, the system of, perhaps based historically on superstition, ii. 117

Promathion's *History of Italy*, ii. 196, 197

Prometheus, his theft of fire, ii. 260

Propertius, on the Vestals, i. 18 *n.*[5] ; on the throwing of stones at a grave, ix. 19 *sq.*

Property, rules as to the inheritance of, under mother-kin, vi. 203 *n.*[1] ; landed, combined with mother-kin tends to increase the social importance of women, vi. 209

Prophecy, Hebrew, distinctive character of, v. 75 ; spirit of, acquired by eating certain food, viii. 143 ; the Norse Sibyl's, x. 102 *sq.*

Prophet regarded as madman, v. 77. *See also* Prophets

Prophetess of Apollo at Patara, ii. 135

Prophetesses inspired by dead chiefs, vi. 192 *sq.* ; inspired by gods, vi. 207

Prophetic inspiration through the spirits of dead kings and chiefs, iv. 200 *sq.*, vi. 171, 172, 192 *sq.* ; under the influence of music, v. 52 *sq.*, 54 *sq.*, 74

—— marks on body, v. 74

—— powers conferred by certain springs, ii. 172

—— water drunk on St. John's Eve, v. 247

Prophets in relation to *ḳedeshim*, v. 76 ; or mediums inspired by the ghosts of dead kings, iv. 200 *sq.*, vi. 171, 172

—— Hebrew, their ethical religion, i. 223 ; on the burnt sacrifice of children, iv. 169 *n.*[3] ; their resemblance to those of Africa, v. 74 *sq.*

—— of Israel, their religious and moral reform, v. 24 *sq.*

Propitiation essential to religion, i. 222 ; of the souls of the slain, iii. 166 ; of spirits of slain animals, iii. 190, 204 *sq.* ; of ancestors, iii. 197, v. 46 ; of the spirits of plants before partaking of the fruits, viii. 82 *sq.* ; of wild animals by hunters, viii. 204 *sqq.* ; of vermin by farmers, viii. 274 *sqq.* ; of ancestral spirits, ix. 86 ; of demons, ix. 93, 94, 96, 100

Proserpine River in Queensland, the aborigines of the, their dread of women's cut hair, iii. 282 ; the Kia

Blacks of the, seclusion of girls at puberty among the, x. 39

Prosopis spicigera, used in kindling fire by friction, ii. 248, 249, 250 *n.*

Prostitution before marriage, practice of, ii. 282, 285, 287

——, sacred, before marriage, in Western Asia, v. 36 *sqq.* ; suggested origin of, v. 39 *sqq.*; practised for the sake of the crops, v. 39 *n.*[3] ; in Western Asia, alternative theory of, v. 57 *sqq.* ; in India, v. 61 *sqq.*; in Africa, v. 65 *sqq.*

—— of unmarried girls in the Pelew Islands, vi. 264 *sq.* ; in Yap, one of the Caroline Islands, vi. 265 *sq.*

Prothero, G. W., as to a May-pole, ii. 71 *n.*[1]; on the passage of sick women through a church window, xi. 190 *n.*[3]

Provence, priests thought to possess the power of averting storms in, i. 232 ; rain-making by means of images of saints in, i. 307 ; May-trees in, ii. 69 ; Mayos on May Day in, ii. 80 ; mock execution of Caramantran on Ash Wednesday in, iv. 227 ; bathing at Midsummer in, v. 248 ; Midsummer fires in, x. 193 *sq.* ; the Yule log in, x. 249 *sqq.*

Prpats, boy employed in rain-making ceremony in Dalmatia, i. 274

Prporushe, young men employed in a rain-making ceremony in Dalmatia, i. 274

Prunus padus, L., branches of, used to avert evil influences, ii. 344

Prussia, contagious magic of clothes in, i. 206 *sq.* ; customs at driving the herds out to pasture for the first time in, ii. 340 *sq.* ; wolves not to be called by their proper name during December in, iii. 396; harvest customs in, v. 238, vii. 136, 137, 139, 150 *sq.*, 209, 219, 280, 281 *sq.*, 289, 292 ; divination at Midsummer in, v. 252 *sq.* ; women's race at close of rye-harvest in, vii. 76 *sq.* ; the Corn-goat in, vii. 281 *sq.* ; the Bull at reaping in, vii. 292 ; " Easter Smacks " in, ix. 268 ; custom before first ploughing in spring in, x. 18 ; Midsummer fires in, x. 176 *sq.* ; mullein gathered at Midsummer in, xi. 63 *sq.* ; witches' Sabbath in, xi. 74. *See also* Prussians

——, Eastern, the Kurs of, their custom at sowing, i. 137 ; dances of girls on Shrove Tuesday in, i. 138 *sq.* ; "to chase out the Hare" at harvest in, vii. 280 ; herbs gathered at Midsummer in, xi. 48 *sq.*; divination by flowers on Midsummer Eve in, xi. 53, 61 ; belief as to mistletoe growing on a thorn in, xi. 291 *n.*[3]

Prussia, West, pretence of birth of child on harvest-field in, vii. 150 *sq.*, 209 ; sticks or stones piled on graves of suicides in, ix. 17

Prussian rulers, formerly burnt, ix. 391

Prussians, the heathen, sacrificed to Pergrubius on St. George's Day, ii. 347

——, the old, their worship of trees, ii. 43 ; their funeral feasts, iii. 238 ; supreme ruler of, iv. 41 *sq.*; their prayers and offerings for the flax crop, iv. 156 ; their custom at sowing, vii. 288 ; their offerings of first-fruits, viii. 133 ; their worship of serpents, xi. 43 *n.*[3]

Pruyssenaere, E. de, on the privations of the Dinka in the dry season, iv. 30 *n.*[1] ; on the reverence of the Dinka for their cattle, viii. 38 *sq.*

Prytaneum at Athens, ii. 137, vii. 32 ; perpetual fire in the, ii. 260

Psalmist (cvi. 35-38) on Hebrew idolatry, iv. 168 *sq.*

Psammetichus I., king of Egypt, dedicates his daughter to Ammon, ii. 134

Pshaws of the Caucasus, their rain-charm, i. 282 ; taboos observed by an annual official among the, iii. 292 *sq.*

Pskov, Government of, holy oak on the borders of, ii. 371 *sq.*

Psoloeis, the, at Orchomenus, iv. 163, 164

Psylli, a Snake clan, make war on the south wind, i. 331 ; expose their infants to snakes, viii. 174 *sq.*

Ptarmigans and ducks, dramatic contest of the, among the Esquimaux, iv. 259

Pterelaus and his golden hair, xi. 103

Pteria, captured by Croesus, v. 128

Ptolemy Auletes, king of Egypt, offered by Cato the priesthood of Aphrodite at Paphos, v. 43

Ptolemy and Berenice, annual festival in honour of, vi. 35 *n.*[2]

Ptolemy I. and Serapis, vi. 119 *n.*

—— II., king of Egypt, iv. 15

—— III. Euergetes, his attempt to correct the vague Egyptian year by intercalation, vi. 27

—— V. on the Rosetta Stone, vi. 152 *n.*

Ptolemy Soter, v. 264 *n.*[4]

Puberty, girls' hair torn out at, iii. 282 ; ceremonial pollution of girl at, viii. 268 ; girls secluded at, x. 22 *sqq.* ; fast and dream at, xi. 222 *n.*[5] ; pretence of killing the novice and bringing him to life again during initiatory rites at, xi. 225 *sqq.*

Public expulsion of evils, ix. 109 *sqq.*

—— magic, i. 215

Public scapegoats, ix. 170 *sqq.*

Pueblo Indians of Arizona and New Mexico, their annual festival of the dead, vi. 54 ; their observation of the Pleiades, vii. 312 ; use of bull-roarers among the, xi. 230 *n.*, 231

Puḥru, "assembly," ix. 361

Puithiam, sorcerer, among the Lushais, ix. 94

Pul, an astrologer, vii. 125 *sq.*

Pulayars of Travancore, their seclusion of girls at puberty, x. 69

Pulling each other's hair, a Lithuanian sacrificial custom, viii. 50 *sq.*

Pulque, Mexican wine made from aloes, iii. 249, 250 *n.*[1] ; continence at brewing, iii. 201 *sq.*

Pulse cultivated in Bengal, vii. 123

Pulverbatch, in Shropshire, the Yule log at, x. 257 ; belief in the bloom of the oak on Midsummer Eve at, xi. 292

Pumi-yathon, king of Citium and Idalium, v. 50

Pumpkin, external soul in a, xi. 105

Puna Indians add stones to cairns in the Andes, ix. 9

Punchkin and the parrot, story of, xi. 97 *sq.*, 215, 220

Punjaub, rain-making in the, i. 278 ; General Nicholson worshipped in his lifetime in the, i. 404 ; human sacrifices to cedar-tree in the, ii. 17 ; no grass or green thing to be cut in the, till after the festival of the ripening grain, ii. 49 *n.*[3] ; wells resorted to by barren women for the sake of offspring in the, ii. 160 ; belief as to tattooing in the, iii. 30 ; belief as to the shadow of a pregnant woman in the, iii. 83 ; belief among the Hindoos of the, as to length of residence in heaven, iv. 67 ; belief as to a man's star in the, iv. 68 ; belief in the reincarnation of infants in the, v. 94 ; children at birth placed in winnowing-fans in the, vii. 7 ; the Mother-cotton in the, vii. 178 ; customs as to the first-fruits of sugar and cotton in the, viii. 119 ; worship of snakes in the, viii. 316 *sq.* ; the Snake tribe in the, viii. 316, 317 ; human scapegoats in the, ix. 196 ; supernatural power ascribed to the first-born in the, x. 295 ; passing unlucky children through narrow openings in the, xi. 190

Puplem, general council, among the Indians of San Juan Capistrano, vii. 125

Puppet made of branches representing the tree-spirit, ducked in water, ii. 75, 76 ; substituted for human victim, v. 219 *sq.* ; made out of last sheaf, vii.

137, 138, 231 ; at threshing, vii. 148, 149 ; at harvest, vii. 150 ; representing the corn-spirit, vii. 224

Puppet-shows as a rain-charm, i. 301 *n.*

Puppets or dolls employed for the restoration of souls to their bodies, iii. 53 *sqq.*, 62 *sqq.* ; of rushes thrown into the Tiber, viii. 107 ; used to attract demons of sickness from living patients, ix. 187.   *See also* Dolls, Effigies, Images

Puppies, red-haired, sacrificed by the Romans to the Dog-star, vii. 261, viii. 34

Puppy, blind, stomachic complaint transferred to a, ix. 50

Pur in the sense of "lot," ix. 361

Purest person cuts the last corn, vii. 158

Purgation, ceremonial, before partaking of new fruits, viii. 72 *n.*², 73, 75 *sq.*, 76, 83, 90.   *See also* Purification

Purgatory, popular beliefs as to souls in, iv. 66, 67

Purge as mode of ceremonial purification, iii. 175

Purification by passing between the pieces of a sacrificial victim, i. 289 *n.*⁴ ; by pig's blood, ii. 107, 108, 109, v. 299 *n.*², ix. 262 ; of hunting dogs and hunters, ii. 125 ; by fire, ii. 327, 329, v. 115 *n.*¹, 179 *sqq.*, x. 296, xi. 16 *sqq.* ; of city, iii. 188 ; of hunters and fishers, iii. 190 *sq.* ; of moral guilt by physical agencies, iii. 217 *sq.* ; by cutting the hair, iii. 283 *sqq.* ; by swinging, iv. 282 *sq.* ; things used in, how disposed of, vii. 9 ; after contact with a pig, viii. 24 ; by washing, ceremonies of, viii. 27 *sq.* ; before partaking of new fruits, viii. 59, 60, 63, 69 *sq.*, 71, 73, 75 *sq.*, 82, 83, 135 ; by emetics, viii. 73, 75 *sq.*, 83 *sq.* ; for slaughter of a serpent, viii. 219 *sq.* ; by leaping through fire, viii. 249 ; before eating the first salmon, viii. 253 ; by bathing or washing, ix. 3 *sq.* ; by means of stone-throwing, ix. 23 *sqq.* ; religious, intended to keep off demons, ix. 104 *sq.* ; of mourners intended to protect them from the spirits of the dead, ix. 105 *n.*¹ ; by standing on sacrificed human victim, ix. 218 ; by beating, ix. 262, x. 61, 64 *sqq.* ; by stinging with ants, x. 61 *sqq.* ; after a death, xi. 178 ; by passing under a yoke, xi. 193 *sqq. See also* Purificatory *and* Expiation

———, ancient Greek, ritual of, iii. 312 ; by laurel and pig's blood, ix. 262

——— of Apollo at Tempe, iv. 81, vi. 240 *sq.*

Purification, Chinese ceremonies of, in spring and autumn, ix. 213 *n.*¹

———, Feast of the (Candlemas), ix. 332

——— festival among the Cherokee Indians, ix. 128

———, the Great, a Japanese ceremony, ix. 213 *n.*¹

——— of manslayers, i. 26, iii. 165 *sqq.*, viii. 148 *sq.*, ix. 262 ; intended to rid them of the ghosts of the slain, iii. 186 *sq.*

——— of the matricide, Orestes, i. 26, ix. 262

——— of Pimas after slaying Apaches, iii. 182 *sqq.*

Purificatory ceremonies at reception of strangers, iii. 102 *sqq.* ; on return from a journey, iii. 111 *sqq.* ; after a battle, vi. 251 *sq.*

——— rites, for sexual crimes, ii. 107 *sqq.*, 115, 116 ; designed to raise a barrier against evil spirits, ii. 128

——— theory of the fires of the firefestivals, x. 329 *sq.*, 341, xi. 16 *sqq.* ; more probable than the solar theory, x. 346

Purim, in relation to Zakmuk, ix. 359 *sqq.* ; the Jewish festival of, ix. 360 *sqq.* ; in relation to the Sacaea, ix. 362 *sqq.* ; custom of burning effigies of Haman at, ix. 392 *sqq.* ; compared to the Carnival, ix. 394 ; its relation to Persia, ix. 401 *sqq.*

Purity, ceremonial, observed by incensegatherers in ancient Arabia, ii. 106 *sq.* ; observed in war, iii. 157.   *See also* Chastity *and* Continence

Purple loosestrife (*Lythrum salicaria*) gathered at Midsummer, xi. 65

Purra or *poro*, secret society in Sierra Leone, xi. 260 *sq.*

Puruha, a province of Quito, sacrifice of first-born children among the Indians of, iv. 185

Pururavas and Urvasi, ancient Indian story of, ii. 250, iv. 131

Purushu, great primordial giant, in the Rig Veda, ix. 410

Pûs, an Indian month, ix. 230

Putanges, canton of, in Normandy, pretence of tying up landowner in last sheaf at, vii. 226

Puttenham, George, on the Midsummer giants, xi. 36 *sq.*

Puwe-wai, god of the rice-fields, in Poso, ii. 104

Puy-de-Dôme, saying as to binder and reaper in, vii. 292

Puyallup Indians, taboo on the names of the dead among the, iii. 365

Pyanepsia, an Attic festival, vii. 52

Pyanepsion, Attic month (October), vi. 41, vii. 52 ; the season of the autumn sowing, vii. 45 *sq.*, 116

Pygmalion, king of Citium and Idalium in Cyprus, v. 50

——, king of Cyprus, father-in-law of Cinyras, v. 41, 49; his love for an image of Aphrodite, v. 49 *sq.*

——, king of Tyre, v. 50

Pygmies of Central Africa said not to know how to kindle fire, ii. 255; their continence before hunting, iii. 197; burn their cut hair, iii. 282

Pylos, burning the Carnival at, iv. 232 *sq.*

Pymaton of Citium, v. 50 *n.*[2]

Pyramid of King Pepi the First, ii. 4 *n.*[1]

Pyramid Texts, vi. 4 *sqq.*, 9 *n.*; intended to ensure the life of dead Egyptian kings, vi. 4 *sq.*; Osiris and the sycamore in the, vi. 110; the mention of Khenti-Amenti in the, vi. 198 *n.*[2]

Pyramids at Sakkara, inscriptions on the, vi. 4; Egyptian texts of the, ix. 340, 341 *n.*[1]

Pyramus, river in Cilicia, v. 165, 167, 173

Pyre at festivals of Hercules, v. 116; at Tarsus, v. 126; of dead kings at Jerusalem, v. 177 *sq.*; traditional death of Asiatic kings and heroes on a, ix. 387, 388, 389 *sqq.*

—— or Torch, name of great festival at the Syrian Hierapolis, v. 146, ix. 392

Pyrenees, prehistoric cave-paintings in the, i. 87 *n.*[1]; tree burned on Midsummer Eve in the, ii. 141; Midsummer fires in the French, x. 193

Pyrites, iron, fire made by means of, ii. 258

Pythagoras, his maxim about footprints, i. 211; his maxim as to bodily impressions on bed-clothes, i. 213; superstitious nature of the maxims attributed to, i. 213 *sq.*, iii. 314 *n.*[2]; his epitaph on the tomb of Apollo at Delphi, iv. 4; his reincarnations, viii. 263, 300; his doctrine of transmigration, viii. 300, 301; his saying as to swallows, ix. 35 *n.*[3]

Pythaists at Athens, their observation of lightning and their sacrifices at Delphi, i. 33

Pythian games at Delphi, iv. 80 *sq.*; originally identical with the Festival of Crowning, iv. 80, vi. 242 *n.*[1]; crown of oak leaves at first the prize in the, iv. 80; celebrated in honour of the dragon or Python, iv. 80, 93; originally celebrated every eight years, iv. 80, vii. 80, 84; their period, vi. 242 *n.*[1]

Python at Delphi, the Pythian games celebrated in his honour, iv. 93

——, sacred, associated with the fer-

tility of the earth, ii. 150; punishment for killing a, iii. 222; worshipped by the Baganda, v. 86. *See also* Pythons

Python clan, a python expected to visit every newborn child of the, viii. 174

—— -god, human wives of the, v. 66

Pythons, dead kings turn into, iv. 84; worshipped in West Africa, v. 83 *n.*[1]; dead chiefs reincarnated in, vi. 193

Qua, near Old Calabar, sacred palm-tree at, ii. 51

Quack, the, a Whitsuntide Mummer, ii. 81

Quadrennial period of Greek games, vii. 77 *sqq.*

Quail, omens as to price of corn from cry of, vii. 295; corn-spirit as, vii. 295, 296

" Quail-hunt," legend on coins of Tarsus, v. 126 *n.*[2]

Quails sacrificed to Hercules (Melcarth), v. 111 *sq.*; migration of, v. 112

Quarrelling at home forbidden in absence of husband, i. 120, 130

Quarter-ill, a disease of cattle, need-fire used as a remedy for, x. 296

Quartz used at circumcision instead of iron, iii. 227

Quartz crystals, magic of, i. 176 *sq.*; used in rain-making, i. 254, 255, 304

—— stones, white, in rain-making, i. 346

Quatuordecimans of Phrygia celebrate the Crucifixion on March 25th, v. 307 *n.*

Quatzow, village of Mecklenburg, taboo on names of animals at, iii. 397

Quauhtitlan, city in Mexico, women sacrificed to the fire-god in, ix. 301

Quedlinburg, in the Harz Mountains, need-fire at, x. 276

Queen, name given to the last sheaf, vii. 146; name given to the last corn cut at harvest, vii. 153

——, the Harvest, in England, vii. 146 *sq.*, 152

—— of Athens married to Dionysus, ii. 136 *sq.*, vii. 30 *sq.*

—— of the Bean on Twelfth Night, ix. 313, 315

—— of the Corn-ears, drawn in procession at the end of harvest, vii. 146

—— of Egypt the wife of Ammon, ii. 131 *sqq.*, v. 72

—— of Heaven, great Oriental goddess, v. 303 *n.*[5]; incense burnt in honour of the, v. 228; the wife of the Sky-god, xi. 303

—— of May, representative of the spirit of vegetation, ii. 79, 84; in France, ii. 87; in England, ii. 87 *sq.*; in the Isle of Man, iv. 259; married to the King of May, iv. 266

Queen of the Roses at Grammont, x. 195
—— of Summer on St. Peter's Day in Brabant, x. 195
—— of Winter in the Isle of Man, iv. 258
Queen Charlotte Islands, the Haida Indians of, i. 70, 133, 168, iii. 72 n.¹, vii. 20, x. 44 ; their propitiation of slain animals, viii. 226. See Haida Indians
—— Charlotte Sound, mourning customs among the Indians of, iii. 143 sq.
Queen sister in Uganda, licence accorded to the, ii. 275 sq.
Queen's County, Midsummer fires in, x. 203 ; divination at Hallowe'en in, x. 242
Queens, licence accorded to, in Central Africa, ii. 277
Queensland, beliefs as to the afterbirth in, i. 183 sq. ; rain-making in, i. 254 sq. ; the Turrbal tribe of, iii. 156 n.¹, iv. 60 ; namesakes of the dead change their names in some tribes of, iii. 355 sq. ; the Gudangs of, iii. 359 ; Maryborough in, iii. 424 ; the Yerrunthally tribe of, iv. 64 ; exposure of first-born children among some tribes of, iv. 180 ; cannibalism in, viii. 151 ; sorcery in, x. 14 ; seclusion of girls at puberty in, x. 37 sqq. ; dread of women at menstruation in, x. 78 ; use of bull-roarers in, xi. 233
——, aborigines of, custom of knocking out teeth among the, i. 99 ; their belief as to scratching and rain, iii. 159 n. : their superstition as to personal names, iii. 320 ; their beliefs as to the birth of children, v. 102 sq. ; their belief as to the bones of dugong, viii. 258 n.²
——, Central, expulsion of a demon among the tribes of, ix. 172
——, natives of, their superstitions as to falling stars, iv. 60 ; their mode of ascertaining the fate of an absent friend, xi. 159 sq.
Quellendorff in Anhalt, custom at sowing at, i. 139
Quercus aegilops, its acorns eaten in Greece, ii. 356
—— ballota, its acorns eaten in Greece, ii. 356
—— ilex, the evergreen oak, its acorns eaten in Spain, ii. 356
—— robur, the British oak, its diffusion in Europe, ii. 355
Querquetulani, Men of the Oak, a tribe of the Latin League, ii. 188
Quetzalcoatl, a Mexican god, ix. 281, 300 ; personated by a priest, viii. 90 ;

man sacrificed in the character of, ix. 281 sq.
Quiches of Central America, their offerings of first-fruits, viii. 134
Quicken-tree, an English name for the rowan or mountain-ash, ix. 267 n.¹
"Quickening" heifers with a branch of rowan, ix. 266 sq.
Quilacare, in South India, suicide of the kings of, iv. 46 sq.
Quimba, a secret society on the Lower Congo, xi. 256 n.
Quimper, Midsummer fires at, x. 184
Quinoa-mother, among the Indians of Peru, vii. 172
Quirinal hill, temple of Quirinus on the, ii. 182, 185 ; villa of Atticus on the, ii. 182 n.¹
Quirinus, Romulus worshipped after death under the name of, ii. 182, 193 n.¹; sanctuary of, on the Quirinal at Rome, ii. 185 ; Patrician and Plebeian myrtle-trees in the sanctuary of, xi. 168
—— and Hora, vi. 233
Quiteve, title of the king of Sofala, revered as a god by his people, i. 392, iv. 37 sq.
Quito, the kings of, vii. 236
Quivering of the body in a rain-charm, i. 260, 261
Quixos Indians, their belief in the transmigration of human souls into animals, viii. 285 ; cause themselves to be whipped with nettles before a hunting expedition, ix. 263
Quonde in Nigeria, custom of king-killing at, iv. 35
Quop district of Borneo, ceremony at securing the soul of the rice in the, vii. 188

Ra, the Egyptian sun-god, i. 418, 419, vi. 6, 8, 12, viii. 30, ix. 341 ; how Isis discovered his name, iii. 387 sqq. ; identified with many originally independent local deities, vi. 122 sqq.
Rabbah, in Ammon, captured by King David, iii. 273, v. 19
Rabbis, burnings for dead Jewish, v. 178 sq.
Rabbit used in stopping rain, i. 295
Rabbit-kangaroo in homoeopathic magic, i. 154
Rabbits in homoeopathic magic, i. 155
Race, charm to secure victory in, i. 150 ; to May-tree to determine the Whitsuntide king, ii. 84 ; succession to kingdom determined by a, ii. 299 sqq. ; for a bride, ii. 300 sqq. ; for the kingdom at Olympia, iv. 90 ; to sheaf on harvest-field, vii. 137 ; of reapers to last sheaf, vii. 291. See also Races

Races at Whitsuntide, ii. 69, 84 ; on horseback to the May-pole to determine the Whitsuntide King, ii. 89 ; to determine the successor to the kingship, iv. 103 *sqq.* ; at harvest, vii. 76 *sq.* ; in connexion with agriculture, vii. 98 ; to ensure good crops, ix. 249 ; at fire-festivals, x. 111 ; to Easter bonfire, x. 122 ; at Easter fires, x. 144 ; with torches at Midsummer, x. 175. *See also* Chariot-races, Foot-races, Horse-races *and* Torch-races

Racoons, prayers for rain to skulls of, i. 288

Radica, a festival at the end of the Carnival at Frosinone, iv. 222

Radigis, king of the Varini, marries his stepmother, ii. 283

Radium, atomic disintegration of, viii. 305 ; bearing of its discovery on the probable duration of the sun, xi. 307 *n.*[2]

Radloff, W., on a Mongolian way of stopping rain, i. 305 *sq.*

Radnorshire, the tug-of-war at Presteign in, ix. 182

Radolfzell, in Baden, the Rye-sow or Wheat-sow near, vii. 298

Rafts, evils expelled on, ix. 199, 200 *sq.*

Rag well in the Aran Islands, ii. 161

Ragnit, in East Prussia, sacred oak near, ii. 371

——, in Lithuania, the Old Woman in the last standing corn at, vii. 223

Rags hung on trees, ii. 16, 32, 42

Ragusa, in Sicily, effigy of dragon carried on St. George's Day at, ii. 164 *n.*[1]

Rahab or Leviathan, a dragon of the sea, iv. 106 *n.*[2]

Rahu, a tribal god in India, xi. 5

Raiatea, deified king of, i. 387 *sq.*

Rain, extraction of teeth in connexion with, i. 98 *sq.* ; the magical control of, i. 247 *sqq.* ; made by homoeopathic or imitative magic, i. 247 *sqq.* ; charms to prevent or stop rain, i. 249, 252, 252 *sq.*, 262, 263, 270 *sqq.*, 290, 295 *sqq.*, 305 *sq.* ; prayers for, i. 285, 286, 287, 288, 346, ii. 46, iv. 20, x. 133 ; kings expected to give, i. 348, 350, 351 *sq.*, 353, 355, 356, 392 *sq.*, 396 ; supposed to fall only as a result of magic, i. 353 ; sacrifices for, ii. 44 ; excessive, supposed to be an effect of sexual crime, ii. 108, 111, 113 ; Zeus as the god of, ii. 359 *sq.* ; prevented by the blood of a woman who has miscarried in childbed, iii. 153 ; caused by cut or combed out hair, iii. 271, 272 ; word for, not to be mentioned, iii. 413 ; procured by bones of the dead, v. 22 ;

excessive, ascribed to wrath of God, v. 22 *sq.* ; instrumental in rebirth of dead infants, v. 95 ; regarded as the tears of gods, vi. 33 ; thought to be controlled by the souls of dead chiefs, vi. 188, viii. 109 ; prayer for, at Eleusis, vii. 69 ; charms to produce, ix. 175 *sq.*, 178 *sq.* ; or drought, games of ball played to produce, ix. 179 *sq.* ; dances to obtain, ix. 236 *sq.*, 238 ; festival to produce, ix. 277 ; divinities of the, ix. 381 ; Midsummer bonfires supposed to stop, x. 188, 336 ; bull - roarers used as magical instruments to make, xi. 230 *sqq. See also* Rain-charm

Rain, Mother of the, in rain-making ceremony among the Arabs of Moab, i. 276

Rain-bird, i. 287

—— -bride in Armenia, i. 276

" —— -bush," ii. 46

—— -charm, by throwing water on leaf-clad mummers, i. 272 *sqq.*, iv. 211 ; by ploughing, i. 282 *sq.* ; by pouring water, iii. 154 *sq.* ; in rites of Adonis, v. 237 ; by throwing water on the last corn cut, v. 237 *sq.*, vii. 134, 146, 170 *n.*[1], 268 ; by pouring water on flesh of human victims, vii. 250, 252. *See also* Rain-making

—— clan of the Dinka, iv. 30, 31

—— -clouds, smoke made in imitation of, x. 133. *See also* Clouds

—— Country, the, in Central Australia, i. 259

—— -doctor among the Toradjas of Celebes, his procedure and the taboos which he observes, i. 271 *sq.*

—— -dragon banished in time of drought, i. 298

—— -drops from eaves in magic, i. 253

—— -god, as dragon, i. 297, 298 ; of the Ewe negroes, iv. 61 ; American Indian, represented with tears running from his eyes, vi. 33 *n.*[3]

—— gods compelled to give rain by threats and violence, i. 296 *sqq.* ; appeal to the pity of the, i. 302 *sq.* ; of Mexico, ix. 283

—— King, leaf-clad mummer sprinkled with water at Poona, i. 275 ; on the Upper Nile, killed in time of drought, ii. 2

—— -maker among the Arunta, costume of the, i. 260 ; assimilates himself to water, i. 269 *sqq.*

—— -makers, their importance in savage communities, i. 247 ; in Africa, their rise to political power, i. 342 *sqq.*, 352 ; on the Upper Nile, i. 345 *sqq.*, ii. 2 ; unsuccessful, punished or killed, i. 345,

352 *sqq.* ; killed in time of drought, ii. 2, 3 ; their hair unshorn, iii. 259 *sq.* ; among the Dinka not allowed to die a natural death, iv. 32, 33 ; (mythical), x. 133

Rain-making by imitative magic, i. 247 *sqq.* ; by means of human blood, i. 256 *sqq.*, iii. 244 ; by wetting flower-clad or leaf-clad mummers, i. 272 *sqq.* ; by bathing and sprinkling of water, i. 277 *sq.* ; by ploughing, i. 282 *sq.* ; by means of the dead, i. 284 *sqq.* ; by means of animals, i. 287 *sqq.* ; by means of stones, i. 304 *sqq.* ; ceremonies of the Shilluks, iv. 20

—— song, sung by women, ii. 46

" —— -stick," in Queensland, i. 254

—— -stones, for procuring rain, i. 254, 305, 345, 346

—— -temple, in Angoniland, i. 250

—— totem in the Kaitish tribe, ceremony performed by the headman of the totem to procure rain, i. 258 *sq.*

—— -water in Morocco, magical virtues ascribed to, x. 17 *sq.*

Rainbow, a net for souls, iii. 79

—— in rain-charm, picture of, i. 258 ; imitation of, i. 288

—— totem in the Nullakun tribe of Northern Australia, v. 101

Rainless summer on the Mediterranean, v. 159 *sq.* ; in Greece, vii. 69

Rains, autumnal, in Greece, vii. 52

Rainy season, general clearance of evils at the beginning or end of the, ix. 224 ; expulsion of demons at the beginning of the, ix. 225

Raipoor, the ancient Mandavie, iv. 132 *n.*[1]

Raipur, in India, ix. 44

Rajah of Bilaspur, custom after the death of a, iv. 154, ix. 44 *sq.*

—— of Manipur, his sins transferred to a criminal, ix. 39.

—— of Tanjore, his sins after death transferred to twelve Brahmans, ix. 44

—— of Travancore, his sins at death transferred to a Brahman, ix. 42 *sq.*

——, temporary, after death of rajah, iv. 154

Rajahs among the Malays, supernatural powers attributed to, i. 361 ; two, in Timor, the civil rajah and the fetish or taboo rajah, iii. 24

Rajamahall, in India, persons who have died of dropsy thrown into river among hill tribes near, i. 79 ; sacrifices of first-fruits among hill tribes near, viii. 117 *sq.* ; ceremony at killing tiger among hill tribes near, viii. 217

Rajaraja, king, dancing-girls in his temple at Tanjore, v. 61

Rajbansis of Bengal, their rain-making ceremony, i. 284 *n.*

Rajputana, gardens of Adonis in, v. 241 *sq.*

Rakelimalaza, a Malagasy god, taboos observed at his sanctuary, viii. 46

Raking a rick in the devil's name, x. 243 ; the ashes, a mode of divination at Hallowe'en, x. 243

Raleigh, Sir Walter, his colonists on Roanoke Island, iii. 357

Rall, the fair of, in the Kanagra district of India, iv. 265

Ralston, W. R. S., on the Russian house-spirit Domovoy, ii. 233 *n.*[1] ; on sacred fire of Perkunas, xi. 91 *n.*[3]

Ram with golden fleece, iv. 162 ; as vicarious sacrifice for human victim, iv. 165, 177 ; sacrificed to Ammon, viii. 41 ; Tibetan goddess riding on a, viii. 96 ; killing the sacred, viii. 172 *sqq.* ; consecration of a white, viii. 313. *See also* Rams

——, black, in rain-making, iii. 154 ; sacrificed to Pelops, iv. 92, 104, viii. 85

Ram-god of Mendes, iv. 7 *n.*[3]

Ram's skull in charm to avert demons, viii. 96

Rama, his wife Sita, ii. 26 ; his battle with the King of Ceylon, xi. 102

Ramadan, the fast of, vii. 316

Ramanga, men who eat up the nail-parings and lick up the spilt blood of nobles among the Betsileo, iii. 246

Rambree, sorcerers dressed as women in the island of, vi. 254

Rameses II., king of Egypt, his treaty with the Hittites, v. 135 *sq.* ; his order to the Nile, vi. 33

Ramin, in Stettin, harvest custom at, vii. 230

Ramirez manuscript on Mexican religion, ix. 283 *n.*[1]

Ramman, Babylonian and Assyrian god of thunder, v. 163 *sq.*

Rampart, old, of Burghead, x. 267 *sq.*

Rams, testicles of, in the rites of Attis, v. 269

Rams' horns attached to pillars, viii. 117

Ramsay, John, of Ochtertyre, on Bridget's bed on the night before Candlemas, ii. 94 *n.*[3] ; on the Highland custom of beating a man in a cow's hide on the last day of the year, viii. 322 *sq.* ; on Beltane fires, x. 146 *sqq.* ; on Midsummer fires, x. 206 ; on Hallowe'en fires, x. 230 *sq.* ; on burying cattle alive, x. 325 *sq.*

Ramsay, Sir William M., on the worship of unmarried goddesses in Western Asia, i. 36 *n.*[2] ; on Hittite hieroglyphs, i. 87 *n.*[1] ; on rock-hewn sculptures at Boghaz-Keui, v. 134 *n.*[1], 137 *n.*[4] ; on priest-dynasts of Asia Minor, v. 140 *n.*[2]; on the god Tark, v. 147 *n.*[3]; on the name Olba, v. 148 *n.*[1]; on *Hierapolis* and *Hieropolis*, v. 168 *n.*[2]; on Attis and Men, v. 284 *n.*[5]; on cruel death of the human representative of a god in Phrygia, v. 285 *sq.*; on the early spread of Christianity in Pontus, ix. 421 *n.*[1]

Ranchi, district of Chota Nagpur, annual expulsion of disease in, ix. 139

Rangoon, scruples with regard to the human head at, iii. 253; Chins at, ix. 123

Rao of Kachh, the, his sacrifice of a buffalo, i. 385 *n.*[1]

Raoul-Rochette, D., on Asiatic deities with lions, v. 138 *n.*; on the burning of doves to Adonis, v. 147 *n.*[1]; on apotheosis by death in the fire, v. 180 *n.*[1]

Rape of Persephone, vii. 66

Rapegyrne, old Scottish name for the harvest Maiden, vii. 155 *n.*[2]

Raratonga, in the Pacific, custom as to children's cast teeth in, i. 179; custom of succession in, iv. 191

Rarhi Brahmans of Bengal, their seclusion of girls at puberty, x. 68

Rarian plain at Eleusis, vii. 36, 234, viii. 15; corn first sown by Triptolemus in the, vii. 70, 74; expiation for the defilement of the, vii. 74; the Sacred Ploughing on the, vii. 108

Raskolnik, Russian Dissenter, i. 285

Raskolniks, their hatred of mirrors, iii. 96

Raspberries, wild, ceremony at gathering the first, viii. 80 *sq.*

Rat, the "god rat," an idol to which sacrifices are offered when rats infest the fields, viii. 283; transmigration of sinner into, viii. 299; external soul of medicine-man in, xi. 199.   *See also* Rats

Rat's hair as a charm, i. 151

Rathcroghan, in Roscommon, site of the palace of the kings of Connaught, iii. 12 *n.*[1]

Rats asked to give new teeth, i. 179; superstitious precautions of farmers against, viii. 277, 278, 283; ravages committed by, viii. 282 *n.*[8]   *See also* Rat

—— and mice, in magic concerned with teeth, i. 178 *sqq.*

Rattan, creeping through a split, to escape a malignant spirit, xi. 183

Rattle, wooden, swung by twins to make fair or foul weather, i. 263; of deer-hoofs used by shaman, iii. 58; shaken before human victim, ix. 286; used at a festival in East Africa, x. 28

Rattles in myth and ritual of Dionysus, vii. 13, 15; to accompany dance, vii. 205; to frighten or keep out ghosts, ix. 154 *n.*, x. 52

Rattlesnake dance to secure immunity from snake-bites, i. 358

Rattlesnakes, attempt to deceive the spirits of, iii. 399; respected by the North American Indians, viii. 217 *sqq.*

Ratumaimbulu, Fijian god of fruit-trees, v. 90

Ratzeburg, harvest custom near, vii. 229

Rauchfiess, a Whitsuntide mummer, in Silesia, carted out of village and thrown into water, iv. 207 *n.*[1]

Raven, prophetic vision ascribed to the, i. 197; used in wind-charm, i. 320; soul as a, iii. 34; transformation into a, iii. 324; the great black (*Corvus umbrinus*), respected by Sudanese negroes, viii. 221

Raven clan among the Niska Indians, xi. 271

—— legends among the Esquimaux, ix. 380

Raven's eggs in homoeopathic magic, i. 154

Ravensberg, in Westphalia, the Fox in the corn at, vii. 296

Raw flesh, Flamen Dialis forbidden to touch or name, iii. 13, 239; Brahman teacher not to look on, iii. 239; relations of slain man not to touch, iii. 240

Ray, S. H., on the names for fire-sticks in the Torres Straits Islands, ii. 209 *n.*[3]

Ray-fish, cure for wound inflicted by a, i. 98 *n.*[1]

Raymi, a festival of the summer solstice, among the Incas of Peru, x. 132

Readjustment of Egyptian festivals, vi. 91 *sqq.*

Reaper of the last sheaf, called the Wolf, vii. 273; called Goat, Corn-goat, Oats-goat, or Rye-goat, vii. 283; called the Cow, Barley-cow, or Oats-cow, vii. 289

Reapers, special language or words employed by, iii. 410 *sq.*, 411 *sq.*, vii. 193; contests between, vii. 136, 140, 141, 142, 144, 152, 153 *sqq.*, 164 *sq.*, 219, 253; throw their sickles at the last standing corn, vii. 136, 142, 144, 153, 154 *sq.*, 155 *n.*[1], 267, 268, 279, 296; blindfolded, vii. 144, 153 *sq.*; pretend to mow down visitors to harvest-field, vii. 229 *sq.*; of rice use a special form of speech in order to deceive the rice-spirit, vii. 184; cries of, vii. 263 *sqq.*; their remedies for pains in the back, vii. 285; race of, to last corn, vii. 291; throw sickles blindfold at last sheaf, xi. 279 *n.*[4]

Reapers, Egyptian, their lamentations, v. 232, vi. 45, vii. 261, 263 ; invoke Isis, vi. 117

Reaping, tug-of-war at, ii. 100 ; Indonesian mode of, vii. 181 *sq.*, 184 ; contests in, vii. 218 *sqq.* ; pains in back at, vii. 285 ; girdle of rye a preventive of weariness in, x. 190

Reaping-match of Lityerses, vii. 217

Reaping rice, homoeopathic magic at, i. 139 *sq.*

Reasoning, definite, at the base of savage custom, iii. 420 *n.*[1]

Reay, in Sutherland, the need-fire at, x. 294 *sq.*

Rebirth from a golden cow, ceremony of, iii. 113 ; of ancestors in their descendants, iii. 368 *sq.* ; of a father in his son, iv. 188 *sqq.* ; of the parent in the child, iv. 287 (288, in Second Impression) ; of infants, means taken to ensure the, v. 91, 93 *sqq.* ; of Egyptian kings at the Sed festival, vi. 153, 155 *sq.* *See also* Birth

—— of the dead, according to Pindar, iv. 70, vii. 84 ; precautions taken to prevent, v. 92 *sq.* *See also* Reincarnation

Recall of the soul, iii. 30 *sqq.*

Reckoning intervals of time, Greek and Latin modes of, iv. 59 *n.*[1]

Red, bodies of manslayers painted, iii. 175, 179 ; faces of manslayers painted, iii. 185, 186 *n.*[1] ; the colour of Lower Egypt, vi. 21 *n.*[1] ; girl's face painted red at puberty, x. 49 *sq.*, 54 ; women at menstruation painted, x. 78

—— and black, faces of bear-hunters painted, viii. 226 ; effigy of snake painted, viii. 316

—— and white, manslayers painted, iii. 186 *n.*[1] ; leopard-hunters painted, viii. 230 ; girls at puberty painted, x. 35, 38, 39, 40 ; women at menstruation painted, x. 78

—— and yellow paint on human victim to represent colours of maize, vii. 261, ix. 285

Red Altar, the, on Snowdon, i. 307

—— colour in magic, i. 79, 81, 83

—— earth or paint smeared on girls at puberty, x. 30, 31

—— feathers of parrot worn as a protection against a ghost, iii. 186 *n.*[1]

—— -haired men sacrificed by ancient Egyptians, vi. 97, 106, vii. 260, 261, 263, viii. 34

—— -haired puppies sacrificed by the Romans, vii. 261, viii. 34

—— horse sacrificed as a purification of the land by the Battas, ix. 213

—— hot iron chain, passing persons

possessed by evil spirits through a, xi. 186

Red Island, Torres Straits, seclusion of girls at puberty in, x. 39 *sq.*

—— Karens of Burma, their festival in April, ii. 69 *sq.*

—— ochre round a woman's mouth, mark of menstruation, x. 77

—— oxen sacrificed by ancient Egyptians, viii. 34

—— sealing-wax a cure for St. Anthony's fire, i. 81

—— thread in popular cure, ix. 55

—— wool in magic, iii. 307

—— woollen threads, a charm against witchcraft, ii. 336

Reddening the faces of gods, custom of, ii. 175 *sq.*

Reddis or Kapus in the Madras Presidency, their women procure rain by means of frogs, i. 294

Redemption of firstling men and asses among the Hebrews, iv. 173 ; from the fire in Lent, x. 110

Reed, W. A., on the religion of the Negritos, ix. 82 ; on a superstition as to a parasitic plant in the Philippines, xi. 282 *n.*[1]

Reed, split, used in Roman cure for dislocation, xi. 177

Reef, plain of, in Tiree, witch as black sheep on the, x. 316

Reef Islands, avoidance of relations by marriage in, iii. 344 ; ceremony at eating the new fruits in the, viii. 52 *sq.*

Reflection, the soul identified with the, iii. 92 *sqq.*

Reflections in water or mirrors, supposed dangers of, iii. 93 *sq.*

Reform, the prophetic, in Israel, v. 24 *sq.*

Reformations of Hezekiah and Josiah, v. 25

Refuse of food burnt by magician to cause disease, i. 341 ; magic wrought by means of, iii. 126 *sqq.*

Regaby, in the Isle of Man, November 1st as New Year's Day at, x. 224

Regalia propitiated with prayer and sacrifice, i. 363 ; carried to battle, i. 363 ; smeared with blood, i. 363 ; treated as fetishes, i. 363 ; employed as instruments of divination, i. 365 ; regarded as a palladium, i. 365 ; sanctity of, in Celebes, iv. 202

—— of Malay kings regarded as powerful talismans, i. 362 *sqq.* ; supernatural powers of, i. 398

Regeneration from a golden cow, ceremony of, iii. 113

Regia, the king's palace at Rome, ii. 201, 228

Regicide among the Slavs, iv. 52 ; modified custom of, iv. 148
Regifugium at Rome, ii. 290, iv. 213 ; perhaps a relic of a contest for the kingdom, ii. 308 *sqq.*
Regillus, appearance of Castor and Pollux at the battle of Lake, i. 50
Regina nemorum, an epithet of Diana, i. 40 *n.*[3]
Regnitz, the River, puppets representing Death thrown into, iv. 234
Rehoboam, King, his family, v. 51 *n.*[2]
Reichenbach, in Silesia, the last sheaf called the Old Man at, vii. 138
Reinach, Salomon, on Hippolytus, i. 27 *n.*[6] ; on prehistoric cave-paintings, i. 87 *n.*[1] ; on Greek custom of carrying infants round the hearth, ii. 232 *n.*[2] ; on virgin priestesses among the Celts, ii. 241 *n.*[1] ; on the death of the Great Pan, iv. 7 *n.*[2] ; on the benefits of a thrashing, ix. 264 *n.*[2] ; on Jesus Barabbas, ix. 420 *n.*[1]
Reincarnation, belief of the aboriginal Australians in, i. 96, 99 *sq.*, v. 99 *sqq.* ; the initiatory rites of the Australians perhaps intended to ensure, i. 101, 106 ; certain funeral rites perhaps intended to ensure, i. 101 *sqq.* ; of ancestors in their descendants, iii. 368 *sqq.* ; of human souls, belief in, a motive for infanticide, iv. 188 *sq.* ; of animals, viii. 247, 249, 250
—— of the dead, iii. 365 *sqq.*, v. 82 *sqq.* ; in newly born infants, i. 103 *sqq.* ; in America, iii. 365 *sqq.*, v. 91 ; in Australia, v. 99 *sqq. See also* Rebirth
Reindeer, blood of, smeared on fireboards, ii. 225 ; protected by sacred fire-boards, ii. 225 ; taboos concerning, iii. 208 ; propitiation of the spirit who controls the, viii. 245 *sq.* ; dogs not allowed to gnaw the leg-bones of, viii. 246 ; sacrificed to the dead, xi. 178
Reinegg, J., on a sacrament of the Abchases, viii. 312 *n.*[1]
Reinsberg-Düringsfeld, O. Frh. von, on the Yule log, x. 249
Reipus, payment made on the remarriage of a widow in Salic law, ii. 286 *n.*[1]
Reiskius, Joh., on the need-fire, x. 271 *sq.*
Rekub-el, Syrian god, v. 16
Relations, names of, tabooed, iii. 335 *sqq.* ; of the dead take new names for fear of the ghost, iii. 356 *sqq.* ; spirits of near dead, worshipped, iv. 175, 176 ; at death become gods, vi. 180
Relationship, terms of, used as terms of address, iii. 324 *sq.* ; classificatory system of, xi. 234 *n.*[1], 314 *n.*[4]

Release of prisoners at festivals, iii. 316
Relics of dead princes preserved as regalia, i. 363 ; of tree-worship in modern Europe, ii. 59 *sqq.* ; corporeal, of dead kings confer right to throne, iv. 202
Relief, archaic Greek, at Nemi, i. 11 *n.*[1]
Religion defined, i. 222 ; two elements of, a theoretical and a practical, i. 222 *sq.* ; opposed in principle to science, i. 224 ; transition from magic to, i. 237 *sqq.*, ii. 376 *sq.* ; combined with magic, i. 347 ; passage of animism into, iii. 213 ; volcanic, v. 188 *sqq.* ; how influenced by mother-kin, vi. 202 *sqq.* ; influenced by agriculture, vii. 93, 108 ; movement of thought from magic through religion to science, xi. 304 *sq.*
——, the Age of, iv. 2
—— and magic, i. 220-243, 250, 285, 286, 347, ii. 376 *sq.* ; Hegel on, i. 423 *sqq.* ; combination of, v. 4
—— and music, v. 53 *sq.*
Religions, the great historical, less permanent than the belief in magic and witchcraft, in ghosts and goblins, ix. 89 *sq.*
Religious associations among the Indians of North America, xi. 266 *sqq.*
—— dramas sometimes originate in magical rites, ii. 142 *sq.*
—— ideals a product of the male imagination, vi. 211
—— systems, great permanent, founded by great men, vi. 159 *sq.*
Reluctance to accept sovereignty on account of taboos attached to it, iii. 17 *sqq.*
Remedies, magical, not allowed to touch the ground, x. 14
Remission of sins through the shedding of blood, v. 299
Remnants of food buried as a precaution against sorcery, iii. 118, 119, 127 *sq.*, 129
Remon branch of the Ijebu tribe, chief of the, formerly killed after a rule of three years, iv. 112 *sq.*
Remulus, ii. 180. *See* Romulus
Remus and Romulus, the birth of, vi. 235. *See* Romulus
Renan, Ernest, on the danger underlying civilization, i. 236 *n.*[1] ; on Tammuz and Adonis, v. 6 *n.*[1] ; his excavations at Byblus, v. 14 *n.*[1] ; on Adom-melech, v. 17 ; on the vale of the Adonis, v. 29 *n.* ; on the burnings for the kings of Judah, v. 178 *n.*[1] ; on the discoloration of the river Adonis, v. 225 *n.*[4] ; on the worship of Adonis, v. 235 ; on custom of sticking pins into a saint's statue, ix. 70

Renewal, annual, of king's power at Babylon, iv. 113, 115, ix. 356, 358
—— of fire, annual, in China, x. 137. *See also* Fire
Rengen, in the Eifel Mountains, Midsummer flowers at, xi. 48
Renouf, Sir P. le Page, on the divinity of Egyptian kings, i. 418 ; on Osiris as the sun, vi. 126
Representative of tree-spirit clad in leaves and blossoms, ii. 75, 76, 79 *sqq.*
Reproductive powers, beating people to stimulate their, ix. 272
Reptile clan of the Omaha Indians, their belief as to the effect of touching a snake, viii. 29
Repulsion and attraction, forces of, viii. 303 *sqq.*
Resemblance of children to their parents, how explained by savages, i. 104 ; of child to father, supposed danger of, iii. 88 *sq.*, iv. 287 (288, in Second Impression) ; of the rites of Adonis to the festival of Easter, v. 254 *sqq.*, 306
Resemblances of paganism to Christianity explained as diabolic counterfeits, v. 302, 309 *sq.*
Reshef, Semitic god, v. 16 *n.*[1]
Resoliss, parish of, in Ross-shire, burnt sacrifice of a pig in, x. 301 *sq.*
Rest for three days, compulsory, among the Esquimaux after the capture of a ground seal, walrus, or whale, viii. 246
Resurrection, cut hair and nails kept for use at the, iii. 279 *sq.* ; of the god, iv. 212, vii. 1, 12, 14, 15, ix. 400 ; of the tree-spirit, iv. 212 ; of a god in the hunting, pastoral, and agricultural stages of society, iv. 221 ; enacted in Shrovetide or Lenten ceremonies, iv. 233 ; of the gods, viii. 16 ; of animals, viii. 200 *sq.*, 256 *sqq.* ; of fish, viii. 250, 254 ; bones of men preserved for the, viii. 259 ; in popular tales, viii. 263 *sq.* ; the divine, in Mexican ritual, ix. 288, 296, 302 ; of Semitic gods, ix. 398 ; of Eabani, ix. 399 ; ritual of death and resurrection at initiation, xi. 225 *sqq.*
—— of Attis at the vernal equinox, v. 272 *sq.*, 307 *sq.*
—— of the Carnival, iv. 252
—— of the dead effected by giving their names to living persons, iii. 365 *sqq.* ; conceived on the pattern of the resurrection of Osiris, vi. 15 *sq.*
—— of the effigy of Death, iv. 247 *sqq.*
—— of Hercules (Melcarth), v. 111 *sq.*
—— of Kostrubonko at Eastertide, iv. 261
—— of Osiris dramatically represented in his rites, vi. 85 ; depicted on the monuments, vi. 89 *sq.* ; date of its

celebration at Rome, vi. 95 *n.*[1] ; symbolized by the setting up of the *ded* pillar, vi. 109
Resurrection of Tylon, v. 186 *sq.*
—— of the Wild Man, iv. 252
Retaliation in Southern India, law of, iv. 141 *sq.*
Retoroños, the, of Bolivia, ate the powdered bones of their dead, viii. 157
Reuzes, wicker giants in Brabant and Flanders, xi. 35
Revelry at Purim, ix. 363 *sq.*
Revels, Master of the, at the English court, ix. 333 *sq.*
Revenge, suicide as a mode of, iv. 141
Revin, Midsummer fires at, x. 188
Revolution, social, from democracy to despotism, i. 371
Revolve from left to right, small fir-trees made to, on Midsummer Day, ii. 66
Revolving image, viii. 322 *n.*
Rex Nemorensis, the King of the Wood at Nemi, i. 11
Rhamnus catharticus, buckthorn, used as a protection against witches, ix. 153 *n.*[1]
Rhea and Cronus, iv. 194, ix. 351
Rhegium in Italy, founded in consequence of a vow to Apollo, iv. 187 *n.*[5]
Rhenish Prussia, Lenten fires in, x. 115
Rhetra, religious capital of the Western Slavs, inspired priest at, i. 383
Rheumatism in homoeopathic magic, i. 155 ; ascribed to magic, i. 207 *sq.*, 213 ; popular remedy for, by means of pepper, iii. 106 ; popular remedy for, by means of bees, iii. 106 *n.*[2] ; crawling under a bramble as a cure for, xi. 180
Rhine, dramatic contest between Winter and Summer on the middle, iv. 254 ; bathing in the, on St. John's Eve, v. 248
——, the Lower, need-fire on, x. 278 ; St. John's wort on Midsummer Day on, xi. 54
Rhinoceros' horn and hide, shavings of, swallowed by warriors to make them strong, viii. 143
Rhinoceros hunters not allowed to wash, i. 115
Rhinoceroses, souls of the dead transmigrate into, iv. 85
Rhins, J. L. Dutreuil de, on ceremony of beating an effigy of an ox in spring at Kashgar, viii. 13
Rhodes, Lindus in, i. 281 ; the Telchines of, i. 310 ; rolling on the grass on St. George's morning in, ii. 333 ; human sacrifices to Baal in, iv. 195 ; described by Strabo, v. 195 *n.*[3] ; worship of Helen in, v. 292
Rhodesia, the Winamwanga of, viii. 112,

xi. 297 ; the Yombe of, viii. 112 ; the Wemba of, viii. 158 ; the Awemba of, viii. 272 *sq.*

Rhodesia, Northern, the Bantu tribes of, their worship of ancestral spirits, vi. 174 *sqq.*; their worship of dead chiefs or kings, vi. 191 *sqq.*

Rhodians worship the sun, i. 315 ; dedicate chariot and horses to the sun, i. 315, 316, viii. 45 ; the Venetians of antiquity, v. 195 ; their annual sacrifice of a man to Cronus, ix. 353 *sq.*, 397

Rhodomyrtus tomentosus, used to kindle fire by friction, xi. 8

Rhön Mountains, Lenten custom in the, x. 117

Rhyndacos, the river, boundary of Bithynia, ix. 421 *n.*[1]

Rhys, Professor Sir John, on Coligny calendar, i. 17 *n.*[2], ix. 343 *n.* ; on the relation of Irish Druidism to Christianity, ii. 363 ; as to *The Book of Rights*, iii. 12 *n.*[2] ; on personal names, iii. 319 ; on Lammas, iv. 101 ; on custom of sticking pins in a saint's statue, ix. 70 *sq.* ; on Beltane fires, x. 157 ; on driving cattle through fires, x. 159 ; on old New Year's Day in the Isle of Man, x. 224 ; on Hallowe'en bonfires in Wales, x. 239 *sq.* ; on burnt sacrifices in the Isle of Man, x. 305 *sqq.* ; on alleged Welsh name for mistletoe, xi. 286 *n.*[3]

Riabba, in Fernando Po, residence of the native king, iii. 8

Ribald jests at the Eleusinian mysteries, vii. 38

—— songs in rain-charm, i. 267

Ribble, Hallowe'en cakes on the banks of the, x. 245

Ribhus, Vedic genii of the seasons, ix. 325

Ribwort gathered at Midsummer, xi. 49

Ricci, S. de, on the Coligny calendar, ix. 343 *n.*

Rice, homoeopathic magic at sowing, i. 136 ; homoeopathic magic at reaping, i. 139 *sq.* ; charm to make rice grow, i. 140 ; homoeopathic magic at planting, i. 143 ; in bloom treated like pregnant woman, ii. 28 *sq.*, vii. 183 *sq.* ; chastity at sowing, ii. 106 ; used to attract the soul conceived as a bird, iii. 34 *sqq.*, 45 *sqq.* ; strewn on bridegroom's head, iii. 35 ; used to attract wandering souls, iii. 62 ; used in exorcism, iii. 106 ; in water, divination by, iii. 368 ; special language employed at harvest in order not to frighten the spirit of the, iii. 412 ; Dyak story as to the first planting of, iv. 127 *sq.* ; cultivated in Assam, vii. 123 ; cultivated

in New Guinea, vii. 123 ; the first rice cut, ceremony at bringing home, vii. 185 *sq.* ; spirituous liquor distilled from, vii. 242 ; spirits that cause the growth of, thought to be in goat form, vii. 288 ; ''eating the soul of the rice,'' viii. 54 ; the first, sowed and reaped by priest, viii. 54 ; the new, ceremonies at eating the, viii. 54 *sqq.*

Rice (paddy), Father and Mother of the, among the Szis of Burma, vii. 203 *sq.*

——, Rajah or King of the, in Mandeling (Sumatra), vii. 197

——, soul of, vii. 180 *sqq.* ; not to be frightened, iii. 412 ; in the first sheaf cut, vi. 239 ; as bird, vii. 182 *n.*[1]; caught or detained, vii. 184 *sqq.* ; recalled, vii. 189 *sq.* ; in a blue bird, vii. 295

Rice barn, homoeopathic magic at building a, i. 140

—— -bride and -bridegroom, marriage of, at rice-harvest in Java, vii. 199 *sq.*

—— -cakes, sacrificial, as substitutes for human beings, viii. 89 ; mystically transformed into bodies of men by manipulation of priest, viii. 89

—— -child at harvest in the Malay Peninsula, vii. 197 *sqq.*

—— -ears, the young, fed like children, ii. 29

—— -fields, sacred, among the Kayans, vii. 93, 108

—— -goddess in Lombok, vii. 202

—— -harvest, special language employed by reapers at, iii. 410 *sq.*, 411 *sq.* ; marriage ceremony in Java at, vii. 199 *sq.* ; ceremony of the Horse at, viii. 337 *sqq.* ; carnival at the, ix. 226 *n.*[1]

—— -mother in the East Indies, vii. 180 *sqq.* ; A. C. Kruyt on the, vii. 183 *n.*[1]; among the Minangkabauers of Sumatra, vii. 191 *sqq.* ; in the Malay Peninsula, vii. 197 *sqq.*

—— -sieve, infant at birth placed in, vii. 8

—— -spirit conceived as husband and wife, vii. 201 *sqq.*

Richalm, Abbot, his fear of devils, ix. 105 *sq.*

Richard Cœur-de-Lion at Rouen, ii. 164, 165

Richter, O., on the valley of Egeria, i. 18 *n.*[4]

Rickard, R. H., on the seclusion of girls at puberty in New Ireland, x. 34

Rickets, children passed through cleft ash-trees as a cure for, xi. 168 ; children passed through cleft oaks as a cure for, xi. 170 ; children passed through a holed stone as a cure for, xi. 187

2 F

Rickety children passed through a natural wooden ring, xi. 184

Riddles in rain-making ceremony, iii. 154; asked while the people watch the crops in the fields, vii. 194; asked at certain seasons or on certain occasions, ix. 121 *n.*[3]

"Ride of the Beardless One," a Persian New Year ceremony, ix. 402 *sq.*

Ridgeway, Professor William, as to Homeric kings, i. 366 *n.*[3]; on a Whitsuntide custom, ii. 103 *n.*[3]; on the magical virtue of iron, iii. 230 *n.*[7]; on the marriage of brothers and sisters, vi. 216 *n.*[1]; on the Thracian Carnival ceremonies, vii. 29 *n.*[2]; on the marriage of Zeus and Demeter at Eleusis, vii. 65; on Dionysus Bassareus, viii. 282 *n.*[5]; on Lycaean Zeus, ix. 353 *n.*[4]; on the origin of Greek tragedy, ix. 384 *n.*[2]

Ridley, Rev. W., on the annual expulsion of ghosts in Australia, ix. 123 *sq.*

Riedel, J. G. F., on the belief in the spirits of the dead in Timor, ix. 85; on the Kakian association in Ceram, xi. 249

Rif, province of Morocco, Midsummer fires in, x. 214 *n.*, 215; bathing at Midsummer in, x. 216

Rig Veda, hymn about frogs in the, i. 294; hymns of the, in honour of Parjanya, ii. 368 *sq.*; on the slaying of Vṛtra by Indra, iv. 106 *sq.*; the sun called "the golden swing in the sky" in the, iv. 279; story of creation in the, ix. 410; how Indra cured Apala in the, xi. 193

Riga, Midsummer festival at, x. 177

Right foot foremost, iii. 189, vii. 203

—— hand, luckiness of the, x. 151 *n.*

—— -hand turn (*deiseal, dessil*) in the Highlands of Scotland, x. 150 *n.*[1], 154

—— shoe of bridegroom to be untied, iii. 300 *n.*[2]

Ring, golden, worn as a charm, i. 137; broken, iii. 13; on ankle as badge of office, iii. 15; competition for, at harvest supper, vii. 160; suspended in Purim bonfire, ix. 393; divination by a, x. 237; crawling through a, as a cure or preventive of disease, xi. 184 *sqq.*; worn by initiates as token of the new birth, xi. 257. *See also* Rings

Ringhorn, Balder's ship, x. 102

Ringing church bells on Midsummer Eve, custom as to, xi. 47 *sq. See also* Bells

"—— out the grass," ii. 154

Rings used to prevent the escape of the soul, iii. 31; as spiritual fetters, iii. 313 *sq.*; as amulets, iii. 235, 314 *sqq.*, x. 92; not to be worn, iii. 314; not

to be worn in the sanctuary of the Mistress at Lycosura, viii. 46; headache transferred to, ix. 2; mourners creep through, xi. 178, 179. *See also* Ring

Rings and knots tabooed, iii. 293 *sqq.*

Rio de Janeiro, ordeal of girls at puberty among the Indians about, x. 59

—— Enivra, the Tauaré Indians of, viii. 157

—— Grande in Brazil, the Carayahis, Indian tribe on the, iii. 348

—— Negro in Brazil, ashes of the dead drunk by Indians of the, viii. 157; ordeals of young men among the Indians of the, x. 63

Risley, Sir Herbert H., on Indian firewalk, xi. 5 *n.*[3]

Rites of irrigation in Egypt, vi. 33 *sqq.*; of sowing, vi. 40 *sqq.*; of harvest, vi. 45 *sqq.*

—— of Plough Monday, viii. 325 *sqq.*

Ritual, children of living parents in, vi. 236 *sqq.*; of the Bechuanas at founding a new town, vi. 249; primitive, marks of, vii. 169; magical or propitiatory, vii. 169, 170; myths dramatized in, x. 105; of death and resurrection at initiation, xi. 225 *sqq.*

—— of Adonis, v. 223 *sqq.*

—— of Attis, v. 263 *sqq.*

—— of Dionysus, vii. 14 *sq.*

Ritual dance in honour of Demeter and Persephone, viii. 339

—— murder, accusations of, brought against the Jews, ix. 394 *sqq.*

River of Good Fortune, in West Africa, ix. 28

Rivers, Dr. W. H. R., on the confusion of magic and religion among the Todas, i. 230 *n.*; on the sacred milkmen of the Todas, i. 403 *n.*[1], vi. 228; on the differentiation of medicine-men from sorcerers among the Todas, i. 421 *n.*[1]; on restrictions imposed on holy dairymen among the Todas, iii. 17; as to Melanesian theory of conception in women, v. 97 *sq.*; on *tamaniu*, xi. 199 *n.*[1]

Rivers, hair offered to, i. 31; girls sacrificed in marriage to, i. 151 *sq.*; horses sacrificed to, ii. 16 *sq.*; as lovers of women in Greek mythology, ii. 161 *sq.*; prohibition to cross, ii. 9 *sq.*; hair dedicated to, iii. 261, 261 *n.*[5]; as the seat of worship of deities, v. 160; bathing in, at Midsummer, v. 246, 248, 249, xi. 30; gods worshipped beside, v. 289; used to sweep away evils, ix. 3 *sq.*, 5; offerings and prayers to, ix. 27 *sq.*; menstruous women not allowed to cross or bathe in, x. 77, 97 ; claim human victims at Midsummer, xi. 26 *sqq.*

Rivos, harvest-god of Celts in Gaul, i. 17

Rivros, a Celtic month, i. 17 *n.*², ix. 343

Rizano, in Dalmatia, the Yule log at, x. 263

Rizpah and her sons, v. 22

" Road of Jerusalem," iv. 76

Roasted food prescribed for man-slayers, iii. 169

Robber caste in South India, the law of retaliation among a, iv. 141 *sq.*

Robbers, charm used by, vii. 235

Robertson, Sir George Scott, on the dances of Kafir women in the Hindoo Koosh, i. 133 *sq.* ; on ceremonial purity among the Kafirs of the Hindoo Koosh, iii. 14 *notes*

Robertson, Rev. James, on the Beltane fires in the parish of Callander, x. 150 *sqq.*

Robigo or *Robigus*, mildew, worshipped by the Romans, viii. 282 *n.*⁷

Robinson, C. H., on human life bound up with that of an animal, xi. 209

Robinson, Edward, on the vale of the Adonis, v. 29 *n.*

Robinson, Captain W. C., on human victims among the Khonds, iv. 139 *n.*¹

Roccacaramanico, in the Abruzzi, Easter ceremonies at, v. 256 *n.*²

Rochholz, C. L., on need-fire, x. 270 *n.*

Rock-crystal in charm to prevent rain, i. 290 ; used to stop rain, i. 305

—— -crystals in rain-charms, i. 346 *sq.* ; at Boghaz-Keui, v. 129 *sqq.*

—— -hewn sculptures at Ibreez, v. 121 *sqq.*

Rockhill, W. W., on the custom of swinging in Corea, iv. 284 *sq.* ; on dance of eunuchs in Corea, v. 270 *n.*² ; on the annual expulsion of the devil at Lhasa, ix. 221 *n.*¹

Rocks in rain-making, i. 306, 309 ; sick people passed through holes in, xi. 186 *sq.*, 189 *sq.*

Rodents, souls of dead in, viii. 291

Rods, iron, in magic, i. 346 *sq.*

Roepstorff, F. A. de, on the Nicobar custom of not mentioning the names of the dead, iii. 362 *sq.*

Roeskilde, in Zealand, the last sheaf called the Rye-beggar near, vii. 231

Rogations, ancient Mexican festival compared to, ix. 277 ; Monday of, ii. 166

Rohde, Erwin, on purification by blood, v. 299 *n.*² ; on Hyacinth, v. 315 ; on an argument for immortality, vii. 91 *n.*² ; on the Anthesteria, ix. 153 *n.*¹

Röhrenbach, in Baden, the Corn-sow or Oats-sow at making up the last sheaf at, vii. 298

Roko Tui, the Sacred King of Fiji, iii. 21

Rolling on the fields as a fertility charm, ii. 103 ; at harvest, ii. 104

—— cakes on the ground for omens on St. George's Day, ii. 338, on May Day, x. 153

—— down a slope on May Day, ii. 103

—— Easter eggs down hill, ix. 269

Rollo, how he learned the speech of animals, viii. 146

Röllshausen, in Hesse, the Little Whitsuntide Man at, ii. 81

Romagna, belief as to falling stars in the, iv. 66 ; Befana (Epiphany) in the Tuscan, ix. 167

Roman calendar, vii. 83 *sq.*

—— celebration of the *Nonae Caprotinae*, ii. 313 *sq.*, ix. 258

—— custom of keeping a perpetual fire in every house, ii. 260 ; of presenting women with key as symbol of easy delivery, iii. 296 : of sacrificing human beings at the grave, iv. 143

—— deities called " Father " and " Mother," vi. 233 *sqq.* ; of the corn, vii. 210 *n.*³

—— emperor, funeral pyre of, v. 126 *sq.*

—— emperors, fire carried before, ii. 264

—— financial oppression, v. 301 *n.*²

—— Forum, temple of Vesta in the, i. 13. *See also* Forum

—— funerals, personation of the illustrious dead at, ii. 178

—— game of Troy, iv. 76 *sq.*

—— *genius* symbolized by a serpent, v. 86

—— gods, their names not to be mentioned, iii. 391 *n.*¹ ; the marriage of the, vi. 230 *sqq.* ; compared to Greek gods, vi. 235

—— husbandman, his prayers to Mars, ix. 229

—— king and queen as representatives of Jupiter and Juno in a Sacred Marriage, ii. 192

—— kings as deities in a Sacred Marriage, ii. 172 *sq.*, 192, 193 *sq.*, 318 *sq.* ; as personifications of Jupiter, ii. 174 *sqq.*, 266 *sq.* ; as public rain-makers, ii. 183 ; list of, ii. 269 *sq.* ; rule of succession among, ii. 270 *sq.* ; plebeians, not patricians, ii. 289 ; how nominated, ii. 295 *sq.* ; as personifications of Saturn, ii. 311, 322 ; their mysterious or violent ends, ii. 312 *sqq.* ; their obscure birth, ii. 312 *sq.*

—— kingship, descent of, in the female line, ii. 270 *sq.* ; abolition of the, ii. 289 *sqq.* ; a religious office, ii. 289

—— law, revival of, v. 301 ; as to knocking a nail into a wall on 13th September, ix. 66

Roman maxim about cutting hair and nails at sea, iii. 271
—— mode of execution, iv. 144
—— mythology, fragments of, vi. 235
—— personal names derived from cattle, ii. 324 n.[1]
—— priests shaved with bronze, iii. 226
—— religion, rule as to knots in, iii. 294
—— rule as to wine offered in libations, iii. 249 n.[2]
—— Saturnalia, ix. 306 sqq.
—— soldiers, celebration of the Saturnalia by, ix. 308 sq.
—— writers on curses at sowing, i. 281
—— women washed their heads on Diana's day, iii. 253
—— year, the old, began in March, ix. 229
Romans, sacrificed pregnant victims to ensure fertility, i. 141 ; their punishment of parricide, ii. 110 n.[2] ; their fire-customs compared to those of the Herero, ii. 227 sqq. ; their superstition as to egg-shells, iii. 129 ; believed the soul to be in the blood, iii. 241 ; vows of the, iii. 262 n.[2] ; their evocation of gods of besieged cities, iii. 391 ; their funeral customs, iv. 92, 96 ; their indifference to death, iv. 143 sq. ; their custom of vowing a "Sacred Spring," iv. 186 sq. ; their custom of catching the souls of the dying, iv. 200 ; adopt the worship of the Phrygian Mother of the Gods, v. 265 ; correct the vague Egyptian year by intercalation, vi. 27 sq. ; their expiation for prodigies, vi. 244 ; their marriage custom, vi. 245 ; their sacrifice of red-haired puppies to avert blighting influence of Dog-star, vii. 261, viii. 34 ; their observation of the Pleiades, vii. 318 ; sacrificed the first-fruits of corn and wine to Ceres and Liber, viii. 133 ; their worship of mildew, viii. 282 ; their cure for fever, ix. 47 ; their cure for epilepsy, ix. 68 ; their festival in honour of ghosts, ix. 154 sq. ; their seasons of sowing, ix. 232 ; their mode of reckoning a day, ix. 326 n.[2] ; their belief as to menstruous women, x. 98 n.[1] ; their cure for dislocation, xi. 177 ; deemed sacred the places which were struck by lightning, xi. 299
——, the ancient, their ceremonies for procuring rain, i. 309, 310 ; their belief as to the wasting effect of incest, ii. 115 ; their superstitious objection to clasped hands and crossed legs, iii. 298 ; their religion, full of relics of savagery, ix. 234. See also Rome
Romanus Lecapenus, emperor, how he took the life of Simeon, prince of Bulgaria, xi. 156
Rome, the Porta Capena at, i. 18 ; temple of Concordia at, i. 21 n.[2] ; the Sacrificial King at, i. 44, 46, ii. 1 ; rain-making ceremony at, i. 310, ii. 183 ; sacred trees in, ii. 10 ; the kings of, ii. 171 sqq. ; founded by settlers from Alba Longa, ii. 178 ; Capitoline hill at, ii. 184, 189 ; Capitoline Jupiter at, ii. 187 ; "fig-town," ii. 218 ; founded by shepherds and herdsmen, ii. 324 ; founded at the Parilia, April 21st, ii. 325, 326 ; name of guardian deity of Rome kept secret, iii. 391 ; funeral games at, iv. 96 ; Regifugium at, iv. 213 ; custom observed by boys at Mid-Lent in, iv. 241 ; masks hung on trees at time of sowing at, iv. 283 ; Phrygian Mother of the Gods brought to, v. 265 ; temple of Victory at, v. 265 ; high-priest of Cybele at, v. 285 ; resurrection of Osiris celebrated at, vi. 95 n.[1] ; sacrifice of she-goat to Vedijovis at, vii. 33 ; annual sacrifice of October horse at, viii. 42 sqq. ; the festival of the Compitalia at, viii. 94, 107 ; the Mother or Grandmother of Ghosts at, vii. 94, 96, 107 ; the Sublician bridge at, viii. 107 ; vintage inaugurated by Flamen Dialis at, viii. 133 ; Piazza Navona at, ix. 166 sq. ; colleges of the Salii at, ix. 232 ; the Saturnalia at, ix. 307 sq. ; the sacred fire of Vesta at, ii. 207, x. 138, xi. 91 ; myrtle-trees of the Patricians and Plebeians at, xi. 168 ; oak of the Vespasian family at, xi. 168 ; the Sister's Beam at, xi. 194 ; the Porta Triumphalis at, xi. 195
——, ancient, oak woods on the site of, ii. 184 sqq. ; the knocking of nails in, ix. 64 sqq. ; human scapegoats in, ix. 229 sqq. ; Midsummer Day in, x. 178
Romove, Romow, or Romowe, its sacred oak and perpetual fire of oak-wood, ii. 366 n.[2], xi. 91, 286
Romsdal, Norway, the Old Hay-man at haymaking in the, vii. 223
Romulus, fig-tree of, ii. 10, 318 ; Capitoline temple of Jupiter built by, ii. 176 ; death of, ii. 181 sq., 313 ; worshipped after death as Quirinus, ii. 182, 193 n.[1] ; married to Hersilia, ii. 193 n.[1] ; legend of his birth from the fire, ii. 196, vi. 235 ; hut of, ii. 200 ; son of a Vestal virgin, ii. 228 ; his children, ii. 270 n.[3] ; the name thought by some to mean "fig-man," ii. 318 ; celebrates the Parilia, ii. 329 ; cut in pieces, vi. 98 ; birth of, vi. 235 ; his disappearance at the Goat's

Marsh on the *Nonae Caprotinae*, ix. 258 ; said to have been cut to pieces by the patricians, ix. 258

Romulus or Remulus, king of Alba, his rivalry with Jupiter, ii. 180

—— and Remus, said to be sons of the fire, ii. 196 ; their legend perhaps a reminiscence of a double kingship, ii. 290 ; suckled by she-wolf under a fig-tree, ii. 318 ; reputed sons of Mars by a Vestal Virgin, vi. 234 *sq.*

—— and Tatius, ii. 290

Rongrong village in Assam, hobby-horse at, viii. 337

Roocooyen Indians of French Guiana, their tug-of-war, ix. 181 ; their custom of stinging young people with ants and wasps, ix. 263. *See* Rucuyennes

Roof, children's cast teeth deposited on the, i. 178 *sq.*, 180 ; hole in, used in ritual, iii. 316 ; spirits enter through the, viii. 123 ; remains of slain bear let down through the, viii. 189 *sq.*, 196 ; dances on the, ix. 315 ; the external soul in, xi. 156

Roofing the king's palace in Uganda, custom as to, iii. 254

Roofs of new houses, sacrifices offered on, ii. 39

Rook, island of, custom of killing all first-born children in the, iv. 180 ; expulsion of devil in the, ix. 109 ; initiation of young men in the, xi. 246

Roots, the first of the season, ceremonies before eating, viii. 80 *sqq.*

—— and seeds, wild, collected by women, vii. 124 *sqq.*

Rope, ceremony of sliding down a, ix. 196 *sqq.*

Roper River, in Australia, gum-tree full of spirit-children on the, v. 101

Ropes used to keep off demons, ix. 120, 149, 154 *n.* ; used to exclude ghosts, ix. 152 *sq.*, 154 *n.*

Roro district of British New Guinea, women after childbirth tabooed in the, iii. 148

—— -speaking tribes of British New Guinea, seclusion of homicides among the, iii. 168 ; taboos observed before a hunt among the, iii. 193

Roscher, Dr. W. H., on the Sacred Marriage, ii. 137 *n.*[1], 143 *n.*[1]; on Janus as the god of doors, ii. 383 *n.*[3]; on the death of the Great Pan, iv. 7 *n.*[2]; on Pan, viii. 2 *n.*[9]; on the beating of Mamurius Veturius, ix. 231 *n.*[3]; on the Salii, ix. 231 *n.*[3]; on the Roman ceremony of passing under a yoke, xi. 194 *n.*[2]

Roscoe, Rev. John, on rite of adoption among the Bahima, i. 75 ; on descent of the totem in Uganda, ii. 276 *n.*[2]; on the belief of the Baganda in conception caused by a wild banana-tree, ii. 318 *n.*[1]; on succession to the kingship among the Banyoro, ii. 322 *n.*[2]; on avoidance of wife's mother in Uganda, iii. 85 *n.*[1]; on the Baganda belief as to shadows, iii. 87 *n.*[5]; as to menstruation customs in Uganda, iii. 145 *n.*[4]; on taboos observed by Baganda fishermen, iii. 195 *n.*[1]; as to roofing the king's palace in Uganda, iii. 254 *n.*[5]; on disposal of cut hair and nails in Uganda, iii. 277 *n.*[10]; on change of vocabulary caused by fear of naming the dead among the Basagala, iii. 361 *n.*[2]; on the bearing of the human victims in Uganda, iv. 139 ; on the custom of strangling first-born males in Uganda, Koki, and Bunyoro, iv. 182 *n.*[2]; on consultation of souls of dead kings of Uganda, iv. 201 *n.*[1]; on serpent-worship among the Baganda and Banyoro, v. 86 *n.*[1]; on the Baganda belief in conception without sexual intercourse, v. 92 *sq.* ; on potters in Uganda, vi. 135 ; on the religion of the Bahima, vi. 190 *sq.* ; on the worship of the dead among the Baganda, vi. 196 ; on Mukasa, the chief god of the Baganda, vi. 196 *sq.* ; on massacres for sick kings of Uganda, vi. 226 ; on woman's share in agriculture among the Baganda, vii. 118 ; on human sacrifices for the crops among the Wamegi, vii. 240 *n.*[4]; on the transference of abscesses among the Bahima, ix. 6 ; on the worship of the river Nakiza, ix. 27 *sq.* ; on the use of scapegoats among the Baganda and Bahima, ix. 32 ; on life-trees of kings of Uganda, xi. 160 ; on passing through a cleft stick or a narrow opening as a cure in Uganda, xi. 181

Roscommon, Twelfth Night in, ix. 321 *sq.*; divination at Hallowe'en in, x. 243

Rose, H. A., on the sacrifice of the first-born in India, iv. 181

Rose, the Little May, ii. 74

——, the Sunday of the, fourth Sunday in Lent, iv. 222 *n.*[1]

——, the white, dyed red by the blood of Aphrodite, v. 226

Rose-bushes a protection against witches, ii. 338 ; used by mourners, probably to keep off the ghost, iii. 143

—— -tree, death in a blue, xi. 110

Rosemary burnt on May Day as a protection against witches, ix. 158 *sq.* ; branches of, used to beat people with in the Christmas holidays, ix. 270, 271

Rosenheim, district of Upper Bavaria, the Straw-bull at harvest in, vii. 289 *sq.*

Roses, the smoke of, a protection against witchcraft, ii. 339 ; festival of the Crown of, x. 195 ; the King and Queen of, x. 195

Rosetta stone, the inscription, vi: 27, 152 *n.*

Roslin, the last sheaf called the Bride at, vii. 163

Rosmapamon, in Brittany, Renan's home at, ix. 70

Ross, Isabella, on the harvest Maiden in Sutherlandshire, vii. 162 *n.*[3]

Ross-shire, the *corp chre* in, i. 69 ; Beltane cakes in, x. 153 ; burnt sacrifice of a pig in, x. 301 *sq.*

Rostowski, S., on the heathen religion of the Lithuanians, ii. 366 *n.*[2]

Rostra, the, in the Forum, ii. 178

Rotation of crops, vii. 117

Rotenburg on the Neckar, offering to the river on St. John's Day at, xi. 28 ; the wicked weaver of, xi. 289 *sq.*

Roth, H. Ling, on Tasmanian modes of making fire, ii. 258 *n.*[1]

Roth, W. E., on changes of names caused by fear of ghosts among the natives of Queensland, iii. 356 ; on belief in conception without sexual intercourse among the natives of Queensland, v. 103 *n.*[2]

Rotomahana in New Zealand, pink terraces at, v. 207, 209 *n.*

Rottenburg in Swabia, burning the Angel-man at, x. 167 ; precautions against witches on Midsummer Eve at, xi. 73

Rotti, an East Indian island, treatment of the navel-string in, i. 191 ; compensation to tree-spirit for felling tree in, ii. 36 ; spiritual ruler in, iii. 24 ; custom as to cutting child's hair in, iii. 276, 283 ; custom as to knots at marriage in, iii. 301 ; story of the type of Beauty and the Beast in, iv. 130 *n.*[1]

Rottweil, the Carnival Fool at, iv. 231

Rotuma, treatment of navel-string in, i. 184

Rouen, St. Romain at, ii. 164 *sqq.* ; church of St. Ouen at, ii. 165 ; ceremony of pardoning a prisoner on Ascension Day at, ii. 166 *sqq.*, ix. 215 *sq.*

Roumania, rain-making ceremonies in, i. 273 *sq.* ; festival of Green George among the gipsies of, ii. 75 *sq.* ; the Jews of, their custom at hard labour in childbirth, iii. 298

Roumanians of Transylvania, their precautions against witches on St. George's Day, ii. 338 ; their dread of

noon, iii. 88 ; their fear as to their shadows at building, iii. 89 *sq.* ; their fear of wounding ghosts, iii. 238 ; pile branches on certain graves, ix. 16 ; their belief in demons, ix. 106 *sq.* ; their belief as to the sacredness of bread, x. 13

Round temple of Diana, i. 13 ; temple of Vesta, i. 13, ii. 206 ; temple of the Sun, ii. 147 ; huts of the ancient Latins, ii. 200 *sqq.*

Rouse, Dr. W. H. D., on the blessing of the fruits in Greece on August 15th, i. 15 *n.*[3] ; on Jack-in-the-Green, ii. 82 ; on image of Demeter, vii. 208 *n.*[1]

Rowan or mountain-ash, hoops wreathed with, carried on May Day, ii. 63 ; used as a charm, ii. 331 ; pastoral crook cut from a, ii. 331 ; herd-boy's wand of, ii. 341 ; parasitic, esteemed effective against witchcraft, xi. 281 ; superstitions about a, xi. 281 *sq.* ; how it is to be gathered, xi. 282 ; not to be touched with iron and not to fall on the ground, xi. 282

Rowan tree, a protection against witches, ii. 53, 54, ix. 267, x. 154, 327 *n.*[1], xi. 184 *n.*[4], 185 ; cattle beaten with branches of, on May Day, ix. 266 *sq.* ; hoop of, sheep passed through a, x. 184. *See also* Mountain-ash

Rowmore, Garelochhead, vii. 158 *n.*[1]

Roxburgh in Queensland, rain-making at, i. 255

Royal blood not to be shed on the ground, iii. 241 *sqq.*

—— disease, jaundice called the, i. 371 *n.*[4]

—— families, two, supplying a king alternately, in the Matse tribe of Togoland, ii. 293 ; animals sacred to, iv. 82

—— family, in four branches, providing a king in turn, among the Igaras of the Niger, ii. 294 ; divided into two branches, in the Langrim State of the Khasis, ii. 295

—— personages conceived as charged with spiritual electricity, i. 371

Royalty, conservative of old customs, ii. 288 ; the burden of, iii. 1 *sqq.*

Rubens, head of giant effigy at Douay said to have been painted by, xi. 33

Rucuyennes of Brazil, ordeal of young men among the, x. 63. *See* Roocooyennes

Rue, curses at sowing, i. 281 ; houses fumigated with, as a protection against witches, ix. 158 ; burnt in Midsummer fire, x. 213

Rue aux Ours at Paris, effigy of giant burnt in the, xi. 38

Rugaba, supreme god in Kiziba, vi. 173

Rügen, holy shrine in, ii. 241 *n.*[4] ; the

binder of the last sheaf called Rye-wolf, Wheat-wolf, or Oats-wolf in, vii. 274 ; sick persons passed through a cleft oak in, xi. 172

Ruhla, in Thüringen, the Little Leaf Man at, ii. 80

Rukmini, wife of Krishna, ii. 26

Rukunitambua, a heathen temple in Fiji, iii. 264

Rulers expected to have power over nature, i. 353 *sq.*

Rules of life observed by sacred kings and priests, iii. 1 *sqq.* ; based on a theory of lunar influence, vi. 132 *sqq.*, 140 *sqq.*

Rum, island of, and the Lachlin family, xi. 284

Rumina, a Roman goddess, unmarried, vi. 231

Runaway slaves, charms to catch, i. 152, 317, iii. 305 *sq.*

Runaways, knots as charm to stop, iii. 305 *sq.*

Runes, magic, i. 241 ; how Odin learned the, v. 290

Running, contests in, at New Year festival among the Kayans, vii. 98. *See also* Foot-races *and* Races

Rupert's Day, effigy burnt on, x. 119

Rupt in the Vosges, Lenten fires at, x. 109 ; the Yule log at, x. 254

Rupture, cured by plugging a snail into a tree, ix. 52 ; nailed into oaks, ix. 60 ; children passed through cleft ash-trees or oaks as a cure for, xi. 168 *sqq.*, 170 *sqq.*

Rurikwi, river in Mashonaland, chiefs not allowed to cross, iii. 9

Rush, the small (*Juncus tenuis*), in homoeopathic magic, i. 144

Rush-cutter (*Binsenschneider*), a mythical being supposed to mow down the crops on St. John's Day, vii. 230 *n.*[5]

Russell, F., on purification of man-slayers among the Pimas, iii. 183 *sq.*

Russia, thieves' candles in, i. 236 ; rain-making in, i. 248 ; bathing as a rain-charm in, i. 277 ; rain-making by means of the dead in, i. 285 ; St. George's Day in, ii. 79, 332 *sqq.* ; priest rolled on the fields to fertilize them in, ii. 103 ; sect of the Skoptsy in, ii. 145, 145 *n.*[2]; belief as to the souls of ancestors in the fire on the hearth in, ii. 232 *sq.* ; fear of having one's like-ness taken in, iii. 100 ; use of knots as amulets in, iii. 306 *sq.* ; funeral ceremonies of Kostrubonko, etc., in, iv. 261 *sqq.* ; annual festivals of the dead in, vi. 75 *sqq.* ; harvest cus-toms in, vii. 146, 215, 233 ; the Wot-yaks of, ix. 155 *sq.* ; the Cheremiss of, ix. 156 ; Midsummer fires in,

x. 176, xi. 40 ; need-fire in, x. 281, xi. 91 ; treatment of the effigy of Kupalo in, xi. 23 ; the Letts of, xi. 50 ; purple loose-strife gathered at Midsummer in, xi. 65 ; fern-seed at Midsummer in, xi. 65, 66, 287 *sq.* ; birth-trees in, xi. 165. *See also* Russian *and* Russians

Russia, the Jews of South, their custom as to cast teeth, i. 178

——, South-Eastern, the Cheremiss of, ii. 44

——, White, worship of Leschiy, a woodland spirit in, ii. 125 ; charm to protect corn from hail in, vii. 300

Russian celebration of Whitsuntide, ii. 64, 79 *sq.*, 93

—— feast of Florus and Laurus, x. 220

—— girls, their mock burial of flies on the 1st of September, viii. 279 *sq.*

—— Midsummer custom, v. 250 *sq.*

—— villagers, their precautions against epidemics, ix. 172 *sq.*

—— wood-spirits, viii. 2

Russians, sect of the Christs among the, i. 407 *sq.*; their dread of noon, iii. 88 ; religious suicides among the, iv. 44 *sq.*; the heathen, their sacrifice of the first-born children, iv. 183 ; their custom on Palm Sunday, ix. 268 ; their story of Koshchei the deathless, xi. 108 *sqq.*

Rust of knife in homoeopathic magic, i. 158

Rustem and Isfendiyar, x. 104 *sq.*

Rustic Calendars, the Roman, vi. 95 *n.*[1]

Rustling of leaves regarded as the voice of spirits, ii. 30

Ruthenia, Midsummer bonfires in, x. 176

Ruthenian burglars, their charms to cause sleep, i. 148

Ruthenians, their treatment of the after-birth of cows, i. 198 ; St. George's Day among the, ii. 335

Rutuburi, a dance of the Tarahumare Indians, ix. 237

Rye, girdles of, a preventive of weariness in reaping, x. 190

Rye-beggar, name given to last sheaf in Zealand, vii. 231

—— -boar, name given to last sheaf among the Esthonians of Oesel, vii. 298, 300

—— -bride, name given to last sheaf in the Tyrol, vii. 163

—— -dog, said to be killed at end of reaping, vii. 272

—— -goat, said to be in the corn, vii. 282 ; name given to reaper of last corn, vii. 283

—— -harvest, women's race at, vii. 76 *sq.*

—— -mother, said to be in the rye, vii.

132 ; name given to wreath made out of the last rye, vii. 135

Rye - pug, name given to thresher of last rye, vii. 273

—— -sow, name given to reaper or binder of last rye, vii. 270 ; name given to last rye cut, vii. 298 ; name given to thresher of last rye, vii. 298

—— -wolf, name given to reaper or binder of last rye, vii. 270, 273, 274 ; caught in the last sheaf, vii. 271, 273 ; moves in the standing rye, vii. 271 ; children warned against the, vii. 272

—— -woman, the Old, said to sit in the corn, vii. 133 ; reaper of last rye said to kill the, vii. 223 ; the Old, said to live in the last stalks of rye and to be killed when they are cut, vii. 223

Saa, one of the Solomon Islands, offerings of first-fruits to the dead in, viii. 127 ; souls of dead in sharks at, viii. 297

Saale, the river, claims a human victim on Midsummer Day, xi. 26

Saaralben in Lorraine, simples collected on Midsummer Day near, xi. 47

Saaz district of Bohemia, the Shrovetide Bear in the, viii. 326

Sabaea or Sheba, the kings of, confined to their palace, iii. 124

Sabarios, a Lithuanian festival, about the time of the autumn sowing, viii. 49

Sabatei-Sevi, a pretended Jewish Messiah, iv. 46

Sabazius, a Thracian and Phrygian god identified with Dionysus, vii. 2 n.¹; mysteries of, v. 90 n.⁴

Sabbath, breach of, supposed to cause the disappearance of herring, viii. 251

Sabbaths, agricultural, vii. 109; of witches on the Eve of May Day and Midsummer Eve, x. 171 n.³, 181, xi. 73, 74

Sabi, taboo, in western tribes of British New Guinea, iii. 343

Sabine country, the oak woods of the, ii. 354

—— priests to be shaved with bronze, iii. 226

Sable-hunters, rules observed by, viii. 238

Sacaea, a Babylonian festival, iv. 113 *sqq.*; the mock king of, perhaps represented Tammuz, vii. 258 *sq.* ; in relation to Purim, ix. 359 *sqq.*; celebrated by the Persians, ix. 402

—— and Zakmuk, ix. 355 *sqq.*, 399, 402

Sacer, taboo, iii. 225 n.

Sacrament in the rites of Attis, v. 274 *sq.*; in the Eleusinian mysteries, vii. 161 *sq.* ; of swine's flesh, viii. 20, 24 ; of first-fruits, viii. 48 *sqq.*; combined with a sacrifice of them, viii. 86 ; totemic,

viii. 165 ; of eating a god, viii. 167 ; types of animal, viii. 310 *sqq.*

Sacramental bread, at Aricia (Nemi), viii. 95, xi. 286 n.²

—— character of harvest supper, vii. 303

—— eating of corn-spirit in animal form, viii. 20

—— meal of new rice, viii. 54 ; at initiation in Fiji, xi. 245 *sq.*

Sacraments among pastoral tribes, viii. 313

Sacred and unclean, correspondence of rules regarding the, iii. 145

Sacred beasts in Egypt, i. 29 *sq.* ; held responsible for the course of nature, i. 354

—— chiefs and kings regarded as dangerous, iii. 131 *sqq.*, 138 ; their analogy to mourners, homicides, and women at menstruation and childbirth, iii. 138

—— dramas, as magical rites, ix. 373 *sqq.*

—— feather girdle of king of Tahiti, i. 388

—— flutes played at initiation, xi. 241

—— groves, in ancient Greece and Rome, ii. 121 *sqq.* ; apologies for trespass on, ii. 328

—— harlots, in Asia Minor, v. 141 ; at Zela, ix. 370, 371 ; in the worship of Ishtar, ix. 372

—— herds of cattle at shrines, iv. 20, 25

—— kings put to death, x. 1 *sq.*

—— Marriage, the, ii. 120 *sqq.* ; of Roman kings, ii. 172 *sq.*, 192, 193 *sq.*, 318 *sq.* ; of king and queen, iv. 71 ; of actors disguised as animals, iv. 71, 83 ; of gods and goddesses, iv. 73 ; of Zeus and Hera, iv. 91 ; of priest and priestess as representing god and goddess, v. 46 *sqq.* ; represented in the rock-hewn sculptures at Boghaz-Keui, v. 140 ; in Cos, vi. 259 n.⁴ ; at Eleusis, vii. 65 *sqq.* See also Marriage

—— men, inspired by image of Apollo, i. 386 ; at Andania, ii. 122, v. 76 n.³ ; (*ḳedeshim*), at Jerusalem, v. 17 *sq.* ; and women, v. 57 *sqq.* ; in West Africa, v. 65 *sqq.* ; in Western Asia, v. 72 *sqq.*

—— persons not allowed to set foot on the ground, x. 2 *sqq.*; not to see the sun, x. 18 *sqq.*

—— ploughings in Attica, vii. 108

—— prostitution, v. 36 *sqq.*; suggested origin of, v. 39 *sqq.* ; in Western Asia, alternative theory of, v. 55 *sqq.*; in India, v. 61 *sqq.* ; in West Africa, v. 65 *sqq.*

—— slaves, v. 73, 79, ix. 370

—— spears used to stab sacrificial victims, iv. 19, 20, v. 274, ix. 218

" —— spring, the," among the ancient Italian peoples, iv. 186 *sq.*

Sacred sticks and stones (*churinga*) among the Arunta, xi. 234. *See* Churinga
—— sticks representing ancestors, among the Herero, ii. 222 *sqq.*
—— stocks and stones among the Semites, v. 107 *sqq.*
—— stool among the Shilluk, iv. 24
—— things deemed dangerous, viii. 27 *sqq.*
—— Way, the, at Rome, ii. 176, viii. 42
—— women among the ancient Germans, i. 391; the fourteen, at Athens, ii. 137, vii. 32; in India, v. 61 *sqq.*; in West Africa, v. 65 *sqq.*; in Western Asia, v. 70 *sqq.*; at Andania, v. 76 *n.*[3]
Sacrifice, gods become immortal by, i. 373 *n.*[1]; of the king's son, iv. 160 *sqq.*; of the first-born, iv. 171 *sqq.*, 179 *sqq.*; of finger-joints, iv. 219; of virginity, v. 60; of virility in the rites of Attis and Astarte, v. 268 *sq.*, 270 *sq.*; of virility in ancient Egypt, among the Ekoi of Nigeria, etc., v. 270 *n.*[2]; nutritive and vicarious types of, vii. 226; not to be touched, viii. 27; annual, of a sacred animal, iii. 31; of first-fruits, viii. 109 *sqq.*; human, successive mitigations of, ix. 396 *sq.*, 408; the Brahmanical theory of, ix. 410 *sq.*; of cattle at holy oak, x. 181; of heifer at kindling need-fire, x. 290; of an animal to stay a cattle-plague, x. 300 *sqq.*; of reindeer to the dead, xi. 178. *See also* Sacrifices
Sacrificer, the Brahman, consecration of, i. 380; becomes Vishnu, i. 380; simulated new birth of, i. 380 *sq.*
Sacrifices offered to ancestors, i. 286 *sq.*, 290 *sq.*; offered to souls of ancestors, i. 339; offered to regalia, i. 363, 365; offered to king's crown, i. 365; offered to king's sceptre, i. 365; offered to king's throne, i. 365; to trees, i. 366; offered to kings, i. 417; offered to a sacred sword, ii. 5; offered to trees, ii. 15, 16 *sq.*, 19, 30, 31, 32, 33, 34, 35, 36, 42, 44, 46, 47, 48; offered on roofs of new houses, ii. 39; at cutting down trees, ii. 44; for rain, ii. 44, iv. 20; to water-spirits, ii. 155 *sqq.*; to ghosts, iii. 56, 166; to the dead, iii. 88, iv. 92, 93, 94, 95, 97; at foundation of buildings, iii. 89 *sqq.*; to ancestral spirits, iii. 104, vi. 175, 178 *sq.*, 180, 181 *sq.*, 183 *sq.*, 190; offered to souls of slain enemies, iii. 166; for the sick, iv. 20, 25; to totems, iv. 31; of children among the Semites, iv. 166 *sqq.*; to earthquake god, v. 201, 202; to volcanoes, v. 218 *sqq.*; to the dead distinguished from sacrifices to the gods, v. 316 *n.*[1]; offered at the rising of Sirius,
vi. 36 *n.*; offered in connexion with irrigation, vi. 38 *sq.*; to dead kings, vi. 101, 162, 166 *sq.*; of animals to prolong the life of kings, vi. 221; without shedding of blood, vi. 222 *n.*[2]; offered to nets, viii. 240 *n.*[1]; offered to wolves, viii. 284; to a toad, viii. 291. *See also* Sacrifice
Sacrifices, human, offered to man-gods, i. 386, 387; to trees, ii. 15, 17; at laying foundations, iii. 90 *sq.*; in ancient Greece, iv. 161 *sqq.*, ix. 253 *sqq.*, 353 *sq.*; mock human, iv. 214 *sqq.*; offered at earthquakes, v. 201; offered to Dionysus, vi. 98 *sq.*; at the graves of the kings of Uganda, vi. 168; to dead kings, vi. 173; to dead chiefs, vi. 191; to prolong the life of kings, vi. 220 *sq.*, 223 *sqq.*; for the crops, vii. 236 *sqq.*; at festivals of new yams in Ashantee, viii. 62, 63; in Mexico, viii. 88, ix. 275 *sqq.*; of men and women as scapegoats, ix. 210 *sqq.*, 217 *sq.*; their influence on cosmogonical theories, ix. 409 *sqq.*; of deified men, ix. 409; at fire-festivals, x. 106; traces of, x. 146, 148, 150 *sqq.*, 186, xi. 31; offered by the ancient Germans, xi. 28 *n.*[1]; among the Celts of Gaul, xi. 32 *sq.*; the victims perhaps witches and wizards, xi. 41 *sqq.*; W. Mannhardt's theory of human sacrifices among the Celts, xi. 43
——, vicarious, iv. 117; in ancient Greece, iv. 166 *n.*[1]
"Sacrificial fonts" in Sweden, x. 172 *n.*[2]
—— King at Rome, i. 44, 46, ii. 2
—— victims carried round city, iii. 188; the tongues of, cut out, viii. 270; beating people with the skins of, ix. 265
Sada, Saza, Persian festival of fire at the winter solstice, x. 269
Sadana, rice-bridegroom in Java, vii. 200 *sq.*
Saddle Island, Melanesia, superstition as to reflections in water in, iii. 93 *sq.*
Sadyattes, son of Cadys, viceroy of Lydia, v. 183
Saffron in charm to make the wind blow, i. 320; at the Corycian cave, v. 154, 187
Saffron Walden, in Essex, May garlands at, ii. 60
Sagaing district of Burma, tamarind-tree worshipped for rain in the, ii. 46
Sagami, in Japan, rain-making at, i. 305
Sagar in India, use of scapegoat at, ix. 190 *sq.*
Sagard, Gabriel, on resurrections of the dead among the Indians of Canada, iii. 366 *sq.*; on preachers to fish among the Hurons, viii. 250 *sq.*
Sage, divination by sprigs of red, on Midsummer Eve, xi. 61 *n.*[4]

Saghalien, the Ainos of, i. 114, viii. 180, 188 ; opening everything to facilitate childbirth in, iii. 297 ; the Gilyaks of, iii. 370, viii. 190 n.[1]

Sagittarius, mistletoe cut when the sun is in the sign of, xi. 82

Sago, magic for the growth of, vi. 101

Sahagun, B. de, on old Mexican view of intoxication, iii. 249 sq. ; on the ancient Mexican calendar, vi. 29 n. ; Franciscan monk, his work on the Indians of Mexico, vii. 175 ; on the sacrifice of the human representative of Tezcatli-poca, ix. 276 ; on the Mexican dances, ix. 280 ; on the sacrifice of human victims to the fire-god in Mexico, ix. 301 n.[1] ; on the treatment of witches and wizards among the Aztecs, xi. 159

Sahara, the Tuaregs of the, iii. 117, 122, 353

Saibai, island of Torres Strait, magical images to procure offspring in, i. 72 ; seclusion of girls at puberty in, iii. 147, x. 40 sq.

Sail Dharaich, Sollas, in North Uist, need-fire at, x. 294

Sailors at sea, special language employed by, iii. 413 sqq.

"Saining," a protection against spirits, ix. 168

St. Andrews, witch burned at, iii. 309

St. Angelo ill-treated in drought in Sicily, i. 300

St. Anthony's fire treated by homoeo-pathic magic, i. 81 sq.

St. Antony, wood of, x. 110

St. Barbara's Day (the 4th of December), custom of putting rods in pickle on, ix. 270

St. Brandon, church of, in Ireland, sick women pass through a window of the, xi. 190

St. Bride, her Day (February 1st) in the Highlands of Scotland, ii. 94 ; an old goddess of fertility, ii. 95 ; at Kildare, ii. 242

St. Bridget, ii. 94 sq., 242. See St. Brigit

St. Brigit, holy fire and nuns of, at Kildare, ii. 240 sqq.

St. Catherine's Day (December 6th), festival of weasels on, viii. 275

St. Christopher, name given to Mid-summer giant at Salisbury, xi. 38

St. Columb Kill, festival of, x. 241

St. Columba worshipped as an embodi-ment of Christ, i. 407 ; on the oaks of Derry, ii. 242 sq.

St. Columba's tomb in Iona, i. 160

St. Corona, church of, at Koppenwal, holed stone in the, xi. 188 sq.

St. Dasius, martyrdom of, at Durostorum, ii. 310 n.[1], ix. 308 sqq. ; his tomb at Ancona, ii. 310 n.[1], ix. 310

Saint-Denis-des-Puits, the oak of, xi. 287 n.[1]

St. Denys, his seven heads, vi. 12

Saint Donan, in Brittany, superstition as to the wren at, vfii. 318

St. Eany's well in the Aran Islands, women desirous of offspring pray at, ii. 161

St. Edmund's Day in November, Lord of Misrule elected at Merton College, Oxford, on, ix. 332

St. Eloi, Bishop of Noyon, his denuncia-tion of heathen practices, xi. 190

St. Estapin, festival of, on August the 6th, xi. 188

St. Eustorgius, church of, at Milan, ix. 331

St. Fillan's well at Comrie, resorted to by women who wish to become mothers, ii. 161

St. Flannan, chapel of, in the Flannan Islands, iii. 393

St. Francis of Paola, the giver of rain, i. 300, 301 n.

St. Gall, the Canton of, the Corn-goat at harvest in, vii. 283

St. Gens, his image used in rain-making, i. 307

St. George and the Dragon, ii. 163 sq., iv. 107 ; and the Parilia, ii. 324 sqq., v. 308, 309 ; patron saint of cattle, horses, and wolves, ii. 330, 332, 336, 337, 338 ; chapel of, ii. 337 ; repre-sented by a living man on horseback, ii. 337 ; as a spirit of trees or vegeta-tion, ii. 343 sq. ; as giver of offspring to women, ii. 344 sqq., v. 78, 79, 90 ; in relation to serpents, ii. 344, 344 n.[4] ; in Syria, ii. 346, v. 78 ; perhaps the modern equivalent of Tammuz or Adonis, ii. 346 ; Cappadocian saint and martyr, ii. 347 ; swinging on the festival of, iv. 283

St. George's Day (23rd April), fertiliza-tion of barren women by fruit-trees on, ii. 56 sq., 344 ; Green George on, ii. 75, 76, 79 ; ceremony to fertilize the fields on, ii. 103 ; cattle crowned on, as a protection against witchcraft, ii. 126 sq., 339 ; effigy of a dragon carried at Ragusa on, ii. 164 n.[1] ; great popular festival of herdsmen and shepherds in Eastern Europe, ii. 330 sqq., x. 223 n.[2] ; the power of witches thought to be at its greatest height on, ii. 336 ; love charms on, ii. 345 sq. ; among the South Slavs, ix. 54 ; bells rung on, to make the grass grow, ix. 247

—— Eve, a time when witches steal milk

from the cows, ii. 334 *sq.*; snake's tongue cut on, viii. 270; witches active on, ix. 158

St. Gervais, spring of, used in rain-making, i. 307

St. Guirec, in Brittany, his statue stuck with pins, ix. 70

St. Hippolytus, a resuscitation of the Greek Hippolytus, i. 21

St. Hitzibouzit, a Persian martyr, ix. 412 *n.*[2]

St. Hubert blesses bullets with which to shoot witches, x. 315 *sq.*

St. James, on faith and works, i. 223; on pure religion, i. 224; name of, bestowed by Peruvian Indians on one of twins, i. 266

St. James's Day (July the 25th), the flower of chicory cut on, xi. 71

St. Jean, in the Jura, Midsummer fire-custom at, x. 189 ,

St. Jerome on the Celtic speech of the Galatians, ii. 126 *n.*[2], xi. 89 *n.*[2]

St. Johann, in Salzburg, the *Perchten* at, ix. 245

St. John blesses the flowers on Midsummer Eve, x. 171; his hair looked for in ashes of Midsummer fire, x. 182 *sq.*, 190; fires of, in France, x. 183, 188, 189, 190, 192, 193; prayers to, at Midsummer, x. 210; claims human victims on St. John's Day (Midsummer Day), xi. 27, 29; print of his head on St. John's Eve, xi. 57; oil of, found on oak leaves at Midsummer, xi. 83, 293

—— the Baptist, bathing on his day, i. 277; his Midsummer festival, ii. 273; his chapel at Athens, ix. 53; associated by the Catholic Church with Midsummer Day, x. 160, 181

—— (the Evangelist), festival of, ix. 334

——, gossips of, in Sicily, v. 145, 251

——, the Knights of, x. 194; Grand Master of the Order of, x. 211

——, Sweethearts of, in Sardinia, ii. 92, v. 244 *sq.*, 251

St. John, Spenser, on reasons for head-hunting in Sarawak, v. 296

St. John's blood found on St. John's wort and other plants at Midsummer, xi. 56, 57

—— College, Oxford, the Christmas candle at, x. 255

—— Day (Midsummer Day), barren fruit-trees threatened on, ii. 22; swinging on, iv. 157, 280; or Eve (Midsummer Day or Eve), custom of bathing on, v. 246 *sqq.*; the Rush-cutter supposed to mow down the crops on, vii. 23; in Abyssinia, ix. 133; Midsummer fires on, x. 167 *sqq.*, 171 *sqq.*, 178, 179;

fire kindled by friction of wood on, x. 281; fern-seed blooms on, xi. 287. *See also* Midsummer

St. John's Eve (Midsummer Eve), in Sweden, ii. 65; Russian ceremony on, iv. 262; in Malta, x. 210 *sq.*; wonderful herbs gathered on, xi. 45 *sqq.*; sick children passed through cleft trees on, xi. 171

—— fires among the South Slavs, x. 178; among the Esthonians, x. 180. *See also* Midsummer fires

—— flower at Midsummer, xi. 50; gathered on St. John's Eve (Midsummer Eve), xi. 57 *sq.*

—— girdle, mugwort, xi. 59

—— herbs gathered at Midsummer, xi. 46 *sq.*, 49; a protection against evil spirits, xi. 49

—— Midsummer festival in Sardinia, v. 244 *sq.*

—— Night (Midsummer Eve), precautions against witches on, xi. 20 *n.*

—— root (*Johanniswurzel*), the male fern, xi. 66

—— wort (*Hypericum perforatum*), gathered at Midsummer, v. 252 *sq.*; a protection against witchcraft, ix. 160; garlands of, at Midsummer, x. 169 *n.*[3], 196; gathered on St. John's Day or Eve (Midsummer Day or Eve), xi. 49, 54 *sqq.*; a protection against thunder, witches, and evil spirits, xi. 54, 55, 74; thrown into the Midsummer bonfires, xi. 55

St. Joseph ill-treated in drought in Sicily, i. 300; feast of, ix. 297

St. Juan Capistrano, in California, ordeal of nettles and ants among the Indians of, x. 64. *See* San Juan Capistrano

St. Julien, church of, at Ath, xi. 36

St. Just, in Cornwall, Midsummer fire-custom at, x. 200

St. Kilda, not to be named in the Flannan Islands, iii. 393; All Saints' Day in, vi. 80; beating man clad in a cow's hide in, viii. 322, 323

St. Lawrence, the fire of, children thought to suffer from, if they touch young wrens in the nest, viii. 318; family of, their lives bound up with an old tree at Howth Castle, xi. 166

St. Leonard, patron of cattle, horses, and pigs, i. 7 *sq.*; blesses women with offspring, i. 8; patron of prisoners, i. 8; his shrines asylums, i. 8

Saint-Lô, the burning of Shrove Tuesday at, iv. 228 *sq.*

St. Louis, gift of healing by touch said to be derived by French kings from, i. 370

St. Luke, the festival of, on October

18th, souls of the dead thought to return on that day, vi. 55

Saintes-Maries, Midsummer custom at, v. 248, x. 194

St. Martin invoked in Switzerland to disperse a mist, x. 280

S. Martinus Dumiensis, on the date of the Crucifixion in Gaul, v. 307 *n.*

St. Mary, wells of, at Whitekirk and in the Isle of May, resorted to by women who wish to become mothers, ii. 161 ; *in Araceli*, the church of, at Rome, ii. 184

—— at Lübeck, church of, x. 100

——, Isle of, custom of whalers in the, viii. 235

St. Matthew's Day (August 21st), festival of weasels on, viii. 275

St. Maughold, gives the veil to St. Bridget, ii. 95

St. Michael ill-treated in drought, i. 300

—— in Alaska, annual festival of the dead among the Esquimaux at, vi. 51 ; bladder-festival of the Esquimaux at, viii. 249

St. Michael's cake, made at Michaelmas in the Hebrides, x. 149, 154 *n.*[3]

St. Neot's, in Huntingdonshire, ii. 71 *n.*[1]

St. Nicholas, patch of oats left at harvest for, vii. 233

St. Nicholas's Day (the 6th of December), the election of the Boy Bishop on, ix. 337, 338

St. Ninian, sacred trees near a chapel of, ii. 44

St. Nonnosius, relics of, in the cathedral of Freising, Bavaria, xi. 188 *sq.*

St. Olaf's Day (July 29th), lamb sacrificed by the Karels on, viii. 258 *n.*[2]

St. Ouen, his church at Rouen, ii. 165 ; early lives of, ii. 168

St. Patrick, canon attributed to, i. 367

—— and the Beltane fires, x. 157 *sq.*

St. Patrick's Chair, pilgrimage to, on Midsummer Eve, x. 205

—— Mount, near Downpatrick, x. 205

St. Paul, the Paulicians appeal to the authority of, i. 407 ; on immortality, vii. 91

St. Paul's, London, the Boy Bishop at, ix. 337

St. Peter, prayed to for rain, his image dipped in water, i. 307 *sq.*

—— and St. Paul, celebration of their day in London, x. 196

St. Peter's, Canterbury, the Boy Bishop at, ix. 337

—— at Rome, new fire at Easter in, x. 125

—— Day (29th June), poplar burnt on, ii. 141 ; the " Funeral of Kostroma " in Russia on, iv. 262 ; bonfires in

Belgium on, x. 194 *sq.* ; bonfires at Eton on, x. 197 ; fires in Scotland on, x. 207

St. Peter's Day (22nd February), ashes exchanged as presents on, vii. 300 ; expulsion of butterflies in Westphalia on, ix. 159 *n.*[1]

—— Eve, bonfires on, x. 195, 198, 199 *sq.* ; Midsummer fires in Ireland on, x. 202 ; gathering herbs on, xi. 45 *n.*[1]

St. Pierre d'Entremont, in Normandy, game of ball on Shrove Tuesday at, ix. 183

St. Pons, his image used in rain-making, i. 307

St. Rochus's Day, need-fire kindled on, x. 282

St. Romain and the dragon of Rouen, ii. 164 *sqq.* ; the shrine (*fierte*) of, ii. 167, 168, 170 *n.*[1], ix. 216

St. Sécaire, Mass of, i. 232 *sq.*

St. Simon and St. Jude's Day (October 28th), the dead feasted among the Letts on, vi. 74

St. Stephen, church of, at Beauvais, Festival of Fools in the, ix. 336

St. Stephen's Day (December 26th), the hunting and burial of the wren on, viii. 319 *sq.* ; custom of beating young women on, ix. 270 ; Lord of Misrule appointed in the Inner Temple on, ix. 333 ; Festival of Fools on, ix. 334

St. Sylvester's Day (New Year's Eve), superstition as to shadows on, iii. 88 ; precautions against witches on, ix. 164 *sq.*

—— Eve, evil spirits driven out of the houses at Trieste on, ix. 165

St. Tecla, the falling sickness cured in her church at Llandegla in Wales, ix. 52

St. Thomas's Day (21st December), the Twelve Days counted from, in some parts of Bavaria, ix. 327 ; election of the Boy Bishop on, ix. 337 *n.*[1] ; bonfires on, x. 266 ; witches dreaded on, xi. 73

—— Eve, witches active on, ix. 160

—— Mount, near Madras, the fire-walk at, xi. 8 *n.*[1]

St. Tredwels, chapel of, in one of the Orkney Islands, heap of stones to which each comer adds at, ix. 29

Saint-Valery in Picardy, torches carried through the fields on the first Sunday in Lent at, x. 113

St. Vitus, festival of, omens drawn from barley and wheat sown a few days before the, v. 252

St. Vitus's dance, supposed to be caused by demoniac possession or the shadow of an enemy, iii. 83 ; mistletoe a cure for, xi. 84

St. Vitus's Day, "fire of heaven" kindled on, x. 335

St. Wolfgang, Falkenstein chapel of, cleft rock through which pilgrims creep near, xi. 189

Saintonge, Feast of All Souls in, vi. 69 ; the Yule log in, x. 251 n.[1] ; wonderful herbs gathered on St. John's Eve in, xi. 45 ; St. John's wort in, xi. 55 ; vervain gathered at Midsummer in, xi. 62 n.[4] ; four-leaved clover at Midsummer in, xi. 63

—— and Aunis, burning the Carnival in, iv. 230 ; Midsummer fires in, x. 192

Saints, violence done to images of saints in Sicily to procure rain, i. 300 ; images of saints dipped in water as a rain-charm, i. 307 sq. ; as the givers of children to women, v. 78 sq., 91, 109 ; cairns near shrines of Mohammedan, ix. 21, 22

Sais, in Egypt, the festival of Osiris at, vi. 49 sqq. ; the grave of Osiris at, vi. 50

Sakai, the, of the Malay Peninsula, power of medicine-men among, i. 360 ; difference of dialect between husbands and wives among the, iii. 348

Sakalavas (Sakkalavas) of Madagascar, the worshipful sovereign of the, i. 397 sq.; their chiefs not allowed to sail the sea or cross rivers, iii. 10 ; taboos observed by their chiefs, iii. 10 sq.; taboo on mentioning personal names among the, iii. 327 ; customs as to names of dead kings among the, iii. 379 sq. ; sanctity of relics of dead kings among the, iv. 202 ; their worship of a black bull, viii. 40 n.

Sakarang Dyaks of Borneo, their euphemisms for smallpox, iii. 416

Sakkalava. See Sakalavas

Sakkara, in Egypt, pyramids at, vi. 4

Sakvarī song, ancient Indian hymn, supposed to embody the might of the thunderbolt, i. 269 sq.

Sâl tree, festival of the flower of the, among the Oraons, ii. 76 sq., 148, v. 47

—— trees, sacred groves of, among the Khonds, ii. 41 ; evil spirits of, among the Parahiya of Mirzapur, ii. 42

Salacia and Neptune, vi. 231, 233

Salagrama, fossil ammonite, an embodiment of Vishnu, ii. 26, 27 n.[2] ; married to the tulasi plant, ii. 26 sq.

Salamis in Cyprus, human sacrifices at, iv. 166 n.[1], v. 145 ; dynasty of Teucrids at, v. 145

Saldern, near Wolfenbuttel, the Corn-maiden at, at the end of reaping the rye at, vii. 150

Sale, nominal, of children, to deceive dangerous spirits, vii. 8

Salee, in Morocco, Midsummer fires at, x. 214, 216

Salem, Melchizedek, king of, v. 17

Saleyer, island off Celebes, certain words tabooed to sailors of, iii. 413 sq.

Salian Franks, custom as to the re-marriage of a widow among the, ii. 285

Salic law, re-marriage of widow under, ii. 285

Saligné, Commune de, Canton de Poiret, pretence of threshing the farmer's wife in, vii. 149 sq.

Salih, a prophet, annual festival of Bedouins at his grave in the Sinaitic Peninsula, iv. 97

Salii, the hymns of the, ii. 383 n.[4] ; the dancing priests of Mars, ix. 231 sqq. ; rule as to their election, vi. 244

Salisbury, May garlands at, ii. 62 ; the Boy Bishop at, ix. 337, 338 ; Midsummer giants at, xi. 37 sq.

Salish or Flathead Indians, artificial deformation of the head among the, ii. 298 ; recovery of lost souls among the, iii. 66 ; their sacrifice of their first-born children to the sun, iv. 184 ; ceremonies observed by them before eating the first wild berries or roots of the season, viii. 80 sq.

Salmon, twins thought to be, i. 263 ; shamans responsible for supply of, i. 358 ; taboos concerning, iii. 209 ; resurrection of, viii. 250 ; ceremonies at catching the first salmon of the season, viii. 253 sq., 255

Salmoneus, king of Elis, his mock thunder and lightning, i. 310, iv. 165 ; personated Zeus, ii. 177 ; killed by a thunderbolt, ii. 181

Salono, a Hindoo festival, v. 243 n.[1]

Salop (Shropshire), fear of witchcraft in, x. 342 n.[4]

Salsette, island near Bombay, use of iron as a talisman in, iii. 234, 236 ; locks unlocked at childbirth in, iii. 296

Salt, abstinence from, i. 124, 266, ii. 98, 105, 149, 248, viii. 75, 93 ; burnt to disperse fog, i. 314 ; as a charm, ii. 331 ; not to be eaten, iii. 10, 167, 182, 184, 194, 195, 196, viii. 190, 195, x. 19, 20, 60, 68, 69 ; name of, tabooed, iii. 401 ; the Mexican goddess of, ix. 278, 283 ; used in a ceremony after marriage, x. 25 sq. ; abstinence from, associated with a rule of chastity, x. 26 sqq.; not to be handled by menstruous women, x. 81 sq., 84 ; divination by, x. 244

Salt cake, divination by, at Hallowe'en, x. 238 *sq.*
—— -makers worship the goddess of Salt, ix. 283 ; their dance, ix. 284
—— -pans, the divinity of, incarnate in a woman, i. 410 ; continence observed by workers in, iii. 200
Saluting the rising sun, a Syrian custom, ix. 416
Salvation of the individual soul, importance attached to, in Oriental religions, v. 300
Salza district, ashes of pig's bone mixed with seed-corn in the, vii. 300
Salzburg, processions round the fields on St. George's Day in, ii. 344 ; harvest custom in, vii. 146 ; Queen of the Corn-ears in, vii. 146 ; the *Perchten* maskers in, ix. 240, 242 *sqq.*
Salzwedel, Whitsuntide king at, ii. 84 ; in the Altmark, the He-goat at harvest near, vii. 287
Samagitians, their sacred groves, ii. 43 ; deemed birds and beasts of the woods sacred, ii. 125 ; their annual festival of the dead, vi. 75
Samal, in North-Western Syria, Barrekub king of, v. 15 *sq.*
Samarai Archipelago, off New Guinea, Logea in the, iii. 354. *See* Logea
Samarcand, homoeopathic charms applied to babies in, i. 157 ; ceremonies to cause cold weather at, i. 329 *n.*[1] ; New Year ceremony at, iv. 151 ; temporary king at, iv. 151
Samaria captured by Shalmaneser, king of Assyria. iv. 169 ; the fall of, v. 25
Samaveda, the, ancient Indian collection of hymns, i. 269
Samban tribe of Dyaks, their belief as to the influence of Rajah Brooke on the crops, i. 362
Sambawa, East Indian island, human foundation-sacrifices in, iii. 91
Sambee, title signifying god, applied to the king of Loango, i. 396
Sambucus ebulus, dwarf elder, in rain-making, i. 273
Samhain, All Saints' Day (November 1st), New Year's Day in Ireland, x. 225
—— Eve of (Hallowe'en), new fire kindled in Ireland on, x. 139, 225 ; Irish New Year dated from, x. 139, 225 ; fiends and goblins let loose on, x. 226
Samhanach, Hallowe'en bogies, x. 227
Samhnagan, Hallowe'en fires, x. 230
Sami wood (*Prosopis spicigera*), used by the fire-priests of the Brahmans in kindling fire, ii. 248, 249, 250 *n.*
Samland, the Old Woman at harvest in, vii. 139 ; " Easter Smacks " in, ix.

269 ; fishermen will not go to sea on Midsummer Day in, xi. 26
Samnites, marriage custom of the, ii. 305 ; guided by a bull, iv. 186 *n.*[4] ; traced their origin to a " sacred spring," iv. 186
Samoa, mode of determining a child's guardian god in, i. 100 *n.*[1] ; gods of, in animal and human form, i. 389 ; special terms used with reference to persons of the blood-royal in, i. 401 *n.*[3] ; bleeding trees in, ii. 20 ; the turtle clan in, their custom at cutting up a turtle, iii. 122 ; persons who have handled the dead not allowed to touch food with their hands in, iii. 140 ; names of chiefs not to be pronounced in, iii. 382 ; expiation for disrespect to a sacred animal in, iv. 216 *sq.* ; circumcision practised in, iv. 220 ; conduct of the inhabitants in an earthquake, v. 200 ; butterfly god in, viii. 29 ; the Wild Pigeon family in, viii. 29. *See also* Samoan *and* Samoans
Samoan nobility, their perpetual fires, ii. 261
—— story of the recovery of a sick man's soul, iii. 65 ; of woman who was impregnated by the sun, x. 74 *sq.*
Samoans, their sacrifices of first-fruits, viii. 132 ; reckon their time by the periodic appearance of a sea-slug, ix. 142 *n.*[1]
Samon, a month of the Gallic calendar, ix. 343
Samorin, title of the kings of Calicut, iv. 47 *sq.*
Samos, sacred marriage of Zeus and Hera in, ii. 143 *n.*[1] ; the month of Cronion in, ix. 351 *n.*[2]
Samothrace, Cadmus in, iv. 89 *n.*[4]
Samothracian mysteries, iv. 89
Samoyed shamans, their familiar spirits in boars, xi. 196 *sq.*
—— story of the external soul, xi. 141 *sq.*
—— women thought to pollute things by stepping over them, iii. 424
Samoyeds of Siberia reluctant to name the dead, iii. 353 ; cut out the eyes of the wild reindeer which they kill, viii. 268
Sampson, Agnes, a Scotch witch, ix. 38
Samsi-Adad, king of Assyria, husband of Shammuramat (Semiramis), ix. 370 *n.*[1]
Samson, his burning the crops of the Philistines, vii. 298 *n.* ; effigy of, carried in procession of giants, xi. 36 ; an African, xi. 314
Samuel, the prophet, consulted about asses, v. 75 ; meaning of the name, v. 79
—— and Saul, v. 22

Samyas monastery near Lhasa, the King of the Years annually detained for seven days in the, ix. 220

San Cristoval, in the Solomon Islands, ghosts supposed to imprison souls in, iii. 56 ; mode of sacrificing a pig in, iii. 247

San Juan Capistrano, in California, Spanish mission at, viii. 169, 171 *n*.[1]

——, Indians of, their ceremony at the new moon, vi. 142 ; women's work among the, vii. 125 ; their calendar, vii. 125 *sq.*; ordeal of nettles and ants among the, x. 64

San Pellegrino, church of, at Ancona, the sarcophagus of St. Dasius in the, ix. 310

San Salvador in West Africa, native belief as to the soul of the king of, xi. 200

Sanctity, uncleanness, and taboo, their equivalence in primitive thought, iii. 285

—— of the head, iii. 252 *sqq.* ; of the corn, viii. 110

—— or pollution, their equivalence in primitive religion, iii. 145, 158, 224

—— and uncleanness not clearly differentiated in the primitive mind, x. 97 *sq.*

Sanctuary of Balder on the Sogne fiord in Norway, x. 104

Sand, souls of ogres in a grain of, xi. 120

Sanda-Sarme, a Cilician king, father-in-law of Ashurbanipal, v. 144

Sandacus, a Syrian, father of Cinyras, v. 41

Sandal of Perseus, at Chemmis in Upper Egypt, iii. 312 *n*.[2]

Sandan, legendary or mythical hero of Western Asia, v. 125 *sqq.*, ix. 368, 388 *sqq.* ; the burning of, v. 117 *sqq.*; identified by the Greeks with Hercules, v. 125, 143, 161, ix. 388 ; said to have founded Tarsus, v. 126 ; burnt in effigy on a pyre at Tarsus, v. 126, ix. 389 ; monument of, at Tarsus, v. 126 *n*.[2]; his figure on coins of Tarsus, v. 127

—— (Sandon, Sandes), Cappadocian and Cilician god of fertility, v. 125

—— and Baal at Tarsus, v. 142 *sq.*, 161

Sandanis the Lydian, dissuades Croesus from marching against the Persians, ii. 315

Sanderval, O. de, on dances at sowing in West Africa, ix. 235

Sandes, identified with Hercules, ix. 389. *See* Sandan

Sandflies imitated by maskers, ix. 381

Sandhill, in Northumberland, Midsummer fires at, x. 198

Sandon, or Sandan, name of the Lydian and Cilician Hercules, v. 182, 184, 185 ; a Cilician name, v. 182. *See* Sandan

Sandu'arri, a Cilician king, v. 144

Sandwich Islands (Hawaii), the king personated the god in the, i. 377 ; precaution as to the spittle of chiefs in the, iii. 289; belief in transmigration among natives of the, viii. 292 *sq.* *See also* Hawaii

Sanga, in Angola, all fires extinguished at death of king of, ii. 262

Sangerhausen, Midsummer fires near, x. 169

Sangi group of islands in the East Indies, Siaoo in the, ii. 33, iii. 288, iv. 218. *See* Siaoo

—— Islanders use a special language at sea, iii. 414

Sangro, river, in Italy, x. 210

Saning Sari, rice-goddess, among the Minangkabauers of Sumatra, represented by certain stalks or grains of rice, vii. 191, 192

Sanitation improved through superstition, iii. 130

Sankara and the Grand Lama, iii. 78

Sankuru River, in the Belgian Congo, xi. 264

Santa Catalina Istlavacan, birth-names of the Indians of, xi. 214 *n*.[1]

Santa Cruz, Melanesian island, wind-charm in, i. 321 ; avoidance of relations by marriage in, iii. 344

—— and Reef Islands, the rain-doctor in the, i. 272

Santa Felicita, successor of Mefitis, v. 205

Santa Maria Piedigrotta at Naples, church of, illuminated on the Nativity of the Virgin, x. 221

Santals, their belief as to the absence of the soul in dreams, iii. 38 ; swinging as a religious or magical rite among the, iv. 279

Santiago (St. James), name given by the Peruvian Indians to one of twins, i. 266 ; the horse of, i. 267

—— Tepehuacan, Indians of, their homoeopathic magic at sowing, planting, and fishing, i. 143 ; propitiate a tree before felling it, ii. 37 ; recovery of child's lost soul among the, iii. 67 *sq.*; their dread of noon, iii. 88 ; their custom at sowing, v. 239 ; their annual festival of the dead, vi. 55 ; transfer sickness to a well, ix. 4 ; their fast at sowing, ix. 347 *n*.[4]

Santorin, island of, its volcanic activity, v. 195

Santos, J. dos, on custom of putting kings of Sofala to death, iv. 37 *sq.*

Sâone-et-Loire, the last sheaf called the Fox in, vii. 296, 297

Saparoea, East Indian island, fishermen's magic in, i. 109 ; hunter's magic in, i. 114 ; treatment of the afterbirth in, i. 187

Sapoodi Archipelago, the name Sapoodi tabooed to sailors at sea, iii. 414

Sapor, king of Persia, how he took the city of Atrae, x. 82 *sq.*

Sappho, on the mourning for Adonis, v. 6 *n.*[2] ; on Adonis and Linus, vii. 216

Saqqarah, ancient Egyptian relief from, ix. 260 *n.*[3]

Saracus, last king of Assyria, v. 174

Saragacos Indians of Ecuador, their seclusion of women at childbirth, iii. 152

Sarah and Abraham, ii. 114

Sarajevo, need-fire near, x. 286

Sarawak, the Berawans of, i. 74 ; taboos observed by women during the search for camphor in, i. 124 *sq.* ; the Sea Dyaks of, i. 127, ix. 154 ; the Dyaks of, i. 361, iii. 67, 339, iv. 277, vii. 314, viii. 152 ; custom at making a clearing in the forest in, ii. 38 *sq.* ; head-hunting in, v. 295 *sq.*

Sarcolobus narcoticus, deceiving the spirit of the plant, ii. 23 *sq.*

Sardan or Sandan, the burning of, at Nineveh, ix. 389 *sq.* *See* Sandan

Sardanapalus, legendary Assyrian monarch, his monument at Tarsus, v. 126 *n.*[2]; his monument at Anchiale, v. 172 ; his death on the pyre, v. 172 *sqq.*, ix. 387 ; confounded with Ashurbanipal, v. 173 *sq.*, ix. 387 *sq.* ; his effeminacy, vi. 257, ix. 387 *sq.* ; perhaps personated by the king of the Sacaea, ix. 368, 387 *sq.* ; his epitaph, ix. 388

—— and Hercules, v. 172 *sqq.*

Sardes in Lydia, ix. 389, 391 ; captured by Cyrus, v. 174 ; lion carried round acropolis of, v. 184, vi. 249

Sardines worshipped by the Indians of Peru, viii. 250

Sardinia, Sweethearts of St. John at Midsummer in, ii. 92, v. 244 *sq.* ; blood-revenge in, ii. 321 ; gardens of Adonis in, v. 244 *sq.* ; Midsummer fires in, v. 245, x. 209

Sargal, in India, gardens of Adonis at, v. 243

Sariputi, village in Ceram, first-fruits of the rice offered to dead ancestors at, viii. 123

Sarmata Islands, marriage of the Sun and Earth in the, ii. 98 *sq.*

Sarmatian tribe moulded the heads of their children artificially, ii. 297

Sarn, valley of the, in Salzburg, the *Perchten* maskers in the, ix. 245

Sarna, the sacred grove of the Oraons, ii. 76

Sarna Burhi, goddess of the sacred grove, among the Oraons, ii. 76 *sq.*

Saron, ancient king of Troezen, perhaps a duplicate of Hippolytus, i. 26 *n.*[3]

Saronic Gulf, Hippolytus on the shore oι the, i. 19

Sarpedonian Artemis, in Cilicia, v. 167, 171

Sarum use, service-books of the, ix. 338

Sasabonsun, earthquake god of Ashantee, v. 201

Sassaks, the, of Lombok, their conception of the rice-spirit, vii. 201

Satan annually expelled by the Wotyaks, ix. 155 *sq.* ; annually expelled by the Cheremiss, ix. 156 ; preaches a sermon in the church of North Berwick, xi. 158 ; brings fern-seed on Christmas night, xi. 289

Satapatha Brâhmana, on the consecration of the sacrificer, i. 380 ; on the confession of sins, iii. 217 ; on transubstantiation, viii. 89 ; on the sun as Death, xi. 174 *n.*[1]

Satirical poems, Arab curses conveyed in, iii. 312

Saturday, persons born on a, can see ghosts, iii. 89, x. 285

——, Easter, new fire on, x. 121, 122, 124, 127, 128, 130

——, Holy, effigy of Queen of Lent beheaded on, iv. 244

Saturn, Roman god, his temple at Rome, i. 10 *sq.* ; personified at the Saturnalia, ii. 310 *sq.* ; the god of the seed, ii. 311 ; his festival the Saturnalia, ii. 311, ix. 306 *sqq.* ; perhaps personified by Roman kings, ii. 311, 322 ; the husband of Ops, vi. 233 ; the old Roman and Italian god of sowing, ix. 232, 306, 307 *n.*[1], 346 ; (Cronus), sacrifice to, at Cyrene, ix. 253 *n.*[3]; man put to death in the character of, ix. 309 ; dedication of the temple of, ix. 345 *n.*[1] ; perhaps represented by a dynasty of sacred kings, ix. 386

—— and the Golden Age, ix. 306, 344, 386

—— and Jupiter, ii. 323

—— and Lua, vi. 233

——, the planet, malignant influence of, iii. 315 ; its period of revolution round the sun, vi. 151 *sq.*

Saturnalia, the Roman, ii. 310 *sqq.*, ix. 306 *sqq.* ; how celebrated by Roman soldiers on the Danube, ii. 310, ix. 308 *sq.* ; Saturn personified at the, ii. 310 *sq.*, ix. 309 ; the festival of sowing, ii. 311 *sq.* ; the

King of the, ii. 311, ix. 308, 311, 312; licence granted to slaves at, ii. 312, ix. 307 *sq.*; its relation to the Carnival, ix. 312, 345 *sqq.*; its relation to Lent, ix. 345 *sqq.*

Saturnalia, licentious festival in general, at the marriage of Sun and Earth in Leti, Sarmata, and other East Indian islands, ii. 99; traces of, at May Day and Whitsuntide, ii. 272; preceding the trial and execution of kings at Fazolglou on the Blue Nile, iv. 16; at ceremonies of the new yams in Ashantee, viii. 62 *sq.*; at ceremonies of new fruits among the Pondos, viii. 66 *sq.*; at New Year among the Iroquois, ix. 127; at harvest among the Hos and Mundaris of North-Eastern India, ix. 136 *sq.*; such licentious festivals generally precede or follow an annual expulsion of evils, ix. 225 *sq.*; modern European analogies in Twelfth Night, the Festival of Fools, the Lord of Misrule, etc., ix. 312 *sqq.*; in ancient Greece, ix. 350 *sqq.*; in Western Asia, ix. 354 *sqq.*; wide prevalence of such festivals, ix. 407 *sqq.*; at celebration of puberty of a princess royal among the Zulus, x. 30 *sq.*; at New Year among the Swahili, x. 135; traces of, at Christmas, xi. 291 *n.*[2]

Saturnine temperament of the farmer, vi. 218

Satyrs in relation to goats, viii. 1 *sqq.*

Saucers, divination by seven, on Midsummer Eve, x. 209

Sauks, an Indian tribe of North America, their fast before war, iii. 163 *n.*[2]; effeminate sorcerers among the, vi. 255

Saul, burial of, v. 177 *n.*[4]

—— and David, v. 21

Saul's madness soothed by music, v. 53, 54

Savage, the, hidebound by custom, i. 217; a slave to the spirits of his dead forefathers, i. 217; his awe and dread of everything new, iii. 230; our debt to, iii. 419 *sqq.*; not illogical, viii. 202; his belief that animals have souls, viii. 204 *sqq.*; unable to discriminate clearly between animals and men, viii. 206 *sqq.*, 310; his faith in the immortality of animals, viii. 260 *sqq.*; observational powers of, ix. 326; secretiveness of, xi. 224 *sq.*; his dread of sorcery, xi. 224 *sq.*

Savage community, the, ruled by a council of elders, i. 216 *sq.*

—— conception of deity different from ours, i. 375 *sq.*

—— custom the product of definite reasoning, iii. 420 *n.*[1]

Savage Island, contagious magic of footprints in, i. 208; kings killed on account of dearth in, i. 354 *sq.*; cessation of monarchy in, iii. 17; castaways and returned natives killed in, iii. 113; mimic rite of circumcision in, iv. 219 *sq.*

—— philosophy, iii. 420 *sq.*

Savagery, the rise of monarchy essential to the emergence of mankind from, i. 217; underlying civilization, i. 236

Savages believe themselves naturally immortal, iv. 1; not to be judged by European standards, iv. 197 *sq.*; lament for the animals and plants which they eat, vi. 43 *sq.*; apologize to the animals which they kill, viii. 221 *sqq.*; their regulation of the calendar, ix. 326

Savile, Lord, his excavations at Nemi, i. 3 *n.*[2]

Saviour Gods, title bestowed by the Athenians on Demetrius Poliorcetes and Antigonus, i. 390

Savo, one of the Solomon Islands, sharkghost in, viii. 297

Savou, island of, treatment of the afterbirth in, i. 190; dread of children who resemble their parents in, iv. 287 (288, in Second Impression)

Sâwan, Indian month, v. 242; corresponding to August, ii. 149

"Sawing the Old Woman," a Lenten ceremony, iv. 240 *sqq.*

Saws at Mid-Lent, iv. 241, 242

Saxe-Coburg, the Old Woman at harvest in, vii. 139

Saxo Grammaticus, old Danish historian, x. 102 *n.*[1]; as to ceremony of standing on stones, i. 160; on kingship obtained by marriage, ii. 280 *sq.*; on the story of Hamlet, ii. 281 *n.*[2]; on understanding the speech of animals, viii. 146; his account of Balder, x. 103

Saxons, marriage with a stepmother among the, ii. 283; their vow, iii. 262

—— of Transylvania, precautions against witches on St. George's Eve among the, ii. 337 *sq.*; loose knots and unlock locks at childbirth, iii. 294, 296; the hanging of an effigy of Carnival among the, iv. 230 *sq.*; "Carrying out Death" among the, iv. 247 *sqq.*; their custom at maize harvest, iv. 254; harvest custom of the, v. 238; gird themselves with corn at reaping to prevent pains in the back, vii. 285; their belief as to a quail in the last corn, vii. 295; their customs at sowing, viii. 274 *sq.*; story of the external soul among the, xi. 116

Saxon cure for rupture, ix. 52

Saxon kings, their marriage with their step-mothers, iv. 193
—— story of soul as mouse, iii. 39 *n.*[1]
Saxony, May or Whitsuntide trees in, ii. 68 *sq.*; the Bridal Pair at Whitsuntide in, ii. 91 ; sacred oaks in, ii. 371 ; Whitsuntide mummers in, iv. 208 ; custom of "carrying out Death" in, iv. 236 ; Westerhüsen in, vii. 134 ; harvest customs in, vii. 134, 149 ; the last sheaf called the Old Man in, vii. 137 ; Oats-bride and Oats-bridegroom at harvest in, vii. 163 ; fires to burn the witches in, x. 160
——, Lower, the need-fire in, x. 272
——, the Wends of, ii. 69, vii. 149, xi. 297 ; their precautions against witches, ix. 163
Sayce, A. H., on kings of Edom, v. 16 ; on name of David, v. 19 *n.*[2]
Sayids in India think that a snake should never be called by its proper name, iii. 401 *sq.*
Scaloi, Drought, effigy of, used by the Roumanians in a rain-making ceremony, i. 274
Scamander, the river, supposed to take the virginity of brides, ii. 162
Scanderbeg, Prince of Epirus, his bones used as talismans by the Turks, viii. 154
Scandinavia, female descent of the kingship in, ii. 279 *sq.*
Scandinavian custom of the Yule Boar, vii. 300 *sqq.*; of the Yule Goat, viii. 327
Scania, province of Sweden, Midsummer fires in, x. 172
Scapegoat, plantain-tree as a, ix. 5 ; decked with women's ornaments, ix. 192 ; Jewish use of, ix. 210 ; a material vehicle for the expulsion of evils, ix. 224
Scapegoats, he-goats employed as, among the Akikuyu, iii. 214 *sq.* ; inanimate objects as, ix. 1 *sqq.* ; animals as, ix. 31 *sqq.*, 190 *sqq.*, 208 *sqq.* ; birds as, ix. 35 *sq.* ; public, ix. 170 *sqq.* ; divine animals as, ix. 216 *sq.*, 226 *sq.* ; divine men as, ix. 217 *sqq.*, 226 *sq.* ; in general, ix. 224 *sqq.*
——, human, ix. 38 *sqq.*, 194 *sqq.*, 210 *sqq.*; in classical antiquity, ix. 229 *sqq.*; in ancient Greece, ix. 252 *sqq.*; beaten, ix. 252, 255 ; stoned, ix. 253, 254 ; cast into the sea, ix. 254 *sq.*; reason for beating the, ix. 256 *sq.*
Scarification as a mode of exorcizing demons and ghosts, iii. 105 *sqq.* ; of warriors, iii. 160 *sq.*; of manslayer, iii. 180 ; of bodies of whalers, iii. 191 ; as a religious rite, viii. 75 ; as a mode of conferring swiftness of foot, viii. 159 ; of Zulu heaven-herds with heaven, viii. 160 *sq.*

"Scaring away the devil" at Penzance on the Eve of May Day, ix. 163 *sq.*
—— away the ghosts of the slain, iii. 168, 170, 171, 172, 174 *sq.*
Scarlet thread in charm against witchcraft, ix. 267
Scarli, poplar-trees burnt on Shrove Tuesday in Piedmont, iv. 224 *n.*[1]
Sceptre of Agamemnon worshipped as a god at Chaeronea, i. 365
Schäfer, H., on the tomb of Osiris at Abydos, vi. 198 *n.*[1]
Schaffhausen, the canton of, the cow at threshing in, vii. 291 ; St. John's three Midsummer victims at, xi. 27
Schar Mountains in Servia, "living fire" kindled in time of epidemics in the, ii. 237 ; the Slavs of the, ii. 238; need-fire in the, x. 281
Scharholz, Midsummer log in Germany, xi. 92 *n.*[1]
Schaumburg, Easter bonfires in, x. 142
Schechter, Dr. S., on Purim, ix. 364 *n.*[1]
Scheil, Father, on Elamite inscriptions, ix. 367 *n.*[3]
Scheroutz, in Russia, rain-making at, i. 277
Scheube, B., on the bear-festivals of the Ainos, viii. 185 *sqq.*
Schinz, Dr. H., on the huts of the Herero, ii. 213 *n.*[2]; on the firesticks of the Herero, ii. 218, 218 *n.*[1]
Schlanow, in Brandenburg, custom at sowing at, v. 238 *sq.*
Schlegel, G., on Chinese festival of fire, xi. 5 *n.*[1]
Schleswig, custom at threshing in, vii. 230 ; custom at rape-seed threshing in, vii. 287
Schlich, W., on mistletoe, xi. 315 *sq.*; on *Loranthus europaeus*, xi. 317
Schlochau, district of, witches' Sabbath in the, xi. 74
Schloss, Francis S., on the rule as to the felling of timber in Colombia, vi. 136 *n.*[4]
Schlukenau, in Bohemia, "burying the Carnival" at, iv. 209
Schmeckostern, "Easter Smacks," in Germany and Austria, iv. 268 *sq.*
Schmidt, A., on Greek mode of reckoning intervals of time, iv. 59 *n.*[1]; on the octennial cycle, vii. 82 *n.*[2]
Schmidt, W., on the superstitions of the Roumanians of Transylvania, ix. 107 *n.*[1]
Schmiedel, Professor P., on the burning of Winter at Zurich, iv. 261 *n.*[1]
Schöllbronn in Baden, "thunder poles" at, x. 145
Schonen, Southern, the last sheaf called the Beggar in, vii. 231 *sq.*
Schönthal, the abbot of, his fear of demons, ix. 105 *sq.*

Schönwert, village of Bohemia, expulsion of-witches on Walpurgis Night at, ix. 161

Schoolcraft, H. R., on the secrecy of personal names among the North American Indians, iii. 325 ; on North American Indian indifference to death, iv. 137 *sq.* ; on human sacrifices among the Pawnees, vii. 239 *n.*[1] ; on renewal of fire among the Iroquois, x. 134 *n.*[1]

Schörzingen, the Carnival Fool at, iv. 231

Schrader, O., on the Twelve Days, ix. 326 *n.*

Schrenck, L. von, on the bear-festivals of the Gilyaks, viii. 191 *sqq.*

Schürmann, C. W., on the Port Lincoln tribe of South Australia, xi. 216 *sq.*

Schüttarschen, in Bohemia, custom at threshing at, vii. 150 ; the mythical Wood-woman at harvest at, vii. 232

Schuyler, E., on the "Love Chase" among the Kirghiz, ii. 301 ; on a human scapegoat in Turkestan, ix. 45

Schvannes, bonfires, on the first Sunday in Lent, x. 111 *n.*[1]

Schwalm, the river, in Hesse, "the Little Whitsuntide Man" at Röllshausen on the, ii. 81

Schwaz, on the Inn, in the Tyrol, St. George's Day at, ii. 343 *sq.* ; the "grass-ringers" at, ix. 247

Schwegler, A., on Servius Tullius, ii. 196 *n.* ; on the "sacred spring," iv. 187 *n.*[4] ; on the death of Romulus, vi. 98 *n.*[2]

Schweina, in Thuringia, Christmas bonfire at, x. 265 *sq.*

Schweinfurth, G., on the reverence of the Dinka for their cattle, viii. 37 *sq.*

Schwenda, witches burnt at, x. 6

Science, the way for, paved by magic, i. 219 ; generalizations of, inadequate to cover all particulars, viii. 37 ; movement of thought from magic through religion to, xi. 304 *sq.* ; and magic, different views of natural order postulated by the two, xi. 305 *sq.*

Scipio, his fabulous birth, v. 81

Scira, an Athenian festival, x. 20 *n.*[1]

Scirophorion, an Attic month, viii. 5 *n.*[1], 8 *n.*[1]

Scirum, in Attica, Sacred Ploughing at, vii. 108 *n.*[4]

Scissors, in a charm to render a bridegroom impotent, iii. 301

"Scoring above the breath," cutting a witch on the forehead, x. 315 *n.*[2]; counter-spell to witchcraft, x. 343 *n.*

Scorpion, Arab treatment of a man stung by a, iii. 95 *n.*[8]

Scorpion's bite, the pain of it transferred to an ass, ix. 49 *sq.*

Scorpions, homoeopathic charm against, i. 153 ; Isis and the, vi. 8 ; a bronze image of a scorpion a charm against, viii. 280 *sq.* ; image of bird with scorpion in its mouth a charm against, viii. 281 ; souls of dead in, viii. 290

Scotch crannogs, oak timber in the, ii. 352

—— cure by knotted thread, iii. 304 *sq.*

—— fishermen, their use of iron as a talisman, iii. 233 ; their superstitions as to herring, viii. 252

—— fowlers and fishermen, words tabooed by, iii. 393 *sqq.*

—— witch, ix. 38 *sq.*

Scotland, magical images in, i. 68-70, 236 ; witches raise winds in, i. 322 ; notion as to whirlwinds in the Highlands of, i. 329 ; magical virtues ascribed to chiefs in the Highlands of, i. 368 ; the Highlanders of, their precautions against witchcraft, ii. 53 ; St. Bride's Day in the Highlands of, ii. 94 ; fertilizing virtue ascribed to wells in, ii. 161 ; new-born children passed through the smoke of fire in, ii. 232 *n.*[2]; race on horseback at a marriage in, ii. 304 ; oaks in the peat-bogs of, ii. 350 *sq.*; mirrors covered after a death in, iii. 95 ; fear of portraiture in, iii. 100 ; need-fire in, iii. 229, x. 289 *sqq.* ; iron as a talisman after a death in, iii. 236 ; sickness thought to be caused by knots in, iii. 302 ; common words tabooed in, iii. 392 *sqq.*; words tabooed by fishermen and others in, iii. 394 *sq.* ; harvest customs concerning the last corn cut in, v. 237, vii. 140 *sqq.*; the Highlanders of, sow in the moon's increase, vi. 134 ; the last corn cut at harvest called the Maiden in, vii. 155 *sqq.* ; custom of "dumping" at harvest in, vii. 226 *sq.*; corn left unreaped at harvest for "the aul' man" in, vii. 233 ; sayings as to the wren in, viii. 318 ; custom of casting stones on cairns in the Highlands of, ix. 20 ; cure for warts in, ix. 48 ; witches burnt in, ix. 165 ; Abbot of Unreason in, ix. 331 ; sacred wells in, x. 12 ; Celts called "thunder-bolts" in, x. 14 *sq.* ; Snake Stones in, x. 15 *sq.*, xi. 311 ; worship of Grannus in, x. 112 ; Beltane fires in, x. 146 *sqq.*; Midsummer fires in, x. 206 *sq.*; divination at Hallowe'en in, x. 229, 234 *sqq.*; bonfires at Hallowe'en in the Highlands of, x. 230 *sqq.*; animals burnt alive as a sacrifice in, x. 302 ; "scoring above the breath," a counter-charm for witchcraft in, x. 315 *n.*[2]; witches as hares in, x. 315 *n.*[1]; St. John's wort in,

xi. 54; the divining-rod in, xi. 67.
See also Highlands *and* Highlanders
Scotland, North-East, precautions against witches on May Day in, ii. 53
Scots pine, mistletoe on, xi. 315
Scott, Sir Walter, on witch at Stromness, i. 326; on the fear of witchcraft, x. 343; oaks planted by, xi. 166
Scottish Highlanders on the influence of the moon, vi. 132, 134, 140; their belief in bogies at Hallowe'en, x. 227; their belief as to Snake Stones, xi. 311
Scourging the man-god before death, a mode of purification, ix. 257; girls at puberty, x. 66 *sq.*
Scourgings, mutual, of South American Indians, ix. 262
Scouvion, x. 108. See *Escouvion*
Scratching the person with the fingers forbidden, i. 254, x. 38, 39, 41, 42, 44, 47, 50, 53, 92; as a magical rite to procure rain, i. 254 *sq.*; rules as to, iii. 146, 156, 158, 159 *n.*, 160, 181, 183, 189, 196; as a religious rite, viii. 75
Scrofula, kings thought to heal scrofula by their touch, i. 368 *sqq.*; chiefs of Tonga thought to heal scrofula by their touch, i. 371; thought to be caused and cured by touching a sacred chief or king, iii. 133 *sq.*, viii. 28; vervain a cure for, xi. 62 *n.*[1]; creeping through an arch of vines as a cure for, xi. 180; passage through a holed stone a cure for, xi. 187
Sculpin, the fish, called the rain-maker, i. 288
Scurrilities exchanged between vine-dressers and passers-by, vii. 258 *n.*[1]
Scurrilous language at the Eleusinian mysteries, vii. 38
Scylla, daughter of Nisus, the story of her treachery, xi. 103
Scythe used to behead cock on harvest-field, vii. 277, 278
Scythes whetted by reapers as if to mow down strangers in the harvest-field, vii. 229 *sq.*; and bill-hooks set out to cut witches as they fall from the clouds, x. 345 *sq.*
Scythian kings, their regalia, i. 365; human beings and horses sacrificed at their graves, v. 293; married the wives of their predecessors, ix. 368 *n.*[1]
Scythians put their kings in bonds in times of dearth, i. 354; their oath by the king's hearth, ii. 265; their belief in immortality, v. 294; their treatment of dead enemies, v. 294 *n.*[3]; set store on heads of enemies, vii. 256 *n.*[1]; revellers disguised as, ix. 355

Sdach Méac, title of annual temporary king of Cambodia, iv. 148
Sea, navel-string and afterbirth thrown into the, i. 184, 185, 190, 191; chief supposed to rule the, i. 337; virgins married to the jinnee of the, ii. 153 *sq.*; phosphorescence of the, ii. 154 *sq.*; prohibition to look upon the, iii. 9, 10; horror of the, iii. 10; offerings made to the, iii. 10; names of priests thrown into the, iii. 382 *sq.*; special language employed by sailors at, iii. 413 *sqq.*; scapegoats cast into the, ix. 254 *sq.*; menstruous women not allowed to approach the, x. 79; demands a human victim on Mid-summer Day, xi. 26
——, bathing in the, on St. John's Day or Eve, v. 246, 248; at Easter, x. 123; at Midsummer, x. 208, 210, xi. 30
"—— of Erechtheus" on the Acropolis at Athens, iv. 87
Sea beasts, taboos observed by the Esquimaux in regard to the dead bodies of, iii. 205 *sqq.*; Esquimau rules as to eating, viii. 84; their bladders restored to the sea by the Esquimaux, viii. 247 *sqq.*
—— Dyaks of Banting, rules observed by women during the absence of warriors among the, i. 127 *sq.*
—— Dyaks or Ibans .of Borneo, beat gongs in a storm, i. 328; their worship of serpents, v. 83; their festivals of the dead, vi. 58 *sq.*; effeminate priests or sorcerers among the, vi. 253, 256; their Head-feast in honour of the war-god, ix. 383 *sq.*
—— Dyaks of Sarawak, their sacred trees, ii. 40 *sq.*; their stories of the origin of omen birds, iv. 126, 127 *sq.*; their reasons for taking human heads, v. 295 *sq.*; their Festival of Departed Spirits, ix. 154
—— -eagle in homoeopathic magic, i. 152
—— -god, human sacrifice to, ix. 255
—— -mammals, Esquimau atonement for killing, iii. 207; taboos observed by the Esquimaux after the killing of, iii. 207 *sqq.*; myth of their origin, iii. 207, viii. 246; the goddess Sedna the mother of the, iii. 210
—— -slugs, ceremonies at the annual appearance of, in Fiji and Tumleo, ix. 141 *sqq.*
Seal, descendants of the, in Sutherland-shire, xi. 131 *sq.* *See also* Seals
Sealing up eyes, nose, and mouth of the dying to prevent the escape of the soul, iii. 31

Seals, supposed influence of lying - in women on, iii. 152 ; taboos observed after the killing of, iii. 207 *sq.*, 209, 213 ; supposed to have sprung from the severed fingers of the goddess Sedna, iii. 207, viii. 246 ; care taken of the bladders and bones of, viii. 247 *sqq.*, 257 ; the bones of, returned to the sea, viii. 258 *n.*[2]

Sealskins in sympathy with the tides, i. 167

Season of festival a clue to the nature of a deity, vi. 24

Seasons, Athenian sacrifices to the, i. 310 ; magical and religious theories of the, v. 3 *sq.*

Seats placed for souls of dead at the Midsummer fires, x. 183, 184

Seb (Keb or Geb), Egyptian earth-god, father of Osiris, by the sky-goddess Nut, v. 283 *n.*[3], vi. 6

Seclusion of travellers after a journey, iii. 113 ; of those who have handled the dead, iii. 138 *sqq.* ; of women at menstruation, iii. 145 *sqq.*, x. 76 *sqq.*; of women at childbirth, iii. 147 *sqq.*; of tabooed persons, iii. 165 ; of manslayers, iii. 166 *sqq.*; of cannibals, iii. 188 *sqq.*; of men who have killed large game, iii. 220 *sq.* ; of girls at puberty, x. 22 *sqq.*; of girls at puberty in folktales, x. 70 *sqq.* ; reasons for the seclusion of girls at puberty, x. 76 *sqq.* ; of novices at initiation, xi. 233, 241, 250, 253, 257 *n.*[1], 258, 259, 261, 264, 266

Second sight enjoyed by persons born with a caul, i. 187 *sq.*

Secret graves of kings, chiefs, and magicians, vi. 103 *sqq.*

—— language learnt at initiation, xi. 253, 255 *n.*[1], 259, 261 *n.*

—— names among the Central Australian aborigines, iii. 321 *sq.*

—— societies in the Bismarck Archipelago, jurisdiction exercised by, i. 340 ; among the Indians of British Columbia, vii. 20 ; in North-Western America, ix. 377 *sq.*; on the Lower Congo, xi. 251 *sqq.*; in West Africa, xi. 257 *sqq.*; in the Indian tribes of North America, xi. 267 *sqq.*; and totem clans, related to each other, xi. 272 *sq.* *See also* Belli-Paaro, Dukduk, Kakian, *Ndembo*, *Nkimba*, *Purra*, and *Semo*

Secretiveness of the savage, xi. 224 *sq.*

Sed festival in ancient Egypt, vi. 151 *sqq.*; its date perhaps connected with the heliacal rising of Sirius, vi. 152 *sq.* ; apparently intended to renew the king's life by identifying him with the dead and risen Osiris, vi. 153 *sq.*

Sedanda, an African king, his suicide, iv. 38

Sedbury Park oak, in Gloucestershire, mistletoe on the, xi. 316

Sedna, an Esquimau goddess of the lower world, iii. 152, 207, 208, 209, 211, 213, viii. 84, 246 ; mother of the sea-mammals, iii. 210 ; her annual expulsion by the Esquimaux, ix. 125 *sq.*

Sedum telephium, orpine, used in divination at Midsummer, xi. 61

Seed sown over weakly children to strengthen them, vii. 11 ; sown by women, vii. 113 *sqq.* ; sown by children, vii. 115 *sq.* *See also* Sowing

Seed - corn, fumigated with wood of sacred cedar, ii. 49 ; fertilized at the Thesmophoria, vii. 63 ; grain of last sheaf mixed with the, vii. 135 ; holy grains mixed with the, to fertilize it, vii. 205 ; taken from the last sheaf, vii. 278 ; feathers of cock mixed with the, vii. 278, viii. 20 ; ashes mixed with the, vii. 300 ; bones of pigs mixed with the, vii. 300, viii. 20 ; the Yule Boar mixed with the, vii. 301, viii. 20 ; grain taken from the Corn - mother mixed with the, vii. 304 ; pig's flesh sown with the, viii. 18, 20 ; cakes made out of the last sheaf mixed with the, viii. 328 ; charred remains of Midsummer log mixed with the, xi. 92

—— -rice, seed sown ceremonially mixed with the, iv. 149 ; precautions at reaping the, vii. 181 ; soul of the rice caught and mixed with the, vii. 189

—— -time, annual expulsion of demons at, ix. 138

Seeds and roots, wild, collected by women, vii. 124 *sqq.*

Seeman, Berthold, on St. John's blood, xi. 56

Seers, their ears licked by serpents, viii. 147 *n.*[1]

Segera, a sago magician of Kiwai, dismembered after death, vi. 101, 102

Seirkieran, perpetual fire in the monastery of, ii. 241 *sq.*

Seitendorf, in Moravia, custom of " carrying out Death" at, iv. 238 *sq.*

Seker (Sokari), title of Osiris, vi. 87

Selangor, Malay State, rice-crop supposed to depend on the district officer in, i. 361 ; durian trees threatened near Jugra in, ii. 21 ; bringing home the Soul of the Rice at Chodoi in, vii. 198 ; demons of disease expelled in a ship from, ix. 187 *sq.*

Selemnus, the River, its water a cure for love, ix. 3

Seler, Professor Eduard, on the ancient Mexican calendar, vi. 29 *n.* ; Aztec text of Sahagun partially translated by, vii. 175 ; on the Mexican festival of Toxcatl, ix. 149 n.[2], 277 ; on nagual, xi. 213 n.

Seleucia, plague blocked up in hole at, ix. 64

Seleucus, a grammarian, v. 146 n.[1]

Seleucus Nicator, king, his buildings at the temple of Zeus in Olba, v. 151

Seleucus the Theologian, v. 146 n.[1]

Self-mutilation of Attis and his priests, v. 265

Seligmann, Dr. C. G., on the meaning of helaga in the Motu tribe of New Guinea, ii. 106 n.[2] ; on the custom of putting Shilluk kings to death, iv. 17 sqq., vi. 163 ; on the danger of allowing Shilluk kings to grow old, iv. 21 ; on the right of candidates for the kingship to attack the Shilluk kings, iv. 22 ; on the willingness of Shilluks to accept the fatal sovereignty, iv. 23 ; on sickness as supposed to be caused by the soul of a dead Shilluk king, iv. 26 ; on the divine spirit supposed to animate Shilluk kings, iv. 26 sq. ; on the Dinkas, iv. 30 sqq. ; on the custom of putting Dinka rain-makers to death, iv. 33 ; on the five supplementary Egyptian days, vi. 6 n.[3] ; on the worship of dead Shilluk kings, vi. 161 n.[2] ; on the name of the Supreme Being of the Dinkas, viii. 40 n., 114 n.[2]

Selkit, Egyptian goddess, patroness of matrimony, ii. 131

Selwanga, python-god of the Baganda, v. 86

Semang tribes of the Malay Peninsula, power of medicine-men among the, i. 360 ; think that the souls of their dead chiefs transmigrate into wild beasts, iv. 85

Semangat, Malay word for the soul, iii. 28, 35, vii. 181, 183

Semele, mother of Dionysus, iv. 3 ; how Zeus got Dionysus by, vii. 14 ; descent of Dionysus into Hades to bring up, vii. 15

Semic in Bohemia, beheading the king on Whit-Monday at, iv. 209

Seminole Indians, souls of the dying caught among the, iv. 199 ; their Green Corn Dance, viii. 76 sq. ; their fear of rattle-snakes, viii. 217

Semiramis, lustful Assyrian queen, ii. 275 ; at Hierapolis, v. 162 n.[2] ; as a form of Ishtar (Astarte), v. 176 sq. ; said to have burnt herself, v. 176 sq., ix. 407 n.[2] ; the mythical, a form of the great Asiatic goddess, vi. 258 ; mythical and historical, ix. 369 sqq. ; the mounds of, ix. 370, 371,

373, 388 n.[1] ; her love for a horse, ix. 371, 407 n.[2] ; the sad fate of her lovers, ix. 371 ; perhaps supposed to be incarnate in a series of women, ix. 386

Semites, moral evolution of the, iii. 219 ; sacrifices of children among the, iv. 166 sqq. ; agricultural, worship Baal as the giver of fertility, v. 26 sq. ; sacred stocks and stones among the, v. 107 sqq. ; traces of mother - kin among the, vi. 213

Semitic Baal in relation to the Minotaur, iv. 75

—— gods, uniformity of their type, v. 119

—— kings, the divinity of, v. 15 sqq. ; as hereditary deities, v. 51

—— language, Egyptian language akin to the, vi. 161 n.[1]

—— personal names indicating relationship to a deity, v. 51

—— worship of Tammuz and Adonis, v. 6 sqq.

Semlicka, festival of the dead among the Letts, vi. 74

Semo, a secret society of Senegambia, xi. 261

Sena, island of, virgin priestesses in, ii. 241 n.[1]

Sena-speaking people to the north of the Zambesi transfer sickness to effigy of pig, ix. 7

Senal Indians of California, their notion as to fire stored in trees, xi. 295

Sencis, the, of Peru, their ceremony at an eclipse of the sun, i. 311

Seneca, on sacred groves, ii. 123 ; as to the soul on the lips, iii. 33 n.[3] ; on the offerings of Egyptian priests to the Nile, vi. 40 ; on the marriage of Roman gods, vi. 231 ; on Salacia as the wife of Neptune, vi. 233

Senegal, Cayor in, iii. 9 ; Walo on the river, iii. 118 ; precaution as to spittle in, iii. 289 ; belief as to conception without sexual intercourse in, v. 93 n.[2] ; myth of marriage of Sky and Earth in, v. 282 n.[2] ; custom of throwing stones on cairns in, ix. 30 n.[2]

Senegal and Niger region of West Africa, the wild fig-tree regarded as a fetish-tree in, ii. 317 n.[1]

Senegambia, the Feloupes of, i. 297 ; the Walos of, i. 370, xi. 79 ; the Sereres of, iii. 70 ; the Wolofs of, iii. 323 ; the Mandingoes of, vi. 141 ; Python clan in, viii. 174 ; the Foulahs of, viii. 214 ; stones thrown on graves of murderers in, ix. 16 ; the Banmanas of, ix. 261 ; secret society among the Soosoos of, xi. 261 sq.

Senjero, sacrifice of first-born sons in, iv. 182 *sq.*

Sennacherib, his siege of Jerusalem, v. 25; said to have built Tarsus, v. 173 *n.*[4]

Sennar, a province of the Sudan, human hyaenas in, x. 313

Senseless Thursday, the last Thursday in Carnival, ceremony with whips and brooms in the Tyrol on, ix. 248

Seoul, capital of Corea, custom on New Year's Day at, iii. 283; tiger eaten at, to make eater brave, viii. 145

Separation of children from their parents among the Baganda, x. 23 *n.*[2]

—— of earth and sky, myth of the, v. 283

Sepharvites, their sacrifices of children, iv. 171

September, month of the maize harvest in modern Greece, vii. 48; the 1st of, mock burial of flies by Russian girls on, viii. 279 *sq.*; the 13th of, Roman custom of knocking a nail into a wall on, ix. 66; expulsion of evils by the Incas of Peru in, ix. 128; eve of the 1st of, new fire in villages near Moscow on the, x. 139; the 8th of, feast of the Nativity of the Virgin, x. 220; the fire-walk in, xi. 9

Seranglao archipelago, custom as to children's cast teeth in the, i. 179; rule as to gathering coco-nuts in the, iii. 201

Serapeum at Alexandria, vi. 119 *n.*; its destruction, vi. 217

Serapis, the later form of Osiris, vi. 119 *n.*; the rise of the Nile attributed to, vi. 216 *sq.*; the standard cubit kept in his temple, vi. 217

Sereres of Senegambia, detention of souls by sorcerers among the, iii. 70

Seriphos, custom of swinging on Tuesday after Easter in, iv. 283 *sq.*

Serpent in homoeopathic magic, i. 154 *sq.*; dried, in ceremony for stopping rain, i. 295 *sq.*; hung up as a wind-charm, i. 323; or dragon of water, ii. 155 *sqq.*; or dragon personated by kings, iv. 82; the Brazen, worshipped to the time of Hezekiah, iv. 86; sacred, on the Acropolis at Athens, iv. 86; as the giver of children, v. 86; at rites of initiation, v. 90 *n.*[4]; fed by a woman out of a saucer, type in Greek art, viii. 18 *n.*[2]; killing the sacred, viii. 174 *sq.*; ceremonies performed after killing a, viii. 192 *sq.*; the Brazen, set up by the Israelites in the wilderness, viii. 281; girls at puberty thought to be visited by a, x. 31; supposed to swallow girl at puberty, x. 57; ten-headed, external soul in a, xi. 104 *sq.*; twelve-headed, external soul of demon in a, xi. 143; external soul of chief in a, xi. 201. *See also* Serpents, Snake, *and* Snakes

Serpent-god, married to human wives, v. 66 *sqq.*; thought to control the crops, v. 67

Serpent's fat a charm against witches on St. George's Day, ii. 335

—— flesh eaten to learn the language of animals, viii. 146

Serpents impart a knowledge of the language of birds, i. 158; in relation to St. George, ii. 344 *n.*[4]; purificatory ceremonies observed after killing, iii. 221 *sqq.*; not to be called by their proper names, iii. 398, 399, 401 *sq.*, 407, 408, 411; transmigration of the souls of the dead into, iv. 84; reputed the fathers of human beings, v. 80 *sqq.*; as embodiments of Aesculapius, v. 80 *sq.*; worshipped in Mysore, v. 81 *sq.*; as reincarnations of the dead, v. 82 *sqq.*, xi. 211 *sq.*; fed with milk, v. 84 *sqq.*, 87; thought to have knowledge of life-giving plants, v. 186; souls of dead kings incarnate in, vi. 163, 173; offerings to, viii. 17 *sq.*; in the "chasms of Demeter and Persephone," viii. 17 *sq.*; lick the ears of seers, viii. 147 *n.*[1]; inspired human mediums of, viii. 213; charms against, viii. 281; souls of the dead in, viii. 291; and lizards supposed to renew their youth by casting their skins, ix. 302 *sqq.*; burnt alive at the Midsummer festival in Luchon, xi. 38 *sq.*, 43; witches turn into, xi. 41; worshipped by the old Prussians, xi. 43 *n.*[3]; in the worship of Demeter, xi. 44 *n.*; the familiars of witches, xi. 202. *See also* Serpent, Snake, *and* Snakes

Serpents' eggs (glass beads) in ancient Gaul, x. 15

Servia, rain-making ceremony in, i. 273; mode of kindling fire by friction of wood in, ii. 237; divination on St. George's Day in, ii. 345; Midsummer fire custom in, x. 178; the Yule log in, x. 258 *sqq.*; need-fire in, x. 281, 282 *sqq. See also* Servian *and* Servians

Servian forest, the great, ii. 237, 237 *n.*[1]

—— stories of the external soul, xi. 110 *sqq.*

—— women, their charm to hoodwink their husbands, i. 149

Servians, their belief as to souls in the form of butterflies, iii. 41; their precaution against vampyres, ix. 153 *n.*[1] ; house-communities of the, x. 259 *n.*[1]

Servitude of Apollo and Cadmus for eight years for the slaughter of dragons, iv. 70 *n.*[1], 78

Servius, Virgilian commentator, on the grove of Egeria, i. 18 *n.*[4]; on Virbius, i. 20 *sq.*, 40, ii. 129; on the worship of Virbius, i. 20 *n.*[3]; on Virbius as the lover of Diana, i. 21, 40 ; on Dido's costume, iii. 313; on the magical virtue of knots, iii. 313 *n.*[1]; · on the legend of Erigone, iv. 282 ; on the death of Attis, v. 264 *n.*[4]; on the marriage of Orcus, vi. 231 ; on Salacia as the wife of Neptune, vi. 233; on Lityerses, vii. 217 *n.*[1]

Servius Tullius, Roman king, his innovation in Roman currency, i. 23 *n.*[5]; laws of, ii. 115, 129; and Fortuna, ii. 193 *n.*[1], 272 ; legend of his birth from the fire, ii. 195 *sq.*,·vi. 235 ; said to have been an Etruscan, ii. 196 *n.* ; succeeded by his son-in-law, ii. 270 ; his descent, ii. 270 *n.*[6]; his death, ii. 320 *sq.*

Sesostris, so-called monument of, in Lydia, v. 185

Set, or Typhon, brother of Osiris, vi. 6, viii. 30 ; murders Osiris, vi. 7 *sq.* ; accuses Osiris before the gods, vi. 17 ; brings a suit of bastardy against Horus, vi. 17 ; his combat with Horus, vi. 17 ; reigns over Upper Egypt, vi. 17 ; torn in pieces, vi. 98 ; the Egyptian devil, viii. 30 ; the birth of, ix. 341. *See also* Typhon

Setonje, village in Servia, need-fire at, ii. 237, x. 282 *sqq.*

Sety I., king of Egypt, represented in the hall of the Osirian mysteries at Abydos, vi. 108

Seven or multiples of seven in offerings to the dead, ii. 32

Seven bonfires, lucky·to see, x. 107, 108
—— ears of last year's crop to attract the corn, vii. 190 ; of rice to form the Soul of the Rice at harvest, vii. 198
—— knots in magic, iii. 303, 304, 305, 308
—— leaps over Midsummer fire, x. 213
—— -legged effigy of Lent, iv. 244 *sq.*
—— months' child, vii. 26, 29
—— rice-stalks cut and brought home with the King of the Rice in Mandeling, vii. 197
—— sorts of plants gathered at Midsummer, xi. 51 *sq.*
—— years, a were-wolf for, x. 310 *n.*[1], 316 *n.*[2]
—— youths and maidens, tribute of, to the Minotaur, iv. 74 *sqq.*

Sevenoaks, in Kent, May garlands at, ii. 62

Seventh month of pregnancy, ceremony performed in the, i. 72 *sq.*

Sewing forbidden to women in absence of whalers, i. 121 ; forbidden to women in absence of warriors, i. 128 ; as a charm to blind wolves, ii. 330 ; as a charm to render wolves powerless, iii. 307

Sex totems among the natives of South-Eastern Australia, xi. 214 *sqq.* ; called "brother" and "sister" by men and women respectively, xi. 215

Sexes, of plants, recognized by some savages and by the ancients, ii. 24 ; influence of the, on vegetation, ii. 97 *sqq.* ; division of labour between the, vii. 129 ; danger apprehended from the relation of the, xi. 277 *sq.*

Sextus Pompeius, his consultation of the Thessalian witch, iii. 390

Sexual communism, tradition of, ii. 284, 287
—— crime, blighting effects attributed to, ii. 107 *sqq.*
—— intercourse practised to make the crops and fruits grow, ii. 97, 98 *sqq.*
—— orgies as a fertility charm, ii. 98 *sqq.*

Seyf el-Mulook and the jinnee, the story of, xi. 137

Sgaus, Karen tribe of Burma, will not mention their parents' names, 337

Sgealoir, the burying-ground of, in North Uist, x. 294

Sgreball, three pence, tax paid to the king of Munster for each fire in Ireland, x. 139

Shades of dead animals, fear of offending, iii. 205, 206, 207

Shadow, the soul identified with the, iii. 77 *sqq.* ; injury done to a man through his, iii. 78 *sqq.* ; diminution of shadow regarded with apprehension, iii. 86 *sq.* ; loss of the, regarded as ominous, iii. 88 ; not to fall on a chief, iii. 255

Shadow Day, a gipsy name for Palm Sunday, iv. 243
—— -plays as a rain-charm in Java, i. 301 *n.*
—— Queen, the, thought to pass under ground in spring and reappear in autumn, iv. 243

Shadows of sacred trees not to be trodden on by women, ii. 34 ; of people drawn out by ghosts, iii. 80 ; animals injured through their, iii. 81 *sq.* ; of trees sensitive, iii. 82 ; of certain birds and people viewed as dangerous, iii. 82 *sq.* ; of people built into the foundations of edifices, iii. 89 *sq.* ; of mourners dangerous, iii. 142 ; of certain persons dangerous, iii. 173

Shahpur district of the Punjaub, rain-making in the, i. 278

Shakespear, Lt.-Colonel J., on the belief in demons among the Lushais, ix. 94

Shakespeare on death at the turn of the tide, i. 168

Shaking of victim as sign of its acceptance, i. 384 *sq.*

Shalmaneser, king of Assyria, captures Samaria, iv. 169 ; carries the Israelites into captivity, iv. 171

Sham - fights at installation of Shilluk kings, iv. 24 ; in honour of the dead, iv. 96 *sq.*; at annual festival in Hawaii, iv. 117 *sq.*; at the first bringing in of the rice among the Kayans, vii. 98 ; at the festival of new fruits among the Creek Indians, viii. 75 ; (mimic battles) before going to war, viii. 207 ; at festival of New Year among the Tenggerese of Java, ix. 184 ; at the sacrifice of a woman among the Mexicans, ix. 289 ; at festival of New Year among the Swahili, x. 135

—— graves and corpses to deceive demons, viii. 98 *sqq.*

Shaman, function of the, ix. 79 *sq.*

Shamanism, magical ritual of the Vedas akin to, i. 229 ; among the Koryaks, ix. 101

Shamanistic faith and magic, period of, among the forefathers of the Indo-Germanic race, ix. 91

Shamans, the importance of, among the Maidu, i. 357 *sq.* ; expected to drive away demons and disease from the village, i. 358 ; expected to inflict death and disease on hostile villages, i. 358 ; bones of dead, placed in trees, ii. 32 ; Buryat, their mode of recovering lost souls, iii. 56 *sq.* ; among the Thompson Indians, their mode of recovering lost souls, iii. 57 *sq.* ; Yakut, their mode of recovering lost souls, iii. 63 ; among the Haidas kill the souls of foes, iii. 72 *n.*[1] ; thought to swallow people's souls, iii. 76 *sq.* ; among the Navajos, ceremony performed by them over a returned captive, iii. 113 ; in Corea, their control of demons, ix. 99, 100 ; among the Koryaks, enjoy the favour of demons and pull out their invisible arrows, ix. 101, 126 ; expel demons at the winter solstice, ix. 126 ; among the Esquimaux, their grotesque masks of supernatural beings, ix. 379 ; their second sight, ix. 380 ; of the Yakuts and Samoyeds, keep their external souls in animals, xi. 196

Shamash, Babylonian sun-god, xi. 80 *n.*[3] ; his human wives, v. 71

——, Semitic god, v. 16 *n.*[1]

Shamashshumukin, king of Babylon, burns himself, v. 173 *sq.*, 176

Shammuramat, Assyrian queen, and Semiramis, v. 177 *n.*[1], ix. 370 *n.*[1]

Shampoo, the fatal, ix. 42

Shan custom on return from a funeral, iii. 51 ; modes of disposing of cut hair and nails, iii. 277. *See also* Shans

Shanga, city in East Africa, story of an African Samson at, xi. 314

Shanghai, geomancy at, i. 170

Shans of Burma, rules observed by wife of absent warrior among the, i. 128 ; obtain rain by drenching images of Buddha, i. 308 ; their theory of earth-quakes, v. 198 ; cut bamboos for building in the wane of the moon, vi. 136 ; custom of executioners among the, viii. 155

—— of Indo-China, their human sacrifices for the crops, vii. 243

—— of Kengtung, their expulsion of demons, ix. 116 *sq.*

—— of Southern China, their annual expulsion of the fire-spirit, ix. 141

Shape, magical changes of, vii. 305

Shark, king of Dahomey represented with body of a, iv. 85

Shark Point, priestly king at, iii. 5, 123

—— -shaped hero named Sigai in the island of Yam, v. 139 *n.*[1]

Sharks, ancestral spirits in, viii. 123, 127 ; offerings of flying-fish set before images of, viii. 127; temples dedicated to, viii. 292 ; souls of dead in, viii. 292 *sq.*, 297

Sharp instruments, use of, tabooed, iii. 205, 237 *sqq.*

Shaving forbidden, iii. 194 ; prisoners, reason of, iii. 273

Shawms blown to ban witches, ix. 160

Shawnee prophet, xi. 157

Sheaf buried as a magical rite, i. 69

—— of corn dressed up to represent Death, iv. 248

——, the first cut, thought to contain the soul of the rice, vi. 239, vii. 197 *sq.*; lamentations over, vii. 215; called the "Cross of the Horse" and trodden by the youngest horse on the farm, vii. 294

——, the largest and finest, buried in corn-field from seed-time to harvest, vii. 174 *sq.*

——, the last cut at harvest used to make Brüd's bed in the Highlands of Scotland, ii. 94 *n.*[2]; the Corn-mother in, vii. 133 *sqq.*; thresher tied up in, vii. 134, 147, 148 ; dressed or made up as a woman,

vii. 134, 135, 136, 137, 139 *sq.*, 140, 141, 145, 146, 148, 150, 153, 154, 155, 157, 159, 160, 162, 163, 166, 190 *sq.* ; drenched with water, vii. 134, 137, 145, 297 ; given to cattle, vii. 134, 155, 158, 161, 170 ; stones fastened to, vii. 135 *sq.*, 138, 139 ; harvester tied up in, vii. 134, 139, 145, 221, 222 ; called the Harvest-mother, vii. 135 ; called the Great Mother, vii. 135, 136 ; called the Old Woman or Old Man, vii. 136 *sqq.* ; called the Grandmother, vii. 136 ; person identified with, vii. 138 *sq.* ; corn-spirit caught in, vii. 139 ; called the *Cailleach* (Old Wife), vii. 140 *sqq.* ; burnt and its ashes strewed on fields, vii. 146 ; called the Bastard, vii. 150 ; called the Child, vii. 151 ; given to the cattle at Christmas, vii. 155, 158, 160 *sq.* ; cut by the youngest girl on the field, vii. 157, 158 ; kept till Christmas, then given to a mare in foal, vii. 160, 161 *n.*[1] ; given to the first mare that foals, vii. 160, 162 ; called the Bride, vii. 162 *sq.* ; supposed to ward off fairies, vii. 165 ; representative of the corn-spirit, vii. 168, viii. 48 ; in Lower Burma, vii. 190 *sq.* ; called the Old Man, vii. 218 *sqq.* ; an object of desire and emulation, vii. 218 *n.*[2] ; in India, vii. 222 *sq.*, 234 *n.*[2] ; called the Neck, vii. 266, 267, 268 ; called the Head, vii. 268 ; the corn-spirit caught in, vii. 270 ; thresher of the last sheaf treated as an animal, vii. 271 ; called the Bitch, vii. 272 ; called the Wolf, vii. 273 ; shaped like a wolf, vii. 274 ; called the Cock, vii. 276 ; live cock bound up with, vii. 278 ; called the Hare, vii. 279 ; called the Cat, vii. 280 ; called the Goat, vii. 282, 283 ; shaped like a goat, vii. 283 ; made up in form of horned ox, vii. 289 ; called the Buffalo-bull, vii. 289 ; called the Cow, vii. 289 ; race of reapers to, vii. 291 ; called the Mare, vii. 292 *sq.* ; called the Fox, vii. 297 ; made in form of fox, vii. 297 ; called the Rye-boar, vii. 298 ; called the Rye-sow, Wheat-sow, Corn-sow, or Oats-sow, vii. 298 ; corn of, used to bake the Yule Boar, vii. 300 *sq.* ; the corn-spirit immanent in, vii. 301, viii. 48, 328 ; loaves baked from, viii. 48 ; used to bake cakes in form of goats, rams, and boars at Christmas, viii. 328 ; the Yule log wrapt up in, x. 248 ; reapers blindfold throw sickles at the, xi. 279 *n.*[4]. See also *Clyack, Kirn, Mell,* Maiden

Sheaf, the last threshed called the Corn-goat, Spelt-goat, or Oats-goat, vii. 286 ; shaped like a goat, vii. 287 ; called the Fox, vii. 297

Sheaf of oats made up to represent St. Bride or Bridget, ii. 94 *sq.*

Sheaves of wheat or barley burnt in Midsummer fires, x. 215

Sheba or Sabaea, the kings of, not allowed to quit their palace, iii. 124 ; their priestly character, iii. 125 *n.*

Sheep torn by wolf in homoeopathic magic, i. 157 ; driven through fire, ii. 327, xi. 11 *sqq.* ; bred by people of the Italian pile villages, ii. 353 *n.*[3] ; used in purificatory ceremonies, iii. 174, 175 ; shoulder-blades of, used in divination, iii. 229 ; to be shorn when the moon is waxing, vi. 134 ; to be shorn in the waning of the moon, vi. 134 *n.*[3] ; reason for not eating, viii. 140 ; ghosts of, dreaded, viii. 231 ; used as scapegoat among the ancient Arabs, ix. 35 ; made to tread embers of extinct Midsummer fires, x. 182 ; driven over ashes of Midsummer fires, x. 192 ; burnt to stop disease in the flock, x. 301 ; burnt alive as a sacrifice in the Isle of Man, x. 306 ; omens drawn from the intestines of, xi. 13 ; passed through a hole in a rock to rid them of disease, xi. 189 *sq.*

——, black, sacrificed for rain, i. 290 ; wetted as a rain-charm, i. 290 ; witch in shape of a, x. 316

Sheep-headed women, statuettes of, found at Lycosura, viii. 21 *n.*[4]

—— -skin, fumigation with, viii. 324

—— -skins, candidates at initiation seated on, vii. 38 ; people beaten with, ix. 265

Sheitan dere, the Devil's Glen, in Cilicia, v. 150

Shell called "old man," homoeopathic magic of, i. 158

Shells used in ritual of death and resurrection, xi. 267 *n.*[2], 269

—— of eggs preserved, viii. 258 *n.*[2]

Shenty, Egyptian cow-goddess, vi. 88

Shepherd beloved by Ishtar, ix. 371

Shepherd's Isle, exorcism of strangers in, iii. 104

—— pouch thrashed as a protection against witchcraft, ii. 338

—— prayer, ii. 327 *sq.*

Shepherds, Roman, fumigate their flocks, ii. 327, viii. 42

Shepherds' festival, ancient Italian, ii. 326 *sqq.*

Sherbro, Sierra Leone, sacred society in the, ix. 259 *sqq.*

Shervaray Hills in Travancore, the Mala-yalies of the, iii. 402

Shetland, tying up the wind in knots in, i. 326 ; witches in, i. 326 ; Yule in, ix. 167 *sqq.*
—— fishermen, their use of magical images, i. 69 *sq.* ; their tabooed words, iii. 394
Shields of manslayers struck to make them resound, iii. 178 ; of the Salii struck with staves, iii. 233
Shifting cultivation, vii. 99
—— dates of Egyptian festivals, vi. 24 *sq.*
Shilluk kings animated by the divine spirit of Nyakang, iv. 18 ; put to death before their strength fails, iv. 21 *sq.*, vi. 163 ; worshipped after death, iv. 24 *sqq.*, vi. 161 *sqq.*
Shilluks, a tribe of the White Nile, iv. 17 *sqq.* ; custom of putting to death the divine kings, iv. 17 *sqq.*, 204, 206 ; their worship of Nyakang, the first of the Shilluk kings, iv. 18 *sqq.*, vi. 162 *sqq.* ; ceremony on the accession of a new king of the, iv. 23 *sq.*, 26 *sq.*, 204 ; their worship of dead kings, iv. 24 *sqq.*, vi. 161 *sq.* ; transmission of soul of divine founder of dynasty to all successors among the, iv. 198, 204
Shin, Loch, Hugh Miller on, iii. 40
Shinto rain-making ceremony, i. 297 ; priest exorcizes demons of plague, ix. 118
Shinty, the Scotch name for hockey, viii. 323, 324 *n.*[1]
Ship, sicknesses expelled in a, ix. 185 *sqq.* ; demons expelled in a, ix. 201 *sq.*
Ships sunk by witches, i. 135 ; ancient processions with, perhaps rain-charms, i. 251 *n.*[3]
Shire River, the Makanga on the, viii. 287
Shirley Heath, cleft ash-tree at, xi. 168
Shirt worn by the effigy of Death, its use, iv. 247, 249
——, wet, divination by, at Hallowe'en, x. 236, 241
Shiverings and shakings as signs of inspiration, i. 377
Shoa, belief as to the shadow of an enemy in, iii. 83 ; a province of Abyssinia, customs observed at eating in, iii. 116
Shoe untied at marriage, iii. 300 ; custom of going with one shoe on and one shoe off, iii. 311 *sqq.* ; divination by thrown, x. 236
Shoes of priestess not to be made from skin of animal that died a natural death, iii. 14 ; not to be brought into the sanctuary of Alectrona, viii. 45 ; not to be worn in sanctuary of the Mistress at Lycosura, viii. 46 ; of boar's skins worn by king at inauguration, x.

4 ; magical plants at Midsummer put in, xi. 54, 60, 65
Shogun's palace in Japan, ix. 144
Shooter, Rev. J., on the agricultural labours of women among the Zulus, vii. 113 *sq.* ; on breaking a calabash and sacrifice of bulls at Zulu festival of first-fruits, viii. 68 *n.*[3]
Shooting at the sun on Midsummer Day, xi. 291
" —— the Witches " on St. Sylvester's Day in Bohemia, ix. 164 ; at witches in the clouds among the South Slavs, x. 345
Shooting stars, superstitions as to, iv. 58 *sqq.*
Shorea robusta, the *sâl* tree, sacred groves of, among the Khonds, ii. 41
Shortland, E., on taboo in New Zealand, iii. 134 *n.*[3]
" Shot-a-dead " by fairies, x. 303
Shoulder-blades of sheep used in divination, iii. 229, 229 *n.*[4], viii. 234
Shoulders of medicine-men especially sensitive, v. 74 *n.*[4]
Shouting as a means of stopping earthquakes, v. 197 *sqq.*
Shravan, an Indian month, iv. 55
Shrew-ash, how prepared, i. 83
—— -mouse in magic, i. 83
Shrine (*fierte*) of St. Romain at Rouen, ii. 167, 168, 170 *n.*[1] ; of Aesculapius at Sicyon, v. 81
——, golden models of, found in royal graves at Mycenae, v. 33
Shrines of dead Shilluk kings, iv. 24 *sq.* ; of shark-shaped and crocodile-shaped heroes in Yam, v. 139 *n.*[1]
Shropshire, Feast of All Souls in, vi. 78 ; cutting "the neck" at harvest in, vii. 268 ; "to loose the goose " at harvest in, vii. 277 *n.*[3] ; "crying the Mare" at harvest in, vii. 293 *sq.* ; the sin-eater in, ix. 44 ; the tug-of-war at Ludlow in, ix. 182 ; fires on Twelfth Night in, ix. 321 ; the Yule log in, x. 257 ; fear of witchcraft in, x. 342 *n.*[4] ; the oak thought to bloom on Midsummer Eve in, xi. 292, 293
Shrove Tuesday, dances on, to make the hemp or flax grow tall, i. 138 *sq.* ; straw puppet burnt by the Slovenes on, ii. 93 ; Burial of the Carnival on, iv. 221 *sqq.* ; mock death of, iv. 227 *sqq.* ; drama of Summer and Winter on, iv. 257 ; pig's flesh boiled on, vii. 300 ; dances to make the flax thrive on, viii. 326 ; the tug-of-war on, ix. 182 *sq.* ; game of ball on, ix. 183 ; dances to promote the growth of the crops on, ix. 239, 347 ; effigies burnt on, x. 120 ; straw-man burnt on, xi.

22 ; wicker giants on, xi. 35 ; cats burnt alive on, xi. 40 ; the divining-rod cut on, xi. 68 ; custom of striking a hen dead on, xi. 279 *n.*

Shrovetide Bear, the, iv. 230, viii. 325 *sq.*

—— custom in the Erzgebirge, iv. 208 *sq.* ; in Bohemia, iv. 209

Shu, Egyptian god of light, v. 283 *n.*[3]

Shumpaoli, god of the Makalaka, first-fruits offered to him, viii. 110 *sq.*

Shurii - Kia - Miau, aboriginal tribe in China, annual human sacrifice among the, iv. 145

Shushan (Susa), fast of the Jews in, ix. 397

Shuswap Indians of British Columbia, their contagious magic of foot-prints, i. 210 ; their beliefs and customs concerning twins, i. 265 ; their way of bringing on cold weather, i. 319 ; their recovery of lost souls, iii. 67 *n.* ; their belief as to the shadows of mourners, iii. 83 ; customs observed by mourners among the, iii. 142 ; girls at puberty forbidden to scratch themselves among the, iii. 146 *n.*[1] ; continence of hunters among the, iii. 198 ; eat nutlets of pines, v. 278 *n.*[2] ; their propitiation of slain bears, viii. 226 *sq.* ; their regard for the bones of beavers, viii. 238 ; seclusion of girls at puberty among the, x. 53 *sq.* ; girls at puberty forbidden to eat anything that bleeds among the, x. 94 ; fence themselves with thorn bushes against ghosts, xi. 174 *n.*[2] ; personal totems among the, xi. 276 *n.*[1] ; their belief as to trees struck by lightning, xi. 297 *n.*[3]

Shway Yoe (Sir George Scott), on the worship of *nats* in Burma, ix. 96

Sia Indians, chastity of hunters among the, iii. 197 *sq.*

Siam, use of fire kindled by lightning in, ii. 256 *n.*[1] ; modes of executing royal criminals in, iii. 241 *sq.* ; forbidden to walk over the head of a superior in, iii. 254 ; tigers and crocodiles not named in their haunts in, iii. 403 *sq.* ; annual temporary kings in, iv. 149 *sqq.* ; catafalque burnt at funeral of king of, v. 179 ; annual festival of the dead in, vi. 65 ; sickness transferred from sick man to image in, viii. 103 ; the Laosians in, ix. 97 ; annual expulsion of demons in, ix. 149 *sqq.* ; human scapegoats in, ix. 212 ; tree-spirit in serpent form in, xi. 44 *n.*[1] *See also* Siamese

——, king of, divinity of, i. 401 ; his perpetual fire, ii. 262 ; not allowed to set foot on ground, x. 3

——, kings of, their bodies not to be touched under pain of death, iii. 226 ;

names of, concealed from fear of sorcery, iii. 375

Siamese, the, do violence to the gods in time of drought or excessive rain, i. 299 ; fear to fell fine trees, ii. 41 ; kindle a sacred fire by means of a metal mirror or burning-glass, ii. 245 *n.* ; their belief as to foundation sacrifices, iii. 90 ; their superstition as to passing under a rope, iii. 250 ; their belief as to a guardian spirit in the head, iii. 252 *sq.* ; mock human sacrifices among the, iv. 218 ; their explanation of a first menstruation, x. 24 ; their story of the external soul, xi. 102

Siamese children, ceremony at cutting their hair, iii. 265 *sqq.* ; disposal of their cut hair, iii. 275

—— monks, their respect for trees, ii. 13

—— objection to stamping coins with the image of the king, iii. 98 *sq.*

—— year of twelve lunar months, ix. 149 *n.*[2]

Siaoo, or Siauw, East Indian island, belief as to sylvan spirits in, ii. 33 ; magic wrought by means of spittle in, iii. 288 ; puppets substituted for human sacrificial victims in, iv. 218 ; children sacrificed to volcano in, v. 219

Sibaia, a good spirit in Nias, viii. 276

Siberia, the Jukagirs of, i. 122 ; the Buryats of, ii. 32 ; the Orotchis of, iii. 232 ; the Samoyeds of, iii. 353 ; the natives of, will not call bears by their proper name, iii. 398 ; Eastern, the Gilyaks of, viii. 190 ; North-East, the Chuckchees of, viii. 221 ; North-East, the Koryaks of, viii. 232 ; marriage custom in, x. 75 ; external souls of shamans in, xi. 196 *sq.*

Siberian sable-hunters, their respect for dead sables, viii. 238

Sibitti-baal, king of Byblus, paid tribute to Tiglath-pileser, v. 14

Sibree, Rev. J., on divinity of Betsileo chiefs, i. 397

Sibyl, the, and the Golden Bough, i. 11 ; and Aeneas, i. 11 ; the Grotto of, at Marsala, v. 247 ; the Norse, her prophecy, x. 102 *sq.*

Sibyl's wish, the, x. 99

Sibylline Books, v. 265

Sicilians, Demeter's gift of corn to the, vii. 56 *sq.*; their lamentations at being robbed of an image of Demeter, vii. 65

Sicily, stones tied to fruit-trees in, i. 140 ; attempts to compel the saints to give rain in, i. 299 *sq.* ; barren fruit-trees threatened in, ii. 21 *sq.* ; date of the artificial fertilization of fig-trees in, ii. 314 ; Syrian prophet in, v. 74 ; fossil bones in, v. 157 ; hot springs in, v.

213 ; gardens of Adonis in, v. 245, 253 *sq.* ; divination at Midsummer in, v. 254 ; Good Friday ceremonies in, v. 255 *sq.* ; worship of Demeter and Persephone in, vii. 56, 65 ; Ascension Day in, ix. 54 ; Midsummer fires in, x. 210 ; St. John's Day (Midsummer Day) regarded as dangerous and unlucky in, xi. 29 ; bathing at Midsummer in, xi. 29 ; St. John's wort as a balm in, xi. 55

Sick, sacrifices for the, iv. 20, 25 ; thought to be possessed by the spirits of kings, iv. 25 *sq.*

Sick man, attempts to prevent the escape of the soul of, iii. 30 *sqq.*

—— and old people put to death, iv. 14

—— people passed through a hole in an oak, ii. 371 ; not allowed to sleep, iii. 95 ; sprinkled with pungent spices, iii. 105 *sq.* ; resort to cave of Pluto, v. 205 *sq.* *See also* Sickness

—— -room, mirrors covered up in, iii. 95

Sickles thrown at last standing corn, vii. 136, 142, 144, 153, 154, 165, 267, 268, 279, 296

Sickness, homoeopathic magic for the cure of, i. 78 *sqq.* ; explained by the absence of the soul, iii. 42 *sqq.* ; caused by ancestral spirits, iii. 53 ; ascribed to possession by demons and cured by exorcism, iii. 105 *sq.* ; thought to be caused by demons or ghosts, viii. 100 *sqq.*, ix. 88, 94, 100, 102, 103, 109 *sqq.* ; cured or prevented by effigies, viii. 100 *sqq.* ; transferred to things, ix. 2 *sq.*, 4 *sq.* ; transferred to people, ix. 6 *sq.* ; transferred to animals in Africa and other parts of the world, ix. 31 *sqq.*, xi. 181 ; transferred to animals in Europe, ix. 49 *sqq.* ; bonfires a protection against, x. 108, 109. *See also* Disease

Sicknesses expelled in a ship, ix. 185 *sqq.*

Sicyon, the wooing of Agariste at, ii. 307 ; shrine of Aesculapius at, v. 81 ; the sanctuary of Wolfish Apollo at, viii. 283 ; wolves at, viii. 283, 284

Sidon, kings of, as priests of Astarte, v. 26

Siebold, H. von, on the bear-festivals of the Ainos, viii. 185 *n.*

Sieg, the Yule log in the valley of the, x. 248

Siem, king, among the Khasis of Assam, vi. 210 *n.*[1]

Siena, the, of the Ivory Coast, their totemism, xi. 220 *n.*[2]

Sierck, town on the Moselle, the mayor of, officiates at the lighting of the Midsummer fire, x. 164

Sierra Leone, the Grebo people of, iii. 14 ; custom of beating a king before proclaiming him in, iii. 18 ; the Pleiades observed by the natives of, vii. 317 *sq.* ; birth-trees in, xi. 160 ; secret society in, xi. 260 *sq.*

Sierra Nevada in Colombia, the Aurohuaca Indians of the, iii. 215, 216

Sieves in homoeopathic magic, i. 157 ; in rain-making, i. 251 ; water poured through, as a rain-charm, i. 285 ; children at birth placed in, vii. 6 *sqq.* ; divination by, x. 236

Sigai, hero in form of shark, v. 139 *n.*[1]

Sigurd and the dragon Fafnir, iii. 324, viii. 146

Sihanaka, the, of Madagascar, funeral custom of the, vi. 246 ; transference of sickness to things among the, ix. 2 *sq.*

Sikhim, kings of, puppets in the hands of priests, iii. 20 ; villagers in, their fear of being photographed, iii. 98 ; the people of, believe that ores and veins of metal are the treasure of earth-spirits, iii. 407 *n.*[2] ; offerings at cairns in, ix. 26 ; demonolatry in, ix. 94 ; custom after a funeral in, xi. 18

Silberberg, in Bohemia, custom at flax-dressing in, vii. 194

Silence observed by women in making pottery, ii. 204 ; enforced during absence of fisher, viii. 256 ; at transferring fever to willow, ix. 58 ; compulsory, to deceive demons, ix. 132 *sq.*, 140 ; compulsory on girls at puberty, x. 29, 57 ; at bathing on Easter Saturday night, x. 123 ; at fetching water on Easter Saturday night, x. 124 ; at digging the root of the yellow mullein at midnight on Midsummer Eve, xi. 63 ; at cutting a branch of hazel to form a divining-rod by night on Midsummer Eve, xi. 67 ; in passing a ruptured or rickety child through a cleft tree, xi. 171 ; in creeping through a hoop of willow as a cure, xi. 184

Silenuses, minor deities associated with Dionysus, viii. 1 *sq.*

Silesia, custom as to children's cast teeth in, i. 181 ; precautions against witches on May Day in, ii. 54 *sq.* ; Whitsuntide King in, ii. 84 ; contest for the kingship at Whitsuntide in, ii. 89 *sq.* ; St. George's Day in, ii. 336 *sq.* ; Whitsuntide mummers in, iv. 207 *n.*[1] ; "Carrying out Death" in, iv. 236 *sq.*, 239 *sq.*, 250 *sq.*, 264 *sq.*, x. 119 ; bringing in Summer in, iv. 246 ; athletic sports at harvest in, vii. 76 ; the Grandmother sheaf at harvest in, vii. 136 ; the last sheaf called the Old Woman or Old Man in, vii. 138, 148 *sq.* ; Girlachsdorf in, vii. 138 ; Hermsdorf in, vii. 139 ; woman binder of last sheaf tied up in it in, vii. 139, 222 ; loaf baked from corn of last sheaf in, vii. 148 *sq.*; Langen-bielau in, vii. 148 ; the Wheat-bride, Oats-bride, Oats-king, and Oats-queen at harvest in, vii. 163 *sq.* ; Neisse in, vii. 164; man who binds the last sheaf called the Beggar-man in, vii. 231 ; Alt Lest in, vii. 231 ; corn-stalks left on harvest-field in, vii. 233 ; man who cuts or binds last sheaf called Wheat-dog or Peas-pug in, vii. 272 ; reaping the last corn called "catching the Wolf" in, vii. 273 ; the Harvest-cock in, vii. 277 ; reaping the last corn called "catching the Cat" in, vii. 280; reaper of last corn called the Tom-cat in, vii. 281 ; Grüneberg in, vii. 281 ; last sheaf shaped like a horned ox in, vii. 289 ; Bunzlau in, vii. 289 ; "catching the quail" at harvest in, vii. 295 ; expulsion of witches on Good Friday in, ix. 157 ; precautions against witches on Walpurgis Night in, ix. 162 *sq.* ; precautions against witches at Christmas and New Year in, ix. 164 ; "Easter Smacks" in, ix. 268, 269 ; mode of reckoning the Twelve Days in, ix. 327 ; Spachendorf in, x. 119 ; fires to burn the witches in, x. 160 ; Midsummer fires in, x. 170 *sq.*, 175 ; need-fire in, x. 278 ; witches as cats in, x. 319 *sq.* ; divination by flowers on Midsummer Eve in, xi. 53

Sililí, a Babylonian goddess, ix. 371

Silius Italicus, on the fire-walk of the Hirpi Sorani, xi. 14 *n.*[3]

Silk-cotton trees reverenced, ii. 14 *sq.*

Silkworms, taboos observed by breeders of, iii. 194

Sill of door, unlucky children passed under the, xi. 190

Silvanus, the Roman wood-god, his representations in art, ii. 45 *n.*[2]; associated with Diana, ii. 121 ; god of cattle as well as woods, ii. 124 ; associated with the Fauns, viii. 2

Silver and gold as totems, iii. 227 *n.*

Silver poplar a charm against witchcraft, ii. 336

—— sixpence or button used to shoot witches with, x. 316

Silvia and Mars, story of, xi. 192

Silvii, the family name of the kings of Alba, ii. 178 *sqq.*, 192, 379

Silvius, first king of Alba, ii. 179

Simbang, in German New Guinea, belief in the transmigration of human souls into crocodiles at, viii. 295

Simbirsk, Government of, in Russia, the "Funeral of Kostroma" in, iv. 262

Simeon, prince of Bulgaria, his life bound up with the capital of a column, xi. 156 *sq.*

Similarity in magic, law of, i. 52, 53

Similkameen Indians, of British Columbia, eat hearts of bears to make them brave, viii. 146

Simla, annual fair and dance near, x. 12

Simplification, danger of excessive simplification in science, i. 332 *sq.*

Simpson, W., as to Emperors of China, iii. 125 *n.*[3]

Simurgh and Rustem, in Firdusi's *Epic of Kings*, x. 104

Sin regarded as something material, iii. 214, 216, 217 *sq.* ; transferred to things, ix. 3. *See also* Sins

Sin-eater, the, ix. 43 *sq.*

—— -eating in Wales, ix. 43 *sq.*

—— -offering, x. 82

Sinai, "Mistress of Turquoise" at, v. 35

Sinaitic Peninsula, annual festival of Bedouins in the, iv. 97

Sinaugolo tribe of British New Guinea, women after childbirth not allowed to handle food in, iii. 147 *sq.*

Sinew of the thigh, customs and myths as to, viii. 264 *sqq.*

Sinews of sacrificial ox cut, vi. 252 ; of dead men cut to disable their ghosts, viii. 272

Singa Bonga, spirit who dwells in the sun, the first-fruits of the harvest dedicated to him by the Hos of Bengal, viii. 117

Singalang Burong, a Dyak war-god, invoked in a long liturgy at the Head-feast, ix. 383, 384 *n.*[1]; the Ruler of the Spirit World, story of the marriage of his daughter to a mortal man, iv. 127 *sq.*

Singarmati Devi, Indian goddess, worshipped by breeders of silkworms in Mirzapur, iii. 194

Singer, charm to become a good, i. 156 ; navel-string used to make a boy a fine, i. 197 *sq.* ; the best, chosen chief, ii. 298 *sq.*

Singhalese, their fear of demons, iii. 233 *sq.* ; their use of iron as a talisman against demons, iii. 233 *sq.* ; unlock locks to facilitate childbirth, iii. 297 ; their custom of tying a knot as a charm on a threshing-floor, iii. 308 *sq.* ; seclusion of girls at puberty among the, x. 69. *See also* Cingalese

Singhalese custom as to cast teeth, i. 180

—— sorcerers, their use of magical images, i. 65

Singing to the moon by wives and sisters in the absence of the men, i. 125

Singleton, Miss A. H., on hunting the wren in Ireland, viii. 320 *n.*[1]; on an Irish cure for whooping-cough, xi. 192 *n.*[1]

Sink or swim, in divination, i. 196 ; test

used to determine a new incarnation, i. 413

Sins, the remission of, through the shedding of blood, v. 299 ; transferred to a buffalo calf, ix. 36 *sq.* ; transferred vicariously to human beings, ix. 39 *sqq.* ; of people transferred to animals, ix. 210 ; the Jewish confession of, over the scapegoat, ix. 210 ; the absolution of, pronounced by the Mikado, ix. 213 *n.*[1] ; Delaware Indian remedies for, ix. 263

——, confession of, i. 266, iii. 114, 191, 195, 211 *sq.*, 214 *sqq.*, ix. 31, 36, 127 ; originally a magical ceremony, iii. 217

Sinsharishkun, last king of Assyria, burned himself in his palace, v. 174

Sintang, district of West Borneo, use of rice to attract souls in, iii. 35

Sinuessa, in Campania, its waters thought to fertilize women, ii. 161

Siouan tribes of North America, names of clans not used in ordinary conversation among the, xi. 224 *n.*[2]

Sioux Indians ate the hearts of brave enemies to make themselves brave, viii. 150 ; their respect for turtles, viii. 243 ; ritual of death and resurrection among the, xi. 268 *sq.*

—— girl sacrificed for the crops, vii. 238 *sq.*

Siphnos, titular kings in, i. 46 *n.*[4] ; ceremonies at felling a tree in the island of, ii. 37

Siphoum, in Laos, taboos observed by salt-workers at, iii. 200

Sipi in Northern India, annual fair and dance at, x. 12

Sipylus, Mother Plastene on Mount, v. 185

Siriac or Sothic period in ancient Egypt, vi. 36

Sirius (the Dog-star), the soul of Isis in, iv. 5 ; observed by Egyptian astronomers, vi. 27 ; called Sothis by the Egyptians, vi. 34 ; date of its rising in ancient Egypt, vi. 34 ; heliacal rising of, on July 20th, vi. 34 *n.*[1], 93 ; the star of Isis, vi. 34, 119 ; its rising marked the beginning of the sacred Egyptian year, vi. 35 ; its rising observed in Ceos, vi. 35 *n.*[1] ; sacrifices offered at its rising on the top of Mount Pelion, vi. 36 *n.* ; in connexion with the Sed festival, vi. 152 *sq.* ; associated with Ishtar, ix. 359 *n.*[1] ; how the Bushmen warm up, x. 332 *sq.*

Sis in Cilicia, v. 144

Sister, marriage with, in royal families, iv. 193 *sq.*

—— and brother not allowed to mention each other's names, iii. 344

—— of a god, v. 51

Sister's Beam (*Sororium tigillum*) at Rome, xi. 194, 195 *n.*[4]

—— children preferred to man's own children, mark of mother-kin, ii. 285

Sisters, taboos observed by, in the absence of their brothers, i. 122, 123, 125, 127 ; kings marry their, v. 316

—— of king, licence accorded to, ii. 274 *sqq.*

—— of hunters, taboos observed by, i. 122

Sisters-in-law, their names not to be pronounced, iii. 338, 342, 343

Sisyphus, the stone of, x. 298

Sit (Set), malignant Egyptian god, iii. 68. *See* Set

Sita, wife of Rama, the Holy Basil (*tulasi*) regarded as an embodiment of, ii. 26

Sithon, king of the Odomanti, and his daughter Pallene, ii. 307

Sitting on the ground prohibited to warriors, iii. 159, 162, 163

Situa, annual festival of the Incas, ix. 128

Siu, a Sea Dyak, and his bird wife, iv. 127 *sq.*

Siva, one of the persons of the Hindoo Trinity, i. 404 ; his wife Gauri, ii. 77 *sq.*

—— and Pârvati, marriage of the images of, iv. 265 *sq.*

Six hundred and sixty-six, the number of the Beast, iv. 44

Sixpence, silver, witches shot with a, x. 316

Sixth day of the moon, mistletoe cut on the, xi. 77

Sixty years, cycles of, xi. 77 *n.*[1]

Siyins of North-Eastern India, their belief in demons, ix. 93

Sizu in Cilicia, v. 144

Skates worshipped by the Indians of Peru, viii. 250

Skatsantzari, fiends or monsters in Macedonia, ix. 320

Skeat, W. W., on Malay rain-making, i. 262 ; on the sanctity of the regalia among the Malays, i. 398 ; on the Rice-mother and Rice-child among the Malays, vii. 197 *sqq.*

—— and Blagdon, C. O., on the power of medicine-men among the wild tribes of the Malay Peninsula, i. 360 *sq.*

Skein, tangled, as a talisman to keep off ghosts, ix. 153 *n.*[1]

Skeleton drenched with water as a rain-charm, i. 284

Skene, W. F., on the Picts as Celts, ii. 286 *n.*[2]

Skin of slain animal placed on a dead man to recruit his strength, iii. 68 *sq.* ; of sacrificial victim in Greek ritual, iii.

312; of ox stuffed and set up, v. 296 *sq.*, viii. 5; body of Egyptian dead placed in a bull's, vi. 15 *n.*²; of sacrificial victim used in the rite of the new birth, vi. 155 *sq.*; of sacrificed ram placed on statue of Ammon, viii. 41, 172; of sacrificed bird or animal, uses of, viii. 170, 173 *sq. See also* Skins

Skin-disease, bathing in dew at Midsummer as remedy for, v. 247, 248, x. 208; caused by eating a sacred animal, viii. 25 *sqq.*; supposed remedy for, ix. 266; Mexican remedy for, ix. 298; leaping over ashes of fire as remedy for, xi. 2; traditional cure of, in India, xi. 192

Skinner, Principal J., on the burnt sacrifice of children, vi. 219

Skins of sacrificed animals hung in sacred groves, ii. 11; of horses stuffed and set up at graves, v. 293, 294; of sacrificed animals stuffed or stretched on frameworks, viii. 5, 257 *sq.*; of sacrificial victims used to beat people, ix. 265; creatures that slough their, supposed to renew their youth, ix. 302 *sqq.*

—— of human victims, uses made of, v. 293; worn by men in Mexico, ix. 265 *sq.*, 288, 290, 294 *sq.*, 296 *sqq.*, 301 *sq.*

Skipping-rope played by Gilyaks at bear-festival, viii. 192

Skoptsi or Skoptsy, the, a fanatical Russian sect, mutilate themselves, ii. 145 *n.*¹, iv. 196 *n.*³

Skull of dead king, drinking out of, as a means of inspiration, iv. 200, vi. 171; drinking out of a human, in order to acquire the qualities of the deceased, viii. 150; of enemy, lad at circumcision seated on, viii. 153. *See also* Skulls

Skull-cap worn by girls at their first menstruation, iii. 146; worn by Australian widows, iii. 182 *n.*²

Skulls used as charms to cause invisibility, i. 150; of racoons prayed to for rain, i. 288; of bears nailed to sacred firs, ii. 11; of dead used as drinking-cups among the Australian aborigines, iii. 372; of dead kings of Uganda removed and kept, iv. 202 *sq.*, vi. 169; human, as protection against powers of evil, vii. 241; the Place of, vii. 243; spirits of ancestors in their, viii. 123; of bears worshipped by the Ainos, viii. 181, 184; of foxes consulted as oracles, viii. 181; of bears as talismans, viii. 197; of turtles propitiated by turtle-fishermen, viii. 244; of enemies destroyed, viii. 260

——, ancestral, used in magical cere-

monies, i. 163; in rain-charm, i. 285; rubbed as a propitiation, iii. 197; offerings set beside, viii. 127

Sky, twins called the children of the, i. 267, 268; appeal to the pity of the, as a rain-charm, i. 302 *sq.*; Aryan god of the, ii. 374 *sq.*; observation of the, for omens, iv. 58; conceived by the Egyptians as a cow, v. 283 *n.*³; girls at puberty not allowed to look at the, x. 43, 45, 46, 69

—— and earth, myth of their violent separation, v. 283

Sky-god, Attis as a, v. 282 *sqq.*; married to Earth-goddess, v. 282, with *n.*²; mutilation of the, v. 283; invoked at Eleusis, vii. 69

—— -god Zeus, vii. 65

—— -goddess, the Egyptian, ix. 341

—— -spirit, sacrifice of children to, iv. 181

Skye, x. 289; sacred wood in the island of, ii. 44; the need-fire in, ii. 238, x. 148; the last sheaf called the Cripple or Lame Goat at harvest in, vii. 164, 284

Sladen, Colonel, expulsion of fire-spirit among the Shans witnessed by, ix. 141

Slain, fear of the ghosts of the, iii. 165 *sqq.*

Slane, the hill of, Paschal fire lit by St. Patrick on the, x. 158

Slaughter of the Dragon, drama of the, at Delphi and Thebes, iv. 78 *sqq.*, 89; myth of the, iv. 105 *sqq.*

—— of prisoners often a sacrifice to the gods, v. 290 *n.*²

Slave, charm to bring back a runaway, i. 152, 317; whipped for rain or sunshine, i. 297; treated as the representative of heaven, i. 399 *sq.*

Slave Indians will not taste blood, iii. 241; do not pare nails of female children, iii. 263

—— priests at Nemi, i. 11

—— women, religious ceremony performed by, ii. 313, ix. 258

Slave Coast of West Africa, custom observed by the mother of stillborn twins on the, i. 269 *n.*¹; the Ewe negroes of the, i. 317, iii. 263; the Ewe-speaking peoples of the, ii. 15, 149, iii. 9, 116, 119, 222, 323, v. 83 *n.*¹, ix. 74; negroes of the, their story of a fungus which revealed a murder, ii. 33; negroes of the, allure the tree-spirit from the tree, ii. 35; exorcism of demons from children on the, iii. 106; Jebu on the, iii. 121; children protected against demons by iron on the, iii. 235; the Yoruba-speaking negroes of the, iii. 252, viii. 149; custom at end of mourning on the, iii. 286 ; precaution as to the spittle of kings on the, iii. 289 ; Porto Novo on the, iv. 117 ; Whydah on the, iv. 188 ; sacred men and women on the, v. 65, 68 ; the Adeli of the, viii. 116 ; custom of widows on the, xi. 18 *sq.* ; use of bullroarers on the, xi. 229 *n.* *See also* Ewe negroes

Slaves succeed to kingdom in Ashantee in default of sons and sisters' sons, ii. 275 ; succeed to kingdom in the Fantee country to exclusion of sons, ii. 275 ; licence granted to, at Saturnalia, ii. 312, ix. 307 *sq.*, 350 *sq.*, 351 *sq.* ; female, licence accorded to, at the *Nonae Caprotinae*, ii. 313 *sq.* ; runaway, charm for recovering, iii. 305 *sq.* ; sacrificed as substitutes for their masters at the funeral of a king, iv. 117 ; sacred, in Western Asia, v. 39 *n.*[1] ; feasted by their masters, ix. 308, 350 *sq.* ; feasted by their mistresses, ix. 346. *See also* Slave

—— of the Earth Gods among the Ewe negroes; viii. 61, 62 *n.*[1]

Slavonia, " Carrying out Death " in, iv. 240 ; Good Friday custom in, ix. 268 ; the Yule log in, x. 262 *sq.* ; needfire in, x. 282

—— (South), peasants of, threaten fruittrees to make them bear fruit, ii. 21 ; crown their cattle on St. George's Day as a protection against witchcraft, ii. 126 *sq.* ; the measures they take to bring down witches from the clouds, x. 345. *See also* Slavonians *and* Slavs

Slavonian bride led thrice round the fire of her new home, ii. 230

—— custom of throwing a knife or a hat at a whirlwind, i. 329

Slavonians, South, housebreaker's charm to cause sleep among the, i. 148 ; thief's charm among the, i. 153 ; their custom as to cast teeth, i. 178 ; their belief as to trees growing on graves, ii. 32 *sq.* ; their belief as to the fertilization of barren women by fruit-trees, ii. 56 *sq.*, 344 ; wash their cows in dew on Midsummer morning, ii. 127 ; their custom of impregnating a woman by sparks of fire, ii. 231 ; their belief as to stepping over a person, iii. 424 ; transfer their laziness to a cornel-tree, ix. 54 *sq.* *See also* Slavonia *and* Slavs

Slavonic countries, the corn-spirit as a dog or wolf in, vii. 271

—— custom of " Carrying out Death," ix. 230

—— peoples, harvest customs concerning the last sheaf among the, vii. 144 *sqq.* ;

" Easter Smacks " among the, ix. 268 ; need-fire among the, x. 280 *sqq.*, 344

Slavonic stories of the external soul, xi. 108 *sqq.*

—— year, the beginning of the, ix. 228

Slavs, tree-worship among the heathen, ii. 9 ; love charms and divination on St. George's Day among the, ii. 345 *sq.* ; the thunder-god Perun of the, ii. 365 ; custom of regicide among the, iv. 52 ; festival of the New Year among the old, iv. 221 ; the old, began their year with March, iv. 221 *sq.* ; " Sawing the Old Woman " among the, iv. 242 ; the Corn-mother among the, vii. 132, 135 ; black god and white god among the, ix. 92 ; the oak a sacred tree among the, xi. 89 ; oak-wood used to kindle sacred fires among the, xi. 91

—— of the Balkan Peninsula, their mode of kindling fire by friction, ii. 237 ; will not blow on fire of hearth with their mouths, ii. 241 ; locks and keys as amulets among the, iii. 308

—— of Carinthia, Green George on St. George's Day among the, ii. 75, 343

——, South, their magic of footprints, i. 211 ; St. George's Day the chief festival of spring among the, ii. 339 *sq.* ; divine by the shoulder-blades of sheep, iii. 229 *n.*[4] ; names of relations tabooed among the, iii. 337 ; practice of childless women among the, in order to obtain children, v. 96 ; children of living parents at marriage among the, vi. 246 ; Midsummer fires among the, x. 178 ; the Yule log among the, x. 247, 258 *sqq.* ; divination from flowers at Midsummer among the, xi. 50 ; their belief in the activity of witches at Midsummer, xi. 74 *sq.* ; need - fire sometimes kindled by the friction of oak-wood among the, xi. 91

——, the Western, religious capital of, i. 383

Slayers of leopards, rules of diet observed by, viii. 230 *sq.*

Slaying of the Dragon, annual drama at Furth in Bavaria, ii. 163 *sq.* ; of the king in legend, iv. 120 *sqq.* ; of the Dragon by Apollo at Delphi, vi. 240 *sq.*

Sleeman, General Sir William, on the use of scapegoats in India, ix. 190 *sq.*

Sleep, homoeopathic magic of the dead used to produce, i. 147 *sqq.* ; charms employed by the shoulder-blades to cause, i. 148 *sq.* ; absence of soul in, iii. 36 *sqq.* ; forbidden in house after a death, iii. 37 *sq.* ; sick people not allowed to, iii. 95 ; on the ground forbidden, iii. 110 ; in bed forbidden, iii. 194 ; forbidden to unsuccessful eagle-hunter, iii. 199 ; magic, at initiation, xi. 256 *sq.*

Sleep of the god in winter, according to the Phrygians, vi. 41

" —— of war," among the Blackfoot Indians, i. 147

Sleeper not to be wakened suddenly, iii. 39 *sqq.* ; not to be moved nor his appearance altered, iii. 41 *sq.*

Sleeping by day forbidden to women during the absence of warriors, i. 127 *sq.* ; on the ground, custom observed by certain priests, ii. 248

Sligo, County, the Druids' Hill in, x. 229

Sloe, twigs of the, burnt on May Day as a protection against witches, ix. 158 *sq.*

Slope of Big Stones in Harris, x. 227

—— of Virbius on the Esquiline hill at Rome, i. 4 *n.*[5], ii. 321

Sloth, the animal, imitated by masker, ix. 381

Sloughing the skin supposed to be a mode of renewing youth, ix. 302 *sqq.*

Slovenes, their custom of Green George on St. George's Day, ii. 79, 343

—— of Overkrain burn a straw puppet on Shrove Tuesday, ii. 93

Slovenians, their belief in the activity of witches on Midsummer Eve, xi. 75

Slow-footed animals not eaten by some savage tribes lest they make the eaters slow also, viii. 139 *sq.* ; eaten by preference by the Bushmen, viii. 140 *sq.*

Small Bird clan of the Dinkas, iv. 31

Smallpox not mentioned by its proper name, iii. 400, 410, 411, 416 ; Chinese cure for, by means of beans and a winnowing-sieve, vii. 9 *sq.*; clay figures offered as substitutes for living persons to the spirit of, viii. 106 ; transference of, in Mirzapur, ix. 6 ; demon of, transferred to a sow, ix. 33 ; attempt to deceive the spirit of, ix. 112 *n.*[2] ; blood of monkey used to exorcise the devil of, ix. 117 ; spirit of, dismissed with tokens of respect and good-will, ix. 119 ; spirit of, driven out of village by drumming and dancing, ix. 120 ; flight from the evil spirit of, ix. 122 *sq.*; barricade of cutting weapons erected against the evil spirit of, ix. 122 ; demon of, expelled by means of an image, ix. 172 ; expelled in a proa from Buru, ix. 186 ; sent away in a canoe by the Yabim of New Guinea, ix. 188 *sq.*

Smearing the body as a means of imparting certain qualities, viii. 162 *sqq.*

—— blood on the person as a purification, iii. 104, 115 ; on persons, dogs, and weapons as a mode of pacifying their souls, iii. 219 ; on worshippers as a mode of communion with the deity, viii. 316

Smearing fat on person after a long absence, iii. 112

—— gall of eagle on eyes of blear-sighted persons, i. 154

—— lampblack on forehead to avert the evil eye, vi. 261

—— porridge on the face before and after a journey, iii. 112 ; on the bodies of manslayers, iii. 176

—— red paint on girls at puberty, x. 31

—— sheep's entrails on body as mode of purification, iii. 174

—— white clay on people after festival of first-fruits, viii. 75 ; on novices at initiation, xi. 255 *n.*[1], 259

Smell, evil, used to drive demons away, vi. 261, ix. 112

Smeroe, Mount, volcano in Java, idols worshipped on, v. 221

Smet, J. de, on human sacrifices among the Pawnees, vii. 239 *n.*[1]

Smintheus Apollo, his worship said to have been instituted in order to avert mice, viii. 283 ; image of mouse in his temple in the Troad, viii. 283

Smith, George Adam, on fertility of Bethlehem, v. 257 *n.*[3]

Smith, Professor G. C. Moore, on the Straw-bear at Whittlesey, viii. 329

Smith, W. Robertson, on rain thought to be caused by defilement, i. 301 *n.*[2] ; on the hunting of souls, iii. 77 *n.*[1] ; on the Raskolniks, iii. 96 *n.*[1] ; on the covenant formed by eating together, iii. 130 *n.*[1] ; on the Mosaic laws compared with savage customs, iii. 219 *n.*[1]; on Arab legend of king bled to death, iii. 243 *n.*[7]; on the original sanctity of domestic animals, iii. 247 *n.*[5]; on a vintage piaculum, iv. 8 *n.*[1] ; on the date of the month Tammuz, v. 10 *n.*[1] ; on anointing as consecration, v. 21 *n.*[3] ; on Baal as god of fertility, v. 26 *sq.* ; on caves in Semitic religion, v. 169 *n.*[3]; on Tophet, v. 177 *n.*[4]; on the predominance of goddesses over gods in early Semitic religion, vi. 213 ; on the sacrifice of children to Moloch, vi. 220 *n.*[1] ; on the date of the month Lous at Babylon, vii. 259 *n.*[1] ; on the *bouphonia*, viii. 5 *n.*[2]; on the sacrifice of wild boars in Cyprus, viii. 23 *n.*[3]; on ceremonial purification, viii. 27 *n.*[5]; on the annual sacrifice of a sacred animal, viii. 31 *n.*[1]; on the reverence of pastoral peoples for their cattle, viii. 35 *n.*[2]; as to disrespect for herring, viii. 251 *n.*[5]; on the sinew of the thigh, viii. 266 *n.*[1]; on a Syrian remedy for caterpillars, viii. 280 *n.* ; on an Arab cure for melancholy, ix. 4 n.²; on Semiramis, ix. 369 sq.

Smith, a spectral, x. 136

Smith Sound, the Esquimaux of, iii. 32 n.²

Smith's craft regarded as uncanny, iii. 236 n.⁵

Smiths sacred, i. 349; viewed as inspired, iii. 237 n.

Smoke used in rain-making, i. 249, 291; of cedar inhaled as means of inspiration, i. 383 sq.; as a charm against witchcraft, ii. 330; made in imitation of rain-clouds, x. 133; used to stupefy witches in the clouds, x. 345; used to fumigate sheep and cattle, xi. 12, 13

—— of bonfires, omens drawn from the, x. 116, 131, 337; intended to drive away dragons, x. 161; allowed to pass over corn, x. 201, 337

—— of Midsummer bonfires a preservative against ills, x. 188; a protection against disease, x. 192; beneficial effects of, x. 214 sq.

—— of Midsummer herbs a protection against thunder and lightning, xi. 48; used to fumigate cattle, xi. 53

—— of need-fire used to fumigate fruit-trees, nets, and cattle, x. 280

Smoke-hole, remains of slain bear at festival brought into the house through the, viii. 189 sq., 196, 256, 256 n.¹

Smoking as a means of inducing prophetic trance or inspiration, iv. 201, vi. 172; as a means of inducing state of ecstasy, viii. 72; to appease a rattlesnake, viii. 219; in honour of slain bears, viii. 224, 226

Smoking first tobacco of season, ceremony at, viii. 82

Smolensk Government, St. George's Day in the, ii. 333 sq.

Smut in wheat, ceremony to prevent, ix. 318

Smyth, R. Brough, on fire customs of the Australian aborigines, ii. 257; on menstruous women in Australia, x. 13

Snail supposed to suck blood of cattle, iii. 81 sq.

Snails as scapegoats, ix. 52, 53

Snake, used in rain-making, i. 287 sq.; rajahs of Manipur descended from a, iv. 133; white, eaten to acquire supernatural knowledge, viii. 146; worshipped, viii. 316 sq.; said to wound a girl at puberty, x. 56; seven-headed, external soul of witch in a, xi. 144; external soul of medicine-man in a, xi. 199. See also Snakes and Serpent

—— or lizard in annual ceremony for the riddance of evils, ix. 208

Snake-bites, homoeopathic charms against, i. 152 sq.; cured by snake-stones, i. 165; rattlesnake dance to ensure immunity from, i. 358; inoculation against, viii. 160

Snake clan exposed their infants to snakes, viii. 174 sq.

—— -entwined goddess found at Gournia in Crete, v. 88

—— -priest, his ceremonies to appease spirit of slain serpent, viii. 219

—— skin a charm against witchcraft, ii. 336

—— -stones thought to cure snake-bites, i. 165; superstitions as to, x. 15 sq.; belief of the Scottish Highlanders concerning, xi. 311

—— tribe in the Punjaub, their worship of snakes, viii. 316 sq.; their treatment of dead snakes, viii. 317

Snake's tongue on St. George's Day or Eve, a charm to ensure talkativeness, ii. 345 n., viii. 270

Snakes, magical ceremony for the multiplication of, i. 90; human wives of, ii. 149, 150; not called by their proper names, iii. 399, 401 sq., 407, 408, 411; as fathers of human beings, v. 82; fed with milk, v. 84 sqq.; respected by North American Indians, viii. 217 sqq.; sacred at Whydah, viii. 287; souls of dead princes in, viii. 288; souls of dead in, viii. 293, 294 sq.; dead, accorded a regular funeral, viii. 317; fat of, used as a hair-restorer, x. 14; thought to congregate on Midsummer Eve or the Eve of May Day, x. 15 sq.; rain-water used as a charm against, x. 17; spirits of plants and trees in the form of, xi. 44 n.; sympathetically related to human beings, xi. 209 sq. See also Snake, Pythons, Rattlesnakes, and Serpents

Snapping the thumbs to prevent the departure of the soul, iii. 31

Snares set for souls, iii. 69

Snipe, fever transferred to a, ix. 51

Snorri Sturluson, on the dismemberment of Halfdan the Black, vi. 100

Snow, external soul of a king in, xi. 102

Snowdon, rain-making on, i. 307

"Sober" sacrifices, offered without wine by the ancient Greeks, i. 311 n.¹

Sobk, a crocodile-shaped Egyptian god, identified with the sun, vi. 123

Sochit or Sochet, epithet of Isis, vi. 117

Social progress, i. 420

—— ranks, inversion of, at festivals, ix. 350, 407

—— revolution from democracy to despotism, i. 371

Societies, secret, in North-Western

America, ix. 377 *sqq.* ; and clans, totemic, related to each other, xi. 272 *sq.* *See also* Secret societies

Society, uniformity of occupation in primitive, i. 245 ; ancient, built on the principle of the subordination of the individual to the community, v. 300 ; stratification of religion according to types of, viii. 35 *sqq.* ; three stages of, the hunting, the pastoral, and the agricultural, viii. 35, 37

Society Islanders, their observation of the Pleiades, vii. 312

—— Islands, offering of first-fruits in the, viii. 132 *sqq.*

Socrates, church historian, on sacred prostitution, v. 37 *n.*[2] ; on a reported murder of a Christian child by Jews, ix. 394 *sq.*

Söderblom, N., on an attempted reform of the old Iranian religion, vi. 83 *n.*[2]

Sodewa Bai and the golden necklace, story of, xi. 99 *sq.*

Sodom and Gomorrah, the destruction of, v. 222 *n.*[1]

Sods, grassy, a protection against witches, ii. 54 ; of turf, a protection against witchcraft, ii. 335, 338 ; freshly cut, a protection against witches, ix. 163

Sodza, a lightning goddess, among the Hos of Togoland, ii. 370

Soemara, in Celebes, were-wolf at, x. 312

Soerakarta, district of Java, conduct of natives in an earthquake, v. 202 *n.*[1]

Soest, customs at flax-pulling near, vii. 225

Sofala in East Africa, the Caffres of, their objection to be struck with anything hollow, i. 157 ; king of, revered as a god by his people, i. 392 ; kings of, put to death, iv. 37 *sq.* ; dead kings of, consulted as oracles, iv. 201 ; the Makalanga near, x. 135 *n.*[2]

Sogamoso or Sogamozo, in South America, the pontiff of, supernatural powers ascribed to, i. 416 ; heir to the throne of, not allowed to see the sun, x. 19

Sogble, a lightning god, among the Hos of Togoland, ii. 370

Sogne Fiord in Norway, Balder's Grove on the, x. 104, xi. 315

Soissons, the Boy Bishop at, ix. 337 *n.*[1]

Sokari (Seker), a title of Osiris, vi. 87

Soku, West Africa, cut hair buried in cairns at, iii. 274 *sq.*

Sol invictus, title of Mithra, v. 304 *n.*[1]

Solanum campylanthum, burned by Nandi women in the cornfields, vi. 47

Solaparuta in Sicily, custom on Palm Sunday at, i. 300

Solar festival in spring, xi. 3

Solar and lunar years, early attempts to harmonize, iv. 68 *sq.*, vii. 80 *sq.*, ix. 325 *sq.*, 339, 341 *sqq.*

—— myth theory, i. 333

—— theory of the fires of the fire-festivals, x. 329, 331 *sqq.*, xi. 15 *sq.*, 72

Soldiers, foods tabooed to, in Madagascar, i. 117 *sq.* ; Roman, celebration of the Saturnalia by, ii. 310, ix. 308 *sq.* *See also* Warriors

Solms-Laubach, Graf zu, on the artificial fertilization of fig-trees, ii. 314 *n.*[2]

Solok district of Sumatra, rain-making in, i. 278

Solomon, King, his name used by Malay fowlers in snaring pigeons, iii. 408, 418 ; puts Adoni-jah to death, v. 51 *n.*[2]

——, the Baths of, in Northern Palestine, resorted to by childless wives in the hope of obtaining children, v. 78 ; in Moab, visited by barren women in order to get children, v. 215 *sq.*

Solomon Islanders, their expulsion of demons, ix. 116

—— Islands, Florida, one of the, iii. 80, viii. 85, 126, 297 ; places sacred to ghosts in the, iii. 80 ; pigs sacrificed to ghosts in the, iii. 247 ; San Cristoval in the, iii. 247 ; fear of passing under a fallen tree in the, iii. 250 ; Ugi, one of the, iii. 250, 277 ; cut hair buried in the, to prevent it falling into the hands of sorcerers, iii. 277 ; ghosts of gardens feared in the, viii. 85 ; Guadalcanar, one of the, viii. 126 ; first-fruits offered to the dead in the, viii. 126 *sq.* ; Saa, one of the, viii. 127, 297 ; belief in the transmigration of human souls into animals in the, viii. 296 *sqq.* ; Savo, one of the, viii. 297 ; Ulawa, one of the, viii. 297, 298 ; fatigue transferred to sticks, stones, or leaves in the, ix. 9

Solör, in Norway, harvest custom at, vii. 225

Solstice, the summer, and the Olympic festival, iv. 90 ; swinging at, iv. 280 ; the Nile rises at, vi. 31 *n.*[1], 33 ; Basuto chiefs regulate the calendar at, vii. 117 ; rain-making ceremony of the Zuni at, viii. 179 ; new fire kindled by the Zuni at, x. 132, 133 ; its importance for primitive man, x. 160 *sq.*

——, the winter, reckoned by the ancients the Nativity of the Sun, v. 303, x. 246 ; Egyptian ceremony at, vi. 50 ; Aztec festival of killing and eating a god at, viii. 90 ; dramatic processions representing the corn spirit at, viii. 325 ; festival of the Koryaks after, ix. 126 *sq.*; new fire kindled by the Zuni at, x. 132 ; Persian festival of fire at, x. 269

Solstices observed by Californian Indians, vii. 125 ; festivals of fire at the, x. 132 *sq.*, 246, 247, 331 *sq.*; the old pagan festivals of the two, consecrated as the birthdays of Christ and St. John the Baptist, x. 181 *sq.*; fern-seed gathered at the, xi. 290 *sq.* ; mistletoe gathered at the, xi. 291 *sq.*

Solstitial fires perhaps sun-charms, xi. 292

Soma, Hindoo deity, x. 99 *n.*[2] ; sacrifice of, in Vedic India, iii. 159 *n.* ; worship of the stone which presses out the juice of the, ix. 90

Somali, marriage custom of the, vi. 246, 247

Somersetshire, Midsummer fires in, x. 199

Somerville, Professor William, on the time for coupling ewes and rams, ii. 328 *n.*[4] ; on the agricultural term " to stool," vii. 193 *n.*

Somme, the river, ceremony of carrying lighted torches on the first Sunday in Lent in villages on, x. 113 ; the department of, mugwort at Midsummer in, xi. 58

Sommerberg, the Grass King at Whitsuntide on the, ii. 86

Somosomo, a Fijian island, sacredness of priests and chiefs in, i. 389

Son, father thought to be reborn in his, iv. 188 *sqq.*, 287 (288 in Second Impression) ; abdication of father on birth of a son in Polynesia, iv. 190 ; abdication of father when his son comes of age, in Fiji, iv. 191 ; father fought and dispossessed by his son among the Corannas, iv. 191 *sq.*

" —— of the Father," ix. 419 *sq.*

—— of God, alleged incarnation of the, in America, i. 409

—— of a god, v. 51. *See also* Sons

—— of the king sacrificed for his father, iv. 160 *sqq.*

Son-in-law, his name not to be pronounced, iii. 338 *sq.*, 344, 345

Songish or Lkungen tribe of Vancouver Island, their formal reception of the first salmon caught in the season, viii. 254

Songs of the corn-reapers, vii. 214 *sqq.*; liturgical, revealed by gods, ix. 381

—— and dances, religious, of North-West American Indians, ix. 378 *sq.*

Sonnenberg, gout transferred to fir-trees in, ix. 56

Sonnerat, French traveller, on the fire-walk in India, xi. 6 *sqq.*

Sons, Roman kings not succeeded by their, ii. 270 ; of king's sister preferred to king's own sons under female kinship, ii. 274 *sq.*

Sons of God, v. 78 *sqq.*

—— of gods, iv. 5

Soosoos of Senegambia, their secret society, xi. 261 *sq.*

Sopater accused of binding the winds, i. 325

Sophocles, on the calamities entailed by the crimes of Oedipus, ii. 115 ; on the wooing of Dejanira by the river Achelous, ii. 161 *sq.* ; on the burning of Hercules, v. 111 ; his play *Triptolemus*, vii. 54

Soracte, Mount, ix. 311 ; sanctuary of Feronia at, iv. 186 *n.*[3] ; fire-walk of the Hirpi Sorani on, xi. 14 *sq.*

" Soranian Wolves " (*Hirpi Sorani*), at Soracte, iv. 186 *n.*[4], xi. 14, 91 *n.*[7]

Soranus, Italian god of Mount Soracte, xi. 14 ; etymology of his name, xi. 15 *n.*[1], 16

Sorcerers regarded as chiefs, i. 337 *sq.*, 342 *sq.* ; souls extracted or detained by, iii. 69 *sqq.* ; influence wielded by, iii. 107 ; make use of cut hair and other bodily refuse, iii. 268 *sq.*, 274 *sq.*, 278, 281 *sq.* ; injure men through their names, iii. 320, 322, 334 ; as protectors against demons, ix. 94 ; exorcize demons, ix. 113 ; Midsummer herbs a protection against, xi. 45 ; detected by St. John's wort, xi. 55 ; detected by fern root, xi. 67. *See also* Magic, Magicians, Medicine-men

—— or priests, order of effeminate, vi. 253 *sqq.*

Sorcery, the dread of, iii. 268 ; pointing sticks or bones in, x. 14 ; bonfires a protection against, x. 156 ; sprigs of mullein protect cattle against, xi. 190 ; mistletoe a protection against, xi. 85 ; savage dread of, xi. 224 *sq. See also* Magic, Witchcraft

—— and witchcraft, Midsummer plants and flowers a protection against, xi. 45, 46, 49, 54, 55, 59, 60, 62, 64, 65, 66, 67, 72

Sorcha, the King of, in a Celtic tale, xi. 127 *sq.*

Sori, a person of the Batta Trinity, ix. 88 *n.*[1]

Sorrentine Peninsula, puppet representing Lent sawn in two in the, iv. 245

Sorrowful One, the vaults of the, opened by the Boeotians in the month of sowing, vi. 41

Sorrows, the Master of, at funerals among the Chams, i. 280

Sositheus, his play *Daphnis*, vii. 217

Sothic or Siriac period in ancient Egypt, vi. 36

Sothis, Egyptian name for the star Sirius, vi. 34. *See* Sirius

Sotih, the, of Burma, revere a priestly king, iii. 237
Soul, belief in the pre-existence of the human, i. 104; the perils of the, iii. 26 *sqq.*; conceived as a mannikin, iii. 26 *sqq.*; ancient Egyptian conception of the, iii. 28 *sq.*; representations of the soul in Greek art, iii. 29 *n.*[1]; as a butterfly, iii. 29 *n.*[1], 41, 51 *sq.*; absence and recall of the, iii. 30 *sqq.*; attempts to prevent the soul from escaping from the body, iii. 30 *sqq.*; sickness attributed to the absence of the, iii. 32, 42 *sqq.*; tied by thread or string to the body, iii. 32 *sq.*, 43, 51; conceived as a bird, iii. 33 *sqq.*; absent in sleep, iii. 36 *sqq.*; in form of fly, iii. 36, 39; in form of mouse, iii. 37, 39 *n.*[2]; in form of lizard, iii. 38; caught in a cloth, iii. 46, 47, 48, 52, 53, 64, 67, 75 *sq.*; identified with the shadow, iii. 77 *sqq.*; identified with the reflection in water or a mirror, iii. 92 *sqq.*; supposed to escape at eating and drinking, iii. 116; in the blood, iii. 240, 241, 247, 250; identified with the personal name, iii. 319; of rice not to be frightened, iii. 412; of man-god transferred to his successor, iv. 10; of a tree in a bird, vi. 111 *n.*[1]; of the rice in the first sheaf cut, vi. 239; of the rice captured in a basket or box, vii. 185; of rice in a blue bird, vii. 295; thought to be seated in the liver, viii. 147 *sq.*; the notion of, a quasi-scientific hypothesis, xi. 221; the unity and indivisibility of the, a theological dogma, xi. 221. *See also* Souls
—— of chief in sacred grove, xi. 161
—— of child deposited in a coco-nut, xi. 154 *sq.*; deposited in a bag, xi. 155; bound up with knife, xi. 157
——, external, in afterbirth (placenta) or navel-string, i. 200 *sq.*; in folk-tales, xi. 95 *sqq.*; in parrot, xi. 97 *sq.*; in bird, xi. 98 *sq.*; in necklace, xi. 99 *sq.*; in a fish, xi. 99 *sq.*, 122 *sq.*; in cock, pigeon, starling, spinning-wheel, pillar, xi. 100 *sq.*; in a bee, xi. 101; in a lemon, xi. 102; in a tree, xi. 102; in a barley plant, xi. 102; in a box, xi. 102, 117, 143 *n.*[4], 149; in a firebrand, xi. 103; in hair, xi. 103 *sq.*; in snow, xi. 103 *sq.*; in two or three doves, xi. 104; in a ten-headed serpent, xi. 104 *sq.*; in a pumpkin, xi. 105; in a spear, xi. 105; in a dragon, xi. 105; in a gem, xi. 105 *sq.*; in an egg, xi. 107, 125, 127, 140 *sq.*; in a duck's egg, xi. 109 *sq.*, 115 *sq.*, 116, 119 *sq.*, 120, 126, 130, 132; in a blue rose-tree, xi. 110; in a bird, xi. 111, 119, 142, 150;

in a pigeon, xi. 112 *sq.*; in a light, xi. 116; in a flower, xi. 117 *sq.*; in grain of sand, xi. 120; in a stone, xi. 125 *n.*[1], 156; in a thorn, xi. 129; in a gem, xi. 130; in a pigeon's egg, xi. 132, 139; in a dove's egg, xi. 133; in a box-tree, xi. 133; in the flower of the acacia, xi. 135 *sq.*; in a sparrow, xi. 137; in a beetle, xi. 138, 140; in a bottle, xi. 138; in a golden cockchafer, xi. 140; in a dish, xi. 141 *sq.*; in a precious stone, xi. 142; in a bag, xi. 142; in a white herb, xi. 143; in a wasp, xi. 143 *sq.*; in a twelve-headed serpent, xi. 143; in a golden ring, xi. 143; in seven little birds, xi. 144; in a seven-headed snake, xi. 144; in a quail, xi. 144 *sq.*; in a vase, xi. 145 *sq.*; in a golden sword and a golden arrow, xi. 145; in entrails, xi. 147 *sq.*; in a golden fish, xi. 147 *sq.*, 220; in a hair as hard as copper, xi. 148; in a cat, xi. 150 *sq.*; in a bear, xi. 151; in a buffalo, xi. 151; in a hemlock branch, xi. 152; in folk-custom, xi. 153 *sqq.*; in inanimate things, xi. 153 *sqq.*; in a mountain scaur, xi. 156; in ox-horns, xi. 156; in roof of house, xi. 156; in a tree, xi. 156; in a spring of water, xi. 156; in capital of column, xi. 156 *sq.*; in a portrait statue, xi. 157; in plants, xi. 159 *sqq.*; in animals, xi. 196 *sqq.*; of shaman or medicine-man in animal, xi. 196, 199; kept in totem, xi. 220 *sqq.*
Soul of iron, xi. 154
" —— of Osiris," a bird, vi. 110
—— of rice, vii. 180 *sqq.*; eating the, viii. 54
—— of ruptured person passes into cleft oak-tree, xi. 172
——, succession to the, iv. 196 *sqq.*
—— of woman at childbirth deposited in a chopping-knife, xi. 153 *sq.*
Soul-boxes, amulets as, xi. 155
—— -cakes eaten at the Feast of All Souls in Europe, vi. 70, 71 *sq.*, 73, 78 *sqq.*
—— -stones, xi. 156
—— -stuff in the East Indies, vi. 182 *sq.*; of ghosts, ix. 182
Soule, a ball contended for in Normandy, ix. 183
"Souling," custom of, on All Souls' Day in England, vi. 79
" —— Day" in Shropshire, vi. 78
Soulless King, whose soul was in a duck's egg, Lithuanian story of the, xi. 113 *sqq.*
Souls strengthened with iron, i. 159 *sq.*; ascribed to trees, ii. 12 *sqq.*; of ancestors in trees, ii. 29 *sq.*, 30, 31, 32; of ancestors supposed to be in fire

on the hearth, ii. 232 ; every man thought to have four, iii. 27, 80 ; light and heavy, thin, and fat, iii. 29 ; transference of, iii. 49, 51 ; impounded in magic fence, iii. 56 ; abducted by demons, iii. 58 *sqq.*; transmigrate into animals, iii. 65, viii. 285 *sqq.*; brought back in a visible form, iii. 65 *sqq.*; caught in snares or nets, iii. 69 *sqq.*; extracted or detained by sorcerers, iii. 69 *sqq.* ; enclosed in tusks of ivory, iii. 70 ; conjured into jars, iii. 70 ; shut up in boxes, iii. 70, 76 ; shut up in calabashes, iii. 72 ; gathered into a basket, iii. 72 ; transferred from the living to the dead, iii. 73 ; wounded and bleeding, iii. 73 ; supposed to be in portraits, iii. 96 *sqq.*; of slain enemies propitiated, iii. 166 ; of beasts respected, iii. 223 ; immortal, attributed by savages to animals, viii. 204 ; of people at a house-warming collected in a bag, xi. 153 ; male and female, in Chinese philosophy, xi. 221 ; the plurality of, xi. 221 *sq.*

Souls of the dead, trees animated by the, ii. 29 *sqq.*; in certain fish, ii. 30 ; all malignant, iii. 145 ; cannot go to the spirit-land till the flesh has decayed from their bones, iii. 372 *n.*[5]; supposed to resemble their bodies, as these were at the moment of death, iv. 10 *sq.*; associated with falling stars, iv. 64 *sqq.*; transmitted to successors, iv. 198 ; reincarnation of the, v. 91 *sqq.*; brought back among the Gonds, v. 95 *sq.*; in caterpillars, viii. 275 *sq.*; received once a year by their relations, ix. 150 *sqq.*; sit round the Midsummer fire, x. 183, 184

——, feasts of All, vi. 51 *sqq.*

——, human, attracted by rice, iii. 34 *sqq.*, 45 *sqq.* ; transmigrate into totemic animals, xi. 223

South America. *See* America, South

—— American Indians, their insensibility to pain, iv. 138 ; their indifference to death, iv. 138 ; women's agricultural work among the, vii. 120 *sqq.*; their practice of bleeding themselves to relieve fatigue, ix. 12 *sq.* ; attribute fatigue to a demon, ix. 20 ; their mutual scourgings at ceremonies connected with the dead, ix. 262

—— Sea Islands, human gods in the, i. 387 ; continence of fishermen in the, iii. 193 ; the Pleiades worshipped in the, vii. 312

—— Slavonian housebreakers, their charm to cause sleep, i. 148. *See also* Slavonians, South

—— Slavs, devices of women to obtain offspring among the, v. 96 ; marriage customs of the, vi. 246. *See also* Slavs, South

Southey, R., on women's agricultural work among the Brazilian Indians, vii. 122 ; on custom of consuming the ashes of relations among the Brazilian Indians, viii. 157

Sovereignty, reluctance to accept the, on account of its burdens, iii. 17 *sqq.*

Sovkou, ancient Egyptian deity, represented by a masker, ii. 133

Sow, the white, of Alba Longa, ii. 187 *n.*[4]; corn-spirit as a, vii. 298 *sqq.*; as scapegoat, ix. 33 ; the cropped black, at Hallowe'en, x. 236, 240

Sower, the Wicked, driven away on the first Sunday in Lent, x. 107, 118

Sowerby, James, on mouse-ear hawkweed, xi. 57 ; on orpine, xi. 61 *n.*[4]; on yellow hoary mullein, xi. 64 ; on the Golden Bough, xi. 284 *n.*[3]; on mistletoe, xi. 316 *n.*[5]

Sowers carry locks as charm to keep off birds, iii. 308 ; and ploughmen drenched with water as a rain-charm, v. 238 *sq.*

Sowing, homoeopathic magic at, i. 136 *sqq.* ; curses for good luck at, i. 281 ; sexual intercourse before, ii. 98 ; periods of abstinence observed before, ii. 98, 105 ; tug-of-war before, ii. 100 ; continence at, ii. 105, 106 ; in Italy and Sicily, time of, ii. 311 *n.*[5]; Prussian custom at, v. 238 *sq.*; rites of, vi. 40 *sqq.*; in Greece, time for, vii. 45, 50, 318 ; festival of Demeter at, vii. 46 *n.*[2]; sacrifice to Demeter at, vii. 57 ; festival of the Kayans of Borneo at, vii. 93 *sqq.*, 111 ; masquerade of the Kayans at, vii. 186 *sq.*; time of, determined by observation of the sun, vii. 187 ; goat killed at, vii. 288 ; the corn-spirit as a pig at, vii. 300 ; cake called Christmas Boar eaten by farm-servants and cattle at time of barley sowing, vij. 303 ; at Magnesia in the Greek month Cronion, viii. 7, 8 *n.*[1]; ceremonies at, among the Chams, viii. 57 ; offerings at, in the North-Western provinces of India, viii. 117 ; offerings at, among the Kachins of Burma, viii. 120 *sq.*; customs observed by Saxons of Transylvania at, viii. 274 *sq.* ; prayer at, among the Khonds, ix. 138 ; expulsion of demons at, ix. 225 ; Saturn the god of, ix. 232, 346 ; dances at, ix. 234 *sqq.*; in Italy, season of the spring, ix. 346 ; fast from flesh, eggs, and grease at, ix. 347 *n.*[4]

——, goddesses of, personated by old women, ix. 238

Sowing and planting, time of, determined by the observation of the Pleiades, vii. 309, 313 *sqq.*; regulated by the phases of the moon, vi. 133 *sqq.*

—— and ploughing, ceremony of, in the rites of Osiris, vi. 87, 90, 96 ; rite of, at the Carnival, vii. 28

Sowing corn, Ovambo custom at, ii. 46

—— the fields, human sacrifices at, vii. 236, 238 *sq.*, 240 *sq.*

—— hemp seed, divination by, at Hallowe'en, x. 235

—— seed, to make children grow, vii. 11 ; done by women, vii. 113 *sqq.* ; done by children, vii. 115 *sq.*

—— the winter corn, goat killed at, vii. 288

Sown fields, fire applied to, on Eve of Twelfth Night, ix. 316, 318, 321

Sozomenus, church historian, on sacred prostitution, v. 37

Spachendorf, in Silesia, " the Burying of Death," effigy burnt at, iv. 250, x. 119

Spades and hoes, human victim killed with, vii. 239, 251

Spae-wives and Gestr, Icelandic story of the, xi. 125 *sq.*

Spain, belief as to death at ebb-tide in, i. 167; acorns used as food in, ii. 355, 356; "Sawing the Old Woman" at Mid-Lent in, iv. 240, 242 ; seven-legged effigies of Lent in, iv. 244 ; custom of swinging at Christmas in, 284 ; bathing on St. John's Eve in, v. 248 ; the Iberians of, vii. 129 ; sticks or stones piled on scenes of violent death in, ix. 15 ; the three mythical kings on Twelfth Day in, ix. 329 ; Midsummer fires and customs in, x. 208 ; bathing at Midsummer in, xi. 29 ; vervain gathered at Midsummer in, xi. 62

Spanish cathedrals, the Boy Bishop in, ix. 338

Spark Sunday in Switzerland, x. 118

Sparks of fire supposed to impregnate women, ii. 197, 231 ; of Yule log prognosticate chickens, lambs, foals, calves, etc., x. 251, 262, 263, 264

Sparrow, external soul of a jinnee in a, xi. 137

Sparrows, charms to keep them from the corn, viii. 274

Sparta, the two kings of, i. 46 *sq.* ; their relation to Castor and Pollux, i. 48-50

——, state sacrifices offered by the kings at, i. 46 ; warned by oracle against a "lame reign," iv. 38 ; funeral games in honour of Leonidas and Pausanias at, iv. 94 ; destroyed by an earth-

quake, v. 196 *n.*[4] ; octennial tenure of kingship at, vii. 82, 85

Spartan king, his fire-bearer, ii. 264

—— kings, supposed divinity of, i. 48 *sq.* ; not to be touched, iii. 226

Spartans, their sacrifice of horses to the sun, i. 315 *sq.* ; their kings liable to be deposed every eighth year, iv. 58 *sq.* ; their attempt to stop an earthquake, v. 196 ; their flute-band, v. 196 ; their red uniform, v. 196 ; at Thermopylae, v. 197 *n.*[1] ; their regard for the full moon, vi. 141 ; their brides dressed as men on the wedding night, vi. 260

Spear in magic, i. 347; custom of wounding the dying with a, iv. 13 *sq.* ; sacred, used to slay human victim, ix. 218 ; used to help women in hard labour, xi. 14 ; external soul in a, xi. 105

Spearing taro stalks, as a charm, vii. 102, 103

Spears, sacred, used to slaughter sacrificial victims, iv. 19, 32, v. 274 ; used to expel demons, ix. 115, 116

Spectral Huntsman, iv. 178

Speech, particular forms of, used in addressing social superiors, i. 402 *n.* ; special form of, used between a man and his wife's mother, iii. 346 ; special form of, used by rice-reapers to deceive the rice-spirit, vii. 184. *See also* Language *and* Words

Speicher, in the Eifel, St. John's fires at, x. 169

Speke, Captain J. H., his experience of the distrust of strangers in Africa, iii. 108 *sq.*

Spell recited at kindling need-fire, x. 290 ; of witchcraft broken by suffering, x. 304

—— and prayer, vii. 105

Spells cast by strangers, iii. 112 ; at hair-cutting, iii. 264 *sq.* ; for growth of crops, vii. 100 ; narrative, vii. 104 *sqq.*; imperative, vii. 105 ; and incantations used in arts and crafts, ix. 81 ; cast on cattle, x. 301, 302 ; cast by witches on union of man and wife, x. 346

Spelt-goat, name given to the last sheaf threshed at harvest in Baden, vii. 286

Spencer, Baldwin, on reincarnation of the dead, v. 100 *n.*[3]

Spencer, B., and F. J. Gillen, on a ceremony for the multiplication of white cockatoos, i. 89 ; on the confusion of a man with his totem, i. 107 *n.*[4] ; on infanticide among the Australian aborigines, iv. 180 *n.*[1], 187 *n.*[6] ; on Australian belief in conception without sexual intercourse, v. 99 ; on an Australian cure for headache, ix. 2 ; on initiation of Australian medicine-men, xi. 238

Spencer, Herbert, his theory of the material universe compared to that of Empedocles, viii. 303 *sqq.*

Spenser, Edmund, on an Irish custom as to blood of friends, iii. 244 *sq.*

Sperchius, River, hair of Achilles devoted to the, iii. 261

Spermus, king of Lydia, marries the widow of his predecessor, ii. 281 ; his wickedness, v. 183

Spices used in exorcism of demons, iii. 105 *sq.*

Spider imitated by actor or dancer, ix. 381

Spiders in homoeopathic magic, i. 152 ; ceremony at killing, viii. 236 *sq.* ; used to extract vicious propensity, ix. 34

Spieth, J., on human gods among the Hos of Togoland, i. 397 ; on the Ewe peoples, v. 70 *n.*[2] ; on the ceremonies at eating the new yams among the Hos, viii. 59 *sqq.* ; on the religion of the Ewe negroes, ix. 76 *n.*[1]

Spindle, woman winds thread on, while sugar-cane is planted, viii. 119

Spindles not to be carried openly on the highroads, i. 113 ; not to be twirled while men are in council, i. 114

Spinning forbidden to women under certain circumstances, i. 113 *sq.*

—— on highroads forbidden in ancient Italy, i. 113, viii. 119 *n.*[5]

—— of mummer at Carnival, viii. 333

Spinning-wheel, external soul of ogress in a, xi. 100

Spinning acorns or figs as a charm to promote the growth of the crops, vii. 102, 103

—— tops at sowing festivals, vii. 95, 97, 187

Spirit of Beans, Iroquois, vii. 177

——, Brethren of the Free, i. 408

—— of the Corn, Iroquois, vii. 177. *See* Corn-spirit

—— of dead apparently supposed to decay with the body, iii. 372

—— or god of vegetation, effigies of, burnt in spring, xi. 21 *sq.* ; reasons for burning, xi. 23 ; leaf-clad representative of, burnt, xi. 25

——, the Great, of the American Indians, iv. 3 ; his gift of corn to men, vii. 177

—— of Squashes, Iroquois, vii. 177

—— of vegetation brought to houses, ii. 74. *See also* Vegetation

Spirit animals supposed to enter women and be born from them, v. 97 *sq.*

—— -children left by ancestors, v. 100 *sq.*

—— -house shut during absence of warriors, i. 129

Spirits of dead fathers thought to attend warriors, i. 129 ; of plants in shape of animals, ii. 14 ; of trees threatened, ii. 20 *sqq.* ; of wild beasts killed in the chase, hunting dogs protected against, ii. 128 ; women married to water-spirits, ii. 150 *sqq.* ; sacrifices to water-spirits, ii. 155 *sqq.* ; of slain enemies conciliated, iii. 182 ; of slain animals propitiated by savages, iii. 190 ; averse to iron, iii. 232 *sqq.* ; evil, fear of attracting the attention of, iii. 334 ; of tin mines and gold mines treated with deference, iii. 407, 409 *sq.* ; taboos on common words based on a fear of, iii. 416 *sqq.* ; of ancestors in the form of animals, v. 83 ; supposed to consort with women, v. 91 ; of forefathers thought to dwell in rivers, vi. 38 ; evil, averted from children, vii. 6 *sqq.* ; of the dead supposed to influence the crops, vii. 104 ; distinguished from gods, vii. 169 ; imitation of, vii. 186 ; retreat of the army of, ix. 72 *sq.* ; guardian, ix. 98 ; good and evil, personated by children, ix. 139 ; Festival of Departed, ix. 154 ; of water propitiated at Midsummer, xi. 31 ; of plants and trees in the form of snakes, xi. 44 *n.*[1] *See also* Ancestral spirits, Dead, *and* Souls

—— of dead chiefs worshipped by the whole tribe, vi. 175, 176, 177, 179, 181 *sq.*, 187 ; thought to control the rain, vi. 188 ; prophesy through living men and women, vi. 192 *sq.* ; reincarnated in animals, vi. 193

—— of the hills, their treasures, xi. 69

—— of land, conciliation of the, iii. 110 *sq.*

Spiritual economy, mysterious law of, i. 405

—— husbands among the Akamba, ii. 316 *sq.*

—— power, its divorce from temporal power, iii. 17 *sqq.*

Spitting in contagious magic, i. 201 ; in a purificatory rite, iii. 175 ; forbidden, iii. 196 ; as a protective charm, iii. 279, 350, 395 ; upon knots as a charm, iii. 302 ; to avert evil omens, iv. 61 ; at sight of falling stars, iv. 61, 63, 65 ; to avert demons, iv. 63 ; as a mode of transferring evil, ix. 3, 10, 11, 41 *sq.*, 187 ; at ceremony for expulsion of evils, ix. 208

Spittle, used in magic, i. 57, iii. 268, 269, 287 *sqq.* ; divination from, i. 99 ; tabooed, iii. 287 *sqq.* ; effaced or concealed, iii. 288 *sqq.* ; used in making a covenant, iii. 290 ; magical virtue of, vii. 247, 250 ; as a protection against demons, ix. 118

Spoil taken from enemy purified, iii. 177
Spoletium, sacred grove near, ii. 122
Spoons used in eating by tabooed persons, iii. 141, 148, 189
Sports, athletic, at harvest, vii. 76 *sq.* *See also* Contests, Games
Spottiswoode, in Berwickshire, harvest customs at, vii. 153 *sq.*
Sprachbrücken, in Hesse, the Harvest-goat at, vii. 283
Sprained leg, Scotch cure for, by means of nine knots in a black thread, iii. 304 *sq.*
Spree, the river, requires its human victim on Midsummer Day, xi. 26
Spreewald, the Wends of the, their wreaths at Midsummer, xi. 48
Sprenger, the inquisitor, his practice of shaving the heads of witches and wizards, xi. 158
Sprigs, green, placed on stumps of felled trees, ii. 37 *sq.*
Spring, magical ceremonies for the revival of nature in, iv. 266 *sqq.* ; called Persephone, vi. 41 ; ceremony at beginning of, in China, viii. 10 *sqq.* ; rites to ensure the revival of life in, ix. 400
‘‘——, the Sacred,” among the ancient Italian peoples, iv. 186 *sq.*
—— and summer, myths of divinities and spirits to be told only in, iii. 384
Spring customs and harvest customs compared, vii. 167 *sqq.*
—— equinox, drama of Summer and Winter at the, iv. 257 ; custom of swinging at the, iv. 284 ; (vernal), sacrifice to Cronus at the, ix. 352
—— festival of Dionysus, vii. 15
Spring. oracular, at Dodona, ii. 172 ; sacrificial, at Upsala, ii. 364 ; external soul in a, xi. 156. *See also* Springs
Springbok, why Bushman hunters will not eat, viii. 141
Springs troubled to procure rains, i. 301 ; hot, resorted to by women in order to get offspring, ii. 161, v. 213 *sqq.* ; which confer prophetic powers, ii. 172 ; oracular, iv. 79 *sq.* ; worship of hot, v. 206 *sqq.* ; bathing in, at Midsummer, v. 246, 247, 248, 249 ; underground, detected by divining-rod, xi. 67 *sq.*
Springwort, mythical plant, procured at Midsummer, xi. 69 *sqq.* ; reveals treasures, opens all locks, and makes the bearer invisible and invulnerable, xi. 69 *sq.*
Sprinkling with holy water, iii. 285 *sq.*
Sproat, G. M., on seclusion of girls at puberty, x. 43 *sq.*
Spruce trees free from mistletoe, xi. 315

Squashes, the spirit of, conceived by the Iroquois as a woman, vii. 177
Squeals of pigs necessary for fruitfulness of mangoes, x. 9
Squills used to beat human scapegoats and image of Pan, ix. 255 *sq.*
Squirrels in homoeopathic magic, i. 155 ; asked to give new teeth, i. 180 ; souls of dead in, viii. 291 *sq.*; burnt in the Easter bonfires, x. 142, xi. 40
Squirting water as a rain-charm, i. 249 *sq.*, 277 *sq.*; on people at Midsummer, v. 248, x. 193
Sri, Hindoo goddess of crops, vii. 182
Srongtsan Gampo, king of Tibet, introduced Buddhism into Tibet, iii. 20
Stabbing men's shadows in order to injure the men, iii. 78, 79
—— reflections in water to injure the persons reflected, iii. 93
—— a transformed witch or were-wolf in order to compel him or her to reveal himself or herself, iii. 315
Stade, Hans, captive among Brazilian Indians, on their distrust of books, iii. 231
Stadium, the Olympic, iv. 287
Staffordshire, All Souls' Day in, vi. 79 ; the Yule log in, x. 256
Stag, emblem of longevity, i. 169 *n.*[1]
Stamfordham, in Northumberland, need-fire at, x. 288 *sq.*
Stammering, homoeopathic charm to cure, i. 156
Standard of conduct shifted from natural to supernatural basis, iii. 213
——, Egyptian, resembling a placenta, vi. 156 *n.*[1]; Egyptian cubit, deposited in the temple of Serapis, xi. 217
Standing on one foot, custom of, iv. 149, 150, 155, 156 ; on sacrificed human victim as a purificatory rite, ix. 218
Stanikas, male children of sacred prostitutes in Southern India, v. 63
Star, falling, in magic, i. 84 ; falling, as totem, iv. 61
—— of Bethlehem, v. 259, ix. 330
——, the Evening, in Keats's last sonnet, i. 166
——, the Morning, said to have enjoined human sacrifices on the Pawnees, vii. 238 ; personated by a man, ix. 238
—— of Salvation, v. 258
Star-spangled cap of Attis, v. 284
Starling, external soul of ogress in a, xi. 100
Stars, time when the stars are vanishing, i. 83 *n.*[2]; the souls of Egyptian gods in, iv. 5 ; shooting, superstitions as to, iv. 58 *sqq.* ; shooting, associated with the souls of the dead, iv. 64 *sqq.* ;

their supposed influence on human destiny, iv. 65 *sq.*, 67 *sq.* ; effect of agriculture in stimulating a knowledge of the, vii. 307 ; their supposed influence on the weather, vii. 318

Starvation as a mode of executing royal criminals, iii. 242, 243

Statius, on the festival of Diana at Nemi, i. 12 *n.*[2] ; on the grove of Egeria, i. 18 *n.*[4]

Statue beheaded instead of man, iv. 158

Stebbing, E. B., on *Loranthus vestitus* in India, xi. 317 *n.*[2]

Steele, Sir Richard, on titular kings in the Temple, ix. 333

Steiermark, Marburg in, the corn-spirit as wolf and bear at, viii. 327

Steinau, in Kurhessen, the Fox in the corn at, vii. 296

Steinen, Professor K. von den, on the discovery of fire by friction, ii. 257 *n.*[1] ; on the bull-roarer, xi. 233 *n.*[2]

Steinn in Hringariki, barrow of Halfdan at, vi. 100

Stelis, a kind of mistletoe, xi. 317, 318

Stella Maris, an epithet of the Virgin Mary, vi. 119

Stengel, P., on sacrificial ritual of Eleusis, v. 292 *n.*[3]

Stepmother, marriage with a, as a title to the throne, ii. 283, iv. 193

Stepping over persons or things forbidden, iii. 159 *sq.*, 194, 423 *sqq.* ; over dead panther, iii. 219 ; or jumping over a woman, viii. 70 *n.*[1] *See also* Jumping

Sterile beasts passed through Midsummer fires, x. 203, 338

Sterilizing influence ascribed to barren women, i. 142

Sternberg, Leo, on the bear-festivals of the Gilyaks, viii. 196, 199 *n.*[1], 201 *sq.* ; on attitude of the Gilyaks towards animals, viii. 206 ; on the belief in demons among the Gilyaks, ix. 101 *sq.*

Sternberg, in Mecklenburg, need-fire at, x. 274

Stettin, the Old Man at harvest in the villages near, vii. 220 *sq.*

Stevens, Captain John, on a temporary substitute for a Shah of Persia, iv. 158 *sq.*

Stevens, H. Vaughan, on fire-making among the Djakuns, ii. 236

Stevenson, Mrs. Matilda Coxe, on the Zuni custom of killing tortoises from a sacred lake, viii. 179

Stewart, Balfour, on the conservation of energy, viii. 262 *n.*[1]

Stewart, C. S., on Polynesian *atua*, i. 387 *n.*[1]

Stewart, Jonet, a wise woman, xi. 184

Stewart, W. Grant, on witchcraft in the Highlands, x. 342 *n.*[4]

Stheni, near Delphi, old chestnut trees at, xi. 317

Sticks, fertilizing virtue attributed to certain, ix. 264 *sq.* *See also* Digging-sticks

——, charred, of bonfires, protect fields against hail, x. 144

——, charred, of Candlemas bonfires, superstitious uses of, x. 131

——, charred, of Easter fire, superstitious uses of, x. 121 ; preserve wheat from blight and mildew, x. 143

——, charred, of Midsummer bonfires, planted in the fields, x. 165, 166, 173, 174 ; a charm against lightning and foul weather, x. 174, 187, 188, 190 ; kept to make the cattle thrive, x. 180 ; thrown into wells to improve the water, x. 184 ; a protection against thunder, x. 184, 192

——, sacred, representing ancestors, ii. 214, 216, 222 *sqq.* *See also* Churinga

—— and stones, evils transferred to, ix. 8 *sqq.* ; piled on the scene of crimes, ix. 13 *sqq.* *See also* Throwing

—— whittled, in religious rites, viii. 185, 186 *n.*, 192, 196, 278, ix. 261, x. 138 *n.*[1]

Stiens of Cambodia propitiate the souls of the animals which they kill, viii. 237

Stiffness of back set down to witchcraft, x. 343 *n.*, 345

Stigand, Captain C. H., on the sacrifice of the first-born among tribes to the south of Abyssinia, iv. 182

Stinging young people with ants and wasps, custom of, ix. 263, x. 61, 62 *sq.* ; as a form of purification, x. 61 *sqq.*

Stipiturus malachurus, emu-wren, men's " brother " among the Kurnai, xi. 216

Stlatlum Indians of British Columbia respect the animals and plants which they eat, vi. 44

Stockholm, leaf-market on the Eve of St. John at, ii. 65

Stocks, sacred, among the Semites, v. 107 *sqq.*

Stolen kail, divination by, at Hallowe'en, x. 234 *sq.*

Stomach of eater, certain foods forbidden to meet in, viii. 83 *sqq.*

Stone used in ceremony to facilitate childbirth, i. 74 ; supposed to cure jaundice, i. 80 ; bitten by a dog in homoeopathic magic, i. 157 ; treading on a, as a homoeopathic charm, i. 160 ; magic of heavy, vii. 100 ; toothache nailed into a, ix. 62 ; look of a girl at puberty thought to turn things to, x. 46 ; external soul in a, xi. 125 *n*.[1], 156 ; precious, external soul of khan in a, xi. 142 ; magical, put into body of novice at initiation, xi. 271

Stone, the Hairy, at Midsummer, x. 212

——, holed, in magic, to make sunshine, i. 313

——, sacred, used in purification of murderer, i. 26 ; (*lapis manalis*), used in rain-making at Rome, i. 310, ii. 183

Stone Age in Denmark, ii. 352 ; agriculture in the, vii. 79, 132

—— -curlew as a cure for jaundice, i. 80

—— knives and arrow - heads used in religious ritual, iii. 228

—— -throwing as a fertility charm, i. 39 ; at Mecca, rite of, ix. 24 ; in ancient Greece, ix. 24 *sq.*

Stonehaven, the last sheaf called the Bride at, vii. 163

Stones anointed in order to avert bullets from warriors, i. 130 ; tied to trees to make them bear fruit, i. 140 ; magical, which cause boils, i. 147 ; homoeopathic magic of, i. 160 *sqq.* ; oaths upon, i. 160 *sq.* ; employed to make fruits and crops grow, i. 162 *sqq.* ; thrown on grave as a rain-charm, i. 286 ; rain-making by means of, i. 304 *sqq.*, 345, 346 ; in charms to make the sun shine, i. 312, 313, 314 ; put in trees to prevent sun from setting, i. 318 ; placed in trees to indicate height of sun, i. 318 ; in wind charms, i. 319, 322 *sq.* ; oiled as a rain - charm, i. 346 ; human souls conveyed into, iii. 66, 73 ; ghosts in, iii. 80 ; on which a man's shadow should not fall, iii. 80 ; fastened to last sheaf, vii. 135 *sq.*, 138, 139 ; criminal crushed between, at Mexican harvest-festival, vii. 237 ; worshipped, viii. 127 *sq.* ; heaped up near shrines of saints, ix. 21 *sq.* ; communion by means of, ix. 21 *sq.* ; thrown at demons, ix. 131, 146, 152 ; thrown into Midsummer fire, x. 183, 191, 212 ; placed round Midsummer fires, x. 190 ; carried by persons on their heads at Midsummer, x. 205, 212 ; at Hallowe'en fires, divination by, x. 230 *sq.*, 239, 240 ; used for curing cattle, x. 324, 325 ; magical, inserted by spirits in the body of a new medicine-man, xi. 235

——, the Day of, the day of the new moon in the month of Bhadon (August), i. 279

Stones, holed, custom of childless women passing through, v. 36, xi. 187 ; to commemorate the dead, vi. 203 ; sick people passed through, xi. 186 *sqq.*

——, precious, homoeopathic magic of, i. 164 *sq.*

——, sacred, anointed, v. 36 ; among the Semites, v. 107 *sqq.* ; among the Khasis, v. 108 *n.*[1]. *See also* Churinga

—— and sticks, evil transferred to, ix. 8 *sqq.* ; piled on the scene of crimes, ix. 13 *sqq.* *See also* Throwing

Stoning, execution by, ix. 24 *n.*[2]

Stoning human scapegoats, ix. 253, 254

Stool at installation of Shilluk kings, iv. 24

Stoole, near Downpatrick, Midsummer ceremony at, x. 205

Stopfer, maskers in Switzerland, ix. 239

Storeroom (*penus*), sacred, ii. 205 *sq.*

Stories told as charms, vii. 102 *sqq.*

Storm fiend exorcized by bells, ix. 246 *sq.*

Storms, Catholic priests thought to possess the power of averting, i. 232 ; thought to be caused by the spirits of the dead, ii. 183 ; caused by cutting or combing the hair, ii. 271, 282

Stourton, in Warwickshire, the Queen of May at, ii. 88

Stout, Professor G. F., on an argument for immortality, viii. 261 *n.*[1]

Stow, in Suffolk, witch at, i. 210

Stow, John, on Lords of Misrule, quoted, ix. 331 *sq.* ; on Midsummer fires in London, x. 196 *sq.*

Strabo, on a marriage custom of the Samnites, ii. 305 ; on the use of acorn-bread in Spain, ii. 355 ; on the concubines of Ammon, v. 72 ; on Albanian moon-god, v. 73 *n.*[4] ; on Castabala, v. 168 *n.*[6] ; his description of the Burnt Land of Lydia, v. 193 ; on the frequency of earthquakes at Philadelphia, v. 195 ; his description of Rhodes, v. 195 *n.*[3] ; on Nysa, v. 206 *n.*[1] ; on the priests of Pessinus, v. 286 ; on the Sacaea, ix. 355, 369, 402 *n.*[1] ; on the sacred slaves at Comana, ix. 370 *n.*[4] ; on the worship of the goddess Ma at Comana, ix. 421 *n.*[1] ; on the sanctuary at Zela, ix. 421 *n.*[1] ; on the Hirpi Sorani, xi. 14 ; on the human sacrifices of the Celts, xi. 32

Strack, H. L., on the accusations of ritual murder brought against the Jews, ix. 395 *n.*[3]

Strackerjan, L., on fear of witchcraft in Oldenburg, x. 343 *n.*

Strange land, ceremonies at entering a, iii. 109 *sqq.*

Strangers, taboos on intercourse with, iii. 101 *sqq.*; suspected of practising magical arts, iii. 102; ceremonies at the reception of, iii. 102 *sqq.*; dread of, iii. 102 *sqq.*; spells cast by, iii. 112; killed, iii. 113; excluded from religious rites, vii. 94, 111, 187, 249; slain as representatives of the corn-spirit, vii. 217; regarded as representatives of the corn-spirit, vii. 225 *sqq.*, 230 *sq.*, 253; preferred as human victims, vii. 242

Strangulation as a mode of executing royal criminals, iii. 242, 243

Strap of wolf's hide used by were-wolves, x. 310 *n.*[1]

Strata of religion and society, viii. 36 *sq.*

Strath Fillan, the harvest *Cailleach* (Old Wife) in, vii. 166

Strathpeffer, in Ross-shire, Beltane bannocks near, x. 153

Strathspey, sheep passed through a hoop of rowan on All Saints' Day and Beltane in, xi. 184

Stratification of religion according to types of society, viii. 35 *sqq.*; of religious beliefs among the Malays, ix. 90 *n.*[1]

Stratonicea in Caria, eunuch priest at, v. 270 *n.*[2]; rule as to the pollution of death at, vi. 227 *sq.*

Straubing, in Lower Bavaria, the Corngoat at cutting the last corn at, vii. 282

Straw, the Yule, vii. 301 *sq.*; of Shrovetide Bear used to make geese and hens lay eggs, viii. 326; wrapt round fruit-trees as a protection against evil spirits, ix. 164; tied round trees to make them fruitful, x. 115

Straw-bear at Whittlesey, viii. 329

—— -bull, effigy placed on land of laggard farmer at harvest, vii. 289 *sq.*

—— -goat at threshing in Bavaria, vii. 286

—— -man placed on apple-tree on April 24th or 25th, viii. 6

Stream, burial under a running, iii. 15

Streams, menstruous women not allowed to cross running, x. 97; need-fire kindled between two running, x. 292

Strehlitz, in Silesia, athletic sports at harvest near, vii. 76; driving away witches on Good Friday near, ix. 157

Strength of people bound up with their hair, xi. 158 *sq.*

Strepsiades in Aristophanes, on the cause of rain, i. 285

Striking or throwing blindfold at corn, cocks, and hens, xi. 279 *n.*[4]

String or thread used to tie soul to body, iii. 32 *sq.*, 43, 51

String music in religion, v. 54

Strings, knotted, as amulets, iii. 309.

See also Cords, Knots, *and* Threads

Striped Petticoat Philosophy, The, x. 6

Stromberg Hill, burning wheel rolled down the, at Midsummer, x. 163

Stromness in the Orkneys, witch at, i. 326

"Strong names" of kings of Dahomey, iii. 374

Strudeli and Strätteli, female spirits of the wood, driven away on Twelfth Night at Brunnen, ix. 165

Strutt, Joseph, on Midsummer fires in England, x. 196

Struys, John, on dances of women during war in Madagascar, i. 131

Stseelis Indians of British Columbia, dread and seclusion of menstruous women among the, x. 89

Stuart, Mrs. A., on withered mistletoe, xi. 287 *n.*[1]

Stuart Lake in British Columbia, Tinneh Indians about, x. 47

Stubbes, Phillip, his *Anatomie of Abuses*, ii. 66; on May-poles, ii. 66 *sq.*

Stubble-cock, name of harvest-supper in Silesia, vii. 277

Students of Fez, their mock sultan, iv. 152 *sq.*

Stuhlmann, Fr., on ceremony at entering a strange land, iii. 109

Stukeley, W., on a Christmas custom at York, xi. 291 *n.*[2]

Stumps of felled trees, green sprigs on, ii. 37 *sq.*

Stuttgart, saying as to wind in corn near, vii. 292

Styria, belief as to falling stars in, iv. 66; the Corn-mother in, vii. 133; the Corn-goat at harvest in, vii. 283; fern-seed on Christmas night in, xi. 289

Styx, oath by the, iv. 70 *n.*[1]; the passage of Aeneas across the, xi. 294

Su-Mu, a tribe of Southern China, said to be governed by a woman, vi. 211 *n.*[2]

Sub-totems in Australia, xi. 275 *n.*[1]

Subincision, use of blood shed at, i. 92, 94 *sq.*; among the aborigines of Central Australia, i. 92, 93, 95, 97, 154; in South-Eastern Australia, i. 202; at initiation of lads in Australia, xi. 227 *sq.*, 234, 235

Sublician bridge at Rome, puppets of rushes annually thrown from the, viii. 107

Subordination of the individual to the community, the principle of ancient society, v. 300

Substitutes put to death instead of kings, iv. 56 *sqq.*, 115, 160, 194 *sq.*; slaves killed as substitutes for their masters at a king's funeral, iv. 117; for human sacrifices, iv. 124, 214 *sqq.*, v. 146 *sq.*, 219 *sq.*, 285, 289, vi. 99, 221, ix. 396

sq., 408 ; voluntary, for capital punishment in China, iv. 145 *sq.*, 273 *sqq.* ; temporary, for the Shah of Persia, iv. 157 *sqq.* ; voluntary, for corporal punishment in China, iv. 275 *sq.* ; for animal sacrifices, viii. 95 *n.*[2]

"Substitutes for a person" in China, puppets burnt to avert misfortune, viii. 104

Substitution of souls as a remedy for sickness, iii. 57 ; of puppet for soul of a sick man, iii. 62 *sq.* ; of animals for human victims, iv. 124, 165, 166 *n.*[1], 177, vii. 24, 33 *sq.*, 249 ; of child for parent in sacrifice, iv. 188, 194 ; of criminals for innocent victims in human sacrifices, iv. 195 ; of effigies for human victims in sacrifice, iv. 215, 217 *sq.*, viii. 94 *sqq.* ; of rice-cakes for human victims, viii. 89 ; of cakes for animal victims, viii. 95 *n.*[2]

Subterranean Zeus, title of Pluto as god of fertility, vii. 66

Subugo tree revered by the Masai, ii. 16

Subura at Rome, viii. 42, 43, 44

Succession to the chieftainship or kingship alternating between several families, ii. 292 *sqq.* ; in Polynesia, customs of, iv. 190 *sq.* ; to the crown under mother-kin (female kinship), v. 44, vi. 18, 210 *n.*[1]

—— to the kingdom, in ancient Latium, ii. 266 *sqq.* ; determined by a race, ii. 299 *sqq.* ; determined by mortal combat, ii. 322 ; through marriage with the king's widow, ii. 283, iv. 193 *sq.* ; through marriage with a sister, iv. 193 *sq.* ; conferred by personal relics of dead kings, iv. 202 *sq.*

—— to the soul, iv. 196 *sq.*

Sucla-Tirtha in India, expulsion of sins in, ix. 202

Sudan, the, the negroes of, their regard for the phases of the moon, vi. 141 ; ceremony of new fire in the, x. 134 ; human hyaenas in the, x. 313

Sudanese, their conduct in an earthquake, v. 198 ; their respect for ravens, viii. 221

Sudeten Mountains in Silesia, bonfires on Midsummer Eve on the, x. 170

Suffering, principle of vicarious, ix. 1 *sq.* ; intensity of, a means to break the spell of witchcraft, x. 304

Sufferings and death of Dionysus, vii. 17

Suffetes of Carthage, v. 116

Suffocation as a mode of executing royal criminals, iii. 242

Suffolk, anointing the weapon instead of the wound in, i. 203 ; contagious magic of footprints in, i. 210 ; May Day custom as to hawthorn in bloom in, ii. 52 ; cure for ague in, ix. 68 ;

belief as to menstruous women in, x. 96 *n.*[2] ; duck baked alive as a sacrifice in, x. 303 *sq.*

Sufi II., Shah of Persia, temporary substitute for, iv. 158

Sugar-bag totem in Australia, v. 101

—— -cane cultivated, vii. 121, 123 ; custom at planting, viii. 119 ; firstfruits of, offered to the sugar-cane god, viii. 119

Suicide of Buddhist monks, iv. 42 *sq.* ; epidemic of, in Russia, iv. 44 *sq.* ; as a mode of revenge, iv. 141 ; by hanging, iv. 282

——, hand of, cut off, iv. 220 *n.*

——, religious, iv. 42 *sqq.*, 54 *sqq.* ; in India, iv. 54 *sq.*

Suicides, ghosts of, feared, iv. 220 *n.*, v. 292 *n.*[3], ix. 17 *sq.* ; custom observed at graves of, v. 93

Suk, the, of British East Africa, power of medicine-men among the, i. 344 *sq.* ; their belief in serpents as reincarnations of the dead, v. 82, 85 ; women's work among the, vii. 117 *sq.* ; their rule as to partaking of meat and milk, viii. 84 ; give children the fat and hearts of lions to eat, viii. 142 ; their dread of menstruous women, x. 81

Sukandar River, in Mirzapur, ghosts shut up in a tree on the, ix. 60 *sq.*

Sulka (Sulkas), the, of New Britain, their way of stopping rain, i. 252 *sq.* ; their rain-making by means of stones, i. 304 ; their sacred stones, ii. 148 ; their notion as to the phosphorescence of the sea, ii. 155 *n.*[1] ; their dread of a woman in childbed, iii. 151 ; will not speak of their enemies by their proper name, iii. 331 ; tell stories only at evening or night, iii. 384 *sq.* ; their belief as to meteors, iv. 65

Sulla at the temple of Diana on Mount Tifata, ii. 380 ; at Aedepsus, v. 212

"Sultan of the Oleander," magical efficacy attributed by the Moors to the, x. 18

"—— of the Scribes," an annual mock sultan at Fez, iv. 152 *sq.*

Sultan Bayazid and his soul, iii. 50

Sultans veiled, iii. 120

Sumatra, images used in evil magic in, i. 58 ; magical images to obtain offspring in, i. 71 ; pregnant woman not to stand at the door in, i. 114 ; homoeopathic magic at sowing rice in, i. 136 ; rain-charm by means of a black cat in, i. 291 ; rain-charm by means of a stone in, i. 308 *sq.* ; ceremony at felling a tree in, ii. 37 ; special language used in searching for camphor in, iii. 406 *n.*[2] ; spirits of gold mines treated with deference in,

iii. 409 ; personification of the rice in, vii. 191 *sq.*, 196 *sq.* ; observation of the Pleiades in, vii. 315 ; kinship of men with crocodiles in, viii. 212 ; tigers respected in, viii. 215 *sqq.* ; use of bull-roarers in, xi. 229 *n.*

Sumatra, the Battas (Bataks) of, i. 71, 193, 330, 398, ii. 41, 108, iii. 34, 45 *sq.*, 104, 116, 296, 338, 405, v. 199, vi. 239, viii. 216, ix. 34, 87, 213 ; totemism among, xi. 222 *sqq.*

——, Central, treatment of the after-birth in, i. 193

——, Gayo, a district of, ii. 29, viii. 33

——, the Gayos of, ii. 125, iii. 409 *n.*[3], 410

——, Jambi kingdom in, iv. 154

——, the Karo-Bataks of, i. 277 *sq.*, iii. 52, 263

——, the Kooboos of, xi. 162 *n.*[2]

——, Lampong in, iii. 10

——, the Loeboes or Looboos of, vi. 264, xi. 182 *sq.*

——, Mandeling in, i. 192 *sq.*, vii. 197, viii. 216

——, the Mandelings of, ii. 36, iii. 296

——, the Minangkabauers of, i. 58, 140, 193, iii. 32, 36, 41, vii. 191, viii. 211 *sq.*, 215, x. 79

——, Northern, the Gayos of, ii. 36

——, Passier in, iv. 51

——, the Solok district of, i. 278

Sumba, East Indian island, custom as to the names of princes in, iii. 376 ; annual festival of the New Year and of the dead in, vi. 55 *sq.*

Sumerians, their origin and civilization, v. 7 *sq.*

Summer, bringing in the, ii. 74, iv. 233, 237, 238, 246 *sqq.* ; myths of gods and spirits not to be told in, iii. 385 *sq.* ; on the Mediterranean rainless, v. 159 *sq.* ; in Greece rainless, vii. 69

—— called Aphrodite, vi. 41

——, King of, chosen on St. Peter's Day, x. 195

—— and winter, personal names different in, iii. 386 ; dramatic battle of, iv. 254 *sq.*

Summer festival of Adonis, v. 226, 232 *n.*

—— solstice in connexion with the Olympic festival, iv. 90 ; swinging at the, iv. 280. *See also* Solstice

—— trees, carried from house to house in Silesia, iv. 246 ; compared to May-trees, iv. 251 *sq.*

Sun, prayers for children offered to the spirit of the, i. 72 ; prayers of women to the, after the departure of the warriors, i. 130 ; charm of the setting, i. 165 *sq.* ; asked to give a new tooth, i. 181 *sq.* ; magical control of the, i. 311 *sqq.* ; charms to cause the sun to shine, i.

311 *sqq.* ; prayers to the, at an eclipse, i. 312 ; ancient Egyptian ceremonies for the regulation of the, i. 312 ; human sacrifices offered by the Mexicans to the, i. 314 *sq.* ; chief deity of the Rhodians, i. 315 ; supposed to drive in chariot, i. 315 ; chariots and horses dedicated by the Rhodians and kings of Judah to the, i. 315, viii. 45 ; horses sacrificed to the, i. 315 *sq.* ; caught by net or string, i. 316 ; worshipped by the Lithuanians, i. 317 *sq.* ; the father of the Incas, i. 415 ; Parthian monarchs the brothers of the, i. 417 *sq.* ; incense deposited in sanctuaries of the, ii. 107 ; marriage of a woman to the, ii. 146 *sq.* ; worshipped by the Blackfoot Indians, ii. 146 ; virgins of, in Peru, ii. 243 *sqq.* ; not allowed to shine on sacred persons, iii. 3, 4, 6 ; sacrifices to, in ancient Egypt, iii. 227 *n.* ; represented by a bull, iv. 71 *sq.* ; represented as a man with a bull's head, iv. 75 ; perhaps personated by the Olympic victors, iv. 91, vii. 86 ; sacrifice of first-born children to the, iv. 183 *sq.* ; called " the golden swing in the sky," iv. 279 ; Adonis interpreted as the, v. 228 ; Osiris interpreted as the, vi. 120 *sqq.* ; called " the eye of Horus," vi. 121 ; worshipped in Egypt, vi. 122, 123 *sqq.* ; the power of regeneration ascribed to the, vi. 143 *n.*[4] ; time of sowing determined by observation of the, vii. 187 ; Japanese deities of the, vii. 212 ; first-fruits offered to the, vii. 237, viii. 117 ; temple of the, at Cuzco, vii. 310 ; primitive mechanisms for observation of the, vii. 314 ; festival of new fruits said to have been instituted by the, viii. 75 ; origin of the Yuchi Indians from the mother of the, viii. 75 ; the great chief of the Natchez descended from the, viii. 135 ; appeal to the, at confession of sins, ix. 3 ; reappearance of, in the Arctic regions, ceremonies at, ix. 124 *sq.*, 125 *n.*[1] ; spirit who lives in the, ix. 186 ; hearts of human victims offered to the, ix. 279, 280 *sq.*, 298 ; Mexican story of the creation of the, ix. 410 ; rule not to see the, x. 18 *sqq.* ; not to shine on girls at puberty, x. 22, 35, 36, 37, 41, 44, 46, 47, 68 ; not to be seen by Brahman boys for three days, x. 68 *n.*[2] ; impregnation of women by the, x. 74 *sq.* ; made to shine on women at marriage, x. 75 ; sheep and lambs sacrificed to the, x. 132 ; symbolized by a wheel, x. 334 *n.*[1], 335 ; in the sign of the lion, xi. 66 *sq.* ; magical virtues of plants at Midsummer de-

rived from the, xi. 71 *sq.* ; in the sign of Sagittarius, xi. 82 ; calls men to himself through death, xi. 173, 174 *n.*[1] ; fern-seed procured by shooting at, on Midsummer Day, xi. 291 ; the ultimate cooling of the, xi. 307

Sun, the birth of the, at the winter solstice, heathen festival of, v. 303 *sqq.*, x. 246, 331 *sq.* ; Christmas, an old pagan festival of, v. 303 *sqq.*, x. 246, 331 *sq.*

—— and Earth, marriage of the, ii. 98 *sq.*, 148, v. 47 *sq.*

——, eclipses of the, ceremonies at, i. 311, 312 ; beliefs and practices as to, iv. 73 *n.*[2], 77, x. 162 *n.* ; defilement or poison thought to be caused by, x. 162 *n.*

——, father of Alectrona, viii. 45

——, the Great, title of head chief of Natchez Indians, ii. 262, 263, viii. 77 *sqq.*

—— and Moon, their marriage celebrated by the Blackfoot Indians, ii. 146 *sq.* ; mythical and dramatic marriage of, iv. 71, 73 *sq.*, 78, 87 *sq.*, 90, 92, 105 ; conjunction of, viii. 15 *n.*[1]

——, moon, and stars represented by globes at the Laurel-bearing festival at Thebes, iv. 88 *sq.* ; human victims sacrificed to, by the heathen of Harran, vii. 261 *sq.*

——, priest of the, among the Blackfoot Indians, ii. 146 *sq.* ; Athenian, uses a white umbrella, x. 20 *n.*[1]

——, the rising, salutations to, vi. 193, ix. 416

——, the setting, homoeopathic magic of, i. 165 *sq.* ; charms to prevent, i. 316 *sqq.*, ix. 30 *n.*[2]

——, temple of the, round, among Blackfoot Indians, ii. 147 ; at Cuzco, ii. 243, ix. 129, x. 132 ; at Baalbec, v. 163 ; among the Natchez, viii. 135

——, the Unconquered, Mithra identified with, v. 304

Sun-charms, i. 311 *sqq.*, x. 331 ; the solstitial and other ceremonial fires perhaps sun-charms, xi. 292

—— clan of the Bechuanas, their magic to cause the sun to shine, i. 313

—— -dial of the Dyaks, vii. 314 *n.*[4]

—— -god, the, Egyptian ceremony to aid, i. 67 *sq.* ; sacrifice for sunshine to, i. 291 ; no wine offered to, i. 311 ; the titles of, transferred to the kings of Egypt, i. 418 ; the Egyptian, i. 418, 419, vi. 123 *sqq.*, ix. 341 ; draws away souls, iii. 64 *sq.* ; supposed to drive in a four-horse car, iv. 91 ; annually married to Earth-goddess, v. 47 *sq.* ; hymns to, vi. 123 *sq.* ; Sûrya,

the Indian, xi. 1 ; wakened from his sleep by the fires of the Pongol festival, xi. 46

Sun goddess, the Mikado an incarnation of the, i. 417, iii. 2 ; of the Hittites, v. 133 *n.* ; the Japanese, ix. 213 *n.*[1]

—— -stone used in making sunshine, i. 314

Sunda, names of father and mother not to be mentioned in, iii. 341 ; names of princes or chiefs not to be uttered in, iii. 376 ; names of certain animals tabooed in, iii. 415. *See also* Sundanese

Sundal, in Norway, need-fire in, x. 280

Sundanese, their belief in the homoeopathic magic of house timber, ii. 146 ; expel tree-spirit before they fell the tree, ii. 36. *See also* Sunda

Sunday, children born on a Sunday can see treasures in the earth, xi. 288 *n.*[5]

—— of the Firebrands, the first Sunday in Lent, x. 110

—— in Lent, the first, fire-festival on the, x. 107 *sqq.*

—— of the Rose, the fourth Sunday in Lent, iv. 222 *n.*[1]

Sunderbans, tigers called jackals in the, iii. 403

Sunderland, cure for cough in, ix. 52

Sunflower roots, revered by the Thompson Indians, ii. 13 ; ceremony at eating the, viii. 81

Sung-yang, were-tiger in, x. 310

Suni Mohammedans of Bombay cover mirrors at a death, iii. 95

Sunkalamma, a goddess, her effigy made of rice and eaten sacramentally by the Malas of Southern India, viii. 93

Sunless, Prince, Acarnanian story of, x. 21

Sunset, stories not to be told before, iii. 384

Sunshine, use of fire as a charm to produce, x. 341 *sq.*

Süntevögel or *Sunnenvögel*, butterflies, expelled in Westphalia on St. Peter's Day, ix. 159 *n.*[1]

Superb warbler, called women's "sister" among the Kurnai, xi. 215 *n.*[1], 216, 218

Superhuman power supposed to be acquired by actors in sacred dramas, ix. 382, 383

Superiority of the goddess in the myths of Adonis, Attis, Osiris, vi. 201 *sq.* ; of goddesses over gods in societies organized on mother-kin, vi. 202 *sqq.* ; legal, of women over men in ancient Egypt, vi. 214

Supernatural basis of morality, iii. 213 *sq.*

—— beings, their names tabooed, iii. 384 *sqq.*

Superstition a crutch to morality, iii. 219 ; spring pageants originate in, iv. 269

Superstitions as to the making of pottery, ii. 204 *sq.* ; as to shooting stars, iv. 60 *sqq.* ; associated with the Twelve Nights, ix. 326 *sqq.* ; as to women at menstruation, x. 76 *sqq.* ; associated with May Day and Hallowe'en, x. 224 ; Index of, x. 270 ; about parasitic rowans, xi. 281 *sq.* ; about trees struck by lightning, xi. 296 *sqq.*

Superstitious practices to procure good crops, vii. 100 ; at the Midsummer festival of St. John the Baptist, xi. 45

Supper, the harvest, vii. 134, 138. *See* Harvest-supper

Supplementary days in the Egyptian year, vi. 6, ix. 340 *sq.* ; in the ancient Mexican year, vi. 28 *n.*[3] ; in the old Iranian year, vi. 67, 68 ; in the year of the Mayas of Yucatan, ix. 171, 340 ; in the Aztec year, ix. 339 *sq. See also* Intercalary

Supply of kings, iv. 134 *sqq.*

Supreme Being of the Ewe negroes, ix. 74 *sq.*, 76 *n.*[1]

—— Beings, otiose, in Africa, iv. 19 *n.*

—— God of the Oraons, ix. 92 *sq.*

—— gods in Africa, vi. 165, 173 *sq.*, 174, 186, with note [5], 187 *n.*[1], 188 *sq.*, 190

Surenthal in Switzerland, new fire made by friction at Midsummer in the, x. 169 *sq.*

Surinam, the Bush negroes of, ii. 385, viii. 26

Surrey, the weald of, ii. 7

Survival of the fittest, the principle of, apparently enunciated by Empedocles, viii. 306 ; stated by Aristotle, viii. 306

Sûrya, the Indian sun-god, xi. 1

Susa, to the south of Abyssinia, the king of, eats behind a curtain, iii. 119

——, in Persia, scene of the Book of Esther laid at, ix. 360, 366

Sussex, belief as to cast teeth in, i. 177 *sq.* ; the weald of, ii. 7 ; belief in, as to ground on which blood has been shed, iii. 244 ; superstition as to clipped hair in, iii. 270 *sq.* ; cleft ash-trees used for the cure of rupture in, xi. 169 *sq.*

Sutherland, the *corp chre* in, i. 69

Sutherlandshire, the harvest Maiden in, vii. 162 ; custom at eating new potatoes in, viii. 51 ; the need-fire in, x. 294 *sq.* ; sept of the Mackays, "the descendants of the seal," in, xi. 131 *sq.*

Suzees of Sierra Leone, kings among the, iii. 18

Svayamvara, ancient Indian mode of determining a husband, ii. 306

Swabia, homoeopathic magic at sowing in, i. 138 ; stones tied to fruit-trees in, i. 140 ; the Harvest-May in, ii. 48 ; May-trees in, ii. 68 ; church bells rung on Midsummer morning in, to drive away witches, ii. 127 ; disposal of cut hair in, iii. 276 ; Whitsuntide mummers in, iv. 207 ; Shrovetide or Lenten ceremonies in, iv. 230, 233 ; the Old Woman at harvest in, vii. 136 ; Altisheim in, vii. 136 ; the Oats-goat at harvest in, vii. 282 ; Gablingen in, vii. 282 ; last standing corn called the Cow in, vii. 289 ; the Cow at threshing in, vii. 290 ; Obermedlingen in, vii. 290 ; the thresher of the last corn called the Sow in, vii. 298 *sq.* ; Friedingen in, vii. 298 ; Onstmettingen in, vii. 299 ; the "Twelve Lot Days" in, ix. 322 ; "burning the witch" on the first Sunday in Lent in, x. 116 ; custom of throwing lighted discs on the first Sunday in Lent in, x. 116 *sq.* ; Easter fires in, x. 144 *sq.* ; custom at eclipses in, x. 162 *n.* ; the Midsummer fires in, x. 166 *sq.* ; witches as hares and horses in, x. 318 *sq.* ; the divining-rod in, xi. 68 *n.*[4] ; fernseed brought by Satan on Christmas night in, xi. 289

Swabian custom as to child's teething, i. 180

—— story of soul in form of mouse, iii. 39 *n.*[1]

Swahili of East Africa, their New Year's Day, ix. 226 *n.*[1] ; their ceremony of the new fire, x. 140 ; birth-trees among the, xi. 160 *sq.* ; their story of an African Samson, xi. 314

Swahili charm by means of knotted cords, iii. 305 *sq.*

Swallow, wooden effigy of, carried about the streets on the first of March, viii. 322 *n.*

Swallow dance among the Kobeua and Kaua Indians of Brazil, ix. 381

—— Song, the Greek, viii. 322 *n.*

Swallowing of souls by shamans, iii. 76 *sq.*

Swallows as scapegoats, ix. 35 ; stones found in stomachs of, x. 17

Swami Bhaskaranandaji Saraswati, Hindoo gentleman worshipped as a god, i. 404

Swan, J. G., on the masked dances of the Indians of North-Western America, ix. 376 *sq.*

Swan, guardian spirit of a woman as a, i. 200

Swan-woman, Tartar story of the, xi. 144

Swan's bone, used by menstruous women to drink out of, x. 48, 49, 50, 90, 92
Swans, transmigration of bad poets into, viii. 308
Swans' song in a fairy tale, xi. 124
Swanton, J. R., on the seclusion of girls at puberty among the Haida Indians, x. 45 *n.*[1]
Swastika, carved on Hittite monument at Ibreez, v. 122 *n.*[1]
Swazieland, knots as charms in, iii. 305
Swazies, the, of South-Eastern Africa, their rain-making, i. 249 ; their king a rain-maker, i. 350 *sq.*
Swearing on stones, i. 160 *sq.*
Sweat, contagious magic of, i. 206, 213 ; of famous warriors drunk, viii. 152
Sweating as a purification, iii. 142, 156, 184
Sweden, guardian-trees in, ii. 58 ; birch-twigs on the eve of May Day in, ii. 64 *sq.* ; bonfires and May-poles at Midsummer in, ii. 65 ; Midsummer Bride and Bridegroom in, ii. 92, v. 251 ; cattle crowned in spring in, ii. 127 *n.*[2] ; Frey and his priestess in, ii. 143 *sq.* ; customs observed in, at turning out the cattle to graze for the first time in spring, ii. 341 *sq.* ; oaks and pines in the peat-bogs of, ii. 352 ; dramatic contest between Winter and Summer on May Day in, iv. 254 ; Maypole or Mid-summer-tree in, v. 250 ; kings of, answerable for the fertility of the ground, vi. 220 ; marriage custom in, to ensure the birth of a boy, vi. 262 ; custom at threshing in, vii. 149, 230 ; " Killing the Hare " at harvest in, vii. 280 ; the Yule Boar in, vii. 300 *sqq.* ; Christmas customs in, vii. 301 *sq.* ; belief as to eating white snake in, viii. 146 ; magpies' eggs and young carried from house to house on May Day in, viii. 321 *n.*[3] ; the Yule Goat in, viii. 327 *sq.*; heaps of stones or sticks to which passers-by add in, ix. 14 ; sticks or stones piled on scenes of violent death in, ix. 15, 20 *sq.* ; offerings at cairns in, ix. 27 ; customs observed on Yule Night in, x. 20 *sq.* ; Easter bonfires in, x. 146 ; bonfires on the Eve of May Day in, x. 159, 336 ; Midsummer fires in, x. 172 ; the need-fire in, x. 280 ; bathing at Mid-summer in, xi. 29 ; " Midsummer Brooms " in, xi. 54 ; the divining-rod in, xi. 69, 291 ; mistletoe to be shot or knocked down with stones in, xi. 82 ; mistletoe a remedy for epilepsy in, xi. 83 ; medical use of mistletoe in, xi. 84 ; mistletoe used as a protection against conflagration in, xi. 85, 293 ;

mistletoe cut at Midsummer in, xi. 86 ; mystic properties ascribed to mistletoe on St. John's Eve in, xi. 86 ; Balder's balefires in, xi. 87 ; children passed through a cleft oak as a cure for rup-ture or rickets in, xi. 170 ; crawling through a hoop as a cure in, xi. 184 ; superstitions about a parasitic rowan in, xi. 281
Swedes, the heathen, their mimicry of thunder, i. 248 *n.*[1] ; sacrifice their kings in times of dearth, i. 366 *sq.*
Swedish kings, traces of nine years' reign of, iv. 57 *sq.*
—— peasants stick leafy branches in corn-fields, ii. 47
—— popular belief that certain animals should not be called by their proper names, iii. 397
Sweeping misfortune out of house with brooms, ix. 5
—— out the town, annual ceremony of, ix. 135
Sweet potatoes cultivated in Africa, vii. 117 ; cultivated in South America, vii. 121 ; cultivated in Assam, vii. 123 ; cultivated in New Britain, vii. 123 ; offering of, to the god of sweet pota-toes among the Maoris, viii. 133
Sweethearts of St. John at Midsummer in Sardinia, ii. 92, v. 244 *sq.*
Swelling and inflammation thought to be caused by eating out of sacred vessels or by wearing sacred garments, iii. 4
Swiftness in running, charm to ensure, i. 155
Swim or sink, in divination, i. 196 ; test used to determine a new incarnation, i. 413
Swine, herds of, in ancient Italy, ii. 354; a tabooed word to fishermen, iii. 394, 395 ; not eaten by people of Pessinus, v. 265 ; not eaten by worshippers of Adonis, v. 265 ; not allowed to enter Comana in Pontus, v. 265 ; souls of the dead in, viii. 296
——, wild, their ravages in the corn, viii. 31 *sqq. See also* Pigs
Swine's flesh sacramentally eaten, viii. 20, 24 ; not eaten by worshippers of Attis, viii. 22 ; not eaten by Egyp-tian priests, viii. 24 *n.*[2] *See also* Pig's flesh *and* Pork
Swineherds, their horns, ii. 354 ; for-bidden to enter Egyptian temples, viii. 24
Swing in the Sky, the Golden, descrip-tion of the sun, iv. 279
Swinging, festival of, at Athens, i. 46 *n.*[1] ; at ploughing rite in Siam, iv. 150, 151, 156 *sq.* ; as a ceremony or magical rite, iv. 277 *sqq.* ; on hooks

run through the body, Indian custom, iv. 278 *sq.* ; as a cure for sickness, iv. 279, 280 *sq.* ; as a mode of inspiration, iv. 280 ; images as a funeral rite, iv. 282 ; as a ceremony of purification, iv. 282 *sq.* ; as a festal rite in modern Greece, Spain, and Italy, iv. 283 *sq.* ; for good crops, vii. 101, 103, 107

Swiss superstition as to knots in shrouds, iii. 310

Switzerland, the lake-dwellings of, ii. 353 ; the Corn-goat, Oats-goat, and Rye-goat at harvest in, vii. 283 ; the Wheat-cow, Corn-cow, Oats-cow, Corn-bull, etc., at harvest in, vii. 289, 291 ; omens from the cry of the quail in, vii. 295 ; weather forecasts in, ix. 323 ; Lenten fires in, x. 118 *sq.* ; new fire kindled by friction of wood in, x. 169 *sq.* ; Midsummer fires in, x. 172 ; the Yule log in, x. 249 ; need-fire in, x. 279 *sq.*, 336 ; people warned against bathing at Midsummer in, xi. 27 ; the belief in witchcraft in, xi. 42 *n.*[2] ; divination by orpine at Midsummer in, xi. 61

Sword, biting a, as a charm, i. 160 ; girls married to a, v. 61

——, a magical, possessed by Fire King, ii. 5 ; sacrifices offered to it, ii. 5

Sword-fish thanked for being killed by the Ainos, viii. 251

Swords to frighten evil spirits, i. 186 ; used to ward off or expel demons, ix. 113, 118, 119, 120, 123, 203 ; carried by mummers, ix. 245, 251

——, golden, iv. 75

Sycamore at doors on May Day, ii. 60 ; effigy of Osiris placed on boughs of, vi. 88, 110 ; sacred to Osiris, vi. 110

Sycamores worshipped in ancient Egypt, ii. 15 ; sacred among the Gallas, ii. 34

Syene, held by a Roman garrison, iv. 144 *n.*[2] ; inscriptions at, vi. 35 *n.*[1]

Syleus, a Lydian, compelled passers-by to dig in his vineyard, vii. 257 *sq.* ; killed by Hercules, vii. 258

Sylvan deities in classical art, ii. 45

Symbolism, coarse, of Osiris and Dionysus, vi. 112, 113

Symmachus on the festival of the Great Mother, v. 298

Sympathetic magic, i. 51 *sqq.*, iii. 164, 201, 204, 258, 268, 287, iv. 77, vii. 102, 139, viii. 33, 271, 311 *sq.*, ix. 399 ; its two branches, i. 54 ; examples of, i. 55 *sqq.* *See also* Magic

—— relation between cleft tree and person who has been passed through it, xi. 170, 171 *n.*[1], 172 ; between man and animal, xi. 272 *sq.*

Sympathy, magical, between a man and severed portions of his person, i. 175, iii. 267 *sq.*, 283

Synonyms adopted in order to avoid naming the dead, iii. 359 *sqq.* ; in the Zulu language, iii. 377 ; in the Maori language, iii. 381

Syntengs of Assam, iv. 55. *See* Jaintias

Syracuse, funeral games in honour of Timoleon at, iv. 94 ; the Blue Spring at, v. 213 *n.*[1]

Syrakoi chose as king the man with the longest head, ii. 297

Syria, charm to make fruit-trees bear in, i. 140 ; oak-tree worshipped in, ii. 16 ; St. George in, ii. 346, v. 78, 79, 90 ; belief as to stepping over a child in, iii. 424 ; Adonis in, v. 13 *sqq.* ; " holy men" in, v. 77 *sq.* ; hot springs resorted to by childless women in, v. 213 *sqq.* ; subject to earthquakes, v. 222 *n.*[1] ; the Nativity of the Sun at the winter solstice in, v. 303 ; turning money at the new moon in, vi. 149 ; bones of sacrificial victim not broken in, viii. 258 *n.*[2] ; precaution against caterpillars in, viii. 279 ; stones piled on graves of robbers in, ix. 17 ; practice of raising cairns near sacred places in, ix. 21 ; Aphrodite and Adonis in, ix. 386 ; restrictions on menstruous women in, x. 84

Syrian bridegroom must have no knots on his garments, iii. 300

—— custom of saluting the rising sun, ix. 416

—— god Hadad, v. 15

—— goddess at Hierapolis, hair offered to the, i. 29

—— mother, her vow, iii. 263

—— peasants believe that women can conceive without sexual intercourse, v. 91

—— witch, her procedure described by Lucian, iii. 270

—— women bathe in the Orontes to procure offspring, ii. 160 ; resort to hot springs to obtain offspring, ii. 161, v. 213 *sqq.* ; apply to saints for offspring, ii. 346, v. 78, 79, 90, 109

—— writer on the reasons for assigning Christmas to the twenty - fifth of December, v. 304 *sq.*

Syrians, their religious attitude to pigs, viii. 23 ; esteemed fish sacred, viii. 26

Syrmia, the Yule log in, x. 262 *sq.*

Syro-Macedonian calendar, iv. 116 *n.*[1], ix. 358 *n.*[1]

Szagmanten, in Tilsit district, the last sheaf at harvest called the Old Rye-woman at, vii. 232

Szis, the, of Upper Burma, the Father

and Mother of the Paddy (unhusked rice) among, vii. 203 *sq.*

Ta-cul-lies, native name of the Carrier Indians, iii. 215 *n.*[2]

Ta-ta-thi tribe of New South Wales, their mode of making rain by crystals, i. 304

Tâ-uz (Tammuz), mourned by Syrian women in Harran, v. 230

Taanach, in Palestine, burial of children in jars at, v. 109 *n.*[1]

Taara, the thunder-god of the Esthonians, ii. 367

Tabali, in South Nigeria, precaution as to the spittle of chiefs at, iii. 289

Tabari, Arab chronicler, his story how King Sapor took the city of Atrae, x. 82 *sq.*

Tabaristan, rain-producing cave in, i. 301

Table, leaping from, a charm to make crops grow high, i. 138, 139 *n.*

Tablets of destiny wrested by Marduk from Ningu, iv. 110

Taboo, or negative magic, i. 111 *sqq.*, 143; of chiefs and kings in Tonga, iii. 133 *sq.*; of chiefs in New Zealand, iii. 134 *sqq.*; Esquimau theory of, iii. 210 *sqq.*; the meaning of, iii. 224; conceived as a dangerous physical substance which needs to be insulated, x. 6 *sq.*

——, sanctity, and uncleanness, their equivalence in primitive thought, iii. 285; sanctity and uncleanness not differentiated in the notion of, viii. 23

Taboo rajah and chief, iii. 24 *sq.*

Tabooed acts, iii. 101 *sqq.*

—— hands, iii. 133, 134, 138, 140 *sqq.*, 146 *sqq.*, 158, 159 *n.*, 174, 265

—— men at festival of wild mango in New Guinea, x. 7 *sq.*

—— persons, iii. 131 *sqq.*; fed by others, iii. 133, 134 *n.*[1], 138, 138 *n.*[1], 139, 140, 141, 142, 147, 148 *n.*[1], 166, 167, 265; secluded, iii. 165; kept from contact with the ground, x. 2 *sqq.*

—— things, iii. 224 *sqq.*; kept from contact with the ground, x. 7 *sqq.*

—— village, viii. 122

—— women at festival of wild mango in New Guinea, x. 8

—— words, iii. 318 *sqq.*

Taboos, homoeopathic, i. 116; contagious, i. 117; on food, i. 117 *sqq.*, iii. 291 *sqq.*; laid on the parents of twins, i. 262, 263 *sq.*, 266; royal and priestly, iii. 1 *sqq.*; on intercourse with strangers, iii. 101 *sqq.*; on eating and drinking, iii. 116 *sqq.*; on showing the face, iii. 120 *sqq.*; on quitting the house, iii. 122 *sqq.*; on leaving food

over, iii. 126 *sqq.*; on persons who have handled the dead, iii. 138 *sqq.*; on mourners, iii. 138 *sqq.*; on lads at initiation, iii. 141 *sq.*, 156 *sq.*; on warriors, iii. 157 *sqq.*; on man-slayers, iii. 165 *sqq.*; on murderers, iii. 187 *sq.*; on hunters and fishers, iii. 190 *sqq.*; transformed into ethical precepts, iii. 214; survivals of, in morality, iii. 218 *sq.*; as spiritual insulators, iii. 224; on sharp weapons, iii. 237 *sqq.*; on blood, iii. 239 *sqq.*; relating to the head, iii. 252 *sqq.*; on hair, iii. 258 *sqq.*; on spittle, iii. 287 *sqq.*; on knots and rings, iii. 293 *sqq.*; on words, iii. 318 *sqq.*, 392 *sqq.*; on personal names, iii. 318 *sqq.*; on names of relations, iii. 335 *sqq.*; on the names of the dead, iii. 349 *sqq.*; on names of kings and chiefs, iii. 374 *sqq.*; on names of supernatural beings, iii. 384 *sqq.*; on names of gods, iii. 387 *sqq.*; on common words, iii. 392 *sqq.*; on common words based on a fear of spirits or of animals supposed to be endowed with human intelligence, iii. 416 *sqq.*; communal, vii. 109 *n.*[2]; agricultural, vii. 187; relating to milk, viii. 83 *sq.*; regulating the lives of divine kings, x. 2

Taboos observed in fishing and hunting on the principle of sympathetic magic, i. 113 *sqq.*; by children in the absence of their fathers, i. 116, 119, 122, 123, 127, 131; by wives in the absence of their husbands, i. 116, 119, 120, 121, 122 *sqq.*, 127 *sqq.*; by sisters in the absence of their brothers, i. 122, 123, 125, 127; by parents of twins, i. 262, 263 *sq.*, 266; after house-building, ii. 40; for the sake of the crops, ii. 98, 105 *sqq.*; by fathers of twins, ii. 102, iii. 239 *sq.*; by Brahman fire-priests, ii. 248; by the Flamen Dialis, ii. 248, iii. 13 *sq.*; by herd-boys while watching the herds, ii. 331; by the Mikado, iii. 3 *sq.*; by headmen in Assam, iii. 11; by ancient kings of Ireland, iii. 11 *sq.*; by the Bodia or Bodio, iii. 15; by sacred milkmen among the Todas, iii. 16 *sqq.*; by a priest in Celebes, iii. 129; by mourners, iii. 235 *sq.*; by searchers for *lignum aloes*, iii. 404; at the sowing festival among the Kayans, vii. 94, 187; by enchanters of crops among the Kai, vii. 100; at the sanctuary of Alectrona in Rhodes, viii. 45; at the sanctuary of the Mistress at Lycosura, viii. 46; after the capture of a ground seal, walrus, or whale among the Esquimaux, viii. 246;

by priest of Earth in Southern Nigeria, x. 4

Tabor, in Bohemia, custom of "Carrying out Death" at, iv. 237 *sq.*

Tacitus, Germans in the time of, ii. 285 ; on the sacred groves of the Germans, ii. 363 *n.*[6]; as to German observation of the moon, vi. 141 ; on human sacrifices offered by the ancient Germans, xi. 28 *n.*[1]; on the goddess Nerthus, xi. 28 *n.*[1]

Taenarum in Laconia, Poseidon worshipped at, v. 203 *n.*[2]

Tagales of the Philippines, their excuse to tree-spirit for felling the tree, ii. 36 *sq.*

Tagalogs of the Philippines, their reverence for flowers and trees, ii. 18 *sq.*

Tagbanuas of the Philippines, their custom of sending spirits of disease away in little ships, ix. 189

Tahiti, seclusion of women after childbirth in, iii. 147 ; kings and queens of, not to be touched, iii. 226 ; sanctity of the head in, iii. 255 *sq.*; remarkable rule of succession in, iv. 190 ; funeral custom to prevent return of ghost in, viii. 97 ; offerings of first-fruits in, viii. 132 ; transference of sins in, ix. 45 *sq.*; king and queen of, not allowed to set foot on the ground, x. 3 ; the fire-walk in, xi. 11. *See also* Tahitians

——, kings of, deified, i. 388 ; abdicate on birth of a son, iii. 20 ; their names not to be pronounced, iii. 381 *sq.*

Tahitians buried their cut hair at temples, iii. 274 ; burned or buried their shorn hair for fear of witchcraft, iii. 281 ; their notions as to eclipses of the sun and moon, iv. 73 *n.*[2]; their belief in the action of spirits, ix. 80 *sq.*; the New Year of the, xi. 244

Tahuata, human god in the island of, i. 387 *n.*[1]

Tai-chow, district of China, voluntary martyrdom of Buddhist monks in, iv. 42

Tâif, custom of polling the hair after a journey at, iii. 261

Taigonos Peninsula, the Koryaks of the, ix. 126

Tail of corn-spirit, vii. 268, 272, 300, viii. 10, 43 ; of sacrificial horse cut off, viii. 42, 43. *See also* Tails

"Tail-money" given to herdsmen on St. George's Day, ii. 331

Tailltenn, pagan cemetery at, iv. 101

Tailltiu or Tailltin, in County Meath, now Teltown, the fair of, iv. 99, 101 ; pagan cemetery at, iv. 101

Tailltiu, foster-mother of Lug, iv. 99

Tails of cats docked as a magical precaution, iii. 128 *sq.*

Tails of cattle, fire tied to, in rain-charm, i. 302

Tain tribe of Dinkas, influence of rainmaker over the, iv. 32

Taiping rebellion, i. 414

Tajan, the Dyaks of, forbidden to mention the names of parents and grandparents, iii. 340

—— and Landak, districts of Dutch Borneo, bride and bridegroom not allowed to touch the earth among the Dyaks of, x. 5 ; birth-trees among the Dyaks of, xi. 164

Tak, mountain in Tabaristan, rainmaking cave on, i. 301

Takhas, the, worship of the cobra, i. 383 *n.*[4]; on border of Cashmeer, inspired prophets among, i. 383

Takilis or Carrier Indians, succession to the soul among the, iv. 199. *See* Carrier Indians

Takitount, in Algeria, rain-making at, i. 250

Talaga Bodas, volcano in Java, sulphureous exhalations at, v. 204

Talaings, the, of Lower Burma, their customs as to the last sheaf at riceharvest, vii. 190 *sq.*

Talbot, P. Amaury, on self-mutilation among the Ekoi, v. 271 *n.*; on external human souls in animals in West Africa, xi. 208 *n.*[1], 209 *n.*[1]

Talegi, Motlav word for external soul, xi. 198

Taleins, the, of Burma, their worship of demons, ix. 96

Tales, wandering souls in popular, iii. 49 *sq.*; told as charms, vii. 102 *sqq.*; the resurrection of the body in popular, viii. 263 *sqq.*; of maidens forbidden to see the sun, x. 70 *sqq.*; the external soul in popular, xi. 95 *sqq.*

Tāli tied to bride, Hindoo marriage symbol, ii. 57 *n.*[4]

Talismans possessed by the Fire King of Cambodia, ii. 5 ; crowns and wreaths as, vi. 242 *sq.*; of cities, x. 83 *n.*[1] *See also* Amulets

——, public, iii. 317 *n.*[1]; in antiquity, i. 365 *n.*[7]

Talmud, the, on Purim, ix. 363 ; on menstruous women, x. 83

Talos, a bronze man, perhaps identical with the Minotaur, iv. 74 *sq.*

Tamanachiers, Indian tribe of the Orinoco, their story of the origin of death, ix. 303

Tamanaks of the Orinoco, their treatment of girls at puberty, x. 61 *n.*[3]

Tamanawas or *tamanous*, guardian spirits, ix. 376 *n.*[3]; dramatic performances of myths, ix. 376, 377

Tamaniu, external soul in the Mota language, xi. 198 *sq.*, 220

Tamara, island off New Guinea, belief in the transmigration of human souls into pigs in, viii. 296

Tamarind married to a mango in India, ii. 25

Tamarind-trees sacred, ii. 42, 44, 46

Tamarisk, sacred to Osiris, vi. 110 *sq.* ; Isfendiyar slain with a branch of a, x. 105

Tamarisk branches used to beat people ceremonially, ix. 263

Tambaran, demons, among the Melanesians of New Britain, ix. 82, 83

Tami, the, of German New Guinea, their theory of earthquakes, v. 198 ; their rites of initiation, xi. 239 *sqq.*

Tamil temples, dancing-girls in, v. 61

Tamirads, a family of diviners in Cyprus, v. 42

Tammuz or Adonis, v. 6 *sqq.* ; in the East perhaps replaced by St. George, ii. 346 ; the summer lamentations for, iv. 7 ; his relation to Adonis, v. 6 *n.*[1] ; his worship of Sumerian origin, v. 7 *sq.*; "true son of the deep water," v. 8, 246 ; laments for, v. 9 *sq.* ; mourned for at Jerusalem, v. 11, 17, 20, ix. 400 ; as a corn-spirit, v. 230 ; his bones ground in a mill, v. 230, vii. 258 ; perhaps represented by the mock king of the Sacaea, vii. 258 *sq.*; the lover of Ishtar, ix. 371, 373 ; annual death and resurrection of, ix. 398. *See also* Adonis

—— and Ishtar, v. 8 *sq.*, ix. 399, 406

Tammuz, a Babylonian month, v. 10 *n.*[1], 230, vii. 259

Tana (Tanna), one of the New Hebrides, contagious magic of clothes in, i. 206 ; power of the disease-makers in, i. 341 ; magic practised on refuse of food in, iii. 127 *sq.* ; dead ancestors worshipped as gods in, viii. 125 ; first-fruits offered to ancestors in, viii. 125 *sq.*

Tanala, the, of Madagascar, their custom at circumcision, iii. 227 ; their mode of averting ill-luck from children, vii. 9 ; believe that the souls of the dead transmigrate into animals, viii. 290

Tanaquil, the Queen, wife of Tarquin, story of the birth of Servius Tullius in connexion with, ii. 195

Tanatoa, deified king of Raiatea, i. 387 *sq.*

Tang dynasty of China, custom of marrying girls to the Yellow River under the, ii. 152

Tanga Coast of East Africa, belief as to mischievous spirits of trees on the, ii. 34

Tanganyika, Lake, Urua to the west of, i. 395 ; human victims thrown into, ii. 158 ; Winamwanga tribe to the south of, ii. 293, viii. 112 ; the Awemba to the west of, vii. 115 ; custom of carriers on the plateau between Lake Nyassa and, ix. 10 ; seclusion of girls at puberty among the tribes of the plateau to the west of, x. 24

—— plateau, custom as to the planting of bananas among the natives of the, vii. 115

Tangier, the Barley Bride among the Berbers near, vii. 178

Tangkhuls of Manipur, licence before sowing among the, ii. 100

Tangkul Nagas of Assam, their annual festival of the dead, vi. 57 *sqq.* ; their tug-of-war, ix. 177

Tani, a god in the Society Islands, first-fruits presented to, viii. 132 *sq.*

Tanjore, dancing - girls at, v. 61 ; the Rajah of, his sins transferred to Brahmans, ix. 44

Tanner, John, and the Shawnee sage, xi. 157

Tanneteya, in Celebes (?), vii. 196 *n.*

Tano, a fetish, on the Ivory Coast, viii. 287

Tanoe, River, on the Ivory Coast, viii. 287

Tantad, Midsummer bonfire, in Lower Brittany, x. 183

Tantalus, king of Sipylus, ancestor of the Pelopidae, ii. 279 ; murders his son Pelops, v. 181

Taoism, religious head of, i. 413 *sqq.* ; defined as " exorcising polytheism," ix. 99

Taoist treatise on the soul, xi. 221

Tapajos, tributary of the Amazon, the Mauhes on the, x. 62

Taphos besieged by Amphitryo, xi. 103

Tapia, a malignant ghost in San Cristoval, iii. 56

Tapio, woodland god in Finland, ii. 124

Tapir, custom of Indians after killing a, viii. 236

Tapirs, souls of dead in, viii. 285

Tapping a palm-tree for wine in Java, ceremony at, ii. 100 *sq.*

Tapuiyas, the, of Brazil, worshipped the Pleiades, vii. 309

Tar as a protection against witchcraft, ii. 53 ; to keep out ghosts and witches, ix. 153 *n.*[1] *See also* Pitch

Tar - barrels burnt at Up-helly-a' in Lerwick, ix. 169 ; burning, swung round pole at Midsummer, x. 169 ; burnt at Midsummer among the

Esthonians, x. 180; burnt on Hogmanay at Burghead, x. 266 *sq.*; procession with lighted, on Christmas Eve in Lerwick, x. 268

Tara, the capital of ancient Ireland, the sun not to rise on the king of Ireland in his bed at, iii. 11; no king with a personal blemish allowed to reign over Ireland at, iv. 39; pagan cemetery at, iv. 101; new fire kindled in spring in the King's house at, x. 158

Tarahumares of Mexico, their charm to secure victory in race, i. 150; their homoeopathic charm to make them fleet of foot, i. 155; their rain-making by making smoke, i. 249; their rain-charm by dipping a plough in water, i. 284; their worship of water-serpents, ii. 156 *sq.*; their belief as to shooting stars, iv. 62; ceremonies performed by them at hoeing, ploughing, and harvest, vii. 227 *sq.*; sacrifice to the Master of Fish, viii. 252; their custom of adding sticks or stones to heaps, ix. 10; their dances for the crops, ix. 236 *sqq.*

Tarascon, the dragon of, ii. 170 *n.*[1]

Tarashchansk district of Russia, rain-making in the, i. 285

Tarbolton, in Ayrshire, annual bonfire at, x. 207

Tari Pennu, Earth Goddess of the Khonds, human sacrifices offered to her for the crops, vii. 245

Tarianas, the, of the Amazon, their custom of drinking the ashes of the dead, viii. 157

Tarija, in Bolivia, Earth-mothers at, vii. 173 *n.*

Tark, Tarku, Trok, Troku, syllables in names of Cilician priests, v. 144; perhaps the name of a Hittite deity, v. 147; perhaps the name of the god of Olba, v. 148, 165

Tarkimos, priest of Corycian Zeus, v. 145

Tarkondimotos, name of two Cilician kings, v. 145 *n.*[2]

Tarkuaris, priest of Corycian Zeus, v. 145; priestly king of Olba, v. 145

Tarkudimme or Tarkuwassimi, name on Hittite seal, v. 145 *n.*[2]

Tarkumbios, priest of Corycian Zeus, v. 145

Tarnow, district of Galicia, wreath made out of last sheaf called the Wheat-mother, Rye-mother, or Pea-mother in, vii. 135

Taro, magical stones to promote the growth of, i. 162; charms·for growth of, vii. 100, 102

Taro plants beaten to make them grow, ix. 264

Tarquin the Elder, husband of Tanaquil, ii. 195; succeeded by his son-in-law, ii. 270; his sons, ii. 270 *n.*[3]; his descent, ii. 270 *n.*[6]; murdered, ii. 320

Tarquin the Proud, sacred precinct on the Alban Mount dedicated by, ii. 187; uncle of L. Junius Brutus, ii. 290; his attempt to shift the line of descent of the Roman kingship, ii. 291 *sq.*

Tarquitius Priscus, on unlucky trees, iii. 275 *n.*[3]

Tarsus in Cilicia, climate and fertility of, v. 118; school of philosophy at, v. 118; Sandan and Baal at, v. 142 *sq.*, 161; priesthood of Hercules at, v. 143; Fortune of the City on coins of, v. 164; divine triad at, v. 171

——, the Baal of, v. 117 *sqq.*, 162 *sq.*

——, coins of, representing Sandan on the pyre, ix. 388 *n.*[2]

——, Sandan of, v. 124 *sqq.*, ix. 388, 389, 391, 392

Tartar Khan, ceremony at visiting a, iii. 114

—— stories of the external soul, xi. 142 *sq.*, 144 *sq.*

Tartars, their belief in living Buddhas incarnate in Grand Lamas, i. 410 *sq.*; divine by the shoulder-blades of sheep, iii. 229 *n.*[4]; do not break bones of the animals they eat, viii. 258 *n.*[2]; after a funeral leap over fire, xi. 18

—— of the Middle Ages, names of the dead not uttered till the third generation among the, iii. 370

Tasmania, the aborigines of, reluctant to name the dead, iii. 353

Tasmanians carried fire about with them, ii. 257 *sq.*; seem to have changed common words after a death, iii. 364 *n.*[1]

Tat or *tatu* pillar. See *Ded* pillar

Tate, H. R., on serpent-worship among the Akikuyu, v. 85

Tatia, wife of Numa, ii. 270 *n.*[5]

Tatius, king of Rome, succeeded by his son-in-law Numa, ii. 270 and *nn.*[1,5]; the Sabine colleague of Romulus, killed with sacrificial knives, ii. 320

Tattoo-marks, tribal, in Dahomey, v. 74 *n.*[4]; of priests in Dahomey, v. 74 *n.*[4]; of priests of Attis, v. 278; on slave or prisoner of war, ix. 47

Tattooing in the Punjaub, belief as to, iii. 30; of bride in Fiji, x. 34 *n.*[1]; medicinal use of, x. 98 *n.*[1]; at initiation, xi. 258, 259, 261 *n.*

Tauaré Indians, of the Rio Enivra, eat the ashes of their dead, viii. 157

Taui Islanders, their custom as to a falling star, iv. 61

Taungthu, the, of Upper Burma, their

way of securing the soul of the rice, vii. 190

Taunton, expedients for facilitating death at, iii. 309

Taupes et Mulots, fire ceremony on Eve of Twelfth Night in the Bocage of Normandy, ix. 317

Taura, priest, in Southern Pacific, i. 377, 378

Taurians of the Crimea, their use of the heads of prisoners, v. 294

Tauric Diana, her image brought by Orestes to Italy in a faggot of sticks, i. 10 *sq.* ; her image only to be appeased with human blood, i. 24

Taurobolium, sacrifice of a bull in the rites of Cybele, v. 274 *sqq.* ; or *Tauropolium*, v. 275 *n.*[1]

Taurus, Mount, the Yourouks of, ii. 43

Taurus mountains, pass of the Cilician Gates in the, v. 120

Tavernier, J. B., on the annual expulsion of demons in Tonquin, ix. 148 *n.*[1]

Taxation perhaps derived from offerings of first-fruits, viii. 116

Tay, Loch, Hallowe'en fires on, x. 232

Taygetus, Mount, sacrifices to the sun on, i. 315 *sq.*

Taylor, Isaac, on the relation of the Italian and Celtic languages, ii. 189 *n.*[3]

Taylor, Rev. J. C., on the annual expulsion of evils at Onitsha, ix. 133 ; on human scapegoat at Onitsha, ix. 211

Taylor, Rev. Richard, on human scapegoats in New Zealand, ix. 39 ; on the Maori gods, ix. 81

Tcheou dynasty of China, change of calendar under the, x. 137

Tchiglit Esquimaux, their belief as to falling stars, iv. 65

Teak, *Loranthus* on, xi. 317

Teanlas, Hallowe'en fires in Lancashire, x. 245

Tears of Isis thought to swell the Nile, vi. 33 ; rain thought to be the tears of gods, vi. 33 ; of human victim signs of rain, vii. 248, 250 ; of oxen as rain-charm, viii. 10

Teasing animals before killing them, viii. 190

Tebach, bear-festival of the Gilyaks at, viii. 191 *sqq.*

Teberans, spirits, among the Melanesians of New Britain, i. 340

Teeth, ceremony of knocking out teeth at initiation among the tribes of Australia, i. 97 *sqq.* ; extraction of teeth in connexion with rain, i. 98 *sq.* ; tribute of, i. 101 ; homoeopathic magic of, i. 137 ; homoeopathic charms to strengthen, i. 153, 157 ; contagious magic of, i. 176-182 ; of rats and mice

in magic, i. 178 *sqq.* ; of foxes and kangaroos in sympathetic magic, i. 180 ; of ancestor in magical ceremony, i. 312 ; loss of, supposed effect of breaking a taboo, iii. 140 ; loosened by angry ghosts, iii. 186 *n.*[1]; as a rain-charm, iii. 271 ; extracted, kept against the resurrection, iii. 280 ; children whose upper teeth appear before the lower exposed, iii. 287 *n.* ; filed as preliminary to marriage, x. 68 *n.*[2] *See also* Tooth

Teeth and nails of sacred kings preserved as amulets, ii. 6

Teething, charms to help, i. 180

Tegea, tombstones at, v. 87 ; Demeter and Persephone worshipped at, vii. 63 *n.*[14]

Tegner, Swedish poet, on the burning of Balder, xi. 87

Tein Econuch, "forlorn fire," need-fire, x. 292

Tein-eigin (teine-eigin, tin-egin), need-fire, in the Highlands of Scotland, x. 147, 148, 289, 291, 293

Teine Bheuil, fire of Beul, need-fire, in the Highlands of Scotland, x. 293

Telamon, son of Aeacus, king of Salamis, ii. 278, v. 145

Telchines, the, of Rhodes, legendary magicians, i. 310

Telepathy, magical, i. 119 *sqq.* ; in hunting and fishing, i. 120 *sqq.*; in voyages, i. 126 ; in war, i. 126 *sqq.*

Telephus at Pergamus, rule as to persons who had sacrificed to, viii. 85

Telingana, euphemistic name for snake in, iii. 402

Tell Ta'annek (Taanach), in Palestine, burial of children in jars at, v. 109 *n.*[1]

Tell-el-Amarna, the new capital of King Amenophis IV., vi. 123 *n.*[1], 124, 125 ; tablets, iv. 170 *n.*[5] ; letters, v. 16 *n.*[5], 21 *n.*[2], 135 *n.*

Tellemarken in Norway, cairns to which passers-by add stones in, ix. 14

Teltown, in County Meath, the fair at, iv. 99

Telugu remedy for a fever, ix. 38

Telugus, their way of stopping rain, i. 253 ; their precaution as to spittle, iii. 289

Tembadere, rain-maker at, ii. 3

Tempe, the Vale of, Apollo purged of the dragon's blood in, iv. 81, vi. 240

Temple, Sir R. C., on the fear of spirits and ghosts among the Nicobarese, ix. 88

Temple at Jerusalem built without iron, iii. 230

Temple, the Inner and the Middle, Lords of Misrule in the, ix. 333

Temple church, Lord of Misrule in the, ix. 333

Temple-tombs of kings, vi. 161 *sq.*, 167 *sq.*, 170 *sqq.*, 174, 194 *sq.*

Temples built in honour of living kings of Babylon, i. 417 ; built in honour of living kings of Egypt, i. 418 ; of dead kings in Africa, vi. 161 *sq.*, 167 *sq.*, 170 *sqq.*, 194 *sq.* ; dedicated to sharks, viii. 292

Temporary king, ix. 403 *sq.* ; in Cambodia, iv. 148 ; in Siam, iv. 149 *sqq.*, ix. 151

—— kings, taking the place of the real kings for a time, iv. 148 *sqq.* ; their divine or magical functions, iv. 155 *sqq.*

—— reincarnation of the dead in their living namesakes, iii. 371

Ten Thousand, the march of the, iii. 124

Tench, jaundice transferred to a, ix. 52

Tendi, Batta word for soul, iii. 45, 263. *See also* Tondi

Tendo, lagoon of, on the Ivory Coast, souls of dead in bats on the, viii. 287

Tenedos, sacrifice of infants to Melicertes in, iv. 162 ; human beings torn in pieces at the rites of Dionysus in, vii. 24 ; calf shod in buskins sacrificed to Dionysus in, vii. 33

Teneriffe, the Guanches of, i. 303

Tengaroeng in Borneo, swinging of priests and priestesses as a mode of inspiration at, iv. 280, 281

Tenggerese of Java, their story of the type of Beauty and the Beast, iv. 130 *n.*[1]; sacrifice to volcano, v. 220 ; their sham fight at New Year, ix. 184

Tenimber Islands, treatment of the afterbirth in the, i. 186 ; first-fruits offered to spirits of ancestors in the, viii. 123

—— and Timor-laut Islands, new-born children passed through the smoke of fire in the, ii. 232 *n.*[3]

Tenos, the calendar of, viii. 6 *n.*

Tent of widow burnt at Midsummer in Morocco, x. 215

Tentyra (Denderah), temple of Osiris at, vi. 86

Teos, public curses in, i. 45 *n.*[7]

Tepehuanes of Mexico afraid of being photographed, iii. 97 ; personal names kept secret among the, iii. 325 ; their belief as to stepping over persons, iii. 424 ; their custom of adding sticks or stones to heaps, ix. 10

Tephrosia, devil's shoestring, in homoeopathic magic, i. 144

Termonde in Belgium, Midsummer fires at, x. 194

Terms of relationship used as terms of address, iii. 324 *sq.*

Ternate, in the Indian Archipelago, ii.

111 ; the natives of, names of objects tabooed to them at sea, iii. 414 ; the sultan of, his sacrifice of human victims to a volcano, v. 220

Tertullian on Christians worshipping each other, i. 407 ; on the Etruscan crown, ii. 175 *n.*[1] ; human sacrifices in the lifetime of, iv. 168 ; on the fasts of Isis and Cybele, v. 302 *n.*[4] ; on the date of the Crucifixion, v. 306 *n.*[5]

Teshu Lama, the, ix. 203

—— Lumbo in Tibet, celebration of Tibetan New Year's Day at, ix. 203

Teshub or Teshup, name of Hittite god, v. 135 *n.*, 148 *n.*

Teso, the, of Central Africa, medicinemen dressed as women among the, vi. 257 ; their use of bells to exorcize fiends, ix. 246 *sq.*

Tessier, on the burning wheel at Konz, x. 164 *n.*[1]

Test of the reincarnation of the Heavenly Master, i. 413 ; of virginity by a flame, ii. 239 *sq.*, x. 139 *n.* *See also* Tests

Testicles of rams in the rites of Attis, v. 269 *n.* ; of bull used in rites of Cybele and Attis, v. 276 ; of goats eaten by lecherous persons, viii. 142 ; of brave enemy eaten, viii. 148

Tests of the reincarnation of Grand Lamas, i. 411 ; of the reincarnation of the dead in the Niger Delta, i. 411 *n.*[1] ; undergone by girls at puberty, x. 25. *See also* Test

Têt, New Year festival in Annam, vi. 62

Tet pillar. *See Ded* pillar

Teti, king of Egypt, mentioned in the Pyramid Texts, vi. 5

Teton Indians, their attempt to deceive the ghosts of the spiders which they kill, viii. 236 *sq.*

Tettnang, in Würtemburg, the He-goat at threshing at, vii. 286

Tetzcatlipoca or Tezcatlipoca, great Mexican god, viii. 165, ix. 276 ; man killed and eaten as the representative of, viii. 92 *sq.* ; young man annually sacrificed in the character of, ix. 276 *sqq.*

Teucer, son of Aeacus, king in Cyprus, ii. 278

—— and Ajax, names of priestly kings of Olba, v. 144 *sq.*, 148, 161

- ——, son of Tarkuaris, priestly king of Olba, v. 151, 157

——, son of Telamon, ii. 278 ; founds Salamis in Cyprus, v. 145 ; said to have instituted human sacrifice, v. 146

——, son of Zenophanes, high priest of Olbian Zeus, v. 151

Teucrids, dynasty at Salamis in Cyprus, v. 145

Teutates, Celtic god, xi. 80 *n.*[3]

Teutonic kings as priests, i. 47
—— peoples, bride race among the, ii. 303 *sqq.*
—— stories of the external soul, xi. 116 *sqq.*
—— thunder-god, ii. 364
—— year reckoned from October 1st, vi. 81
Texas, the Tonkawe Indians of, iii. 325 ; the Toukaway Indians of, xi. 276
Tezcatlipoca. *See* Tetzcatlipoca
Tezcuco, statue of the god Xipe from, ix. 291 *n.*[1]
Thahu, curse or pollution, among the Akikuyu, x. 81
Thakombau, Fijian chief, the War King, iii. 21 ; family who enjoyed the privilege of scratching him, iii. 131
Thalavettiparothiam, custom observed in Malabar, a competition for the privilege of being decapitated after a five years' reign, iv. 52 *sq.*
Thales on spirits, ix. 104
Thamus, an Egyptian pilot, and the death of the Great Pan, iv. 6 *sq.*
Thanda Pulayans, in India, their notion as to the phosphorescence of the sea, ii. 155 *n.*[1]
Thann, in Alsace, the Little May Rose at, ii. 74
Tharafah, on a custom of the heathen Arabs as to a boy's fallen tooth, i. 181
Thargelia, human scapegoats at the Greek festival of the, ix. 254, 255, 256, 257, 259, 272, 273
Thargelion, Greek harvest month, i. 32, vi. 239 *n.*[1], viii. 8
Thatch of roof, children's cast teeth deposited in, i. 179 ; burnt as a charm against witchcraft, ii. 53 ; shorn hair hidden in, iii. 277
Thays of Indo-China, their offerings of first-fruits to their ancestors, viii. 121 ; their worship of spirits, ix. 97 *sq.* ; their customs after a burial, xi. 177 *sq.*
Theal, G. McCall, on the worship of ancestors among the Bantus, vi. 176 *sq.* ; on fear of demons among the Bantu tribes of South Africa, ix. 77 *sq.*
Theban priests, in Egypt, their determination of the solar year, vi. 26
Thebes, the Boeotian, grave of Eteocles and Polynices at, ii. 33 ; the women of, muffled their faces, iii. 122; festival of the Laurel-bearing at, iv. 78 *sq.*, 88 *sq.*, vi. 241 ; founded by Cadmus, iv. 88 ; stone lion at, v. 184 *n.*[3]; grave of Dionysus at, vii. 14 ; Dionysus torn to pieces at, vii. 14, 25 ; the Thesmophoria at, viii. 17 *n.*[2]; effigies of Judas burnt at Easter in, x. 130 *sq.*

Thebes in Egypt, temple of the sun-god at, i. 67 *sq.* ; the human consort of Ammon at, ii. 130 *sq.* ; priestly dynasty at, ii. 134 ; high priests of Ammon at, ii. 134 ; priestly kings of, iii. 13 ; temple of Ammon at, v. 72 ; the Memnonium at, vi. 35 *n.* ; the Valley of the Kings at, vi. 90 ; annual sacrifice of ram to Ammon at, viii. 41, 172
Theckydaw, annual expulsion of demons in Tonquin, ix. 147 *sq.*
Theddora tribe of South-East Australia ate the hands and feet of their foes, viii. 151
Theebaw, king of Burma, his relations beaten to death, iii. 242
Theias, a Syrian king, father of Adonis, v. 43 *n.*[4], 55 *n.*[4]
Theism late in human history, vi. 41
Then, spirits, among the Thay of Indo-China, ix. 97
Thensae, sacred cars at the Circensian games in Rome, ii. 175 *n.*[1]
Theocracies in America, iii. 6
Theocracy, government by human gods, i. 386 ; in the Pelew Islands, tendency to, vi. 208
Theocritus, witch in, i. 206 ; on an image of Demeter, vii. 43 ; on the harvest-home in Cos, vii. 46 *sq.*
Theodore, Archbishop of Canterbury, his denunciation of a heathen practice, xi. 190 *sq.*
Theodosius and Honorius, decree of, against the burning of effigies of Haman by the Jews, ix. 392
Theogamy, divine marriage, ii. 121
Theology distinguished from religion, i. 223 ; the gods at first mortal in Brahman, i. 373 *n.*[1]; vague thought of a crude, iii. 3 *n.*; cruel ritual diluted into a nebulous, ix. 411
Theophrastus, on the woods of Latium, ii. 188 ; on the woods used by the Greeks in kindling fire, ii. 251 ; on the artificial fertilization of fig-trees, ii. 314 *n.*[2]; on the flowering of squills, vii. 53 *n.*[1]; on the custom of ploughing the land thrice, vii. 73 *n.*[1]; on the different kinds of mistletoe, xi. 317
Theopompus, on sexual communism among the Etruscans, ii. 207 ; wins prize of eloquence at Halicarnassus, iv. 95 ; on the names of the seasons, vi. 41
Theory of sacrifice, the Brahmanical, ix. 410 *sq.*; solar theory of the European fire-festivals, x. 329, 331 *sqq.*; purificatory theory of the European fire-festivals, x. 329 *sq.*, 341 *sqq.*
Thera, worship of the Mother of the Gods in, v. 280 *n.*[1]

Therapia, near Constantinople, effigies of Judas burnt at Easter in, x. 131

Thermopylae, the Spartans at, v. 197 n.[1]; the hot springs of, v. 210 sqq.

Theseus offers his hair to Apollo at Delphi, i. 28

—— and Ariadne, iv. 75

—— and Hippolytus, i. 19

Thesmophoria, ancient Greek festival celebrated by women in October, viii. 17 sqq.; release of prisoners at the, iii. 316; chastity of women at the, v. 43 n.[4], vii. 116; sacrifice of cakes and pigs to serpents at the, v. 88, viii. 17 sq.; pine-cones at the, v. 278; fast of the women at the, vi. 40 sq.; seeds of pomegranates not eaten at the, vii. 14; indecencies at the, vii. 63; descent and ascent of Persephone at the, viii. 17; its analogy with folk-customs of Northern Europe, viii. 20 sq.

Thessalian witch, her love-charm, iii. 270; consulted by Sextus Pompeius, iii. 390

Thessalians, their festival of the Peloria, resembling the Saturnalia, ix. 350

Thessaly, kings of, i. 47 n.; rain-making among the Greeks of, i. 272 sq.; Crannon in, i. 309

Thetis and her infant son, how she tried to make him immortal by fire, v. 180

Thevet, F. A., on the importance of medicine-men among the Indians of Brazil, i. 358 sq.

Thief wears a toad's heart to escape detection, x. 302 n.[2]. See also Thieves

Thief's charm among the South Slavs, i. 153; garments beaten instead of thief, i. 206 sq.; name boiled, iii. 331

Thiers, J. B., on the Yule log, x. 250; on gathering herbs at Midsummer, xi. 45 n.[1]; on belief concerning wormwood, xi. 61 n.[1]

Thieves, transmigration of souls of, into animals, viii. 299; detected by diving-rod, xi. 68

Thieves' candles, i. 148, 149, 236

Thigh, sinew of the, customs and myths as to, viii. 264 sqq.

Thighs of diseased cattle cut off and hung up as a remedy, x. 296 n.[1]

Things, homoeopathic magic of inanimate, i. 157 sqq.; tabooed, iii. 224 sqq.

Thinis, in Egypt, the mummy of Anhouri at, iv. 4 sq.

Thiodolf, the poet, on King Aun's sacrifice of his sons at Upsala, iv. 161

Third marriage regarded as unlucky, ii. 57 n.[4]

Thirst, transference of, in ancient Hindoo ritual, ix. 38

Thirty years, the Sed festival held nominally at intervals of, vi. 151

—— years' cycle of the Druids, xi. 77

—— Years' War, plague during the, ix. 64

Thistles, as a charm to keep off witches, ii. 339, 340

Thlinkeet or Tlingit Indians, the, viii. 253; think that stormy weather may be caused by combing hair, iii. 271. See Tlingit

—— shamans, their use of the tongues of otters and eagles, viii. 270

Thomas, N. W., as to the doctrine of souls among the Angass, xi. 210 n.[2]

Thomas, W. E., on human god of the Makalakas, i. 394 n.[3]

Thomas the Rhymer, verses ascribed to, on the mistletoe at Errol, xi. 283 sq.

Thompson Indians of British Columbia, ceremonies performed by girls at puberty among the, i. 70; dances of women during absence of warriors among the, i. 132 sq.; their custom as to children's cast teeth, i. 181; their treatment of the navel-string, i. 197; their contagious magic of footprints, i. 212; their way of stopping rain, i. 253; their beliefs and customs concerning twins, i. 264 sq.; their belief as to the loon and rain, i. 288; their superstition as to killing a frog, i. 293; their reverence for sunflower roots, ii. 13; the fire-drill of the, ii. 208; their custom of not sleeping the night after a death, iii. 37 sq.; recovery of lost souls by shamans among the, iii. 57 sq.; think that the setting sun draws away men's souls, iii. 65; their fear of witchcraft at meals, iii. 117; customs of mourners among the, iii. 142 sq.; their custom after killing an enemy, iii. 181; their continence and other observances before hunting, iii. 198; their disposal of their loose hair, iii. 278 sq.; burned their nail-parings for fear of witchcraft, iii. 282; their children may not name the coyote in winter, iii. 399; their ceremonies before eating the first berries or roots of the season, viii. 81 sq.; offered first berries of season to the earth or the mountains, viii. 133 sq.; will not eat the fool-hen lest they grow foolish, viii. 140; their belief in the assimilation of men to their guardian animals, viii. 207; their propitiation of slain bears, viii. 226; their superstitions in regard to killing deer, viii. 242; custom observed by man whose daughter has just reached puberty among the, viii. 268; their charms against ghosts, ix. 154 *n.* ; seclusion of girls at puberty among the, x. 49 *sqq.* ; their dread of menstruous women, x. 89 *sq.* ; prayer of adolescent girl among the, x. 98 *n.*[1] ; supposed invulnerability of initiated men among the, xi. 275 *sq.* ; their ideas as to wood of trees struck by lightning, xi. 297

Thomsdorf, in Germany, story of an immortal girl told at, x. 99

Thomson, Basil, on circumcision in Fiji, xi. 244 *n.*[1] ; on the *Nanga* in Fiji, xi. 244 *n.*[2]

Thomson, Joseph, on the fear of photography among the Wa-teita, iii. 98

Thonga, Bantu tribe of South Africa, their belief in serpents as reincarnations of the dead, v. 82 ; their presentation of infants to the moon, vi. 144 *sq.* ; worship of the dead among the, vi. 180 *sq.* ; seclusion of girls at puberty among the, x. 29 *sq.* ; will not use the wood of trees struck by lightning, xi. 297 ; think lightning caused by a bird, xi. 297 *n.*[5]. *See also* Ba-Thonga

Thonga chiefs buried secretly, vi. 104 *sq.*

Thongs, legends as to new settlements enclosed by, vi. 249 *sq.*

Thor, the Norse thunder god, equivalent to the Teutonic Donar or Thunar, ii. 364 ; his hammers, i. 248 *n.*[1] ; fought for Balder, x. 103

Thorn, external soul in a, xi. 129 ; mistletoe on a, xi. 291 *n.*[3]

Thorn-bushes as charms against witches, ii. 338 ; to keep off ghosts, iii. 142, xi. 174 *sq.*

Thorns, wreaths of, hung up as a sign to warn off strangers, ix. 140

Thorny branches used to keep out witches, ix. 161

—— shrubs, a protection against witches, ii. 338

Thoth, Egyptian god of wisdom, at the marriage of the Queen of Egypt to Ammon, ii. 131 ; how he added five days to the Egyptian year, vi. 6 ; teaches Isis a spell to restore the dead to life, vi. 8 ; restores the eye of Horus, vi. 17 ; how he outwitted the Sun-god Ra, ix. 341

Thoth, the first month of the Egyptian year, vi. 36, 93 *sqq.*

Thothmes I., king of Egypt, the god Ammon in the likeness of, ii. 131, 132

—— IV., king of Egypt, the god Ammon in the likeness of, ii. 131, 132

Thought, the web of, xi. 307 *sq.*

Thrace, the Edonians of, i. 366 ; the grave of Ares in, iv. 4 ; worship of

Dionysus in, vii. 3 ; the Bacchanals of, vii. 17 ; modern Carnival customs in, vii. 25 *sqq.*, viii. 331 *sqq.* ; Abdera in, ix. 254

Thracian gods ruddy and blue-eyed, iii. 387

—— villages, custom at Carnival in, vi. 99 *sq.*

Thracians threatened the thunder-god, ii. 183 *n.*[2] ; funeral games held by the, iv. 96 ; their contempt of death, iv. 142

Thrashing people to do them good, ix. 262 *sqq.* *See also* Beating *and* Whipping

Thread, red, in popular cure, ix. 55

—— or string used to tie soul to body, iii. 32 *sq.*, 43, 51

Threads hung on trees, ii. 134 ; knotted, in magic, iii. 303, 304 *sq.*, 307 ; used to transfer illnesses to trees, ix. 55

——, red, tied to cattle as a protection against witchcraft, ii. 336

Threatening the thunder god, ii. 183 *n.*[2]

—— the spirits of fruit-trees, ii. 20 *sqq.*, x. 114

Three days, taboos observed for, at bringing home the Soul of the Rice, vii. 198 *sq.*

—— Holy Kings, the divining-rod baptized in the name of the, xi. 68

—— Kings on Twelfth Day, ix. 329 *sqq.*

—— knots in magic, iii. 304, 305

—— leaps over bonfire, x. 214, 215

—— years, chief killed at end of reign of, iv. 113. *See also* Thrice

Thresher tied up in last sheaf, vii. 134, 147, 148 ; of last sheaf treated as an animal, vii. 271

—— of the last corn called the Corn-pug, vii. 273 ; called Goat or Oats-goat, vii. 286 ; called the Cow, vii. 291 ; called the Bull, vii. 291 ; called the Sow, vii. 298, 299 ; disguised as a wolf, viii. 327

Threshers, contests between, vii. 147 *sqq.*, 218, 219 *sq.*, 221 *sq.*, 223 *sq.*, 253 ; pretend to throttle or thresh people on threshing-floor, vii. 149 *sq.*, 230 ; tied in straw and thrown into water, vii. 224 *sq.*

Thresher-cow, name given to man who threshes the last corn, in the Canton of Zurich, vii. 291

Threshing, customs at, vii. 134, 147 *sqq.*, 203, 221 *sq.*, 223, 223 *sq.*, 225 *sq.*, 230, 271, 273, 274 *sq.*, 277, 281, 286 *sq.*, 290 *sqq.*, 297, 298 *sq.* ; contests in, vii. 218 *sqq.* ; corn-spirit killed at, vii. 291 *sq.*

—— in Attica, date of, viii. 4

—— in Greece, date of, vii. 62

Threshing-dog, name given to man who gives the last stroke with the flail, vii. 271

—— -floor, stalks of corn knotted as a charm on a, iii. 308 *sq.* ; Demeter associated with the, vii. 41 *sq.*, 43, 47, 61 *sq.*, 63, 64 *sq.* ; the festival of the, at Eleusis, vii. 60 *sqq.* ; of Triptolemus at Eleusis, vii. 61, 72, 75 ; strangers treated as embodiments of the corn-spirit on the, vii. 230 ; sanctity of the, viii. 110 *n.*[4]

Threshing corn by oxen, vi. 45

Threshold, shells on, i. 158 ; the caul (chorion) buried under the, i. 200 ; personal relics buried by witch under the, i. 206 *n.*[4] ; guarded against witches on Walpurgis Night by flowers, sods, and thorny branches, ii. 52, 54, 55, ix. 163 ; protected against witches on Walpurgis Night by knives, ii. 55, ix. 162 ; cut hair buried under the, iii. 276 *sq.* ; burial of infants under the, v. 93 *sq.* ; nail knocked into, to prevent death entering, ix. 63 *n.*[4] ; shavings from the, burnt, xi. 53

Thrice, custom of spitting thrice to avert evil, iv. 63 ; Greek custom of ploughing land thrice, vii. 72 *sq.* ; to crawl thrice under a bramble as a cure, xi. 180 ; to pass thrice through a wreath of woodbine, xi. 184

—— born, said of Brahmans, i. 381

Thrice-ploughed field, Plutus begotten on a, vii. 208

Throne, sanctity of the king's, i. 365 ; reverence for the, iv. 51

Throttling, a punishment for incest, ii. 110 ; farmer's wife at threshing, pretence of, vii. 150 ; strangers at threshing, pretence of, vii. 230

Throwing of sticks or stones interpreted as an offering or token of respect, ix. 20 *sqq.*, 25 *sqq.* ; as a mode of riddance of evil, ix. 23 *sqq.* ; or striking blindfold, xi. 279 *n.*[4]

Thrumalun, a mythical being in Australia who kills and resuscitates novices at initiation, xi. 233. *See also* Daramulun *and* Thuremlin

Thrushes deposit seeds of mistletoe, xi. 316 *n.*[1]

Thucydides on military music, v. 196 *n.*[3] ; on the sailing of the fleet for Syracuse, v. 226 *n.*[4]

Θύειν distinguished from ἐναγίζειν, v. 316 *n.*[1]

Thule, ceremony in Thule at the annual reappearance of the sun, ix. 125 *n.*[1]

Thumbs snapped to prevent the de-

parture of the soul, iii. 31 ; of dead enemies cut off, viii. 272

Thunar or Donar, the German thunder god, ii. 364

Thunder, imitation of, in a Russian rain-charm, i. 248 ; kings expected to make, ii. 180 *sq.* ; thought to be the roll of the drums of the dead, ii. 183 ; rain, sky, and oak, god of the, ii. 349 *sq.* ; Esthonian prayer to, ii. 367 *sq.* ; expiation for hearing, iii. 14 ; the first heard in spring, offering of grain to guardian ancestral spirit at, viii. 121 ; the first peal heard in spring, peas cooked and eaten at, ix. 144 ; demon of, exorcized by bells, ix. 246 *sq.* ; associated with the oak, x. 145 ; Midsummer fires a protection against, x. 176 ; charred sticks of Midsummer bonfire a protection against, x. 184, 192 ; ashes of Midsummer fires a protection against, x. 190 ; brands from the Midsummer fires a protection against, x. 191 ; certain flowers at Midsummer a protection against, xi. 54, 58, 59 ; the sound of bull-roarers thought to imitate, xi. 228 *sqq.* *See also* Lightning

—— and lightning, imitation of, in rain-making ceremonies, i. 248, 309 *sq.* ; sacrifices to, v. 157 ; the Syrian, Assyrian, Babylonian, and Hittite god of, v. 163 *sq.* ; the Yule log, a protection against, x. 248, 249, 250, 252, 253, 254, 258, 264 ; bonfires a protection against, x. 344 ; smoke of Midsummer herbs a protection against, xi. 48 ; vervain a protection against, xi. 62 ; name given to bull-roarers, xi. 231 *sq.*

—— and oak, the Aryan god of the, ii. 356 *sqq.*, x. 265

Thunder-beings, among the Teton Indians, viii. 237

" —— -besom," name applied to mistletoe and other bushy excrescences on trees, xi. 85, 301 ; a protection against thunderbolts, xi. 85

—— -bird in rain-making, i. 309 ; the mythical, painted on screens behind which girls at puberty hide, x. 44

—— god, threatening the, ii. 183 *n.*[2] ; black victims sacrificed for rain to the, ii. 367 ; conceived as a deity of fertility, ii. 368 *sqq.* ; of the Hittites, with a bull and an axe as his emblems, v. 134 *sqq.*

" —— -poles," oak-sticks charred in Easter bonfires, x. 145

—— totem, in the Mungarai tribe of Northern Australia, v. 101

Thunderbolt as emblem of the Hittite

thunder-god, v. 134, 136 ; as emblem of the Syrian, Babylonian, and Assyrian thunder-god, v. 163

Thunderbolt and ears of corn, emblem of the Syrian god Hadad, v. 163

—— of Indra, i. 269

——, Zeus, surnamed the, worshipped at Olympia and elsewhere, ii. 361

Thunderbolts, kings killed by, ii. 181 ; flint implements regarded as, ii. 374 ; prehistoric celts called thunderbolts, x. 14 *sq.*

Thunderstorms, death or disappearance of Roman kings in, ii. 181 *sqq.* ; thought to be caused by the spirits of the dead, ii. 183, 183 *n.*[2] ; caused by cut hair, ii. 271, 282 ; caused by hair-cutting, iii. 265 ; and hail caused by witches, x. 344 ; Midsummer flowers a protection against, xi. 48

Thuremlin, a mythical being who kills lads at initiation and restores them to life, xi. 227. *See also* Daramulun

Thurgau, the Canton of, man who cuts the last corn called the Corn-goat at harvest in, vii. 283 ; last sheaf called Cow in, vii. 289 ; man who threshes the last corn called the Corn-bull in, vii. 291

Thüringen (Thuringia), homoeopathic magic at sowing flax in, i. 136 ; the Little Leaf Man in, ii. 80 *sq.* ; May King at Whitsuntide in, ii. 84 *sq.* ; wolves not to be named between Christmas and Twelfth Night in, iii. 396 ; Whitsuntide mummers in, iv. 208 ; Carrying out Death in, iv. 235 *sq.* ; the Old Corn-woman at threshing in, vii. 147, 276, 290, 291 ; custom at threshing in, vii. 222 ; the mythical Rush-cutter (*Binsenschneider*) in, vii. 230 *n.*[5] ; the Little Wood-woman at harvest in, vii. 232 ; last sheaf called the Harvest-cock at Wünchensuhl in, vii. 276 ; man who gives the last stroke at threshing called the Cow at Wurmlingen in, vii. 290 ; treatment of farmer who is last at threshing at Herbrechtingen in, vii. 291 ; saying as to the wind in the corn in, vii. 298 ; expulsion of witches in, ix. 160 ; Halberstadt in, ix. 214 ; custom of beating people on Holy Innocents' Day in, ix. 271. *See also* Thuringia

Thuringia (Thüringen), custom at eclipses in, x. 162 *n.* ; Midsummer fires in, x. 169, xi. 40 ; Schweina in, x. 265 ; belief as to magical properties of the fern in, xi. 66 *sq. See* Thüringen

Thurn, Sir E. F. im, on the objection of the Indians of Guiana to tell their names, iii. 324 *sq.* ; on Indian want

of discrimination between animals and men, viii. 204 ; on the fear of demons among the Indians of Guiana, ix. 78

Thursday, Thunar's Day, ii. 364 ; Maundy, church bells silenced on, x. 125 *n.*[1]

Thurso, witches as cats at, x. 317

Thurston, Edgar, on votive images of the Kusavans, i. 56 *n.*[3] ; on dancing-girls in India, v. 62 ; on the transference of sins to a buffalo calf among the Badagas, ix. 36 *sq.* ; on the fire-walk of the Badagas, xi. 9

Thyatira, hero Tyrimnus at, v. 183 *n.*

Thyestes and Atreus claimed the throne of Mycenae in virtue of a golden lamb, i. 365

Thyiads, college of women at Delphi, devoted to worship of Bacchus, i. 46

Thymbria, sanctuary of Charon at, v. 205

Thyme burnt in Midsummer fire, x. 213 ; wild, gathered on Midsummer Day, xi. 64

Tiaha, Arab tribe of Moab, shave the prisoners whom they release, iii. 273

Tiamat, dragon, embodiment of the watery chaos, mythical Babylonian monster, iv. 105, 108, ix. 410

—— and Marduk, iv. 105 *sq.*, 107 *sq.*

Tiber, grove of Dia on the, ii. 122 ; puppets annually thrown from the Sublician bridge into the, viii. 107 ; in flood, ix. 65

Tiberius, the Emperor, refused the oak crown, ii. 177 *n.*[2] ; dedicated a chapel to the Julii at Bovillae, ii. 180 *n.* ; his inquiries as to the death of Pan, iv. 7 ; his attempt to put down Carthaginian sacrifices of children, iv. 168 ; persecuted the Egyptian religion, vi. 95 *n.*[1]

Tibet, the Grand Lamas of, i. 411 *sq.* ; incarnate human gods in, i. 413 ; vicarious use of images to save sick people in, viii. 103 ; heaps of stones or sticks in, ix. 12 ; prayers at cairns in, ix. 29 ; demonolatry in, ix. 94 ; human scapegoats in, ix. 218 *sqq.* ; sixty years' cycle in, xi. 78 *n.*

Tibetan New Year, ceremonies at the, ix. 197 *sq.*, 203, 218 *sqq.*

Tibetans put effigies at doors of houses to deceive demons, viii. 96 *sq.*

Tibullus on the rising of Sirius, vi. 34 *n.*[1]

Tibur, Vestals at, i. 13 *sq.*

Ticunas of the Amazon, ordeal of young men among the, x. 62 *sq.*

—— of Brazil tear out the hair of girls at puberty, iii. 282

Tide, Cimbrians take arms against the, i. 331 *n.*[3]

Tides, homoeopathic magic of the, i. 166 *sqq.*

Tidore, i. 125

Tiegenhof, in Prussia, custom of reapers at binding the corn near, vii. 137

Tiele, C. P., on the deification of Egyptian kings, i. 419 *sq.* ; on rock-hewn sculptures at Boghaz-Keui, v. 140 *n.*[1]; on the death of Saracus, vi. 174 *n.*[2] ; on Isis, vi. 115 ; on the nature of Osiris, vi. 126 *n.*[2]

Tien-tai Mountains, in China, voluntary deaths of Buddhist monks on the, iv. 42

Tiengum-Mana, a tribe of New Guinea, their mode of making fire, ii. 254

Tifata, Mount, the oak woods of, ii. 280 ; temple of Diana on, ii. 280

Tiger, gall-bladder of tiger eaten to make eater brave, viii. 145 *sq.*

——, a Batta totem, xi. 223

Tiger clan, in Mandeling, viii. 216 ; members of, pay honour to dead tigers, viii. 293

—— -spirits expelled in a raft, ix. 199

Tiger's flesh eaten to make eater brave, viii. 145

—— ghost, deceiving a, vi. 263, viii. 155 *n.*[4] ; appeasing a, viii. 293

—— skin at inauguration of a king, x. 4

Tigers not called by their proper names, iii. 401, 402, 403 *sq.*, 408, 411, 415; called dogs for euphemism, iii. 402 ; called jackals for euphemism, iii. 402, 403 ; souls of the dead transmigrate into, iv. 85, viii. 293 ; ceremonies at killing, viii. 155 *n.*[5], 215, 216 *sq.* ; respected in Sumatra, viii. 215 *sq.* ; kinship of men with, viii. 216

Tiglath-Pileser III., king of Assyria, v. 14, 16, 163 *n.*[3]

Tigre-speaking tribes to the north of Abyssinia, their fear to fell fruit-trees, ii. 19

Tii, Egyptian queen, mother of Amenophis IV., vi. 123 *n.*[1]

Tikopia, island of, epidemic sickness sent away in a small canoe from, ix. 189

Tille, A., on beginning of the Teutonic winter, vi. 81 *n.*[3]

Tilling the earth treated as a crime, viii. 57

Tillot, canton of, in Lothringen, "killing the Old Woman" at threshing in the, vii. 223

Tilsit district, the last sheaf left for the Old Rye-woman in the, vii. 232

Tilton, E. L., on burning the Carnival at Pylos, iv. 232 *sq.*

Timber used in house-building, homoeopathic magic of, i. 146 ; of houses, tree-spirits propitiated in, ii. 39 *sq.* ; not to be cut while the corn is green, ii. 49 ; felled in the waning of the moon, vi. 133, 135 *sq.*, 137

Timbo, in French Guinea, dances at sowing at, ix. 235

Time, Greek and Latin modes of reckoning intervals of, iv. 59 ; personification of periods of time too abstract to be primitive, ix. 230

Timekeepers, natural, vii. 53

Timmes, the, of Sierra Leone beat their kings before their coronation, iii. 18 ; their secret society, xi. 260 *n.*[1]

Timoleon, funeral games at Syracuse in his honour, iv. 94

Timor, island of, telepathy of high-priest of, in war, i. 128 *sq.* ; treatment of the placenta in, i. 190 ; the marriage of the Sun and Earth deemed the source of all fertility in, ii. 99 *n.*[1] ; sacrifice to crocodiles in, ii. 152 ; fetish or taboo rajah in, iii. 24 ; speaker holds his hand before his mouth in, iii. 122 ; customs as to war in, iii. 165 *sq.* ; theory of earthquakes in, v. 197 ; burial of woman who has died in childbed in, viii. 98 ; kinship of men with crocodiles in, viii. 212 ; transference of fatigue to leaves in, ix. 8 ; belief in the spirits of the dead in, ix. 85. *See also* Timorese

Timor fecit deos, ix. 93

Timorese, their sacrifices for rain and sunshine, i. 291

Timorlaut Islands, treatment of the afterbirth in the, i. 186 ; married men may not poll their hair in the, iii. 260 ; first-fruits offered to spirits of ancestors in the, viii. 123 ; mourners rub themselves with the juices of the dead in the, viii. 163 ; dead turtles propitiated by fishermen in the, viii. 244 ; the tug-of-war in the, ix. 176 ; demons of sicknesses expelled in a proa from the, ix. 185 *sq.*

Timotheus on the death of Attis, v. 264 *n.*[4]

Tin-egin, forced fire (need-fire) among the Highlanders of Scotland, ii. 238

Tin ore, Malay superstitions as to, iii. 407

Tinchebray in Normandy, ix. 183

Tinguianes of the Philippines reluctant to name the dead, iii. 353

Tinneh or Déné Indians, the power of medicine-men among the, i. 357 ; recall of lost souls among the, iii. 45 ; taboos observed by those who have handled a corpse among the, iii. 143 ; their fear and avoidance of menstruous women, iii. 145 *sq.*, x. 91 *sqq.* ; their refusal to taste blood, iii. 240 *sq.*; their belief as to falling stars, iv. 65 ; their magical ceremony to procure game, iv. 278 ; seclusion of girls at puberty among the, x. 47 sqq.

Tinneh Indians of Alaska, their ceremonies at killing a wolf, viii. 220

—— Indians of North-West America, ceremonies observed by them before eating the first wild berries or roots of the season, viii. 80 sq.

Tinnevelly, the Kappiliyans of, x. 69

Tipperary, county of, were-wolves in, x. 310 n.[1] ; woman burnt as a witch in, x. 323 sq.

Tiraspol, in Russia, collective suicide in, iv. 45 n.[1]

Tiree, Hebridean island, vii. 140 ; the need-fire in, x. 148 ; the Beltane cake in, x. 149 ; witch as sheep in, x. 316

Tiru-kalli-kundram, dancing-girls at, v. 61

Tirunavayi temple, near Calicut, attack on the King of Calicut every twelfth year at the, iv. 49 sq.

Titane, shrine of Aesculapius at, v. 81

Titans attack and kill Dionysus, vii. 12 sq., 17, 32

Tithe-offering dedicated to Apollo, iv. 187 n.[5]

Tithorea, festivals of Isis at, viii. 18 n.[1]

Titicaca, Lake, thunder - god of the Indians about, ii. 370

Tivor, god or victim, in Norse, x. 103 n.

Tiyans of Malabar, their seclusion of girls at puberty, x. 68 sq.

Tjingilli tribe of Central Australia, their cure for headache, ix. 2

——, the, of Northern Australia, their way of making rain by means of a bandicoot, i. 288

Tjumba, island of, harvest festival in the, viii. 122

Tlacaxipeualiztli, "The Flaying of Men," a Mexican festival, ix. 296

Tlacopan, city of Mexico, idol of paste eaten as a sacred food in, viii. 91

Tlactga or Tlachtga in Ireland, pagan cemetery at, iv. 101 ; new fire annually kindled on Hallowe'en at, x. 139

Tlaloc, the Mexican water-god, girls drowned in his honour, ii. 158 sq. ; Mexican god of thunder and rain, vii. 237 ; temple of, in Mexico, ix. 284, 292

Tlaxcallan in Mexico, the goddess Xochiquetzal worshipped at, vii. 237

Tlemcen, in Algeria, rain-making at, i. 250 sq. ; orgies of the Aïsawa order at, vii. 22 n.[1] ; fowl used to divert jinn from pregnant women at, ix. 31

Tlingit (Thlinkeet) Indians of Alaska, their respectful treatment of the first halibut of the season, viii. 253 ; seclusion of girls at puberty among the, x. 45 sq. See also Thlinkeet

Tlokoala, a secret society of the Nootka Indians, xi. 271

Tmolus, Mount, the Birthplace of Rainy Zeus on, ii. 360

Toad in charm to avert a storm, i. 325 ; soul in form of, iii. 42 n. ; figure of, at bear-feasts of the Gilyaks, viii. 193, 194 ; soul of dead man in a, viii. 291 ; as scapegoat, ix. 135, 193, 206 sq. ; witch in form of a, x. 323. See also Toads

Toad clan among the Carrier Indians, xi. 273

—— -stools thrown into Midsummer bonfires as a charm, x. 172

Toad's heart worn by a thief to prevent detection, x. 302 n.[2]

Toads in relation to rain, i. 292, 292 n.[3] ; burnt alive in Devonshire, x. 302

Toaripi or Motumotu, of New Guinea, magical telepathy among the, i. 125 ; sorcerers regarded as chiefs among the, i. 337 sq. ; their rule as to menstruous women, x. 84. See Motumotu

Toba, Lake, in Sumatra, prince worshipped as a deity on the shore of, i. 398

Tobacco thrown on troubled water, i. 321 ; smoke, priest inspired by, i. 384 ; used as an emetic, viii. 73 ; first of season, ceremony at smoking, viii. 82

Tobarrath-Bhuathaig, a magical well in the island of Gigha, i. 323

Tobas, Indian tribe of the Gran Chaco, their custom of secluding girls at puberty, x. 59

Tobelorese of Halmahera, their rites of initiation, xi. 248

Tobolbel, custom of putting chiefs to death in the Pelew Islands, vi. 266

Toboongkoo (Toboengkoe), the, of Central Celebes, their treatment of the afterbirth, i. 189 ; careful not to frighten away the spirit of the rice, ii. 28 ; their offerings to tree-spirits before felling timber, ii. 35 ; their recall of lost souls, iii. 48 ; forbid children to play with their shadows, iii. 78 ; mock human sacrifices among the, ix. 219 ; riddles among the, ix. 122 n. ; custom observed by widower among the, xi. 178 sq.

Tocandeira, native name for the Cryptocerus atratus, F., ant, used by the Mauhes to sting boys as an ordeal, x. 62

Tocantins River, the Chavantes Indians on the, iv. 12 n.[5]

Toci, Mexican goddess, sacrifice of woman in the costume and ornaments of, ix. 289 *sqq.*

Tod, J., on rites of goddess Gouri, v. 241 *sq.*

Todas, a tribe of Southern India, offer silver images of buffaloes, i. 56 ; confusion of magic with religion among the, i. 230 *n.* ; divine milkmen of the, i. 402 *sq.*, iii. 15 *sqq.* ; magic and medicine among the, i. 421 *n.*[1] ; hide their clipped hair and nails, iii. 271 ; names of relations tabooed among the, iii. 337 *sq.*; reluctant to name the dead, iii. 353 ; custom as to the pollution of death observed by sacred dairyman among the, vi. 228 ; their sacrament of buffalo's flesh, viii. 314 ; let loose a calf at a funeral, ix. 37 ; their ceremony of the new fire, x. 136

Todtenstein, hill at Königshain in Silesia, ceremony of driving out Death at, iv. 264

Toepffer, J., on Triptolemus, vii. 73

Toeratayas, or Toradjas, of Celebes, vii. 196 *n. See* Toradjas

Tofoke, the, of the Congo State, woman's share in agriculture among, vii. 119

Togo, in West Africa, wind-fetish in, i. 327 ; the Bassari of, ii. 102 *n.*[1]; Mount Agu in, iii. 5

Togoland, the Hos of, i. 265, 365, ii. 19, iii. 259, 301, 304, vi. 104, vii. 130, 234, viii. 59, 115 *sq.*, ix. 134, 206 ; the Matse of, ii. 293, viii. 115, ix. 3 ; festival of Earth in, iii. 247 ; magic modes of facilitating childbirth in, iii. 295 ; the Ewe-speaking peoples of, iii. 369, v. 282 *n.*[2], viii. 105, 228 ; the Yewe religious order in, iii. 383 *sq.*; the Bassari of, viii. 116 ; ceremony performed by Ewe hunters in, viii. 244 ; the negroes of, their remedy for influenza, ix. 193

Toh Sri Lam, a crocodile goddess among the Malays, offerings and prayers to, viii. 212

Tokio, annual expulsion of demons at, ix. 213 ; the fire-walk in temple at, xi. 9 *sq.*

Tokoelawi of Central Celebes, custom observed by mourners among the, xi. 178

Tolalaki, the, of Central Celebes, their treatment of the afterbirth, i. 188 *sq.* ; their punishment of incest, ii. 111 ; drink blood of foes to make themselves brave, viii. 152

Tolampoos, the, of Central Celebes, their belief as to written names, iii. 319

Toledo, Elipandus of, i. 407

Tolindoos of Central Celebes, offence to tread on a man's shadow among the, iii. 78

Tolucan, Mount, in Mexico, human sacrifices offered to the water-god on, ii. 158 *sq.*

Tomas or Habes, a tribe of Nigeria, revere a fetish doctor, iii. 124

Tomb of chief, sacrifices at, viii. 113

—— of Hyacinth, v. 314

—— of Midas, v. 286

—— of Moses, ix. 21

—— of Osiris, vi. 18 *sq.*, 20 *sqq.*

Tombs of the ancient kings of Egypt, vi. 19 ; of the kings of Uganda, vi. 168 *sq.* ; of kings sacred, vi. 194 *sq.*

Tomil, village in Yap, taboos observed by men for the sake of girls under puberty at, iii. 293

Tomori, the, of Central Celebes, their treatment of the afterbirth, i. 189 ; feed the ripening rice, ii. 29 ; their ceremonies at felling a tree, ii. 35 ; their punishment and expiation of incest, ii. 110 *sq.*; use a special vocabulary when at work in the fields, vii. 193 ; their customs as to the Rice-mother, vii. 193 ; their use of riddles at harvest, vii. 194 ; their conception of rice-spirits as shaped like goats, vii. 288

——, the Gulf of, in Celebes, x. 312

Tonan, Mexican goddess, ix. 287; woman sacrificed in the character of, ix. 287 *sq.*

Tonapoo, the, of Central Celebes, offer human sacrifices on roofs of new houses, ii. 39

Tondi, Batta word for soul, iii. 35, 116, vii. 182. *See also* Tendi

Tonga, chiefs of, thought to heal scrofula and indurated liver by their touch, i. 371 ; special vocabularies employed with reference to divine chiefs in, i. 402 *n.*; veneration paid to divine chiefs in, iii. 21 ; the taboo of chiefs and kings in, iii. 133 *sq.* ; chiefs not to touch food with tabooed hands in, iii. 138 *n.*[1] ; tabooed persons not allowed to handle food in, iii. 140 ; taboos connected with the dead in, iii. 140 ; circumcision practised in, iv. 220 ; ceremony performed after contact with a sacred chief in, viii. 28 ; offerings of first-fruits in, viii. 128 *sqq. See also* Tongans

——, the king of, not to be seen eating, iii. 119 ; no one allowed to be over his head, iii. 255

Tongans, their theory of an earthquake, v. 200 *sq.*

Tongue of dead king eaten by his successor, iv. 203 ; of sacrificial ox cut out, vi. 251 *sq.* ; of medicine-man, hole in, xi. 238, 239. *See also* Tongues

Tongues of birds eaten, viii. 147 ; of slain men eaten, viii. 153 ; of dead animals cut out, viii. 269 *sqq.* ; of animals worn as amulets, viii. 270

Tonkawe Indians of Texas, their superstition as to personal names, iii. 325 *sq.*

Tonocotes. *See* Lules

Tonquin, image of Buddha whipped in time of drought in, i. 297 *n.*[7]; guardian spirits of villages in, i. 401 *sq.* ; division of monarchy in, iii. 19 *sq.* ; royal criminals strangled in, iii. 242 ; the tiger spoken of respectfully in, iii. 403 ; annual festival of the dead in, vi. 62 ; livers of brave men eaten in, as a means of acquiring bravery, viii. 151 *sq.* ; demon of sickness expelled in, ix. 119 ; annual expulsion of demons in, ix. 147 *sq.* ; the Thays of, their burial customs, xi. 177 *sq.* *See also* Tonquinese

——, kings of, blamed for drought, dearth, floods, storms, cholera, etc., i. 355 ; screened from public gaze, iii. 125

Tonquinese, their test of a sacrificial victim, i. 384 *sq.* ; their custom of catching the soul of the dying, iv. 200

Tonsure, the clerical, viii. 105 *n.*[1]

Tonwan, magical influence of medicine-bag, xi. 268, 269

Tooitonga, divine chief of Tonga, iii. 21, viii. 128, 129, 130, 131, 140

Toorateyas of Southern Celebes hold their princes responsible for the rice-crop, i. 361

Tooth knocked out as initiatory rite, iii. 244, xi. 227, 235 ; of dead king kept, iv. 203. *See also* Teeth

Toothache, tooth of an ounce a homoeopathic remedy for, i. 153 ; transferred to enemies, ix. 6 ; transferred to a frog, ix. 50 ; transferred to trees, ix. 57, 58, 59 *sq.*; nailed into a door or a wall, ix. 62, 63 ; cured by sticking needles into a willow, ix. 71

Töpffer, J., on the Eudanemi at Athens, i. 325 *n.*[1]

Tophet, at Jerusalem, children burnt in sacrifice in, iv. 169, 170, 171, v. 177

Töppen, M., on the Lithuanian god Perkunas, ii. 365 *n.*[5]

Tops spun at sowing festival, vii. 95, 97, 187

Toradjas, meaning of the name, i. 109 *n.*[1]; their mode of annulling an evil omen, i. 170 ; employ a special language in passing through a forest, iii. 412 *sq.*

—— of Central Celebes, their magical use of jawbones, i. 109 ; their rule not to loiter in the doorway of a pregnant woman, i. 114 ; telepathy in war among the, i. 129 ; their use of iron in hómoeopathic magic, i. 159 ; their rain-making, i. 253 ; customs observed by the rain-doctor among the, i. 271 *sq.* ; their rain - making by means of the dead, i. 286 ; their way of making rain by an appeal to the pity of the gods, i. 303 ; their sacrifice at building a new house, ii. 39 ; use the incest of animals as a rain-charm, ii. 113 ; rules observed by them on entering an enemy's country, iii. 111 ; their custom as to cutting a child's hair, iii. 263 ; names of relations tabooed among the, iii. 340 ; disinter the bones of the dead at a festival, iii. 373 *n.* ; their field-speech, iii. 411 *sqq.*; their theory of rain, vi. 33 ; their conception of the rice-soul as a blue bird, vii. 182 *n.*[1], 295 *sq.* ; attribute souls to men, animals, and rice, vii. 183 ; their customs as to the Mother of the Rice, vii. 194 *sq.* ; their offerings to the souls of the dead at planting a new field, vii. 228 ; their custom at circumcision, viii. 153 ; cure for kleptomania among the, ix. 34 ; hide themselves from the demon of small-pox, ix. 112 *n.*[2]; their cure by beating, ix. 265 ; were-wolves among the, x. 311 *sq.*; their custom at the smelting of iron, xi. 154

Toradjas of Poso, in Central Celebes, recovery of souls abducted by demons among the, iii. 62 ; use a secret language in the harvest-field, iii. 411 *sq.*; ask each other riddles while they watch the crops in the field, vii. 194

Torch-bearer, the Eleusinian, vii. 54, 55, 59

—— -races at Athens presided over by the king, ii. 44 *sq.*; at Easter, x. 142 ; at Midsummer, x. 175

Torches offered by women to Diana, i. 12 ; fight with, as a ceremony, i. 94 ; used to mimic lightning, i. 310 ; in relation to Demeter and Persephone, vii. 57 ; lighted, used in purification, viii. 249 ; used in the expulsion of demons, ix. 110, 117, 120, 130, 131, 132, 133 *sq.*, 139, 140, 146, 157, 171 ; used in the expulsion of witches, etc., ix. 156, 157, 158, 159, 160, 163, 165, 166 ; carried in procession by maskers in Salzburg, ix. 243 ; carried by dancers in Mexico, ix. 285 ; applied to fruit-trees on Eve of Twelfth Night, ix. 316 *sq.*; carried about the sowed fields on the Eve of

Twelfth Night, ix. 316, 317; interpreted as imitations of lightning, x. 340 *n.*[1]

Torches, burning, carried round folds and lands at Midsummer, x. 206; applied to fruit-trees to fertilize them, x. 340

—— of Demeter, x. 340

——, processions with lighted, x. 141, *sq.*, 233 *sq.*; through fields, gardens, orchards, and streets, x. 107 *sq.*, 110 *sqq.*, 113 *sqq.*, 179, 339 *sq.*; at Midsummer, x. 179; on Christmas Eve, x. 266

Torchlight dance of the Natchez Indians at the festival of new corn, viii. 79; procession at Eleusis, vii. 38

Torgot, province of China, rain-dragon banished in time of drought to, i. 298

Torquemada, J. de, Spanish historian of Mexico, ix. 286 *n.*[1]; on the eating of the flesh of the human representative of Tezcatlipoca, ix. 279 *n.*[1]; on the flaying of human victims in Mexico, ix. 300 *n.*[1]

Torres Straits Islands, use of magical images in the, i. 59, 72; magic to catch dugong and turtle in the, i. 108; raising the wind in the, i. 322; wind raised by bull-roarer in the, i. 324; magicians in the, i. 420 *n.*[2]; the fire-drill in the, ii. 209; ritual flight of man who has decapitated a corpse in the, ii. 309 *n.*[2]; names of relations by marriage tabooed in the, iii. 343 *sq.*; funeral custom in the, iv. 92 *sq.*; worship of animal-shaped heroes in the, v. 139 *n.*[1]; death-dances in the, vi. 53 *n.*[2]; cat's cradle in the, vii. 103 *n.*[1]; the natives of the, their observation of the Pleiades, vii. 313; modes of acquiring courage in the, viii. 152 *sq.*; seclusion of girls at puberty in the, x. 36 *sq.*, 39 *sqq.*; dread and seclusion of women at menstruation in the, x. 78 *sq.*; use of bull-roarers in the, xi. 228 *n.*[2], 232

Tortoise, emblem of longevity, i. 169 *n.*[1]; deemed ill-omened in China, i. 170; fever transferred to, ix. 31

Tortoises in homoeopathic magic, i. 151; land, in homoeopathic magic, i. 155; reasons for not eating, viii. 140; external human souls lodged in, xi. 204. *See also* Turtles

Torture, judicial, of criminals, witches, and wizards, xi. 158 *sq.*

Tossing successful reaper in Berwickshire, vii. 154

Totec or Xipe, Mexican god, ix. 297, 298; personated by a man wearing the skin of a human victim, ix. 300. *See also* Xipe

Totem confounded with the man himself, i. 107; custom observed at eating the, iii. 127; skin-disease supposed to be caused by eating, viii. 25 *sq.*; transference of man's soul to his, xi. 219 *n.*, 225 *sq.*; supposed effect of killing a, xi. 220; the receptacle in which a man keeps his external soul, xi. 220 *sqq.*; the individual or personal, xi. 222 *n.*[5], 224 *n.*[1], 226 *n.*[1] *See also* Totems *and* Sex totem

Totem animal, artificial, novice at initiation brought back by, xi. 271 *sq.*; transformation of man into his, xi. 275

—— animals and plants, custom of eating, i. 107

—— clans and secret societies, related to each other, xi. 272 *sq.*

—— names kept secret, iii. 320, 330, xi. 225 *n.*

—— plants among the Fans, xi. 161

—— sacrament, viii. 165

Totemic animals, purification for killing, viii. 28; dances in imitation of, viii. 76; represented by masks, ix. 380

Totemism defined, viii. 35; in Central Australia not a religion, i. 107 *sq.*; characteristics of early Australian, i. 107; of the Dinkas, iv. 30 *sq.*; the source of a particular type of folk-tales, iv. 129 *sqq.*; possible trace of Latin, vi. 186 *n.*[4]; in Kiziba, vi. 173, 174 *n.*[1]; not proved for the Aryans, viii. 4; probably originated in the hunting stage of society, viii. 37; in Australia and America, viii. 311; suggested theory of, xi. 218 *sqq.*

Totems in Central Australia, magical ceremonies for the multiplication of the, i. 85 *sqq.*, 335; custom of eating the, i. 107; descent of the, in Uganda, ii. 288; sacrifices to, iv. 31; stories told to account for the origin of, iv. 129; honorific, of the Carrier Indians, xi. 273 *sqq.*; personal, among the North American Indians, xi. 273, 276 *n.*[1]; multiplex, of the Australians, xi. 275 *n.*[1]

Totonacs, their worship of the corn-spirit, ix. 286 *n.*[1]

Tototectin, men clad in skins of human victims in Mexico, ix. 298

Touch of menstruous women thought to convey pollution, x. 87, 90

Touch-me-not (*Impatiens sp.*), bundle of, representative of goddess Gauri, ii. 77

Touching for the King's Evil (scrofula), i. 368 *sqq.*

—— sacred king or chief, supposed effects of, iii. 132 *sqq.*

Toukaway Indians of Texas, ceremony of mimic wolves among the, xi. 276

Toulon, custom of drenching people with water at Midsummer at, v. 248 *sq.*

Toulouse, adoration paid to each other by the Albigenses noticed in the records of the Inquisition at, i. 407 ; torture of sorcerers at, xi. 158

Toumbuluh tribe of Celebes, taboos observed during wife's pregnancy in the, iii. 295, 298

Toumon, Egyptian god, the mummy of, iv. 5

Touraine, Midsummer fires in, x. 182

Town, charm to protect a, vi. 249 *sqq.*

Toxcatl, fifth month of old Mexican year, ix. 149 *n.*[2] ; old Mexican festival, ix. 149 *n.*[2], 276

Tozer, H. F., on Mount Argaeus, v. 191

Trachinian Women, The, play of Sophocles, ii. 161

Trading voyages, continence observed on, iii. 203

Tradition, the thraldom of, i. 219 ; historical, hampered by the taboo on the names of the dead, iii. 363 *sqq.*

Traditions of kings torn in pieces, vi. 97 *sq.*

Train, Joseph, on St. Bridget in the Isle of Man, ii. 95 ; on Beltane fires in the Isle of Man, x. 157

Trajan, Pliny's letter to, ix. 420

Tralles in Lydia, sacred prostitution at, v. 38

Transference of human souls to other bodies, iii. 49 ; from the living to the dead, iii. 73

—— of Egyptian festivals from one month to the preceding month, vi. 92 *sqq.*

—— of evil, ix. 1 *sqq.*; to other people, ix. 5 *sqq.*; to sticks and stones, ix. 8 *sqq.*; to animals, ix. 31 *sqq.*; to men, ix. 38 *sqq.*; in Europe, ix. 47 *sqq.*

—— of a man's soul to his totem, xi. 219 *n.*, 225 *sq.*

—— of sins, iii. 214 *sqq.*, ix. 39 *sqq.*, 42 *sqq.*

Transformation of men into animals, iv. 82 *sqq.*, xi. 207 ; of men into women, attempted, in obedience to dreams, vi. 255 *sqq.* ; of women into men, attempted, vi. 255 *n.*[1]; of woman into crocodile, viii. 212 ; of animals into men, ix. 380 ; of men into wolves at the full moon, x. 314 *n.*[1] ; of witches into animals, x. 315 *sqq.*, xi. 311 *sq.*; of man into his totem animal, xi. 275

Transgressions, need of confessing, iii. 211 *sq.* *See also* Sins

Transition from mother-kin to father-kin, vi. 261 *n.*[3]

Transmigration, belief in, a motive for infanticide, iv. 188 *sq.*

—— of soul of ruptured person into cleft oak-tree, xi. 172

Transmigration of human souls, into animals, iii. 65, iv. 84 *sq.*, viii. 141, 285 *sqq.* ; into turtles, viii. 178 *sq.* ; into bears, viii. 191; doctrine of, in ancient India, viii. 298 *sq.*; doctrine of, in ancient Greece, viii. 300 *sqq.*, 307 *sq.*; into totem animals, xi. 223

Transmigrations of human deities, i. 410 *sqq.*; of Buddha, viii. 299 ; or Buddha in the *Jataka,* ix. 41

Transmission of soul to successor, iv. 198 *sqq.*

Transubstantiation among the ancient Aryans, viii. 89 *sq.* ; among the ancient Mexicans, viii. 89 ; ridiculed by Cicero, viii. 167

Transvaal, the Bawenda of the, i. 351, 401 *n.*[3] ; the Malepa of the, iii. 241

Transylvania, rain-making in, i. 282 ; festival of Green George among the gipsies of, ii. 75 *sq.* ; precautions against witches on St. George's Eve or Day in, ii. 337 *sq.*; saying as to sleeping child in, iii. 37 ; story of a witch's soul in the shape of a fly in, iii. 38 *sq.*; belief as to falling stars in, iv. 66 ; "Sawing the Old Woman" among the gipsies of, iv. 243 ; crown made of last ears cut at harvest in, v. 237 *sq.*, vii. 221 ; the Cock at reaping the last corn at Braller in, vii. 276 ; cock beheaded on harvest-field near Klausenburg in, vii. 278 ; live cock killed in last sheaf near Udvarhely in, vii. 278 ; the Hare at reaping the last corn at Birk in, vii. 280 ; catching the quail in the last corn reaped in the Bistritz district of, vii. 295 ; customs at sowing to keep off birds and insects in, viii. 274 *sq.*; belief as to children born on a Sunday in, xi. 288 *n.*[5]. *See also* Transylvanian

——, the Germans of, iii. 296, 310

——, the Roumanians of, iii. 88, 89, 238, ix. 16, 106 *sq.*, x. 13 ; harvest custom among, v. 237

——, the Saxons of, iii. 294, iv. 230, 248, 254, vii. 285, 295, viii. 274 ; harvest customs among, v. 237 *sq.* ; story of the external soul among, xi. 116

Transylvanian gipsies, their way of stopping rain, i. 296

—— Saxons, their homoeopathic magic at sowing, i. 138

—— sowers carry locks as a charm to keep off birds, iii. 308

Traps for devils, iii. 59, 69 *n.*[4] ; set for souls, iii. 70 *sq.*

Trasimene Lake, battle of, iv. 186

Traunstein, district of Upper Bavaria, the Oats-goat at harvest thought to be in the last sheaf of oats in, vii. 287 ;

the last standing corn called the Sow in, vii. 298

Travail, women in, knots on their garments untied, iii. 294. *See also* Childbirth

Travancore, special terms used with reference to persons of the blood-royal in, i. 401 *n.*³ ; serpents spoken of respectfully in, iii. 402 ; dancing-girls in, v. 63 *sqq.* ; infants placed in winnowing-fans in, vii. 8 *sq.* ; customs at executions in, viii. 272 ; the Rajah of, his sins transferred to a Brahman, ix. 42 *sq.*; demon-worship in, ix. 94 ; women deemed liable to be attacked by demons in, x. 24 *n.*² ; the Pulayars of, x. 69

Travellers make knots in their garments as a charm, iii. 306

Travexin, in the Vosges, witch as hare at, x. 318

Treason, old English punishment of, v. 290 *n.*²

Treasures guarded by demons, xi. 65 ; found by means of fern-seed, xi. 65, 287 ; discovered by divining-rod, xi. 68 ; revealed by springwort, xi. 70 ; revealed by mistletoe, xi. 287, 291 ; bloom in the earth on Midsummer Eve, xi. 288 *n.*⁵

Treasury of Minyas at Orchomenus, iv. 164

Treasury Islanders, their observation of the Pleiades, vii. 313

Treaty, blood of contracting parties sprinkled on their footprints in making a, i. 211

Trebius on the springwort, xi. 71

Tree thought to cause blindness, i. 147 ; extracted teeth placed in a, i. 176 ; child's life thought to be bound up with the tree which was planted with its navel-string, i. 182, 184 ; embraced by barren women in hopes of obtaining offspring, i. 182 ; the navel-string planted with or under a, i. 182, 184, 186, 196 ; navel-string hung on a, i. 185, 186, 190, 198 ; the afterbirth buried under a, i. 186, 187, 188, 194, 195 ; the afterbirth hung on a, i. 186, 187, 189, 190, 191, 194, 198, 199 ; that has been struck by lightning, i. 319 ; on which an eagle has built its nest deemed holy, ii. 11 ; culprits tied to sacred, ii. 112 *sq.* ; origin of men and cattle from a sacred, ii. 219 ; fire kindled from ancestral, ii. 221 ; decked with bracelets, anklets, etc., v. 240 ; soul of a, in a bird, vi. 111 *n.*¹ ; disease transferred to, ix. 6 ; use of stick cut from a fruitful, ix. 264 ; burnt in the Midsummer bonfire, x. 173 *sq.*, 180, 183 ; external

soul in a, xi. 102, 156. *See also* Trees

Tree of life in Eden, v. 186 *n.*⁴

Tree-agates, homoeopathic magic of, i. 164 *sq.*

—— -bearers (*Dendrophori*) in the worship of Cybele and Attis, v. 266 *n.*², 267

—— -creeper (*Climacteris scandens*), women's "sister" among the Yuin, xi. 216

—— -gods banned at building a house, ix. 81

—— -spirit in the shape of a bull, ii. 14 ; represented simultaneously in vegetable and human form, ii. 73 *sqq.* ; representative of, thrown into water to ensure rain, ii. 75, 76 ; killing of the, iv. 205 *sqq.* ; resurrection of the, iv. 212 ; in relation to vegetation-spirit, iv. 253 ; Osiris as a, vi. 107 *sqq.* ; effigies of, burnt in bonfires, xi. 21 *sqq.* ; human representatives of, put to death, xi. 25 ; human representative of the, perhaps originally burnt at the fire-festivals, xi. 90

—— -spirits, ii. 7 *sqq.* ; threatened, ii. 20 *sqq.* ; in house-timber propitiated, ii. 39 *sq.* ; beneficent powers of, ii. 45 *sqq.* ; give rain and sunshine, ii. 45 *sq.*; make crops grow, ii. 47 *sqq.*; make cattle and women fruitful, ii. 50 *sqq.*, 55 *sqq.*, xi. 22 ; in human form or embodied in living people, ii. 71 *sqq.* ; fear of, iii. 412 *sq.* ; in the form of serpents, xi. 44 *n.*¹

—— -stone, marvellous virtue of a, i. 165 *n.*¹

—— -worship in ancient Rome, ii. 8 ; among the ancient Germans, ii. 8 *sq.*; among the European families of the Aryan stock, ii. 9 *sqq.* ; among the Lithuanians, ii. 9 ; in ancient Greece and Italy, ii. 9 *sq.*; among tribes of the Finnish-Ugrian stock in Europe, ii. 10 *sq.* ; notions at the root of, ii. 11 *sqq.* ; in modern Europe, relics of, ii. 59 *sqq.*

Trees married to men and women, i. 40 *sq.*, ii. 57 ; foreskins placed in, i. 95 *sq.*; extracted teeth deposited in, i. 98 ; the dead deposited in, i. 102 *sq.*; navel-strings placed in, i. 182, 183, 185, 186 ; afterbirth (placenta) placed in, i. 182, 187, 190, 191, 194, 198, 199 ; stones placed in, to prevent sun from setting, i. 318 ; worship of, ii. 7 *sqq.* ; oracular, ii. 9 ; regarded as animate, ii. 12 *sqq.* ; sacrifices offered to, ii. 15, 16 *sq.*, 19, 30, 31, 32, 33, 34, 35, 36, 42, 44, 46, 47, 48 ; rags hung on, ii. 16, 32 ;

sensitive, ii. 18 ; apologies offered to trees for cutting them down, ii. 18 *sq.*, 36 *sq.* ; bleeding, ii. 18, 20, 33 ; threatened to make them bear fruit, ii. 20 *sqq.* ; married to each other, ii. 24 *sqq.* ; in blossom treated like pregnant women, ii. 28 ; animated by the souls of the dead, ii. 29 *sqq.* ; planted on graves, ii. 31 ; bones of dead shamans placed in, ii. 32 ; as the abode of spirits, ii. 33 *sqq.* ; ceremonies at cutting down, ii. 34 *sqq.* ; demons of, ii. 42 ; drenched with water as a rain-charm, ii. 47 ; grant women an easy delivery, ii. 57 *sq.* ; cut hair deposited on or under, iii. 14, 275 *sq.*, 286 ; the shadow of trees sensitive, iii. 82 ; lucky and unlucky, iii. 275 *n.*[3] ; struck by lightning used in magic, iii. 287 ; masks hung on, iv. 283 ; spirit-children awaiting birth in, v. 100 ; sacrificial victims hung on, v. 146 ; represented on the monuments of Osiris, vi. 110 *sq.* ; felled in the waning of the moon, vi. 133, 135 *sq.*, 137 ; growing near the graves of dead kings revered, vi. 162, 164 ; in relation to Dionysus, vii. 3 *sq.* ; spirits of the dead in, viii. 124 ; evils transferred to, ix. 52, 54 *sqq.* ; evils nailed into, ix. 59 *sqq.*; men changed into, by look of menstruous women, x. 79 ; burnt in spring fires, x. 115 *sq.*, 116, 142 ; burnt in Midsummer fires, x. 173 *sq.*, 185, 192, 193, 209 ; burnt at Holi festival in India, xi. 2 ; burnt in bonfires, xi. 22 ; lives of people bound up with, xi. 159 *sqq.* ; hair of children tied to, xi. 165 ; the fate of families or individuals bound up with, xi. 165 *sqq.* ; creeping through cleft trees as cure for various maladies, xi. 170 *sqq.* ; fire thought by savages to be stored like sap in, xi. 295 ; struck by lightning, superstitions about, xi. 296 *sqq. See also* Tree *and* Fruit-trees

Trees and plants, attempts to deceive the spirits of, ii. 22 *sqq.* ; as life-indices, xi. 160 *sqq.*

—— and rocks, Greek belief as to birth from, v. 107 *n.*[1]

——, sacred, ii. 40 *sqq.* ; smeared with blood, ii. 367

Tréfoir, the Yule log, x. 249

Tréfouet, the Yule log, x. 252 *n.*[2], 253

Tregonan, in Cornwall, Midsummer fires on, x. 199

Trench cut in ground at Beltane, x. 150, 152

Trespass on sacred groves, apologies for, ii. 328

Trevelyan, G. M., on the custom of a temporary king in Cornwall, v. 154 *n.*[1]

Trevelyan, Marie, on Midsummer fires in Wales, x. 201 ; on Hallowe'en in Wales, x. 226 *n.*[1]; on St. John's wort in Wales, xi. 55 *n.*[2]; on burnt sacrifices in Wales, xi. 301

Treveri, a Celtic tribe on the Moselle, their name preserved in *Treves*, ii. 126 *n.*[2]

Trèves, "cutting the goat's neck off" at harvest near, vii. 268 ; the Corn-wolf killed at threshing in the district of, vii. 275 ; the Archbishop of, gives wine for burning wheel rolled down hill, x. 118

Triad, divine, at Tarsus, v. 171

Trial of the axe at Athens, viii. 5

Trials, judicial, of animals and inanimate things by the king at Athens, i. 45, viii. 5 *n.*[1]

Triangle of reeds, passage of mourners through a, xi. 177 *sq.*

Tribes reported to be ignorant of the art of making fire, ii. 253 *sq.*

Tribute (presents) brought to rainmakers, i. 338, 342, 346, 348, 349, 351, 353, ii. 3 ; of youths and maidens sent to the Minotaur, iv. 74 *sqq.*

Trident, emblem of Hittite thunder-god, v. 134, 135 ; emblem of Indian deity, v. 170

Trie-Chateau, dolmen near Gisors, xi. 188

Triennial tenure of the kingship, iv. 112 *sq.*

Trieste, St. Sylvester's Eve at, ix. 165

Τριετηρίς, vii. 15 *n.*

Trilles, Father H., on the theory of the external soul among the Fans, xi. 201

Trimouzette, the, a flower-crowned girl in the Ardennes on May Day, ii. 80 *n.*[4]

Tring, a Tonquinese general, restores the king, iii. 19

Trinidad, the fire-walk in, xi. 11

Trinities, the ancient Egyptian gods arranged in, iv. 5 *n.*[3]

Trinity, Christian doctrine of the, iv. 5 *n.*[3]

——, the Batta, ix. 88 *n.*[1]

——, the Hindoo, i. 225, 404 ; the Norse, ii. 364

Trinity College, Cambridge, Lord of Misrule at, ix. 332

Trinouxtion, in the Coligny calendar, seems to mark summer solstice, ix. 343 *n.*

Tripoli, fighting the wind in, i. 331 ; ghosts of murdered men nailed into the earth in, ix. 63

Triptolemus, prince of Eleusis, vii. 37 ; shown the corn by Demeter, vii. 38 ; the agent of Demeter in disseminating corn over the world, vii. 54, 72 *sq.* ; victims sacrificed to him at Eleusis, vii. 56, 72 ; his Threshing-floor at Eleusis, vii. 61, 72, 75 ; in Greek art, vii. 68 *n.*[1], 72 ; sows seed in Rarian plain, vii. 70, 74 ; the corn-hero, vii. 72 *sq.* ; etymology of his name, vii. 72 *sq.* ; receives corn from Demeter, viii. 19

Triptolemus, play of Sophocles, vii. 54

Tristram, H. B., on date of corn-reaping in Palestine, v. 232 *n.* ; on wild boars in Palestine, viii. 31 *sq.*

Triumph, costume worn by Roman generals in celebrating a, ii. 174 *sqq.*

Triumphal arch, suggested origin of the, xi. 195

Troad, temple of Mouse (Smintheus) Apollo in the, viii. 283

Trobriands, Kiriwina, an island of the, v. 84

Trocadero Museum, statues of kings of Dahomey in the, iv. 85

Troezen, sanctuary of Hippolytus at, i. 24 *sq.*

Troezenians sacrificed first-fruits to Poseidon, viii. 133 ; their festival resembling the Saturnalia, ix. 350

Trojeburg, labyrinths for children's games called, iv. 77

Trokoarbasis, priest of Corycian Zeus, v. 145

Trokombigremis, priest of Corycian Zeus, v. 145

Trolls, efforts to keep off the, x. 146 ; and evil spirits abroad on Midsummer Eve, x. 172 ; Midsummer flowers a protection against, xi. 54 ; rendered powerless by mistletoe, xi. 86, 283, 294

Trophonius at Lebadea, iv. 166 *n.*[1]

Troppau, in Silesia, "Carrying out Death" at, iv. 250 *sq.*

Trows, certain mythical beings in Shetland, ix. 168

Troy, sanctuary of Athena at, ii. 284 ; the game of, iv. 76 *sq.*

"True of speech," epithet of Osiris, vi. 21

"True Man, the," official title of the head of Taoism in China, i. 413

—— Steel, whose heart was in a bird, xi. 110 *sq.*

Trumpets, blowing of, in the rites of Attis, v. 268 ; in rites of Dionysus, vii. 15 ; blown to expel demons, ix. 116, 117, 156 ; blown at the feast of Purim, ix. 394 ; sounded at initiation of young men, xi. 249

——, penny, blown at Befana (Twelfth Night) in Rome, ix. 166 ; at the feast of the Nativity of the Virgin, x. 221, 222

Trumpets, sacred, blown to make palm-trees bear fruit, ii. 24

Truth the hypothesis which is found to work best, iii. 422

Tschudi, J. J. von, his communication of a Spanish tract to W. Mannhardt, vii. 172 *n.*[2]

Tschwi, the, of West Africa, their custom after the death of a twin, viii. 98

Tsetsaut Indians of British Columbia, fasting and chastity of hunters among the, iii. 198 ; men among the, do not cut their hair, iii. 260 ; seclusion of girls at puberty among the, x. 46

Tshi-speaking peoples of the Gold Coast, rules observed by wives during absence of their husbands at war, i. 132 ; descent of kingship among the, ii. 274 *sq.* ; their stories to explain their totemism, iv. 128 *sq.* ; dedicated men and women among the, v. 69 *sq.* ; ordeal of chastity among the, v. 115 *n.*[2] ; their annual festival of the dead, vi. 66 *n.*[2]

Tsimshian Indians of British Columbia, their beliefs as to twins, i. 262 *sq.* ; cannibal rites among the, vii. 19, 20 ; their ceremonies after catching the first olachen fish of the season, viii. 254 *sq.* ; rules observed by their girls at puberty, x. 44 *n.*[2]

Tsong-ming, Chinese island, mode of procuring rain in, i. 298

Tsuen-cheu-fu, in China, geomancy at, i. 170

Tsuina, expulsion of demons in Japan, ix. 212 *sq.*

Tsûl, the, a Berber tribe of Morocco, their tug-of-war, ix. 179

Tuaran district of British North Borneo, the Dusuns of, their annual expulsion of demons, ix. 200 *sq,*

Tuaregs of the Sahara, their seclusion at meals, iii. 117 ; their men veil their faces, iii. 122 ; reluctant to name the dead, iii. 353 ; their fear of ghosts, iii. 353

Tubilustrium, purification of trumpets at Rome, v. 268 *n.*[1]

Tübingen, "Burying the Carnival" near, iv. 230

Tubuan or Tubuvan, man disguised as cassowary in Duk-duk ceremonies, xi. 247

Tubuériki, a god in the Kingsmill Islands, first-fruits offered to, viii. 127 *sq.*

Tucanos, the, of the Amazon, their custom of drinking the ashes of the dead, viii. 157

Tud or Warrior Island, Torres Straits, sweat of warriors drunk in, viii. 152 *sq.*

Tug-of-war before sowing and at reaping

of rice, ii. 100 ; probably in origin a magical rite, vii. 103 *n.*[1], 110 *n.* ; as a religious or magical rite, ix. 173 *sqq.* ; as a charm to produce rain, ix. 175 *sq.*, 178 *sq.*

Tugeri or Kaya-Kaya of Dutch New Guinea, their use of bull-roarers, xi. 242 *sq.*

Tuhoe tribe of Maoris, their belief as to the fertilization of barren women, ii. 56

Tui Nkualita, a Fijian chief, founder of the fire-walk, xi. 11

Tuič tribe of the Upper Nile, lion-tamer as chief of the, i. 347 *sq.*

Tuikilakila, a Fijian chief, claims to be a god, i. 389

Tukaitawa, a Mangaian warrior, whose strength waxed and waned with his shadow, iii. 87

Tul-ya's e'en, seven days before Christmas, the Trows let loose on, in Shetland, ix. 168

Tulasi, or Holy Basil, worshipped in India, ii. 26 ; married to Krishna, ii. 26 ; married to the *Salagrama*, ii. 26 *sq.*

Tulava, sacred prostitution in, v. 63

Tulle, in Berry, "Sawing the Old Woman" at Mid-Lent at, iv. 242

Tullus Hostilius, king of Rome, ii. 193 ; killed by lightning, ii. 181, 320 ; said to have instituted the Saturnalia, ix. 345 *n.*[1]

Tully River, in Queensland, natives of, their ideas as to falling stars, iv. 60 ; belief of the natives as to conception without sexual intercourse, v. 102

Tulsi plant, its miraculous virtue, xi. 5

Tum of Heliopolis, an Egyptian sun-god, i. 419, vi. 123

Tumbucas of South Africa, their notion as to whirlwinds, i. 331 *n.*[2]

Tumleo, island of, treatment of spilt blood and rags in, i. 205 ; contagious magic of bodily impressions in, i. 213 ; seclusion of women after childbirth in, iii. 150 ; annual fight in, ix. 142 *sq.*

Tummel, the valley of the, Hallowe'en fires in, x. 231

Tuña, a spirit, expulsion of, among the Esquimaux, ix. 124 *sq.*

Tundja River, the Orotchis of the, viii. 197

Tung ak, a powerful spirit, dreaded by the Esquimaux, ix. 79 *sq.*

Tunghät, wandering genii of the Esquimaux, ix. 379

Tunguzian people, the Gilyaks a, viii. 190 ; the Orotchis a, viii. 197

Tunis, New Year fires at, x. 217 ; gold sickle and fillet said to be found in, xi. 80 *n.*[3]

Tunja, capital of the Chibchas, in Colombia, i. 416

Tunnel, creeping through a, as a remedy for an epidemic, x. 283 *sq.*

Tupi Indians of Brazil, their customs as to eating captives, iii. 179 *sq.* ; cut off the thumbs of dead enemies, viii. 272

Tupinambas of Brazil, their superstition as to planting earth-almonds, i. 142 ; woman's share in agriculture among the, vii. 122

Turban, soul caught in a, iii. 75

Turcoman cure of fever by means of knotted thread, iii. 304

Turf, sick children and cattle passed through holes in, xi. 191

Turiks of Borneo, soul hooked fast to body among the, iii. 30

Turkana, the, of British East Africa, the power of medicine-men among, i. 344 *sq.*

Turkestan, human scapegoat in, ix. 45 ; Ferghana in, ix. 184

Turkey, feathers of a, in homoeopathic magic, i. 155 ; soul in form of, iii. 42 *n.*

Turkish tribes of Central Asia, girls propound riddles to their wooers among the, ix. 122 *n.*

—— village, oak-tree worshipped in, ii. 16

Turks, exorcism practised by the, iii. 102 ; preserve their nail-parings for use at the resurrection, iii. 280 ; their belief as to the bones of Scanderbeg, viii. 154

—— of Armenia, their rain-charm by means of pebbles, i. 305

—— of Central Asia give birds' tongues to backward child to eat, viii. 147

—— of Siberia, marriage custom of the, x. 75

Turmeric cultivated, vii. 245, 250

Turner, Dr. George, on the power of the disease-makers in Tana, i. 341 *sq.* ; on sacred stones, v. 108 *n.*[1]

Turner, L. M., on the fear of demons among the Esquimaux of Labrador, ix. 79 *sq.*

Turner's picture of "The Golden Bough," i. 1

Turning or whirling round, custom of, observed by mummers, i. 273, 275, ii. 74, 80, 81, 87

"Turquoise, Mistress of," at Sinai, v. 53

Turrbal tribe of Queensland, rule observed by boys at initiation in the, iii. 156 *n.*[1]

—— River in Queensland, natives of the, their ideas as to falling stars, iv. 60

Turrinus, P. Clodius, coin of, i. 12 *n.*[3]

Turtle, magical models of, i. 108

Turtle - catching, taboos in connexion with, iii. 192

—— -dove, consumption transferred to a, ix. 52

—— family in Samoa, their rule as to eating and cutting up turtles, iii. 122

—— -shell badges of homicide, iii. 168

Turtles, ancestral spirits in, in the Tenimber and Timor-laut Islands, viii. 123 ; killing the sacred, among the Zuni, viii. 175 *sqq.* ; transmigration of human souls into, among the Zuni, viii. 178 *sq.*

Turukhinsk region, Samoyeds of the, xi. 196

Tusayan, an ancient province of Arizona, vii. 312

——, the Pueblo Indians of, their custom at planting, v. 239 ; their observation of the Pleiades, vii. 312

Tuscan Romagna, Befana (Epiphany) in the, ix. 167

Tuscany, oak forests on the coast of, ii. 354 ; volcanic district of, v. 208 *n.*[1] ; omens from the cry of the quail in, vii. 295

Tusculum, Egerius Baebius or Laevius, of Tusculum, a Latin dictator, i. 22, 23 *n.*[3] ; King of the Sacred Rites at, i. 44 *n.*[1]

Tusks of ivory, souls shut up in, iii. 70

Tusser, Thomas, on planting peas and beans, vi. 134

Tutu, island of Torres Strait, treatment of girls at puberty in, x. 41

Tver Government in Russia, charm to keep wolves from cows in, iii. 307

Twana Indians of Washington State, recovery of lost souls by medicine-men among the, iii. 58 ; prohibition to mention the names of the dead among the, iii. 365

Twanyirika, an Australian spirit whose voice is heard in the sound of the bull-roarer, xi. 233 *sq.* ; kills and resuscitates lads at initiation, xi. 234

Twelfth Day, dances on, i. 138 ; ceremony of the King at Carcassone on, viii. 321 ; mummers representing a Goat and a Bear on, viii. 327 ; dances on the roof on, to make the hemp grow tall, ix. 315 ; serious significance of, ix. 315 ; the Three Kings on, ix. 329 *sqq.* *See also* Twelfth Night

—— Day, the Eve of, expulsion of witches, etc., on, ix. 166 *sq.* ; twelve fires in Gloucestershire and Herefordshire on, ix. 318 ; the bonfires of, x. 107 ; processions with torches on, x. 340

—— Night, fruit-trees girt with straw ropes between Christmas and, ii. 17 ; certain animals not to be called by their proper names between Christmas and, iii. 396 *sq.* ; expulsion of the powers of evil on, ix. 165 *sqq.* ; dances for the crops on, ix. 238 ; Perchta's Day, ix. 244 ; (Epiphany), the King of the Bean on, ix. 313 *sqq.*, x. 153 *n.*[2] ; divination on, ix. 316 ; cake, x. 184 ; the Yule log on, x. 248, 250, 251 ; the divining-rod cut on, xi. 68. *See also* Twelfth Day

Twelfth Night, the Eve of, old Mrs. Perchta on, ix. 240, 241 ; ceremonial fires on, ix. 316 *sqq.*

Twelve Days from Christmas to Twelfth Night (Epiphany), precautions against witches during the, ix. 158 *sqq.*, 164 *sqq.* ; in Macedonia, superstitions as to the, ix. 320 ; weather of the twelve months supposed to be determined by the weather of the, ix. 322 *sqq.* ; in ancient India, ix. 324 *sq.* ; accounted a miniature of the year, ix. 324 ; in the Highlands of Scotland, ix. 324 ; difference of opinion as to the date of the, ix. 324, 327 ; probably an old intercalary period at midwinter, ix. 325 *sq.*, 328, 338 *sq.*, 342

—— Days or Twelve Nights not of Christian origin, ix. 326 *sqq.*

—— fires on Eve of Twelfth Day, ix. 318 *sq.*, 321 *sq.*

—— Gods, images of the, carried in procession at Magnesia, viii. 8

—— Nights, remains of Yule log scattered on fields during the, x. 248 ; between Christmas and Epiphany, were-wolves abroad during the, x. 310 *n.*[1]

—— years, king's reign limited to, in South India, iv. 46 *sqq.*

" Twice-born " Brahman, xi. 276

Twin, name applied by the Baganda to the navel-string, i. 195, 196, vi. 170 ; the navel-string of the king of Uganda called his, vi. 147. *See also* Twins

——, ghost of a, lodged in a wooden figure, viii. 98

Twin brothers in ritual, x. 278

—— girl charged with special duty, viii. 280

—— -producing virtue ascribed to a kind of mistletoe, xi. 79

Twining thread forbidden to women and children during absence of warriors, i. 131

Twins in war, i. 49 *n.*[3] ; produced by eating two mice, two bananas, or two grains of millet, i. 118, 145 ; taboos laid on parents of, i. 262, 263 *sq.* ; supposed to possess magical powers, especially over the weather and rain, i. 262-269, ii. 183 ; supposed to be salmon, i. 263 ; thought to be related to grizzly bears, i. 264 *sq.* ; thought to be related to apes, i. 265 ; thought to be the sons of lightning, i. 266 ; called the children of the sky, i. 267, 268 ; water poured on graves of, i. 268, iii. 154 *sq.* ; custom observed by mother of still-born, i. 269 *n.*[1] ; parents of, thought to be able to fertilize plantain-trees, ii. 102 ; mothers of, not allowed to go near farm at sowing and reaping, ii. 102 *n.*[1] ; customs of the Baganda in regard to, ii. 102 *sq.* ; precautions taken by women at the graves of, v. 93 *n.*[1] ; precautions against the ghosts of, viii. 98 ; deemed a great misfortune in Kamtchatka, viii. 173 *n.*[4], ix. 178 ; crocodiles thought to be born as the twins of human children, viii. 212 ; Baganda women throw sticks or stones on the graves of, ix. 18

Twins and their afterbirths counted as four children, xi. 162 *n.*[2]

——, father of, taboos observed by the, iii. 239 *sq.* ; his hair shaved and nails cut, iii. 284 ; no male except the, allowed to enter hut of girl in her seclusion at puberty, x. 24

Two bananas eaten produce twins, i. 145

—— Brothers, ancient Egyptian story of the, xi. 134 *sqq.*

—— days, heathen festivals displaced in the Christian calendar by, i. 14

—— -faced statue set up by the mother of still-born twins, i. 269 *n.*[1] ; mask worn by image of goddess, ix. 287

—— Goddesses, the, Demeter and Persephone at Eleusis, vii. 56, 59, 73, 90

—— grains of millet eaten produce twins, i. 145

—— -headed bust at Nemi, portrait of the King of the Wood, i. 41 *sq.*

—— -headed deity on a Cilician coin, v. 165 *sq.*

—— mice eaten produce twins, i. 118

Tyana, Hittite monument at, v. 122 *n.*[1]

Tybi, an Egyptian month, vi. 98 *n.*[2]

Tycoons, the, long the temporal sovereigns of Japan, iii. 19

Tydeus marries the daughter of the king of Argos, ii. 278

Tyers, Lake, in Victoria, reluctance to mention personal names among the blacks about, iii. 321

Tying up the winds in knots, i. 326 ; the soul to the body, iii. 32 *sq.*, 43

Tylon or Tylus, a Lydian hero, v. 183 ; his death and resurrection, v. 186 *sq.*

Tylor, Sir Edward B., on fertilization of date-palm, i. 25 *n.* ; on magic, i. 53 *n.*[1] ; on the fire-drill, ii. 208 ; on Garcilasso's account of the Peruvian priestesses of fire, ii. 244 *n.*[1] ; on the association of flints with lightning, ii. 374 *n.*[2] ; on reincarnation of ancestors, iii. 372 *n.*[1] ; on fossil bones as a source of myths, v. 157 *sq.* ; on names for father and mother, v. 281 ; on a theory of totemism, viii. 298 *n.*[2]

Tyndarids (Castor and Pollux) thought to attend the Spartan kings, i. 49

Types of animal sacrament, viii. 310 *sqq.*

Typhon, or Set, the brother of Osiris, vi. 6 ; the sea called the foam of, iii. 10 ; invoked by his true names, iii. 390 ; the soul of, in the Great Bear, iv. 5 ; murders Osiris, vi. 7 *sq.* ; mangles the body of Osiris, vi. 10, viii. 30 ; interpreted as the sun, vi. 129 ; the enemy of Osiris, vii. 262, 263, viii. 100 ; his injury of the eye of Horus, viii. 30 ; as a pig or boar, viii. 30, 31, 33, 34 ; the birth of, ix. 341. *See also* Set

——, in Greek mythology, slays Hercules, v. 111 ; Corycian cave of, v. 155 *sq.* ; his battle with the gods, v. 193, 194 ; the gods flee before, vi. 18

—— and Zeus, battle of, v. 156 *sq.*

Tyre, Melcarth at, v. 16 ; burning of Melcarth at, v. 110 *sq.* ; festival of "the awakening of Hercules" at, v. 111 ; king of, his walk on stones of fire, v. 114 *sq.*

——, kings of, their divinity, v. 16 ; as priests of Astarte, v. 26

—— and Sidon, ix. 17

Tyrie, parish of, in Aberdeenshire, the cutting of the *clyack* sheaf in, vii. 158

Tyrimnus, axe-bearing hero at Thyatira, v. 183 *n.*

Tyrol, sacred larch-tree in the, ii. 20 ; "ringing out the grass" on St. George's Day in the, ii. 343 *sq.* ; witches in the, their magic use of cut hair, iii. 271 ; disposal of loose hair in the, iii. 282 ; wedding rings as amulets in the, iii. 314 ; Feast of All Souls in the, vi. 73 *sq.* ; the Wheat-bride and Rye-bride at harvest in the, vii. 163 ; treatment of man who gives last stroke at threshing at Volders in the, vii. 224 ; last thresher said to "strike down the Dog" at Dux in the, vii. 273 ; the last thresher called the Goat at Oberinntal in the, vii. 286 ; annual "Burning out of the Witches" on May Day in the, ix. 158 *sq.*, x. 160 ; the *Perchten* in the, ix. 240, 242 *sq.* ; Senseless Thursday in the, ix. 248 ; burning the witch on the first Sunday in Lent at Voralberg in the, x. 116 ; Midsummer fires in the, x. 172 *sq.* ; magical plants culled on Midsummer Eve in the, xi. 47 ; St. John's wort in the, xi. 54 ; mountain arnica gathered at Midsummer in the, xi. 58 ; four-leaved clover gathered on Midsummer Eve in the, xi. 62 *sq.* ; dwarf-elder gathered at Midsummer in the, xi. 64 ; the divining-rod in the, xi. 68 ; mistletoe used to open all locks in the, xi. 85 ; belief as to mistletoe growing on a hazel in the, xi. 291 *n.*³

Tyrolese peasants use fern-seed to discover buried gold and to prevent money from decreasing, xi. 288

—— story of a girl who was forbidden to see the sun, x. 72

Tyropoeon, ravine at Jerusalem, v. 178

Tyrrel, Colonel F., as to the story of Sultan Bayazid and his external soul, iii. 51 *n.*

Tzentales, the, of Mexico, propitiate dead deer, viii. 241

Tzultacca, a mythical being of the Central American Indians, viii. 241

Ualaroi, the, of the Darling River, their belief as to initiation, xi. 233

Uap (Yap), one of the Caroline Islands, taboos observed by fishermen in, iii. 193 ; custom as to cutting hibiscus tree in, iii. 227 ; the natives of, burn or throw into the sea their cut hair and nails for fear of witchcraft, iii. 281 *sq.* *See also* Yap

Uaupes of Brazil, seclusion of girls at puberty among the, x. 61

—— River, woman's share in agriculture among the tribes of the, vii. 121 *sq.*

Ubemba, a royal family in Central Africa, ii. 277

Ucayali river in Peru, the Conibos of the, ii. 183 *n.*², v. 198 ; the Indians of the, their greetings to the new moon, vi. 142

Ucria, in Sicily, barren fruit-trees threatened at, ii. 21 *sq.*

Udvarhely in Transylvania, wreath made out of the last ears cut at harvest at, vii. 221 ; cock killed in last sheaf at, vii. 278

Uea, one of the Loyalty Islands, recall of a lost soul in, iii. 54

Uelzen in Hanover, the Harvest-goat at, vii. 283

Uffizi, the temple of Vesta represented on a relief in the gallery of the, at Florence, ii. 186

Uganda, priest inspired by tobacco smoke in, i. 384 ; ceremonies observed by the parents of twins in, ii. 102 ; the king's perpetual fire in, ii. 261 ; licence accorded to the Queen-Dowager and Queen-Sister in, ii. 275 *sq.*; descent of the totems in, ii. 288 ; avoidance of wife's mother in, iii. 84 *sq.* ; rule as to the Queen-mother of, iii. 86 ; ceremony on return from a journey in, iii. 112 ; uncleanness of women at menstruation and childbirth in, iii. 145 ; seclusion of brides in, iii. 148 *n.*¹ ; intercourse of chiefs with their wives before going to war in, iii. 164 *n.*¹; taboos observed by fishermen in, iii. 194 *sq.*; weapons removed from room at childbirth in, iii. 239 ; taboos observed by fathers of twins in, iii. 239 *sq.* ; king's brothers burnt in, iii. 243 ; custom as to roofing the king's palace in, iii. 254 ; rule as to cutting child's hair in, iii. 263 ; disposal of cut hair and nails in, iii. 277 ; custom as to the hair and nails of fathers of twins in, iii. 284 ; reluctance of people to name their totems in, iii. 330 ; spirits of ancestors reincarnate in their namesakes in, iii. 369 ; etiquette at the court of the king of, iv. 39 *sq.*; human sacrifices in, iv. 139 ; first-born sons strangled in, iv. 182 ; dead kings of, give oracles through inspired mediums, iv. 200 *sq.*, vi. 167, 171 *sq.* ; priest drinks beer out of skull of dead king in, iv. 200, viii. 150 ; temples of the dead kings of, vi. 167, 168 *sq.*, 170 *sqq.* ; human sacrifices offered to dead kings of, vi. 168, 172 *sq.* ; human sacrifices offered to prolong the lives of the kings of, vi. 223 *sqq.* ; men inspired by the spirits of lions, leopards, and serpents in, viii. 213 ; funeral ceremony in, ix. 45 *n.*²; human scapegoats in, ix. 242, 194 *sq.* ; kings of, not allowed to set foot on ground, x. 3 *sq.* ; life of the king of, bound up with barkcloth trees, xi. 160 ; passage of sick man through a cleft stick or a narrow opening in, xi. 181 *sq.* ; cure for lightning-stroke in, xi. 298 *n.*² *See also* Baganda

Uganda Protectorate, the Bahima of the, iii. 183 *n.*, ix. 6

Ugi, one of the Solomon Islands, fear of passing under a fallen tree in, iii. 250 ; cut hair buried in, iii. 277 ; observation of the Pleiades in, vii. 313

Uisnech, in County Meath, great fair at, x. 158

Uist, in the Hebrides, rain-making in, i. 308 ; Beltane cakes in, x. 154

——, North, the harvest *Cailleach* in, vii. 166 ; need-fire in, x. 293 *sq.*

——, South, fairies at Hallowe'en in, x.

226 ; salt cake at Hallowe'en in, x. 238 sq.

Uiyumkwi tribe, in Red Island, their treatment of girls at puberty, x. 39 sq.

Ujjain, the old capital of Malwa, in Western India, iv. 132, 133 ; tradition as to killing kings after one day's reign in, iv. 122 sq. ; Vikramaditya's Gate at, iv. 124

Ukami, in German East Africa, xi. 313

Ukpong, external soul in Calabar, xi. 206

Ukraine, ceremony to fertilize the fields on St. George's Day in the, ii. 103

Ulad Bu Aziz, Arab tribe in Morocco, their Midsummer fires, x. 214

Ulawa, one of the Solomon Islands, soul of dead man in a shark at, viii. 297 ; soul of dead man in bananas in, viii. 298

Uliase, East Indian island, fear to lose the shadow at noon in, iii. 87 ; sick people sprinkled with pungent spices in, iii. 105

Ullensvang, Hardanger, Norway, Whitsuntide Bride and Bridegroom at, ii. 92

Ulster, taboos observed by the ancient kings of, iii. 12 ; tombs of the kings of, iv. 101

Ulysses wins Penelope in a foot-race, ii. 300 sq.

—— and Aeolus, i. 326

Umbandine, king of the Swazies, expected to make rain for his people, i. 350

Umbrella, white, carried over Athenian priests and priestess, x. 20 n.[1] ; carried over bride in procession, x. 31

Umbrellas in ritual, x. 20 n.[1]

Umbrians, ordeal of battle among the, ii. 321

Unalashka, one of the Aleutian Islands, stones piled on a grave in, ix. 16

Uncle, dead, worshipped among the Awemba, vi. 175

——, maternal, preferred to father, mark of mother-kin, ii. 285 ; in marriage ceremonies in India, v. 62 n.[1]

Unclean and sacred, correspondence of the rules regarding the, iii. 145

Unclean animals originally sacred, viii. 24

Uncleanness regarded as a vapour, iii. 152, 206 ; of man-slayers, of menstruous and lying-in women, and of persons who have handled the dead, iii. 169 ; of whalers, iii. 191, 207 ; of lion-killer, iii. 220 ; of bear-killers, i. 221 ; caused by contact with the dead, vi. 227 sqq. ; ceremonial, among the Indians of Costa Rica, x. 65 n.[1] ;

of women at menstruation, x. 76 sqq. ; and sanctity not clearly differentiated in the primitive mind, x. 97 sq.   See also Menstruous

Uncles named after their nephews, iii. 332

Unconquered Son, Mithra identified with the, v. 304

Uncovered in the open air, prohibition to be, iii. 3, 14

Underground Zeus, Greek ploughman prayed to, vii. 45, 50

Undiara in Central Australia, magical stones at, i. 147

Ungarisch Brod, in Moravia, dramatic contest between Summer and Winter among the Slavs near, iv. 257 sq.

Unguent of lion's fat, magic virtue of an, viii. 164 ; made from fat of crocodiles and snakes, x. 14

Uniformity of occupation in primitive society, i. 245 ; of nature, ii. 376

Unis, king of Egypt, mentioned in the Pyramid Texts, vi. 5

Universal healer, name given to mistletoe, xi. 77

Unkareshwar, the goddess of cholera at, ix. 194

Unkulunkulu, "the Old-Old-one," the first man in the traditions of the Zulus, vi. 182

Unleavened bread baked with new corn at the harvest festival of the Natchez Indians, viii. 136

Unlucky, intercalary days regarded as, ix. 339 sq. ; Midsummer Day regarded as, xi. 29

—— children passed through narrow openings, xi. 190

—— marriages in India, ii. 57 n.[4]

Unmasking a were-wolf or witch by wounding him or her, x. 315, 321

Unmatjera tribe of Central Australia, their disposal of foreskins at circumcision, i. 95 sq. ; burial customs of the, i. 102 ; their charm to ensure wakefulness, i. 154 ; their contagious magic of footprints, i. 208 ; their rites of initiation, xi. 234 ; initiation of a medicine-man in the, xi. 238

Unna, in Westphalia, treatment of the last sheaf at, vii. 138

Unnefer, "the Good Being," a title of Osiris, vi. 12

Unreaped corn, patches of, left at harvest, viii. 233

Unreason, Abbot of, in Scotland, ix. 331

"Unspoken water" in marriage rites, vi. 245 sq.

Unyoro, king of, his custom of drinking milk, iii. 119 ; not to be seen drinking, iii. 119 ; cowboy of the king of,

iii. 159 *n.* ; diet of the king of, iii. 291 *sq.* ; kings of, put to death, iv. 34

Up-helly-a', popular festival on January 29th in Shetland, ix. 168 *sq.*, x. 269 *n.*

Up-uat, Egyptian jackal-god, vi. 154

Upias, King, father of Bormus, vii. 216

Upis, a Hyperborean maiden, i. 34 *n.* ; a name of Artemis, i. 34 *n.*

Upsala, popular assembly at, i. 366 *sq.* ; sacred grove at, ii. 9, 364, 365 ; temple of Frey at, ii. 144 ; images of Thor, Odin, and Frey at, ii. 364 ; sacrificial spring at, ii. 364 ; great temple and festival at, ii. 364 *sq.*, iv. 58 ; sepulchral mound at, iv. 57, 161 ; sacrifice of king's sons at, iv. 160 ; human sacrifices in the holy grove at, v. 289 *sq.*, vi. 220 ; the reign of Frey at, vi. 100

Upulero, the spirit of the sun, in the Babar Archipelago, prayers for off-spring to, i. 72

Ur, the fourth dynasty of, i. 417

Urabunna tribe of Central Australia, their fire-drill, ii. 209 ; their rites of initiation, xi. 234

Uranium, atomic disintegration of, viii. 305

Uranus mutilated by his son Cronus, iv. 192, v. 283

Uraons. *See* Oraons

Urewera, in New Zealand, magic use of spittle in, iii. 288

Uri-melech or Adom-melech, king of Byblus, v. 14

Urns, funereal, in shape of huts, ii. 201 *sq.*

Urquhart, Sir Thomas, on the Lord of Misrule, ix. 332

Urua, in Central Africa, divinity claimed by the chief of, i. 395

Urvasi and King Pururavas, Indian story, ii. 250, iv. 131

Usagara hills in German East Africa, the Wamegi of the, vii. 240

Usener, H., on Befana at Rome, ix. 167 *n.*[1] ; on the etymology of Veturius, ix. 229 *n.*[2]

Ushnagh, in Ireland, pagan cemetery at, iv. 101

Usirniri, temple of, at Busiris, vi. 151

Usondo, the lord of rain, in Zululand, i. 303

Ussingen, in Nassau, saying as to wind in corn at, vii. 296

Ussukuma (Usukuma), district on the southern bank of Lake Victoria Nyanza, sultans of, expected to make rain and drive away locusts, i. 353 ; heads not to be shaved till corn is sown in, iii. 260

Ustrels, a species of vampyre in Bulgaria, supposed to attack cattle, x. 284

Utch Kurgan, in Turkestan, human scapegoat at, ix. 45

Uttoxeter, May garlands at, ii. 61

Ututwa, sultan of, expelled for drought, i. 353

Uuayayab, demon of evil in Yucatan, ix. 171

Uwet, tribe on the Calabar River, their excessive use of the poison ordeal, iv. 197

Vagney, in the Vosges, Christmas custom at, x. 254

Vagueness and inconsistency of primitive thought, xi. 301 *sq.*

Val di Ledro, effigy burnt in the, at Carnival, x. 120

Valais, the canton of, Midsummer fires in, x. 172 ; cursing a mist in, x. 280

Vale of Tempe, Apollo purified from the dragon's blood in the, iv. 81, vi. 240

Valenciennes, Lenten fire-custom at, x. 114 *n.*[4]

Valentines at bonfires, x. 109 *sq.*

Valerius Soranus, said to have divulged the name of Rome, iii. 391

Valesius, on the standard Egyptian cubit, vi. 217 *n.*[1]

Valhalla, the dead in battle received by Odin in, iv. 13

Vallabhacharyas or Maharajas, a Hindoo sect, believe that barren women can be fertilized by bathing in a sacred well, ii. 160 ; men assimilated to women in the, vi. 254. *See also* Maharajas

Vallancey, General Charles, on Hallowe'en customs in Ireland, x. 241 *sq.*

Vallée des Bagnes, cursing a mist in the, x. 280

Vallericcia, near the Alban Lake, archaic Greek relief found in the, i. 11 *n.*[1]

Valley of Hinnom, sacrifices of children to Moloch in the, iv. 169, v. 178

—— of the Kings of Thebes, vi. 90

—— of Poison, in Java, v. 203 *sq.*

Vampyres, charms against, ix. 153 *n.*[1] ; need-fire kindled as a safeguard against, x. 284 *sqq.*, 344

Vancouver Island, the Lkungen Indians of, i. 145 ; wind-stones in, i. 322 ; the Ahts of, vi. 139 *n.*[1], x. 43 ; the Songish or Lkungen tribe of, viii. 254

Vanua Lava, in the Banks Islands, avoidance of wife's mother at, iii. 85

Vapour thought to be exhaled by lying-in women and hunters, iii. 152, 206, 213 ; supposed, of blood and corpses, iii. 210 *sq.* ; supposed to be produced by the violation of a taboo, iii. 212

Vapour bath taken by girls at puberty, x. 40

Vapours, worship of mephitic, v. 203 sqq.

Var, Midsummer fires in the French department of, x. 193

Varanda, in Armenia, rain-charm at, i. 306

Varé, African kingdom, power of rain-making ascribed to the kings of, i. 348

Varini, a tribe akin to the Saxons, marriage with a step-mother among the, ii. 283

Varro, on the oak groves of Rome, ii. 185; on the so-called temple of Vesta, ii. 200; on the foundation of Rome by shepherds and herdsmen, ii. 324 n.¹; on Pales, ii. 326; on Janus as a sky-god, ii. 381; on a Roman funeral custom, iv. 92; on suicides by hanging, iv. 282; on the marriage of the Roman gods, vi. 230 sq., 236 n.¹; his derivation of Dialis from Jove, vi. 230 n.²; on Salacia, vi. 233; on Fauna or the Good Goddess, vi. 234 n.⁴; on the rites of Eleusis, vii. 88; on killing oxen in Attica, viii. 6; on annual sacrifice of goat on the Acropolis of . Athens, viii. 41; on the fire-walk of the Hirpi Sorani, xi. 14 n.³

Varuna, festival of, wife of the sacrificer obliged to name her paramours at the, iii. 217

Vase, external soul of habitual criminal in a, xi. 145 sq.

Vase - paintings of Cadmus and the dragon, iv. 78, 79; of Croesus on the pyre, v. 176

Vashti, derivation of the name, ix. 366
—— and Esther, temporary queens, ix. 365, 401
—— and Haman the duplicates of Esther and Mordecai, ix. 406

Vasse River in Western Australia, mourners cut themselves for the dead on the, i. 91

Vaté, in the New Hebrides, the aged buried alive in, iv. 12

Vatican, worship of Cybele and Attis on the site of the, v. 275 sq.

Vatican hill, evergreen oak on the, ii. 186
—— statue of Ephesian Artemis, i. 38 n.¹

Vaughan Stevens, H., on the wild tribes of the Malay region, ii. 236 n.¹

Veal eaten by Egyptian kings, iii. 13, 291

Veckenstedt, E., i. 326 n.⁵

Vecoux, in the Vosges, cattle believed to talk on Christmas Eve at, x. 254

Vedas, the magical ritual of the, akin to shamanism, i. 229

Vedic age, the Aryans of the, their calendar, ix. 342
—— hymns, the fire-god Agni in the, xi. 295 sq.
—— India, consecration of the sacrificer of soma in, iii. 159 n.; belief and custom as to meteors in, iv. 63; swinging as a religious rite in, iv. 279 sq.
—— rites, magical nature of, i. 229
—— times, charm to restore a banished prince in, i. 145; transference of sin in, ix. 3; cure for consumption in, ix. 51; the creed of the, ix. 90; riddles asked at sacrifice of horse in, ix. 122 n.; the Aryans of the, ix. 324

Vedijovis, she-goat sacrificed like human victim to, vii. 33. See also Vejovis

Vegetable and animal life associated in primitive mind, v. 5
—— food prescribed for man-slayers, iii. 167

Vegetables at Midsummer, their fertilizing influence on women, xi. 51

Vegetation, homoeopathic influence of persons on, i. 142; spirit of, newly awakened in spring, ii. 70; spirit of, brought to houses, ii. 74; spirit of, represented by mummers dressed in leaves, branches, and flowers, ii. 74 sqq., 78 sqq., 97; spirit of, represented by a tree and a living man, ii. 76; spirit of, represented in duplicate by a girl and an effigy, ii. 78; spirit of, represented by a king or queen, ii. 84, 87, 88; influence of the sexes on, ii. 97 sqq.; men and women masquerading as spirits of, ii. 120; marriage of the powers of, ii. 142, 171; death and revival of the spirit of, iv. 212, 252, 263 sqq.; perhaps generalized from a tree-spirit, iv. 253, v. 233; mythical theory of the growth and decay of, v. 3 sqq.; annual decay and revival of, represented dramatically in the rites of Adonis, v. 227 sqq.; gardens of Adonis charms to promote the growth of, v. 236 sq., 239; Midsummer fires and couples in relation to, v. 250 sq.; Attis as a god of, v. 277 sqq.; Osiris as a god of, vi. 112, 126, 131, 158; decay and growth of, conceived as the death and resurrection of gods, vii. 1 sq.; Mars a deity of, ix. 229 sq.; outworn deity of, ix. 231; processions representing spirits of, ix. 250; spirit of, burnt in effigy, xi. 21 sq.; reasons for burning a deity of, xi. 23; leaf-clad representative of the spirit of, burnt, xi. 25; W. Mannhardt's view that the victims burnt by the Druids represented spirits of, xi. 43

Vegetation - god, Easter an old vernal

festival of the death and resurrection of the, ix. 328

Vehicle, expulsion of evils in a material, ix. 185 *sqq.*, 198 *sqq.*, 224

Vehicles, material, of immaterial things (fear, misfortune, disease, etc.), ix. 1 *sqq.*, 22 *n.*[2], 23 *sqq.*

Veil over mouth worn by Parsee priests, ii. 241, 241 *n.*[4]

Veiling faces to avert evil influences, iii. 120 *sqq.*

Veils worn by candidates for initiation at Eleusis, vii. 38

" Veins of the Nile," near Philae, offerings of money and gold thrown into the, vi. 40

Vejovis, the Little Jupiter, ii. 179, 180 *n. See also* Vedijovis

Velamas, in India, their belief as to third marriages being unlucky, ii. 57 *n.*[4]

Veleda, deified woman among the Bructeri, i. 391

Vellalas, of Southern India, their custom at marrying a second, third, or fourth wife, ii. 57 *n.*[4]

Velten, C., on an African Balder, xi. 312 *sq.*

Vendée, custom at threshing in, vii. 149 *sq.*

Veneti sacrifice white horses to Diomede, i. 27 ; on the Atlantic coast of Brittany, their boats of oak, ii. 353

Venezuela, province of Coro in, viii. 157 ; sticks or stones piled on scenes of violent death in, ix. 15

Venison, taboos concerning, iii. 208 *sq.* ; Esquimau rules as to eating, viii. 84 ; eaten as a protection against fever, viii. 143 ; not eaten by young men lest it make them timid like deer, viii. 144 ; not brought into hut by door, viii. 242 *sq.* ; not eaten because the souls of the dead are believed to be in deer, viii. 286, 293

Ventriloquism a basis of political power, i. 347

Ventriloquist as chief of his tribe, i. 347

Venus (Aphrodite) and Adonis, i. 21, 25, 40, 41, ix. 406. *See also* Adonis, Aphrodite

——, the bearded, in Cyprus, vi. 259 *n.*[3]

—— and Vulcan, vi. 231

Venus, the planet, identified with Astarte, v. 258, vi. 35

Venus' fly-trap (*Dionaea*), homoeopathic magic of, i. 144

Vera Cruz, in Mexico, the Indian tribes of, dated the beginning of their years by the setting of the Pleiades, vii. 310

Verbascum, mullein, gathered at Midsummer, xi. 63 *sq.* ; its relation to the sun, xi. 64

Verbena officinalis, vervain, gathered at Midsummer, xi. 62

Verdun, "killing the dog" at harvest near, vii. 272

Verges, in the Jura, Lenten fire-custom at, x. 114 *sq.*

Vermilion applied to bride in Hindoo marriage ceremony, ii. 25 ; faces of Roman generals at a triumph reddened with, ii. 175

Vermin from hair returned to their owner, iii. 278 ; propitiated by farmers, viii. 274 *sqq.* ; images of, made as a protection against them, viii. 280 *sq.* ; exorcized with torches, x. 340

Vernal festival of Adonis, v. 226

Verrall, A. W., as to Mohammed's prohibition of the artificial fertilization of the palm, ii. 25 *n.*[1] ; on the *Anthesteria*, v. 235 *n.*[1] ; on the pyre of Hercules, ix. 391 *n.*[4]

Verres, C., carried off image of Demeter from Henna, vii. 65

Versipellis, a were-wolf, x. 314 *n.*[1]

Vertumnus and Pomona, vi. 235 *n.*[6]

Vervain, root of, in homoeopathic cure, i. 84 ; garlands or chaplets of, at Midsummer, x. 162, 163, 165 ; burnt in the Midsummer fires, x. 195 ; used in exorcism, xi. 62 *n.*[4] ; gathered at Midsummer, a protection against thunder and lightning, sorcerers, demons, and thieves, xi. 62

Vesoul, the Cat at cutting the last corn at, vii. 280

Vespasian, monument of, at Nemi, i. 5 *sq.* ; German woman worshipped as a deity in the reign of, i. 391

Vespasian family, the oak of the, xi. 168

Vesper-bell on Midsummer Eve, xi. 62

Vessels used by tabooed persons destroyed, iii. 4, 131, 139, 145, 156, 185, 284 ; new or specially reserved, to hold new fruits, viii. 50, 53, 65, 66, 72, 81, 83

——, special, employed by tabooed persons, iii. 138, 139, 142, 143, 144, 145, 146, 147, 148, 160, 167, 185, 189, 197, 198 ; reserved for eating bear's flesh, viii. 196, 198 ; used by menstruous women, x. 86, 90 ; used by girls at puberty, x. 93

Vesta, her round temple, i. 13, ii. 200 *sq.* ; her sacred fires in Latium, i. 13 *sq.* ; worshipped at Lavinium, i. 14 ; her festival in June, ii. 127 *n.*[3] ; at Rome, the grove of, ii. 185 ; her fire at Rome fed with oak wood, ii. 186, xi. 91, 286 ; called Mother, not Virgin, ii. 198, 229 ; as Mother, ii. 227 *sqq.* ; a goddess of fecundity, ii.

229 *sq.* ; sacred fire in the temple of, annually kindled, x. 138

Vestal fire at Alba, i. 13 ; at Rome a successor of the fire on the king's hearth, ii. 200 *sqq.* ; rekindled by the friction of wood, ii. 207 ; at Nemi, ii. 378 *sq.*, 380

—— Virgin, mother of Servius Tullius, ii. 196 ; mother of Romulus and Remus, ii. 196, vi. 235

—— Virgins, in Latium, i. 13 *sq.* ; become mothers by the fire, ii. 196 *sq.* ; regarded as wives of the fire-god, ii. 198, 199, 229 ; relit the sacred fire of Vesta, ii. 207, x. 138 ; their function at the Parilia, ii. 229, 326 ; an order of, among the Baganda, ii. 246 ; their address to the King of the Sacred Rites, ii. 265 ; daughters of the Latin kings, ii. 271 ; their shorn tresses hung on a lotus-tree, iii. 275 ; rule as to their election, vi. 244 ; ceremonies performed by them on April 21st, viii. 42 ; their rule of celibacy, x. 138 *n.*[5]

Vestals fetch water from the spring of Egeria, i. 18 ; African, ii. 150 ; house of the, at Rome, ii. 201 ; their coarse earthenware, ii. 202 ; of the Herero, ii. 213, 214 ; custom of burying alive unfaithful Vestals, ii. 228 ; at Rome the wives or daughters of the kings, ii. 228 ; adore the male organ, ii. 229 ; rites performed by them for the fertility of the earth and the fecundity of cattle, ii. 229, 326 ; Celtic, ii. 241 *n.*[1]; Peruvian, ii. 243 *sqq.* ; in Yucatan, ii. 245 *sq.*

—— and pontiffs threw puppets annually into the Tiber at Rome, viii. 107

Vestini, the ancient, Midsummer fires in the territory of, x. 209

Veth, P. J., on the Golden Bough, xi. 319

Vi River, the Orotchis of the, viii. 197

Vicarious and nutritive types of sacrifice, vi. 226

—— sacrifices in ancient Babylon and on the Slave Coast, iv. 117 ; in ancient Greece, iv. 165, 166 *n.*[1] ; for kings, iv. 220 *sq.*

—— suffering, principle of, ix. 1 *sq.*

—— use of images, viii. 96 *sqq.*

Victim, passing between the pieces of a sacrificial, i. 289, 289 *n.*[4]

——, human, taken in procession from door to door, vii. 247

Victims give signs of inspiration by shaking themselves, i. 384 *sq.*

——, human, sacrificed to man-gods, i. 386, 387 ; treated as divine, vii. 250 ; assimilated to gods, vii. 261 *sq.* ; personating gods and goddesses in ancient Mexico, ix. 275 *sqq.* ; claimed by St. John on St. John's Day (Midsummer Day), x. 27, 29 ; claimed by water at Midsummer, xi. 26 *sqq. See also* Human sacrifices

Victims, sacrificial, hung on trees, v. 146 ; carried round city, iii. 188

——, white, sacrificed for sunshine, i. 291, 292, 314

Victoria, the late Queen, worshipped as a deity in Orissa, i. 404

Victoria, the Wotjobaluk of, i. 206, 251 *sq.* ; rain-making in, i. 251, 252 ; the Wurunjeri tribe of, iii. 42 ; the Kurnai of, iii. 83, 84 ; the Bad Country in, iii. 109 ; human hair used to cause rain by the tribes of, iii. 272 ; avoidance of wife's mother among the tribes of, iii. 345 *sq.* ; difference of language between husbands and wives in some tribes of, iii. 347 *sq.* ; the Gowmditch-mara tribe of, iii. 348 ; personal names rarely perpetuated among the tribes of, iii. 353 *sq.* ; kinsfolk of the dead change their names in some tribes of, iii. 357 ; the natives of, their observation of Canopus and the Pleiades, vii. 308 ; sex totems in, xi. 217

——, aborigines of, use of magical images among the, i. 62 ; their custom as to teething, i. 180 ; contagious magic of footprints among the, i. 212 ; mourning custom among the, iii. 182 *n.*[2] ; concealment of personal names among the, iii. 321 ; fear of naming the dead among the, iii. 350, 365 ; changes in their vocabulary caused by their fear of naming the dead, iii. 359 *sq.* ; women's share in the search for food among the, vii. 127 *sq.* ; their custom as to emu fat, x. 13 ; their dread of women at menstruation, x. 77 *sq.*

——, in Vancouver's Island, wind-stones at, i. 322

Victoria Nyanza, Lake, Kadouma near, i. 328 ; Ussukuma, on the southern bank of, i. 353, iii. 260 ; Mukasa, the god of the, ii. 150, vi. 257 ; customs of Baganda fishermen on, iii. 194 *sq.* ; the Wanyamwesi, to the south of, vii. 118 ; Kiziba, to the west of, viii. 219

Victory, temple of, on the Palatine Hill at Rome, v. 265

Vicuña, reason for not eating the, viii. 140

Vidovec in Croatia, Midsummer fires at, x. 178

Viehe, Rev. G., on the huts of the Herero, ii. 213 *n.*[2] ; on the fire-sticks of the Herero, ii. 218 *n.*[1] ; on sacred sticks representing ancestors among the Herero, ii. 222, 223 *sq.* ; on the worship of the dead among the Herero, vi. 187 n.[1]

Vienne, the Boy Bishop at, ix. 337 n.[1]; Midsummer fires in the department of, x. 191; the Yule log in, x. 251

Vieux-Pont, in Orne, game of ball at, ix. 183 n.[3]

Vigil, the all-night, in the mysteries of Eleusis, vii. 38

Vikramaditya, legendary king of Ujjain in Western India, iv. 122 sqq., 132

Vilavou, New Year's Men, the name given to newly initiated lads in Fiji, xi. 244

Village, double-headed idol set up as guardian at entrance of, ii. 385; continence at building a new, iii. 202; tabooed at feast of first-fruits in Borneo, viii. 122; surrounded with a ring of fire as a protection against an evil spirit, x. 282

Village May-poles in England, ii. 66 sqq.

Villages, expulsion of demons from, ix. 111 sqq. See also Pile-villages

Villagomez, Pedro de, on the Peruvian Maize-mother, etc., vii. 172 n.[2]

Vimeux, Lenten fires at, x. 113

Vine, Flamen Dialis not allowed to walk under a, iii. 14, 248; the cultivation of, introduced by Osiris, vi. 7, 112; in relation to Dionysus, vii. 2. See also Vines

——, wild, used in kindling fire by friction, ii. 251

Vine-branches used to beat people with at Easter, ix. 269

Vines blessed on the Assumption of the Virgin (15th August), i. 14 sq.; Festival of the Threshing-floor held at the pruning of the, vii. 61

Vineyards dedicated to Artemis, i. 15

Vintage, first-fruits of, offered to Icarius and Erigone, iv. 283, viii. 133; inaugurated by priests, viii. 133; omens of, x. 164

—— in Greece, time of, vii. 47

Vintage festival, Oschophoria, at Athens, vi. 258 n.[6]

—— rites at Athens, vi. 238

—— song, Phoenician, vii. 216, 257

Vintagers and vine-diggers, treatment of strangers by, vii. 257 sq.

Violence done to the rain-powers in drought, i. 296 sqq.

Violent deaths of the Roman kings, ii. 313 sqq.

Violets sprung from the blood of Attis, v. 267

Vipers sacred to balsam trees in Arabia, xi. 44 n.[1]

Viracocha, name applied by the Peruvian Indians to the Spaniards, i. 56, 57 n.

Virbius, the mate of Diana at Nemi, i. 19-21, 40 sqq., ii. 129, 378, v. 45; the mythical predecessor or archetype of the Kings of the Wood at Nemi, i. 40 sq., ii. 129; perhaps annually married to Diana at Nemi, ii. 129; perhaps a local form of Jupiter, ii. 379; etymology of the name, ii. 379 n.[5]; restored to life by Aesculapius, iv. 214; interpreted as an oak-spirit, xi. 295

—— or Hippolytus killed by horses, iv. 214

—— and the horse, viii. 40 sqq.

——, the slope of, i. 4 n.[5], ii. 321

Virgil, the witch in, i. 206 n.[4]; the story of Polydorus in, ii. 33; on the oak-crowned kings of Alba, ii. 178; an antiquary as well as a poet, ii. 178; on the Capitoline hill, ii. 184; on the primitive inhabitants of Rome, ii. 186; on the Golden Bough, ii. 379, xi. 284 sq., 286, 293 sq., 315 sqq.; the enchantress in, iii. 305; on the rustic militia of Latium, iii. 311; on Dido's magical rites, iii. 312; on the game of Troy, iv. 76; on the creation of the world, iv. 108 sq.; as an enchanter, viii. 281; on the fire-walk of the Hirpi Sorani, xi. 14

Virgin, the Assumption of the, in relation to Diana, i. 14-16; festival of the, in the Armenian Church, i. 16; in relation to Ephesian Artemis, i. 38 n.[1]; blesses the fruits of the earth, x. 118; the hair of the Holy, found in ashes of Midsummer fire, x. 182 sq., 191; feast of the Nativity of the, x. 220 sq.

—— and child supposed to sit on the Yule log, x. 253 sq.

——, the Heavenly, mother of the Sun, v. 303

Virgin birth of Perseus, v. 302 n.[4]

—— Mary and Isis, vi. 118 sq.

—— Mary of Kevlaar, the pilgrimage to, i. 77

—— Mother, the Phrygian Mother Goddess as a, v. 281

—— mothers, tales of, v. 264; of gods and heroes, v. 107

—— priestesses of Ephesian Artemis, i. 38; in Peru, Mexico, and Yucatan, ii. 243 sqq.

Virginia, rites of initiation among the Indians of, xi. 266 sq.

Virginity offered to rivers, ii. 162; test of, by blowing up a flame, ii. 239 sq., x. 139 n.; sacrifice of, v. 60; recovered by bathing in a spring, v. 280

Virgins plant and gather olives, ii. 107; sacrificed to serpents, dragons, or other monsters, folk-tales of, ii. 155; supposed to conceive through eating certain food, v. 96 ; sacrificed to goddess in Mexico, vii. 237

Virgins of the Sun at Cuzco, x. 132

——, the Vestal, and the sacred fire, x. 136. *See also* Vestal Virgins *and* Vestals

Virility, hierophant at Eleusis temporarily deprived of his, ii. 130 ; sacrifice of, to Cybele, ii. 144 *sq.* ; sacrifice of, in the rites of Attis and Astarte, v. 268 *sq.*, 270 *sq.* ; other sacrifices of, v. 270 *n.*² ; supposed to be lost by contact with menstruous women, x. 81

Viscum album, common mistletoe, xi. 315 *sqq.*

—— *quernum*, xi. 317

Vishnu invoked at rain-making, i. 283 ; a Brahman sacrificer supposed to become, i. 380 ; embodied in the *Salagrama*, a fossil ammonite, ii. 26, 27 *n.* ; supposed to pervade the Holy Basil (*tulasi*), ii. 26 ; mock human sacrifice in the worship of, iv. 216

Vision, charm by means of eagle's gall to ensure good, i. 154 ; sharpness of, conferred by dragon-stone, i. 165 *n.*⁶

Visiter, the Christmas, among the Servians, x. 261 *sq.*, 263, 264

Visve Devah, the common mob of deities, a pap of boiled grain offered to, in ancient Hindoo ritual, viii. 120

Vitellius at Nemi, i. 5

—— and Otho, iv. 141

Viti Levu, the largest of the Fijian Islands, the drama of death and resurrection at initiation in, xi. 243

Vitrolles, bathing at Midsummer at, v. 248, x. 194

Vitruvius, on the origin of fire among men, ii. 257 *n.*

Vituperation thought to cause rain, i. 278

Vitzilipuztli or Vitzilopochtli, Mexican god, dough image of him made and eaten sacramentally, viii. 86 *sqq.* ; young man annually sacrificed in the character of, ix. 280 *sq.*

Viza in Thrace, Carnival customs at, vi. 91, vii. 26, 28

Vizagapatam, in the Madras Presidency, human god at, i. 405 ; the Kudulu tribe near, vii. 244

Vizyenos, G. M., on a Carnival custom in Thrace, vii. 25 *n.*⁴, 26

Vogel Mountains, burning wheels on the first Sunday in Lent near the, x. 118

Vohumano or Vohu Manah, a Persian archangel, ix. 373 *n.*¹

Voigtland, leaping as a charm to make flax grow tall in, i. 139 *n.* ; locks unlocked at childbirth in, iii. 296 ; toothache nailed into trees in, ix. 59 ; belief

in witchcraft in, ix. 160 ; witches driven away in, ix. 160 ; "Easter Smacks" in, ix. 268 ; young people beat each other at Christmas in, ix. 271 ; bonfires on Walpurgis Night in, x. 160 ; tree and person thrown into water on St. John's Day in, xi. 27 *sq.* ; divination by flowers on Midsummer Eve in, xi. 53 ; mountain arnica gathered at Midsummer in, xi. 57 *sq.* ; wild thyme gathered at Midsummer in, xi. 64 ; precautions against witches in, xi. 73 *sq.*

Volcanic eruptions supposed to be caused by incest, ii. 111

—— region of Cappadocia, v. 189 *sqq.*

—— religion, v. 188 *sqq.*

Volcano, criminals thrown into, ii. 111 ; sacrifice of child to, iv. 218. *See also* Volcanoes

Volcano Bay, in Yezo, viii. 185

Volcanoes, fire perhaps first procured from, ii. 256 ; the worship of, v. 216 *sqq.* ; human victims thrown into, v. 219 *sq.*

Volders, in the Tyrol, custom at threshing at, vii. 224

Volga, sacred groves among the tribes of the, ii. 10 ; the Cheremiss of the, viii. 51, x. 181

Volksmarsen in Hesse, Easter fires at, x. 140

Volos, the beard of, name given to unreaped patches of corn in Russia, vii. 233

Voluntary human victims at religious rites, iv. 140 *sq.*, 143 *sq.*, 145 ; substitutes for capital punishment in China, iv. 145 *sq.*, 273 *sqq.*

Voluspa, the Sibyl's prophecy in the, x. 102 *sq.*

Vomiting, homoeopathic cure for, i. 84 ; as a religious rite, viii. 73, 75

Voralberg, in the Tyrol, "burning the witch" on the first Sunday in Lent at, x. 116

Vorges, near Laon, Midsummer fires at, x. 187

Vorharz, the Oats-man and Oats-woman at the harvest feast in the, vii. 163

Voroneje, in Russia, patch of rye left for Elijah at harvest at, vii. 233

Vosges, peasants of the, preserve their extracted teeth against the resurrection, iii. 280 ; disposal of cut hair and nails in the, iii. 281 ; "the Dog of the harvest" in the, vii. 272 ; toothache nailed into trees in the, ix. 59 ; Midsummer fires in the, x. 188, 336 ; the Yule log in the, x. 254 ; cats burnt alive on Shrove Tuesday in the, xi. 40

Vosges, the Upper, rule as to the shearing of sheep in, vi. 134 *n.*[3]
Vosges Mountains, homoeopathic magic at sowing in the, i. 137 ; May custom in the, ii. 63 ; French peasants of the, their belief in St. George as protector of flocks, ii. 334 *n.*[2] ; belief as to shooting stars in the, iv. 67 ; Feast of All Souls in the, vi. 69 ; "to catch the Hare " at harvest in the, vii. 279 ; " catching the cat " at haymaking and harvest in the, vii. 281 ; dances on Twelfth Day in the, ix. 315 ; the Three Kings of Twelfth Day in the, ix. 330 ; Lenten fires in the, x. 109 ; witches as hares in the, x. 318 ; magic herbs culled on Eve of St. John in the, xi. 47
Votaries, female, of Marduk, ix. 372 *n.*[2]
Votiaks (Wotyaks) of Russia, annual festivals of the dead among the, vi. 76 *sq.* *See also* Wotyaks
Votive images among the Kusavans, i. 56 *n.*[3]
—— offerings at Nemi, i. 4, 6, 12, 19, 23 ; to St. Leonhard, i. 7 *sq.* ; to the Virgin Mary, i. 77 *sq.*
Vow, hair kept unshorn during a, iii. 261 *sq.*, 285
Voyage, charm to make or mar a, i. 163 ; in boats of papyrus in the rites of Osiris, vi. 88
Voyagers, fire kept burning at home in absence of, i. 121 ; sympathetic taboos observed by girls in absence of, i. 126
Voyages, telepathy in, i. 126
Vrid-eld, need-fire in Sweden, x. 280
Vrigne-aux-Bois, in the Ardennes, mock execution of Carnival at, iv. 226
Vrtra, the dragon, conquered by Indra, in the Rigveda, iv. 106 *sq.*
Vulcan, the fire-god, father of Caeculus, ii. 197, vi. 235 ; the husband of Maia or Majestas, vi. 232 *sq.* ; his Flamen, vi. 232
—— and Venus, vi. 231
Vulci, Etruscan tomb at, ii. 196 *n.*
Vulsinii, in Etruria, nails annually knocked into the temple of Nortia at, ix. 67
Vulture, wing-bone of, in homoeopathic magic, i. 151 ; in divination, i. 158 ; transmigration of sinner into, viii. 299. *See also* Vultures
——, the black, mimicked by actor or dancer among the Kobeua and Kaua Indians of Brazil, ix. 381
Vulture's feather in a charm, viii. 167
Vultures not to be called by their proper names, iii. 408 ; lives of persons bound up with those of, xi. 201, 202
Vunivalu, the War King of Fiji, iii.

21

Wa, the Wild, a tribe of Upper Burma, their custom of head-hunting for the sake of the crops, vii. 241 *sqq.*
Wa-teita, the, of East Africa, their fear of being photographed, iii. 98
Wabisa, Bantu tribe of Rhodesia, their great god, vi. 174
Wabondei of East Africa, their sacrifices to baobab-trees, ii. 47 ; preserve the hair and nails of dead chiefs as charms, iii. 272 ; their belief in serpents as reincarnations of the dead, v. 82 ; their rule as to the cutting of posts for building, vi. 137 ; eat hearts of lions and leopards to become brave, viii. 142
Wachsmuth, C., on Easter ceremonies in the Greek Church, v. 254
Wachtl in Moravia, drama of Summer and Winter at, iv. 257
Wadai, the Sultan of, conceals his face, iii. 120 ; the Sultan of, must have no bodily defect, iv. 39 ; ceremony of the new fire in, x. 134, 140
Waddell, L. A., on the kings of Sikhim, iii. 20 ; on demonolatry in Sikhim and Tibet, ix. 94
Wade, Sir Thomas, formerly Professor of Chinese at Cambridge, iv. 273 *sq.*
Wadowe, the, of German East Africa, woman's share in agriculture among, vii. 118 ; their story of an African Balder, xi. 312
Wafiomi, of East Africa, seclusion of girls at puberty among the, x. 128
Waga-waga, in British New Guinea, changes of vocabulary caused by fear of naming the dead at, iii. 362
Wageia, the, of German East Africa, purification of man-slayers among the, iii. 177
Waggum, in Brunswick, the May Bride at Whitsuntide at, ii. 96
Wagogo, of German East Africa, chastity of women during absence of warriors among the, i. 131 ; their rain-making by means of black animals, i. 290 *sq.*; chiefs as rain-makers among the, i. 343 ; custom observed by man-slayers among the, iii. 186 *n.*[1] ; their ceremony at the new moon, vi. 143 ; their belief in the effect of eating a totemic animal, viii. 26 ; eat the hearts of lions to become brave, viii. 142 ; eat the hearts of enemies to make them brave, viii. 149 ; their way of getting rid of birds that infest gardens, viii. 276 ; their transference of sickness, ix. 6 *sq.*
Wagogo hunters, taboos observed by wives in absence of, i. 123
Wagstadt in Silesia, Judas ceremony on Wednesday before Good Friday at, x. 146 *n.*[3]

Wagtail, the yellow, in magic, i. 79
Wahehe, a Bantu tribe of German East Africa, custom before marriage among the, iii. 86 *n.*; the worship of the dead among the, vi. 188 *sqq.*; their belief in a supreme god Nguruhe, vi. 188 *sq.*; their belief that skin disease is caused by eating a totemic animal, viii. 26
Waheia, the, of German East Africa, their belief that skin disease is caused by eating a totemic animal, viii. 26
Wahoko, the, of Central Africa, their disposal of their cut hair and nails, iii. 278
Wahrstedt, in Brunswick, Whitsuntide King at, ii. 85
Wahuma, the, of the Albert Nyanza Lake, their rain-making, i. 250
Wailing of women for Adonis, v. 224
Waizganthos, an old Prussian god, prayers and offerings for the growth of the flax for, iv. 156
Wajagga, the, of German East Africa, their treatment of the corpses of childless women, i. 142 ; their charm for runners, i. 151 ; their rain-making, i. 250 ; mourners cut their hair among the, iii. 286 ; their covenant by means of spittle, iii. 290 ; their custom of leaping over a grandfather's corpse, iii. 424 ; their way of appeasing ghosts of suicides, v. 292 *n.*[3] ; their human sacrifices at irrigation, vi. 38 ; their way of diverting locusts from the fields, viii. 276 ; plants planted at birth of infants among the, xi. 160
Wajagga warriors swallow shavings of rhinoceros hide and horn to make them strong, viii. 143
Wak, a sky-spirit of the Borans, children and cattle sacrificed to, iv. 181
Wakamba, the, of East Africa, sacrifice to baobab-trees, ii. 46. *See* Akamba
Wakan, in the Dacotan language, mysterious, sacred, taboo, iii. 225 *n.*, viii. 180 *n.*[2]
Wakanda, a spirit recognized by the Omahas, iii. 187
Wakefulness, homoeopathic charms to ensure, i. 154, 156
Wakelbura, the, of Australia, their way of disabling ghosts, iii. 31 *sq.*; dread and seclusion of women at menstruation among the, x. 78
Wakondyo (Wakondjo), the, of Central Africa, their way of obtaining rain by means of a stone, i. 305 ; their custom as to the afterbirth, xi. 162 *sq.*
Walachia (or Wallachia), precautions against witches on St. George's Day

in, ii. 338 ; crown of last ears of corn worn by girl at harvest in, v. 237
Walachians, herdsman's festival on St. George's Day among the, ii. 338 *sq.*
Walber, a tree and a man disguised in corn-stalks, on May 2nd in Bavaria, ii. 75, 78
Walburgis Day, the 2nd of May in the Franken Wald mountains of Bavaria, ii. 75 *n.*[2]
Waldemar I., king of Denmark, magical powers attributed to, i. 367
Wales, belief as to death at ebb-tide in, i. 167 *sq.*; All Souls' Day in, vi. 79 ; harvest customs in, vii. 142 *sqq.*; the last sheaf called the Hag in, vii. 142 *sqq.*; Snake Stones in, x. 15 *sq.*; Beltane fires and cakes in, x. 155 *sq.*; Beltane fire kindled by the friction of oak-wood in, x. 155, xi. 91 ; Midsummer fires in, x. 200 *sq.*; divination at Hallowe'en in, x. 229, 240 *sq.*; Hallowe'en fires in, x. 239 *sq.*; the Yule log in, x. 258 ; burnt sacrifices to stop cattle-disease in, x. 301 ; witches as hares in, x. 315 *n.*[1]; belief as to witches in, x. 321 *n.*[2]; bewitched things burnt in, x. 322 ; divination by flowers on Midsummer Eve in, xi. 53 ; St. John's wort used to drive away fiends in, xi. 55 ; mistletoe to be shot or knocked down with stones in, xi. 82 ; mistletoe gathered at Midsummer in, xi. 86, 293 ; mistletoe used to make the dairy thrive in, xi. 86 ; mistletoe used to dream on at Midsummer in, xi. 293. *See also* Welsh
Walhalla, mistletoe growing east of, x. 101. *See also* Valhalla
Walking over fire as a rite, xi. 3 *sqq.*
Wall, Roman ceremony of knocking nails into a, ix. 65 *sqq. See also* Walls
Wallace, A. R., on women's work among the tribes of the Uaupes River, vii. 121 *sq.*
Wallace, Sir Donald Mackenzie, on the Russian sect of the Christs, i. 407 *sq.*
Wallachia. *See* Walachia
Wallis Island, tabooed persons not allowed to handle food in, iii. 140
Walls of houses beaten to expel ghosts, iii. 170 ; maladies and devils nailed into, ix. 62 *sqq.*; fortified, of the ancient Gauls, x. 267 *sq.*
Walnut, branches of, passed across Midsummer fires and fastened on cattle-sheds, x. 191
Walo, on the Senegal, the king of, not to be seen eating, iii. 118
Walos of Senegambia, their royal family thought to possess the power of healing by touch, i. 370 *sq.*; their belief as to a sort of mistletoe, xi. 79 *sq.*

Walpi, Pueblo Indian village, use of bull-roarers at, xi. 231

Walpurgis Day, the 1st of May, charred sticks of Judas fire planted in the fields on, x. 143

—— Night (the Eve of May Day), dances on, to make flax grow tall, i. 138, 139 *n.*; precautions against witches on, ii. 52, 54, 55, xi. 20 *n.*; milk and butter stolen by witches on, ii. 127; witches abroad on, ix. 158 *sqq.*, x. 159 *sq.*; annual expulsion of witches on, ix 159 *sqq.*; dances for the crops on, ix. 238; a witching time, x. 295; witches active on, xi. 73, 74

Walrus, taboos concerning, among the Esquimaux, iii. 208 *sq.*

Walton, Izaak, on Lapland witches, i. 326 *n.*[2]

Wamara, a worshipful dead king in Kiziba, vi. 174

Wambuba, the, of Central Africa, carry fire on the march, ii. 255

Wambugwe of East Africa, their rain-charm by means of black animals, i. 290; sorcerers as chiefs among the, i. 342; their belief as to falling stars, iv. 65

Wamegi, the, of German East Africa, their human sacrifices at harvest and sowing, vii. 240

Wand, magic, made from a tree growing on a grave, ii. 33

Wandorobbo, of East Africa, their con-tinence at brewing poison, iii. 200 *sq.*

Wangala, harvest-festival of the Garos, viii. 337 *sq.*

Wangen in Baden, bonfire and burning discs on the first Sunday in Lent at, x. 117

Wanigela River, in New Guinea, purifi-cation of manslayers among tribes on the, iii. 167 *sq.*; preparations for fish-ing turtle and dugong among the tribes of the, iii. 192

Waniki, the, of East Africa, their belief in the spirits of trees, ii. 12; their reverence for coco-nut palms, ii. 16; their mode of killing their cattle, iii. 247

Waning of the moon, theories to account for the, vi. 130; time for felling timber, vi. 135 *sqq.*

Wannefeld, in the Altmark, the last stalks at reaping left for the He-goat at, vii. 287

Wanyamwesi, the, of Central Africa, iii. 109; their belief in the associa-tion of twins with water, i. 268 *sq.*; ceremony observed by them on return from a journey, iii. 112; their custom as to personal names, iii. 330; woman's share in agriculture among the, vii. 118; their propitiation of slain ele-phants, viii. 227; their practice of adding to heaps of sticks or stones, ix. 11 *n.*[1]; their belief as to wounded crocodiles, xi. 210 *n.*[1]

Wanyoro (Banyoro), the, of Central Africa, their disposal of their cut hair and nails, iii. 278. *See* Banyoro

Wanzleben, near Magdeburg, man called the Wolf at threshing at, vii. 274 *sq.*

War, use of twins in, i. 49 *n.*[3]; tele-pathy in, i. 126 *sqq.*; continence in, iii. 157, 158 *n.*[1], 161, 163, 164, 165; rules of ceremonial purity observed in, iii. 157 *sqq.*; hair kept unshorn in, iii. 261; sacrifice of a blind bull before going to, vi. 250 *sq.*

" ——, the sleep of," among the Black-foot Indians, ii. 147

War chief, or war king, iii. 20, 21, 24

—— -dance of villagers round victor, iii. 169; of manslayers on their return, iii. 170, 178; of old men round man-slayer, iii. 182; of king before the ghosts of his ancestors, vi. 192; at festival of new corn among the Natchez Indians, viii. 79

—— -god, dog sacrificed to, i. 173

Ward, Professor H. Marshall, on the respective hardness of ivy and laurel, ii. 252; on the artificial fertilization of the fig, ii. 315 *n.*[1]

Ward, Professor James, as to Hegel's views on magic and religion, i. 423

Warlock, the invulnerable, stories of, xi. 97 *sqq.*

Warm food tabooed, iii. 189

Warner, Mr., on Caffre ideas about lightning, vi. 177 *n.*[1]

Warramunga, the, of Central Australia, their magical ceremonies for the multi-plication of their totems, i. 89; their custom at subincision, i. 93; custom observed by Warramunga women while the men are fighting each other with torches, i. 94; knocking out of teeth among the, i. 99; their homoeo-pathic charm to catch euros, i. 162; their custom as to extracted teeth, i. 181; their treatment of the navel-string, i. 183; believe certain trees to be inhabited by disembodied human spirits, ii. 34; their propitiation of a mythical water-snake, ii. 156; will not call the mythical snake Wollunqua by its proper name, iii. 384; their belief in the reincarnation of the dead, v. 100; their tradition of purification by fire, v. 180 *n.*[2]; their cure for headache, ix. 2

Warrior Island, Torres Straits. *See* Tud

Warriors tabooed, iii. 157 *sqq.*, x. 5 ; worship their weapons, ix. 90

Warts supposed to be affected by the moon, vi. 149 ; transferred to other people, ix. 48 *sq.* ; transferred to the moon, ix. 54 ; transferred to an ash-tree, ix. 57

Warua, their seclusion at meals, iii. 117 ; unwilling to tell their names, iii. 329

Warundi, the, of East Africa, custom as to girls at puberty among the, iii. 225 *n.*

Warwickshire, Arden in, ii. 7 *sq.* ; the Queen of May in, ii. 88 ; the Yule log in, x. 257

Washamba, the, of German East Africa, dance and deposit stones at dangerous places, ix. 29 ; their custom at circumcision, xi. 183

Washing forbidden for magical reasons during a rhinoceros-hunt, i. 115, during husband's absence, i. 122, during search for sacred cactus, i. 124, during heavy rain, i. 253 ; practised as a rain-charm, i. 253 ; practised as a ceremonial purification by the Jews after reading the scripture, viii. 27, by the Jewish high priest after the sin-offering, viii. 27, by the Greeks after expiatory sacrifices, viii. 27, 85, by the Parjas after killing a totemic animal, viii. 27 *sq.*, by the Matabele at eating the new fruits, viii. 71, by the Esquimaux before a change of diet, viii. 84, 85, by the Basutos after the slaughter of foes, viii. 149. *See also* Bathing

—— and bathing forbidden to rain-doctor when he wishes to prevent rain from falling, i. 271, 272

—— the feet of strangers, iii. 108

—— the head, customs as to, in Siam, Burma, ancient Persia, ancient Rome, and Peru, iii. 253

Washington group of the Marquesas Islands, seclusion of man-slayers in the, iii. 178. *See also* Marquesas

—— State, rain-charm in, i. 309 ; the Twana Indians of, iii. 58 ; the Klallam Indians of, iii. 354 ; the Twana, Chemakum, and Klallam tribes of, iii. 365 ; seclusion of girls at puberty among the Indians of, x. 43

Wasmes, processions with torches on the first and second Sundays in Lent at, x. 108

Wasp, external soul of enchanter in a, xi. 143

Wasps in homoeopathic magic, i. 152 ; young men stung with, as an ordeal before marriage among the Roocooyen Indians, ix. 263, x. 63

Wassailing on Eve of Twelfth Day in Herefordshire for the sake of the crops, ix. 319

Wassgow mountains, the need-fire as a remedy for cattle-plague in the, x. 271

Wata, a caste of hunters in East Africa, children of the Borans sent away to be reared by the, iv. 181

Wataturu, the, of East Africa, their chiefs sorcerers, i. 342 *sq.* ; their rule as to partaking of flesh and milk, viii. 84

Watchandie woman, in Australia, her fear of naming the dead, iii. 350

Watchdogs, charm to silence, i. 149

Water not to be touched by people at home in absence of hunters, i. 120 ; splashed by wife in absence of her husband, i. 120 *sq.* ; sprinkled as rain-charm, i. 248 *sqq.*; poured on graves as a rain-charm, i. 268, 286 ; puppet representing the tree-spirit thrown into, ii. 75, 76 ; serpent or dragon of, ii. 155 *sqq.*; conspicuous part played by, in the Midsummer festival, ii. 273, v. 246 *sqq.*, x. 172, 205 *sq.*, 216, xi. 26 *sqq.* ; poured as a rain-charm, iii. 154 *sq.* ; not allowed to touch the lips, iii. 160 ; to be called by another name in brewing, iii. 395 ; effigies of Death thrown into the, iv. 234 *sqq.*, 246 *sq.* ; thrown on the last corn cut as a rain-charm, v. 237 *sq.*; marvellous properties attributed to, at Mid-summer (the festival of St. John), v. 246 *sqq.*, x. 172, 205 *sq.*, 216, xi. 29 *sqq.* ; used to wash away sins, ix. 39 ; not to cross, in ritual, ix. 58 ; from sacred wells, x. 12 ; menstruous women not to go near, x. 77 ; consecrated at Easter, x. 122 *sqq.*, 125 ; turned to wine at Easter, x. 124 ; improved by charred sticks of Mid-summer fires, x. 184 ; at Midsummer, people drenched with, x. 193 *sq.*; heated in need-fire and sprinkled on cattle, x. 289 ; claims human victims at Midsummer, xi. 26 *sqq.* ; haunted and dangerous at Midsummer, xi. 31

—— and Fire, kings of, in the back-woods of Cambodia, ii. 3 *sqq.*

——, holy, sprinkling with, iii. 285 *sq.*; a protection against witches, ix. 158, 164 *sq.*

—— of Life, Ishtar sprinkled with the, in the lower world, v. 9 ; prince restored to life by the, in a folk-tale, xi. 114 *sq.*

——, prophetic, drunk on St. John's Eve, v. 247

——, rites of, at Midsummer festival in Morocco, x. 216 ; at New Year in Morocco, x. 218

—— of springs and wells thought to

acquire medicinal qualities on Midsummer Eve, x. 172, 205 *sq.*

Water-bird, a Whitsuntide mummer, iv. 207 *n.*[1]

" —— -carriers," maidens called, at Athens, viii. 5

—— -cross, a stone cross in Uist, used in rain-ceremonies, i. 308

—— -dragon, drama of the slaying of the, at Delphi and Thebes, iv. 78

—— -fowl, migratory, as representatives of the Old Woman of maize, vii. 204 *sq.*

—— -lilies, charms to make water-lilies grow, i. 95, 97, 98

—— nymphs, fertilizing virtue of, ii. 162

—— -ousel, heart of, eaten to make the eater wise and eloquent, viii. 144

—— -spirits, propitiation of, ii. 76; women married to, ii. 150 *sqq.*; sacrifices to, ii. 155 *sqq.*; as beneficent beings, ii. 159; bestow offspring on women, ii. 159 *sqq.*; danger of, iii. 94; offerings to, at Midsummer, xi. 28

—— totem among the Arunta, rain made by men of the, i. 259 *sq.*

Waterbrash, a Huzul cure for, vi. 149 *sq.*

Waterfalls, spirits of, ii. 156, 157

Watford, in Hertfordshire, May garlands at, ii. 61

Watubela Islands, treatment of the afterbirth in the, i. 187

Watuta, the, an African tribe of freebooters, iii. 109

Wave accompanying earthquake, v. 202 *sq.*

Waves, water from nine, in cure, xi. 186 *sq.*

Wawamba, the, of Central Africa, their way of making rain by means of a stone, i. 305

Wawanga, tribe of Mount Elgon, in British East Africa, their kings not allowed to die a natural death, iv. 287 (in Second Impression)

Wax melted to cause love, i. 77

Wax figures in magic, i. 66, 67, iii. 74, ix. 47

Waxen models of the human body or of parts of it as votive offerings, i. 77 *sq.*

Wayanas of French Guiana, ordeals among the, x. 63 *sq.*

Waziguas of East Africa do not call the lion by his proper name, iii. 400

Wealds of Kent, Surrey, and Sussex, ii. 7

Wealth acquired by magicians, i. 347, 348, 351, 352

Weaning of children, belief as to the, in Angus, vi. 148

Weapon and wound, contagious magic of, i. 201 *sqq.*

Weapons, prayers to, i. 132; sharp,

tabooed, iii. 237 *sqq.*; of man-slayers, purification of, iii. 172, 182, 219; turned against spiritual foes, ix. 233

Weariness transferred to stones or sticks, ix. 8 *sqq.*; attributed to an evil spirit in the body, ix. 12; magical plants placed in shoes a charm against, xi. 54, 60. *See also* Fatigue

Weasels, superstition of farmers as to, viii. 275

Weather, the magical control of the, i. 244 *sqq.*; of the twelve months determined by the weather of the Twelve Days, ix. 322 *sqq.*

Weather doctors in Melanesia, i. 321

Weaver, the wicked, of Rotenburg, xi. 289 *sq.*

Weavers, the Kaikolans, a caste of, v. 62

Weaving forbidden during absence of warriors, i. 131; homoeopathic charm to ensure skill in, i. 154 *sq.*

Weber, A., on origin of the Twelve Days, ix. 325 *n.*[3]

Wedau, in New Guinea, the chief of, a sorcerer, i. 338

Wedding rings amulets against witchcraft, iii. 314, 314 *sq.*

Weeks, Rev. J. H., on inconsistency of savage thought, v. 5 *n.*; on the names for the supreme god among many tribes of Africa, vi. 186 *n.*[5]; on the fear of the spirits of the dead among the Boloki, ix. 76 *sq.*; on the fear of witchcraft among the natives of the Congo, ix. 77 *n.*[2]; on rites of initiation on the Lower Congo, xi. 255 *n.*[1]

Weeping of the women of Jerusalem for Tammuz, vi. 11; for the gods, Xenophanes on the custom of, vi. 42; of savages for the animals and plants they kill, vi. 43; of sowers, vi. 45; of Karok Indians at hewing sacred wood, vi. 47 *sq.*; of oxen an omen of good crops, viii. 9; at slaughter of worshipful bear, viii. 189; at thanksgiving for the crops, ix. 293; of girls at puberty, x. 24, 29. *See also* Tears

Weevils, spared by Esthonian peasants, viii. 274

Weiden, in Bavaria, cutter of last sheaf tied up in it at, vii. 139

Weidenhausen, in Westphalia, the Yule log at, x. 248

Weidulut, heathen priest among the old Prussians, vii. 288

Weights and measures, false, corrected after an earthquake, v. 201 *sq.*; corrected in time of epidemic, ix. 115

Weihaiwei, in Northern China, ceremony of "the Beginning of Spring" in the cities nearest to, viii. 11

Weinhold, K., as to the sacrifice of a king's son every ninth year, iv. 57 *n.*[2] ; on the superstitions connected with the Twelve Nights, ix. 327 *n.*[4]

Weitensfeld, in Carinthia, bride-race at, ii. 304

Wellalaick, festival of the dead among the Letts, vi. 74

Wellhausen, J., on Arab rain-charm, i. 303

Wells cleansed as rain-charm, i. 267, 323 ; married to the holy basil, ii. 26 *sq.* ; bestow offspring on women, ii. 160 *sq.* ; divination by means of, ii. 345 ; sacred, in Scotland, x. 12 ; menstruous women kept from x. 81, 96 *sq.* ; charred sticks of Midsummer fires thrown into, x. 184 ; crowned with flowers at Midsummer, xi. 28

—— , goddess of, married to a wooden image of a god, ii. 146

—— , holy, resorted to on Midsummer Eve in Ireland, x. 205 *sq.*

—— , the Lord of the, at Fulda on Midsummer Day, xi. 28

Welsh, Miss, on the custom of the *churn* in the north of Ireland, vii. 155 *n.*[1]

Welsh cure for cough by transferring it to a dog, ix. 51 ; by crawling under a bramble, xi. 180 ; by passing under an ass, xi. 192 *n.*[1]

—— custom of sin-eating, ix. 43 *sq.*

—— name, alleged, for mistletoe, xi. 286 *n.*[3]. *See also* Wales

Wemba, the, of Rhodesia, punishment of adultery among, viii. 158. *See* Awemba

Wen-Ammon, Egyptian traveller, at Byblus, v. 14, 75 *sq.*

—— -chow, city in China, iv. 43

Wend cure for jaundice, i. 81. *See also* Wends

Wendland, P., on the crucifixion of Christ, ix. 412 *sq.*, 415, 418 *n.*[1]

Wends, their superstition as to oaks, ii. 55 ; their ancient custom of killing and eating the old, iv. 14 ; call the last sheaf the Old Man, vii. 138 ; the Harvest-cock among the, vii. 276 ; their faith in Midsummer herbs, xi. 54

—— of Saxony, their custom of the May-tree, ii. 69 ; say that the man who gives the last stroke at threshing "has struck the Old Man," vii. 149 ; their precautions against witches on Walpurgis Day, ix. 163 ; their idea as to wood of trees struck by lightning, xi. 297

—— of the Spreewald gather herbs and flowers at Midsummer, xi. 48 ; their

belief as to the divining-rod, xi. 68 *n.*[4]

Wensleydale, in Yorkshire, the Yule log in, x. 256

Werboutz, in Russia, rain-making at, i. 277

Were-tigers in China and the East Indies, x. 310 *sq.*, 313 *n.*[1]

—— -wolf, how a man becomes a, x. 310 *n.*[1] ; story in Petronius, x. 313 *sq.*

—— -wolves in Livonia, belief as to, iii. 42 ; active during the Twelve Days, ix. 164 ; compelled to resume their human shape by wounds inflicted on them, x. 308 *sqq.* ; put to death, x. 311 ; and the full moon, x. 314 *n.*[1] ; and witches, parallelism between, x. 315, 321

Wermland, in Sweden, treatment of strangers on the threshing-floor in, vii. 230 ; grain of last sheaf baked in a girl-shaped loaf in, viii. 48

Werner, Miss Alice, on the sanctity of the wild fig-tree in Africa, ii. 317 *n.*[1] ; on a soul-box in Africa, xi. 156 *n.*[1] ; on African Balders, xi. 314

Wernicke, on the character of Artemis, i. 35 *sq.*

West, Oriental religions in the, v. 298 *sqq.*

West Indian Islands, precaution as to spittle in the, iii. 289

Westenberg, J. C., on the Batta theory of souls, xi. 223 *n.*[2]

Westerhüsen in Saxony, last corn cut at harvest made up like a woman at, vii. 134

Westermann, D., on the worship of Nyakang among the Shilluks, vi. 165

Westermarck, Dr. E., as to king-killing on the Blue Nile, iv. 16 *n.*[1] ; on annual mock sultans in Morocco, iv. 153 *n.*[1] ; on the reason for killing the first-born, iv. 189 *n.*[2] ; on the hereditary holiness of kings, iv. 204 *n.*[2] ; on the tug-of-war in Morocco, ix. 180 ; on New Year rites in Morocco, x. 218 ; on Midsummer festival in North Africa, x. 219 ; his theory that the fires of the fire-festivals are purificatory, x. 329 *sq.* ; on water at Midsummer, xi. 31

Westphalia, the Whitsuntide Bride in, ii. 96 ; the Femgericht in, ii. 321 ; sacred oaks in, ii. 371 ; the last sheaf called the Great Mother in, vii. 135 *sq.*, 138 ; the *hörkelmei* at harvest in, vii. 147 *n.*[1] ; the Harvest-cock in, vii. 276 *sq.*, 277 *sq.* ; children warned against the Fox in the corn at Ravensberg in, vii. 296 ; fox carried from house to house in spring in, vii. 297 ; custom of "quickening " cattle on May Morning in, ix. 266 ; Easter fires in, x. 140 ; the Yule log in, x. 248 ; divination by orpine at Midsummer in, xi. 61 ; camomile gathered at Midsummer in, xi. 63 ; the Midsummer log of oak in, xi. 92 n.[1]

Westphalian form of the expulsion of evil, ix. 159 n.[1]

Wetar (Wetter), East Indian island, stabbing people's shadows in, iii. 78 ; fear of women's blood in, iii. 251 ; leprosy supposed to be caused by eating of a sacred animal in, viii. 25

Wetter, East Indian island, no fire after a death in, ii. 268 n. See also Wetar

Wetteren, wicker giants carried in procession at, xi. 35

Wetterpfähle, oak sticks charred in Easter bonfires, x. 145

Wetting people with water as a rain-charm, i. 250, 251, 269 sq., 272, 273, 274, 275, 277 sq., ii. 77, v. 237 sqq. ; the last corn cut, as a rain-charm, v. 237 sq. ; ploughmen and sowers as a rain-charm, v. 238 sq.

Weverham, in Cheshire, May-poles at, ii. 70 sq.

Wexford, in Leinster, great fair formerly held at, iv. 100 ; Midsummer fires in, x. 203

Whakatane valley in New Zealand, hinau tree thought to make barren women fertile in the, i. 182

Whale, solemn burial of dead, iii. 223 ; represented dramatically as a mystery, ix. 377. See also Whales

Whale-fishing, telepathy in, i. 121

Whale's ghost, fear of injuring, iii. 205

Whalers, taboos observed by, iii. 191 sq., 205 sqq. ; their bodies cut up and used as charms, vi. 106

Whales not mentioned by their proper names, iii. 398 ; ceremonies observed after the slaughter of, viii. 232 sqq. ; worshipped by the Indians of Peru, viii. 249

Whalton, in Northumberland, Midsummer fires at, x. 198

Wheat, charm at sowing, i. 137 ; offerings of, at Lammas, iv. 101 ; forced for festival, v. 243, 244, 251 sq., 253 ; thrown on the man who brings in the Christmas log, x. 260, 262, 264 ; protected against mice by mugwort, xi. 58 sq.
—— and barley, the cultivation of, introduced by Osiris, vi. 7 ; discovered by Isis, vi. 116

Wheat-bride, name given to the last sheaf of wheat and to the woman who binds it, vii. 162, 163

Wheat-cock, the last sheaf at harvest called the, vii. 276
—— -cow, the man who cuts the last ears of wheat at harvest called the, vii. 289
—— -dog, the man who cuts or binds the last sheaf called the, vii. 272
—— -goat, at cutting the last corn, vii. 282
—— -harvest, time of, in ancient Greece, vii. 48
—— -mallet, the man who gives the last stroke at threshing called the, vii. 148
—— -man, said to be killed by the last stroke at threshing, vii. 223
—— -mother, name given to wreath made out of last stalks at harvest, vii. 135
—— -pug, name given to man who gives the last stroke at threshing, vii. 273
—— -sow, name given to the last sheaf, vii. 298
—— -sowing, ceremony at, among the tribes of Gilgit, ii. 49, 50 sq.
—— -wolf, thought to be in the last bunch of standing corn, vii. 273 ; effigy of wolf made out of the last sheaf of wheat, vii. 274

Wheaten flour, the Flamen Dialis not allowed to touch, iii. 13

Wheel, magic, spun by witch in an enchantment, iii. 270 ; effigy of Death attached to a, iv. 247 ; fire kindled by the rotation of a, x. 177, 179, 270, 273, 289 sq., 292, 335 sq., xi. 91 ; as a symbol of the sun, x. 334 n.[1], 335 ; as a charm against witchcraft, x. 345 n.[3]

Wheels, burning, rolled down hill, x. 116, 117 sq., 119, 141, 143, 161, 162 sq., 163 sq., 166, 173, 174, 201, 328, 334, 337 sq., 338 ; thrown into the air at Midsummer, x. 179 ; rolled over fields at Midsummer to fertilize them, x. 191, 340 sq. ; perhaps intended to burn witches, x. 345

Wherry, Mrs., as to Lenten fires in Belgium, x. 108 n.[2] ; as to processions with effigies of giants, xi. 36 n.[1]

Whetham, W. C. D., on atomic disintegration, viii. 305 n.[2]

Whip made of human skin used in ceremonies for the prolongation of the king's life, vi. 224, 225. See also Whips

Whipping people on Senseless Thursday in the Tyrol, ix. 248 sq. ; to rid them of ghosts, ix. 260 sqq. See also Beating

Whips used in the expulsion of demons and witches, ix. 156, 159, 160, 161, 165, 214 ; used by maskers, ix. 243,

244 ; cracked to make the flax grow, ix. 248 ; cracked to drive away witches, xi. 74

Whirling or turning round, custom of, observed by mummers, i. 273, 275, ii. 74, 80, 81, 87

Whirlwind, attacking the, i. 329 *sqq.*

Whirlwinds thought to be demons or spirits, i. 331 *n.*²

Whit-Monday, custom observed by Russian girls on, ii. 80 ; the Leaf King at Hildesheim on, ii. 85 ; the King in Bohemia on, ii. 85 ; the king's game on, ii. 89, 103 ; custom of rolling down a slope on, ii. 103 ; pretence of beheading leaf-clad man on, iv. 207 *sq.* ; pretence of beheading the king on, iv. 209 *sqq.* See also Whitsuntide

Whitby, All Souls' Day at, vi. 79 ; the Yule log at, x. 256

White, Rev. G. E., on dervishes of Asia Minor, v. 170 ; on passing through a ring of red-hot iron, xi. 186 ; on passing sheep through a rifted rock, xi. 189 *sq.*

White, Miss Rachel Evelyn (Mrs. Wedd), on the position of women in ancient Egypt, vi. 214 *n.*¹, 216 *n.*¹

White, faces and bodies of man-slayers painted, iii. 175, 186 *n.*¹ ; widows painted, iii. 178 *n.*¹ ; lion - killer painted, iii. 220 ; the colour of Upper Egypt, vi. 21 *n.*¹ ; as a colour to repel demons, ix. 115

—— and black in relation to human scapegoats, ix. 220 ; figs worn by human scapegoats, ix. 253, 257, 272

White birds, souls of dead kings incarnate in, vi. 162 ; ten, external soul in, xi. 142

—— bull, soul of a dead king incarnate in a, vi. 164

—— bulls sacrificed to Jupiter, ii. 188 *sq.* ; sacrificed by Druids at cutting the mistletoe, ii. 189, xi. 77

—— chalk, bodies of newly initiated lads coated with, xi. 241

—— clay, Caffre boys. at circumcision smeared with, iii. 156 ; people smeared with, at festival, viii. 75 ; bodies of novices at initiation smeared with, xi. 255 *n.*¹, 257

—— cloth, fern-seed caught in a, x. 65, xi. 291 ; springwort caught in a, x. 70 ; mistletoe caught in a, xi. 77, 293 ; used to catch the Midsummer bloom of the oak, xi. 292, 293

—— cloths in homoeopathic magic, i. 137

—— cock buried at boundary, iii. 109 ; disease transferred to, ix. 187 ; as

scapegoat, ix. 210 *n.*⁴ ; burnt in Midsummer bonfire, xi. 40

White crosses made by the King of the Bean, ix. 314

—— Crown of Upper Egypt, vi. 20, 21 *n.*¹ ; worn by Osiris, vi. 87

—— dog, Iroquois sacrifice of a, viii. 258 *n.*², ix. 127, 209

—— god and black god among the Slavs, ix. 92

—— herb, external souls of two brothers in a, xi. 143

—— horse, effigy of, carried through Midsummer fire, x. 203

—— horses sacrificed to Diomede, i. 27 ; used to draw triumphal car of Camillus, ii. 174 *n.*² ; sacred among the Aryans, ii. 174 *n.*²

—— Maize, Goddess of the, in Mexico, lepers sacrificed to her, vii. 261

—— mice spared by Bohemian peasants, viii. 279, 283 ; under the altar of Apollo, viii. 283

—— Nile, the Dinkas of the, ix. 193

—— ox, sacrament of, among the Abchases, viii. 313 *n.*¹

—— poplar, the, at Olympia, ii. 220, xi. 90 *n.*¹, 91 *n.*⁷

—— ram, consecration of a, among the Kalmucks, viii. 313 *sq.*

—— and red wool in ceremony of the expulsion of evils, ix. 208

—— roses dyed red by the blood of Aphrodite, v. 226

—— sails that turned black, ix. 202

—— snake eaten to acquire supernatural knowledge, viii. 146

—— Sunday, the first Sunday in Lent and the first Sunday after Easter, x. 11 *n.*¹

—— thorn, a charm against witches, ii. 53, 191

—— victims sacrificed for sunshine, i. 291, 292, 314

Whiteborough, tumulus near Launceston, Midsummer fires on, ii. 141, x. 199

Whitekirk, St. Mary's well at, ii. 161

Whitethorn a protection against witches, ii. 53, 191

Whiteway, R. S., on custom of regicide in Bengal and Sumatra, iv. 51 *n.*²

Whitsun-bride in Denmark, ii. 91 *sq.*

Whitsunday, dragon carried in procession at Tarascon on, ii. 170 *n.*¹

Whitsuntide, rain-charms at, ii. 47 ; races, ii. 69, 84 ; contests for the kingship at, ii. 84, 89 ; rolling down a slope at, ii. 103 ; cattle first driven out to pasture at, ii. 127 *n.*², iv. 207 *n.*¹ ; drama of Summer and Winter at,

iv. 257 ; ceremonies concerned with vegetation at, ix. 359

Whitsuntide Basket in Frickthal, ii. 83

—— Bride, the, ii. 89, 91 sq., 96

—— Bridegroom, the, ii. 91

—— customs in Brunswick, ii. 56 n.³, 85, 96 ; in Holland, ii. 80, 104 ; in Russia, ii. 64, 79 sq., 93

—— crown, the, ii. 64, 89 sq., 91

—— Flower, ii. 80

—— King, ii. 84 sqq., 89, 90, iv. 209 sqq. See also Whit-Monday

—— -lout, the, ii. 81

—— Man, the Little, ii. 81

—— Mummers, iv. 206 sqq.

—— Queen, ii. 87, 89 sq., iv. 210

Whittled sticks in religious rites, viii. 185, 186 n., 192, 196, 278, ix. 261

Whittlesey in Cambridgeshire, the Straw-bear at, viii. 328 sq.

Whooping-cough cured by crawling under a bramble, xi. 180 ; Bulgarian cure for, by crawling under the root of a willow, xi. 181 ; child passed under an ass as a cure for, xi. 192

Whydah, on the Slave Coast, human sacrifices by drowning at, ii. 158 ; expiation for the slaughter of a sacred python at, iii. 222 ; the doctrine of reincarnation at, iv. 188 ; serpents fed with milk at, v. 86 n.¹ ; snakes sacred at, viii. 287

—— (Fida), in Guinea, king of, rule as to his drinking, iii. 129 ; his worship of serpents, v. 67 ; the hoeing and sowing of his fields, ix. 234

Wicked after death, fate of the, in Egyptian religion, vi. 14

Wicked Sower, driving away the, on the first Sunday in Lent, x. 107, 118

Wicken (rowan) tree, a protection against witchcraft, x. 326, 327 n.¹ See also Rowan

Wicker giants at popular festivals in Europe, xi. 33 sqq. ; burnt in summer bonfires, xi. 38

Widow, claim to kingdom through marriage with the late king's, ii. 281 sqq. iv. 193 ; re-marriage of, in Salic law, ii. 285 sq.

——, bald-headed, in cure, ix. 38

Widow-burning in Greece, v. 177 n.³

Widowed Flamen, the, vi. 227 sqq.

Widows painted white, iii. 178 n.¹ ; wear skull-caps of clay, iii. 182 n.² ; cleansing of, ix. 35 sq. ; drag plough round village in time of epidemic, ix. 172

—— and widowers, mourning customs observed by, iii. 142 sq., 144 sq. ; not

allowed to eat fresh salmon, viii. 253 sq.

Wied, Prince of, on the objection of Indians to have their portraits taken, iii. 96 sq.

Wiedemann, Professor Alfred, on the confusion of religion and magic in ancient Egypt, i. 230 sq. ; on Wen-Ammon, v. 76 n.¹ ; on the Egyptian name of Isis, vi. 50 n.⁴, viii. 35 n.⁴

Wiedingharde, in Schleswig, custom at threshing at, vii. 230

Wieland's House, name given to certain labyrinths used for children's games in Northern Europe, iv. 77

Wiesensteig, in Swabia, witch as horse at, x. 319

Wiesent, the valley of the, in Bavaria, the last sheaf called Goat in, vii. 282 sq.

Wife, the Old, name given to the last corn cut, vii. 140 sqq.

Wife's infidelity thought to injure her absent husband, i. 123, 124 sq., 128. See also Wives

—— mother, the savage's dread of his, iii. 83 sqq. ; her name not to be pronounced by her son-in-law, iii. 337, 338, 343

—— name not to be pronounced by her husband, iii. 337, 338, 339

Wiglet, king of Denmark, killed his predecessor and married the widow, ii. 281, 283

Wigtownshire, water thrown on last wagon-load of corn at harvest in, v. 237 n.⁴

Wiimbaio tribe of South-Eastern Australia, bleeding in the, i. 91 ; their medicine-men, v. 75 n.⁴

Wilamowitz-Moellendorff, U. von, on the Sacred Marriage of Dionysus, ii. 137 n.¹

Wild animals propitiated by hunters, viii. 204 sqq.

—— beasts not called by their proper names, iii. 396 sqq.

—— Dog clan of the Arunta, i. 107

—— fig-trees held sacred as the abodes of the spirits of the dead, viii. 113. See also Fig-Tree

'' —— fire,'' the need-fire, x. 272, 273, 277

—— fruits and roots, ceremonies at gathering the first of the season, viii. 80 sqq.

—— Huntsman, ix. 164, 241

—— Man, a Whitsuntide mummer, iv. 208 sq., 212

—— parsnip stalks burnt for ceremonial fumigation, viii. 248, 249

—— seeds and roots collected by women, vii. 124 sqq.

Wild Wa, the, of Burma, vii. 241 *sqq.*
See Wa
Wilde, Lady, her description of Midsummer fires in Ireland, x. 204 *sq.*
Wilhelmina, a Bohemian woman, worshipped, i. 409
Wilken, G. A., on the transmigration of human souls into animals as a base of totemism, viii. 298 *n.*[2]; on the external soul, xi. 96 *n.*[1]
Wilkes, Charles, on seclusion of girls at puberty among the Indians of Washington State, x. 43
Wilkinson, Sir J. G., on corn-stuffed effigies of Osiris, vi. 91 *n.*[3]
Wilkinson, R. J., on different dialectic names for the same animal in the Malay language, ii. 383 *n.*[1]; on the Malay's attitude to nature, iii. 416 *n.*[4]; on the Indonesian conception of the rice-soul, vii. 181 *sq.*
Will-fire, or need-fire, x. 288, 297
Willcock, Rev. Dr. J., on Up-helly-a' at Lerwick, ix. 169 *n.*[2]
William III. refuses to touch for scrofula, i. 369 *sq.*
William of Wykeham, his provisions for a Boy Bishop, ix. 338
Williams, Sir Monier, on the divinity of Brahmans, i. 403 *sq.*; on the fear of demons in modern India, ix. 91 *sq.*
Willkischken, in the district of Tilsit, man who cuts the last corn called "the killer of the Rye-woman" at, vii. 223
Willoughby, Rev. W. C., on the purification of Bechuana warriors, iii. 173
Willow used to beat people with at Easter and Christmas, ix. 269, 270; mistletoe growing on, xi. 79, 315, 316; children passed through a cleft willow-tree as a cure, xi. 170; crawling under the root of a willow as a cure, xi. 181; crawling through a hoop of willow branches as a cure, xi. 184; Orpheus and the, xi. 294
Willow-tree at festival of Green George among the gipsies, ii. 76
—— -trees, maladies transferred to, ix. 56, 58, 59; needles stuck into, as a cure for toothache, ix. 71
—— wands as disinfectants, iii. 143
—— -wood used against witches, ix. 160
Willstad, the Yule-goat at, viii. 328
Wilson, Colonel Henry, on a custom at hop-picking, vii. 226 *n.*[6]
Wilson, C. T., and R. W. Felkin, on the worship of the dead kings of Uganda, vi. 173 *n.*[2]
Wilson, Rev. J. Leighton, on the annual expulsion of demons in Guinea, ix. 131
Wilton, near Salisbury, May garlands at, ii. 62

Wimmer, F., on the various sorts of mistletoe known to the ancients, xi. 318
Winamwanga of East Africa, their custom as to fire kindled by lightning, ii. 256 *n.*[1], xi. 297 *sq.*; alternate dynasties among the, ii. 293; their offerings of first-fruits to the spirits of the dead, viii. 112; seclusion of girls at puberty among the, x. 24 *sq.*
Winchester College, Boy Bishop at, ix. 338
Winckler, H., his excavations at Boghaz-Keui, v. 125 *n.*, 135 *n.*
Wind, magical control of the, i. 319 *sqq.*; charms to make the wind drop, i. 320; fighting and killing the spirit of the, i. 327 *sqq.*; charm to produce a rainy or dry, ix. 176, 178 *sq.*; bull-roarers sounded to raise a, xi. 232. See also Winds
—— in the corn, sayings as to the, vii. 132, 271, 281 *sq.*, 288, 292, 296, 298, 303
—— of the Cross, Finnish wizards supposed to ride on the, i. 325
Wind clan of the Omahas, their way of starting a breeze, i. 320
—— -doctor among the Caffres of South Africa, his mode of procedure, i. 321 *sq.*
Windessi, in Dutch New Guinea, customs observed by head-hunters on their return, iii. 169 *sq.*
Winding thread on spindle at planting sugar-cane, viii. 119
Window, skins of slain bears brought in through the, viii. 193; dead game brought in through the, viii. 256; magic flowers to be passed through the, xi. 52
Winds, charms to calm the, i. 320 *sqq.*; thought to be caused by a fish, i. 320 *sq.*; sold to sailors, i. 325, 326; tied up in knots, i. 326; kept in jars, iii. 5. See also Wind
Wine not offered to the sun-god, i. 311; poured on head of sacrificial victim, i. 384; considered as a spirit, iii. 248; the blood of the vine, iii. 248; called milk, iii. 249 *n.*[2]; tabooed in certain Egyptian, Roman, and Greek rites, iii. 249 *n.*[2]; new, offered to Liber, viii. 133; the sacramental use of, viii. 167; thought to be spoiled by menstruous women, x. 96
Wine-jars, Dionysiac festival of the opening of the, ix. 352
Winenthal in Switzerland, new fire made by friction at Midsummer in the, x. 169 *sq.*
Wing-bone of vulture in homoeopathic

magic, i. 151 ; of eagle used to drink through, iii. 189

Winged deities in Cilicia and Phoenicia, v. 165 *sq.*

—— disc as divine emblem, v. 132

Winnebagoes, ritual of death and resurrection among the, xi. 268

Winnowing done by women, vii. 117, 128

Winnowing-basket, image of snake in, viii. 316 ; beaten at ceremony of expulsion of poverty, ix. 145 ; divination by, x. 236

—— -fan in rain-making, i. 294 ; in magic rites, iii. 55 ; used to scatter ashes of human victims, vi. 97, 106, vii. 260, 262 ; an emblem of Dionysus, vii. 5 *sqq.*, 27, 29 ; as cradle, vii. 6 *sqq.* ; used at reception of "the bridal pair" at rice-harvest in Java, vii. 200

—— -fork in rain-making, i. 276

Winter, myths of gods and spirits to be told only in, iii. 385 *sq.* ; effigy of, burned at Zurich, iv. 260 *sq.* ; called Cronus,· vi. 41 ; name given to man who cuts the last sheaf, vii. 142 ; name of harvest-supper, vii. 160 ; mummer personating, viii. 326 *n.*[1] ; ceremony at the end of, ix. 124 ; general clearance of evils at the beginning or end of, ix. 224 ; dances performed only in, ix. 376 ; ceremony of the expulsion of, ix. 404 *sq.* ; effigies of, destroyed, ix. 408 *sq.*

——, Queen of, in the Isle of Man, iv. 258

—— and Summer, dramatic battle of, iv. 254 *sqq.*

Winter festival of Dionysus, vii. 16 *sq.*

—— sleep of the god, vi. 41

—— solstice, reckoned the Nativity of the Sun, v. 303, x. 246 ; Egyptian ceremony at the, vi. 50 ; Aztec festival of the, viii. 90 ; corn-spirit represented dramatically in processions about the, viii. 325 ; ceremony after the, ix. 126 ; Persian festival of fire at the, x. 269

"Winter's Grandmother," burning the, x. 116

Winterbottom, Thomas, on a secret society of Sierra Leone, xi. 260

Wintun, Indian tribe of California, fear of naming the dead among the, iii. 352 ; seclusion of girls at puberty among the, x. 42 *sq.*

Wiradjuri or Wirajuri tribe of South-East Australia, the headman always a magician, i. 335 *sq.* ; their belief as to sorcery, iii. 269

Wissowa, Professor G., on Manius Egerius, i. 22 *n.*[5] ; on altar at Nemi, i. 23 *n.*[2] ; on sacrifices to Janus, ii. 382 *n.*[1] ; on Janus as the god of doors, ii. 383 *n.*[3] ; on introduction of Phrygian rites at Rome, v. 267 *n.* ; on Orcus, vi. 231 *n.*[5] ; on Ops and Consus, vi. 233 *n.*[6] ; on the marriage of the Roman gods, vi. 236 *n.*[1]

Wit, Miss Augusta de, on the importance of rice for Java, vii. 200 *n.*[1]

Witch, Mac Crauford, the great arch, x. 293

Witch burnt in Ireland, i. 236, x. 323 *sq.* ; soul departs from her in sleep, iii. 39, 41, 42 ; burned at St. Andrews, iii. 309 ; name given to the last corn cut after sunset, vii. 140 ; effigy of, burnt on first Sunday in Lent, x. 116, 118 *sq.* ; effigy of, burnt on Walpurgis Night, x. 159 ; compelled to appear by burning an animal ˏor part of an animal which she has bewitched, x. 303, 305, 307 *sq.*, 321 *sq.* ; in form of a toad, x. 323. *See also* Witches

——, Old, burning the, on the last day of harvest in Yorkshire, vii. 224 ; on Twelfth Day in Herefordshire, ix. 319

"Witch-shot," a sudden stiffness in the back, x. 343 *n.*, 345

Witch's herb, St. John's wort, xi. 56 *n.*[1]

"—— nest," a tangle of birch-branches, xi. 185

Witchcraft, precautions against, on May Day, ii. 52 *sqq.* ; the rowan a protection against, ii. 53, 54, ix. 267, x. 154, 327 *n.*[1], xi. 184 *n.*[4], 185, 281 ; strangers suspected of practising, iii. 102 ; almost universal dread of, iii. 281 ; the harvest Maiden a protection against, vii. 156 ; singed sheepskin a protection against, viii. 324 ; practised in cures in Scotland, ix. 38 *sq.* ; on the Congo, dread of, ix. 77 *n.*[2] ; the belief in, persists under the higher religions, ix. 89 *sq.* ; in Moravia, precautions against, ix. 162 ; bonfires a protection against, x. 108, 109 ; holy water a protection against, x. 123 ; cattle driven through Midsummer fire as a protection against, x. 175 ; burs and mugwort a preservative against, x. 177, xi. 59 *sq.* ; Midsummer fires a protection against, x. 185, 188 ; a broom a protection against, x. 210 ; need-fire kindled to counteract, x. 280, 292 *sq.*, 293, 295 ; in Devonshire, x. 302 ; great dread of, in Europe, x. 340 ; the fire-festivals regarded as a protection against, x. 342 ; stiffness in the back attributed to, x. 343 *n.*, 345 ; colic and sore eyes attributed to, x. 344 ; a wheel a charm against, x. 345 *n.* ; thought to be the source of almost all calamities, xi. 19 *sq.* ; leaping over bonfires as a protection against, xi. 40; its treatment by the Christian Church, xi. 42 ; and sorcery, Midsummer herbs and flowers a protection against, xi. 45, 46, 49, 54, 55, 59, 60, 62, 64, 65, 66, 67, 72 ; St. John's wort a protection against, xi. 54 ; dwarf-elder used to detect, xi. 64 ; fern root a protection against, xi. 67 ; mistletoe a protection against, xi. 85 *sq.*, 282, 283, 294 ; fatal to milk and butter, xi. 86 ; oak log a protection against, xi. 92 ; children passed through a ring of yarn as a protection against, xi. 185 ; a "witch's nest" (tangle of birch-branches) a protection against, xi. 185. *See also* Witch, Witches, *and* Sorcery

Witches sink ships, i. 135 ; raise the wind, i. 322, 326 ; in the wind, knives thrown at, i. 329 ; souls of dead, said to pass into trees, ii. 32 ; buried under trees, ii. 32 ; steal milk of cows on May Day or Walpurgis Night, ii. 52 *sqq.*, ix. 267 ; precautions against, ii. 52 *sqq.* ; in the shape of hares suck the milk of cows, ii. 53 ; steal butter, ii. 53 ; burned out on May Day, ii. 54 ; driven away by the sound of church bells, ii. 127 ; steal milk from cows on Midsummer Eve, ii. 127, x. 176, xi. 74 ; steal milk on Eve of St. George, ii. 334 *sqq.* ; as cats and dogs, ii. 334, 335 ; make use of cut hair, iii. 270, 271, 279, 282 ; wedding rings a protection against, iii. 314, 314 *sq.* ; steal cows' milk, iii. 314 *sq.*, x. 343 ; burnt alive in Africa, ix. 18, 19 ; special precautions against, at certain seasons of the year, ix. 157 *sqq.* ; annually expelled in Calabria, Silesia, and other parts of Europe, ix. 157 *sqq.* ; active during the Twelve Days from Christmas to Twelfth Night, ix. 158 *sqq.* ; the burning out of the, in the Tyrol, ix. 158 *sq.*, in Bohemia, ix. 161, in Silesia and Saxony, ix. 163 ; shooting the, ix. 164 ; driving out the, ix. 164 ; burnt in Scotland, ix. 165 ; beaten with rods of buckthorn on Good Friday, ix. 266 ; not allowed to touch the bare ground, x. 5 *sq.* ; burnt and beheaded, x. 6 ; effigies of, burnt in bonfires, x. 107, 116 *sq.*, 118 *sq.*, 342, xi. 43 ; charm to protect fields against, x. 121 ; Beltane fires a protection against, x. 154 ; cast spells on cattle, x. 154 ; steal milk from cows at Beltane, x. 154 ; in the form of hares and cats, x. 157, 315 *n.*1, 316 *sqq.*, 317, 318, 319 *sq.*, xi. 41, 311 *sq.* ;

burnt on May Day, x. 157, 159, 160 ; fires to burn the witches on the Eve of May Day (Walpurgis Night), x. 159 *sq.*, xi. 20 *n.* ; abroad on Walpurgis Night, x. 159 *sq.* ; kept out by crosses, x. 160 *n.*2 ; driving away the, x. 160, 170, 171 ; resort to the Blocksberg, x. 171 ; Midsummer fires a protection against, x. 176, 180 ; steal milk and butter at Midsummer, x. 185 ; active on Midsummer Eve, x. 210, xi. 19 ; abroad at Hallowe'en, x. 226, 245 ; burnt in Hallowe'en fires, x. 232 *sq.* ; the Yule log a protection against, x. 258 ; thought to cause cattle disease, x. 302 *sq.* ; at Ipswich, x. 304 *sq.* ; transformed into animals, x. 315 *sqq.* ; as cockchafers, x. 322 ; come to borrow, x. 322, 323, xi. 73 ; cause hail and thunder-storms, x. 344 ; brought down from the clouds by shots and smoke, x. 345 *sq.* ; burning missiles hurled at, x. 345; active on Hallowe'en and May Day, xi. 19, 73 *sqq.*, 184 *n.*4, 185 ; burnt or banned by fire, xi. 19 *sq.* ; gather noxious plants on Midsummer Eve, xi. 47 ; gather St. John's wort on St. John's Eve, xi. 56 ; purple loosestrife a protection against, xi. 65 ; tortured in India, xi. 159 ; animal familiars of, xi. 202. *See also* "Burning the Witches"

"Witches, Burning the," a popular name for the fires of the festivals, xi. 43
—— and hares in Yorkshire, xi. 197
—— and were-wolves, parallelism between, x. 315, 321
—— and wizards thought to keep their strength in their hair, xi. 158 *sq.* ; put to death by the Aztecs, xi. 159
—— and wolves the two great foes dreaded by herdsmen in Europe, ii. 330 *sqq.*, x. 343
Witches' Sabbath on the Eve of St. George, ii. 335, 338 ; on the Eve of May Day and Midsummer Eve, x. 171 *n.*3, 181, xi. 73, 74
Witchetty grubs, ceremony for the multiplication of, among the Arunta, i. 85
"Withershins," against the sun, in curses and excommunication at Hallowe'en, x. 234
Wittichenau, in Silesia, custom at end of threshing at, vii. 149
Witurna, a spirit whose voice is heard in the sound of the bull-roarer, xi. 234
Wives, taboos observed by, in the absence of their husbands, i. 116, 119, 120, 121, 122 *sqq.*, 127 *sqq.* ; exchanged at the appearance of the Aurora Australis, iv. 267 *n.*1 ; of dead kings sacrificed at their tombs, vi. 168 ; of a king

taken by his successor, ix. 368 *n.*[1]
See also Wife

Wives, human, of gods, v. 61 *sqq.*, vi. 207 ; in Western Asia and Egypt, v. 70 *sqq.*

" —— of Marduk," at Babylon, ii. 130

Wiwa, the, of East Africa, their custom as to fire kindled by lightning, ii. 256 *n.*[1]

Wiwa chiefs reincarnated in pythons, vi. 193

Wizards in Melanesia, the variety of their functions, i. 227 *sq.* ; who raise winds, i. 323 *sqq.* ; Finnish, i. 325 ; capture human souls, iii. 70, 73 ; gather baleful herbs on the Eve of St. John, xi. 47 ; gather purple loosestrife at Midsummer, xi. 65 ; animal familiars of, xi. 196 *sq.*, 201 *sq.* *See also* Medicine-men *and* Sorcerers

Woden, Odin, or Othin, the master of spells, iii. 305 ; the father of Balder, x. 101, 102, 103 *n.*[1] *See also* Odin

Wogait, Australian tribe, their belief in conception without cohabitation, v. 103

Woguls, sacred groves of the, ii. 11

Wohlau, district of Silesia, custom of "Carrying out Death" in, iv. 237

Wolf, charm to make a wolf disgorge his prey, i. 135 ; imitation of, as a homoeopathic charm, i. 155 ; track of, in contagious magic, i. 211 ; transformation into, iv. 83 ; said to have guided the Samnites, iv. 186 *n.*[4] ; corn-spirit as, vii. 271 *sqq.*, viii. 327 ; the last sheaf at harvest called the, vii. 273 ; the woman who binds the last sheaf called the, vii. 273 *sq.* ; the last sheaf shaped like a, vii. 274 ; man after threshing wrapt in threshed-out straw and called the, vii. 274 *sq.* ; stuffed, carried about, vii. 275 ; the beast-god of Lycopolis in Egypt, viii. 172 ; figure of, kept throughout the year, viii. 173 *n.*[4] ; ceremonies at killing a, viii. 220 *sq.*, 223 ; name given to thresher of last corn, viii. 327. *See also* Wolves

——, Brotherhood of the Green, at Jumièges in Normandy, x. 185 *sq.*, xi. 15 *n.*, 25

Wolf clan among the Moquis, viii. 178 ; in North-Western America, xi. 270, 271, 272 *n.*[1]

—— -god, Zeus as the, iv. 83

—— masks worn by members of a Wolf secret society, xi. 270 *sq.*

—— -mountain (Lycaeus) in Arcadia, iv. 83

—— society among the Nootka Indians, rite of initiation into the, xi. 270 *sq.*

Wolf-worshippers, cannibal, iv. 83

Wolf's heart eaten to make eater brave, viii. 146

—— hide, strap of, used by were-wolves, x. 310 *n.*[1]

—— skin, man clad in, led about at Christmas, vii. 275

Wolfeck, in Austria, leaf-clad mummer on Midsummer Day at, xi. 25 *sq.*

Wolfenbüttel, need-fire near, x. 277

Wolfish Apollo, viii. 283 *sq.* ; his sanctuary at Sicyon, viii. 283

Wollaroi, the, of New South Wales, rubbed themselves with the juices of the dead, viii. 163

Wolletz in Westphalia, the last sheaf called the Old Man at, vii. 238

Wollunqua, a mythical serpent, iii. 384

Wolofs of Senegambia, their superstition as to their names, iii. 323

Wolves in relation to horses, i. 27 ; feared by shepherds, ii. 327, 329, 330 *sq.*, 333, 334, 340, 341 ; charms to protect cattle from, iii. 308 ; not to be called by their proper names, iii. 396, 397, 398, 402 ; sacrifices offered to, viii. 284 ; transmigration of sinners into, viii. 308

——, the place of (Lyceum), at Athens, viii. 283 *sq.*

——, Soranian, iv. 186 *n.*[4]

—— and witches, the two great foes dreaded by herdsmen in Europe, ii. 330 *sqq.*, x. 343

Woman representing the Moon and married to the Sun, ii. 146 *sq.* ; feeding serpent in Greek art, v. 87 *sq.* ; as inspired prophetess of a god, vi. 257 ; burnt alive as a witch in Ireland, i. 236, x. 323 *sq.*

——, Sawing the Old, a Lenten ceremony, iv. 240 *sqq.*

Woman's bracelets and earrings worn by man who has been stung by a scorpion, iii. 95 *n.*[8]

—— dress assumed by men to deceive dangerous spirits, vi. 262 *sq.*

—— ornaments, scapegoat decked with, ix. 192

—— part in primitive agriculture, vii. 113 *sqq.*

Women forbidden to spin under certain circumstances, i. 113 *sq.* ; observe certain rules while the men are away hunting, i. 120 *sqq.* ; forbidden to sew in the absence of whalers and warriors, i. 121, 128 ; observe certain rules while the men are away fighting, i. 127 *sqq.* ; forbidden to sleep by day in the absence of warriors, i. 127 *sq.* ; forbidden to cover their faces in the absence of warriors, i. 128 ; dance while the men are at war, i. 131 *sqq.* ; dance to make crops grow tall, i. 139 *n.*; employed to sow the fields on the principle of homoeopathic magic, i. 141 *sq.* ; who have borne many children employed to fertilize fruit-trees, i. 141 ; plough as a rain-charm, i. 282 *sq.* ; chief makes women fruitful, i. 347 ; worshipped by the ancient Germans, i. 391 ; married to gods, ii. 129 *sqq.*, 143 *sq.*, 146 *sq.*, 149 *sqq.* ; fertilized by water-spirits, ii. 159 *sqq.* ; impregnated by fire, ii. 195 *sqq.*, 230 *sq.*, vi. 235 ; alone allowed to make pottery, ii. 204 *sq.* ; tabooed at menstruation, iii. 145 *sqq.*, x. 76 *sqq.* ; tabooed at childbirth, iii. 147 *sqq.*, x. 20 ; abstinence of men from, during war, iii. 157, 158 *n.*[1], 161, 163, 164 ; in childbed holy, iii. 225 *n.* ; dying in childbed, precautions against the return of their ghosts, iii. 236, viii. 97 *sq.* ; blood of, dreaded, iii. 250 *sq.* ; not allowed to see the drawing of men's blood, iii. 252 *n.*; not allowed to mention their husband's names, iii. 333, 335, 336, 337, 338, 339 ; impregnated by dead saints, v. 78 *sq.* ; impregnated by serpents, v. 80 *sqq.* ; fear to be impregnated by ghosts, v. 93 ; impregnated by the flower of the banana, v. 93 ; excluded from sacrifices to Hercules, v. 113 *n.*[1], vi. 258 *n.*[5]; their high importance in the social system of the Pelew Islanders, vi. 205 *sqq.* ; the cultivation of the staple food in the hands of women (Pelew Islands), vi. 206 *sq.* ; their social importance increased by the combined influence of mother-kin and landed property, vi. 209 ; their legal superiority to men in ancient Egypt, vi. 214 ; priests dressed as, vi. 253 *sq.* ; dressed as men, vi. 255 *n.*[1], 257, 262 *sqq.*, 263 ; milk cows, vii. 118 ; influence of corn-spirit on, vii. 168 ; swear by the Pleiades, vii. 311 ; thought to have no soul, viii. 148 ; ceremonies performed by, to rid the fields of vermin, viii. 279 *sq.*; impregnated by ghosts, ix. 18 ; as exorcizers, ix. 200 ; personating goddesses, ix. 238 ; fertilized by effigy of a baby, ix. 245, 249 ; fertilized by mummers, ix. 249 ; put to death in the character of goddesses in Mexico, ix. 283 *sqq.* ; in hard labour, charm to help, x. 14 ; who do not menstruate supposed to make gardens barren, x. 24 ; impregnated by the sun, x. 74 *sq.* ; impregnated by the moon, x. 75 *sq.*; dread of menstruous, x. 76 *sqq.* ; at menstruation painted red, x. 78 ; leap over Midsummer bonfires to ensure an easy delivery, x. 194, 339 ; fertilized by tree-spirits, xi. 22 ; creep through a rifted rock to obtain an easy delivery, xi. 189 ; not allowed to see bull-roarers, xi. 234, 235, 242. *See also* Barren, Childless, Menstruous, Pregnant, *and* Sacred women

Women, barren, thought to sterilize gardens, i. 142; tied to wild fig-trees to be fertilized by them, ii. 316 ; passed through holed stones as cure for barrenness, v. 36, with *n.*[4], xi. 187; fertilized by being struck with stick which has been used to separate pairing dogs, ix. 264 ; hope to conceive through fertilizing influence of vegetables, xi. 51

——, living, regarded as the wives of dead kings, vi. 191, 192 ; reputed wives of gods, vi. 207

——, pregnant, employed to fertilize crops and fruit-trees, i. 140 *sq.* ; taboos on, i. 141 *n.*[1]; wear garments made of bark of sacred tree, ii. 58 ; mode of protecting them against dangerous spirits, viii. 102 *sq.*

—— as prophetesses inspired by dead chiefs, vi. 192 *sq.* ; inspired by gods, vi. 207

Women's clothes, supposed effects of touching, iii. 164 *sq.*

—— hair, sacrifice of, v. 38

—— race at harvest, vii. 76 *sq.*

'' —— speech '' among the Caffres, iii. 335 *sq.*

Wonghi or Wonghibon tribe of New South Wales, ritual of death and resurrection at initiation in the, xi. 227

Wonkgongaru tribe of Central Australia, their magical ceremony for the multiplication of fish, i. 90

Wood, fire kindled by the friction of, ii. 207 *sqq.*, 235 *sqq.*, 243, 248 *sqq.*, 258 *sq.*, 262, 263, 336, 366, 372. *See also* Fire

——, King of the, at Nemi, i. 1 *sqq.*, ii. 1 *sq.*, 378 *sqq.*, iv. 28, x. 2, xi. 285, 286, 295, 302, 309 ; at Aricia, ix. 409

——, Lord of the, prayed to by the Gayos before they clear the forest, ii. 36 ; prayed to by the Gayos before they hunt in the woods, ii. 125

Wood-spirits in goat form, viii. 2 *sq.*

—— woman, stalks of corn left on the harvest field for the, vii. 232

Woodbine as a charm to keep witches from cows on May Day, ii. 53, ix. 267; sick children passed through a wreath of, xi. 184

Woodford, C. M., on offering of canarium nuts to ghosts, viii. 126 *sq.*

Woodmen, sacrifices offered by, at felling trees, ii. 14, 15 ; ask pardon · of trees at felling them, ii. 18, 19 ; form blood-brotherhood with the trees which they fell ii. 19 *sq.* ; ceremonies observed by at felling trees, ii. 37 *sqq.*

Woodpecker (*picus*) said to have guided the Piceni, iv. 186 *n.*[4] ; sacred among the Latins, iv. 186 *n.*[4] ; brings the mythical springwort, xi. 70 *sq.*

Woods (forests), of ancient Europe, ii. 7 *sq.*, 350 *sqq.* ; of England, the old, ii. 7 *sq.* ; of ancient Italy and Greece, ii. 8 ; of ancient Latium, ii. 188

Woods used in house-building, homoeopathic magic of, i. 146 ; species of, used in making fire by friction, ii. 248-252

Wootton-Wawen, in Warwickshire, the Yule log at, x. 257

Words tabooed, iii. 318 *sqq.* ; savages take a materialistic view of words, iii. 331. *See also* Language *and* Speech

——, common, changed because they are the names of the dead, iii. 358 *sqq.*, 375, or the names of chiefs and kings, iii. 375, 376 *sqq.* ; tabooed, iii. 392 *sqq.*

——, special, applied to the person and acts of a sacred chief or king, i. 398, 401, 401 *n.*[3] ; used by Scotch fowlers, iii. 393 *sq.* ; used by Scotch fishermen, iii. 393 *sqq.* ; used by German huntsmen, iii. 396 ; used by Nandi warriors, iii. 401 ; used by elephant-hunters in Laos, iii. 404 ; used by searchers for eagle-wood and *lignum aloes* in Indo-China, iii. 404 ; used by searchers for camphor in the Malay Peninsula, Sumatra, and Borneo, iii. 405 *sqq.* ; used by Malay tin-miners, iii. 407 ; used by Malay fowlers, iii. 407 *sq.* ; used by Malay fishermen, iii. 408 *sq.* ; used by Achinese fishermen, iii. 409 ; used by gold-miners in Sumatra, iii. 409 ; used by reapers in Nias, iii. 410 *sq.* ; used by the Javanese at night and in gathering simples, iii. 411 ; used by workers in the harvest-fields in Celebes, iii. 411 *sq.* ; used by the Toradjas of Celebes in the forest, iii. 412 *sq.* ; used by the Bugineese and Macassars of Celebes at sea, iii. 413 ; used by the Sangi Islanders at sea, iii. 414 ; used by the Kenyahs of Borneo in poisoning fish, iii. 415 ; used by reapers among the Tomori of Celebes, vii. 193

Wordsworth, W., on the pre-existence of the human soul, i. 104

Work in huts of absent whalers tabooed, i. 121 ; on holy days, the Flamen Dialis not allowed to see, iii. 14

"Working for need-fire," a proverb, x. 287 *sq.*

World regarded by early man as the product of conscious will and personal agency, i. 374; conceived as animated, ix. 90 *sq.* ; daily created afresh by the self-sacrifice of the deity, ix. 411

Worm, transmigration of sinner into, viii. 299

Wormeln, holy oak of, ii. 371

Worms, charm against, i. 152 ; souls of dead in, viii. 289 ; popular cure for, x. 17

Wormwood (*Artemisia absinthium*), xi. 58 *n.*[3]; burnt to stupefy witches, x. 345; superstitions concerning, xi. 61 *n.*[1]

Wororu, man supposed to cause conception in women without sexual intercourse, in West Australia, v. 105

Worship of trees, ii. 7 *sqq.* ; of the oak, ii. 349 *sqq.*, xi. 298 *sqq.* ; of mephitic vapours, v. 203 *sqq.* ; of hot springs, v. 206 *sqq.* ; of volcanoes, v. 216 *sqq.* ; of cattle, viii. 35 *sqq.* ; of animals, two forms of the, viii. 311 ; of snake, viii. 316 *sq.* ; paid to human representatives of gods in Mexico, ix. 278, 282, 289, 293 ; of ancestors in Fiji, xi. 243 *sq.*

—— of ancestral spirits among the Bantu tribes of Africa, vi. 174 *sqq.* ; among the Khasis of Assam, vi. 203

—— of the dead, magic blent with the, i. 164 ; perhaps fused with the propitiation of the corn-spirit, v. 233 *sqq.* ; founded on the theory of the soul, vii. 181 ; among the Thay of Indo-China, ix. 97

—— of dead kings and chiefs, iv. 24 *sq.* ; in Africa, vi. 160 *sqq.* ; among the Shilluks, vi. 161 *sqq.* ; among the Baganda, vi. 167 *sqq.* ; among the Barotse, vi. 194 *sq.* ; an important element in African religion, vi. 195 *sq.*

—— of frogs by the Newars, i. 294 *sq.*

Worshipful animal killed once a year, viii. 322

Worshippers of Osiris forbidden to injure fruit-trees and to stop up wells, vi. 111

Worth, R. N., on burnt sacrifices in Devonshire, x. 302

Worthen, in Shropshire, the Yule log at, x. 257

Wotjobaluk tribe in Victoria, contagious magic of clothes among the, i. 206 ; their rain-making, i. 251 *sq.*; their notion as to falling stars, iv. 64 ; their sorcery by means of spittle, iii. 288 ; sex totems among the, xi. 215 *sq.*

Wotyaks (Votiaks), the, of Russia, sacred

groves of the, ii. 43 *sq.* ; their marriage of Keremet to the Earth-wife, ii. 145 *sq.* ; their custom of leading a bride to the hearth, ii. 231 ; their annual festivals of the dead, vi. 76 *sq.* ; annual expulsion of Satan among the, ix. 155 *sq.*

Wound and weapon, contagious magic of, i. 201 *sqq.*

Wounded men not allowed to drink milk, iii. 174 *sq.*

Wounding the dead or dying, custom of, iv. 13 *sq.*

—— were-wolves in order to compel them to resume their human shape, x. 308 *sqq.*

Wounds at reaping, customs and sayings as to, vii. 281, 285, 288, 296 ; self-inflicted, of inspired men, ix. 117 *sq.* ; St. John's wort a balm for, xi. 55

" —— between the arms " of Hebrew prophets, v. 74 *n.*[4]

" —— of the Naaman," Arab name for the scarlet anemone, v. 226

Wrach (Hag), name given to last corn cut in Wales, vii. 142 *sqq.*

Wreath of woodbine, sick children passed through a, xi. 184

Wreaths of flowers thrown into water, divination from, ii. 339 ; as amulets, vi. 242 *sq.* ; of corn made out of last sheaf at harvest, vii. 134, 135 ; of flowers thrown across the Midsummer fires, x. 174 ; superstitious uses made of the singed wreaths, x. 174 ; hung over doors and windows at Midsummer, x. 201

Wren, hunting the, viii. 317 *sqq.*, in the Isle of Man, viii. 318 *sq.*, in Ireland, viii. 319 *sq.*, in England, viii. 320, in France, viii. 320 *sq.* ; called the king of birds, viii. 317 ; superstitions as to the, viii. 317 *sq.*, 319

Wrestling-matches in honour of the dead among the Kirghiz, iv. 97 ; at New Year festival among the Kayans, vii. 98 ; at festival of first-fruits in Tonga, viii. 131

Wright, Dr. Joseph, on *hockey*, vii. 147 *n.*[1] ; on the *mell*-sheaf, vii. 152 *n.*

Wrist-bands as amulets, iii. 315

Wrists tied to prevent escape of soul, iii. 32, 43, 51

Wukari, in Nigeria, custom of king-killing at, iv. 35

Wunenberger, Ch., on kings as rain-makers in Africa, i. 348

Wünsch, R., on the *Anthesteria*, v. 235 *n.*[1] ; on modern survivals of festivals of Adonis, v. 246 ; on Easter ceremonies in the Greek Church, v. 254 *n.*

Wünschensuhl, in Thüringen, the Harvest-cock at, vii. 276

Wurmlingen in Swabia, pretence of beheading a leaf-clad mummer at Whitsuntide at, iv. 207 *sq.* ; the Carnival Fool at, iv. 231 *sq.*

——, in Thüringen, man who gives the last stroke at threshing called the Barley-cow, Oats-cow, Peas-cow, etc., at, vii. 290

Würtemberg, bushes set up on houses on Palm Sunday in, ii. 71 ; the Lazy Man on Midsummer Day at Ertingen in, ii. 83 ; thresher of last corn called the He-goat at Tettnang in, vii. 286 ; effigy of goat made out of last corn threshed at Ellwangen in, vii. 287 ; Midsummer fires in, x. 66 ; leaf-clad mummer at Midsummer in, xi. 26

Wurunjeri tribe of Victoria, recovery of lost soul in the, iii. 42 *sq.*

Würzburg, Midsummer fires at, x. 165

Wuttke, A., on the superstitions connected with the Twelve Nights, ix. 327 *n.*[4]

Wyingurri, tribe of Western Australia, their contagious magic of footprints, i. 208

Wyld, E., on shrieks of tree-spirits, ii. 18

Wyse, Miss A., on May Day custom at Halford in Warwickshire, ii. 89 *n.*[1]

Wyse, William, as to circumcision in the Old Testament, i. 101 *n.*[2] ; as to the Greek custom of sacrificing to the dead on their birthdays, i. 105 *n.*[5] ; as to edible acorns in *Don Quixote*, ii. 356 *n.*[3] ; as to Cretan sacrifices without the use of iron, iii. 227 *n.*[2] ; on a reported Roman custom, iv. 144 ; on the causes of the downfall of ancient civilization, v. 301 *n.*[2] ; as to the fixed and movable Egyptian festivals, vi. 35 *n.*[2] ; as to an Egyptian festival of lights, vi. 51 *n.*[1]

Wyttenbach, D., his emendation of Plutarch, ix. 341 *n.*[1]

Xanthicus, a Macedonian month, vii. 259 *n.*[1]

Xenophanes of Colophon, on the creation of the gods in the likeness of men, iii. 387 ; on the Egyptian rites of mourning for gods, vi. 42, 43

Xenophon, his rural home, i. 7 ; on Triptolemus, vii. 54

Xeres, Fr., Spanish historian, on the sacrifice of children among the Indians of Peru, iv. 185

Xerxes in Thessaly, iv. 161, 163 ; identified with Ahasuerus, ix. 360

Xilonen, Mexican goddess of the Young Maize, ix. 285 ; woman annually sacrificed in the character of, ix. 285 *sq.*

Ximanas, an Indian tribe of the Amazon, kill all their first-born children, iv. 185 *sq.*

Xipe, "the Flayed One," Mexican god, ix. 297, 298, 299 ; statuette of, ix. 291 *n.*[1] ; his festival of the flaying of men, ix. 296 *sqq.* ; his image clad in the skin of a flayed man, ix. 297

Xixipeme, men clad in skins of human victims, in ancient Mexico, ix. 298, 299

Xnumayo tribe of Zulus, change of word to avoid the use of chief's name in the, iii. 377

Xochiquetzal, wife of Tlaloc, the Mexican thunder-god, human sacrifices offered to, vii. 237

Xomanas, an Indian tribe of the Rio Negro in Brazil, drink the ashes of their dead as a mode of communion, viii. 157

Yabim (Jabim), tribe of German New Guinea, their treatment of the navel-string, i. 182; their custom at childbirth, iii. 151 ; drive away the ghosts of the murdered, iii. 170 ; precaution against the ghost of a murdered man among the, iii. 186 *n.*[1] ; their use of magic knots in fishing-boats, iii. 306 ; avoidance of parents-in-law among the, iii. 342 ; unwilling to name the dead, iii. 354 ; tell stories to promote the growth of the crops, iii. 386 ; propitiate the souls of the dead for the sake of the crops, vii. 104 ; tell tales to get good harvests, vii. 104 *sq.*; their offerings to the souls of the dead for the sake of the crops, vii. 228 ; their way of getting rid of caterpillars and worms, viii. 275 *sq.*; their belief in the transmigration of some human souls into swine, viii. 295 *sq.*; their custom of sending disease away in a small canoe, ix. 188 *sq.*; girls at puberty secluded among the, x. 35 ; use of bull-roarers among the, xi. 232 ; rites of initiation among the, xi. 239 *sqq.*

Yaguas, Indians of the Amazon, girls at puberty secluded among the, x. 59

Yakut shamans, their descent into the lower world to recover lost souls, iii. 63 ; keep their external souls in animals, xi. 196

Yakuts, their charm to make the wind blow, i. 319 ; inspired sacrificial victims among the, i. 384 ; leap over fire after a burial, xi. 18

Yakutsk, rain-making by means of bezoar stones at, i. 305

Yam, island of Torres Straits, heroes worshipped in animal forms in, v. 139 *n.*[1] ; treatment of girls at puberty in, x. 41

Yam vines, continence observed at the training of, ii. 105 *sq.*

Yams, magical stones to promote the growth of, in New Caledonia, i. 163 ; feast of, at Onitsha on the Niger, iii. 123 ; charm for the growth of, among the Kai of New Guinea, vii. 100, 101 ; cultivated in Africa, vii. 119 ; cultivated in South America, vii. 120, 121 ; cultivated in New Britain, vii. 123 ; dug by Australian aborigines, vii. 126 *sq.*

——, ceremonies at eating the new, in New Caledonia, viii. 53 ; in West Africa, viii. 58 *sqq.*, ix. 134

——, festivals of the new, in West Africa, viii. 115 *sq.*; in Tonga, viii. 128 *sqq.*

Yang-Seri, prayers for the crops offered by the Banars of Cambodia to, viii. 33

Yaos, the, of British Central Africa, their fear of being photographed, iii. 97 *sq.*; their offerings of first-fruits to the dead, viii. 111 *sq.*

Yap (Uap), one of the Caroline Islands, precaution as to the spittle of important people in, iii. 290 ; taboos observed by men for the sake of immature girls in, iii. 293 ; prostitution of unmarried girls in, vi. 265 *sq.*; seclusion of girls at puberty in, x. 36. *See also* Uap

Yaraikanna, the, of Northern Queensland, seclusion of girls at puberty among, x. 37 *sq.*

Yarilo, the funeral of, celebrated in Russia on June 29th, iv. 261, 262 *sq.* ; a personification of vegetation, v. 253

Yarn, divination by, at Hallowe'en, x. 235, 240, 241, 243 ; sick children passed through a ring of, xi. 185

Yarra river in Victoria borders the Bad Country, iii. 109 ; treatment of girls at puberty among the aborigines of the Upper, x. 92 *n.*[1]

Yasawu Islands of Fiji, reverence for coco-nuts in the, ii. 12 *sq.*

Yassin, king of Fazoql, put to death, iv. 16

Yawning, soul supposed to depart in, iii. 31

Year, beginning of, marked by appearance of Pleiades, vii. 309, 310, 312, 313, 314, 315 ; divided into thirteen moons, viii. 77 ; burning out the Old, ix. 165, 230 *n.*[7] ; supposed representatives of the old, ix. 230 ; called a fire, x. 137. *See also* New Year

——, the fixed Alexandrian, vi. 28, 49,

Year, the Caffre, beginning of, marked by festival of new fruits, viii. 64 *sq.*
——, the Celtic, reckoned from November 1st, vi. 81
——, the Egyptian, a vague year, not corrected by intercalation, vi. 24 *sq.*
—— of God, a Sothic period, in ancient Egypt, vi. 36 *n.*[2]; began with the rising of Sirius, vi. 35
——, the Great, in ancient Greece, iv. 70
——, the old Iranian, vi. 67
——, the Julian, vi. 28
——, lunar, of old Roman calendar, ix. 232; equated to solar year by intercalation, ix. 325, 342 *sq.*
——, the old Roman, began in March, ix. 229
——, the Slavonic, beginning of, ix. 228
——, solar, length of, determined by the Theban priests, vi. 26; intercalation of the, ix. 407 *n.*[1]
——, the solar and lunar, early attempts to harmonize, ix. 325 *sq.*, 339, 341 *sqq.*
——, the Teutonic, reckoned from October 1st, vi. 81
Year-man, the, in Japan, ix. 144
Years, cycle of eight, in ancient Greece, iv. 68 *sqq.*, vii. 80 *sqq.*; mode of counting the, in Manipur, iv. 117 *n.*[1]; named after eponymous magistrates, ix. 39 *sq.*
——, the King of the, in Tibet, ix. 220, 221
Yegory or Yury, Russian name for St. George, ii. 332, 333. *See* St. George
Yehar-baal, king of Byblus, v. 14
Yehaw-melech, king of Byblus, v. 14
Yellow the royal colour among the Malays, i. 362, ix. 187
—— and black, face of human representative of goddess painted, ix. 287
Yellow birds in magic, i. 79 *sq.*
—— colour in magic, i. 79 *sqq.*
—— Day of Beltane, x. 293
—— Demeter, vii. 41 *sq.*
—— River, girls married to the, ii. 152
—— snow, the year of the, x. 294
—— things supposed to cure jaundice, i. 79 *sqq.*
Yerkla - mining tribe of South - Eastern Australia, their belief in the contagious magic of wounds, i. 202; the headmen medicine-men in the, i. 336
Yerrunthally tribe of Queensland, their ideas as to falling stars, iv. 64
Yewe order, secret society in Togo, iii. 383
Yezidis, their belief as to New Year's Day, iv. 117
Yezo or Yesso, Japanese Island, the Ainos of, viii. 180, 185
Yibai, tribal subdivision of the Coast Murring tribe, xi. 236

Yluta, in Mexico, bones of the dead preserved for the resurrection in, viii. 259
Ynglingar family, members of the, obtain kingdoms in Norway through marriage, ii. 279 *sq.*
Ynglings, a Norse family, descended from Frey, vi. 100
Yoke, purification by passing under a, xi. 193 *sqq.*; ancient Italian practice of passing conquered enemies under a, xi. 193 *sq.*
Yokuts, a tribe of Californian Indians, influence of rain-makers among the, i. 358
Yombe, the, of Rhodesia, their sacrifice of first-fruits to the dead, vi. 191, viii. 112 *sq.*
Yopaa, in southern Mexico, governed by a sacred pontiff, iii. 6
Yopico, temple in Mexico, ix. 299
York, the Boy Bishop at, ix. 337, 338; custom formerly observed at Christmas, in the cathedral at, xi. 291 *n.*[2]
Yorkshire, custom as to the placentas of mares at Cleveland in, i. 199; May garlands (hoops) in, ii. 62 *sq.*; the *mell*-sheaf in, vii. 151 *sq.*; "burning the Old Witch" on the last day of harvest in, vii. 224; first corn cut at harvest by clergyman in, viii. 51; Plough Monday in, viii. 330 *n.*[1]; belief as to menstruous women in, x. 96 *n.*[2]; Bealfires on Midsummer Eve in, x. 198; the Yule log in, x. 256 *sq.*; needfire in, x. 286 *sqq.*; witch as hare in, x. 317, xi. 197
Yoruba, West Africa, fear of strangers in, i. 103
—— -land, the paramount king of, iv. 203
—— race in the province of Lagos, iv. 112
—— -speaking negroes of the Slave Coast eat the hearts of men to make themselves brave, viii. 149 *sq.*
Yorubas of West Africa, sanctity of the king's crown among the, i. 364 *sq.*; rule of succession to the chieftainship among the, ii. 293 *sq.*; their theory of a guardian spirit in the head, iii. 252; rebirth of ancestors among the, iii. 369; their custom of putting their kings to death, iv. 41; their custom after the death of a twin, viii. 98; their use of human scapegoats, ix. 211 *sq.*; use of bull-roarers among the, xi. 229 *n.*
Young, Arthur, on "hurling" for a bride in Ireland, ii. 305 *sq.*
Young, E., on the ceremony of the first ploughing in Siam, iv. 150 *n.*

Young, Hugh W., on the rampart of Burghead, x. 268 *n.*[1]

Young, Issobell, buries ox and cat alive, x. 325

Youngest person cuts the last corn, viii. 158, 161

—— son, his name changed after his mother's death in order to deceive her ghost, iii. 358

Younghusband, Sir Francis, in the desert of Gobi, ix. 13

Yourouks of Asia Minor, their sacred trees, ii. 43

Youth restored by the witch Medea, v. 180 *sq.*; supposed to be renewed by sloughing of skin, ix. 302 *sqq.*

Youths and maidens, tribute of, sent to Minos, iv. 74 *sqq.*

Ypres, wicker giants at, xi. 35

Yu-ă, spirits of the elements believed in by the Esquimaux, ix. 379, 380

Yucatan, Indians of, their way of detaining the sun, i. 318 ; Vestals in, ii. 245 *sq.* ; fire-worship among the Indians of, ii. 246 *n.*[1]; calendar of the Indians of, vi. 29 *n.* ; the Mayas of, ix. 171, 340 ; human blood smeared on face of idol at sacrifices in, ix. 256 *n.*[3]; fire-walk among the Indians of, xi. 13 *sq.*, 16

Yuchi Indians of Oklahoma, their festival of new fruits, viii. 75 ; their respect for their totems, viii. 311 *n.*[1]

Yuin tribe of South-East Australia, political power of medicine-men in the, i. 336 ; avoidance of wife's mother among the, iii. 84 ; totem names among the, iii. 320 ; their sex totems, xi. 216 ; totem names kept secret among the, xi. 225 *n.*

Yuki Indians of California, dances of their women while the men were away fighting, i. 133

Yukon River, the Lower, in Alaska, the Esquimaux of, their fear of being photographed, iii. 96 ; their festivals of the dead, vi. 51 *sq.* ; their double-faced masks, ix. 380 ; seclusion of girls at puberty among them, x. 55

—— territory, Indians of the, place their cut hair and nails in crotches of trees, iii. 276

Yule, Colonel Henry, on modes of executing royal criminals in the East, iii. 242

Yule Boar, a loaf baked in the form of a boar-pig in Sweden and Denmark, vii. 300 *sqq.*, viii. 328 ; often made out of the corn of the last sheaf, vii. 300 *sq.*, viii. 328 ; part of it mixed with the seed-corn, part given to the ploughmen and plough-horses or

plough-oxen to eat, vii. 301, viii. 43, 328

Yule cake, x. 257, 259, 261

—— candle, x. 255, 256, 260

—— Goat, the, personated by a man wearing goat's horns at Christmas in Sweden, viii. 327 *sq.*

—— Island, Torres Straits, magical telepathy in, i. 121

—— log, x. 247 *sqq.*; in Germany, x. 247 *sqq.*; made of oak-wood, x. 248, 250, 251, 257, 258, 259, 260, 263, 264 *sq.*, xi. 92 ; a protection against conflagration, x. 248 *sq.*, 250, 255, 256, 258 ; a protection against thunder and lightning, x. 248, 249, 250, 252, 253, 254, 258, 264 ; in Switzerland, x. 249 ; in Belgium, x. 249 ; in France, x. 249 *sqq.*; helps cows to calve, x. 250, 338 ; in England, x. 255 *sq.*; in Wales, x. 258 ; among the Servians, x. 258 *sqq.*; a protection against witches, x. 258 ; in Albania, x. 264 ; privacy of the ceremonial of the, x. 328 ; explained as a sun-charm, x. 332 ; made of fir, beech, holly, yew, crab-tree, or olive, xi. 92 *n.*[2]

—— Night in Sweden, customs observed on, x. 20 *sq.*

—— ram, the, straw-effigy at Christmas in Dalarne, viii. 328

—— straw in Sweden, magical virtues ascribed to, vii. 301 *sq.*

Yules, the, in Shetland, ix. 168

Yumari, a dance of the Tarahumare Indians, ix. 237 *sq.*

Yung-chun, city in China, i. 170

Yungman tribe of Australia, their belief as to the birth of children, v. 101

Yuracares, the, of Bolivia, their superstitions as to the making of pottery, ii. 204 ; their propitiation of the apes which they have killed, viii. 235 *sq.*; take great care of the bones of the animals and fish which they eat, viii. 257 ; their practice of bleeding themselves to relieve fatigue, ix. 13 ; seclusion of girls at puberty among the, x. 57 *sq.*

—— of Peru threaten the thunder-god, ii. 183 *n.*[2]

Yuruks, pastoral people of Cilicia, v. 150 *n.*[1]

Zabern, in Alsace, May-trees at, ii. 64 ; the goat or fox at threshing at, vii. 287, 297

Zadrooga, Servian house-community, x. 259

Zafimanelo, the, of Madagascar, their seclusion at eating, iii. 116

Zagreus, a form of Dionysus, murdered by the Titans, vii. 12 *sq.*

Zakmuk or Zagmuk, the Babylonian festival of the New Year, iv. 110 sq., 113, 115 sq., ix. 356 sqq.
—— and the Sacaea, iv. 113, 115 sqq., ix. 355 sqq., 399, 402
Zambesi, the River, the Angoni to the north of, i. 291, iii. 174; short-handled hoes used by Caffres above the, vii. 116; the Makanga of the, viii. 287; belief in transmigration among the Caffres of the, viii. 289; Sena-speaking people to the north of the, ix. 7; heaps of sticks and stones to which passers-by add on the, ix. 11
——, the Lower, rain-maker at Boroma on, iii. 259
——, the Upper, the Barotse of, i. 310 n.[7], 392, vi. 193, x. 28; the Maraves or Zimbas of, i. 393 n.[2], viii. 111; tribes of, their belief in the homoeopathic magic of a flesh diet, viii. 141
Zanzibar, custom at sowing in, vii. 233
Zaparo Indians of Ecuador, their belief in the homoeopathic magic of animal flesh, viii. 139
Zapotecs of Mexico, their harvest customs, vii. 174 sq.; their belief that their lives were bound up with those of animals, xi. 212
——, the pontiff of the, rule of continence observed by, iii. 6 sq.; not allowed to set foot on ground, iii. 6, x. 2; the sun not allowed to shine on him, iii. 6, x. 19
Zaramamas, Maize-mothers, name given to certain maize-stalks or stones carved in the likeness of maize-cobs among the Indians of Peru, vii. 173 n.
Zas, name of priest of Corycian Zeus, v. 155
Zealand, the Rye-beggar at harvest in, vii. 231; treatment of strangers at the madder-harvest in, vii. 231
Zechariah on the mourning of or for Hadadrimmon, v. 15 n.[4]; on wounds of prophet, v. 74 n.[4]
Zekar-baal, king of Byblus, v. 14
Zela in Pontus, priestly kings at, i. 47; Anaitis and the Sacaea at, ix. 370, 372, 373, 421 n.[1]; Omanos and Anadates at, ix. 373 n.[1]
Zemis of Assam, parents named after their children among the, iii. 333
Zemmur, the, of Morocco, their Mid-summer custom, x. 215
Zend-Avesta, the, on cut hair and nails, iii. 277; on the Fravashis, vi. 67 sq.
Zengwih, in Burma, priestly king near, iii. 237
Zenjirli in Syria, Hittite sculptures at, v. 134; statue of horned god at, v. 163
Zer, old Egyptian king, his true Horus name Khent, vi. 20 n.[1], 154. See Khent
Zerdusht and Isfendiyar, story of, in Firdusi's Epic of Kings, x. 104
Zerka, river in Moab, the ancient Callirrhoe, v. 215 n.[1]
Zeus, at Panamara in Caria, sacrifice of men's hair to, i. 29; mated with Artemis, i. 36; Spartan kings descended from, i. 48; Castor and Pollux the sons of, i. 49; rids himself of his love for Hera, i. 161; rain made by, i. 285; the priest of, makes rain by an oak branch, i. 309; mimicked by King Salmoneus, i. 310; crowned with chaplet of oak leaves at Dodona, ii. 177; Greek kings called, ii. 177, 361; at Olympia, the sacred white poplar of, ii. 220; priests of, at Dodona, ii. 248; Spartan kings sacrifice to, ii. 264; as god of the oak, the rain, the thunder, and the sky, ii. 358 sqq.; his oracular oak at Dodona, ii. 358; prayed to for rain by the Greeks, ii. 359; father of Aeacus, ii. 359; the sign-giving, on Mount Parnes, ii. 360; his resemblance to Donar and Thor, ii. 364; his resemblance to Perun and Perkunas, ii. 365, 367; as sky-god, ii. 374; his sanctuary on Mount Lycaeus, iii. 88; the fleece of, Διὸς κώδιον, iii. 312 n.[3]; the grave of, in Crete, iv. 3; oracular cave of, on Mount Ida in Crete, iv. 70; father of Minos, iv. 70; festival of, on Mount Lycaeus, iv. 70 n.[1]; his transformations into animals, iv. 82 sq.; the Olympic victors regarded as embodiments of, iv. 90 sq.; swallows his wife Metis, iv. 192; saved by a trick from being swallowed by his father Cronus, iv. 192; his marriage with his sister Hera, iv. 194; god of Tarsus assimilated to, v. 119, 143; Cilician deity assimilated to, v. 144 sqq., 148, 152; the flower of, v. 186, 187; identified with Attis, v. 282; castrates his father Cronus, v. 283; the father of dew, vi. 137; the Saviour of the City, at Magnesia on the Maeander, vi. 238; his intrigue with Persephone, vii. 12; father of Dionysus by Demeter, vii. 12, 14, 66; said to have transferred the sceptre to the young Dionysus, vii. 13; said to have swallowed the heart of Dionysus, vii. 14; his intrigue with Demeter, vii. 66; his temple at Olympia, viii. 85; his appearance to Hercules in the shape of a ram, viii. 172; cake with twelve knobs offered to, ix. 351; an upstart at Olympia, ix. 352; identified with the Babylonian Bel, ix. 389; and his

sacred oak at Dodona, xi. 49 *sq.*; wood of white poplar used at Olympia in sacrificing to, xi. 90 *n.*[1], 91 *n.*[7]

Zeus, Corycian, priests of, v. 145, 155; temple of, v. 155

—— and Cronus, ii. 323

—— and Danae, how he visited her in a shower of gold, x. 74

—— and Demeter, viii. 9; their marriage perhaps dramatically celebrated in the Eleusinian mysteries, ii. 138 *sq.*, vii. 65 *sqq.*

—— the Descender, places struck by lightning consecrated to, ii. 361

——, Dictaean, his sacred precinct in Crete, ii. 122

—— and Dione at Dodona, ii. 189, 381

—— and Europa, iv. 73

—— the Fly-catcher, viii. 282

——, the Fruitful One, ii. 360

——, Heavenly, at Sparta, i. 47

—— and Hecate at Stratonicea in Caria, v. 270 *n.*[2], 227

—— and Hephaestus, x. 136

—— and Hera, sacred marriage of, ii. 140 *sq.*, 142 *sq.*, 359, iv. 91; sacrifices for rain to, ii. 360

—— and Hercules, viii. 172

—— the Husbandman, ii. 360

——, Labrandeus, the Carian, v. 182

——, Lacedaemon, at Sparta, i. 47

——, Laphystian, his sanctuary at Alus, iv. 161; associated with human sacrifices, iv. 162, 163, 164, 165, vii. 25; his sanctuary on Mount Laphystius, iv. 164

—— the Leader, Spartan king sacrifices to, ii. 264

——, Lightning, the hearth of, at Athens, i. 33, ii. 361

——, Lycaean, on Mount Lycaeus, human sacrifices to, ix. 353, 354

——, Olbian, ruins of his temple at Olba, in Cilicia, v. 151; his cave or chasm, v. 158 *sq.*; his priest Teucer, v. 159; a god of fertility, v. 159 *sqq.*

——, Olybrian, of Anazarba in Cilicia, v. 167 *n.*[1]

——, Olympian, his temple at Athens, ix. 351

——, Panhellenian, at Aegina, ii. 359

—— Papas, in Phrygia, v. 281 *n.*[2]

——, Pelorian, in Thessaly, iii. 350

——, Polieus in Cos, ox sacrificed to, viii. 5 *n.*[2]; on the Acropolis of Athens, viii. 5, 7

——, Rainy, the birthplace of, ii. 360; sacrifices for rain to, ii. 360

——, Showery, on Hymettus, ii. 360

—— Sosipolis at Magnesia on the Maeander, ox sacrificed to, viii. 7

——, Subterranean, vii. 66, viii. 9;

sacrifices for the crops offered to, at Myconus, vii. 66

Zeus, surnamed Thunderbolt at Olympia and elsewhere, ii. 361

—— and Typhon, battle of, v. 156 *sq.*, 160

——, surnamed Underground, Greek ploughman's prayer to, vii. 45, 50

—— the Wolf-god, on the Wolf-mountain (Mount Lycaeus) in Arcadia, transformation of men into were-wolves at his festival, iv. 83

Zileh, the modern successor of Zela, ix. 370 *n.*[2]

Zimbales, a province of the Philippines, superstition as to a parasitic plant in, xi. 282 *n.*[1]

Zimbas or Muzimbas, of South-East Africa, regard their king as a god, i. 392

—— or Maraves offer the first-fruits to the spirits of the dead, viii. 111

Zimmer, H., on the Picts, ii. 286 *n.*[2]

Zimmern, Professor H., as to the myth celebrated at the Babylonian Zakmuk, iv. 111 *n.*[1]; on Mylitta, v. 37 *n.*[1]; as to Nabu and Marduk, ix. 358 *n.*; on the distinction of Sacaea from Zakmuk, ix. 359 *n.*[1]; on the derivation of the name Purim, ix. 361 *n.*[4]; on the principal personages in the Book of Esther, ix. 406 *n.*[2]

Zimri, king of Israel, burns himself, v. 174 *n.*[2], 176

Zion, Mount, traditionally identified with Mount Moriah, vi. 219 *n.*[1]

Zoganes, temporary king at Babylon, put to death after a reign of five days, iv. 114, ix. 355, 357, 365, 368, 369, 387, 388, 406

Zoilus, priest of Dionysus at Orchomenus, iv. 163

Zombo-land, traps to catch the devil in, iii. 69 *n.*[4]

Zonares, on the triumphal crowns, ii. 175 *n.*[1]

Zoroaster, gods worshipped by the Persians before, ix. 389; on the uncleanness of women at menstruation, x. 95

Zoroastrian fire-worship in Cappadocia, v. 191

Zoznegg, in Baden, Easter fires at, x. 145

Zulu custom of putting the king to death when his strength failed, viii. 68

—— fancy as to eating forehead and eyebrow of enemy, viii. 152

—— hunters, their use of magic knots, iii. 306

—— king, dance of the, viii. 66

—— kings put to death, iv. 36 *sq.*

—— language, its diversity, iii. 377

Zulu medicine - men or diviners, their shoulders sensitive to the Amatongo (ancestral spirits), v. 74 *n.*[4], 75 ; their charm to fertilize fields, vi. 102 *sq.*

—— women may not utter their husbands' names, iii. 333

Zululand, rain-making by means of the dead in, i. 286 ; children buried to the neck as a rain-charm in, i. 302 *sq.* ; hoes used by women in, vii. 116

Zulus, use made by them of twins in war, i. 49 *n.*[3] ; foods tabooed among the, i. 118 *sq.* ; employ pregnant women to grind corn, i. 140 ; their contagious magic of footprints, i. 212 ; their belief as to twins, i. 268 ; their rain-making by means of a "heaven - bird," i. 302 ; their superstition as to reflections in water, iii. 91 ; names of chiefs and kings tabooed among the, iii. 376 *sq.* ; their belief in serpents as reincarnations of the dead, v. 82, 84 ; their observation of the moon, vi. 134 *sq.* ; the worship of the dead among the, vi. 182 *sqq.* ; their sacrifice of a bull to prolong the life of a king, vi. 222 ; women's part in agriculture among the, vii. 113 *sq.* ; their fences to keep wild boars from gardens, viii. 32 ; their festival of first - fruits, viii. 64 *sqq.* ; eat leopards, lions, etc., in order to become brave like the beasts, viii. 142 ; their charm for attaining old age, viii. 143 ; their inoculation, viii. 160 *sq.* ; seclusion of girls at puberty among the, x. 22, 30 ; fumigate their gardens with medicated smoke, x. 337 ; their custom of fumigating sick cattle, xi. 13 ; their belief as to ancestral spirits incarnate in serpents, xi. 211

Zülz, in Silesia, Midsummer fires at, x. 170

Zündel, G., on demonolatry in West Africa, ix. 74 *sqq.*

Zungu tribe of Zulus, special words used by them in order to avoid mentioning the name of their chief, iii. 376

Zuni Indians of New Mexico, their custom of killing sacred turtles, viii. 175 *sqq.*, ix. 217 ; their totem clans, viii. 178 ; their ritual at the summer solstice to ensure rain, viii. 179 ; their new fires at the solstices, xi. 132 *sq.* ; use of bull-roarers among the, xi. 230 *n.*, 231

Zürcher Oberland, Switzerland, charm to make a cherry-tree bear in, i. 141

Zurich, effigies of Winter burnt after the spring equinox at, iv. 260 *sq.*, x. 120 ; the Canton of the Corn-mother in, vii. 232 ; the Thresher-cow at threshing in, vii. 291 ; the last sheaf called the Fox in, vii. 297

Zygadenus elegans, Pursch., roots of, inserted in eyes of dead grouse by father of pubescent girl among the Thompson Indians, viii. 268

Žytniamatka, the Corn-mother, represented by a woman who pretends to give birth to the Corn-baby on the harvest field (Prussian custom), vii. 209

THE END

Printed by R. & R. Clark, Limited, *Edinburgh.*